On March 4, 1905, the day of
Theodore Roosevelt's inauguration,
the skies over the Capitol were
sunny and clear; "Roosevelt luck"
had brought "Roosevelt weather,"
Washingtonians remarked.

ALSO BY DORIS KEARNS GOODWIN

Team of Rivals: The Political Genius of Abraham Lincoln

Wait Till Next Year: A Memoir

*No Ordinary Time: Franklin & Eleanor Roosevelt:
The Home Front in World War II*

The Fitzgeralds and the Kennedys

Lyndon Johnson and the American Dream

Theodore Roosevelt,

William Howard Taft,

AND THE

Golden Age of Journalism

THE
BULLY
PULPIT

DORIS KEARNS GOODWIN

SIMON & SCHUSTER

NEW YORK   LONDON   TORONTO   SYDNEY   NEW DELHI

Simon & Schuster
1230 Avenue of the Americas
New York, NY 10020

First Simon & Schuster hardcover edition November 2013

SIMON & SCHUSTER and colophon are registered trademarks
of Simon & Schuster, Inc.

For information about special discounts for bulk purchases,
please contact Simon & Schuster Special Sales at
1-866-506-1949 or business@simonandschuster.com.

The Simon & Schuster Speakers Bureau can bring authors to your
live event. For more information or to book an event contact the
Simon & Schuster Speakers Bureau at 1-866-248-3049 or visit our
website at www.simonspeakers.com.

Interior design by Joy O'Meara
Jacket design by Jackie Seow
Jacket art by Getty Images

Manufactured in the United States of America

10   9   8   7   6   5   4   3   2   1

Library of Congress Cataloging-in-Publication Data

Goodwin, Doris Kearns.
    The bully pulpit : Theodore Roosevelt, William Howard Taft, and the
golden age of journalism / Doris Kearns Goodwin. — First Simon & Schuster
hardcover edition.
        pages   cm
    Includes bibliographical references and index.
    1. Roosevelt, Theodore, 1858–1919.   2. Taft, William H. (William Howard),
1857–1930.   3. United States—Politics and government—1901–1909.
4. United States—Politics and government—1909–1913.   5. Progressivism
(United States politics)—History—20th century.   6. Press and politics—
United States—History—20th century.   7. Republican Party (U.S. :
1854–)—History—20th century.   I. Title.
    E757.G66 2013b
    973.91'1—dc23
                                                            2013032709

ISBN 978-1-4165-4786-0
ISBN 978-1-4516-7379-1 (ebook)

To Alice Mayhew and Linda Vandegrift

CONTENTS

PREFACE

I BEGAN THIS BOOK SEVEN YEARS ago with the notion of writing about Theodore Roosevelt and the Progressive era. This desire had been kindled nearly four decades earlier when I was a young professor teaching a seminar on the progressives. There are but a handful of times in the history of our country when there occurs a transformation so remarkable that a molt seems to take place, and an altered country begins to emerge. The turn of the twentieth century was such a time, and Theodore Roosevelt is counted among our greatest presidents, one of the few to attain that eminence without having surmounted some pronounced national crisis—revolution, war, widespread national depression.

To be sure, Roosevelt had faced a pernicious underlying crisis, one as pervasive as any military conflict or economic collapse. In the wake of the Industrial Revolution, an immense gulf had opened between the rich and the poor; daily existence had become more difficult for ordinary people, and the middle class felt increasingly squeezed. Yet by the end of Roosevelt's tenure in the White House, a mood of reform had swept the country, creating a new kind of presidency and a new vision of the relationship between the government and the people. A series of anti-trust suits had been won and legislation passed to regulate railroads, strengthen labor rights, curb political corruption, end corporate campaign contributions, impose limits on the working day, protect consumers from unsafe food and drugs, and conserve vast swaths of natural resources for the American people. The question that most intrigued me was how Roosevelt had managed to rouse a Congress long wedded to the reigning concept of laissez-faire—a government interfering as little as possible in the economic and social life of the people—to pass such comprehensive measures.

The essence of Roosevelt's leadership, I soon became convinced, lay in his enterprising use of the "bully pulpit," a phrase he himself coined to describe the national platform the presidency provides to shape public sentiment and mobilize action. Early in Roosevelt's tenure, Lyman Abbott, editor of *The Outlook*, joined a small group of friends in the president's library to offer advice and criticism on a draft of his upcoming message to Congress. "He had just finished a paragraph of a distinctly ethical character," Abbott recalled, "when he suddenly stopped, swung round in his swivel chair, and said, 'I suppose my critics will call that preaching, but I have got such a bully pulpit.'" From this bully pulpit, Roosevelt would focus the charge of a national movement to apply an ethical framework, through government action, to the untrammeled growth of modern America.

Roosevelt understood from the outset that this task hinged upon the need to develop powerfully reciprocal relationships with members of the national press. He called them by their first names, invited them to meals, took questions during his midday shave, welcomed their company at day's end while he signed correspondence, and designated, for the first time, a special room for them in the West Wing. He brought them aboard his private railroad car during his regular swings around the country. At every village station, he reached the hearts of the gathered crowds with homespun language, aphorisms, and direct moral appeals. Accompanying reporters then extended the reach of Roosevelt's words in national publications. Such extraordinary rapport with the press did not stem from calculation alone. Long before and after he was president, Roosevelt was an author and historian. From an early age, he read as he breathed. He knew and revered writers, and his relationship with journalists was authentically collegial. In a sense, he was one of them.

While exploring Roosevelt's relationship with the press, I was especially drawn to the remarkably rich connections he developed with a team of journalists—including Ida Tarbell, Ray Stannard Baker, Lincoln Steffens, and William Allen White—all working at *McClure's* magazine, the most influential contemporary progressive publication. The restless enthusiasm and manic energy of their publisher and editor, S. S. McClure, infused the magazine with "a spark of genius," even as he suffered from periodic nervous breakdowns. "The story is the thing," Sam McClure responded when asked to account for the methodology behind his publication. He wanted his writers to begin their research without preconceived notions, to carry their readers through their own process of discovery. As they educated themselves about the social and economic inequities rampant in the wake of teeming industrialization, so they educated the entire country.

Together, these investigative journalists, who would later appropriate Roosevelt's derogatory term "muckraker" as "a badge of honor," produced a series of exposés that uncovered the invisible web of corruption linking politics to business. McClure's formula—giving his writers the time and resources they needed to produce extended, intensively researched articles—was soon adopted by rival magazines, creating what many considered a golden age of journalism. Collectively, this generation of gifted writers ushered in a new mode of investigative reporting that provided the necessary conditions to make a genuine bully pulpit of the American presidency. "It is hardly an exaggeration to say that the progressive mind was characteristically a journalistic mind," the historian Richard Hofstadter observed, "and that its characteristic contribution was that of the socially responsible reporter-reformer."

PERHAPS MOST SURPRISING TO ME in my own process of research was the discovery that Roosevelt's chosen successor in the White House, William Howard Taft, was a far more sympathetic, if flawed, figure than I had realized. Scholarship has long focused on the rift in the relations between the two men during the bitter 1912 election fight, ignoring their career-long, mutually beneficial friendship. Throughout the Roosevelt administration, Taft functioned, in Roosevelt's own estimation, as the central figure in his cabinet. Because it was seen as undignified for a sitting president to campaign on his own behalf, Taft served as the chief surrogate during Roosevelt's 1904 presidential race, the most demanded speaker on the circuit to explain and justify the president's positions. In an era when presidents routinely spent long periods away from Washington, crisscrossing the country on whistle-stop tours or simply vacationing, it was Taft, the secretary of war—not the secretary of state or the vice president—who was considered the "acting President." Asked how things would be managed in his absence, Roosevelt blithely replied: "Oh, things will be all right, I have left Taft sitting on the lid."

Long before Taft's 1908 election, Roosevelt had disclosed his passionate wish that Taft be his successor. There was no man in the country, he believed, better suited to be president, no man he trusted more to carry out his legacy of active moral leadership and progressive reform. Yet, left alone at the helm when Roosevelt embarked on a yearlong African expedition, Taft questioned whether he was suited for the office. For all of Taft's admirable qualities and intentions to codify and expand upon Roosevelt's progressive legacy, he ultimately failed as a public leader, a failure that underscores the pivotal importance of the bully pulpit in presidential leadership.

From the start of his administration, Taft's relationship with journalists was uneasy. He was never able to seek the counsel they offered or harness the press corps to broadcast a coherent narrative concerning his legislative goals. As a former judge, he assumed that his decisions would speak for themselves. Eventually, he recognized the handicap of his inability to engage the press as his predecessor had done, conceding after he left office that he had been "derelict" in his use of the bully pulpit. He had failed to educate the country about his policies and programs. He was simply "not constituted as Roosevelt" to expound upon his thoughts and vent his feelings with the members of the press. It was, Taft came to realize, a matter of temperament.

Finally, my own process of discovery led me to the realization that the story I wanted to tell had three interwoven strands. One was the story of Theodore Roosevelt, whose crusade to expand the role of government in national life required the transformation of the presidency itself. The next strand was the story of William Howard Taft, whose talents and skills played a more significant role in the Roosevelt administration than is generally understood. When Taft attained the presidency, however, he found himself at sea, in large part because he was temperamentally unsuited to make use of the story's third strand—the bully pulpit that had provided the key to his predecessor's success.

As S. S. McClure well understood, the "vitality of democracy" depends on "popular knowledge of complex questions." At the height of *McClure's* success, observed the philosopher William James, the investigative journalists McClure had assembled and their counterparts in other leading magazines had embarked on nothing less than "the mission of raising the tone of democracy," exerting an elevating influence on public sentiment.

It is my greatest hope that the story that follows will guide readers through their own process of discovery toward a better understanding of what it takes to summon the public to demand the actions necessary to bring our country closer to its ancient ideals. "There is no one left," McClure exhorted his readers as he cast about for a remedy to America's woes at the turn of the twentieth century, "none but all of us."

THE
BULLY
PULPIT

CHAPTER ONE

The Hunter Returns

Theodore Roosevelt receives a hero's welcome in New York on
June 18, 1910, following his expedition to Africa.

ROOSEVELT IS COMING HOME, HOORAY! Exultant headlines in
mid-June 1910 trumpeted the daily progress of the *Kaiserin*, the luxury
liner returning the former president, Theodore Roosevelt, to American shores
after his year's safari in Africa.

Despite popularity unrivaled since Abraham Lincoln, Roosevelt, true to his
word, had declined to run for a third term after completing seven and a half
years in office. His tenure had stretched from William McKinley's assassination in September 1901 to March 4, 1909, when his own elected term came to
an end. Flush from his November 1904 election triumph, he had stunned the
political world with his announcement that he would not run for president
again, citing "the wise custom which limits the President to two terms." Later,
he reportedly told a friend that he would willingly cut off his hand at the wrist
if he could take his pledge back.

Roosevelt had loved being president—"the greatest office in the world." He had relished "every hour" of every day. Indeed, fearing the "dull thud" he would experience upon returning to private life, he had devised the perfect solution to "break his fall." Within three weeks of the inauguration of his successor, William Howard Taft, he had embarked on his great African adventure, plunging into the most "impenetrable spot on the globe."

For months Roosevelt's friends had been preparing an elaborate reception to celebrate his arrival in New York. When "the Colonel," as Roosevelt preferred to be called, first heard of the extravagant plans devised for his welcome, he was troubled, fearing that the public response would not match such lofty expectations. "Even at this moment I should certainly put an instant stop to all the proceedings if I felt they were being merely 'worked up' and there was not a real desire . . . of at least a great many people to greet me," he wrote one of the organizers in March 1910. "My political career is ended," he told Lawrence Abbott of *The Outlook*, who had come to meet him in Khartoum, the capital of Sudan, when he first emerged from the jungle. "No man in American public life has ever reached the crest of the wave as I appear to have done without the wave's breaking and engulfing him."

Anxiety that his star had dimmed, that the public's devotion had dwindled, proved wildly off the mark. While he had initially planned to return directly from Khartoum, Roosevelt received so many invitations to visit the reigning European sovereigns that he first embarked on a six-week tour of Italy, Austria, Hungary, France, Belgium, Holland, Denmark, Norway, Germany, and England. Kings and queens greeted him as an equal, universities bestowed upon him their highest degrees, and the German Kaiser treated him as an intimate friend. Every city, town, and village received him with a frenzied enthusiasm that stunned the most sophisticated observers. "People gathered at railway stations, in school-houses, and in the village streets," one journalist observed. They showered his carriage with flowers, thronged windows of tenement houses, and greeted him with "Viva, viva, viva Roosevelt!" Newspapers in the United States celebrated Roosevelt's triumphant procession through the Old World, sensing in his unparalleled reception a tribute to America's newfound position of power. "No foreign ruler or man of eminence could have aroused more universal attention, received a warmer welcome, or achieved greater popularity among every class of society," the *New York Times* exulted.

"I don't suppose there was ever such a reception as that being given Theodore in Europe," Taft wistfully told his military aide, Captain Archie Butt. "It illustrates how his personality has swept over the world," such that even "small villages which one would hardly think had ever heard of the United States should seem to know all about the man." The stories of Roosevelt's "royal progress" through Europe bolstered the efforts of his friends to ensure, in Taft's words, "as great a demonstration of welcome from his countrymen as any American ever received."

In the week preceding his arrival in America, tens of thousands of visitors from all over the country had descended upon New York, lending the city's hotels and streets "a holiday appearance." Inbound trains carried a cast of characters "as diversely typical of the American people as Mr. Roosevelt himself . . . conservationists and cowboys, capitalists and socialists, insurgents and regulars, churchmen and sportsmen, native born and aliens." More than two hundred vessels, including five destroyers, six revenue cutters, and dozens of excursion steamboats, tugs, and ferryboats, all decked with colorful flags and pennants, had sailed into the harbor to take part in an extravagant naval display.

An army of construction workers labored to complete the speaker's platform and grandstand seating at Battery Park, where Roosevelt would address an overflow crowd of invited guests. Businesses had given their workers a half-holiday so they could join in the festivities. "Flags floated everywhere," an Ohio newspaper reported; "pictures of Roosevelt were hung in thousands of windows and along the line of march, buildings were draped with bunting."

The night before the big day, a dragnet was set to arrest known pickpockets. Five thousand police and dozens of surgeons and nurses were called in for special duty. "The United States of America at the present moment simulates quite the attitude of the small boy who can't go to sleep Christmas Eve for thinking of the next day," the *Atlanta Constitution* suggested. "And the colonel, returning as rapidly as a lusty steamship can plow the waves, is the 'next day.' It is a remarkable tribute to the man's personality that virtually every element of citizenship in the country should be more or less on tiptoes in the excitement of anticipation."

SHORTLY AFTER 7 A.M. ON June 18, as the bright rising sun burned through the mists, Theodore Roosevelt, as jubilant with anticipation as his country, stood on the bridge of the *Kaiserin* as the vessel headed into New York Harbor. Edith, his handsome forty-eight-year-old wife, stood beside him. She had journeyed halfway around the world to join him in Khartoum at the end of his long African expedition. Edith had found their year-long parting, the longest in their twenty-three years of marriage, almost unbearable. "If it were not for the children here I would not have the nervous strength to live through these endless months of separation from Father," she wrote her son Kermit after Theodore had been gone only two weeks. "When I am alone & let myself think I am done for."

Edith was no stranger to the anxiety of being apart from the man for whom she "would do anything in the world." They had been intimate childhood friends, growing up together in New York's Union Square neighborhood. She had joined "Teedie," as he was then called, and his younger sister Corinne, in a private schoolroom arranged at the Roosevelt mansion. Even as children, they missed each other when apart. As Teedie was setting off with his family on a Grand Tour of Europe when he was eleven years old, he broke down in tears at the thought of leaving eight-year-old Edith behind. She proved his most faithful correspondent over the long course of the trip. She had been a regular guest at "Tranquillity," the Roosevelts' summer home on Long Island, where they sailed together in the bay, rode horseback along the trails, and shared a growing passion for literature. As adolescents, they were dancing partners at cotillions and constant companions on the social scene. Roosevelt proudly noted that his freshman college classmates at Harvard considered Edith and her friend Annie Murray "the prettiest girls they had met" when they visited him in New York during Christmas vacation.

In the summer of 1878, after his sophomore year, however, the young couple had a mysterious "falling out" at Tranquillity. "One day," Roosevelt later wrote, "there came a break" during a late afternoon rendezvous at the estate's summerhouse. The conflict that erupted, Roosevelt admitted, ended "his very intimate relations" with Edith. Though neither one would ever say what had happened, Roosevelt cryptically noted to his sister Anna that "both of us had, and I suppose have, tempers that were far from being of the best."

The intimacy that Edith had cherished for nearly two decades seemed lost forever the following October, when Roosevelt met Alice Hathaway Lee. The beautiful, enchanting daughter of a wealthy Boston businessman, Alice lived in Chestnut Hill, Massachusetts, not far from Cambridge. The young Harvard junior fell in love with his "whole heart and soul." Four months after his graduation in 1880, they were married. Then, in 1884, only two days after giving birth to their only child, Alice died.

A year later, Theodore resumed his friendship with Edith. And the year after that they were married. As time passed, Edith's meticulous and thoughtful nature made her an exemplary partner for Theodore. "I do not think my eyes are blinded by affection," the president told a friend, "when I say that she has combined to a degree I have never seen in any other woman the power of being the best of wives and mothers, the wisest manager of the household, and at the same time the ideal great lady and mistress of the White House."

Their boisterous family eventually included six children. Three of the six were standing next to their parents on the bridge of the ocean liner: twenty-year-old Kermit, who had accompanied his father to Africa; eighteen-year-old Ethel; and twenty-six-year-old Alice, the child born to his first wife.

The girls had joined their parents in Europe. Along the rails of the four upper decks, their fellow passengers, some 3,000 in all, formed a colorful pageant as they waved their handkerchiefs and cheered.

Although wireless telegrams on board the ship had alerted Roosevelt to some of the day's planned activities, he was surprised to learn that President Taft had assigned the massive battleship *South Carolina* as his official escort. "By George! That's one of my ships! Doesn't she look good?" an overwhelmed Roosevelt exclaimed when he saw her gray bulk pulling near. "Flags were broken out from stem to stern in the ceremony of dressing the ship," reported the *Boston Daily Globe*, while "a puff from the muzzle of an eight-pounder" signaled the start of a 21-gun salute, the highest ceremonial honor, generally reserved for heads of state. Sailors clad in blue lined the decks of the warship, as the scarlet-uniformed Marine Band played "The Star-Spangled Banner." The cannon roar of the *South Carolina* was followed by the rhythmic volley of salutes and whistles from the dozen or more additional naval ships in the bay. President Taft had clearly gone to great lengths, Captain Butt proudly noted, "to add dignity to the welcome and to extend a warm personal greeting to his predecessor."

From the deck, Roosevelt spotted the tugboat carrying the reporters whose eyewitness accounts of the spectacular scene would dominate the news the following day. As he leaned over the rail and vigorously waved his top hat back and forth to them, they stood and cheered. To each familiar face, he nodded his head and smiled broadly, displaying his famous teeth, which appeared "just as prominent and just as white and perfect as when he went away." Then, recognizing the photographers' need to snap his picture, he stopped his hectic motions and stood perfectly still.

During his presidency, Roosevelt's physical vigor and mental curiosity had made the White House a hive of activity and interest. His "love of the hurly-burly" that enchanted reporters and their readers was best captured by British viscount John Morley, who claimed that "he had seen two tremendous works of nature in America—the Niagara Falls and Mr. Roosevelt." One magazine writer marveled at his prodigious stream of guests—"pugilists, college presidents, professional wrestlers, Greek scholars, baseball teams, big-game hunters, sociologists, press agents, authors, actors, Rough Riders, bad men, and gun-fighters from the West, wolf-catchers, photographers, guides, bear-hunters, artists, labor-leaders." When he left for Africa, the "noise and excitement" vanished; little wonder that the members of the press were thrilled to see him return.

Shortly after the *Kaiserin* dropped anchor at Quarantine, the revenue cutter *Manhattan* pulled alongside, carrying the Roosevelts' youngest sons, sixteen-year-old Archie and twelve-year-old Quentin, both of whom had remained at home. Their oldest son, twenty-two-year-old Theodore Junior, who was set to marry Eleanor Alexander the following Monday, joined the group along with an assortment of family members, including Roosevelt's sisters, Anna and Corinne; his son-in-law, Congressman Nicholas Longworth; his niece Eleanor Roosevelt; and her husband, Franklin. While Edith anxiously sought a glimpse of the children she had not seen for more than two months, Roosevelt busily shook hands with each of the officers, sailors, and engineers of the ship. "Come here, Theodore, and see your children," Edith called out. "They are of far greater importance than politics or anything else."

Roosevelt searched the promenade deck of the *Manhattan*, reported the *Chicago Tribune*, until his eyes rested on "the round face of his youngest boy, Quentin, who was dancing up and down on the deck, impatient to be recognized," telling all who would listen that he would be the one "to kiss pop first." At the sight of the lively child, "the Colonel spread his arms out as if he would undertake a long-distance embrace" and smiled broadly as he nodded to each of his relatives in turn.

When Roosevelt stepped onto the crimson-covered gangplank for his transfer to the *Manhattan*, "pandemonium broke loose." The ship's band played "America," the *New York Times* reported, and "there came from the river craft, yachts, and ships nearby a volley of cheers that lasted for fully five minutes." Bugles blared, whistles shrieked, and "everywhere flags waved, hats were tossed into the air, and cries of welcome were heard." Approaching the deck where his children were jumping in anticipation, Roosevelt executed a "flying leap," and "with the exuberance and spirit of a school boy, he took up Quentin and Archie in his arms and gave them resounding smacks." He greeted Theodore Junior with a hearty slap on the back, kissed his sisters, and then proceeded to shake hands with every crew member.

Around 9 a.m., the *Androscoggin*, carrying Cornelius Vanderbilt, the chairman of the reception, and two hundred distinguished guests, came alongside the *Manhattan*. As Roosevelt made the transfer to the official welcoming vessel, he asked that everyone form a line so that he could greet each individual personally and then went at the task of shaking hands with such high spirits, delivering for each person such "an explosive word of welcome," that what might have been a duty for another politician became an act of joy. "I'm *so* glad to see you," he greeted each person in turn. The *New York Times* reporter noted that "the 'so' went off like a firecracker. The smile backed it up in a radiation of energy, and the hearty grip of the hand that came down upon its respondent with a bang emphasized again the exact meaning of the words."

When Roosevelt grasped the hand of Joe Murray, the savvy political boss who had first nominated him for the state legislature years before, it must have seemed as if his public life had come full circle. "This takes me back 29 years," he said, "to the old Twenty-first Assembly district when I was getting a start in politics." Earlier he had warmly welcomed Massachusetts senator Henry Cabot Lodge, his closest friend for more than a quarter of a century, and Archie Butt, who had served as his devoted military aide before taking up the same position with President Taft. Jacob Riis, the Danish immigrant whose book, *How the Other Half Lives*, had greatly influenced Roosevelt when he was police commissioner of New York City, received a fraternal welcome and "the broadest of smiles." Roosevelt clasped him with both hands, exclaiming, "O, Jake. I've got so much to tell you." His face grew somber as he glimpsed Beverly Robinson, who conjured memories of McKinley's assassination. "This boy was with me on top of Mount Mary," he mused, "when the sudden news came that I had become President." Nothing, however, could dampen his innate joviality for more than a moment. "Why, hello, Stimson, old sugar trust," he laughed, his eyes twinkling, as he approached Henry Stimson, the government's special counsel in the famous trust case. "Oh, friend, this is good. I can't tell you how I feel," he confided to Frank Tyree, the Secret Serviceman who had protected him loyally for years. On and on he went, his personal greetings for all interspersed with expressions of outright delight: "Fine! Fine! Oh, it's simply great!" "George, this is bully!"

When Vanderbilt suggested it was time to go up to the bridge to acknowledge the thousands of people massed solidly on both the New Jersey and the Manhattan sides of the river, Roosevelt hesitated. "But here are the reporters," he said, turning to the members of the press eagerly taking down his words. "I want to shake hands with them." Indeed, at every stop during the long day, he made sure to deliver a special welcome to the members of the press. "Boys, I am *glad* (emphasis on the glad) to see you. It does me good to see you, boys. I am glad to be back." Clearly, that pleasure was reciprocated. "We're mighty glad to have you back," shouted one exuberant reporter.

From the time reporters had accompanied the Colonel to Cuba—helping transform him and his intrepid Rough Riders into a national icon—Roosevelt had established a unique relationship with numerous journalists. He debated points with them as fellow writers; regardless of the disparity in political rank, when they argued as authors, they argued as equals. He had read and freely commented upon their stories, as they felt free to criticize his public statements and speeches. Little wonder, then, that these same journalists celebrated Roosevelt's return from Africa, flocking to lower Manhattan to welcome him home. For the members of the press, the story of Roosevelt's homecoming was not merely an assignment—it was personal.

Reporters present at the festivities remarked how "hale and hearty" the fifty-one-year-old Roosevelt looked, tanned and extremely fit. "It is true that the mustache, once brown, has grown grayer, but the strong face is not furrowed with deep wrinkles and the crows feet have not changed the expression which is habitual to the man who is in robust health and has a joy in living." After the long African expedition he displayed a leaner physique, but overall, he seemed "the same bubbling, explosively exuberant American as when he left." Archie Butt, however, detected "something different," though at first he could not put his finger on it. After talking with Lodge, the two men speculated that as a citizen of the world, not simply an American, Roosevelt had developed "an enlarged personality," with a "mental scope more encompassing."

At Battery Park, where the *Androscoggin* was due to dock at around 11 a.m., an immense crowd had gathered since early morning, straining for sight of the ship that would bring Roosevelt onto American soil. A reporter captured this mood of anticipation in his story of a stevedore who, in the midst of unloading cargo off another ship, laid aside his hook in hopes of glimpsing Roosevelt. His foreman shouted at him: "You come back here or I'll dock you an hour." The stevedore, undaunted, retorted: "Dock me a week. I'm going to have a look at Teddy."

"There he is!" rose the cry, soon confirmed as a beaming Roosevelt came ashore to a rendition of "Home, Sweet Home" by the Seventy-first Regimental Band. The uplifted cheers that greeted "the man of the hour" as he disembarked were said to exceed the "echoing boom of saluting cannon and the strident blast of steam whistles."

Straightaway, Roosevelt headed from the pier to the speaker's platform. He was in the midst of shaking hands with cabinet members, senators and congressmen, governors and mayors when his daughter Alice cried, "Turn around, father, and look at the crowd." Outspread before him was "one vast expanse of human countenances, all upturned to him, all waiting for him." Beyond the 600 seated guests, 3,500 people stood within the roped enclosure, and beyond them "unnumbered thousands" on the plaza. Still more crammed together on the surrounding streets. It was estimated that at least 100,000 people had come to Battery Park, undeterred by the crushing throngs and the oppressive heat and humidity. From a ninth-floor window of the nearby Washington Building, "a life-size Teddy bear" belted with a green sash was suspended. A large white banner bearing Roosevelt's favorite word, "Delighted," was displayed on the Whitehall Building, where "from street level to skyline every window was open and every sill held as many stenographers and office boys and bosses as the sills could accommodate." Clearly, this was not a day for work!

"Is there a stenographer here?" Roosevelt asked, as he prepared to speak. Assured that one was present, he began, his voice filled with emotion: "No man could receive such a greeting without being made to feel very proud and humble. . . . I have been away a year and a quarter from America and I have seen strange and interesting things alike in the heart of the wilderness and in the capitals of the mightiest and most highly polished civilized nations." Nonetheless, he assured the crowd, "I am more glad than I can say to get home, back in my own country, back among the people I love. And I am ready and eager to do my part so far as I am able in helping to solve problems which must be solved. . . . This is the duty of every citizen but it is peculiarly my duty, for any man who has ever been honored by being made president of the United States is thereby forever after rendered the debtor of the American people." For those who wondered whether Roosevelt would remain active in public life, his brief but eloquent remarks were telling.

The address at Battery Park only served to set off the real celebration. A five-mile parade up Broadway to 59th and Fifth followed, with an estimated 1 million spectators lining the streets. "The sidewalks on both sides of Broadway were jammed with people, from curb to building fronts," the *Chicago Tribune* noted. "There were people in all the windows, people on the housetops, and people banked up in the side streets." As Roosevelt took his place in the open carriage leading the procession, an additional surprise lay in store for him: 150 members of his Rough Rider unit, whom he had led so brilliantly in the Spanish-American War, appeared on horseback to serve as his escort of honor. Beyond the Rough Riders, there were 2,000 additional veterans from that same war who had come to participate in the celebration. The demonstration was "incomparably the largest affair of its kind on record," the Washington, D.C., *Evening Star* claimed, "characteristic of the man himself, the man of superlatives, and of intense moods."

Placards with friendly inscriptions, familiar cartoons, and exhortations for Roosevelt to once again run for the presidency in 1912 hung in shop windows all along the way. At 310 Broadway, an immense Teddy bear stared down an enormous stuffed African lion. At Scribner's, a ten-foot-high portrait of the Colonel in full hunting gear graced the front of the building. Peddlers were everywhere. "You could not move a step," one reporter observed, "without having shoved in your face a remarkable assortment of Teddy souvenirs. There were jungle hats with ribbons bearing the word De-lighted, there were Roosevelt medals, Teddy's teeth in celluloid, miniature Teddy bears, gorgeous flags on canes, with a picture of the Rough Rider, buttons, pins and many other reminders of the Colonel's career." Even along Wall Street, where it was jokingly predicted black crepe would signal Roosevelt's return (given his storied fights with "the malefactors of great wealth"), flags waved and colored streamers were tossed from upper windows.

"Teddy! Teddy! Bully for you, Teddy," the crowd yelled, and he responded with "unconcealed delight" to the gleeful chants. "One could see that he enjoyed every moment of the triumphal progress," the *New York Times* reported, and " those who cheered cheered the louder when they saw how their cheers delighted him." Near the end of the route, a reporter shouted: "Are you tired?" His answer was clear and firm despite the long day, the hot sun, and the perspiration dripping down his face. "Not a bit."

Around 1 p.m., when the parade finally concluded at the 59th Street Plaza, Roosevelt, with tears in his eyes, flashed his dazzling smile and headed toward a private residence for a family lunch. No sooner had the Colonel reached his destination than a frightening storm began. Lightning, thunder, and ferocious winds accompanied a heavy downpour. Uprooted trees littered the ground with fallen limbs. In all, seventeen lives were lost. It seemed the sky had stayed peaceful and blue only for the sun-splashed hours of the celebration for Roosevelt.

"Everyone began talking about Roosevelt luck," Captain Butt observed. While the pelting rain continued, Roosevelt relaxed in the Fifth Avenue home belonging to the grandfather of his son's fiancée and enjoyed a festive meal of chicken in cream sauce with rice while catching up on the news of the day. In the late afternoon, he boarded a special train for his hometown of Oyster Bay, Long Island. Once again, the Roosevelt luck came into play. The severe rainstorm miraculously ceased just as his train pulled in. He was met by "the whole town," complete with a 500-member children's choir, a display of devotion that nearly "swept the former President from his feet as he stepped to the ground." Walking beneath "triumphal arches" constructed by his neighbors, Roosevelt reached a nearby ballpark where grandstands had been raised to seat 3,000 people. There, he spoke movingly of what it meant to be home once more, "to live among you again as I have for the last 40 years." Reporters who had followed Roosevelt since he began shaking hands on the *Kaiserin* that morning marveled at the energy with which he continued to grasp the hands of his neighbors, finding something personal to say to one and all, without revealing "the slightest trace of fatigue in voice or manner."

In their lengthy coverage of the historic day, the press corps brought to light scores of colorful anecdotes. The story they failed to get, however, was the story they wanted above all—Roosevelt's response to the major political issue of the day: the growing disenchantment of progressive Republicans with the leadership of President Taft.

As HIS SECOND TERM NEARED its end, Roosevelt had handpicked from his cabinet the trusted friend he desired to succeed him: William Howard Taft. The two men had first met in their early thirties, when Roosevelt headed the Civil Service Commission and Taft was U.S. Solicitor General. "We lived in the same part of Washington," Taft recalled, "our wives knew each other well, and some of our children were born about the same time." Over the years, this friendship had deepened, becoming what Taft described as "one of close and sweet intimacy." During his first presidential term, Roosevelt had invited Taft, then governor general of the newly acquired Philippine Islands, to serve as his secretary of war. Initially reluctant to leave a post to which his talents were ideally suited, Taft had finally been persuaded to join his old friend's administration as "the foremost member" of his cabinet, his daily "counsellor and adviser in all the great questions" that might confront them.

Roosevelt had thrown all his inexhaustible energy behind the drive to make Taft president. "I am quite as nervous about your campaign as I should be if it were my own," he had told Taft. He had edited Taft's speeches, relayed a constant stream of advice, and corralled his own immense bloc of supporters behind Taft's candidacy. When Taft was elected, Roosevelt reveled in the victory, both delighted for a "beloved" friend and confident that America had chosen the man best suited to execute the progressive goals Roosevelt had championed—to distribute the nation's wealth more equitably, regulate the giant corporations and railroads, strengthen the rights of labor, and protect the country's natural resources from private exploitation.

At the start of Roosevelt's presidency in 1901, big business had been in the driver's seat. While the country prospered as never before, squalid conditions were rampant in immigrant slums, workers in factories and mines labored without safety regulations, and farmers fought with railroads over freight rates. Voices had been raised to protest the concentration of corporate wealth and the gap between rich and poor, yet the doctrine of laissez-faire precluded collective action to ameliorate social conditions. Under Roosevelt's Square Deal, the country had awakened to the need for government action to allay problems caused by industrialization—an awakening spurred in part by the dramatic exposés of a talented group of investigative journalists he famously labeled "muckrakers."

By the end of Roosevelt's tenure, much had been accomplished. The moribund 1890 Sherman Anti-Trust Act had been revived, vast acres of lands had been protected from exploitation, and railroads had been prevented from continuing long-standing abuses. Congress had passed workmen's compensation, a pure food and drug law, and a meat inspection act. Nevertheless, much remained to be done. Roosevelt's legacy would depend upon the actions of his chosen successor—William Howard Taft. "Taft is as fine a fellow as ever sat in the President's chair," Roosevelt told a friend shortly after the election, "and I cannot express the measureless content that comes over me as I think that the work in which I have so much believed will be carried on by him."

While he was abroad, however, Roosevelt had received numerous disturbing communications from his progressive friends. Word that his closest ally in the conservation movement, Chief Forester Gifford Pinchot, had been removed by Taft, left Roosevelt dumbfounded: "I do not know any man in public life who has rendered quite the service you have rendered," he wrote to Pinchot, "and it seems to be absolutely impossible that there can be any truth in this statement." When the news was confirmed, he asked Pinchot to meet him in Europe in order to hear his firsthand account. Pinchot had arrived with a number of letters from fellow progressives, all expressing a belief that Taft had aligned himself with old-line conservatives on Capitol Hill and was gradually compromising Roosevelt's hard-won advances.

Roosevelt found it difficult to believe he had so misjudged the character and convictions of his old friend. On his final day in Europe, he confided his puzzlement to Sir Edward Grey as the two outdoorsmen tramped through the New Forest in southern England in pursuit of the song or sight of several English birds Roosevelt had only read about. "Roosevelt's spirit was much troubled by what was happening in his own country since he left office," Grey recalled. "He spoke of Taft and of their work together with very live affection; he had wished Taft to succeed him, had supported him, made way for him. How could he now break with Taft and attack him?" Yet the concerted voice of his progressive friends was urging him to do precisely that.

All through the spring of 1910, as the date of his return approached, one question had dominated political discourse and speculation: "What will

Mr. Roosevelt do?" Which side would he take in the intensifying struggle that was dividing the Republican Party between the old-line conservatives and a steadily growing number of "insurgents," as the progressive faction was then known. Aware that anything he said would be construed as hurtful or helpful to one side or the other, Roosevelt determined to remain silent on all political matters until he could more fully absorb and analyze the situation. "There is one thing I want, and that is absolute privacy," he told reporters as the day's celebration came to an end. "I want to close up like a native oyster . . . I am glad to have you all here; but . . . I have nothing to say."

THE WEEKS PRECEDING ROOSEVELT'S HOMECOMING had been especially difficult for President Taft. "He looks haggard and careworn," Captain Butt told his sister-in-law, Clara. His characteristic ruddy complexion had faded to a sickly pale, his weight had ballooned to 320 pounds, and his jovial temperament had turned mournful. "It is hard on any man to see the eyes of everyone turn to another person as the eyes of the entire country are turning to Roosevelt," Butt speculated. Nonetheless, Butt acknowledged that Taft's low spirits had little to do with jealousy. Never once had he heard Taft "murmur against the fate" that kept him, "a man of tremendous personality himself . . . in the shadow" of his predecessor. "He is so broad as to show no resentment" of his "secondary role," Butt marveled. Rather, Taft's anxiety stemmed, he thought, from the fact that "he loves Theodore Roosevelt," and the specter of a potential rupture in their friendship was causing great emotional distress.

No shadow of such troubles was in evidence when Taft's presidency began. "He is going to be greatly beloved as President," Roosevelt had predicted. "He has the most lovable personality I have ever come in contact with." A big man with a big heart, clear blue eyes, and a thoughtful nature, Taft was portrayed as "America incarnate—sham-hating, hardworking, crackling with jokes upon himself, lacking in pomp but never in dignity . . . a great, boyish, wholesome, dauntless, shrewd, sincere, kindly gentleman."

The time had come, even Roosevelt's most ardent admirers agreed, for a different kind of leader—a quieter, less controversial figure. Roosevelt, with his fiery temperament, inexhaustible supply of arresting quips, and demagogic appeals, had given powerful voice to the Progressive movement. Now, Roosevelt's journalist friend William Allen White argued, the country needed a man who could "finish the things" Roosevelt had begun, who could work with Congress to consolidate the imperfect statutes and executive orders generated in the tumultuous previous years. Although Taft would "say little," White acknowledged, he would "do much." His mind would not, like Roosevelt's, move "by flashes or whims or sudden impulses," another journalist wrote, but rather with steady efficiency, "in straight lines and by long, logical habit."

Taft agreed with this assessment of the situation he faced. He likened Roosevelt's administration to "a great crusade" that had aroused the people to the need for greater federal regulation of the economy. Now it was the work of his administration to make these expanded powers "permanent in the form of law." In contrast to Roosevelt, a career politician whose "intense desire to reach practical results" had led him occasionally to chafe under "the restraint of legal methods," Taft had trained as a lawyer and a judge, disciplines that had instilled "the necessity for legal method." Roosevelt had ended his presidency "in an ugly fight" with a Congress he had sought to bypass through a direct appeal to the public. With a very different yet complementary temperament, Taft insisted that he must work "with the tools and the men . . . at hand." It was his misfortune to take office at a time marked by a bitter rift within the Republican Party, when progressives viewed compromise with conservatives as treachery.

Taft had not openly sought the presidency. Since his appointment as a superior court judge at the age of twenty-nine, he had aspired to one day become chief justice of the United States. He had moved swiftly up the judicial ladder, becoming U.S. Solicitor General at age thirty-two and a federal circuit judge at thirty-four. When President McKinley asked him to go to the Philippines, it was with the implied promise that he would return to a Supreme Court appointment. When Roosevelt became president, he honored his predecessor's promise, twice offering Taft a position on the Supreme Court. With great reluctance, Taft had declined both opportunities; in the first instance, he felt he could not leave his work in the Philippines unfinished; in the second, his wife and closest adviser, Nellie, persuaded him not to bury himself on the Court at the very moment when, as secretary of war, he was being touted throughout the country as Roosevelt's most likely successor. Indeed, were it not for his wife's White House dreams, Taft would likely never have agreed to a presidential run.

Taft had found little joy in campaigning for the presidency in 1908. He had "great misgivings" about every speech he was forced to make. For months, the thought of his acceptance speech loomed over him "like a nightmare." He feared that his efforts to forge a middle ground on issues would "make many people mad." Unlike Roosevelt, who regularly perused articles about himself and found pleasure in responding to critics, Taft acknowledged that negative press left him "very, very discouraged." After a while, despite Nellie's urg ings, he refused to read unfavorable articles altogether. His speeches, Nellie warned, tended to be much too long. "But I am made this way and 'I can do no other,' " he told her. "That is the kind of an old slow coach you married." In the end, with his "campaign manager" (as he called Nellie) by his side to edit his speeches and offer advice, comfort, and encouragement, he won a magnificent victory over William Jennings Bryan.

Taft took office in 1909 with commingled exhilaration and trepidation. "I pinch myself every little while to make myself realize that it is all true," he told a friend. "If I were now presiding in the Supreme Court of the United States as Chief Justice, I should feel entirely at home, but with the troubles of selecting a cabinet and the difficulties in respect to the revision of the tariff, I feel just a bit like a fish out of water." More than a year later, such misgivings had not subsided. When asked if he liked being president, he replied that he "would rather be Chief Justice," for the "quieter life" on the Court would prove "more in keeping with my temperament." However, he reflected, "when taken into consideration that I go into history as a President, and my children and my children's children are the better placed on account of that fact, I am inclined to think that to be President well compensates one for all the trials and criticisms he has to bear and undergo."

Taft well knew how fortunate he was to have a natural politician in his devoted and intelligent wife, one whose superb judgment and political acumen could help him "overcome the obstacles that just at present seem formidable." They had been partners from the earliest days of their married life in Cincinnati. Like Edith and Theodore, Nellie and Will had grown up together in the same city. Their sisters had been "schoolmates," and their fathers, Nellie wrote, had "practiced law at the same bar for more than forty years." Nellie and Will had been friends for six years when their relationship began to deepen into love.

Young Nellie was an unconventional woman. From early adolescence, she craved a more expansive life. She liked to smoke, drink beer, and play cards for money. She was an avid reader with a passion for classical music, a talented writer, and a dedicated teacher. In her early twenties, she had organized a weekly salon, with Will and his brother Horace among the regular participants. Every Saturday night their circle of six or seven friends presented essays and discussed literature and national politics "with such high feeling and enthusiasm," Nellie recalled, that the history of the salon "became the history of our lives during that period." The more time he spent with Nellie, Will told his father, "the deeper grew my respect for her, the warmer my friendship until it unconsciously ripened into a feeling that she was indispensable to my happiness. . . . Her eagerness for knowledge of all kinds puts me to shame. Her capacity for work is wonderful."

For her part, Nellie found in Will a husband who adored her and highly valued her intelligence. Their union provided a channel for her to pursue her intense ambition to accomplish something vital in life. Will also proved a loving father for their three children, Robert, Helen, and Charlie, who were eighteen, sixteen, and eleven when Taft became president. Throughout their marriage, Taft looked to Nellie as a "merciless but loving critic," depending on her advice at every crucial juncture. They labored together over his speeches and discussed political strategy in a manner, one observer recalled, much like "two men who are intimate chums." Their partnership gave Taft confidence that he would learn to navigate the uncharted waters of the presidency.

The *New York Times* predicted that with Nellie Taft as first lady, "the Taft Administration will be brilliant beyond any similar period in America's social history." Over the years, she had established a sterling reputation as a democratic hostess, opening her doors to people from all backgrounds. In the Philippines, she had stunned the conservative military establishment by rejecting their strict segregation of whites and native Filipinos, instead insisting "upon complete racial equality" at the governor's palace. As first lady, she brought the same egalitarian ethos to her position. She spoke out against the unhealthy working conditions of government employees and embarked upon several civic projects. She helped design a beautiful public park along the Tidal Basin where concerts could be held every week during the summer months, and made arrangements to bring the same flowering cherry trees she had admired in Japan to the nation's capital.

Nellie Taft was swiftly becoming one of the most respected and powerful first ladies in history. Then, only ten weeks after the inauguration, terrible misfortune shattered these auspicious beginnings. On board the presidential yacht with her husband and some guests, Nellie suffered a devastating stroke that left her temporarily paralyzed and unable to speak. At the sight of his half-conscious wife, only forty-seven years old, Taft turned "deathly pale." Taft's "great soul," Archie Butt empathized, was "wrapped in darkness." Although Nellie gradually recovered the ability to walk, she would continue to struggle with her speech the rest of her life.

A year after Nellie's stroke, shortly before Roosevelt was due to return to America, Taft sent him a plaintive handwritten letter weighing his accomplishments and failures as president. "I have had a hard time," he confided. "I do not know that I have had harder luck than other presidents but I do know that thus far I have succeeded far less than have others. I have been conscientiously trying to carry out your policies but my method of doing so has not worked smoothly." In closing, he told his old friend, "it would give me a great deal of pleasure if after you get settled at Oyster Bay, you could come over to Washington and spend a few days at the White House."

Taft had been tempted to go to New York and personally welcome Roosevelt home. According to one report in the *Indianapolis Star*, his advisers had suggested that "this demonstration of amity would be appreciated by Col. Roosevelt and would do more than anything else to drive away the suspicion that seems to have gained ground that the relations between the chief executive and his predecessor are strained." Upon reflection, however, Taft concluded that it would diminish the status of the presidential office "if he were to 'race down to the gangplank,' to be the first to shake hands with the former President." He explained to his military aide that he was "charged with the dignity of the Executive" and was determined to "say nothing that will put a momentary slight even on that great office." No matter how much he would rather be Will, welcoming his friend Theodore, he was now *President* Taft. "I think, moreover, that [Roosevelt] will appreciate this feeling in me," he concluded, "and would be the first one to resent the slightest subordination of the office of President to any man."

Instead, he planned a journey of his own that day—a train trip to Villanova, Pennsylvania, to deliver the commencement address at the Catholic university, followed by a visit to the small town of West Chester, and a second commencement address at a celebrated black institution, Lincoln University. "When you are being hammered," Taft explained, "not only by the press, but by members of your own party in Washington, and one feels there isn't anything quite right that he can do, the pleasure of going out into the country, of going into a city that hasn't seen a president for twenty years, and then makes a fuss over him to prove to him that there is somebody that doesn't know of his defects, is a pleasure I don't like to forego."

He boarded the train at Union Station in Washington for a departure to Philadelphia at 7 a.m., the very hour at which Roosevelt's ocean liner reached New York. Before the train left, it was noted that he "read with deep interest the latest news of the homecoming of Col. Roosevelt." Arriving at Philadelphia shortly before ten thirty, he was taken by special locomotive to Villanova, where he was met by a delegation of over five hundred professors and students. The college had arranged to bring all "the members of the faculty, the entire student body and all the townspeople that could get to the station in traps, autos and on foot." As the president stepped from the locomotive, "the Villanova band played 'Hail to the Chief' and the college boys let out one concentrated, prolonged and tremendous yell." Charmed by the rousing welcome, Taft broke into a beaming smile.

The entire visit to Villanova proved a gratifying relief from the besieging trials of the presidency. The commencement exercises took place in the college auditorium, gaily decorated with bunting and flags. Since the auditorium held only 2,500 invited guests, arrangements had been made for Taft to deliver his address outside, so that an overflow crowd of 5,000 people who had been gathering on the grounds since early morning might hear him. "The Roosevelt luck" that graced the former president's celebration in New York with sunny skies did not hold for Taft, however; the sky blackened with thunderclouds just as he was set to start his address, prompting a reluctant decision to speak indoors.

Despite the sudden change, Taft's address was received with enthusiasm. He applauded the Augustinians' missionary work in the Philippines and spoke wistfully of his years as governor general—perhaps the most fulfilling of his political career. An outburst of applause greeted every positive reference to the Catholic Church, and when he finished his speech, the entire audience rose in loud acclamation.

With lifted spirits, Taft boarded a special train to West Chester, home to Republican congressman Thomas S. Butler. Butler had remained loyal to Taft through all the difficult days of his presidency. Now Taft graciously repaid him by making a "flying visit" to the little town to deliver two short speeches extolling his steadfast supporter. "He came to me at the beginning of my administration," Taft said of Butler, "and declared he was going to stand by me to the end—he probably didn't know how much that meant." The townspeople were thrilled to see the president. "Banks, office buildings, residences and the post office were a mass of colors," one correspondent wrote, "while displayed on a number of buildings were the ten foot high letters T-A-F-T."

The president continued on to the campus of Lincoln University, arriving just as "a terrific electrical storm raged overhead." Undeterred, 2,000 people patiently stood on the grounds in the pouring rain without even the protection of umbrellas. "I thank you sincerely for coming out to greet me," he humbly told the cheering crowd. "I understand that it is to the President of the United States, and I accept it as such." In his well-received address, Taft referred to Booker T. Washington as "one of the greatest men of the century" and called on the black community to develop its own educated leaders to help solve the nation's racial problems.

Despite Taft's heartfelt reception all along his route, the press could not resist drawing comparisons between the outright jubilation that marked Roosevelt's sunlit homecoming on the seacoast and the decorous approval accorded the president in the rain-drenched interior. Furthermore, while Roosevelt seemed as fresh and buoyant at day's end as when he disembarked, Taft was "travel-stained" and exhausted when he boarded the train back to Washington. One reporter went so far as to portray the overweight Taft "in a free state of perspiration . . . suffering from so much prickly heat that it pushes his clothes out from him," making it impossible for him to keep his shirt buxom in place. On his way home, Taft read the afternoon newspaper accounts of Roosevelt's homecoming reception, doubtless taking note of the Colonel's remark that he stood "ready and eager" to do his part in solving the country's ills.

When the president reached the White House shortly before ten o'clock, his weariness abruptly vanished with news that his bill to expand the federal government's power to prevent arbitrary increases in railroad rates had passed Congress that day and was awaiting his signature. Even in the worst of times, when bombarded by criticism in insurgent newspapers for his willingness to deal with the conservative bloc in the Congress, Taft had retained "an abiding faith" that if he could secure legislation the country needed, "the credit would take care of itself ultimately." Now, with the passage of his railroad bill, he could allow himself a bit of optimism. In the previous session, he had secured a corporation tax bill, hailed as "the first positive step toward the National supervision of great corporations," as well as an amendment to the Interstate Commerce Act that gave the commission "for the first time, the power to prevent stock-watering."

In addition to the railroad bill, two important progressive measures were about to receive his signature: the first confirmed presidential authority to withdraw millions of acres of land for conservation; the second, a postal savings bill "fought at every step by powerful interests," provided the poor a secure place to deposit their money. That very afternoon, in fact, the lead editorial in the Philadelphia *Evening Bulletin* suggested that Taft "had unquestionably strengthened his position in the public esteem, within the last thirty days," as the country was "beginning to realize more clearly the essential force that lies behind his quiet, persistent methods. . . . His policy throughout has been that of a resolute defender of the public interest who preferred to work without parade or ostentation."

As he went to sleep that night, Taft could take heart that Roosevelt, too, would recognize the necessity that led him to deal with the conservatives. He was working in his own, unspectacular way to accomplish the progressive goals that both shared with equal fervor. That morning, he had dispatched Captain Butt to deliver a second handwritten letter to Roosevelt as he landed in New York. He warmly reiterated the invitation tendered to Roosevelt three weeks earlier, to join him at the White House. Once reunited, despite the swirling tensions and innuendo, they might enjoy the camaraderie of the old days, when, as Roosevelt's sister Corinne recalled, they had so enjoyed one another's company that "their laughs would mingle and reverberate through the corridors and rooms, and Edith would say, 'It is always that way when they are together.' "

The restoration of their old friendship—a matter more in Roosevelt's hands than in Taft's—was not simply a private concern: "No other friendship in our modern politics has meant more to the American people," William Allen White wrote, "for it has made two most important and devoted public servants wiser, kindlier, more useful men."

"The whole country waits and wonders," the *Baltimore Sun* noted in a prescient editorial. Roosevelt "seems to hold the future of his party in the hollow of his hand. Taft looks to him for succor. The Insurgents know if they can win his support the Regulars will be swept away. Old leaders tremble, new aspirants take hope. His decision is important to the country, and even more important to himself. Many another has risen to the heights of popularity to be dethroned in a day. Has Roosevelt reached the pinnacle of his fame, or is he to move forward to fresh conquests? It rests with him. He is at the height of his mental and physical powers. He possesses a great influence over the masses of his countrymen. Such power is a tremendous weapon for good or evil. How will he wield it?"

To understand the complex contours of this consequential friendship, however, we must go backward in time to analyze the similarities in experience that initially drew Roosevelt and Taft together and the differences in temperament that now threatened to split them apart.

CHAPTER TWO

Will and Teedie

"Teedie" Roosevelt, age four, and Will Taft, age seven.

WILLIAM HOWARD TAFT WAS BORN on September 15, 1857, in a two-story yellow brick house in a fashionable neighborhood on Mt. Auburn, one of the hills surrounding Cincinnati. Six days after his birth, his father, Alphonso, proudly noted to a friend: "Louise is getting along astonishing well and the baby is fat & healthy." In the hours after the birth, he explained, Louise "had a fair prospect of milk and on the 3d day the boy had plenty," but a few days later, the infant's "clamorous appetite" necessitated a wet nurse to supplement his mother's milk supply. The plump, ravenous new baby provided welcome relief to his parents. Their first child, Samuel, had been frail from birth and had died of whooping cough at fourteen months, the year before Will was born.

At two months, his mother recorded, Will was "very large for his age, and grows fat every day." Indeed, she noted with amazement and pride, "he has such a large waist, that he cannot wear any of the dresses that we made with belts." While his rapid growth kept her busy making ever larger clothes, she "took great comfort" in his "perfect good health" and his fullness of flesh. "The care of him fills in some measure the void left by Sammy's death," she wrote her mother, "but I am constantly thinking how interesting [Sammy] would be now if he had lived and how pleasant to have two little boys growing up together."

Will's sweet, open nature was evident from infancy. "He spreads his hands to anyone who will take him and his face is wreathed in smiles at the slightest provocation," Louise told her sister, Delia Torrey. His parents admired his cherubic face, "a solitary dimple in one cheek," his eyes "deeply, darkly, beautifully blue." Finding great pleasure and solace in her "healthy, fast-growing boy," Louise happily acquiesced to his insistence "upon being held whenever he is awake," even if she felt her "hands and feet were tied" to the child. "Mother would think it poor management," she confided in Delia, "but I do not understand making him take care of himself." Her torment at losing her firstborn had convinced her that children "are treasures lent not given and that they may be recalled at any time." Parents, she firmly believed, could never "love their children too much."

Louise Torrey came from a line of strong, intelligent women. Her mother, Susan Waters Torrey, had studied philosophy and astronomy at Amherst Academy and possessed a vibrant intellectual curiosity, an interest in anti-slavery politics, and an appreciation for art. After her marriage to merchant Samuel Torrey, they settled in Boston, where she relished the rich culture and lively debates over the critical issues of the day. To her "great disappointment," her husband, hopeful that country air would improve his health, moved the family to the small town of Millbury, Massachusetts. In Millbury, her spirits plummeted. "She has great mental and physical activity," her daughter Delia noted, "and there is not a man or woman in town with whom she can have any satisfactory intellectual conversation." Lacking any immediate outlet for her talents and energy, she shared the frustration of many educated women in the mid-nineteenth century. "Mother, you know, is very ambitious," Delia dryly wrote Louise, "and ambition in a woman is synonymous with unhappiness."

Resolved to give her daughters opportunity for intellectual development and involvement in a broader world, Susan Torrey exposed Louise and Delia to good literature, lyceum lectures in Boston, theatre in New York. They studied for a time in New Haven, Connecticut, and attended Mount Holyoke College in South Hadley, Massachusetts. Cherishing their freedom, they taught at Monson Academy in Maine, studied music, attended opera, and traveled together through Canada, New England, and New York. Both rejected eligible suitors in favor of their own liberated lives. When one disappointed young man upbraided Delia for willfulness, she retorted: "If 'ladies of strong minds seldom marry,' I suppose the reverse proves true and ladies with weak minds usually do. I prefer to belong to the first class even though it precluded me from marrying."

Louise was twenty-six when she was introduced to forty-three-year-old Alphonso Taft at the home of her uncle, Reverend Samuel Dutton, pastor of North Church in New Haven, a meeting that would alter her existence in an unexpectedly domestic direction. Alphonso had grown up on a small farm in West Townsend, Vermont, the only child of Peter Rawson Taft and Sylvia Howard. "One day in an oat field," he later recalled, he "first told his father of his dream of going to college." The expense would be a hardship for the family, but "to the boy's intense delight," his parents decided to support his education. To help out, Alphonso taught school in Vermont for several years before entering Yale. He made the 140-mile trek from Vermont to New Haven on foot. After graduating Phi Beta Kappa, he taught in a boarding school for two years and then returned to Yale, where he became a tutor and studied law. "He had sacrificed so much and had been so earnest in his pursuit of an education," his youngest son Horace observed, "that everything that he learned in college was sacred in his eyes."

Although Alphonso had initially hoped to practice law in New York, a short stay there changed his mind: "I feel well assured I might make a living in that city, but I dont think it the place for me," he concluded. "I dislike the character of the New York Bar exceedingly. . . . Money is the all in all . . . nothing else brings honor." He decided instead to go west, finding "the Queen City" of Cincinnati a far more congenial place. "There are no such high partition walls here, between different classes," he wrote his mother. "Here & there a family is beginning to stiffen up & assume consequential airs, but they are comparatively few." Perhaps most significant to a man who had striven so hard for his own education, Alphonso found Cincinnati "honourably famous for its free schools," as the visiting Charles Dickens noted, "of which it has so many that no person's child among its population can by possibility want the means of education."

While studying for the Ohio bar, Alphonso clerked in the office of a fellow Vermonter with an established practice. In these early years, he depended for his livelihood on the small sums his parents could send. "I have not spent one dollar," he assured them in 1839, "not a farthing for any amusement, or for anything which was not a matter of immediate, & necessary use." With hard work and untiring discipline, he succeeded in building a successful practice that allowed him to buy the substantial two-story house on Mt. Auburn set back from the street on a stretch of green lawn. There he lived with his first wife, Fanny, an intelligent, scholarly young woman, until tuberculosis took her life at twenty-nine. She left him with two sons, Charley, ten, and Peter, six.

Though Alphonso was seventeen years older than Louise Torrey when they met in New Haven, his handsome face, muscular physique, and abundant energy bridged the years between them. She agreed to marry in 1853 and moved with him to Cincinnati, where she grew to love her "noble husband" with a heart "full of a deep and quiet joy." For his part, Alphonso rejoiced in the affection Louise showed his two older sons, who came to love her as if she were their own mother. "I do feel under the greatest obligation to you, my dear Louise, for the great care and attention you have given to the lads," he wrote to her several years before Will's birth.

Within months of her marriage, Louise confided to Delia that she had "the best husband in the United States." For Delia, the loss of her sister's companionship was devastating. "Oh, Louise, Louise how can I live the rest of my life without you?" she lamented. "I am but half of a pair of scissors." As the months passed, however, the gentle Alphonso made Delia an integral part of her sister's new family.

The family expanded rapidly after Will's birth, eventually containing six children including Charley and Peter. Henry Waters (always called Harry) was born two years after Will, followed quickly by Horace Dutton, and finally by a long-desired girl named Fanny in honor of Alphonso's first wife. As the children grew, good-natured Will remained the center of his parents' affection. "I had more pride in Willie than in all the rest," Louise acknowledged. "Willie is foremost," agreed Alphonso, "and I am inclined to think he will always be so." Rather than displaying the jealousy this favored status might easily have provoked, Will's siblings responded to his "simplicity, courage, honesty, and kindliness"—qualities he shared with his father—with devoted affection. "If flattery or admiration could have spoiled him he would have been ruined before he emerged from childhood," Horace recalled, but "his personality made him a favorite everywhere." The younger brother's fond dedication to Will never wavered. "It was very hard for anybody to be near him without loving him," Horace recollected when he had passed his eightieth birthday.

Even as his family grew and his career flourished, Alphonso Taft was rarely able to relinquish the rigid self-discipline that had enabled him to forge a comfortable existence. "Scarcely a night would pass that he was not bent over a table deep in papers or books he had brought from his office," William's biographer Henry Pringle notes. "We might almost as well ask a train of cars to go out of its course to carry a passenger," Delia lovingly observed, "as to expect Mr. Taft to turn aside from his business for the pursuit of pleasure." To Alphonso, work and family were paramount, and in that order.

Living on the wooded slope of Mt. Auburn with the entire city below "spread out before you like a map" gave the children "the advantages of both city and country," Horace recalled. Left to their own devices, the children rambled and explored. In the nearby pond, "we learned to swim, but not because anybody taught us. . . . We went fishing or on long hikes . . . we had plenty of games, but they were not organized." Looking back years later, Horace wished that they "had been taught to sail, or to rough it," been exposed more to the woods, been challenged by experiences that would have broadened their education. If not adventurous, the life he remembered seemed "wholesome and natural."

Many citizens of Cincinnati, linked to the South through commerce, sympathized with the Confederacy when the Civil War broke out, but Alphonso had long held anti-slavery views. He had been a delegate to the first Republican Convention in 1856, and after Ohio's Salmon Chase failed to secure the presidential nomination in 1860, he supported Abraham Lincoln. He sold government bonds, delivered speeches promoting emancipation, and argued government cases against the Copperhead faction at the request of Secretary of War Edwin Stanton. When news of General Lee's surrender came, "the city fairly blossomed with flags, and everybody turned out to join in a rejoicing which included all parties," Louise told her sister. "Almost every house on Mt. Auburn was lighted to its utmost extent and many were luxuriously ornamented." Hours after the celebration came word of Lincoln's assassination. "The transition from such a jubilee to the unlooked-for calamity of the next morning seemed too great to be believed," she lamented. "The symbols of joy which had been universal were turned into mourning, and the city is draped and creped from one end to the other."

Eight months after the war ended, Alphonso was appointed to fill a vacancy on the Cincinnati Superior Court bench. The following year, he was elected to a full term on the Republican ticket, and two years afterward, he was nominated and elected to the court by both Republicans and Democrats. "He was . . . a born judge," his son Horace proudly remembered. "He had the judicial temperament, the moral courage, the ability and patience."

The most important opinion Judge Taft rendered on the superior court upheld the right of the local school board to prohibit the reading of the Bible in public schools. He argued in a dissenting opinion that "the Constitution of the State did not recognize the Christian religion any more than it recognized the religions of any other citizens of the state" and that "the school board had an obligation as well as a right to keep religious partisanship out of the public schools." Alphonso was forever proud of his opinion, even though it prompted fierce opposition from conservatives.

For Alphonso, nothing equaled the honor of his judicial calling; indeed, he could envision no office higher than a seat on the Supreme Court. "To be Chief Justice of the United States," he told Salmon Chase after Lincoln had announced Chase's appointment to the Court, "is more than to be President, in my estimation." Nonetheless, after six years on the superior court, Alphonso recognized that his judicial salary could not meet the expenses involved in educating his large family. Reluctantly, he resigned his judgeship and returned to private practice. "No leader of the Bar ever left the court feeling that his case had been too difficult or deep for the Judge's understanding and learning," a distinguished lawyer wrote at the time of his resignation. "No beginner at the Bar ever left feeling that the case had been too small and unimportant for the Judge's patience and kindness."

Over the years, Alphonso became increasingly involved in the community life of Cincinnati. As a city councilman, he fought to extend the city line to annex a newly built section so that "rich real estate holders" living there would have to pay "their just share of taxes." He joined future president Rutherford B. Hayes, future Supreme Court justice Stanley Matthews, and lawyer John W. Herron, Nellie's father, as charter members of the Literary Club. And Alphonso and Louise were instrumental in founding the House of Refuge, a progressive reform school designed to return delinquent children to "the path of virtue and integrity." Taking a liberal perspective, Alphonso argued that "these children are unfortunate rather than criminal." Their delinquency, he maintained, was "not the product of nature" but rather of the "cruel circumstances" into which they were born.

At the suggestion of a group of prominent Republicans, Alphonso allowed his name to be put forward as a candidate for governor of Ohio. Though he lost at the convention to his friend Rutherford Hayes, in large part because of widespread opposition to his position on school prayer, his unblemished reputation for being "as honest as the day is long" caught the attention of President Ulysses S. Grant, who brought him into his cabinet. He served first as secretary of war and then as attorney general during Grant's final months in office, where he was seen as a representative of the "reform element" against the "old regime." While he enjoyed his short stint in Washington, he was happy to return to his beloved Cincinnati and resume the practice of law.

Alphonso and Louise supported and expected excellence in their children, pushing them at every level to succeed in their studies. Charley attended Yale and went on to Columbia Law School. Peter followed his brother to Yale, graduating first in his class with the best record ever achieved to that time. The pressure upon Will, his parents' favorite child, to match the sterling records of his older half brothers created anxiety. From his grammar school days, he had to work harder than his fellow students to succeed. His tendency to procrastinate when anxious about assignments further intensified his nervousness. In the afternoons he was frequently seen reading under a tree on the grassy lawn in the front of his house. He was ridiculed by passing neighborhood boys for not playing ball, mocked because he was a "fatty," a "lubber" who could not keep up in their rough-and-tumble games. "If you can't walk," they taunted, "we'll roll you, old butter ball." Refusing to be provoked, he merely smiled and returned to his book.

The desire to please his parents became central to young Taft's temperament and development. At the age of seven he was reading, but his mother had to work with him in "arithmetic and writing." "He means to be a scholar and studies well," Alphonso proudly recorded. "I have never had any little boy show a better spirit in that respect." When he fell to fifth in his class, Alphonso tersely declared: "Mediocrity will not do for Will." By the age of twelve, his last year in grammar school, he ranked first in his class, earning both his school's highest medal and his father's praise. "His average was 95," Alphonso told Delia, "and the nearest to him averaged 85. This was doing uncommonly well, and makes us all very happy." His younger brothers were conscientious students as well, placing second and third in their respective classes. "We felt that the sun shone brighter if we brought home good reports," Horace recalled. Yet each successful performance only fueled higher expectations, giving Will, who drove himself intensely to perform, little peace. Years later, his mother realized the mechanism they had unwittingly fostered: "Love of approval," she acknowledged, became her adored son's "besetting fault."

In the summer of 1869, when Will was eleven, Alphonso and Louise sailed to Europe to join their older sons, Charley and Peter, who were studying and traveling abroad with the aid of $50,000 bequeathed to each upon the death of their maternal grandfather, Judge Phelps. For Charley, Europe proved life-altering, awakening a love of music, art, and theatre that would continue to deepen in the years ahead. Of all the Taft boys, Charley seemed best able to balance study and relaxation. For Peter, the most brilliant yet brittle of the brothers, the desire to meet his father's expectations produced a chronic state of nervous exhaustion, marked by headaches and eye trouble. His family hoped that the year in Europe would restore his spirits.

Will and his younger siblings remained behind during this European sojourn, missing excursions to historical sites in England, Italy, and Germany that would likely have provided far more vivid and spacious lessons than the daily round of class work in their local grammar school. In their letters from abroad, the parents suggested readings that would connect their sons to their various stops along the way. When they reached Liverpool, Louise advised Will to "read up in the Gazetteer and Encyclopedia of this the greatest harbor in the world," trusting that the knowledge his parents were there would "make his geography real & impressive to him." Writing from Rome, where he had visited the supposed site of Julius Caesar's assassination at the base of Pompey's colossal statue, Alphonso re-created for Will the story of Caesar's rivalry with Pompey and the struggle with the senators that led to his death.

In the fall of 1870, Will entered rigorous Woodward High, a public school for college-bound students in downtown Cincinnati. His years there were marked by the same pattern of hard work, procrastination, and an anxiety driven by his need to maintain the family standard of excellence. In his study of Taft's early education, the historian David Burton concludes that Will left high school with "a mastery of fact and a commitment to disciplined study, rather than a sense of an intellectual adventure." Horace Taft, who eventually became a celebrated educator, recalled the learning environment of their childhood home and concluded that "the most conspicuous thing about it was its limitations. My father was very ambitious for all of his children but, like most Americans of that day, thought of education as a school affair and as connected almost exclusively with the school curriculum. . . . We had no music, no art, no mechanical training, and our reading was done with very little guidance." So long as his children worked hard and performed well, Alphonso believed his obligation regarding their education had been met.

The winter of Will's senior year, his brother Charley, who was then practicing law in Cincinnati, married Annie Sinton, the only daughter of the city's wealthiest man, iron king David Sinton. Charley's wedding to Annie Sinton was "the great social event" of the year. Long afterward, Nellie Herron Taft, who was twelve at the time, recalled the excitement of the gala staged at the splendid Sinton mansion situated at the top of her street. A long and happy marriage commenced when the young couple moved into that mansion with Annie's widowed father. Charley would eventually leave the law to become publisher of the *Cincinnati Times*, which merged into the *Evening Star* to form the *Times-Star*, a Taft family holding for the next seven decades. Over the years, Charley accrued considerable wealth that would help provide a foundation for Will's public service career.

Even as a high school student, Will began to develop a progressive sensitivity informed by the feminist teachings of his mother and grandmother. His inclinations for social justice were reflected in a thoughtful essay he wrote during his senior year. "The result of coeducation of the sexes shows clearly that there is no mental inferiority on the part of the girls," he asserted. These views echoed the liberal views of his mother, who was incensed by an article in the *New York Times* suggesting that "from their constitutional peculiarities girls cannot be pushed in school as rapidly as can boys." Moving beyond coeducation, Will argued for woman's suffrage. "Give the woman the ballot, and you will make her more important in the eyes of the world." The right to vote, he optimistically predicted, would beget other benefits. "Every woman would then be given an opportunity to earn a livelihood. She would suffer no decrease in compensation for her labor, on account of her sex. . . . It becomes this country, as a representative of liberty, to lead in this great reform."

Will graduated second in his high school class, with an average of 91, earning him an acceptance at Yale. Still, his father expressed concern about his work habits, citing a teacher who believed the only obstacle to Will's achieving great success was laziness. Despite the affection his parents showered on young Will, the impression remains that he never experienced their love as a steady force, but rather as a conditional reward dependent upon his achievements.

When he entered Yale, Will stood over six feet tall and weighed 225 pounds, quickly earning him the admiring nickname "Big Bill." His affable disposition and genial companionship with students of all backgrounds combined to make him the most popular man in the freshman class. "To see his large bulk come solidly and fearlessly across the campus," one classmate enthused, "is to take a fresh hold on life." Observing him walk through the college auditorium was "like seeing a dreadnaught launched." When the sophomore class challenged the freshmen to a tug-of-war, the freshman team proved seriously outmatched, its members "dragged bodily down the field" until Big Bill entered the fray, anchored the rope, and hauled his classmates back, inch by inch, to victory.

Academics came less easily for Will; he found his courses in Latin, Greek, and mathematics especially difficult. "I begin to see how a fellow can study all the time and still not have perfect [marks]," he warned his father only days after the semester had begun. Nevertheless, when grades were posted after six weeks, his tireless efforts placed him in the first division, where he was joined by his good friend from Cincinnati, Howard Hollister. "It is not more than we expected," Louise told Delia. "Now that the best scholars are in one division, the motive for effort, incited by constant comparison with each other is very strong, inspiring them with unflagging ambition." The added pressure only aggravated Will's distress. There was no respite so long as self-esteem depended on the approval of his parents. "Another week of this 'dem'd horrid grind,' has passed by . . . I am somewhat embarrassed in this first division," Taft confessed to his father. "You expect great things of me but you mustn't be disappointed if I don't come up to your expectations." Despite the worry of such expectations, the fact that Will was able to speak openly to his father about his fears indicates the depth of their relationship.

He did not try out for football, baseball, or crew. His father "had other ideas," Taft recalled years later, insisting he focus solely on his class work. Nor was Alphonso pleased to hear that his social son had been elected president of Delta Kappa and taken into Skull and Bones. "I doubt that such popularity is consistent with high scholarship," he warned. Will disagreed: "If a man has to be isolated from his class in order to take a high stand I dont want a high stand. The presidency of Delta Kap takes none of my time except so much as I spend on Saturday night which I sh'd use any how. There's got to be some relaxation." This brief spark of rebellion was quickly doused as Will settled into a structured regimen that produced the expected academic distinction. Rising at half past six, he studied before breakfast, followed by prayers, morning recitation, lunch, and afternoon recitation until three o' clock. Then he went to the gym for half an hour and studied until his last recitation at five. If he had time before dinner he would stop by the post office in hopes of finding letters from home, and then work until ten or even eleven at night.

"As a scholar, he stood high," a fellow classmate, Herbert Bowen, recalled; more important, "he towered above us all as a moral force." He was the class leader, directing all manner of college activities, from the literary board to the junior prom. He listened sympathetically to the troubles of his fellow students, who regularly sought his counsel. His classmates found him "safe and comforting," always ready to "come up with a cheery bit of wholesome discourse." Without a single dissenting vote, Taft's colleagues affectionately appointed him "father" of their graduating year and long remembered his perpetual smile and rumbling, hearty laugh. In sum, Bowen writes, he "was the most admired and respected man not only in my class, but in all Yale."

Nonetheless, David Burton concludes, "there was little in his academic training at Yale to suggest that learning was exciting for him, a galvanizing experience." Rather, Will was conditioned to regard his subjects "as hurdles to be taken on the way to a degree." When a younger student inquired about setting himself "a course of outside reading" to facilitate a deeper immersion in French and German literature and culture, Will Taft advised: "Don't do it. Get over it. You mustn't try to be too independent, just yet. These University professors have laid out a course, and it's the result of their long experience, while you—well, this is just your first trial at educating anybody. . . . You'd just better stick to the course."

In the spring of his sophomore year, Will delivered an oration on the continued vitality of the Democratic Party, tracing its history from Thomas Jefferson and Andrew Jackson to the present day. Despite his own strong Republican leanings, he could appreciate and praise various Democratic leaders, noting in particular Jackson's "hard common sense which is only acquired by knocking about among the masses." Even at this young age, his biographer observes, "Taft was judicial beyond the comprehensions of a Theodore Roosevelt," who not long thereafter would write a paper at Harvard accusing Jefferson of "criminal folly" and labeling Jackson "a spoilsman before anything else."

Taft would recall one professor above all, the political economist William Graham Sumner, who, he said, "had more to do with stimulating my mental activities than any one under whom I studied during my entire course." Considered one of the most gifted educators of his generation, Sumner lectured to classes packed not only with eager students but with professors from various universities "seeking the secret of his success." An impassioned advocate of laissez-faire and social Darwinism, of property rights and economic freedom, Sumner was an apostle for the gospel of wealth, the reigning philosophy of the Industrial Revolution and the Gilded Age that followed the Civil War.

Sumner passionately rejected concerns about the consolidation of business and the excessive concentration of wealth in the hands of a few, arguing on the contrary that wealthy business leaders like John Rockefeller, Andrew Carnegie, J. P. Morgan, and Cornelius Vanderbilt should be lionized. Through their enterprise, ingenuity, and capital, America had become the world's leading industrial power, capable of building more railroads, producing more oil and steel, manufacturing more clothing, appliances, and consumer goods than any other nation on earth. "If we should set a limit to the accumulation of wealth," he argued, "we should say to our most valuable producers, 'We do not want you to do us the services which you best understand how to perform, beyond a certain point.' It would be like killing off our generals in war."

Will absorbed Sumner's central teaching—that property rights demanded protection against the onslaught of radical theories and socialist ideals. Like Sumner, he argued that "princely profits" represented the just reward for "the men of judgment, courage and executive ability who have conceived and executed the great enterprises." Unlike Sumner, however, he did not place the businessman at "the highest pinnacle of honor and trust." Nor did he regard property rights as absolute, deserving precedence at every turn over human rights. From his father he had learned that the man who devoted himself to his community—"the lawyer who makes man's peace with man; the doctor who makes his peace with Nature; the minister who makes his peace with God"—deserved greater praise than the man who pursued wealth for its own sake. Wealth was honorable only to the extent that it contributed to the well-being of the community.

Honors were showered upon Will Taft during his senior year. His proud father boasted to Delia in late October 1877 that Will had been chosen by his classmates to be class orator, "the greatest prize in college," valedictorian not-withstanding. "He has in this respect surpassed his older brothers," Alphonso noted. "The honor too is of the historical kind which will not be forgotten by his class." He would "have his hands full, however," Alphonso explained, for the chosen student was expected to deliver "a long speech of half an hour to the class, carefully written & committed, & practiced."

Almost immediately, as Will anticipated his performance, anxiety set in. Two months after his selection, with more than five months left to prepare, he so agonized over his insufficient progress that he determined to forgo Christmas vacation in Cincinnati. "We shall regret that Willie cannot come home, but believe he does right in giving time to the great work," Alphonso wrote Delia. "I rely on his strength of purpose, & of intellect to accomplish it all and raise his reputation every time." As spring approached, Will lamented that his oration was "coming on slowly." Though he had settled upon his theme, he had not formulated how to present it. A month later he was still struggling, "finding it rather difficult to adapt its tone to the occasion." Another vacation was spent toiling in New Haven alone.

In the end, young Taft delivered a splendid oration before an overflow crowd at the Battell Chapel. "The sound of approaching music was heard," the *New York Times* reported, "followed by the measured tramp of the Class of '78, as in long line they filed up the aisle and took their places for the last time in their accustomed seats, where they would listen to the address of the Class Orator." No accolade could have pleased Taft more than the comparisons to his father drawn by the *Times*. "The orator in physique, in the method of handling his subject, and in style of oratory, presented some strong resemblances to his distinguished father. The address was characterized throughout by a transparency of thought, a clearness of statement, and an appearance of manly sincerity."

In the weeks before his graduation, Will had grown increasingly alarmed and troubled by news that his brother Peter had suffered a nervous breakdown and been committed to a private hospital for the insane in College Hill, Ohio. "I wish you could get Peter to come to Commencement," he beseeched his father. "We might turn his thoughts back to his college days and ease his mind considerably. President [Noah] Porter asked about him. I told him that we thought he was suffering from some mental disease."

Before his breakdown, Peter had begun practicing law in Cincinnati. There he met and married Tillie Hulbert, daughter of another prominent and wealthy local family. Unfortunately, his marriage did not share the productive harmony of Charley's. The union shortly proved disastrous, and his old anxieties multiplied. "Peter continues so strange," his mother confided to her sister. "He is very cross to Tillie and quarrels about everything in the arrangement of the house. He . . . puts in partitions, buys paper, carpets & furniture and changes the position of everything in the house in opposition to Tillie's wishes." Tormented by a series of ailments, including wild mood swings and a recurrence of the mysterious eye trouble that rendered him unable to read, Peter began the first of several treatments at the sanitarium.

"I am doing my best to be reconciled to the treatment in this institution," he wrote his father. "You have thought it best, and whatever your judgment thinks best I shall obey. But the course here is very hard. The Doctor gives me a kind of tonic that heats my head very much, and makes my mind so sensitive that any exercise of it deprives me of rest at night. . . . You are proceeding on a mistaken theory in my case. What I need is, not to be shut off from you and the family, but to be drawn to you and made to feel your love. . . . It seems to me that I am on a downward path. Whatever is the result of treatment, remember always that I, your son, love you more than I do any living mortal, and I respect your will above all others." Despite the entreaties of both Will and Peter himself, Alphonso decided that Peter should remain in the hospital rather than join the family at Yale.

On June 27, 1878, Will Taft was honored as salutatorian of his class, having surpassed all of his 132 classmates save Clarence Hill Kelsey, who would become a lifelong friend.

Even as he prepared to enter Cincinnati Law School the following fall, much of Will's motivation continued to stem from his father's high expectations rather than from any strong internal drive. Indeed, years later, Taft would credit his father's indomitable will and lofty aspirations in prompting his own achievements. When his father lay dying, he described this enveloping paternal spirit to Nellie: "I have a kind of presentiment that Father has been a kind of guardian angel to me in that his wishes for my success have been so strong and intense as to bring it, and that as his life ebbs away and ends I shall cease to have the luck which has followed me thus far."

☞ ☜

THEODORE ROOSEVELT WAS BORN THIRTEEN months after Will Taft, on October 27, 1858, in a four-story town house at 28 East 20th Street in Manhattan. "Teedie," as he was nicknamed, was by his own admission "a sickly and timid boy . . . a wretched mite," whose childhood was shaped by an assortment of troubling ailments, the most dangerous of which was asthma. When these agonizing attacks came, he found himself frantically gasping for breath, terrified he would suffocate. "Nobody seemed to think I would live," he recalled. His younger sister, Corinne, remarked on the irony that "Theodore Roosevelt, whose name later became the synonym of virile health and vigor, was a fragile, patient sufferer in those early days of the nursery." His fierce determination to escape an invalid's fate led him to transform his body and timid demeanor through strenuous work; Taft, on the other hand, blessed from birth with robust health, would allow his physical strength and energy to gradually dissipate over the years into a state of obesity.

During the worst of Teedie's asthmatic attacks, when the constriction in his chest made sleep impossible, his father comforted him with "great and loving care." "Some of my earliest remembrances are of nights when he would walk up and down with me," Roosevelt later wrote. "I could breathe, I could sleep, when he had me in his arms." If carrying the gasping child from room to room around the house proved inadequate, Theodore Senior drove him with horse and carriage through the gaslit city streets, hoping that the chill gusts of wind would fill the boy's lungs with air. "My father—he got me breath, he got me lungs, strength—life."

Teedie's father, known as "Thee," was the youngest of five sons born to Margaret and Cornelius Van Shaack Roosevelt, a glass merchant who had amassed a substantial fortune in real estate and banking. Considered "one of the five richest men in New York," C.V.S. hired tutors to educate his sons in the basement study of his imposing brick mansion on Union Square. Instead of enrolling Thee in college, which he feared would "spoil" him, C.V.S. sent him on a Grand Tour of Europe when he turned nineteen. Returning from the year abroad, Thee followed his older brother, James, into the family business. As the years went by, however, his keen sense of social justice began to shift his focus from the firm. Increasingly, he was drawn to philanthropic efforts to improve the lives of the poor at a time when extravagant wealth and abject poverty stood side by side.

In 1853, at age twenty-one, Thee married seventeen-year-old Martha "Mittie" Bulloch, daughter of a high-spirited family from Roswell, Georgia. Mittie had been raised in Bulloch Hall, a white-columned antebellum plantation mansion, where every need was attended to by a dozen slaves. The story of their courtship suggests an intense attraction from the moment they met in Roswell when Mittie was only fifteen. They renewed their acquaintance when she came north to visit relatives in the spring of 1853, and within weeks they were engaged. A southern beauty with delicate features, blue eyes, black hair, and radiant skin, Mittie possessed a quick mind and playful sense of humor. She proved irresistible to a young man raised amid the staid gentility of the Roosevelts' ordered social world.

In June, Thee came to Roswell to meet the members of the large Bulloch clan. "I am trying to school myself to coolly shaking hands with you when we meet—before the family," Thee told her. After his visit, Mittie assured him she was now "confident" of her "own deep love," confessing that "everything now seems associated with you. Even when I run up the stairs going to my own room, I feel as if you were near, and turn involuntarily to kiss my hand to you. I feel, dear Thee—as though you were part of my existence, and that I only live in your being." Her words so thrilled Thee that he felt "the blood rush" to his temples, forcing him "to lay the letter down, for a few minutes to regain command" of himself. "O, Mittie," he declared, "how deeply, how devotedly I love you!" Within four months, the young couple settled into their new 20th Street home, one of two adjoining houses that C.V.S. had purchased for Thee and his brother Robert.

Here, in the eight years that followed, four children were born: Anna, who was nicknamed "Bamie"; Theodore, Elliott, and Corinne. The advent of the Civil War, however, blasted the idyllic days of Thee and Mittie's marriage. While Thee passionately supported the Union cause, Mittie remained loyal to her homeland. Her brother, two stepbrothers, and all the young men she had known in Georgia had enlisted in the Confederate Army. Before the outbreak of war, Mittie's widowed mother, Martha, and her sister, Anna, had left Georgia and moved in with Thee and Mittie. Their plantation eventually fell into the hands of Union soldiers. "If I may judge at all of the embittered feeling of the South against the North by myself," Martha told her daughter, "I would say they would rather be buried in one common grave than ever again live under the same government. I am confident I should." The strain of a divided household took a toll on Mittie's health. "I shudder to think of what she must have suffered," Bamie later said. "I remember that Mother for a long time never came to the dinner table." Unable to bear the inevitable arguments, she withdrew more and more to the sickroom, plagued by an assortment of ills: palpitations, stomach troubles, and debilitating headaches.

Thee suppressed his impulse to volunteer for the Union Army, fearing that it would destroy his fragile wife "for him to fight against her brothers." Reluctantly, he decided to purchase a substitute. Although it seemed the only choice at the time, he "always afterwards felt that he had done a very wrong thing," recalled Bamie, "in not having put every other feeling aside and joined the absolute fighting forces." Thee worked tirelessly on behalf of the Union cause, devoting all his time and abundant energy to the great work of the U.S. Sanitary Commission, the Union League, the U.S. Allotment Commission, and the U.S. Employment Bureau, which found work for soldiers who had lost limbs, yet the decision not to enlist caused an indelible regret.

All four Roosevelt children idolized their father, "the most dominant figure" in their childhood, especially since their mother's fragility absented her from so many of their activities. He was "the most intimate friend of each of his children," Corinne recalled, "and we all craved him as our most desired companion." Theodore described the joyful anticipation when "we used to wait in the library in the evening until we could hear his key rattling in the latch of the front hall, and then rush out to greet him." Bamie was convinced "there was never anyone so wonderful" as her father, while Elliott marveled that "he was one of those rare grown men who seem never to forget that they were once children themselves." He took the children sailing on the swan boats in Central Park and brought them to museums. He tutored them in riding (first on Shetland ponies and then saddle horses) and in tree-climbing, pointing out "the dead limbs" to avoid.

In contrast to Alphonso Taft, who was rarely able to "turn aside from his business for the pursuit of pleasure," the elder Theodore Roosevelt skillfully balanced work and leisure in his family's life. "I never knew anyone who got greater joy out of living than did my father," Theodore declared, "or any one who more whole-heartedly performed every duty." His hard work in both business and philanthropic activities never precluded a rich social life. He reveled in the company of friends at dinner parties, relished a good cigar, danced into the early morning hours, and raced his four-in-hand coach through the streets. While acknowledging the often cruel class divisions that drove Alphonso from New York, he saw the city "not so much for what it was as for what it might become" under enlightened leadership. In an era when assistance to the poor remained mainly in the hands of private charity, Thee developed a sterling reputation for his dedication to improving the lives of tenement children through his work with the Newsboys' Lodging House, the Children's Aid Society, Miss Sattery's School for Italian Children, and the Five Points Mission. "Father was the finest man I ever knew, and the happiest," Roosevelt later told his journalist friend Jacob Riis.

Their father's affection and vitality compelled the Roosevelt children to surmount serious physical ailments. Bamie was deformed at birth by a severe curvature of the spine which gave her a hunchbacked appearance. Elliott was afflicted by what were considered epileptic attacks. Corinne, like Teedie, suffered from asthma, though her illness was not as severe as her brother's. Concern with the children's health prompted Thee to arrange home tutoring rather than send them to school. They were taught the fundamentals of reading, writing, and arithmetic by Mittie's sister, Anna, but their lifelong love of learning, their remarkable wide-ranging intellectual curiosity, was fostered primarily by their father. He read aloud to them at night, eliciting their responses to works of history and literature. He organized amateur plays for them, encouraged pursuit of their special interests, prompted them to write essays on their readings, and urged them to recite poetry. In addition, their mother provided a romantic and engaging perspective on history through accounts of her childhood in the vanished world of plantations, slaves, and chivalrous codes.

Even at a young age, Teedie held a distinct place among his siblings; the asthma that had weakened his body seemed to have inordinately sharpened his mind and sensibilities. "From the very fact that he was not able originally to enter into the most vigorous activities," Corinne noted, "he was always reading or writing" with a most unusual "power of concentration." He especially loved animal stories, adventure tales, and inspiring chronicles of "men who were fearless" in battle. His voracious reading gave him a rich cache of ideas for stories of his own to entertain his younger sister and brother. "I can see him now struggling with the effort to breathe," Corinne recalled, describing her eight-year-old brother's winding serial narratives, "which never flagged in interest for us" though at times they "continued from week to week, or even from month to month."

In the summers, Thee sought a broader field of educational activities for his children in the country, moving the family first to the Hudson Valley, and then to Oyster Bay, in the rambling house called Tranquillity—although Corinne wryly observed that "anything less tranquil than that happy home," crowded with cousins and friends of all the children, "could hardly be imagined." Her

friends Edith Carow and Fanny Smith were regular visitors every summer. To
Fanny Smith, these summer sojourns to Oyster Bay seemed a blissful round of
"riding, driving, boating, picnicking, games and verse-writing—no day was
long enough." Fanny was so taken with "the extraordinary vitality and gusto
with which the Roosevelt family invested life" that she felt as if they had all
been "touch[ed] by the flame of the 'divine fire.'"

In the woodlands surrounding the Roosevelts' summer retreat, young
Theodore's avocation as a naturalist took shape. As he roamed the forest trails,
he began to observe the birds, listening to their distinctive songs, carefully
noting flight patterns, beak and bill shapes, and coloration. When his interest expanded to a wide range of animals, he studied in scientific books, and
then took lessons, which his father arranged, from a professional taxidermist.
He began to collect, prepare, and mount hundreds of meticulously labeled
specimens. Encouraged by Thee, he set about establishing his own "Roosevelt
Museum of Natural History," with the fervent aspiration to become the next
J. J. Audubon or Spencer Baird.

The expansive education the Roosevelt children enjoyed, with boundaries
stretching far beyond the classroom, closely resembled the ideal of learning
envisioned by Horace Taft, when he wished that he and his siblings had been
exposed to the natural world, to the arts and music, to reading unconfined
by pedantic needs and standards. Years later, when Roosevelt was president,
he tried to interest Taft in birds and nature. "He loves the woods, he loves
hunting," Taft said of Roosevelt; "he loves roughing it, and I don't." On one
occasion, when Taft served as Roosevelt's secretary of war, he entered the Oval
Office while Roosevelt was speaking with an ornithologist. Taft was anxious
to talk about the Philippine tariff bill, but Roosevelt tried to engage Will in
his discussion. "Sit down, Will, and we will talk about something more interesting; we'll tell you something about birds," the president exclaimed. Taft
responded with a laugh: "I don't believe that you can interest me in natural
history, and I don't want you to send me any more such books as you sent me
the other day. I read it because you asked me to, and it took me nearly all night.
What do I care about dog-wolves, and whether they help she-wolves in pro-
curing food for their young. I don't think I ever saw a wolf, and certainly . . .
I am not interested in their domestic affairs."

The same year that Alphonso and Louise traveled abroad, without Will
and their younger children, Thee and Mittie took ten-year-old Teedie and the
entire family to Europe for a twelve-month journey through England, Scotland, Holland, Germany, Switzerland, Italy, and France. Although Teedie,
affectionately known within the family as "a great little home-boy," surely

missed his childhood friends, particularly eight-year-old Edith, his faithful diary entries reveal scores of invigorating adventures. He traversed fields where the Wars of the Roses were fought, inspected the tombs at Westminster Abbey, stood astride the boundary of France and Italy, ascended Mt. Vesuvius, and admired the art treasures of the Vatican.

And always, the children were accompanied by books, allowing Teedie the occasional opportunity to withdraw into his own world. At the end of four months, before the trip was half over, he proudly announced that "we three" (the three younger children, Bamie being considered part of the "big people" world) had read fifty novels. Beyond works of popular fiction, the family carried a small library of classic history and literature, which Thee read aloud to stir discussion.

Although the European voyage answered Thee's hopes "that a real education for his children would be acquired more easily through travel," he feared that Teedie, whose asthma and stomach troubles had necessitated frequent days of bed rest, was becoming too familiar with illness, timidity, and frailty, too prone to retreat into invalidism. When they returned home, he took his young son aside. "Theodore, you have the mind but you have not the body, and without the help of the body the mind cannot go as far as it should," he admonished. "You must *make* your body. It is hard drudgery to make one's body, but I know you will do it." Teedie responded immediately, according to Corinne, giving his father a solemn promise: "*I'll make my body.*"

The boy threw himself into a strict regimen of strength and endurance training; week after week, month after month, he lifted weights and pulled himself up on horizontal bars. Methodically, he sought to expand "his chest by regular, monotonous motion—drudgery indeed," first at Wood's Gymnasium and then in the home gym his father constructed on the second floor. The fierce determination that had propelled Teedie to become a serious student of nature, a voracious reader, and a sensitive observer was now directed toward expanding his physical capabilities by refashioning his body. Years would pass before the potential of these labors would be actualized in an adult capacity and physique that made him an exemplar of "the strenuous life."

In the meantime, his physical inferiority made him vulnerable to a humiliating experience that remained fresh in his mind forty years later. In his *Autobiography*, he recounted a stagecoach ride to Maine where he was set upon by two "mischievous" boys, who "proceeded to make life miserable" for him. Attempting to fight back, he discovered that either boy alone could handle him "with easy contempt." The injury to his self-respect was such that he was determined never again to be so helpless. In addition to his regular exercise regimen, he began taking boxing lessons. "I was a painfully slow and awkward pupil," he recalled, "and certainly worked two or three years before I made any perceptible improvement whatever."

Transforming his body was only one step in the psychological struggle against what Teedie shamefully considered his "timid" nature. "There were all kinds of things of which I was afraid at first," he acknowledged, "but by acting as if I was not afraid I gradually ceased to be afraid." As a childhood friend observed, "by constantly forcing himself to do the difficult or even dangerous thing," he was able to cultivate courage as "a matter of habit, in the sense of repeated effort and repeated exercise of will-power."

When Teedie was fourteen, his family went abroad again. Rather than repeat the heady pace of their first sweep through the Continent, they spent an entire winter in Egypt, three weeks in Palestine, two weeks in Lebanon and Syria, three weeks in Athens, Smyrna, and Constantinople, and five months in Germany. None of the children benefited more from this remarkable journey than Teedie, whose romantic nature conjured visions of ancient lives entwined with his own. "We arrived in sight of Alexandria," he wrote in his diary. "How I gazed on it! It was Egypt, the land of my dreams; Egypt the most ancient of all countries! A land that was old when Rome was bright, was old when Babylon was in its glory, was old when Troy was taken! It was a sight to awaken a thousand thoughts, and it did."

In addition to the cultural sites, young Theodore was thrilled by the chance to observe and catalogue exotic species he had hitherto known only in books. This was his "first real collecting as a student of natural history." During their two-month journey along the Nile in a private vessel, staffed by a thirteen-man crew, furnished with comfortable staterooms and a dining saloon, he was able clearly to perceive the habits of these entirely new birds and animals at close range, for finally, he had been fitted with spectacles that corrected his severe nearsightedness. "I had no idea," he later said, "how beautiful the world was until I got those spectacles." In the mornings he and his father would go out shooting along the banks of the Nile, retrieving specimens to be skinned, dissected, preserved with chemicals, and labeled. "My first knowledge of Latin was obtained by learning the scientific names of the birds and mammals which I collected and classified." His early dedication to such pursuits revealed "an almost ruthless single-mindedness where his interests were aroused," one biographer, Carleton Putnam, observed, "suggestive of a purposeful, determined personality."

Summer found the children in Dresden, where their father had arranged for them to live with a German family. Throughout that summer of 1873 and into the early fall, the daughter of the hosts was hired to teach them the German language, literature, music, and art. Teedie was so earnestly focused upon his studies, which occupied six hours of the day, that he asked to extend the lessons further. "And of course," his younger brother Elliott complained, "I could not be left behind so we are working harder than ever in our lives."

In the course of the year abroad, young Theodore had traveled by ship and by train, by stagecoach and on foot; he had stayed in hotels, inns, tents, and private homes. Armed with an innate curiosity and a discipline fostered by his remarkable father, he had obtained firsthand knowledge of the peoples and cultures in Europe, the Middle East, and Africa. Forty years later, Roosevelt remained appreciative of the opportunity afforded him. "This trip," he wrote in *An Autobiography*, "formed a really useful part of my education."

The family returned to a new home at 6 West 57th Street, a stately mansion with a fully equipped gymnasium for the children and a large space set aside in the garret to house Teedie's ever-expanding taxidermy collection. Although the fifteen-year-old's travels abroad had given him an unusually strong foundation in natural science, history, geography, and German, he was, in his own words, "lamentably weak in Latin and Greek and mathematics." If he wished to enter an Ivy League school, he could not compete with students like Will Taft, who had mastered the strenuous program at Woodward High that fully prepared him for Yale. To fill the gaps in Teedie's learning and prepare him for Harvard's rigorous entrance examinations, his father hired a recent Harvard graduate, Arthur Cutler. Under Cutler's tutelage, Teedie worked long hours every day and completed three years of college preparation in two. "The young man never seemed to know what idleness was," marveled Cutler, "and every leisure moment would find the last novel, some English classic or some abstruse book on natural history in his hands."

Elliott also studied under the guidance of a tutor, but lacking his brother's inner motivation and self-confidence, he proved unable to master subjects on his own. Even at thirteen, he worried about his future. "What will I become when I am a man," he plaintively demanded of his father. Acknowledging that Teedie was "much quicker and [a] more sure kind of boy," he pledged that he would "try to be as good . . . if [it] is in me, but it is hard." Desiring perhaps to separate himself from daily competition with his brother, Elliott entreated his father to send him to St. Paul's preparatory school. The summer before his entry, however, he suffered a series of mysterious seizures rooted, doctors believed, in a nervous disorder. Thee decided to postpone St. Paul's, choosing instead to take his son to Europe on a business trip. In Liverpool, Elliott suffered another attack, more severe than any previous incident. "It produced congestion of the brain with all its attendant horrors of delirium," Thee reported to Mittie. Two weeks later, Elliott remained ill. "I jump involuntarily at the smallest sound," he confided in a letter to Teedie, "and have a perpetual headache (and nearly always in low spirits)."

Upon returning home, Elliott resumed working with his tutor, but his hopes were still set on St. Paul's, where, he wrote his father, he "could make more friends" than studying at home. "Oh, Father will you ever think *me* a 'noble boy.' You are right about Teedie he is one and no mistake a boy I would give a good deal to be like in many respects." That fall, Thee agreed to let Elliott go to boarding school, but only a few weeks after arriving, he again fell ill. "During my Latin lesson, without the slightest warning," he told his father, "I had a bad rush of blood to my head it hurt me so that I can't remember what happened. I believe I screamed out." The boarding school experiment ended two months later when he "fainted just after leaving the table and fell down." Teedie was sent to St. Paul's to bring him home. Believing that a vigorous physical regimen would help, Thee sent his son to an Army post in Texas that built up his body but did little to cure his nervous disorder.

Meanwhile, Teedie's systematic effort to prepare himself for Harvard paid off. "Is it not splendid about my examinations," he triumphantly wrote Bamie. "I passed well on all the eight subjects I tried." If he was intellectually prepared for college, however, he lacked the social skills of many of his fellow students. Years of ill health and home schooling had isolated him from regular contact with boys and girls outside his family circle. He entered Harvard at scarcely five feet eight inches tall and only 130 pounds, "a slender nervous young man with side-whiskers, eyeglasses, and bright red cheeks." While Will Taft's sturdy physique, genial disposition, and empathetic manner won immediate popularity at Yale, Theodore Roosevelt took longer to establish a core group of friends at Harvard. He worried initially about the "antecedents" of the people he met, maintaining distance from classmates until he could determine whether their families shared the Roosevelts' station in life.

One contemporary remembers him as "studious, ambitious, eccentric—not the sort to appeal at first." He filled the shelves in his room with snakes and lizards, stuffed birds and animals; the smell of formaldehyde followed him from one class to the next. At a time when indifference toward one's studies was in vogue, Theodore was blatantly enthusiastic. "It was not often that any student broke in upon the smoothly flowing current" of their professors' lectures, one classmate recalled, "but Roosevelt did this again and again," posing questions and requesting clarification until finally one professor cut him short. "Now look here, Roosevelt, let me talk. I'm running this course." He also had a curious habit of dropping into classmates' rooms for conversation; then, rather than joining in, he would retreat to a corner and immerse himself in a book as if seated alone on a tree stump in the middle of the forest. Furthermore, he scorned fellow students who drank or smoked.

"No man ever came to Harvard more serious in his purpose to secure first of all an education," recalled one classmate, Curtis Guild, Jr.; "he was forever at it, and probably no man of his time read more extensively or deeply, especially in directions that did not count on the honor-list or marking-sheet." Whereas Taft discouraged the young Yale student from extracurricular reading, fearful it would detract from required courses, Roosevelt read widely yet managed to stand near the top of his class. The breadth of his numerous interests allowed him to draw on knowledge across various disciplines, from zoology to philosophy and religion, from poetry and drama to history and politics.

"My library has been the greatest possible pleasure to me," he wrote to his parents during his freshman year, "as whenever I have any spare time I can immediately take up a book. Aunt Annie's present, the 'History of the Civil War,' is extremely interesting." From early childhood, he had regarded books as "the greatest of companions." And once encountered, they were never forgotten. Much later, greeting a Chinese delegation when he was president, he suddenly remembered a book about China read many years before. "As I talked the pages of the book came before my eyes," he said, "and it seemed as though I were able to read the things therein contained." Taft was continually amazed at how Roosevelt found time to read, snatching moments while waiting for lunch or his next appointment. "He always carried a book with him to the Executive Office," Taft noted, "and although there were but few intervals during the business hours, he made the most of them in his reading." Charles Washburn, a classmate at Harvard, considered Roosevelt's ability to concentrate a signal ingredient to his success. "If he were reading," observed Washburn with astonishment, "the house might fall about his head, he could not be diverted."

The habits of mind Roosevelt developed early in his academic career would serve him well throughout his life. As soon as he received an assignment for a paper or project, he would set to work, never leaving anything to the last minute. Preparing so far ahead "freed his mind" from worry and facilitated fresh, lucid thought. During the last months of his presidency, aware that he was committed to speak at Oxford University following his yearlong expedition to Africa, he finished a complete draft of his lengthy address. "I never knew a man who worked as far in advance of what was to be done," marveled Taft. "Perhaps I value this virtue more highly because I lack it myself."

While posting honor grades each semester, Roosevelt cultivated a boggling array of social activities. He persevered in the promise to *"make my body,"* exercising rigorously day after day. He spent hours in the gym vaulting and lifting weights. He competed for the lightweight cup in boxing and wrestling, rowed on the Charles River, played strenuous games of lawn tennis, and ran three or four miles a day. Like his father, he pursued his chosen pastimes with the same zeal he devoted to his work. He organized a whist club and a finance club at which William Graham Sumner appeared; he wrote for *The Advocate*, joined the rifle club and the arts club, taught Sunday school, and took a weekly dancing class. With his explosive energy "he danced just as you'd expect him to dance if you knew him," a contemporary recalled—"he hopped." And despite this overcharged agenda, he maintained his passionate interest in birds, watching and shooting them in the field during the days, stuffing and labeling them in his room at night.

"His college life broadened every interest," Corinne observed, "and did for him what had hitherto not been done, which was to give him confidence in his relationship with young men of his own age." If he lacked Will Taft's immediate charisma, gradually his classmates could not resist the spell of his highly original personality. "Funnily enough, I have enjoyed quite a burst of popularity," he told his mother after his election into several social clubs, including the Hasty Pudding Club, the D.K.E. Society, and the prestigious Porcellian Club.

Theodore's burgeoning self-assurance and involvement in the Harvard community came at a critical time. He would need all the resilience and support he could muster to cope with a shattering blow during his sophomore year when his forty-six-year-old father came down with a fatal illness. An intense love had continued to bind father and son while Teedie was in college. "As I saw the last of the train bearing you away the other day," Roosevelt had written his son after seeing him off for his freshman year, "I realized what a luxury it was to have a boy in whom I would place perfect trust and confidence who was leaving me to take his first independent position in the world." Teedie's reply reflected his own profound respect and devotion: "I do not think there is a fellow in College who has a family that love him as much as you all do me, and I am *sure* that there is no one who has a Father who is also his best and most intimate friend, as you are mine." With unabashed affection, Teedie addressed his frequent letters to his "darling father" or his "dearest father," and Thee returned the tenderness in kind.

Two months before Roosevelt Senior was taken ill, he had been nominated by President Rutherford Hayes to replace incumbent Chester A. Arthur as

Collector of Customs for the Port of New York. His nomination was seen as a triumph for civil service reformers over New York senator Roscoe Conkling, who had run the port as his special fiefdom for years. The distinguished position required the approval of the U.S. Senate, however, where a fierce battle raged for weeks between the reform element of the Republican Party, represented by Hayes and Roosevelt, and the machine politicians, represented by Conkling and Arthur. In the end, the machine politicians won. The Senate rejected Roosevelt's nomination, insisting instead on the reappointment of Arthur. "The machine politicians have shown their color," a disappointed Thee wrote Teedie. "I fear for your future. We cannot stand so corrupt a government for any great length of time."

Six days after his rejection by the Senate, Theodore Senior collapsed. Doctors diagnosed an advanced stage of bowel cancer. Over Christmas vacation, when Teedie was home, his father seemed "very much better," sparking the false hope that he was beginning to recover. As Teedie was leaving to return to Harvard, he had a conversation with him that he would long remember: "Today he told me I had never caused him a moments pain. I should be less than human if I ever had, for he is the best, wisest and most loving of men, the type of all that is noble, brave, wise & good."

The final days of the forty-six-year-old Thee's two-month bout with cancer produced excruciating pain. His groans reverberated through the house and his dark hair turned gray. Elliott stayed by his father's side, ready to bring a handkerchief drenched in ether to his face. But when he screamed, neither the ether nor the sedatives could still the pain, and the fear in his father's eyes was terrible for the sixteen-year-old boy to behold.

On Saturday, February 9, 1878, the family, who had shielded Teedie from the worsening situation, sent an urgent message for him to come home. He raced to catch the overnight train, but reached New York on Sunday morning to find his father had died late Saturday night. His grief was "doubly bitter," he wrote. "I was away in Boston when the man I loved dearest on earth died." Remembering how his father's devoted strength had comforted him throughout the worst of his childhood attacks, he was filled with unbearable remorse: "I never was able to do anything for him during his last illness."

"The death of Mr. Roosevelt was a public loss," stated the *New York Times*. "Flags flew at half-mast all over the city," reported Jacob Riis. "Rich and poor followed him to the grave, and the children whose friend he had been wept over him." Newsboys from the lodging house, orphans for whom he had found homes, and Italian girls he had taught in Sunday school all grieved for their kind benefactor. "There was truly no end to a life that had been devoted to such philanthropy," Reverend William Adams declared at his funeral, "for the work he had laid out would remain and grow in power long after his death."

"He has just been buried," Theodore wrote in his diary. "I felt as if I had been stunned, or as if part of my life had been taken away; and the two moments of sharp, bitter agony, when I kissed the dear, dead face and realized he would never again on this earth speak to me or greet me with his loving smile, and then when I heard the sound of the first clod dropping on the coffin. . . . " Ten days later, back at Harvard, his loss still struck him "like a hideous dream." Semi-annual examinations offered some distraction to get through the days, but the restless nights were filled with misery. "It has been a most fortunate thing for me that I have had so much to do," he wrote in his diary. "If I had very much time to think I believe I should almost go crazy." He was grateful for the small margin of relief his insular college world offered, realizing that his mother and siblings had nothing to assuage their grief.

Returning home to Oyster Bay that summer was difficult, for "every nook and corner about the place, every piece of furniture about the house is in some manner connected with him." Only frenzied activity managed to keep his sorrow at bay. In late June, however, Theodore confided to his diary a surprising recognition of his own character: "Am leading the most intensely happy & healthy, out of doors life & spending my time riding on horseback, making long tramps through woods and fields after specimens, or else on the bay rowing or sailing—generally in a half naked condition and with my gun along. I could not be happier, except at those bitter moments when I realize what I have lost. Father was himself so invariably cheerful that I feel it would be wrong for me to be gloomy, and besides, fortunately or unfortunately, I am of a very buoyant temper being a bit of an optimist." Nevertheless, the young man remained painfully aware of the magnitude of his loss. His father had been "the only human being to whom I told *everything*," he wrote. "Never failing to get loving advice and sweet sympathy in return; no one but my wife, if ever I marry, will ever be able to take his place."

Perhaps this fundamental loneliness contributed to Theodore's ardent pursuit of seventeen-year-old Alice Hathaway Lee during his junior year at Harvard. He later claimed that when they first met at the home of his college friend, Richard Saltonstall, "it was a real case of love at first sight—and my first love too." Like the first flush of his father's infatuation with Mittie, it seemed as if Theodore's passion for Alice far exceeded his genuine knowledge of her. While his diary is rife with descriptions of her bewitching beauty, scant space is devoted to shared sympathies or interests that might lead to lasting companionship. Within four weeks of their introduction, he vowed "to win her." Seven months later, when he was only twenty, he proposed and initially, she rejected him. He was undeterred.

The campaign he launched to gain Alice's love necessitated a full-blown battle plan. Theodore later told a friend he "made everything subordinate to winning her." Weekend after weekend, he rode his horse six miles to her country home in Chestnut Hill. He took her sledding and skating, read to her, accompanied her on long walks in the woods, and escorted her to dances. He worked to ingratiate himself with her parents and mesmerized her young brother with exciting tales of adventure. Meanwhile, he made every attempt to integrate her into his sphere, introducing her to his friends at the Porcellian and inviting her to join his family for a round of parties in New York. Still, she hesitated to make a commitment at such a young age. Only in the privacy of his diary did young Theodore acknowledge "the tortures" he was suffering. His wooing of Alice had the aspect of an epic quest in which he was the hero, a crusade in which he would succeed or die. "I have hardly had one good night to rest and night after night I have not even gone to bed. I have been pretty nearly crazy over my wayward, wilfull darling."

Finally, in late January of his senior year, she agreed to become his wife, and they set a wedding date for the following autumn. "I am so happy that I dare not trust in my own happiness," he wrote. "I do not believe any man ever loved a woman more than I love her." Captivated by his first love, he believed there was "nothing on earth left to wish for."

Despite the absorption in his engagement, Theodore continued to wrestle and box. He joined a hunting expedition in Maine and had a "royally good time" with his club mates. He completed a thesis on "Equalizing Men and Women Before the Law" that shared the same progressive attitude toward women as Will Taft's senior essay. "As regards the laws relating to marriage there should be the most absolute equality preserved between the two sexes," Theodore wrote. "I do not think the woman should assume the man's name . . . I would have the word 'obey' used not more by the wife than by the husband." Unlike young Taft, however, he was not ready to recommend women's suffrage.

Nor did he neglect his regular class work, applying himself sufficiently to graduate magna cum laude and Phi Beta Kappa, twenty-first in a class that opened with 230 students. Still dividing his classmates according to their family's standing, he boasted that "only one gentleman stands ahead of me." As he approached graduation, he reflected on his college years with self-satisfaction. "I have certainly lived like a prince," he wrote in his diary. "I have had just as much money as I could spend; belonged to the Porcellian Club; have had some capital hunting trips; my life has been varied; I have kept a good horse and cart; I have had half a dozen good and true friends in college, and several very pleasant families outside; a lovely home . . . and to crown all infinitely above everything else put together—I have won the sweetest of girls for my wife. No man ever had so pleasant a college course."

The prospect of marriage altered his long-cherished plan to become a naturalist, a career that would require years of study abroad and was unlikely to provide a substantial income. Instead, he decided to enter Columbia Law School, vowing to "do my best, and work hard for my own little wife."

From that point on, as Carleton Putnam writes, "Natural history was to remain a genuine avocation, but it never loomed again as a feasible career."

By the age of twenty-one, Theodore had known, in his own words, "great sorrow and great joy," and while he believed "the joy has far overbalanced the sorrow," his early suffering had deepened his self-knowledge, intensified his powers of concentration, and heightened his sensibilities.

☙ ❧

BOTH WILL AND TEEDIE HAD the good fortune of growing up as favored children in close-knit, illustrious families where affection and respect abounded. Both inherited from their fathers legacies of honorable and distinguished careers, as well as a commitment to public service and a dedication to the Republican Party. Where Will developed an accommodating disposition to please a living father who cajoled him to do more and do better, Teedie forever idolized a dead father who had paid for a substitute for himself during the Civil War to placate his wife, yet had fostered military and historical tales of heroism in his beloved son.

Will had the stronger physical endowment but the weaker self-control; Teedie the weaker body but the greater strength of will. The enormously powerful Will abused his physical gift; the smaller Teedie, a heroic compensator, toughened and transformed his body. Will tended to stay indoors; Teedie tested himself outdoors, against nature. Taft was easygoing and even-tempered; Roosevelt perpetually in motion, as if to keep self-inquiry at bay.

Will, by temperament warmer and more sociable than Teedie, found common ground with one and all; others instinctively responded to his smiling countenance and kindly demeanor. Teedie was less approachable at first blush, limiting his associations to those who shared his class and station in life.

Where Teedie was an intellectual adventurer with a passion for reading and a wide-ranging curiosity engendered by a broad set of experiences, Will worked methodically, within the defined frameworks outlined by his instruc tors. The one was self-assured, guided by his own ferocious determination; the other more subject to the entreaties of others, steering his course out of the desire to please. Will was more modest and straightforward; Teedie more boastful and complex. Common to both was a sober good sense and a willingness to work hard that led to high distinction in college and the promise of success as they looked forward to law school.

If there are splendid traits in abundance in the characters of both young men, the one major distinction at this stage is that Teedie had shown he could come through agonizing misfortune. Will had not yet been tested by adversity.

CHAPTER THREE

The Judge and the Politician

Will Taft, rising Cincinnati attorney, in the early 1880s.

FOR WILLIAM HOWARD TAFT, LAW school fortified his life's ambition to become a judge, fixing upon him "a judicial habit of thought
and action" that marked the rest of his life as he moved from the bench to the
far less congenial world of politics. For Theodore Roosevelt, the study of law
merely facilitated his diverse ventures as historian, assemblyman, rancher, civil
service commissioner, police commissioner, assistant secretary of the Navy,
soldier, governor, and vice president. Each experience would eventually contribute vitally to a memorable presidency.

Cincinnati Law School, where Taft matriculated in 1878, was among the
oldest in the country. Situated at that time in the Mercantile Library Building
at the city center, it remained an "old style" institution untouched by the modern case method of instruction introduced at Harvard earlier in the decade.
While Taft might easily have gained admission to Harvard or Yale, he chose

to return to his hometown, to be enveloped by the warmth of his close-knit family. His brothers Charley and Peter were practicing law in his father's firm; Harry was a student at Yale; Horace a senior at Woodward High; and Fanny was still a girl at thirteen. Furthermore, Will's best friend and Yale classmate, Howard Hollister, entered Cincinnati Law in the same class.

For two hours every day, Taft and sixty-six fellow students listened to professors expound broad legal principles derived from standard texts. The curriculum, far less demanding than his courses at Yale, allowed students to work as well as study. Although most law students gained their first practical experience apprenticing in law offices, Taft decided he could learn "more about the workings of the law" as a court reporter for Murat Halstead's local newspaper, the *Cincinnati Commercial*. Once his morning lectures were completed, he began his rounds to the police court, the probate court, the district court, and the superior court. At each venue, he took notes, listed the cases on the various dockets each day, and wrote up short accounts of the half-dozen most compelling cases.

Readers of "The Courts" column followed the cases of a husband suing for divorce after discovering his wife had two husbands; a buxom woman ensnared by a livery-stable keeper who failed to reveal that he suffered from a contagious private disease; a husband alleging that his wife had "struck and scratched him in a vicious manner" and had so ill-treated their children that their lives were endangered. He chronicled criminal trials for larceny, domestic abuse, and assault and battery and followed malpractice suits, contested wills, bastardy cases, contract disputes, and mortgage foreclosures. He wrote in a clear, straightforward style, emphasizing the facts of the cases without embellishment. Usually, he managed to complete these accounts before dinner, allowing him time to relax in the evenings.

In his early twenties, Will found himself the center of a lively set of young friends, enjoying to the fullest the wealth of social activities Cincinnati provided. With a population of 250,000, the "Queen City" had come of age in the 1870s, boasting an array of cultural events that included classical music, opera festivals, theatrical performances, literary societies, and art exhibits. "Washington will remain our political and New York our commercial capital," Murat Halstead predicted in 1878, but cosmopolitan Cincinnati would become "the social center and musical metropolis of America."

Will Taft cut quite a figure in this bustling society: "large, handsome and fair, with the build of a Hercules and the sunny disposition of an innocent child," one local newspaper described him. Women were drawn by his open engaging manner and he, in turn, was completely at ease conversing with them. He listened sympathetically to their concerns, valued their intelligence, and displayed an unself-conscious candor. At dancing parties he sparkled, surprisingly light on his feet. He and his compatriots enjoyed picnics on the Ohio River, sledding parties, debutante balls, nights at the theatre, whist parties, tennis matches, baseball games, and songfests at the beer gardens in "Over-the-Rhine," the German section.

With growing apprehension, Alphonso observed his son's diversions, convinced that without the structured environment that had compelled diligence at Yale, Will was simply marking time. Tensions between father and son only grew when Will went to work in his father's office in the summer of 1879 between his first two years in law school. In late June, Will departed for several days to visit one of his college friends in Cleveland. In his absence, a woman sought legal help in a small case involving the destruction of $300 worth of property. Seeing this as "a capital opportunity" for Will to handle a jury trial with several witnesses to be sworn, Alphonso sent him a letter requesting his immediate return. "I had the case laid over to next Saturday so that you might prepare & try it," he told his son. "I shall be sorry to have you lose it."

The next day, Alphonso wrote again, venting his irritation. Will should disregard the previous letter, for he had "agreed on a settlement of the case . . . a thing which you cd. have done if you had been here, & carried a nice little fee for yourself." Alphonso's exasperation and disappointment were clear. "This gratifying your fondness for society is fruitless," he admonished. "I like to have you enjoy yourself, so far as it can be consistent with your success in life. But you will have to be on alert for business, and for influence among men, if you would hope to accomplish success." Alphonso had not exhausted his censure, for yet a third letter followed the next day. "I do not think you shd make arrangements for a second visit at Cleveland, or for anything, but close application to study and business. There is no day in wk. you will not have as much as you are able to do. You must acquire a mastery of the German Language, as well as of the law and you should be forming valuable business acquaintance, if not political. I do not think that you have accomplished as much this past year as you ought, with your opportunities. You must not feel that you have time enough to while a way with every friend who comes."

Alphonso worried too much. Will finished law school in good standing. Then, heeding his father's advice, he shuttered himself in the law office for the month leading up to the bar examination, combing the shelves of standard legal tomes. Will informed his friends that "he would not be seen in public again until after the tests." He easily passed and was admitted to the bar. His solid work as a court reporter for the *Cincinnati Commercial* had, meanwhile, earned Halstead's esteem and a full-time job offer at a salary of $1,500 a year. Although his calling was to the law rather than journalism, he remained on the newspaper staff through the summer and fall of 1879. There, his coverage of a dramatic embezzlement trial against Cy Hoffman, a Democratic auditor for the city, led to an unexpected opportunity.

Counsel for the defendant in the Hoffman case was the criminal attorney Thomas C. Campbell, head of a political ring said to have dug "its talons deep in the judiciary." Campbell reputedly owned court officers, regularly bribed witnesses and juries, and "was able to secure any verdict" he desired. The Hoffman case took "a sensational turn" when Miller Outcault, the assistant prosecuting attorney, charged that his chief prosecutor, Samuel Drew, had conspired with the unscrupulous Campbell to fix the jury and assure Hoffman's acquittal.

For the idealistic young Taft, the picture of judicial corruption was deeply disturbing. He later acknowledged that he "fell in" with Miller Outcault, providing reports that aided his efforts to expose both the chief prosecutor and the disreputable attorney. The *Cincinnati Commercial* stories about the dramatic proceedings created widespread interest in the case. Large crowds packed the courthouse, spectators "standing upon the railing, desks and chairs" as day after day, Outcault leveled a "nasty torrent of abuse" against both Campbell and his boss. After two weeks of "the bitterest invective" from all parties in this singular "three-cornered fight," the judge was compelled to dismiss prosecutor Drew from the case. Proceedings were suspended until the district court sustained the judge's action. The jury finally received the case but could not reach an agreement; a mistrial was declared.

When Outcault replaced Drew as prosecuting attorney, he offered the post of assistant prosecuting attorney to Will Taft, who had just passed his twenty-third birthday. Nellie Taft later declared that "the experience he had in the rough-and-ready practice in criminal trials, in preparing cases for trial, in examining witnesses, in making arguments to the court and in summing up to the jury, was the most valuable experience he could possibly have in fitting him for trial work at the bar." He prepared indictments for grand juries; he took depositions, interviewed witnesses, and independently conducted a number of criminal trials, including a dramatic murder case. After only four months on the job, Will opened the prosecution's case in the state's second attempt to put the city auditor Cy Hoffman behind bars. Once again, the celebrated criminal defense lawyer Tom Campbell defended Hoffman; once again Campbell secured a hung jury, and suspicions of jury tampering abounded.

Considering the marked contrast of disposition between Taft and Roosevelt, Henry Pringle speculates that "a Theodore Roosevelt might have won renown, glory and headlines in this post of assistant district attorney." He might have publicly pledged to root out the corrupt dealings between officers of the court and the city's political machine, but Will Taft "was no showman, nor was he, to the same extent, personally or politically ambitious." He valued the post solely as a vital contribution to his legal education. "He was on his legs day after day before judge and jury," Horace recalled, and consequently "became so expert in regard to the laws of evidence as to surprise the older lawyers when he mounted the bench."

Although he harbored no political ambitions for himself, Taft took an active role in local Republican politics. During his father's race for governor, he canvassed the city in search of delegates to the state convention and remained involved from that point forward. "I attended all the primaries and all the conventions," he later recalled, "and attempted to do what I could to secure respectable nominees for the party, especially for judicial places." He worked in his ward to defeat disreputable machine candidates "by hustling around among good people to get them out." He never hesitated to attack "the gang methods" whenever he witnessed corruption at the polls, but while attacking their methods, he always stayed "on good terms" with all the various factions. His amiability and reluctance to hold a grudge made him, in the estimation of Republican congressman Benjamin Butterworth, "the most popular young man in Hamilton County."

Beneath Will's benign nature, however, lay a sharp temper, especially where his family's honor was concerned. A weekly tabloid published an anonymous letter ridiculing Alphonso, along with the insidious suggestion that Louise Taft herself had authored the attack. Determined to seek revenge for this slander against both his parents, Will sought out the tabloid's editor, Lester A. Rose. Charley cautioned restraint since Rose "was known to be a bruiser of considerable physical courage and great endurance." Undaunted, Will confronted Rose on a street corner and administered what the newspapers termed a "terrible beating." He reportedly "lifted him up and dashed him to the pavement," executing continuous blows and hammering the man's head against the ground until Rose promised to leave town that very night. The story of the thrashing made news across the country. "The feeling among all classes of citizens," observed the *Bismarck Tribune*, "is that Mr. Taft did a public service and ought to have a medal."

At his father's urging, Will began stumping for Republican candidates in his county. "I want him to accustom himself to speaking from the beginning," Alphonso told Delia Torrey, explaining that as a lawyer, "he is to make speaking a business, & he should do it well." Will was sick with anxiety before his maiden political speech, aghast to see his name, the Hon. William H. Taft, plastered on posters throughout the city. "Don't allow yourself to be discouraged," his father urged him. "It is a great undertaking, but it is the best thing that can happen to you. . . . It will be worth a fortune to you if you can conquer the difficulties & speak well in public. I know it is hard work to get adequate preparation. . . . You will find it difficult to commit literally a long speech. I do not attempt it. You will have your memory helped by notes of the points." Will followed his father's advice, and the speech, which he delivered three times in three different venues, went well. "He finds the farmers make attentive listeners, and he is not embarrassed," Louise noted. "There is every prospect that he will be a first class speaker," Alphonso wishfully predicted, "and a first class lawyer, too."

In January 1882, Taft's popularity with the discordant factions of the Republican Party led Congressman Butterworth to recommend him to President Chester Arthur as Collector of Internal Revenue for the Cincinnati District. The sitting collector, affiliated with a coalition considered unfriendly to the president, had been dismissed. His removal threatened to escalate political strife unless a replacement was found who could mollify all sides. "If you will appoint Will Taft to this important position, everybody will be satisfied," Butterworth told President Arthur. Taft's mother opposed the idea. "I did not wish Will to go into politics," she said. "I wished him to engage in nothing not in the line of his profession." His father, too, questioned the appointment, fearing that Taft was "too young" to lead a staff of more than a hundred employees in the task of collecting over $10 million from the sales of whiskey and tobacco.

Taft later acknowledged that he was offered the post, making him the youngest collector in the country, predominantly because he "had no political enemies." It is likely that this decision to interrupt his emerging legal career was less a function of ambition than of desire to satisfy Congressman Butterworth and President Arthur. Indeed, this unwillingness to disappoint others would continue to shape the course of his professional life. While Taft possessed a highly developed social intelligence, he was less discerning of his own strengths and weaknesses.

Still, it did not take him long to realize that the work was decidedly ill-suited to his temperament. He detested the prominence of the position and could not bear the criticism that inevitably came with the job, acknowledging years later that he was too "thin-skinned" for "public life." Moreover, his moderate reformist tendencies were at odds with the prevailing customs of the day. At a time when civil service reform was still in its infancy, when political patronage, rather than merit, filled the majority of positions, government employees were expected to contribute part of their salaries to the party in power. Horace recalled that when the local Republican Party circulated a subscription list demanding money from each of the department employees, Taft made a contribution in his own name "but announced that he would not look at the subscriptions made by any of his employees." Ruffled party members charged that "he was wrecking the party by the course he followed."

Taft's troubles multiplied during a bitter contest for the congressional nomination in the Second District between Governor Tom Young and Amor Smith. Young sent a letter to Taft demanding the removal of a number of men in the Revenue Department who he claimed were allied with his opponent. Taft refused, resenting the "bulldozer" tone of the letter. The half-dozen men whose removal the governor demanded, he countered, "are among the best men in this District in the energy, skill and faithfulness with which they discharge their duties. If removed they must be simply and solely removed because they would prefer Amor Smith's nomination to yours." As for Young's implied threat to involve President Arthur in the situation, Taft argued that "the popularity of the present Administration in this county has been strengthened by the fidelity with which we have tried to follow the President's moderate course in National Affairs in regard to Civil Service."

In a letter to his father, Taft defiantly declared: "I would much rather resign and let some one else do Tom Young's service and dirty work." In an effort to avoid public dissension, he decided to write to the president directly. "The men whose removal he seeks," Taft told the president, "are such men as practical and conscientious politicians delight to find, men of political power and of ability to discharge their official duties." He promised President Arthur that these employees supported the administration; they simply preferred Smith to Young. Although Governor Young eventually backed down, the disagreeable conflict intensified Taft's desire to resume the practice of law. "I long to get out of politics," he told his father in October 1882, "and get down to business." A month later, after less than a year on the job, he journeyed to Washington and asked the president to accept his resignation. "I am mighty glad he is going to resign," Horace told his mother. With clear admiration for his older brother, he added: "I'll bet one thing & that is they won't get a man in that place very soon who knows more about the law & business of the office than he does or who abstains more carefully from the dirty parts of politics. Will makes fun of me for being so radical theoretical & impractical in my opinions but when it comes to the point I think he is a thorough Civil Service Reformer in practice."

Palpably relieved to be free of political discord, Taft penned a long letter to his father, who was then enjoying a pleasant stint in Vienna as the American foreign minister to Austria-Hungary at the behest of President Arthur. Will happily reported his intent to go into partnership with his father's former law partner, Major Harlan Page Lloyd, a widely respected figure in Cincinnati. "It is the opening of what I hope will be my life's work," he said. "Of course I shall have to work hard but that will agree with me and I shall have that sweetest of all pleasures the feeling of something accomplished, something done in the life that I have marked out for myself." It was a rare moment of insight into his own feelings and desires. Alphonso was gratified to hear that his son was leaving politics "to work at the law, with all his might," he told Charley. "That is his destiny."

By early 1883, Taft was settled in his new job. Charley's wife Annie believed that since leaving the politically embroiled revenue department Will looked "younger by several years." In January, Taft wrote his sister Fanny with evident satisfaction: "I wish you could look in on me now, seated in my cozy library with a cheerful soft coal fire and lots of easy chairs with the familiar old pictures looking down on me from every wall." That summer, he planned to take his first trip abroad to visit his parents. "I hope you will make yourselves comfortable and elegant even if it is a little expensive," he teased them. "You're off on a lark and we are willing to extend your allowance a little to insure your having a good time." But after three months in Europe he was "glad to get home" and resume his law practice. "Will is working well & seems very happy," Major Lloyd reported to Alphonso.

Will and Horace roomed together on the west side of Broadway when Horace, after graduating from Yale, also returned to Cincinnati to study law. Tall, spare, with a refreshing sense of humor, Horace relished politics more than his brother did and would become a fervent advocate for reform. Horace "makes friends wherever he goes," Will reported to his sister, "because his honest good nature and straight forward character shines out of him."

Will also confided in Fanny his hope that his own law practice would "grow large enough in some years to warrant my making an ass of myself in regard to some girl." By his twenty-fifth birthday, however, he confessed that he was "no nearer matrimony than I was when I first went into society. In the loneliness that I sometimes feel stealing over me, the temptation in that direction is strong but with no object to satisfy the feeling, the thought passes like many other castles in the air."

If Will felt he lacked the proper foundation to marry, he was certainly entertaining eligible candidates. When the Opera Festival came to Cincinnati during the first week in February, Taft reported to his mother and sister that he was planning to take a different girl each evening: Nellie Herron on Monday night, Edith Harrison on Tuesday, Miss Lawson on Wednesday, Miss Tomlin on Thursday, Alice Keys on Saturday afternoon, and Agnes Davis on Saturday night. "I see Father shake his head when he reads this list and hear him say that a thorough knowledge of the law is not obtained in that way."

THE REVIVAL OF TAFT'S LEGAL career reignited a clash with his old nemesis: Tom Campbell. A wave of ghastly murders in 1883, including a husband and wife killed for the $30 their bodies would be worth to a dissection class at the medical school, had created panic throughout Cincinnati. And amid this widespread anxiety, a particularly vicious killing of a liveryman on Christmas Eve of 1883 set in motion "a series of events that shook the foundation of Cincinnati."

The prosecution charged that seventeen-year-old William Berner and an accomplice had robbed and killed their employer, William Kirk, by beating him savagely on the head with a blacksmith's hammer and club. They hid the body in a covered wagon, fled with $345, and enjoyed a night of revelry in numerous saloons. When the victim's body was discovered, the pockets of his jacket "were filled with Christmas presents he was taking home to his family." Evidence implicated Berner, who confessed six times to six different people, detailing the planning and execution of the "cold-blooded butchery." Before the trial commenced, Berner, in order to avoid hanging, agreed "to plead guilty to murder in the second degree." The prosecution refused, certain that the evidence for first-degree murder "was absolute and unquestioned," and that the heinous nature of the crime deserved punishment by death.

Tom Campbell was enticed to defend Berner with the hefty fee of $5,000, offered by the father of the accused young man. It proved a sage investment; with the powerfully connected Campbell leading the defense, the jury delivered a shocking verdict. After deliberating but twenty-four hours, they rejected both the first- and second-degree murder charges, finding Berner guilty only of murder in the third degree. Cincinnati residents were stunned and outraged, convinced that the father of the murderer had purchased the verdict through a cunning lawyer who had corrupted the jury. While not the first miscarriage of justice that Cincinnati had witnessed, it was certainly the most infamous.

"The people of Cincinnati are abundantly warned that the law furnishes no protection to life," declared the *Cincinnati Commercial Gazette*. "Justice," the *New York Times* reported, "was poisoned at its source. The peace and safety of society were betrayed by the agency chosen to defend them. It is a terrible fact . . . that money outweighs human life and that the land of the law is palsied by bribes." A number of papers grimly noted that the lower courts in too many cities across the country had "become the mere agents of unscrupulous attorneys, who dictate acquittals or convictions at will. So scandalous and notorious has it become that lawyers now openly boast that they own this or that court."

A mass meeting was held at the Music Hall on March 29, 1884, to protest both the verdict and the corrupting influence of the Campbell organization. Speakers addressed the crowd, and a committee was formed to revise the rules governing the selection of juries. The proceedings were repeatedly interrupted by outbursts of "Hang the jury!," "Hang Tom Campbell!," "Hang Berner!," and a large "boisterous element remained" after the meeting adjourned.

After some excited deliberation, they thronged to the jail, determined to find Berner and deliver by lynching the justice denied by the court. Gathering strength on every corner, the crowd grew to nearly 1,000 by the time it reached the jail. There the mob divided into three groups. The first division stormed the courthouse, ran through the tunnel leading to the jail, and managed to break through the heavy iron doors at the end of the tunnel. The second group shattered the south windows and demolished the chapel on the way to the rotunda. With a heavy ram, the third group battered down the iron entrance to the jail and raced up a winding stairway to reach the cells. But Berner was nowhere to be found; for his safety, he had already been transferred to another jail. In their fury, the mob set the courthouse ablaze.

Order was finally restored with the arrival of the police and the state militia, but in the course of the struggle, forty-five men were killed and more than a hundred injured. Many thousands of dollars of property was lost. The *New York Times* declared it "the bloodiest affair that ever occurred in Cincinnati."

A few weeks later, a grand jury brought an indictment against Tom Campbell for bribing several of the jurors. Taft rightly surmised that it would be impossible "to obtain testimony because the only witnesses of Campbell's rascalities are men who were as deeply implicated in them as he was." Campbell chose for his counsel Joseph Foraker, a rising political ally, and was acquitted by a jury unable to reach a verdict. Taft complained to his father that Foraker had "conducted the defense in a most shystering and ungentlemanly way." In the future, he pledged, "I shall do everything I can against Foraker in every political fight."

The Cincinnati Bar Association, meanwhile, decided to create a committee to prepare sufficient evidence for a disbarment suit against Campbell in the district court. Taft was chosen by the senior members of the bar to serve as junior counsel for the nine-person committee. This appointment, Horace noted years later, "was an extraordinary honor, considering his youth, and was not to be accounted for by smiling good nature." Alphonso worried about the consequences of a direct collision with Campbell and the insidious forces behind him, fearing even for his son's physical safety. Will, however, relished the chance to confront the man who had "thrown the bar of Hamilton County into disrepute." He stridently announced to his father that it was time "for men to have backbone and drive away the scourge that has been such an infliction on this community for so many years. Those who tamely cower in the face of attack I have no use for. I have gone into this thing fully realizing the danger- ous enemy we have to encounter."

The committee presented its findings before the district court in July 1884, and a trial date was set for November. Horace proudly recalled that his brother was instrumental in building the case for senior members of the committee. Will had traveled throughout Ohio compiling evidence and interviewing wit- nesses to document a pattern of disreputable behavior that had persisted for years. While his law practice suffered and his father feared that Campbell's stranglehold on the judicial system would make "a thankless task" of all his endeavors, Will found the work exhilarating.

The intensity of his pursuit drained young Taft of any remnant of zeal for political campaigning. "I find that the Campbell case has robbed politics of any interest for me," he told his father at the start of the 1884 presidential race between Republican James Blaine and Democrat Grover Cleveland. "If I can assist to get rid of Campbell, I think that I shall have accomplished a much greater good than by yelling myself hoarse for Blaine."

As the election neared, however, he succumbed to pressure from Con- gressman Butterworth and agreed to serve as chief supervisor of elections in the city. He was charged with organizing forces to man the polling places, where intimidation and fraud were rampant, repeat voters numbered in the thousands, and hundreds of men "voted the cemetery." Taft had done his job well. Republicans carried the city and the state, though Cleveland won the presidential election. "Your son Will did splendid service in the campaign," Butterworth informed Alphonso. "He is a magnificent fellow. If he has a flaw in him I don't know where it is. He is not only brainy, but brave, honorable and honest." Despite such accolades, the political world held little appeal for Taft. "This is my last election experience I hope for some years to come," he told his mother.

Campbell's disbarment trial opened before three district court judges on

November 6, 1884, two days after the election. "The investigation," Taft ex-plained to his father, would undertake "to prove acts at the different periods of [Campbell's] professional career to show a consistent course of unprofessional conduct down to the present time." Taft sat beside the senior attorneys who argued the case, providing documents, facts, and affidavits. The trial contin-ued through December, with closing arguments slated for January 5, 1885.

On that crucial day, the senior attorney scheduled to present the prosecu-tion's closing summary fell ill, and William Taft was selected to take his place, "suddenly emerging from obscurity," as Henry Pringle notes, " to play the part of a leading actor." He took the floor for four hours and ten minutes, revealing an absolute mastery of the complex case. Point by point, Taft enumerated the charges against Campbell, reviewing the evidence presented over the previous twenty days. Emphasizing that the members of the Cincinnati Bar Association were "actuated by no other motive than a desire that the profession should be purged of a man whose success in this community threatens every institution of justice that is dear to us or necessary to good governance," Taft offered a powerful concluding summary: "We have presented the case which we think calls for the action of your Honors in saying that the profession must be kept pure. We deny nothing to Mr. Campbell except integrity, and we say that that is the essential, the indispensable quality of a member of the Bar."

On the final day, Campbell took the stand, delivering an impassioned and eloquent plea on his own behalf. "There was not a vindictive word uttered, and one looked in vain for any of the characteristics or manner of speech of the Thos. C. Campbell of one year ago," the *Commercial Gazette* reported. "Tears were welling in his eyes, and there was a look of keen mental suffering upon his face," as he described the pain and humiliation endured "from the first filing of these charges to the present moment." He ascribed the "smoke of suspicion" that shadowed him largely to his active engagement in bitter political wranglings through the years in which "he had blindly made enemies who had multiplied." He acknowledged that "the public had been worked up to the highest pitch of feeling" during the Berner case and that his decision to defend Berner had cost him greatly. He closed with a sentimental flourish, directly impugning Taft as the assassin of his character: "Mr. Taft has said that the relators deny me nothing save integrity. That is like saying, let me wound you just once with a rapier, and I will be merciful and thrust you not through the arm or the leg, but through the heart. Integrity is to a man what chastity is to a woman. When that is gone, all is gone."

Taft anxiously waited week after week while the three judges deliberated. He believed both the reputation of the legal profession and the confidence of the public in the judicial system were at stake. Congressman Butterworth warned that "Tom Campbell controls one of the Judges absolutely and one of the others partially." Nonetheless, few were prepared for the stunning verdict, delivered on February 3, 1885, that exonerated Campbell of all charges save a minor one which merited no suspension from the bar. "It was disastrous and disgraceful," Taft reported to his father. "I am glad to say that this is the universal opinion." Indeed, Butterworth observed that "whatever may be said of the full, clear, complete, technical legal certainty, the moral proof is absolutely overwhelming that Campbell and his ring represent the social, moral, political, legal rot of Cincinnati."

"I am very glad now that I spoke," Taft told his father. "The labor was very great and it is discouraging to have such an ending," he avowed, but "the Public generally and the Bar are disposed to think that we tried the case as well as it could be tried." From his faraway perch in St. Petersburg, Russia, where he had been appointed a second ministerial job, Alphonso agreed. "I was very much pleased with your argument," he assured his son. "I think you must have a great majority of the community on your side; and you will find it will be remembered in your favor. You must not allow yourself to be discouraged by the folly and perverseness if not wickedness of men who have by some accident come into a little brief Authority."

As the weeks went by, Taft managed to recover a measure of optimism. "It is the beginning of an era of reform," he excitedly told his father. "The trial of his case has shorn [Campbell] of that veneer of respectability. . . . Everybody knows he was guilty. He and the Court have gone down together." He also reported a curious shift in his own perception of the matter and the man: "I can hardly explain to you the change in my feeling in regard to him. I have no personal animus toward him. He is no more to me than one of the thieves or bunks men whom I know. He hates me with a perfect hatred but I am indifferent to his feeling toward me."

Taft's satisfaction with his own performance in the case was certainly justified. And in an ironic turn of events, his involvement also aided his judicial ambitions. Taft's unlikely benefactor would be Campbell's ally, Joseph Foraker, who, much to Taft's disgust, became the Republican gubernatorial nominee several months after the trial. "I should not bow my head in tears," Taft confessed, "if the Democratic candidate defeated him." Despite Taft's grave reservations about the "double-faced Campbell man," Foraker won the election and was returned to the governor's office two years later.

In May 1887, during Foraker's second term, a vacancy arose in the Ohio Superior Court when Judge Judson Harmon decided to retire with fourteen months left on his elected term. To Taft's astonishment, Foraker offered to appoint him to fill the temporary vacancy until he could run for a full term. Considering Taft's manifest antipathy toward Foraker, Foraker's choice of a young man who was not yet thirty remains an enigma. In a memoir written after Taft became president, Foraker's wife, Julia, claims that an "instant sympathy" had developed between the two men when Taft, a cub reporter for the *Cincinnati Commercial*, covered cases over which her husband presided. "Foraker liked Taft's smile, liked his agreeable manner, liked his type of mind," she wrote. Foraker also recalled his own prescient respect for the young man after Taft had risen to eminence. Despite his youth, Foraker avowed, he "knew him well enough to know that he had a strong intellectual endowment, a keen, logical, analytical, legal mind, and that all the essential foundations for a good Judge had been well and securely laid."

Taft would surely have denied this "instant sympathy" with a man he roundly disliked. It is more likely that in appointing a young lawyer with Taft's reputation for honesty and sincerity, Foraker sought to mollify reformers who called for the restoration of integrity on the Ohio bench. The *Weekly Law Bulletin* praised the appointment, noting that despite a mere seven years before the bar, Taft was "a very bright young man, who already enjoys great popularity and personal respect." In a letter to Foraker, Taft acknowledged his profound appreciation. "Considering the opportunity so honorable a position offers to a man of my age and circumstances, my debt to you is very great," he wrote. "The responsibility you assume for me in making this appointment will always be a strong incentive to an industrious and conscientious discharge of my duties."

To Taft, who would become the youngest judge in the state of Ohio, this appointment represented "the welcome beginning of just the career he wanted." His work as court reporter, prosecuting attorney, litigator, and counsel for the Bar Association had prepared him well, giving him an intimate acquaintance with varied aspects of the law. The golden chance to sit on the superior court represented the establishment of a judicial career that would eventually lead, after a painful detour as president, to his ultimate destination—chief justice of the United States.

⌒ ⌒

WHEN THEODORE ROOSEVELT TOOK UP the study of law, he was not sure where it would lead, nor whether he even wanted to be a lawyer. Foremost, he was about to be married and had a responsibility, despite the inheritance his father left him, to support his wife and family. Within two weeks of entering Columbia Law School on October 6, 1880, he acknowledged that he had his "hands full attending to various affairs." While mornings were spent in school, his afternoons and evenings were devoted to wedding arrangements. The marriage was scheduled to take place at Chestnut Hill on October 27, his twenty-second birthday. "It almost frightens me, in spite of my own happiness," he revealed in his diary, "to think that perhaps I may not make her happy; but I shall try so hard; and if ever a man love woman I love her."

The wedding was celebrated at noon on a balmy autumn day at the Unitarian church in Brookline before a large crowd, including Theodore's childhood friend Edith Carow. After a sumptuous reception at the Lee mansion, the young couple spent the night in a hotel suite and then headed to Oyster Bay. They remained two weeks at the family's country home, where their every need was attended to by a cook, maid, and groom. "Our intense happiness is too sacred to be written about," Roosevelt asserted in his diary, then proceeded to detail idyllic days spent driving their buggy, roaming through the woods and fields, playing "equally matched" lawn tennis, and reading poetry before blazing fires at night.

On November 17, Roosevelt resumed his law school classes. He set forth shortly after 7:30 a.m. from his mother's house on 57th Street, where he and Alice would spend the winter, to begin the three-mile walk to the four-story law building on Great Jones Street at the corner of Lafayette Place. At Columbia, as at Harvard, he stood out as "an energetic questioner of the lectures," his intensity provoking a mixture of resentment and admiration in his classmates. Though the pleasure he took in his studies is amply expressed in his journal, he was troubled that "some of the teaching of the law books and of the classroom seemed to me to be against justice." He noted critically that "we are concerned with [the] question of what law is, not what it ought to be." Nevertheless, more than 1,000 pages of handwritten notes during his two years of study testify to his diligence, and he impressed professors with his amazingly deft grasp of materials.

During his first year in law school, Roosevelt assumed several positions formerly held by his father on the boards of charitable organizations. Hopeful this philanthropic work might prove fulfilling, he found himself ill-suited to follow in his father's footsteps. "I tried faithfully to do what father had done," he confessed to his reporter friend, Jacob Riis, "but I did it poorly. . . . [I] joined this and that committee. Father had done good work on so many; but in the end I found out that we have each to work in his own way to do our best." Despite his relative youth, Roosevelt demonstrated a confidence and clear-minded assessment of his own interests and capabilities, making him far more successful than Taft in refusing endeavors he found uncongenial.

During this hectic phase of his life, Roosevelt even managed to try his hand as an author. As a senior at Harvard, he had embarked on a project that would become his first published work, *The Naval War of 1812*. His interest in the war had been sparked by a volume in the Porcellian Club library by the reigning British authority on the subject, William James. Angered by the biased, boastful approach of the author, who appeared "afflicted with a hatred toward the Americans," Roosevelt searched out American historians of the war, only to find their accounts equally distorted by jingoism.

With the goal of writing an impartial history, he began research into the official papers and records on both sides of the conflict. By the spring semester of his first year at Columbia, he noted: "I spend most of my spare time in the Astor Library on my 'Naval History.' " In the reading room—"a wonderfully open two-story-high hall surrounded by gilded balconies and books arranged in double-height alcoves"—he pored over official letters, logbooks, original contracts, and muster rolls.

With the same inordinate concentration he gave to law lectures in the mornings, Theodore spent his afternoons at the library compiling figures to compare warring ships in terms of tonnage and guns, and researching the number of officers and men on each side as the war began and ended. He concluded that in most of the battles at sea, the American fleets overpowered the British, but that American historians, desiring to embellish the valor of the commanders, minimized the difference; British historians retaliated with even greater exaggerations. With his fierce utilization of every waking moment, Roosevelt stole time to write both before and after a full round of social engagements, including formal balls, nights at the theatre, large receptions, and more intimate parties. "We're dining out in twenty minutes," Alice lightheartedly complained, "and Teedy's drawing little ships!"

On May 12, 1881, the day after classes ended, Theodore and Alice sailed off on their delayed honeymoon to Europe. His diary tells of joyous days crowded with visits to castles, cathedrals, and museums, with sailing excursions on inland rivers and carriage rides through the Alps. "Alice is the best traveling companion I have ever known," Theodore marveled. "Altogether it would be difficult to imagine any two people enjoying a trip more." But when they reached Zermatt, Theodore pursued a solo adventure: the irresistible challenge of climbing the dangerous Matterhorn. "I was anxious to go up it," he acknowledged to Bamie, "because it is reputed very difficult and a man who has been up it can fairly claim to have taken his degree as, at any rate, a subordinate kind of mountaineer." In the company of two guides, finding the climb "very laborious" but with "enough peril to make it exciting," he reached the summit.

Roosevelt managed to work on his naval history throughout the trip, lugging his books and papers from country to country. "You would be amused to see me writing it here," he told Bamie. "I have plenty of information now, but I can't get it into words; I am afraid it is too big a task for me. I wonder if I won't find everything in life too big for my abilities. Well, time will tell."

Returning home from Europe, he resumed his law courses in early October. "Am working fairly at my law," he reported a few weeks later, "and hardest of all at my book." In early December, he delivered a 500-page manuscript to Putnam's. Recalling this maiden literary voyage, Roosevelt acknowledged years later that some of the chapters "were so dry that they would have made a dictionary seem light reading by comparison." Nonetheless, uniformly favorable reviews hailed his accomplishment, noting flashes of the muscular tone and vigor that would mark his mature prose. "The volume is an excellent one in every respect," noted the reviewer for the *New York Times*, "and shows in so young an author the best promise for a good historian—fearlessness of statement, caution, endeavor to be impartial, and a brisk and interesting way of telling events."

It was an auspicious beginning. He learned early on the rewards attendant upon painstaking research and the meticulous deployment of facts. The boldness with which he challenged entrenched opinion was refreshing to critics, although one reviewer remarked that his running criticisms of the British authority suggested "a comparison with those zealous sailors who 'overloaded their carronades so as to very much destroy the effect of their fire.' "

In the years ahead, even as he turned his prodigious energies and talents to the world of politics, Theodore Roosevelt never stopped writing. Though he may never have realized his dream of writing a book that would rank "in the very first class," he produced a substantial body of excellent work, forty books in all, in addition to hundreds of magazine articles and book reviews. He covered an astonishing range of subjects, including narratives of hunting expeditions, meditations and natural histories on wolves, the grizzly bear, and the black-tailed deer, biographies of public figures, literary essays, commentaries on war and peace, and sketches of birds. His four-volume history of the American frontier would win high praise from the eminent historian Frederick Jackson Turner, who termed it "the first really satisfactory history of the field . . . a wonderful story, most entertainingly told,"

Roosevelt's many-sided writings would prove an invaluable resource during his presidency, passionately linking him with hunters, naturalists, bird lovers, historians, biographers, conservationists, educators, sailors, soldiers, and sportsmen. "Everything was of interest to him," marveled the French ambassador, Jean Jules Jusserand, "people of today, people of yesterday, animals, minerals, stones, stars, the past, the future."

THE ROAD THAT WOULD LEAD Roosevelt into public life began at Morton Hall, the "barn-like room over a saloon" at 59th Street and Fifth Avenue that served as the Republican headquarters for the Twenty-first District. That district encompassed both the elegant neighborhoods along Madison Avenue and the more populous tenement sections on the West Side of Manhattan. While Roosevelt had found philanthropic administration ill-suited to his restless temperament, he longed to honor his father and family through his own efforts "to help the cause of better government in New York." When he began inquiring about the local Republican organization, he was warned by his privileged circle that district politics were "low," the province of "saloon-keepers, horse-car conductors, and the like," men who "would be rough and brutal and unpleasant to deal with." Their caution did nothing to deter Roosevelt. "I answered that if this were so it merely meant that the people I knew did not belong to the governing class," he observed, "and that the other people did—and that I intended to be one of the governing class."

In addition to attending the monthly meetings, Roosevelt stopped by in the evenings at the smoke-filled room with its benches, cuspidors, and poker tables that functioned as a club room. "I went around there often enough to have the men get accustomed to me and to have me get accustomed to them," he explained, "so that we began to speak the same language, and so that each could begin to live down in the other's mind what Bret Harte has called 'the defective moral quality of being a stranger.' "

To the machine politicians who represented the tenement population, Roosevelt initially appeared very much an alien. "He looked like a dude, side-whiskers an' all, y' know," one of them commented. Over time, however, as he had done at Harvard, he won over his comrades with the warmth, unabashed intensity, and pluck of his personality. He grew particularly close to Joe Murray, the thickset, red-haired Irish boss with "a fine head, a fighter's chin, and twinkling eyes," the man whom Roosevelt later credited with launching his political career. "He was by nature as straight a man, as fearless and as stanchly loyal, as any one whom I have ever met," Roosevelt wrote in his *Autobiography*.

When Murray determined that the incumbent Republican assemblyman for the Twenty-first District could not hold his seat in the fall elections in 1881, having recently been linked to corruption, he surprised his compatriots by nominating the twenty-three-year-old Roosevelt, unknown to anyone in Morton Hall eight months earlier. The shrewd boss calculated that victory over the Democratic candidate would be assured if the Republican machine mustered its regular totals while Roosevelt mobilized the college-educated men and "the swells" who rarely voted in local elections. Murray's instincts proved correct. On November 1, a list of eminent New Yorkers, including future Secretary of War Elihu Root and Columbia law professor Theodore W. Dwight, heartily endorsed Roosevelt as a man "of high character . . . conspicuous for his honesty and integrity." A week later, Theodore Roosevelt was elected as the youngest member of the New York State Assembly, launching an unprecedented political career, one that would culminate less than two decades later in his becoming the youngest president in the history of the United States.

On January 2, 1882, Theodore Roosevelt was sworn in, along with 127 other assemblymen. "My first days in the Legislature were much like those of a boy in a strange school," he recalled. "My fellow legislators and I eyed one another with mutual distrust. . . . The Legislature was Democratic. I was a Republican from the 'silk-stocking' district." Assemblyman Isaac Hunt, who later became a close friend, would never forget the first time he saw Roosevelt. "He came in as if he had been ejected by a catapult," Hunt recalled. "He pulled off his coat; he was dressed in full dress, he had been to dinner somewhere." With hair parted in the middle, eyeglasses suspended by a silk cord, and elegant gloves, he cut a unique figure.

For the first six weeks, according to Hunt, Theodore Roosevelt was uncharacteristically taciturn. "He was like Moses in the Wilderness," but all the while watching and learning. One night in his private diary, Roosevelt delineated "an analysis of the character of each man in that Legislature." His initial reactions to the other assemblymen revealed that he was still far from overcoming Harte's "defective moral quality of being a stranger." His Republican colleagues, he wrote, were "bad enough; but over half the democrats, including almost all of the City Irish, are vicious, stupid looking scoundrels with apparently not a redeeming trait." The men who belonged to the New York City Tammany Hall Democratic machine, furthermore, seemed "totally unable to speak with even an approximation to good grammar; not one of them can string three intelligible sentences together to save his neck."

Clearly, the Tammany men were as contemptuous of and antagonistic to Roosevelt as he was of them. Tammany lieutenant John McManus, a practical joker nearly twice Roosevelt's size, let it be known that he intended to toss the young upstart in a blanket. Outwardly uncowed, a belligerent Roosevelt confronted McManus: "By God! If you try anything like that, I'll kick you, I'll bite you, I'll kick you in the balls. I'll do anything to you—you'd better let me alone." And he did.

The more serious altercation took place at Hurst's Roadhouse, a popular gathering place for assemblymen and reporters six miles out of Albany. Late one winter afternoon Roosevelt entered Hurst's and was greeted by three jeering bullies, who raucously mocked his appearance and lack of a winter coat. "Why don't your mother buy you an overcoat? Won't Mama's boy catch cold?" A reporter present noted that Roosevelt ignored them until it was clear they would not let up. Finally, he confronted the three. "You—little dude," taunted one, while his companion took a swipe at Roosevelt. "But, quick as lightning, Roosevelt slipped his glasses into his side pocket, and in another second he had laid out two of the trio on the floor. The third quit cold." The story soon made the rounds in the statehouse, along with the significant fact that once the men got off the floor, Roosevelt invited them to join him in a glass of ale.

The lively natures displayed by young Taft and Roosevelt remained with them throughout their lives. The aftermath of their anger, however, was handled very differently. "When Taft gives way to his," one reporter observed, "it is to inflict a merciless lashing upon its victim, for whom thereafter he has no use whatever. With Roosevelt it is a case of powder and spark; there is a vivid flash and a deafening roar, but when the smoke has blown away, that is the end."

Roosevelt quickly determined that his colleagues could be divided into three groups: a small circle of "very good men," fellow reformers like Isaac Hunt, William O'Neil, and Mike Costello, anxious to fight against corrupt political machines, made up the first; the second group, the majority, "were neither very good nor very bad, but went one way or the other, according to the strength of the various conflicting influences acting around, behind, and upon them"; finally, the "very bad men" in both parties, ever susceptible to bribery, made up a rough third of the assembly and were essentially owned by various business interests. Good legislation could be passed only if the conscience of the public was awakened, exerting pressure on the passive majority. Immediately, Roosevelt understood that the most effective means of circumventing the machines and transforming popular sentiment was to establish a good rapport with the press corps.

About thirty reporters from across the state covered the legislature in Albany, where a rigid hierarchy governed their assigned seats. In front-row box seats, facing the assemblymen, sat George F. Spinney of the *New York Times*, Hugh Hastings of the *Albany Express*, H. Calkins of the New York *World,* and A. W. Lyman of the New York *Sun*. Reporters for the *New York Herald*, the *New York Tribune*, and the *Brooklyn Times* sat in the second and third rows. Journalists representing smaller papers were consigned to the bleachers in the back of the chamber. Roosevelt's expansive demeanor, manic energies, and often original, always articulate and quotable statements made him a favorite among the journalists. A mutually productive alliance was forged between these journalists and Roosevelt that would boost his political career at every stage.

The *New York Times* reporter George Spinney took an immediate liking to Roosevelt, calling him a "good-hearted man," with "a good, honest laugh." Spinney, who would later become editor and publisher of the *Times*, was considered then one of the best reporters in the state, lauded for the "vigor, thoroughness and intelligence of his daily dispatches" from Albany. Spinney marveled at the speed with which the rookie assemblyman mastered every aspect of the state legislature. "He grew like a beanstalk," he recalled in a conversation with Assemblyman Hunt forty years later. "He would just stand a man up against the wall and interview him and ask: 'How do you do this in your district and county' and 'What is this thing and that thing.' He went right to the bottom of the whole thing. He knew more about State politics at the end of that first session than ninety percent of them did."

Isaac Hunt himself, described by a contemporary as "a mighty tree that stood out in the forest," had never encountered anyone like Roosevelt. "He would go away Friday afternoon," Hunt remembered, "and Monday he would throw out new things he never had before, just like a child that you see grow from day to day, that is the way he grew. He increased in stature and strength materially all the time." In that first session, Hunt wrote, "I thought I knew more than he did . . . but before we got through, he grew right away from me."

Brooklyn Eagle reporter William C. Hudson, who resided at the same hotel as Roosevelt, was boggled by the young legislator's early morning routine. "It was Roosevelt's habit to come into the breakfast room with a rush, copies of all the morning papers he could lay his hands on under his arm, and, seating himself, to go through those papers with a rapidity that would have excited the jealousy of the most rapid exchange editor. He threw each paper, as he finished it, on the floor, unfolded, until at the end there was, on either side of him, a pile of loose papers as high as the table for the servants to clear away. And all this time he would be taking part in the running conversation of the table. Had anyone supposed that this inspection of the papers was superficial, he would have been sadly mistaken. Roosevelt saw everything, grasped the sense of everything, and formed an opinion on everything which he was eager to maintain at any risk."

Roosevelt's prodigious learning curve was tested after only two months in Albany, when he took a leading role in the battle to impeach a corrupt state supreme court judge, Theodore Westbrook. The battle pitted Roosevelt against a similar insidious alliance to the one Taft had uncovered in the Campbell debacle in Cincinnati. In December 1881, shortly before Roosevelt was sworn in, the *New York Times* had published a nine-column piece condemning Judge Westbrook's collusion with the notorious Wall Street financier Jay Gould in an elaborate scheme to gain control of the elevated railway system in New York. "We went after him with yards of space," recalled Spinney, who conducted several phases of the investigation.

Over the years, the swashbuckling Gould had amassed railroads, steamship lines, telegraph companies, and newspapers in a series of well-planned raids, stitching together an empire that stretched from coast to coast. In 1881, he moved to appropriate the Manhattan Elevated Railway Company, one of the first outfits to engineer and develop a steam-powered rapid-transit system for the city. A burdensome lawsuit devised by Gould's accomplices was brought against the company, forcing it into receivership. Judge Westbrook, who had been Gould's legal counsel, was selected to preside over the bankrupt company. Holding court in Gould's private offices, Westbrook issued a series of onerous rulings calculated to panic stockholders into throwing their shares on the market, depressing the stock to almost nothing. At that point, the Gould syndicate began buying. Once Gould had gained control of the valuable property, Judge Westbrook mysteriously decreed the company solvent, and the stock rose sharply. This simple, perfidious maneuver cost thousands of innocent stockholders their life savings.

The comprehensive account of this stock-jobbing scheme created a stir in the newspaper world. At issue, the *Brooklyn Eagle* proclaimed, were not simply the transgressions of a justice who "prostituted" himself, but the fact that the "State Government in all its branches" has prostrated itself before the robber barons. "These things show where the wealth of the country is going; they show that the farmer, the artisan, and the merchant are sweating their lives out to enrich a little coterie of blooded knaves who regard their fellowmen as the spider does the fly or the wolf the sheep." If the charges were substantiated, the *Auburn* (New York) *Advertiser* argued, nothing less than Westbrook's impeachment would restore the "dignity and respect" of the state supreme court. "Officials should be taught that they are the servants of the people," chided the *Times*, "not of rings and cliques." All agreed that Westbrook could not "remain silent under the severe arraignment of the *Times*."

In fact, that is precisely what Westbrook did; his strategic silence on these charges had nearly extinguished interest in the entire matter when Theodore Roosevelt picked up the case in March 1882. Isaac Hunt had prompted Roosevelt's involvement after a second, unrelated article appeared in the *New York Herald* accusing Judge Westbrook of a flagrant abuse of power and conflict of interest. He had appointed receivers for defunct insurance companies and granted excessive fees to select lawyers (including his cousin and son) who handled the cases. Hunt suggested that Roosevelt introduce a resolution to investigate Judge Westbrook. Roosevelt agreed to consider the action "but would not take it up until he was sure there was evidence sufficient to warrant such a resolution."

Recalling the Westbrook article in the *New York Times* three months earlier (as he seemed to remember anything he had read), Roosevelt approached the city editor, Henry Loewenthal, and asked to examine the corroborating evidence behind the December exposé. The editor later described "an energetic young man" who "questioned and cross-questioned him" throughout the entire night. George Spinney, who had worked for Loewenthal before becoming the Albany correspondent, heard that "the presses in the basement were finishing that day's edition in the early morning hours, when the young Assemblyman emerged with an armful of ammunition" that included an incriminating letter in which Judge Westbrook told Gould, "I am willing to go to the very verge of judicial discretion to serve your vast interests."

On March 29, 1882, Roosevelt rose from his seat in the assembly. Noting that the newspaper charges made against Westbrook in relation to the Manhattan Elevated Railway Company had "never been explained or fairly refuted," he offered a resolution empowering the Judiciary Committee to begin an investigation. This bold action created a sensation in the chamber. "By Jove!" Hunt recalled. "It was like the bursting of a bombshell." Supporters of Westbrook and Gould quickly rallied, demanding a debate that automatically tabled the motion and threatened its indefinite postponement. The next day an editorial in the *New York Times* praised Roosevelt's resolution: "Mr. Roosevelt correctly states that these charges have never been explained or fairly rebutted. . . . Those who believe that Judge Westbrook has been unjustly assailed ought to welcome so good a chance of vindicating his character."

A week later, Spinney recalled, "Roosevelt suddenly interrupted the humdrum routine, with the demand that all business be laid aside and his resolution of investigation be taken up." The move was "so unexpected and so

sudden that dilatory tactics were out of the question." When Roosevelt began
to speak, "the House, for almost the only time during the session grew silent."
Though Roosevelt was not then an accomplished speaker, he delivered his
speech "slowly and clearly and his voice filled the chamber, abominable as were
its acoustics. A frequent gesture of his determination was the resounding blow
of his right fist as he smacked it in the palm of his left hand."

"The men who were mainly concerned in this fraud," Roosevelt began
(alluding to Jay Gould, Russell Sage, and Cyrus Field), "were men whose
financial dishonesty is a matter of common notoriety," requiring of the judiciary extreme efforts to assure the appearance of probity. Instead, the judge
answered petitions in the offices of one of the trio of investors and held court
in the office of another who was "nothing but a wealthy shark." To address
one aspect of the case, Westbrook appointed a man who was employed by Jay
Gould. Every decision was rendered to enable Gould and his conspirators to
seize control of the railway at a baldly manipulated bargain price. "We have a
right to demand that our judiciary should be kept beyond reproach," Roosevelt ardently continued, "and we have a right to demand that if we find men
against whom there is not only suspicion, but almost a certainty that they have
had collusion with men whose interests were in conflict with the interests of
the public, they shall, at least, be required to bring positive facts with which
to prove there has not been such collusion; and they ought themselves to have
been the first to demand such an investigation."

"Beyond a shadow of doubt," Spinney believed, "a vote at that juncture
would have insured the passage of his resolution." But former Governor
Thomas Alvord took the floor and filibustered until the scheduled adjournment at two o'clock in the afternoon. Speaking in "disjointed sentences and
fragmentary thoughts," Alvord advised the rookie assemblyman to find proof
for his accusations rather than stoop to "slanderous utterances or newspaper
stories," because "human reputation and human characters were too sacred
to be trifled with."

Though Roosevelt was temporarily outmaneuvered by veteran opposition,
"the day's proceedings," Spinney observed, "made the youngest member of
the Assembly the most talked of man in the State." That night, from his room
at the Kenmore Hotel, Roosevelt wrote to Alice with no small gratification:
"I have drawn blood by my speech against the Elevated Railway judges, and
have come in for any amount both of praise and abuse from the newspapers.
It is rather the hit of the season so far, and I think I have made a success of
it. Letters and telegrams of congratulation come pouring in on me from all
quarters. But the fight is severe still."

Roosevelt's speech to the assembly garnered widespread coverage, as he well knew it would. "Mr. Roosevelt has a most refreshing habit of calling men and things by their right names," the *Times* editorialized, "and in these days of judicial, ecclesiastical and journalistic subserviency to the robber barons of the Street it needs some little courage in any public man to characterize them and their acts in fitting terms. There is a splendid career open for a young man of position, character and independence like Mr. Roosevelt."

Not surprisingly, Jay Gould's New York *World* castigated him in equal measure. "Before any official shall be subjected to the vexation and discredit of an investigation, some responsible person or association must prefer a charge accompanied with allegations of wrong-doing." Yet in this instance, the *World* complained, "an inexperienced legislator gets up [from] his seat and recites in a somewhat intemperate speech sundry hearsay charges against Judge West-brook based upon statements published in a newspaper."

Roosevelt dismissed these attacks, according to Hunt, shedding criticism "like water poured on a duck's back." He held his ground, even when an old family friend gently insisted that while "it was a good thing to have made the 'reform play,' " he should not "overplay" his hand. "I asked," Roosevelt recalled, "if that meant I was to yield to the ring in politics. He answered somewhat impatiently that I was entirely mistaken (as in fact I was) about there being merely a political ring," for the "inner circle" was, in truth, a miasma, an enormous knot of "big businessmen, and the politicians, lawyers, and judges who were in alliance with and to a certain extent dependent upon them, and that the successful man had to win his success by the backing of the same forces, whether in law, business, or politics."

The day before the House adjourned for Easter recess, Roosevelt was again frustrated in his attempt to bring the issue to a vote. During the break, how-ever, newspapers continued to headline the story. "By the time the Legislature came back again," Hunt explained, "the Legislators had evidently heard from their home folks, because the vote was overwhelmingly in favor of the inves-tigation." This first skirmish awakened Roosevelt to the massive persuasive capacity of the press to stir public resolve and exert pressure on otherwise unassailable insiders.

The investigation was entrusted to the Judiciary Committee which, over the course of seven weeks, conducted hearings in both New York and Albany. Despite an accumulation of damaging evidence, a majority declared that Judge Westbrook's behavior, although indiscreet, did not warrant impeachment. Hunt later alleged that three decisive votes in favor of impeachment were lost in the middle of the night when the legislators were offered $2,500 each to sign the majority report. When the Judiciary Committee's decision was announced, Hunt recalled, Roosevelt "was dancing and jumping about and full of fire and full of fury and full of fight."

"Mr. Speak-ah! Mr. Speak-ah," he called out, with a strident plea for his colleagues to accept the minority report calling for impeachment: "To you, members of the Legislature of the greatest commonwealth in this great Federal Union, I say you cannot by your votes clear the Judge. He stands condemned by his own acts in the eyes of all honest people. All you can do is to shame yourselves and give him a brief extension of his dishonored career. You cannot cleanse the leper. Beware lest you taint yourselves with his leprosy."

Roosevelt's dramatic exhortation brought "deathless silence" to the chamber, but the assembly nonetheless voted on May 31, 1882, to accept the majority report exonerating the judge. "It was apparent to those familiar with politics," Spinney concluded, "that every wire that could be pulled in both the dominant political parties to prevent impeachment was stretched to the tautest."

"The action of the Assembly last night in voting to exonerate Judge Westbrook is simply disgraceful," declared the *New York Herald*. "We venture the assertion that the entire Bench and nine-tenths of the Bar of the State are convinced that Judge Westbrook ought to be impeached." The *New York Times* titled its editorial "A Miscarriage of Justice"; the *Brooklyn Eagle* called the vote "an open avowal of contempt for public sentiment, for public intelligence and common honesty." The *Buffalo Express* quoted from Roosevelt's speech, and predicted that the young man's indictment expressed "the general verdict."

Though Roosevelt's first joust at entrenched corruption had failed, he emerged as a champion of reform both within the assembly and in the court of public opinion. Hunt maintained that Roosevelt "won his spurs in that fight." While he had been derided as "a society man and a dude" prior to the Westbrook debate, he was now "looked upon as a full-fledged man and worthy of anybody's esteem." When the session came to a close in early June, claimed Spinney, "Roosevelt's name was known to every nook and corner of the State."

⌒ ⌒

"I ROSE LIKE A ROCKET," Roosevelt remembered, proudly noting his reelection the following November with "an enormous majority" despite a Democratic sweep in the state elections. As a further sign of his swift and brilliant ascent, when the legislature convened in January 1883, his Republican colleagues selected him, the youngest member of the New York State Assembly, as their minority leader. Thereafter, he acknowledged, "I immediately proceeded to lose *my* perspective . . . I came an awful cropper, and had to pick myself up after learning by bitter experience the lesson that I was not all-important."

"My head was swelled," he conceded, looking back upon his self-indulgent behavior in the aftermath of such sudden fame. "I would listen to no argument, no advice." In that second session, Hunt recalled, Roosevelt became "a perfect nuisance," interrupting the business of the House in a manner "so explosive, and so radical and so indiscreet" that even fellow reformers worried that he was becoming "a damn fool." When contesting an issue, "he yelled and pounded his desk," firing back "with all the venom imaginary." Without restraint he castigated the New York *World* "as a paper of limited circulation and unlimited scurrility"; he denounced the "rotten" Democratic Party, belittling the political lineage that ran "down the roll from Polk, the mendacious, through Pierce, the Copperhead, to Buchanan, who faced both ways." His colorful language invariably made headlines, spurring him to progressively more outlandish outbursts. His antics kept his name in print, but he finally acknowledged that he was "absolutely deserted" and lamented that "every bit of influence I had was gone. The things I wanted to do I was powerless to accomplish."

This grim, isolate reality prompted a radical reassessment: "I thereby learned the invaluable lesson that in the practical activities of life no man can render the highest service unless he can act in combination with his fellows, which means a certain amount of give-and-take between him and them." Restraining his histrionic rhetoric and making overtures to his fellow legislators, Roosevelt was able to establish common grounds of agreement. "I turned in to help them, and they turned to and gave me a hand," he reflected, "and so we were able to get things done."

Roosevelt's developing sensibilities did not initially embrace the cause of labor seeking greater protection against the abusive onslaughts of the flourishing industrial order. Rather, he regarded union leaders as "exceedingly unattractive persons," and considered the majority of labor bills introduced in the legislature "foolish." The reigning laissez-faire doctrine—inculcated at Harvard as well as Yale, and accepted categorically by those within his privileged circle—had "biased" him, he later acknowledged, "against all governmental schemes for the betterment of the social and industrial conditions of laborers." With unexamined confidence, he voted against increasing the minimum wage to 25 cents an hour, spoke in opposition to a bill that would limit streetcar conductors to twelve-hour workdays, and fought against legislation to raise the salaries of New York's policemen and firemen.

When the Cigar-Makers' Union introduced a bill to prohibit the manu-facture of cigars in tenement houses, Roosevelt presumed from the outset he would vote against it. He had always believed that tenement owners had an absolute right to do as they wished with their own property. As he examined more closely the conditions leading to the bill, however, he began to question his inherited resistance to social legislation.

The labor leader Samuel Gompers had long considered the production of cigars in unsanitary tenements "one of the most dreadful, cancerous sores" on the city of New York. Realizing that the only hope of eradicating a system that employed nearly 10,000 people lay in exposing the "actual character of the evils," he conducted a personal inspection of the tenements, gaining entrance in the guise of a book agent peddling copies of Charles Dickens. Gompers made detailed notes of his observations and published comprehensive reports of his findings. He discovered that the capitalists who owned the tenement factories demanded grueling hours from their workers, mainly Jewish im-migrants, and charged absurd rents for their filthy, ill-ventilated apartments.

In one tenement house, fifteen families crowded into three floors. Fathers, mothers, and children were at work stripping, drying, and wrapping cigars from six in the morning until midnight. In the yard, "a breeding ground of disease" with "no drain to a sewer," lay large mounds of decaying tobacco. Another building housed ninety-eight people from twenty families, with several families living and working together in one room. Everywhere piles of tobacco and fetid tobacco scraps littered the floors, filling the air with an overwhelming stench. The hallways were so "dark and gloomy" that even at midday it seemed like night.

Roosevelt was shaken by these reports. He agreed to accompany Gomp-ers on an inspection tour, pledging that "if the conditions described really existed he would do everything in his power to secure the passage of the bill." He admitted that he was "a good deal shocked" at what he found. While a few of the tenements provided living space for the workers apart from the sweatshops, the "overwhelming majority" had no separate accommodation. He long remembered one tenement in which five adults and several children were confined to a single room for sleeping, eating, and making cigars. "The tobacco was stowed about everywhere, alongside the foul bedding, and in a corner where there were scraps of food." After two additional forays into this dark underworld, Roosevelt was "convinced beyond a shadow of doubt" that the manufacture of cigars in tenement houses "was an evil thing from every standpoint, social, industrial and hygienic." Though the proposed bill was "a dangerous departure from the laissez-faire doctrine in which he thoroughly believed," he championed its passage and joined a group of supporters urging Governor Grover Cleveland to sign it.

Once the bill became law in March 1883, the cigar makers straightaway brought suit, arguing their right to hold property, guaranteed by the state constitution, was violated by the new regulations. The case, *In re Jacobs*, eventually made its way to the New York Court of Appeals, where the justices declared that the law indeed deprived the cigar makers of their "fundamental rights of liberty . . . without due process of law." Furthermore, the court argued, the legislation did not constitute a legitimate use of the state's police power to regulate behavior detrimental to the public welfare, for tobacco was in no way "injurious to the public health." On the contrary, it was "a disinfectant and a prophylactic."

"It was this case," Roosevelt later said, "which first waked me to . . . the fact that the courts were not necessarily the best judges of what should be done to better social and industrial conditions." While the justices were well intentioned, they interpreted law solely from the vantage point of the propertied classes. "They knew nothing whatever of tenement house conditions," he charged, "they knew nothing whatever of the needs, or of the life and labor, of three-fourths of their fellow-citizens in great cities." In the years that followed, the court's defense of free enterprise in this case would be repeatedly cited to block governmental regulation of industry. "It was," Roosevelt observed, "one of the most serious setbacks which the cause of industrial and social progress and reform ever received."

Roosevelt soon demonstrated his broadening perspective as a legislator in the fight for civil service reform. Members of the Democratic Party he had lately termed "rotten" now became his allies in the construction of a civil service bill that would, he said, "do for the City of New York what the Pendleton bill has done for the United States. Its aim is to take the civil service out of the political arena, where it now lies festering, a reproach and a hissing to all decent men, and the most terrible source of corruption." Recognizing Roosevelt's ability to galvanize the reform element in the assembly, Governor Grover Cleveland summoned him and promised that "he would deliver the Cleveland Democrats in the House" if Roosevelt would corral his own faction. The deal was struck and genuine civil service reform came to New York.

Easily winning a third term in November 1883, when the Republicans recaptured a majority in the assembly, Roosevelt announced he would run for Speaker. With the Republican bosses lined up against him, he calculated that his "only chance lay in arousing the people in the different districts." Never one for half-measures, Theodore Roosevelt campaigned tirelessly. He sent out letters to potential supporters and personally visited dozens of assembly members, traveling by horse, train, or on foot to remote villages and towns. His open pursuit of the post dismayed his patrician circle of friends, who insisted that "the office should seek the man and not the man the office." Roosevelt countered that "if Abraham Lincoln had not sought the Presidency he never would have been nominated."

Though his spirited campaign failed to break the hold of the machine, Roosevelt's attempt to run independent of patronage from the bosses reinforced his leadership of the burgeoning reform element. His autonomy, he later maintained, enabled him "to accomplish far more than [he] could have accomplished as Speaker." Selected as chairman of the influential Committee on the Cities, Roosevelt promptly introduced a series of bills aimed at dismantling the dominion of the Tammany Hall machine. The primary measure would invest greater power in the mayor rather than the aldermen, who were solely "the creatures of the local ward bosses." To enlist public backing in the struggle to reorganize city government, Roosevelt launched investigations into various city departments, reaping headlines with dramatic exposés of venality and abuse of the public trust. "I feel now as though I had the reins in my hand," he assured Alice in January 1884.

Years later, George Spinney fondly recalled that despite the punishing work hours Roosevelt kept, he found time for festive dinners and shared pints of ale with reporters and colleagues where conversation and song stretched into the early morning hours. Spinney would never forget the "great night" when Roosevelt challenged him for the title of amateur boxing champion. With the entire assembly watching, Spinney, taller and heavier than Roosevelt, conceded after three rounds that "he'd had enough." Amid general good cheer, Roosevelt was declared victor.

⤳ ⤲

EVERY WEEKEND, ROOSEVELT HASTENED HOME to be with his wife, who was expecting their first child in mid-February 1884. A year earlier, Theodore and Alice had moved from his mother's house to a comfortable brownstone on West 45th Street. In diary entries, Roosevelt extolled the pleasure of being "in my own lovely little home, with the sweetest and prettiest of all little wives— I can imagine nothing more happy in life than an evening spent in my cozy little sitting room before a bright fire of soft coal, my books all around me."

Confident that this baby would be the first of many, Theodore bought a spectacular piece of property on Oyster Bay and hired an architect to build a country home amid the fields and forests that had fostered his imagination and spurred his passion for nature. During their weekends together, the young couple spent hours poring over the architect's designs for the spacious ten-bedroom house entirely skirted by a porch. He proposed to christen their nest "Leeholm," in honor of Alice. "How I did hate to leave my bright, sunny little love," Theodore lamented in early February after their weekend had drawn to a close. "I love you and long for you all the time, and oh *so* tenderly; doubly tenderly now, my sweetest little wife. I just long for Friday evening when I shall be with you again."

During the winter months, Theodore decided to sublet his little brownstone and move back to his family's spacious home on West 57th Street. There, his mother, his unmarried sister Bamie, and a host of family servants could watch over Alice while he was in Albany. His sister Corinne, married two years earlier to Douglas Robinson and mother to a baby boy, had also returned to the family home for the winter season. Clearly, Alice would not lack loving support in Theodore's absence.

On Monday afternoon, February 11, with the arrival of the baby imminent, Theodore left for Albany to attend to several city bills then in progress. Alice had assured him that while she "hated" to see him leave, she was "feeling well." The doctor did not expect her labor to begin until Thursday at the earliest. In fact, her gravest concern lay with Mittie, who had suffered for several days with what appeared to the family a severe cold, but which the doctor suspected might be typhoid.

"I do love my dear Thee so much," Alice told him. "I wish I could have my little new baby soon." Twenty-four hours later, at 8:30 p.m. on Tuesday evening, February 12, she gave birth to a healthy eight-and-three-quarter-pound girl. According to the handwritten account that Mittie's sister Anna kept for the child to read when she grew up, Alice was thrilled that her baby was a little girl. A nurse took the newborn to be washed and dressed before returning her to her mother, who cradled and kissed her.

Roosevelt received the welcome news in a telegram from New York the following morning. Isaac Hunt would long recall the joyful scene in the assembly that morning when all present congratulated him on the news. "He was full of life and happiness." Despite an ambivalent report that his mother was "only fairly well," Theodore had no reason to suspect her condition was anything out of the ordinary.

The family at 57th Street, however, was rapidly becoming aware of considerable cause for worry. The attending doctor recognized the symptoms Alice was developing as signs of acute Bright's disease, perhaps resulting from an infection that had inflamed her kidneys. Alice could easily have attributed the complications of the disease—back pain, vomiting, puffiness of the face, and distention of the body—to her advanced pregnancy. By the time the diagnosis was made, fluid had likely accumulated in Alice's lungs, restricting her ability to breathe.

Mittie, meanwhile, slipped in and out of consciousness. The enervating advance of what was indeed acute typhoid racked Theodore's mother with high fever, diarrhea, vomiting, and a worsening dehydration. As in many cases, the disease had progressed "somewhat insidiously," with early symptoms of headache, lassitude, and feverishness that gave way to prostration, delirium, internal hemorrhage, and a "coma vigil" when less than a day of life remained.

A second telegram was dispatched to Albany, advising Theodore to come home at once. The thickening fog that stalled the progress of his train ride to New York mirrored his despair. For nearly two weeks, New Yorkers had endured a string of what the *Times* called "suicidal" days, "dark, foggy, depressing, and dismal." Visibility was drastically diminished in the pervasive fog, which stalled traffic on the river and railways when signals became invisible. Ferryboats were unable to run; horses jostled one another on the streets; the elevated railway ran off its tracks. "There is," the *Times* remarked, "something suggestive of death and decay in the dampness that fills the world, clings to the house door, drips from the fences, coats the streets with liquid nastiness, moistens one's garments, and paints the sky lead-color."

The fog that forced Theodore's train to creep along also delayed the return of Corinne and Douglas Robinson from a brief visit to Baltimore. Elliott met them at the door. "There is a curse on this house!" he said. "Mother is dying, and Alice is dying, too." It was nearly midnight when Theodore finally reached home. Racing up to the third floor, he found Alice in a state of semi-consciousness. He held her gently, refusing to leave her side, until he was informed that if he wished to see his mother one last time, he had better come downstairs. At three o'clock that morning, surrounded by her children, Mittie died. She was only forty-nine. Returning to the third floor, Theodore once more enfolded his wife in an embrace. By two o'clock that dismal St. Valentine's Day afternoon, twenty-two-year-old Alice Lee Roosevelt was also dead. Roosevelt's private diary for that day contains a single, desolate entry. Beneath a large X he wrote: "The light has gone out of my life."

"Seldom, if ever, has New York society received such a shock," observed the New York *World* when word spread that Roosevelt's wife and mother had died in a single day. When the news of the twin deaths reached Albany, the assembly took an action "wholly unprecedented in the legislative annals of the State or country," voting unanimously to adjourn until the following

Monday evening in recognition of "the desolating blow" suffered by its revered colleague. One assemblyman after another rose to show Roosevelt that he had companions in grief. "It has never been my experience to stand in the presence of such a sorrow as this," said one speaker. Isaac Hunt's voice filled with affection as he spoke of his "particular friend." He called upon his colleagues to appreciate "the uncertainty of human life" and use their remaining hours "to improve the opportunities of the present—to act well our part upon this stage of action." Witnessing the overwhelming emotions in the chamber, one reporter stated that "no sadder meeting of the Legislature has ever been held."

Theodore remained "in a dazed, stunned state" throughout the double funeral at the Fifth Avenue Presbyterian Church and the burial at Green-Wood Cemetery in Brooklyn. "He does not know what he does or says," observed his former tutor, Arthur Cutler. "I fear he sleeps little, for he walks a great deal in the night," Corinne told Elliott, "and his eyes have that strained red look."

Six years earlier, his father's death had taught Theodore that frantic activity was the only way to keep sorrow at bay. "If I had very much time to think," he had said then, "I should almost go crazy." Now he determined to return to the assembly as soon as possible. "I shall come back to my work at once," he told one friend. "There is now nothing left for me except to try to so live as not to dishonor the memory of those I loved who have gone before me."

He returned "a changed man," Hunt recalled. "From that time on there was a sadness about his face that he never had before." When Hunt tried to console his friend, he soon discovered that Theodore "did not want anybody to sympathize with him. It was a grief that he had in his own soul." He recorded his pain only in his private diary, and even there the account was spare: "We spent three years of happiness greater and more unalloyed than I have ever known fall to the lot of others. For joy or sorrow my life has now been lived out."

Roosevelt's inability to express and share his grief over the loss of his wife finally locked into an obsessive refusal to speak of her at all. As planned, he allowed the baby to be christened Alice, but in letters to his sister Bamie, with whom the child had gone to live, he referred to her simply as "Baby Lee." "There can never be another Alice to me," he confessed to a friend, "nor could I have another, not even her own child, bear her name." Almost all his love letters to Alice from Harvard were destroyed, along with most of the pictures and mementoes of their courtship. To dwell on the loss, he believed, was "both weak and morbid."

Roosevelt had at first been thrilled to realize that his baby shared her birthday with Abraham Lincoln, one whose high and profound character he considered without parallel. Yet the manner in which his hero had dealt with the death of his ten-year-old son Willie from a typhoid epidemic that swept Washington in 1862 could hardly have differed more from Roosevelt's response to the loss of his wife and the needs of their child. Rather than dispose of all reminders and mementoes, Lincoln cherished every vestige of his son's life: a painting by the child adorned his mantelpiece; he spent hours leafing through a scrapbook in which Willie had followed the various battles of the war; and he told countless stories about his son to visitors and friends. Believing that the dead continue only in the minds of the living, Lincoln willfully maintained an intense connection with his dead son. In starkest contrast to Lincoln's fervent determination to consecrate a part of his daily life to his child is Roosevelt's systematic suppression of his wife's memory. Indeed, Roosevelt's *Autobiography*, written three decades later, failed even to recognize that his first wife had ever lived. And years later, when his niece had lost her fiancé, he likewise advised her "to treat the past as past, the event as finished and out of her life. . . . Let her never speak one word of the matter, henceforth."

UPON HIS RETURN TO ALBANY, Roosevelt immersed himself in the long hours of work. The routine of the daily sessions and the camaraderie of his fellow legislators worked to mitigate his misery, just as the circumscribed world of Harvard had offered refuge from the pain of his father's death. "We are now holding evening sessions and I am glad we are," he told Bamie; "indeed the more we work the better I like it." In the weeks that followed, his Committee on the Cities conducted a series of dramatic investigations, and eventually nine reform bills were reported to the floor. He was able to secure passage of the most vital of these, including his bill to diminish the scope of the machine-controlled Board of Aldermen by centralizing responsibility in the hands of the mayor. The brilliant cartoonist Thomas Nast celebrated Roosevelt's success in a *Harper's Weekly* caricature of the young Republican legislator holding out reform bills to receive the signature of Democratic governor Grover Cleveland. Entitled "Reform Without Bloodshed," the cartoon juxtaposed the bipartisan "Law and Order" triumph in New York with the corruption warping Cincinnati's legal system. Cincinnati's woes were illustrated by headlines announcing the deadly riots and destruction in the wake of the shocking verdict in William Berner's murder trial.

Yet Roosevelt was thwarted in other reform measures, according to

William Hudson of the *Brooklyn Eagle*, because his bills were badly constructed. Cleveland felt compelled to veto them, certain they would embroil
the state in "prolonged and expensive litigation." Roosevelt was furious. "You
must not veto those bills," he told Cleveland. "I can't have it, and I won't have
it." The governor could not be dissuaded. "As debate is his strong point," an
editorialist observed of the young Roosevelt, "so parliamentary procedure
is his weak one." Too often, the critique concluded, he dives into legislative
waters "without considering whether broken bottles or blue water are below
him. With more attention to these necessary preliminaries and several years'
additional experience, he will be fitted for the larger field of national politics."

That involvement in national politics, however, came sooner than even
Roosevelt anticipated. During the weeks before the Republican Convention
in June 1884, he had joined a group of reformers that included a new friend,
Massachusetts state legislator Henry Cabot Lodge. The reformers backed
the presidential candidacy of George F. Edmunds, an honorable but little-
known senator from Vermont, over the two leading contenders, President
Chester Arthur and James Blaine. While Arthur's admirable performance
as president in the wake of Garfield's assassination had surprised reformers,
Roosevelt could never forgive the man who had defeated his father for the
collectorship. And Blaine, to his mind, was "by far the most objectionable,
because his personal honesty, as well as his faithfulness as a public servant,
are both open to question."

At the convention, Roosevelt and the small band of reformers fought
tirelessly to bring in votes for Edmunds, but in the end widespread popular
support for Blaine carried the nomination. "Our defeat is an overwhelming
rout," Roosevelt admitted to Bamie. The choice of Blaine "speaks badly for the
intelligence of the mass of my party," he ruefully continued. "It may be that
'the voice of the people is the voice of God' in fifty one cases out of a hundred;
but in the remaining forty nine it is quite as likely to be the voice of the devil,
or, what is still worse, the voice of a fool." Still, he concluded, "I am glad to
have been present at the convention, and to have taken part in its proceedings;
it was a historic scene."

"Although not a very old man, I have yet lived a great deal in my life,"
the twenty-six-year-old Roosevelt confided to a reporter friend during the
Edmunds campaign, "and I have known sorrow too bitter and joy too keen
to allow me to become either cast down or elated for more than a very brief
period over any success or defeat." Despite an almost pathological reticence in
his personal life, it seemed the recent devastating losses had put the vagaries
of politics into perspective.

His three terms in the New York State Assembly had provided Roosevelt with considerable reason for pride and satisfaction in his accomplishments. He had led the fight against Judge Westbrook and been instrumental in the passage of both the cigar bill and civil service reform. He had steered landmark governmental reform bills through his committee and on the floor. Passion and pridefulness might have occasioned some arrogant foolishness, but his perceptiveness and diligence allowed him to develop broader, more effective strategies in the wake of these mistakes. His rigorous honesty and independence inspired adulation in young reformers, and old-timers began to treat him with grudging respect.

The assembly had proved a "great school" for Roosevelt. He had learned to cooperate with colleagues far removed from his patrician background, even those he had initially dismissed as "stupid looking scoundrels" and illiterate thugs. He had come a long way from the Harvard prig who found it necessary to ascertain if a prospective friend's social standing was equal to the status of his own family. "We did not agree in all things," he later said of his colleagues, "but we did in some, and those we pulled at together. That was my first lesson in real politics. . . . If you are cast on a desert island with only a screwdriver, a hatchet, and a chisel to make a boat with, why, go make the best one you can. It would be better if you had a saw, but you haven't. So with men."

Though he insisted that he would stay in public life only if he could remain true to his principles, his singular success in the rough-and-tumble world of the state assembly revealed a temperament supremely suited for politics, strife, and competition. He thrived in the cauldron, functioning best when dramatic moral issues were at stake. He fought with gusto against fraud and corruption, delivering speeches studded with bold and original turns of phrase. "Words with me are instruments," Roosevelt said, and so they were—instruments to galvanize the emotions of the people in spirited battles for reform. "There is little use," he liked to say, "for the being whose tepid soul knows nothing of the great and generous emotion, of the high pride, the stern belief, the lofty enthusiasm, of the men who quell the storm and ride the thunder." When his critics fought back, he relished the fight, believing that "only through strife, through hard and dangerous endeavor," would victory be won.

TAFT STEADFASTLY SHUNNED THE VERY spotlight Roosevelt craved. He preferred to fight his battles from the inside, trusting logic, reason, and the careful recitation of facts. A conciliator by nature, Taft was never comfortable when called upon to deliver partisan diatribes at political rallies. Though reluctant to stir controversy, or give avoidable offense, Taft was not ready to compromise his principles for approval or expediency. He had demonstrated quiet courage in his fight against Tom Campbell and his refusal to fire conscientious workers simply because of their political preferences.

William Taft's amiable disposition and jovial countenance, evident from his earliest days, earned the goodwill and cooperation of family, friends, and colleagues alike. Within the family, Horace recalled, his brother often assumed the role of mediator. His keen perception and empathy allowed him to resolve the little conflicts that inevitably arose among parents and siblings. In his professional world, Taft's skill in developing relationships proved vital to his ascent. He established a rapport with a diverse cadre of mentors, from Murat Halstead and Miller Outcault to Benjamin Butterworth, Major Lloyd, and finally, Joseph Foraker.

Always plagued by procrastination and insecurity, Taft struggled to turn this intuitive emotional intelligence inward to access his own desires and use that knowledge to steer his life and career accordingly. Had he been able accurately to analyze the root of his unhappiness in the collector's office, he might have understood that his temperament was not suited for the turbulent world of politics. He detested political gamesmanship, found no pleasure in giving speeches, and chafed at public criticism. Yet, just as his desire to please Benjamin Butterworth had led him to take the collector's job, so, in the years ahead, his anxiety to please Nellie Herron—the complex woman who would become his wife—would eventually lead him away from his beloved law into the often scathing vortex of political life.

CHAPTER FOUR

Nellie Herron Taft

Nellie Herron, ca. 1886, the year she married
William Howard Taft.

EIGHTEEN-YEAR-OLD NELLIE HERRON was enjoying her debutante season when she was introduced to twenty-two-year-old Will Taft.
"It was at a coasting party," she wrote years later, recalling a merry gathering
where young people went sledding down a steep snow-covered Mt. Auburn
hill. Though their parents were acquainted and their younger sisters, Maria
and Fanny, were close friends, Nellie and Will had not met before this festive
night. "Tall and slender with fine gray eyes and soft brown hair," Nellie was
described as handsome rather than beautiful, with a smile that "lights up her
whole countenance."

Nellie was the fourth of eleven children born to Harriet Collins and John
Herron. She was raised with five sisters and two brothers, while three other
siblings had died in infancy. Although her mother, Harriet, was born in

Lowville, New York, a hamlet in the Adirondack foothills, the family was connected with a larger world of culture and politics. Harriet's father, Eli Collins, had served in the New York State Assembly and the U.S. Congress before his sudden death when she was eleven. Six years later, Harriet moved to Ohio to reside with her older brother. There, she met and married twenty-six-year-old lawyer John Herron.

John Herron had been a Miami University of Ohio schoolmate of future president Benjamin Harrison. When Herron opened his law practice in Cincinnati, he shared an office with another man who would be president, Rutherford B. Hayes. "Quite like living my college life over again," Hayes recorded in his diary. "We sleep on little hard mattresses in a little room cooped off from one end of our office." The lifelong friendship that developed between Herron and Hayes would eventually include their wives, Harriet and Lucy. Years later, Harriet said of Lucy that she "had no other friend with whom there has been such freedom of intimacy, none other so ready to respond with generous sympathy." This bond between the two couples would play a significant role in shaping Nellie Herron's ambitions.

When Hayes became governor of Ohio in 1869, he nominated his good friend Herron to the superior court. Herron hungered for the post but could not afford to relinquish his law practice. His wife's hankering for high society and insistence on private schooling for their children meant that he was forced "to go for money and leave glory to others." Hayes tried again a few years later. "I wish I could accept it. I may never have such another chance," Herron replied. "Like other things when I want them, I can't get them. And when I can get them I can't take them. At present I haven't one dollar coming in from a single investment that I have made & so I must look to my profession to support my family."

While Nellie remembered the three-story gray brick house where she grew up as "not particularly distinguished," she took pride that her home shared the same street as the Sinton mansion where Will's brother Charley and Annie Taft lived. Nellie marveled at the elegant facade of the white colonial dwelling; its Doric portico and bay windows, set amid "green lawns and finely kept shrubbery," reminded her of the White House.

At "The Nursery," as the exclusive Miss Nourse's school was known, Nellie excelled. A voracious reader, she carried a book everywhere she went. She read in the afternoons after completing her household chores, read at night in the quiet of her room and on rocky beaches during summer vacations. "A book," Nellie confided in her diary, "has more fascination for me than anything else." She possessed a sensibility for the beauty of language. Reading aloud with her girlfriends, she was attracted to the sound of words and the rhythms of passages. The curriculum at The Nursery included literature, history, science, music, French, German, Latin, and Greek, a comprehensive course of study to prepare students for entry into the best colleges. Nellie yearned to continue her education when she graduated, hoping especially to study music, which she considered "the inspiration of all my dreams and ambitions." While her brothers departed for Harvard and Yale, however, Nellie was informed that her father could not afford to send her to college. Instead, she was expected to "come out" into society and find herself a good husband.

Nellie was sixteen in 1877 when she accompanied her parents on a week-long visit to the White House at the invitation of Rutherford and Lucy Hayes. The president and first lady planned to celebrate their silver wedding anniversary among the friends who had stood with them at their marriage in 1852. The invitation included the prospect of a christening ceremony for the Herrons' seven-week-old baby in the Blue Room. The child had been named Lucy in honor of Harriet's closest friend. Harriet was reluctant at first to accept, protesting that "her baby has no fine clothes fit for such a place . . . & that she herself has only the same dresses that she had last March, hasn't bought a stitch since & hasn't time now to do it, even if she had any money to pay for them." But John insisted, and Nellie was thrilled to be included.

"I feel very much complimented that you should have remembered me in the preparations for the holiday festivities," Nellie wrote her "Aunt Lucy." "I have been in some doubts as to whether it would do for me to emerge from the chrysalis of school girl existence even for a short time into the butterfly life of young ladyhood, but the temptation has proved too strong for me, and it will give me great pleasure to accept your invitation."

Because Nellie had yet to make her official debut, she was not included at the anniversary dinner in the East Room attended by cabinet officers, generals, and justices of the Supreme Court. She could hear the music of the Marine Band from her room and spy the elegant gowns amid the splendor of the Blue, Red, and Green parlors, "profusely decorated with choice flowers from the conservatory." Hayes stated in his diary that Nellie brought "the house alive with laughter, fun, and music."

She was so elated by the visit that she rapturously confided to "Uncle Rutherford" that she intended "to marry a man who will be president." With a smile, Hayes replied: "I hope you may, and be sure you marry an Ohio man." Thirty years later, even as her husband sat in Roosevelt's cabinet, the allure of that first stay at the White House had not dimmed. In interviews with journalists, she recalled every detail. "Nothing in my life," she confessed, "reaches the climax of human bliss, which I felt as a girl of sixteen, when I was entertained at the White House." The vision of that expansive world spurred her sense of purpose. "She was intoxicated by what she saw and heard there," observed one reporter, "the bigness and breadth of the life."

For as long as she could remember—Nellie revealed in her diary—she had dreaded the prospect of leaving school, turning eighteen, and "coming out" into society. In the fall before her first season, she and her best friend, Alice (Allie) Keys, shrank from the prospect of becoming young women according to the traditional rituals, obliged to "receive attentions and offers and to wait around calmly to see if any future life will adjust itself." When the season drew to a close the following spring, though, she noted with surprise that she had "exceedingly" enjoyed herself in the "perfect whirr of gaiety" of the young Cincinnati set. She and her girlfriends Allie, Agnes, Laura, and Mary "stuck valiantly to each other" as they joined their male friends at Gilbert and Sullivan operettas, theatre parties, poker games, and German dances at Clifton Hall.

As summer came, her mood shifted. The cumulative months without intellectual or purposeful activity had grown enervating. "I am blue as indigo," she wrote on July 13, 1880, from a hammock at Yellow Springs, Ohio, a popular summer resort where she was vacationing with her family. "We are all rusticating up here, doing absolutely nothing, and I am reduced to a queer state of mind. . . . I am sick and tired of my life. I would rather be anyone else, even some one who has not some advantages I have and I am only nineteen. I feel often as if I were fifty." She yearned to "be busy and accomplish something." Even her attempts to pursue musical instruction were stymied. While she practiced diligently on her own to become a more accomplished pianist, she required guidance and lessons to achieve genuine virtuosity—lessons that cost more than her father would pay to accommodate what he considered simply a pastime.

"I would much rather give up some of the dresses I am getting," she wrote, "but Mama thinks I must have them." Harriet was determined that her daughters should "enjoy all the comforts and privileges of the wealthy class," even if John had to work long hours and weekends to stay out of debt. Nellie's biographer Carl Anthony conjectures that "a repressed nervousness" was instilled in the young woman by the chronic strain of the family's drive to maintain their place in a circle of greater wealth and privilege.

"I am beginning to want some steady occupation," she confided in her diary. "I read a good deal to be sure . . . but I should have some occupation that would require active work moving around—and I don't know where to find it. I believe my greatest desire now is to write a book. . . . I do so want to be independent."

Nellie's stifled energy and curiosity were quickened by the arrival of "that adorable Will Taft" at Yellow Springs. "Unfortunately I did not recover from my surprise and delight soon enough," she wrote Allie, "to make that impression which I would have wished." Will's solicitous, chivalric nature made a great effect upon Nellie. She was touched when he offered to cut up the meat for her six-year-old sister at a picnic on the Fourth of July, and charmed when he helped the women over brooks as they tramped through the woods the following day. "We had a lovely walk," she reported, and at an evening dance, Will "was enchanting as ever. You see what a splendid chance I had at Will, but alas!" she noted regretfully, "he strikes me with awe."

Later that summer, Nellie accompanied her father to Rhode Island's Narragansett Pier, where she was joined by several friends. Though her days were filled with tennis, croquet, and sailing, she could not rouse herself from her "stupid state." The thrill of forbidden activities provided some respite from her torpor. She hid in the rocks at dusk to smoke cigarettes with her girlfriend Sallie, gambled at cards, and drank milk punches laced with whiskey late at night.

As fall approached, convinced that her rebellious unconventional nature would forever preclude a great success in society, Nellie pledged to devote five or six hours a day to the piano. She begged her mother to intercede with her father and facilitate the music lessons she craved. She realized, however, that no decision could be made until her parents returned from a two-month trip with the president and first lady to California, a historic voyage that marked the first visit by a president to the west coast. Nellie was left behind with her four younger siblings to take charge of the household, to dust and tidy, sew and darn, set the table for dinner, and wash the dishes. "I have not read one good book, novel excepted, but Schiller's Life by Carlyle," she complained.

Nellie gained some leisure time when her parents returned, but the music lessons never materialized. Desperate for a measure of genuine intellectual engagement, she enrolled in less expensive chemistry and German classes at the University of Cincinnati. Her spirits lifted. She relished her studies and joined a walking club that included Annie Taft, several of her girlfriends, John Mack, and Howard Hollister, Will's best friend. "He is very sympathetic," Nellie wrote of Hollister. Seated next to him at a supper following one of their hikes, she was "all afire" when he launched into a sentimental debate on the glory of dying for one you loved. Being "exceedingly romantic" herself, Nellie leapt into the conversation. Then, suddenly overcome by self-consciousness, she worried that he was simply drawing her out to "make fun" of her. "Make fun of you," he exclaimed. "Why Miss Herron there is no one whose good opinion I value as much as yours."

After a brief flirtation, Nellie and Howard settled down to become good friends. "I am perfectly delighted in the hope that a very ordinary love affair may perhaps have become what I always longed for," she wrote in her diary, "a warm friendship between two quite congenial people—which is very rare, and so much more to be desired than the other. . . . Such a friendship is infinitely higher than what is usually called love, for in it there is a realization of each other's defects, and a proper appreciation of their good points, without that fatal idealization which is so blind. . . . From my point of view a love which is worthy of the name should always have a beginning in the other, and should this friendship turn into something higher it is a blessed happiness."

Nellie counseled Howard through a tumultuous relationship with her friend Agnes Davis while he, in turn, supported Nellie's struggle to find purpose in her life. In her diary, she recorded diverting evenings in the German section of town where they "drank beer and ate Wiener Wurst." Mixing with laborers and merchants in raucous beer halls might be unsuitable behavior for a society girl, but Nellie loved the atmosphere. Indeed, the fact that such surroundings "greatly horrified" her proper friends intensified her pleasure. "There being something Bohemian about it which delighted me," she wrote, "I really felt quite like a comrade & man."

In the spring of 1883, contrary to her mother's wishes, Nellie accepted an offer to teach in a private school for boys. "Do you realize you will have to give up society, as you now enjoy it," Harriet reminded her. "Certainly late hours and dancing parties do not promote the patience and physical endurance required by a teacher. And then is it quite the thing for a young girl in your position to teach in a boys school—and where there are no other ladies? . . . I shrink from thinking of you as making your own way in the world in any inconsequential manner." Nellie was shaken by the opposition that her mother expressed in "two dreadful letters." Though several friends admired her decision, the majority questioned her "queer taste." Disconcerted by her inability to "get along as other girls do," she was determined to move forward, envisioning a future as headmistress of a school. "Of course a woman is happier who marries, if she marries exactly right, but how many do," she reasoned. "Otherwise I do think that she is much happier single, and doing some congenial work."

Harriet Herron's conviction that her daughter's decision would inhibit her social life proved unfounded. In fact, Nellie's occupation bolstered her confidence and buoyed her mood, making her a far more engaging companion. Her insecurity in Will Taft's presence evaporated as he joined her regular circle of friends. On numerous occasions, she accompanied Will and Howard Hollister to concerts and German dances at Clifton Hall, returning the hospitality with whist parties at her house. "The meeting at Miss Herron's was a great success," Will told his sister Fanny, describing an evening of cards, supper, charades, and games. "We made the Herron mansion ring with the merry peals of the young ladies and the harsher but joyous tone of the men until the hands of the clock were pushing us home by pointing towards two o'clock."

Sustained by this new sense of direction, Nellie no longer found the long summer days depressing. In July 1883, she joined Allie and a group of their friends at "Sea Verge," the Keys' summer mansion at Little Boar's Head in North Hampton, New Hampshire. Alongside the customary swimming and sailing, tennis and card games, she and Allie determined to embark on an ambitious reading program. They resolved daily to read aloud fifty pages of Henry Buckle's three-volume *History of Civilization in England*; they shared "long and very tough" readings of John Stuart Mill, and immersed themselves in German and Italian. To "repair" their "exhausted intellects," they took long walks through the countryside, picked berries, read a little poetry, and watched the tide break around the rocks. In the evenings they plunged into the bracing water of the North Atlantic to stimulate their appetites before dinner.

Returning to her teaching job in the fall, Nellie struggled with her mother's increasingly strident opposition. "Mamma thinks I am wrong," she told her diary. "I hope that I am not . . . I should be a miserable apathetic woman without an interest in life unless I bettered myself now while I am young and courageous and engaged in some real work. The usual pottering which an un-married woman calls work would never satisfy me." Still, she could not easily disregard her mother's admonition that a society girl entered the workforce at her peril. "Why should I take life so hard? Other people seem to get through all right without inconvenient ideas," she lamented. "All week I have been in that state when my eyes fill with tears at the least provocation," she admitted, "and I take refuge in silence."

Despite these private misgivings, Nellie was self-possessed and animated among her friends, emerging as the leader of their social circle. The Saturday night salons she hosted, anticipated by her coterie the week long, offered an enlivening combination of entertainment and intellectual pursuits. The regu-lars included Allie Keys, Will Taft and his brother Horace, Howard Hollister, Agnes Davis, and Maria Herron, Nellie's younger sister. The group selected a different topic each week and the members of the salon were expected to prepare for discussion with all the reading and research they could muster. For the session on the French Revolution, Will read Thomas Carlyle's *The French Revolution, a History*; when the topic was Russia, he read Donald MacKenzie's *Russia*. When Rousseau, Cavour, Edmund Burke, Matthew Arnold, and Isaac Newton were selected as subjects, he scoured the public library for their works. The Yale graduate who had refused to read outside the course curriculum suddenly found himself inspired.

"Nellie Herron has made a great success of her salon," Will reported to his sister. "I feel as if I had really profited greatly by the reading which I have done for it. The pleasure of it has grown as we go on. I value the friendships which have grown out of it very highly. Nobody is absent when he can help it." Indeed, forced to travel out of town one Saturday, Will sent Nellie roses to express his regret at missing "that sweet school of Peripatetic philosophy in which I am an humble but enthusiastic disciple."

Writing of one salon session, focused on Edmund Burke, Will wryly remarked to his mother that the discussion became "very heated especially between the men, who knowing less about the subject than the ladies, are naturally more certain of their position." Burke was not the only topic to stir dissension among these passionate young people; in the aftermath of a debate on slavery, the volatile mixture of historical inquiry and individual points of view left Will much chagrined. "I am not satisfied at all with my bearing in the slavery discussion," he wrote to Nellie. "I deeply regret that my manner was such as to leave the impression on your mind that I held your suggestions or arguments lightly or regarded them with contempt. . . . So far as holding your opinions lightly, I know no one who attaches more weight to them or who more admires your powers of reasoning than the now humbled subscriber."

The attachments forged in the salon deepened as the friends consoled each other in difficulties and together celebrated triumphs. The group spent weekends together at the Keys' mansion in Walnut Hills and escorted each other to the regular Thursday German dances. The girls organized card parties and picnics for which the men provided both the punch and the repast. They put on amateur theatricals for charity. Nellie long remembered the burlesque production of *Sleeping Beauty* in which Will played the beautiful princess, while Horace, who had fallen in love with Nellie's sister, Maria, performed as Puck.

With increasing frequency, Nellie's name appeared in Will's letters to his family in Vienna. He lauded her as "the only notable exception" among superficial society girls who viewed "a suitable marriage as a proper ending of their social career." He proudly relayed the news that she had been offered a teaching position at Miss Nourse's school, declaring that she deserved "the greatest credit" for persevering despite censure from friends and family alike. "It is easy enough to talk about woman's widening her sphere and being something more than an ornament or a housekeeper but it is not so easy in the present state of society for her to act on that theory."

In the summer of 1884, Will was invited to spend a long weekend with Nellie and Allie at Sea Verge, the summer mansion at Little Boar's Head. During those sunlit days, filled with picnics, swims, and ventures into Boston, Will first began to recognize the central place Nellie had come to hold in his life. "After awhile I found myself deferring to her opinion in everything I did or said," he later told Allie. "Finally what she thought became of much more importance to me than what I thought myself."

Largely to gain Nellie's approbation, Will began to carry a book as a matter of course. "Trollope is a great favorite of mine because of the realistic every day tone which one finds in every line he writes," he told her. "His heroes have failings human character is heir to, and we like them none the less on that account." He became increasingly solicitous of Nellie's happiness. When the German opera festival was in town, he accompanied her to hear *Tannhäuser*, admitting to his mother that while "my own appreciation of Wagner is not intense . . . [I] shall derive most if not all of my pleasure from her enjoyment of the music."

Eager to acknowledge Nellie's own desire to accomplish something worthy, he spoke with disdain of two wealthy acquaintances whose chief literary nourishment was drawn from stock reports. "It seems to me that with their money and opportunities they could do so much good in this country where we are in such need of disinterested public work that their listlessness and idleness is little better than a sin. . . . If all the wealthy were of their kind I should become a communist." He found validation for the more progressive ideals he and Nellie shared in reports from the East that "young men of wealth who do not have to devote their time to making a livelihood, are taking an interest in politics." This is "a good augury," he maintained, for it would infuse a generation's political life with a growing zeal for public service. He was likely referring directly to Theodore Roosevelt and Henry Cabot Lodge, whose reform efforts on behalf of George Edmunds were then making news.

By winter, he later confessed, "I was wakened to the fact that I loved her." The truth of his feelings struck him "with overwhelming force," and in late April 1885, he finally asked her to marry him. The proposal stunned Nellie, who feared that his precipitous declaration would compromise a friendship that had become vital to her. Moreover, she feared that marriage would destroy her hard-won chance to accomplish something worthy in her own right. She turned him down and told him never to speak of it again.

Undeterred, Will remained certain that in time he could bring her to love him as he loved her. Only five days later, he penned a long letter, assuring her that the hesitation she felt about the institution of marriage was perfectly understandable. "I never have been certain that marriage was the happier state for women. I know it is for a man. Then too a mistake with him does not involve his entire life. With a woman a mistake is worse than death for in marriage she gives her all." During a long walk a few days after that, he pressed his case, following up with another heartfelt letter. "I love you Nellie," he declared. "I love you for all that you are. I love you for your noble consistent character . . . for all that you are, for all that you hope to be. . . . Oh how I will work and strive to be better and do better, how I will labor for our joint advancement if only you will let me. You will be my companion, my love and my life."

Her initial resistance to his entreaties only confirmed his admiration and intensified his own determination. "My love for you grew out of a friendship, intimate and of long standing," he noted, methodically laying out his appeal. "That friendship of course was founded on a respect and admiration for your high character, your sweet womanly qualities and your intellectual superiority over any woman I know and for that quality in you which is called sympathy but I call it self forgetting companionableness. . . . Much as I should love to have you love me now and say so now, there is proud satisfaction I feel in that such a heart as yours can not be won in a moment."

Finally, Nellie agreed to an engagement. Far from curtailing her ambitions, she sensed that marriage to a man of Will's enlightened temperament would create enhanced opportunities for them both. With her direction and support, he could be her emissary to the wider world she craved. "You know," she told her mother soon after the engagement, "a lot of people think a great deal of Will. Some people even say that he may obtain some very important position in Washington." Although her ambitions for her fiancé had a worldly aspect, Nellie clearly expected far more from him and from herself than mere status and stability.

Will was ready to shout the news of their betrothal from every street corner. Nellie insisted that it remain a secret from all but their parents until she was ready for a public announcement. Forced to maintain a pretense of mere friendship before Howard, Allie, Horace, and all his friends, Will had to content himself with long letters to his parents, who were still in Europe. "The more I knew her," Will told his father, "the deeper grew my respect for her, the warmer my friendship until it unconsciously ripened into a feeling that she was indispensable to my happiness. . . . I know you will love her when you come to know her and will appreciate as I do her noble character and clear cut intellect and well informed mind. She has been teaching for three years and has been no expense at all to her father. She has done this without encouragement by her family who thought the work too hard for her because she chafed under the conventionalities of society which would keep a young lady only for evening entertainments. She wanted something to do in life. . . . Her eagerness for knowledge of all kinds puts me to shame. Her capacity for work is wonderful."

That summer of 1885, when Nellie left for the Adirondacks with her family, Will experienced an unfamiliar sense of desolation. "Your sweet smile today as you stood on the stoop, I shall carry in my memory as something to console me with your absence," he wrote only hours after she departed. "And now Nellie I fold you in my arms and imprint on your lips the kisses I was cheated out of by Fate today." Solace came in the form of the daily letters he wrote. "The only real pleasure I take is in writing you," he told her, "and in the hope, so often in vain, that the mail carrier's appearance inspires in me. When I don't get a letter I read all the old ones over again." His familiar surroundings only exacerbated his restless loneliness. Everywhere he went—the library, the homes of their friends, the corner of Pike and Fifth—heightened his awareness of her absence. "It is the one who stays at home that feels the parting. New scenes, new interests, quickly dispel the pleasant sadness of the parting for the one who leaves."

To mollify his impatience for her return, he narrated the minutiae of the day without her, filling pages with political news, gossip about their friends, and images of the life they would lead once they were married. "I long to settle down in a home of our own," he told her, adding, "we must continue the salon." Nellie's father had promised them a plot of land in Walnut Hills, where they planned to construct their home. "I shall have the greatest pride in entertaining my classmates, Bonesmen, under our roof where you and they can know each other." Although Will's vision of domestic bliss included social entertainment, it focused on the bond of marriage. His letters conjured evenings seated "comfortably and cosily before a bright fire," reading and talking "with such demonstrations of affection as the unruly husband can not restrain." While he acknowledged that his ideal might seem "commonplace" or "prosaic," he fondly anticipated a married life resembling those depicted in Victorian novels, "where the husband was working hard, materially assisted and buoyed up by the earnest sympathy and intelligence of the wife."

He repeatedly assured Nellie that he would strive to make himself worthy of her. He had labored diligently in college to satisfy his parents; now he would persevere and please his wife. "His temperament," one insightful journalist later reflected, "requires settled authority." With Nellie to replace his father's role of "guide, counsellor and friend," he would find far greater success than he could ever have secured on his own. "You are becoming responsible for the actions of two persons now," he frankly admitted to Nellie. "I feel a weight lifted from my shoulders." While they might never be wealthy, they would build a rich life together. With her encouragement, he promised to overcome his reluctance and exact suitable payment for his legal work. "It is hard for me to learn to charge a fee without apologizing for its amount," he confessed. "That is one of the defects in my character you must remedy. You must stiffen me in the matter of fees." He pledged that theirs would be "an equal partnership. You earn half of everything that comes in just as much as if you wrote the briefs or honeyfugled a jury. You may write the briefs, who knows?" He proudly reported that "business had been brisker" and that he had "done twice as much work" in the months since their engagement, a circumstance which his partner Major Lloyd attributed directly to Nellie's influence.

He conceded a natural tendency toward laziness and procrastination, a condition Nellie's influence was certain to remedy in order to make him "a good and just member of society." Indeed, just two weeks before his proposal, he had delivered "a very hastily prepared paper before the Unity Club on Pontifical Rome," which, he acknowledged, did him "no credit." Horace agreed. "As usual," he told his mother, "he put the thing off until he had only two or three days to prepare it and then he had to toil like a slave. I told him I thought it would be a lesson worth a fortune to him if he were to make one complete & ignominious fizzle at this early period of his life from want of preparation. He did not do it this time but it was enough to serve as a warning. His was the best piece of the evening, but that is not saying much and he might have done much better. He has a wonderful power of work when he once gets started and the only danger is in his trusting to it too much." Will's own recognition of these deficits, and of the corresponding drive in Nellie's character, contributed to his profound admiration for the woman he loved and to his deep-seated reliance upon her judgment and resolve.

Will joined Nellie in the Adirondacks for two weeks in early August 1885. "Each day has found Nellie and me on the lake and in the woods," he joyously reported to his mother. "She sews or sketches while I read aloud to her. We finished *Their Wedding Journey* by Howells and have begun *The Mill on the Floss* by George Eliot." At summer's end, Nellie finally assented to make public the engagement.

"I knew you would be delighted to hear," Will wrote to Allie Keys. "Didn't

I know that you were hoping for this for so many months? Didn't I tingle to my finger tips with gratitude to you for the many little schemes which you concocted to help me on in my suit, you little conspirator. . . . Oh, Alice, you do know the prize I have won . . . that no more perfect character than Nellie's is among all our friends. You know what a constant source of comfort and strength she is to everyone who seeks it from her. . . . She has already made me a better man. My ideals of life are higher and I believe my purpose to attain them is stronger. Certainly there could not be given to a man a stronger motive for upright consistent, hardworking and kindly living than the approval and intelligent sympathy of such a wife."

"How much I appreciate your confidence in me," Allie elatedly replied, "your telling me so much of what is in your heart. To have had either you or Nellie marry anyone I did not know or even did not love would have been hard for me, but I should have been happy in your happiness and tried not to be selfish. But to have you marry one another is such a joy to me that the sky has been bluer and the sunlight brighter ever since I heard. Yes, Will, I do know her, and it makes me so happy to think that some one is to have her who appreciates what she is who has known her long enough to understand her, for I do not think she is soon known or easily understood. . . . You and Howard—you have been the two best new friends I ever had, and I hope and believe I shall never lose you." Allie's fervent wishes were soon realized: she and Howard became engaged, and the two couples would remain devoted friends to the end of their lives.

Certainly, Will and Nellie's match met with resounding approval from friends and family. "What a pair you will be!" Horace told Will. "In all my acquaintance she is the girl I would have picked for you long ago & ever since and you are the one I would have chosen for her." Indeed, it had appeared for a time that the two brothers might marry two Herron women, but Horace could not persuade Nellie's beautiful sister Maria to accept his proposal of marriage. Nevertheless, their lives would intersect frequently in the years ahead.

In late February 1886, Nellie and Allie traveled east together for two weeks. In New York, they stayed with Allie's wealthy Aunt Phoebe, mistress of Sea Verge, the summer home where Will first realized the depths of his feelings for Nellie. The two old friends enjoyed their time together, walking around the city, shopping for books and clothes. They perused furniture stores and curiosity shops, looking for tables, sideboards, lamps, and etchings for their new homes. From Cincinnati, Will wrote frequently to Nellie, describing his daily routine in detail only a lover would not find exhausting. "I went to the gymnasium today wholly because of you," he proudly reported. "It was

Washington's birthday and I felt lazy," he admitted, but the thought of his fiancée mobilized him. Four days later, he returned to the gym, though he acknowledged, "I have given up weighing myself each day. 'A watched pot never boils,' and I shall try to surprise myself by waiting until you get home before I weigh again."

Proceeding to Washington, Nellie selected her wedding dress, "a superbly-fashioned satin robe with embroidered front." Pining at home, Will tried to inject some levity into his letter: "I hope you will think of me tomorrow when you take your Sunday afternoon walk along the beautiful streets of Washington. I wonder, Nellie dear, if you and I will ever be there in any official capacity? Oh yes, I forgot, of course we shall when you become Secretary of the Treasury." A few days later he wrote again, musing on the ten short months which had affected a sea change in both their lives since she had finally accepted his proposal: "The parlor is unchanged, the street is unchanged, the new custom house as it was then, but to me they all wear a different look, so different indeed that I almost forget how they did look before you made silent promise to be mine. . . . In that ten months we have had very few differences of any kind."

Nellie Herron and William Taft were married on June 19, 1886, in the parlor of the Herron house on Pike Street. Alphonso and Louise, who had returned from Europe the previous October, were present to celebrate their son's marriage. Maria Herron and Fanny Taft served as bridesmaids. Horace was his brother's best man. After what the *Cincinnati Enquirer* described as "a brilliant reception," the young couple traveled to New York and prepared to embark for Europe and the honeymoon Nellie called "my first taste of the foreign travel of which I had always dreamed."

Aboard ship, they read aloud from Oliver Goldsmith's *Vicar of Wakefield* and the collected poems of Coleridge and Shelley in preparation for their visit to the English countryside. They visited Shakespeare's house in Stratford-on-Avon, reveled at the sight of Gladstone's Welsh castle in Hawarden, and dined in English country inns. Nellie pored through reports of parliamentary speeches by Gladstone and Parnell and hungered to hear live orations and debates. They continued through Scotland, Holland, and France, managing to travel for a hundred days on "just one thousand dollars," thanks to Nellie's unremitting budget.

They returned to a home still under construction in Cincinnati and spent their first month living with Will's parents. Nellie developed a strong attachment to Alphonso, whom she considered "gentle beyond anything I ever knew . . . one of the most lovable men that ever lived." Both Alphonso and Louise, she wrote, "had created a family atmosphere in which the children breathed in the highest ideals, and were stimulated to sustained and strenuous intellectual and moral effort in order to conform to the family standard." She marveled at the "strong minds, intellectual tastes, wide culture and catholic sympathies" that generated the loving yet rigorous environment of the Taft household.

In January 1887, Nellie and Will moved into their redwood-shingled home overlooking a splendid stretch of the Ohio River and the lush hills and valleys on both the Ohio and Kentucky sides. The library, lined with bookshelves of solid walnut, housed Will's accumulating legal texts, which he would continue to accrue until he had proudly amassed a catalogue of scholarly volumes that was estimated among the foremost in the country.

⤆ ⤇

No sooner were the newlyweds settled in their new home on McMillan Street than Will was surprised by Governor Foraker's decision to appoint him to the bench. Hurrying home to share the astonishing news with his wife, he tried to appear casual. "Nellie," he coyly questioned, "what would you think if I should be appointed a Judge of the Superior Court?" "Oh, don't try to be funny," Nellie answered. "That's perfectly impossible." A twenty-nine-year-old, she reasoned, would never receive an appointment over much more experienced lawyers. Quickly realizing that Will was not teasing, she was stunned and gratified by "the honour which came to us so unexpectedly." Horace was thrilled. "Wasn't it immense," he wrote Nellie. "How does his Honor bear it? You'll have to help him work with a vengeance now Nellie. Tie wct towels around his head. You & I know what kind of a judge he will make. We can afford to let the world find out."

Nellie's elation soon gave way to misgivings, however, as she reflected that the appointment "was not a matter for such warm congratulation after all." Indeed, the more she considered his new post and colleagues, the more unsettled she felt. "I saw him in close association with men not one of whom was less than fifteen years older than he, and most of whom were much more than that. He seemed to me suddenly to take on a maturity and sedateness quite out of keeping with his actual years and I dreaded to see him settled for good in the judiciary and missing all the youthful enthusiasms and exhilarating difficulties which a more general contact with the world would have given him. . . . I began even then to fear the narrowing effects of the Bench." For the young woman who had hoped her husband's career would carry them both to an exciting life in Washington, the superior court in Cincinnati assumed the aspect of a stumbling block rather than a stepping-stone.

Nevertheless, Nellie grudgingly acknowledged that her husband "did not share this feeling in any way. His appointment on the Superior Court was to him the welcome beginning of just the career he wanted." Upon completion of Will's interim appointment, Foraker successfully backed him for election to a full five-year term. This ballot marked Taft's only bid for elected office until he became a candidate for president of the United States. He flourished as a judge, proud to sit on the bench where his father had once presided. He immersed himself in work entirely suited to his temperament, enjoying legal research and finding precedents for a broad range of cases covering contracts, wills, trademarks, suits for libel and negligence, disputes between the rights of property and the rights of labor. His profound satisfaction and facility in his vocation were evident to all.

Will Taft's most significant action as a superior court judge was a ruling in 1890 that addressed the balance of power between the burgeoning labor movement and industrial interests. The case involved a secondary boycott, a sanction intended to punish one business by wielding pressure against another business unrelated to the original cause of grievance. In this instance, the Bricklayers' Union had declared a boycott against the contracting firm of Parker Brothers on grounds that the company had discriminated against its members. The union called on all suppliers of the firm's building materials to honor the boycott. When the Moore Lime Company continued to supply Parker Brothers, the union declared it would no longer use lime supplied by Moore's. Moore's & Co. sued the Bricklayers' Union for damages caused by the secondary boycott. Their suit was upheld by the lower court in Hamilton County, which awarded a verdict of $2,250 to the plaintiffs. When *Moore's & Co. v. Bricklayers' Union et al.* reached the superior court on appeal, Taft sustained the lower court decision, affirming that a secondary boycott against a firm with whom there was no dispute was illegal. His decision was upheld by the Ohio Supreme Court. Decades later, it remained a leading case on the law of secondary boycotts.

While his decision worked to limit the power of organized labor, Taft revealed a sympathy for the rights of workers that his more conservative colleagues did not share. He was careful to underscore the union's prerogative in withdrawing its members from Parker Brothers; when the union turned on an unrelated company, however, it had exceeded its legal bounds. Though Taft refused to condone the union's action in this case, he argued strongly for a laborer's "right to work for such wages as he chooses, and to get as high a rate as he can." He maintained that an individual "may lawfully notify his employers of his objection and refuse to work," and concluded that "what one workman may do . . . many may combine to do."

Taft sought to delineate union rights at a hazardous time in Cincinnati, when the memory of a violent general strike was still raw. Calling for an eight-hour day, 32,000 Cincinnati workers had joined workers in other cities in a crippling general strike commencing on May Day, 1886. Singing a version of the *Marseillaise*, they marched through the city, brandishing Springfield rifles and red flags. For days, "no freight moved in or out of the city; garbage went uncollected; laundresses, streetcar conductors, waitresses and machinists cooperated in shutting down the city." The militia was called out and the workers returned to their posts, but the horror of the strikers' "revolutionary fervor" had impressed itself upon Cincinnati's propertied classes. It was in this context that Taft, in his judicial sphere, tried to balance the rights of labor with the rights of capital.

NELLIE'S CAREFUL ALLOCATION OF WILL'S $6,000 annual salary allowed the couple to furnish their new home and still save enough to fund a second trip to Europe the following summer. With the house fully settled, Nellie returned to work, taking a teaching position at the kindergarten recently opened by Miss Nourse to serve the children of the poor. Earlier in the decade, Louise Taft had served as the first president of the Cincinnati Free Kindergarten Association. In the 1880s, Ohio laws had forbidden public funding of education for children younger than six. Public kindergartens would eventually be established, but meanwhile Louise and a group of her friends helped raise money to open a series of charity kindergartens. "If the little ones who wander neglected in our streets are to be reached," she proclaimed, "private benevolence must come to the rescue. We therefore appeal to the friends of education and humanity to help us in this effort." The first kindergarten was established in 1880, followed by others, including Miss Nourse's school. There, Nellie devoted herself to teaching, experimenting with colored balls, cylinders, cubes, and spheres to convey concepts of number, color, and geometric forms to younger children. Determined to allow her young charges every avenue she could devise to quicken their understanding and facilitate its expression, she explored all manner of mediums, hoping to engage them through music, art, and play.

The first serious breach in the close-knit Taft family occurred in early June 1889. Following a divorce from his wife Tillie, the mental condition of Peter, Will's older brother, had seemed much improved. He resumed his law practice and appeared to be leading a quiet life, devoting his leisure time to his young son, Hulbert. His agitation and paranoia gradually returned, however, rendering him incapable of work. He complained that mysterious forces "were conspiring against him," preventing the medicine from taking effect. Throughout his illness, his father's support never wavered. "You may rely upon one thing," Alphonso lovingly assured him, "and that is that my heart is always with you." The deterioration of Peter's mind was accompanied by a progressive wasting of his body, most likely from consumption. Though the family knew he was unwell, his death early that summer came as a shock.

The funeral was conducted at the home of Charles and Annie. One of Peter's Yale classmates delivered the eulogy, recalling the halcyon days when Peter achieved "the highest rank in scholarship ever reached at Yale," bringing "lasting honor on himself, his family, his class." Annie found solace in the knowledge that young Hulbert was able to hear "what sort of a man his father was."

"Poor Peter!" Harry Taft wrote to his father, remembering the brother who was once "the sunniest of us all." In the end, he reflected, "his was a sad life and while I had hoped that life near the old home would add much to his comfort and perhaps to his happiness, it could never have restored him to what he was and perhaps the Lord has done wisely to remove him." Harry had moved to Manhattan after his marriage to Julia Smith, daughter of a wealthy lawyer from Troy, New York. He had begun his legal career at Simpson, Thacher, & Barnum but had recently joined Cadwalader's, a leading corporate law firm that would eventually bear his name. His absence from Cincinnati contributed to an increasing sense of distance at the dispersal of the Taft family.

Will worried about the impact of Peter's death on his father, who was still suffering from the effects of typhoid pneumonia contracted in St. Petersburg. The disease had thickened Alphonso's lungs and affected the right ventricle of the heart, making it difficult for him to breathe. In recent months, he had seemed to improve, but the trauma of Peter's death brought on a marked deterioration in his health. "Every time the telephone rings I am fearful lest it be a sudden summons," Will confided to Horace.

Horace, meanwhile, harbored anxiety and a measure of guilt that he had added to his father's sadness. Disconsolate after Maria Herron refused his marriage offer, he had abandoned Cincinnati and the practice of law, which he had never enjoyed, for a teaching position in Kansas City. "My chief regret about it," he acknowledged, "came from my father's disappointment, for his heart was set on my going on in the law." He had taught in Kansas City only briefly when he was offered a faculty position at Yale, where he conceived the plan of founding a boys' school. The year after Peter's death, he opened a private school in a redbrick house in Watertown, Connecticut, instructing ten boarders and seven day students. In those early years, Horace taught nearly all the classes himself; but in time the institution, known as the Taft School, would become a prestigious preparatory school, boasting a distinguished faculty and more than five hundred students.

On September 10, 1889, Nellie gave birth to an eight-pound son christened Robert Alphonso to carry the patriarch's name into the next generation. "Nellie took the pain bravely," Will reported to his father. "It is a treat to see how happy she is." Will was ecstatic at the arrival of his first son. "On the whole, sitting as I do judicially in this case, I am obliged to give judgment for those who contend that the boy is one of the most remarkable products of this century," he jauntily pronounced. "I have been accused of the unjudicial conduct of rushing out into the street after the boy came and yelling, 'Hurrah!' For a man is born unto me." As Will only presided in court on Tuesdays and Saturdays, he was able to spend prolonged stretches at home, surrounded by the books of his own library, writing opinions. Horace heckled him over this arrangement with a friendly jibe: "I suppose you wish me to deny the report that you adjourn Court whenever Robert Alphonso has the colic. I am trying to keep it out of the papers."

These were happy days for Taft. A *New York Times* correspondent, analyzing his work on the bench, noted: "He breathes good will and suggests mental, moral, and physical wholesomeness. Yet, with all his pleasant informality and his frequent laughter, he has a dignity of manner and carriage that commands respect and attention." In his opinions, he presented the facts and his well-reasoned conclusions in a cogent, if sometimes verbose style. Ohio court records reveal that his thorough, thoughtful decisions were "upheld by the State Supreme Court to a gratifying extent."

Taft's equanimity and penchant for research deeply impressed his two older colleagues, Judges Hiram Peck and Frederick E. Moore. When the death of Stanley Matthews left a vacancy on the Ohio Supreme Court in 1889, they joined other Ohioans in recommending their thirty-two-year-old colleague Taft to President Benjamin Harrison, despite his youth and mere two years on the bench. Governor Foraker concurred, assuring Harrison that Taft's appointment "would be satisfactory to an unusually high degree to the Republicans of this state and no Democrat could justly criticize it." From New Haven, Horace reported a conversation with Will's classmate John Porter, now editor of the *Hartford Post*. His well-connected friends in Washington called Taft's prospects "pretty hopeful." Porter had recently spoken with Congressman

Butterworth, who suggested that Will, if passed over for the supreme court, should run for governor. Horace was less enthusiastic about that possibility, much preferring that his brother become "a fine old Justice."

When President Harrison visited Cincinnati that August, Taft joined the welcoming party at the train. Asked later if he had noticed Taft, Harrison replied: "O Yes, what a fine looking man he is. What a fine physique he has." Although Taft dined with the presidential party that night at the city's leading hotel, the Burnet House, he had no opportunity to speak with the president again. He reported to his father that his "chances of going to the Moon and of donning a silk gown at the hands of President Harrison are about equal. I am quite sure if I were he, I would not appoint a man of my age and position to that Bench." Taft felt some disappointment yet small surprise when, in December 1889, Harrison nominated circuit court judge David Brewer, a twenty-eight-year veteran on the bench.

Harrison had not forgotten the imposing young man. A month later, when U.S. Solicitor General Orlon Chapman suddenly died from pneumonia, Harrison nominated William Howard Taft for the prestigious post of chief barrister for the government. "It is a great event in your career, & you should accept without hesitation," Alphonso counseled from San Diego, where he and Louise were spending the winter. Louise was also enthusiastic. Alphonso had been certain the news would leave him sleepless, she wrote, "but it was I who lay awake . . . it is so hard not to be with you in this excitement." She too emphasized the importance of the appointment—not just for Will but for Alphonso as well, whom the news had imbued with "a new interest in life."

For Nellie, the appointment offered a chance to realize her goals both for herself and her husband. "I was very glad," she later wrote, for it offered Will "an opportunity for exactly the kind of work I wished him to do; work in which his own initiative and originality would be exercised and developed." They would escape the confining world of the Cincinnati Superior Court, where Will fraternized with much older men and dinner conversations too often focused on tedious legal questions. Moreover, she fondly anticipated life in the capital, where her husband's eminence would gain admission to an exciting world of cabinet officials, congressmen, and senators, and where she would attend White House receptions, observe legislative debates, and discuss the vital topics of the day. She was immediately willing to find and furnish a new house, leave behind supportive parents and relatives, and uproot their small son from his routine—all in search of a more fulfilling and exciting existence.

Only Will was reluctant. As solicitor general, he would argue cases as an advocate, standing to present "one side of a case" rather than weighing evidence and rendering judgment, temperamentally a far more congenial role. In his early days as a lawyer, arguing before the court had quickly become his least favorite aspect of the job; his affinity was for administering justice with fairness and integrity. Moreover, he was "entirely unfamiliar with the rules of practice" before the federal court, and had "very little familiarity" with federal statutes. And he knew he would have little time to orient himself. Straightaway upon his arrival, a backlog of cases to be argued would greet him. Furthermore, he took no pleasure in the prospect of leaving behind the close friendships and comfortable life he had built in Cincinnati.

"Go ahead, & fear not," his father advised. "You will have a full library at your service, in your own room, with messengers to get the books, besides Assistant Atty Generals to examine law points & make briefs for you; and you will have a short hand reporter take down & write out with type writing what you wish to have written." He continued to encourage and prod his reluctant son in a string of letters. "To a large extent the legal field of inquiry will be new," Alphonso wrote, "but you can master it, as you have mastered other things." His mother agreed: "You have learned the duties of a Judge so soon you can certainly hope to acquire those of an advocate." Alphonso was intent on stamping out any doubt his son might experience, faced by a change of such magnitude. "I believe you are equal to it," the father proclaimed with confidence, "although I do not believe the experiment has ever before been tried with so young a man. I receive more compliments than I know what to do with for having such a son. I try to behave with becoming modesty. . . . We are intensely proud of you."

The formidable combination of his father's high expectations and his wife's desires proved irresistible for Taft. He wrote to President Harrison, accepting the position. His confirmation was celebrated with a "brilliant reception" at the Lincoln Club. Four days later, Taft set out alone on a sleeper train for Washington, determined to find proper lodging before Nellie and the baby joined him.

Nellie's depiction of Will's anxiety upon reaching the nation's capital evinces a novelist's empathy: "He arrived at six o'clock on a cold, gloomy February morning at the old dirty Pennsylvania station. He wandered out on the street with a heavy bag in his hand looking for a porter, but there were no porters. Then he stood for a few moments looking up at the Capitol and feeling dismally unimportant in the midst of what seemed to him to be very formidable surroundings. . . . He was sure he had made a fatal mistake in exchanging a good position and a pleasant circle at home, where everybody knew him, for a place in a strange and forbidding city where he knew practically nobody." Nellie's account clearly reveals, beneath her insistence that he establish himself in Washington, a compassionate knowledge of her husband's nature. She relates that he dropped his bag off at the Old Ebbit House and walked to the Department of Justice for his swearing-in. Then he went to examine his office, where he "met the most dismal sight of the whole dismal day. His 'quarters' consisted of a single room, three flights up." Nor was the busy hive of assistants his father had forecast waiting to greet him. The sole shorthand reporter on the premises did not work for Taft. He was a telegrapher in the chief clerk's office and could only take Taft's dictation when not engaged in his primary duties. "Altogether it must have been a very disheartening outlook," Nellie wrote. "He wondered to himself why on earth he had come."

Taft's mood brightened considerably once Nellie arrived with Robert. They happily settled into a rented three-story town house at 5 Dupont Circle, which was easily affordable on his yearly salary of $7,000. "It is not a large house, but it is very pleasantly situated," Taft told Judge Peck, "with an out-look on a delightful little park, and is very convenient to the street cars, which are constantly passing to and fro in front of the house." His satisfaction with both their temporary home and the neighborhood, "one of the nicest and most convenient in the City," is evident in a letter to his father: "Our house is what is called a swell front, so that we are able from the front windows to look up and down the street and get such a view and so much light as to make the three front rooms of the house charming. The front room on the first floor is a reception room; the front room on the second floor is a library and sitting-room and the guest room is on the third floor immediately back of the nursery." The dining room was completed with a new table and eight new mahogany chairs, a Chippendale sideboard, and a new rug. For Will, the most important feature of the house was the sanctuary of a large library, lined with shelves sufficient to accommodate his treasured law books. "I find that without a place to work, it is difficult to work. I look forward with the greatest pleasure to the use of my books at night at home."

The most fortuitous and enduring aspect of the new Taft residency, how-ever, lay neither in cheerful accommodations nor access to the city center. Rather, 5 Dupont Circle stood only 1,000 feet away from the modest house at 1820 Jefferson Place which Theodore Roosevelt, newly appointed member of the Civil Service Commission, and his second wife, Edith Carow, had rented, and where they had come to live just two months earlier. The proximity of those two addresses in northwest Washington, both within walking distance of the White House, would give rise to the legendary friendship between Theodore Roosevelt and William Howard Taft.

CHAPTER FIVE

Edith Carow Roosevelt

Edith Carow in 1885, a year before her marriage
to the widower Theodore Roosevelt.

I N THE DESOLATE MONTHS AFTER Alice Lee's death, Theodore
Roosevelt could never have conceived that within two years he would be
secretly engaged to his childhood friend Edith Carow. Retreating to the "vast
silent spaces" and "lonely rivers" of the Badlands following the tumultuous
Republican Convention in the summer of 1884, he remained certain that his
allotment of domestic bliss was "lived out." The ecstatic love he had shared
with Alice came only once in a lifetime. His own capacity for passionate feeling
was exhausted, he believed, and he resolved never to dishonor the wife he had
loved more than "any man ever loved a woman." With an inexorable romantic
idealism, he resigned himself to a bleak and isolate existence.

Leaving his four-month-old daughter with Bamie, who had sold the family's New York town house and moved into her own home at 689 Madison

Avenue, Theodore sought refuge from sorrows both personal and public. Privately, memories of his wife haunted every corner of the city. In the political arena, his support of the failed reform candidate against the triumphant machine nominee, James Blaine, had diminished his prospects and informed his decision not to run for a fourth term in the New York State Assembly.

He had fallen in love with the rugged landscape surrounding the Dakota Territory's Little Missouri River during a hunting trip the previous September. He had hoped to return with "the head of a great buffalo bull" to hang in the home he and Alice were building in Oyster Bay, but while there, he had decided to invest in two open-range cattle ranches, the Elkhorn and the Chimney Butte. His purchase of 1,400 head of cattle for $85,000 reduced by more than half the sum his father bequeathed to him. He went into partnership with two local cowboys, Bill Merrifield and Sylvane Ferris, and convinced William Sewall and William Dow, two wilderness guides he had hunted with in Maine, to join the enterprise. As his vision of family happiness died with Alice, he seriously considered a career as a full-time rancher, residing and writing in the West, with only occasional visits back east.

When he first returned to the Badlands in the summer of 1884, the austere landscape seemed to mirror his melancholy. "The plains stretch out in death-like and measureless expanse," he wrote. "Nowhere, not even at sea, does a man feel more lonely than when riding over the far-reaching, seemingly never-ending plains." In the "noontide hours" of a scorching summer day, he remarked, "there are few sounds to break the stillness." With every living thing immobile in the stifling heat, he heard only the "soft, melancholy cooing of the mourning-dove, whose voice always seems far away and expresses more than any other sound in nature the sadness of gentle, hopeless, never-ending grief."

Just as he had frantically thrown himself into his labors in the assembly to alleviate the immediate anguish of Alice's death, so he now immersed himself in the daily work of the ranch. He was often on his horse sixteen hours a day, riding after stray horses, hunting game, joining his men in the "hardest work," that of "the spring and fall round-ups, when the calves are branded or the beeves gathered for market." During roundups that covered over two hundred miles in four to five weeks, the cook began "preparing breakfast long before the first glimmer of dawn." Shortly after three o'clock the men were roused from sleep and the day's toil delegated. "These long, swift rides in the glorious spring mornings are not soon to be forgotten," Theodore marveled. "As we climb the steep sides of the first range of buttes, wisps of wavering mist still cling in the hollows of the valley; when we come out on top of the first great plateau, the sun flames up over its edge, and in the level, red beams the galloping horsemen throw long, fantastic shadows."

Relentless physical activity served him well. "Black care," he wrote, "rarely sits behind a rider whose pace is fast enough." Once, constant activity had assuaged the pain of his father's death; now, he hoped that by occupying every minute of his waking day, he could simply outride his depression. A two-week hunting trip in September, he reported to Bamie, had provided "enough excitement and fatigue to prevent over much thought"; he had "at last been able to sleep well at night."

In Medora, he had a spacious ranch house built to share with his friends, Sewall and Dow, and eventually their wives. "The story-high house of hewn logs is clean and neat, with many rooms," he wrote, "so that one can be alone if one wishes to." The central room featured a massive stone hearth with trophy heads gazing down from the walls and buffalo robes covering the couches. His own chamber held a rubber tub for bathing and rough shelves for his favorite books—"Parkman and Irving and Hawthorne and Cooper and Lowell"—along with a growing assortment of volumes sent from New York by his devoted sister.

As the months passed and Roosevelt started to recover himself, he approached *Century* magazine with the idea of presenting a series of sketches highlighting hunting experiences on the Great Plains. In fits and starts at first, he began to compose during breaks in his work. Before long, he was writing steadily before "the flickering firelight" of the enormous fireplace. Organizing his manuscript around the different game he hunted—black-tailed deer, antelope, bull elk, buffalo, and grizzly bear—he fused a naturalist's interest in the unique characteristics of each animal with a hunter's thrill of the chase.

Daily labor on the ranch had given Roosevelt an acute awareness of the natural cycles and unique pleasures each season held. On summer evenings, he relaxed in his rocking chair on the wide porch of the ranch house, reading in the shade of the cottonwood and enjoying the "cool breeze" from the nearby river. As the crisp autumn temperatures began to transform the landscape, he particularly savored the long days in the saddle, whether hunting or rounding up cattle. "Where everything before had been gray or dull green there are now patches of russet red and bright yellow," he noted. "The clumps of ash, wild-plum trees, and rosebushes in the heads and bottoms of the sloping valleys become spots of color that glow among the stretches of brown and withered grass."

Even when the winter days "dwindled to their shortest" and the yapping wailing songs of coyotes echoed through the "never-ending" nights, Roosevelt took comfort in the camaraderie of housemates gathered round the fireplace to read, relax, or play chess. Soon enough, spring brought earlier daybreak to the Badlands and his morning rides took on "a charm all their own," the bleached landscape becoming "a vivid green, as the new grass sprouts and the trees and bushes thrust forth the young leaves." On those clear mornings, he thrilled to the sounds of "bird songs unknown in the East"—the lilting melodies of the Missouri skylark, the "rich, full notes" of the white-shouldered lark-bunting, the tuneful sweetness of the lark-finch. The green thickets and groves encircling his ranch house teemed with the songs of hermit thrushes and meadowlarks. This quickening of life in the Badlands awakened a corresponding energy in Theodore Roosevelt.

As his fits of depression subsided and publication of his book, *Hunting Trips of a Ranchman*, drew near, Roosevelt's thoughts turned east, toward the home and the people he had left behind. Memories of joyful days spent with his childhood friend Edith Carow increasingly intruded on his consciousness. The desire to renew their old and deep friendship, however, was coupled with a surge of guilt and anxiety when he contemplated anything that might compromise Alice's memory. This thought lay on his conscience like a crime, and he instructed his sisters, who were still close to Edith, that she never be present during his visits. He traveled to New York in July 1885, when his book was published to excellent reviews. This work "will take a leading position in the literature of the American sportsman," the *New York Times* reported. "Mr. Roosevelt writes most happily, tells naturally what he sees and does."

Roosevelt remained in New York that summer, living for the first time in his recently finished country home at Oyster Bay, the planning and design for which had filled many happy hours with Alice. Completed and furnished under Bamie's devoted supervision, the rambling twenty-two-room Queen Anne house stood atop a hill, surrounded by forests and grassy clearings, commanding a clear view of the Long Island Sound. Returning to Cove Neck must have recalled vivid memories of childhood summers at nearby Tranquillity, where "no day was long enough" to contain the myriad pursuits of Roosevelt's lively family and friends.

Replicating those crowded childhood days, Bamie orchestrated a steady stream of houseguests to Oyster Bay, including Corinne's childhood friend Fanny Smith. Fanny found Theodore's new house, which he rechristened "Sagamore Hill," as enchanting as she had once found Tranquillity. The Roosevelt homestead again became a social hub, but Theodore now assumed the central position his father had once occupied. "Especially memorable," Fanny recalled, "were the battles, ancient and modern, which were waged relentlessly

on the white linen tablecloth with the aid of such table-silver as was available."
Stunned by Theodore's "familiarity with historical details of long past cen-
turies," Fanny admiringly noted that he made her "feel that Hannibal lived
just around the corner." Roosevelt's Aunt Annie and her husband had recently
completed a country house accessible to his by a dirt path through the woods,
and nearby lived his cousin Dr. West Roosevelt, who had accompanied him to
Maine when he first met Bill Sewall. Despite this renewed consolidation of the
Roosevelt clan, Theodore managed to avoid one old friend. Although Edith
had spent a week with Aunt Annie at "Gracewood" earlier that summer, she
was noticeably absent from the group that gathered at Theodore's new home.

These summer weeks were the most extended time Theodore had spent
with his daughter, Alice, who was now nearly eighteen months old. Under
Bamie's loving guardianship, Alice had emerged as a lively, blond, blue-eyed
toddler. Indeed, the warmth and affection that bound Bamie and her niece
could not have been stronger if they were mother and child. "She was the
only one I really cared about when I was a child," Alice later remembered.
Though crippled by curvature of the spine and seriously overweight, Bamie
seemed to Alice marvelously larger than life, "a great big handsome man of
a woman . . . but oh so attractive!" Even as a young child Alice observed that
Bamie "had an extraordinary gift with people." Her numerous friends adored
her and felt completely at ease in her presence. Had "she been a man," Alice
believed, "she would have been the one to be President."

Roosevelt returned to the Badlands in late August, but two months later
he was back in New York. He arrived at Bamie's Madison Avenue town
house, where he routinely stayed while visiting the city, to find Edith Carow
about to depart. Whether Theodore's failure to signal his impending return
or her delay in taking leave of Bamie brought about the reunion, long-hidden
feelings surfaced before day's end. Less than three weeks later, the two were
secretly engaged. "You know all about me darling," Edith told Theodore. "I
never could have loved anyone else. I love you with all the passion of a girl
who has never loved before."

❥ ❥

THE RESURRECTION OF HER RELATIONSHIP with Theodore offered Edith the
prospect of happiness and security that had eluded her since childhood. Her
father, Charles Carow, became an alcoholic after his family's once-thriving
shipping business fell into bankruptcy. The seventh of eight children born
to wealthy merchant prince Isaac Quentin Carow, Charles had lacked no
privilege growing up in his family's St. Mark's Place mansion. He dwelled

in a world of private tutors, dancing lessons, and access to New York's most exclusive clubs. At twenty-five, he had just begun work at Kermit & Carow, the family firm, when his father suddenly passed away.

Charismatic and eligible, Charles Carow seemed a perfect match for Gertrude Tyler. At nineteen, she had lately returned from two years in a fashionable Parisian girls' school. Gertrude's father, Daniel Tyler IV, had graduated from West Point and served in the Army before amassing a fortune in iron manufacturing. Following his marriage to Emily Lee, they moved to the sumptuous mansion in Norwich, Connecticut, where Gertrude was raised.

Intent that she become a poised and well-bred young lady, Gertrude's father had insisted she attend boarding school in Paris. On the Continent, in contrast to America, he assured her, she would "find great attention paid to deportment and manners." She would be schooled in "matters of carriage, such as walking, entering a room, sitting down and rising"; comportment that would signify a proper upbringing. "Do not my dear Gertrude undervalue or despise these matters," he admonished. "They are important and it will be my pride to know and feel that both your mind and manners are formed on good and true standards. Now is the time for you to finish an education, mental and physical which will make you an ornament to society." While Gertrude was often homesick and could not bear to spend the Christmas season abroad, she pledged to work hard at music lessons, study of French, and riding lessons. "Do not doubt," she promised her mother, "that I shall do everything in my power to improve the advantages that you and Father have given me."

Encountering Gertrude in New York soon after her return, Charles pursued her avidly. On March 7, 1859, he formally declared his intentions to her father: "My dear Sir, I have to ask of you the greatest favor that one man can ask of another. I have won Gertrude's heart. Will you give me her hand?" The wedding took place two months later in the Christ Episcopal Church in Norwich, Connecticut, followed by a brilliant reception in the Tyler mansion.

The couple's first child, a boy, died at six months. Then, the year the war began, the Carows welcomed their first daughter, Edith. Gertrude's father rejoined the Army as a general, while Charles remained in New York endeavoring to steer the family shipping business through an abrupt decline precipitated by the Civil War. He had inherited the family enterprise on the brink of a crisis that made "the risk of sailing under the American flag . . . so great as to divert a large share of the carrying trade into foreign bottoms." Buffeted by drastic financial reverses, Charles began drinking heavily and gambling. Soon he was no longer able to afford his own home and the family was forced to move in with his widowed sister, Ann Eliza Kermit. As the war came to an end, the Carow's second daughter, Emily, was born in Ann's large town house at 12 Livingston Place near Union Square.

When Charles was not drinking, he was an affectionate husband and an effusive, doting father. "My dear little girl," he wrote Edith when he and Gertrude left to visit the Tylers in Norwich, "Papa hopes his dolly has been very good since he has been gone. . . . Papa & Mamma always say, before they go to sleep, 'God bless little Edie,' and again before they get up in the morning." From the time she was young, Charles had sought to communicate to his "precious little monkey" his fascination with the theatre and love of literature. Edith proved an apt pupil. "Almost the first thing I remember," she later told Theodore, "is being told about Sinbad the Sailor when I was a tiny girl and used to climb up on my father's knee every evening and beg him to 'spin me a yarn.' " As her father read aloud from the *Arabian Nights*, "a new world" opened up, "full of glowing Eastern light and colour." Her early exposure to such frightful and wonderful stories spurred "a passion for fairy tales" later concisely distilled into her own verse: "Oh fairy tales, my fairy tales / Fantastic, weird and wild / I love you with a changeless love / A mother gives her child."

When father and daughter were apart, Charles urged her to write him her thoughts and feelings without the monitor of self-consciousness, without worry over corrections. "I got your letter about 3 o'clock yesterday," he wrote. "It was so nice & long. No matter about the spelling when you write to me. Say what you want to say and don't lose time thinking how to spell the words. If I want I can beat you with a big stick when you come back—so just write whatever comes into your head." When they were together, he took Edith on long walks, pointing out various wildflowers and teaching her to know them by color, shape, and habitat. This shared pursuit fostered an interest in the natural world that remained with her the rest of her life.

When Charles Carow was drinking, however, recrimination and tension permeated the household. Gertrude began to suffer bouts of melancholy coupled with a mysterious series of nervous disorders. Still, the Carows managed to maintain a public facade of elegance and ease, spending their winters in New York with Mrs. Kermit and their summers at General Tyler's country estate in New Jersey. Gertrude's finishing school lessons in proper carriage and deportment helped her conceal private anxiety behind a veneer of propriety. And she imparted these lessons to her uncommonly poised little girl, Edith.

Edith was a toddler when she first met Theodore Roosevelt. The Kermit house on Livingston Place stood directly behind the 14th Street mansion of Theodore's grandfather, Cornelius Van Schaak Roosevelt. Edith and Corinne

Roosevelt were almost exactly the same age and they soon became, in Corinne's words, "pledged friends." Edith's earliest memories revolved around the Roosevelts' 20th Street household, where she frequently played with Corinne and developed a particular affection for Teedie, three years her senior. Far less did she enjoy their visits to her own house, where she anxiously struggled to hide her "old and broken toys."

When she was five, Edith was invited to join the Roosevelt children in the home school taught by Mittie's sister, Annie Gracie. Years later, Edith fondly recalled "the school room, the children around the table, and dear Mrs. Gracie training clumsy little fingers to write and teaching the earliest lessons in the primer." She and Teedie cherished an illustrated children's magazine called *Our Young Folks*, a compilation of stories, poems, and illustrations by celebrated writers and artists, including Harriet Beecher Stowe, Winslow Homer, Henry Longfellow, and Charles Dickens. Later, "at the cost of being deemed effeminate," Roosevelt confessed an early fascination with "girls' stories," such as *Little Men* and *Little Women* and *An Old-Fashioned Girl*. His ability to focus and withdraw into a book was equaled only in his friend, Edith Carow. "I think imagination is one of the greatest blessings of life," Edith later wrote, "and while one can lose oneself in a book one can never be thoroughly unhappy."

Thoughts of Edith provoked an intense yearning in Teedie during his family's yearlong trip to Europe. "It was verry [sic] hard parting from our friend," he confided in his diary. Six months into the Grand Tour, when the family was in France, he dramatically revealed to his diary that a glance at Edith's picture provoked "homesickness and longings for the past which will come again never, alack never." Edith eagerly awaited his return, promising to keep all Teedie's letters so they could read them over back in New York and relive his adventure together.

Edith's parents considered sending Edith to school when Mrs. Gracie's lessons ceased during the Roosevelts' time abroad. In the end, they decided to postpone her entry until the following fall, fearful she was already damaging her eyes by constant reading. "Whenever they see a book in my hands," she told Corinne, "they give me no peace till I lay it down."

Edith was nine years old when a bankruptcy warrant was issued against her father's estate. The *New York Times* followed the proceedings for weeks, reporting creditor meetings and the auction sale of several ships, including the *Edith*, named after his daughter. Charles quickly realized he had no choice but to seek more frugal living arrangements. That summer, his family moved with Aunt Kermit to a more modest house on West 44th Street.

The Carows' reduced means did not prevent them from enrolling Edith in Miss Comstock's renowned private school for girls at West 40th Street. Nor did Gertrude scrimp on the stylish clothes her daughter required to join her classmates for regular forays to the symphony or theatre. Miss Comstock, headmistress of the fashionable school, was a formidable figure to the young girls. Edith's schoolmate Fanny Smith described the "terrifying charm" of that "impressive-looking woman with flashing dark eyes and clear-cut features." The curriculum included history, languages, arithmetic, zoology, botany, poetry, drama, and literature. Edith proved to be a diligent and exceptional student. "When I come home, I study my lessons, and when I think I know them I read," she told Corinne, who was still being schooled by private tutors. "I like my composition class very much," she confided, and "I am trying hard for the Arithmetic and Department prizes and hope to get them."

At Miss Comstock's, Edith developed a lifelong devotion to drama and poetry. "I have gone back to Shakespeare, as I always do," she would write to her son Kermit seven decades later. "Usually the Historical plays, or *Hamlet* or *Macbeth*. *Lear* is too tragic. This time I read *As You Like It*. There can be nothing more delightful! I believe if it were lost I could write it out." She could memorize and recite numerous poems, including John Milton's *Lycidas* in its entirety, and was able to quote extensively from Wordsworth, Coleridge, and other Romantic poets.

Edith also cultivated a defensive air of detachment during her schooldays, declining to participate in the costumed tableaux and girlish gossip that so fascinated her classmates. Her beloved books often took precedence over friends, leading schoolmates to reproach her for "indifference." Years later, Edith explained that her aloofness was simply "a trick of manner" to obscure her own perceived defects. While it may have deprived her of camaraderie, her tactic succeeded in establishing the distance and mystery that prevented humiliation. "Girls," one of her fellow classmates observed, "I believe you could live in the same house with Edith for fifty years and never really know her."

Edith's friendship with the Roosevelt family remained her lodestar, helping her navigate a troubled girlhood as her father became more and more unstable and her mother descended into hypochondria and depression. When the Roosevelts returned from their first trip abroad, Edith joined Corinne, Theodore, and Elliott in a weekly dancing class taught by the demanding Mr. Dodsworth. The dance lessons were "the happiness of many New York children of those years," Edith remembered. A half century later Edith could still recall her pride as she and Corinne, "the only two who had satisfied our difficult and critical teacher," were called onto the floor to dance the minuet all alone. Fanny Smith never forgot the pleasure of belonging to that "little group of girls and boys wearing special badges and pledged either definitely or otherwise only to dance with one another."

During the summers at Tranquillity, Edith was a regular houseguest. In particular, she excelled in the word games the young people loved to play, " 'Consequences,' 'Truth,' and nearly always 'Crambo,' when each one would draw from a hat a folded question and from another hat a word, and then in the few minutes allotted would answer the question in verse which should include the word we had drawn." In the afternoons, "the happy six" would row across the bay: Theodore with Edith, Elliott with Corinne, their cousin West Roosevelt with Fanny, whom he "much worshipped." They would carry their books to the woods and read aloud to one another. At picnic lunches near Cooper's Bluff, they recited their favorite poems. "In the early days," Fanny recalled, "we all delighted in Longfellow and Mrs. Browning and Owen Meredith." Later, they turned to Swinburne, Kipling, Shelley, and Shakespeare.

The Roosevelts celebrated Edith's birthdays as if she were a member of the family. "I cannot believe that my sweet little fair, golden-haired friend, whom I have loved since she was three years old is really fifteen today," Aunt Gracie wrote. Edith was included in small family dinners and visits to the theatre. On New Year's Day, 1877, she stood by Corinne's side to receive guests. At dancing parties, continuing the partnership begun under Mr. Dodsworth's tutelage, she regularly paired off with Theodore. At one of Aunt Gracie's sociables, Corinne and a friend deliberately wandered into the "dimly and suggestively lit" morning room "for the express purpose of interrupting Thee and Edith, who had gone there for a cosy chat." The party was "far too merry," Corinne chided, "for a sentimental tete-a-tete."

Theodore's departure for Harvard produced the first unraveling in the close-knit circle of family and friends. Refusing to let their cherished scholarly and social coterie vanish with him, Corinne and Edith formed a literary society in which Corinne served as president and Edith as secretary. The group, which included Fanny Smith, Maud Elliott, and Grace Potter, expected members to contribute original poems and short stories to be read aloud and criticized at weekly meetings. As secretary, Edith was charged with copying and organizing the submissions into a "Weekly Bulletin."

Edith personally produced dozens of poems, short stories, and essays, which she carefully preserved in her papers. The Roosevelt family biographer Betty Boyd Caroli observes that in her writings for this intimate circle, "Edith revealed about as much about herself as she ever permitted anyone to see."

Her poem entitled "My Dream Castles," written during Theodore's freshman year at Harvard, suggests the lonely distance she maintained despite her inclusion in the Roosevelt household. While she might join in their games and celebrations, loving friendship and charity could not entirely ease an outsider's sense of loss, of alienation:

> *To my castles none may enter*
> *But the few*
> *Holding to my inmost feelings*
> *Love's own clue.*
> *They may wander there at will*
> *Ever welcome finding still,*
> *Warm and true.*
>
> *Only one, one tiny room*
> *Locked they find,*
> *One thin curtain that they ne'er*
> *Gaze behind.*
> *There my lost ambitions sleep,*
> *To their tear-wept slumber deep*
> *Long consigned.*
>
> *This my lonely sanctum is;*
> *There I go*
> *When my heart all worn by grief*
> *Sinketh low.*
> *Where my baseless hopes do lie*
> *There to find my peace, go I.*
> *Sad and slow . . .*

Romantic longing and a self-dramatizing nostalgia resonate in her words, an elegy for the warm companionship of the dream family she feared would be left behind with their childhoods. In another poem, "Memories," she once again reveals the profound anxiety of a melancholy girl confronting adulthood at the end of her day:

> *I sit alone in the twilight*
> *In the twilight gloomy grey*
> *And think with a sad regretting*
> *For the days that have passed away.*

Both Corinne and Fanny recognized a superior quality in Edith's writings. "She reads more and writes better than any girl I know," Corinne noted in her diary. For Corinne, whose literary ambitions would drive her to become an accomplished poet, this was not easy to admit. Indeed, she often found Edith's criticism of her work overwhelming and her personality inscrutable. Still, she could not help loving best of all her "clever" friend, "tall and fair, with lovely complexion and golden hair." She confided in her journal: "I have a feeling for Edith which I have for no one else, a tender kind of feeling. I am always careful of her and then I know quite well that I love her much more than she does me in fact."

In the spring of Theodore's freshman year, Theodore Senior brought a small party of young people to visit him at Harvard, including Bamie, Corinne, and Elliott, along with Edith Carow and Maud Elliott. "What fun we did have," Corinne remembered, describing lively lunches and dinners with her brother and his friends, Johnny Lamson and Harry Jackson. They played hide-and-seek, attended the theatre, and enjoyed long carriage rides through the surrounding countryside. Edith and Theodore again found themselves partners, riding in one carriage, while Corinne and Maud were paired with Lamson and Jackson.

"The family all went home, leaving me disconsolate," Theodore recorded in his diary. "The last three days have been great fun." Arriving in New York, Edith immediately wrote to Theodore, echoing his sentiment. She had "enjoyed to the utmost" every moment of "three perfectly happy days." Theodore admitted to Corinne that he had never seen "Edith looking prettier; everyone, and especially Harry Chapin and Minot Weld admired her little Ladyship intensely, and she behaved as sweetly as she looked."

Edith's cherished relationship with Theodore remained constant in the following months, as did her friendship with Corinne. When Theodore Senior lay dying, Corinne confided her grief and frustration to her oldest friend. "Oh Edith, it is the most frightful thing to see the person you love best in the world in terrible pain, and not be able to do a thing to alleviate it." The following summer, Edith joined Theodore and Corinne at Oyster Bay as the Roosevelt children tried to distract themselves from the sorrow of the patriarch's death.

In his diary, Theodore described days spent sailing with Edith or rowing with her to the harbor where the steamboats from the city landed. He wrote of "spending a lovely morning with her" driving to Cold Spring Harbor to pick water lilies.

The next day, August 22, 1878, he took Mittie, Elliott, Corinne, and Edith on a long sail, followed by tea at his cousin West's house. The mysterious severance in their relationship occurred that same evening. In his diary, Theodore merely notes: "Afterwards Edith & I went up to the summer house." What transpired there would become the subject of much speculation by Roosevelt's family and friends. Some postulated that Edith had refused Theodore's offer of marriage, although her intense devotion makes such a scenario unlikely. Furthermore, an initial refusal would hardly have deterred Theodore, who would shortly prove his tenacity in his courtship of Alice. Corinne suggested a different reason, indicating that her dying father had expressed concern about Theodore's intimacy with Edith, given Charles Carow's fiscal and temperamental instability. If Theodore discussed the issue with Edith that night, he might well have triggered the volatility that he would obscurely explain to Bamie as a clash of tempers "that were far from being of the best." This, too, is mere conjecture. Neither Edith nor Theodore ever talked about what happened.

We know only that eight weeks later, Theodore met Alice Hathaway Lee, fell in love "at first sight," and launched the spirited campaign "to win her" that concluded successfully in the winter of 1880. Before the engagement was announced in mid-February, Theodore wrote to Edith. Years later, Corinne spoke of the "shock" Edith experienced when she heard the news. The summer months that year must have been lacerating for Edith; another woman would be Theodore's constant companion, displacing her on morning drives to Cold Spring, afternoon sailing and rowing excursions, and private evening tête-à-têtes in the summerhouse.

Edith was long accustomed to mastering her private sorrows. She schooled herself to participate in the engagement and wedding festivities of the man she adored. Arriving at the Brunswick Hotel in Boston two nights before the marriage, she crowded into an upstairs chamber with Fanny and Grace, while the Roosevelt family occupied two suites downstairs. "We had great fun," Fanny recorded in her diary. They explored the town and shared meals at a large table, where "wild spirits" prevailed. The next morning, Edith, Grace, and Fanny drove to the church together. At the reception following the ceremony, Edith reportedly "danced the soles off her shoes."

Her brave attempt to affect gaiety was not the only trial Edith would face. The death of Mrs. Kermit, with whom Edith had lived since she was a small child, was soon followed by the final days of her gentle grandfather, General Tyler. Initially, she continued to see a great deal of Corinne, Fanny, and Aunt Gracie, who held a weekly sewing class for the girls once their formal schooling ended. Soon, however, she found herself quite forsaken as both Corinne and Fanny became engaged. Edith and Fanny served together as bridesmaids at Corinne's wedding. "All yesterday I thought of nothing but you from morning to night," she explained to her oldest friend. "I do not mean I was sad or grieving for that would be impossible when I know how happy you are going to be, but I kept realizing that you were leaving your old life behind, and if we live to be ninety years old we can never be two girls together again."

In 1883, yet another death seemed to complete the disintegration of Edith's support system. Charles Carow, his body weakened by decades of drinking, collapsed and died that spring. He left his wife and daughters without sufficient means to maintain their accustomed life. Recognizing that they could live abroad more cheaply than in New York, Gertrude made plans for an extended sojourn in Europe with Edith and Emily. While rumor circulated that Edith might marry "for money," such gossip proved groundless. Even as more and more of her friends were engaged or married, Edith maintained her solitude. As the circle of her friends diminished, she sought consolation in her treasured books, keeping a careful record of the hundreds of volumes she completed. During this desolate period, Edith purportedly held on to the belief that "someday, somehow, she would marry Theodore Roosevelt." She certainly never anticipated the grim coincidence that left Theodore's wife and mother dead on the same day. Though Edith joined the family at the funeral service and frequently saw Corinne, Bamie, and Aunt Gracie in the months that followed, there is no evidence that she and Theodore connected until their chance encounter at Bamie's house in October 1885.

THEODORE WAS REMARKABLY ALTERED FROM the young man Edith had last seen. Months laboring under the Badlands sun had hardened his body and bronzed his skin, but he had the same bright eyes, the same splendid smile. Edith herself had become a handsome young woman, still "the most cultivated, best read girl" he knew. In the days that followed, he became a regular visitor, enlivening the parlor of her 36th Street town house. Perhaps their old friendship and mutual losses quickened the relationship. On November 17, 1885, they pledged themselves to marry. The engagement opened a world of joy for Edith, an emergence from five years of bleak nightmare. If the love Theodore developed for Edith lacked the extreme sentimental idealism of his love for Alice, their complex, ever-strengthening bond would sustain a mature and lifelong growth and happiness.

The early months of his reunion with Edith, however, were clouded by Theodore's Victorian belief that second marriages "argued weakness in a man's character." He insisted upon a sufficient interval before informing anyone, even their families, about their intention to marry. Acutely aware of the importance of appearances, Edith decided to accompany her mother and sister to Europe that spring as planned, allowing time to elapse before any public announcement of the engagement. In the meantime, they felt there was nothing wrong with two old friends keeping company during the winter social season. Once again, Edith joined the Roosevelts at the Essex County Hunt Ball, theatre parties at Aunt Annie's, and dinners at Bamie's. Respecting their secret even in his private diary, Theodore never wrote out Edith's full name, though the capital E appears day after day, reflecting the extensive time they spent together.

In the spring of 1886, Edith sailed to Europe and Theodore returned to the Badlands. In New York, he had begun work on a biography of Missouri senator Thomas Hart Benton, which he hoped to complete at his ranch in Medora. Though separated by nearly 5,000 miles, the couple sustained their relationship month after month through the exchange of long letters. In early June, just five weeks after Edith's arrival in London, she had already received seventeen letters from Theodore and written almost as many in return. "How fond one is of old letters and how one prizes them," Edith had written in her composition book at Miss Comstock's. "I never wish to destroy even a note." Though she cherished each word, the intensely private Edith would one day burn nearly their entire correspondence from this period. Only one full letter remains—the same letter in which she declared to Theodore that she loved him "with all the passion of a girl who has never loved before."

Written from London on June 8, 1886, this letter made the strength of Edith's feelings for Theodore abundantly clear, even as she appealed to him to be patient while she tried to put her "heart on paper." Never having troubled much about her appearance, Edith admitted she was suddenly anxious "about being pretty" in order to please him. "I perfectly love your description of the life out west for I almost feel as if I could see you and know just what you are doing, and I do not think you sentimental in the least to love nature; please love me too and believe I think of you all the time and want so much to see you."

Edith's diffident and beseeching tone disappears the moment she turns to literature, whether expressing her fascination with Coleridge's *Kubla Khan* or noting the "digging" required to excavate meaning from Browning's poems. Her critique of the lead singer's performance in a production of *Carmen*, which she had heard the previous night, displays a confident, acerbic wit: "He is middle aged, ugly and uninteresting with not enough voice to redeem his bad acting. His one idea of making love is to seize the prima donna's arm and shake her violently. I am so glad it is not your way."

As ever, books remained a medium through which Theodore and Edith connected and interpreted the larger world. Like Edith, Theodore filled pages of his letters with talk of authors and their creations. He had carried *Anna Karenina* with him during this trip west and told Corinne that he "read it through with very great interest." Although he considered Tolstoy "a great writer," he found his work deeply unsettling. "Do you notice how he never comments on the actions of his personages? He relates what they thought or did without any remark whatever as to whether it was good or bad, as Thucydides wrote history—a fact which tends to give his work an unmoral rather than an immoral tone, together with the sadness so characteristic of Russian writers."

Roosevelt read this novel of multiple marriages, broken marriages, and an assortment of adulteries at a time when the nature of marriage and remarriage, its moral and ethical reverberations, was of signal importance to the newly betrothed widower. From its very first sentence—"Happy families are all alike; every unhappy family is unhappy in its own way"—Tolstoy's *Anna Karenina* confronted Theodore in an intensely personal fashion and his comments upon it illuminate his own nature more brightly than Tolstoy's novel.

"I hardly know whether to call it a very bad book or not. There are two entirely distinct stories in it," he observed. The history of Levin and Kitty "is not only very powerfully and naturally told, but is also perfectly healthy. Annas most certainly is not, though of great and sad interest; she is portrayed as being a prey to the most violent passion, and subject to melancholia, and her reasoning power is so unbalanced that she could not possibly be described otherwise than as in a certain sense insane. Her character is curiously contradictory; bad as she was however she was not to me nearly as repulsive as her brother, Stiva." Roosevelt's revulsion at Tolstoy's infantile, pathetic, endearing *bon vivant*—his categorical interpretation of healthy relationships versus unhealthy relationships—reveals a deep-seated disgust with physical and moral slackness that would remain with him for the rest of his life.

While he continued to enjoy the simple, invigorating routine of his life at the ranch, with long days free to read and write, ride and hunt, his engagement to Edith provided a welcome sense of clarity about his future. He began to muse on the satisfactions and exhilaration of political life that he had abandoned in New York. He contemplated an offer from Mayor William Grace to assume the presidency of the Board of Health, but it ultimately fell through. Still, he admitted to Henry Cabot Lodge in August, "I would like a chance at something I thought I could really do."

In late August and early September, Roosevelt accompanied his ranching partner Bill Merrifield on a hunting trip in Idaho. When he returned, he was appalled to find that news of the engagement had leaked into the social columns of the *New York Times* and that Bamie, assuming the report must be unfounded gossip, had demanded a retraction. Theodore faced the difficult and necessary prospect of revealing the truth to his sister after months of deceit.

"Darling Bamie," he wrote on September 20, 1886, "On returning from the mountains I was savagely irritated by seeing in the papers the statement that I was engaged to Edith Carow; from what source it could have originated I can not possibly conceive. But the statement itself is true. I am engaged to Edith and before Christmas I shall cross the ocean and marry her. You are the first person to whom I have breathed one word on the subject." He proceeded to reiterate his condemnation of second marriages. "You could not reproach me one half as bitterly for my inconstancy and unfaithfulness, as I reproach myself," he maintained. "Were I sure there were a heaven my one prayer would be I might never go there, lest I should meet those I loved on earth who are dead. No matter what your judgement about myself I shall most assuredly enter no plea against it. But I do very earnestly ask you not to visit my sins upon poor little Edith. It is certainly not her fault; the entire blame rests on my shoulders." He was particularly anxious that his family never question their long history of affection toward Edith, that none should mistake her in any fashion for a schemer or interloper.

"As regards yourself, my dearest sister," he continued, "I can only say you will be giving me the greatest happiness in your power if you will continue to pass your summers with me. We ourselves will have to live in the country almost the entire year; I thoroughly understand the change I will have to make in my life. As I have already told you, if you wish to you shall keep Baby Lee, I, of course paying the expense. . . . I will explain everything in full when I see you. *Forever your loving brother*." This arrangement for the child of his previous marriage would prove more problematic than he anticipated.

His plans to return home were delayed by troubles at the Elkhorn ranch. A calamitous drop in the price of cattle had persuaded Sewall and Dow that the ranch was no longer a viable operation. "It looked to me as if we were throwing away his money," Sewall reported, deeply distressed by the prospect of failing his friend Roosevelt. The two men and their wives reluctantly returned to Maine, later reflecting that despite "all of the hardships and work it was a very happy life [they] had lived all together," indeed, "the happiest time" they had ever known.

Roosevelt, too, never forgot his years in the Badlands. Though he would ultimately lose a sizable portion of his fortune when a blizzard decimated his cattle herd, he considered his experience with "fellow ranchmen on what was then the frontier" to be "the most educational asset" of his entire life, instrumental to his success in becoming president. "It is a mighty good thing to know men, not from looking at them, but from having been one of them," Roosevelt explained. "When you have worked with them, when you have lived with them, you do not have to wonder how they feel, because you feel it yourself." Just as his daily work in the assembly had taught him to live down "the defective moral quality of being a stranger" among colleagues with whom he initially had little in common, so his years in the Badlands taught him "to speak the same language" as men who spent their days herding cattle, roping steer, and hunting game in the open country. Men who routinely faced danger and hardship recognized no superiority in social class or family background. His ranching days enabled him "to interpret the spirit of the West," fostering a genuine national perspective foreign to most eastern politicians.

With his wedding planned for December 1886, however, Theodore returned to the city and his preparations for a renewed life with his oldest friend. Immediately upon his arrival in New York, he "was visited by a succession of the influential Republicans of the city to entreat [him] to take the nomination for Mayor." He understood that it was "of course a perfectly hopeless contest," since Democrats outnumbered Republicans by 50,000 votes. Nevertheless, he agreed to make the sacrificial three-week run, knowing that it would elevate his stature within the party.

The race pitted twenty-eight-year-old Roosevelt against both the Democratic candidate, Abraham Hewitt, a socially conscious industrialist, and the independent labor candidate Henry George, a radical, whose hugely popular book *Progress and Poverty* had become a bible for reformers. In powerful prose that struck a chord throughout the country and made the book one of the top ten best sellers in American history, George argued that the "enormous increase in productive power" during the previous decades had not diminished poverty nor lifted "the burdens of those compelled to toil." On the contrary, the progress that accompanied the Industrial Revolution had produced ever harsher lives for the masses of the people. He contended, in opposition to the social Darwinists, that "the want and injustice of the present social state are not necessary." The gap between the rich and the poor was not a consequence of unchanging natural laws or the survival of the fittest, but of environments made by man and changeable by man. Under the right laws, George insisted, "a social state is possible in which poverty would be unknown."

Roosevelt responded that "the mass of the American people are most emphatically not in the deplorable condition of which you speak, and the 'statesmen and patriots of to-day' are no more responsible for some people being poorer than others than they are for some people being shorter, or more near-sighted, or physically weaker than others. If you had any conception of the true American spirit you would know we do not have 'classes' at all on this side of the water. . . . Some of the evils of which you complain are real and can be to a certain degree remedied; others, though real, can only be gotten over through the capacity for steady individual self-help which is the glory of every true American, and can no more be done away with by legislation than you could do away with the bruises which you received when you tumbled down, by passing an act to repeal the laws of gravitation."

"The best I can hope for is to make a decent run," Roosevelt conceded in a letter to Fanny Smith Dana. "The simple fact," he explained, alluding to a famous painting, "is that I had to play Curtius and leap into the gulf that was yawning before the Republican party." As the days progressed, how-ever, with George firing up audiences across the city, Roosevelt worried that the gulf into which he had leapt was even deeper than he had first thought. He feared that many of his "should-be supporters" in the Republican Party would desert him in the end, voting for Hewitt to prevent the election of a radical mayor. Nonetheless, he committed to the campaign with his customary zeal. From sunup to sundown, tirelessly canvassing the city, he roused audi-ences with his fighting spirit, heartily shook endless hands, and freely granted interviews to reporters. He brought overflow crowds to their feet, pledging, "I am a strong party man myself [but should] I find a public servant who is dishonest, I will chop his head off even if he is the highest Republican in this municipality."

Friends and family were thrilled to see Roosevelt again step into the pub-lic arena. "It is such happiness to see him at his very best once more," Bamie wrote to Edith in London. "Ever since he has been out of politics in any active form; it has been a real heart sorrow to me, for while he always made more of his life than any other man I knew, still with his strong nature it was a permanent source of poignant regret that even at this early age he should lose these years without the possibility of doing his best and most telling work . . . this is the first time since the [assembly] days that he has enough work to keep him exerting all his powers. Theodore is the only person who had the power except Father who possessed it in a different way; of making me almost wor-ship him."

Despite the excitement generated by Roosevelt's return to public life, the Democratic candidate, Abraham Hewitt, won the election. Moreover, since thousands of Republicans voted for Hewitt in fear of the radical George, Roosevelt came in a distant third. Nonetheless, the press praised Roosevelt for a spirited campaign. "Fighting is fun for him, win or lose," the New York *Sun* editorialized.

Three days after the election, Theodore set sail for England, accompanied by his faithful sister Bamie. Three weeks later, on December 2, 1886, he married Edith Carow in a simple ceremony at St. George's Chapel in London. Theodore and Edith swiftly departed for a three-month honeymoon that would take them across England, France, and Italy. Typically, even as they explored Florence, Venice, and Paris, Theodore managed to complete a half-dozen articles on ranching life for the *Century* magazine. "I read them all over to Edith," he reported to Corinne, "and her corrections and help were most valuable to me."

During these halcyon days, Edith realized hopes and longings harbored since she was a girl. More than a decade after her honeymoon, she claimed to "remember them all one by one, and hour by hour." Her marriage to Theodore commenced what appears to have been a rich sensual life. Many years later, her biographer Sylvia Morris reports, Edith amazed a granddaughter by openly mentioning "that wonderful silky private part of a woman." When the Roosevelts returned home in March 1887, Edith was already three months pregnant.

The young couple returned from this idyllic interlude to face complications in uniting their daily lives. When Edith learned that Theodore was planning to leave three-year-old Alice in Bamie's care, she surprised him with powerful opposition, insisting they incorporate the little girl into their new household. Edith's reaction created a painful dilemma for Theodore, who well knew the devotion his childless older sister had shown her "blue-eyed darling." "I hardly know what to say about Baby Lee," he uncomfortably informed Bamie. "Edith feels more strongly about her than I could have imagined possible." For Bamie, the loss was devastating. "It almost broke my heart to give her up," she confessed. Although she maintained her composure, conceding that it was best for Alice to be with her father, she avoided further emotional attachments for some time thereafter.

The situation must have been terribly confusing for Alice, whose happiest memories revolved around Bamie's warm and loving home, where "the lovely smell of baking bread coming from the kitchen" heralded "the pleasure of English-style afternoon tea with piping-hot Earl Grey's tea and lots of paper-thin bread and butter." Alice never forgot the wrenching and bewildering day Theodore returned with his new wife: "I in my best dress and sash, with a huge bunch of pink roses in my arms, coming down the stairs at my aunt's house in New York to meet my father and my new mother."

The small child was expected simultaneously to transfer her affections to a new mother and pray each night for her "mother who is in heaven," though her father kept steadfastly mute about the beautiful woman who had been his first love. "In fact," Alice lamented, "he never ever mentioned my mother to me, which was absolutely wrong. He never even said her name . . . I think my father tried to forget he had ever been married to my mother. To blot the whole episode out of his mind. He didn't just never mention her to me, he never mentioned her name, to *anyone*. . . . He obviously felt tremendously guilty about remarrying. . . . The whole thing was really handled very badly. It was awfully bad psychologically."

Edith, too, had to adjust her conception of domestic bliss to the new realities of married life. As mistress of Sagamore Hill, she had envisioned a quiet life in the country with her husband and children, filled with books, writing, and a few like-minded friends. Unlike her husband, she was not a naturally gregarious person. "Where she was reserved," Theodore's cousin Nicholas Roosevelt recalled, "he overflowed with exuberance and enthusiasm." Their divergent natures would require both Theodore and Edith to balance private family life and public pursuits, necessitating compromise and cooperation.

Initially, Theodore focused intently upon his new wife. She happily recalled "rowing over to a great marsh, filled with lagoons and curious winding channels," reading aloud from Browning and Matthew Arnold. The household seemed complete when she gave birth to a son, Theodore Junior, on September 12, 1887. "She was extremely plucky all through," Theodore reported to Bamie. "I am very glad our house has an heir at last!"

For a time, the placid existence suited Theodore. After completing his book on Senator Benton, he had embarked on a short biography of founding father Gouverneur Morris and was beginning research on what would be his major work, *The Winning of the West*. "I have a small son now," he wrote to a friend, "and am settling down more and more to country life for all but a couple of months of the year. My literary work occupies a good deal of my time; and I have on the whole done fairly well at it; I should like to write some book that would really take rank as in the very first class, but I suppose this is a mere dream."

It was not long, however, before his abundant energy and expansive nature required an outlet that tranquil family life could not provide. Even his conception of domestic satisfaction included a continuous stream of houseguests arguing over books or politics at dinner, hiking together in the woods, enjoying canoe races and competitive games of tennis or polo. He assumed that his entire family, which had always been a kind of self-contained universe, would spend weeks together in his rambling home.

For a time, Edith tried to isolate her new household and create a more secluded family life. "Theodore," she would quietly say, "I think this winter we've seen a great deal of Douglas and Corinne and I don't think we'll ask them down for a little while—yet. We may ask them later." At first he would agree: "Very well, very well, Edie, we'll have them later." But soon he "put his foot down" and insisted upon opening their home to the company, stimulation, and activity he needed. Clearly, two very different temperaments had to be reconciled. Edith later acknowledged to Theodore Junior that it had been a great "temptation" to withdraw from society, but "Father would not allow it." Slowly, she began to open her house to her husband's family and friends, while wisely turning the drawing room into her sanctuary, "the place where she kept her own books and treasures." In this elegant room, furnished with bookcases, chairs, and sofas that had been in her family, she found the privacy she craved. Children and guests were told to knock and await permission to enter.

The accommodations Edith made in her manner of life at Sagamore Hill were insignificant beside the transformations occasioned by her husband's impulsive move to Washington, D.C., to become a member of the Civil Service Commission. The 1888 presidential campaign between Benjamin Harrison and Grover Cleveland had revived his interest in politics. A loyal Republican, he had agreed to stump for Harrison, traveling through the Midwest for twelve days, speaking before large crowds, discovering once again the pride and pleasure an enthusiastic audience could bestow. His reintroduction to national politics was "immense fun," he told Henry Cabot Lodge, who would join him in Washington as a new congressman from Massachusetts.

When Republicans captured both the presidency and the U.S. Congress, Roosevelt hoped he might be appointed assistant secretary of state. Despite intense lobbying by his friends, however, the new secretary, James Blaine, was hesitant to have a man of "Mr. T.R.'s temperament" in such an important post. "I do somehow fear that my sleep at Augusta or Bar Harbor would not be quite so easy and refreshing," Blaine admitted, "if so brilliant and aggressive a man had hold of the helm."

After absorbing this disappointing news, Roosevelt finally received word that President Harrison would offer him the less exalted post of civil service commissioner, where he would be charged with enforcing the 1883 Pendleton Act, mandating that one quarter of all federal jobs be filled by competitive examination rather than party affiliation. Roosevelt's family and friends cautioned against accepting the post, believing it beneath his talents, but Roosevelt leapt at the chance to return to political life.

For Edith, pregnant with their second child after a miscarriage the previous summer, the move to Washington signaled an unwelcome disruption of domestic order. Politics held scant interest for her compared with an abiding love of literature, a passion she could share with her husband while he was at work writing. Moreover, as the manager of the family's finances, she worried that his meager annual salary of $3,500 would not cover both the rental in Washington and the maintenance of Sagamore Hill. To economize, Roosevelt decided to stay with Henry Cabot Lodge until Edith could join him after the baby's birth in October.

Whereas Edith dreaded the long separation from her husband, Roosevelt was thrilled to be actively involved in the ferment of the capital. Within minutes of his arrival at the commission offices in the City Hall building, it was clear that he would bring impetus and authority to his new role. Matthew Halloran, who served as a certification clerk for thirty-five years, recalled his first indelible glimpse of Roosevelt. The morning quiet was instantly shattered by his ringing introduction: "I am the new Civil Service Commissioner," he proclaimed, his energetic, penetrating voice and brusque demeanor setting his new staff scrambling. "Have you a telephone? Call up the Ebbit House. I have an engagement with Archbishop Ireland. Say that I will be there at ten o'clock." His appearance had immediate effect. "I jumped up with alacrity," Halloran recalled. "Behind large-rimmed eye-glasses flashed piercing blue-gray eyes, Theodore Roosevelt impressed me as a fine specimen of vigorous manhood. The dazzling smile with its strong white teeth, which was later to become famous all over the world, is still a most vivid recollection. It seemed to mirror the wholesomeness and geniality of the man and it put me wholly at ease. . . . Our friendship and my admiration for him began at that moment."

Indeed, it seemed that a favorable impression of the new commissioner was widespread. In an editorial praising Roosevelt's appointment, the *Decatur* (Illinois) *Republican* observed, "He is equally at home in the drawing rooms of New York or Paris, in the halls of legislation or amid the exciting scenes of a national convention, and when he plays the cowboy on the ranch in Montana he is as far from a tenderfoot as when he takes up the pen to paint in glowing language the glories of a sunset in the Rockies or describes in a magazine article the interest of a fight with the hungry coyotes of the plains." The legend of this intrepid young man and his multifarious talents was beginning to grow.

Theodore spent most of the summer in Washington, with only occasional weekend visits to Sagamore Hill. "It has been a hopeless kind of summer to look back on," Edith wrote in mid-August, "and all I can think of are the times you have been here; our lovely rows and that long drive and our drives to and from the station. . . . My darling you are all the world to me. I am not myself when you are away. Do not forget me or love me less."

On October 10, 1889, Edith gave birth to a second son. She named him Kermit, carrying forward the name of her Aunt Kermit and her father's old mercantile house, Kermit & Carow. Two months later, she finally joined her husband in their newly rented town house at 1820 Jefferson Place. "Edie has occasional fits of gloom," Theodore reported to Bamie on January 4, 1890, "but the house is now getting to look very homelike and comfortable, such a contrast to when I was alone in it! I can hardly realize it is the same place; and I am thoroughly enjoying the change."

So it was that the spring of 1890 saw both the Roosevelts and the Tafts settled in the same Washington neighborhood. Both men had accepted positions in the capital that were far from their ideal vocations, though Roosevelt stepped into his job as commissioner with characteristic verve, while Will approached the role of solicitor general with trepidation. Their two wives also responded very differently to the prospect of life in Washington. Nellie had been an active proponent of the move, undeterred by the idea of uprooting her growing family in order to expand her experience and influence alongside her husband. Edith shuddered at the tumult and social demands of the city, a disruption imposed on the family circle she had waited so long to establish. In many ways, the two women complemented and balanced their respective partners. Nellie spurred Will Taft to greater confidence and action, her expectations and support driving him to greater engagement in the important work of the time. Edith, meanwhile, worked to restrain the impetuous will that drove her husband to ceaseless activity.

Despite—or perhaps because of—their dissimilar natures, Theodore Roosevelt and William Taft would forge a historic friendship. Nellie and Edith, despite their proximity and clear parallels in their interests and upbringings, never made a deep connection. In fact, their commonalities were far more superficial than their disparities. Both had grown up in the shadow of wealthier, more eminent families and had eventually married into them. The social ambitions that dictated private schools, proper wardrobes, and advantageous marriages for both girls were internalized in very different ways. Nellie, exposed to the scintillating world of national politics and society as a girl, was determined to marry a future president (or create one of the man she married).

She had watched her father sacrifice personal ambitions and satisfaction for material comfort and longed to find personal fulfillment, a more vivid and expansive existence. Edith, on the other hand, who had seen the dissipation of her family's empire in the hands of an alcoholic father, craved security and domestic coherence above all else.

Both women were scholars after their fashion. Each had avidly pursued her education, read widely for pleasure, and developed her closest friendships in a circle with similar literary inclinations. For Nellie, literature was a way to engage the larger world, to explore the social issues of the day; reading and writing were intensely personal pursuits for Edith, a way to isolate herself and create a private world to share with those she let in. When Edith married, she believed that she and Theodore could withdraw and build a life centered on books and family, sustained by reading and writing. Nellie, whose relationship with Will evolved in the heated discussions of her salon, agreed to a marriage she believed would expand the boundaries of her existence and her opportunities for involvement and impact.

Nellie always chafed at the conventions that circumscribed her role in the world. The same iconoclastic impulse that drove her to sneak cigarettes or dance in German beer halls made her ache to pursue higher education, as her brothers had, or to find purpose as a pioneer in early childhood schooling despite the opposition of her family. Seeing nothing but ennui in the "favorable" matches that were the crowning achievement for women of her time and station, she sought something different in her union with Will Taft. Solicitous and respectful, he accepted and needed her as a partner in public as well as in domestic pursuits. In London on her honeymoon, she was thrilled to hear Gladstone speak in Parliament. In Cincinnati, she savored newspapers and enjoyed discussions of current events. She was elated that they would now find themselves in Washington, at the epicenter of American political life.

Edith desperately longed for the staid home life that Nellie was fighting to escape. She sought always to make the Roosevelt home a refuge for herself and her family. "A very long way after her husband and children," one friend observed, "came a small group of chosen friends." Like Nellie, she was accomplished and competent, pursuing her intellectual passions while astutely managing her household. She did not, however, share her new neighbor's interest in the social and political agendas that dominated the consciousness of Washington, D.C. While Edith and Nellie lacked a basic affinity and understanding, the unique support each woman gave her husband was indispensable, allowing William Taft and Theodore Roosevelt to find common cause and succeed in ways neither could have alone.

CHAPTER SIX

The Insider and the Outsider

Theodore Roosevelt, U.S. Civil Service Commissioner, ca. 1889.

WASHINGTON IS JUST A BIG village, but it is a very pleasant big village," Theodore Roosevelt reported in the 1890s. Accustomed to the clamor of New York, "where everything throbs with the chase for the almighty dollar," Roosevelt must have been amazed to find that in the nation's capital, "pleasure takes precedence over work." Government officials enjoyed unhurried breakfasts, arriving at their desks between nine and ten, often leaving the office by four. Even Roosevelt, with his singular disciplined drive, managed to quit work early four or five afternoons each week for a game of tennis or jog through Rock Creek Park before heading off to a dinner party.

To illustrate the marked atmospheric contrast between the two cities, the writer Frank Carpenter observed that in New York, "a streetcar will not wait for you if you are not just at its stopping point. It goes on and you must stand there until the next car comes along. In Washington people a block away signal the cars by waving their hands or their umbrellas. Then they walk to the car at a leisurely pace, while the drivers wait patiently and the horses rest." While the capital might lack "the spirit of intense energy" that animated New York, Carpenter concluded that Washington, with its broad, clean streets and fine marble buildings (and its shanties generally hidden from view), offered "the pleasanter place in which to live."

Roosevelt and Taft apparently met within days of Taft's arrival in town, possibly through their mutual friendship with Congressman Benjamin Butterworth. "Common views and sympathies," Taft recalled, made them immediate allies, particularly in the cause of "Civil Service reform." Roosevelt had been chagrined to find that many influential senators, congressmen, and cabinet officials "hated the whole reform and everything concerned with it and everybody who championed it." For sixty years, politicians in both parties had been complicit in a spoils system where officials (postal carriers, typists, stenographers, and clerks) were appointed, promoted, or fired according to their politics rather than their merit. Uprooting that system would prove a far more strenuous endeavor than Roosevelt had realized when he accepted the post of civil service commissioner.

In William Howard Taft, however, Roosevelt recognized a staunch comrade, a steadfast advocate of advancement due not to cronyism but to competence. Indeed, Taft had been willing to resign his post as revenue collector rather than bow to demands that he fire the best men in his department due to their political affiliations. This experience had given Taft some intimation of the hardships his new friend would face. "It will be a long, hard, discouraging struggle," Taft acknowledged during Roosevelt's tenure as commissioner, "but the right *must* win."

In the mornings, Roosevelt and Taft would often walk together to work. Although a streetcar stopped at nearby Farragut Square, they preferred to go on foot, as did most Washingtonians of the time. "One of the first observations that a New-Yorker makes on coming to Washington," the *New York Times* recorded, "is the difference in the way people walk. Here they usually walk slowly, deliberately always, and one rarely sees the rushing, hurrying, preoccupied walking that lends so much life to New York streets." The two friends soon became familiar figures as they strolled along Connecticut Avenue. More than half a foot shorter and 70 pounds lighter than Taft, Roosevelt busily scanned "everything and everybody" as he pursued a lively conversation. Taft trudged more ponderously, focused intently upon his companion. Taft reached the Justice Department first, which stood one block from the White House, opposite the northern front of the Treasury Department. Roosevelt continued ten blocks east to his destination, Judiciary Square, where the Civil Service Commission was housed.

Increasingly, they relied upon one another for advice and camaraderie, often meeting for leisurely lunches. Roosevelt did most of the talking, finding scant pleasure in his food, while Taft relished generous portions. Whether "absorbed in work or play," one reporter observed, Roosevelt "would eat hay and not know it," whereas Taft savored his meals with care. Profound differences in manner and metabolism never diminished the delight they found in each other's company.

"Externally Taft is everything Roosevelt is not," commented the journalist William Allen White. "Roosevelt's mental processes are quick, intuitive and sure," while "Taft grapples a proposition, wrestles with it without resting and without fatigue until it is settled or solved." Taft had no interest in hunting, boxing, or playing polo, no affinity for the often violent contests of strength and endurance, those manifestations of male prowess that so obsessed Roosevelt. His one passion was for the game of golf, which Roosevelt found excruciatingly dull and slow. Nonetheless, White concluded, the two had no sooner become acquainted than "they established one of those strong friendships that may be established only by men whose exteriors form such antipathetical sutures that they unite by a spiritual affinity."

From the outset, each man recognized the rare character and unique talent of the other. "Mr. Taft," a *Boston American* reporter expounded, "is the kind of man you would expect to find in the president's office of a bank if you went in to start an account. His appearance would give you confidence in the bank. You would say to yourself, 'This man will not let the bank fail if he can possibly help it.' " His kind and ingenuous nature was instantly apparent, inspiring the trust and amity of all he encountered. "If the boat were sinking, and he could swim and you couldn't, you'd hand him your $50,000—if you had it—saying, 'Give this to my wife,' and she'd *get* it."

"One loves him at first sight," Roosevelt acknowledged of Taft. "He has nothing to overcome when he meets people. I realize that I have always got to overcome a little something before I get to the heart of people. . . . I almost envy a man possessing a personality like Taft's." Taft, Roosevelt said, "can get along with some men that I can't get along with." While Roosevelt had difficulty suppressing his contempt and irritation toward men he did not like, Taft's "good nature, his indifference to self, his apparently infinite patience, enables him to get along with men, however cold or acerb or crotchety."

A reporter well acquainted with both men noted that Taft possessed "a capacity, indeed, for personal intimacy which a self-centered man like Roosevelt never could have." Perhaps, he suggested, "Roosevelt could see that sweetness of character in Mr. Taft and he could admire it, as we so often admire the faculties we do not possess." Taft felt a similar wonder at Roosevelt's aggressive self-confidence. His friend's talent for publicity, delight in confrontation, and rousing rhetorical manner were gifts he would never share.

ROOSEVELT WOULD NEED ALL THESE attributes and more if he hoped to win his war against the entrenched spoils system. "Each party profited by the offices when in power," Roosevelt explained, "and when in opposition each party insincerely denounced its opponents for doing exactly what it itself had done and intended again to do." Although long aware that corruption was endemic in the country's political and judicial systems, Roosevelt was sustained by his sometimes overweening belief in the rectitude of his cause and the prospect of a rousing struggle. "For the last few years politics with me has been largely a balancing of evils," he explained to a friend, "and I am delighted to go in on a side where I have no doubt whatever, and feel absolutely certain that my efforts are wholly for the good; and you can guarantee I intend to hew to the line, and let the chips fly where they will."

For Roosevelt, civil service reform presented a historic opening to ensure that "the fellow with no pull should have an even chance with his rival who came backed; that the farmer's lad and the mechanic's son who had no one to speak for them should have the same show in competing for the public service as the son of wealth and social prestige." Allowing party officials to ensconce unqualified friends and kinsmen in public positions, he argued, was not merely "undemocratic"; it ensured inefficient public service that impacted the poor and vulnerable most of all. The smug axiom "To the victor belongs the spoils" was a "cynical battle-cry" he denounced as "so nakedly vicious" that no honorable man could condone it.

Roosevelt's crusade prompted immediate attention from reporters in Washington. Although he was only one of three commissioners, he soon became the public face of the Civil Service Commission. "Yes, TR is a breezy young fellow," a New York *Sun* correspondent commented with patronizing approbation, "and we do not find fault with him because he fancies that he knows it all. The quality of self-confidence is not bad in youth. We rather like to see it, for it indicates usually the possession or the motive power which makes a man aggressive and enterprising. He works more vigorously if he is sure that he is nearer right than other people, and has no misgivings as to his ability to accomplish his ends. The self distrustful, self-critical young man, who is always looking for direction from somebody else, and in whom what the old phrenologists used to call the bump of approbativeness is out of proper proportion, is pretty sure to be left behind in the race."

From the start, Roosevelt understood that public opinion was the single most effective prod for recalcitrant party leaders in the cabinet and the Congress. "Until he began to roar," his biographer Henry Pringle maintained, "the merit system had been a subject that interested a small fraction of the intelligent minority" whom powerful politicians could safely afford to ignore. In order "to secure proper administration of the laws," the task before Roosevelt was nothing less than "to change the average citizen's mental attitude toward the question." In order to battle this entrenched spoils system, it was necessary to instill something of his own sense of outrage into the people, to popularize the reformist cause and foment change from the bottom up.

In his campaign to muster publicity and elicit indignation, Theodore Roosevelt adapted techniques that had served him well in the New York State Assembly, and developed new tactics he would perfect in the years ahead. For his opening salvo, he launched an on-the-spot investigation into the New York Customs House, where rumors indicated that clerks were leaking examination questions to favored party candidates for a fee of $50. When he determined the identity of the guilty clerks, Roosevelt issued a scathing report demanding their dismissal and prosecution. Headlines and editorials broadcast his message across the country, serving notice that civil service law was "going to be enforced, without fear or favor."

Roosevelt's investigation into the New York Customs House furnished evidence that despite the new regulations prohibiting mandatory contributions to the party in power by government employees, party leaders were still demanding "so-called voluntary contributions" from low-level clerks and stenographers as the price for retaining their positions. An identical tithing system had incensed Taft in Ohio, prompting party officials to claim "he was wrecking the party by the course he followed." Cannily appealing to the sympathy and sentiment of his audience, Roosevelt observed that "to a poor clerk just able to get along the loss of three per cent of his salary may mean just the difference between having and not having a winter overcoat for himself, a warm dress for his wife or a Christmas tree for his children."

Straightaway, it was evident to Roosevelt that the corruption he had observed in New York was rampant nationwide, a blight far exceeding the resources of his own staff. To conduct the investigations necessary to expose illegal practices across the country, he cultivated a network of progressive journalists and editors "to point out infractions of the law in their localities."

Recognizing that the foundation of his unwelcome campaign of reform depended on sound information, Roosevelt took especial care to confirm the accuracy of the reports he received.

From Lucius Burrie Swift, editor and publisher of the crusading *Civil Service Chronicle*, he learned that the Indianapolis postmaster, William Wallace, a good friend of President Harrison's, had made a number of irregular appointments that violated civil service standards. "Give me all the facts you can," Roosevelt implored Swift. "I have to be sure that every recommendation I make of any kind or sort can be backed by the most satisfactory evidence. It would be irritating if it were not amusing to see the eagerness with which so many of the people here in power watch to catch me tripping in any recommendation, and their desire to find me making some recommendation, whether for removal or indictment, which I cannot sustain." Initially, Wallace's indignant response generated headlines, but the charges were ultimately verified. "We stirred things up well," Roosevelt gloated to his friend Lodge, "but I think we have administered a galvanic shock that will reinforce [Wallace's] virtue for the future." His hopes were realized. In fact, the newspaper exposure did chasten the Indianapolis postmaster; within two years, his administration was deemed "a model of fairness and justice."

Buoyed by this early success, Roosevelt turned his spotlight on Milwaukee, where informants claimed that Postmaster George Paul was systematically manipulating examination scores in order to appoint favored party members. Evidence in hand, Roosevelt issued a blistering public report and demanded Paul's removal from office. "If he is not dismissed, as we recommend, it will be a black eye for the Commission," Roosevelt told Lodge, "and practically an announcement that hereafter no man need fear dismissal for violating the law; for if Paul has not violated it, then it can by no possibility be violated." Roosevelt's report and the ensuing publicity infuriated President Harrison's postmaster general, John Wanamaker. He charged that Roosevelt was overstepping his authority, intruding on matters that were the province of his own department. A wealthy contributor to Harrison's campaign fund, Wanamaker fully adhered to the time-honored spoils system and harbored contempt for civil service reformers. Wanamaker appealed to the president, who forged a weak compromise by accepting Paul's resignation. "It was a golden chance to take a good stand," Roosevelt lamented, "and it has been lost."

The apparent rebuff from President Harrison did not deter Roosevelt from initiating another, more controversial investigation into violations and irregularities in the Baltimore Post Office. On the basis of information supplied by Charles Bonaparte, a civil service reformer who would one day become a member of his own cabinet, Roosevelt charged officials with using postal appointments as "a bribery chest." Wanamaker countered by conducting his own investigation, submitting the results to a committee in the House of Representatives. Wanamaker's report absolved the employees of any wrongdoing and accused Roosevelt of pursuing an inquisition both "unfair and partial in the extreme." Roosevelt countered by publishing an open letter to Postmaster General Wanamaker, whom he called the "head devil" of the spoilsmen, demanding that he renounce the "gross impertinence and impropriety" of his statements.

The escalating hostility between Roosevelt and Wanamaker delighted the press. "It is war, open, avowed, and to the knife," *The Washington Post* reported. The *New York Times* could "not remember an instance in the history of our Government" when one member of a president's administration made "statements so damaging to the character of another officer of the Government of still higher rank."

Critics assailed Roosevelt's tactics, recommending that he "put a padlock on his restless and uncontrollable jaws." *The Washington Post* claimed that he spoke "like a person suffering from an overdose of nerve tonic," expressing their scorn with savage clarity: "He came into official life with a blare of trumpets and a beating of gongs, blared and beat by himself. He immediately announced himself the one man competent to take charge of the entire business of the Government. To his mind every department of the Government was under the management of incompetent and bad men. He said to himself, to his barber, to his laundryman, and to all others who would listen to his incoherent gibberish: 'I am Roosevelt; stop work and look at me.' For a short time he had clear sailing. As he sailed he took in wind. As he took in wind he became more puffed up. As he became more puffed up he became insolent, arrogant, and more conceited."

As Roosevelt continued to commandeer center stage, relationships with his fellow commissioners, once quite amicable, grew increasingly contentious. He complained to Lodge that Charles Lyman was "utterly useless . . . utterly out of place as a Commissioner," and that Hugh S. Thompson, though an "excellent" fellow, lacked the fortitude to pursue enemies of civil service with the necessary zeal. He much preferred to proceed unilaterally. "My two colleagues are now away and I have all the work of the Civil Service Commission to myself," he told his sister Bamie. "I like it; it is more satisfactory than having a divided responsibility; and it enables me to take more decided steps."

More troubling than friction within the commission was Roosevelt's deteriorating relationship with President Harrison. "I have been continuing my civil service fight, battling with everybody," he groused to Bamie, " the little gray man in the White House looking on with cold and hesitating disapproval." Never once throughout his service in the Harrison administration was Roosevelt invited to dine at the White House. Despite the president's "high regard" for the young commissioner's abilities, he was often irked by Roosevelt's uncompromising, aggressive temperament. "Roosevelt seemed to feel," Harrison remarked, "that everything ought to be done before sundown." Rumors abounded that Roosevelt would be removed. With most of the influential newspapers supporting him, however, and with public indignation about violations of the civil service law at an inflamed pitch, Harrison dared not take action.

Although Roosevelt's impetuous offensives frayed personal relationships, his public triumph over Postmaster General Wanamaker was soon complete. After hearing testimony from both sides, the House committee concluded that incontrovertible evidence backed up every single charge of fraud and misconduct. "Mr. Roosevelt is a regular young Lochinvar," the Boston *Evening Times* remarked. "He isn't afraid of the newspapers, he isn't afraid of losing his place, and he is always ready for a fight. He keeps civil-service reform before the people and as the case often is, his aggressiveness is a great factor in a good cause."

To HER GREAT SURPRISE, EDITH Roosevelt found that she thoroughly enjoyed Washington. Through her husband's friendship with Massachusetts congressman Henry Cabot Lodge, she entered a circle of literary-minded men and women whose engaging conversations centered on the books, art, and music that she loved. "Cabot has been a real comfort to her," Theodore reported to Bamie. "He is one of the few men I know who is as well read as she is in English literature, and she delights to talk with him." Edith also developed a close relationship with Nannie Lodge, a charming woman guided by a quick mind and a warm heart. Both women loved poetry and could recite Shakespeare "almost by heart." The Lodges and the Roosevelts lived close enough to easily frequent each other's homes. "You know, old fellow," Roosevelt confided to Lodge, "you and Nannie are more to me than any one else but my own immediate family."

Together with the Lodges, Theodore and Edith were frequent guests at the Lafayette Square town house of the historian Henry Adams. The distinguished group that congregated there included the Lincoln biographer John Hay and his wife, Clara; Senator Don Cameron with his exquisite wife,

Elizabeth; the sculptor Augustus Saint-Gaudens; and the Winthrop Chanlers. Adams felt an immediate fondness for Edith, who struck him as especially "sympathetic." His encouragement and admiration put her quickly at ease in the group's discussions of literature, drama, and poetry. "Her taste in books and judgment of their merit *qua* literature were always far more reliable than were Theodore's," noted a town house regular.

"Edith is really enjoying Washington," Roosevelt reported to Bamie. "One night we dined at Cabots to meet the Willy Endicotts; another night I gave a dinner to some historical friends; last evening we went to the theatre, and a supper afterwards with John Hay. . . . Of course Hay was charming, as he always is; and Edith enjoyed it all as much as I did." She had even developed a small taste for talk of political events, so long as she could rely on her inner circle for company and conversation. At a breakfast hosted by Secretary of State James Blaine, she was delighted to find herself seated between Elizabeth Cameron and Clara Hay. Her deepening friendships did much to assuage Edith's dread anxiety of Washington's social world. New Year's Day entailed an exhausting series of calls on the wives of government officials, but she was heartened by the company of Nannie Lodge. "Nannie has been a dear about sending me her carriage & this afternoon I have found courage to go out & pay hundreds of calls."

While Edith made an effort to overcome her natural reserve, her husband happily immersed himself in the social whirl of the nation's capital. The Roosevelts hosted casual dinners that made an enduring impression on their circle of friends. "Sunday-evening suppers where the food was of the plainest and the company of the best," Margaret Chanler recalled. "Theodore would keep us all spellbound with tales of his adventures in the West. There was a vital radiance about the man—a glowing, unfeigned cordiality towards those he liked that was irresistible." Edith was "more difficult of access. . . . Just as the camera is focused, she steps aside to avoid the click of the shutter." Despite this elusive quality, "one felt in her a great strength of character, and ineluctable will power."

During those first years in Washington, the Roosevelts successfully established themselves among the city's social and intellectual elite. "Edith and I meet just the people we like to see," Theodore told Bamie. "We dine out three or four times a week, and have people to dinner once or twice; so that we hail the two or three evenings when we are alone at home, and can talk and read. . . . The people we meet are mostly those who stand high in the political world, and who are therefore interested in the same subjects that interest us; while there are enough who are men of letters or of science to give a pleasant and needed variety."

Rudyard Kipling, whom Theodore had first met at the Cosmos Club in New York, was a guest on a number of occasions. Kipling later described that first encounter when he "curled up" on a chair across from Roosevelt "and listened and wondered until the universe seemed to be spinning around and Theodore was the spinner." If Roosevelt initially resented Kipling's "tendency to criticise America," he nonetheless recognized the author's "genius" and found the man himself "very entertaining."

Roosevelt sometimes worried that his political career suffered as he devoted time and attention to his social pursuits. After two years, his war on the spoils system had produced singular successes but little systemic change. While he had managed to reduce the practice of forcing salary contributions from government clerks, he had not "succeeded in stopping political assessments outright." He had "harassed the wrong-doers" who manipulated examination results without eliminating the endemic corruption that fueled the practice.

If Roosevelt fretted that his gains had been modest, he had accomplished more than any of his predecessors in the Civil Service Commission. Through his dramatic investigations of unscrupulous officials, his alliances with reformist journalists and immense skill in generating publicity, he had alerted Americans to the flagrant iniquities of the spoils system. The process Roosevelt had set in motion by shining the light of publicity on these practices would prove crucial in any attempt to create a system of government based upon good work rather than political influence.

TAFT EMBARKED UPON HIS TENURE in Washington with a very different style of leadership; meticulous habits and an affable disposition helped him build accord among colleagues and superiors at every level, including the executive.

Recalling their time together in Washington, Roosevelt wryly conceded Taft's success in gaining Harrison's cooperation while he so "got on Harrison's nerves," that his very presence set the president's "fingers drumming on the desk before him as though it were a piano." Roosevelt marveled that despite Taft's ability to foster cooperation among all manner of men, "he was always a man of highest ideals."

William Howard Taft's stolid demeanor prevented the sort of aggressive, confident debut in Washington that Roosevelt had enjoyed. He confessed to his father that his first oral argument before the Supreme Court had left him despondent. "I did not find myself as fluent on my feet as I had hoped to," he explained. "I forgot a great many things I had intended to say." He worried that his deliberate speaking style would fail to capture the justices' attention.

"They seem to think when I begin to talk that that is a good chance to read all the letters that have been waiting for some time, to eat lunch, and devote their attention to correcting proof, and other matters that have been delayed until my speech," he grumbled. While the solicitor general's position might offer great "opportunities for professional experience," he doubted his own ability to capitalize on those opportunities. "I find it quite embarrassing to change from the easy position of sitting on the bench to the very different one of standing on your legs before it," he told one friend, "and I do not find myself at home as I hoped to do in presenting one side of a case at Court." Called to make a quick business trip home, he was delighted to spend "a few days in Cincinnati, which it seems to me I left ten years ago, such a change has come over my mode of life."

"Don't be discouraged," his father counseled. "I have no doubt that you will soon come to understand them & their ways perfectly, & that they will be as anxious to hear what you have to say, as you will to say it." His mother also tried to assuage his anxieties. "Members waste their eloquence in the House and the Senate on empty benches or disorderly parties who never listen," she reminded him. Taft assured his parents that he remained steadfastly "philosophical," stoically framing his lack of immediate success as "the strongest reason for . . . having this experience and improving it." Indeed, he acknowledged, "the very fact that I find it difficult, and not particularly agreeable is evidence that the medicine is good for me."

His second appearance before the Court gave him "somewhat more satisfaction" and made him feel "more at home." Unfortunately, his speaking style, at least in his own estimation, seemed to exert "the same soporific power" on the justices. He refused to be discouraged, declaring he would "gain a good deal of practice in addressing a lot of mummies and experience in not being overcome by circumstances."

The sudden death of his predecessor the previous January had left him with a "rather overwhelming" workload; nearly a dozen unfinished cases had to be argued before the Court that spring of 1891. Midnight often found him still methodically reading through briefs, looking up precedents, drafting opinions, and editing proofs in his home library. His hard work secured victories in his first eleven cases. But even then, he could not share Roosevelt's sanguine outlook. "Each time a case of mine is now decided, I look for defeat," he anxiously wrote. "It is my turn. It ought to come, and doubtless will." In fact, of seventeen cases argued in his first year, Taft was gratified to find he had won fifteen. "So," he told his father, "you see that Fortune has been good to me on the whole." Although reluctant to proclaim his own accomplishments, he concluded that "the year's experience has been valuable." He no longer considered "the inattention of the judges" a personal affront. "Everyone suffers the same way," he realized. "It is the custom of the Bench." As he mastered his initial insecurities, Taft appreciated that his position had opened an entirely "new field of federal practice, law and decisions, with which I had no familiarity before."

Perhaps even more central to his success, Taft had "made some very valuable acquaintances" in his year's time. "It would be difficult for the Department of Justice to be organized with officers who are pleasanter to get along with than it has been since I have been here," he happily reported. "The Attorney General [William Miller] is a very satisfactory man to work under. . . . I like him very much, and am conscious that he has been in every way considerate of me."

While Roosevelt reveled in any opportunity to exercise sole power in the absence of his fellow commissioners, Taft took no pleasure in suddenly assuming the role of attorney general. "The novelty of it wore off in just about a day," he admitted, "and no man will be happier than I shall be when he returns to his desk." In the following months, as Attorney General Miller suffered recurring intestinal attacks, Taft became more comfortable wielding authority. But he was careful not to overstep or compromise his relationship with Miller. "The first duty of a subordinate," he strongly believed, "is courteous respect to his superior officer."

Taft's regard for the attorney general went beyond mere professional courtesy. On one occasion, Miller fell ill while his wife was out of town and Taft proposed that he stay overnight: "I shall sleep in a room next to his," he related to Nellie. "I know what it is to be attacked in the stomach at night all alone, and even though I could probably do no good the fact of the presence of a friend is reassuring."

Taft's kind and ingenuous nature defined not only his bond with Miller but a growing intimacy with President Harrison, one of Miller's closest friends. Visiting the attorney general's household, Taft often found the president himself relaxing in the parlor. In the course of their conversations, Harrison in turn found Taft so amiable that he issued an open invitation to call on him at the White House "every evening if convenient." Louise was delighted to learn of the proffered hospitality, regarding the unusual invitation "as not only a great compliment, but as a great privilege."

Furthermore, Taft was happy to note that by year's end he had "come into exceedingly pleasant relations with the Supreme Court," the bench he one day ardently hoped to join. He developed a genuine friendship with Justice John

Harlan and, at Harlan's request, agreed to write a short sketch of his life for publication in a commemorative history of the Supreme Court. "It has been a work of considerable labor, because it involved an examination of a great many cases," Taft related to his father. "However, Judge Harlan has been very kind to me, and I feel as if anything I could do for him was only repaying the friendly interest he has taken in me." Indeed, the trust and affection generated by Taft's good nature made him welcome in the city's most eminent company. He became a regular whenever the attorney general hosted dinners for members of the Supreme Court.

Taft was equally popular among his subordinates and immediate colleagues, quickly earning the confidence and friendship of the assistant attorneys general. His administrative skills enabled him to organize the department's functions in a manner that expedited everyone's work. Under his predecessors, business had been "scattered over the Department," but Taft had methodically taken control of the docket. "Every paper that comes to the Department with reference to Supreme Court business comes to me," he proudly explained to his father. "I have a general idea of all the cases that are to be argued in the Supreme Court." Taft's dedication earned him great esteem in the capital, and word spread that he was "the heaviest weight intellectually of any men in the Department of Justice."

For Nellie, life in Washington settled into a gratifying routine. She had been in town only six weeks when she received her first invitation to a White House dinner for the Supreme Court. "There were fifty at the table," Taft reported to his father, "and it made a very brilliant assemblage." The company included a number of senators and congressmen from the judiciary committees of both Houses, as well as the justices themselves. Nellie's seatmate was "exceedingly conversational and pleasant, and Nellie had a good time," Taft continued, immersing himself in the details of this social landscape. "You may tell Mother that Nellie's dress which she got in Paris she had made over in New York, and that it is exceedingly becoming to her." News of the festivities elicited great excitement in Cincinnati. "Do write me details," Nellie's friend Agnes Davis implored. "I feel so proud of our Cin. friends."

Nellie was back at the White House for the traditional reception on New Year's Day 1891, where the Marine Band's performance must have evoked memories of her first visit as a young girl. "In the East Room," *The Washington Post* reported, "the electric lights were used for the first time, the twelve great crystal suns set in the center of as many medallions on the ceiling gleaming with white light." In the Red Parlor and the Blue Room, government officials and their wives mingled until the invited guests moved into the private dining room for lunch. "She had a very pleasant time," Taft told his father, "and met a great many people—all the diplomats, and most of the prominent officials." Later that afternoon, she stood in the receiving line at a party hosted by the attorney general and his wife. Days later, the Tafts attended a reception hosted by Vice President Levi Morton for the president and the cabinet. Nellie and her husband had established a place in the bright constellation of Washington that she had yearned for since childhood.

The house on Dupont Circle was large enough to accommodate guests, allowing Nellie to entertain her parents, her sister Maria, Taft's brothers and sisters-in-law, and a number of her old friends from home. "Tom Mack is with us now," Taft reported in January 1891, "and he and Nellie go every day to the Senate and House to hear the debates. They have been quite interesting during the past few days." Finally, Nellie Herron Taft was privy to the intellectual and political discourse at the summit of Washington's society.

The Roosevelts and Tafts were frequent guests at the home of Ohio congressman Bellamy Storer and his wealthy wife, Maria Longworth. Nellie and Edith both shopped at the Center Market, considered a Washington institution. On market day, the two women joined "throngs of buyers of all classes of society, fashionable women of the West End, accompanied by negro servants, mingling with people of less opulent sections." They made the rounds of the carts, selecting fresh fruits and vegetables, fish, chicken and other meats. "The true Washingtonian," the historian Constance Green wrote, "regarded marketing in person as much a part of well-ordered living as making calls or serving hot chocolate to morning visitors."

Curiously, despite a constant proximity, the bond between these two impressive women "never ripened into intimacy." In fact, Nellie later confessed to her younger son that "I don't like Mrs. Roosevelt at all. I never did."

DURING HIS SECOND YEAR AS solicitor general, Taft extended his string of victories in three celebrated cases. In the first, he successfully defended the constitutionality of the McKinley tariff, which raised duties on imports competing with American products. His second case, in which he convinced the Supreme Court to sustain Speaker Thomas Reed's new method of counting a quorum, had profound implications for partisan politics in the legislative process. Reed's procedure ended the old practice that demanded a voice vote rather than a simple tally of "those who were actually present in the room" to establish a quorum. This traditional method, in place since the first Congress, had enabled the minority party to prevent the transaction of business by simply hiding in the cloakrooms and refusing to answer the roll call. Reed's new rule, unanimously affirmed by the Court, greatly increased the power of the Speaker, allowing him to push through sweeping legislation.

Taft's most resounding triumph involved a dispute between Great Britain and the United States over fishing rights in the Bering Sea. Initially, the international attention focused on the case disconcerted Taft. "I suppose I ought to feel that it is a great privilege to take part in it," he confessed, "but I look forward with considerable trepidation to making an argument orally before that court in a case which will be so conspicuous." If Taft had gained confidence in the quality of his preparation, he remained uneasy about his oratorical skills. In such an important case, the work was customarily divided between the attorney general and the solicitor general. But another episode of Miller's chronic illness left Taft responsible for the entire brief, a task he welcomed: "I do not object to this, at all, because I like the work," he told his father. In the end, his conscientious planning and competent presentation yielded a unanimous ruling in the government's favor. His three significant victories, announced at the same time, made headlines across the country.

Taft's pleasure in his success as solicitor general was magnified by the joy he knew it would bring to his father. In 1890, the elder Tafts had moved to California, hoping the climate would improve Alphonso's diseased lungs. For a time, it seemed his health had improved, but he soon began to suffer from a range of ailments, including asthma and bladder infections. "Your letters are what we live upon here," Alphonso told his son. "Your success has been wonderful." Despite his exhaustion at the end of each working day in Washington, Will took the time to write to his father, describing his cases in detail. "I am greatly exhilarated by your letters," returned Alphonso wistfully. "They carry back 14 years when I was able to act a man's part & enjoy life as it passed."

In November 1890, Charley Taft traveled to the west coast to spend a week with their father. "The morning is his best time," he reported to Will. "But the afternoon tires him out with pain and suffering. He is ready to go to bed at eight o'clock. His power of enduring suffering is wonderful. I could see traces of pain on his features during the afternoons, when he sits in his chair, but he never complained at all." Louise confirmed Charley's report. "Except when he is actually suffering his happy temperament surmounts all discouragements preserving a cheerfulness equal to Mark Tapley's," she explained, alluding to the irrepressible servant in Dickens's *Martin Chuzzlewit* who sought out all manner of obstacles to surmount and miseries to transcend, and yet maintained a joyful aplomb. While Alphonso's body deteriorated, his mind remained sufficiently lucid to find pleasure when his wife read to him. "What a resource is a cultivated mind!" Louise told her son. "What can people do when old and sick without intellectual resources. I can always entertain him."

Nothing mattered more to Alphonso in his last days, Charley reported, than the accomplishments of his boys—and Will's foremost. "Can you not in your long summer vacation of next year come & see us?" Alphonso beseeched Will. "Think of it, & the fate of one old man who has to be across the continent from the best children in the world."

In early May 1891, Will received word that his father had begun to hemorrhage internally and little time remained. He left work immediately and traveled by train to California. Though doctors had given up any hope for recovery by the time Will arrived, the chance to be with his father at the end was a gift that Theodore had been denied. "His vitality is fighting with death," Will recounted to Nellie ten days later. "Each day might end his life and yet he has breathed on." No longer able to take nourishment, Alphonso had lost some 75 pounds; still, his body clung to life. Only Will could persuade him to take anything to drink: "He seems to trust me. After I had given him some brandy he looked up at me in the sweetest way and said to me 'Will I love you beyond expression.'"

A few mornings later, before Will had risen, Alphonso asked the nurse to fetch his "noble boy." Agonizingly short of breath, he struggled to tell his son that "he ought to have avoided this by suicide." Three days later, with Will by his side, Alphonso Taft died. He was eighty years old.

The funeral was held in the old Taft home on Mt. Auburn. In Washington, the Justice Department flag was flown at half-mast, though Taft rejected the attorney general's proposal to close the department on the day of the funeral. Appreciative of the honor, Taft nonetheless insisted he did not want the general public to be inconvenienced.

All four sons returned to Cincinnati for the funeral. Taft worried that Charley and Annie, who had recently lost their twelve-year-old son David to typhoid fever, could scarcely absorb this new grief. "I trust you may never have this experience to go through," Charley had written Will. "It takes one's heart right out of a person." For the rest of the Taft children, life was proceeding more smoothly. Harry's law business was growing and Julia had given birth to a son. Horace's school was beginning to prosper and he had fallen in love with Winifred Thompson, a teacher in New Haven. Fanny was happily settled in California, having married her father's doctor, William Edwards. And Nellie had returned from Washington pregnant with her second child.

After the funeral, Nellie remained in Cincinnati with her family to await the birth of the baby. Taft returned alone to Washington, well aware that he made a "ludicrous" picture as he raced to catch the train at the Cincinnati station without the benefit of his wife's management. Apparently, Taft had forgotten to safety-pin his drawers to his trousers, and as he began to run, his drawers "began to work themselves clear down into the legs of the trousers and [his] legs were thus shackled so as to prevent any rapidity of movement." To close this comic vignette, just as the train departed the platform, he somehow managed to climb aboard.

Taft returned to a city that was gradually emptying as women and children escaped the insufferable summer heat and humidity, leaving the men behind. With Edith and the children at Sagamore Hill, Theodore and his British diplomat friend, Cecil Spring Rice, roomed together. "Springy and I have had a pleasant time," Roosevelt told Bamie. "He is a good fellow; and really cultivated; in the evenings he reads Homer and Dante in the originals! I wish I could. . . . Of course I miss Edith and the children frightfully. But it is pleasant to be engaged in a work which I know to be useful and in which I believe with all my heart." In July, they moved into Lodge's vacant house while Cabot and Nannie were abroad. "We are just as comfortable as possible," Roosevelt informed Lodge, "and are excellently taken care of by nice black Martha; and we think very gratefully of our absent host and hostess."

On August 1, 1891, Nellie gave birth to a daughter, Helen. Twelve days later, Edith gave birth to Ethel. "I see that I got ahead of Mrs. Roosevelt and feel quite proud," Nellie remarked to Will.

Without the domestic order imposed by the presence of wives and children, the men who worked through the long Washington summer established an intimate camaraderie. With Springy's "nervous and fidgety" assistance, Theodore hosted several dinners, proudly reporting to Lodge that no guest had yet died. In Nellie's absence, he invited Will to one of these bachelor meals. On this occasion, the invitation to Taft revealed an affectionate and casual humor: "Can you dine with me, in the *most* frugal manner Friday night at 8 o'clock. . . . No dress suit—I haven't got any."

At the time of their dinner, Roosevelt was wrestling with the headlong deterioration of his brother Elliott's mental health, a situation that echoed Taft's painful experience with his brother Peter. Elliott had gone to work for his Uncle Gracie's real estate firm, but heavy drinking and mental instability prevented him from contributing to the enterprise. At twenty-three, he had married the socialite Anna Hall. She bore him three children—Eleanor, Elliott Junior, and Hall—but the responsibilities of fatherhood never slowed his drinking. "It is a perfect nightmare about Elliott," Theodore had informed Bamie. "Elliott must be put under some good man, and then sent off on a sea voyage, or made to do whatever else he is told. Half measures simply put off the day, make the case more hopeless, and render the chance of public scandal."

The disgrace Roosevelt feared surfaced that summer. One of Elliott's maids, Katy Mann, threatened to file suit against him, claiming that he was the father of her newborn child. Theodore initially counseled against giving in to blackmail, but changed his mind when the family determined the likely truth of her story. "He is evidently a maniac, morally no less than Mentally," Theodore gravely declared to Bamie. "How glad I am I got his authorization to compromise the Katy Mann affair!" When negotiations stalled and Theodore learned new details of Elliott's increasingly violent behavior at home, he secured Anna Hall's consent to have him institutionalized. His petition to declare his brother legally insane made headlines the very week of his dinner with Taft. ELLIOTT ROOSEVELT DEMENTED BY EXCESSES, proclaimed the *New York Herald*. Two days later, Elliott retaliated in an open letter to the *Herald* "emphatically" denying he was "a lunatic or that any steps have been taken to adjudge him one." Theodore was beside himself. "The horror about Elliott broods over me like a nightmare," he told his sister.

In the end, Elliott agreed to seek a cure for his alcoholism and the family withdrew their petition to declare him insane. The treatment failed, as did several other interventions. Two years later, suffering from delusions, Elliott "jumped out of the parlor window of his house, had a seizure and died." Just as the Tafts had sought solace in memories of the time when Peter was "the sunniest" child in the family, so Theodore found "great comfort" in the realization that he no longer had to dwell on his brother's degradation: "I only need to have pleasant thoughts of Elliott now," he reflected. "He is just the gallant, generous, manly boy and young man whom everyone loved."

While Theodore rarely talked with anyone about his private sorrows, the public nature of the struggle, combined with Taft's empathetic nature raises the possibility that he was able to discuss some portion of the situation with his friend. In a letter to Bamie, Roosevelt spoke of another dinner party in his home that included Taft, "of whom we are really fond." At such gatherings, one observer noted, Taft's "merry blue eyes, his heavy mop of dark-brown hair, and the cherubic look of his big face, conspired with his soft, sibilant, self-deprecatory voice" and booming laugh to make him an ideal companion.

☞ ☜

WILLIAM TAFT'S WIDESPREAD POPULARITY IN Washington would prove an invaluable resource when he sought one of nine new circuit court judgeships created by Congress to relieve congestion in the courts. At thirty-four, Taft was young for the prestigious appointment, the second highest in the nation's judicial system. The reduction in pay from his salary as solicitor general mattered little to Taft when he considered that a seat on the Sixth District's court of appeals would put him "in the line of promotion" for the Supreme Court. His old friend Howard Hollister and Yale classmate Rufus Smith both worked tirelessly to build support for the appointment. They "have stirred up matters in my behalf in Cincinnati," he gratefully observed, "so that a great number of letters have come from the leading members of the bar there."

The affinity Taft had developed with Attorney General Miller and Justice Harlan served him well when the two men wholeheartedly endorsed him for the post. In a joint interview with the president, Harlan called Taft "the man whom . . . of all others, you should appoint"; Miller agreed, telling Harrison that he believed Taft possessed "in an eminent degree the judicial faculty" and that his "age was such as to secure to the people of the circuit a great many years of hard work." Justice Henry Billings Brown affirmed that he "would be very glad" if Taft received the appointment. Despite such resounding, prestigious endorsements, Taft remained "entirely philosophical" about his chances, aware that the number of qualified candidates was "legion." The Sixth District covered Ohio, Michigan, Tennessee, and Kentucky, each state offering a favorite son to compete for the position. Indeed, the flood of applicants to the new judicial posts necessitated a nine-month selection process, stretching from March until December. Though Alphonso Taft had been thrilled by the possibility of his son's appointment, he did not live to hear who had received the coveted post.

As the Tafts awaited a decision, Nellie endeavored to discourage Will from actively pursuing the post. She had finally secured the life she had long desired and dreaded a return to the staid, tranquil existence in Cincinnati. Just as she had objected to his superior court appointment years earlier, fearing he would be "settled for good," she now resisted a promotion that would keep him "fixed in a groove for the rest of his life" among colleagues "almost twice his age." Since her life was now completely bound to his, she insisted that she should weigh in on the decision.

Taft was disheartened to find his wife "very much opposed" to a course of action he ardently desired. After five years of marriage, his love for her transcended the passion of courtship days. "It seems to me now," he told her, "as if more completely than ever, we have become one." He was alarmed by her warning: "If you get your heart's desire My darling it will put an end to all the opportunities you now have of being thrown with bigwigs." And he was disquieted when she spoke of her great affection for Washington and her qualms that outside her family there was "hardly a soul" in Cincinnati she cared to see. "You will regard my failure to get the Circuit Judgeship as only another stroke of good luck and perhaps you may be right, though I can not think so," he acknowledged. "In any event my Darling, we can be happy as long as we live, if we only love each other and the children that come to us."

Such assurances notwithstanding, the long delay as President Harrison made up his mind was as tense for Nellie as it was for Will. Though the prospect ran counter to her own desires, she realized how deeply her husband was invested in the appointment. Each week a different rumor surfaced heralding a different name for the post, though Will remained the top candidate. "I hate that you should be disappointed," Nellie cautioned him. "It would be very easy for the Pres. to change his mind, even if it had been made up." The years of their marriage had only served to intensify her own devotion to Will. While she had left him craving the slightest expression of affection during their courtship days, her letters during their recent summer separation were filled with tenderness.

"I am not a bit happy without you," she confessed. "I love you ever and ever so much." Every day they were apart, she penned a letter to him and was disappointed when he missed a day in replying, reminding him that "when we were first married you often wrote twice a day." She felt his anxiety acutely, commingled with her own reluctance to embrace his hopes.

Perhaps the satisfaction she had found in motherhood had given Nellie a measure of equanimity as she faced an uncertain future. She wrote at length about the doings of their children. When Robert was a year old, she noted that he was "simply crazy about people—will go to any one and even run into their rooms if he sees the door open. The moment he sees anyone he knows, he sets up a shout at the top of his voice, which makes him a great favorite." She declared him "the dearest child that ever was," happily noting his devotion toward baby Helen as well as herself.

Nevertheless, her husband remained the primary focus of her love and concern. His eating habits and lack of exercise were constant sources of worry for her. When colleagues praised him, Nellie reveled in the accolades. "I seem to care much more that people should like and appreciate you than that they should care about me," she admitted. And whatever the situation, she never stopped giving him clever and frank counsel. "Don't make your brief too long, dearest," she admonished on one occasion. "The court will appreciate it much more if they don't grow weary over reading it. Many a good thing is spoiled by there being too much of it."

On December 16, 1891, the president announced his nominations for the nine new judgeships. His nomination of William Howard Taft for the Sixth District won widespread approbation. "The press notices have been as flattering as anyone could desire," Harry wrote to his brother. *The Washington Post* called Taft "one of the most popular officials in public life," citing a senior Ohio judge's opinion that "no man could have been named who would be more acceptable to the bar of that circuit." Horace teased that he could no longer afford to keep sending Will telegrams with each new success his brother achieved, but earnestly assured him that he was ideally suited for the post: "Aside from your especially liking the work and being fitted for it, there has always seemed to me a dignity about the office and a chance for fine service. . . . Somehow Father's brave & conscientious career on the bench always pleased me more than any other part of his professional or public life."

Taft viewed the return to his home city of Cincinnati with great high spirits. "One of the sweetest things connected with the appointment," he wrote Howard Hollister, "is the pleasure I anticipate in coming back to our old associations," to renew "the enthusiastic affection and intimacy which we had during our college days, and after. When we are in Cincinnati together, we must see as much of each other as possible." Suppressing her disappointment, Nellie dutifully packed up the house on Dupont Circle and moved back with the children. Taft remained in Washington for three additional months as solicitor general until the Senate confirmed the nominations on March 17, 1892. "I feel so good over the confirmation and the prospect of seeing you and the babies that I could hurrah for joy," he enthusiastically told Nellie.

Once established in his new post, Taft did not forget the kind support he had received in Washington. He wrote with warm appreciation to Attorney General Miller. "The two years which I have spent under you in Washington have been full of pleasure and profit to me. No man ever received more considerate treatment from another than I have from you. . . . Our relations have refined into affectionate friendship and I shall cherish the memory of it always. . . . I know to whom I owe my present appointment to the Bench. But for you, I should not have attained what has been my life's ambition and I am deeply grateful."

⤙ ⤚

LIKE NELLIE, EDITH HAD BECOME accustomed to Washington and was loath to relinquish the "pleasant life" she had built, which seemed likely when the Democrat, Grover Cleveland, defeated Benjamin Harrison in 1892. Roosevelt handed in his resignation, but Cleveland did not immediately accept it. "Our places are still uncertain," she told her sister Emily. She wished that her husband could be "elected by the people" to Congress, rather than dependent on presidential whim for his position and livelihood. She feared, however, this was "a dream never to be realized." It was an anxious time for Theodore as well; they had stretched their finances during their stay in the capital, and his inheritance was dwindling. "He is now in one of his depressed conditions about the future," Edith remarked, "and says the children will have reason to reproach him for not having insisted upon taking a money making profession." Edith understood that such histrionics were essentially "nonsense," a mere diversion from his true concerns. Theodore revealed his deeper troubles to Bamie, insisting that he had no permanent prospects in the political world, where he believed he "could do most." With overdetermined fatalism, he consigned himself to more modest pursuits: "But I shall speedily turn back to my books and do my best with them; though I fear that only a very mild & moderate success awaits me."

Decisions about the future were happily postponed when Cleveland asked Roosevelt to stay at his post for another year or two. News that "the moving spirit of the Commission" would remain was certain to be "received with joy by all reformers, and with equal dismay by spoilsmen throughout the country," the New York *Evening Post* observed. "Through the Harrison Administration, he pursued the spoilsmen 'with a sharp stick,' although they belonged to his own party, and he will not be any easier with them now that he will have to deal with Democrats."

In fact, despite the Democratic administration, the ensuing months brought contentment to the Roosevelts. Theodore got along better with Cleveland than he had with Harrison. Edith happily reported to Bamie that they had finally been invited to a White House dinner. "It was practically a family affair," she noted, and she was "certainly glad to dine once at the White House." Increasingly, however, Edith was occupied by the demands of her growing family. That spring of 1894, she gave birth to her fourth child, named Archibald Bulloch in honor of Theodore's maternal relatives.

The pleasant routine of life in Washington was interrupted in the fall when Roosevelt was approached by the New York Republican bosses to run for mayor. In contrast to his earlier token run, this time the Republicans stood a good chance of winning in both the city and the state. Theodore was elated by the sudden turn of events, he told Lodge, which renewed his "hope of going on in the work and life for which I care far more than any other." But Edith recoiled from the uncertainty, believing "they simply could not afford to take the chance," and asking, "What if Theodore resigned his commissionership in order to run and then lost the election?" Furthermore, she was alarmed that a costly campaign might drain their already diminished resources when their growing family required more stability. And in addition, she hated to leave her good friends for "big, bustling New York."

Edith did not argue with her husband; she simply withdrew "into one of her reserved and disapproving silences, that often, Bamie knew, had more of a disturbing effect on Theodore than anything she said." Both Corinne and Bamie urged their brother to run. In the end, the weight of Edith's opposition and the difficulty of funding the campaign led him to decline the offer. The bosses turned to William L. Strong, a reform-minded businessman, who ran and won on a fusion ticket of Republicans and anti-Tammany Democrats.

Contemplating his lost opportunity, Roosevelt fell into a profound depression. "The last four weeks, ever since I decided not to run, have been pretty bitter ones for me," he admitted to Lodge. "I would literally have given my right arm to have made the race, win or lose. It was the one golden chance, which never returns; and I had no illusions about ever having another opportunity. . . . At the time, with Edith feeling as intensely as she did, I did not see how I could well go in; though I have grown to feel more and more that in this instance I should have gone counter to her wishes and made the race anyhow. It is not necessary to say to you that the fault was mine, not Edith's; I should have realized that she could not see the matter as it really was, or realize my feelings."

Edith was horrified when she fathomed the magnitude of her husband's disappointment. "I cannot begin to describe how terribly I feel at having failed him at such an important time," she confided to Bamie. "He never should have married me, and then would have been free to take his own course quite unbiased. I never realized for a minute how he felt over this, or that the mayoralty stood for so much to him . . . if I knew what I do now I should have thrown all my influence in the scale with Corinne's and helped instead of hindering him. You say that I dislike to give my opinion. This is a lesson that will last my life, never to give it for it is utterly worthless when given—worse than that in this case for it has helped to spoil some years of a life which I would have given my own for."

Both Edith's fierce self-reproach and Theodore's despondent conviction that he had botched his sole opportunity in life, his "one golden chance," proved overwrought. Though his political path might be more circuitous, Roosevelt's restless drive would hardly allow him to retire from public life. The following spring, he was on his way to New York to accept Mayor Strong's offer to serve as police commissioner, a job that would utilize all his intrepid energies.

CHAPTER SEVEN

The Invention of *McClure's*

S. S. McClure *(left)* and John S. Phillips *(right)*, in the offices
of *McClure's* magazine, 1895.

I N THE MID-1890S, THE GENTEEL world of patrician reformers
and civil service enthusiasts that Taft and Roosevelt initially typified
had begun a seismic shift. Widespread discontent with the industrial order,
building for over a decade, threatened now to flare into open revolution. The
growth of colossal corporations in the aftermath of the Civil War had produced immense, consolidated wealth for business owners, but the lives of
the working people, western farmers and eastern factory workers alike, had
become increasingly difficult. "We plow new fields, we open new mines, we
found new cities," Roosevelt's mayoral rival, Henry George, observed; "we
girdle the land with iron roads and lace the air with telegraph wires; we add
knowledge to knowledge and utilize invention after invention." Yet despite
such vaunted progress, he declared, "it becomes no easier for the masses of our
people to make a living. On the contrary, it is becoming harder."

The captains of industry, George acknowledged, had fueled unprecedented innovations: "the steamship taking the place of the sailing vessel, the railroad train of the wagon, the reaping machine of the scythe." To confirm the positive changes wrought by the Industrial Revolution, he continued, one need only visit "the great workshops where boots and shoes are turned out by the case with less labour than the old fashioned cobbler could have put on a sole; the factories where, under the eye of a girl, cotton becomes cloth faster than hundreds of stalwart weavers could have turned it out with their hand-looms." With this transfiguring mechanization and the development of mass production, however, "the gulf between the employed and the employer is growing wider; social contrasts are becoming sharper; as liveried carriages appear, so do barefooted children."

Far from heralding an age of plenty, these wondrous savings of time and labor served only to diminish the ability of many Americans to procure the goods they needed to sustain their families. So long as the frontier remained open, restless Americans could escape hardships by moving west, lured by promises of free land and equal opportunity. By the 1890s, this option had withered. As Frederick Jackson Turner observed in a seminal paper delivered during the American Historical Association meeting in Chicago in 1893, the frontier had closed, and a distinctive phase of American history had thereby come to an end.

A mood of rebellion began to spread among the laboring class. The late eighties and nineties witnessed an unprecedented number of violent strikes in the nation's factories, mines, and railroads. The combination of meager wages for twelve-hour working days in unsafe, unsanitary conditions had spurred millions of workers to join unions. "It was a time of strikes and riots, pitting troops against desperate workers," the historian Frank Latham observed, "of tense meetings where businessmen talked fearfully of 'a coming revolution.' "

In the year 1886 alone, more than 600,000 workers walked out on strike, disrupting thousands of businesses and railroad lines for weeks at a time. At the McCormick Reaper plant in Chicago, police were called in to break up a confrontation between strikers and scabs. In the brutal clash, four workers were killed. On May 4, a group of anarchists gathered in Chicago's Haymarket Square to protest those deaths. The peaceful demonstration turned violent when police ordered the protesters to disperse. A bomb thrown into the officers' formation killed eight policemen and four protesters and wounded more than seventy others.

Although police never determined who threw the bomb, they promptly arrested eight anarchists, several of whom had not even attended the demonstration. At their trial, the judge ruled that the anarchists' belief in violence made them as guilty as the murderous bomb thrower. Four were put to death by hanging, the others sentenced to jail. Citing an unprecedented miscarriage of justice, Illinois governor John Peter Altgeld pardoned the remaining prisoners. History has vindicated Altgeld, but the pardon was widely condemned at the time.

News of the Haymarket riot reached Roosevelt at his ranch in Medora. Drawing no distinction between the strikers and the anarchist protestors, Roosevelt railed against the breakdown of law and order. "My men here are hardworking, laboring men, who work longer hours for no greater wages than many of the strikers; but they are Americans through and through," he told Bamie. "I believe nothing would give them greater pleasure than a chance with their rifles at one of the mobs. When we get the papers, especially in relation to the dynamite business they become more furiously angry and excited than I do. I wish I had them with me, and a fair show at ten times our number of rioters; my men shoot well and fear very little."

While some union supporters regarded the condemned anarchists as heroes, Roosevelt judged them the "foulest of criminals, the men whose crimes take the form of assassination." He denounced Governor Altgeld, along with all those who followed Leo Tolstoy's collectivist longings, Edward Bellamy's Utopian socialism, and Henry George's "wild and illogical doctrines," men who mistakenly believed "that at this stage of the world's progress it is possible to make every one happy by an immense social revolution, just as other enthusiasts of similar mental caliber believe in the possibility of constructing a perpetual-motion machine."

In 1893, the most serious depression the nation had yet experienced settled over the land. The downturn began when the railroads, having borrowed heavily from banks, rashly expanded their operations beyond current demand. More than seventy overbuilt railroads fell into bankruptcy, compromising banks unable to recoup their loans. Scrambling to shore up capital, these institutions called in the loans of all their borrowers. Small businesses and heavily mortgaged farmers unable to cover their notes followed railroads into bankruptcy. As the economic situation deteriorated, frightened depositors rushed to withdraw funds and hundreds of insolvent banks were forced to close their doors. Within twelve months, more than 4 million jobs had been lost. At the nadir of this collapse, nearly one in four workers was unemployed. Jobless men begged for food; homeless families slept on streets; farmers burned their crops rather than send them to market at a loss. Millions feared that in the wreckage of the Gilded Age, democracy itself would crumble.

⌐ ⌐

AMID SUCH PANGS OF RAMPANT anxiety and latent insurrection, *McClure's* magazine was born. This acclaimed muckraking journal would play a signal role in
rousing the country to the need for political and economic reform, animating
the Progressive movement with which Theodore Roosevelt's name would
forever be linked.

The descriptions of thirty-six-year-old Samuel S. McClure, the magazine's
founder, bear an uncanny resemblance to accounts of Theodore Roosevelt
himself. McClure was termed a "genius," with "a highly creative mind, and
a great deal of excitable energy." He impressed all who knew him as a prodigious character, "a vibrant, eager, indomitable personality that electrified
even the experienced and the cynical." His frenetic style, though, made him
often appear "a bundle of tensions, keyed up, impetuous, impatient, impulsive." While Roosevelt's tumultuous energy elicited comparison to that force
and marvel of nature, Niagara Falls, McClure, ever threatening to erupt in
"a stream of words," was likened to a volcano. Indeed, McClure cut such a
compelling figure that novelists as varied as Robert Louis Stevenson, Willa
Cather, Upton Sinclair, William Dean Howells, and Alice Hegan Rice all
incorporated him as a character in their fiction.

McClure was capable of wild bursts of creative productivity, episodes during which his mind tumbled from one idea to the next while he prowled the
room "like a caged lion." Rudyard Kipling later recalled that his first conversation with McClure "lasted some twelve—or it may have been seventeen—
hours." But such euphoria was often punctuated by periods of exhaustion and
depression when he could not bring himself to eat, sleep, or concentrate. For
months at a time, he was forced into sanitariums, where he was kept in total
isolation, on continuous bed rest.

Born the same year as Taft, on a struggling farm in County Antrim, Northern Ireland, Sam McClure faced obstacles unimaginable to Roosevelt or Taft.
The first of four sons, he was raised in a stone house with a dirt floor and a
straw-covered roof. His father, Thomas, was a rough carpenter; his mother,
Elizabeth, worked the fields of their farm. While the coddled childhoods
enjoyed by Roosevelt and Taft were calculated to launch them on the road to
achievement, the pain and penury of McClure's early life make his convoluted
journey to success more unexpected and striking.

Even as a toddler, Sam displayed unusual curiosity, a fierce precocity that
convinced his parents to send him to school when he was only four years of age.
"That was the first important event in my life," he later wrote. "It was then
that I first felt myself a human entity." Teachers recognized his astonishing

aptitude and were soon furnishing materials suited for boys twice his age. "For a long while," he recalled, "I was convinced that long division was the most exciting exercise a boy could find." Several times each year, a large box of new books was delivered to his school. For a child whose family possessed a scant three works—the Bible, *Pilgrim's Progress*, and Foxe's *Book of Martyrs*—the experience of "opening those boxes and looking into the fresh books that still had the smell of the press, was about the most delightful thing that happened during the year." Weekends often found the boy depressed; the excitement of his studies "seemed to die down" the moment he returned home.

Sam was seven when his father fell through an open ship's deck where he worked and suffered a fatal head injury. His death left the family destitute, bereft of the small wages his carpentry work had provided. Sam "began for the first time to be conscious of the pressure of poverty." His mother returned temporarily to her father's home as the family debated how to divide the four boys among relatives. Determined to keep her sons together, Elizabeth used her remaining funds to purchase steerage passage across the Atlantic. From Quebec, she shepherded her children to Indiana, where two of her brothers and a married sister with six children had settled. For a time, she stayed with her sister, but the home proved too small to accommodate four additional children. In desperation, she moved with her boys into an empty room in a commercial building undergoing repairs. Before long, the owner evicted them; twice more, they were forced to move until, finally, she found a home for her children by marrying a struggling local farmer, Thomas Simpson.

Sam and his brothers spent so many hours toiling from planting until harvest on his stepfather's farm that they could attend school only during the winter months. Furthermore, the county school was unable to accommodate Sam's searching intellect. Hearing of "a kind of 'arithmetic' in which letters were used instead of figures," the avid pupil asked his teacher to tutor him in algebra. The teacher "had never studied it and had no text-book." The years passed slowly for Sam until, at fourteen, he learned of a new high school opened in Valparaiso. Straightaway, his mother decided that to have a chance in life, he must venture out on his own. If he could find work to pay for room and board, Sam had her blessing to leave. He departed that very day with one dollar in his pocket.

Learning that Dr. Levi Cass was Valparaiso's wealthiest citizen, Sam knocked on his door and inquired if he could exchange work for room and board. Cass accepted the enterprising young man, but his terms were not especially generous: in return for food and a basement room, Sam was expected to build up the fires before dawn, feed the livestock, and do the household laundry. Once the school day was over, a second round of arduous chores left him only a few hours late in the evening to study. In his cellar room, he recalled, "I used to waken up in the night and cry from the sense of my loss." It was in these straitened circumstances that Sam initially suffered "attacks of restlessness," when he "simply had to run away for a day, for half a day, for two days," a compulsion he "seemed to have no control over." Indeed, he acknowledged forty years later, "I have had to reckon with it all my life." Sam persevered in his schooling for two years, until his stepfather's death from typhoid fever forced his return home to help his mother manage the farm.

Sam and his brothers worked the farm well, producing a profit for the first time in years. Still, his mother wanted her eldest son to continue his education. Her brother Joseph Gaston was studying at Knox College in Galesburg, Illinois, about two hundred miles away. In September 1874, as Taft traveled east to Yale, McClure headed west to Galesburg. Upon his arrival, he was informed that his prior fragmentary schooling would require the completion of three full years at Knox Academy before he could even begin college. The news did not deter him. "I was seventeen," he recalled, "and it was a seven years' job that I was starting upon, with fifteen cents in my pocket." Finally realizing the opportunity to pursue a serious education, he "felt complete self-reliance." Once again, he had to work hard for room and board but managed to keep up with his studies, moving toward the day when he would become a freshman at the college.

At seventeen, a shock of blond hair over his forehead and blue eyes bright and clear, the painfully thin Sam had reached his full height of five feet six inches. One classmate remarked that he had "never seen so much enthusiasm and life in such a small carcass." All his subjects interested him, Greek and mathematics most of all. "Everything went well with me until Friday night," he recalled, when the "blank stretch" of the weekend rendered him disconsolate. Without the focal point of classes, he felt lonely and isolated.

During his second preparatory year, Sam fell in love with eighteen-year-old Harriet Hurd, considered by many "the most beautiful and gifted girl in town." The willowy, blue-eyed daughter of Knox College's star professor, Albert Hurd, Hattie, as she was called, was then a sophomore in the college. A brilliant student, she would graduate at the top of her class with the highest academic record ever obtained at Knox. "Don't cry for the moon," the kindly wife of the town's minister told Sam. Hattie had been her father's assistant since childhood, working by his side as he gathered geological specimens and prepared materials for his classes in science, religion, and Latin. Professor Hurd, a graduate of Middlebury College, had studied under Louis Agassiz at Harvard before embarking upon a long and distinguished career at Knox. A commanding figure in Hattie's life, Professor Hurd adamantly opposed his daughter's relationship with an impoverished immigrant. The professor's opposition seemed to embolden rather than discourage Sam. "My feeling for her," he later recalled, "became a despairing obsession, as fixed as my longing to get an education had been."

From the start, Hattie was drawn to Sam's peculiar intensity. After a series of furtive meetings and a surreptitious exchange of romantic letters, she agreed to a secret engagement. Torn between her father's implacable disapproval and her adoration for Sam, she repeatedly broke the engagement, only to realize that she couldn't resist the magnetism of Sam's personality. But when she graduated from Knox and prepared for graduate school in Canada, her father forbade Hattie to disclose her destination to Sam. Secrecy was the price for her continued education. "You mustn't write to me or expect to hear from me, as long as I am dependent on my father," she told Sam. "If I should bring his displeasure on me it would kill me. Oh, Sam, it is very hard to bear." For nearly four years, all communication in this odd and fervent relationship ceased.

Sam immersed himself in his studies, eventually graduating second in his college class. More important, he developed lifelong friendships with two classmates, John S. Phillips and Albert Brady, that one day would be instrumental to the success of *McClure's* magazine. Sam was closer to John Phillips, the quiet, steady, and intellectual son of a respected local physician and a relative of the abolitionist Wendell Phillips. Phillips, McClure proudly noted, "was easily the best read student in the college, a boy with a great natural aptitude for letters." At Phillips's house, McClure first encountered a copy of *Scribner's*, the sophisticated literary magazine that would soon become the *Century*. Returning numerous times to his friend's home, he was thrilled to read the new serialized novel by William Dean Howells, *A Modern Instance*, from start to finish.

Sam McClure's enterprising spirit and unique knack for finding partners with complementary abilities was already evident. In the summer between his junior and senior years, the young man canvassed the Great Lakes region, peddling microscopes with Albert Brady, the son of the editor of the *Davenport* (Iowa) *Daily Times*. Enabled by Brady's shrewdness, the two Knox students bought microscopes wholesale at $25 each and turned them at a profit. McClure would later credit this experience of traveling through villages and knocking on doors with fostering a "close acquaintance with the people of the small towns and the farming communities, the people who afterward bought *McClure's Magazine*."

In his senior year, McClure was chosen as editor-in-chief of the student newspaper. His unconventional working style both troubled and amazed his colleagues on the paper. "He works by fits and starts," a fellow student noted; "weeks, almost months go by, and he does no work to amount to anything and then crowds all into a few days and nights." With Phillips providing daily editorial support and Brady as the advertising virtuoso, the publication produced quality articles and successfully solicited an abundance of advertising from local businesses. In the years ahead, observed the journalist Ray Stannard Baker, this same triumvirate would be responsible for the triumph of *McClure's*. While McClure provided the foundation work of creative genius, the magazine would never have realized its historic status without the insightful editing of Phillips and the business acumen of Albert Brady. "The three together," Baker marveled, "who had been friends since their college days—made the perfect publishing organization."

After an absence of four years, Hattie returned briefly to Galesburg in 1881. She had completed her graduate training and was preparing to depart for Massachusetts, where she had accepted a teaching position at Abbott Academy in Andover. A chance encounter with Sam apparently summoned old feelings, and the young couple recommitted themselves to one another. "My present and future are completely changed," Sam told her. "My soul is filled with love and peace and joy." Although she soon left for Massachusetts, they revived their secret correspondence. Sam filled his letters with grandiose intentions, entertaining various careers as diplomat, philosopher, and writer/publisher. As the date of his June graduation approached, however, Hattie's letters stopped coming. Sensing that something was wrong, Sam consulted Phillips, who recommended that he head for Massachusetts the moment his graduation ceremonies ended. A letter from Hattie arrived just after Sam left Galesburg. "Mr. McClure," it formally declared, "I have come to the unalterable conclusion that I have not and never can have any respect or affection for you . . . I wish never to meet you again."

Once again, Hattie had succumbed to pressure from her father, who vowed that he "would never receive [McClure] as his son-in law," and that if Hattie chose to marry him, he would never be allowed into the house. Everything about McClure was anathema to Professor Hurd, who objected to "his personal appearance, his bearing, his address," adding for good measure that he found Sam "conceited, impertinent, meddlesome." In sum, he concluded, "I regard it as a misfortune that you ever made his acquaintance." Forced to choose between her father and Sam, Hattie could not betray her father. Unaware of the reception that awaited him, McClure knocked on the door where Hattie was staying. Told that she did not wish to see him, he refused to leave the parlor until she finally came down. "I do not love you," she said flatly, adding icily, "and I never can. Please be good enough to return to me any of my letters that you may still have."

"This dismissal," McClure recounted later, "I accepted as final." With no definite plans and no place to stay, he took a train to Boston, where the offices of the Pope Manufacturing Company were located. This company had recently produced a newfangled sensation with the Columbia Roadster, America's first bicycle. The owner, Colonel Albert Pope, had purchased advertising space in Sam's student publication, furnishing him with an opening to meet the entrepreneur. Finding McClure's enthusiasm and determination irresistible, Pope put him in charge of the bicycle rink where beginners came to learn how to ride. Although McClure himself had never ridden a bicycle, he was soon teaching others to operate the unwieldy contraption with a high front wheel nearly twice the size of the rear wheel.

When Pope revealed to McClure his determination to publish a magazine devoted to bicycling, fire was touched to kindling. On the basis of his experience at the *Knox Student*, McClure convinced Pope that he could edit the magazine Pope envisioned, to "weave the bicycle into the best in literature and art." Just at this time, McClure received a fortuitous letter from his friend John Phillips, who was struggling to plot his own future career. "You are the surest fellow I ever saw," Phillips wrote McClure. "You always alight on your feet. I wish I had one half your push and business ability. Great Heavens, I wish I was with you. If you think I can make a living . . . I'll come." So Phillips joined McClure as co-editor of the *Wheelman*, as the surprisingly professional, illustrated monthly magazine was titled.

Reviews of the new magazine, which included short stories, articles, and book reviews, were positive; the *Nation* rated it "among the most attractive of the monthly magazines." While Phillips ran the office, McClure took to the road, hoping to persuade New England writers such as Oliver Wendell Holmes, Harriet Prescott Spofford, and Thomas Bailey Aldrich to barter articles for a new bicycle. "I was in the big game, in the real business of the world," he recalled. "Up to this time I had always lived in the future and felt that I was simply getting ready for something. Now I began to live in the present."

Wheelman was the first professional enterprise into which McClure poured his astounding energy. Ascending the steps to that office at 597 Washington Street in Boston, he bid a final farewell to his youthful self. "When I have passed that place in later years," he recalled in his autobiography in a haunting passage, "I have fairly seen him standing there—a thin boy, with a face somewhat worn from loneliness and wanting things he couldn't get, a little hurt at being left so unceremoniously. When I went up the steps, he stopped outside; and it now seems to me that I stopped on the steps and looked at him, and that when he looked at me I turned and never spoke to him and went into the building. I came out with a job, but I never saw him again, and now I have no sense of identity with that boy."

McClure had not seen Hattie since her brutal rejection; then, as he worked hard to produce *Wheelman* in the fall, she reached out to him, insisting that she had deceived him because she simply "*could not*" bring herself to disobey her father. "I felt that you would take nothing as a reason for our separation," she endeavored to explain, "as long as you believed that I loved you—and so I gave you, falsely, the only reason that I knew would be valid in your eyes . . . I perjured myself . . . I loved you then, and love you still." In September 1883, they were quietly married, with John Phillips serving as McClure's best man. Sam and Hattie began their married life in Boston, but only three months later, when Sam was offered a position as an editorial assistant with the prestigious *Century* magazine, they moved to New York.

The following summer, after the birth of the first of his four children, Sam found himself increasingly restless in his new job. He yearned for independent control of some venture and finally hit upon an idea he shared with Roswell Smith, the editor of the *Century*. He proposed that the *Century* underwrite a Literary Associated Press, a syndicate that would purchase stories and articles from well-known authors and then sell them at reduced rates to numerous newspapers for simultaneous publication, usually in their new Sunday supplements. "I saw it, in all its ramifications, as completely as I ever did afterward," McClure later explained, "and I don't think I ever added anything to my first conception." Roswell Smith liked the idea but thought it unsuitable for his magazine. He offered McClure "a month's vacation with full pay" to see if he could launch the project on his own, with the opportunity to return to the *Century* should the venture fail.

In a matter of weeks, McClure's syndicate was up and running. His first sale was a short story by the popular writer Hjalmar H. Boyesen, which he bought for $150 and promptly sold to a sufficient number of newspapers to make "a handsome profit." He then utilized the proceeds to send a thousand circulars to editors across the nation. This flyer explained how "a dozen, or twenty, or fifty newspapers—selected so as to avoid conflict in circulation— can thus secure a story for a sum which will be very small for each paper, but which will in the aggregate be sufficiently large to secure the best work by the best authors."

The syndicate grew so steadily that by 1887, his biographer Peter Lyon estimates, McClure was "distributing fifty thousand words a week to well over one hundred newspapers." John Phillips, after three years in graduate school, first at Harvard and then in Leipzig, Germany, once again joined his friend and assumed responsibility for the daily management of the syndicate, a role for which he was "much better fitted" than McClure. "He had an orderly and organizing mind—which I had not," McClure acknowledged. "I usually lost interest in a scheme as soon as it was started, and had no power of developing a plan and carrying it out to its least detail, as Mr. Phillips had." With his trusted friend at the helm, McClure was free to travel "from one end of the country to the other" and eventually "from one end of Europe to the other—always seeking new material, and always, like the retriever, coming back with a treasure-trove in his teeth."

"McClure was a Columbus among editors," proclaimed the writer and critic Jeannette L. Gilder. "I doubt if there is any man in his profession who has to his credit the discovery of more big writers." At the time, three principal literary journals—*Century*, *Atlantic*, and *Harper's*—had a stranglehold on America's literary market. They were defenders of everything "dignified and conservative in the magazine world." Young writers, particularly those who embraced the new realistic style scorned by established critics, had difficulty publishing their stories. McClure gave them a chance. "My qualifications for being an editor," he explained, "were that I was open-minded, naturally enthusiastic, and not afraid to experiment with a new man."

McClure, who had adopted the designation "S. S." rather than Sam, is credited with introducing Robert Louis Stevenson, Rudyard Kipling, J. M. Barrie, and Arthur Conan Doyle to American readers. "He secured the best writers in the world," one reviewer noted. "He had the discernment in some cases and the good luck in others to establish connections with rising authors at the happy moment when they were about to step across the threshold of fame. He helped them and they helped him. His treatment of them was both honorable and generous." McClure noted proudly that he had purchased Kipling's work "before the name of Kipling had been printed in a newspaper in this country." After reading one of Conan Doyle's short stories, McClure promptly purchased a dozen Sherlock Holmes mysteries at the bargain price of $60 apiece. "To find the best authors," he boasted, "is like being able to tell good wine without the labels."

The McClure syndicate serialized *The Quality of Mercy*, a novel by the controversial champion of realism, William Dean Howells; they printed stories by Thomas Hardy and Émile Zola which shocked genteel readers, and published a series of polemics by William Morris on socialism, Hamlin Garland on wheat farmers, and Henry Harland on life in the slums of New York's Jewish East Side. Even as he provided a platform for new voices and radical topics, McClure filled the preponderance of his pages with stories and poems from established writers and more staid articles on standard subjects of interest—religion, adventure, travel, Abraham Lincoln, and the Civil War.

By the early 1890s, the success of the McClure syndicate was assured. "I propose to down *all* competition, and in a short time I can dominate the *world* in my line," he bragged headily. "My blood is like champagne." Such unqualified success, however, seemed a harbinger to the restlessness that had plagued him since childhood, the compulsive drive to stave off depression through ceaseless activity. He felt compelled to tackle something new lest depression, always waiting in the wings, resume center stage. In 1892, he and Phillips began discussing the creation of a new low-priced, high-quality illustrated magazine. "I would rather edit a magazine," McClure told Hattie, "than be President of the United States a hundred thousand times over."

Conventional wisdom held that 35 cents was the lowest price a publisher of a quality magazine could charge and still anticipate "a reasonable profit." At 35 cents, a magazine was necessarily targeted to the "moneyed and well-educated classes," a parameter which kept the contents "leisurely in habit, literary in tone, retrospective rather than timely, and friendly to the interests of the upper classes." McClure's resolve to put a quality magazine "within reach of all who care about good literature" at 15 cents per copy was tantamount to revolution.

New technology made his rash endeavor to compete with publications like the *Century* or the *Atlantic* feasible. "The impregnability of the older magazines," McClure explained, "was largely due to the costliness of wood-engraving. Only an established publication with a large working capital could afford illustrations made by that process." Photo engraving was the innovation that fundamentally altered the printing industry. At a fraction of the cost of wood engraving, the new process allowed publishers "to make pictures directly from photographs, which were cheap, instead of from drawings, which were expensive."

McClure envisioned a new magazine containing four sections: "The Edge of the Future" would feature interviews in which scientists such as Thomas Edison or Alexander Graham Bell discussed their recent inventions; "Human Documents" would showcase portraits of famous people at different ages;

"The Real Conversations" would present one distinguished person interviewing another; and the final section would offer short stories initially drawn from the best fiction already published in the syndicate, thereby costing him almost nothing to reprint. McClure hoped to use syndicate profits to support the new magazine until it could stand on its own. One of his trips west to garner support for the magazine included a visit to Davenport, Iowa, where he reconnected with his Knox classmate Albert Brady and persuaded him to come on board as his advertising manager.

For all his plans, McClure could not have anticipated the Panic of 1893, the run on the banks, and the burgeoning unemployment that bankrupted some newspapers and forced others to slash expenses. In this climate, the syndicate became one of the first things struggling newspapers jettisoned. "There was certainly never a more inopportune time to launch a new business," McClure lamented. He had little personal capital to invest in the venture, having paid syndicate authors handsomely and incurred heavy expenses searching out new world-class writers. He had built up an invaluable asset, however: "the good will of thousands of people"—friends, fellow editors, and writers. Phillips persuaded his father to place a mortgage on his Galesburg home, bringing in $4,500; Conan Doyle invested $5,000; Colonel Pope supplied $6,000; and the geologist Henry Drummond, whose articles would frequently appear in the new journal, invested $2,000 and volunteered an additional loan of $1,000.

The first issue, appearing on the stands in June 1893, received uniformly favorable reviews. "It is not often that a new periodical begins its career with prestige enough to make its success a certainty from the very first number," noted the *Review of Reviews*, but "the wisest judges concede it a place among the winners." The *Providence Journal* rated the magazine "no little of a triumph," applauding its freshness and originality: "It is not an imitation of anything existing in this country." The Philadelphia *Public Ledger* placed it in the "front rank at once," while the *Atlanta Constitution* hailed it as "unusually brilliant." From Theodore Roosevelt came a letter of congratulations on "the first issue of your excellent magazine."

McClure immediately understood that his magazine must have "a unity" beyond a mere compilation of freelance articles suiting the individual tastes of miscellaneous authors. He dreamed of creating a full-time staff of writers who would be guaranteed salary and generous expense accounts. The job of staff writer was a new concept; in years to come, McClure would claim he himself "almost invented" it—a justifiable assertion at a time when few magazines subsidized their writers. He wished a writing staff to collaborate with him and with each other, treating mutually agreed-upon topics "in line with the general attitude of the publication." He wanted "to deal with important social, economic and political questions, to present the new and great inventions and discoveries, to give the best in literature," and above all, to become "a power in the land . . . a power for good."

Indeed, the ultimate success of *McClure's*—its literary worth, its major contributions to Progressive era reforms, and its significant role in the rise of Theodore Roosevelt—can be directly traced to the prodigiously gifted writing staff McClure assembled. Along with the nucleus consisting of Ida Tarbell, Ray Stannard Baker, Lincoln Steffens, and William Allen White, the *McClure's* staff intermittently included Burton Hendrick, Mark Sullivan, George Kibbe Turner, Will Irwin, Willa Cather, Stephen Crane, and Frank Norris. This talented pool of writers produced hundreds of influential pieces which played a major role in shaping public discourse around the most pressing economic and social issues of the day.

⌒ ⌒

IDA MINERVA TARBELL, THE FIRST to join McClure's stable of writers, became the "mother hen" of the group. The story of the first meeting between McClure and Tarbell in the summer of 1892 would be told and retold in the years ahead. McClure had briefly stopped in Paris on one of his whirlwind tours in search of material for his new magazine. Thirty-four and unmarried, Tarbell had been living on the Left Bank for twelve months, struggling to support herself with freelance articles for American newspapers. Her free hours were spent in the manuscript room of the Bibliothèque Nationale researching the life of Mme Roland, a celebrated figure in the French Revolution. One of her newspaper articles, "The Paving of the Streets of Paris by Monsieur Alphand," had landed on McClure's desk. "This girl can write," McClure told Phillips. "I want to get her to do some work for the magazine." The piece, he later said, "possessed exactly the qualities" he desired—a clear narrative style alive with human interest, sound judgment, and trustworthy facts.

Tarbell was then lodging in a boardinghouse on an obscure, crooked street "unknown to half the *cochers* of Paris." Yet, somehow, McClure managed to locate the place one Monday evening, "bareheaded, watch in hand, breathless" from racing up the eighty steps to her fourth-floor chamber. "I've just ten minutes," he gasped; "must leave for Switzerland tonight to see [John] Tyndall." Those minutes stretched to nearly three hours as McClure regaled her with childhood tales in Ireland, his struggles at Knox College and desperate pursuit of Hattie, his creation of the syndicate and friendship with Phillips. Finally, he laid out his plans for the new magazine and her involvement in it.

Captivated by his "outrightness, his enthusiasm and confidence," Tarbell, in turn, confided her own experiences, her hopes and ambitions.

Though less extreme than McClure's, Ida's history was shaped by an equally fierce resolution to succeed. The oldest of four children, she was born the same year as McClure and raised in northwestern Pennsylvania, where the discovery of oil had transformed wilderness areas into bustling cities and towns. Her father, Franklin Tarbell, was making "more than he could ever have dreamed" as an independent oil producer. Titusville, where Franklin built a substantial home for his growing family, was flourishing, "confident of its future," boasting graded roads, handsome homes, college preparatory high schools, and a newly built opera house. "Things were going well in father's business," Ida recalled; "there was ease such as we had never known, luxuries we had never heard of."

For the local oilmen, who drilled the wells and sustained a booming local economy, it seemed there was "nothing they did not hope and dare." The triumph of optimism in Titusville was destined to end, however: "Suddenly, at the very heyday of this confidence, a big hand reached out from nobody knew where, to steal their conquest and throttle their future." That mysterious hand belonged to none other than John D. Rockefeller, as Tarbell would boldly elucidate years later in her chronicle of the history of the Standard Oil Company for *McClure's* magazine—the landmark series that would affirm her reputation as the leading investigative journalist of her day.

At the time, all that Ida's father and his colleagues knew was that the railroads arbitrarily doubled their published rates for carrying petroleum—crude and refined—to the east coast, a huge inflation heralding ruin for the entire region. The local oilmen eventually discovered that Rockefeller had forged an alliance between the railroads and a small group of privileged refiners. His "big scheme" enabled those in the newly formed South Improvement Company to receive secret rebates on every barrel shipped, while outside companies would be charged increased rates to make up for the insiders' discount. This deal, meant to destroy small competitors, Tarbell later explained, "started the Standard Oil Company off on the road to monopoly."

The local producers joined together to retaliate. "There were nightly antimonopoly meetings," Ida recalled, "violent speeches, processions; trains of oil cars loaded for members of the offending corporation were raided, the oil run on the ground." The tensions of these confrontations were reflected in the Tarbell household. Franklin Tarbell no longer entertained his family with "the funny things he had seen and heard during the day" or relaxed with an after-dinner cigar to the music he loved. If the machinations behind the conflict were "all pretty hazy" to young Ida, she gleaned enough from her father's conversation to comprehend that "what had been undertaken was *wrong*." From that painful, disruptive period, she wrote, "there was born in me a hatred of privilege"—in this case, the powerful oilmen preying on the independents, but eventually "privilege of any sort."

As her father fought against monopoly, her mother struggled with a painful "readjustment of her status in the home and in society." Esther Tarbell, Ida later wrote, "had grown up with the Woman's Rights movement." She had taught for a dozen years before her marriage and had planned on "seeking a higher education." Had she remained single, Ida believed, "she would have sought to 'vindicate her sex.' . . . The fight would have delighted her." But after marriage she "found herself a pioneer in the Oil Region, confronted by the sternest of problems," which compelled the investment of her energies into the well-being of her family. Witnessing her mother's frustration, Ida determined early on that she "would never marry." She was certain that having a husband and children would thwart her freedom and curtail her nascent ambition. At fourteen, she fell to her knees and entreated God to prevent her ever marrying.

Captivated by the natural world, Ida had spent the long afternoons of her childhood wandering around the countryside to gather leaves and plant specimens in her area, "classifying them by shapes, veins, stalks, color." She began her high school years already intent upon a career as a biologist. Graduating at the top of her class at Titusville High, she enrolled in Allegheny College in Meadville, Pennsylvania, in the fall of 1876, the same year that Roosevelt matriculated at Harvard. At eighteen, Ida had reached her commanding height of five feet ten inches. She was not considered pretty. Her nose and ears were too big, but her "luminous eyes" indicated unusual sensitivity and intelligence.

As the sole woman in the freshman class, and one of four in the entire college, she felt herself "an invader." But in the college library she found "the companionship there is in the silent presence of books." Though she may have been "shy and immature," Ida was a tenacious student, and she had the good fortune of studying under "a great natural teacher," Jeremiah Tingley, the chair of the science department. Like Professor Hurd, Tingley had studied under Louis Agassiz and absorbed the celebrated scientist's "faith in observation and classification, as well as his reverence for Nature." Sensing Ida's enthusiasm and native intelligence, he took particular interest in her progress. Coupled with her own fierce drive, this support helped her excel once again. "She would arise at four A.M. and get to work studying," a classmate recalled.

"She was never satisfied with anything less than perfection . . . but she was no grind. She was too interested in people."

After graduation, Ida taught for two years at Poland Union Seminary in Poland, Ohio, hoping to save enough money to "go abroad and study with some great biologist." But her wages were low, and two years later she had managed to save nothing to further her dream of studying in Europe. She returned to Meadville, where she took a temporary job annotating articles for *The Chautauquan*, the official publication of the recently founded Chautauqua Institution, a summer camp that provided Bible studies and lectures on science, the arts, and humanities. What began as a temporary assignment became a full-time job as she rose to become managing editor of *The Chautauquan*, discovering in the process a great fascination with storytelling and the delineation of character. "My early absorption in rocks and plants had veered to as intense an interest in human beings," she reported. "I was feeling the same passion to understand men and women, the same eagerness to collect and classify information about them . . . I recognized that men and women were as well worth notes as leaves, that there was a science of society as well as of botany."

She and her colleagues on the liberal monthly magazine were "ardent supporters" of the inclusive labor organization the Knights of Labor and their fight for an eight-hour workday. "We discussed interminably the growing problem of the slums, were particularly strong for cooperative housing, laundries and bakeshops," she recalled. She came to the conclusion that "a trilogy of wrongs" was responsible for the maldistribution of wealth: "discriminatory transportation rates, tariffs save for revenue only, and private ownership of natural resources."

"My life was busy, varied, unfolding pleasantly in many ways, but it also after six years was increasingly unsatisfactory," she later wrote. "I was trapped—comfortably, most pleasantly, most securely, but trapped." While she stayed up nights working out several ideas for a novel, her days were occupied with the myriad demands of editing the magazine. Furthermore, the design she had brought to the "disorderly fashion" in which the editor-in-chief, Dr. Theodore L. Flood, had formerly managed the magazine was never truly credited. Inevitably, she found herself "secretly, very secretly, meditating a change." She envisioned herself in Paris, researching and writing a biography of Mme Roland, an alluring character she had included in a series of sketches for *The Chautauquan* on women of the French Revolution. Though she still had little money saved, Ida aspired to earn a living writing articles on Parisian life for several of the newspaper syndicates in the United States.

Dr. Flood was stunned when Ida revealed that she was leaving for Paris. "How will you support yourself?" he demanded. When she replied that she would make her way by writing, his retort was memorably cruel and condescending. "You're not a writer," he announced. "You'll starve." Flood struck deep-seated anxieties in Ida about her vocation as a writer, yet she would not be deterred. She persuaded two of her friends from *The Chautauquan* to join her, and the three set sail for Europe in August 1891. After searching several days for affordable lodgings, they found a boardinghouse in the Latin Quarter run by Mme Bonnet, a cheerful, welcoming landlady. Though their rooms were tiny, they shared a salon with an amiable group of Egyptian students. Before long, they had developed close friendships.

Ida set to work immediately, outlining a series of articles on the daily life of Paris. She astutely guessed that people back home would want to know the very things she herself was curious about: what Parisians did for entertainment; what they ate and drank; how the city preserved the beauty of its parks and sidewalks; whether it was safe for women to walk the streets at night. For an article on the poor, she worked for a time in a soup kitchen. She haunted the shops in the Jewish section for a story on Parisian Jews. "There were a multitude of things I thirsted to know," Ida wrote. "And if I could get my bread and butter finding out, what luck! What luck!"

"There were few mornings that I was not at my desk at eight o'clock," she remembered; "there were few nights that I went to bed before midnight, and there was real drudgery in making legible copy after my article was written." On weekends, she allowed time for expeditions to the cathedrals and the museums, as well as Versailles and Fontainebleau. Before seven weeks had passed, she had sent a dozen articles to various papers at home but had heard nothing in return. It seemed as if Dr. Flood's prediction would prove correct. Finally, in early November, she received her first check, from the *Cincinnati Times-Star*, the paper edited by Will Taft's brother Charles. "It was not much, $6.00," she reported to her family. "How the doctor would scorn it! But I was glad to get it because it's a start."

In the meantime, she and her friends managed to enjoy their "bohemian poverty." They dined two nights a week with Mme Bonnet, who provided "a good dinner of 6 courses with cider and wine for 40 cents." These were "happy evenings," Ida recalled, "for the Egyptians loved games, tricks, charades, play of any sort." They found a local restaurant that catered to Americans and offered a noonday meal for 23 cents. "Think of us," she wrote home, "going into a place where there is sawdust on the floor, a bar in one corner, every table with wine and many men smoking cigarettes, but there are lots of ladies, American artists, and then everybody does it." For their remaining meals, they pledged to spend only 12 cents to offset the expense of the dinners, buying "not a morsel more" than they absolutely required—"a single egg, one roll or croissant, a gill of milk, two cups apiece of café au lait, never having a drop left in the pot."

Winter came early to Paris that year. "It is the most heartless weather I ever experienced," she told her family. "It is clear and dry but the wind cuts like a knife." With only one little heating grate in the room where she wrote, she sat at her desk with one shawl wrapped around her legs, another over her head, and a hand stove to keep her feet warm. At night she wore everything but her sealskin coat to bed. Still, she was convinced that no one in Paris was having more fun. "It isn't money after all that makes the best of things," she assured them.

A breakthrough came in December when *Scribner's* accepted a piece of short fiction pending her agreement on several changes. "I think after 'mature deliberation' for about 1/50 of a second that I'll allow the changes to be made," she excitedly told her parents. "That it has been accepted at all is a tremendous encouragement to me. It gives me heart and hope." *Scribner's* paid $100 for the story, nearly the amount she had brought to cover her passage to Europe and her first months in Paris. "What excitement in our little salon when I showed my companions that check!" Her success freed her to attend courses at the Sorbonne on French history and literature, to spend time at the library going through the papers of Mme Roland, relax with friends in the cafés, and buy a new pair of shoes.

In the months that followed, more and more newspapers accepted her articles. "Writing $5 and $10 articles" was admittedly "an awful slow way of making one's living," but Ida had proved Dr. Flood wrong and banished her own doubts. She was a working woman, living in a city she adored, surviving on her own as a published writer.

McClure's invitation to join him as he launched his new magazine intrigued Ida, but she was unwilling to leave for New York before her research on Mme Roland was complete. She happily agreed, however, to contribute freelance articles from Paris once the magazine was under way. His mission that summer evening in 1892 accomplished, McClure suddenly jumped to his feet. "I must go," he said. "Could you lend me forty dollars? It is too late to get money over town, and I must catch the train for Geneva." As it happened, Ida had exactly that sum stashed in a drawer, saved for a long-awaited vacation. "It never occurred to me to do anything but give it to him," she recalled, though the next day she suffered "some bad moments," fearing he would "simply never think of it again." The following day, a forty-dollar check was sent from McClure's office in London.

Work for the new magazine opened up a broad new world of intellectual adventure. She studied microbe theory and interviewed Louis Pasteur in his home, examined the psychology of legerdemain, investigated the new Bertillon system of criminal identification, surveyed public health practices in French cities, and secured contributions from Émile Zola, Alphonse Daudet, and Alexandre Dumas. McClure was thrilled with her work. "We all hope you are not planning to get married and cut short your career," he told her. "All of the articles which you have sent to us recently are most admirably done . . . I have always liked your work, as you know, but of late you have been surpassing yourself."

The only snag in this propitious arrangement was that McClure had no money to compensate her efforts. Despite rave reviews, the new magazine was struggling to survive in the midst of the severe depression. Indeed, the situation at home was so bleak, Esther Tarbell informed her daughter, that people were "actually starving by hundreds and thousands." The alarming circumstances had convinced her mother that "monopolies are fearful evils," a plague to confront by peaceful means or "by force, if it must be."

Irrepressible Ida, "on the ragged edge of bankruptcy," nonetheless insisted she was "gay as a cricket." She continued to believe in McClure. "The little magazine is sure to live," she assured her family; "they are honest and energetic and young and they'll pull through." Her prediction proved on the mark. Month by month, *McClure's* circulation continued to increase. In April 1894, McClure returned to Paris, this time securing Ida's commitment to begin full-time work on the magazine in the fall. But first she would spend the summer with her parents in Titusville, where she hoped to complete her book on Mme Roland.

Tarbell had been home for only six weeks when she received an urgent wire from McClure, begging her to come to New York. An intense fascination with Napoleon Bonaparte had recently swept Europe and McClure believed that America, too, would be captivated anew by the French emperor. McClure had made connection with Gardiner Green Hubbard, father-in-law to Alexander Graham Bell and owner of a valuable collection of Napoleon portraits. McClure secured Hubbard's permission to reproduce the portraits alongside a short biography of Napoleon by an English author, Robert Sherard. The illustrated series, set to begin in November, had been heavily promoted. When the manuscript arrived, Hubbard found the tone "so contemptuously anti-

Napoleon" that he withdrew permission to let his pictures accompany the text. In desperation, McClure turned to Ida.

Though the task of producing the first installment in six weeks seemed impossible, Ida agreed to try. She left at once for Washington, where she was given a suite in Hubbard's magnificent country estate on Woodley Lane, not far from Roosevelt's modest Dupont Circle home. In addition to Hubbard's immense library, she had access to the State Department archives, which held printed copies of all Napoleon's official correspondence. Granted a desk at the Library of Congress, Tarbell was able to summon books and pamphlets from what turned out to be an exceptional collection covering the Napoleonic era.

Despite her embarrassment at constructing "biography on the gallop," Ida not only met the deadline but produced a work of quality. When the seven installments were completed, the *New York Press* hailed the series as "the best short life of Napoleon we have ever seen." From the reigning Napoleon expert came the welcome, heartening comment: "I have often wished that I had had, as you did, the prod of necessity behind me, the obligation to get it out at a fixed time, to put it through, no time to idle, to weigh, only to set down. You got something that way—a living sketch." An additional benefit of her accomplishment was Scribner's agreement to publish her book on Mme Roland.

On the strength of the Napoleon series, the circulation of *McClure's* doubled, reaching nearly 100,000 by publication of the final installment. Even before it was finished, McClure conjured another series for Tarbell—a short life of Abraham Lincoln. "His insight told him that people never had had enough of Lincoln," explained Tarbell later; he was certain that thirty years after Lincoln's death, hundreds of people remained whose reminiscences were still untapped. Characteristically, once having conceived of the project, McClure "could think of nothing but Lincoln, morning, noon, and night."

"Out with you," he ordered Ida. "Look, see, report." Before her departure, she called on John Nicolay, whose monumental biography had recently been serialized in the *Century*. Nicolay greeted her coldly. He assured her that he and his co-author John Hay had discovered "all there was worth telling of Lincoln's life." She would be well advised "not to touch so hopeless an assignment." When the *Century*'s editor, Richard Watson Gilder, was questioned about his opinion of *McClure's* magazine, he scoffed: "They got a girl to write a Life of Lincoln."

Nicolay's disdain influenced her "plan of campaign." Rather than start her inquiry "at the end of the story with the great and known," she would begin "in Kentucky with the humble and unknown." She would trace Lincoln's life chronologically, through the little towns and settlements where he had lived and worked. Tarbell's approach unearthed scores of people who had known him in those early days. She scoured local histories, probed court records and newspaper clippings. Combining the skills of an investigative reporter with those of a detective, artist, and biographer, she coaxed reluctant people and jogged their memories with the hard evidence she had discovered. McClure covered all her expenses and kept her on salary during the three-year period of her research and writing. She completed her project in a charming Washington boardinghouse on I Street between Ninth and Tenth, a lodging shared by Massachusetts senator and Mrs. George Hoar. McClure scrutinized multiple drafts of every installment, assuring that the narrative retained its momentum.

The series proved a popular and critical triumph. "It is not only full of new things," the *Chicago Tribune* wrote, "but is so distinct and clear in local color that an interest attaches to it which is not found in other biographies." When the first installment appeared, *McClure's* circulation increased by 40,000 copies to 190,000. A month later, it reached a quarter of a million, exceeding both the *Century* and *Harper's Monthly*.

With the completion of the Lincoln series, McClure brought Tarbell to New York as the desk editor of the magazine. The publication was then housed on the sixth floor of the Lexington Building on 25th Street. Working in the office each day, Tarbell soon understood the critical role that John S. Phillips, whom they called "JSP," played in the success of the magazine. If McClure was the wind in the sails, with "great power to stir excitement by his suggestions, his endless searching after something new, alive, startling," the stabilizing ballast was the steady, unflappable Phillips. "Here's a man," Tarbell wrote, "who knows the power of patience in dealing with the impatient." Phillips lived in the city during the week so that he could be available day and night; on weekends, he joined his wife, Jennie, and their small children in Goshen, New York, a small town in the foothills of the Catskills. It was said in the office "that Sam had three hundred ideas a minute, but only JSP knew which one was not crazy."

"I found the place so warmly and often ridiculously human," Tarbell remembered. Her genial temperament allowed her to get on "capitally" with the brilliant but volatile art director, August Jaccaci, whose towering fits of anger "came and went like terrible summer thundershowers." She developed a lifelong friendship with Viola Roseboro, the cigarette-smoking, wisecracking former actress in charge of reading the thousands of unsolicited manuscripts that arrived month after month. Without doubt, Ida was enamored with McClure himself. Years later, she remembered how his blue eyes "glowed and sparkled" when the peripatetic publisher prowled the newsroom spouting a tumult of thoughts and projects, any one of which might harbor "a stroke of genius."

For Ida Tarbell, the most alluring aspect of *McClure's* was "the sense of vitality, of adventure, of excitement," the feeling of "being admitted on terms of equality and good comradeship" with an extraordinary group of people. They perched on one another's desks, they lunched together at the Ashland House, they drank together after hours. Each was an integral component of a team that was creating what would soon become the most exciting and influential magazine the country had ever seen.

⌒ ⌒

THE NEXT "PERMANENT ACQUISITION" TO join Ida Tarbell on McClure's writing staff was Ray Stannard Baker. Baker had spent six years reporting for the *Chicago Record*, a publication he proudly called "an honest paper" that played "no 'inside game,' but wanted to tell the truth, whatever it might be." His distinguished work at the *Record* included an extensive and memorable series on the growing tension between labor and capital. Baker had always enjoyed talking with "farmers, tinkers, blacksmiths, newsdealers, bootblacks, and the like," and firmly believed that "every human being has a story in him—how he has come to be what he is, how he manages, after all, to live, just to live."

At the age of twenty-seven Baker felt he had exhausted the possibilities of the newspaper format. He craved "a wider field of activity," a vehicle for in-depth research, a space for longer stories of lasting "import and value." An avid reader of *McClure's* from its inception, he had quickly become "a devoted admirer." The magazine's long and thoroughly researched articles, he noted with admiration, "were not merely about people . . . the people seemed to be there in person, alive and talking." The innovative publication, in his opinion, was simply "something fresh and strong and living in a stodgy literary world." After reading Tarbell's series on Lincoln, Baker sent *McClure's* a proposal for an article on his uncle, Colonel Lafayette C. Baker, the Secret Service member who had led the party that captured John Wilkes Booth. Tarbell promised to give it serious attention, and within days of its arrival, the piece was accepted for immediate publication. Intuiting that Baker might be a good fit for the magazine, McClure suggested that he come to New York and discuss ideas for further contributions.

"To say that I was awed at having a letter from the founder and editor of such a magazine was to put it mildly," Baker related a half century later. Soon he received a letter from John S. Phillips with an enclosed "pass" on the New York Central Railroad. "It took my breath away," he remembered. "So this was the magical way they did things in New York." Of that first foray into New York, he related that "Mr. McClure had suddenly dashed off to Europe, as was his custom, but I had long and delightful talks with John Phillips and August Jaccaci, the art director, and Ida Tarbell and others of the staff. I went out with them to the jolly table at the old Ashland House where they lunched together, a spot that still glimmers bright in my memory. It all seemed like a marvelous new world, with a quality of enthusiasm and intellectual interest, I had never before encountered. Even with S. S. McClure absent, I suppose I was in the most stimulating, yes intoxicating, editorial atmosphere then existent in America—or anywhere else."

In the months that followed, Baker submitted a half-dozen additional articles to *McClure's* while continuing to work at the *Chicago Record*. When the coveted invitation to join the *McClure's* staff finally arrived, he accepted at once, though he would miss his cohorts at the *Record*. "It 'breaks me all up' to leave after having been so long and so intimately connected with the paper," he told his father. "I suppose the regret is natural and that it will wear off as I bend to other work. I hope so." Once in New York, he never looked back. "This is a magnificent old town," he assured his father. "I never worked so hard in my life as I am doing now." He got along exceedingly well with the entire *McClure's* staff. "I like them and they like me," he proudly noted.

Baker was "a capital team worker," Tarbell recalled. "He had curiosity, appreciation, a respect for facts. You could not ruffle or antagonize him. He took the sudden calls to go here when he was going there, with equanimity; he enjoyed the unconventional intimacies of the crowd, the gaiety and excitement of belonging to what was more and more obviously a success. He was the least talkative of us all, observant rather than garrulous, the best listener in the group, save Mr. Phillips. He had a joyous laugh which was more revealing of his healthy inner self than anything else about him."

Baker's cheerful, balanced temperament could likely be traced to a devoted father and a peaceful childhood in the frontier village of St. Croix, Wisconsin. The oldest of six sons, he shared his father's love for "fishing and hunting" amid "the forests and the swift rivers and the lumber camps." Joseph Stannard Baker, his father, had been educated at Oberlin and the University of Wisconsin. An honored member of the Secret Service during the Civil War, he married Alice Potter, a minister's daughter from Lansing, and became the "resident agent" of a timber-rich swath of Wisconsin Territory owned by absentee landlords.

"Ours was a house of books," Ray fondly recalled, noting with pride that his father's library was the largest in the entire county. Every night, Baker would read aloud to his boys. "How well I remember the little gatherings just before bedtime," Ray later wrote, "the lamp in the middle of the table, the book, whatever it was, open before him and the small audience, tousle-headed, with grimy legs drawn up under them, sitting with mouths open and eyes fixed upon the reader's face! Whatever Father did, he did with gusto." Baker's animation and expressive voice made him "a prodigious story-teller, the best I ever knew. . . . We teased incessantly for stories and it was not un-usual in the earlier days, for my father to have a roomful of people for his audience."

Ray was still a child when his father gave him a silver dollar for completing *Pilgrim's Progress*. No further bribery was ever required to fuel his passion for all manner of tales. By the time he was eleven, the boy loved nothing more than entering "into the lives and sorrows and joys" of others through books. "My reading was always a kind of living," he explained later, "a longing to know some man or men stronger, braver, wiser, wittier, more amusing, or more desperately wicked, than I was, whom I could come to know well and sometimes be friends with."

The eldest child and his father's favorite, Ray was expected to help shape the behavior of his younger siblings. Both in the classroom and at home he strove to be worthy of that trust. He was the top student in his grammar school class, performed household chores without complaint, and diligently partici-pated in Sunday school classes. When his mother's ill health briefly forced her into a sanitarium, Ray assumed responsibility for provisioning the household with food and supplies. For a time after her return, her condition seemed to improve, but the year Ray turned thirteen, Alice Baker died. Ray would never forget the shock of witnessing his father's grief: "It went through me like the thrust of a sharp knife: it was more terrible than anything else that had hap-pened. My father, that strong man, that refuge of safety and fearlessness, my father shaken with weeping."

After only one year in high school, Ray passed the entrance examinations for college, allowing him to enter Michigan Agricultural College (later Michi-gan State) as a fifteen-year-old freshman. Like Ida Tarbell, Ray enjoyed the invaluable benefit of an inspired botany professor, William Beal, yet another acolyte (like Professors Hurd and Tingley) of Harvard's Louis Agassiz. Ray's first experience in Professor Beal's laboratory made an indelible impression. Instructed to study a single plant specimen for several days under a compound microscope, he initially deemed the assignment "a great waste of time" when he could simply research the specimen in a botany text and enumerate its characteristics. Baker soon came to understand that Beal wanted his students to learn by investigating for themselves, by compiling "details and facts before principles and conclusions." Beal, he would come to realize, taught "the one thing I needed most of all to know. This was to *look* at life before I talked about it: not to look at it second-hand, by way of books, but so far as possible to examine the thing itself." The friendship he developed with his professor and mentor would last a lifetime; indeed, Baker would eventually marry Beal's daughter, Jessie. And Beal's methodology would serve as Baker's lodestar throughout his long journalistic career.

The personable Baker was well liked in college. He stood five feet ten inches tall, with handsome features: blue eyes behind round spectacles, a straight nose, and a cleft chin. The intent scholarship that kept him at the top of his class did not preclude joining a fraternity, playing rugby, or serving as editor-in-chief of the school newspaper. He was a leader in student government and was selected to deliver one of the commencement orations.

That his father hoped he would return to St. Croix after college, learn the land business, and ultimately become his partner was long understood. "When the time comes I shall give you advice," his father told him, "but I shall never attempt to force or urge you into any position or calling which is at all distasteful to you." Tears filled young Ray's eyes as he read those words, and he resolved "never to fail" his beloved father; upon graduation, he dutifully returned home to apprentice in Baker's office. Sadly, he soon discovered that he "was not adapted to a business life." He traveled with his father, keeping the books and bank accounts, but "did not *live* in it, as one must do if he is to be happy and truly successful in any employment." Despite his efforts, he found his occupation increasingly distasteful: "I felt as though I were being crowded back into a kind of cocoon from which I had long ago worked free, and flown."

Ray consoled himself by writing poems and stories and by recording thoughts in a journal, a habit he would continue all his life. Decades later, he wrote of the tremendous importance this private chronicle held for him: "Experience soon fades, thought degenerates into musing, even love may presently wither, but the honestly written expression, hot from the penpoint, of the contents of one's mind, its observations, desires, doubts, faith, ambition, and the like, becomes at length a kind of immortality." Ray endured two cheerless years in the office until his brother Harry, who found the land business far more congenial, replaced him. Harry's decision to join their father freed Ray to continue his education.

Having enrolled in the University of Michigan Law School in Ann Arbor, Ray soon found himself drawn instead to courses in the English department.

A gifted professor, Fred Newton Scott, became his mentor. Unlike traditional surveys of the literary canon, Scott's seminar focused on a limited number of writers, subjecting their works to in-depth literary criticism. The progressive young professor believed, as did Howells and the realist school, that authors had a social responsibility to address the problems of their era. The test of a writer's work, he told his students, must be its contribution to the "good working order" of society as a whole.

Baker signed up for a second seminar with Scott called "Rapid Writing," one of the country's earliest college programs to teach journalism. The popular class required that students pick one newspaper to follow daily and focus on a particular subject. Baker chose the *Chicago Record*, concentrating on the struggles between laboring men and employers in that city. Immersed in coverage of the fight to establish workers' rights in the new industrial order, he began to question the laissez-faire economic principles inherited from his Republican father. Though he already had read Henry George's *Progress and Poverty*, the book's remedy—a single tax on land—was "anathema" to his father, whose very livelihood was founded upon the ownership of land. Ray was still trying to reconcile these conflicting ideas when he encountered Professor Scott.

Numerous stories in the *Chicago Record* that semester reflected the growing tension between labor and capital, as well as an economic stagnation that signaled the impending depression of 1893. Every morning, Ray read and analyzed news articles and editorials, writing his own reports "with the greatest fervor," eagerly anticipating Scott's exacting appraisals. "For the first time in my life I was getting honest and direct criticism," he recalled, "and it was like a draught of clear water to a thirsty spirit."

By the semester's close, Baker realized that his desire to study law had evaporated, and he was certain his future lay in journalism. "I did not make this break-away without many hesitations," he admitted. "I knew how disappointed my father would be." Unable to confront Joseph, he set out for Chicago, ostensibly seeking summer employment as a reporter, though in actuality he already hoped to make journalism his career. When he presented himself to the editor of the *Chicago Record*, Baker was told that there were no regular openings, but he could await possible assignments in the city room. After many weeks, his opportunity arrived. The regular labor reporter was out on a story one afternoon when word came that the waiters in a popular restaurant had gone out on strike. Baker received the assignment. When he turned the article in, the assistant night editor delivered words he would never forget. "Great stuff, Baker," he exclaimed, "great stuff." With bolstered confidence, Baker canvassed the neighborhoods of Chicago. His explorations resulted in a series of human interest stories, "glimpses, street scenes, common little incidents of the daily life of a great city, which could be treated more or less lightly or humorously." Pleased with Baker's work, the *Record* offered him a regular position that fall.

But in December 1892 he received an urgent summons from his father. Baker's hearing, damaged in the war many years earlier, was deteriorating into deafness. It was Harry's turn to enroll in college courses, and he needed his oldest son to come home. Ray tried to convince his father that his aspirations as a writer were neither pretentious nor frivolous, but his father's needs prevailed and Ray found himself back in St. Croix. For nearly a year, he remained to assist his father until Harry's winter break allowed a return to Chicago.

The depression was taking a grim toll on the city that winter. Baker was welcomed back to the *Record* to cover the plight of the unemployed. "There are thousands of homeless and starving men in the streets," he told his father. "I have seen more misery in this last week than I ever saw in my life before." This destitute urban population was unlike anything he had encountered. While there were "plenty of people on the frontier who were poor," he noted, they had means of subsistence. "Land was to be had almost for the asking, logs were at hand for their houses, all the streams were full of fish, and all the hills full of game. . . . There was everywhere plenty of work." The city offered no such opportunities. "The miserable living conditions, the long hours, the low wages, the universal insecurity, tended to tear down the personality, cheapen the man."

As Harry prepared for the spring semester, Baker appealed once again to his oldest son. Ray had promised to return home "in the event of absolute necessity" to protect the family business, but leaving the newspaper would force him "to begin all over again at the bottom of the ladder" when he returned to Chicago. Moreover, he insisted, "there is no use in trying to run a business with your heart elsewhere." While reluctant to return, he reassured his father of his loyalty: " I shall regard it as my first duty, whatever may happen to see that your business is protected and I think every one of the six boys feels in the same way." Realizing his son's devotion to his chosen vocation, Baker relented. Ray should remain in Chicago, and he would manage at home.

Supplied with a typewriter for the first time, Ray was sent to Massillon, Ohio, in mid-March 1894 to cover a crusade that would become known as Coxey's Army. The fiery reformer Jacob Coxey planned a massive march on Washington to demand a government-sponsored public works program to put thousands of unemployed men to work building roads. Baker's first articles reflected his paper's editorial stance against the march—venting concern that a horde of vagrants and derelicts would wreak havoc as they marched through the countryside en route to the capital.

Yet as Baker trudged alongside the men, his attitude shifted. "I began to know some of them as Joe and Bill and George," he related. "I soon had them talking about their homes in Iowa and Colorado and Illinois and Chicago and Pittsburgh—and the real problems they had to meet." These were not "bums, tramps, and vagabonds" but "genuine farmers and workingmen," driven in a time of depression by their inability to "earn a living." Baker's sympathetic articles brought hundreds of additional recruits to Coxey's Army and revealed to him the incredible "power of the press." Skeptics had predicted that the Army, outfitted with supplies for only a few days, would soon disintegrate. But at each scheduled stop "there appeared an impromptu local committee, sometimes including the mayor and other public men, with large supplies of bread, meat, milk, eggs, canned goods, coffee, tea."

Following Coxey's improbable army was "a grand adventure" for Baker and his fellow correspondents. Crossing the Allegheny Mountains, they found themselves in snow at least a foot deep. Although some marchers with ragged boots dropped out, the majority persevered, and at last, six weeks after they began, the motley Army reached Washington, D.C. Massive crowds thronged the streets as the procession headed toward the Capitol. Senators and congressmen looked on from the Capitol portico. A large mounted police guard awaited and, as the marchers spilled onto the lawn, Baker reported, "the police seemed to lose their heads completely as they dashed into the crowds on their horses and slashed out with their clubs." Coxey gained the Capitol steps and was beginning to address the crowd when he was arrested for trespassing and roughly carried away.

"Coxey's eventful march from Massillon to the marble steps of the national Capitol closed today in riot and bloodshed," Baker recorded, leaving in its wake public works bills "no nearer passage than they were a month ago." A remark by a Massachusetts politician reflected the widespread hostility to the reforms among legislators. "The bill," he claimed, "was immoral, for unemployment was an act of God." With the arrest of Coxey, the Army "vanished in thin air," and with it, hope for a political solution to unemployment. It would take the Great Depression of the 1930s to convince the New Deal Congress that Coxey's approach had merit.

Immediately upon his return to Chicago, Baker was sent to Pullman, Illinois, the model town founded by the railroad industrialist George M. Pullman, developer of both the sleeping car and the dining car and president of the Pullman Palace Car Company. Baker had read rhapsodic descriptions of the experimental community where Pullman's workers lived in Pullman-owned homes, shopped in Pullman stores, and worshipped in Pullman churches. He had long wanted to meet the "benevolent-looking, bearded man," but he arrived in Pullman in 1894 to discover a scene of "the wildest confusion." Three thousand factory workers were striking to protest substantial wage cuts. The company argued that it was losing money in the hard times, but workmen pointed out that regular dividends were still being paid out to stockholders. Indeed, it was later proved that the company's dividend payouts were in excess of $2 million annually, while profits held steady at $25 million per year.

The Pullman workers appealed for support to the American Railway Union (ARU), headed by Eugene Debs. Initially reluctant to help, Debs was finally convinced by reports of the excessive prices workers were forced to pay for rent, utilities, and food; the predatory hold of the Pullman monopoly must be broken. Baker took an immediate liking to Debs, believing him unselfishly committed to the cause. The ARU gave the company five days to arbitrate a settlement, but Pullman declared that there was "nothing to arbitrate." He insisted that "workers have nothing to do with the amount of wages they shall receive; that is solely the business of the company." The powerful union responded with a boycott of all Pullman cars, disrupting railroad traffic across the nation. When railroad managers attempted to replace the strikers with non-union men, riots broke out.

The managers then requested and received a federal injunction against the boycott, ostensibly on grounds of protecting the delivery of mail. Despite the injunction, the boycott continued until President Grover Cleveland, over the objection of Illinois governor Altgeld, sent in federal troops, thereby escalating the violence. Trains were overturned and fires started. The federal troops opened fire. Dozens were killed and wounded. Debs was jailed for ignoring the injunction. By the end of August 1894, more than three months after it had begun, the strike collapsed with nothing gained for the workers.

Baker well understood that mobs could not run amok, "putting the torch to millions of dollars' worth of property," yet his feelings of support remained firm for the striking workers whose stories he had come to know. Clearly, Joseph Stannard Baker did not share his son's empathy for the strikers. "It does seem to me as if the laboring classes were possessed of the devil," he wrote in early July. "I believe in the free application of rifle balls, grape and canister to mobs." Ray held his ground. Asked to testify before a federal panel that fall, he asserted that he was "in the midst of the mob" when the violence began and that "at no time" did he witness the involvement of a member of the railway union or a striker. On the contrary, the men who overturned the cars were "toughs and outsiders." Moreover, when the federal troops arrived, they fired into the crowd with no warning, killing and wounding innocent spectators. While most of the newspapers blamed the strikers and created the impression that the federal troops had saved Chicago from anarchy, Baker carefully recounted what he had observed.

The young journalist believed that his "honeymoon as a newspaper reporter ended with the Pullman strike." He "had been wonderfully fortunate" to that point, he realized: "I had been able to work on subjects that interested me profoundly ever since my days in the university—the new problems of unemployment and the relationships of labor and capital." But in the aftermath of the protracted and distressing Pullman strike, even those editors sensitive to labor issues sensed that their readers "were profoundly relieved to have the trouble ended," no longer wishing to hear about labor's struggles. Baker found himself covering murders, fires, and robberies. He felt that he was stifling.

The dramatic 1896 campaign between Democrat William Jennings Bryan and Republican William McKinley provided a welcome diversion. After witnessing Bryan's famous "Cross of Gold" speech at the Chicago Wigwam, Baker concluded that the candidate was "the greatest popular orator [he] had ever heard." Though his father vociferously derided Bryan and his Populist followers, Baker was deeply impressed when he went to see him at the Palmer House. "The essential impression he made," Baker later recalled, "was one of deep sincerity." McKinley won a convincing victory, claiming every state outside the West and the South, and Baker found himself once again covering "the commonplace" rather than "the spectacular."

Two years earlier, Ray had married Jessie Beal, with whom he had corresponded since their college days. He was feeling "somewhat low" as he contemplated how he might support his wife and new child on his newspaper salary and doubted if he "was getting anywhere at all as a writer." At this stressful juncture, the fortuitous offer from S. S. McClure prompted elation. "Suddenly and joyously" Ray Stannard Baker was transported to a world "full of strange and wonderful new things," and he was "at the heart of it, especially commissioned to look at it, hear about it, and above all, to write about it."

☞ ☜

Twenty-nine-year-old William Allen White, editor of a small country newspaper in Emporia, Kansas, ironically came to the attention of S. S. McClure through a scathing anti-Populist editorial that he would later disavow when he became an ardent progressive. "What's the Matter with Kansas?," written in the heat of the election between McKinley and Bryan, ridiculed his home state for endorsing Bryan's "wild-eyed" rhetoric that pitted the rich against the poor and was sure to drive out capital and extinguish the possibility of progress. "That's the stuff!" he jeered. "Give the prosperous man the dickens! Legislate the thriftless man into ease, whack the stuffing out of the creditors. . . . Whoop it up for the ragged trousers; put the lazy, greasy fizzle, who can't pay his debts, on the altar, and bow down and worship him."

White's editorial was republished in dozens of newspapers throughout the country. The sardonic tone caught the fancy of Mark Hanna, McKinley's campaign manager, who had it reprinted and distributed "more widely than any other circular in the campaign." Speaker of the U.S. House of Representatives Tom Reed, without even knowing White's name, sent a laudatory note to the editor of the little paper. "I haven't seen as much sense in one column in a dozen years," he declared. Suddenly, the rotund, florid young man who had labored at his obscure midwestern newspaper became a national figure.

McClure jotted down the name William Allen White; some weeks later, having also read a small volume of short stories White had recently published, he brought the young man to New York. "I had seen cities," White later recalled, "Kansas City, St. Louis, Denver, Chicago, but even in 1897 the New York sky line as I ferried across to the Twenty-third Street slip, made my country eyes bug out with excitement."

At first sight, White was totally smitten too by the *McClure's* staff. McClure himself seemed "a powerhouse of energy," a dynamo "full of ideas," who "talked like a pair of scissors, clipping his sentences, sometimes his words." White's mother, Mary Ann Hatton, they discovered, had been Professor Hurd's student at Knox College. And White connected at once with "fellow midwesterner" John Phillips, who invited him, along with Ida Tarbell, to a "gorgeous dinner" at a cozy restaurant way uptown. "These people knew Rudyard Kipling," he noted with amazement. "They knew Robert Louis Stevenson. . . . The new English poets were their friends."

McClure's original staff members, for their part, were enchanted by the country editor with "the smile of a roguish little boy" and "the eyes of a poet." Tarbell liked "his affection and loyalty for his state, his appreciation and understanding of everything that she does—wise and foolish." Baker relished White's "love of life" and contagious "high spirits." McClure deluged him with concepts for new magazine pieces, and Phillips helped him distinguish the fool's gold from the gold. Before leaving New York, White pledged to send the lion's share of his future stories and articles to *McClure's*. They reciprocated his good faith, urging him to "call on them whenever he needed help," a promise kept when he mentioned he was trying to raise $5,000 to pay for a new home. *McClure's* magazine instantly remitted White a check for all construction costs, plus an additional $1,000.

"The McClure group became for ten or fifteen years my New York fortress, spiritual, literary and, because they paid me well, financial," White later wrote. McClure "was always Sam to me and John Phillips was always John, Miss Tarbell was always Ida M., and Jaccaci was always Jack. And I loved them all. There was no New England repression in our relations. They were cordial to the point of ardent. . . . They talked the Mississippi Valley vernacular. They thought as we thought in Emporia about men and things. They were making a magazine for our kind—the literate middle class. This group had real influence."

Baker was struck with admiration that White "never yielded to the temptation" of leaving Emporia, "the country and the people he knew best." He frequently visited New York, "stayed as long as he wanted to stay . . . worked out plans for new articles and stories, and then went back to Kansas." Yet the rapport and fellowship with the McClure group profoundly influenced his thinking: the provincial editor became cosmopolitan; the young conservative a progressive.

William Allen White's youthful conservatism was nourished by the comfortable world of his childhood. His family lived in "the best house" in the small central Kansas town of El Dorado, where his father, a successful doctor and shopkeeper, enlarged the family fortunes by operating the town's grandest hotel and speculating in real estate. "I look back upon my boyhood there in the big house," White later said, "with a sense of well-being." The "White House," as it was called, boasted eleven rooms and a wraparound porch designed "to get a breeze from every angle." Dr. White was elected to the city council and later served as mayor. He was "somebody," White later said, fostering William's "sense of belonging to the ruling class."

His college-educated mother was thirty-six when she married forty-eight-year-old Doc White. Will, their only surviving child, was, by his own account, terribly spoiled. His "devoted and adoring" parents "bowed down" to accommodate his every desire. "In that Elysian childhood," he recalled, "I was shielded from pain and sorrow and lived, if ever a human being did live, in a golden age." In his local school, everyone liked him. "He was so good-natured," one classmate recalled, "they could not do otherwise." Summer days were spent diving and going fishing in the nearby river; autumn promised hunting in the surrounding woods; the onset of winter meant setting traps for birds and game, and ice-skating on the frozen river. It was a boy's paradise, one that later he would work to faithfully re-create in nostalgic fiction.

White's house, like Baker's, was filled with books, and every night his mother read to him. "I remember as a child sitting in the chair, looking up to her while she read Dickens and George Eliot, Trollope, Charles Reed, and the Victorian English novels. My father, I remember, used to growl a good deal at the performance, and claimed that if my mother read to me so much I would never get so I would read for myself. But his prediction was sadly wrong. It was to those nights of reading and to the books that my mother had always about the house that I owe whatever I have of a love for good reading."

Dr. White was a gentle and jovial man, fond of entertaining guests in his spacious house. Will particularly remembered those cheerful evenings when his family hosted friends, neighbors, and frequently "distinguished citizens— the politicians of the time, the governors, congressmen, senators, and judges who came to the town on their political pilgrimages." The doctor's geniality and the whirl of his social and professional activity obscured a chronic illness: Dr. White was suffering from severe diabetes, and after a two-week illness in the fall of 1882, he died. Will was fourteen. The entire town attended the funeral, with crowds of mourners converging on the house and congesting the surrounding sidewalks and streets. "I was not without my pride," White recalled, "looking back as we made the turn half a mile from home and headed for the East Cemetery, to see the long line of carriages and wagons and carts still moving into the procession on Main Street."

Upon his high school graduation, White enrolled in the College of Emporia, sixty miles away. There he first encountered the new literature of realism through the serialization of William Dean Howells's *A Modern Instance,* the same novel McClure had devoured at John Phillips's home. "Here," White recalled, "was a novel different from the Dickens I adored." The young freshman "read it and reread it" that spring, feeling that "a new door" had opened. When he returned home that summer, White got a job with the local paper, the *El Dorado Democrat*. His responsibilities were limited to sweeping floors, doing odd jobs, and helping the typesetters, but he was enchanted by the world of journalism, certain he had found his "life's calling."

The following year, White transferred to the University of Kansas, and his mother rented out their El Dorado house so she could "establish a home" for her beloved son in Lawrence. White thoroughly enjoyed his years at the university, where he developed a lifelong friendship with his political science professor, Dr. James H. Canfield. A gifted teacher who taught history, sociology, and economics as well as political science, Canfield encouraged "a babble of clamoring voices" in classes built on discussion rather than lectures. In these classes, White first understood the inequities wrought by the high protective tariff, the standard of the Republican Party. In the years ahead, Canfield encouraged White to read books on socialism and to follow the works of the Progressive economist Richard Ely, father of Reform Darwinism. Ely argued that what businessmen claimed to be the "natural laws" of economics were in fact tools "in the hands of the greedy and the avaricious for keeping down and oppressing the laboring classes." Had White focused more on his schoolwork, he might have absorbed more of Canfield's philosophy, but he readily acknowledged that his extracurricular passions—his social life and after-hours work for the *Lawrence Journal*—consumed far more time and attention than his classes. "As I look back at it, classroom pictures blur in my memory of the university," White wrote. "Fraternity meetings are clear; political excursions are etched deeply; parties, little dances, picnics and what, in the student nomenclature of the time, was called 'girling,' I recall vividly. Also, I was downtown much of the time writing my news items for the Lawrence Journal, taking my copy for the Weekly University Courier to the printer, covering local events for the St. Louis and Kansas City papers." He found himself cutting class after class and realized he had somehow "ceased to be a student and had become a reporter." Failing to pass a required mathematics exam for the third time, he left the university without a degree.

Despite his mother's chagrin, she accompanied William back to El Dorado, where he went to work at the *El Dorado Republican*. Though his father had been a Democrat, White had by this time adopted his mother's allegiance to the Republican Party, a commitment he would ardently maintain throughout his life. Charged with generating local stories and editorials, the twenty-two-year-old reporter found himself in the midst of the Populist uprising.

The boom times that had accompanied White's childhood years had vanished for the majority of Kansas farmers, who found themselves caught between usurious interest rates on debts to eastern bankers and the predatory, monopolistic practices of both the grain elevator companies that stored their crops and the railroads that carried them to market. In many sections of the West and Midwest, where only one elevator company or railroad served the area, farmers were forced to pay whatever price these companies demanded. "We have three crops," a Nebraska newspaper editor lamented, "corn, freight rates, and interest. The farmers farm the land, and the businessmen farm the farmers."

The grim hardships endured by farming families galvanized the so-called Grangers movement. They successfully pressured state legislatures to regulate exorbitant elevator and railroad rates, but these laws were swiftly challenged in the courts, where corporate influence was pervasive. The Grangers secured a spectacular, albeit temporary, triumph in the 1877 case of *Munn v. Illinois*. The U.S. Supreme Court confirmed the constitutionality of an Illinois state law regulating excessive elevator rates. The Court agreed that Illinois was simply exercising its "police power" to regulate private property "affected with a public interest." Nine years later, however, in *Wabash, St. Louis & Pacific Railway Co. v. Illinois*, the Supreme Court effectively reversed its decision. The justices denied the state's regulatory power in a case concerning inflated railroad rates on grounds that only Congress had the right to dictate commerce between states. In the years that followed, the Court would remain an uncompromising barrier to state regulation of business in the public interest.

Responding to the public outcry that followed the *Wabash* decision, Congress filled the regulatory void in 1887 by passing the Interstate Commerce Act, which created an Interstate Commerce Commission (ICC) to ensure that railroad rates were "reasonable and just." The practice of granting rebates to favored big shippers, which essentially destroyed smaller competitors, was outlawed. But the legislation did not authorize the commission to set specific rates, a fatal omission that allowed railroad barons to challenge the ICC rulings in the courts at every turn, thereby rendering the law largely ineffective. In time, railroad executives actually found the law useful. "It satisfies the public clamor for a government supervision of railroads," one corporate lawyer, Richard Olney, wrote, "at the same time that the supervision is almost entirely nominal."

Though widespread bitterness against the concentration of economic power led to the passage of the Sherman Anti-Trust Act in 1890, that law likewise remained a paper tiger while the trusts continued to grow. "Liberty produces wealth, and wealth destroys liberty," Henry Demarest Lloyd wrote in *Wealth Against Commonwealth*, an influential 1902 indictment of the trusts. "The flames of a new economic evolution run around us, and we turn to find that competition has killed competition, that corporations are grown greater than the State . . . and that the naked issue of our time is with property becoming master, instead of servant."

In 1890, the Farmers' Alliance, which had succeeded the Grangers, successfully fielded slates of radical candidates in the West and Midwest. Mary Lease, a formidable proponent of reform, traveled around Kansas on behalf of Alliance candidates. "Wall Street owns the country," she charged. "It is no longer a government of the people, by the people and for the people, but a government of Wall Street, by Wall Street and for Wall Street." She angrily dismissed claims that the farmers' troubles stemmed from a surfeit of produce. "Overproduction!—when 10,000 little children, so statistics tell us, starve to death every year in the United States, and over 10,000 shop-girls in New York are forced to sell their virtue for the bread their niggardly wages deny them!"

Buoyed by successes in the midterm elections of 1890, the Farmers' Alliance sent delegates to a national convention in Omaha, Nebraska. There, in 1892, a new party, the People's or Populist Party, was born. "We meet in the midst of a nation brought to the verge of moral, political and material ruin," the platform began. "The fruits of the toil of millions are boldly stolen to build up colossal fortunes for a few, unprecedented in the history of mankind." The Populists called for a graduated income tax to shift the heavier burden to the wealthy, a silver standard to facilitate an easier discharge of their debts, and a federally administered system of postal savings banks where people could safely deposit their earnings. To circumvent the collusion of corporate interests and political bosses who, in turn, controlled the state legislatures, they demanded a constitutional amendment to elect U.S. senators by a direct vote of the people, as well as new techniques—the initiative and the referendum—which would enable voters to directly initiate or reject legislation.

Realizing the necessity of a coalition with more urban areas, organizers of the largely agrarian party tried to appeal to industrial workers. The platform endorsed labor's fight for an eight-hour day and opposed the use of Pinkerton guards as strikebreakers. Finally, arguing that "the railroad corporations will either own the people or the people must own the railroads," the Populists called for government ownership of the railroads. Though their 1892 presidential candidate, James Weaver, proved unable to unify support beyond the western states, the Populist message remained a rallying point for America's working poor.

At first, the ruling classes—the bankers, the businessmen, and the lawyers—paid little attention to the members of the Farmers' Alliance and the new Populist Party. "We prideful ones," White later admitted, "considered the Alliance candidates as the dregs of Butler County society; farmers who had lost their farms, Courthouse hangers-on . . . political scapegraces." White wrote stinging editorials to ridicule the uprising, convinced that the grassroots movement was "demagogic rabble-rousing" without any tie to reality. "A child of the governing classes, I was blinded by my birthright," he later acknowledged. When the local Populists burned him in effigy, he proudly noted that their actions served only to aggrandize his standing with the local leaders of the Republican Party.

Like White, Theodore Roosevelt dismissed the members of the Farmers' Alliance as "pinheaded, anarchistic crank[s]" and castigated the Populists as grandstanding demagogues. While Tarbell sympathized with the Populists' outcry against monopoly after experiencing her father's struggle with Standard Oil, and while Baker came to know personally the members of Coxey's Army, the Pullman strikers, Governor Altgeld, and William Jennings Bryan, Roosevelt categorically denounced them all as "representatives of those forces which simmer beneath the surface of every civilized community, and which, if they could break out, would destroy not only property and civilization but finally even themselves."

For genteel reformers like Theodore Roosevelt and William Howard Taft, "good government," not economic reform, was the benchmark. "The 'best citizens,' " White explained, "were supposed to desire honest men in office, men who would not take bribes, men who would appoint high-minded men as their subordinates, men who would look after the public interests, see that public charities were well supported." The appearance of the Farmers' Alliance, "the first wave of the shock troops of a revolution that was to gather force as the years went by," reported White, "all this did not disturb either the Spring Chickens or their parents at the high-five clubs, the formal dances at the opera house given for the firemen, and the town charities."

White's jeering editorials against the Populists attracted widespread notice and prompted a job offer from the *Kansas City Journal*, a conservative Republican paper. During the next three years, from 1892 to 1895, he wrote for the *Journal* and then for the *Kansas City Star*. During these tumultuous years, as "the black hand of despair" fell over the countryside, he remained, by his own admission, "a supercilious young Pharisee, blinder than a bat to the great forces that were joining issue in our politics, forces that would be in combat for fifty years." Although his attacks on the Populists did not abate, he also began to write short stories based on his early life in Kansas that would eventually attract the attention of Sam McClure.

In 1895, having married schoolteacher Sallie Lindsay, White decided to quit big city life and return to the small town of Emporia, with its population of 15,000, a Main Street and college, and simple neighborly life. Intent on becoming his "own master," White purchased the *Emporia Gazette*, a local paper with a circulation of less than five hundred. He hoped to streamline the paper's production and dedicate most of his time to writing poetry and fiction. Most important, he told a skeptical city friend at the time, "I want to live and work some place where I can sit down with the mayor on the edge of the sidewalk and we can let our feet hang off and can discuss local politics and the state of the nation and what we must do to be saved till it's time to go home to dinner."

In his very first editorial for the *Gazette*, White spelled out a manifesto that would define the rest of his life. "The new editor hopes to live here until he is the old editor," he began. "He hopes always to sign 'from Emporia' after his name when he is abroad, and he trusts that he may so endear himself to the people that they will be as proud of the first words of the signature as he is of the last words." The young idealist would make good on his pledge, living out his years in his beloved country town, even as he became "the best-known and most often quoted country journalist in the United States."

While White never capitulated to Sam McClure's repeated invitations to relocate to New York, the warm friendships he developed with McClure, Phillips, Tarbell, and Baker fundamentally altered his social and political attitudes. He began to understand the profound inequities that had produced the Populist uprising: how the growth of colossal corporations had strangled competition in one field after another; how these corporations blatantly wielded their power through venal politicians, widening the gap between the rich and the poor. Belatedly but surely, he came to recognize that Bryan's platform in 1896 "was the beginning of a long fight for distributive justice, the opening of a campaign to bring to the common man . . . a larger and more equitable share in the commonwealth of our country."

⌒ ⌒

THE FINAL MEMBER OF THE celebrated quartet at the heart of *McClure's* was Lincoln Steffens. As a police reporter for the New York *Evening Post*, Steffens covered Theodore Roosevelt's activities as police commissioner. Early on, McClure had identified Roosevelt as a man of unusual potential: he "seems big from here," McClure confided to Phillips, indicating his resolve to cultivate a connection with a public figure "just our size." Aware of Steffens's intimacy with Roosevelt, the editor hoped to secure that conduit to New York's dynamic commissioner by adding Steffens to his staff.

When first approached by *McClure's*, Steffens was reluctant to abandon the newspaper industry and the reputation he had built as "one of the best journalists New York ever had." A long lunch with Phillips, followed by a visit to the bustling *McClure's* office, began to conquer his hesitancy. McClure was out of town, but Steffens met with the rest of the staff and was particularly captivated by the art director, August Jaccaci. "Jaccaci probed me hard, took me to his home, talked with and drew me out," he recalled. "That was his way. He could not be a friend, he had to be a lover." Their discussions convinced Steffens that the format of a monthly magazine would allow him to "tell the whole, completed story," providing time and space for details and implications he could not explore in a daily newspaper. That conversation "clinched" the deal.

Arriving at *McClure's*, Steffens later recalled, was "like springing up from a bed and diving into the lake—and life." S. S. McClure's sheer, irrepressible drive astounded Steffens. "He was a flower that did not sit and wait for the bees to come and take his honey and leave their seeds," observed the new staff writer. "He flew forth to find and rob the bees." Tensions invariably arose when McClure returned from his trips and assembled the staff to allocate new assignments gleaned from his travels. It was Ida Tarbell, Steffens recalled, who helped sort things out. Time and again, she managed to placate the staffers, to avoid battles, and find a path "to compromise and peace."

Tarbell in turn came to consider the "young, handsome, self-confident" Steffens "the most brilliant addition to the McClure's staff." Though "incredibly outspoken" and "never doubtful of himself," he demonstrated a disconcerting ability to analyze events and detect the underlying patterns, illuminating "the relations of police and politicians, politicians and the law, law and city officials, city officials and business, business and church, education, society, the press." Tarbell found it "entirely in harmony with the McClure method of staff building that this able, fearless innocent should be marked for absorption."

More reserved by nature than the cocksure Steffens, Ray Baker acknowledged they would not likely have been friends had they not been "associates in the same enterprise, eagerly engaged in similar tasks, meeting familiarly every day, discussing ideas and projects." Nevertheless, the more he worked with Steffens, the greater his respect and affection grew. Staff luncheons and dinners, visits to each other's homes, confidences shared, and letters exchanged combined to "make up the texture of a long friendship." Baker thought of Steffens "as a kind of Socratic skeptic, asking deceptively simple questions . . . striving first of all to understand." Indeed, his biographer Robert Stinson observes that throughout Steffens's long career, "his most consistent pose was that of a student." Projecting an earnest, unbiased, and questioning nature, he was able to gain the confidence and elicit the secrets of his subjects.

The qualities that made Steffens a first-rate reporter—his immense curiosity and self-assurance, his social ease and storytelling gifts—were perceptible even in his youth. "My story is of a happy life," he observed in his famous *Autobiography*, beginning with a childhood surrounded by doting parents and three affectionate younger sisters. His mother, Elizabeth Symes, was a cheerful, quick-witted, warmhearted woman who adored him. His father, Joseph, owned a successful business dealing in "paints, oils and glass." Later, as vice president of the California National Bank, president of the Board of

Trade, and a Republican stalwart, he would become a leading figure in Sac-
ramento, California. The "palatial residence" where Lincoln was raised was
subsequently turned into the governor's mansion.

Both intrepid and inquisitive, eight-year-old Steffens quickly capitalized
on his newfound freedom when his parents gave him a pony. He could explore
the countryside so long as he returned home in time for dinner. "If I left home
promptly after breakfast on a no-school day and right after school on the other
days," Lincoln recalled, "I could see a good deal of the world." His questing,
precocious nature attracted a various and colorful assortment of acquaintances.
He befriended a bridge-tender who let him follow along as he walked the
tracks to extinguish the burning coals spewed by passing locomotives. In the
course of their conversations, the bridge-tender shared his dreams of striking
it rich as a gold miner. Watching an artist render a drab, leached-out river
channel, he saw the scene transformed by small choices of color and light.
Hanging out at the racetrack, the boy struck up a relationship with a jockey
who dampened his ardor for horse racing by confiding that the races were
frequently fixed—so that those "in on the know" would realize "big killings."
A friendly page at the state capitol took him to the smoke-filled committee
rooms and hotel apartments where legislators and lobbyists hammered out
compromises on the price to be paid for votes in a particular piece of legislation. "Bribery! I might as well have been shot," he lamented. "Nothing was
what it was supposed to be."

Organized schooling frustrated young Lincoln's quest for knowledge and
information. Though he read more books than were required, he resisted the
standardized curriculum that he perceived as irrelevant to his experience.
Graduating at the bottom of his class from grammar school, he was sent to
a military boarding school to remedy the problem. When he still failed the
entrance examinations for the University of California at Berkeley, he required
an additional year at "the best private school in San Francisco" and the aid of
a private tutor in order to matriculate.

In his autobiography, Steffens blithely claimed that the enormous liberties
he enjoyed as a child had not made him one of those boys "brought up to do
their duty," boys for whom the American educational system was designed.
Knowledge at Berkeley, he complained, was "stored in compartments, categorical and independent." He resented the requirements in higher mathematics, wishing only to pursue his passion for philosophy. "No one," he insisted,
"ever brought out for me the relation of anything I was studying to anything
else." Then, during his junior year, when a history professor demanded re-

search in original documents, he discovered that the past was not a list of dates to be memorized but a series of questions to be continually debated. By the time he graduated from college, Steffens believed himself finally prepared to be a genuine student, an authentic intellectual, and decided to pursue graduate study in Europe.

"My father listened to my plan, and he was disappointed," Steffens recalled. The older man had harbored hopes that his son would take over the business: "It was for that that he was staying in it. When I said that, whatever I might do, I would never go into business, he said, rather sadly, that he would sell out his interest and retire." Facing the same irreconcilable demands of familial duty and personal desire that had plagued Baker, Lincoln Steffens was considerably more self-indulgent. He later postulated that having received love "so freely" as a child, he had never learned to reciprocate. Not until his own son was born, as Steffens approached sixty years old, did he feel any intimation of what unconditional love required.

A three-year interlude in Europe allowed Steffens to continue his philosophic study of man and society, first in Germany, then France, and finally in England. Through the works of Marx and Engels, he was exposed to the idea that the state had a responsibility to foster social welfare. He studied music and art, psychology and philosophy, attending lectures if and when he chose. He spent his days reading in cafés, wandering through museums, attending concerts, playing cards, drinking beer, and debating politics and philosophy with fellow students.

European social and sexual mores offered Steffens greater latitude to pursue unconventional relationships as well. In Leipzig, he became involved with Josephine Bontecou, a liberated woman ten years his senior. The daughter of a wealthy New York surgeon, she was studying psychology and anatomy to further her ambitions as both a scientist and a novelist. "She stands next to me as my equal in all respects," he wrote at the time. "She will have a life and a life's work of her own." After a clandestine marriage in London, concealed to ensure his father would continue sending remittances, the two moved together to Paris. They found lodgings in the Latin Quarter where Ida Tarbell struggled to maintain her meager but exciting livelihood during those same months. Steffens savored a carefree intellectual existence for the better part of a year until summoned by his father's letter: "My dear son: When you finished school you wanted to go to college. I sent you to Berkeley. When you got through there, you did not care to go into my business; so I sold out. You preferred to continue your studies in Berlin. I let you. After Berlin it was Heidelberg; after that Leipzig. And after the German universities you wanted

to study at the French universities in Paris. I consented, and after a year with
the French, you had to have half a year of the British Museum in London.
All right. You had that too. By now you must know about all there is to know
of the theory of life, but there's a practical side as well. It's worth knowing."

So at last, determined to heed his father's edict to find work and support
himself, Steffens crossed the ocean, landed in New York, and found employment as a reporter. Armed with a letter of introduction from a friend of his
father's to Joseph B. Bishop, an editor at the New York *Evening Post*, he was
given a chance to prove himself "on space" in an unsalaried position that
paid by the word once a piece was accepted for publication. Within weeks,
he made good. Assigned to interview the partner of a stockbroker who had
suddenly disappeared, he soon gained the man's confidence: "I told him the
story of my life; he told me his," Steffens later related. Before long, he learned
that the missing banker had absconded with all the firm's funds. More work
quickly followed this successful investigation, and soon Steffens was put on
salary.

"I came to love New York," he wrote. "In the course of a few months I
had visited all parts of the city, called on all sorts of men (and women), politicians, business men, reformers; described all sorts of events, fires, accidents,
fights, strikes, meetings. It was happy work for me." Suddenly, "science and
philosophy, like the theaters and books, seemed tame in comparison with the
men and women, the unbelievable doings and the sayings of a live city." Like
Baker and Tarbell, whose early enthusiasm for science gave way to a fascination with human beings, Steffens had found his calling, a focus for his diverse
intellectual interests in journalism.

Just as the Panic began during the winter of 1892–93, the city editor assigned Steffens to cover Wall Street. He was directed to develop relationships
with leading financiers that would allow the conservative *Evening Post* to explain insolvent banks and railroads in "cool, dull, matter-of-fact terms," rather
than resort to the fearmongering and sensationalism practiced by competing
papers. Recognizing that the Panic of 1893 "was a dismal time of radiating
destruction" for millions of people, Steffens nevertheless noted that "it had its
bright side, inside; it was good for the bears." From the sidelines of the Stock
Exchange, he dispassionately witnessed "the wild joy" of men who shorted
stocks and "rejoiced in the ruin." In later years, he would come to despise "successful men who seize such opportunities," but "the practices of big business"
were still a mystery, and he "was not thinking in those days; life was too, too
interesting, the world as it was too fascinating, to stop to question."

Steffens gained a reputation as "the gentleman reporter," one who could

be relied upon to present the news with "accuracy and politeness." In a letter
to his father, he proudly described the close relationships he had cultivated
with the big bankers. They "confide in me," he reflected, "saying they know
I will report them accurately and without exaggeration." The equanimity
and clarity of his writing was gaining notice. "Above all," he confessed to his
father, "I want that you should be convinced that you were right in giving me
the long training of college and that I am worthy of your long, patient help to
a son who did not ever seem worth it all."

In November 1893, a challenging new assignment inspired both elation
and unease: "The Evening Post has never given any space to police news: fires,
suicides, murders, and other crimes," Steffens explained to his father. "Now
I am to be tried." He would be head of a new *Post* police bureau, "with an
office on Mulberry Street across the street from Police Headquarters, fitted
up with a desk, bookcase, paper racks and telephone, and an assistant and a
boy." From the outset, Steffens understood that he faced "beastly work, police,
criminals and low-browed 'heelers' in the vilest part of the horrible East Side
amid poverty, sin and depravity," but he regarded the challenge with eager
anticipation. "Will it degrade me? Will it make a man of me? Here is my
field, my chance."

Dr. Charles H. Parkhurst, a respected minister, was responsible for the
Post's decision to cover the activities of the police department. Head of the
Society for the Prevention of Crime, Parkhurst had undertaken an investigation into the relationship between Tammany Hall and the police force. He
exposed a system of ubiquitous bribery and coercion that governed all aspects
of municipal operation: appointments, promotions, liquor licenses, protection
for houses of prostitution, gambling operations, and saloons operating illegally
on Sundays. Long opposed to the Tammany regime, the *Post* editors were
delighted to document Parkhurst's findings in full detail.

Parkhurst's allegations forced the state legislature in Albany to authorize its own investigating commission, headed by Republican state senator
Clarence Lexow. The hearings of the Lexow Committee splashed headlines
throughout the state, ultimately revealing a system of corruption even more
widespread than Parkhurst had guessed. The shocking revelations produced
a surge of support for reform candidates, precipitating the defeat of Tammany
in the 1894 elections, the triumph of reform mayor William L. Strong, and
the choice of Theodore Roosevelt as the new police commissioner. By the time
Roosevelt arrived in New York, Steffens had learned a great deal about the
workings of the police department, insights he readily shared in return for
access to the new commissioner and his department. A complicated friendship

was born that would give Steffens the unique perspective he would bring to *McClure's*, where the "Big Four"—Ida Tarbell, Ray Baker, William Allen White, and Lincoln Steffens—would become the heart of the muckraking movement.

≈ ≈

UNLIKE MCCLURE, WHO HAD BECOME acquainted with the crueler side of American prosperity through a childhood scarred by poverty and instability, the Big Four were the children of prominent and enterprising businessmen. Each of them had encountered the corrosive effects of the industrial system. Ida Tarbell had witnessed the economic ruin of her father and his fellow independent oil producers at the hands of an all-powerful monopoly. Ray Stannard Baker, in his dedicated pursuit of the human stories behind the Chicago labor conflicts, had developed a sympathetic attitude toward the workingman's struggles that set him apart from his father's laissez-faire views. Lincoln Steffens had absorbed radical social ideas during his intense interdisciplinary studies in Europe and would bring an open, inquisitive, analytic mind to his work as police reporter. Even William Allen White, despite a coddled, conservative upbringing, had begun to recognize injustices in the farming and freight industries that had crippled the regional economy and compromised a community he cared for deeply.

All four were extraordinary, independent thinkers. Tarbell defied the conventions of her gender, steadfastly refusing the path of marriage and braving poverty and alienation to pursue her ambitions as a writer. Baker, too, resisted the pressure of social and familial expectation, declining to make his father's business his own life's work. Steffens's difficulty in conforming to a normal course of study allowed him to develop the rigorous and comprehensive understanding of human nature that rendered networks of power transparent. White's passionate devotion to his state's progress may have assumed a pugnacious form in the blistering editorials that brought him into prominence, but that same devotion led him to a progressive metamorphosis as he came to see the neglected underside of the new industrial order.

Each of the four journalists was deeply influenced by a teacher. Both Tarbell and Baker had pursued studies in biology, learning investigative principles and procedures they would later apply to human society. Steffens had discovered the joy of working with original documents and the exhilarating freedom when one is allowed to question established authorities. White had found a mentor whose influence would continue to grow in the years ahead. All passionately believed, with S. S. McClure, that "a vigilant and well-informed press, setting forth the truth," could become "an infinitely greater guard to the people than any government officials." The new fusion of journalism, literature, exposé, and human interest that emerged in the pages of *McClure's* would turn the microscope on humanity, on the avarice and corruption that stunted the very possibility of social justice in America.

This revolutionary cadre of writers would soon play a vital role in Theodore Roosevelt's political future as well, helping to generate the critical mass of public sentiment to implement progressive policies. Though the *McClure's* team had not yet articulated a distinct progressive agenda, their novel, vivid, and fearless explorations of the American condition would sound a summons and quicken the Progressive movement.

CHAPTER EIGHT

"Like a Boy on Roller Skates"

Theodore Roosevelt at work in the Navy Department,
Harper's Weekly, May 7, 1898.

ON MAY 6, 1895, LINCOLN Steffens was relaxing with fellow reporters on the front steps of the newsmen's building across the street from police headquarters when a shout from veteran police reporter Jacob Riis heralded the story of the day. Theodore Roosevelt had been sworn in as police commissioner earlier that morning at City Hall. Accompanied by the three other board members, he was approaching his new headquarters at 300 Mulberry Street in the heart of Little Italy.

As the foursome came into view, Steffens noted that the new commissioner surged past the other gentlemen, "head forward, jaw set and looking straight and sharp out of his big round glasses." Roosevelt greeted Jacob Riis, a friend of several years, with exuberance. "Hello, Jake," he exclaimed, then continued to race up the stairs, signaling for all reporters to follow. "T.R. seized Riis, who introduced me," Steffens recalled, "and still running, he asked questions: 'Where are our offices? Where is the board room? What do we do first?' "

As agreed, the first order of business was to elect Roosevelt president of the four-man board (comprising two Republicans—Roosevelt and Frederick D. Grant, son of General Ulysses S. Grant—and two Democrats—West Pointer Avery D. Andrews and lawyer Andrew D. Parker). With this accomplished, Roosevelt pulled Riis and Steffens aside into his office. "It was all breathless and sudden," Steffens recalled in *The Autobiography*, "but Riis and I were soon describing the situation to him, telling him which higher officers to consult, which to ignore and punish; what the forms were, the customs, rules, methods. It was just as if we three were the police board."

Roosevelt could not have found two more valuable tutors than Jacob Riis and Lincoln Steffens. For nearly twenty years, Riis had covered police activities for the *New York Tribune* and the *Evening Sun*. An immigrant from Denmark, he had landed at Castle Garden the same year that the cosseted eleven-year-old Roosevelt docked in Manhattan after his family's Grand European Tour. For three years, Riis had scraped together a living doing everything from carpentry and peddling to hunting and trapping. Finally, he found an opportunity to pursue his "life-work" in journalism, initially serving for several years as a general reporter. At the age of twenty-eight, he was assigned to the police department, where he remained for most of his professional life. "Being the 'boss reporter' in Mulberry Street," Riis later wrote, was "the only renown I have ever coveted or cared to have." The years spent covering fires, murders, and robberies in the immigrant slums fostered a keen awareness of the devastating conditions confronting families in these tenement districts. "The sights I saw there," he recalled, "gripped my heart until I felt that I must tell of them, or burst, or turn anarchist, or something."

In newspaper exposés, Riis described overcrowded, unsanitary tenements with insufficient light and air, often the properties of absentee owners who neglected "repairs and necessary improvements." Riis had witnessed these conditions in the course of his daily work as a police reporter. Although he documented the same criminal incidents that fellow journalists covered, his perspective was unique. "Only Riis wrote them as stories, with heart, humor, and understanding," Steffens remarked, and "beautiful stories they were . . . for Riis could write." When he narrated a suicide, fire, or outbreak of disease, Jacob Riis took down every detail of the building or the city block where it occurred, relentlessly pursuing the negligent landlords, holding them responsible for the abhorrent conditions and threatening further stories until the problems were redressed. "Why," he asked, "should a man have a better right to kill his neighbor with a house than with an axe in the street?" "The remedy," he concluded, "must proceed from the public conscience."

How the Other Half Lives, Riis's first book, was published in 1890. This visceral account traced the daily struggles he witnessed in the Italian tenements, the Jewish quarters, and the Bohemian ghetto. Riis guided readers to fetid corners of the city they had never visited—to Mulberry Bend, Bandit's Roost, and Bottle Alley. The catchy title, Riis modestly acknowledged, had contributed to the book's phenomenal success. "Truly, I lay no claim to eloquence," he noted, "so it must have been the facts." Humility notwithstanding, readers were captured by the power and empathy of the writing. "I cannot conceive how such a book should fail of doing great good, if it moves other people as it has moved me," wrote the critic James Russell Lowell. "I found it hard to get asleep the night after I had been reading it."

Theodore Roosevelt had read *How the Other Half Lives* while he was civil service commissioner. Calling it "both an enlightenment and an inspiration," he was convinced the book would "go a long way toward removing the ignorance" of comfortable New Yorkers about the hardships confronting their less fortunate neighbors. Furthermore, he was hopeful that Riis's disclosures would help engender a new spirit of reform. Roosevelt found the tone of the writing particularly admirable, lauding the manner in which Riis revealed social ills without stridency, never descending into "hysterical" negativity or "sentimental excess."

When intrigued by the work of a writer or journalist, Roosevelt often endeavored to establish a personal connection; he called on Riis at the *Evening Sun*. Finding him out of the office, Roosevelt left a card, with a succinct message that he had read the book and "had come to help." Riis had long tracked Roosevelt's progress from his days as a young silk stocking legislator "exposing jobbery, fighting boss rule," and "rattling dry bones" disinterred from the city's closets. "I loved him from the day I first saw him," Riis later wrote. Over the course of Roosevelt's tenure as police commissioner, this affection and mutual respect would intensify until Roosevelt regarded Riis as "one of my truest and closest friends."

Roosevelt later recalled "two sides" of his role as police commissioner: first, the daily work of managing the police department; second, the opportunity to use his position, which also encompassed membership on the health board, to make "the city a better place in which to live and work for those to whom the conditions of life and labor were hardest." To comprehend the practical possibility for real change, Roosevelt relied on Jacob Riis. "He had the most flaming intensity of passion for righteousness," Roosevelt recalled.

Never a "mere preacher," he was among the few whose convictions proved a touchstone to action. In Riis, Roosevelt found a man "who looked at life and its problems from substantially the same standpoint" as he did: a moderate reformer seeking to rectify social ills through moral conviction and suasion.

☞ ☜

ROOSEVELT'S RELATIONSHIP WITH THE INTELLECTUAL Lincoln Steffens was more complex. They shared an irrepressible self-confidence, an immense curiosity, a driving ambition, and a sharp intelligence. Later, as Steffens entertained more radical ideas and began to question capitalism itself, Roosevelt lost patience with him. During the decade of Roosevelt's boggling ascent from commissioner to governor and then president, however, they enjoyed a rich friendship that benefited both men substantially. After only four months' acquaintance, Roosevelt gave Steffens an enthusiastic letter of recommendation. "He is a personal friend of mine; and he has seen all of our work at close quarters," Roosevelt assured Horace Scudder, the editor of the *Atlantic Monthly*. "He speaks at first hand as an expert."

While Steffens later acknowledged that he might have overstated his influence in claiming that he and Riis functioned as working members of Roosevelt's police board, he maintained that the statement had truly reflected his "state of mind." So willing was Roosevelt to bring the two journalists into his inner circle, so candid was he in admitting ignorance about his new job, that both men naturally assumed the aura of "wise" mentors to the newcomer.

Steffens had begun his job on the police beat with the simplistic belief that if good men replaced dishonest men at the top of the organization, corruption would be defeated. Only after two years—through numerous days spent with the crusading Dr. Parkhurst and months of coverage devoted to the sensational Lexow Committee hearings documenting the relationship between Tammany Hall and the police department—would Steffens fathom a vast entrenched system of police corruption that would not yield so easily to reform.

Steffens's initial interviews with Dr. Parkhurst began with a series of deceptively innocent questions, a technique that developed into his mode of operating. For what reason, when gambling enterprises and houses of prostitution were illegal, did the police officers of the law allow them to exist? Why were some saloons permitted to stay open beyond the designated hours while others were not? "With astonishment" Steffens learned that pervasive, systematic bribery allowed those businesses willing to pay Tammany Hall's substantial monthly charge to operate unmolested, while those who refused to furnish protection money were closed down.

New police recruits were forced to pay Tammany a fixed fee for their appointments. The fee was well beyond the means of most, but every officer understood he would make the money back with plenty to spare once inside the system. Policemen who secured the confidence of Tammany were promoted, though each advancement required hefty additional fees. "One police captain," Steffens told his father, "has confessed to having paid $15,000 for his promotion and said that, though he had to borrow the money," he was able to repay his debt within two years. With each higher rank a policeman attained, his percentage of the blackmail fund grew. Superintendent Tom Byrnes had amassed what was then a sizable fortune of $350,000, while his chief inspector, Alec "Clubber" Williams, could not explain the unusual size of his bank account when forced to testify before the Lexow Committee.

Observers would later credit Steffens's success as a journalist to his "supreme gift of making men tell—or try to tell—him the truth." He always seemed able to coax people to "explain themselves," even when their explanations implicated rather than vindicated them. After the Lexow Committee hearings, Steffens approached Captain Max Schmittberger, a pivotal witness who had made "a clean breast" of everything. As the two men became friends, Schmittberger explained how, as an "honest" young policeman, he had been drawn into "the whole rotten business." The substance of these long conversations would prove most instructive when Steffens later recounted them with Roosevelt. Immersed so gradually in the venality of the department, Schmittberger never realized the shamelessness of his actions until the Lexow Committee called upon him to testify. After many hours with Schmittberger, Steffens concluded that he was "on the square," a decent man entangled in a crooked system. He persuaded Roosevelt to keep him on the force, a decision resulting in both a trusted ally and an insider who could teach the new commissioner things he could never have learned alone.

Joseph Bishop, the *Evening Post*'s editorial writer to whom Steffens had initially carried his letter of introduction, noted that Roosevelt opened the battle for reform wielding the same weapons he had used in his previous fights against corruption: "full publicity, strict enforcement of the law, and utter disregard of partisan political considerations." Like Steffens, Bishop was "in almost daily confidential conference" with Roosevelt during his tenure as police commissioner. "There began between him and myself," Bishop recalled a quarter century later, "a close personal friendship which continued unbroken throughout his career, growing steadily in mutual confidence and affection with time."

At his first press conference, Roosevelt announced that henceforth appointments and promotions would be made on merit alone: "No political influence could save a man who deserved punishment and none could win an unworthy promotion." The police force had heard such rhetoric before, but they soon began to realize the unique weight of Roosevelt's pledge. Within three weeks of his swearing-in, he summoned Superintendent Byrnes and Inspector Williams to his office and forced them to resign. These stunning departures broadcast clearly that the reform police board "would spare no man" in its campaign to root out corruption.

Genuine reform, however, hinged upon the patrolmen on the beat. Riis suggested that Roosevelt accompany him on a series of unannounced inspections between midnight and sunrise to determine whether the officers on the beat were faithfully safeguarding their designated posts. Concealing his evening clothes beneath a long coat and donning a floppy hat to obscure his face, Roosevelt set out with Riis at 2 a.m. from the steps of the Union League Club. Over the next three to four hours, they would follow a route mapped out in advance by the veteran reporter to encompass a dozen police patrol areas. If he found an officer dutifully patrolling his beat, Roosevelt patted him on the back; but those whom he discovered sleeping or enjoying a meal at an all-night restaurant were summoned to appear before him as soon as the department opened that morning. One startled policeman was chatting with a prostitute when Roosevelt confronted him and asked him to account for himself. Not recognizing the commissioner of the New York City Police, the officer belligerently replied: "What's that to you? Shall I fan him, Mame?" The woman nodded in agreement. "Sure, fan him to death."

The police reporters all attended the morning roundup when the delinquent men appeared before the commissioner. "A sorrier-looking set of men never came to police headquarters," Steffens reported in the *Evening Post*. The New York *Sun* provided details of the new commissioner's midnight forays with the dramatic headline: "Roosevelt on Patrol: He Makes Night Hideous for Sleepy Policemen." Under Bishop's guidance, the editorial page praised the "patrolman hunt" as "the beginning of a new epoch." Roosevelt continued his surprise inspections on subsequent nights with different companions, including Steffens, the celebrated reporter Richard Harding Davis, and the novelist Hamlin Garland.

These predawn missions attracted press attention across the country. "Police Commissioner Roosevelt finds that he can secure more information in one night," observed the *San Antonio Daily Light*, "than he would in a year in broad daylight." As tales of his unorthodox maneuvers spread, Roosevelt became an alluring subject for cartoonists, spawning caricatures of startled policemen cowering at the sight of an enormous set of teeth and round, metal-rimmed eyeglasses. "A pair of gold-mounted spectacles is a mark of authority more to be feared in police circles," one reporter quipped, "than the biggest badge that ever glittered on a uniformed coat." Roosevelt relished seeing his caricature. "Few men," he remarked, "live to see their own hieroglyph."

"These midnight rambles are great fun," Roosevelt admitted to Bamie, "though each meant my going forty hours at a stretch without any sleep." Riis and Steffens guided him through sections of the city he had never explored. "It is one thing to listen in perfunctory fashion to tales of overcrowded tenements," Roosevelt conceded, "and it is quite another actually to see what that overcrowding means, some hot summer night, by even a single inspection during the hours of darkness." Progress was slow, but with the attention Roosevelt helped focus on conditions in the most abject neighborhoods, the city eventually "tore down unfit tenements, forced the opening of parks and playgrounds."

Conversations with Riis and Steffens convinced Roosevelt that the only way to pry out what Riis described as "the tap-root" of corruption in the police force was through strict enforcement of the law requiring that saloons be closed on Sundays. Passed by the state legislature nearly four decades earlier to satisfy rural constituents, the Sunday law had warped into a massive vehicle of police and political blackmail. In more than 10,000 saloons operating in the city, owners and managers understood that so long as they continued to make monthly payments to the police and politicians, they were free to flout the statute on the Lord's Day, often the most lucrative day of the week. If they refused or fell out of favor with Tammany, they were promptly shut down and arrested for violating the law.

Roosevelt fully anticipated the political fallout of rigorously enforcing a law both unpopular and immensely lucrative. "The corrupt would never forgive him," remarked Steffens, "and the great mass of the people would not understand." For the workingmen of the city, the saloon was a place to drink with friends, play cards, and shoot pool on their only day off. Roosevelt sympathized with the statute's critics, allowing that it "is altogether too strict." Until the legislature changed the law, however, he was responsible for enforcing it fairly and squarely. Still, he deliberated long and hard before taking action. "Is there any other way," he implored Steffens and Riis, "to do the work I was sent here to do?" Assured that no alternative existed, he resolutely targeted June 23, 1895, to commence a new policy of regulation that would harbor "no protected class."

Each Sunday proved dryer than the one before. By the third Sunday in

August, Roosevelt and Riis combed the city and discovered more than 95 percent of the saloons shut down. Those that took the risk of remaining open operated "to a most limited extent," with no money changing hands for the privilege. "The tap-root" of corruption had been extracted. "The police force became an army of heroes," Riis noted, at least "for a season."

As expected, Roosevelt's uncompromising enforcement policy drew forth violent resentment. "I have never been engaged in a more savage fight," Roosevelt told Lodge. Vitriolic telegrams flooded his office: "You are the biggest fool that ever lived"; "What an ass you have made of yourself"; "You have wrecked the Republican Party." Reports surfaced that a box containing dynamite had been sent to the commissioner's office. Though it proved a hoax, "the next bomb," warned the *World*, "will be deposited in the ballot-box in November and be loaded with popular indignation at his uncalled-for, unjust, discriminating, oppressive and superlatively foolish execution of the Sunday excise law." Rumors circulated that both the Republican bosses and Mayor Strong were dissatisfied with the new commissioner. "Roosevelt is like a boy with his first pair of skates," one prominent Republican boss lamented, "and the Republican Party is sure to be held responsible for what he does."

"This was a fight after Roosevelt's own heart," remarked Joseph Bishop. When he received a mocking invitation to what promised to be a massive parade protesting his policy, the commissioner astounded the organizers by accepting. Along the parade route more than 150,000 cheering people were gathered, standing "in windows, on steps and poles and wagons, and even lampposts. . . . There were gilded floats, decorated and peopled in a manner most pleasing to the eye," reported the *World*, "and long lines of men in shining uniforms and all the glitter and splendor of mounted paraders." As more than 30,000 marchers paraded along Lexington Avenue, there was Roosevelt, the signal object of derision, smiling and waving for hours from the reviewing stand.

The commissioner "laughed louder than any one else" as the scathing banners and placards came into view: "Send the Police Czar to Russia"; "Rooseveltism is a farce and a humbug." Sighting one banner emblazoned with the words: "Roosevelt's Razzle Dazzle Reform Racket," he asked the bearer if he could keep the banner as a souvenir. "Certainly," replied the man. "That is the best yet," Roosevelt chuckled, pointing to a wagon entitled "The Millionaire's Club." The float sported three gentlemen in frock coats and tall hats, with one bearing "a striking resemblance to Theodore Roosevelt." The trio sipped champagne at a "private club," while at the rear of the wagon a mock arrest of a beer-drinking laborer was staged. "That is really a good stroke," Roosevelt burst forth with admiration.

Even the New York *World*, which had been "shrieking with rage" against Roosevelt, conceded that the crowd was delighted by his appearance: "It looked almost as if the whole affair were in his honor, and the long lines to whom he bowed, took off their hats in salute." All along the way, marchers shouted, "Bully for Teddy!" and "Teddy, you're a man!" His ability to turn the tables, to relish his protracted self-mockery in public, was compressed into the headline of a Chicago newspaper: "Cheered by Those Who Came to Jeer."

Good feelings soon faded, however, when Roosevelt announced that, despite his thorough enjoyment of the festivities, "a hundred parades . . . would not make me change the position I have taken." As the November 1895 elections approached, Roosevelt feared that his unpopular stance on the Sunday closing law might usher in a revival of Tammany. The Republican bosses "are on the verge of open war with me," Roosevelt told Lodge, adding that Mayor Strong "has actually been endeavoring to make me let up on the saloon, and impliedly threatened to try to turn me out if I refused! It is needless to say that I told him I would not let up one particle; and would not resign either." The city elections confirmed Roosevelt's worst misgivings. The Tammany slate routed the Republican slate, and the Republican bosses placed the blame squarely on Roosevelt's uncompromising policy. Rumblings from the state legislature in Albany suggested machinations afoot to sweep him out of his job.

Open dissension in the bipartisan police board multiplied Roosevelt's woes. "Thinks he's the whole board," grumbled Democrat Andrew Parker. "He talks, talks, talks, all the time," Parker complained to the *Evening Post*'s Joseph Bishop: "Scarcely a day passes that there is not something from him in the papers about what he is doing . . . and the public is getting tired of it. It injures our work." In defense of his friend, Bishop replied, "Stop Roosevelt talking? Why you would kill him. He has to talk. The peculiarity about him is that he has what is essentially a boy's mind. . . . I don't know as he will ever outgrow it. But with it he has great qualities . . . inflexible honesty, absolute fearlessness and devotion to good government." Parker "said nothing further," Bishop recalled, "and we parted rather coldly." Parker's hostility toward Roosevelt eventually congealed into hatred, and the structure of the bipartisan board allowed him to paralyze Roosevelt's further ambitions for reform. Not surprisingly, the newspapers delighted in the running feud, likening the battle between Roosevelt and Parker to "armed combat."

During these trying days, Roosevelt's growing family provided indispens able respite. "His wife and children gave him," one friend observed, "a kind of spiritual bath that sent him back to the city refreshed and ready for what might come." Roosevelt spent two or three nights in town at Bamie's pied-à-terre on Madison Avenue, but during the rest of the week he commuted by bicycle and train from the loving home Edith had created at Sagamore Hill. Their five children, now ranging in age from eleven to two, inhabited a world far removed from the intrigue and animosity of his public career. "Their gay doings, their odd sayings," one family friend, Hermann Hagedorn, remarked, "cleansed him of the smoke and the grime of the battle."

When forty-year-old Bamie stunned the family by announcing her engagement and marriage to naval officer William S. Cowles, Theodore and Edith rented her Madison Avenue apartment for the winter months. While Edith preferred the domestic seclusion of Sagamore Hill, city life allowed her to provide the children with wider social and cultural opportunities, including lessons at Mr. Dodsworth's, the dance school she had adored as a young girl.

Despite the restorative presence of his family, Roosevelt seemed "overstrained & overwrought" to Lodge, who confided in Bamie that Theodore's "wonderful spring and interest in all sorts of things is much lowered. He is not depressed but he is fearfully overworked & insists on writing history & doing all sorts of things he has no need to do. He has that morbid idée fixe that he cannot leave his work for a moment else the world should stop."

The 1896 presidential contest between McKinley and Bryan provided a welcome outlet, allowing Roosevelt to leave behind his multitude of problems in the city, traveling through the state and country to stump for the Republican nominee. While he had passionately hoped that his friend Speaker Tom Reed would be the candidate, he campaigned vigorously for the Republican ticket. He retained serious reservations about McKinley, whom he considered to have "a chocolate éclair backbone," but convinced himself that the Republican fight against the Democrats was crucial for the soul of America. If victory came to Bryan and the mob of populists and socialists "who want to strike down the well-to-do, and who have been inflamed against the rich," the United States would face "years of social misery, not markedly different from that of any South American Republic."

Beyond his overwrought dread of a Democratic triumph, Roosevelt also determined that lending his energetic voice to McKinley's campaign represented his best hope for regaining the confidence of the Republican bosses. He spoke before huge audiences everywhere he went. "The halls were jammed," he reported to Bamie, "people standing in masses in the aisles." His adventures in New York, captured in stories, headlines, and cartoons across the nation, had made him a compelling, national figure. Roosevelt capitalized on this interest and his efforts did not go unrecognized. "He gave all of his time, all of his energy, and all of his towering ability to the work of the campaign," recalled Republican National Committee member Albert B. Cummins.

McKinley's victory resulted in Roosevelt's appointment as assistant secretary of the Navy, providing a graceful exit from his mounting troubles as police commissioner. His departure left both Riis and Steffens downcast. Indeed, Jacob Riis considered the two years he spent with Roosevelt on Mulberry Street "the happiest by far" of his entire career. "Then was life really worth living," he recalled, confessing that once Roosevelt departed, he "had no heart in it." Beyond his personal despondency, Steffens for his part feared that "reform was beaten." And in short order, "Tammany did come back."

Still, the impact of Roosevelt's vigorous tenure would not be forgotten. "The end of the reign of Mr. Roosevelt is not the end of Rooseveltism," Steffens wrote in the *Evening Post*, predicting that his impress would exert "an active influence in the force for a generation at least, till the youngest 'reform cop' is retired." Even after Roosevelt became a national hero during the Spanish-American War and was elected governor of New York, Steffens deemed his controversial reign as police commissioner "the proudest single achievement of his life," insisting that no other challenge "called for so much courage, energy, labor or brain and will power." Steffens would also leave Mulberry Street in short order to serve as editor of New York's oldest newspaper, the *Commercial Advertiser*, yet the relationship established with Roosevelt would flourish in the years ahead.

Just as Roosevelt's three years in the New York Assembly had taught him to work with colleagues far removed from his cloistered patrician background, so his two years as police commissioner in New York City had deepened and broadened his outlook on social and economic issues. Jacob Riis had introduced him to the realities of immigrant life in the slums, though Roosevelt found it hard to relinquish his conception of the poor as people who had "failed in life." He had walked through ill-ventilated, dilapidated tenements where wealthy landlords used every legal device to evade regulation and responsibility. Observing this widespread failure to rectify conditions, Roosevelt recalled, "I became more set than ever in my distrust of those men, whether business men or lawyers, judges, legislators, or executive officers, who seek to make of the Constitution a fetish for the prevention of the work of social reform."

The mentoring of Riis and Steffens and the intimate exposure to the hardships confronting the city's poor had begun to work a marked change in Roosevelt, loosening the "steel chain" of conservative opposition to government intervention in the economic and social processes that had been his birthright.

⌒ ⌒

THE FRENETIC PACE AND STRESS of Roosevelt's years as New York police commissioner stand in perfect counterpoint to William Howard Taft's ruminative, congenial eight-year-tenure on the circuit court. Two decades later, Nellie would reflect that Taft savored his work on the federal bench "more than any he has ever undertaken," more than his years as governor general of the Philippines, secretary of war, or president. "Perhaps it is the comfort and dignity and power without worry I like," Taft told his brother Horace.

Life on the circuit ideally suited a man of Taft's gregarious temperament. Traveling to Cleveland, Toledo, Memphis, Nashville, Detroit, and Louisville, he quickly made friends in every city that comprised the Sixth District. Though he missed Nellie and the children when he was away from Cincinnati, he delighted in the camaraderie of the circuit. His daily letters home describe a continuous round of banquets and receptions hosted by leading members of the bar, as well as invitations to private clubs. "I have been in court every day from nine until five o'clock and I have been out every night to dine and have not tumbled into bed any night before twelve o'clock," he wrote to Nellie from the Russell House in Detroit, concluding, "I have had no trouble with sleeping except for want of time." In Memphis, he described a ball at the Tennessee Club, a meeting of the Shakespearean circle, and a banquet he attended. "The Bar here is said to be the finest in the circuit," he told Nellie. "Certainly it is a most delightful body of men." He was equally enchanted by three evenings at the palatial Lake Shore home of the Cleveland industrialist Mark Hanna. "They have eight bedrooms besides those required for his family," he explained to his wife, "and he gives house parties lasting a week when he has twenty or twenty five guests at a time."

In these most agreeable settings, Taft was totally at ease, sharing stories, drinks, and conversation. While Roosevelt's indomitable, often contentious nature stirred discord with colleagues at both the Civil Service Commission and the police board, Taft enjoyed warm professional relationships from the outset, bonding effortlessly with his fellow circuit justices, William R. Day and Horace H. Lurton, both of whom would eventually sit on the Supreme Court—the former appointed by Roosevelt, the latter by Taft himself.

No one on the circuit was more widely respected or better loved than Taft. "He is absolutely the fairest judge I have ever seen on the bench," a fellow attorney remarked. Countless stories circulated of his kind and even-handed actions in the courtroom. When a prosecuting attorney persistently hectored a witness who had already disclosed his shame of being illiterate, Taft brought a quick end to the attorney's line of questioning: "Stop that!" he admonished. "You have brought out that this man cannot read; that is enough. I will not have you humiliate this witness any further, because it has no relation to the case." In another incident, an inexperienced lawyer had filed a badly drawn petition on behalf of a young girl whose foot had been severed in a railroad accident; Taft edited the document himself, knowing that otherwise the railroad attorney would easily secure a dismissal of the case.

The work itself was intellectually challenging, requiring him to reach decisions and write opinions on far-reaching issues regarding labor strikes, injunctions, workplace injuries, street railways, and monopolies. He was allowed the time necessary to study cases thoroughly, reviewing precedents and refining his positions. Most important, he was able to draft, revise, and edit his decisions "over again and again" until he had honed the language to his satisfaction. His opinions earned the admiration of lawyers across the nation, building a reputation that bolstered his dream of one day sitting on the Supreme Court.

Presiding on the bench through the turbulent 1890s, Taft was called upon to adjudicate a number of highly controversial cases that shadowed the rest of his career. The most noteworthy, *In re Phelan*, had boiled over from the 1894 Pullman strike. While the strike stirred turmoil in Chicago, Frank Phelan, an authorized representative of Eugene Debs, arrived in Cincinnati to organize railway employees in Ohio and Kentucky for a general boycott of all Pullman trains. With the Cincinnati Southern Railroad nearly paralyzed by the boycott, the company's manager successfully petitioned the court for an injunction, enjoining Phelan from inciting workers—who themselves had no grievance against the Pullman Company—to join a strike preventing the flow of interstate traffic. When Phelan defied the injunction and union members continued to stop trains, Taft issued a warrant for his arrest.

Taft told Nellie, who had taken the children to Canada for that summer of 1894, that the case worried him more than any other. Each day, newspapers carried sensationalized accounts of the tumult in Chicago, claiming that mobs were "holding that city by the throat." Like Roosevelt, Taft feared that demagogic leaders had resolved "to provoke a civil war" and that some of the agitators would have to be killed "to make an impression." Dozens of marshals were posted throughout Cincinnati in anticipation of similar violence. When news broke of Phelan's arrest, Taft received death threats. His decision was loudly denounced at raucous meetings held throughout the city, and his courtroom was ominously crowded with strikers. "I hate the publicity that this brings me into," he complained to Nellie, explaining that his days were occupied "trying to say nothing to reporters."

The mayor of Cincinnati and the chief of police tried to persuade Taft to draw out the trial until the tumult and bloodletting in Chicago had subsided, but with Phelan under arrest and his sympathizers packing the court "to suffocation," Taft's sense of duty obliged him to move the case forward. After hearing the arguments on both sides, he spent two long nights writing his opinion, just managing, he told Nellie, to have "the last sentence copied when twelve oclock struck, the time fixed for its announcement." Attired in the silk judicial robe he donned for important occasions, Taft took almost an hour to read out his long opinion.

At the core of his argument lay the same distinction he had drawn in *Moore's & Co. v. Bricklayers' Union* between a legal strike and an illegal secondary boycott. He began by emphasizing that the employees of the railroad "had the right to organize into or to join a labor union which should take joint action as to their terms of employment." With strong language, he clearly delineated the vital role of unions in industrial society: "It is of benefit to them and to the public that laborers should unite in their common interest and for lawful purposes," Taft began, further explaining that "if they stand together, they are often able, all of them, to command better prices for their labor than when dealing singly with rich employers. . . . The accumulation of a fund for the support of those who feel that the wages offered are below market prices is one of the legitimate objects of such an organization." Furthermore, Taft recognized the legitimacy of union leadership and their right to maintain solidarity. He explained that officers of a union might order members "on pain of expulsion from their union, peaceably to leave the employ of their employer because any of the terms of their employment are unsatisfactory."

Had Phelan arrived in Cincinnati to protest a wage cut by the Cincinnati Southern and "urged a peaceable strike," Taft maintained, "the loss to the [railroad] would not be ground for recovering damages, and Phelan would not have been liable to contempt even if the strike much impeded the operation of the road." In this case, however, "the employees of the railway companies had no grievance against their employers." Nor did they have cause to obstruct the Pullman Company, which had nothing to do with their compensation or working conditions. Phelan, therefore, had conspired to bring about an illegal boycott. Taft found him guilty and sentenced him to six months in jail.

Lost in the ensuing uproar, Taft's clear and forceful defense of labor's right to strike was perhaps the most definitive pronouncement on the subject to that date. Nine years later, when the Wabash Railroad issued an injunction against the striking Brotherhood of Railroad Trainmen and Firemen, the labor union relied on Taft's statement on labor rights to dissolve the injunction and win their case.

Yet Taft's failure to explicate his decision more fully to reporters and his refusal to court public opinion left him vulnerable to charges of an anti-union bias. As police commissioner, Theodore Roosevelt had faced similar accusations from labor leaders following repeated arrests of union picketers involved in violent scuffles with employers and scabs. Unlike Taft, however, Roosevelt had responded with aplomb, realizing that such charges must not go unanswered. At the suggestion of Jacob Riis, Roosevelt had invited union leaders to meet at a beer hall and speak to him, not "as Police Commissioner, but just as plain 'me.' " During a three-hour exchange of views, Roosevelt had insisted that no genuine friend of labor could condone violence. When the marathon session came to a close, the union audience "applauded him to the echo."

While Taft lacked Roosevelt's political savvy and press connections, his advocacy for the workingman and desire for an even-handed policy in a rapidly industrializing nation made his nascent progressivism increasingly evident. Following the Phelan controversy, two additional railroad cases demonstrated Taft's support for the cause of labor. The swift expansion of railroads in the last quarter of the nineteenth century had generated a shocking increase in accidents causing death or severe physical harm to industrial workers. Statistics revealed that annually "one railroad worker in every three hundred was killed on the job," while one out of fifty American laborers sustained an injury. In an era when courts consistently favored property rights over individual rights, railroad employees found it nearly impossible to recover damages. Under the doctrine of assumed risk, railroad attorneys successfully argued that employees assumed all risk of injury, even if railroad negligence was involved. In some cases, railroads demanded that employees sign formal contracts releasing the company from liability in the event of injury or death.

In the case of *Voight v. Baltimore*, Taft held the Baltimore Railroad liable for permanent injuries to a worker. Although the man had signed a contract agreeing to hold the railroad harmless, Taft held that this document did not divest the company of responsibility to employees in the case of negligence. The conservative Supreme Court reversed Taft's ruling, citing the sanctity of contract, but he would later be vindicated when in 1908 President Theodore Roosevelt signed a law specifically outlawing such oppressive contracts.

Taft further challenged the doctrine of assumed risk in the *Narramore* case. A recently passed Ohio law required railroads to install safety devices that would protect workers from getting caught in guard rails and frogs—switch mechanisms that allowed a train to cross from one track to another. One brakeman was working on the tracks when his foot became stuck in an unsecured frog. Unable to escape as the train approached, he suffered horrific injuries, including the loss of one leg. The federal district court heard his case, but refused damages on grounds that Narramore had assumed the risk when he continued to work despite his knowledge that the frogs lacked safety devices. Taft reversed the lower court decision, arguing that any safety law would be "a dead letter" if companies were permitted to defend themselves in this way. In the years ahead, injured employees successfully cited Taft's ruling, allowing them to receive damages when the hazards of their employment resulted from a corporation's failure to meet safety regulations.

Of William Taft's hundreds of rulings in the 1890s, the most consequential involved an anti-trust suit against the Addyston Steel and Pipe Company, which had joined with five other cast-iron pipe manufacturers to fix prices under a contract of association. Since the 1890 passage of the Sherman Anti-Trust Act, corporations had openly defied the law's restrictions against combinations in restraint of trade. Anti-trust suits brought in pro-business state courts were invariably lost, and monopolies continued to grow. In the 1895 *Knight* case, the Supreme Court delivered what seemed a death knell to the Sherman Act, refusing to break up a sugar company that controlled 98 percent of the country's sugar refineries.

When Taft received the government's case against the Addyston Company combination on appeal in 1898, it was widely assumed that he would follow the lower court's ruling and dismiss the suit. Instead, he held that the association was indeed an attempted monopoly designed "to give the defendants power to charge unreasonable prices." Taft's order for the association's dissolution made national news, emboldening those who fought to stay the growth of colossal combinations. The *New York Times* headlined the importance of the decision: "Iron Pipe Trust Illegal: The First Case in Which Manufacturing Combination Had Been Found Guilty." Enumerating the facts of the pipe case, the New York *World* suggested that "precisely the same things are true of hundreds of other trusts, and they can be smashed if the people's attorneys and the courts will do their duty." Still, there was little concerted action against monopolies until 1902, when President Roosevelt brought suit against the Northern Securities Company, a giant holding company combining three railroads in an attempt to control rail prices throughout the Northwest. Roosevelt's suit relied, in part, on Taft's opinion in the *Addyston Pipe* case.

These were productive, invigorating years for William Taft, who also agreed to serve as dean of the new Cincinnati Law School, where he was teaching two courses. "The deanship is going to involve considerable work," he told Nellie, "but I think I can systematize it." He was elected president of the Cincinnati Civil Service Reform Association and was overjoyed to be made a trustee of Yale College, where he regularly presided over reunions with his fellow Bonesmen. Indeed, the only drawback of his burgeoning reputation was the increasing number of invitations to deliver speeches at banquets and meetings.

"I wish I could make a good speech," he confided to Nellie before a banquet in Memphis, "but I fear it must be desultory and haphazard." Another disappointing performance in Grand Rapids, he confessed with chagrin, had left "a bad taste in my mouth but I am used to that." Nellie tried to buoy his confidence, reminding him that whenever he spent time in preparation, he invariably found "something to say that is worthwhile." When he agreed to address the annual meeting of the American Bar Association in Detroit at the end of August 1895, he promised Nellie that he would work on the speech for an hour every day and would submit drafts to her throughout the summer. "I shall use you as my merciless but loving critic," he assured her. Still, when he saw "the prominent names" of the other speakers, including Supreme Court justice David Brewer and Harvard professor James Thayer, it made him "tremble lest I shall make a fizzle of mine."

That same summer, Horace spent a month with his brother at Murray Bay in Canada, where Will and Nellie had expanded a small cottage into "a happy summer home." The little resort village of Murray Bay, situated on the St. Lawrence River one hundred miles north of Quebec, had become a gathering place for the entire Taft clan. In the early days, Charles Taft recalled, the "whole cargo of Tafts," twenty-one in all, shared a six-room house, with thin partitions dividing the rooms. Eventually each of the brothers had purchased or rented cottages of their own, all within easy walking distance of one another, the golf course, the tennis courts, the river, the hills, and the small village.

Horace recalled that although Taft's weight had ballooned by 1895 to 280 pounds, he maintained a preposterous schedule with unflagging vitality: "He played eighteen holes on a very hilly golf course in the morning, came home, ate his lunch, read his mail, and then went down to a tennis court, where he played a rather elephantine game," after which he went rowing on the river until it was time for a picnic supper. One night, Horace found Howard Hollister, Will's old friend, stretched out on the sofa. Asked about plans for the next day, Hollister laughingly replied, "The Lord knows. I doubt whether I shall live till tomorrow. I have been following Bill around today." Provided his weight did not become so onerous as to impede his activities, Taft was able to jest about it. Horace remembered sitting with Harry and Will in an overcrowded theatre with narrow seats. "Horace," Will said, "if this theater burns, it has got to burn around me."

During these years, Nellie Taft, originally reluctant to leave Washington, had immersed herself in the civic life of Cincinnati. She instituted a current events salon where she and her friends studied the administration's Hawaiian policy and the Chinese exclusion question, reading congressional debates and legal briefs. She attended the theatre regularly, took music lessons, and published an essay on Schumann. She also resumed her leadership role in promoting access to early education for the city's children, an advocacy that resulted in the kindergarten movement.

Despite her eclectic pastimes, Nellie found time to undertake the enormous project of founding the Cincinnati Symphony Orchestra, which gave its first concert series in 1895, with nationally recognized Frank Van der Stucken conducting. Previous orchestral associations had failed, but with the permanent dedication of a new Music Hall, Nellie was determined to create a symphony orchestra to rival those in Boston and New York. As president of the Orchestral Association, she raised funds, organized committees to sell subscriptions and advertising space, and negotiated contracts for the conductor and musicians, working with their labor union to protect local musicians against foreign imports. She even managed to persuade the major railroads to offer reduced rates for out-of-town passengers attending concert performances and inaugurated a series of free summer concerts.

Taft was immensely proud of Nellie's work with the orchestra. He kept up with every detail, encouraging her through difficult days and exulting at her great success. "My love for you, Dear, grows each year," he remarked. "This is not the enthusiasm of the wedding journey but it is the truth deliberately arrived at after full opportunity for me to know." He ardently defended Nellie when her mother charged that she fancied herself "the new woman," citing her unseemly public pursuits and the fact that she had borne but two children (though a third, named after Taft's brother Charley, would be born in 1897). Yet, in some ways, Nellie Taft did represent the new woman. She continued to frequent German beer halls, enjoyed smoking, played cards for money, followed the Cincinnati Reds baseball team, and was among the first in her hometown to wear a short skirt. "It is so delightful that I shall live in it," she told Will. "It makes me feel very young and frisky to be so unencumbered." Her manner may have seemed unorthodox to some, but the mutual affection and admiration she shared with her husband allowed her to pursue diverse interests even as she raised healthy, intelligent, confident children.

During his fruitful years on the bench, Taft's friendship with Roosevelt continued to grow. While still civil service commissioner, Roosevelt visited Cincinnati to deliver a lecture and attend a dinner at the St. Nicholas Hotel in honor of their mutual friend Bellamy Storer. During his stay, Roosevelt collaborated with Taft to create the Civil Service Reform Club in Cincinnati, to which Taft was elected president. In the years that followed, Taft worked hard to nominate and elect candidates committed to reform. The two men also met in Washington and New York for lunches, dinners, and long conversations about advancing their reform cause. On one trip to New York, Taft was disappointed when a previous engagement prevented him from dining with Roosevelt. "I should have much preferred to go to the R's," he wrote to Nellie, "because I wanted to have a full political talk with R."

The vision of reform shared by Roosevelt and Taft was still far removed from the Populists' call for fundamental economic change. Yet their experiences as police commissioner and circuit judge had awakened both to the harsh circumstances confronting the nation's working poor and sensitized them to the avarice and power of industrial interests. As social and economic issues increasingly consumed each man's attention, both were beginning to question the laissez-faire doctrine that had guided them since their days in college.

Neither Roosevelt nor Taft could have anticipated that an insurgent rebellion against Spanish rule on the small island of Cuba would soon redirect their energies, and alter both their destinies.

⌒ ⌒

THE POST OF ASSISTANT SECRETARY of the Navy proved difficult to secure for Theodore Roosevelt. Taft and Lodge lobbied intensely for his appointment and were joined in their campaign by Maria Storer, a prominent Washington socialite whose husband, Bellamy, had contributed $10,000 to a private fund so that McKinley could retire his debts. The new president was hesitant to appoint the young New Yorker. "I want peace," he told Maria Storer, "and I am told that your friend Theodore—whom I know only slightly—is always getting into rows with everybody. I am afraid he is too pugnacious." When Taft pressed Theodore's case, McKinley remained unconvinced. "The truth is, Will, Roosevelt is always in such a state of mind," he replied. Roosevelt's friends refused to give up. "Judge Taft, one of the best fellows going, plunged in last week," Lodge reported to Roosevelt. He enlisted the help of both John Addison Porter, his fellow Bonesman at Yale, who would soon become the president's secretary, and Myron T. Herrick, one of the president-elect's clos-est Ohio friends. "Give him a chance to prove that he can be peaceful," Maria Storer begged. McKinley finally relented, though Taft later speculated that "more than once, when [Roosevelt] was joining with those who demanded war with Spain and almost attacking the Administration for not declaring it, I think McKinley wished he had been anywhere else than where he was."

Even before assuming his post in the Navy Department, Roosevelt had insisted that he "would rather welcome a foreign war." He feared that Ameri-cans had lost their "soldierly virtues" in the race for material gain and were becoming "slothful, timid," and sedentary. "The victories of peace are great; but the victories of war are greater," he maintained. "No merchant, no banker, no railroad magnate, no inventor of improved industrial processes, can do for any nation what can be done for it by its great fighting men." While McKinley, who had "seen the dead piled up" at Antietam, prayed for peace, Roosevelt, who had never seen combat, absurdly romanticized war. "Every man who has in him any real power of joy in battle," he blithely wrote, "knows that he feels it when the wolf begins to rise in his heart; he does not shrink from blood and sweat, or deem that they mar the fight; he revels in them, in the toil, the pain and the danger, as but setting off the triumph." No sooner had Roosevelt settled into his office in the Navy Department than he "became convinced" that war with Spain over Cuba was imminent.

For more than two years, Cuban freedom fighters had engaged in a guer-rilla war against their Spanish occupiers. Spanish authorities had retaliated by imposing martial law throughout the island, incarcerating nearly a third of the Cuban population in unsanitary concentration camps without sufficient food, water, or medical treatment. Led by William Randolph Hearst and Joseph Pulitzer, yellow journals carried daily, often exaggerated reports of Spanish treachery that aroused humanitarian outrage. These concerns combined with economic interests in the island to fuel jingoist sentiment in favor of interven-tion. In November 1897, Roosevelt confided to a friend that he recommended going to war with Spain "on the ground of both humanity and self-interest," also citing "the benefit done to our people by giving them something to think of which isn't material gain."

Working under the elderly Navy secretary, John Davis Long, Roosevelt did everything in his power to prepare the U.S. Navy for war. During the long summer months when his boss vacationed in New England, Roosevelt exercised a "free hand" to purchase guns, ammunition, and supplies. He gen-erated war plans, scheduled additional gunnery drills, stocked distant supply stations with coal, consulted Captain Alfred Mahan about the need for new battleships, and succeeded in having Admiral George Dewey placed in command of the Asiatic Fleet. "I am having immense fun running the Navy," he boasted to Bellamy Storer.

Henry Pringle notes that "it is not easy to draw a line between Roosevelt's anxiety to build up the navy, which was legitimate preparedness, and his lust for war." In a comical stream of letters, Roosevelt repeatedly urged Secretary Long to prolong his vacation. "There isn't the slightest necessity of your returning," he told Long on June 22, 1897. "Nothing of importance has arisen." More obviously solicitous a fortnight later, he wrote again: "You must be tired, and you ought to have an entire rest." Three weeks later, he recommended that Long "stay there just exactly as long as you want to. There isn't any reason you should be here before the 1st of October." If Long had any thought of ending his vacation, Roosevelt reminded him that he was fortunate to avoid Washington and the hottest summer in memory.

In January 1898, McKinley agreed to station the battleship USS *Maine* in Havana Harbor as "an act of friendly courtesy" to the Cuban people. Steadfastly, however, he continued to resist mounting pressure for intervention. Then, on February 15, the *Maine* exploded, killing 262 Americans. Though the cause of the explosion was never determined with certainty, Roosevelt immediately labeled the sinking "an act of dirty treachery on the part of the Spaniards," declaring that as prelude to war, he "would give anything if President McKinley would order the fleet to Havana tomorrow."

꩜ ꩜

THE VERY MORNING AFTER THE explosion of the *Maine* in Havana Harbor, Ida Tarbell was scheduled to meet with Army chief General Nelson Miles, the subject of a planned *McClure's* article. Upon hearing the news, she assumed her appointment would be canceled. "It seemed as if the very air of Washington stood still," she recalled. But when she arrived at his office, she was surprised to find that "the routine went on as usual." She would long admire "the steadiness of General Miles" during those troublesome hours, as orderlies periodically interrupted their interview to deliver updated casualty reports.

In the weeks that followed, Tarbell "vacillated between hope that the President would succeed in preventing a war and fear that the savage cries coming from the Hill would be too much for him." While Roosevelt derided McKinley's insistence upon a thorough investigation, Ida respected the president's "suspension of judgment" until it could be determined if the blast was an accident or sabotage. Her esteem for McKinley's restraint was matched by her disgust at Roosevelt's "excited goings-on," which she witnessed during her frequent appointments with General Miles—the departments of War, Navy, and State then being housed together in the Old Executive Office Building. While others worked with steadfast composure to address the crisis, Roosevelt "tore up and down the wide marble halls," she contemptuously recalled, "like a boy on roller skates." War had not yet been declared, yet "already he saw himself an important unit in an invading army."

Though Tarbell was later drawn to the compelling energy of Roosevelt's "amazing" personality, her initial assessment of his unseemly, overwrought avidity for war was wholly accurate. "I am more grieved and indignant than I can say at there being any delay on our part in a matter like this," he told his brother-in-law, William Sheffield Cowles. "A great crisis is upon us, and if we do not rise level to it, we shall have spotted the pages of our history with a dark blot of shame." He had no patience with President McKinley, whose "weakness and vacillation" he considered "even more ludicrous than painful." He summarily rejected all who argued against intervention, dismissing any possibility of legitimate objection. "The only effective forces against the war are the forces inspired by greed and fear," he categorically proclaimed, "and the forces that tell in favor of war are the belief in national honor and common humanity."

As Tarbell feared, the "warlike element" on the Hill, the yellow press, and an aroused public sentiment exerted a combined pressure that proved "too much" for McKinley to resist: "He steadily grew paler and thinner, and his eyes seemed more deep-set than ever," she noted. On April 11, 1898, he finally summoned Congress to authorize armed intervention in Cuba. Two weeks later, the United States formally declared war against Spain. Later that same day, Secretary Long cabled Admiral Dewey to "proceed at once to Philippine Islands," using "utmost endeavor" to attack the Spanish fleet.

That Dewey was equipped to win the famous Battle of Manila Bay was largely due to Roosevelt's exertions months earlier. As acting secretary, he had ordered the squadron to Hong Kong at the beginning of the year. "Keep full of coal," Roosevelt had cabled Dewey when Long was out of the office: "In the event of declaration of war Spain, your duty will be to see that the Spanish squadron does not leave the Asiatic coast." Indeed, Taft later asserted, "if it had not been for Theodore Roosevelt, we would never have been in a position to declare war, for it was he and only he who got from Congress sufficient ammunition to back any bluff we might make with actual play."

The war marked a turning point in the lives of Roosevelt and Taft, and signaled a transformation in the nature of *McClure's* magazine. "In all its earlier years," Tarbell explained, the publication had sought "to be a wholesome, enlivening, informing companion for readers." It strove to provide "an eager welcome" to newly discovered fiction writers and poets, introducing recent inventions in science, while illuminating "the best of the old" in its extended series on Napoleon, Lincoln, and the Civil War. In the spring of 1898, however, McClure jettisoned plans for the June issue to create a special war edition, which, in the months ahead, led to "a continuous flow of war articles." Tarbell was assigned to cover McKinley's White House, Baker to analyze how the press reported the war, and White to gauge the heartland's response to the president's call for 125,000 volunteers. Stephen Crane and Frank Norris were recruited as correspondents from the warfront. "The editors of *McClure's* Magazine, in common with thousands of other American citizens, have to face new conditions and new interests," McClure told his readers. "We hope to obtain a record that will have absorbing human and dramatic interest," he explained, "and one that will prove to be of permanent historical value."

The shift from historical research to current affairs had a profound effect upon Ida Tarbell. She had contemplated returning to Paris after completing her Lincoln series, but realized, she later wrote, that she "could not run away to a foreign land" and become "a mere spectator." Her new assignment allowed an intimate perspective on the hard choices confronting McKinley: "I was learning something of what responsibility means for a man charged with public service," she recalled, "of the clash of personalities, of ambitions, judgments, ideals. And it was not long before I was saying to myself, as I had not for years, You are a part of this democratic system they are trying to make work. Is it not your business to use your profession to serve it?" While others inflamed public sentiment with sensational reports, Tarbell relied upon documentary evidence and dozens of interviews with cabinet officers, White House staff members, congressmen, and senators; using these sources Tarbell analyzed the pressures brought to bear upon McKinley in those two months between the destruction of the *Maine* and his decision to intervene. She revealed a president who struggled gallantly for a peaceful resolution until he was finally overwhelmed by the popular call for war. Her absorbing portrait of the political and psychological strains on a president in wartime created an enduring new model of political journalism.

McClure's also afforded Ray Baker the opportunity for a novel investigation of the newspaper industry itself—a definitive analysis of the unprecedented torrent of news generated by the Cuban conflict. This extensive war coverage, which vastly increased newspaper circulation, was considered "a triumph of the new journalism." College-educated reporters and writers with literary ambitions vied to be dispatched as correspondents. Newspapers spent anything necessary to scoop their rivals. Baker calculated the daily costs incurred by publications that maintained scores of correspondents in both Cuba and Florida: he added up rental fees for the private vessels carrying messages from Havana to Key West; he discovered covert signals indicating the receipt of important intelligence; he followed waiting cabs from the wharf to offices where the messages were cabled to New York; he computed the expense of every transmitted word. "It is a little short of stupendous, the amounts of money being spent in getting up a newspaper which sells for a penny," he told his father. In fact, Arthur Brisbane, the editor of the *New York Evening Journal*, later remarked that had the war not come to a swift conclusion, his paper and many other major dailies would have collapsed into insolvency.

In "When Johnny Went Marching Out," William Allen White described the nationalistic zeal that swept the country with the declaration of war. "Populists stopped watching the money power, Republicans ceased troubling themselves over repudiation, Democrats forgot the deficit," he observed. The indelible marks of regionalism were all but obliterated as northerners and southerners joined to fight under the same flag. "A simple but great emotion, that of patriotic joy, was stirring the people," White felt, "and they moved as men move under stress of strong passion." Children who once staged skirmishes between cowboys and Indians now waged war against the Spanish, adopting "Remember the Maine!" as their rallying cry. Immense crowds greeted the trains rushing soldiers to the front: "Everywhere it was flags: tattered, smoke-grimed flags in engine cabs; flags in buttonholes; flags on proud poles; flags fluttering everywhere."

While *McClure's* special war issue mirrored popular fascination with the Spanish conflict, a concluding article, "The Cost of War," sounded a compelling cautionary note. The generation who lived through the Civil War, the journalist George Waldron tellingly observed, "have not been the most ardent to join in the clamor for war. They know the havoc it wrought, and are not eager to repeat the experience. The thousands slain in battle, the tens of thousands afflicted with wounds which often resulted in death after days of agony, the losses of relatives and friends, the anxious waiting for news, the want and distress of body and mind following in the train of warfare, all have left impressions so vivid that thirty-three years of peace have not sufficed to wear them away." And beyond the social and emotional toll, Waldron calculated that the financial outlay of the Civil War "would have bought the freedom of every slave, and left enough to pay all the peace expenses of the Federal Government for half a century. The divided nation expended money enough during the struggle to supply every man, woman and child with ample food for the entire four years."

This balance of vivid, responsible war coverage and comprehensive analysis made *McClure's* one of the most respected magazines in the country. With a circulation now approaching 400,000, the pressroom and bindery had to operate "day and night" to meet increased demand. The advent of the Spanish-American War fueled the magazine's evolution toward a new role, a crucial engagement in American society. "Having tasted blood," Tarbell recalled, "it could no longer be content with being merely attractive, readable. It was a citizen and wanted to do a citizen's part."

DURING THE WINTER AND EARLY spring of 1898, as the country moved inexorably toward war, Edith Roosevelt was gravely ill. She had never recovered from the birth of her fifth child, Quentin, the previous fall. "For weeks we could not tell whether she would live or die," Roosevelt told a friend. Finally, in early March, doctors diagnosed a massive abscess in a muscle near the base of her spine. A dangerous operation was performed that would require many weeks of slow recovery. During this same spring, ten-year-old Theodore Roosevelt, Jr., underwent treatment for what appeared to be "kind of a nervous breakdown."

Despite the fragility of his family, Roosevelt later acknowledged, he could not forgo the opportunity to go to Cuba. "You know what my wife and children mean to me," he told Archie Butt, "and yet I made up my mind that I would not allow even a death to stand in my way; that it was my one chance to do something for my country and for my family and my one chance to cut my little notch on the stick that stands as a measuring-rod in every family. I know now that I would have turned from my wife's deathbed to have answered the call."

Roosevelt was offered a position as colonel but wisely requested to serve as a lieutenant colonel under his friend Leonard Wood, an Army surgeon and Medal of Honor recipient. The press found the story of the so-called Rough Riders irresistible from the start—a volunteer regiment in which cowboys, miners, and hunters served on an equal footing with Ivy League graduates, Somerset Club members, polo players, tennis champions, and prominent yachtsmen. And no journalist was better suited to cover Theodore Roosevelt and his colorful regiment than Richard Harding Davis, a war correspondent so legendary "that a war hardly seemed a war if he didn't cover it."

Indeed, at the outset of the war, Richard Harding Davis enjoyed far wider recognition than Theodore Roosevelt himself. The son of the feminist novelist Rebecca Harding Davis, thirty-four-year-old Richard was a man of many talents—an award-winning correspondent, best-selling fiction writer, successful playwright, and editor of *Harper's Weekly*. His handsome face and athletic physique had adorned countless magazine covers as Charles Dana Gibson's ideal exemplar of masculine beauty. "We knew his face as we knew the face of the President of the United States," the novelist Booth Tarkington remarked, "but we infinitely preferred Davis's. . . . Of all the great people of every continent, this was the one we most desired to see."

Roosevelt and Davis first met in New York in 1890. After reading "Gallegher," the short story that made Davis a household name, Roosevelt invited the young author to dinner at his sister's Madison Avenue home. Two years later, they encountered each other at a dinner party hosted by members of the British legation. This time, a caustic interchange was sparked by Roosevelt's recent *Cosmopolitan* essay deriding rich Americans who evinced a "queer, strained humility" toward Englishmen and failed to take pride in their own statesmen, soldiers, and scholars. Rebuked by Davis, who affected an aristocratic British accent and admired British customs, Roosevelt later reported the testy exchange to his friend James Brander Matthews. "He apparently considered it a triumphant answer to my position to inquire if I believed in the American custom of chewing tobacco and spitting all over the floor," Roosevelt noted sarcastically, continuing to insist that "I did; and that in consequence the British Minister, who otherwise liked me, felt very badly about having me at the house, especially because I sat with my legs on the table during dinner."

Any resentment either man might have harbored swiftly dissipated in the first days of the Spanish-American War. No public figure of the time understood better than Roosevelt the importance of cultivating reporters. As with Steffens and Riis, Roosevelt granted Davis unusual access. Writing from the headquarters of the Rough Riders, Davis assured his brother that his situation was "absolutely the very best . . . nothing they have they deny us." Davis realized from the start that the Rough Riders were likely to provide the most picturesque story of the war. "This is the best crowd to be with—they are so well educated and so interesting," he reported to his father. "To-day a sentry on post was reading 'As You Like It,' and whenever I go down the line half the men want to know who won the boat race." Indeed, he concluded, "being with such a fine lot of fellows is a great pleasure."

Roosevelt also forged a relationship with the *New York Journal*'s best known correspondent, Edward Marshall. The two men had met in New York when Roosevelt was police commissioner and Marshall was Sunday editor of the *New York Press*. In 1893, Marshall served as the secretary of the

Tenement House Commission, which brought him into close contact with Roosevelt. Like Davis, Marshall managed to write successful novels, short stories, and plays in his spare time. For a time, he edited the Sunday *World*, but when the war broke out, William Randolph Hearst engaged him as a war correspondent.

Both Davis and Marshall accompanied the Rough Riders during their first engagement at Las Guásimas, a confusing ninety-minute battle conducted in a dense tangle of tall grass and twisted brush. Las Guásimas was situated at the intersection of two trails on the way to Santiago de Cuba, an inland town where the Spaniards were known to be concentrated. As the Rough Riders made their way along the steep trail, they encountered fierce fire from an enemy they could not see. Within minutes, a half-dozen men were killed and nearly three dozen wounded. Marshall recorded a defining moment as Roosevelt "jumped up and down," his "emotions evidently divided between joy and a tendency to run," as he awaited Wood's order to lead his troops across a cut wire fence and into a thicket on the right.

Marshall's description continues to recount Roosevelt's pivotal transformation from idealistic, romantic warmonger to composed, levelheaded soldier: "Ushering a dozen men before him, Roosevelt stepped across the wire himself, and from that instant, became the most magnificent soldier I have ever seen. It was as if that barbed-wire strand had formed a dividing line in his life, and that when he stepped across it he left behind him . . . all those unadmirable and conspicuous traits which have so often caused him to be justly criticized in civic life, and found on the other side of it, in that Cuban thicket, the coolness, the calm judgment, the towering heroism, which made him, perhaps, the most admired and best beloved of all Americans in Cuba."

Before long, a bullet tore through Marshall's spine. "He was suffering the most terrible agonies," Davis recalled, yet he "was so much a soldier to duty that he continued writing his account of the fight until the fight was ended." Doctors doubted Marshall would live. He suffered permanent paralysis and the amputation of one leg but survived to write the regimental history of the Rough Riders and to be presented with a medal for valor by Theodore Roosevelt. Davis, too, was honored with a medal for bravery under fire. In the midst of the ambush, the intrepid reporter had picked up a carbine and begun firing at the Spaniards. "If the men had been regulars I would have sat in the rear," Davis explained to his family, "but I knew every other one of them, had played football, and all that sort of thing, with them, so I thought as an American I ought to help." When the Spanish finally retreated, Roosevelt promised to make Davis a captain in his unit, informing the Associated Press that "no officer in his regiment . . . had 'been of more help or shown more courage' " than Richard Harding Davis.

The Las Guásimas skirmish prepared Roosevelt for the decisive battle of the conflict the following week. Large Spanish forces were massed along the ridgeline of two large hills. The Rough Riders were ordered to march on Kettle Hill, while the regulars attacked San Juan Hill. With Roosevelt in the colonel's customary position at the back of the column, the troops advanced slowly under a hail of bullets. Mounted on horseback, Roosevelt suddenly charged toward the front, rallying his men and propelling them onward. When he reached the head of the regiment, he was a short distance from the Spanish rifles. "No one who saw Roosevelt take that ride expected he would finish it alive," Davis reported. "As the only mounted man, he was the most conspicuous object in the range of the rifle-pits. . . . It looked like foolhardiness, but, as a matter of fact, he set the pace with his horse and inspired his men."

Watching Roosevelt "charging the rifle-pits at a gallop and quite alone," Davis marveled, "made you feel that you would like to cheer. He wore on his sombrero a blue polka-dot handkerchief . . . which, as he advanced, floated out straight behind his head, like a guidon." Roosevelt's dauntless leadership, and the unit's remarkable esprit de corps, galvanized the men to storm the hill with near-reckless abandon. The Spaniards were forced to retreat.

Jacob Riis was at his Long Island home when the morning paper blared the Rough Riders' triumph. For days, he and his wife had rushed to get the paper, eager to confirm that their friend Roosevelt was alive and well. At last, on the Fourth of July, the anxiously awaited report arrived, detailing the successful charge under a hail of Spanish fire. "Up, up they went in the face of death," the story read, "men dropping from the ranks at every step. The Rough Riders acted like veterans. It was an inspiring sight and an awful one. . . . Roosevelt sat erect on his horse, holding his sword and shouting for his men to follow him" until they gained the summit at last.

"In how many American homes was that splendid story read that morning with a thrill never quite to be got over," mused Riis. Taking their cue from Davis's account, the newspapers portrayed a battle in which Roosevelt "had single-handedly crushed the foe." He quickly found himself the most popular man in the nation. The war burnished Davis's reputation as well; critics reckoned his writings among the very best of the war. "Except for Roosevelt," Davis's biographer Arthur Lubow observes, "no one had a better war." The Spanish surrendered thirteen days later. By the middle of August, four months after the war began, Roosevelt and his Rough Riders were on their way to a triumphal homecoming.

Jacob Riis was with Edith Roosevelt in Montauk, Long Island, when the ship bearing the Rough Riders came into shore. Although Edith had fully recovered from her operation, she had lived in constant anxiety, steeling herself against possible loss. "These dreadful days must be lived," she told Corinne in June, "and whatever comes Theodore and I have had more happiness in eleven years than most people in long lives." She understood that she must show strength "for the sake of the children," resolutely assuring her husband, "I do not want you to miss me or think of me for it is all in a day's work." Never again, after her unfortunate efforts to dissuade him from an 1894 mayoral run, would Edith interfere in her husband's career decisions. Only with his safe return could she acknowledge the terror she had suffered.

As the bedraggled troops marched down the pier—some limping, others on stretchers, a number stricken with yellow fever—reporters noted that Roosevelt "looked the picture of health," the only man disembarking who "gave no evidence of having passed through the tortures of the Cuban campaign." He "bubbled over with spirits," the *World* observed. Asked how he felt, Roosevelt responded with characteristic verve: "I'm in a disgracefully healthy condition. I feel ashamed of myself when I look at the poor fellows I brought with me." He momentarily fell silent, then added: "I've had a bully time and a bully fight. I feel as big and strong as a bull moose. I wish you all could have been with us."

S. S. McClure, who had identified Roosevelt as a man to watch more than a year before the battle at San Juan heights, was now especially eager to pursue an extended biographical piece on the returning hero. The first editor to commission an in-depth profile, McClure chose Ray Baker for the task.

Like Ida Tarbell, Baker had felt misgivings about the war, initially remaining hopeful that "the sober judgment" of the people would prevail over the yellow journals "to keep the nation from any bloodshed." Before long he found himself swept up in the adventure of the war. "War excitement here runs a great deal higher than it does at any other place I've seen," he reported to his father from New York. "Bulletins are displayed all over the city and the street before them is always filled with jostling crowds." He clearly recollected "the thrill" when he was asked to write a series of war articles, including the character sketch of Theodore Roosevelt.

Baker had met Roosevelt briefly twice before, at the Hamilton Club in Chicago and again at Roosevelt's Mulberry Street office in New York. "It was the personality of the man that chiefly attracted me," he recalled. Never before had he encountered such vitality or such inimitable "concentration of purpose." Entering Roosevelt's large office in the police department as a previous visitor departed, Baker noted with astonishment that "in the few seconds that I took to reach his desk," Roosevelt had picked up a book about the culture of Sioux Indian tribes and appeared totally engrossed in the work. "It is surprising," Roosevelt explained, "how much reading a man can do in time usually wasted."

Researching the Roosevelt piece, Baker spent substantial time with his subject. Roosevelt invited him to the "roomy, comfortable house" at Sagamore Hill, where the host's "prowess as a hunter" was abundantly evident "in the skins of bears and bison, and the splendid antlers of elk and deer." More impressive to a man of Baker's scholarly and artistic bent, the library was "rich" with works of history and literature, and the wide front veranda afforded "a view unsurpassed anywhere on Long Island Sound." The two men spoke at length about Roosevelt's childhood, his days in the legislature, his experiences in the Wild West, and the challenges he faced in the Civil Service Commission and police department. Roosevelt expressed his growing disgust for the predatory rich, "the mere money-getting American, insensible to every duty, regardless of every principle, bent only on amassing a fortune."

From Oyster Bay, Baker journeyed with Roosevelt to Camp Wikoff in Montauk, where the Rough Riders were still in quarantine to prevent a further outbreak of yellow fever. "I talked with a number of officers and troopers in Mr. Roosevelt's regiment," Baker wrote, "and I found their admiration for their colonel to be boundless. 'Why, he knows every man in the regiment by name,' said one. 'He spent $5,000 of his own money at Santiago to give us better food and medicine.' "

The finished article profiled "a magnificent example of the American citizen of social position, means, and culture devoting himself to public affairs." In every phase of Roosevelt's life, Baker detected a "rugged, old-fashioned sense of duty," the legacy of a civic-minded father who "had great strength and nobility of character, combined with a certain easy joyousness of disposition." In Roosevelt, Baker discerned a "rare power of personal attraction," a man possessed of "immense vitality and nervously active strength." Writing to his father as he completed the piece, the journalist predicted that Roosevelt could well be "president of the United States within ten years."

"I want to thank you for the article in 'McClure's,' " Roosevelt wrote Baker. "It has pleased me more than any other sketch of my life that has been written, and especially because of the way in which you speak of my father." In the years ahead, the friendship between the politician and reporter would have significant consequences for progressive policy. "I was to write about him many times afterward," Baker later reflected, "not always so uncritically." Nevertheless, Roosevelt generally took the reporter's criticisms in good stride. Personal loyalty was "one of his finest characteristics," Baker observed. "Once a friend with him, always a friend, and a warm friend, too."

In the months that followed, Baker was commissioned to write on a staggering array of subjects. McClure had an intuitive feel for "what was really interesting to people," Baker recalled. And nothing fascinated the reading public more at the end of the nineteenth century than the spectacular "outpouring of marvelous new inventions and scientific wonders"—the automobile, the incandescent lightbulb, the moving picture, the radio, the phonograph. His peregrinations even took Baker on a voyage to the bottom of the sea, in the most amazing invention "since the days of Jonah"—a submarine boat. He visited automobile manufacturers to assess two competing vehicles: the electric car and the gasoline-powered car. The electric vehicle, Baker concluded, was much quieter, "simpler in construction and more easily managed." Acknowledging that it "could run only a limited distance without recharging," he envisioned a string of festive roadhouses where car owners could relax as their batteries charged.

McClure's uncanny sense for "the new," Baker believed, bordered on genius. No sooner had he got wind of an Italian inventor experimenting with wireless telegraphy than he dispatched Baker to Signal Hill, Newfoundland. There, Baker was among the first to witness Guglielmo Marconi's historic reception of signals from across the Atlantic. Straightaway, Baker produced "the first fully verified account of the new invention and its revolutionary possibilities." Informed that the world's largest steamship was under construction by the Hamburg-American line, McClure sent Baker to Germany. There he remained for six months and completed twelve additional articles, including a long interview with the illustrious German biologist Ernst Haeckel, who was "one of the few thinkers of Europe who supported the theories set forth in 'that extravagant book,' the *Origin of Species*."

Yet, although Baker continued to invest great effort in crafting thorough and polished articles, he was becoming unraveled and despondent. "My life was being ordered," he felt, "not by myself, but by other people; not for my purposes, but for theirs." His reputation was steadily growing, but the focus that gave meaning and clarity to his work had begun to elude him. "I have been spreading too much, trying to do the impossible," he explained. "It seemed to me that I was no longer doing anything of any account. I was not more than half alive." Broken in health and profoundly depressed, Baker decided to resign from *McClure's* and move with his family to the countryside.

There, he hoped to commence work on a serious novel that would tackle the struggle between capital and labor, an issue of vital interest since his first days as a reporter.

Baker's colleagues at *McClure's* fought hard to prevent his departure. Ida Tarbell repeatedly reminded him of McClure's "affectionate interest" and warm feelings. "I cannot think for a moment of your severing your connection with our house," John Phillips told him. "I believe that you can do better than you have ever done and I believe that we can help you to that end." McClure raised his salary by a large margin, made the increase retroactive, and proposed that he take a long break with his wife and young family at the magazine's expense. He encouraged Baker to recover himself fully, urging, "Do only what you yourself want to do, get well physically, and we'll talk it over when you get back." The generosity "quite bowled me over," Baker wrote. "What good friends they were."

Intent on getting "as far away as possible from New York," Baker withdrew to the Santa Catalina Mountains in Arizona. "At first," he recalled, "the desert wastes, the great bare mountains, the wild and rocky arroyos seemed forbidding and even hostile." In time the rugged beauty of the desert exerted a restorative power. Riding for hours in the warm winter sun "across bare ridges and open spaces," Baker enjoyed a "sense of freedom" unknown since his childhood. He delighted in the sight of jackrabbits bounding before him, small desert creatures darting into their holes, birds sheltering under the cacti. For the first few weeks, he deliberately refrained from writing, opting for more physical pursuits. "I rode or tramped to weariness every day. I ate prodigiously. I slept soundly."

As his mind cleared and his strength returned, Baker tried to make sense of his breakdown. "I began again to write in my neglected notebooks, trying to understand what all the things I saw and thought and felt might really mean," he recorded. There could be no return, he realized, to the pioneer days of his youth. The frontier had vanished in a teeming urban landscape marked by a fierce battle for survival, voracious competition, and a hurried pace of life. "This being true, what am I to do about it?" he mused. "What is my function as a writer in a crowded world," he wondered, endeavoring to reconcile his artistic inclinations with popular demands—"that is, a writer not wishing merely to amuse people, but in the practice of his art, to make them see and think."

Reviewing his own inclinations and abilities, Baker determined that he was "not a leader, not an organizer, not a preacher, not a businessman," and probably not a novelist. "*I was a reporter*," he reflected. "I had certain definite gifts for seeing, hearing, understanding, and of reporting afterward what I had seen and heard and, so far as might be, what I understood." This realization hastened his return to *McClure's*, where he focused his journalistic skills on the economic issues that interested him most intensely, employing his gifts "to help people understand more clearly and completely" how they might "live together peaceably." True to his ambition, in the years that followed, Ray Baker would produce a series of landmark articles on labor and capital that would play a pivotal role in shaping public sentiment toward the development of a progressive public policy.

⤇ ⤆

LINCOLN STEFFENS, WHO HAD NOT yet left the *Commercial Advertiser* for *McClure's*, joined the throng of friends and reporters at Montauk to greet Roosevelt upon his return from Cuba. They buttonholed Roosevelt, Steffens reported, and "one by one they whispered to him: 'You are the next Governor of New York.' " Drawing Steffens aside, Roosevelt sought his gauge of the situation. "Should I run?" Aware that the Colonel was debating aloud rather than posing a question, Steffens nevertheless offered a resounding "yes" and, furthermore, predicted victory.

Political conditions in New York were not so simple, as Roosevelt well understood. Without the support of Senator Thomas Collier Platt, head of the state Republican machine, he would never secure the Republican nomination. Although Platt detested reformers like Roosevelt, the powerful old boss was in a bind. The party's image was seriously damaged in the aftermath of an exposé of corruption in the current Republican administration in Albany. The hero of San Juan was perhaps the antidote, the sole candidate who could save the party from defeat in the fall.

Steffens and his reformer friends in the Citizens' Union and the Good Government Clubs believed Roosevelt could outwit the Republican machine by running as an independent. Two leading reformers made the pilgrimage to Montauk to offer Roosevelt the independent nomination. "Take an independent nomination, and the machine will have to support you," they maintained. "You are of us, you belong to us. If you don't, you are a ruined man." With the machine weakened, reformers believed that this was the moment to crush Platt. "He's down now," they crowed. "One more blow will end him." Steffens himself had long since forsworn allegiance to either party, convinced both were irredeemably dishonest. "I am not a Republican," he told his father. "I am also not a Democrat. I am a mugwump or independent." He believed that the independent vote represented the best hope for dismantling the system of governmental corruption, perpetuated by machine control of both the

Democratic and Republican parties. If Roosevelt won as an independent, his victory would fundamentally alter the political culture of New York.

Roosevelt disputed Steffens's analysis. Even in the unlikely event of victory without the organization's endorsement, he would still have to work with the legislature in order to accomplish anything, and the legislature was absolutely controlled by the machine. "I'm a practical man," he insisted. If the Republican nomination were offered to him, he confided to Steffens, he would happily accept and work to reconcile disillusioned independents with the Republican Party, proving that "good public service was good practical politics." His goal was "to strengthen the party by bettering it," to build a decent progressive record for the good of both the state and the Republican Party.

Never content until he had exhausted every angle of a matter, Steffens pressed Roosevelt for further elaboration. Would he approach Platt or wait for the boss to make an overture? "What's the difference?" Roosevelt countered: "Can you see how it matters whether I call on Platt or Platt calls on me? I can't." He had small patience for points of etiquette: "I have to see the leaders. I want to, anyway. . . . I mean to go as far as I can with them. Of course I may have to break away and fight, and in that case I will fight hard, as they know." To the question of whether he would initiate a meeting with Platt, Roosevelt replied confidently. "Yes I'll see him now," he told Steffens, "and I'll see him after election; I'll see him when I'm governor."

Accordingly, on September 17, 1898, four days after the Rough Riders were mustered out of service, Roosevelt went to meet with Platt at the Fifth Avenue Hotel. Emerging from their session, Platt announced that he would support Roosevelt for the nomination. Later the same day, a machine spokesman declared that "Roosevelt most positively will not accept the independent nomination" for governor. "Oh, what a howl there was then!" Steffens recalled. Reformers felt betrayed, certain that a deal had been struck, that in return for Platt's endorsement, Roosevelt had agreed to reject the independent nomination. Rumors surfaced that the Colonel had bowed before the boss. One newspaper suggested that he had "received with becoming meekness the collar that marks him serf and regular, and that all talk of a people's candidate is rubbish." Democrats leaped at the opportunity: "Rough Rider Roosevelt made a charge up the backstairs of the Fifth Avenue Hotel," the Democratic paper jeered, adding that on this occasion, unlike his famous charge up San Juan Hill, "he was taken prisoner."

Platt relished being portrayed as "the master mind playing with the simple foolish soldier, who could lead a regiment into the jaws of death, but could not alone stand up against a domineering politician." Asked what had transpired in the meeting, the old boss cryptically remarked that "the conversation was interesting and satisfactory." Realizing that these "damning words" would convince independents that a sordid deal had indeed been struck, Roosevelt invited Steffens to his sister Corinne's Madison Avenue house for a confidential conversation. "He was pacing, like a fighting man, up and down the dining room," Steffens recalled. "His pride up, his jaw out, and his fist clenched," Roosevelt insisted that no deals had been made, no concessions exacted outside a reasonable promise to consult regularly with the organization and consider their views concerning decisions and appointments. Repeatedly, he emphasized that not "one iota of his independence" had been yielded.

The following day, *Commercial Advertiser* readers perused "an inspired account" of the secret meeting with Platt. Steffens revealed that "no one asked or even suggested to the Rough Rider" that he reject the independent nomination, a decision which was the Colonel's alone. Upon shaking hands with Platt, Steffens reported, Roosevelt made his position clear. "Before you say anything, Mr. Platt," he declared, "let me say this: that if I accept the nomination of the Republican organization I will stand with the ticket. Any support that is not for the rest of the ticket I will not seek, and an independent nomination of myself without my colleagues I will refuse. Now I am ready to listen." Roosevelt had concluded, Steffens explained, "that he would be unable to accomplish as much as he would wish unless he had a majority of the legislature. To insure that, he must do all in his power to discourage separate tickets that would divide the Republican vote for legislators."

While Steffens's account of the meeting satisfied some independent reformers, many who would naturally have been Roosevelt's allies sulked on the sidelines and refused to help in the canvass. Grudgingly admitting that they would probably have to vote for him against Augustus Van Wyck, the Democratic candidate chosen by Tammany Hall boss Richard Croker, they remained disaffected. "It is hard," they complained, "and we cannot advise others to follow our example."

Encumbered by such grumbling, doubt, and rancor, the campaign got off to a cold start. "It looked as though defeat were ahead of Mr. Roosevelt," Steffens reported, "and he was bitterly disappointed." Unwilling to accept failure without putting forth his utmost effort, Roosevelt demanded a statewide push. Machine leaders, who customarily controlled the entire campaign, initially resisted his requests; candidates rarely took the stump on their own behalf. Amid troubling reports of widespread apathy in the final weeks, however, the bosses realized that "the Rough Rider personally would have to win it, for he alone would be able to warm the rank and file to enthusiasm. So Mr. Roosevelt was allowed to go his way."

"He stumped the State up and down and across and zigzag," Steffens wrote, "speaking by day from the end of his special train and at night at mass meetings, in the towns and cities." Immense crowds greeted his train at every station along the way. "The fire and school bells rang," the *New York Times* reported, "and the children were dismissed from the schools so that they could see the hero of San Juan. Cannon fired and a band played, while the people cheered." Some spectators were disappointed, puzzled by their first impression of the Colonel. Newspaper accounts of his startling exploits in Cuba had led them to imagine a colossus, "seventeen feet high and his teeth a foot long." Nevertheless, his old friend William O' Neil reflected, when Roosevelt began to speak, his "presence was everything. It was electrical, magnetic." Before he was done, listeners discovered "that indefinable 'something' which led men to follow him up the bullet-swept hill of San Juan."

Jacob Riis joined Roosevelt as the train sped home from the western part of the state during the final night of the canvass. Over a belated midnight supper, they debated the "probable size" of the impending triumph or defeat. Riis predicted a Roosevelt victory margin of more than 100,000 votes. Roosevelt was less sanguine, believing that if he won, it would be by a mere "ten or fifteen thousand votes." While they sat together at the table, a knock was heard on the door, "and in came the engineer, wiping his oily hands in his blouse, to shake hands and wish him luck." Roosevelt rose, grabbing the engineer's hands with eagerness. "I would rather have you come here," he assured the man, "than have ten committees of distinguished citizens bring pledges of support." Roosevelt, Riis noted with admiration, was "genuinely fond of railroad men, of skilled mechanics of any kind, but especially of the men who harness the iron steed and drive it with a steady eye and hand through the dangers of the night." The engineer's enthusiasm seemed to Riis "an omen of victory."

When the votes were tallied the following day, Roosevelt's forecast proved more accurate than Riis's projection of sweeping victory. He had been elected governor by a relatively narrow margin of fewer than 18,000 votes.

As Steffens contemplated Roosevelt's successful campaign, he recalled the yardstick set forth by his reform-minded political science professor at Berkeley. "Young gentlemen," he had told the class, "you can get the measure of your country by watching how far Theodore Roosevelt goes in his public career." An honest man trying to work in a dishonest system, Roosevelt would never survive the machine politicians, the professor mournfully predicted.

CHAPTER NINE

Governor and Governor General

Governor Roosevelt at work in Albany, New York, ca. 1900;
Governor General Taft at his desk in Manila, ca. 1901.

A FOOT OF SNOW COVERED THE streets of Albany on January 2, 1899, the day Roosevelt was inaugurated as governor of New York. The thermometer registered several degrees below zero, but the bright sun and jingling sleigh bells lent a jubilant air to the thousands gathered at the statehouse. "There never was such a mass of people out to see a Governor installed," the New York *World* reported. In the assembly chamber where the ceremony would take place, "the desks and seats of the members had been removed, and in their places were hundreds of camp chairs for the accommodation of the audience."

"A deafening outburst of applause" greeted Roosevelt as he reached the flag-draped platform. He "stood for a moment in stern-faced dignity," one journalist observed, "but the cheers continued, and then, like a sunburst the familiar Roosevelt smile broke forth." His gaze was drawn to the Ladies' Gallery where Edith and his six children stood, the boys desperately flapping both hands to attract his notice. When he threw his family a kiss, the "touch of human nature" spurred another round of thunderous applause.

Roosevelt's brief inaugural address sketched out the creed he would follow as governor. "He is a party man," a *New York Tribune* editorial remarked, one who "intends to work with his party and be loyal to it in all things that belong to it." Nevertheless, he made it clear that he would "never render to party what belongs to the State, and the State is the first consideration." Addressing fellow reformers who demanded renunciation of Boss Platt and the machine, Roosevelt emphasized that nothing would be accomplished "if we do not work through practical methods and with a readiness to face life as it is, and not as we think it ought to be." Yet Mr. Platt would have to accept that "in the long run he serves his party best who helps to make it instantly responsive to every need of the people."

"It was a solemn & impressive ceremony," Edith told her sister Emily, confessing, "I could not look at Theodore or even listen closely or I should have broken down." That afternoon, she stood by her husband's side to greet more than 5,000 guests attending the festive reception in the executive mansion. But as soon as her public duties were fulfilled, she escaped to her room, where she could quietly read, write letters, and keep her diary. For this inordinately private woman, who seemed "physically to cringe" in the glare of "the public searchlight," the prospect of life in Albany was intimidating. Reporters had already intrusively chronicled every aspect of the "general exodus" that carried "Mrs. Roosevelt, Miss Roosevelt, and the five little Roosevelts, the governesses, the nurses, the maid and the coachman, the mongrel but gentlemanly dog Susan, a new French Bulldog El Carney, the war horse Texas, and the other horses and the pony, as well as the guinea pigs" from Oyster Bay to the governor's three-story mansion. Fanny Smith, who visited her old friend soon after her arrival, noted that Edith, "usually an extremely calm and self-controlled person," paced "nervously up and down the room."

Faced with the imposing task of transforming the cavernous governor's mansion into a comfortable family home, Edith was understandably anxious. After securing the admittance of twelve-year-old Theodore Junior and ten-year-old Kermit to a local boys' academy, she established a schoolroom in the basement for the younger children, Ethel and Archie. A nursery was created for little Quentin, a governess hired for fifteen-year-old Alice, and a third-floor billiard room remodeled to become the gymnasium. A competent staff orchestrated drawing-room receptions, musical entertainments, and large dinner parties, but Edith remained ill at ease on such elaborate occasions. She much preferred the sort of dinner parties and literary discussions she had once enjoyed with her intimate Washington circle. "If only I could wake up in your library," she told Henry Cabot Lodge, "how happy I would be." Edith soon began to adjust to her new role, however, just as she had settled into her new home. "Edith will never enjoy anywhere socially as much as she enjoyed Washington, nor make friends whom she cares for as much as she did for you and a few others," Roosevelt confided to Maria Storer, "but she enjoys the position here greatly and has made some very good friends and is altogether having an excellent time. She is picking up in health and is looking very pretty."

In February, a candid photograph of Edith appeared in newspapers. The image reveals a slender woman of medium height, dressed in plain but "perfect taste." Although she had steadfastly refused interviews and declined to furnish a photograph for publication, reporters considered her neither "haughty, nor excessively modest." She simply disliked personal publicity and proved as intractable as her husband once "her mind is made up." Despite her habitual reticence, she never made reporters feel unwelcome in her home. Her family life was just not an appropriate subject for their stories. "Everything about her speaks of grace," an Iowa journalist remarked. "There's honor even among reporters, or at least there's gratitude," another explained. "We knew Mrs. Roosevelt's wish to keep herself and the children out of the papers, and after her courtesy to us we were glad to respect that wish."

Yet she was always prepared to entertain reporters and friends with humorous stories about the new governor. In a special scrapbook, she meticulously assembled every caricature relating to her husband, whether they "represented him as riding a hobby-horse or dispensing peanuts in paper bags from a corner stand." While other wives were known to burn papers and magazines that burlesqued their husbands, Edith had perfect confidence in Theodore's good humor and relished the laughter they shared over the cartoons.

⌒ ⌒

NEWSPAPER READERS SOON LEARNED THAT Theodore Roosevelt was unlike any governor New York had known. He arrived in his office long before the usual hour of nine o'clock to begin the baffling task of sorting through his mail. Three or four hundred letters arrived each morning, a far larger volume than any previous governor had contended with. At 10 a.m., his official day commenced, with an hour reserved for assemblymen and senators, followed by rapid-fire meetings with political delegations, members of his administration, and individual petitioners. Roosevelt was "ever on his feet" during these sessions, ranging restlessly as he talked, laughed, or scowled. He punctuated sentences with his fists, "filling the entire room with his presence." The stately desk, where his staid predecessors had "judicially" received visitors, might as well have been removed, one observer noted, for "it hardly knows the Governor."

Despite Roosevelt's often combustible and seemingly impulsive nature, he maintained a schedule so precise that he could reliably meet an individual slated for 12:20 to 12:25 and conclude business just in time to usher in his 12:25 appointment. Visitors were encouraged to "plunge at once" into their subject, for the governor deftly yet positively closed the interview after the allotted time. Roosevelt's official day ended at 5 p.m., though he frequently remained in his office until seven o'clock. Once the governor departed the capitol for the short walk to the executive mansion, he was "not to be disturbed" unless by an emergency. "These evening hours," wrote a correspondent who profiled the governor, "are set apart for his literary work, his reading and social converse with his family, the Roosevelt youngsters having a decided claim, even in the midst of the most pressing affairs of the State."

Honoring his promise to regularly consult organization leaders, Roosevelt soon announced that he would visit New York City every weekend during the legislative session to meet with Boss Platt and Benjamin Odell, chairman of the Republican State Committee, an announcement that incensed staunch reformers. The New York *Evening Post*, an influential independent paper which had supported Roosevelt's bitter fight against Tammany Hall as police commissioner, now decried his willingness to "touch Platt both politically and socially." Never had a governor "so belittled the dignity of the office," opined the *Albany Argus*: "Imagine for a moment William Seward, Samuel Tilden or Grover Cleveland running down to New York, like a capitol district messenger boy, to bring back the orders of some party boss."

While Roosevelt absorbed attacks from Democratic papers with equanimity, he could barely contain his fury at "the irrational independents and the malignant make-believe independents" who remained aloof, never engaging genuine political issues for fear of sullying themselves. These "solemn reformers of the tom-fool variety," Roosevelt complained, stridently assumed that any contact with the bosses indicated some "sinister" collusion. "I have met many politicians whom I distrust and dislike," he told a friend, "yet there are none whom I regard as morally worse than the editors of the *Post*." His indignation was aggravated by a conviction that the *Post*'s denunciation might cause some of his friends, the sincere reformers as opposed to the lunatic fringe, to misconstrue his actions.

Once again Roosevelt reached out to Steffens, proffering what the reporter termed "an understanding." Steffens would meet the governor each Friday afternoon when he arrived in Manhattan for his weekly consultation with the bosses, keeping "in close touch with him all the time he was there," and escorting him to the train station for his return to Albany on Sunday evening. "I was to know all the political acts he was contemplating, with his reasons for them," Steffens recounted. By sharing the full context of each decision and appointment before it became public, Roosevelt trusted that Steffens would credit and document the complex, pragmatic maneuvering behind an ethical and effective approach to leadership. Roosevelt's trust was well placed. Steffens kept the governor's confidences until he determined a course of action, providing an authoritative account of the decision-making process for the *Commercial Advertiser.* "T.R. was a very practical politician," Steffens recalled, "and it was partly from watching him sympathetically that I lost some of my contempt for politicians and practical men generally."

Steffens was not the sole journalist to whom Roosevelt granted such inside access. The governor understood that however courteously he might handle Platt and the organization, he would inevitably clash with them on a range of salient issues. When the battles began, he would need the persuasive power of the press to marshal public sentiment for his reformist agenda. Only by "appealing directly to the people," by "going over the heads" of party leaders, did he have any chance of pushing significant reform through the legislature.

To that end, Roosevelt soon declared that he would hold two press conferences each day he was in town. His unprecedented announcement thrilled the twenty-five statehouse correspondents, who quickly labeled the morning session "the séance" and the afternoon session "the pink tea." The governor generally opened these informal conferences "with a smile and nearly always with a joke, generally at his own expense." In the course of fifteen minutes, one reporter marveled, he would explain his objectives and the rationale behind them. He outlined his "future movements" and intentions regarding various controversial issues, clearly indicating which statements were on the record and which were simply shared confidences, not meant for publication. These lively forums impressed the journalists with "the wonderful mental activity of the man." With his "marvelous fund of general information to draw upon," Roosevelt never haltingly answered or appeared at a loss.

One of Roosevelt's first acts as governor was to convene a meeting with Jacob Riis and three leading trade unionists to determine the most constructive labor legislation to sponsor. The labor leaders agreed that while some new laws were in order, workers would most benefit from the application of laws that already had been enacted to cover maximum hours of work, sweatshop conditions, prevailing wages, and safety requirements. In too many instances, such laws had been put on the books simply to satisfy public demand; as soon as publicity and interest faded, they became dead letters, and companies did as they pleased.

To dramatize these flagrant violations, Roosevelt requested that Riis accompany him one day on a series of surprise visits to tenement sweatshops, ostensibly under the supervision of state inspectors. "I think that perhaps if I looked through the sweatshops myself," Roosevelt told Riis, "we might be in a condition to put things on a new basis, just as they were put on a new basis in the police department after you and I began our midnight tours."

Riis never forgot the appalling conditions they unearthed during their inspection tour. "It was on one of the hottest days of early summer," he recalled. "I had picked twenty five-story tenements, and we went through them from cellar to roof, examining every room and the people we found there." In building after building, the minimum requirements for licensing home work—"no bed in the room where the work was done, no outsider employed, no contagious disease, and only one family living in the rooms"—were found wanting or neglected entirely. As soon as the tour concluded, Roosevelt proceeded to the factory inspector's office. "I do not think you quite understand what I mean by enforcing a law," he admonished, insisting that inspectors "make owners of the tenements understand that old, badly built, uncleanly houses shall not be used for manufacturing in any shape." Day's end found Riis spent but Roosevelt percolating with new ideas and eager for extended discussion over a good meal. Immediately, he would increase the number of tenement inspectors, and when the legislature convened the following winter, he would successfully introduce a bill to revise the code of tenement house laws.

Years later, Roosevelt recalled his labor record as governor with satisfaction. Although his effort to pass an employers' liability act failed, he did manage to obtain "the grudging and querulous assent" of the bosses for legislation establishing an eight-hour day for state employees, limiting the maximum hours women and children could work in private industry, improving working conditions for children, hiring more factory inspectors, and mandating air brakes on freight trains. At a time when laissez-faire attitudes reigned, even such limited measures represented considerable progress.

Roosevelt also took pride in a remarkably innovative conservation record. Within weeks of taking office, he invited an old friend, the architect Grant La Farge, along with the head of the U.S. Forestry Division, Gifford Pinchot, to spend the night at the governor's mansion. Pinchot, like Roosevelt, had been born into a moneyed New York mercantile family but had chosen to dedicate his life to public service. A devoted naturalist and wilderness enthusiast, he had studied forestry conservation in France after graduating from Phillips Exeter Academy and Yale College. The tall, confident thirty-three-year-old brought great originality and ambition to his position when McKinley appointed him to head the Forestry Division.

Pinchot's visit with Roosevelt was unforgettable from the outset: "We arrived just as the Executive Mansion was under ferocious attack from a band of invisible Indians," he wrote in his autobiography, "and the Governor of the Empire State was helping a household of children to escape by lowering them out of a second-story window on a rope." After rescuing his young pioneers, Roosevelt settled down to a long evening of food, drink, and conversation, punctuated by a spirited boxing match in which Pinchot "had the honor of knocking the future President of the United States off his very solid pins," though the governor emerged victorious from the wrestling contest that concluded their visit. The alliance established that night would play a central role in future conservation policy.

In the months that followed, Roosevelt convinced the state legislature to preserve tens of thousands of forested acres in the Catskills and the Adirondacks. He appointed a single superintendent to replace the five-man Fisheries, Game and Forest Commission, which had become a haven for machine spoilsmen. He created the Palisades Park and used his bully pulpit to promote awareness of the state's unique natural resources and the pressing need to conserve them. Roosevelt's second annual message, the historian Douglas Brinkley argues, "was the most important speech about conservation ever delivered by a serious American politician up to that time." Pinchot committed whole passages to memory "as if it were the Gettysburg Address," while ornithologists considered its call for the protection of endangered birds "the tipping point for the Audubon Movement."

"I need hardly say how heartily I sympathize with the purposes of the Audubon Society," Roosevelt maintained, expressing his profound emotional investment in the matter. "When the bluebirds were so nearly destroyed by the severe winter a few seasons ago, the loss was like the loss of an old friend, or at least like the burning down of a familiar and dearly loved house. . . . When I hear of the destruction of a species I feel just as if all the works of some great writer had perished; as if we had lost all instead of only part of Polybius or Livy." This lifelong sympathy proved instrumental in preserving natural lands and wildlife habitat in his state and would become a driving force to protect the entire nation's wilderness.

⌐ ⌐

THE GOVERNOR WAS INITIALLY SURPRISED that on many issues, even those involving labor and conservation, he "got on fairly well with the machine." Indeed, his endeavors to placate Platt through weekly pilgrimages to the city seemed so successful that he was unprepared for "the storm of protest" when he came out in favor of a new franchise tax on corporations. Until this moment, Roosevelt acknowledged, he had "only imperfectly understood" the intricate web linking the Platt machine to the corporate world. Unlike other political bosses, Senator Platt "did not use his political position to advance his private fortunes." He lived simply and had few interests beyond the powerful network he had meticulously constructed and nurtured over the decades. To keep control of the political organization he required regular revenue from the corporate world "in the guise of contributions for campaign purposes" and donations for "the good of the party." These sums were distributed to his select candidates for the state legislature with the "gentlemen's understanding" that they could be counted upon for important votes, particularly when an issue touched upon the corporations that fueled the machine. The public had small awareness and less understanding of this threat that Roosevelt labeled the "invisible empire."

For decades, the state of New York had granted exclusive franchises to corporations to operate immensely lucrative electric street railways, telephone networks, and telegraph lines. These franchises, often secured by outright bribery, had been awarded with no attempt to obtain tax revenues from the corporations in return. After investigating the issue, Roosevelt concluded "that it was a matter of plain decency" for these corporations to pay their share of taxes for privileges worth tens or even hundreds of millions. In fact, a bill to tax such franchises had previously been introduced by John Ford, a Democratic state senator from New York City. The measure "had been suffered to slumber undisturbed" in the machine-dominated assembly until the governor's surprise announcement brought the issue "into sudden prominence."

At their next breakfast meeting, Platt furiously warned Roosevelt that the Ford bill would never be permitted to pass. If he persisted in pushing it forward, the governor risked an open break with the machine. This "radical legislation," Platt argued, had no serious public support "until you sprang forward as its champion." In its stead, Platt suggested that a joint legislative committee "consider the whole question of taxation," with the obligation to report back the following year. Realizing that the tax bill had dim prospects for success without Platt's support, Roosevelt agreed to postpone consideration until the commission issued its report. Reformers recognized the commission as a cynical effort to kill the bill and roundly derided the governor for bending to the subterfuge of the machine. "The time to tax franchises is now, not next year," goaded the *Tribune*. "Roosevelt Stops Franchise Tax," the *Herald* blared.

Stung by the swarm of criticism from reformers, Roosevelt altered his approach, explaining to reporters that despite his reservations about the Ford bill, he would like to see it become law. Well aware of the blackmailing power Tammany Hall would gain, he was particularly concerned by the provision allowing cities to determine tax assessments instead of the state. Nevertheless, a flawed bill was better than none, and Roosevelt concluded that if he "could get a show in the Legislature the bill would pass, because the people had become interested and the representatives would scarcely dare to vote the wrong way." Through a complicated series of maneuvers, the bill was finally brought to a vote in both chambers just before the legislative session ended. While many Republicans in the lower chamber heeded Platt's directive to vote against the measure, Roosevelt secured enough Republican support that, combined with a heavy Democratic vote, he was able to produce a majority.

"It was said to-day," Steffens declared in the *Commercial Advertiser*, "that many of the men who supported the measure have been threatened with political destruction by the party leaders for their action in the matter. These men may rest assured," Steffens knowingly asserted, "that they will have the sympathy and support of the governor for their courage in openly declaring themselves. He appreciates courage."

Asked how the tax would affect his company, the counsel for one affected corporation was blunt: "Right in the solar plexus," he replied. In the days that followed, the stock market suffered a significant drop. "You will make the mistake of your life if you allow that bill to become a law," Platt warned Roosevelt at the close of a bitter letter. He promised the governor that an ugly confrontation was imminent unless Roosevelt summoned that "very rare and difficult quality of moral courage not to sign" the bill after endeavoring to pass it. "When the subject of your nomination was under consideration, there was one matter that gave me real anxiety," Platt noted. "I had heard from a good many sources that you were a little loose on the relations of capital and labor, on trusts and combinations, and indeed, on those numerous questions which have arisen in politics affecting the security of earnings and the right of a man to run his own business in his own way, with due respect of course to the Ten Commandments and the Penal Code. Or, to get at it even more clearly, I understood from a number of business men, and among them many of your own personal friends, that you entertained various altruistic ideas." In Platt's lexicon, Roosevelt clearly understood, *altruistic* meant "Communistic or Socialistic." The governor, Platt acknowledged, had lately adjourned a legislative session that "created a good opinion throughout the State." Then, "at the last minute and to my very great surprise, you did a thing which has caused the business community of New York to wonder how far the notions of Populism, as laid down in Kansas and Nebraska, have taken hold upon the Republican party of the State of New York."

"I do not believe that it is wise or safe for us as a party to take refuge in mere negation and to say that there are no evils to be corrected," Roosevelt countered. "It seems to me that our attitude should be one of correcting the evils and thereby showing that, whereas the populists, socialists and others really do not correct the evils at all, or else only do so at the expense of producing others in aggravated form, that we Republicans hold the just balance and set our faces as resolutely against improper corporate influence on the one hand as against demagogy and mob rule on the other." Their disagreement on this salient issue troubled him, he confessed to Platt, especially since "you have treated me so well and shown such entire willingness to meet me halfway." Nevertheless, he firmly believed that the Republican Party "should be beaten, and badly beaten, if we took the attitude of saying that corporations should not, when they receive great benefits and make a great deal of money, pay their share of the public burdens."

Corporate representatives descended on Roosevelt, warning that if he signed the bill, "under no circumstances could [he] ever again be nominated for any public office, as no corporation would subscribe to a campaign fund if [he] was on the ticket." Refusing to be bullied, yet well aware that a break with the organization would be fatal, Roosevelt made one concession. Before signing the bill, he told Platt, he would call a special legislative session and try to pass an amendment that would substitute a state board of assessors for local authorities. He also agreed to hold a hearing with corporate representatives and solicit suggestions for additional improvements in the bill. In the event the extra session produced amendments that would weaken the tax, however, he would simply sign the Ford bill in its present form.

"Some of the morning newspapers repeat the expression of astonishment that Governor Roosevelt has consulted the attorneys of corporations," Steffens reported in the *Commercial Advertiser*. "Some yellow minds cannot seem to understand that the governor is willing to fight the corporations to make them do right and yet be ready to negotiate just terms of peace—nay to fight for the corporations against wrong." In fact, when Roosevelt learned that corporations in some communities had already paid local taxes, he agreed to an amendment providing that "any taxes already payable for public rights could be deducted from the franchise valuation."

The passage of this amendment, along with the shift to state assessors, allowed Platt to make the best of a difficult situation when Roosevelt signed the bill. "Persistent efforts have been made by the Democratic newspapers," the boss told reporters, "to have it appear that there are serious divisions in the Republican Party." Such claims he blithely dismissed: "All agreed," he now maintained, "that franchises were a proper and necessary subject of taxation." While the original bill had been "carelessly drawn and thoughtlessly enacted," these "just and reasonable" amendments enabled Platt and his organization to save face and support the bill.

"Passage of the amended franchise tax bill is a distinct personal triumph for Governor Roosevelt," the *Commercial Advertiser* asserted in its lead editorial. "By exercise of tact and by concessions where no sacrifice of principle was involved, the governor achieved his ends. His integrity of motive and his eagerness to prevent party rupture were so apparent that Republican legislators were left no choice but to support him."

IN THE SUMMER OF 1899, following his successful push for the franchise tax, Roosevelt prepared to head west to New Mexico for the first reunion of his beloved Rough Riders. "Would you let me ask a great favor," he wrote William Allen White several weeks before the trip, "and that is that you should try to join me on the train and ride three or four hours with me. There is very much that I have to talk over with you. As you know, you have got the ideas of Americanism after which I am striving."

White and Roosevelt had met two years earlier during the reporter's first journey to the east coast at the invitation of Sam McClure. Before proceeding to New York, White spent a few days in the nation's capital, where he was informed that "a young fellow named Roosevelt" in the Navy Department had read his famous editorial and book of short stories about Kansas and was eager to meet him. White was deeply impressed by his first glimpse of the man who would become a close friend, confidant, and correspondent: "a tallish, yet stockily built man, physically hard and rugged, obviously fighting down the young moon crescent of his vest; quick speaking, forthright, a dynamo of energy, given to gestures and grimaces, letting his voice run its full gamut from base to falsetto." Roosevelt seemed, White's description concluded, "to be dancing in the exuberance of a deep physical joy of life."

"We walked from the Navy Department under the shade of the young trees that lined the streets that Summer day to the Army and Navy Club, had lunch, talked and talked, and still kept talking," White recollected. Roosevelt was just then beginning to comprehend "the yearnings" of America's working poor for social and economic justice, "to see clearly that our problems were no longer problems of production, but problems affecting the distribution of wealth and income." For White, still adhering to conservative predilections, Roosevelt's progressive ideas were a revelation. "He sounded in my heart the first trumpet call of the new time that was to be," White recalled, stressing that such notes represented "youth and the new order" and "the passing of the old into the new." The young journalist was overcome by "the splendor" of Roosevelt's personality. "I had never known such a man as he," White wrote more than a quarter of a century after Roosevelt's death, "and never shall again."

Roosevelt for his part felt an immediate kinship with the ebullient writer. Both men were blessed with confidence and energy, both ready to engage in the political and ideological contests that would define their country. While the rotund White had no interest in the physical challenges and trials that Roosevelt adored, preferring to spend his leisure time reading poetry or playing piano, his nimble, perceptive mind perfectly matched Roosevelt's, and they shared a vigorous style of speaking and writing. Doubtless, Roosevelt also recognized that the celebrated journalist was an influential leader of middle-class opinion. "Between his newspaper editorials, magazine articles and a growing list of books," one historian suggests, "White could claim one of the largest audiences of any writer in America at the turn of the century."

Following their initial encounter, the two men had continued to exchange letters, articles, and books. Roosevelt purchased an out-of-town subscription to the *Emporia Gazette*, and sent his new friend a copy of his recently published work, *American Ideals and Other Essays*. "I read it with feelings of mingled astonishment and trepidation," White recalled, confessing that "it shook my foundations, for it questioned things as they are. It challenged a complacent plutocracy."

By the time Roosevelt's train steamed through Kansas en route to New Mexico that summer of 1899, White was working "with the zeal of a converted disciple" to help his friend become president in 1904—assuming that McKinley would run again in 1900. Paul Morton, vice president of the Santa Fe Railroad, had offered Roosevelt his private car so the governor and his invited guests (including White and H. H. Kohlsaat, publisher of the *Chicago Times-Herald*) could relax and talk. On short notice, White had done his utmost to ensure that reporters and enthusiastic supporters greeted Roosevelt's train at every stop.

In Topeka, 3,000 people gave the New York governor "a rousing reception." At the Newton station, "cannon boomed, whistles were blown and the crowd cheered." In Kansas City, men wore cards in their hatbands promoting Roosevelt in 1904. The largest audience gathered in White's hometown of Emporia. "No public man who has come into Kansas during the last ten years has stirred as much personal enthusiasm as Roosevelt," White's *Emporia Gazette* proclaimed. Roosevelt made a short fighting speech that roused supporters. "Governor Roosevelt may be said to be an Eastern man with a Western temperament," the *Kansas City Star* noted. "His sympathy with the people of the Transmississippi country and the power he has displayed in appealing to their fancy marks him as a person of unusual breadth." Despite a mere forty-eight hours' notice of his arrival, White rhapsodized, Roosevelt "had a larger crowd at the Kansas stations than McKinley had with the state central committee back of him. Reporters with both trains concede this. . . . There is no man in America today whose personality is rooted deeper in the hearts of the people than Theodore Roosevelt."

Kohlsaat, who had never met Roosevelt before, was stunned by the fervor of the crowds. On travels with his close friend McKinley, he had witnessed nothing comparable to the New York governor's reception. The night the train left Emporia, he and Roosevelt stayed up talking until midnight. Roosevelt was curious to learn about Kohlsaat's relationship with McKinley. For seven years, Kohlsaat proudly noted, McKinley did not once give a speech to the nation "without either wiring, telephoning, or writing me, and sending me his speeches to read before delivering them." When Kohlsaat the next day begged pardon for having sounded arrogant, Roosevelt put his mind at ease: "Do you know what I thought after I went to bed?" Roosevelt asked. "I wondered if you would do the same thing for me."

Delighted to find that Roosevelt welcomed his advice, Kohlsaat suggested that he issue a pledge of support for McKinley's renomination. McKinley's friends, he had learned, were irritated by premature talk of the governor's presidential ambitions. Recognizing the value of Kohlsaat's counsel, Roosevelt immediately telegraphed the president, "telling of the sentiment he had found in the West for his renomination," and provided a similar statement to the press for publication. Shortly afterward, Roosevelt received a telegram from President McKinley inviting him to the White House. "Oh mentor!" Roosevelt addressed Kohlsaat. "Was my McKinley interview all right? . . . Didn't we have a good week together?"

Roosevelt wrote a warm letter to White as well, expressing deep gratitude for their trip together. His absolute trust in White allowed him to share
his hopes and intentions unguardedly. Even in that summer of 1899, White
recalled, "we were planning for 1904." Before they parted, White promised
to send Roosevelt a map analyzing the strengths of various factions in each
western state, helping to determine which political leaders should be approached—and by whom. Meanwhile, he assured the governor that the trip
through Kansas was already "bearing great fruit," as evidenced by laudatory
clippings from Kansas newspapers that White enclosed. He recommended
that Roosevelt send a personal note to each editor and publisher he met along
the way. "All of these men have endorsed you emphatically since your departure, and spoke of you not only as possibility, but as probability for 1904,"
White assured him, adding that a personal acknowledgment "would convince
those men of their wisdom."

Increasingly, White began to identify the trajectory of Roosevelt's success
with nothing less than the nation's prospects. "When the war with Spain broke
out, I wanted to go the worst kind [of way]," White confided to Roosevelt,
"but my wife was sick and I felt that my first duty was to her. Then when your
regiment had such remarkable success and when you came home and were
made governor and acquitted yourself so admirably, I formed a great desire
to help you to be president of the United States. It has seemed to me that if
I could perform some service for you that would land you in the presidency,
I would perform as great a service for my country as I could perform upon
the battlefield."

In the years that followed, the two men exchanged more than three hundred letters. White reacted to Roosevelt's speeches and Roosevelt religiously
read White's stories and articles as they appeared. "I think the 'Man on Horseback' almost your strongest bit of work," he wrote, in response to White's tale
of an honest man corrupted by wealth as he builds a street railway empire and,
in the process, loses his idealistic son. "There is a certain iron grimness about
the tragedy with its mixture of the sordid and the sublime that made a very
deep impression on me," Roosevelt told his friend. After finishing another
of White's stories about a populist senator who hammers away at trusts and
money power while building his own fortune through shady deals, Roosevelt
penned a 2,000-word reply. "You are among the men whose good opinion I
crave and desire to earn by my actions," he frankly avowed. "I rank you with,
for instance Judge Taft of Cincinnati and Jim Garfield of Cleveland, and with
the men whom I am trying to get around me here, men of high ideals who

strive to achieve these ideals in practical ways, men who want to count for decency and not merely to prattle."

⌒ ⌒

ROOSEVELT WAS PARTICULARLY INTRIGUED BY White's views on the problem of the trusts, finding himself "in a great quandary what position to advocate about them." His struggle for the franchise tax had sensitized him to the "growth of popular unrest and popular distrust" over the increasing concentration of power in large corporations. He told Lodge he was "surprised to find" that many workingmen who had supported McKinley and the Republicans in 1896 now insisted that William Jennings Bryan was "the only man who can control the trusts; and that the trusts are crushing the life out of the small men." He feared that so long as Republicans failed to develop a cogent policy regarding trusts, those workers who suffered "a good deal of misery" would gravitate toward "the quack," whose dangerous remedies would undo the benefits of the Industrial Revolution.

In the months that followed, Roosevelt consulted a variety of experts to develop a reasonable proposal for regulating the trusts, which he intended to present in his second annual message to the legislature when it reconvened in January. When a draft of the message was completed, he sent it to his old friend Elihu Root, a successful corporate lawyer who had just joined McKinley's cabinet as war secretary. Root's vehement opposition to the franchise tax measure had strained their friendship for a time, but he was "such a good fellow," Roosevelt told Lodge, "that I was sure it would not last, and now I think every shade of it has vanished." Root read the draft carefully, making a number of changes to tone down the governor's rhetoric and moderate his condemnation of those who amassed their riches "by means which are utterly inconsistent with the highest rules of morality." Roosevelt gratefully accepted most of Root's suggestions. "Oh, Lord! I wish there were more of you," he wrote; "you have the ideas to work out whereas I have to try to work out what I get from you and men like you."

The lengthy message, delivered on January 3, 1900, opened with praise for the legislative achievements in the previous year, taking special note of the passage of the franchise tax law. More remained to be done to address the state's industrial problems. "In our great cities there is plainly in evidence much wealth contrasted with much poverty and some of the wealth has been acquired or is used in a manner for which there is no moral justification," Roosevelt said. Then, taking heed of Root's advice, he carefully qualified this indictment, noting that "wealth which is expended in multiplying and elaborating real comforts, or even in pleasures which produce enjoyment at all proportionate to their cost will never excite serious indignation."

"We do not wish to discourage enterprise," Roosevelt stressed; "we do not desire to destroy corporations; we do desire to put them fully at the service of the State and the people." He acknowledged that anti-trust legislation vengefully designed to punish the mere acquisition of wealth would be destructive but insisted that it would be "worse than idle to deny" the existence of abuses "of a very grave character." Consequently, "we must set about finding out what the real abuses are, with their causes and to what extent remedies can be applied."

"The first essential," Roosevelt maintained, "is knowledge of the facts, publicity." Such exposure would open the trusts to investigation for "misrepresentation or concealment regarding material facts" and reveal a corporation's involvement in "unscrupulous promotion, overcapitalization, unfair competition, resulting in the crushing out of competitors" or the "raising of prices above fair competitive rates." He recognized that "care should be taken not to stifle enterprise or disclose any facts of a business that are essentially private" but insisted on the state's right to protect the public from monopoly and even from the "colossal waste" of resources in "vulgar forms of social advertisement." With the facts in hand, measures—including taxation—could be devised to regulate the trusts. Most immediately, Roosevelt reiterated, "publicity is the one sure and adequate remedy which we can now invoke."

Advocating "the adoption of what is reasonable in the demands of reformers" as "the surest way to prevent the adoption of what is unreasonable," Roosevelt hoped to propel "the party of property" toward a more "enlightened conservatism." The bosses had no interest in Roosevelt's musings about a transformed Republican Party. On the contrary, Tom Platt and Benjamin Odell considered the message, even with Root's modifications, dangerously provocative toward business. Odell warned that Roosevelt's call to increase publicity surrounding corporate activities would spur manufacturers to leave New York State. Tensions with the party bosses escalated further when the governor threw his support behind a bill that would compel corporations to disclose information on "their structure and finance."

To Roosevelt's great disappointment, the public did not rally behind the bill. The danger of the trusts, apparent to farmers and wage earners, had not yet penetrated the consciousness of middle-class America. In three years' time, Ida Tarbell and her fellow muckrakers would reach that important audience through their narrative abilities, putting faces and names to the giant corporations, shining a bright light on the sordid maneuvers that were crushing independent businessmen in one sector after another, dramatizing the danger in a way the voting population could no longer ignore. In 1900, however, the trusts remained amorphous entities, arousing vague apprehension but insufficient outrage to exert pressure on the political machines operating as their protectors. And in the absence of public demand, it was not difficult for Platt to prevent the legislature from acting on Roosevelt's proposal.

DISSENSION BETWEEN PLATT AND ROOSEVELT continued to intensify. The three-year term of the state's superintendent of insurance was coming to a close in February 1900. Lou Payn, the current superintendent, was Platt's "right-hand" man. His reappointment was a foregone conclusion. Reading newspaper reports of Payn's cozy relationships with the very companies he was supposed to oversee, Roosevelt issued an announcement that he would seek a new superintendent. Straightaway, the party countered with a statement that Payn would continue at his post "no matter what the opposition to him may try to do." At a contentious breakfast, Platt "issued an ultimatum" to the governor, warning "that if he chose to fight," he would most certainly lose, for "under the New York constitution the assent of the Senate was necessary not only to appoint a man to office, but to remove him from office." There was no need to remind Roosevelt who controlled the senate. "I persistently refused to lose my temper," he recalled. "I merely explained good-humoredly that I had made up my mind."

Though he steadfastly refused to consider Payn's reappointment, Roosevelt moved to conciliate the organization. At the next breakfast meeting, he gave Platt a list of good machine men and told him to select any name on it. Still, Platt refused to compromise. While independent newspapers endorsed Roosevelt's decision to remove Payn, they criticized his attempt to mollify Platt. "Why does he not fight in the open?" the *Evening Post* queried. "He could openly say that he found a rogue in office whom all the powers of political corruption in both parties were banded together to keep there, and that he, the people's Governor, must appeal to the good citizens to sustain him in his fight against the whole confederate crew. That would be real war, and how the people would volunteer for it! That would be raising a standard to which honest men could repair. But what sort of banner is it on which the chief insignia are muffins and coffee devoured by Roosevelt and Platt, sitting cheek by jowl?"

The impasse persisted until Roosevelt, with the help of a newspaper investigation, uncovered a loan of more than $400,000 that Payn had received from a trust company controlled by an insurance firm under the superintendent's jurisdiction. Unwilling to risk a scandal and extended scrutiny, Platt finally capitulated. He agreed to the nomination of Francis Hendricks, one of the men on Roosevelt's list, whom the governor considered "thoroughly upright and capable."

"I have always been fond of the West African proverb: 'Speak softly and carry a big stick; you will go far,' " Roosevelt exultantly told a friend. "If I had not carried the big stick the organization would not have gotten behind me." At the same time, he pointed out, had he "yelled and blustered," he would not have been able to muster 10 votes in the senate for Hendricks's nomination. Indeed, following the righteous recommendations of the *Evening Post* "would have ensured Payn's retention" and facilitated "a very imposing triumph for rascality."

"The outcome of the Payn contest is a complete vindication of the governor's way of accomplishing results," Steffens's *Commercial Advertiser* declared. "Could the governor have accomplished any more than he has if he had declared open war on the organization?" The *Evening Post* remained dissatisfied. Although Hendricks's appointment promised an "honest administration of the Insurance Department," the *Post* declared, the governor should have selected his own man "without consulting the organization, and he could thus have dealt the Republican machine such a blow as it has never suffered. The moral courage of the Governor at Albany was not equal to the physical courage of the Colonel before Santiago."

Roosevelt's stormy relationship with Senator Platt troubled him far less than the perpetual hail of invective from fellow reformers. "Could they assail such a man more viciously and persistently than they have assailed him?" the *Commercial Advertiser* queried in his defense. "Are they not making it possible for the politicians to say: 'We gave the reformers a governor who secured reforms and who would not do what we wished him to do: they fell upon him because he did not get reforms in *their* way, not because he did not get reforms.' Why not simply choose one of our own machine men from here on in? They surely won't attack him more fiercely than they have Roosevelt."

Even as he excoriated "the dogs of the *Evening Post*" for their attacks, Roosevelt preserved his friendship with the *Post*'s longtime editorial writer, Joseph Bucklin Bishop. "I value you too much to go into recrimination," he wrote to Bishop in the wake of another derogatory *Post* editorial. "Now, I have a proposal to make. Wouldn't you like to come up here and meet some of the 'wild beasts'?" During his weekends in New York, Roosevelt encouraged

Bishop to visit at Bamie's Madison Avenue town house so they could air their disagreements. "I will explain to you the merits of the police bill, if it passes," he suggested, "and you shall explain to me its demerits, if it fails." Their lively correspondence mollified rancor that might have hardened into lasting hostility. After being quoted that he was uncertain which he regarded "with the most unaffected dread—the machine politician or the fool reformer," Roosevelt hastily assured Bishop that he was "emphatically not one of the 'fool reformers.' "

In late 1899, after sixteen years at the *Post*, Bishop made the wrenching decision to leave the newspaper. His standing there had deteriorated after he declined to follow "positive orders to suppress the truth" concerning Roosevelt's accomplishments. "The policy of the *Evening Post*," he was informed, "is to break down Roosevelt." Consequently, Roosevelt was thrilled when Bishop joined Steffens at the *Commercial Advertiser*. "You are about fourteen different kinds of a trump," Roosevelt told him. "I thank Heaven for the Advertiser continually." With both Bishop and Steffens writing for the well-regarded paper, Roosevelt now had two advocates who might promote vital support among the practical reformers.

In the months that followed, the friendship between Bishop and Roosevelt deepened. Roosevelt sought Bishop's advice on speeches, appointments, and legislation. He invited him to stay overnight in the governor's mansion, met with him regularly over meals in Manhattan, and exchanged letters two or three times a week. "Good Lord, what an interesting correspondence we have had at times!" Roosevelt remarked. Their friendship remained strong even when Bishop publicly disagreed with the governor and told his readers why. "I need not tell you that no criticism of yours can alter in the least my affectionate regard for you," Roosevelt assured Bishop. "You have shown yourself a friend indeed, and above all, when you differ I know you differ because you honestly think you must."

Roosevelt's ability to countenance criticism in the interest of friendship also marked his relationship with the humorist Finley Peter Dunne. Dunne's weekly columns in the *Chicago Times-Herald*, featuring his adopted persona, the irreverent Irish bartender Martin Dooley, placed him among the nation's most popular and influential literary figures. Dunne later recalled that his "first acquaintance with Col. Roosevelt grew, strangely enough, out of an article that was by no means friendly to him." In the fall of 1899, a copy of *The Rough Riders*, Roosevelt's wartime memoir, came across Dunne's desk. "Mr. Dooley's" book review in *Harper's Weekly* mocked Roosevelt's propensity for placing himself at the center of all the action: "'Tis Th' Biography iv a Hero be Wan who Knows. Tis Th' Darin' Exploits iv a Brave Man be an Actual Eye Witness," Mr. Dooley observes. "If I was him, I'd call th' book, 'Alone in Cubia.'" Three days after this satirical assessment amused readers across the country, Roosevelt wrote to Dunne: "I regret to state that my family and intimate friends are delighted with your review of my book. Now I think you owe me one; and I shall exact that when you next come east you pay me a visit. I have long wanted the chance of making your acquaintance."

"I shall be very happy to call on you the next time I go to New York," Dunne replied. "At the same time the way you took Mr. Dooley is a little discouraging. The number of persons who are worthwhile firing at is so small that as a matter of business I must regret the loss of one of them. Still if in losing a target I have, perhaps, gained a friend I am in after all." The humorist never had to make the choice he feared; he continued to lampoon the nation's premier target without losing Roosevelt's friendship. "I never knew a man with a keener humor or one who could take a joke on himself with better grace," Dunne recalled. For years, Roosevelt told and retold the story of meeting a charming young lady at a reception: "Oh, Governor," she said, "I've read everything you ever wrote." "Really! What book did you like best?" "Why that one, you know, *Alone in Cuba*."

❧ ❧

In June 1900, as Roosevelt's first term as governor began to wind down, Lincoln Steffens wrote a lengthy political analysis for *McClure's*. He described Roosevelt's tenure as "an experiment"—a test to determine whether a leader could serve both the party machine and the good of the state, whether he could simultaneously maintain his ideals and get things done. Steffens vividly depicted the fights over the insurance commissioner and the franchise tax, both of which ended in Roosevelt victories. It remained unclear, however, whether the Roosevelt experiment itself would succeed. Despite an ostensible truce between the governor and Boss Platt, wrote Steffens, "the organization doesn't like Mr. Roosevelt as Governor, neither does 'Lou' Payn, neither do the corporations. The corporations cannot come out openly to fight him; they have simply served notice on the organization that if he is renominated they will not contribute to campaign funds."

Publicly to deny the popular governor a second term would cast the organization in a starkly negative light. The "obvious solution," Steffens predicted, "would be to promote" Roosevelt to "the most dignified and harmless position in the gift of his country"—the vice presidency. "Then everybody could say, 'We told you so,' for both the theorists and the politicians have said that it is impossible in practical politics to be honest and successful too." This astute piece, together with several of Steffens's previous articles on Roosevelt, initially attracted Sam McClure's attention. "Your TR article is a jim-dandy," McClure told Steffens, resolving then and there to bring him from the *Commercial Advertiser* to his own publication. "I could read a whole magazine of this kind of material. It is a rattling good article."

Roosevelt first became aware of Platt's unwelcome "solution" in late January 1900, when three high-ranking representatives from the Republican National Committee came to Albany. They cautioned that he "would be tempting Providence to try for two terms" as governor, emphasizing the near certainty that he would "hopelessly" lower his standing "with either the independents or the party men" before a second term was out. Only "great luck," they claimed, had enabled him to get by thus far "without cutting [his] own throat." On the other hand, the vice-presidential nomination was a fait accompli if he decided within the next few weeks. Disconcerted by the drift of the conversation, Roosevelt informed the committeemen that he had absolutely no interest in the position. The vice presidency, he told Platt the next day, is "not an office in which a man who is still vigorous and not past middle life has much chance of doing anything. As you know, I am of an active nature." He had "thoroughly enjoyed being Governor" and strongly desired a second term. "As Governor," Roosevelt added, "I can achieve something, but as Vice-President I should achieve nothing."

Henry Cabot Lodge questioned Roosevelt's rationale, concurring with the committeemen that his friend was "tempting Providence" by remaining in New York. He would be wiser to accept the political haven of the vice presidency, "the true stepping stone . . . either toward the Presidency or the Governor Generalship of the Philippines." Roosevelt conceded that "in New York with the republican party shading on the one hand into corrupt politicians, and on the other hand, into a group of impracticables . . . the task of getting results is one of incredible difficulty, and the danger of being wrecked very great." Nevertheless, this very challenge rendered the work both more important and absorbing. He could not bear to be a mere "figurehead," with no other task than presiding over the Senate.

Moreover, he confided to Lodge, "the money question is a serious one with me." As governor, he made $10,000 a year and was "comparatively well paid, having not only a salary but a house which is practically kept up all winter." Between the remnant of his inheritance and the few expenses in Albany, he had been able to save money for the first time in years. For Edith, perpetually worried about family finances, this stability was a great "comfort," especially since their older children would soon start private school. The vice president's salary was $2,000 less and no house was provided. Furthermore, the Roosevelts would be expected to entertain as lavishly as their predecessors, men frequently selected based on their resources and affinity for the social side of the office. Even if his family lived simply, Roosevelt concluded, the position "would be a serious drain" for him, causing both him and his wife "continual anxiety."

In addition, Roosevelt did not perceive the vice presidency as a likely avenue to the White House; a student of history, he was well aware that over sixty years had passed since a sitting vice president had been elected to the presidency. His chances in 1904 would be far better if he served as governor of the most populous state in the Union than if he languished in "oblivion" as vice president.

Despite these objections, Roosevelt reasoned, "if the Vice-Presidency led to the Governor Generalship of the Philippines, then the question would be entirely altered." That post was the one he desired above all others, even a second gubernatorial term. From the moment the United States acquired the islands as a provision of the treaty in 1899 ending the Spanish-American War, Roosevelt had coveted the job of creating a new government in a Philippines free of Spanish tyranny. The vigorously paternal leadership he envisioned would "prove to the islanders that [his country] intended not merely to treat them well, but to give them a constantly increasing measure of self-government" until they could "stand alone as a nation."

During the acrimonious Senate debate over ratification of the peace treaty, Roosevelt had expressed nothing but contempt for anti-imperialists who justly argued that acquisition of the Philippines would signal "a violent departure from the established traditions and principles of our republic." They are "little better than traitors," Roosevelt flatly told Lodge, while his public rhetoric made the alternatives stridently clear. "We shall be branded with the steel of clinging shame if we leave the Philippines to fall into a welter of bloody anarchy," he proclaimed, "instead of taking hold of them and governing them with righteousness and justice, in the interests of their own people even more than in the interests of ours."

Serving as the civilian leader on the islands "would not be pleasant," Roosevelt told Maria Storer, "for I should have to cut myself off from my family," who would surely not relocate to the war-torn Philippines. Yet he considered the task "emphatically worth doing" and was increasingly convinced that "the chief pleasure really worth having for any man is the doing well of some work that ought to be done." Moreover, Roosevelt's evolving doctrine of sacrifice and satisfaction applied to nations as well as individuals. In a widely quoted speech delivered in Chicago in April 1900, he insisted that "if we shrink from the hard contests where men must win at hazard of their lives and at risk of all they hold dear, then the bolder and stronger peoples will pass us by, and win for themselves the domination of the world. . . . It is only through strife, through hard and dangerous endeavor, that we shall ultimately win the goal of true national greatness."

McKinley had assured Lodge that Roosevelt was "the ideal man to be the first pioneer Governor" but explained that the appointment would not be made until American troops stationed in the Philippines suppressed the native uprising that had followed the treaty. Known as the Philippine Insurrection, that conflict had erupted when the Filipinos learned, after decades of fighting for independence, that they had been betrayed into exchanging the rule of Spain for American occupation. With 35,000 additional troops authorized by Congress, Roosevelt projected that within two years the rebellion would be crushed, a necessary step before the United States could execute its avowedly beneficent intentions. As governor of New York, he would be free to instantly resign and assume the pioneering post, whereas he would be irreversibly "planted" in the vice presidency for four years. Although he hated to counter Lodge's judgment on a matter of such importance, Roosevelt decided to "declare decisively" that he did not want the post of vice president.

Lodge reluctantly accepted Roosevelt's decision but warned that if he attended the Republican Convention in June, continued refusal in the face of popular clamor for his nomination would damage his future prospects. "There are lots of good men who are strongly for you now who will not like it," Lodge cautioned. Though Roosevelt acknowledged his friend's admonitions, he was constitutionally incapable of forgoing involvement. He allowed himself to be chosen as one of four delegates-at-large from New York and made plans to bring Edith, Corinne, and her husband, Douglas, to Philadelphia.

Three weeks before the convention opened, Judge Alton Brooks Parker was a guest of the Roosevelts at the governor's mansion. Over dinner, Edith expressed her excitement over her first national convention. "You will have the most wonderful time of your life," Judge Parker promised. "You will see almost all the Republican Senators and Members of Congress, many of them with brilliant careers in the public service. And . . . you will see your handsome husband come in and bedlam will at once break loose, and he will receive such a demonstration of applause from the thousands of delegates and guests as no one else will receive. . . . Then, some two or three days later, you will see your husband unanimously nominated for the office of Vice-President."

"You disagreeable thing," Edith interrupted. "I don't want to see him nominated for the vice-presidency." Parker, who regarded Edith highly, instantly regretted his words when he saw how "very anxious" she was that his "prophecy should not come true." For Edith, the vice presidency foretold only burdensome expenses and a stilted social life filled with formal receptions and idle chatter. Most important, she and Theodore had had more time together in the gubernatorial mansion than they had in years. She was by his side when he made his rounds to local fairs and Pioneer picnics. "I really think she enjoyed it as much as I did," Roosevelt proudly reported to Lodge after an eight-day stretch of "the county fair business." Sagamore Hill beckoned when the legislature adjourned in summer and was close enough to Albany to provide a romantic escape, even in the fall.

Judge Parker joined the Roosevelts at another dinner party a few days after his disconcerting conversation with Edith. "You gave my wife a bad quarter of an hour the other night," Roosevelt told him. "Did you mean all you said to her?" Parker replied that he meant "every word," adding that Roosevelt's only possibility of evading the vice-presidential nod was to avoid Philadelphia altogether and deliver elsewhere a categorical refusal of the nomination.

By the time the convention opened in late June, Roosevelt was no longer certain how to proceed. As he pondered his future, his doubts grew: even if he secured the gubernatorial nomination for a second term, there was at least "an even chance" that he would be beaten. And even if he did win, he could easily "come a cropper" with any subsequent misstep that would signal "in all probability the end of any outside ambition." Nevertheless, he continued to prefer the hazardous pursuit of a second term to being buried alive in the vice presidency.

The moment Roosevelt arrived in Philadelphia, the stampede for his nomination began—just as Lodge and Judge Parker had predicted. Entering the crowded lobby of the Hotel Walton around 6 p.m., he was met by "vociferous applause" and thunderous cries of "Teddy, Teddy, Teddy." When the raucous crowd launched into a chorus of "There'll Be a Hot Time in the Old Town Tonight," journalists noted, "Roosevelt blushed, doffed his hat and bowed his acknowledgments as he recognized the tune played after his charge up San Juan Hill."

He had scarcely finished breakfast the following morning, the *New York Tribune* reported, when "he had reason to suspect that something of importance affecting his political fortunes had happened in the course of the night": one state delegation after another "invaded" his room, announcing that he was their unanimous choice for vice president. Throughout the western states, where Roosevelt was regarded as one of their own, the enthusiasm was overwhelming. Corinne was with her brother when the Kansas delegation arrived. "Round and round the room they went," she recalled, chanting, "We want Teddy, We want Teddy, We want Teddy," to the accompaniment of "fife, drum and bugle." Similar demonstrations of support came from California, Colorado, the Dakotas, and Nevada.

The bosses of the eastern states followed suit. To a man, they pledged the full support of their delegations. Platt had done his work well. The only resistance had come from the conservative party chairman, Ohio's Mark Hanna. "Don't you realize," Hanna famously objected, "that there's only one life between this madman and the White House?" In the end, even Hanna conceded that Roosevelt would add more strength to the ticket than any other candidate. "There is not a man, woman, or child in the hotels of Quakertown tonight," the *Washington Times* reported, "who does not believe that TR is to be nominated as President McKinley's running mate."

"These fellows have placed me in an awful position," Roosevelt complained. "If I refused it, people will say that 'Roosevelt has a big head and thinks he is too much of a man to be Vice-President.' " Lodge had little patience with Roosevelt's continued reluctance: "If you decline the nomination," he informed his friend, "you had better take a razor and cut your throat."

Roosevelt eventually resigned himself to the inevitable nomination. The next morning, "the sun shone brightly" for the first time in several days as the formal proceedings began. When the chair recognized Roosevelt to second McKinley's nomination, "the magic" of his personality "sent the multitude into convulsions of enthusiasm." From the gallery, Edith watched her husband stride toward the platform amid "the sea of waving, cheering humanity." The jubilation continued while Roosevelt commanded the stage. "He made no acknowledgements, no salutations to the plaudits, but like a hero receiving his due, calmly awaited the subsidence of the tumult." His expression relaxed only once, the *New York Tribune* correspondent remarked, "when he caught a glimpse of his wife in the gallery and waved his hand to her." At last, with his uplifted hand, the demonstration subsided.

Finally, Roosevelt addressed the adoring crowd: "We stand on the threshold of a new century big with the fate of mighty nations," he proclaimed. "We face the coming years high of heart and resolute of faith that to our people is given the right to win such honor and renown as has never yet been vouchsafed to the nations of mankind." It was not a speech, observed one reporter, "of rounded periods, such as Senator Lodge could deliver, nor did it have the fervor or the rich metaphor of the Wolcotts and Dollivers." Nevertheless, no other speech proved "so effective, none so full of character and none which found so responsive an audience. It carried everything before it, and old campaigners sighed that such energy was beyond them."

Once the frenzy of the convention had waned Roosevelt admitted to a friend that he felt "a little melancholy." While he "should be a conceited fool" not to appreciate such resounding support, the thought of four years in the restrictive office of the vice presidency remained abhorrent. "His friends were in despair," Jacob Riis wrote, "his enemies triumphed. At last they had him where they wanted him."

His family shared Roosevelt's aversion to the prospect. "Oh, how I hate this Vice Presidency," Corinne told Fanny Parsons. "Poor Edith feels it tremendously too." Indeed, Edith admitted to Emily that she "had hoped to the last moment that some other candidate would be settled upon." Her only comfort was the prospect that her husband might "get the rest that he sadly needs and for the next four years he will have an easy time."

⌒ ⌒

WHILE THEODORE ROOSEVELT TRIED TO reconcile himself to the unhappy combination of events resulting in his nomination as vice president, William Howard Taft would embark on the most gratifying period of his long public career. In late January 1900, a telegraph boy knocked on the door of the consultation room at the circuit court in Cincinnati. He handed Judge Taft a telegram, summoning him to the White House for "important business" with President McKinley. "What do you suppose that means?" he excitedly asked Nellie that evening. She had no answer. Had there been an opening on the Supreme Court, the summons might have foretold his long-desired appointment to the bench, but no vacancy then existed.

Secretary of War Elihu Root and Navy Secretary Long had joined McKinley in the Oval Office when the president informed Taft that he intended to appoint him to a new Philippine Commission, charged with formulating a civilian code for governance. "He might as well have told me," Taft remembered, "that he wanted me to take a flying machine." Taft protested that he was not the right man for the task. He was emphatically not an expansionist and had been "strongly opposed to taking the Philippines," believing the United States should not take on a responsibility "contrary to our traditions and at a time when we had quite enough to do at home." Such objections were "beside the question," McKinley countered; now that the Philippines had fallen to the United States, "it behooved the United States to govern them until such time as their people had learned the difficult art of governing themselves."

Taft agreed that once the islands were occupied, we were "under the most sacred duty to give them a good form of government" but insisted he was not the man best equipped for that important responsibility. He did not speak Spanish, which would hamper easy relationships with the Filipino people. Furthermore, he was loath to relinquish his long-cherished lifetime appointment as a judge. "Well," said McKinley, "all I can say to you is that if you give up this judicial office at my request you shall not suffer. If I last and the opportunity comes, I shall appoint you." Long confirmed that the president was speaking of a place on the Supreme Court. "Yes," McKinley assured him, "if I am here you'll be here."

War Secretary Root offered the decisive argument. "You have had a very fortunate career," he told Taft. "You are at the parting of the ways. Will you take the easier course, the way of least resistance . . . or will you take the more courageous course and, risking much, achieve much?" Taft asked for a week to ponder the matter with his wife and brothers.

On the overnight train heading back to Cincinnati, Taft "didn't sleep a wink." Root's words about courage frequented his thoughts, and the president's implied promise of a Supreme Court appointment beckoned powerfully. Despite his mounting excitement, Taft was certain that the long distance and "the atrocious climate of Manila" would not prove a happy prospect for Nellie. Unlike Roosevelt, he could not imagine a protracted absence from his family. By the time he reached home, his countenance was "so grave" that Nellie "thought he must be facing impeachment."

Will explained the president's proposal to his wife, doubtful she would consider joining him. Much to his surprise, Nellie never hesitated: "Yes, of course," she exclaimed, the opportunity gave her "nothing but pleasure." She later admitted that perhaps she should have given the prospect of moving three children under ten years old more than 8,000 miles from home more consideration, but her excitement overcame all anxiety. "I knew instantly," she recalled, "that I didn't want to miss a big and novel experience."

Taft's brothers echoed Nellie's enthusiasm. "You can do more good in that position in a year than you could do on the bench in a dozen," Horace maintained, acknowledging, "I hated to have us take the Philippines, but I don't see how in the world we can give them up." Harry agreed, certain that both Will and Nellie would profit "the rest of [their] lives" from "the educational effect of the experience." Harry added that his brother should ask to be made president of the commission so he "could have a voice in selecting some of [his] colleagues."

Three days later, Taft wrote to Root, accepting the post with the stipulation that he be made head of the commission, "responsible for success or failure" of the venture. Root readily agreed; he and McKinley had assumed that Taft would be granted that authority. Notwithstanding, Taft's resignation from his beloved bench was, Nellie believed, "the hardest thing he ever did."

News of Taft's appointment must have disquieted Roosevelt, who nurtured a slim hope that "the Philippines business" could wait a few years, that the fighting would not abate before he was in a position to serve as the first governor general. Though Taft's appointment to the presidency of the commission did not ensure that McKinley would make him civilian governor when hostilities ended, Roosevelt undoubtedly realized that Taft was now the obvious and logical choice.

The two men had kept in close contact over the years, and Taft remained a loyal friend. At the close of "a very hard month" in the governor's office, Roosevelt had found solace in an encouraging letter from Taft. "Need I tell you how your letter pleased me, and how much touched I was by it?" he wrote back, explaining that he had endeavored to follow Taft's counsel and "make the good of the State [his] prime consideration, and yet not follow any impractical ideas." Still, Roosevelt noted, it was "not always easy to strike the just middle," and he inevitably made mistakes. "The thing I should most like," he revealed to Taft, "would be to have someone here just like yourself to advise with." In a letter to their mutual friend Maria Storer, Roosevelt wistfully reiterated his affection and respect: "I wish there was someone like [Taft] here in New York, for I am very much alone. I have no real community of principle or feeling with the machine. So far I have gotten along very well with them, but I never can tell when they will cut my throat." For his part, Taft habitually tracked Roosevelt's battles closely and had wholeheartedly rejoiced in his "final triumph" over Lou Payn.

Though Roosevelt received news of Taft's appointment with ambivalence, his happiness for his friend soon overcame any personal disappointment. "Curiously enough," Roosevelt told him, "I had just written you a note, but I will tear it up, for now I see that you are going on the new Philippine Commission. . . . You are to do a great work for America, and of all the men I know I think you are best fitted to do it."

While Will traveled to Washington to discuss the composition of the commission with the president and the secretary of war, Nellie began to prepare for the odyssey ahead. "That it was alluring to me I did not deny to anybody," she happily remembered. "I read with engrossing interest everything I could find on the subject of the Philippines." Meanwhile, within eight weeks, she managed to vacate their house, store their belongings, and pack for shipment

what they would need. "Robert was ten years old, Helen eight, while Charlie, my baby, was just a little over two. It did not occur to me that it was a task to take them on such a long journey, or that they would be exposed to any danger through the experience," she recalled matter-of-factly.

In mid-April 1900, the five commission members and their families, along with a translator, five secretaries, a stenographer, and an Army surgeon, gathered in San Francisco to board the *Hancock* and begin their two-week journey to the Philippines. "We soon became well acquainted, as people do on shipboard," Nellie recalled, "and proceeded at once to prove ourselves to be a most harmonious company." This close-knit group, with whom Nellie would spend "the most interesting years" of her life, included a former Confederate general, "one of the ablest lawyers in Tennessee"; a New England judge who had served as chief justice of Samoa; a professor from the University of Michigan who had been on two scientific expeditions to the Philippines; and a historian from the University of California who had written on politics and economics. Nellie relished "the bonds of friendship" that developed over drinks, meals, political discussions, and continuous rounds of cards. They learned Spanish together and shared books on British colonization and the history of the Philippines. And their children became fast friends.

No sooner had the *Hancock* landed in Manila Bay than the complexity of Taft's mission was immediately apparent. "The populace that we expected to welcome us was not there," recalled Taft, "and I cannot describe the coldness of the army officers and army men who received us any better than by saying that it somewhat exceeded the coldness of the populace." The Filipinos' lack of faith in the advent of the blue-ribbon commission was unsurprising. Brutal fighting still raged in scattered regions of the islands. Further, reports circulated of water torture and other cruelties practiced by American soldiers against the Filipinos, and condescending suggestions that the Filipinos were not yet fit for self-government roused deep resentment.

Taft had expected to be met by General Arthur MacArthur, who had occupied the Philippines for nearly two years and was serving as military governor. But MacArthur was nowhere to be seen. The general regarded the commission's arrival with displeasure, for it compromised the absolute authority he had exercised in the governance of the islands. According to the president's new instructions, the military governor would retain executive powers until the termination of hostilities, while the new Philippine Commission would become the legislative body. Taft and his colleagues had authority to appropriate money, determine taxes, create political departments, and establish courts. MacArthur bluntly informed Taft that he regarded the appointment of the commission "as a personal reflection on him, and that while he was of course obliged to submit to [its] presence there, he resented it nevertheless."

In his first public statement, Taft appealed to the people of the islands, declaring that the commission's arrival signaled a better day and presaged the beginning of the end of military rule. "We are civil officers. We are men of peace. We are here to do justice to the Philippine people, and to secure to them the best government in our power," he reassured them, explaining that the people would retain "such a measure of popular control as will be consistent with stability and the security of law, order and property." He promised to build schools and roads, to open clinics and improve harbors, to establish a system of justice based on the American model, and eventually to create a political structure run by the Filipinos. He explained that "the field" of his work could not yet include those regions where insurgents remained active. Once the rebels laid down their arms they could rely "on the justice, generosity, and clemency of the United States" to accord them "as full a hearing upon the policy to be pursued and the reforms to be begun, as to anyone."

Harper's Weekly deemed Taft's address "the precise kind of speech" demanded by the situation, suggesting that when a man like Taft made promises, he could be believed. "He is not a New York politician who would sacrifice his soul for office; he is not an anxious member of Congress who would promise anything to get a second term," *Harper's* maintained, heartily endorsing Taft and his agenda. "He is Judge Taft and when we say that he is Judge Taft, we mean to imply that he represents all that is best in American manhood, involving integrity of character, a sane mind, and the loftiest of motives."

As chief executive, General MacArthur occupied the official Malacañan Palace. Left to secure his own housing, Taft finally settled on a comfortable house with a wide veranda overlooking Manila Bay. A central hall separated the large dining room from several roomy bedrooms, and a drawing room was located over the carriage entrance. Three more large downstairs chambers and baths, which Nellie allocated to the children, were equipped with "high canopied and mosquito-netted" beds. The Spanish furniture was "very fine," and electric ceiling fans cooled every room. The house staff included "the cook, the number one boy, the number two boy and the laundryman." The cook, Nellie happily noted, could be given word as late as six or seven o'clock that Taft had eight people coming to dinner and "a perfect dinner would be served." Though their house staff were far outnumbered by the several dozen servants at the Malacañan, the Tafts came to love what Nellie affectionately termed their "homely and unpalatial abode."

Each morning, a coach driven by two horses carried Taft to the old capitol building on Cathedral Plaza in the Walled City, where both military and civilian headquarters were lodged. MacArthur and the military occupied most of the building, forcing the commission to work in tight quarters. Nonetheless, Taft was contented so long as he had space for the large library of books on civil law, history, and government that he had purchased for $2,300 before leaving the States. Taft generally began his workday reading the newspapers and writing letters. At ten o'clock on Mondays, Wednesdays, and Fridays, the commission held executive sessions to hammer out legislation on banking and currency, the courts, public works, civil service, health, and education. The five members were charged with designing—from the foundation up—a new colonial government for a population of nearly 7 million. Once the proposed legislation was drafted, public hearings would be held to solicit contributions from the Filipino people. On Tuesday, Thursday, and Saturday mornings, the door was opened for anyone "who wish[ed] to see them." At one o'clock, Taft drove back to the house for lunch and a Spanish lesson, before returning to preside over the commission's afternoon session. Not until six or seven o'clock would he and a fellow commissioner set out on foot for their homes. "The walk is about two miles and a half and the exercise we get is very good for us," he told his mother-in-law. Dinner was "rather a formidable" affair at which they often entertained guests. Nellie and her sister Maria "put on low-necked gowns" and Will changed into more formal attire. "We begin with soup, have fish, not infrequently an entrée, and the roast and dessert and fruit," he reported in loving detail. Lest his mother-in-law chide him for gaining weight, he rationalized that "in this climate one's vital forces are drawn upon by work so much that one's appetite is very strong at meals."

Taft's "policy of conciliation," his strategy of reaching out to the Filipino people, aroused undisguised antipathy within the insulated regime MacArthur had established. Upon hearing that Taft had referred to the Filipinos as "our little brown brothers," the soldiers promptly composed a marching song "which they sang with great gusto and frequency," climaxing with the jeering refrain: "He may be a brother of William H. Taft, but he ain't no friend of mine!" Believing that it would take ten years to pacify the islands, MacArthur considered Taft's desire to provide education and involve the populace in government as both wrongheaded and ultimately hazardous. As the British colonialists understood, such policies could only lead to "agitation and discontent and constant conspiracy."

The military, Taft sorrowfully reflected, was determined to treat the Filipinos as "niggers." Nellie shared his dismay. "It is a great mistake to treat them as if they were inferiors," she told her husband, "and it really surprises me that the powers that be do not insist upon a different policy." Nellie deplored MacArthur's refusal to entertain anyone in the palace "except a select military circle," and condemned his abhorrence of "even small gestures of social equality among the different races in the Philippines."

In defiance of the established order, Nellie "made it a rule from the beginning that neither politics nor race should influence [their] hospitality in any way." Though her dining room seated only twelve in comfort, she could host parties for hundreds of people in her spacious garden. "We always had an orchestra," she recalled, "and the music added greatly to the festive air of things, which was enhanced too, by a certain oriental atmosphere, with many Japanese lanterns and a profusion of potted plants." While Nellie's insistence "upon complete racial equality" marked a spirit of tolerance far ahead of military attitudes, her guest lists were nonetheless drawn from a narrow segment of the population—educated Filipinos of "wealth and position"—the very class Taft hoped to enlist in the new government.

Although Taft's annual salary of $17,500 was more than he had ever earned, he had to pay his own considerable expenses and could barely sustain his household and lifestyle. Once again, his brother Charley came to his rescue, sending an unexpected $2,500 check. "To say that I was overcome and struck dumb by your generous present is inadequate," Will responded. "Nothing ever diminishes the ardor and enthusiasm of your loyalty to the family." Nellie, too, committed her resources to further her husband's goals, spending a small inheritance she had received to pay for receptions and dinners.

Meanwhile, the Philippine Commission made steady progress. The members revised the Spanish tax code, which had burdened the poor while "giving [the] wealthy comparative immunity." They built a series of schools throughout the islands and brought five hundred recent college graduates from America as teachers. These idealistic young educators, deemed by one historian "precursors of the Peace Corps," arrived carrying "baseball bats, tennis rackets, musical instruments, cameras and binoculars." Under Taft's guidance, the commission built roads, railways, and hospitals, improved harbors and ports, and instituted extensive legal reforms.

Nellie worked side by side with her husband. Upon arrival, he had encouraged her to "enter upon some work of public importance like the organization of a Philippine Orchestra and Philippine bands." She needed no further prompting. Drawing on her love of music and organizational experience, she helped create the Philippine Constabulary Band. Led by an African-American captain, comprised of musicians from all over the islands, the celebrated band would achieve international renown and win a coveted prize at the St. Louis

World's Fair in 1904. While Taft worked on regulatory measures to improve sanitation, Nellie decided her personal cause should be the reduction of infant mortality in Manila. To that end, she instituted an educational campaign on good nutrition and launched a highly successful program to provide the city's children with sterilized milk, a campaign credited with saving many lives. In all her endeavors, she advocated respect for the native culture. When the Army engineers, "in the interest of efficiency and sanitation," threatened to demolish "the medieval walls of the old city of Manila," Nellie successfully campaigned to protect this cherished historical monument.

Taft was immensely proud of his wife. He likened her activism to that of Lady Curzon, who had accompanied her husband to India and achieved worldwide fame for championing women's health. On the eve of their fourteenth anniversary, Will gave Nellie a handwritten note. "I wish to record the fact that it was the most fortunate [day] of my life and every year only confirms me more strongly in that opinion," he wrote. "Every year I feel more dependent on you . . . and every year, my darling, I love you more." Nellie had never been happier. She had welcomed her new living situation "with undisguised surprise and pleasure." The children flourished in their new environment. Bob and Helen were enrolled in one of the new public schools, where they had met "congenial companions." In the evenings and on weekends, they lived outside. In the year-round warm weather, they raced their little ponies on the Luneta, the public stretch of sandy beach bounded on both ends by bandstands, where "everybody in the world came and drove around and around the oval, exchanging greetings and gossip." Two-year-old Charlie, nicknamed "the tornado" for his high-spirited whirl of activity, was petted and simply adored.

Each passing month bolstered Taft's confidence. His judicial training proved indispensable as he labored to draft legislation and regulations. His kind generosity and inclusive style of leadership won the regard of his fellow commissioners. The Filipino people, too, were attracted to the warmth of his personality and his willingness to embrace the native culture. After much practice and intent studying of a diagram indicating the various movements, he and Nellie learned to execute the rigodon, the complicated national dance of the Philippines, "an old fashioned quadrille" that required "graceful and somewhat intricate but stately figures." Observing Taft's impressively large frame, spectators marveled at his surprising agility. This gentle giant, one reporter noted, attended scores of state balls, "literally dancing and smiling his way into the hearts of the people." Indeed, his "unusual size," which required a double rickshaw, created an aura of "superiority."

As Taft became better acquainted with the people of the Philippines, he grew increasingly confident that he would deliver "a good government" and "prosperous" economy to the islands. While he doubted that independence could soon be granted to an illiterate, and in his words, an "ignorant, superstitious people," he trusted that the enlightened colonial rule of the United States would gradually prepare them for self-government. His success depended on McKinley's election, which would ensure consistent support as he constructed new political, educational, and economic institutions. "Not that I am an expansionist," he told a friend, "for I have not changed my mind on that general subject, but only that in the situation into which events have forced us, the Democratic policy of abandonment of these Islands was impossible."

Taft was tremendously heartened by the news of Roosevelt's vice-presidential nomination. The administration had "a good deal to carry" after being in power for four years, he told his brother Charles. Mistakes had "doubtless" been made, and the Democratic nominee, William Jennings Bryan, still enjoyed a formidable following among the working class. Roosevelt's name on the ticket, he explained, added "a following of hero worshippers who [would] give life and vitality to the campaign." Charles agreed, hopeful that Roosevelt would "draw in line all the younger element of the country."

"I could wish that you had continued Governor of New York to do the work thoroughly you have so well begun," Taft told Roosevelt after the Republican National Convention, "but the national election is the more important and you were right to make the sacrifice. The situation here is much more favorable than I had been led to suppose. The back of the Insurrection is broken and the leaders are much discouraged and anxious, most of them, for peace." The remaining insurgents, he claimed, were "restrained from surrender by nothing now but the possibility of Bryan's election." By joining the Republican ticket and rendering "success most probable," he believed Roosevelt "was performing a great service not only to the people of his own country but to the Filipinos as well."

In a warm reply to his friend, Roosevelt acknowledged his regret at forgoing a second gubernatorial term but maintained his satisfaction if he should prove "any help to the ticket this year." Nonetheless, he added wistfully, "I had a great deal rather be your assistant in the Philippines . . . than be vice-president."

Roosevelt's immense contribution to the Republican ticket was beyond question. Telling Mark Hanna that he was "as strong as a bull moose" and should be used "up to the limit," Roosevelt carried the entire campaign on his shoulders. "No candidate for Vice-President in the whole history of this

Republic ever made such a canvass," Boss Platt acknowledged. While McKinley remained at the White House, Roosevelt became "the central figure, the leading general, the field marshal." Breaking every record, "he traveled more miles, visited more States, spoke in more towns, made more speeches and addressed a larger number of people than any man who ever went on the American stump."

Surrounded by his wife and children on November 6, 1900, Roosevelt waited for the results at Sagamore Hill. Throughout the evening, scattered messages arrived from the telegraph operator at the railroad station three miles away. Around ten o'clock, a newspaper correspondent knocked on the door, bringing news of a smashing Republican victory. On the other side of the world, Will and Nellie were on their "tiptoes with excitement." The time difference of thirteen hours between the United States and the Philippines exacerbated their anxiety. "We lived through the day knowing that the United States was asleep, and went to bed just about the time the voters began to go to the polls," Nellie recalled. Finally, just before lunch the next day, a War Department cablegram announced the eagerly anticipated result: "McKinley."

"My dear Theodore," Will saluted his friend in a celebratory letter, "the magnificent victory in the states of the Far West and in New York is eloquent testimony to the good which you have done. The party for whom you made a great sacrifice will not forget it. I have no doubt that you will be the nominee in 1904." Taft felt personal gratitude toward Roosevelt, for McKinley's election allowed him to continue his work, a mission which had come to mean more than he had ever imagined when he reluctantly resigned from the bench.

As Taft had predicted, insurgent activity began to decrease once Bryan's defeat confirmed America's resolve to remain in the Philippines. "Hardly a day passed that did not bring news of the capture or surrender of insurgent officers," Nellie recalled. "The attitude of the native is completely changed," Taft told his brother, "and he is looking around to get in on the 'band wagon.' " By early January 1901, he believed that the momentum had shifted in favor of peace. "The leaders in Manila," he told Senator Lodge, "are hastening to form a party called the 'Federal Party,' which is pushing and pressing for peace and which will have an organization in every province and town in the Islands before many months have passed." The time had come, he continued, to prepare for the transition from General MacArthur and the military authority to the civilian commission. "Their methods of doing things are so very different from ours," he mordantly remarked, "and the people will welcome a change."

To ready the Philippine Commission for full control and responsibility, Taft organized a two-month expedition to the southern provinces, where open hearings would be held to explicate new municipal codes that specified a Filipino governor in every province. Nellie insisted on accompanying the commission. "Of course," Taft told his brother Charles, Nellie would not leave the children behind, so they came along as well. In the end, all the wives and children of the commission were included in the foray, comprising a party of sixty on the Army transport ship. The cluster of wives and children "greatly pleased" the Filipinos, Nellie noted, making the visits far more festive. "Much to the disgust of the military authorities present," she remembered with satisfaction, "we assumed the friendliest kind of attitude."

The desire of the provinces to substitute civil government for military rule was "manifest on every side," Taft reported to his brother Horace. In each provincial capital, "the streets were crowded with men, women and children waving flags and shrilly cheering." Bands playing "The Star-Spangled Banner" and "A Hot Time in the Old Town Tonight" led the commission to the public hall where daylong hearings were held. "Spectacular" festivities followed the working day, Nellie recalled; torchlight parades, fireworks, six-course banquets, and balls celebrated their progress. Altogether, she later wrote, it was "a singular experience, an expedition perhaps unique in history, with which was ushered in a new era, not to say a new national existence, for the people of the Philippine Islands."

At long last, in late February 1901, Congress passed the Spooner Amendment that declared the Insurrection over and called for the transfer of power from military to civilian authorities. Taft informed Roosevelt that he had been selected as the first governor general. "The responsibilities of this position, I look forward [to] with a great deal of hesitation," he confided. "The pitfalls are many and the territory to be traversed is almost unknown." Still, he admitted, "there is a natural gratification in taking control of things."

Roosevelt would have given a great deal to change places with his friend. "I envy you your work," he told Taft eight days after he was sworn in as vice president, bemoaning his own situation. "More and more it seems to me that about the best thing in life is to have a piece of work worth doing and then to do it well." The lull in Roosevelt's customary frenetic activity allowed time for painful reflection: "I did not envy you while I was Governor of New York," he wrote, "nor while I was on the stump last fall taking part in the campaign which I believed to be fraught with the greatest consequences to the Nation; but just at present I do envy you. I am not doing any work and do not feel as though I was justifying my existence."

Roosevelt similarly registered his discontent in a letter to Maria and Bellamy Storer; neither McKinley nor Mark Hanna, he wrote, "sympathize with my feelings or feel comfortable about me, because they cannot understand what it is that makes me act in certain ways at certain times, and therefore think me indiscreet and overimpulsive." Though the president was "perfectly cordial," Roosevelt insisted, "he does not intend that I shall have any influence of any kind, sort or description in the administration from the top to the bottom." Roosevelt longed for some active enterprise in Cuba or the Philippines, but the president had no interest in sending him where real work might be done. The vice presidency "ought to be abolished," he told his friend Leonard Wood. "The man who occupies it may at any moment be everything; but meanwhile he is practically nothing. I do not think that the President wants me to take any part in affairs or give him any advice."

When Congress adjourned for nine months in the spring, suspending the vice president's sole constitutional responsibility of presiding over the Senate, Roosevelt retired to Oyster Bay. "I am rather ashamed to say," he wrote Taft at the end of April, that I do "nothing but ride and row with Mrs. Roosevelt, and walk and play with the children; chop trees in the afternoon and read books by a wood fire in the evening." Despite this peaceful existence, Roosevelt admitted to "ugly feelings," aware that he was "leading a life of unwarrantable idleness."

Taft tried to buoy his friend's spirits with the prospect of a presidential bid in 1904. "I look forward with great confidence to your nomination for President at the next convention," he declared, "and I sincerely hope it may be brought about. Four years in the Vice-Presidential chair will save you from a good many hostilities that might endanger such a result, while the prominence of the position keeps you continually to the front as the necessary and logical candidate." But to Roosevelt it seemed more likely that Taft would get the nod. "I doubt if in all the world there has been a much harder task set any one man during the past year than has been set you," he observed, praising Taft's work under such trying circumstances: "In spite of all the difficulties you have done well, and more than well, a work of tremendous importance. You have made all decent people who think deeply here in this country feel that they are your debtors. . . . It has paid after all, old man."

On the Fourth of July, 1901, William Howard Taft was inaugurated as governor general of the Philippines. The spectacular ceremony featured "music, fireworks, gold lace and glitter, dancing and feasting and oratory." A pavilion had been erected in Cathedral Plaza, the large square in the center of the Walled City, to accommodate the celebration. It was "an occasion of great dignity and interest," Nellie happily remembered. "Americans and Filipinos, all in gala attire, were pressed close together . . . the plaza below was thronged with Filipinos of every rank and condition, in all manner of bright *jusis* and calicos; while above the crowd towered many American soldiers and sailors in spic-and-span khaki or white duck." General MacArthur, who would be departing Manila the next day, stood by as the Filipino chief justice administered the oath of office to Taft. Resplendent in a "crisp white linen suit," Taft appeared "larger even than his natural size."

In his inaugural address, Taft hailed the transfer of authority from the military to the civilian commission as "a new step" toward "Permanent Civil Government on a more or less popular basis." He announced that three leading Filipino citizens would be added to the five-member commission and that educated Filipinos would have voices both in the legislature and in the governance of the provinces. In time, as Stanley Karnow and James Bradley observe, the flaws in Taft's attempt to construct a democracy "from the top down" would become clear. Reliance upon the elite, refusal to sanction any opposition to the Federal Party, and the policy of granting suffrage to a select minority further entrenched the existing "feudal oligarchy," thereby expanding "the gap between rich and poor." On this inaugural day, however, Taft's forthright speech elicited "the wildest of cheering, and the playing of national airs." Such a manifestation "of popular approval," one correspondent noted, "indicates an auspicious beginning for the administration of the new governor."

The next morning, the Tafts relocated their household to the historic Malacañan Palace. "In some ways we regretted that the move was necessary," Nellie recalled, "for we were very comfortable in our 'chalet.'" Until they occupied the palace where MacArthur had presided the Filipinos would not "be convinced that civil government was actually established." Despite her reservations, "the idea of living in a palace . . . appealed to my imagination," Nellie acknowledged. Set on twenty beautifully landscaped acres of trees, flowers, and fountains, the palace stood on a bend in the Pasig River, with windows open all around. There were about twenty rooms on the first floor, "all of them good sized and some of them enormous, and it took a great many servants to keep the place in order," Nellie noted, recollecting the impressive space in detail: "The great living-rooms open one into another, giving a fine perspective, and they lead, through a dozen different doorways, on to a splendid, white-tiled verandah which runs out to the bank of the Pasig." There were a half-dozen houses on the grounds for secretaries and assistants.

Barely established at the palace, Nellie placed an immediate announcement in the newspapers stating that she would hold a reception every Wednesday, open to everyone on an equal basis. Her receptions were soon thronged with "Army and Navy people, civilians of every occupation," and "American school teachers." Never before had the military mixed socially with the islanders, so

Nellie had to cajole the Filipinos to attend "by asking many of them personally and persistently." In short order, she proudly remarked, "there began to be as many brown faces as white among our guests." But Nellie refused to confine herself to the company at the palace and was eager to explore the native culture: she attended local parties and dances, often accompanied by a group of young Army officers, including Archie Butt. Stationed in the Quartermaster Department, Captain Butt was "a great society beau in Washington, and was said to be the handsomest man there," Nellie told her mother. "You would be amused to see Maria and me frisking around with youths years younger than we are, and dancing cotillions with the best of them," she boasted. "Of course the position gives us a great deal of attention which I for one would never have otherwise," she added, "and of course we feel we might as well make the best of it while we have the opportunity."

When news of the triumphant inauguration reached the United States, Roosevelt wrote a long letter to Taft. "It seems idle to keep repeating to you what a lively appreciation not only I but all the rest of us here have of what you are doing. But when you are so far away. . . . I do want you to understand that you are constantly in the thoughts of very many people, and that I have never seen a more widespread recognition of service among men of character than the recognition of the debt we owe you."

Though he rejoiced in his friend's success, Roosevelt was less sanguine about his own prospects. "Here everything is at slack water politically," he continued, addressing Taft's expressed hope for a Roosevelt presidency in 1904. "I should like to be President, and feel I could do the work well," he acknowledged, but "it would be simply foolish for me to think seriously of my chances of getting the office, when the only certain feature of the situation is that my own State will be against me. . . . If the convention were held now, my hold is still so strong both in the west and in New England that I might very well get the nomination without regard to New York. But my present position is one in which I can do absolutely nothing to shape policies, and so looked at dispassionately, I cannot see that there is any but the very smallest chance of my keeping enough hold even to make me seriously spoken of as a candidate." Considering the circumstances, he told Taft, "you are of all the men in this country the one best fitted to give the nation the highest possible service as president. . . . Sometime I want to get the chance to say this in public."

Utterly frustrated and increasingly dispirited, Roosevelt even made plans to begin law school again in the fall, figuring that two additional years of coursework would enable him to pass the bar examinations and launch a legal practice. He also inquired about the possibility of becoming a professor of history at a university. "Of course, I may go on in public life," he reckoned, "but equally of course it is unlikely, and what I have seen of the careers of public men has given me an absolute horror of the condition of the politician whose day has passed; who by some turn of the kaleidoscope is thrown into the background; and who then haunts the fields of his former activity as a pale shadow of what he once was."

On September 6, 1901, that kaleidoscope shifted in a way Roosevelt never anticipated. A young anarchist walked up to shake hands with President McKinley at the Pan-American Exposition in Buffalo. Removing a revolver screened by a handkerchief, the assassin fired two shots into McKinley's chest. Eight days later, the wounds proved fatal. Theodore Roosevelt, at forty-two years of age, became the youngest president in the history of the country.

CHAPTER TEN

"That Damned Cowboy Is President"

"1902 Finds the Helm in Safe Hands," an illustration
in *Puck* magazine, Jan. 1, 1902.

THE SHIP OF STATE IS on its way to unknown ports," the *Nation* declared portentously, warning that the assassination of President McKinley had "violently altered the natural course of events." When Roosevelt took the oath of office on September 14, 1901, questions abounded, unsettling conservatives and reformers alike. "What changes will he make?" "What does the future hold in store?" "Will he continue the policy mapped out by his predecessor?"

Conservatives, who had utterly dominated the Republican Party for three decades, feared the impulsive young president would prove a "bucking bronco," upsetting the alliance between business and government that had delivered unparalleled prosperity at the turn of the century. Reformers hoped Roosevelt's vigorous leadership would refashion the Republican Party into the progressive force it had been under Abraham Lincoln, endeavoring to spread prosperity beyond the wealthy few to the common man.

Comforting themselves that Roosevelt remained a loyal Republican despite occasional fights with the party bosses, conservatives maintained that his "first great duty" was to carry on the policies of the slain president. Throughout the latter part of the nineteenth century, presidents had been captive to their parties: not only did nominations require the approval of party machines, but party platforms also dictated policy preferences. Furthermore, the partisan press became the central organ for mobilizing voters. Recognizing this long-standing subordination of any personal agenda, the New York *Sun* predicted that the new president's actions would "not depend on the possible vagaries of an individual judgment." The Wall Street tycoon Henry Clews made a similar assumption. "The conservative policy of Mr. McKinley has become so settled in the minds of the people," he pronounced, "that it matters not who becomes his immediate successor. . . . No one will dare to experiment or to deviate from such a course of administration."

Throughout his career, Roosevelt had struggled to reconcile party allegiance with the drive to address social problems, a balancing act that became more difficult as the troubling aspects of industrialization intensified. While he considered himself conservative in relation to the Populists, he believed that his party was in thrall to reactionaries who so "dreaded radicalism" that they "distrusted anything that was progressive." Precisely such men dominated both chambers of Congress, Roosevelt lamented. He would work to "push" them forward but recognized that genuine progress would require a direct appeal to the people, "the masters of both of us." To reach the general public, he would enlist the new breed of independent journalists, without whose "active support," he later acknowledged, he "would have been powerless."

Initially he understood the necessity of caution. Warned that the stock market might crash unless he reassured Wall Street that he and his predecessor were "one in purpose," Roosevelt issued a solemn pledge: "In this hour of deep and terrible bereavement, I wish to state that I shall continue absolutely unbroken the policy of President McKinley for the peace, prosperity, and the honor of the country."

Even as he publicly vowed to preserve a comfortable conservative agenda, Roosevelt signaled journalists that a new political era was imminent. On his very first day in the White House, he invited managers of the Associated Press, the Scripps-McRae Press Association (now the United Press), and the New York *Sun* to his office. It was "an unusual request," one historian noted, "for in those days, presidents rarely convened journalists to discuss public matters."

He proposed an unprecedented accessibility, agreeing to "keep them posted" on each evolving plan and policy if they, in return, promised never to "violate a confidence or publish news that the President thought ought not to be published." These parameters established, Roosevelt informed them that despite his public endorsement of the status quo, the Constitution had provided for his succession. "I am President," he bluntly maintained, "and shall act in every word and deed precisely as if I and not McKinley had been the candidate for whom the electors cast the vote for President."

That evening, presiding over his first dinner party as president, Roosevelt openly avowed his intention to differentiate himself from McKinley. A small party had gathered in the modest N Street residence of his sister Bamie and her husband, Will Cowles, where Roosevelt boarded during his first week to allow the grieving Ida McKinley a measure of time to move out of the executive mansion. Two guests, William Allen White and the young president of Columbia University, Nicholas Murray Butler, joined the family. White vividly recalled sitting "pop-eyed with wonder" at the edge of his chair while Roosevelt spoke "with a kind of dynamic, burning candor" about his plans. Though accustomed to Roosevelt's indiscreet talk, White had assumed he would "be different" in his new office, only to find that "he was absolutely unchanged."

The president worried openly that his pledge to follow in McKinley's footsteps, compelled by dire economic predictions, would "embarrass him sorely in the future." He might have forestalled a stock market crash, but if he pursued McKinley's policies to the letter, would it not "give the lie to all he had stood for?" During a "cataract solo of talk" that left White astonished, Roosevelt's thoughts turned to his political future. Should he secure a second term, he would be only fifty years old when it came to a close. "Imagine me as an ex-President, dedicating buildings and making commencement speeches," he mused. The prospect of being "the old cannon loose on the deck in the storm" terrified him. Of more immediate concern, he would likely face Republican Committee chair Mark Hanna in 1904. A powerful adversary much like Boss Platt, Hanna threatened to derail Roosevelt's aspiration for a second term.

White was delighted when conversation turned to Platt, on whom he was gathering material for a long profile in *McClure's*. Roosevelt had promised his assistance, and the two men had planned to meet at Oyster Bay before McKinley's assassination brought them both to Washington. The profile of the New York boss was part of a series White had projected for the magazine. Roosevelt had read White's two earlier pieces on William Jennings Bryan and Tammany boss Richard Croker with great enthusiasm. "Here you are living in a small town out in Kansas, not accustomed to the conditions of life in a seething great city, pay a somewhat hurried visit to New York," he marveled, "and yet you sketch Croker as no one in New York, so far as I know, could sketch him. . . . I immensely admired your Bryan; but then I can entirely understand how you knew Bryan. When it comes to Croker it almost seems as if you must have divined it."

White had interviewed Boss Platt in his downtown office, "a frowzy little cubbyhole that had not been tidied up for years." He had talked with his lieutenants, searched out his rivals, and scoured newspaper files. He believed his study of the Platt machine would have national resonance because its "story of intrigue, corruption and the sordid amalgamation of plutocratic self-interest and political power was typical of American politics in the North at that time." In White's mind, Roosevelt was to be commended for wanting a tough story "about his own party printed" and for believing that "the more people knew" about the corrupt alliance binding big business and elected officials, "the sooner they would wreck the machines." By this time, White was convinced the "untrammeled" greed of the great industrial captains must be checked. He left the dinner that night loaded with ammunition for his profile on Platt.

Lincoln Steffens, who joined William Allen White in Washington the following day, recounted his own exhilaration on learning that Roosevelt would assume the presidency. "We reformers went up in the air when President McKinley was shot, took our bearings, and flew straight to our first president, T.R. And he understood, he shared, our joy." The White House offices, Steffens recalled, "were crowded with people, mostly reformers," amid whom the president "strode triumphant." Despite Roosevelt's attempts to mute his ebullience while Washington and the nation mourned, "his joy showed in every word and movement." When the day's work was done, he grabbed White and Steffens: "Let's get out," he exclaimed, propelling the two men into the streets. "For better than an hour, he allowed his gladness to explode. With his feet, his fists, his face and with free words he laughed at his luck. He laughed at the rage of Boss Platt and at the tragic disappointment of Mark Hanna; these two had not only lost their President McKinley but had been given as a substitute the man they had thought to bury in the vice-presidency. T.R. yelped at their downfall. And he laughed with glee at the power and place that had come to him."

By the time White returned to Emporia to write his profile, he had thoroughly imbibed Roosevelt's resentment toward Platt. "Unconsciously, or perhaps consciously, I used my best and most burning adjectives in that article expressing my scorn of Senator Platt and his machine, and contempt for the things it represented," White later recalled. "It was a bitter piece." Although he warned the editors at *McClure's* that he was afraid it might be "too scorching," they were proud to publish it.

The piece vividly delineated the origin of the Platt machine. Twenty years earlier, every business had maintained its own lobby in Albany, an expensive and often inefficient way of influencing the state legislature. Platt made it his business "to bring order out of confusion," centralizing power in his own hands. He first persuaded corporations to contribute generously to the state central committee rather than field individual lobbyists, and then allocated the money to elect the machine's slate of candidates. Over time, Platt built up a majority of legislators absolutely beholden to his organization. Corporations thrived under the Platt regime; it cost less to support the state committee than to keep individual lobbies. Furthermore, since Platt took none of the money for himself, "there were no longer stories of individual corruption, of bribes and scandals." But the people of New York bore the cost of the system that worked so seamlessly for both the corporations and the politicians. "What we call popular government," White concluded, "is abrogated by purchase of privileges."

White's analysis of the workings of the machine was unsparing but deadly accurate; his portrait of Platt, however, was gratuitously savage. He described the New York boss as an earthworm, "boring beneath the roots of local self-government by cities and States, burrowing silently yet with incalculable power, loosening the soil, sagging foundations." He portrayed a soulless man devoid of any "moral nature," loyal only to his machine and its corporate sponsors; a man transformed into "a machine himself—hard, impulseless, cunning, cute but witless, immovable, inexorable, grinding."

Enraged, Platt immediately declared his intention "to haul both author and publisher into court to answer the charge of criminal libel," threatening that his lawyers had already begun preparing their complaint. "I will get that fellow's scalp if it is the last thing I ever do," he seethed, vowing to employ all his resources "to bring about the punishment of this man." Moreover, White and *McClure's* would not be his only targets. Through depositions, he promised to unearth every one of White's sources, exposing those "who told him the lies," and proceeding equally against them. Suspecting that Roosevelt himself was one of White's sources, he stormed into the president's office, demanding that the journalist be forever barred from the White House. "No friend of mine," Platt insisted, "can be a friend of that man." Wisely, Roosevelt denied having read the article but promised to do so.

"I am perfectly heartbroken at the whole business," White revealed to

Roosevelt, " not for myself, but for the embarrassment to you. I thought I was doing a service to good government in the United States by writing the article. I still believe that I was right, but I seem to have been right at a terrible cost to you." The distraught journalist queried how he might "straighten this business out" but forwarded a second letter to the president's secretary without waiting for an answer. The second letter was to be shown to Senator Platt or made public, as Roosevelt saw fit. "Not one syllable, hint, or inference escaped President Roosevelt's lips while I was a guest in the White House, which might have been used in any way to the discredit of Senator Platt," White asserted. "My opinion of Senator Platt was formed, not by President Roosevelt, but by careful study of conditions in New York politics. Many of my conclusions are probably foreign to those, which everyone knows are held by the president."

Roosevelt thanked White for the potentially mollifying letter, nevertheless insisting he had no intention of letting Platt's indignation dictate his friendships. He sought to ease White's anxiety over their relationship by insisting, "The only damage that could come to me through such articles would be if you refused to continue to champion me!"

No sooner had *McClure's* publicly declared that "they would welcome the suit," claiming to possess a wealth of additional information relating to the boss and his machine, than Platt decided not to go forward. But the incident took a heavy toll on White. He suffered "a kind of nervous collapse," and though he felt "perfectly well physically," he could no longer bear to write, or even to read the papers. "My nerves are gone," he told the editors at *McClure's*, explaining his failure to submit another article that was overdue, admitting that "to as much as dictate this letter throws me in a perspiration." His doctor recommended a protracted rest: "I must leave the state and go to the mountains . . . I am very sorry that I have thrown you all out so." The staff of *McClure's* supported him during the five-month recuperation; equally steadfast during this nadir of White's career was Theodore Roosevelt. White would not forget either.

⌒ ⌒

"PROBABLY NO ADMINISTRATION HAS EVER taken such a curious hold upon the people as that of Theodore Roosevelt," remarked the longtime White House usher Irwin (Ike) Hoover. "While he is in the neighborhood," one critic grudgingly conceded, "the public can no more look the other way than the small boy can turn his head away from a circus parade followed by a steam calliope."

Indeed, Roosevelt's initial months as chief executive were less remarkable for significant political accomplishments than for his impact on the public consciousness. "The infectiousness of his exuberant vitality made the country realize there was a new man in the White House," observed Mark Sullivan, "indeed, a new kind of man. His high spirits, his enormous capacity for work, his tirelessness, his forthrightness, his many striking qualities, gave a lift of the spirits to millions of average men." Among admirers and opponents alike, the president's outsized personality compelled attention.

Newspapers invariably contrasted the vigorous young president with his staid predecessor, a Civil War veteran from a previous generation. "Where Mr. McKinley was patient, cautious, tactful, a very good listener, mindful of the little things which go to put a visitor at ease," observed Walter Wellman of the *Chicago Record-Herald*, "Roosevelt is impetuous, impatient and wholly lacking in tact." When dealing with public officials, Wellman noted, Roosevelt "is so full of energy that he simply runs over. He has no patience with long speeches or extended explanations. He cuts people off in the middle of sentences, tells them he knows all about it, and very often announces his decision before the caller has more than fairly started with his little say. . . . He wants action, action all the time. But he rarely gives offense, and never means to do so." Fortunately, the new president had always tolerated, and even relished, humor at his own expense. It was said that he had "a right good laugh" when told of an epigram circulating widely in Washington: "President McKinley listened to a great many people and talked to but few. President Roosevelt talks to a great many men and listens to nobody."

Roosevelt's frenetic yet disciplined schedule mesmerized the press corps. In a piece for *McClure's*, Lincoln Steffens described a breathless day begun when the president "darts into the breakfast-room with a cheerful hail to those already there," then rushes to his office before the official workday starts to tackle his voluminous correspondence, dictating "one letter after another" to his secretary, "his voice and face reflecting vividly the various emotions which guided his words." From 10 a.m. to 12 p.m., except on cabinet days, the second-floor reception room was crowded with senators, congressmen, Army and Navy officials. "The room is a large one, chairs and sofas are set all about it; but they are filled," Steffens noted, "and many persons are standing."

At noon, the doors opened to ordinary citizens, "an overflowing stream" of people eager to see the most colorful president in their memory. For an hour, Roosevelt moved speedily around the room, giving each person a dazzling smile and a warm handshake. The press of visitors, a *New York Times* reporter observed, never seemed "to try the President's strength or impair his good temper."

At one o'clock, Roosevelt generally excused himself from the crowd for his midday shave. During the "barber's hour," reporters were allowed audience, permitted to question—or more likely listen—as the president expounded upon any number of subjects while the barber desperately tried to ply his trade. "A more skillful barber never existed," newspaperman Louis Brownlow observed, describing how "the President would wave both arms, jump up, speak excitedly, and then drop again into the chair and grin at the barber, who would begin all over." Only "when the barber bent over the presidential head and began to shave the lower lip," Steffens noted, "did he quiet down, giving reporters a few moments to pose their questions."

Lunchtime was always a lively affair, featuring all manner of guests rarely seen in the White House—"Western bullwackers, city prize fighters, explorers, rich men, poor men, an occasional black man, editors, writers." If an article or book piqued Roosevelt's interest, the author received an invitation to lunch. "Whether the subject of the moment was political economy, the Greek drama, tropical fauna or flora, the Irish sagas, protective coloration in nature, metaphysics, the technique of football, or postfuturist painting," the British statesman Viscount Lee remarked, Roosevelt "was equally at home."

Late afternoon was devoted to exercise—a horseback ride or boxing match, a raucous game of tennis or a strenuous hike along the cliffs in Rock Creek Park. Dragging visitors and friends through the wooded sections of the park, Roosevelt had one simple rule: You had to move forward "point to point," never circumventing any obstacle. "If a creek got in the way, you forded it. If there was a river, you swam it. If there was a rock, you scaled it, and if you came to a precipice you let yourself down over it." Journalists delighted in portraying these late afternoon rambles. Jacob Riis described a route that could be traced by the "finger-marks" on "gripped fences, telegraph-poles and trees," where Roosevelt's exhausted companions struggled to follow. Stories multiplied about "this or that general or ambassador or cabinet officer who had dropped out and fallen by the way."

The French ambassador Jules Jusserand left a celebrated account of his first walk with the president. After presenting himself at 1600 Pennsylvania Avenue "in afternoon dress and silk hat, as if we were to stroll in the Tuileries Garden or in the Champs Elysées," he soon found himself in the countryside, following Roosevelt "at breakneck pace" through fields and over rocks. When they approached a broad stream, he assumed the race had finally ended. "Judge of my horror when I saw the President unbutton his clothes and heard him say, 'We had better strip, so as not to wet our things in the Creek.' Then I too, for the honor of France, removed my apparel, except my lavender kid gloves." To be without gloves, he insisted, "would be embarrassing if we should meet ladies."

Reporters soon discovered that the hour when the president returned from these excursions and commenced the daily task of sorting his correspondence was "by far the best time to see him." The *New York Times* reporter Oscar King Davis marveled at Roosevelt's "amazing facility for carrying on a conversation while he was going over the mail. He would glance over a letter, make an addition or alteration with his pen, and sign his name at the same time that he was keeping up a steady fire of talk about whatever subject happened to be under discussion."

Finally quitting his office and the company of his reporter friends, Roosevelt returned to the mansion, where he could relax and dress for dinner. There, in the family quarters, he was "allowed to become again husband, father and playmate." He talked over the day's events with his wife, read to the children or, more often, engaged them in physical games. "I play bear with the children almost every night," he wrote, "and some child is invariably fearfully damaged in the play; but this does not seem to affect the ardor of their enjoyment."

Under Edith's guidance, a vital domesticity returned to the presidential residence. "It was the gloomiest house," she recalled, "with the shadow of death still over it, and a house in which an invalid [McKinley's wife] had lived, why it didn't seem as if the air from Heaven had blown through it." She opened windows, rearranged rooms, brought in fresh flowers, had new carpet laid, and replaced the heavy canopied beds in the children's rooms with their familiar white bedsteads from Oyster Bay.

Not since Willie and Tad Lincoln scampered through hallways and played hide-and-seek in closets had there been such a din in the old mansion. The children, ranging in age from three to seventeen, unabashedly made the White House their own. They dashed across its wooden floors on roller skates. They hid live reptiles in sofa cushions, walked upstairs on stilts, waded through the fountains on the landscaped grounds, and coaxed their pony to ride the elevator to the second-floor bedroom when seven-year-old Archie was sick. "Places that had not seen a human being for years were now made alive with the howls and laughter of these newcomers," observed Ike Hoover. The Roosevelt family has "done more to brighten and cheer the White House than a whole army of decorators," the *Atlanta Constitution* asserted, "and the merry prattle of children echoing through the corridors and apartments impart a homelike atmosphere which every caller is quick to notice and appreciate."

⌢ ⌣

WHILE THE REPUBLICAN ESTABLISHMENT HARBORED misgivings about McKinley's successor, William Howard Taft was certain that Roosevelt possessed every needful quality to be a good president from the outset. In letters home, he rebutted charges of Roosevelt's "impulsiveness and lack of deliberation," citing the fortitude, honesty, and intelligence that characterized his friend's interactions with all manner of men over a wide-ranging career.

Saddened that McKinley had not lived to see "the consummation" of Taft's own endeavors in the Philippines, he nevertheless trusted that Roosevelt would provide the same steadfast support. "In so far as the work in the Philippines was concerned," Nellie noted, "my husband knew where the new President's sympathies were and he had no fears on that score." A week after McKinley's death, *Outlook* magazine published an extraordinary article by Theodore Roosevelt entitled "Governor William H. Taft." Written a month earlier by then Vice President Roosevelt, the extravagantly laudatory article prompted Horace to tease Will that "only a strenuous man like Teddie would put it so strongly in print, unless the subject of the article happened to be dead."

"I dislike speaking in hyperbole," Roosevelt began, "but I think that almost all men who have been brought in close contact, personally and officially, with Judge Taft are agreed that he combines . . . a standard of absolute unflinching rectitude on every point of public duty, and a literally dauntless courage and willingness to bear responsibility, with a knowledge of men, and a far-reaching tact and kindliness." Indeed, Roosevelt observed of his old friend, "few more difficult tasks have devolved upon any man of our nationality during our century and a quarter of public life than the handling of the Philippine Islands just at this time; and it may be doubted whether among men now living another could be found as well fitted as Judge Taft to do this incredibly difficult work."

Roosevelt's support would prove essential for Taft in the weeks that followed as one crisis after another threatened the relative peace and prosperity of the Philippines. Although most of the insurrectionists had surrendered their arms, a brutal uprising in late September 1901 stunned the town of Balangiga on the island of Samar, where a small garrison of American soldiers had set up an outpost at the request of the local mayor. Unbeknownst to the Americans, this request had been a cunning ploy to isolate the troops where they would be vulnerable to a surprise assault.

In the days preceding the ambush, throngs of what appeared to be local mothers and grandmothers in black mourning clothes had assembled at the local church, bearing small caskets said to hold the bodies of their dead children claimed by a recent cholera outbreak. Instead, the coffins held machetelike weapons, and the black-clad figures proved to be guerrilla fighters. Shortly after the church bells rang at 6 a.m. on Sunday morning, September 27, hundreds of insurrectionists suddenly charged into the mess hall and fell upon the unarmed soldiers. One sergeant was decapitated as he sat gripping his breakfast spoon; a private was immersed in the vat of boiling water used to clean utensils. Most of the others were hacked to death. Of seventy-four members of the unit, only twenty escaped with their lives.

"It was a disaster so ghastly in its details," Nellie recalled, "so undreamed of under the conditions of almost universal peace which had been established, that it created absolute panic." As a result, she remembered, attitudes toward the islanders shifted: "Men began to go about their everyday occupations in Manila carrying pistols conspicuously displayed, and half the people one met could talk of nothing else but their conviction that the whole archipelago was a smouldering volcano and that we were all liable to be murdered in our beds any night."

Army officials were quick to place blame for the massacre on Taft's "silly talk of benevolence and civilian rule [and] the soft mollycoddling of treacherous natives." General Jacob W. Smith ordered four companies into Samar with the directive to take "no prisoners. I wish you to kill and burn, the more you kill and burn the better you will please me. I want all persons killed who are capable of bearing arms." When requested to provide a minimum age under which residents of Balangiga might be spared, the general stated clearly: "Ten years." This reprehensible order would eventually lead to Smith's court-martial.

The Samar massacre made headlines in the States: "Disastrous Fight," cried the *New York Tribune*; "Slaughtered by Filipinos," accused the *Houston Daily Post*. The news of "the first severe reverse" in many months prompted a delegation of congressmen to visit the Philippines. Taft called for calm, stressing that the Samar tragedy did not characterize and should not reflect upon the entire Filipino people. "One of the Republicans has made an ass of himself by denouncing the Filipinos as savages and utterly unfit for anything good," Taft told his brother Charles. Contrary to the fearmongering circulated by the military, Taft maintained, "in all other parts of the Islands there is entire peace." If violence escalated, he argued, the military, having roused the native population "to such a pitch of enmity," would bear the blame. At each of the five hundred military posts strung throughout the islands, Taft lamented, they imposed themselves with a dangerous disregard for local communities. "Officers take the good houses in the town and the soldiers live in the church, the 'convento' (which is the priest's house), the schoolhouse or the provincial building," he reported, adding that property owners "are paid an arbitrarily fixed rent and are very fortunate if they get their rent."

The troubles that beset the Philippines were compounded when a highly contagious viral disease called rinderpest laid waste to three quarters of the island's draft cattle. Without these sturdy animals to plow the fields, "a dreadful depression in agriculture" resulted. With the spread of hunger, roving outlaw bands—in a phenomenon known as "ladronism"—preyed on their neighbors. And making matters worse, rats carrying the plague continued to multiply despite an extensive eradication campaign by the new Board of Health. "Altogether," the usually optimistic Taft understated, "we have not passed through the happiest months of our lives out here."

On October 1, Nellie and two of the commissioners' wives departed for a trip to China. That very afternoon, Taft fell seriously ill with what doctors mistakenly diagnosed as dengue fever. He remained bedridden for ten days, and when he returned to work, severe rectal pain prevented him from sitting. At the same time, a fungal infection developed in his groin. "While I have none of Job's comforters," Taft told Horace with grim humor, "I have many of his troubles." On October 25, doctors finally discovered a large perineal abscess, most likely caused by the invasion of bacteria into his system. With gangrene spreading, an immediate operation was necessary. As Taft was carried from the palace on a stretcher, his terrified ten-year-old daughter Helen burst into tears. Taft dispatched a telegram to Nellie: "Come dear am sick." When the ether was administered, he later joked, he deliriously wished that he could "hire a hall and make a speech." A large incision drained the cavity and removed the infected flesh. His doctors worried that the gangrenous tendency and blood poisoning had not been stopped in time, but they became more optimistic as the wound began to heal. The next day, Taft telegraphed Nellie again: "Much better don't shorten trip."

Confined to bed for several weeks, Taft secured an order from Washington appointing commission member Luke Wright as vice governor. This step provided him "peace of mind," assuring that his duties would not be neglected while he convalesced. No sooner had he resumed work than he immediately fell ill again, requiring a second operation. Roosevelt and Root decided that Taft should return to the United States until he was thoroughly recovered and rested. The Filipinos feared they would never see their friend and trusted advocate again. As Taft made ready to depart, he spoke to the large native crowd that surrounded the governor's palace to bid him anxious farewell, promising them he would return as soon as he was well.

WHILE TAFT ENDURED THE MOST discouraging period in his experience as viceroy, Roosevelt worked busily to draft his State of the Union address. Scheduled for early December when the legislature convened, his message would provide the first indication of his position on the most critical issue of the day—how best to address the massive trusts that were rapidly swallowing up competitors in one field after another. The period following McKinley's first election has been labeled "the high summer of corporate influence." Hundreds of small railroads, steamship companies, tobacco firms, copper industries, and collieries consolidated into single corporations that controlled as much as three quarters of the production in their particular fields.

In the year and a half since Roosevelt had failed to secure legislation to regulate the trusts in New York State, corporate consolidation had produced more than a thousand new mergers, including the creation of the world's most colossal trust, United States Steel. And every passing week heralded new combinations, stirring fear in small businessmen and consumers alike. Across the country, mergers brought absentee ownership, disregard for working conditions, higher prices, and lower wages.

Roosevelt believed the future of the Republican Party would be determined by its willingness to confront this malignancy. "I intend to work with my party and to make it strong by making it worthy of popular support," he told Joseph Bucklin Bishop. Despite this resolve, he saw clearly that an open denunciation of the Republican alliance with big business would set the bosses against him. They would deny him the presidential nomination in 1904, just as they had prevented his run for a second term as governor. Moreover, without the support of Republican leadership in Congress, he had no chance of passing even the mildest legislation to regulate the trusts.

The U.S. Senate presented the most powerful obstacle to any progressive reform. Because senators at the time were elected by state legislatures rather than by popular vote, the majority of senators owed their positions to their state machines. These organizations, William Allen White observed, were in thrall to the business interests that filled their coffers through campaign contributions or blatant bribery. In a number of states, the bosses made themselves senators; in others, wealthy individuals purchased their seats outright.

In a scathing editorial, the *New York Times* suggested that a millionaire could buy a Senate seat "just as he would buy an opera box, or a yacht, or any other luxury in which he can afford to indulge himself." In some instances, the *Times* reported, "the sale takes the form of open bribery of the legislators"; more often, the Senate seat was "simply the satisfaction of a 'claim' acknowledged by the leaders of the party and created by large contributions to the Party treasury." A widespread biting anecdote captured the popular view of the Senate: One night, Frances Cleveland, wife of the president, was awakened by a noise in the house. "Wake up," she nudged her husband. "There are robbers in the house." President Cleveland set her mind at ease. "There are no robbers in the House," he reassured her, "but there are lots in the Senate."

Five men comprised the inner circle in the Republican-controlled Senate. Sixty-four-year-old Mark Hanna had only recently joined the Senate after a long and successful business career dealing in coal, iron ore, shipping, and street railways. Architect of McKinley's two victorious campaigns, Hanna had earned the title of "national boss" of the Republican Party. Cartoons and editorials depicted a bloated capitalist, a tool of Wall Street, and a representative of the trusts; though more sympathetic to labor than most capitalists, Hanna had become an emblem of "the liaison between big business and government." Under his influence, not a single anti-trust suit had been prosecuted in two years, even as consolidation escalated beyond anything previously imagined. "In the final analysis," Lincoln Steffens succinctly charged, Hanna's methods "amount to the management of the American people in the interest of the American businessman for the profit of American business and politics."

Much like Platt, Hanna viewed Roosevelt as fundamentally unstable, a political hazard. "I told William McKinley it was a mistake to nominate that wild man at Philadelphia. I asked him if he realized what would happen if he should die," Hanna fumed. "Now look, that damned cowboy is President of the United States!" Early on, Roosevelt was convinced that he would eventually have to wrest party control from Hanna, but if an open break occurred, he told Steffens, "it would be a great calamity to the party and therefore to the public." To assail the powerful Hanna machine, the New York *World* noted, "would be as foolhardy as for a mill hand to fling himself upon a whirling buzz-saw."

Accordingly, Roosevelt reached out to the older man, expressing hope that they might one day share an intimacy similar to the one Hanna had enjoyed with McKinley. In addition, he requested a conference to solicit Hanna's counsel on political strategy and the upcoming message. "Go slow," Hanna cautioned. "It would not be possible to get wiser advice," Roosevelt graciously responded. Such patience would not cost Roosevelt, Mark Sullivan noted, for "his was the rising star; Hanna's was falling."

In addition, Roosevelt sought out the "Big Four," a group of veteran senators who commanded the power to pass, block, or kill any legislation: Nelson Aldrich of Rhode Island, John C. Spooner of Wisconsin, William B. Allison of Iowa, and Orville Platt (no relation to the New York boss) of Connecticut. Aldrich, the leader of the group, had become a multimillionaire through investments in street railways, banking, oil, gas, electricity, and rubber. Elected to the Senate in 1881 after two terms in the House, he was considered the most influential Republican legislator on the Hill. As chairman of the Finance Committee, he wielded absolute control over legislation on tariffs and trusts. Furthermore, Aldrich's only daughter, Abby, had married John D. Rockefeller, Jr., only son of the Standard Oil tycoon.

To each of these influential conservative leaders, Roosevelt made an expansive overture, similar in tone to his September 30 note to Senator Spooner: "I hope to keep in closest touch with you and to profit by your advice in the future as I have profited by it in the past." At regular intervals, he solicited their suggestions, inviting them to the White House for confidential conversations. As he drafted sections of his message, Roosevelt read them aloud to Hanna and the Big Four, appealing to them as valued mentors. He also included members of his cabinet in these sessions, inviting a frank discussion. The press described "a very pretty scene, this young president sincerely and earnestly placing his thoughts before his older counselors and begging them to criticize wherein they thought he was wrong."

Journalists noted in early November that Roosevelt had "made more progress in the preparation of his message to Congress than any of his predecessors ever did so far in advance." This lengthy process allowed him to write the entire message personally rather than simply compile sections submitted by various department heads, as was customary. As page after page accumulated, curiosity about the contents escalated. No subject attracted more interest than the trusts. "Many scribes with many minds, writing for many papers, are guessing and philosophizing as to what the president's message will and will not contain," one newspaper commented, concluding that "the only real thing anybody can guess or predict about with an approximation to truth is that it will be Roosevelt's message and nobody else's."

From the start, Roosevelt determined that he would not retreat "one hair's breadth" from the position on the trusts that he had established in his gubernatorial message, his vice-presidential acceptance speech, and the address he had delivered at the Minnesota State Fair five days before McKinley was shot. "More and more it is evident," he had declared that day in Minneapolis, "that the State, and if necessary, the Nation, has got to possess the right of supervision and control as regards the great corporations." He had repeatedly emphasized the need for corporations to deliver public reports to the government on their capitalization, profits, and financial structures. Now, he intended to highlight that recommendation in his annual message by calling for a cabinet-level Department of Commerce and Industries, an agency empowered to examine the workings of the big corporations.

Orville Platt warned Roosevelt that if Congress passed a law "going so far as to force corporations doing an interstate business to make reports to United States officials," it would likely be ruled unconstitutional. Hanna insisted that the proposition would only "furnish ammunition to the enemy in a political contest" and that "even the labor unions were not greatly interested in corporate control."

Roosevelt held his ground, even after a contentious session with his friends George Perkins and Harvard classmate Robert Bacon, both of whom were partners in J. P. Morgan's firm. While he remained "very fond" of both men, Roosevelt confided to a relative that they argued "like attorneys for a bad case, and at the bottom of their hearts each would know this . . . if he were not the representative of a man so strong and dominant a character as Pierpont Morgan." Not only did they encourage the president "to go back on" his previous demands for disclosure, but Perkins apparently suggested that he "do nothing at all, and say nothing except platitudes; accept the publication of what some particular company chooses to publish, as a favor, instead of demanding what we think ought to be published from all companies as a right." As the historian Eric Goldman observes, the practice of "not prying into business affairs was accepted as part of a prevailing laissez-faire."

Just as Abraham Lincoln would exorcise his frustrations in "hot letters" he would put aside unsent, Roosevelt confined his rancor to private diatribe and followed it with a public letter for Douglas Robinson (Corinne's husband) to share with the two men. "I much enjoyed the visit from Perkins," he amiably wrote. "I am particularly desirous to see him and Bacon as often as possible."

To Paul Dana, conservative editor of the New York *Sun*, Roosevelt spoke more directly. In mid-November, Dana wrote a long, critical letter to Roosevelt admonishing that "the proposition that the Federal Government shall lay its hand on business corporations is revolutionary. . . . It would open the door to an unlimited increase of the powers of the Federal Government." Adding to his argument, Dana insisted that "there is no authority of public opinion for the demand for trust legislation. . . . I deny the political right of the Republican successor of President McKinley to undertake it." Roosevelt acknowledged Dana's warnings but had no intention of altering his course. "Your letter causes me concern," he replied, "to ask me to alter my convictions as to the proper course to be pursued about these big corporations is much like asking me to alter my convictions about the Monroe Doctrine and the need of building a navy. . . . You have no conception of the revolt that would be caused if I did nothing."

On the morning of December 3, 1901, Roosevelt's completed message, totaling more than 20,000 words, was carried to the House and the Senate to be read out by a clerk, as had been the custom since Thomas Jefferson sent the message in writing. "A hush immediately fell over the body as the clerk began in clear, firm, and distinct tones to read the opening paragraphs," the *Washington Times* reported, observing that "he did not read in the usual sing-song monotone, but with emphasis and expression." The recitation took about two hours, but "there was interest in every line, and members of both houses listened with unusual attention." The assembled legislators generally received such messages "with scant courtesy," the Washington correspondent for the *Chicago Record-Herald* noted, retiring to the "allurement of the smoking-room or restaurant. To-day they sat still."

The message opened with an emotional denunciation of McKinley's assassin, "a professed anarchist, inflamed by the teachings of professed anarchists." Such men, "who object to all governments, good and bad alike," only sabotaged progress, Roosevelt declared. This impassioned opening introduced Roosevelt's agenda of moderate, reasoned reform. His tempered approach toward curbing the abuses of industrialism, he asserted, would prove the surest way to combat the alarming rise in anarchism, socialism, and demagoguery.

In the long sentences of the president's message, semicolons followed by "yet" or "but" separated clauses that balanced each side of an issue, reflecting Roosevelt's characteristic "on the one hand, on the other" style of crediting antagonistic views. "The captains of industry who have driven the railway system across the continent, who have built up our commerce, who have developed our manufactures, have on the whole done great good to our people," he proclaimed, "yet it remains true . . . there have been abuses connected with the accumulation of wealth." Repeatedly, he employed this rhetorical display of evenhandedness: "To strike with ignorant violence" at the great trusts "endangers the interests of all . . . and yet it is also true that practical efforts must be made to correct those evils." If he had no patience for those who resorted "to hatred and fear" to denounce the trusts, Roosevelt made it clear that he shared the "wide-spread conviction" that certain invidious practices were "hurtful to the general welfare." While he stopped short of advocating prohibition of the trusts, he demanded that they be "supervised and within reasonable limits controlled."

Roosevelt's strategic deliberations provoked a stinging parody from Finley Dunne's Mr. Dooley: "Th' trusts, says [Roosevelt], are heejoous monsthers built up be th' inlightened intherprise iv th' men that have done so much to advance progress in our beloved counthry. On wan hand I wud stamp thim undher fut; on th' other hand not so fast."

Although Roosevelt's carefully balanced propositions invited accusations of equivocation, the rhetoric of his message allowed him to set the stage for reform without immediately alienating corporate interests. Conservative critics, soothed by language touting the benefits of capitalism and condemning the populist call for the total destruction of the trusts, missed the true implications of Roosevelt's central argument concerning the federal government's responsibility to regulate corporations in the public interest. "It is no limitation upon property rights or freedom of contract," he noted, "to require that when men receive from government the privilege of doing business under corporate form," they assume an obligation to the public. Through the creation of a new Department of Commerce, the government would merely exercise its duty "to inspect and examine" corporate finances as a means to determine whether regulation or taxation was necessary. Should Congress determine that "it lacks the constitutional power to pass such an act," Roosevelt recommended that an amendment to the Constitution "be submitted to confer that power."

Public attention immediately following his message focused on the trusts. Yet Roosevelt had also outlined his plans for the welfare of wageworkers, reciprocity agreements, railway rebates, forest preserves, irrigation of arid lands, and the isthmian canal—as well as his ideas for reorganizing the Army and expanding the Navy. At the close of his address, he returned to the tragedy of McKinley's death, acknowledging the expressions of sympathy and grief "from every quarter of the civilized world" that had touched "the hearts" of every American.

Generally, both the public and the press received Roosevelt's address well. "No other message in ten years past has been read by so many American citizens," claimed *The Independent*. The tenor of the State of the Union was viewed as "characteristic of the man; self-assertive, determined, honest, patriotic, permeated with the spirit of progress." Despite widespread approbation, newspapers remained "skeptical of any important outcome from the president's recommendations regarding trusts," convinced that Roosevelt's primary goal at this juncture was his own nomination and election. "He knows very well that no man can secure the Republican nomination over the trusts," one Indiana paper editorialized. The trusts understood the proposals as mere theatre to satisfy reformers. While it was "refreshing" to see "a bold man struggling with the devil-fish of party intrigue," until the middle-class confusion about corporate consolidation galvanized a demand for positive action, the conservative powers in Congress would have no trouble in preventing Roosevelt's proposals from even reaching the floor.

THE FINANCIAL WORLD WAS STAGGERED on February 19, 1902 when Roosevelt announced the government's intention to bring an anti-trust suit against the Northern Securities Company. This giant holding company had recently merged the rail and shipping lines of James Hill, J. P. Morgan, and Cornelius Vanderbilt in the Northwest with those of E. H. Harriman, the Rockefellers, and the Goulds in the Southwest. Consummated during Roosevelt's watch, this vast new combination, first reported on at length by Ray Baker, touched a nerve in the president.

Baker, who had worked for months on a series of articles profiling the nation's tycoons, was well positioned to cover the spectacular merger. He had returned to New York from his sojourn in Arizona reenergized and eager to tackle the unsettling issues of labor and capital that had preoccupied him since his college days. He felt that he "had come to see and know the workers' side" as he covered the Pullman strike for the *Chicago Record*, conversing at length with Eugene Debs and spending long weeks with a number of other labor leaders. "I knew, or thought I knew, the powerful incentives for organization behind their movements," he wrote, "and their demands for more wages and more freedom." Realizing he must also develop an understanding of "the business and financial side," Baker was thrilled when McClure suggested a series focused on the captains of industry. While he did not consider these articles to be "revolutionary" or "crusading," his research shaped an evolving conception of capitalism's dazzling strengths and troubling weaknesses.

Baker's first article, on J. P. Morgan, published in October 1901, portrayed a Wall Street giant who controlled "a yearly income and expenditure nearly as great as that of Imperial Germany, paid taxes on a debt greater than that of many of the lesser nations of Europe, and by employing 250,000 men, supported a population of over one million souls, almost a nation in itself." While Baker acknowledged that the powerful private banker was "an expert financial doctor," who had rescued the American economy from panic on three separate occasions, he withheld judgment on whether Morgan had employed that "unquestioned genius to the highest purpose."

The alarming dimensions of Morgan's empire were delineated in a second, follow-up article that analyzed the structure of the United States Steel Corporation. This immense enterprise, the first billion-dollar corporation in the world, had been conceived the previous April when J. P. Morgan, Andrew Carnegie, and the leaders of nine other steel companies merged to avoid a ruinous, competitive war. Many of these men, Baker concluded, "were unquestionably forced" into consolidation "against their will." The resulting corporation produced "more than a quarter of the entire [steel] production of the world" and dictated "the destinies of a population nearly as large as that of Maryland or Nebraska." To enumerate its corporate possessions glazes the mind: more than 18,000 coke ovens, 80 blast furnaces, six giant railroad companies, and 115 steamships. "It is difficult to convey any adequate idea of the magnitude of the Steel Corporation," Baker concluded. "Nothing like this has ever been seen before."

Baker's research for these two articles on J. P. Morgan provided clear perspective on the machinations behind the formation of Northern Securities. The merger, Baker explained, stemmed from a costly quarrel the previous spring: two rival railroads that controlled the overwhelming majority of railroad lines in their respective regions had fought for control of a third railroad. In the aftermath, under the leadership of J. P. Morgan, "the contestants gathered themselves together, counted their losses, smoothed over their difficulties," and forged a gargantuan new holding company. On November 13, 1901, Northern Securities became "the second largest corporation in the world," behind only U.S. Steel. With tens of thousands of miles of track spanning the continent and hundreds of ships, Baker declared it "absolute dictator in its own territory, with monarchical powers in all matters relating to transportation."

"None outside the golden coterie know all the details," Baker observed, presciently adding, "the future will find one of its great problems in deciding how big a business enterprise must become before the public is entitled to know the full details of its management." It appeared certain that "the same dozen or more men" would own "nearly all the great railroads of America and the greatest industries besides." Indeed, with this new combination in place, a person might journey "from England to China on regular lines of steamships and railroads without once passing from the protecting hollow of Mr. Morgan's hand." Would the day come, Baker mused, "when an imperial M will repose within the wreath of power?" The implication that these few men were "more powerful than the people, more powerful than Congress, more powerful than the government," observed Mark Sullivan, "presented to Roosevelt a challenge such as his nature would never ignore."

Roosevelt asked his attorney general, Philander C. Knox, if an anti-trust suit against Northern Securities could be sustained. A brilliant lawyer who had enjoyed a successful career in Pittsburgh, Knox calculated the odds for several weeks before reporting to Roosevelt that he believed an anti-trust suit based on the Sherman Anti-Trust Law could be won. Roosevelt kept his decision to proceed from everyone else in his cabinet, including Elihu Root, his closest adviser. Root did not share "the view that Taft and I take about corporations," he later explained to a journalist friend. The unexpected announcement that the government was in the process of preparing a bill "to test the validity of the merger" appeared "like a thunderbolt from a clear sky." Many commentators feared the outbreak of "a wholesale war on industrial trusts."

"Not since the assassination of President McKinley has the securities market been compelled to face news for which it was wholly unprepared," declared the *New York Herald*, under headlines announcing a precipitous fall in stock prices. Financiers could not fathom how Roosevelt lacked the courtesy to provide advance notice. He was, after all, one of them: a Harvard man, a member of their clubs. "If we have done anything wrong," J. P. Morgan complained in a hastily arranged meeting with the president three days later, "send your man to my man and they can fix it up." An agreeable resolution was impossible, Roosevelt countered. "We don't want to fix it up," Knox confirmed, "we want to stop it." Turning to Roosevelt, Morgan inquired if U.S. Steel was in jeopardy. "Certainly not," Roosevelt replied, "unless we find out that in any case they have done something that we regard as wrong." Roosevelt remarked to Knox after Morgan's departure: "That is a most illuminating illustration of the Wall Street point of view. Mr. Morgan could not help regarding me as a big rival operator."

Morgan's partners were appalled at the lack of recognition for their substantial contribution to American progress. "It really seems hard," James Hill complained, "that we should be compelled to fight for our lives against the political adventurers who have never done anything but pose and draw a salary." Members of New York's legal community were scathing in their opinion of Knox, calling him "an unknown country lawyer from Pennsylvania." When these words reached the president, his response was curt: "They will know this country lawyer before this suit is ended."

For a quarter of a century, Roosevelt later observed, "the power of the mighty industrial overlords of the country had increased with giant strides, while the methods of controlling them, or checking abuses by them on the part of the people, through the Government, remained archaic and therefore practically impotent." The anti-trust suit "served notice on everybody that it was going to be the Government, and not the Harrimans, who governed these United States." At the same time, Roosevelt's actions clearly demonstrated to powerful Republican leaders "that he was President in fact as well as in name."

Roosevelt next turned his attention to the beef trust. Allegations had surfaced in the press that the big beef packers, led by Armour & Co. and Swift & Co., had agreed to parcel out territories and fix prices, resulting in a sharp cost increase for families purchasing meat. The advent of refrigerated freight cars had diminished the advantage once held by local butchers, facilitating consolidation among the big national firms. Labeling the beef trust "an atrocious conspiracy of greed against need," one New York newspaper challenged anyone to deny "that such absolute control by a few men over the food supply of a nation is in the highest degree hostile to the public welfare." After the Justice Department investigated the matter, Roosevelt directed Knox to bring suit against the beef trust. "This is the right course," the *World* editorialized, "and the president has proved himself, as he did in directing the similar suit against Northern Securities Co., to be wiser and more resolute than leaders of his party in Congress, who sit supinely in the path of a rising storm of popular indignation and refuse to do anything to 'disturb the business' of protecting monopolies by law!"

For all the accolades that attended his confrontations with these massive combinations, Roosevelt considered the Sherman Act a blunt instrument that might prove "more dangerous to the patient than the disease." In the hands of zealots, unable or unwilling to distinguish *good* trusts that yielded efficient operations, lower prices, and better service, from *bad* trusts that used predatory tactics to gain monopoly, artificially depress production, and extort unreasonable prices, the Sherman Act might destroy the very prosperity it was intended to foster. Roosevelt far preferred the approach recommended in his annual address—new legislation enabling the national government to examine corporate records and determine what remedies, if any, were needed. Nevertheless, "with the path to effective regulation blocked by a stubborn, conservative Congress," the historian George Mowry observes, "the only way for Roosevelt to bring the arrogant capitalists to heel was through the judicious use of the anti-trust laws."

For Nellie and Will Taft, the winter of Roosevelt's skirmishes with the trusts marked "a period of bereavement and protracted illnesses." During the long sea voyage from Manila to San Francisco, doctors discovered that Taft's incision was not healing properly. It was "opened and drained," but months of bed rest the previous fall had weakened his knees and ankles, making it painful for him to stand for any protracted time. To compound matters, Nellie was suffering from what was later diagnosed as malaria. In San Francisco, they were informed that their cross-country trip on the Union Pacific would be interrupted by a severe snowstorm in the Midwest. Having received word that her mother was seriously ill, Nellie insisted on moving forward nonetheless. In Utah, a catastrophic blizzard froze water pipes and broke the train's heating system. Wrapped in blankets, they pressed eastward. Even after enduring these hardships, they were too late: in Omaha, Nellie received a telegram bearing the news that her mother had died the previous day.

Taft remained with Nellie and the children in Cincinnati until he had to leave for Washington to testify before the Senate Committee on the Philippines. From the moment he arrived in the capital, Taft was surrounded by affectionate support. War Secretary Elihu Root and his wife insisted that he board with them during his stay, which eventually stretched to thirty days. No sooner had Taft reached their home on Rhode Island Avenue than the president called with plans to join them that evening. Taft was pleased to find Roosevelt "just the same as ever," writing to Nellie that it was hard "to realize that he is the President. He greatly enjoys being President and shows not the slightest sign of worry or hard work in his looks or manner." Scarcely a night passed for Taft without an invitation to dine with the Roosevelts, the Lodges, the Hays, or the Hannas.

Despite his warm reception in Washington, Taft worried about the hearings. Called by Massachusetts senator George Hoar, an eloquent anti-imperialist who insisted on exposing the truth of events in the Philippines, the proceedings would likely be exhausting and unproductive. "If General Chafee is right," Hoar proclaimed, referring to the Civil War veteran who served as the military governor of the Philippines, "there is not a man in those islands who is not conspiring against the government and eager for liberty." The day before the hearings convened, Taft wrote to his brother Horace, playfully requesting "compassion and merciful judgment, when you shall read of the condemnation to which I shall probably be subjected by anti-imperialists and our democratic brethren. Please do not deny the fact that you are still my brother, though a mortified one."

Yet throughout a long week of testimony Taft acquitted himself exceedingly well, drawing a sharp line between the military's negative estimates of the Filipino people and his own more hopeful perspective. "I have much more confidence in the Filipino and his loyalty than have a good many of the military officers," he assured them. Asked by Democratic senator Joseph Rawlins if the country was not "flying in the face" of Asiatic culture and tradition by imposing a republican form of government, he expressed his conviction that such difficulties could be successfully negotiated. In the course of his governorship, Taft said, he had developed "somewhat intimate relations" with the Filipino people and was certain that the overwhelming majority wanted peace and a stable government.

Taft told the committee, as he had told McKinley, that he had not supported the idea of occupying the Philippines, "but we are there." America's primary responsibility, he maintained, must be to help the Filipinos achieve self-rule, slowly inducting them into the political process. Eventually a determination would be possible regarding the future of the Philippines—whether they should apply for statehood, declare full independence, or perhaps develop a commonwealth connection to the United States similar to that of Canada or Australia to Great Britain. He called on Congress to reduce the tariff on Philippine imports and to establish a popularly elected assembly to constitute a lower branch of the government while the Philippine Commission continued to comprise the upper branch. Taft understood that some senators considered this policy "too progressive and too radical," but he believed it would provide "a great educational school" in the art of democracy.

When pressed about instances of military brutality against the Philippine insurgents, he admitted "that cruelties have been inflicted; that people have been shot when they ought not to have been," and that soldiers had employed water torture to extract information from insurgents. Courts-martial had been ordered to address these abuses. He insisted, however, that the military had largely exercised uncommon "compassion" and "restraint."

"Following his appearance," one reporter noted, "not a speaker on either side but paused a moment to pay at least some small tribute to the man." By speaking freely and openly, Taft "had taken his fellow-citizens into his confidence on the dangers and the doubtful points of our 'experiment' as well as on its rosier aspects." In return, he had earned their confidence "in his sincerity and his ability to meet the task in hand." Extremely pleased, Elihu Root assured Taft that if he continued his great service to the Philippines for another year or more, "there was not anything in the gift of the President" that would be withheld.

The pleasure of Taft's stay in Washington was cut short when doctors determined that yet another operation was required to remove a deep abscess that had developed in the aftermath of his previous surgery. The news that he would be confined to his bed for three weeks left him feeling downcast: "I have been hacked and cut and curetted and etherized so much and have lain so long in bed that a continuance of all this for the better part of a month I do not welcome and should deeply regret if it delayed my return." Nonetheless, he submitted gamely to a third operation in six months, and this time happily recorded that "the cure seems to be complete."

Contemplating his return to the Philippines, Taft decided to stop first in Rome, where he hoped personally to negotiate some solution to the perplexing problem of the Spanish friars, a situation that had plagued him from his first days in the islands. To the Filipino people, Taft understood, the friars represented "the crown of Spain, and every oppression by the Spanish government was traced by them to the men whose political power had far outgrown that exercised by them as priests." Over the years, these clerics had come to operate as political bosses, acquiring 400,000 acres of the best agricultural lands and assuming despotic power over the police, the civil government, and the schools. Once the revolution began, he wrote, they "had to flee for their lives. Fifty of them were killed and three hundred of them were imprisoned." If they should return and attempt to reclaim title to the land, he feared violence would break out. Roosevelt and Root deputized Taft to inform the Holy See that the United States would purchase the lands for a fair price so long as the hated friars never returned to the archipelago. The land would then be redistributed among the poor Filipino farmers.

"What a splendid thing it will be to go to Rome," Nellie exclaimed when she learned of her husband's strategic mission. In the weeks before the planned trip, her own health had improved. Blood tests revealed a reduction in her malarial infection and her spleen had returned to normal. But just before they were scheduled to sail, Robert contracted scarlet fever, making departure impossible for Nellie and the children. "What a disarrangement of our plans!" Taft lamented. "And more than this what a trial for Robert and you."

Louise Taft was in Millbury, Massachusetts, when Will called to explain her grandson's illness and to bid her goodbye. Realizing that Nellie could not travel, Louise offered to accompany her son. Nellie, despite her own disappointment, was relieved that Will would have the comfort and assistance of his mother during the trip. "Within twenty-four hours," Nellie recalled, "the intrepid old lady of seventy-four packed her trunks and was in New York ready to sail." In the years since Alphonso's death, Louise had astonished her family with her unflagging activity. "She went wherever she liked," Nellie noted with admiration, "and it never seemed to occur to her that it was unusual for a woman of her age to travel everywhere with so much self-reliance." Until Nellie arrived in Rome with the children more than a month later, Louise managed affairs with "an energy and an enterprise" that overwhelmed her son with "pleasure and pride."

Several factors complicated Taft's mission. He had to take care throughout the process that his dealings with the Pope never implied diplomatic recognition, which would violate America's separation of church and state and incur the hostility of Protestants. At the same time, he sought to defuse Catholics' fears that he was antagonistic to the Church. His initial meeting with the Pope, still "lively as a cricket" and "bubbling with humor" at eighty-two, went better than he could have hoped. Most significantly, Taft noted, he secured the pontiff's promise to meet all questions "in a broad spirit of conciliation," though the details were left to a group of cardinals who proved far less accommodating. Weeks went by before the cardinals finally issued a statement on June 21, 1902. The Church would consent to sell its property in the Philippines, but would not withdraw the friars currently in residence. With this unsatisfactory conclusion, negotiations were suspended.

When Taft at last prepared to sail for the Philippines, word arrived that a cholera epidemic had struck Manila. He decided Nellie and the children should remain in Europe for an additional month, hoping that by then the outbreak "would have run its course." Writing to Nellie from the steamer, he confessed feeling apprehensive about his reception in Manila. "I don't know how the people will take the result of my visit to Rome. Then they are not in very good humor about the strict cholera regulations . . . I may land with a few handshakings and a dull thud." He regretted her absence but trusted she would soon join him and her indispensable support would help him surmount all difficulties. "I can not tell you what a comfort it is to me to think of you as my wife and helpmeet," he declared. "I measure every woman I meet with you and they are all found wanting. Your character, your independence, your straight mode of thinking, your quiet planning, your loyalty, your sympathy when I call for it (as I do too readily) your affection and love (for I know I have it) all these Darling make me happy only to think about them."

To his amazement, Taft's arrival triggered what was said to be the grandest demonstration of popular support ever recorded in the history of the Philippines. Thirty thousand Filipinos had come from the hills and neighboring provinces to welcome Taft home. Whistles sounded and bells rang as soon as his vessel was spied. From the harbor to the palace, his carriage was met by cheering crowds. Triumphal arches and flags decorated the streets. Children tossed flowers and released doves into the air as Taft went by.

In his speech at the palace, Taft told the people "in a straightforward way of his experiences in Washington and Rome." Though negotiations with the Vatican had been suspended, "the sale of church lands to the government was assured," and he was confident that an agreement to remove the friars would eventually be worked out. Taft took comfort that the natives had clearly interpreted his visit to Rome "as a real effort on the part of the United States to do something which could not have been for any other benefit than the benefit of the Filipino people." Visibly moved, he promised to work unremittingly for the people of the islands. So "universal, earnest, and enthusiastic" was the response, reporters noted, that it left no doubt that Taft had earned "a proud position in the hearts of the Filipino people."

1

Theodore Roosevelt as a Harvard sophomore in 1878. Never content to sit still and listen, he constantly posed questions in class until one professor cut him short: "Now look here, Roosevelt, let me talk. I'm running this course."

2

Known to his admiring Yale classmates as "Big Bill," Taft's affable disposition made him one of the most popular men on campus. His fellow students elected him class orator in 1877, an honor considered "the greatest prize in college."

Young Will Taft, perched on a gatepost in the foreground, grew up with four brothers and one sister in this substantial, two-story yellow brick house in a fashionable neighborhood of Cincinnati.

When the Roosevelt family returned from a yearlong tour of Europe and the Mediterranean in 1873, they moved into a stately mansion on West 57th Street in Manhattan that boasted a magnificent library, pictured, and a fully equipped gymnasium.

Intimate childhood friendships flourished between Edith Carow *(above left, seated on the ground)* and the Roosevelt siblings Teedie, Corinne, and Elliott *(left to right)* during their vacations at Tranquillity *(below),* a beloved summer retreat on Long Island. Teedie and Edith's adolescent romance came to an abrupt end in August 1878. Just eight weeks later the young Harvard student met Alice Hathaway Lee. For Teedie, pictured here *(above right)* with Alice *(seated)* and Corinne, "it was a real case of love at first sight."

As young girls, both Edith Carow and Nellie Herron hungered for intellectual stimulation. Edith formed an all-girl literary society (*above*) with Teedie's sister, Corinne (*seated center*), while Nellie Herron, shown below to the left of twenty-six-year-old Will Taft, organized a lively Saturday night debate society among her circle of friends. Taft's brother Horace is at far right and Nellie's sister Maria at far left (*standing*). Nellie's salon flourished for three years. "Nobody is absent when he can help it," Taft enthusiastically remarked.

Seen here as a twenty-four-year-old New York State legislator, Roosevelt found the
state assembly to be a "great school" for learning the rough-and-tumble of politics
and how to cooperate with colleagues far removed from his patrician background.

11

The years Roosevelt spent visiting this Badlands cabin *(above)* and working as a cattle rancher *(below left)* would become critical to his evolving public image—as in this 1889 cartoon *(below right)*, where Thomas Nast emblazons Roosevelt as a cowboy in the popular imagination.

12

13

As New York City police commissioner, Roosevelt, seen here in his office on Mulberry Street circa 1896, would traverse the city streets at night. Concealing his evening clothes beneath a long coat, he made a series of surprise inspections, checking if policemen on the beat were faithfully safeguarding their posts. He was accompanied on some of these night rambles by Lincoln Steffens *(right)*, then an enterprising crime reporter for the New York *Evening Post*, but who later joined the celebrated team at *McClure's* magazine.

Samuel S. McClure, the indomitable and visionary founder of *McClure's* magazine, faced obstacles unimaginable to Roosevelt or Taft. Raised in poverty in northern Ireland in the thatched cottage shown below, McClure emigrated to America as a young child. Though penniless, his charismatic personality and extraordinary mental abilities earned him a place at Knox College in Galesburg, Illinois. He is pictured here as an undergraduate circa 1878.

16

17

In 1893, McClure *(top left)* launched the magazine that would become the engine of progressive reform. At the time he headed the magazine, McClure was capable of wild bursts of creativity, punctuated by periods of exhaustion and depression. His staff, considered by many the most brilliant gathering of journalists ever assembled, included Ida Tarbell *(top right)*, Ray Stannard Baker *(bottom left)*, and William Allen White *(bottom right)*, as well as Lincoln Steffens.

"I am having immense fun running the Navy," Assistant Secretary Roosevelt boasted from his office in the Navy Department *(top)*. While President McKinley vacillated about intervening in Cuba, TR could not contain his excitement at the prospect of conquest, as this 1898 cartoon suggests *(bottom)*. A more skeptical Ida Tarbell *(center right)*, covering the developing story for *McClure's*, derided Roosevelt's martial enthusiasm as that of "a boy on roller skates." Even before war had been declared, she wrote, Roosevelt "saw himself an important unit in an invading army."

25

26

27

Far from dreading the challenge of moving her three children over 8,000 miles from home, Nellie Taft— shown here *(top)* en route to Manila—"knew instantly" that she "didn't want to miss a big and novel experience." At the Malacañan Palace *(center)*, she blazed a trail by opening her guest lists to Filipinos and Americans on an equal basis. "Neither politics nor race," she insisted, "should influence our hospitality in any way." In Albany, Edith Roosevelt turned a cavernous governor's mansion *(bottom)* into a comfortable home for her six children, adding a nursery, a schoolroom, and a gymnasium.

Will and Nellie Taft seated in the Philippine governor's residence circa 1901 with their children, four-year-old Charlie *(standing in rear)*, ten-year-old Helen *(seated)*, and twelve-year-old Robert *(standing at right)*.

Governor Taft in 1902, somewhat awkwardly riding a carabao, the breed of water buffalo relied upon by Filipino farmers to till fields and haul timber.

Nellie Taft, a tireless hostess during her husband's tenure as governor general of the Philippines, wore a Spanish costume for one official reception.

VICE-PRESIDENTIAL POSSIBILITIES.
THE ROUGH RIDER

After his widely publicized Rough Rider heroics in Cuba, Roosevelt—as seen in this *Harper's Weekly* cartoon from 1900 *(above left)*—was an obvious choice for vice president on the Republican ticket. Stumping for McKinley *(above right)*, Roosevelt became "the central figure, the leading general, the field marshal" of the entire Republican campaign; yet the prize of victory was a do-nothing office that Roosevelt himself believed "ought to be abolished." On September 6, 1901, the kaleidoscope turned: an assassin's bullet made him at forty-two years of age the youngest president in the country's history. Roosevelt is pictured below in 1901, conferring with reporters shortly after McKinley was shot.

During whistle-stop speaking tours across the country in 1902 and 1903, Roosevelt began to test the phrase "the square deal"—the slogan that would come to characterize his entire domestic program. After visiting a majestic grove of giant sequoias in California, he exhorted an audience "to protect these mighty trees, these wonderful monuments of beauty."

Roosevelt's inauguration: After weeks of cloudy skies and heavy snow, the morning of March 4, 1905, broke "blue, flecked with lazily floating white clouds."

To audiences who gathered at the Capitol to watch him take the oath of office, the new president appeared "supremely happy." Roosevelt's election, the journalist William Allen White predicted, was a clear signal that "the Republican party has turned the corner and is now on a new road."

President Roosevelt's dynamic, often collaborative, relationship with a rising class of progressive journalists resulted in a wave of public enthusiasm for political and social reforms. "The Crusaders," a cartoon from the February 21, 1906, edition of *Puck* magazine, portrays Ida Tarbell, Ray Stannard Baker, Lincoln Steffens, S. S. McClure, and others as medieval knights in shining armor, with shields and weapons, waving banners emblazoned with the names of their publications, crusading against corruption and injustice.

Back in the United States, Taft's visit to Rome met with less enthusiasm. "I am in the worst hole politically I have ever been in my life," Roosevelt confided to his newspaper friend Herman Kohlsaat. "The whole Catholic Church is on my back." Though every intelligence from the Philippines established "what a lecherous lot of scoundrels the Spanish friars are," Roosevelt privately railed, Catholics maintained that these reports were "simply propaganda to establish Protestant missions in the Philippines." If such "calumnies" did not cease, the president was cautioned, Catholics would join en masse to thwart his nomination in two years' time.

"As things have turned out, it has probably been unfortunate that we got you to stop at Rome," Roosevelt wrote Taft, lamenting that the Catholic uproar had "rather complicated the political situation" at home. Perhaps, he suggested, they should "let this whole matter go and simply administer the civil government, leaving the friars and other ecclesiastical bodies to get along as best they can."

Taft responded vehemently. "While the result of the visit to Rome may have been bad in the United States," he told Roosevelt, "I do not state it too strongly when I say that the visit to Rome has done us a great deal of good in this country." Taft's letter persuaded the president to continue talks with the Vatican, which eventually produced an agreement. The United States paid $7.5 million for the lands, which were divided into small parcels and sold to natives, creating a new landowning class. Though the Spanish friars were never formally withdrawn, their power dwindled with the appointment of priests and bishops from other countries. Under Taft's deliberate leadership, a solution had been found that eased tensions and, in the end, finally satisfied the islanders, the administration, and the Catholic Church alike.

⌒ ⌒

ON JULY 1, 1902, SPEAKER David Henderson delivered a rousing speech to his colleagues, flattering them before they adjourned that "no house of representatives since the adoption of the Constitution had done so much work as this one." The Speaker's laudatory words "touched a responsive chord" among the members, who saluted both their Speaker and themselves with unrestrained emotion. "While the cheering and applause were still in progress," one reporter noted, "the members on the floor began singing 'My Country, Tis of Thee.' It was taken up by the correspondents in the press gallery, and soon the vast hall was ringing" as spectators joined in for "The Star-Spangled Banner" and other patriotic tunes. The mood of jubilation culminated when General

Charles Hooker of Mississippi, a Confederate veteran who had lost his arm in the war, "took his place by the side of the speaker, and together they sang 'Dixie.'"

Roosevelt's assessment of the work done by the 57th Congress was far less sanguine. Nonetheless, he was delighted by the passage of the bill providing $170 million to acquire land and begin construction of the Panama Canal. "By far the most important action I took in foreign affairs during the time I was President," he later reflected, "related to the Panama Canal." He also took "a keen personal pride" in the Newlands Reclamation Act, which set aside revenue from the sale of western public lands into a national fund for the construction of dams and irrigation projects. The act was structured to enable small farmers to settle previously arid lands. "I regard the irrigation business as one of the great features of my administration," he remarked at the time.

Congress also appropriated more than half a million dollars for badly needed renovations to the White House. Despite its thirty-one rooms, the mansion did not provide comfortable living quarters for a family, especially a large one like the Roosevelts'. The entire first floor, except for the family dining room, was used for state functions; the second floor was divided between a private wing and executive offices, including the president's office, the Cabinet Room, and the telegraph room. The family quarters consisted of only five bedrooms and lacked both closet space and sufficient bathroom facilities. The kitchen was outmoded, and the floors throughout "trembled when one walked on them."

Previous presidents had failed to persuade Congress that a thorough renovation was necessary. The Roosevelts alone, Sylvia Morris writes, "had the determination, in spite of criticism, to forge ahead with the long-overdue changes." The plans, drawn up by the architect Charles McKim, called for the construction of a new West Wing office building connected to the main house by a colonnade, freeing up the old second-floor spaces for conversion into extra bedrooms, bathrooms, and sitting rooms—as well as a boudoir, a library, and a den. The demolition and major renovations were scheduled during the summer months, allowing Edith and the children to escape to Oyster Bay. Roosevelt had originally planned to remain in the White House but was finally persuaded to move into a large town house on Lafayette Square.

Despite his satisfaction with the Canal bill, the Reclamation Act, and the successful appropriations for the White House renovation project, Roosevelt was sorely disappointed by the failure of Congress to take action on the signal economic issue of the day: the trusts. The call to establish a Department of Commerce with the power to demand information and determine necessary regulation of corporate trusts had been at the center of Roosevelt's first annual message. While the bill was debated at the committee level, Republican opposition prevented any real progress. Meanwhile, the Democratic attack on the trusts gathered momentum, heightening Roosevelt's anxiety that Republicans would pay at the polls for their failure to address the issue.

Senators obligated to the sugar trust also had managed to kill a reciprocity bill designed to reduce the tariffs on Cuban exports, including raw sugar, by 20 percent. The reduction of duties, Roosevelt argued in a special message, would boost the young republic's economy and simultaneously open Cuba's markets to the United States. "I ask that the Cubans be given all possible chance to use to the best advantage the freedom of which Americans have such right to be proud," he exhorted, "and for which so many American lives have been sacrificed." Despite his plea, no action was taken. "Their conduct will return to plague them later," Joseph Bishop predicted.

With the adjournment of Congress, Roosevelt headed to Oyster Bay for a six-week vacation with his family before launching a campaign swing to generate popular enthusiasm for Republicans in the upcoming midterm elections. The failure of the Republican Congress to take action on corporate regulation and reciprocity issues had furnished Democrats with powerful proof, despite Roosevelt's anti-trust initiatives, that the Republican Party was "in alliance with the trusts and with all the great monopolies of every description which are preying upon the country." By appealing directly to the people and lending his personal prestige to the fight for trust regulation, Roosevelt hoped to save his party from defeat in November.

Traveling by train and open carriage, accompanied by dozens of reporters, he opened his campaign in New England. In each of the six states, he delivered speeches focused predominantly on the trust issue, emphasizing the distinction between his own reasonable call for oversight of federal regulation of trusts and the Democratic crusade to eradicate all trusts in a manner that would "destroy all our prosperity." Roosevelt understood that many looked back with nostalgia on the pre-industrial era, when "the average man lived more to himself," when "the average community was more self-dependent," and when the gap between rich and poor was less glaring. He conceded that cities could never provide "the same sense of common underlying brotherhood" as country living, but argued that the modern industrial society had substantially raised "the standard of comfort" for most people. Efforts to turn backward he considered not only futile but also wrongheaded. Lending "a sympathetic ear" to "the unfocused discontent" he encountered, Roosevelt forged a powerful connection with his audience and then hammered home his core message: the national government must assume "full power" over the giant trusts and that power must "be exercised with moderation and self-restraint."

From Rhode Island, Connecticut, and Massachusetts, to Vermont, New Hampshire, and Maine, the president was met with overwhelming fervor. "The booming of cannon, the clanging of church bells, the tooting of whistles, the braying of brass bands and the cheering of thousands" marked his progress. When he delivered his prepared speeches in the major cities, "factories shut down, stores put up their shutters, flags were hoisted and the people were out in their holiday clothes." There was not a single moment, observed reporters, "when the streets were not crowded and people were not cheering themselves hoarse." As the train moved from city to city, thousands gathered at local railroad stations to glimpse their vibrant young president. Indeed, it seemed to one journalist that "small towns turned out their entire population."

The heady atmosphere of Roosevelt's tour abruptly ceased on the final day of his New England campaign when a speeding trolley car crashed headlong into the open carriage carrying Roosevelt and his party from Pittsfield, Massachusetts, to Stockbridge. The impact overturned the carriage and hurled its occupants to the ground. The president, his private secretary George Cortelyou, and Governor Winthrop Murray Crane of Massachusetts were thrown clear of the wreck, but Roosevelt's favorite Secret Service agent, William Craig, was caught under the wheels of the rushing trolley car and torn apart. "It was a dreadful thing," Roosevelt grimly observed; "the car was coming at such a terrific speed that I felt sure all in the carriage would be killed." The crowd hastened toward the spot where Roosevelt lay, but despite a blackened eye and deep bruises on his jaw and leg, he insisted that he required no help. "I'm all right," he said. "Some of the others are badly hurt. Look after them." When he saw the body of his loyal guard he dropped on his knee. "Poor Craig," he muttered over and over, "too bad, too bad." Still, he insisted that his tour through Stockbridge, Great Barrington, and Bridgeport, Connecticut, should proceed. Seated in a new carriage, he gave the mounted guard somber instructions: "Gallop ahead, tell the people everywhere along the line that Craig has been killed and I wish no cheering." Edith rushed to meet her husband at Bridgeport and take him back to Oyster Bay, where he remained for only one day before departing on a weeklong campaign swing through Tennessee, West Virginia, and North Carolina.

Returning to Sagamore Hill, Roosevelt convened a "memorable conference" (with Senators Aldrich, Spooner, Hanna, Allison, and Lodge) to resolve how he should handle the divisive issue of tariffs during his upcoming western tour. The Republican establishment viewed the high Dingley tariff, passed during McKinley's first administration, as sacrosanct—the key to the country's economic prosperity. Yet in recent years sharply rising consumer prices had produced growing demand for downward revision of the tariff. Capitalizing on this discontent, Democrats argued that high tariffs not only inflated prices but effectively sustained the hated trusts. The destruction of both trusts and tariffs would be the rallying cry of their fall campaign.

Complicating matters further, the tariff issue threatened to divide the president's own party between western Republicans, who clamored for relief from the highest tariff in history, and eastern manufacturers, who insisted on continued protection. At a state convention in the Republican stronghold of Iowa, a resolution had passed that linked tariffs to trusts and called for the elimination of tariffs on any product manufactured by a monopolistic trust. "The tariff must be revised, for it is barbarous, extortionate, damnable," the *Chicago Record-Herald* journalist Walter Wellman wrote to Roosevelt, insisting, "I want to see you take the lead. It is the biggest work to be done in the country today." Should Republicans launch the fall campaign without lowering the tariff, he warned, "hell will be to pay."

Though Roosevelt found this point of view congenial, he also recognized the "dynamite" in tariff reduction. Tinkering with tariff policy might well produce "a panic or something approaching to it, with consequent disaster to the business community and incidentally to the Republican party." Moreover, Senators Aldrich and Hanna made it clear that if a reciprocity treaty could not pass the protectionist Senate, more general tariff revision had absolutely no chance of success. "As long as I remain in the Senate and can raise a hand to stop you," Mark Hanna pointedly told him, "you will never touch a schedule of the tariff act." Bowing to reality, Roosevelt promised the senators gathered at Oyster Bay that he would "make no attempt to revise the tariff at the coming session of Congress," though he would continue to speak out about the trusts. "I do not wish to split my own party wide open on the tariff question," he conceded, "unless some good is to come." The implications of Roosevelt's retreat on this issue would be far-reaching.

Certain that he carried an unwelcome tariff message to western audiences, Roosevelt anticipated "a three weeks' nerve-shattering trip." He soldiered on from Cincinnati to Detroit to Logansport, Indiana, where the sentiment for downward revision of the tariff was particularly strong. The president's references to the tariff, the *New York Times* editorialized, sound "like that of a man treading a path selected for him by others, not chosen by himself, and pursued only because the situation seemed to require it." His words were absorbed by crowds "in comparative silence" after the noisy acclaim that had greeted his earlier speeches. "There are a good many worse things than the possibility of trolley-car accidents in these trips!" Roosevelt darkly quipped.

Unfortunately, the injuries he sustained in the collision proved far more agonizing than tariff complications. He had tried to ignore the continued pain in his leg but was noticeably limping by the time he reached Logansport. A visit to the hospital revealed "a threatening abscess" that required immediate surgery. The abscess was lanced and a miniature pump attached to drain the bloody serum. Refusing anesthesia, Roosevelt climbed onto the operating table and turned to the doctors with a smile. "Gentlemen, you are formal; I see you have your gloves on." The surgeon jested in answer: "It is always in order to wear gloves at a president's reception." If Roosevelt muttered in pain under his breath a few times during the procedure, he reportedly "said nothing that was distinct except to ask for a glass of water before the needle was removed." Carried out on a stretcher, he received strict orders to stay off his leg for several weeks, forcing cancelation of his remaining campaign itinerary.

As renovations to the executive mansion were still not complete, he was taken to the temporary White House at Lafayette Square. "Tell it not in Gath, but really I have enjoyed this nine days' seclusion," he told Senator Orville Platt the following week. "I see Mrs. Roosevelt all the time, as she has come on here to take care of me. I read everything from *Pendennis* and *Our Mutual Friend* down to the last study of European interests in Asia. I do not have to see the innumerable people whom there is no object in seeing, but whom I would have to see if I were not confined to my room with my leg up, and I am able to do all the important work."

Capitalizing on his enforced leisure, Roosevelt appealed to Herbert Putnam, the librarian of Congress, for books that would feed his wildly eclectic intellectual appetites—a history of Poland or something on early Mediterranean races. "Exactly the books I wished," he told Putnam several days later. "I am now reveling in Maspero and occasionally make a deviation into Sergis' theories about the Mediterranean races. . . . It has been such a delight to drop everything useful—everything that referred to my duty—everything, for instance, relating to the coal strike and the tariff, or the trusts, or my power to send troops into the mining districts, or my duty as regards summoning Congress—and to spend an afternoon in reading about the relations between Assyria and Egypt; which could not possibly do me any good and in which I reveled accordingly."

⌐ ⌐

By EARLY OCTOBER 1902, THE coal strike to which Roosevelt referred had become "the most formidable industrial deadlock in the history of the United
States." The previous spring, more than 140,000 anthracite coal miners had
gone on strike in Pennsylvania to protest low wages, harsh working conditions, and long hours. While the five-month-old strike had caused no serious
problems during the hot summer months, panic was setting in as cold weather
approached. Coal was then the chief fuel source for heating homes, schools,
and businesses. By September's end, schools in the Northeast began closing
due to the shortage. Hospitals and government buildings were threatening to
shut their doors. Confrontations in the coal fields were becoming increasingly
violent, and mobs commandeered coal cars as they trundled through villages
and small towns. An all-out social war seemed imminent.

John Mitchell, the charismatic president of the United Mine Workers
(UMW), believed that if the American people could truly see "the sorrows
and the heartaches of those who spend their lives in the coal mines," they
would sympathize with the strikers' decision to stop work. To "the average
magazine or newspaper reader," however, the lives of those "who delve in the
bowels of the earth; removed from the sight of their fellow-beings," remained
as darkly hidden as the work itself, while the hardships generated by their
strike were too immediately apparent.

Some years earlier, Sam McClure had tried to expose the suffering of the
industry's workers, commissioning the realist author Stephen Crane to write
a piece entitled "In the Depths of a Coal Mine." Crane described a sinister
system that brought children "yet at the spanking period" into the mines as
breaker boys. There, they worked ten hours each day, separating out pieces of
slate and other impurities from streams of coal speeding by on conveyor belts.
Earning 55 cents a day, a breaker boy rarely set foot in a schoolhouse. His highest ambition was to rise to door-boy, then mule-boy, laborer, miner's helper,
and finally full-fledged miner. If he reached that zenith, having survived "the
gas, the floods, the 'squeezes' of falling rocks, the cars shooting through little
tunnels, the precarious elevators," and the peculiar miner's lung disease, he
started "on the descent, going back to become a miner's helper, then a mine
laborer, now a door-boy; and when old and decrepit, he finally returns to the
breaker where he started as a child."

In most collieries, mining families were forced to rent their shacks from
the company and buy their food, clothing, and supplies in the company store,
invariably at higher costs than outside the compound. It was a proverbial

saying that "children were brought into the world by the company doctor, lived in the company house or hut, were nurtured by the company store, baptized by the company parson, buried in a company coffin, and laid away in the company graveyard." Since mine owners generally paid employees in company-printed scrip instead of cash, workers had little recourse but to pay the exorbitant prices the company demanded. Just such conditions led to the founding of the United Mine Workers Union in 1890.

The wave of consolidation that created trusts in steel, oil, and beef had produced a massive coal trust during this same period. The process of combination had begun when coal-carrying railroads began purchasing coal fields. Quickly, they utilized their control over freight rates to destroy independent coal operators, "reaping the reward" of monopolistic power over both production and transportation. While mine owners and operators of earlier eras had lived near the coal fields, gathering some understanding of the miners' situation, the railroad presidents and financiers who now controlled the industry shared no personal connection with their workers. Skilled in high finance, they had little experience with labor unions and scant comprehension of public relations. In the months preceding the strike, the miners had agreed to accept a 5 percent wage increase, a raise which would have amounted to $3 million annually against the operators' estimated profit of $75 million. The operators, represented by George Baer of the Philadelphia & Reading Railroad, flatly refused, confident that public opinion would drive the strikers back to work, crushing the union and Mitchell in the process.

The operators badly miscalculated; as the strike entered its fifth month, opinion had turned in favor of the miners, largely due to the contrasting public impressions of Mitchell and Baer. In early August 1902, Lincoln Steffens had drawn a profile of the compelling young UMW president for *McClure's*. A telling anecdote in his article illustrated the near-mystical hold Mitchell exercised over the miners, many of them immigrants who barely spoke English: "When President McKinley was shot, and the news spread to the coal region, the workmen gathered into a mob, crying, 'Who shot our President?' They dispersed when they learned that it wasn't President Mitchell who was shot."

Subsequent coverage confirmed Mitchell's stature with the workers and the public at large. "No better strike leader than John Mitchell has ever emerged in any time of industrial strife," Walter Wellman remarked. Throughout the summer, Mitchell conducted himself with impressive dignity, never resorting "to bitterness or retort." He allowed pump men and firemen to continue at work protecting the mines. He agreed to meet with anyone at any time to discuss potential areas of agreement, publicly declaring readiness to compromise.

Whereas Mitchell welcomed arbitration, George Baer refused even to meet with the labor leader and flatly denied Mitchell's right to speak for the anthracite miners in the various collieries. To the wealthy, college-educated railroad president, Mitchell "was only a common coal-miner, who had worked with his hands for 15 years, and was now a labor agitator." Any negotiation, Baer felt, would unduly recognize a mere rabble-rouser.

In response to a citizen's plea for compromise, Baer wrote: "I beg of you not to be discouraged. The rights and interests of the laboring man will be protected and cared for—not by the labor agitators, but by the Christian men to whom God in His infinite wisdom has given the control of the property interests of the country, and upon the successful Management of which so much depends." When Baer's correspondent submitted this rejoinder to the newspapers, the railroad president's overweening arrogance was mocked in editorials across the country. "The doctrine of the divine right of kings was bad enough, but not so intolerable as the doctrine of the divine right of plutocrats," remarked one Boston paper. "It will take a load from the consciences of many earnest people to have this authoritative declaration that God, through the kindness of the coal operators, will be able to manage this strike in accordance with the dictates of infinite wisdom," jeered the *New York Tribune*. "But if the medium's acquaintances really are spirits acquainted with the heavenly mysteries why, oh why, do they on earth talk such egregious nonsense?"

In the Northeast, where people suffered the effects of the strike most keenly, opinion began turning against the Republicans, whom many continued to regard as henchmen of the trusts despite Roosevelt's bold action against Northern Securities. "The coal business here is getting rapidly worse," Lodge wrote from Massachusetts. "If no settlement is reached it means political disaster in New England and especially in this state," he warned. "The demand that the Government take the coal fields is rising louder all the time. It is a perilous cry. When the cold weather comes it will be far worse. You have no power or authority of course, that is the worst of it. Is there anything you can appear to do?" Roosevelt himself was increasingly frustrated. "I am at my wit's end how to proceed," he admitted. "Of course, we have nothing whatever to do with this coal strike and no earthly responsibility for it," he wrote to Hanna. "But the public at large will tend to visit upon our heads responsibility for the shortage in coal precisely as Kansas and Nebraska visited upon our heads their failure to raise good crops in the arid belt, eight, ten or a dozen years ago."

In discussions with Attorney General Knox, Roosevelt was told that he had "no warrant" to intervene. The Constitution provided no precedent for a president to mediate disputes between labor and management. He was warned "that he would almost certainly fail if he tried; and that he would injure his prestige and perhaps sacrifice his political future if he essayed to step out-side the role of his constitutional duties." Roosevelt would not be confined by precedent or bound by fear of failure. He held to what he called "the Jackson-Lincoln theory of the Presidency; that is, that occasionally great national crises arise which call for immediate and vigorous executive action, and that in such cases it is the duty of the President to act upon the theory that he is the steward of the people, and that the proper attitude for him to take is that he is bound to assume that he has the legal right to do whatever the needs of the people demand, unless the Constitution or the laws explicitly forbid him to do it."

On October 1, 1902, he sent identical telegrams to the coal operators' board of directors and to the union representative, John Mitchell. Both factions were invited to Washington to discuss "the failure of the coal supply, which has become a matter of vital concern to the whole nation." This singular request from the president captivated newspapermen and magazine writers across the nation.

"For the first time in the history of the country," Walter Wellman wrote, great corporate leaders and union leaders would join "the President of the United States to talk over their differences face-to-face." The large crowd gathered in front of the temporary White House on Lafayette Square earlier that morning was increasing with each passing hour. Confidence spread that an end to the menacing coal strike was near at hand. Reporters eagerly fol-lowed the arrival of the parties, contrasting the "luxurious private cars" that carried the six coal operators to the nation's capital with "the smoking car of a night train" that transported Mitchell and his three district presidents to Union Station, whereupon they "trudged down Pennsylvania Avenue, their grips in their hands, stopping at a cheap hotel." Likewise, the elaborate carriages, staffed by footmen in "plum-colored livery," that deposited the coal barons at Roosevelt's door illustrated a sharp disparity with the common streetcars that bore the union representatives from their hotel. Nonetheless, once in the president's presence, both parties met as equals.

Theodore Roosevelt greeted his guests warmly, explaining that he could not rise from his chair, for his leg was still healing after his recent carriage accident. As the gentlemen took their seats, the president opened the meet-ing with a graceful statement acknowledging the existence of "three parties affected by the situation in the anthracite trade—the operators, the miners, and the general public." He spoke, he assured them, "for neither the operators nor the miners, but for the general public." Rather than adjudicate "respective claims," he would appeal to their shared "patriotism, to the spirit that sinks personal considerations and makes individual sacrifices for the general good."

No sooner had the president finished than Mitchell "literally jumped to his feet." In a voice "clear as a bell," he reiterated his willingness to negotiate with the operators at any time. If they were unable to reach a resolution by themselves, he would willingly abide by the decision of an impartial tribunal that the president might appoint, even if the ruling denied the miners' claims. Mitchell's dramatic statement took both the operators and the president by surprise. "I had not expected such an offer as this," Roosevelt admitted. Turning to the operators, he asked: "What have you gentlemen to say to this proposition?" After a swift consultation, President George Baer stood up. "We cannot agree to it. We cannot agree to any proposition advanced by Mr. Mitchell," he emphatically asserted. "Very well," said the president. "I shall ask you, then, to return at three o'clock and I wish you would present at that time your various positions in writing so we may discuss them."

When they reconvened, tension in the room quickly escalated. Rather than engage in open discussion, the coal barons read a series of typewritten statements that accused the strikers of criminal behavior, including the murder of hundreds of non-union men willing to work the mines during the strike. "The duty of the hour is not to waste time negotiating with the fomenters of this anarchy," Baer declared. Roosevelt was stunned by what he considered the "extraordinary stupidity and bad temper" of the operators, who "did everything in their power to goad and irritate Mitchell," resorting to "insolent" words that were "insulting to the miners and offensive to me." Roosevelt told Mark Hanna that after the operators belittled the union officials, "they insulted me for not preserving order" by sending federal troops to protect their property "and attacked Knox for not having brought suit against the miners' union as violating the Sherman Antitrust Law." Through it all, he marveled, "Mitchell behaved with great dignity and moderation." Not one of the operators, he remarked, "appeared to such advantage as Mitchell," who "towered above" them all. Roosevelt later admitted that after one operator referred to the union as "a set of outlaws," he wanted to take him "by the seat of the breeches and nape of the neck and chuck him out of that window." With great difficulty he managed to keep his anger in check.

Realizing that the operator's high-handed belligerence would negate any direct negotiation, Roosevelt finally repeated Mitchell's proposition that they submit the conflict to a presidential tribunal. Again they refused "to have any dealings of any nature with John Mitchell." Roosevelt was intensely irritated by their stubborn disdain. "If this is the case," he concluded, "I can see no necessity for detaining you gentlemen further."

"Well, I have tried and failed," Roosevelt told Mark Hanna. "I feel down-hearted over the result both because of the great misery made necessary for the mass of our people, and because the attitude of the operators will beyond a doubt double the burden on us who stand between them and socialistic action." Worse still, when the coal barons provided an account of the failed conference to the press, they reveled "in the fact that they had 'turned down' both the miners and the President."

The operators' exultation was short-lived. Roosevelt had made arrangements for a stenographer to record the entire proceedings, and when the statements of both parties were released to the press, public opinion turned sharply against them. While a small number of papers endorsed the operators' view that the public had no rights in the situation and insisted that Roosevelt's "uncontrollable penchant for impulsive self-intrusion" had made "a sorry mess" of the negotiations, the majority held the coal barons totally responsible for the failed Washington conference and the continuing strike. Furthermore, their insolent defiance of the president did not compare favorably with Mitchell's "respectful, placable, and patriotic spirit."

Public condemnation of the operators' intractable behavior fortified Roosevelt as he contemplated a more extreme step. With "ugly talk of a general sympathetic strike" beginning to spread, he considered the situation nothing short of "a state of war." He warned Attorney General Knox and Secretary of War Root that he was considering an action that "would form an evil precedent" but felt "obliged to take it rather than expose our people to the suffering and chaos which would otherwise come." Knox and Root were free to disavow the action he was contemplating, but he had made up his mind. He believed that the operators and their colleagues on Wall Street were "absolutely out of touch with the big world," and the president could not remain idle as "misery and death" threatened masses of the American people.

His undisclosed strategy was to ready "a first-rate general" and 10,000 regular Army troops to enter the coal fields with instructions "to dispossess the operators and run the mines as a receiver" for the government until a settlement could be reached. He secured the agreement of his selected general, John M. Schofield, to pay "no heed to any authority, judicial or otherwise," besides the president in his role as "Commander-in-Chief." According to this stratagem, if "the operators went to court and had a writ served on him, he would do as was done under Lincoln, simply send the writ on to the President." This intrepid plan illustrated one of Roosevelt's favorite maxims: "Don't hit till you have to; but, when you do hit, hit hard."

Whether the president would have implemented this unorthodox design is not clear. "Theodore was a bit of a bluffer," Elihu Root observed. But Mark Sullivan had discussed the measure with Roosevelt on a number of occasions and believed he was prepared to follow through: "The one condition Roosevelt's spirit could not endure," he remarked, "was any situation in which individuals or groups seemed able to defy or ignore the people as a whole and their representative in the White House."

The question proved moot. Secretary Root devised a way to resolve the issue that would not humiliate the mine owners or require massive federal intervention. Certain that public opinion had finally convinced the coal barons to negotiate so long as they did not have to deal directly with union representatives, Root proposed that he travel to New York and meet with J. P. Morgan. If anyone could bring the operators to the table, he believed, it would be the original architect of the coal trust. Morgan's financial genius had unified the railway owners and coalmen together in the gargantuan combination that now controlled 80 percent of the anthracite coal market. Root would make it clear that in speaking with Morgan, he acted independently, without instructions from the president. Roosevelt enthusiastically approved the plan.

Taking the midnight train to New York, Root met with Morgan for five hours on his yacht, the *Corsair*. Together, they composed a memorandum that Morgan carried to the Union Club, where the mine owners were holding a meeting. The memo called for the president to establish an Arbitration Commission, virtually identical to the proposition Mitchell and then Roosevelt had suggested at the Washington conference. In this instance, however, J. P. Morgan was advocating the measure—not John Mitchell—allowing the owners to maintain the fiction that they were not negotiating with representatives of organized labor. "It was a damned lie," Root later said, but it opened the door to a settlement. To his credit, Morgan intervened at this critical juncture, for only eight months earlier he had considered Roosevelt's suit against Northern Securities as a personal attack. The financier's willingness to help the president "was one of the crowning moments of his life," one journalist remarked, observing, "there was to be no littleness in this great hour."

Despite this breakthrough, immediate difficulties emerged over the composition of the panel. The owners insisted that the Arbitration Commission be comprised of five members chosen from specific categories: an officer of the military or naval Engineer Corps, an expert mining engineer unconnected with coal, a Pennsylvania judge, a businessman familiar with mining and selling coal, and an eminent sociologist. Both Roosevelt and Mitchell immediately recognized the pointed absence of a labor representative in this configuration. After a series of hurried meetings with Morgan's men, Bacon and Perkins, Roosevelt hit upon a solution. "Suddenly," he recollected, "it dawned on me that they were not objecting to the thing, but to the name. I found they did not mind my appointing any man, whether he was a labor man or not, so long as he was not appointed *as* a labor man." Roosevelt promptly appointed Edgar E. Clark, the head of the Brotherhood of Railway Train Conductors, to the "eminent sociologist" slot. While the owners "would heroically submit to anarchy rather than have Tweedledum," Roosevelt noted with amusement, "yet if I would call it Tweedledee they would accept with rapture."

Once the owners further agreed to expand the commission to include Bishop L. Spalding of Baltimore, Mitchell brought his miners back to work, peacefully concluding the nation's most serious strike. For three months the commission heard complaints from both sides: the operators presented evidence that strikers had not only threatened but used violence to prevent willing miners from working; the miners spoke of the oppressive hardships of the industry. The Arbitration Commission ultimately awarded the miners a retroactive wage increase of 10 percent as well as a reduction in daily work hours, from ten to nine.

"The American people will not soon forget their debt to Mr. Roosevelt," the *Washington Post* editorialized, proclaiming, "More glorious than winning a battle is this triumph of peace." Both Republican and Democratic journals concurred that the strike "was won by popular sentiment, controlled by the people's chief." Acting as "the people's attorney," William Allen White summarized, Roosevelt had defined the public interest in the previously *private* struggle between labor and capital. Understanding that the laissez-faire philosophy retained a powerful appeal, he had patiently waited through five months of the strike until the "steady pressure of public opinion" accompanying the onset of cold weather created space for his unprecedented call to bring the two sides together. And after the failed conference, he wisely allowed outrage over its published transcript to build until the public was primed to sustain radical measures it would have roundly rejected but months earlier. Though he "was all ready to act" if final negotiations failed, Roosevelt was thrilled when a less disruptive solution prevailed. "It is never well to take drastic action," he later commented, "if the result can be achieved with equal efficiency in less drastic fashion."

Flush with victory, Roosevelt agreeably shared credit for the successful settlement. "My dear sir," he addressed J. P. Morgan, "If it had not been for your going into the matter I do not see how the strike could have been settled at this time . . . I thank you and congratulate you with all my heart." With the coal operators, Roosevelt was less generous. "May Heaven preserve me," he told Bamie, "from ever again dealing with so wooden-headed a set."

ROOSEVELT SPENT NOVEMBER 4, 1902, the day of the midterm elections, at Sagamore Hill. "Mother and I took a walk," he told Kermit, "accompanied by all six dogs, whom we both of us feel are real members of the family." And the election results that evening brought an invigorating day to a satisfying conclusion. In early October, when his risky intervention appeared "doomed to failure through the obduracy of the capitalists," there was widespread conviction that "the new Congress would be overwhelmingly Democratic." But Republicans had defied the midterm curse and retained control of both Houses of Congress. Commentators credited the president's successful settlement of the coal strike with saving "many thousands of votes."

Returning to Washington after the midterms, the president was finally able to move back into the renovated White House. All summer long, Edith had worked with the architects, attending to "a steady stream of little problems"—sorting through "fabric swatches by the dozen, samples of wallpaper, and samples of rugs," selecting sofas, tables, and curtains, poring over detailed plans for every bedroom and bath, designing a garden for the children and a tennis court for her husband. The renovations garnered widespread praise. "If Roosevelt had never done anything else," a Washington insider remarked, "the metamorphosis of the White House from a gilded barn to a comfortable residence that he has accomplished would entitle him to his country's gratitude."

Roosevelt credited Edith's perseverance and instinct for tasteful comfort. A girlhood marked by relocation from one temporary abode to another as her father's resources diminished had shaped what one historian shrewdly identifies as a "remarkable coping mechanism," an ability "to make a home on short notice, then pick up her tent and start again." She had reappointed the executive mansion with the same aptitude and flair that had once transformed their tiny rented town house in Washington and the cavernous governor's mansion in Albany.

Edith never sought recognition for her work. "She is an old-fashioned type of woman who feels that no lady should make herself conspicuous," her secretary Isabella Hagner James explained. "By nature and inclination she should probably have had a life of sheltered seclusion," Hagner James later observed in her memoir, but when devotion to her husband necessitated a public presence, "never did a woman carry herself with more gentle dignity and charm." She was "at home" for the cabinet officers' wives every Tuesday morning in the library, entertained hundreds of governmental officials at afternoon teas, and hosted formal dinner parties with uncommon grace. As Jacob Riis understood, however, "the chief end of her life" lay not in her public duties but in "companionship with husband and children."

The president deserved credit for at least one aspect of the new West Wing building. "For the first time in history," reporters gratefully noted, the president had "set apart a room adjoining his own office for the exclusive use of the press." Formerly crowded together at one end of the general waiting room, journalists now enjoyed immediate access to the president and a room furnished with a large oak table, chairs, and telephones. "The public man who now escapes an interview will have to be a sprinter," one journalist happily remarked.

Taking stock of his first fifteen months in office, Roosevelt told Maria Longworth Storer in early December that he had achieved as much as he "had any right to hope or expect." Though occasionally forced to subordinate his own desires to what was possible "under the given conditions," he found comfort in the knowledge that Abraham Lincoln had often done the same.

With each passing month, the president's hold on the American people grew stronger. "It is very curious," Roosevelt told his newspaper friend Joseph Bucklin Bishop, "ever since I have been in the Presidency I have been pictured constantly as a huge creature with enormous clenched teeth, a big spiked club, and a belt full of pistols—a blustering, roaring swashbuckler type of ruffian, and yet all the time I have been growing in popularity. I don't understand it at all." To Bishop, the reason was perfectly clear: "All the cartoonists at heart liked him, and there was seldom or never anything bitter or really unfriendly in their portrayals of him; they were uniformly good-natured."

Caricatures even transformed his failure during a mid-November bear hunt into a triumph, conjuring an image of the president steadfastly refusing to shoot a small bear furnished for the occasion. As renditions of the original Clifford Berryman cartoon proliferated, the bear dwindled in size until he appeared as a tiny cub, prompting toy store owners to market stuffed bears in honor of Teddy Roosevelt. Soon the Teddy bear became one of the most cherished toys of all time.

Roosevelt's burgeoning public favor augured well for the 1904 presidential race, although no vice president had ever been elected in his own right after succeeding to the presidency as a consequence of his predecessor's death. "I'd rather be *elected* to that office than have anything tangible of which I know," he avowed. Nevertheless, he continued to fear that the Republican establishment would prevent his nomination. "*They* don't want it," he flatly stated, "Hanna and that crowd." Indeed, each time he riled business interests—as with his anti-trust suit or intervention in the coal strike—Hanna's name invariably arose. "I do not think Mr. Roosevelt can win," Alabama senator John Morgan predicted in late November. "I do not believe the wiser heads of the Republican Party want him as the nominee. The trouble is they cannot keep him where they can rely on him. Every now and then he bucks and runs off. They have to lasso him and haul him back." Newspapers reported that "the monied interests" were determined to prevent his election, even if it meant contributing "liberally" to the opposition party.

Delegations pledged to Mark Hanna were considered especially likely in the South, where Roosevelt's quiet attempt to include blacks in party councils had stirred fierce opposition. In addition, southern Republicans had never forgiven Roosevelt for the unprecedented dinner invitation extended the previous fall to the black educator Booker T. Washington. At the time, the vehement reaction in the South had stunned and saddened Roosevelt. Newspaper editorials throughout the region decried the president's attempt to make a black man the social equal of a white man by sharing the same dinner table. "Social equality with the Negro means decadence and damnation," announced one southern official. "The action of President Roosevelt in entertaining that nigger will necessitate our killing a thousand niggers in the South before they will learn their place," declared South Carolina's Ben Tillman. For disaffected Republicans in both North and South, Mark Hanna promised deliverance from Roosevelt's wrongheadedness.

All these factors weighed on the president's mind as he prepared his second annual address. Delivered on December 2, 1902, the message reiterated his call for Congress to create a Department of Commerce with broad powers of supervision over the big corporations. The tone of his message, "not nearly so strong as it was expected to be," proved a great disappointment to reformers. "The plain people," Roosevelt insisted, "are better off than they have ever been before." The majority of the great fortunes were "won not by doing evil, but as an incident to action which has benefited the community as a whole." Although abuse and misconduct were undeniable, he urged, "let us not in fixing our gaze upon the lesser evil forget the greater good." Those who sought removal of the protective tariff "as a punitive measure directed against the trusts," he argued, put the entire nation's productivity in jeopardy.

"It appears that the vested interests of the country have succeeded in scaring the President," one Washington correspondent asserted, "preventing him from expressing in his usual forcible style his convictions." The *Cincinnati Enquirer* deemed it "a very lame message for a president who is chiefly celebrated for his strenuosity," and further lamented that it read "like a surrender to the party leaders who control the senate and house." Other commentators were equally unimpressed. "A milk and water communication," charged the *Indiana Democrat*, "from a man whose chief aim is the presidential nomination two years hence."

Even the more moderate reviews were not optimistic that Roosevelt's message heralded any fundamental progress. "We are bound to believe that Mr. Roosevelt's heart is in his policy of regulating the trusts, yet even here he is singularly vague and inconclusive," editorialized the New York *Evening Post*, predicting that "the result of such an uncertain trumpet can not lead to any serious preparation for battle."

⌒　⌒

IN THE CLAMOR FOLLOWING THE president's message, few perceived that Roosevelt's ideals were always moderated by his pragmatism. Until the Republican establishment felt threatened by an aroused and targeted public opinion, he knew there was little chance of securing legislation to regulate the trusts. His tepid message revealed a conviction that popular outrage was not yet sufficient to threaten the Big Four, those powerful senators who continued to block his path to significant reform.

More than any president since Abraham Lincoln, Theodore Roosevelt was able to shrewdly calculate popular sentiment. He read daily excerpts from scores of newspapers, probed the eclectic assemblage of visitors and guests frequenting the White House, and tested his ideas on reporters. Over time, he developed an uncanny ability to gauge the changeable pulse of the American public. His experience in bringing the suit against Northern Securities and mediating the Pennsylvania coal strike had evinced the signal role that the press could play in rallying the public support essential to achieve substantial reform—just as Ray Baker's series on J. P. Morgan's "monarchical powers" and Stephen Crane's description of the inhumane, abusive practices of the coal barons had proven pivotal in alerting the public to the menace of increasingly concentrated monopolies.

In order to aggressively pursue redress for the abuses and inequity of the industrial age, the president would need to ride a seismic shift in national consciousness. He would need an instrument capable of reaching into the homes of workers, teachers, shopkeepers, and small business people across the country—an instrument that would not just explain but vividly illustrate the human and economic costs of unchecked industrial growth and combination. The complex and sometimes contentious partnerships that Roosevelt had forged with investigative journalists would soon illuminate corruption, as if by heat lightning, and clarify at last a progressive vision for the entire nation.

CHAPTER ELEVEN

"The Most Famous Woman in America"

Ida M. Tarbell, in her office at *McClure's*, 1904.

ROOSEVELT'S FLAGGING HOPES OF CONFRONTING the trusts, purging corrupt political machines, and checking abuses by both capital and labor were rekindled by the January 1903 publication of *McClure's* magazine. In this celebrated issue, the "groundbreaking trio" of Tarbell, Steffens, and Baker produced three exhaustive, hard-hitting investigative pieces that ushered in the distinctive new period of journalism that would later be christened "the muckraking era." First off, Ida Tarbell revealed the predatory, illegal practices of Standard Oil; Lincoln Steffens then exposed the corrupt dealings of Minneapolis mayor Albert "Doc" Ames; and finally, Ray Baker described the complicity of union members manipulating and deceiving their own fellow workers.

The convergence of these three powerful exposés prompted S. S. McClure to attach an unusual editorial postscript to his January issue, exhorting readers to take action against corruption in every phase of industrial life. "Capitalists, workingmen, politicians, citizens—all breaking the law, or letting it be broken," McClure accused, sparing no one in his sweeping denunciation:

> Who is left to uphold it? The lawyers? Some of the best lawyers in this country are hired, not to go into court to defend cases, but to advise corporations and business firms how they can get around the law without too great a risk of punishment. The judges? Too many of them so respect the laws that for some "error" or quibble they restore to office and liberty men convicted on evidence overwhelmingly convincing to common sense. The churches? We know of one [Trinity Church in Manhattan], an ancient and wealthy establishment, which had to be compelled by a Tammany hold-over health officer to put its tenements in sanitary condition. The colleges? They do not understand. There is no one left; none but all of us.

"A lesser editor might have hesitated . . . to print three such contentious papers—arraignments of industry, labor, and government—all in one issue," observes Peter Lyon, McClure's biographer, but McClure was resolute. His exceptional sensitivity to the interests of the American public convinced him that people would not shrink from the truth, however dispiriting. He believed, as Steffens later observed, that "shameful facts, spread out in all their shame," would "set fire to the American pride," that when people fully realized the corrosive national affliction wrought by unchecked industrialism, they would seek remedies. Yet even the remarkably prescient McClure could not have predicted the extraordinary response his exposés would soon receive from readers across the country.

The January 1903 issue sold out within days, faster than any previous issue. The revelatory articles became a leading topic of conversation in cities and towns across the country. With such incriminating information in the hands of *McClure's* vast middle-class audience, one historian observes, "for the first time considerable numbers of small businessmen and white-collar workers were joining factory hands and farmers in a restless questioning." Elated, McClure considered the January issue "the greatest success we have ever had." Editorials in one newspaper after another praised the quality of the research, the dramatic structure of the narratives, the careful documentation. "Of course, every magazine from time to time had published able articles dealing with some phase of wrong and suggesting some needed reform," the *New York World* noted. "What Mr. McClure did was to make this work systematic and persistent, to describe realities with absolute frankness, to avoid preaching, and to let the facts produce their own impression upon the public conscience."

In the months that followed, the circulation of *McClure's* continued to climb as the three writers pursued their investigations. Tarbell's Standard Oil series eventually stretched over a three-year period; Steffens's studies of corrupt political machines in a dozen cities and states generated fourteen articles and two books; and Baker produced more than a dozen seminal articles on labor and capital. Baker later attributed the tremendous impact of these meticulously researched exposés to the fact that they finally verified years of "prophets crying in the wilderness, and political campaigns based upon charges of corruption and privilege which everyone believed or suspected had some basis of truth, but which were largely unsubstantiated." The solid reputation of *McClure's* and its gifted stable of writers assured millions of Americans they could trust what they were reading.

The success at *McClure's* persuaded editors and publishers at a dozen leading magazines—including *Collier's*, *Cosmopolitan*, *Everybody's*, *Leslie's*, *Pearson's*, and *Hampton's*—to launch similar forays into investigative journalism. Like McClure, these publishers began to funnel substantial resources into the extensive research necessary for such in-depth studies, promoting a new breed of investigative reporter dedicated to extensive fact-finding and analysis. Their disclosures of the corrupt linkages between business, labor, and government educated and aroused the public, spearheading the Progressive movement that would define the early years of the twentieth century. "It is hardly an exaggeration to say that the Progressive mind was characteristically a journalistic mind, and that its characteristic contribution was that of the socially responsible reporter-reformer," historian Richard Hofstadter observed. "Before there could be action, there must be information and exhortation. Grievances had to be given specific objects, and these the muckraker supplied. It was muckraking that brought the diffuse malaise of the public into focus."

⌒ ⌒

YEARS OF PREPARATORY WORK AND investigation preceded the publication of *McClure's* landmark January 1903 issue. As early as the spring of 1899, when few middle-class journals would broach the subject, McClure was already endeavoring to determine how the increasingly vital, complex issue of trusts might engage a wide audience. The English journalist Alfred Maurice Low suggested to McClure that if a single trust were traced from its origin through its "gradual rise and growth," an examination of whether malfeasance, wage curtailment, or price inflation had abetted its development would prove "full of intense human interest." McClure enthusiastically agreed. "The great feature is Trusts," he told John Phillips, and the magazine that treats this "great question" will inevitably develop "a good circulation." While Phillips embraced McClure's idea, he insisted the project not be assigned to Low, a reputed sensationalist; better to trust one of their own staff, one trained to rely on substantiated fact rather than overwrought rhetoric.

The McClure team initially considered targeting the sugar or beef trusts, but neither seemed conducive to an extended series. McClure soon struck another approach to the pernicious problem. Several years earlier, after a short story in a small magazine by Frank Norris had attracted his interest, Mc-Clure had brought the struggling young author from California to New York, providing him a steady salary to read manuscripts in the mornings, leaving the afternoons free for his own writing. Norris shared McClure's conviction that writers held a responsibility to the public—not simply to entertain but to address contemporary problems such as corporate avarice and economic injustice. "The Pulpit, the Press, and the Novel," Norris argued, "these indisputably are the great moulders of public opinion and public morals to-day."

One morning, Norris appeared in McClure's office with an idea for a sprawling trilogy chronicling the struggle between wheat growers and the railroad trust. The first book, to be called *The Octopus*, would center on an actual incident in the San Joaquin Valley, where scores of local farmers, dispossessed by the Southern Pacific Railroad, had engaged in a violent altercation with railroad agents that left seven people dead. Both McClure and Phillips were attracted by the young novelist's idea, for in this protracted, harrowing fight against one railroad, the larger struggle of the people versus the trusts would play out. McClure pledged to pay Norris's salary while he returned to the west coast to muster all research materials necessary to begin the novel.

The dramatic saga of *The Octopus* interweaves the stories of a dozen or more men and their families. Struggling to draw a good harvest from the arid land, these hardworking people are compromised and oppressed at every turn by the maddening, predatory policies of the railroad: ruinous increases in highly inflated shipping rates for wheat and hops are announced; arbitrary routing decisions require urgently needed agricultural equipment to travel non-stop past the town and then return at extra cost; greed and peculation make a mockery of the state commission board, supposedly designed to administer fair rates. Meanwhile, the implacable railroad rolls on, leaving behind "the destruction of once happy homes, the driving of men to crime and of women and girls to starvation and ruin." As the lives of the novel's central group of characters are shattered, a powerful fuse is lit against "the iron-hearted Power, the monster, the Colossus, the Octopus."

Published two years later, Norris's novel garnered spectacular reviews. "*The Octopus* is a work so distinctly great that it justly entitles the author to rank among the very first American novelists," claimed *The Arena*. "It is a work that will not only stimulate thought: it will quicken the conscience and awaken the moral sensibilities of the reader, exerting much the same influence over the mind as that exerted by Patrick Henry." Although the widely acclaimed and prodigiously gifted Norris would never complete his trilogy—a ruptured appendix ended his life at the age of thirty-two—*The Octopus* was an unmitigated success for both McClure and its young author.

Indeed, Sam McClure seemed to be moving from one triumph to another. The circulation of the magazine had topped 400,000, the syndicate was turning a profit, and his talented staff of writers, editors, and contributors was considered among the country's very best. But even this catalogue of accomplishments could not satiate his restless ambition for long. "The string of triumphs had to be prolonged," his biographer observes, "for only so would McClure get what he most needed: a steady supply of affection, admiration, and flattery."

Just when all his enterprises were proceeding successfully, McClure overreached, committing his company to purchase the prestigious publishing house Harper & Brothers. Negotiated in a burst of manic energy, the deal would bring five additional magazines under McClure's management (including *Harper's Monthly* and *Harper's Weekly*), as well as a second syndicate service, a second book press, and a lecture bureau. Troubles mounted immediately: Frank Doubleday, angry at his marginalization, broke up the association of Doubleday & McClure. Additional responsibilities for *McClure's* staff stole time and attention from the magazine at the heart of the empire. Most crucially, the capital needed to sustain the purchase was never properly in place. Reluctantly, and at enormous expense, McClure was forced to withdraw from the contract six months after it was signed.

The failed deal crushed McClure, precipitating a nervous breakdown in April 1900 that propelled him to Europe to undergo the celebrated "rest-cure" devised by an American physician, S. Weir Mitchell. Prescribed for a range of nervous disorders, the rest cure required that patients remain isolated for weeks or even months at a time, forbidden to read or write, rigidly adhering to a milk-only diet. Underlying this regimen was the assumption that "raw milk is a food the body easily turns into good blood," which would restore positive energy when pumped through the body.

This extreme treatment was among the proliferating regimens developed in response to the stunning increase in nervous disorders diagnosed around the turn of the century. Commentators and clinicians cited a number of factors related to the stresses of modern civilization: the increased speed of communication facilitated by the telegraph and railroad; the "unmelodious" clamor of city life replacing the "rhythmical" sounds of nature; and the rise of the tabloid press that exploded "local horrors" into national news. These nervous diseases became an epidemic among "the ultracompetitive businessman and the socially active woman."

While McClure had endured troubling mood swings for years, this depressive episode was the most disturbing, transforming even his love for his work into "the repulsion that a seasick man feels toward the food he most enjoys in health." His manic drive had finally sapped him of his strength. "I had never thought of such a thing as economy of effort. When I had an idea, I pursued it; when I wanted anything, I went ahead and got it." By crossing the ocean and committing himself to exclusive sanitarium in France and Switzerland, he hoped to recover the will and vitality that had sustained him since the penniless days of his youth.

Not surprisingly, the steady diet of milk and tedium did little to restore McClure. After six months in the famous spa towns of Aix-les-Bains and Divonne-les-Bains, he felt more enervated than when he left New York. "When I get rested I become very restless, but no place I plan to go interests me for many hours," he admitted. "A walk of a few blocks tires me terribly. Riding in a cab tires me. I cannot see any of the beautiful things here," he complained, lamenting that he had become "half hopeless & half comatose." Although he tried to remain optimistic, observing that "perhaps my condition is normal & this is the way one gets over brain exhaustion," he confessed to feeling doubtful about the state of his recovery. "I sometimes think that it is like taking off a leaky roof before putting on a new one, for a while the condition is worse than ever."

In October, unable to tolerate the isolation, McClure persuaded a nurse to accompany him to Paris to secure the most recent edition of his magazine. Finding little of timely interest in its pages, he fired off a furious critique to Phillips, accusing him of attempting to destroy the magazine. No sooner was the letter posted than he tried to retrieve it. "I am simply heart-broken to have caused you such grief," the contrite McClure told Phillips, assuring him, "You are the most wonderful friend & comrade a man ever had. Destroy the Paris letter. It was the expression of jangled nerves & a crazy brain. . . . In my mad scramble which in one way or another seems to have existed all my life, I have sacrificed much that is most important . . . I feel hopelessly sad to have caused you such terrible & useless pain. I really ought to have died some time ago . . . I wish you would remember the good things about me & forget all the bad."

But in April 1901, exactly one year after leaving for Europe, McClure unaccountably returned to the office bursting with ideas for future articles. "The great issue," he continued to believe, "was the phenomenon of the trusts." He was now even more strongly convinced that "the way to handle the Trust question was, not by taking the matter up abstractly, but to take one Trust, and to give its history, its effects, and its tendencies." If neither the sugar trust nor the beef trust would suffice, perhaps John D. Rockefeller's Standard Oil, "the Mother of Trusts," would serve as the subject of their investigations. As "the creature largely of one man," Standard Oil was perfectly suited to the biographical approach that had proved so successful with Napoleon and Lincoln. The story of the world's wealthiest man would beguile the public into the more complicated exposition of his corporation and the hitherto esoteric question of the trusts. No one, McClure perceived, was better situated to engage that subject than Ida Tarbell, who "had lived for years in the heart of the oil region."

Tarbell initially hesitated, though no subject so captured her imagination. As a child, she had witnessed the anguish the "big trust" had caused in its early development, and "the unfairness of the situation" had troubled her deeply. As a young woman, she had begun a novel focused on the period when "the bottom had dropped out" of the Allegheny oil region. She never completed the work, however, realizing that "there must be two sides to the question." If she hoped to write a work of history rather than propaganda, she would now have to "comprehend the point of view of the other side." She recognized the difficulties, even hazards, this undertaking would present, for Standard Oil officials were notoriously close-mouthed. Even in her hometown of Titusville, she found that men and women were unwilling to talk, fearing "the all-seeing eye and the all-powerful reach of the ruler of the oil industry." In search of telling, intimate details like those at the core of her Lincoln series, she encountered only the same terse warning: "They will get you in the end." Her own father tried to dissuade her. "Don't do it, Ida," he admonished; "they will ruin the magazine." Finally she was tantalized by "the audacity of the thing"—just as when McClure had challenged her to complete the first installment of Napoleon's life in one month's time.

By early September 1901, Ida Tarbell had read everything from articles extolling the growth of trusts to *Wealth Against Commonwealth*, Henry Demarest Lloyd's passionate diatribe against monopolies. Already she had outlined an extensive series that would detail the history of Standard Oil from its earliest days to the present. Phillips was enthusiastic, but only McClure, then in Switzerland, could approve a project of such magnitude. "Go over," Phillips told Tarbell, "show the outline to Sam, get his decision." McClure was thrilled to hear from Tarbell. "Come instantly," he wrote back, suggesting that she stay for several weeks and travel with him to Lucerne and the Italian lakes; "I want a good time." Hattie, too, welcomed Ida's arrival, knowing her soothing influence upon McClure's anxious temperament.

When Tarbell reached Lausanne, Switzerland, in early October, McClure was so overjoyed that he begged her to remain in Europe so they could spend the winter together in Greece. "You've never been there. We can discuss Standard Oil in Greece as well as here," fancifully adding, "if it seems a good plan you can send for your documents and work in the Pantheon." The image of the proper Miss Tarbell, seated at a desk cluttered with papers and documents in the middle of the ancient marble building, struck him as incongruous and hilarious.

Ida happily agreed to join Sam and Hattie. From their first meeting in Paris nearly a decade earlier, she had never stopped loving this brilliant, creative, hectic, exasperating man. In his expansive moods, no one was better company. While he could be irritable and demanding with others, he was invariably kind and loving toward Ida. "I lean on you as no other," he confided to her. "In all great & noble qualities you are peerless to me."

In mid-October, Sam, Hattie, and Ida set out together for Greece by way of the Italian lake region and the cities of Milan and Venice. As usual, the voluble McClure found interest in everything he saw, frequently jotting down notes for future articles. Before reaching Greece, he decided to stop at Salsomaggiore, an exclusive resort spa in northern Italy. There, enjoying relaxing treatments of mud and steam (and conversing with Cecil Rhodes, who had just returned from his exploits in South Africa), the editor and his writer came to an agreement on the shape of her project. So ebullient was McClure that he encouraged Ida to return to New York at once, postponing Greece for another time. Immediately, she set to work on what would become a twelve-part history of the Standard Oil Company—the magisterial series that would spur popular demand to dismantle the rapacious trusts and ensure her legacy as one of the most influential journalists of all time.

When McClure returned to the office a month later, he assembled the entire staff and bombarded them with suggestions for future articles. "It was always so when he came back from a trip," Steffens recalled. His valise was stuffed with "clippings, papers, books, and letters," ranging over the "world-stunning" subjects he wanted his staff to pursue. Some of these "history-making schemes" were brilliant, Steffens acknowledged, but "five out of seven" were foolish, requiring the staff to "unite and fight" against the "wild editor." Only Ida Tarbell could sift through the ideas that tumbled from his mind with patience and respect. Time and again, she tactfully placated both Sam and the staffers, finding "a way to compromise and peace." Unfortunately, Tarbell was in Titusville researching the early chapters of her story when McClure arrived this time, and the office meeting degenerated into a string of fiery confrontations.

Further fueling these tensions, McClure abruptly decided to switch Samuel Hopkins Adams from the syndicate to managing editor of the magazine; such staffing shifts had become a habit with McClure, but this change proved particularly unsettling. The move produced a violent protest from the art director, August Jaccaci, who charged that Adams was "absolutely incompetent to do this job." The accusation ignited "an epic spat" between Jaccaci and McClure: "Fists were hammered down on desks. Unforgiveable words passed." The manuscript reader Viola Roseboro left the room in tears. Mary Bisland, an editor on the syndicate, wrote a distressed letter to Tarbell, begging her to return before something terrible happened. Another tempest provoked yet another distressed letter to Tarbell. Her response provides insight into the peculiar dynamic at the heart of the revolutionary magazine and an acute and intimate assessment of its founder and animating force: "Things will come out all right," Tarbell assured the staff. McClure "may stir up things and interfere with general comfort but he puts the health of life into the work at the same time." More important, Tarbell urged them to remember that "the inimitable nature of McClure's genius greatly outweighed the inconveniences resulting from his eccentricities."

> Never forget that it was he & nobody else who has created that place. You must learn to believe in him & *use* him if you are going to be happy there. He is a very extraordinary creature, you can't put him into a machine and make him run smoothly with the other wheels and things. We don't need him there. Able methodical people grow on every bush but genius comes once in a generation and if you ever get in its vicinity thank the Lord & *stick*. You probably will be laid up now and then in a sanatarium [*sic*] recovering from the effort to follow him but that's a small matter if you really get into touch finally with that wonderful brain.
>
> Above all, don't worry. What you are going through now we've all been through steadily ever since I came into the office. If there was

nothing in all this but the annoyance and uncertainty & confusion—
that is if there were no results—then we might rebel, but there are always results—vital ones. The big things which the magazine has done
always come about through these upheavals. . . . The great schemes,
the daring moves in that business have always been Mr. McC's. They
will continue to be. His one hundredth idea is a stroke of genius. Be
on hand to grasp that one hundredth idea!

FOR IDA TARBELL, McCLURE's DIRECTIVE to approach the trust issue through a
narrative history of Standard Oil proved that "one hundredth idea"—a true
stroke of genius. Her investigations were fortuitously timed. In an era of
heightened, yet unfocused, public concern over increasing corporate consolidation, the growth of the first great industrial monopoly provided a dramatic
blueprint for comprehending how "a particular industry passes from the control of the many to that of the few."

Tarbell began her customary search for primary sources, a task facilitated
by the fact that numerous state and federal authorities had been investigating
Standard Oil since its founding. Defendants' testimony in court, she noted,
exhibited "exactly the quality of the personal reminiscences of actors in great
events, with the additional value that they were given on the witness stand;
and it was fair, therefore, to suppose that they were more cautious and exact in
statement than are many writers of memoirs." Traveling to Washington, New
York, Pennsylvania, Ohio, and Kansas, Tarbell patiently scoured so many
thousands of pages of depositions and testimony that she almost lost her eyesight. She culled old files from defunct newspapers, transcribed single-spaced
congressional reports, examined a large collection of pamphlets published
during various controversies, and studied pages of statistics provided by the
Interstate Commerce Commission.

Such vigorous inquiry soon revealed that critical memos and reports had
vanished from the record. Informed that Standard had destroyed them, Tarbell refused to give up, convinced that if a document had been printed, it
would eventually "turn up." Usually, she was right. In the archives of the
New York Public Library, she found the sole remaining report of an obscure
thirty-year-old investigation; all the other copies had curiously disappeared.
After reaching out to the lawyers and plaintiffs who had conducted the cases,
she gradually found everything she needed. "Her sources of information,"
McClure proudly noted, "were open to any student who had the industry and
patience to study them."

As the immense scope of her project became evident, Tarbell realized she would need an assistant in Cleveland, where Rockefeller had gotten his start and established the early headquarters of Standard Oil. She wanted someone who was not only clever and curious but who would also "get his fun in the chase" and "be trusted to keep his mouth shut." In John M. Siddall she found the ideal comrade. "Short and plump, his eyes glowing with excitement," the twenty-seven-year-old reporter manifested such exuberance during their first interview that she "had a sudden feeling of alarm lest he should burst out of his clothes." Tarbell later reflected that she "never had the same feeling about any other individual except Theodore Roosevelt." In the months that followed, she found the partnership "a continuous joy"; eventually the entire *McClure's* staff looked forward to "Sid's" lengthy letters, fascinated by the revealing statistics he compiled or the curious details he had unearthed of Rockefeller's day-to-day existence in the city where he lived and worked, Cleveland. Their alliance, Tarbell's biographer Kathleen Brady writes, "was as illustrious a meeting as that of Holmes and Watson. Only in this case, each was to be Sherlock and no leap of deduction, only clear evidence, was allowed."

Such evidence could only be gathered through methodical, painstaking research. "Someone once asked me why I did not go first to the heads of the company for my information," Tarbell explained to an interviewer. "This person did not know overmuch of humanity I think, else he would have realized instantly that the Standard Oil Company would have shut the door of their closet on their skeleton. But after one had discovered the skeleton and had scrutinized him at a very close range, why then shut the door? That is the reason I did not go to the magnates in the beginning."

Although Tarbell never did secure an interview with the reclusive Rockefeller, she established a warm relationship with Henry H. Rogers, a Standard Oil partner who staunchly believed in the firm and wanted to present his perspective to the public. Learning of the impending series in *McClure's*, Rogers sent word to Sam McClure through their mutual friend, Samuel Clemens (Mark Twain), offering to meet with Tarbell at his home at 26 East 57th Street. "I was a bit scared at the idea," Tarbell later acknowledged. Previous attempts to arrange personal meetings with company executives had either proven unsuccessful or rendered little beyond generic policy statements: "I had been met with that formulated chatter used by those who have accepted a creed, a situation, a system, to baffle the investigator trying to find what it all means." Despite her prior frustrations, she was eager for another chance. "It was one thing to tackle the Standard Oil Company in documents . . . quite another thing to meet it face to face."

Rogers immediately put her at ease. Sixty-two years old, with "a heavy shock of beautiful grey hair," he struck Tarbell as "by all odds the handsomest and most distinguished figure in Wall Street." Decades later, she could still recall his features: his "aquiline" nose, "blazing" eyes, and the white mustache partially obscuring his mouth, which she imagined to be "flexible, capable of both firm decision and of gay laughter." As they began to converse, Tarbell discovered that Rogers had once lived close to her childhood home in a white house on a neighboring hillside. "Oh, I remember it," Tarbell exclaimed; "the prettiest house in the world, I thought."

They reached an amicable agreement that day to continue their conversation in a regular series of meetings: Tarbell would share with Rogers her evidence concerning the controversial aspects of Standard's history; he, in turn, would offer "documents, figures, explanations, and justifications—anything and everything which would enlarge [her] understanding." From the start, Tarbell made it clear that her own judgment would supersede his on all points. Their talks remained friendly; when the debate grew tense or unproductive, one or the other would simply change the subject. For Tarbell, the interchange proved invaluable, helping her construct work of "unimpeachable accuracy."

The rigorous editing process at *McClure's* and the constant support of her colleagues were both vital to the excellence of Tarbell's finished work. Early on, when she was "deep into appalling heaps of documentary stuff," Jaccaci wrote her in Titusville to assure her that the immense jumble of research "will clear up little by little and you will begin to see the possibilities of your story." And throughout the process, McClure offered reassurance, reading her early letters from the field, counseling her not to "hurt your health or hurt the work by speed." She should not feel compelled "to write on the monthly demand of a magazine," he insisted, for "this work will turn out to be our great serial feature for next fall." This regular exchange of letters sustained Tarbell while she was "separated so completely" from the office colleagues with whom she had shared daily meals and conversation.

By late May 1902, ten months after she began, Ida had completed a rough draft of the first three articles. She wrote to Phillips, then recovering from an illness at his summer home in Duxbury, Massachusetts. She hoped to send the articles and, if he was feeling well enough, plan a visit to discuss them. "They are in such shape that you can see the character of the material and the treatment I propose," she explained. "I want very much to have your criticism and judgment. It is certainly a great deal more to me than anybody else's." Indeed, her deep respect for Phillips's opinion led her to delay publication until she could answer his concerns.

Viola Roseboro marveled at Tarbell's willingness to accept harsh criticism from both Phillips and McClure. Both expected to "be satisfied and thrilled; they pounded her and her stuff to make the best of it page by page," Roseboro recalled. Tarbell absorbed the barrage and never flinched. She kept revising, cutting, organizing, and rewriting to meet their demands that she move the narrative forward and strip the text of inessential material. Finally, when she felt "moderately comfortable" with her opening articles, she decided to put the work aside for her regular summer vacation—hoping to return with clearer perspective and renewed intensity. "It has become a great bugbear to me," she confessed to Siddall. "I dream of the octopus by night and think of nothing else by day, and I shall be glad to exchange it for the Alps."

Tarbell's first installment explores the birth of the oil industry in the region where she was raised. The "irrepressible energy" of the pioneers who settled "this little corner of Pennsylvania" transformed the landscape and created an entire commercial machine. Scores of small businesses flourished: refineries were necessary to distill the oil, storage tanks to hold it, barrels to carry it, and teamsters to haul it to shipping points on the river or the railroad. In twelve years, as hamlets became towns and towns became cities, the region metamorphosed "from wilderness to market-place." The residents "boasted that the day would soon come when they would refine for the world."

As Tarbell's story unfolds, she describes how the enterprising individuals whose energy and independence brought such prosperity to the region finally proved no match for the regimented power of Standard Oil. Her narrative plainly documents how the ascendancy of the company was aided at every stage by discriminatory railroad rates and illegal tactics—bribery, fraud, criminal underselling, and intimidation. While Tarbell acknowledges John D. Rockefeller's "genius for detail" and admires his rare strength "in energy, in intelligence, in dauntlessness," she demonstrates compellingly that he would never have achieved his monopoly without special transportation privileges. At a time when Rockefeller and his partners in Cleveland held only one tenth of the refining business in the county, he certified to the railroads that he had control of the industry. Providing his organization cheaper rates than their competitors, he argued, was in their interests. "You will have but one party to deal with," he inveigled. "Think of the profits!" And so, swayed by the prospect of avoiding rate wars and enduring the "wear and tear" of securing quotas, the railroad owners entered into clandestine contracts providing Rockefeller with substantial rebates from the published prices.

With this insider deal granting him rates far below those of competitors, and simultaneously kicking back "the extra hundred percent" that outsiders were now forced to pay, Tarbell described how Rockefeller "swooped down" on the independent oil men in Cleveland. "There is no chance for anyone outside," he announced, "but we are going to give everybody a chance to come in. You are to turn over your refinery to my appraisers." Resistors soon found they could not compete against the lower freight rates Standard enjoyed. Within three months, twenty-one of the twenty-six refiners in Cleveland had sold their assets to Standard.

Rockefeller next laid siege to the Oil Creek refiners. "They were there at the mouth of the wells," noted Tarbell. "What might not this geographical advantage do in time?" In her suspenseful installment, "The Oil War of 1872," Tarbell chronicles the defiant struggle of independents when they learned freight rates would suddenly double. More than 3,000 people gathered at the Opera House in Titusville to protest the ruinous rate inflation. It had long been understood that since "the railroad held its right of way from the people," it must "be just to the people, treating them without discrimination," regardless of the volume of business. The Creek oilmen formed a Petroleum Producers Union, demanding investigations by state and federal authorities, and instituted a series of lawsuits. Unlike Rockefeller they had neither the patience nor the capital for protracted litigation. In the end, "from hopelessness, from disgust, from ambition, from love of money," the majority of the local oil producers "gave up the fight for principle" and succumbed to Standard Oil.

Nevertheless, a few intrepid independents refused to submit. "To the man who had begun with one still and had seen it grow by his own energy and intelligence to ten, who now sold 500 barrels a day where he once sold five, the refinery was the dearest spot on earth save his home," Tarbell explained. Where persuasion and simple coercion failed, Rockefeller resorted to more iniquitous tactics. Tarbell uncovered a system of espionage by which Standard bribed railroad agents to access confidential shipping records, detailing "the quantity, quality, and selling price of independent shipments."

Information in hand, Rockefeller knew exactly how much to undercut prices in a particular region to guarantee the elimination of small competitors. One woman testified that "her firm had a customer in New Orleans to whom they had been selling from 500 to 1,000 barrels a month, and that the Standard representative made a contract with him to pay him $10,000 a year for five years to stop handling the independent oil and take Standard oil!" If undercutting the refiners proved insufficient, retailers were directly threatened. Indeed, grocery stores selling oil refined by independents were themselves hounded and harassed to the point that their businesses failed. Of all the machinations that enabled Rockefeller to build his monopoly, Tarbell found these measures the most insufferable. "The unraveling of this espionage charge, the proofs of it," she later said, "turned my stomach against the Standard in a way that the indefensible and robust fights over transportation had never done. There was a littleness about it that seemed utterly contemptible compared to the immense genius and ability that had gone into the organization."

By 1887, Tarbell writes, Rockefeller "had completed one of the most perfect business organizations the world has ever seen, an organization which handled practically all of a great natural product." With "competition practically out of the way, it set all its great energies to developing what it had secured." Most important, Rockefeller now had the power to control prices. Rather than use this domination and the efficiencies of scale to reduce costs, Standard Oil sought to maximize profits. Wherever competition was extinguished, Tarbell maintained, the consumer paid more. Under investigative duress Standard would temporarily reduce prices, only to jack them up in the same area once the scrutiny ceased. "Human experience long ago taught us," she warned, "that if we allow a man or a group of men autocratic powers in government or church, they use that power to oppress and defraud the public."

Throughout her series, Tarbell acknowledged Standard Oil's "legitimate greatness" and recognized the extraordinary business acumen of John D. Rockefeller: "Plants wisely located—The smallest detail in expense looked out for—Quick adaptability to new conditions as they arise—Economy introduced by the manufacture of supplies—Profit paid to nobody—Profitable extension of products and by-products—A general capacity for seeing big things and enough daring to lay hold of them." Nevertheless, she concludes, while "these qualities alone would have made a great business . . . it would not have been the combination whose history we have traced."

Tarbell's final assessment of Rockefeller's practices and unethical maneuvering is unsparing: He began his ascent by flouting the common law to secure favorable rates from the railroads, allowing him to drive his rivals out. "At the same time he worked with the railroads to prevent other people getting oil to manufacture, or if they got it he worked with the railroads to prevent the shipment of the product. If it reached a dealer, he did his utmost to bully or wheedle him to countermand his order. If he failed in that, he undersold until the dealer, losing on his purchase, was glad enough to buy thereafter of Mr. Rockefeller." In the end, "every great campaign against rival interests which the Standard Oil Company has carried on has been inaugurated, not to save its life, but to build up and sustain a monopoly in the oil industry."

In her closing paragraph, Tarbell issues a challenge: "And what are we going to do about it?" Echoing McClure's celebrated editorial, she exhorts her readers, the American public, to take action. "For it is OUR business," she insists, "we, the people of the United States, and nobody else, must cure whatever is wrong in the industrial situation, typified by this narrative of the growth of the Standard Oil Company."

                                                   ⸎ ⸎

"YOU ARE TODAY, THE MOST famous woman in America," McClure told the forty-five-year-old Tarbell six months after her sensational series appeared. "People universally speak of you with such a reverence that I am getting sort of afraid of you," he bantered. For the accolades were imposing: A journalist for *The Outlook* proclaimed her "a Joan of Arc among moderns," crusading "against trusts and monopolies." Another journalist declared her "The New Woman," a powerful and independent agent of social change. "At least one American takes rank with the leading biographers and historians of the old world," the *Lowell* (Massachusetts) *Sun* remarked, and "women are proud to know that one is a woman, Miss Ida Minerva Tarbell." The *Los Angeles Times* called her "the strongest intellectual force among the women of the United States," while the *Washington Times* maintained that she had "proven herself to be one of the most commanding figures in American letters."

Tarbell was invited to speak at numerous colleges, clubs, and law schools. Members of the Twentieth Century Club were reportedly enthralled to hear "the woman who talks like a man," while a Missouri newspaperman described an audience enthralled by the tall, stately woman, "so feminine as to appear décolleté in order to make her assault more effective!" Yet, despite her immense professional achievement, influence, and acclaim, Ida Tarbell was the only person in her office not invited to the first annual publishers' dinner. Newspapermen had met annually for several years, but this was the first such official assemblage of magazine publishers and editors together with writers and public officials. President Roosevelt served as the keynote speaker, and the men-only guest list included cabinet and Supreme Court members as well as prominent senators and congressmen. "It is the first time since I came into the office that the fact of petticoats has stood in my way," Ida confessed to Ray Baker, "and I am half inclined to resent it."

The emergence of humorous commentary surrounding "Miss Tarbell" and her exploits only served to underscore her growing popularity. *The Washington Post* facetiously suggested "that Mr. Rockefeller would be glad to pay the expense if some man should win Miss Ida Tarbell and take her on a leisurely tour of the world for a honeymoon." The *Chicago Daily Tribune* noted that "Miss Ida Tarbell goes calmly on jabbing her biographical hat-pin into Mr. Rockefeller." Even on Broadway, the season's biggest hit, *The Lion and the Mouse*, featured a thinly veiled Tarbell character as the mouse that frees the lion Rockefeller from "the net of avarice." The play's young female author enters the magnate's household under the guise of writing a benign biography. In fact, she seeks documents that will clear her father of unjust corruption charges leveled by the Rockefeller character. Once inside, she successfully clears her father's name, changes "Rockefeller's disposition from sordid to benevolent," and, in a final melodramatic twist, is wooed by the tycoon's son!

The *McClure's* series that had inspired this theatrical parable was read and discussed across the nation. Most important for Tarbell, the reaction from critics was overwhelmingly positive. They applauded her "accumulation of facts," stunning "in their significance," her "intimate style," and her ability to tell a complex story "remarkable for being nearly all plot." With each installment, she left the reader "in a state of lively suspense" as to what might follow. Above all, she was praised repeatedly for the fairness of her presentation. "She never rants," one critic observed. "She never howls and waves her arms."

Rockefeller's defenders argued that by focusing her dramatic analysis on one personage, Tarbell ignored the conditions that made consolidation inevitable in scores of industries, including meatpacking, grain elevators, and railroads. Similarly, she failed to acknowledge that rebating was not confined to Standard Oil; it was, on the contrary, "an almost universal practice." Although her work might be "excellent journalism and very good drama," Gilbert Montague wrote in the *Boston Evening Transcript,* "Miss Tarbell does not seem to have guessed the larger bearings of the movement she describes. . . . She prefers to attribute the course of events to a single pervasive, mysterious personality."

It was the "mysterious" Rockefeller, however, who made the series so wildly popular; the story of his life and the creation of his company provided a narrative spine, on which Tarbell could flesh out a more complex and vivid subject. In her portrait of Rockefeller, Tarbell stressed the duality of his nature, presenting "a quiet, modest church-going gentleman, devoted to Sunday school picnics, golf, and wheeling," yet simultaneously "willing to strain every nerve to obtain special and illegal privileges from the railroads which were bound to ruin every man in the oil business not sharing them with him." When she began her series, one newspaper observed, "Rockefeller was known only as a shrewd businessman who had built up an immense business, with a great name for generosity to educational institutions. Now there are very few sane men who would take Rockefeller's millions if his tarnished reputation must go along with them."

As her narrative progresses, Tarbell's indignation at Rockefeller seems to grow, and her language sometimes slips into the same metaphors for soulless mechanical power that cheapened White's portrait of Boss Platt. She describes his eyes "as expressionless as a wall," notes the "downward" droop of "his mouth," his "cruelest" and "most pathetic" feature, and the repellent puffiness of his cheeks. More than a touch of personal vindictiveness colors her representation of Rockefeller as she describes how his pursuit of money renders him no longer "a human man" but rather "a machine—a money machine—stripped by his overwhelming passion of greed of every quality which makes a man worthy of citizenship."

Far more telling insight lies in her argument that "were Mr. Rockefeller the only one of his kind he would be curious, interesting, unpleasant, but in no way vital. . . . But Mr. Rockefeller is not the only one of his kind. He is simply the type preeminent in the public mind of the militant business man of the day." In the end, she insists, there could be "no cure" for the problem of the trusts without "an increasing scorn of unfair play—an increasing sense that a thing won by breaking the rules of the game is not worth the winning. When the businessman who fights to secure special privileges, to crowd his competitor off the track by other than fair competitive methods, receives the same summary disdainful ostracism by his fellows that the doctor or lawyer who is 'unprofessional,' the athlete who abuses the rules, receives, we shall have gone a long way toward making commerce a fit pursuit for our young men."

Though Rockefeller never directly responded to Tarbell's attacks, his friends and associates vented their displeasure by denying McClure membership to the Ardsley Country Club, perched above the Hudson River twenty miles north of Manhattan. Although no protests had been lodged against McClure before the publication of Tarbell's series, he suddenly found himself blackballed through the collusion of board members "closely allied to the Standard Oil interests," including John D. Archbold, William Rockefeller, and Charles Schwab. Such persecution did nothing to subdue McClure's enthusiasm for Tarbell's writing. "Your monumental work on the Standard Oil will never be forgotten," he assured her. In a special editorial, he touted her series as "one of the most remarkable pieces of work ever published in a magazine." Since he fervently believed that it was "up to magazines to rouse public opinion," he was inordinately proud of the fact that her series had mobilized popular sentiment against the trusts as no other writing had done before.

McClure once claimed "that the two things of which he is proudest are, first, that he was the founder of McClure's Magazine; second, that he was the discoverer of Miss Tarbell." Certainly, the peculiar and intimate partnership that they developed was vital to both. McClure may have been more vision-ary, more in tune with the public's shifting interests, but Tarbell possessed a far sturdier temperament, a relentless work ethic, and the ability to mediate conflict. "You cannot imagine how we all love and reverence you," McClure told her shortly after the launch of the Standard Oil series. "What you have been to me no words can tell." For her part, Tarbell repeatedly proclaimed McClure's manic bursts of energy "the most genuinely creative moments of our magazine life." Nor did she ever forget that he was instrumental in every phase of her journey from obscure expatriate writer to foremost journalist in the nation.

As MEMBERS OF THE HOUSE and Senate assembled in the winter of 1903, a newspaper in Oshkosh, Wisconsin, predicted that Ida Tarbell's sensational exposure of Standard Oil had finally generated enough pressure to compel congressional action against monopolies. The Republican Party, another west-ern paper editorialized, "must stand by the people or yield to the demands of the corporations." While big business had been "a tower of strength" to the majority party for years, growing indignation demanded that some anti-trust action be taken—the "only question being as to how long the shrewd and cunning agents of the trust can manage to delay this outcome." Indeed, the stalling commenced as soon as Congress convened.

Republican leaders in the Senate spread the word that there would be "no time for anti-trust legislation at this session." The subject, they argued, was too complex for the short session that would end in early March: ill-considered legislation might lead to financial panic; much wiser to wait until the longer session the following year. On the other side of the aisle, Democrats called for radical proposals that stood little chance of passing constitutional muster.

"I pass my days in a state of exasperation," Roosevelt told his son Ker-mit, "first, with the fools who do not want any of the things that ought to be done, and, second, with the equally obnoxious fools who insist upon so much that they cannot get anything." Emboldened by public support, Roosevelt was determined to prevent the 1903 Congress from playing "the ancient and honorable bunko game" of letting legislation "fall between the two stools" of the House and Senate, with no time left in conference committee to har-monize their differences. "The party had promised antitrust legislation," he maintained, "and it was the party's duty to do something towards fulfilling its obligations." Summoning the leaders of both branches together, he threatened to exercise the president's constitutional power to call an extra session "on extraordinary occasions" unless his anti-trust proposals were brought to the floor before adjournment. "While I could not force anyone to vote *for* these bills," he explained to a friend, "I felt I had a right to demand that there should be *a vote* upon them."

The administration's anti-trust program in 1903 was comprised of three elements: a measure to strengthen existing laws against discriminatory railroad rebates; a bill to expedite legal proceedings against suspected trusts; and of particular interest to the president, a revived proposal to create a cabinet-level Department of Commerce with regulatory powers over the large corporations.

The first measure, sponsored by Congressman Stephen Elkins of West Virginia, rode the crest of popular fury against what had become known as "Rockefeller's rebates." That single word, "rebate," one editorial observed, dominated Tarbell's chronicle of Standard Oil; every successful step Rockefeller took to "corner the oil interests of the country" could be traced to the secret freight rates he obtained from the railroads. For years, farmers and small businessmen had argued that current laws failed to protect them against discriminatory rebating practices. The Elkins bill was designed to remedy weaknesses in the existing regulations, such as the provision that made only railroad agents actually granting the rebates liable to prosecution: under the new bill, corporations would be held responsible for the acts of any of their officers or agents, and failure to follow published rates would subject both railroads and shippers to heavy fines. The courts would be granted increased powers to secure transaction records, demand testimony, and provide summary judgment.

Although secret opposition to the Elkins bill remained, the impact of Tarbell's investigation, Roosevelt told a friend, meant that "no respectable railroad or respectable shipping business can openly object to the rebate bill." By 1903, the railroads themselves actually favored ending cash rebates, which cost them millions of dollars each year in lost revenue. Furthermore, the most powerful corporations offered no objection; as *The Washington Post* noted, they had already "grown beyond any effects the enforcement of the legislation might have." Even with the ban on secret rebates, there remained myriad ways the trusts could exact special concessions from the railroads. The Elkins bill swiftly passed both Houses, promising, in Roosevelt's words, to throw "the highways of commerce open on equal terms to all who use them." The legislation represented small but pragmatic advancement in pursuit of "equal rights for all; special privileges to none."

Growing public sentiment against monopolies also fueled a bill to expedite prosecutions under the Sherman Anti-Trust Act. Initially, this proposed bill to grant anti-trust suits precedence on court calendars had met with what Roosevelt termed "violent opposition"; now, in the face of public rancor, it was "rather sullenly acquiesced in." When the bill passed both Houses with little debate, William Allen White triumphantly declared that "the subconscious moral sense of the people has come to a distinct realization of the fact that crimes are as possible in what we call high finance as they are in lower quarters."

While the trusts reluctantly yielded on the expedition bill, they brought the full force of their influence against the president's proposed Department of Commerce and Labor. The idea of consolidating the various bureaus and offices overseeing immigration, lighthouses, shipping, fisheries, and the census provoked no outcry. When Senator Knute Nelson of Minnesota introduced an amendment crafted by the administration to establish a Bureau of Corporations within the department, however, fierce opposition erupted. Invested with substantial powers to investigate the internal operations of corporations engaged in interstate commerce, the prospective bureau embodied Roosevelt's conviction that publicity was "the first essential" to determine whether individual trusts were guilty of "unfair competition," "unscrupulous promotion," or "overcapitalization." The amendment would provide the bureau with authority to compel testimony, and to subpoena books, papers, and reports. At his discretion, the president could use these findings to determine whether anti-trust laws were being violated and to induce Congress to pass additional regulatory measures to remedy the abuses uncovered.

Long accustomed to operating without effective oversight or federal regulation, corporate interests regarded the prospective Bureau of Corporations as the harbinger of a stifling socialism. "The Standard Oil Company has always regarded anti-trust laws, anti-rebate laws, and such things, as harmless, though, at times annoying," the *Wall Street Journal* explained, "but publicity hurts. And the company will always, at all times, and in all ways, fight publicity." Determined to kill the new bureau, officials of the trusts descended on Washington for private meetings with their loyal allies on Capitol Hill.

Roosevelt's failure the previous year had taught him to carefully monitor every stage of the bill's movement through Congress. Night after night, he convened meetings with leaders of the Senate and the House, impressing on the Speaker, the ranking committee members, and the majority leader that the Nelson amendment was essential to redeem the party's pledge to take action on the trusts. These sessions required all the president's finesse, the press reported, for there was "a disposition in some quarters" to resent his meddling in legislative affairs.

Realizing that he would benefit from the broadest possible consensus, Roosevelt sought to cultivate warm connections with a number of Democrats. Attending the wedding of Missouri's Democratic senator Francis Cockrell's daughter, the president "joked with the girls, shook hands with the matrons and exchanged 'jollying' remarks with the young and old men." At the celebratory breakfast, he announced with sly wit that he could never reside in Missouri, however splendid that state might be: "I think so much of Sen. Cockrell and admire him so greatly that I don't see how I could keep from voting for him, and as he is a Democrat you know that would never, never, do."

"I have been worked until I could hardly stand," the notoriously tireless Roosevelt grumbled to Kermit, "some days twelve hours and over absolutely without intermission." But in fact, his days were not without respite—almost every afternoon he managed the diversion of some mode of exercise. Singlestick, a form of swordplay in which competitors wield wooden sticks, had become his latest obsession. General Leonard Wood, Roosevelt's favorite opponent, bested the president on various occasions, leaving him with a swollen arm, a bruised forehead, and once, a deep cut on his right wrist that required him to shake left-handed at the next White House reception. A comic diagram in the *Minneapolis Journal* pinpointed the numerous injuries Roosevelt had sustained during sundry activities, humorously labeling him "The Most Wounded President in the Nation's History."

When multiplying bruises precluded more singlestick jousts, he rode a horse along snowy streets or split wood for exercise. If his exertions as a woodsman did "not suffice," the *Boston Traveler* quipped, "he might try his hand at lopping off a few of the trust privileges." And indeed, that formidable energy was funneled into a single objective—persuading Congress to pass his pet anti-trust bill.

Saturday, February 7, 1903, would prove critical in the struggle for the Bureau of Corporations. Roosevelt's demeanor, as he discussed literature and international events with the French ambassador Jules Jusserand, revealed nothing of the ruse under way for that evening. As darkness descended, he called together members of the three press associations. Insisting that the source of the information must remain confidential, Roosevelt confided that he had secured proof that John D. Rockefeller was personally orchestrating an underhanded campaign to sabotage the Nelson amendment. A half-dozen senators, he claimed, had received telegrams bearing John D. Rockefeller's signature, with "peremptory" instruction indicating that the corporation was "unalterably opposed" to the bill, and it "must be stopped." The message, one paper reported, was clear: "We own the Republican party and it must do our bidding."

The offending telegrams, Roosevelt assured the assembled journalists—without giving them the exact wording or showing the actual telegrams—had only redoubled his determination to establish the Bureau of Corporations. Unless Congress enacted a satisfactory bill by the March 4 adjournment, he would surely insist on the extra session previously threatened. As anticipated, word of Rockefeller's imperious telegrams inspired headlines and editorials across the country and produced "a decided sensation" on Capitol Hill. One senator after another hastily denied receiving a Rockefeller telegram, "for fear," one Wisconsin paper suggested, that "somebody might think they had intimate relations with the great octopus."

Rockefeller's purported tactic should have occasioned "no surprise," one newspaper sardonically noted: "It is pretty much his senate, anyway. Most of the members of the once august body were elected on a pro-trust understanding, and Deacon John is simply insisting upon fulfillment of the bargain mutually entered into." For years, he and his fellow industrialists had filled Mark Hanna's coffers, the editorial concluded, and Rockefeller was now simply "claiming the privileges he paid for, nothing more."

To combat the pending legislation, Standard Oil sent three of its top lawyers to the Arlington Hotel in Washington. There, they would combine with congressional allies to prepare an emasculating amendment if the bill could not be killed outright. "This is no more than is done every day by managers and attorneys of great business enterprises," the *Los Angeles Times* acknowledged. Companies routinely sent representatives to the nation's capital in an effort to shield themselves from unfavorable legislation. The appearance of the Standard attorneys amid the outrage sparked by Ida Tarbell's exposé and the Rockefeller telegram scandal, however, seemed certain to "inflame the agitator element" in Congress and possibly spur even more radical legislation. "Grasping the whole situation at a glance," Senator Aldrich "wheeled the trio of counsel promptly to right-about," sending them back to New York the next morning.

JUBILANT, ROOSEVELT BOASTED THAT "FROM the standpoint of constructive statesmanship," he considered the Department of Commerce and Labor, with its Bureau of Corporations, "a much greater feat than any tariff law." Well aware of the importance of sharing credit for the victory, he wrote a warm note to

Speaker David Henderson, who had finally conceded that Republicans must take action against the trusts. "Taken as a whole," Roosevelt told him, "no other Congress of recent years has to its credit a record of more substantial achievement for the public good than this over the lower house of which you presided. I congratulate you and it." To head the new department, he chose his private secretary and trusted friend, George Cortelyou, and selected James Garfield, the son of the former president, for Commissioner of Corporations.

After failing for years both as governor and president to pass legislation regulating corporations, Roosevelt had finally succeeded because "a great many people had been thinking and talking" about the problem of the trusts, and "a certain consensus of opinion" had been reached. Ida Tarbell's series had helped foment and articulate a conscious desire for reform in every village, township, and city. In John D. Rockefeller, she had furnished a human face for the bewilderingly intricate and multifaceted problem of the trusts—thereby giving the president an identifiable target that he brilliantly exploited to mobilize public sentiment behind his legislative program.

With the passage of the rebate bill and the expedition bill and the establishment of the Department of Commerce, Roosevelt was convinced that he had "gotten the trust legislation all right," that Democrats could no longer wield the trust issue against his party. Although some charged that even these measures combined were "not sufficiently far-reaching," even these critics acknowledged that Congress had exceeded expectations. Moreover, this trio of bills would provide the basis to determine what further action might be necessary.

Perhaps no forum better illustrated the progressive direction of public opinion than William Allen White's scorecard for the 57th Congress. The country editor who had ridiculed calls for governmental intervention only a few years earlier now heralded Roosevelt's three anti-trust measures as a major step toward rectifying laissez-faire economic policy. He predicted that "no single legislative act since the Missouri Compromise" would impact American business as much as the Department of Commerce and Labor. "Thousands of interests that have known no Federal regulation and control," he wrote, "will be welded to the Government hereafter, and can only grow and develop under the hands of Congress and the President." Some might fear that the country was taking "a step toward socialism," he concluded, but "if so, well and good; the step will not be retracted."

CHAPTER TWELVE

"A Mission to Perform"

"Bigger Than His Party," a Roosevelt cartoon
in *Puck* magazine, May 7, 1902.

O N THE MORNING OF APRIL 1, 1903, Roosevelt embarked in high
spirits upon the longest tour ever taken by a president—a nine-week
transcontinental journey by train that would cover 14,000 miles across twenty-
four states and territories. Freed from the vexations of dealing with Congress,
he jauntily doffed his hat and waved to the hundreds of cheering well-wishers
gathered at the Sixth Street station to see him off. As he boarded the train, he
turned to offer parting advice to George Cortelyou, whom he had appointed
head of the new Department of Commerce and Labor. "Look out for the
trusts," he chuckled. "I hate to leave you here alone with those dreadful corporations, but I can't very well help it. Be careful of them and don't let them
hurt you while I am away."

The specially equipped train, reportedly among "the handsomest ever placed on the tracks by the Pullman Company," consisted of six cars. The lush, mahogany-finished *Elysian* would be the president's home throughout the trip. This "traveling palace" boasted three state rooms, a kitchen staffed by expert chefs, a private dining room, an observation parlor, quarters for the servants, and a rear platform from which to address crowds gathered at little stations along the way. The remaining cars included spacious quarters for the president's guests, stenographers, and Secret Service crew, a sleeping car housing reporters and photographers, and a dining car.

Invited to accompany the presidential party, the naturalist John Burroughs described the train's progress north and west through Maryland, Pennsylvania, Illinois, Wisconsin, the Dakotas, and Montana. The president "gave himself very freely and heartily to the people," he noted, his arrival sparking a festive spirit in each village and town. Whenever Roosevelt spotted a group of men or women waving from a distance, he raced out to lift his hat and return the greeting. He never saw such exchanges with the public as inconvenient or intrusive. Burroughs recalled an occasion when the president was lunching as the train passed by a small schoolhouse where the teacher had ushered her students outside. Clutching his napkin, Roosevelt raced to the platform. "Those children," he said, "wanted to see the President of the United States, and I could not disappoint them. They may never have another chance."

Recognizing that people would come "to see the President much as they would come in to see a circus," Roosevelt also surmised that in many small towns the train—rather than the president—was the marquee attraction: "The whole population of the plains now looks upon the Pullman sleepers and dining cars," he told John Hay, "just as Mark Twain describes the people along the banks of the Mississippi as formerly looking at the Mississippi steamers." Nonetheless, he was convinced that "besides the mere curiosity there was a good feeling behind it all, a feeling that the President was their man and symbolized their government and that they had a proprietary interest in him."

Jostled by frantic crowds as he made his way to crude bandstands erected along the route, Roosevelt never betrayed impatience or irritation. Since active campaigning by a presidential candidate was still considered distasteful, this extended tour represented his best chance to gain "the people's trust" before the coming election. Determined to connect with the people, Roosevelt radiated nothing but delight as he accepted an array of bizarre gifts that included an infant badger, a lizard, a horned toad, a copper vase, an Indian basket, two bears, a horse, and a gold inlaid saddle. Through it all, Roosevelt maintained good humor and gratitude. In Butte, Montana, when presented with a foot-high three-handled silver loving cup capable of holding sixteen pints of beer, he graciously exclaimed, "Great heavens and earth!"

Before embarking on the tour, Roosevelt had prepared a half-dozen policy speeches, each addressing a specific issue—the trusts, the tariff, the Navy, the Philippines, and the Monroe Doctrine. "These were not epoch-making addresses," William White explained. Neither "particularly original" nor profound, they were structured with two simple goals in mind: to outline his policies in straightforward language and to establish an emotional rapport with his audiences.

The further he moved from "the thick of civilization," the more expansive and at ease the president appeared. When he talked informally to "rough-coated, hard-headed, gaunt, sinewy farmers and hired hands," Roosevelt proudly told John Hay, he was "always sure of reaching them" with simple language that his Harvard friends would judge "not only homely, but commonplace." Despite "all the superficial differences," he remarked, "down at bottom these men and I think a good deal alike, or least have the same ideals."

Newspapermen began to compile the aphorisms they termed "Roosevelt Gems"—pithy sayings about citizenship, character, and ordinary virtues that he repeated time and again to the great pleasure of his audiences: farmers in Aberdeen, South Dakota, whistled approval when he declared that no law could ever be framed to "make a fool wise or a weakling strong, or a coward brave." They cheered when he compared the qualities desired in the best kind of public servant to those displayed by a good neighbor or a trustworthy friend—"a man who keep[s] his word and never promise[s] . . . what he knows cannot be done." Oregonians nodded in approval when he affirmed, "I do not like hardness of heart, but neither do I like softness of head." Indianans cheered the now familiar Roosevelt adage "Speak softly and carry a big stick." Such "sudsy metaphors," which reportedly dripped "like water from a clothesline," reached the hearts of citizens at every stop along the way.

It was during this western tour that Roosevelt began to test the phrase "a square deal"—the slogan that would come to characterize his entire domestic program. In a speech the previous summer he had called for "a square deal for every man, great or small, rich or poor." Now, he began to flesh out what this really meant for particular segments of the populace. In Arizona, he spoke of the Indians in his regiment: "They were good enough to fight and to die, and they are good enough to have me treat them exactly as square as any white man. . . . All I ask is a square deal for every man." In Montana, he expressed a similar sentiment about the black troops who fought beside him in Santiago. Still later, he elaborated on the concept, applying it to his policy regarding labor and capital. The appeal of the slogan was immediately evident; even advertisers along the president's route appropriated his phrase, headlining "A Square Deal" in their copy. A real estate company in Butte, Montana, began its pitch with Roosevelt's words: "We must treat each man on his worth and merits as a man. We must see that each is given a square deal, because he is entitled to no more and should receive no less."

Reaching Yellowstone, Roosevelt bid a temporary farewell to the newspapermen, who were instructed to stay behind. Accompanied by John Burroughs, he intended to relax for two weeks, to watch birds and simply observe rather than hunt game—the herds of elk, antelope, and black-tailed deer. Roosevelt had stayed with the older man in his log cabin three years earlier, striking Burroughs then as "a great boy," filled with inexhaustible energy. "He climbed everything on the place," the naturalist recalled with mixed awe and dread. "He shinned up tree after tree, running his arms into every highhole's and woodpecker's nest, while I stood on the ground below shuddering and waiting for him to fall." Their stay at Yellowstone convinced Burroughs that the presidency had altered Roosevelt little: he remained "a man of such abounding energy and ceaseless activity that he sets everything in motion around him wherever he goes. . . . Nothing escaped him, from bears to mice, from wild geese to chickadees, from elk to red squirrels; he took it all in, and he took it in as only an alert, vigorous mind can take it in."

These invigorating days in Yellowstone and a subsequent camping trip in the magnificent forests of Yosemite with the founder of the Sierra Club, John Muir, deeply impressed Roosevelt and informed the tone of his speeches during the remainder of the trip. Turning from trusts and the tariff, he increasingly focused on the importance of preserving the country's national heritage from exploitation. He arrived at the Grand Canyon as a great contest was raging over whether to preserve the landmark as a national monument or open it up to mining for precious metals. "Leave it as it is," he urged his countrymen. "The ages have been at work on it, and man can only mar it. . . . Keep it for your children, your children's children and for all who come after you, as one of the great sights which every American . . . should see." Deeply moved by this "great wonder of nature," the president resolved to ensure the designation of the Grand Canyon as a national park. "If Roosevelt had done nothing else as president," Douglas Brinkley has observed, "his advocacy on behalf of preserving the canyon might well have put him in the top ranks of American presidents."

When the presidential party reached the California coast, Roosevelt took a special detour on a narrow-gauge road into the San Lorenzo Valley, home to a majestic grove of giant sequoias. "I am, oh, so glad to be here," he exclaimed. "This is the first glimpse I have ever had of the big trees." At Stanford University the next day, he exhorted his audience "to protect these mighty trees, these wonderful monuments of beauty." It seemed a desecration to turn "a tree which was old when the first Egyptian conqueror penetrated to the valley of the Euphrates" into house siding or decks or porches. While many would hold that practical progress should trump aesthetic value, Roosevelt argued, "there is nothing more practical, in the end, than the preservation of beauty, than the preservation of anything that appeals to the higher emotions in mankind."

The vital role of these massive redwoods, "the great monarchs of the woods," was confined neither to their commercial value nor to their natural beauty. The primary object of his overall forest policy, Roosevelt insisted, was "not to preserve forests because they are beautiful—though that is a good in itself—not to preserve them because they are refuges for the wild creatures of the wilderness—though that too is a good in itself," but rather, to conserve them in order to guarantee "a steady and continuous supply of timber, grass, and above all, water" that would foster the growth of prosperous communities. Contrary to the prevailing view, Roosevelt foresaw that our natural resources were not inexhaustible. Destructive lumbering practices had already "seriously depleted" the forests. In clear language, he delineated the causal connection between forest protection and water conservation: forests absorb water and slow the melting of snow in the spring; they prevent the rain from "rushing away in uncontrollable torrents"; they "regulate the flow of streams." In every watershed, forests help determine the amount of available water that can transform a wasteland into "a veritable garden of Eden."

In speech after speech, Roosevelt lauded the passage of the 1902 Reclamation Act, which, for the first time, made substantial federal funds available to construct dams, reservoirs, and other irrigation projects in the West. Intended to open "small irrigated farms to actual settlers, to actual home-makers," the legislation stipulated that tracts of land larger than 160 acres would be ineligible for federally sponsored irrigation. In this way, the government sought to ensure that speculators would not commandeer the program's benefits. "We do not ever want to let our land policy be shaped so as to create a big class of proprietors who rent to others," Roosevelt asserted. America's forests and waters must "come into the hands, not of a few men of great wealth, or into the hands of a few men who speculate in them, but be distributed among many men, each of whom intends to make him a home on the land."

Of the five irrigation projects under way in the spring of 1903—in Colorado, Montana, Wyoming, Nevada, and Arizona—the most prominent was a huge masonry arch dam in Arizona's Salt River Valley. When Charles Walcott, director of the U.S. Geological Survey, announced on April 18 that the government had selected the Salt River Valley for its first big enterprise, a banner headline in the *Arizona Republican* hailed the decision: THE DAY OF DELIVERANCE IS AT HAND. The reservoir created by the project, later christened the Roosevelt Dam, would be, excepting the work being done on the Nile, "the greatest in the world." Designed to irrigate 200,000 acres, the dam promised to "make the community near Phoenix [with a population then of 25,000] one of the most prosperous in the country."

The estimated cost of the five projects would total $7 million, which settlers would then repay to the government over a ten-year period. Once completed, Roosevelt predicted, these irrigation projects would more profoundly impact the entire western region over the next half century than "any other material movement whatsoever." He could already envision "a new type" of settler throughout the West who could build homes, roads, businesses, schools, and places of amusement, populating bustling towns and cities that might one day contain "a million inhabitants." Moreover, an arable, enticing West could alleviate some of the social evils caused by overcrowding in the East.

Century magazine suggested that Roosevelt's decision to highlight issues of conservation, irrigation, and preservation would have an "educational effect upon the people," fostering a new determination to protect "the western wonderlands," expand national parks, and institute a sustainable, scientific approach to managing the nation's wilderness areas. Any action to safeguard forest lands was usually delayed until the end of a president's term, the journalist noted, but Roosevelt would not hesitate "to throw the full force of his influence" behind legislation that would halt "the ruinous waste of the great national forests."

From California, the president's train headed north to Portland, Oregon, and Seattle, Washington, before veering east for the long trip home. Roosevelt had delivered 265 speeches, once addressing nine crowds in a single day. He had participated in countless parades, endured long banquets (and gained 11 pounds), met with all manner of local officials, dedicated monuments, and attended military reviews. Sustained by the enthusiastic reception all along his travel route, he returned, according to Edith, "as fresh and unworn as when he left."

Roosevelt had scarcely settled into the White House when reports surfaced of possible governmental corruption over the Salt River reservoir. Objections and accusations swirled around the choice of Salt River for the government's inaugural project. During congressional debates over the Reclamation Act, talk of making desert lands in the public domain "blossom like a rose" abounded; ultimately, the government hoped to open these revitalized lands to individual settlers at a small cost under the Homestead Act. Yet given that almost all the land in the Salt River Valley was already in private hands, such settlements represented a glaring problem. For twenty years, private funds had irrigated the valley; unlike the four smaller projects, this reservoir would "irrigate no public lands, but only those in private ownership, vastly increasing, of course, their value." Indeed, the irrigated lands would likely quadruple in value when the government completed its work. To further complicate matters, some of the tracts—undoubtedly held by speculators—covered upward of 10,000 acres, many times the established limit of 160 acres. Opportunities for corruption seemed boundless.

As Roosevelt struggled to address the complex situation in Arizona, he turned to Ray Baker for insight and counsel. Ever since Baker's early biographical sketch had caught his attention, Roosevelt had followed the reporter's career, occasionally sending him short notes commending his "excellent" work. He had read Baker's now famous January 1903 article on the brutality between union men and the scabs who had continued to work during the coal strike, and gauged the public reaction to Baker's gripping investigative piece. Despite his firm support of trade unions, Roosevelt strongly believed that members who engaged in violent acts such as Baker described should be held accountable. "We intend to do absolute justice to every man," he repeatedly proclaimed, "whether he be capitalist or wageworker, union man or nonunion man."

While Baker shared this conviction, he had initially hesitated when Mc-Clure suggested he study the violence perpetrated against non-striking miners. He was loath to provide "ammunition for mere stupid opposition to all labor organizations" or to compromise the labor leaders he had come to know and respect over the years. Furthermore, the coal strike had erupted during his second leave of absence from the magazine as he began long-postponed work on his novel exploring the nation's grave social and economic plight. Baker had finally moved from New York to East Lansing, a quiet hamlet near the campus of Michigan State College where his father-in-law still taught biology. He calculated that his savings would last at least a year. The change delighted his wife tremendously, drawing their three children close to their grandparents and reuniting her with childhood friends.

Baker would "never . . . forget the feeling of joyful independence" as he settled into his new home and commenced work on his novel. On his study wall, he hung portraits of Walt Whitman, Leo Tolstoy, and his own father. He tacked favorite quotations to the back of the desk, which, he noted with satisfaction, was "the first desk I ever had that was big enough . . . where I could spread out my elbows and work as long as I wanted to without interruption."

"I actually thought my future was settled!" Baker recalled of the brief respite. "I did not count sufficiently upon S. S. McClure." Eager to keep his gifted young reporter, McClure had contacted him in October 1902 as the coal strike was escalating. The magazine, he generously proposed, would pay a weekly stipend throughout the year, while Baker would have to work only six months. The rest of the year he would be free to pursue his own writing, which *McClure's* would publish on liberal terms. "So the serpent in my new Eden!" Baker ruefully jested, the proposition too tempting to reject.

Baker had just arrived at the magazine's New York office when he received word that McClure wanted him in Wilkes-Barre, Pennsylvania, where the coal strike was coming to an end. McClure himself had traveled to the coal region shortly after his summer vacation in Europe, joining dozens of reporters, writers, and publishers gathered to cover the historic strike. Recognizing that the press was saturated with stories about the terrible coal-field conditions that had precipitated the five-month strike, McClure sought a different aspect of the story. Despite the abysmal conditions, some miners had kept on the job, refusing to support their fellow strikers, even at the risk of violent reprisal. "What sort of men were they?" McClure pondered. The story of "the scabs" was yet untold, and McClure felt that no one was better suited to investigate the matter than Ray Baker.

When they met at the Hotel Sterling at the corner of River and Market Streets, the buoyant McClure presented his idea to Baker. The young writer was less sanguine, explaining his concern that so long as public opinion "was generally hostile to labor unionism," it must be emphasized that the strike-breakers' plight was "only one aspect of a highly complex problem." But the longer he considered the proposal, the more curious he grew about the 17,000 out of roughly 140,000 miners who persisted in working. Baker had always been intrigued by the motivation of the few who went against the many, and in the end, to McClure's delight, he agreed to stay in the coal region for a month or more to talk with these men and learn why they refused to support the union.

With the same exacting impartiality that marked his investigation of the Pullman strike, Baker sought out people on all sides of the "scab" issue. He talked with the miners in the kitchens of their homes and descended with them down the shafts into the mines, taking note of the "low wages, company houses, company stores, poor schools, wretched living conditions" in the collieries. He sat in on union meetings where "the scabs" were bitterly denounced and interviewed John Mitchell, whom he found "singularly steady-headed" in the wake of the turbulent strike. In hotel suites thick with cigar smoke, he discussed the conflict with fellow writers and radical leaders, including Henry D. Lloyd and Clarence Darrow. Armed with a range of opinions, he spent weeks with scores of non-striking miners, talking with them and their families, eliciting their perspectives of the realities that led to their decision to continue working even under such treacherous conditions.

"What men I met during those fiery weeks!" he recalled. "What stories they told me: what dramas of human suffering, human loyalty, and human fear." McClure was thrilled with Baker's letters from the field. "Don't, my dear boy, be afraid of space," he urged; "we can give this thing all the space it requires, all the articles it requires. I am glad you have struck such a rich mine." A week later, McClure wrote again. The New York *Sun* had devoted two columns that day to a sermon delivered in Brooklyn on the subject of "the feuds in the coal-fields, the bitterness between union and non-union men, the uncompromising hatred" opening "wounds that only death can heal." Baker's subject had "become the most important question of the day," McClure reassured him. "I am going down to go over the material with you yourself," he added. "You have done magnificently!"

Baker completed his piece, which McClure titled "The Right to Work," just in time for inclusion in the landmark issue. At Baker's insistence, an editor's note preceded the piece to clarify the magazine's support for labor unions. Although the magazine would continue to advocate for the nation's workingmen, the editor explained, the public "is beginning to distinguish between unionism and the sins of unionists, as it is between organized capital and the sins of capitalists." By illuminating the individual lives of the strikebreakers, Baker also stressed in his opening, he intended neither to challenge "the rights of labor to organize" nor to question "the sincerity of the labor leader." Instead, he simply wanted to offer a detailed "series of case histories" exploring why these men "continued to work in spite of so much abuse and even real danger."

The story of John Colson dramatically illustrated the divisive impact of the strike within mining families. An engineer from the small town of Gilberton, Pennsylvania, Colson enjoyed "the best position at the colliery." Although not a member of the union, he initially went out with the strikers. But with no prospect of a settlement after several months, he took a job at a distant colliery while his wife remained at home with the children. The moment spies determined that Colson had gone back to work, his wife was targeted for retaliation: stores would not serve her; former friends repudiated her in the streets; neighbors pelted her with rocks. When she tried to move, no teamster would help her. A mob finally tracked down Colson himself, beating him so badly that he was mistakenly listed among those murdered during the strike. After talking with Colson and his wife, Baker went to visit Colson's elderly parents in Mahonay City, four miles away. Mrs. Colson spoke with pride of her sons, all miners, all union members who had faithfully maintained the strike. She discussed her eldest son, John, reluctantly. "He might better be dead," she declared, "for he's brought disgrace on the name. He deserved all he got. He wasn't raised a scab." Never again would the family acknowledge him. "The strike," Baker wrote, "had wholly crushed all family feeling."

Baker's reporting illustrated how, all too often, lifelong friendships, like familial bonds, became casualties of the conflict. A strong believer in unions, one miner, Hugh Johnson, nonetheless considered this strike, the second in two years, a bad idea. Although he voted against it, he remained out with the strikers until he could no longer afford to pay his family's living expenses. As soon as he returned to work, troubles began: his daughter was fired from her job as a teacher, his son harassed at school, and his wife prevented from buying food and supplies at the local stores. One night, a mob chased and threatened to kill him. "All these things," Baker observed, "were done by his neighbors and friends, among whom he had lived an honorable life for years."

As the strike dragged on, the level of violence escalated. One telling example involved James Winstone, a respected community leader. Winstone, too, had argued against the strike but stayed out to support his fellow workers. Informed that he did not qualify for assistance from the union relief fund because he owned property, Winstone finally returned to work. In late September, only a few days before the strike was settled, he was clubbed to death by three longtime neighbors. Such stories, Baker insisted, constituted "only a few among scores, even hundreds, of similar tragedies of the great coal strike."

Baker returned to East Lansing after completing the article "on fire with the wealth of new material, new characters and, above all, new understandings of the human elements" involved in the labor struggle. He happily anticipated sitting at his desk to work on his novel "gloriously all winter long." As January turned to February, however, he found it increasingly difficult to concentrate. Clippings arrived from all over the country praising his article. "Everything has borne out the truthfulness and value of the article you wrote," McClure congratulated him. His case histories had dramatized a vital aspect of the conflict—the price paid by non-striking miners—better than anything else written. McClure sought to entice him with the prospect of an entire series on labor.

Baker found himself making scant headway on his novel, unable "to write fiction when the world seemed literally on fire with critical, possibly revolutionary, movements in which [he] was deeply interested." Putting the fiction aside, he returned to New York, where "a powerful new interest, a common purpose" was energizing the *McClure's* office. The enthusiasm generated by the magazine's critical and popular success was palpable. "I doubt whether any other magazine published in America ever achieved such sudden and overwhelming recognition," Baker proudly remarked. "We had put our fingers upon the sorest spots in American life."

The staff members at *McClure's* had always worked closely, even while pursuing diverse interests. Now that their respective investigations into the problems of modern industrial society substantially overlapped, they eagerly read one another's works, often suggesting further lines of inquiry. Tarbell's disclosures of John D. Rockefeller's illegal activities resonated with Steffens's endeavor to trace political corruption to the captains of industry. Tarbell looked to Steffens for an understanding of the invisible web that linked businessmen to politicians, politicians to judges. Indeed, the intensity of these reciprocally informing projects and the sense of camaraderie in a momentous cause affected Baker profoundly. "I have wondered," he later wrote, "if there could have been a more interesting editorial office than ours, one with more of the ozone of great ideas, touch-and-go experimentation, magic success." This rare formula, he noted, owed as much to rigorous and honest feedback as to affectionate support. "We were friends indeed, but we were also uncompromising critics of one another." Forty years later, Baker still considered John Phillips "the most creative editor" he had worked with in his entire life. "He could tell wherein an article failed and why," he recalled; "he could usually make fertile suggestions for improving it; he was willing to give the writer all the precious time he needed for rewriting his story."

The office itself, now situated just east of the Flatiron Building on 23rd Street, reflected the collaborative ardor of McClure's staff. The walls in the hallway were a mosaic of original artwork designed for pages of the magazine. Mementoes from individual articles decorated each writer's office. They even had special names for one another: McClure was "the Chief," Steffens was "Stef," and Ida M. Tarbell was affectionately dubbed "I-dare-m." In her office, she proudly displayed a framed note from Finley Peter Dunne: "Idarem— She's a lady but she has the punch." No one, Baker said of Tarbell, lived "so warmly in the hearts of her friends." Never had he known "a finer human spirit," "so generous, so modest, so full of kindness, so able, so gallant—and yet with such good sense and humor."

The exhilarating atmosphere in the office persuaded Baker to accept the Chief's suggestion and embark upon a series of labor articles. "Why bother with fictional characters and plots," he told himself, "when the world was full of more marvelous stories that were true: and characters so powerful, so fresh, so new, that they stepped into the narratives under their own power?"

⌒ ⌒

THE PRESIDENT'S REQUEST FOR BAKER'S help in uncovering possible corruption in Arizona reached the reporter in Chicago, where he was researching the first of five lengthy articles on various aspects of the labor problem. As the celebrated series unfolded, Roosevelt would frequently reach out to Baker for advice and counsel on labor issues. In the summer of 1903, as Roosevelt labored to assess the contentious Salt River situation, he recalled a more obscure series on the Southwest Baker had written for the literary *Century* magazine the previous year. Like Roosevelt, Baker recognized the transformative potential of irrigation. Using language close to Roosevelt's heart, Baker described riding through miles of desert with "no sign of living creatures," only to discover a green stretch of well-watered acreage "with rows of rustling cottonwoods, the roofs of home, and the sound of cattle in the meadows. A wire fence was the dividing line: on this side lay the fruitless desert; on the other green alfalfa, full of blossoms and bees, brimming over the fences." The sight, Baker proclaimed, "was something to stir a man's heart." "My dear Mr. Baker," Roosevelt wrote on June 25, explaining his dilemma and soliciting Baker's guidance. "As you know, I am especially concerned over the irrigation project. At times I hear rumors of crookedness in connection with the Government irrigation work, especially in Arizona. I have been utterly unable hitherto to get any definite statement in reference thereto. It has occurred to me that you may be able privately to tell me something about this."

Baker swiftly responded, promising to share all the information gleaned concerning the Salt River project. He had, in fact, returned to Arizona earlier that spring, contemplating another irrigation article. Moreover, he had been present at the meetings when Charles Walcott of the U.S. Geological Survey delivered his decision in favor of the Water Users Association in Salt River, and had spent time on an alfalfa ranch in order to "get at the exact sentiment of the people." Though he had witnessed no overt corruption, Baker had little doubt that something was wrong; promoters of the Water Users Association, "backed by the government officials," relied on "overbearing" methods that were "suspicious in the extreme." He assured the president that he would gladly call at the White House when he returned to Washington the following week.

"I suppose that the Government officials you speak of must be in the Geological Survey," Roosevelt replied, adding that "in public life as in private life a man of the very highest repute will occasionally go wrong." Still, he recognized that accusations and rumors are readily fabricated, and in such cases "it is most desirable that their falsity be shown." Some criticism of Walcott was undoubtedly political—fueled by Republicans upset with projects recommended in Democratic states, as well as senators and congressmen in the Rocky Mountain region furious over the choice of Arizona (still a territory without representation in Congress). Regardless of the origins, Roosevelt insisted that if Walcott "or any other Government official has gone wrong in Arizona I am more anxious than any other man can be to get at it." He requested that Baker do him the favor of stopping first to see Gifford Pinchot at the Forestry Division and then joining him for lunch at Oyster Bay. "If there is any kind of ground for believing in fraud of any sort by Government officials," he concluded, "I want to consult with you as to the best way of setting men to work so as to be sure of our getting the proof."

Baker was thrilled by the prospect of working closely with the president either to uncover corruption or to dispel malicious career-destroying rumors. "I was so eager to help," he recalled, "that I got together a large package of notes and memoranda—also maps and pictures—and a veritable article of several thousand words on which I spent several days of hard work, setting forth in detail the exact situation in the Salt River Valley as I had seen it." He took another day to compile a memorandum on the coal fields, just in case Roosevelt ventured to discuss labor issues as well. "I was determined to be fully prepared," he explained, "to give the President of the United States several hours of sound enlightenment and instruction!"

Baker's study of the situation in Arizona convinced him that the government's choice of the Salt River Valley was perfectly justified. "If ever men worked miracles," he wrote, it was in Salt River. Sustained by private capital, neighbors had cooperated for decades to dig ditches and build canals in order to divert water. From inhospitable desert, they had wrested three cities replete with electric lights, fine hotels, schools, and churches—all shaded by mature trees and bordered by thriving and productive "orchards of oranges, almonds, olives, and figs." After seven years of insufficient rainfall and reckless deforestation, however, the "implacable desert" was closing in again. homes were reluctantly abandoned as orchards died, fields withered, and land values plummeted. Without the infusion of vast government capital to build a great reservoir, this once-thriving valley would perish. Baker carefully considered how two related factors complicated the situation: vast tracts of land were already under private ownership, and unscrupulous developers might lure more people into the valley than the water project could supply.

On the morning of July 15, Baker boarded a train at Long Island City. En route to Oyster Bay, where the president was spending the summer, he ran into an old Chicago acquaintance, Herman Kohlsaat, publisher of the *Record-Herald*. Treasury Secretary Leslie Mortimer Shaw and Charles J. Bonaparte, a noted attorney who was investigating postal fraud for the Justice Department, also joined them aboard the train. Upon arrival, the four men crowded into a horse-driven public carriage for the three-mile journey to Sagamore Hill.

"The President lives very simply," Baker informed his father. "I thought as I drove over from the station what some modern German or English worthy might say on entering the president's grounds & seeing no guards or military anywhere about." A maid ushered the guests into the library to wait for the president. "Robust, hearty, wholesome, like a gust of wind," he soon burst in, wearing knee-length breeches and an old coat.

The company at lunch included members of the Roosevelt family and the president's old friend Jacob Riis. Theodore Roosevelt, Baker observed, "takes an extraordinary interest in life, gets pleasure out of everything. His mind seems to leap upon every question with boundless enthusiasm." The president first addressed the alleged postal corruption, assuring Bonaparte that he desired an exhaustive investigation. "I don't care whom it hurts," he assured Baker; "we must get to the bottom of these scandals." Shifting the conversation to Arizona, he reiterated that his irrigation development must benefit the individual settler rather than the wealthy landowner or speculator. Baker understood the difficulty of realizing this intention, but a recently promulgated regulation promised to guide the project in that direction. The government had announced that landowners possessing more than 160 acres must put their extra acreage "on the market at reasonable prices" or receive no water from the reservoir.

Unaware of these developments, Roosevelt suddenly turned to Baker: "Who is the chief devil down there in the Salt River valley?" Baker was momentarily unsure how to respond to such a query. When he hesitated, "the President burst into a vigorous, picturesque, and somewhat vitriolic description of the situation, implying that if he could catch the rascals who were causing the trouble he would execute them on the spot." Baker was taken aback by Roosevelt's simplistic diatribe, "but when I tried to break into the conversation—boiling inside with my undelivered articles and memoranda (one of which I tried to draw from my pocket)—the President put one fist on the table beside him, looked at me earnestly, and said: 'Baker, you and I will have to get together on these subjects.' "

Startled by Roosevelt's pugnacity, Baker and the guests adjourned to the library after lunch. "As the time drew near for leaving," Baker recollected, "I began to wonder when the President would ask me for the information upon which I had spent so much time and hard work. I had my heavy brief case in hand when I went up to say good-bye—and my grand plans for enlightening the Government of the United States vanished in a handshake."

Despite the self-deprecatory tone of this account, Baker's meticulous research, later passed on to Gifford Pinchot, eventually proved invaluable. His conclusion that government agents were doing everything possible to carry out the president's purposes in a complex situation cleared Charles Walcott of suspicion. In a letter to Baker, Pinchot expressed great satisfaction that Baker had arrived at his vindicating assessment despite his initial suspicions.

⌒ ⌒

SEVERAL MONTHS LATER, THEODORE ROOSEVELT received an advance copy of Baker's exposé on the corrupt relationship between Sam Parks, the powerful boss of New York's builders' union, and the Fuller Company, the leading contractor in the city. The president quickly penned a long note to the reporter: "I am immensely impressed by your article. While I had known in rather a vague way that there was such a condition as you describe, I had not known its extent, and as far as I am aware the facts have never before been brought before the public in such striking fashion."

Lincoln Steffens had provided Baker with the basis for this first extended study of the role labor racketeering played in the rise of the trusts. Investigating municipal corruption in Chicago and New York, Steffens had unearthed evidence that large building contractors were colluding with corrupt labor bosses to force smaller contractors out of business to eliminate competition. When he shared this material with his colleague, Baker spent months pursuing his own investigation. This research culminated in the stunning charge that the Fuller Construction Company was providing a regular salary to the union leader.

In "The Trust's New Tool—The Labor Boss," Baker focused on one disturbing question: While the great building strike of 1903 paralyzed construction through all of Manhattan, why did one firm, the Fuller Construction

Company, keep on building? In answer, Baker laid out evidence that for years, the Fuller Company had paid Sam Parks to look after *its* interests.

Baker traced Parks's ascent from railroad brakeman to bridge-builder, from "walking delegate" of the Housesmiths' and Bridgemen's Union to undisputed boss of the Board of Building Trades. The board, comprised of the walking delegates who represented workmen in each of three dozen unions affiliated with the building industry, was designed to protect the interests of its members. In theory, Sam Parks was simply a paid agent for his union, receiving the same salary as an ordinary workman in his trade. In reality, Baker tracked him "riding about in his cab, wearing diamonds, appearing on the street with his blooded bulldog, supporting his fast horses, 'treating' his friends." How reminiscent, Baker grimly observed, "of the familiar, affluent aldermen or police captains of our cities building $50,000 residences on salaries of $1500 or less." Indeed, the more he studied the situation, the more parallels emerged between Sam Parks and the Tammany chief Richard Croker.

A half-decade earlier, the Fuller Construction Company had arrived in New York from Chicago; "starting with no business at all," it had swiftly risen to become the "greatest construction company in the world, with the largest single building business in New York, and important branches in Chicago, Baltimore, and Philadelphia." Behind the Fuller Company, Baker found a familiar cast of characters—Charles Schwab represented the steel industry; Cornelius Vanderbilt the railroad industry; and James Stillman, president of Rockefeller's bank, the financial industry. "A gigantic hand had reached into New York," Baker observed, echoing Tarbell's description of Standard Oil's stranglehold on the oil region, "the hand of the Trust."

Baker's article also detailed the events ultimately leading to Parks's arrest. "Curiously enough," he remarked, "the Fuller Company brought Sam Parks from Chicago when it came." The flamboyant labor boss proved helpful in a variety of ways. Offering no explanation to fellow union members, he unilaterally called strikes designed to cripple Fuller's independent competitors. "Worse still," Baker observed, "strikes were often accompanied by a demand for money" before they could be settled. Rumors of blackmail, bribes, and pocketed spoils had circulated for years before District Attorney William Travers Jerome finally indicted Parks. In discovery, Jerome learned that Parks had approached the Hecla Iron Works, threatening to call a strike unless he was paid $1,000. After the company balked, the ensuing strike lasted for several weeks, costing the company $50,000 and keeping over a thousand men out of work. Only when Hecla agreed to Parks's extortion—paying double the amount originally demanded—did the walkout end. When the $2,000 check surfaced, endorsed by Parks and cashed by the Fuller Company, the district attorney finally had sufficient grounds to arrest the labor boss.

Roosevelt told Baker that his exposé illustrated with graphic urgency "the need of drawing the line on *conduct*, among labor unions, among corporations, among politicians, and among private individuals alike!" The president noted sardonically that "the organs of Wall Street men of a certain type are bitter in their denunciations of the labor unions, and have not a word to say against the iniquity of the corporations. The labor leaders of a certain type howl against the corporations, but do not admit that there is any wrong ever perpetrated by labor men." Baker's even-handed investigation and subsequent critique of both labor and capital dovetailed with Roosevelt's own approach. The president invited Baker to the White House to discuss the matter further. "When I get back East again," Baker replied, "I shall be more than pleased to accept your invitation." Roosevelt's commendation, he continued, made him "feel more strongly than ever that there is here a great duty to perform; to bring out these conditions clearly and fairly and above all, truthfully." Furthermore, he added, "Mr. McClure is giving me the best medium in this country to do so."

McClure and Phillips were delighted with the widespread commentary engendered by Baker's labor pieces. The *Wall Street Journal* printed a fierce editorial condemning corporate corruption and demanding change: "When the corporations have their paid agents in the trade unions as they have their paid agents in the legislatures, and in the executive councils of great parties, the necessity for reform in corporate management is clear. . . . The only way the trusts and the labor unions can hope to stand long without harsh restrictive legislation is to play square with the people." And when Harvard professor John Brooks publicly endorsed Baker's analysis, college students across the country flocked to hear the man considered "the greatest reporter" in the country.

"You have gone into a splendid field of material and you are getting the mastery of it," Phillips wrote to his rising star, claiming that "before you are through with this you will know more than any one else about labor questions in America." Steffens congratulated Baker on the greatest triumph "a man can have with a pen," maintaining that the Parks piece had "made both sides see themselves as they are." He confessed his own difficulty in writing after reading Baker's article, finding himself oppressed by a "yellow streak" of jealousy that left him "burning with shame." He finished with a question at once rueful and admiring: "Ever catch yourself at mean thinking? I guess not. I envy you your perfect honesty."

Baker followed up this success with "The Lone Fighter," a biographical piece on the union leader Robert Neidig, who had worked for years to combat

Parks's pernicious influence. Initially, his struggle seemed futile; just as the political bosses kept their power because only a small minority of the public attended party primaries, so despotic union leadership endured when but a small percentage of union members attended meetings. The majority, Baker explained, "were tired at night and wanted to go home and play with their babies." Neidig, a steel builder with a wife and children, decided early on to take his union responsibilities in earnest. He never missed a meeting and gradually built up a following. At election time, however, Parks exercised the full power of his corrupt machine. "We hear of repeaters and purchased votes," Baker reported, "even of fraudulent ballots and fraudulent counts." Neidig was "threatened with personal violence, with loss of his job, and even with expulsion from the union." Nothing, it seemed, could break the labor boss's hold on the union, not even his indictment.

Nevertheless, Neidig refused to abandon his efforts to build an honest union, and Baker's detailed revelations about Parks helped turn the tide. "The 'lone fighter' is not alone," one correspondent observed, "when there are other lone fighters to act at the same time with him." One union member confessed to Baker that before reading the article, he had considered Parks "a true and faithful officer of our Union" and repeatedly supported him in elections. He considered Baker's piece "by far the best exposition of the causes of the present Labor troubles" and recommended that it "be placed in the hands of working-men" everywhere.

Robert Neidig gratefully assured Baker that his "splendid" exposé had "done more to weaken Parks and Parksism than any article that has been published." Within the union itself, its impact had been tremendous. Members finally understood "the wrong that had been done them" and were ready to take action. "To you belongs a large part of the credit," Neidig commended, concluding that "an excellent prospect" now existed of overthrowing Parks and reorganizing "the Union on a sound and honest basis."

"My present work interests me very deeply," Baker reported to his father. "It seems almost as if I had a mission to perform—to talk straight out on a difficult subject." With justifiable pride, he noted that between his own work and that of Tarbell and Steffens, his magazine was "probably doing more now in stirring up the American people than any other publication ever did before."

CHAPTER THIRTEEN

Toppling Old Bosses

The 1904 *Puck* cartoon "More Rough Riding" shows President Roosevelt
galloping the GOP elephant through a crowd of opponents.

OOSEVELT TRIED TO PROLONG HIS 1903 summer vacation,
recognizing that once he returned to the capital, there would be "mighty
little letup to the strain." It was "as lovely a summer as we have ever passed," he
told Corinne, "the happiest, healthiest, most old-fashioned kind of a summer."

Of all the Roosevelt children, only nineteen-year-old Alice was absent,
choosing to spend most of July and August with her fashionable friends in
Newport, Rhode Island. This decision rankled her father, who expressed
distaste for her wealthy companions at the exclusive resort community. "I
suppose young girls and even young men naturally like a year or two of such
a life as the Four Hundred lead," he fretted to a friend, perhaps mindful of his
own youthful snobbery in preferring to associate only with other gentlemen
at Harvard. "But I do not think anyone can permanently lead his or her life
amid such surroundings and with such objects, save at the cost of degenera-

tion in character," he added, revealing how far his attitudes had changed. "I have not a doubt that they would mortally object to associating with me—but they could not possibly object one one-hundredth part as much as I should to associating with them. . . . For mere enjoyment, I would a great deal rather hold my own in any congenial political society—even in Tammany."

The rest of the children blissfully entertained themselves, their siblings, and their cousins with picnics, hikes, and sailboat rides. Fifteen-year-old Ted Junior and thirteen-year-old Kermit were delighted to be home from boarding school at Groton. Eleven-year-old Ethel, who had boarded during the week at the National Cathedral School, happily assumed the role of "little mother" to her younger brothers, Archie and Quentin. "She is a great comfort to them," Roosevelt contentedly remarked, "and they are great comforts to her."

Nothing Edith accomplished as first lady compared with the uncompli-cated joy of long summer days with her husband at their family home. Edith "looks so young and pretty," Theodore beamed to Emily Carow. Both relished this time alone, riding horses together through the woods, carrying lunches and books with them on picnic excursions, and rowing to the end of Lloyd's Neck, where they "watched the white sails of coasters passing up and down the Sound."

Their tranquil family escape came to an end with the season. As soon as Roosevelt returned to Washington, he was bombarded by delegations of party officials, senators, and congressmen. Only thirteen months remained until the presidential election. "Whether I shall be re-elected, I have not the slightest idea," he admitted. "I know there is bitter opposition to me from many different sources. Whether I shall have enough support to overcome this opposition, I cannot tell." While large and enthusiastic crowds at every stop of his summer tour confirmed the president's unprecedented popularity, the American people did not control the nomination process in these days before the direct primary. Machine politicians and party bosses—the very men Roosevelt had opposed throughout his career—determined the candidates, and their selections were then endorsed by the very same financial interests he had antagonized during his two years as president. The public might ap-plaud his anti-trust policies and his intervention in the coal strike, but the big businessmen whose contributions sustained the Republican Party had become, in Roosevelt's words, "determined foes."

"The whole country breathed freer, and felt as if a nightmare had been lifted when I settled the anthracite coal strike," Roosevelt explained to the British historian George Otto Trevelyan, but although public memory of the crisis quickly dissipated, "the interests to which I gave mortal offense will make their weight felt as of real moment." Roosevelt had not forgotten how the same web of political and financial interests had stymied his hope for a second gubernatorial term after he had defied the party with his franchise tax bill and his stubborn refusal to retain Boss Platt's corrupt friend, Lou Payn, as superintendent of insurance. Then, Republican bosses had retaliated by attempting to bury him in the vice presidency; now, he feared, they would deny him the nomination for president.

Roosevelt understood perfectly that party leaders would vastly prefer the Republican Party chairman Mark Hanna, "flesh of their flesh, bone of their bone," who had cemented the party's alliance with the corporations. Hanna had only to "pass the word along," William Allen White observed, and within ten days "the politicians in the Republican party would leave the president." While Roosevelt had successfully established some of his own men in various state positions, the national organization remained firmly in Hanna's control.

The president's best hope lay in the fact that "reform was in the air." All over the country, White noted, "little Roosevelts were appearing in city halls, county courthouses, statehouses and occasionally were bobbing up in Congress." In Toledo, Republican reformer Samuel Jones had been elected mayor over the determined opposition of the Hanna machine. In Cleveland, Hanna's nemesis, reform Democrat Tom Johnson, was serving a second term as mayor. A newly formed Municipal Voters' League in Chicago, led by Republicans William Kent and George Cole, was engaged in a bitter fight against the entrenched corruption fostered by Charles T. Yerkes, the tycoon whose life Theodore Dreiser later fictionalized in his *Trilogy of Desire*. Republican Robert La Follette of Wisconsin had defied the machine to become governor by waging "war on the railroads that ruled his state."

‿ ‿

THESE ROUSING STORIES WERE DRAMATICALLY told in Lincoln Steffens's spectacular series on municipal and state corruption: "Shame of the Cities" and "Enemies of the Republic." Focusing national attention on these local battles, Steffens inspired reformers in other cities to address the corruption that plagued every level of government. His series played a significant role in toppling old bosses, bringing a new generation of Roosevelt-type reformers to positions of power in cities and states across the nation.

As ever, the idea for the acclaimed series had originated with Sam McClure. Returning to the office in late 1901 after several months abroad, McClure encountered Steffens, then serving as managing editor, seated at his desk. "You may be an editor," McClure huffed dismissively, "but you don't know how to edit a magazine. . . . You can't learn to edit a magazine here in this office. . . . Get out of here, travel, go—somewhere. . . . Buy a railroad ticket, get on a train, and there, where it lands you, there you will learn to edit a magazine."

With McClure's support, Steffens embarked on an odyssey. For the better part of three years, he called on people in St. Louis, Minneapolis, Pittsburgh, Chicago, Philadelphia, New York, Cleveland, and Madison. "My business is to find subjects and writers, to educate myself in the way the world is wagging, so as to bring the magazine up to date," he explained to his father. "I feel ready to do something really fine."

Following up on McClure's persistent interest in political corruption, Steffens interviewed city editors, political bosses, crusading district attorneys, and reformist mayors. In each city, he uncovered an invisible web of power linking political bosses to both the criminal world below and the business community above. His investigations convinced him that the misgovernment of American cities would furnish abundant material for a fascinating series, featuring portraits of the bosses and the men who were fighting to expose their corruption. "If I should be entrusted with the work," he told Tarbell, "I think I could make my name." His conjecture proved accurate: *The Shame of the Cities*, the six-part series that began in late 1902, made him an international celebrity.

Everywhere he went during his first weeks of travel, the same questions stirred conversation. Everyone was speculating on the future of a young district attorney named Joe Folk and the investigations he had undertaken in St. Louis. His curiosity aroused, Steffens took a train to St. Louis and, in a lobby corner of the Planters Hotel, met with the idealistic district attorney who was just beginning to lay bare pervasive corruption within the Democratically controlled city council and Board of Aldermen. Mistakenly assuming Folk would be "safe," the Democratic bosses had nominated this "smiling, even-tempered man of thirty-three" for the district attorney post.

The story Folk told fascinated Steffens from the start. An obscure notice in a local newspaper first caught the attorney's eye: a sizable quantity of cash had been deposited in a respected St. Louis banking house with the intention "of bribing certain assemblymen to secure the passage of a street railway ordinance." Folk decided to follow up on the report, even though "no names were mentioned." Suspecting that the legislation in question was a recent bill benefiting the Suburban Railway Company, he pieced their scheme together and issued dozens of subpoenas to assemblymen, councilmen, and the employees and management of Suburban Railway. Evaluating his list to determine who would most likely fold under pressure, he summoned the company president, Charles H. Turner, and the lobbyist rumored to have brokered the deal, Philip Stock.

Turner and Stock were notified that they had three days to cooperate. Facing indictment for bribery and prosecution "to the full extent of the law," they both "broke down and confessed." The ordinance in question, Turner told Folk, would have increased the value of his company by $3 million. To secure its passage, he had first approached Colonel Edward Butler, the longtime boss of St. Louis. When Butler demanded $145,000 to distribute among the assembly members, Turner hired Stock on his promise to get the bill passed for a mere $75,000. As swiftly as that amount was deposited into the bank, the legislation proceeded smoothly. A court decision quickly overturned the franchise ordinance, however, and the Suburban Railway Company refused to turn over the money, claiming it had not secured the franchise. Legislators threatened to sue Turner and Stock, insisting that the money "was theirs because they had done their part."

During this contentious interchange, the newspaper leak occurred. The testimony of Turner and Stock led to numerous confessions, along with the convictions of eighteen municipal assembly members. Folk's investigation eventually revealed that a precise schedule of bribery had been devised, specifying the price of obtaining wharf space, a side track, a switchway, a grain elevator, and so on. "So long has this practice existed," Steffens was told, the members had "come to regard the receipt of money for action on pending measures as a legitimate perquisite of a legislator."

Indefatigable Folk would not be content until he felled "the greatest oak" in this forest of corruption. Colonel Butler, the man who had been saved from indictment in the Suburban scandal simply because he had demanded more money than the company would pay, had controlled nominations and elections in the city for years, becoming a multimillionaire through his schemes. "It was generally understood that he owned Assemblymen before they ever took the oath of office," Steffens wrote, giving him absolute control of legislation and the power to negotiate with businessmen seeking regulations, rulings, or ordinances. When Folk found two members of the Board of Health willing to testify that Butler had promised each of them $2,500 to sign off on a garbage contract, he put the swaggering boss on trial. Folk uncovered documents proving that once the contract was approved, Butler was due to receive over $200,000. In a dramatic closing statement before the jury, Folk argued that the state itself was on trial: "Missouri, Missouri. I am pleading for thee, pleading for thee." Colonel Butler was convicted and sentenced to three years in prison.

After hearing Folk's account, Steffens contacted McClure and Phillips to inform them that he had found an article for the magazine and the person to write it—a local reporter named Claude H. Wetmore. The subject thrilled McClure, but when the first draft arrived, he was displeased that names and places, essential to authenticate and validate the story, had been omitted. Under McClure's guidance, Steffens drafted a new version of the article so that every statement was a matter of record. The names of legislators who fled the state were accompanied by details of their eventual arrests and confessions. A comical anecdote emerged of one House of Delegates member "so frightened while under the inquisitorial cross-fire that he was seized with a nervous chill; his false teeth fell to the floor, and the rattle so increased his alarm that he rushed from the room without stopping to pick up his teeth, and boarded the next train." Satisfied with the revision, McClure proposed the evocative title "Tweed Days in St. Louis." The article, with Wetmore and Steffens listed as co-authors, was a smashing success, prompting the publisher to build an entire series around municipal corruption that would accompany Ida Tarbell's work on corporate corruption.

A newspaper article condemning malfeasance in Minneapolis drew McClure's attention, prompting him to focus Steffens's next project on the Minnesota city. There, testimony before the grand jury had revealed a system of police corruption similar to that Steffens had witnessed in New York during the days of the Lexow Commission. In return for police protection, a host of illegal establishments that included gambling operations, unlicensed saloons, and opium dens paid regular weekly fees. These spoils were divided between the Democratic mayor, his henchmen, and the police captains, all carefully recorded in ledgers each week. After befriending Hovey C. Clarke, the courageous foreman of the grand jury, Steffens received permission to photograph pages from these ledgers. "Your article is certainly a 'corker,' " McClure enthused after reading the first draft. "We'll call it 'The Shame of Minneapolis,' " indicating the piece should be framed as a colossal battle between one crusading individual and the corrupt establishment. "You have made a marvelous success of your Minneapolis article," he assured Steffens. "We fellows are so busy pushing things through that we don't stop to tell each other how much we think of each other's work. But I take this moment to tell you."

The piece, printed in the famous January 1903 issue, made headlines across the country. "Mr. Steffens's stirring story should be read everywhere," advised *Outlook* magazine, "for it strikes at the very heart of both of the twin stupidities which dull the conscience of American municipalities—the optimism which says that all is so good that nothing need be done, and the pessimism which says that all is so bad that nothing can be done." The *Arizona Republic* ardently proclaimed that by exposing corruption in St. Louis and Minneapolis, *Mc-Clure's* magazine was "doing a public service," prodding people to conclude that similar corrupt networks were in scores of other cities not yet "overtaken by a wave of reform."

Steffens giddily recalled a train ride during which he overheard men in the washroom and dining car exclaiming over his story and his writing. The article was a surpassing success: "The newsstand had exhausted the printed supply; subscriptions were coming in; and the mail was bringing letters of praise." Citizens across the country invited him to their localities, promising scandals more sordid than those described in Minneapolis and St. Louis. He proudly told his father that as he entered a New York gentleman's club, members stood and applauded. With lavish promises, a London editor had tried to woo him from *McClure's*, while a cigar manufacturer even asked permission to christen a cigar after him, with his portrait on the box lid.

Flush with success, Steffens was anxious to scientifically test his "dawning theory" that corruption originated from the top, not the bottom, that it "was not merely political; it was financial, commercial, social." He suspected that in every case, the web of corruption radiated out from the captains of industry—the big businessmen running gas and electric companies, street railways, and other public service corporations—who would do anything necessary to acquire lucrative franchises and privileges.

Wary of "philosophical generalizations," McClure feared that Steffens would invariably tint his observations or arrange facts to confirm his theory that businessmen were always to blame. He insisted that Steffens present "facts, startling facts" that would involve the reader one step at a time in his detective work. While Steffens chafed to move on to Chicago or Philadelphia, McClure insisted he return to St. Louis to pursue the story in more detail. "The disagreement became acute," Steffens recalled; "it divided the office." At moments like this, Ida Tarbell was indispensable. "Sensible, capable, and very affectionate, she knew each one of us and all our idiosyncrasies and troubles," he noted. She would sit the fractious parties down, "smiling, like a tall, good-looking young mother, to say, 'Hush, children.' " A compromise was reached: Steffens would return to St. Louis, "stick to facts," and only afterwards proceed to any city he desired.

McClure's stipulation that Steffens must follow up in St. Louis proved most fortuitous. In the months since the first article had appeared, a series of events revealed the corruption in Missouri to run far deeper than either Folk or Steffens had suspected. When Colonel Butler's conviction reached the Missouri Supreme Court on appeal, the decision was reversed. All the aldermen cases were overturned as well. Steffens discovered that over the years Butler had directed the nominations not only of legislators but also of justices on the very bench that heard the graft cases on appeal. Indeed, the presiding justice publicly called for Folk to leave Missouri, implying that his exposures were ruining the reputation of the state. More dispiriting still, when the next election arrived, the citizens of St. Louis blithely kept the Butler ring in power. All the felons were back in the assembly, undaunted by the initial round of convictions.

Though McClure was again delighted with the substance of Steffens's article, he was less impressed with its structure. "Your narrative lacks force," he chided, suggesting that the tale should move forward with inexorable momentum and culminate in the shocking circumstance that Butler and the convicted aldermen remained in office, continuing to enact laws and reap profits. "I am telegraphing you to come East," McClure added, insisting, "You must be here with me when you are working out the article." The finished installment, which McClure entitled "The Shamelessness of St. Louis," once again proved a stunning success. The pride and conscience of St. Louis had finally been kindled; on the city streets, 200,000 people sported "Folk for Reform" buttons. "Your article is bearing fruit," Folk told Steffens, observing, "Every number of your March edition has been sold here and there is still a great demand for them." Finally, people rallied to support Folk's cause. Throughout the city, Folk Clubs were organizing. "The State is commencing to speak," Folk happily reported. "The permanent remedy is in the hands of the people and someday they will apply it. I believe the public conscience is more alive to the situation today and the cause of civic righteousness brighter than for many years."

"I must tell you how tremendously I am pleased with your achievements," McClure generously reassured Steffens in June 1903. "I know of no young man who has such a splendid opportunity of work in front of him as you have." Furthermore, the publisher grandly instructed his reporter to inform Folk that he was "the candidate of McClure's Magazine at the present moment for President in 1908." McClure's closing remark revealed his awareness of the massive influence his publication exerted on the American conscience: "I believe," he flatly told Steffens, "we can do more toward making a President of the United States than any other organ."

After St. Louis, Steffens traveled to Pittsburgh, Philadelphia, Chicago, and New York, perfecting the interview technique that allowed him to elicit a great deal of information by sharing the little he already knew. He regaled Pittsburgh's boss with tales of how his counterparts in Minneapolis worked.

He delighted reformers in Chicago with stories of how Folk had uncovered corruption in St. Louis. He spent hours "just chew[ing] the rag" with the old boss of Philadelphia, fascinated by his rise to power. In conversations with a couple of "wise guys" in Minneapolis, he described the famous burglars and con men he had known in New York. "Thieves, politicians, business men, reformers, and our magazine readers," he commented, "all assumed that I had what I was trying to get: knowledge." His demeanor shrewdly implied that he already knew their secrets, he explained, so "they might as well talk." Steffens's gift of drawing out his subjects soon became the stuff of legend. William Randolph Hearst considered Lincoln Steffens "the best interviewer he ever met," and the New York *World*'s Herbert Bayard Swope "looked up to him as a demi-god."

As Steffens expanded the scope of his inquiry, he became increasingly convinced that corruption in municipal politics was not "a temporary evil" engendered by the need for profitable new transportation and electrical facilities in explosively thriving young cities. Older cities, too, were rife with such dishonesty. Nor could it be attributed to Republicans or Democrats or to the presence of large immigrant populations under the sway of political bosses. Philadelphia, with the largest native population of any major city, suffered an epidemic of corruption. In every city, he now confidently argued, business interests were responsible. He had documented them "buying boodlers in St. Louis, defending grafters in Minneapolis, originating corruption in Pittsburgh, sharing with bosses in Philadelphia, deploring reform in Chicago, and beating good government with corruption funds in New York." Corruption, it seemed, was the hallmark of the age—an age in which "public spirit became private spirit, public enterprise became private greed."

When the articles were collected into the book entitled *The Shame of the Cities*, Steffens was hailed as a moral prophet come to save the republic from sin and a worthy descendant of abolitionist agitator William Lloyd Garrison. Across the country, Lincoln Steffens was lionized as "a new kind" of journalist altogether. "Instead of having his news and his editorial on separate pages," one critic noted, "Steffens welds the two into one so that the fact and the meaning and the portent of it strike you simultaneously." According to *The Outlook*, Steffens had "correctly diagnosed the characteristic disease" of the age—"the itch to make a little more money by illegitimate means than can be made by legitimate industry." Rather than examine the abstract political and legal structures of city charters, William Allen White observed, Steffens had ventured "into the wards and precincts of the towns and townships of this land [in order to] bring in specimens of actual government under actual conditions." These articles, another critic remarked, "have done more to awaken the American conscience to civic duty than anything else written in many years."

Immediately upon completing his series on the cities, Steffens embarked on an equally ambitious study of the states. Wherever he had sought to track "the political corruption of a city ring," he had found that "the stream of pollution" was part of a statewide watershed. Although he could have chosen "almost any State," Missouri seemed the logical starting point. As Joe Folk had learned when his cases were overturned, "the System was indeed bigger than St. Louis; it was the System of Missouri." The state constitution prescribed a governor, a legislature, and a judiciary, he remarked, but "this paper government has been superseded by an actual government"—a network of legislators, bosses, and party leaders answering to the state's major industries.

In addition, an investigation in Missouri would bolster Joe Folk's bid for governor on the Democratic ticket. He would be "appealing his case to the people" on a bold platform "that corruption is treason; that the man, who, elected to maintain the institutions of a government by the people, sells them out, is a traitor; whether he be a constable, a legislator, a judge, or a boss, his act is not alone bribery but treason."

Returning a third time to St. Louis, Steffens again joined with Folk to reveal a sweeping bribery scheme that stretched from the president and agent of the Royal Baking Powder Company, to the House and Senate combines, to the lieutenant governor. Published under the title "Enemies of the Republic"—another one of McClure's "brilliant reductions of a complex situation to slogan size"—the article prompted a new round of vehement editorials across the country. Crediting Folk's work as district attorney, the *New York Times* called Steffens's piece "a striking article" that illuminated the situation "with the utmost plainness," implicating "prominent men in politics and in business" in "specific instances of bribery, defining the purposes, and stating the amounts, the givers, the takers." The *Times* concluded by calling on the public to condemn such pervasive dishonesty. "When Americans really agree that corruption is treason," the editors argued, "the traitors will be punished, not legally alone, but as [Benedict] Arnold was, by the insufferable and blasting scorn of his fellow-men."

Folk's fight for the Democratic nomination tore the state wide open, but Steffens's articles had built the district attorney into such a heroic figure that the party did not dare reject him. "Your last article was magnificent and came in just in time to be of tremendous service," a grateful Folk told Steffens. "You ought to be here and see how the people can run things when they take a mind to," he observed, having witnessed the effect of the article on the public; "my faith in the plain people has not been misplaced." They had achieved a stunning victory, Folk happily noted, "when one thinks of the mighty power arrayed on the other side, the great corporations, the hoodlers, the gamblers, a gigantic political machine, every professional politician in the State." This "bloodless political revolution," he continued, could never have been accomplished without the indefatigable work of Steffens and the support of McClure.

After Missouri, Steffens pursued investigations in five other states. In Wisconsin, he told the story of "Fighting Bob" La Follette. Soon after La Follette's election as governor, it became clear that his real adversaries were the corrupt leaders in his own Republican Party, who had "fixed" the legislature to kill his reform measures and "discredit him with defeat." The failed legislative session taught La Follette that he had to outmaneuver the bosses, creating an organization of his own to beat the system and install trustworthy men in the legislature. This conflict was still raging when Steffens arrived in Wisconsin. "To have you turn your searchlight on Wisconsin politics is better than anything our guardian angel could do for us—on earth at least," La Follette's wife, Belle, confided to the reporter.

Appearing a month before the election, Steffens's article applauded the young reformer's struggle against an entrenched system, asserting that his "long, hard fight" offered the people of Wisconsin a chance to make their government work for the common good rather than private interests. "La Follette's people think it has turned the scale in his favor," Steffens informed his father, "but the other side is howling at it and at me. It has sold out the magazine already." Governor La Follette not only won reelection but finally "met a friendly legislature," comprised of men who had "gone through the fire" with him and would readily enact his reform measures to regulate the railroads, institute the direct primary, address workmen's compensation, and establish tax reform. "No one will ever measure up the full value of your share in this immediate result," an exultant La Follette wrote Steffens. During reelection campaigning, La Follette witnessed the impact of Steffens's article "everywhere," even "out on the farms, away back among the bluffs and coulees of the Mississippi," noting a distinct "difference" in his reception before and after its publication. "The article settled things," he said. "It was like the decision of a court of last resort."

⤜ ⤝

"THE PRESIDENT HAS BEEN VERY interested in your articles," Roosevelt's secretary informed Steffens on August 24, 1903. "He wishes to inquire if you cannot come down here some time to see him." A week later, Steffens joined Roosevelt for lunch at Oyster Bay, renewing a friendship somewhat chilled by Steffens's frequent carping that the president compromised too readily with conservatives in his efforts to move legislation forward. Throughout his complicated relationship with Roosevelt, Steffens worked to maintain his distance "as a political critic," keeping personal affection separate from professional judgment. For his part, Roosevelt managed to overcome his occasional irritation with Steffens in order to maintain a mutually advantageous alliance.

During lunch, the two men spoke of Joseph Folk and his great fight against the Missouri bosses. Shortly thereafter, Steffens followed up with a letter urging the president to meet with the young reformer. "He is a Democrat, but only as you are a Republican, and in motives and purposes you and he would be in perfect accord," the journalist reassured him, adding, "you can get from him a great deal of information about essential facts, and all honestly given. Mr. Folk has gotten no little of his inspiration from you." Roosevelt readily agreed to send a letter of invitation to the young district attorney through Steffens. "I wonder if you realize what a fundamental gratification such a letter will be to this man who has gone a long while along a lonely road with all big men against him," Steffens appreciatively replied to the president.

When Folk appeared at the White House, Steffens related to his father, "he and the President, Democrat and Republican, became confidential at sight, and the President thanked me for bringing Folk to his notice." Writing to a Missouri Republican, Roosevelt later proclaimed that though Folk headed the Democratic ticket, his nomination represented "a complete destroying of the old corrupt machine, and the success of the movement for honesty and decency." He assured the politician that "it would be better for the republicans to endorse his nomination instead of making any nomination against him." Such a step would not only demonstrate "a spirit of true citizenship," the president continued, but would "be wise policy on our part."

The Missouri Republicans ignored Roosevelt's advice, choosing to nominate Cyrus P. Walbridge, a conservative businessman who had been mayor of St. Louis. Although concern for the general Republican ticket in Missouri kept Roosevelt from publicly supporting Folk, he refused to endorse Walbridge and was delighted when William Allen White penned a ringing editorial endorsement of Folk in the *Emporia Gazette*. In plain language, White charged that those who voted against the honest Democrat Folk would be voting "with the boodlers, and their victory, whether it is republican or what not, will be in reality a victory for boodle." He reminded Missouri's citizenry that "parties are means for good government and not its ends," insisting that "it is better to be a bolter to a party than a traitor to a state." White's editorial made headlines across the nation and threw Missouri Republicans into what *The Washington Post* described as "a state of violent excitement, to use a mild phrase."

Folk ran a superb campaign, gaining enough votes from independents and reform-minded Republicans to override the corrupt Democratic machine and win the election by over 30,000 votes. "It must make you feel good," Folk later wrote Steffens, "to know the important part you had in bringing about these results." He reiterated the profound obligation he felt toward the reporter and his magazine for their role in the upset victory.

Folk was not alone in recognizing the publication's growing influence. *McClure's*, the monthly periodical *Arena* proclaimed, was "one of the greatest moral factors in America." Having "discovered that the first step toward curing an evil is to make it known," the magazine had become "a powerful exponent of the national revolt against corrupt and oppressive methods in business, in finance and in government." Month after month, its pages contained "must-read" pieces, spurring a national conversation on contemporary issues.

Just a few years earlier, one critic observed, *McClure's* was "distinctly literary in its character, and its content was given over exclusively to reviews, essays, stories and poems." Both format and function had since undergone a dramatic and influential metamorphosis: "The daily newspaper gives the facts as they occur from day to day, with editorial comment thereon, but it is left for the magazine to come along afterwards with a summary of these facts and their relation to one another." When vital issues were treated with depth and insight, people began "thinking for themselves, and a thinking people, if honest, will seldom go wrong in the end."

⌒ ⌒

AWARE OF *McCLURE'S* BURGEONING POLITICAL clout, Roosevelt invited Sam McClure himself to lunch at the White House on October 9. Steffens joined them for dinner, and the three men talked until midnight. Roosevelt offered to furnish the sources and documents for a potential series of articles outlining his struggles with the trusts and the unions. In the end, however, McClure preferred to continue with Steffens's series on corruption, focusing on a pitched battle being fought in Ohio between a group of young reformers and the Old Guard, led by Mark Hanna. Steffens was energized by the prospect, recognizing that Hanna remained the sole person who could snatch the nomination from Roosevelt—and that if he succeeded, the Republican Party would turn its back on reform.

A preliminary skirmish against Hanna earlier that spring had turned to Roosevelt's advantage. Stirring up trouble, Ohio's senior senator Joseph Foraker had introduced a resolution endorsing Roosevelt's 1904 candidacy at a state convention assembled to nominate candidates for state office in 1903. The development placed Hanna in a bind. As Republican National Convention chairman, he did not want to preclude all other candidacies—including his own—at such an early date, yet he would need administration support to promote his bid for a second Senate term in the fall. In light of his position, Hanna told Roosevelt he felt obliged to oppose the premature endorsement. He did not think it proper for a state convention to "assume the responsibilities" of the following year's national convention. "When you know all the facts," he concluded, "I am sure that you will approve my course." Roosevelt delayed his reply for twenty-four hours. Seeking advice from friends, he ultimately decided that "the time had come to stop shilly-shallying" and inform Hanna that he "did not intend to assume the position, at least passively, of a suppliant to whom he might give the nomination as a boon."

"Your telegram received," Roosevelt finally responded. "I have not asked any man for his support. I have had nothing whatever to do with raising this issue. Inasmuch as it has been raised of course those who favor my administration and my nomination will favor endorsing both and those who do not will oppose." Roosevelt's curt message left Hanna little choice. "In view of the sentiment expressed," Hanna telegraphed back, "I shall not oppose the endorsement of your administration and candidacy by our State Convention."

The publicized exchange of telegrams humiliated Hanna. "It was surrender, unequivocal and certain," declared a California paper. Headlines across the country proclaimed the older man's loss of power: "Hanna Backs Down to Roosevelt and Takes Water Like a Swan"; "Hanna Obeys the President's Wishes." Roosevelt tried to mitigate the sting with a personal letter. "I hated to do it because you have shown such broad generosity and straightforwardness in all your dealing with me," he told the senator, proceeding to offer justifications for his actions. "I do not think you appreciated the exact effect that your interview and announced position had in the country at large. It was everywhere accepted as the first open attack on me." Before closing, he confirmed his intention to attend the wedding of Hanna's daughter in Cleveland a few weeks later and expressed hope that the two of them could have "a real talk—not just a half hours chat" while he was there.

But the damage was already done. The tense interchange had intensified Hanna's reluctance to publicly endorse Roosevelt's candidacy, fueling supporters' confidence that Hanna would eventually announce his own candidacy.

That fall, Hanna launched "the most arduous and exciting stumping tour of his career," rallying the conservative Ohio base behind his chosen slate of candidates for the state legislature. The results were "an overwhelming personal victory" for Hanna, assuring his own reelection to the Senate. The landslide victory, "almost unique in American politics," constituted proof that Hanna was once more "Boss of the Republican party" and Roosevelt "a discredited leader."

"There is alarm in the Roosevelt camp," a Canton, Ohio, newspaper reported. The spectacular showing by Hanna's conservative wing of the party in the Ohio elections, coupled with the defeat of Roosevelt's reform ticket in New York, appeared to signal "the turning point" in the president's career: "Unless Mr. Roosevelt can retrieve his fortunes in a Napoleonic manner," the Omaha *Evening World-Herald* predicted, "the dual elections in Ohio and New York will mark the time that saw the tide begin to ebb from Theodore Roosevelt." The president himself was particularly disturbed by reform mayor Seth Low's defeat in New York. "The wealthy capitalists who practice graft and who believe in graft alike in public and in private life, gave Tammany unlimited money just as they will give my opponent," he grimly told a friend.

Reports multiplied of telegrams and letters of support arriving "by the bushel" in Hanna's office, beseeching him to rally Republican opposition to Roosevelt and build a steady, conservative platform that would foster prosperity and cultivate the pro-business policies begun under McKinley. "It is agreed by leaders of the party that the distinguished gentleman may now have the nomination for the asking," one editorial stated flatly, further suggesting that "Roosevelt may well be apprehensive. The vast following of McKinley will be found back of the Ohio Senator and this together with his own strength will certainly be potent enough to overcome any opposition at the national convention of his party in 1904."

Compounding these difficulties, a campaign financed by the corporations to discredit the president began to gain traction. The Union Pacific's E. H. Harriman dispatched hundreds of letters claiming that Roosevelt had "lost his popularity in the far west" and suggesting that without that region's support, he would be a weak candidate. Criticism of Roosevelt converged on "the general idea that he [was] impulsive, erratic and not to be counted on." Stories were circulated to emphasize his dangerously irresponsible, capricious nature. One disgruntled southerner, still aghast at Roosevelt's dinner invitation to Booker T. Washington, relayed an anecdote of particularly maniacal behavior. "We have a wild boy in the White House," he dismissively observed, painting the president as incompetent and immature: "The other day Roosevelt set out in his yacht from Oyster Bay in the teeth of a hurricane and against warning and advice, and nearly wrecked the vessel before he got to safety; and as he paced up and down the plunging deck and the wild winds blew his coat-tails over his head, there in his pocket was a six-shooter, just as if he were still a boy playing a game out on the plains!"

Rumormongers speculated that Senator Lodge was now "worried lest Hanna should come out at the eleventh hour as a candidate, and wrest the nomination." Roosevelt himself was said to fear that there was "a plot brewing" designed to "rob him of the prize at the last moment." White House lunch guests were reportedly queried about whether there was "any prospect of Hanna getting the delegates" in their respective states, a line of questioning that indicated genuine apprehension on Roosevelt's part.

AMID THIS DISCORD, LINCOLN STEFFENS's foray into Ohio politics could not have been more fortuitous for Roosevelt. The reporter explained to his father that he was "hoping to get Hanna," and that by unmasking the powerful Ohio boss, he might affect the presidential election just as he had transformed the prospects of Joseph Folk. "If I am to have so much influence," he wrote, "I want to make it a power for the possible and worth while." Before embarking on this project, he would return to the capital "for a short confab with the President." To be sure, "Roosevelt may be beaten," Steffens warranted, "but he will not be beaten without some pretty stiff fighting," and in that battle for reform, he added, with both accuracy and characteristic grandiosity, "we expect to deal some of the heaviest blows."

Steffens spent five weeks in Ohio talking with newspaper editors, politicians, bosses, and citizen groups in Cleveland, Toledo, Columbus, and Cincinnati. "Hanna is my villain this time," he informed his father in late January 1904. Acknowledging that the piece was "pretty rough" on the senator, he nevertheless maintained that "it's true and may do good." Hanna might have considered himself "above the danger mark," added Steffens, but a close examination of his career revealed many troubling, even criminal aspects.

The piece depicted Hanna as a businessman who had entered politics for the sole purpose of gaining special privileges for his street railway system. To secure advantages, Steffens explained, Hanna systematically "degraded the municipal legislature" through campaign contributions and outright bribery. Success only inflamed his ambitions. "He wanted to have a President," Steffens wrote, so he engineered the "spontaneous demand" for William McKinley and backed him with the largest campaign fund ever raised. Then Hanna resolved to become a U.S. senator. Since the votes were cast by the state legislature in 1898, Steffens reported, "legislators were kidnapped, made drunk and held prisoners," bribed and threatened with revolvers; in the end, unsurprisingly, Hanna emerged victorious. Steffens concluded that the system Hanna established in Ohio was "government of the people by politicians hired to represent the privileged class . . . the most dangerous form of our corruption." And this malignant operator "was the choice of big business and bad machine politics for President of the United States."

Steffens had nearly completed the first draft of his exposé when Hanna was stricken with typhoid fever. While his doctors hoped for a full recovery, they admitted that "the senator's advanced age and rheumatic conditions [made] the case a more serious one than in a younger man." When Roosevelt was informed of Hanna's illness, he walked over to the Arlington Hotel, where the senator and his wife occupied a large suite. "For some inexplicable reason, this affected him very much," Roosevelt told Elihu Root. After the president left, Hanna asked for paper and pen. "My Dear Mr. President," he wrote. "You touched a tender spot, old man, when you called personally to inquire after me this a.m. I may be worse before I can be better, but all the same, such 'drops' of kindness are good for a fellow." Always gracious at such times, Roosevelt quickly responded: "Indeed, it is your letter from your sick bed which is touching—not my visit. May you very soon be with us again, old fellow, as strong in body and as vigorous in your leadership and your friendship as ever."

Hanna's condition unexpectedly worsened in the days that followed. His temperature shot up to 104 degrees. He developed a congestive chill and the doctors administered strychnine to stimulate his heart. More than fifty correspondents and dozens of congressmen and senators crowded the lobby of the hotel, awaiting news. Steffens also waited, Hanna's precarious condition having left the fate of his article hanging. "The illness of Hanna leaves me in the air," he reported to his father. For a short time, the old senator seemed to rally, asking if the barber could come in to give him a shave. "Today he is better," Steffens wrote on February 14. Although the crisis seemed to have passed, the fever had not yet crested. "Tomorrow," Steffens predicted, "should decide his fate." Indeed, the following day Hanna's pulse rate dropped precipitously, and that evening, after "a brave struggle," he died at the age of sixty-six.

Without Mark Hanna, pundits agreed, "all talk of any real opposition to the nomination of President Roosevelt seems to have ended." Lacking the voice of a potent conservative leader to challenge the incumbent, open resistance to Roosevelt within the party crumbled.

"Of course, Hanna's death knocks out Steffens' article entirely," the managing editor Albert Boyden told Ray Baker. "It's tough luck!" After six months passed, however, Steffens found a way to revive the story. While his material on Hanna would provide the sordid backdrop of Ohio's boss rule, his focus shifted to the fierce contest in the state between a new generation of reformers and the Old Guard. Calling his piece "A Tale of Two Cities," he dramatically juxtaposed two municipal governments: Cleveland was led by Tom Johnson, the street railway tycoon turned radical reformer; and Cincinnati remained in thrall to George Cox, a corrupt party boss and longtime ally of Mark Hanna. Cleveland, he concluded, was "the best-governed city in the United States, Cincinnati, the worst."

Steffens's lengthy analysis appeared in the midst of Tom Johnson's uphill campaign for a third term as mayor. The well-documented and admiring portrait of Johnson's tenure, one observer noted, "appeared just in the nick of time to turn the tide." The reform mayor won reelection by the largest margin he ever achieved and attributed much of his success to Steffens. "My feeling for you, my dear old fellow," Johnson wrote the reporter, "is stronger than that of blood."

That same year, machine politicians were defeated in a number of cities. "The day of the American boss is past," proclaimed the *Baltimore Herald*. "Few men in the country," declared another publication, "have done more to bring to pass last Tuesday's defeat of municipal bosses than S. S. McClure and Lincoln Steffens." Letters of praise flooded the *McClure's* office. "To you, more than any one individual," one writer told McClure, "belongs much of the credit for this week's rout of the grafters. You were one of the first to grasp the real significance of the evil and to inaugurate its comprehensive exposure." It was a rapturous moment for Sam McClure, who had a protective passion for his magazine "very much like what the lioness has for her cubs."

"The story is the thing," McClure responded, when asked to account for the achievement of his publication. "When Mr. Steffens, Mr. Baker, Miss Tarbell write they must never be conscious of anything else while writing other than telling an absorbing story." As his authors began their research, he explained, they knew they had months—or even years—to complete the investigation and "mold it into a story palpitating with interest." The magazine's reputation as an instrument of reform, he insisted, was "due solely to its effective method of telling the truth, of giving stories vital interest." Had his writers begun with preconceived notions, they could not have so persuasively carried readers through their own process of discovery nor produced such visceral reactions to the unfolding narratives. "We were ourselves personally astonished, personally ashamed, personally indignant at what we found," Baker recalled, "and we wrote earnestly, even hotly." The more the public learned, the more engaged people grew by every facet of the complicated struggle for reform. "Month after month," Baker remarked, "they would swallow dissertations of ten or twelve thousand words without even blinking—and ask for more."

If corrupt businessmen, politicians, or labor leaders took offense to the detailed scrutiny of their motives and means, the *Minneapolis Tribune* noted, their hostility should be considered both "a medal of honor" and "an inspiration," irrefutable evidence "that something is being accomplished." Many decades hence, *The Independent* predicted, "when the historian of American literature writes of the opening years of the century, he will give one of his most interesting chapters to the literature of exposure, and he will pronounce it a true intellectual force."

CHAPTER FOURTEEN

"Thank Heaven You Are to Be with Me!"

President Roosevelt with members of his cabinet;
Secretary of War Taft is seated at the far left.

A S *MCCLURE'S* WRITERS LABORED TO expose corruption and monopoly, William Howard Taft was too immersed in the knot of difficulties he faced in the Philippines to keep abreast of this transformative time in his own country. Letters from his brother Horace suggest Taft's isolation in the islands but also make clear *McClure's* essential role in keeping the public informed of key political developments at home. "You have been out of the country, and unless you have read the articles in the New York Times and in McClure's," Horace Taft cautioned his brother, "you will not appreciate how much of a stirring there is in the big cities where the worst corruption is. The progress in Chicago is remarkable and most gratifying." Reformers had "absolutely cut off" the spoils system, he explained, ending all manner of illegal privileges for the trolley companies and the railroads.

No one felt Taft's absence more during this period of profound change than

Theodore Roosevelt. With the Northern Securities case moving slowly toward the Supreme Court, Roosevelt wanted Taft to be a member of the Court when the time for decision came. He believed that "it would be impossible to overestimate the importance" of the suit. If Northern Securities was allowed to stand, the national government would be rendered impotent to control the big corporations. Monopolies would continue to grow, stifling competition and crushing small businessmen. Failure would diminish the presidency, confirming the Morgans and the Harrimans as the true rulers of the country.

Roosevelt's appointments to the Supreme Court would therefore prove critical. Indeed, he told a friend, he would hold himself "guilty of an irreparable wrong to the nation" if he failed to nominate men who shared his understanding of the great questions raised by the industrial age. To fill the first vacancy that arose, he had appointed Oliver Wendell Holmes, chief justice of the Massachusetts Supreme Court, whose sympathies with the labor movement were well known. "The labor decisions which have been criticized by some of the big railroad men and other members of large corporations," Roosevelt remarked at the time, "constitute to my mind a strong point in Judge Holmes' favor." When the appointment was announced, it garnered "the hearty approval of the laboring people of the country," as well as "no small amount of praise from the Republican organs."

A second spot on the Supreme Court opened when Judge George Shiras announced that he would retire on January 1, 1903. Roosevelt considered it "of utmost importance" to replace the conservative Shiras with the right man. He could not afford to make a mistake. Under these circumstances, the president immediately settled on his old friend Taft. He not only admired Taft above any other figure in public life, but he knew that Taft's views on economic matters paralleled his own. Like Roosevelt, Taft was dismayed by what he termed "the blindness and greed of the so-called captains of industry." He had little patience with "the unconscious arrogance of conscious wealth and financial success," yet he recognized the necessity of guiding "the feeling against trusts and the abuses of accumulated capital, in such a way as to remedy its evils without a destruction of the principles of private property and freedom of contract." Moreover, Taft's reasoning in the *Addyston Pipe* decision had encouraged reformers hoping to revitalize the Sherman Act.

Three months before Shiras's retirement, Roosevelt informed Taft of his intention to nominate him for the Supreme Court: "I hesitated long, for Root felt you should not under any circumstances leave the islands, and I was painfully aware that no one could take your place; but I do think it of the very highest consequence to get you on the Supreme Court. I am not at all satisfied with its condition—let us speak this only with bated breath and between you and me. I think we need you there greatly."

The telegram disconcerted Taft. "All his life," Nellie recalled, "his first ambition had been to attain the Supreme Bench. To him it meant the crown of the highest career that a man can seek, and he wanted it as strongly as a man can ever want anything. But now that the opportunity had come acceptance was not to be thought of." From Taft's perspective, the timing of Roosevelt's request could not have been worse. "Great honor deeply appreciated but must decline," he telegraphed. "Situation here most critical . . . Cholera, rinderpest, religious excitement, ladrones, monetary crisis, all render most unwise change of Governor. . . . Nothing would satisfy individual taste more than acceptance. Look forward to the time when I can accept such an offer, but even if it is certain that it never can be repeated I must now decline."

"I am disappointed of course," the president returned, "that the situation is such as to make you feel it unwise for you to leave, because exactly as no man can quite do your work in the islands, so no one can quite take your place as the new member of the Court. But, if possible, your refusal on the ground you give makes me admire you and believe in you more than ever. I am quite at a loss whom to appoint to the bench in the place I meant for you. Everything else must give way to putting in the right man."

Before five weeks had passed, however, Roosevelt sent an emphatic letter reopening the question, pushing Taft to accept the Court appointment with what Nellie termed "unanswerable" finality. "I am awfully sorry, old man," Roosevelt explained, "but after faithful effort for a month to try to arrange matters on the basis you wanted I find that I shall have to bring you home and put you on the Supreme Court. I am very sorry. I have the greatest confidence in your judgment; but after all, old fellow, if you will permit me to say so, I am President and see the whole field. The responsibility for any error must ultimately come upon me, and therefore I cannot shirk this responsibility or in the last resort yield to anyone else's decision if my judgment is against it." In closing, Roosevelt informed his friend that he would promote Commissioner Luke Wright to the position of governor general once Taft was appointed to the Supreme Court.

While this second request was en route to the Philippines, the president had a long talk with Taft's brother Harry. The two had become good friends when Roosevelt served in New York as police commissioner and governor. He now called on Harry to persuade his brother to return to Washington. "He is extremely anxious that you accept the appointment," Harry wrote to Taft, laying out Roosevelt's reasoning at length. "He does not belittle the importance of the problems which you have to contend with, but he feels that there are questions pending here which have to be solved by him which are of even greater importance and perhaps of almost equal difficulty. . . . He evidently thinks he has secured the right man in Holmes and now seeks you, because, as he remarked to me, you will approach all the industrial questions without fear of the affect [*sic*] upon yourself of the influence of either J. P. Morgan or of the labor leaders." Harry also reported an interesting talk on the matter with Elihu Root. Root considered Taft "the surest candidate as Roosevelt's successor, at the end of his second term," and therefore "could not be enthusiastic about your going on the Bench."

Despite Roosevelt's design in urging his letter, Harry admitted that he agreed with Root. "Of course, we all know how you have cherished the ambition to receive this appointment," he acknowledged, "but when it is within your grasp, it is natural to reflect as to whether you want to make that choice, particularly when your career in the Philippines and the reputation you have made there has opened up before you so many alluring possibilities." He added that there was "some diversity of view" within the family: Charley favored acceptance, knowing his brother had long coveted the post, while their mother, Aunt Delia, and Horace remained opposed. "I shall be satisfied with your decision," he assured his brother in closing.

To Taft, as to Nellie, the president's letter seemed unanswerable. The request "really leaves me no option, so far as I can see, but to give up here and go to Washington," he told Charley. The *Washington Times* reported that "within a few months" Taft would resign as governor of the Philippines to take a place on the Court. Nellie "heaved a sigh of resignation" and began making plans for their departure. Still, she recalled, her husband "could not resist the temptation to hazard one more protest."

"Recognize soldiers duty to obey orders," he telegraphed Roosevelt on January 8, 1903. "Before orders irrevocable by action, however, I presume on our personal friendship even in the face of your letter to make one more appeal." Taft proceeded to lay out his argument one final time: "No man is indispensable," he reasoned. "My death would little interfere with progress, but my withdrawal more serious. Circumstances last three years have convinced these people controlled largely by personal feeling, that I am their sincere friend and stand for a policy of confidence in them and belief in their future and for extension of self-government as they show themselves worthy. Visit to Rome and proposals urged there assure them of my sympathy, in regard to Friars, in respect of whose far-reaching influence they are morbidly suspicious. Announcement of withdrawal . . . will, I fear, give impression that change of policy is intended, because other reasons for action will not be understood. My successor's task thus made much heavier." Nevertheless, Taft concluded, "if your judgment is unshaken, I bow to it."

With little confidence that his request would be considered, Taft sadly informed his colleagues of his impending departure. The announcement spurred an overwhelming response and precipitated one of the "proudest and happiest" moments William Taft had experienced. As January 10 dawned, he and Nellie awakened to the din of band music, as 8,000 Filipinos gathered in front of the Malacañan Palace, urging the governor to stay. Stretched out for blocks, with "flags flying," the ranks of people carried handmade signs and placards printed in "all sizes and all colours," some in English, some in Spanish, still others in Tagalog, but all bearing the same message: WE WANT TAFT.

Taft listened in glad surprise as one speaker after another hailed his virtues and accomplishments. "This is a spontaneous demonstration of affection for our Governor," the first speaker announced. The orator who followed, a former insurrectionist, declared that all the hardships facing the islanders ranked "as nothing compared with the evil effect caused by [Taft's] impending departure. . . . The Filipino people trust that the home government will not tear from their arms their beloved governor upon whom depends the happy solution of all Philippine questions." When the speeches concluded, journalists reported, "the thousands of people who filled the grounds of the palace broke into a cheer for the governor."

News of the popular demonstration soon reached Washington, along with hundreds of cables from Taft's colleagues, citizen committees, the Filipino Bar Association, and individuals throughout the archipelago, all urging Roosevelt to reconsider. Three days later, a welcome cable arrived in Manila: "All right stay where you are. I shall appoint some one else to the Court. ROOSEVELT." A more personal letter followed a few days later. Roosevelt admitted he was still "very sorry" Taft would not be joining the Court but assured his friend that all would be well. "In view of the protests from the Philippine people," he conceded, "I do not see how I could take you away."

AFTER HIS STRUGGLE TO PERSUADE Roosevelt that he must remain in the Philippines, William Taft resumed work "with renewed vigour and strengthened confidence." A host of challenges remained, but he was optimistic that the connections he had forged among the Filipino people would allow them to make progress. Absorbed in his daily tasks, Taft found immense gratification in "working for other people and attempting to win their confidence and finally in a measure succeeding." His genuinely cordial temperament was infectious, enabling him to create an effective, collegial team. "I was not a month with Judge Taft until I was shaking hands with everyone I met and greeting them with a laugh," remarked one staff member, noting with admiration that he "never saw anyone who could so thoroughly dominate everybody about him and saturate them, as it were, with his own geniality."

Roosevelt himself continued to laud the many gifts that his friend brought to the difficult task of governing the Philippines. "There is not in this Nation," Roosevelt told an audience, "a higher or finer type of public servant than Governor Taft." Secretary of War Elihu Root, who collaborated with Taft on all issues relating to the Philippines, concurred. He assured Henry Taft that his brother possessed "a personality which made [him] nothing but friends" and that "no man in the country had recently exhibited such unusual ability, both administrative and legislative." When good-natured telegrams between Taft and Root subsequently appeared in newspapers, their obvious camaraderie delighted readers. Taft had cabled Root a description of a long trip to a beautiful resort in the Benguet mountains. "Stood trip well. Rode horseback twenty-five miles to five thousand feet elevation." Root, knowing Taft's weight exceeded 300 pounds, cabled back: "How is the horse?" With typical good humor, Taft released Root's cable to the press, along with his praise for the horse—"a magnificent animal," he told Root, "gentle and intelligent and of great power. He stood the trip without difficulty."

With Nellie and the family happily situated at the palace, Taft envisioned a tenure of at least two years, time in which he could construct the foundation for Filipinos to elect their own assembly and achieve a greater degree of sovereignty. But another letter from the president on March 27 soon disrupted this prospect. "You will think I am a variety of the horse leech's daughter," Roosevelt began, alluding to the biblical parable in which a blacksmith's perpetually dissatisfied daughter demands ever more of him. Twice before, Roosevelt had asked Taft to return home; twice he had reluctantly acquiesced to Taft's resolve to remain in the islands. This third request was an imperative.

"The worst calamity that could happen to me (personally and) officially is impending," Roosevelt informed Taft, "because Root tells me that he will have to leave me next fall." The secretary of war had originally joined McKinley's cabinet, remaining on the understanding that he would return to his legal practice once new governments had been established in Cuba and the Philippines. The time to depart, Root insisted, had now come. For Roosevelt, the alarming prospect of losing "the wisest, the most surefooted, the most far-seeing" member of his administration could be remedied only by recalling Taft to take his place. "I wish to heaven that I did *not* feel as strongly as I do about two or three men in the public service, notably Root and you," the president told his friend. "But as I *do*, I want to ask you whether if I can persuade Root to stay until a year hence, you cannot come back and take his place."

Recognizing the depth of Taft's nation-building commitment, Roosevelt assured his friend that he would not have to abandon his cause. "As Secretary of War you would still have the ultimate control of the Philippine situation," he insisted, "and whatever was done would be under your immediate supervision." Beyond this enticement, Roosevelt felt he had arrived at the point in his presidency where Taft's judicious guidance was indispensable. "Remember too the aid and comfort you would be to me," he urged, "as my counsellor and adviser in all the great questions that come up." While he respected Taft's repeatedly expressed desire to complete his work in the Philippines, he needed him at home. "If only there were three of you!" Roosevelt concluded. "Then I would have one of you on the Supreme Court . . . one of you in Root's place as Secretary of War . . . and one of you permanently Governor of the Philippines. No one can quite take your place as Governor; but no one of whom I can now think save only you can at all take Root's place as Secretary."

This time, although he reiterated his concerns, Taft realized that the president's summons left no room to maneuver. "In view of your desire that I shall be in Washington expressed thus three times, I should feel reluctant to decline again," he replied, "but the change you propose is full of difficulties for me." He endeavored to explain the problem of extricating himself from his Filipino colleagues, particularly after his recent pledge to remain with them. While continued supervision of Philippine policy as secretary of war made the prospect of departure more palatable, Taft maintained that he had "no knowledge of army matters and no taste for or experience in politics." Moreover, the weight of Roosevelt's expectations left him uneasy: "I cannot but be conscious that were I to come to Washington, you would find me wanting in many of the respects in which you are good enough now to think I might aid you." Taft hoped the president would grant him several weeks to talk things over with Nellie and consult his brothers before supplying "a definite answer."

Much as Nellie enjoyed her life in the Philippines, she counseled Will to accept. She had argued strongly against the Supreme Court appointment but had long envisioned an active role for her husband at the highest level of government. The proffered cabinet post, she reflected, fell precisely "in line with the kind of work I wanted my husband to do, the kind of career I wanted for him." Further, Taft's health had become an increasing priority for Nellie; he had already endured two serious illnesses and was currently suffering from amoebic dysentery, a plague throughout the tropics. At the same time, the children were reaching ages when their education had to be given serious consideration. Thirteen-year-old Robert was scheduled to leave for Horace's boarding school in Watertown, Connecticut, later that summer. In three years, he would be prepared to enter the Yale Class of 1910, as his father had proudly "prophesied on the day of his birth." For Nellie and Will, the separation of 8,000 miles from their eldest son was painful to consider.

In a letter to his brothers, Taft acknowledged the difficulty of refusing the president but expressed serious reservations. "If I were to go, I should have to be in the midst of a presidential campaign, which would be most distasteful to me, for I have no love of American politics," he explained. "In addition, I do not see how I could possibly live in Washington on the salary of a Cabinet officer." Cabinet members were expected to entertain lavishly, but their $8,000 salary was far below his compensation as governor general. "My life insurance policy amounts to nearly $2000 a year," he protested, "and I should very much hate to go there and live in a boarding house." On the other hand, if his dysentery did not improve, doctors were likely to recommend his departure from the Philippines in any case.

Taft's mother, intensely anxious about her son's physical condition, urged his return. Indeed, given these growing health concerns, the family was unanimous in advising that Will accept the post. "I should prefer really not to have you get into politics here," Charles admitted, "but under the circumstances I do not see how you can decline the offer." Horace regretted that his brother would have to give up so "great a work" but feared that remaining in the islands would permanently damage Will's health. If acceptance of the secretaryship seemed inconsistent so soon after declining the Court appointment, Harry reasoned, the control he would retain over Philippine policy considerably mitigated this concern. Reassured by the support of his family, Taft wrote a long letter to Roosevelt indicating acceptance. Yet the letter was so circuitous that his intentions remained somewhat inscrutable. Conceding that the president's "earnest desire ought to be controlling," he nevertheless continued to stress his "great reluctance" to desert the Filipino people.

While Taft's indecision over the cabinet appointment may have been difficult to decipher, there was no equivocation over his personal devotion to Theodore Roosevelt. Taft's letter cited recent "intimations that the trust people, and possibly some of the machine politicians, are looking about for someone to center upon in opposition to your nomination" and noted that his own name had been bandied forth. "This is absurd," he declared, because "my loyalty and friendship for you and my appreciation of the manner in which you have stood behind me . . . are such that it would involve the basest ingratitude and treachery for me to permit the use of my name in any way to embarrass your candidacy." Upon receipt of this puzzling letter, Roosevelt dispatched a telegram to Harry Taft, who assured the president that it should be treated as an acceptance. Roosevelt was thrilled, sending Taft a forthright reply: "You don't know what a weight you have taken off my mind."

The president also worked to ease his friend's qualms over maintaining a proper Washington lifestyle. "It would really add immensely to my pleasure as an American to have you, who will be the foremost member of my Cabinet in the public eye, live the simplest kind of life," he wrote. "I hope you will live just exactly as you and I did when you were Solicitor General and I Civil Service Commissioner." Charley Taft, anxious that his brother should face no hardship in his removal to Washington, provided more tangible support. He gave Will 1,000 shares of Cleveland Gas Company stock worth $200,000 and proffered an additional $10,000 a year so that Taft "should feel independent of everybody and able to do as [he] pleased politically or in any other way." The proposal, Will gratefully replied, "struck me all in a heap: The love you manifest, the possibilities you open and the burdens you take away fill my heart with a joy moderated only by a feeling that I do not deserve it and that I cannot sufficiently requite it."

With the matter settled at last, only the timing and details of Taft's return to America remained. "The President is very much gratified," Harry relayed to Will; "he told me that he expected that you would be the strong man of the Cabinet and he should lean upon your counsel and advice." Root was impatient to depart but had agreed to stay until year's end. "Now that it is decided that you are to go," Harry continued, "we think that you might as well take the step at once." But Taft held his ground, promising to return in early January 1904. Despite his lifelong resolve to "keep out of politics," it seemed he would now be thrust in headlong, in the midst of a presidential campaign. Nonetheless, he admitted, the task ahead excited him.

And Roosevelt was unabashedly thrilled to finally have Taft on board, exclaiming, "Thank Heaven you are to be with me!"

"I have an additional and selfish reason for wanting you here," he confessed, as he looked toward the upcoming presidential campaign. "I shall have to rely very much upon you—upon your judgment and upon your making an occasional speech in which you put my position before the people. I should like you to be thoroughly familiar with this position in all its relations; and such familiarity you can only gain by close association with me for some length of time—in other words, by being in the Cabinet." The mood of the country had changed in Taft's absence, he explained. "When you come back I shall have much to tell you."

❦ ❦

WHEN WILLIAM TAFT FINALLY REACHED Washington at 4 p.m. on January 27, 1904, exhausted from a four-week journey by ocean liner and transcontinental train, he was astonished to discover that President Roosevelt had sent the 15th Cavalry to meet him. Escorted to a waiting carriage by a dozen officers in full uniform, Taft was "too amazed for words" when a bugler sounded the call for a hundred cavalry horses to begin their march to the War Department. As the station crowd cheered, journalists marveled that the elaborate ceremony—befitting a tribute to "a sacred potentate" from some faraway land—was unprecedented for an American citizen not yet even sworn in as secretary of war.

The rumpled traveler had barely settled into his rooms at the Arlington Hotel before having to depart for a reception honoring Elihu Root. The evening "was most enjoyable," Taft reported to Nellie, who was still in California with the two younger children. All the members of the Supreme Court and the cabinet were in attendance, and the president stayed for hours to celebrate both his outgoing and incoming war secretaries.

Journalists gleefully contrasted the easygoing new cabinet member, affectionately known as "Big Bill," with his staid predecessor, whom few would dare address by his first name, if indeed they could correctly pronounce it. "Two men were never born who are more unlike," the *Washington Times* observed. "One is the reserved, dignified, scholarly type, admitted by all persons who know him. The other is the hail-fellow well met, with unlimited brain power and the fortunate gift of being able to make a friend of every man who comes near him."

Roosevelt was sad to see Root go, he told his eldest son, but "Taft is a splendid fellow and will be an aid and comfort in every way." Edith worried that Taft was "too much like" her husband to deliver the same detached advice that Root had always provided. Roosevelt did not share his wife's reservations. "As the people loved Taft, so did Roosevelt," Mark Sullivan observed, recalling that "whenever Roosevelt mentioned Taft's name, it was with an expression of pleasure on his own countenance." Moreover, he instinctively perceived in Taft's steady composure "a needed and valuable corrective to his own impetuosity."

On February 1, Taft was sworn in as secretary of war, the position once held by his father. His brothers Harry and Charley stood by his side, along with Annie Taft. "It was good for sore eyes to see them," Will told his wife. Horace had fallen ill that week and "felt like crying" when he realized he could not join his brothers for the ceremony. After their father's death, the devotion and support among the Taft brothers had only strengthened.

It was quickly evident that Taft's innate diplomacy and administrative acumen would bring a jovial, effective leadership to the department. If his spirit of camaraderie, "democratic manner," and "breezy informality" occasionally irritated Army officers, they, too, eventually succumbed to his authentic affability. "I'm mighty glad to see you," he exclaimed as he grasped officers by the shoulders, determined to overcome barriers in Washington as he had done in Manila. As Taft traversed the halls of the War Department, one reporter noted, "he found time to extend a hearty welcome to colored messengers he had known for years." At 320 pounds, his large frame invariably commanded attention. "He looks like an American Bison, a gentle, kind one," the newspaper editor Arthur Brisbane observed of Taft's benign, substantial presence.

Having arrived in Washington at the height of the social season, Taft was bombarded by dinner invitations. A brilliant stag affair at Root's house was followed by the Gridiron Dinner, a Yale Club reception in his honor, a Judiciary Dinner, a cabinet dinner at the new Willard, a formal military banquet, and a White House reception. "I went down behind the Pres. & Mrs. R with Mrs. Shaw [wife of the treasury secretary] and we cut a wide swath," he told Nellie. "Mrs. Shaw is about as big as I am."

Hardly a day passed that Taft did not lunch at the White House, join the Roosevelt family for dinner, or consult privately with the president in the early morning or late evening. "The President seems really to take much comfort that I am in his cabinet," he informed Nellie. "He tells me so and then he tells people so who tell me. He is a very sweet natured man and very trusting man when he believes in one." Aware that Nellie still reserved judgment, he was careful to add: "I hope you will agree with me when you have fuller opportunities of observation."

Despite his hectic schedule, Taft managed to compose long letters to Nellie, detailing choice anecdotes about Washington's social drama: he gossiped over Mrs. Root's disdain when the first lady invited the "coarse and brazen" divorced wife of ex-Senator Wolcott to the White House; explained that Senator Hale of Maine had been dubbed "the Chief of the Pawnees because he has a pleasant habit of putting his hand on the knees of ladies whom he affects, under the dining table"; and recounted the various exploits of nineteen-year-old Alice Roosevelt—her late night partying, unchaperoned motor rides, brazen public smoking and betting on racehorses. She was known to keep a pet snake in her purse, hide small flasks of whiskey in her long gloves, and play poker with men. Will told Nellie that he had consulted Mrs. Lodge, who had also heard "a great deal of criticism of Alice Roosevelt's manners and rather rapid life," and was "much troubled" about it.

"Isn't there anything you can do to control Alice?" a friend asked Roosevelt. "I can do one of two things," he famously replied. "I can be President of the United States, or I can control Alice. I cannot possibly do both!"

When Nellie elected to spend several months in the California sun before traveling east, Taft was bereft. "I do not feel that I am living at all in your absence," he repeatedly lamented; "all that happens to me, all the work I do, every speech I make are all by the way. They are not permanent steps of progress. I am just marking time till you shall come on and real life shall begin again."

He had little time to brood. Roosevelt "loaded tons of work" on his newly appointed secretary and it seemed "the harder he was pushed the better work he did." William Taft became the "veritable pack horse for the Administration," a "trouble-shooter" with duties that extended beyond military matters and the Philippines. The president chose him to supervise the Isthmian Canal Commission, charged with constructing the Panama Canal, and consulted him regularly on labor and capital issues. And, as he had promised, Roosevelt would rely upon Taft heavily for speeches and advice during the presidential campaign. As one reporter observed: "Wherever a tension needed the solvent of good-will, or friction the oil of benevolence; wherever suspicion needed the antidote of frankness, or wounded pride the disinfectant of a hearty laugh— there Taft was sent."

Taft was "extremely popular both in the senate and the house," one Iowa newspaper reported. "He spends more time at the capital than all the other members of the cabinet," the journalist remarked, noting that he had become "an intermediary between the executive and congress, familiar with both ends of Pa. Ave, and as well liked at one end as the other."

Not surprisingly, Taft remained deeply engaged in the progress of the Philippines. Throughout his tenure as war secretary, he maintained close contact with Luke Wright, his successor as governor general, and with dozens of former colleagues in the islands. "Things have quieted down very much since your departure," one friend told him, "and we are all taking a much-needed rest, including the old-fashioned clock that stood in your office, which stopped on the day of your departure and has refused persistently, though much coaxed, to tick."

Taft spent a great deal of his time in February and March on the Hill, testifying and lobbying for a bill to subsidize the construction of a much-needed railroad system in the Philippines. Consultation with railway leaders in New York and a study of Britain's experience with colonial railroads had convinced Taft that capitalists were loath to invest "so far from home," especially where a tropical climate's long rainy season and dense vegetation complicated their prospects. If the Philippine government were authorized to guarantee 5 percent interest on bonds issued for construction, however, he was confident that vital infrastructure projects would be undertaken.

Taft first secured Speaker Joseph Cannon's approval of the railroad bill, knowing its passage in the Republican-controlled House would then be ensured. "All in favor will please say Aye," the powerful Speaker declared when the railroad bill came up for a vote. "There was a gentle piping of 'aye' on the Republican side." When the Speaker called for those opposed, there was "a thunderous burst of 'No!' " from the Democrats. "The 'noes' seem to make the most noise," Cannon brusquely concluded, "but the 'ayes' have it and the bill is passed."

Opposition in the Senate, where individual members could easily block a bill, proved more formidable. "I have been working with Democratic members," Taft told Nellie. "I have been as pretty to them as I can be but it may be love's labor lost, till more flies can be won with molasses than vinegar and I shall continue to coddle them, even if they go back on me." Through Taft's dogged efforts, the bill finally passed, though not until the following congressional session.

Taft's endeavor to secure congressional support for tariff reduction on Philippine products proved far less successful. Reduced tariffs were essential to the future prosperity of the islands, Taft repeatedly argued, insisting furthermore that reducing excessive import taxes was a matter of basic justice. An Indiana editorial concurred: since the United States had undertaken to govern the Philippines, "it would seem to be taking an unfair advantage of a poor, defenseless people" to levy an "exorbitant tax on their business relations with us" in order to satisfy "a few protected interests." Within the Congress, however, allies of the sugar and tobacco industries vowed to use any parliamentary tactic necessary to prevent a tariff reduction bill from reaching the floor.

"I can see in the opposition," Taft complained to Roosevelt, "the fine Italian hand of our dear friend Aldrich of Rhode Island. Whenever there is anything which is likely to injure the tobacco, sugar or silver mining interests under the so-called trust arrangements, that very able and deft manager of the Senate appears long enough in Washington to disturb the even tenor of projected remedial legislation." Lyman Abbott, as editor of *The Outlook*, offered pithy commiseration: "The interest of dollars is more powerful than the interest of conscience."

To Taft's dismay, Roosevelt defended the Senate leader. "You are unjust to Senator Aldrich," he chided Taft. Though the president often differed radically with Aldrich and the other members of the Big Four, he insisted that "taken as a body, they [were] broad-minded and patriotic, as well as sagacious, skillful and resolute." Such words offered scant consolation for Taft; the Senate's inner circle would effectively block any legislative action on the Philippine tariff reduction until Taft himself became president.

∽ ∽

ON MARCH 14, 1904, as word spread that the Northern Securities merger decision was imminent, an immense crowd gathered outside the Supreme Court. For Roosevelt, the outcome loomed with enormous implications for his party, as well as the nation. If the Court sustained the administration's argument that the colossal merger represented a monopoly that restricted trade, the victory would demonstrate a fundamental shift in the Republican Party's relationship with the trusts.

Inside the chamber, seating was filled to capacity. Dozens of senators and congressmen jockeyed for space in the section normally reserved for families of the justices. At the government bench, Attorney General Knox and Secretary Taft sat side by side, their expressions marked by "nervous expectancy." Nearby, ranks of powerful corporate lawyers had assembled. At the back of the chamber, more than fifty newspapermen, "paper and pencil in hands," readied to race to the telegraph wires the moment the ruling came down. "It required but little effort of imagination," one reporter noted, "to see in the vast background millions of American citizens awaiting the outcome of this judicial battle against daring financiers."

The crowd stood as the Court crier opened the session with the traditional cry: "Oyez, Oyez, Oyez." The spotlight on the Supreme Court likely conjured conflicting emotions in William Taft, who would have been among the justices had he accepted the president's appointment offer. That seat was now occupied by Justice William Rufus Day, Taft's good friend and former colleague on the Ohio bench. The moment Roosevelt had appointed Day, Taft realized that "being an Ohio man, and coming from the same court" foreclosed any chance that he might succeed to the bench in the near future. "Of course this is something of a disappointment," he had acknowledged to Joseph Bishop at the time, but maintained, "I am sure it would have made no difference if I had known definitely that this was the alternative." When Bishop shared that excerpt from Taft's letter with the president, it only confirmed Roosevelt's admiration. "How eminently characteristic of Taft those extracts are!" he exclaimed. "What a fine fellow he is!"

As Justice John Harlan began to read the Court's 5–4 opinion, papers reported, "everyone was alert for the significant sentence which should disclose the attitude of the majority." They did not wait long. "No scheme or device could more certainly come within the words of the [Sherman Anti-Trust Act]," Harlan immediately pronounced, "or more effectively and certainly suppress free competition between the constituent companies." Echoing the warning Baker had issued when the giant merger first became public, the Court cautioned that if no limits were placed on railroad mergers and more "holding companies" combined, "a universal merger" might be reached, and "a single man might thus control . . . and sway the transportation of the entire country." With this unambiguous declaration, "it was all over," the *Boston Daily Globe* recorded, recounting how "a score of eager men jumped for the exit and disappeared from the chamber to the waiting wires. Wall Street had lost. The government had won."

Taft enjoyed a moment of personal triumph when Harlan explicated the principles and precedents informing the majority decision. Central among the cases he cited was Taft's decision in *Addyston Pipe and Steel*. "If Congress can strike down a combination between private persons or private corporations that restrains trade among the States in iron pipe," Harlan argued, clearly they were empowered "to strike down combinations among stockholders of competing railroad carriers."

Oliver Wendell Holmes, Roosevelt's first appointee to the Court, proved "the surprise of the day" when he joined the other three dissenting justices. Known as "the friend of the common people" and "the champion of labor," Holmes delivered a stinging rebuttal, claiming that "while the merger was undoubtedly taken with the intention of ending competition between the two railroads," the Sherman Act—as currently constructed—did not apply to a transaction of this kind. Roosevelt was stunned by Holmes's dissent. "I could carve out of a banana a judge with more backbone than that," he angrily charged. Years later, Holmes agreed that the Northern Securities case had derailed his nascent friendship with Roosevelt. "We talked freely later," he recalled, "but it was never the same."

Roosevelt's frustration with Holmes did not diminish his absolute pleasure in the verdict. Upon receiving the news, the president "put aside all else to express his satisfaction" to every caller at the White House. The impact of this decision on Roosevelt's political stature could "hardly be exaggerated," the New York *World* editorialized. "People will love him for the enemies he has made. It cannot now be said that the Republican Party is owned by the trusts. It cannot now be said that Mr. Roosevelt is controlled by them." Minnesota governor Samuel Van Sant went so far as to claim the decision meant "more to the people of the country than any other event since the civil war." The government's triumph, the *Minneapolis Times* declared, had confirmed that "no man, however great, is greater than the law." From that moment, Roosevelt's reputation as the great "trust-buster" was confirmed.

Even as he savored his dramatic victory, Roosevelt nevertheless made clear that the government would not "run amuck." While the nation possessed the right and responsibility to regulate corporations, he maintained, "this power should be exercised with extreme caution." The Northern Securities suit should not be construed as the opening volley of a populist campaign to destroy all big corporations simply because they were big. In fact, Roosevelt viewed the organization of capital as a natural outcome of industrialization and welcomed the lower prices and efficient service made possible by combination. "If a corporation is doing square work I will help it so far as I can," he insisted. But at the same time, he asserted, "if it oppresses anybody; if it is acting dishonestly towards its stockholders or the public, or towards its laborers, or towards small competitors—why, when I have power I shall try to cinch it." With characteristic rhetorical balance, the president made it clear he would abide neither the excesses of "the selfish rich" nor the resentful outrage of the "lunatic fringe."

As he worked to implement this vision for genuine but evenhanded reform into public policy, the president was relieved to have William Howard Taft at his side. The approaching campaign would require powerful advocates for Roosevelt's election and for his progressive agenda. With his affable nature and tempered approach, the new secretary of war would be Roosevelt's indispensable complement.

CHAPTER FIFTEEN

"A Smile That Won't Come Off"

The 1904 Republican National Convention in Chicago, with
Mark Hanna's portrait visible above the speaker's platform.

WHEN ROOSEVELT UPROOTED TAFT FROM the Philippines to make him a pivotal figure in his Washington cabinet, he had warned his friend that he would lean on him heavily. In an era when it was still considered undignified for candidates to stump heavily on their own behalf, Taft would serve as a campaign surrogate, clarifying and promoting Roosevelt's positions. As the president had feared when he called Taft home, the mood of the country was becoming increasingly unstable. In the opening months of the 1904 election year, tensions between labor and capital had escalated to a dangerously volatile point.

No single incident illustrates the severity of this instability better than the Colorado labor wars, a series of conflicts that pushed the region to the brink of revolution. In the spring, labor violence in Colorado threatened to unbalance the carefully calibrated middle ground Roosevelt had forged in his dealings with unions and management. A continuous round of strikes by the Western Federation of Miners had roiled the region for over a year. The previous November, James Peabody, Colorado's conservative Republican governor, had declared martial law and urged Roosevelt to send federal troops to quell the disturbances. Strikers, he reported, had shut down mining activity across most of the state and were threatening a range of other businesses. The safety of Colorado's citizens and the security of their private property were in peril. After consulting with his cabinet, Roosevelt sent a telegram to the governor. While he understood the difficult conditions, he explained that he had "no lawful authority" to intervene unless the situation amounted to "an insurrection . . . beyond the power of the civil police and military forces of the State to control."

As the violence escalated, Ray Baker traveled to Colorado and began researching the history of "corruption & bribery on the part of the corporations & violence on the part of the strikers. I am going to go for them hard," as he told his father. Upon hearing that Baker was preparing an article on the Colorado labor strife, Roosevelt invited him to the White House. Throughout their lunch, Baker wrote his wife, Jessie, the president "had a pad of paper at his hand" and "asked me much in detail about conditions in the West."

As Baker labored to complete his 10,000-word article, "The Reign of Lawlessness: Anarchy and Despotism in Colorado," he sought Roosevelt's permission to quote from a statement in their private correspondence. "I believe in corporations," Roosevelt had written. "I believe in trade unions. Both have come to stay and are necessities in our present industrial system. But where, in either the one or the other, there develops corruption or mere brutal indifference to the rights of others . . . then the offender, whether union or corporation, must be fought." With the president's blessing, Baker used the quote to headline his argument that both capital and labor had broken the law in Colorado, equally contributing to the pervasive disorder and destruction.

Tracing the chronology of the conflict from the 1890s, Baker began with the Western Federation strikes in Cripple Creek, which successfully obtained "everything the men wanted," including higher wages, closed shops, and an eight-hour workday. But in both Colorado City and Denver, Baker noted, a number of mills remained "open shops," and Telluride mill owners refused to grant an eight-hour day. Federation leaders ordered all 3,000 men out in a "sympathetic strike," exercising a nearly "autocratic" authority over their statewide membership, a majority of whom were reluctant to strike. As union mines shut down across the state and unionized workers instigated violent altercations with non-union men in the smelting plants, public opinion began to turn against the Western Federation. Seizing this opportunity to break the union altogether, mine owners called on the governor to bring in state troops and keep the non-union mines open.

The governor needed little persuasion, Ray Baker reported, for he unabashedly "sided with the mine owners" in an effort "not merely to prevent violence, but *to break the strike*." The state militia arrested union members "without charges," suspending the writ of habeas corpus. Soldiers "entered and searched" private homes without warrants, and a local newspaper was shut down after its editor "criticized the methods of the soldiery."

"One of the great underlying reasons for the existing struggle," Baker determined, "was the demand for an eight-hour day in the smelters and mills of Colorado." In 1899, the state legislature had passed a law restricting work in extremely hazardous occupations to eight hours. After Colorado's supreme court declared the law unconstitutional, the unions sponsored an amendment to the state constitution. Passed by a large majority, the measure mandated that the legislature enact an eight-hour law. When lawmakers assembled, however, lobbyists from the Smelter Trust, controlled by John D. Rockefeller, descended upon the capitol. An eight-hour day would require three shifts instead of two, cutting profits. Money for bribes was plentiful. Despite the clear mandate, the legislature ended its session without having acted on the eight-hour law.

Little wonder, Baker mused, that after years of struggling for this legislation, the unions "were discouraged, even desperate." Nonetheless, he emphasized, the chaos in Colorado was the work of all parties: unions had utilized violent means to drive scabs from work; military forces had become despotic; corporations had bribed legislators; and the legislature itself had defied "the will of the people." Only public outrage and pressure could hope to stem the corruption and violence.

In mid-April, Baker sent an advance copy to Roosevelt. "I have endeavored in this article to set down the truth with absolute frankness, no matter who it hit," he wrote the president, "and if the truth were ever needed, it is needed today in Colorado." Baker's investigation and analysis drew widespread praise throughout the country. *The Arena* called it "the most masterly, exhaustive and on the whole judicially impartial account of the reign of anarchy in Colorado." The evenhanded stance evidenced in the Roosevelt quote Baker cited also occasioned favorable comment. "This language is not calculated to please either the extremists on the side of capital, or the extremists on the side of labor," the *Wall Street Journal* asserted, "but it commends itself to the sober thought of the great mass of people, who, while believing in the right of capital and labor to organize, hold that neither capital nor labor shall be permitted to exercise a power of monopoly." Roosevelt not only read the piece but had it circulated among officials in the Labor Department.

On June 6, the long-simmering tensions in Colorado ignited. At two o'clock that morning, twenty-five miners who had just completed a shift in defiance of the union's strike waited at the Cripple Creek station for the 2:15 a.m. train. Suddenly, a massive charge of dynamite detonated near the tracks, rocking the depot. Over a dozen men died instantly in the blast and more were gravely injured. The Western Federation of Miners was blamed for the "dastardly crime." News of this fatal explosion, destructive enough to render the dead unidentifiable by doctors and family members, quickly led to rioting. The governor called out the militia, and soldiers roamed the streets arresting anyone who uttered "the least anarchistic expression." Under orders of the state national guard, more than one hundred union miners were corralled onto a special train and banished from Cripple Creek. Among the thousands who thronged the station, one reporter observed, were "wives and sisters, fathers and mothers of the deported men, and the scenes were affecting."

The Western Federation appealed to the president, "in the name of law and order," pressing him to investigate "the terrible crimes that are being perpetrated in Colorado." The union's plea placed Roosevelt in a difficult position. "Having refused to send them in at the request of one side," he explained, "we are now asked to send them in at the request of the other." Exasperated by inaction, Roosevelt dispatched an investigative team to Colorado. "If it becomes necessary for me to act, or merely lay before Congress a statement of what has occurred, I want to know fully the exact facts," he told labor commissioner Carroll Davis Wright.

Commissioner Wright later informed Ray Baker that his article had served as "the basis of the government investigation in Colorado," which likewise traced the origin and history of the region's labor struggles and analyzed the same incidents, also attributing to both sides responsibility for the confrontation. Reading Wright's preliminary report, Roosevelt concurred with Baker that Governor Peabody had exacerbated the situation, intervening not simply "as the representative of law, order and justice" but "as the supporter and representative of the capitalist against the laborer." Nevertheless, the president believed the miners had erred, leaving strike decisions to an autocratic inner circle and using violence to accomplish their goals. The report validated Roosevelt's initial reluctance to interfere, providing abundant evidence that would justify his decision to Congress and to the public. Once the president had transmitted the final report to the House and the Senate, he again invited Baker to lunch. "He was most gratifyingly complimentary about my work," Baker informed his father. The president's response, he maintained, confirmed that his article "had been absolutely correct & fair."

The turbulence in Cripple Creek eventually subsided, though many of the deported miners never returned. In Telluride, the strike ended when the mine owners finally agreed to an eight-hour day. Governor Peabody was forced out of office, and the state legislature passed a state law limiting working hours for dangerous occupations, including work in mines, smelters, and reduction mills.

As the Republican National Convention opened in Chicago on June 21, 1904, Roosevelt was confident that, "barring a cataclysm," he would secure the nomination. The old bosses who still controlled the delegations might engage in "a great deal of sullen grumbling," but their hope of mounting a successful opposition had died with Marcus Hanna. Rather than "the thunderous demonstration usually attendant upon political conventions," newspapers described "a lifeless gathering," a "sober and unhysterical" affair. An enormous portrait of Hanna had been positioned above the speaker's platform and the first mention of the former chairman's name provoked a wild outburst. Although the majority of the delegates would be voting for Roosevelt, they made it clear from the outset that they supported him "because they had to." Had there been a "shadow of the chance" that any member of the conservative Old Guard could win the presidency, the majority would have "embraced it gladly."

More than any other writer covering the convention, William Allen White perceived the significance of the Republicans' peevish mood. Despite the empty seats, lack of enthusiasm, and "mechanical" twenty-minute cheer when Roosevelt's name was put into nomination, White nevertheless concluded that the convention was the "most successful gathering" in more than a generation. He recognized that "the puppet show" in Chicago was not an accurate reflection of national sentiment: the American people were exerting their will—and the people wanted Roosevelt. "It makes little difference whether the politicians cheered for Roosevelt twenty-three minutes or twenty-four hours," White insisted. Politicians and political machines were "dangerous" only if the people remained passive, but let a reformer like Roosevelt gain public confidence, and "the service of the politicians" would be at his command. "There is no boss so powerful that he can overcome the people."

White believed that this spirit of rebellion, the push to realize "a better world," was fueled by "a new element in political life"—the appearance of progressive newspapers and magazines urging the country to move forward. A decade earlier, men who called for a more equitable distribution of wealth were castigated as socialists or bomb-hurling anarchists. Now reformers were everywhere: small businessmen sought to regulate railroads, merchants demanded new laws to regulate the trusts, skilled laborers were striking for higher wages and shorter hours. All these agents of change, he concluded, now looked to Roosevelt "to speak and act for his times."

The appointment of George Cortelyou to replace Mark Hanna as campaign manager and chairman of the Republican National Committee confirmed that the embattled party needed Roosevelt far "more than he needed the party." A former newspaperman of modest background, Cortelyou had served as private secretary to Cleveland, McKinley, and Roosevelt before becoming head of the Department of Commerce and Labor. Roosevelt's support for Cortelyou drew immediate opposition from "professional politicians," who correctly sensed that they "were losing their grip of power." With his reputation for honesty and dedication, Cortelyou represented a younger, forward-thinking generation that was "taking control of the party," and conservatives "could not bear to abdicate without leaving a monumental growl behind them." Roosevelt moved swiftly to quash the opposition. "People may as well understand that if I am to run for President then Cortelyou is to be Chairman," he told a Massachusetts businessman and politician. "I will not have it any other way," he stated with finality. "The choice of Cortelyou is irrevocable." Delegates were left with no alternative but to ratify Roosevelt's selection.

Roosevelt was less successful in dictating the Republican Party platform. While it largely mirrored the president's public actions and statements on foreign policy, the Panama Canal, trusts, and labor, observers noted that it reflected a difference of opinion on the tariff. Roosevelt argued that failure to revise the tariff would put "a formidable weapon in the hands of our opponents," yet the platform espoused the principle of protectionism as "a cardinal policy of the Republican party." As Roosevelt predicted, the Democrats seized on the issue to proclaim that a Republican victory would herald "four years more of trust domination, of high prices to the consumer and of low prices to the producer." Nevertheless, Roosevelt hesitated to push the issue, fearful that a tariff battle would pit westerners anxious for relief against the eastern industrial and financial establishment, thereby creating a disastrous schism in the party.

Nor did Roosevelt contest the selection of Indiana senator Charles Fair banks as vice president. Although he far preferred Illinois congressman Robert Hitt, "of all men the pleasantest to work with," he accepted the "cautious, slow, conservative" Fairbanks as a concession to the Old Guard. Since his own experience as vice president had convinced him that the office was essentially powerless, there was no need to take a stand. Paramount was winning his party's presidential nomination.

Seated with his family on the south veranda of the White House, Roosevelt received news of his unanimous nomination. They had just finished lunch when his private secretary, William Loeb, brought the anticipated telegram. After "affectionate congratulations" from his wife and children, Roosevelt returned to his office, where members of the press, many of whom he considered "his personal friends," had convened. The president was "in exceptionally good humor" as he handed out cigars, joking that the stern prohibitionist Carrie Nation would not approve. The AP reporter described the scene: "With genial raillery he chatted with one; exchanged comments on men or things with another; laughed heartily at a cartoon of himself to which his attention was drawn; sketched in a free-hand way incidents of the convention; recalled some interesting situations, personal and political; and in conclusion again thanked his friends for expressions of their congratulations."

᙮ ᙮

WHEN THE DEMOCRATS ASSEMBLED IN St. Louis two weeks later, the party's conservative wing had clearly regained control. Though William Jennings Bryan remained the heartfelt choice of the rank and file, the professional politicians were starved for victory. After two consecutive defeats with Bryan, party leaders turned to a "gold Democrat," Judge Alton B. Parker. Bryan's repeated calls for using silver rather than gold as the standard unit of currency value had pleased western debtors who would benefit from inflation but had angered eastern creditors whose money would be devalued. Democratic bosses hoped Parker could both retain Bryan's liberal base in the West and win back eastern conservatives who had broken with the party on the gold issue.

Covering the Democratic Convention for *Collier's*, William Allen White portrayed Bryan as "the hero of the occasion, even though he did not triumph." Though deafening yells and "epileptic spasms" greeted Bryan's every appearance, the delegates had vowed not to let sentiment rule a third time. "They were like men who had been stark mad," observed White, "and the fear of it coming back was in their hearts." Bryan managed to keep the platform from endorsing gold, but the overwhelming vote for Parker's nomination signaled that his "eight-year reign was over." The platform roundly denounced trusts and protectionism as "robbery of the many to enrich the few," demanded large reductions in public spending, decried executive usurpation of legislative functions, called for Philippine independence, and advocated direct election of U.S. senators.

The nomination voting was completed shortly before midnight on Friday, July 8. The reporters gathered in Parker's hometown of Esopus, New York, were disappointed to learn that the judge had retired with orders that he not be awakened. As a result, the nominee was not apprised of his victory until returning from his regular morning swim in the Hudson River. Asked for a statement, Parker replied that he would wait until he received official notification. The delay provided time for a shrewd strategic maneuver: at noon, he dictated a telegram to be read before the convention adjourned, informing delegates that he regarded "the gold standard as firmly and irrevocably established." If his views on this issue "proved to be unsatisfactory to the majority," he should feel it his duty "to decline the nomination." The convention moved swiftly to adopt a resolution stating that the currency question did not appear in the platform simply because it was no longer "an issue at this time." The gold standard would not be challenged, they assured Parker, leaving nothing to prevent him from accepting the nomination.

Parker's move "was most adroit," Roosevelt acknowledged. "He is entitled to hearty praise, from the standpoint of a clever politician," the president observed, adding that the maneuver had gained for Parker "all of Cleveland's strength without any of Cleveland's weakness, and made him, on the whole, the most formidable man the Democrats could have nominated." William Taft disagreed, predicting that the success of Parker's machination would be short-lived, unlike the rift within the party it had perpetuated. He assured Roosevelt that Parker "was stronger the morning the telegram was published than he ever will be again." Nevertheless, Roosevelt fretted that he now faced "a hard and uphill fight" in the general election.

According to his habit, Theodore Roosevelt sought to harness anxiety through action. He had begun crafting his acceptance speech immediately after his nomination, but now he turned to it with a vengeance, determined to sharpen its tone. "I always like to do my fighting in the adversary's corner," he told Lodge. The speech, delivered on July 27 from the sun-splashed veranda at Sagamore Hill, "was received with immense enthusiasm" by the assembled crowd. "It is just such a statement as we should expect Theodore Roosevelt to make," the *Minneapolis Journal* editorialized: "terse, luminous, logical, convincing." His defense of Republican policy, said another paper, was "characteristically forceful," and his satirical commentary on the Democratic Party, noted Lodge, was "keen and polished as a Japanese sword blade."

Parker's acceptance speech had no such luster. Between bouts of heavy rain, the Democratic candidate held forth for forty minutes from the soaked lawn of his Esopus country home. Parker's flat style and lack of oratorical experience were immediately apparent; he "used few gestures," failed to distinguish his positions from Roosevelt's, and mustered no "bugle call." The most vigorous applause reportedly followed his closing declaration that, if elected, he would not run for a second term. Roosevelt was relieved that his rival's "shifty and tricky" gambit had failed to "straddle" the factions within the Democratic Party. Perhaps, Roosevelt told Lodge, Taft's assessment had been correct from the start.

Characteristically, Roosevelt began drafting his formal letter of acceptance weeks before its early September publication date, ensuring ample time for consultation with his advisers. Taft attended numerous breakfasts, lunches, and midnight discussions to dissect each section. "His opponents may attack the letter," Taft told Nellie, "but they will not say it is lacking in snap or ginger." Seeking a broad sounding board, Roosevelt also circulated drafts to Root, Lodge, Knox, Hay, Garfield, and the civil service reformer Lucius Swift—requesting merciless critiques. "I went at the letter hammer and tongs," Swift told his wife, "and got in a good many points."

Published on September 12, Roosevelt's letter received widespread praise. "Remarkable," the New York Times declared, "astonishingly able." The Washington Post observed that he had constructed "a veritable keynote for the stump," in which signal Republican objectives were championed with "enough spirit to arouse the partisan masses." The letter's strength, Taft told Roosevelt, was "the challenge contained in every line of it to the Democrats to be specific in their charges and to deal with facts." He maintained that if Parker produced a letter of acceptance akin to his tepid speech it would be glaringly apparent just "how little real ammunition the Democrats have."

The lackluster piece Taft anticipated from the Democratic candidate did not materialize. Parker's 6,000-word letter presented a spirited attack against centralized government at home and imperialism abroad, along with a robust call for tariff reform and further trust regulation. Republicans frankly acknowledged that now "the issues of the campaign would be more squarely joined." The New York Times deemed Parker's letter "a great paper." Though not designed to stir "the yells of crowds," it would appeal "to men who think," presenting "a first-rate test of the people."

Roosevelt conceded that Parker had cleverly managed to engage disparate factions of his party, giving "heart to his supporters" and halting "the downward movement of his campaign." At such moments, Roosevelt sorely longed to "take the offensive in person" and face his Democratic challenger on the stump. "I could cut him into ribbons if I could get at him in the open," he wrote to Kermit. "But of course a President can't go on the stump and can't indulge in personalities." His only option was to "sit still" and trust that his cabinet officials, traversing the country on his behalf, could make the case for his election.

GIVEN WILLIAM HOWARD TAFT'S MARKED aversion to preparing and delivering public speeches, he surprised even himself by emerging as the most sought-after speaker on the campaign trail. "It seems strange that with an effort to keep out of politics and with my real dislike for it, I should thus be pitched into the middle of it," he told his close friend Howard Hollister. Yet, in letters to Nellie, he confided his irritation at the extent to which "mere political discussion" dominated cabinet meetings. "I suppose it is natural," he lamented, "but it seems to me to be undignified." Nevertheless, as the campaign heated up, he settled into his role as spokesman for the administration. "I rather think I am to do more work than any other member of the cabinet," he noted with pride, "but I don't object to that."

Regardless of his engagement, Taft struggled with his inveterate tendency to procrastinate. Preparing for his first major speech during Harvard's commencement, where he and former Democratic secretary of state Richard Olney would square off on the Philippine issue, he confessed to his brother Charley that he was "right down to almost the last day in the preparation, as is usual with me." The night before departing for Cambridge, he reviewed the speech with the president and James Garfield. The president anticipated that the address would stand as "a great public document." Garfield too rated it "a masterly argument," recording in his diary that he considered Taft "a truly great man."

William Taft presented his speech to the Harvard Law School alumni at Sanders Theatre, presided over by Chief Justice Melville Fuller and Harvard president Charles W. Eliot. For two hours in the morning, Taft simply but clearly recounted the history of America's relationship with the Philippines, beginning with the war against Spain and the decision to exert sovereignty over the islands. He argued that American policy promoted "the Philippines for the Filipinos" and would eventually prepare the people to govern themselves. To promise independence before educating the populace, as many Democrats and independents urged, Taft believed would be a mistake.

Olney's rebuttal openly acknowledged that Taft had rightly earned "the general admiration" of the islanders "by the justice and skillfulness of his rule, and by the tact, patience and humanity of his dealings" with the Filipino people. He insisted, however, that the United States must not "sacrifice American lives and American treasures indefinitely and without stint for the education and elevation of Filipinos." The Constitution did not authorize the government to "turn itself into a missionary to the benighted tribes" or "to tax the toiling masses of this country for the benefit of motley groups of the brown people of the tropics." Simply, continued occupation of the Philippines represented a departure from the traditions and interests of the United States.

Despite their opposing views, both speakers remained impeccably civil. "Their differences," the *Cincinnati Enquirer* observed, "were, of course, stated in terms that prevented any exhibition of acrimony. When such men as Taft and Olney meet, the public can expect enlightenment on high ground." Olney's presentation was "a good thing," the *Enquirer* added, for it allowed "the young men of Harvard to have an opportunity to hear both sides of the question. Otherwise Secretary Taft might have hypnotized them, for they love him."

Taft was emboldened when his first campaign appearance generated nothing but positive notices. "I fired my gun at Cambridge and was pleasantly disappointed to find how well received it was," he drolly wrote to Roosevelt.

Will, Nellie, and the children soon departed Cambridge for their summer home on Murray Bay. Having spent the previous two summers in the Philippines, Taft was overjoyed at their return to this "magical place," where his brothers and their families could readily gather for picnics, trout fishing, and daily rounds of golf. "The air is bracing and delightful," Taft wrote to Roosevelt at Oyster Bay early in July. "I feel a boyish feeling—I'd like to jump up and down and shout." Nellie and the children planned to remain in Murray Bay until late September, but campaign and cabinet duties required Will's return to Washington at the end of July.

In August, Taft delivered two more impressive speeches on the Philippines, one in St. Louis and the other at Chautauqua. Increasingly confident in his area of expertise, Taft nevertheless remained anxious about a campaign appearance in Montpelier, Vermont, at the end of August. "The next ten days I must devote myself to the preparation," he told his wife. For better than twenty years, Taft had not given a purely political speech, and feared he was "a bit rusty on general politics." Indeed, he mused, "the Bench disqualifies one in this respect."

Roosevelt was particularly eager for Taft to speak in Vermont, where the September state elections were considered an important indicator of the vote in the presidential contest. Though the Green Mountain State generally leaned Republican, "the size of her majority" was thought to portend "the trend of public opinion." Rather than presenting an overview of Republican policies, Taft chose to focus on Roosevelt's leadership, mounting a spirited defense against repeated charges that the president was a bully, whose dictatorial demeanor toward Congress transgressed the constitutional separation between executive and legislative powers. "When Theodore Roosevelt is attacked for being a strong-headed tyrant, obstinate in his pride of opinion, and failure to listen to argument, I am in a position to know," he reassured his audience of more than 1,500 Vermonters. "In all my experience I never have met a man in authority with less pride of opinion," he asserted. "I have never met a man who was so amenable to reason, so anxious to reach a just conclusion, and so willing to sacrifice a previously formed opinion." Rather than a litany of clichéd tributes, Taft's vivid, personal testimony concerning the president's nature and character won the interest and enthusiasm of his listeners.

"It was a success," he told Nellie, proudly relaying that he was "told by many that it was thought to be the best political speech delivered in Vermont." The press concurred: "It would be difficult to praise it too highly," one Pennsylvania paper editorialized. "Judge Taft had already attained a high reputation as a jurist and executive officer." Now, he had established himself "as a political orator of the first rank. . . . Probably no member of the President's cabinet will prove more effective in defense and support of his administration." Published in its entirety in the *Boston Transcript*, Taft's speech promised to become "a text-book for Republican orators and writers." Most important, the Vermont vote proved a "glorious" triumph for Republicans, with a larger margin than anyone had predicted. "I am pleased as Punch about Vermont," Roosevelt exclaimed to Taft, adding that the unforeseen magnitude should "cut off some of the money supply of our adversaries."

Taft next proceeded to Portland, Maine; Roosevelt had received "a rather gloomy letter" from Senator Eugene Hale about Republican prospects in the state and hoped that Taft's presence could help energize support. Buoyed by positive reactions, Taft prepared himself "to speak without notes" for the first time. Despite initial anxiety that his memory might fail and leave him floundering, his performance went smoothly.

Taft continued north to Murray Bay for a final two weeks of vacation before the true rigors of the campaign began. To his "great surprise," a large contingent of Murray Bay residents appeared at his house on the night of his forty-seventh birthday. A torchlight parade escorted him to the Bay's largest house, where they feasted and drank, danced the Virginia reel, sang songs, presented gifts, and proposed toasts.

Taft wrote to Roosevelt every other day during his vacation, planning future speeches, exchanging political gossip, discussing Parker's campaign. "Mrs. Taft says that you must be bored by the number of letters that I write you," he jested; "now that I have my Secretary with me you may expect more." Ease and camaraderie mark their correspondence from this period as they discussed matters both personal and political: Roosevelt complained freely about their mutual friend Maria Storer; Taft described a new diet requiring him to refrain from drinking all liquids with his meals; Roosevelt cursed the "infernal liars" in the independent press—"the New York Times, Evening Post, Herald"—with their outrageous claims that he had sent "a corruption fund" to influence the vote in Vermont; Taft recounted "playing golf every day in air that is as invigorating as dry champagne without any evil after effect."

Upon his return to Washington in late September, Taft was immediately dispatched to Ohio, Rhode Island, Connecticut, New York, and New Jersey. "Do not in any speech take any position seeming in the least to be on the defensive," Roosevelt cautioned. "Attack Parker. Show that his proposals are insincere; his statements lacking in candor, and disingenuous. Announce that we have not the slightest apology to make; that we intend to continue precisely as we have been doing in the past; that we shall not abandon building up the navy and keeping up the army, or abandon rural free delivery, or irrigation of the public lands. Either Parker is insincere, or else he must propose to abandon these works and other works like them in order to economize."

On October 1, Taft opened the Republicans' Ohio campaign with a day-long extravaganza in Warren's public square that featured marching bands, songs, and large delegations from neighboring Cleveland, Youngstown, and Akron. With nearly 2,000 people in attendance, the campaign kickoff was considered "the most auspicious in years." Sharing the platform with the state's governor and two U.S. senators, Taft delivered the keynote address. Following Roosevelt's directives, he targeted Parker directly, saving his most stinging condemnation for the gross distortions and outright lies the Democratic candidate had spread about the administration's expenditures in the Philippines. "After reading the statements of Judge Parker concerning the Philippines," Taft repeatedly avowed, "I sometimes wonder whether I was ever there."

Taft would have welcomed Nellie's company on the campaign trail, but she had to settle the family into their new house at 1904 K Street in Washington and prepare the children for school. In daily letters, she related her progress in unpacking cartons of furniture, carpeting floors, setting up beds, working with carpenters, and arranging books in the library. With Robert attending Horace's boarding school in Watertown, Connecticut, only the two younger children remained at home. Thirteen-year-old Helen joined Ethel Roosevelt at the National Cathedral School. Seven-year-old Charlie was enrolled in the local public school, where he became great friends with Quentin Roosevelt. "I hope Charley's first day in school was a success," Taft wrote from Indiana. "I can remember mine. It was not."

As the campaign ground on, Taft's yearning to be home with his wife and children intensified. "I wish I could get on the train and go right to you now," he told Nellie early in October. With each passing day, he grew wearier of presenting the same speech. In Indianapolis, the crowd grew restless, some departing early as he held forth for nearly two hours. "I don't think my style of speaking is calculated to hold the curious," he admitted to Nellie, "but the audience which remained was most attentive." She "could not but smile," Nellie replied, when he mentioned the length of the speech. "If you confine it to an hour," she suggested, "I think people will stay."

A tense situation developed in mid-October, when a delegation of cigar and tobacco manufacturers, irate at Taft's proposed reduction of the tariff on Philippine tobacco, threatened "to control cigar makers enough to defeat Roosevelt in N.Y., Conn, Missouri and almost everywhere else." Enlisting the support of labor organizations in the cigar trade, they petitioned Congress and approached the president, "just at the anxious time when everything assumes distorted proportions." That same day, Taft wrote to the president. "I feel sure you would not wish me to retract anything on that subject," he began, adding that he would willingly cancel his appearances in affected states that might "emphasize the issue." If the president felt it necessary, Taft concluded, he would retire from the cabinet rather than back down on the principle.

"Fiddle-dee-dee!" Roosevelt responded, quickly dismissing Taft's resignation talk as "nerves, or something." While there was certainly no sense in exacerbating the issue by dwelling on the tobacco tariff, the New England states were precisely where his talent was most necessary. With this reassurance, Taft continued his grueling schedule but grumbled to his wife that the issue confirmed his resolve that he "would not run for President if you guaranteed the office. It is awful to be made afraid of one's shadow."

☙ ❧

As summer advanced into fall, the struggles between labor and capital increasingly defined the campaign. Democrats sought to contrast Roosevelt, "a man who never needed to do a day's work," and Parker, "a man who has always had to work to maintain himself and his family." This emblematic opposition sought to distinguish "the party of aristocracy and oligarchy" from "the party of liberty and equality." Democratic newspapers predicted that the rank and file of labor would vote in record numbers against Roosevelt. "It is the culmination of many grievances which union labor has against the party and its leaders," judged one paper. In Pennsylvania, Old Guard Republican senator Boies Penrose had "utterly ignored" union demands relating to construction of the state's new capitol. In the Rocky Mountain states, the bitterness of union miners against conservative Governor Peabody threatened to supply Parker with such overwhelming labor support that Republicans were reportedly conceding the region to Democrats. The rising cost of living fueled these complaints of the working class, undercutting Republican campaign strategies of a "full dinner pail" that had once helped McKinley.

All the while, Roosevelt was hammered by party conservatives for being too friendly with labor. Day after day, the New York *Sun* savaged him for his actions in the coal strike, his temerity in inviting labor men to dinner at the White House, and his honorary membership in the Brotherhood of Locomotive Firemen. "He is on the side of the men who are every day seeking to overthrow the Constitution," the *Sun* stridently charged. "He has joined their organizations, espoused their creed, received their leaders at his dwelling and in his official residence; and as President of the United States has welcomed their delegates." Simultaneously, Roosevelt lamented that populist publications reviled him for breaking bread with the great corporate heads.

As this antagonism intensified, Ray Baker began drafting a piece for *McClure's* to dissect each candidate's point of view on the labor issue. He read every one of Judge Parker's decisions addressing unions and corporations, discovering that "without exception," they were "strongly favorable to the contentions of labor." In one case, Parker had declared that "the state has a right to limit the hours of employment for bakers to sixty a week"; in another instance, he stated "that cities must pay the 'prevailing rate of wages' "; in still another, he ruled in favor of the closed shop.

Baker expected a discussion of labor issues when he was invited to spend the afternoon with the judge at Esopus. "Personally he is a most attractive man—a good type of the comfortable country gentleman," Baker told his father. "I was disappointed in finding him so apparently uninformed on labor affairs, though, of course, his mode of life has given him little opportunity of coming into contact with the great vital forces of the industrial conflict." Indeed, beyond his judicial decisions, Baker was unable to decipher coherent underlying principles governing Parker's approach to the paramount issue of the day.

In contrast, when Baker requested from Roosevelt a clarification of what many considered a contradictory position on the labor issue, Roosevelt promptly produced a nearly 2,000-word reply. "I cannot help feeling," the president testily responded, "that the people who have been 'confused by my action in the various labor cases,' must be of such limited brain power that nothing in the world will make my position clear to them." To comprehend his stance, he insisted, one need only study his words and actions over time. If such "creatures" remained confused, he continued, "I hardly think it will be possible to set them right; for they must be people who do not understand that when I say I wish to give a square deal to every man I mean just exactly that, and that I intend to stand by the capitalist when he is right and by the laboring man when he is right, and will oppose the one if he goes wrong just as fearlessly as I should oppose the other." Those offended by his dinner invitations to labor leaders should understand that the White House door would always swing open for labor leaders "just as easily" as "for the big capitalists, but *no* easier."

In this striking letter, Roosevelt proceeded to articulate his actions in the coal strike, the eight-hour day, the Colorado situation, immigration law, and convict labor. The basic principles and convictions Roosevelt so aggressively outlined spurred Baker to reread carefully all of the president's speeches and writings on the subject of labor. "I am perfectly astonished," he wrote to Roosevelt, "though I thought myself pretty well informed before—at the number and definiteness and breadth of your declarations on the labor question, as well as the record of your acts since your early days in the Legislature. And if I, who represent, perhaps the average busy American, am astonished, I believe a great many other people will be."

Before the election, Baker's article, entitled "Parker and Roosevelt on Labor: Real Views of the Two Candidates on the Most Vital National Problem," appeared in *McClure's*. Without any direct exposition or elaboration from Parker, Baker had relied on the judge's reasoning in the applicable half-dozen cases he had presided over. On the other hand, with access to a lifetime of Roosevelt's statements and decisions, Baker could present "a clear idea of the labor platform upon which he stands." Beginning with Roosevelt's early success as a state legislator against sweatshop conditions in tenement cigar factories, Baker demonstrated that, unlike Old Guard Republicans, the president was "a thoroughgoing believer in labor organization." In contrast to radical

Democrats, however, Roosevelt recognized that "there is no worse enemy of the wage-worker than the man who condones mob violence in any shape, or who preaches class hatred."

The time and attention Roosevelt had devoted to the journalist's request proved most rewarding. The *Los Angeles Times* observed that Baker's "thorough and painstaking" methods provided *McClure's* vast middle-class audience with a clear, illuminating portrait of the president's fair-minded and long-standing attitudes toward labor.

⟨⟩ ⟨⟩

WITH ONLY WEEKS REMAINING UNTIL the election, Roosevelt recognized that while "the bulk of the voters" would "oppose or support" him based on his three years in office, "a sufficient mass of voters" remained who might yet be swayed by a dramatic turn in the campaign. Mid-October delivered just such a development, when the discovery of immense corporate contributions to the Republican Party suddenly threatened to compromise Roosevelt's hopes for victory. "The steady advance in the influence of money in our public life," decried a *New York Times* editorial, works "as a poison on the minds and hearts of men." Such toxicity was abundantly clear, the *Times* added, "when a man of Mr. Roosevelt's native scorn for corruption can be the willing, the eager beneficiary of funds paid into his campaign chest through his former secretary and former cabinet officer [Mr. Cortelyou] with the undisguised hope that it will be repaid in favors to the subscribers."

Lincoln Steffens called on Roosevelt at the White House to suggest that the issue could be lanced if he were to return all corporate contributions and look instead to small donations from the general public to fund his campaign. An informed public of small contributors "would make the millions feel that it was their government, as it is; and that you and your administration were beholden to the many, not to the few." Such a change, Steffens believed, would herald a new era in election politics. "If we must have campaign contributions, this is the way to raise them," he concluded. "If you would start this method now you really would begin a tremendous reform."

Roosevelt "most emphatically" rejected the premise of Steffens's argument, insisting that he already felt "beholden to the many more than to the few." Whether an individual or corporation contributed one dollar or one hundred thousand dollars would never sway him to sponsor legislation or take executive action. It was "entirely legitimate to accept contributions, no matter how large," he contended, so long as "they were given and received with no thought of any more obligation on the part of the National Committee or of the National Administration than is implied in the statement that every man shall receive a square deal."

In the end, Roosevelt willingly received hundreds of thousands of dollars from executives in dozens of corporations, including J. P. Morgan's banking house, New York Central Railroad, Standard Oil, General Electric, and International Harvester. Only when apprised of a check for $100,000 from the Standard Oil Company, "the Mother of Trusts," did Roosevelt draw the line. He instructed Cortelyou to return the money immediately: "In view of the open and pronounced opposition of the Standard Oil Company to the establishment of the Bureau of Corporations, one of the most important accomplishments of my Administration, I do not feel willing to accept its aid." So long as other "big business corporations" believed that the country's well-being could "only be secured through the continuance in power of the republican party," however, he deemed their contributions "entirely proper."

Roosevelt's justification did not satisfy the editorial board of the *New York Times*. "The fact that the chief beneficiary of the process is blind to its gross impropriety," declared the *Times*, "and can see in it only a means to the promotion of the welfare of the Nation dependent beyond question upon his attainment of the Presidential office by election shows how insidious and how irresistible has been the demoralization." The general unseemliness of large corporate contributions made little impact on the campaign, however, since it was widely known that corporations habitually "contributed to both campaign funds."

The scandal that did catch the public's attention and threatened to derail Roosevelt's campaign was the far more lethal accusation that the president and George Cortelyou were engaged "in a conspiracy to blackmail corporations." Judge Parker and fellow Democrats charged the Republicans with extortion—using detailed information on violations obtained from the newly created Bureau of Corporations "like a big stick with the threat of prosecution if a fat contribution to the republican campaign [was] not made." Democratic newspapers insinuated that "the prostitution of an entire federal department to the use of a campaign committee was cleverly planned and carefully executed." First, the papers accused, Roosevelt had appointed Cortelyou head of the cabinet department overseeing the new bureau; then, having amassed the necessary information, Cortelyou was made chairman of the Republican National Committee.

Roosevelt's advisers were divided over how to respond. Initially, Cortelyou and Garfield were reluctant to dignify the infamous accusation with a rejoinder. Taft disagreed. "I don't see why Cortelyou does not deny it but he keeps mum," he wrote Nellie. "Of course Parker cites no evidence to sustain his charge and Cortelyou's position is that until he does so, he is not called upon to answer. But I think it would be better to make a short denial."

Roosevelt concurred with Taft that the charges must be refuted, but resolved, against all precedent, to answer them personally. "I am the man against whom Parker's assaults are really directed and I am the man who can give the widest publicity to the denial," he told Cortelyou. "I should feel an intolerable humiliation if I were beaten because infamous charges had been made against me and good people regarded my silence as acquiescence in them." In characteristic fashion, Roosevelt drafted the statement himself, submitting it to his advisers for criticism. Revised speech in hand, he asked Garfield to take the midnight train to New York and confer with Cortelyou and Root.

All reservations concerning the propriety of the president's personal involvement in the fray vanished when, in an inflammatory speech on November 3, five days before the election, Parker labeled Cortelyou's fund "Blood Money." From the rear of his train in Meriden, Connecticut, Parker spoke "without notes for the first time since the campaign began." The Democratic candidate, reporters suggested, was stirred from his usual reticence by the loud enthusiasm of the immense crowd of 5,000. "His eyes flashed, his clenched hand swung above his head and his voice rang out with a vigor that betrayed his emotion," as he declared that all other issues of the campaign were now subsumed by one great question: "whether it is possible for interests in this country to control the elections with money." Parker scornfully claimed that when "every trust in this country, including the Standard Oil Trust, is doing its best to elect the Republican ticket," it becomes the duty of the American people to determine "once and for all, whether money or manhood suffrage shall control." He described how Cortelyou had exploited his cabinet position to blackmail the trusts for campaign contributions. "This country," he pledged in closing, "shall not pass into the hands of the trusts." The crowd responded "with a thundering cry that lasted until the train drew out of sight."

At ten o'clock the following night, William Loeb summoned members of the press to the White House, where he handed them the president's signed statement. The "direct and fierce" tone of this letter "became the common news of the hotels and streets in a few moments," prompting a flurry of discussion among politicians and the press. "The gravamen of these charges," Roosevelt began, "lies in the assertion that corporations have been blackmailed into contributing," and that in return, "they have been promised certain immunities or favors." Such accusations leveled without any evidence were "monstrous," he maintained. "If true, they would brand both of us forever with infamy, and inasmuch as they are false, heavy must be the condemnation of the man making them." He unequivocally dismissed the charge that Cortelyou had used intelligence gleaned from his cabinet position to coerce contributions as "a *falsehood*" and the insinuations that pledges were offered for contributions as "a *wicked falsehood*." All these allegations, the president flatly concluded, were "*unqualifiedly and atrociously false*."

In the wake of Roosevelt's vigorous and categorical rebuttal, Parker seemed to backpedal, claiming that "he had made no criticism of the President, but had simply called attention to a 'notorious and offensive situation.' " Nor, in response to Roosevelt's direct challenge, did he offer to substantiate his earlier claims. "Parker fails to furnish proofs," headlines blared in response. The president's public rebuttal, Garfield happily observed, "has knocked Parker flat."

The outcome delighted Roosevelt. "Parker's attacks became so atrocious," an ebullient Roosevelt told Kermit, "that I determined—against the counsel of my advisors—to hit; and as I never believe in hitting soft, I hit him in a way he will remember. In spite of loud boasting he made no real return attack at all, and I came out of the encounter with flying colors."

As election day approached, Roosevelt's anxiety escalated. He confessed to his sister Corinne that "he had never wanted anything in his life quite as much as the outward and visible sign of his country's approval." Elevated to the presidency as a result of "a calamity to another rather than as the personal choice of the people," he longed "to be chosen President on his own merits by the people of the United States." Should his campaign end in rejection, he consoled himself in moments fraught with tension that he had enjoyed "a first class run." And if, in defeat, he "felt soured at not having had more, instead of being thankful for having had so much," it would signal "a small and mean mind."

Late on the morning of November 8, Roosevelt cast his vote in Oyster Bay. A crowd of "home folk" greeted him at the train station with flags and banners. Arriving at the polling place, he "sprang briskly from the carriage and ran up the stairs." As soon as his ballot was cast, he caught the 1:14 train back to Washington, reaching the White House at 6:30 p.m. Not expecting returns for several hours, Roosevelt tried "not to think of the result, but to school [himself] to accept it as a man." He had scarcely crossed the threshold when news arrived that he had carried doubtful New York with "a plurality so large as to be astonishing." By the time he sat down with his family at dinner, sufficient returns had been received from key precincts in various states to suggest "a tremendous drift" in his direction.

After dinner, the president joined a group of intimate friends and members of his official family in the Red Parlor to await further results. While Taft had not yet returned from voting in Cincinnati, Nellie and the wives of the other cabinet members were present. Eleven-year-old Archie, "fairly plastered with badges," carried telegrams from the telegraph operator to his father, who read them aloud. At 9 p.m., a personal telegram arrived from Judge Parker conceding the election. It was "the greatest triumph I ever had had or ever could have," Roosevelt wrote, "and I was very proud and happy."

An hour later, Roosevelt greeted the Washington correspondents in the executive mansion office. Following an animated discussion in which he made "no attempt to conceal his gratification," the president leaned back in his chair and dictated a statement to his secretary. "So quiet was everyone in the room," one correspondent noted, "that one could hear the clock tick on the mantel shelf" as he read his startling pronouncement.

> I am deeply sensible of the honor done me by the American people in thus expressing their confidence in what I have done and have tried to do. I appreciate to the full the solemn responsibility this confidence imposed on me, and I shall do all that in my power lies not to forfeit it. On the 4th of March next I shall have served three and one half years and the three and one half years constitute my first term. The wise custom which limits the President to two terms regards the substance and not the form, and under no circumstance will I be a candidate for or accept another nomination.

Roosevelt's statement was not an impulsive gesture made in a moment of delirious joy; he had considered renouncing a third term weeks earlier but decided to wait for the election results lest it seem "a bid for votes." From his first days in office, critics had disparaged Roosevelt's single-minded focus on his own advancement. Such negativity sharpened during the campaign as opponents charged that he would "use the office of President to perpetuate [himself] in power." His simple pledge in the wake of the election-day triumph silenced all such criticism.

"I feel very strongly," Roosevelt explained to the British historian George Trevelyan, that "a public man's usefulness in the highest position becomes in the end impaired by the mere fact of too long continuance in that position." Even if custom had not frowned upon a third term, he maintained, "it would yet be true that in 1908 it would be better to have some man like Taft or Root succeed me in the presidency, at the head of the Republican party, than to have me succeed myself. In all the essentials of policy they look upon things as I do; but . . . what they did and said would have a freshness which what I did and said could not possibly have; and they would be free from the animosities and suspicions which I had accumulated, and would be able to take a new start."

When all the votes were finally tallied, Roosevelt had achieved "the greatest popular majority and the greatest electoral majority ever given to a candidate for President." He had won all the northern states, carried the western states previously claimed by Bryan, and added a totally unexpected coup in Missouri, breaking the Democratic Party's enduring hold on the South. "I am stunned by the overwhelming victory we have won," Roosevelt confessed. "I had no conception that such a thing was possible."

Everyone in the administration, Taft told his brother Charley, "has had a smile that won't come off since the election." William Taft could well take particular satisfaction in his own vital contribution to the victorious campaign. Personal letters and newspaper articles recorded his tireless efforts and powerful speeches in defense of administration policy. "The document that gave the most force to the Roosevelt campaign," journalist Murat Halstead told Taft, "was your utterance on the Philippines on the stump—that had the air and the dignity and the conclusiveness of a decision handed down by the Supreme Court." Howard Hollister proudly noted that his old friend had generated "thousands of votes" by standing "fearlessly" on the issues, making "a contribution much greater probably than you would be willing to admit." Characteristically, Taft refused to take credit, replying to all who congratulated him that "the victory is so overwhelming that I cannot think that anything that was done in the way of speaking had any particular effect." Above all, he insisted, the success was "a tribute to the personal popularity of the President."

Notwithstanding the general elation surrounding the historic election, Taft issued a public warning to the Republican Party: "It is no unheard of thing to have a majority as large and sweeping as this followed by a defeat equally emphatic at the next Presidential election." Without a candidate as compelling and charismatic as Roosevelt, it was very possible that the country would have voted Democratic; the Republican Party must not "diminish in any way the care with which the public interests must be protected." His timely admonition met with widespread approval. "Unless the Republican party is wise and liberal toward all legitimate and right demands of the people in the social and economic controversies which are going on," one respondent agreed, "we must expect sweeping radical victories during the next few years."

For those who hoped to see a more progressive Republican Party, Roosevelt's surprise decision to forgo a third term seemed "pregnant with promise" of a vigorous future for reform. Now that he was "absolutely independent of all party bosses and party machines," the *Minneapolis Journal* predicted, "Theodore Roosevelt is likely to make the administration of 1905–9 one of the two or three most resplendent and beneficial in the history of the republic." The *St. Paul Globe* endorsed this sanguine assessment, proclaiming that if Roosevelt stayed true "to the best that is in him," he could "become one of the great presidents in our history." Even his harshest critics had "nothing but praise" for Roosevelt's declaration. It was "to his everlasting honor," the New York *Sun* proclaimed, that "in the hour of his triumph," the president chose to make his second term his last.

Though he reveled in the acclaim that accompanied his declaration, Theodore Roosevelt would come to bitterly regret his action, later reportedly telling a friend that if he could rescind the pledge, he would willingly cut off his hand at the wrist.

CHAPTER SIXTEEN

"Sitting on the Lid"

"I have left Taft sitting on the lid," Roosevelt remarked before
departing on a western tour, prompting this April 5, 1905,
cartoon in the *Washington Times*.

AFTER WEEKS OF CLOUDY SKIES and heavy snow, the morn-
ing of March 4, 1905, broke "blue, flecked with lazily floating white
clouds"—the day Theodore Roosevelt was inaugurated president in his own
right. Washingtonians happily remarked that once again "Roosevelt luck"
had brought "Roosevelt weather." For the tens of thousands lining the streets
to watch the president's carriage pass from the White House to the Capitol,
"the morning sun gave brilliancy and luster to the fluttering mass of flags and
banners."

Roosevelt appeared "supremely happy," waving and bowing as a record-
breaking crowd hailed him with "the roar of the ocean upon a rockbound
coast." The galleries were filled inside the Senate chamber, where Charles

Fairbanks prepared to take the vice-presidential oath. Raucous cheers broke out when Roosevelt arrived. Stepping onto the floor, he at once scanned the gallery for Edith and the children; spotting them, he did not wave "furtively, nor half-heartedly, nor as if he were afraid someone might see this evidence of his domestic affection but with demonstration frank and full." His demeanor proclaimed simply: "This, my dear wife and children, is the proudest moment of our lives."

Hundreds of spectators perched in trees, crowded on rooftops, and lined the wings of the Capitol building as the president stood before the vast multitude and delivered "a friendly little homily on the duties of the nation and citizen," betraying nothing of the "truculent note" that often marked his speeches. "Much has been given us, and much will rightfully be expected from us," he told the crowd. "We have become a great nation, forced by the fact of its greatness into relations with the other nations of the earth. . . . Our relations with the other powers of the world are important, but still more important are our relations among ourselves." The Industrial Revolution, Roosevelt maintained, had generated both "marvelous material well-being" and the "care and anxiety inseparable from the accumulation of great wealth"—creating a host of problems that government had the responsibility to address. He spoke with characteristic "earnestness," one reporter wrote, stressing every word with such force that it seemed "as if he would like to get hold of each individual person in his audience and pound home the truths which he believes he is uttering, till the wretched man should be forced to admit the error of his ways and agree with the speaker."

Editorialists predicted "tempestuous doings" now that Roosevelt was president in his own right rather than by the happenstance of assassination. Backed by a massive popular mandate, he would no longer be held in check by the conservative bloc in Congress. "The Republican party has turned the corner and is now on a new road," William Allen White proclaimed. "It is hard to believe that the party that eight years ago was advocating the policy of 'hands off' is now ready to lay hands on capital, and such rough hands, too, when capital goes wrong. 'The old order changeth, yielding place to the new.' "

TURBULENT EVENTS WOULD INDEED FOLLOW, but first the newly elected president embarked on a two-month vacation trip through the Southwest and the Rocky Mountain region. A Rough Riders reunion in Texas began the hiatus, followed by a five-day wolf-hunting expedition in Oklahoma and a three-week bear hunt in Colorado. "Everybody rejoices that he is to have some time for recuperation," an Ohio newspaper editorialized. "Only the bears and the mountain lions have occasion for regret." On the morning of April 4, cheered by well-wishers at the Pennsylvania Railroad Station, Roosevelt stepped onto a "handsomely fitted" train consisting of a private car, a Pullman sleeper, and a buffet car. He looked, one reporter noted, "like a small boy let out of school," rejoicing that he would soon enter wild country beyond the reach of official duties and office seekers.

Along the route, Roosevelt followed his customary procedure, emerging onto the platform at every stop to shake hands and deliver brief remarks. It was "much more pleasant than ordinarily," he told his son Kermit, because the presidential race was over and he was finally "free from the everlasting suspicion" a candidate invariably arouses. Even in the traditionally Democratic strongholds of Louisville, Austin, and Dallas, flags waved, cannons thundered, and tens of thousands greeted him with "wild enthusiasm."

Clearly, these hunting expeditions not only afforded Roosevelt a most "genuine pleasure" but provided the opportunity for revitalization. In Oklahoma, he was "in the saddle eight or nine hours every day" helping to track and kill eleven wolves: "It was tremendous galloping over cut banks, prairie dog towns, flats, creek bottoms, everything," he exulted. "One run was nine miles long and I was the only man in at the finish except the professional wolf hunter." In Colorado, he was "up at daybreak" and refused to stop until the sun set, keeping his "little band of huntsmen" in constant motion. As always, Roosevelt found the intense physical trial invigorating; while his face was "roughened by wind and sun and snow," he felt healthier than he had for months.

Reporters questioned how any pressing matters arising in his absence would be handled. "Oh, things will be all right," he emphatically responded. "I have left Taft sitting on the lid." The vivid phrase instantly inspired cartoons and commentary. One widely reprinted caricature depicted Taft wielding a big stick while seated on the lid of a boiling cauldron. Even his impressive bulk appears scarcely able to stem the "grave and exacting problems of the highest interest"—Panama, Santo Domingo, Venezuela, and Morocco—threatening to burst forth. In another cartoon, an outsized Taft spans three chairs. He is firmly planted on the widest, the "Chair of the President," but his legs extend on either side, occupying both the "Chair of the Sec'y of State" and the "Chair of the Sec'y of War."

In the absence of both President Roosevelt and Secretary of State John Hay, who was on a long cruise attempting to recover his health, official Washington considered Taft "acting President" and "the real head of all executive departments." Little mention was made in the press of the sitting vice president, Charles A. Fairbanks, as the press focused all attention on Taft. Reporters noted "the unusual sight" of "foreign diplomats going to the War Department instead of to the State Department to conduct business." Such a proliferation of responsibilities might well have intimidated a weaker man, an Ohio paper commented, but "William Howard Taft is a very large man, mentally and physically."

Panama soon emerged as the most pressing of the trouble spots threatening to boil over. Taft had been 8,000 miles away in November 1903 when Roosevelt sent U.S. ships to support a Panamanian uprising against Colombia. Recognition was swiftly granted to the newly formed Republic of Panama, and a treaty was negotiated that guaranteed Panamanian independence. In return, the United States was allowed to purchase land to build a canal. "I took the Canal Zone," Roosevelt later boasted.

When word first arrived at the *McClure's* office "that Roosevelt had snitched Panama," Viola Roseboro remembered, "there were gasps," accompanied by "amusement and excitement." Ida Tarbell, however, "was very grave." Tarbell considered the president's seizure of the Canal Zone "a dishonorable outrage," according to Roseboro. Ida "got a line on Teddy that she never lost sight of." While she considered him "a delight and a wonderful person and of great value to the country," Tarbell could not overlook the despotic side of Roosevelt's leadership. "You cannot conceive of Lincoln's trifling with his conscience," she had admonished, "even for the sake of an international canal."

Taft had also been absent during the fierce senatorial debate surrounding the treaty that granted the United States permanent rights to a ten-mile strip in exchange for $10 million and a significant annual payment. Assuming responsibility for overseeing the Panama Commission shortly after his return, Taft proved a quick study. "He had an enormous capacity for mastering official detail," one historian observed, "content that the overall direction came from his superior." Under Taft's command, the commission was authorized to establish official guidelines for the Canal Zone; make all engineering, construction, and sanitary contracts; acquire private lands; tabulate all monies spent; and institute a civil service system. This complex supervisory job was "really enough to occupy the whole time of any average executive," Taft's biographer maintains, yet it was just one among the many tasks that fell to Secretary Taft during these "crowded years."

As construction of the Canal got under way in the fall of 1904, a wave of popular discontent swept through Panama. Panamanians began to suspect that the United States intended to establish "an independent colony" within their country, compromising their own sovereignty and economic well-being. A small band of soldiers threatened to seize power. Endeavoring to defuse tensions, Roosevelt dispatched Taft to the isthmus.

Conscious of the need to project goodwill and friendship, Taft asked Nellie to accompany him. Their arrival in Colón, Nellie recalled, felt like coming home. "The whole atmosphere and surroundings, the people, the language they spoke, the houses and streets, the rank earth odours and the very feel of the air reminded me so strongly of the Philippines as to give me immediately a delightful sense of friendly familiarity with everything and everybody," she later wrote. They remained in Panama for two weeks. During the day, Taft held private conferences with Panamanian officials; in the evenings, he and Nellie socialized at receptions, dinners, and balls. As in the Philippines, Taft charmed the local citizens with his surprising skill on the dance floor. Finally, an agreement was forged that encompassed a range of political and economic issues. Panamanian citizens greeted the published text with delight. As small boys hawking newspapers shouted "Extras" from every street corner, Nellie recalled, "excited groups stood about here and there wreathed in smiles and talking with great animation. Everybody seemed wholly satisfied and wherever we went we were met with cheers and cries of 'Viva!' "

A number of problems regarding the construction of the Canal required attention before Roosevelt returned from his hunting trip. A serious dispute had arisen between John Wallace, the chief engineer, and William Gorgas, the chief sanitary officer. Wallace remained highly skeptical of his colleague's work to contain the spread of mosquitoes on the theory that the insect transmitted yellow fever. Castigating Gorgas's ideas as merely "experimental," Wallace failed to carry out safety protocols that recommended mosquito-proof screens in all government offices. When a virulent outbreak of yellow fever sent a majority of American workers retreating back to the States, Gorgas demanded greater independent authority from both Wallace and the commission. "Here again I must trust your judgment," Roosevelt wrote to Taft from Glenwood Springs, Colorado. Taft wisely threw his support to Gorgas and eventually called for Wallace to resign.

With equal insight and acumen, Taft resolved conflicts in Santo Domingo that threatened U.S. interests in Morocco and Venezuela. "You are handling everything just right," Roosevelt praised him on April 8. Two weeks later, Roosevelt again assured Taft he was "keeping the lid on in great shape!" Each letter expressed unconditional confidence and support: "You are on the ground," he reiterated, "you see the needs of the situation, and I shall back up whatever you do." Invariably, Roosevelt's letters reflect profound respect and gratitude for his friend's service. "I wish you knew Taft, whom I have had acting as Secretary of State as well as Secretary of War in Hay's absence," he told George Trevelyan. "To strength and courage, clear insight, and practical common sense, he adds a very noble and disinterested character. I know you would like him. He helps me in every way more than I can say." And to John Hay, Roosevelt confided: "Taft, by the way, is doing excellently, as I knew he would, and is the greatest comfort to me."

ROOSEVELT FINALLY RETURNED TO WASHINGTON on May 12; six weeks later, Taft left for a journey of his own—a three-month cruise to the Philippines and the Far East. Recalling his pledge that the Filipino people would always remain first in his heart, Taft had been troubled by reports from Dr. Pardo de Tavera, one of the three Filipino members of the Philippine Commission. When Taft had departed two years earlier, Tavera wrote, "everything was in good order and every Filipino was confident in the future," but the commission had since lost its "Pole star"—the policy of working together with the Filipino people to shape their destiny. Under Luke Wright, Taft's successor, "discontent [was] general, resentment profound and well-founded." Tavera implored Taft to return to the islands for a visit. The Filipino people regarded the former governor general as "the only man who can and will reestablish justice and liberty here."

Convinced that he must return to assess the situation in person, Taft assembled a party of eighty people to accompany him, including seven senators, twenty-three congressman, and a dozen journalists. His guest list was inclusive and bipartisan, embracing Democrats and Republicans, pro–tariff reduction men and "standpatters," strong supporters of the administration's policy and fierce opponents alike. He hoped that firsthand experience of the islands' rich potential and personal encounters with the Filipino people would beget a more supportive attitude toward legislation to reduce tariffs, build railroads, and speed agricultural development. "I doubt if so formidable a Congressional representation ever went so far," he proudly noted.

Not long after Taft's party embarked for Southeast Asia, Secretary of State John Hay lost his long battle with illness. "Just heard sad news," Taft cabled Roosevelt, wondering if he should postpone his journey and return to Washington. "If it were not that I feel so keenly the great importance of having you in the Philippines," Roosevelt replied, "I should have been tempted to keep you over here, for I shall miss you greatly." He informed Taft that he would likely ask Elihu Root to take Hay's place. Although he confided to Lodge that he "hesitated a little between Root and Taft," noting that Taft was "very close" to him, the prospect of having both men by his side left "no room for doubt." Taft dispelled any qualms Roosevelt might have felt, urging the president to appoint Root to the premier post. "My dear fellow," Roosevelt replied, "I could say nothing higher of you than that it was just exactly characteristic of you, I do not believe that you will ever quite understand what strength and comfort and help you are to me."

Under the sway of Taft's amicable leadership, everyone who had joined the expedition got along surprisingly well. "I do not think that I have ever known any one with the equanimity, amiability, and kindliness of Mr. Taft," Alice Roosevelt reported. "During all that summer, I never once saw him really cross or upset. He was always beaming, genial, and friendly, through all his official duties, and the task of keeping harmony among his varied and somewhat temperamental army of trippers." In the evenings, guests enjoyed formal dances, sleight-of-hand performances, mock trials, and pillow fights. "The party has been a very jolly one," Taft related to Roosevelt, "and Democrats and Republicans have joined alike in praising the fine weather and really delightful voyage."

Friends and family had warned Taft that dealing with Alice—or "Princess Alice," as she had been dubbed by the press—would prove challenging; despite such admonitions, he found her unspoiled and delightfully forthright. "She is quite amenable to suggestion and I have seen nothing about the girl to indicate conceit or a swelled head," he told Nellie, who had elected to spend "a quiet summer in England" with the children following their hectic year. At times, she could be "oblivious to the comforts of other people," he explained, but considering "what she has gone through and who she is," the young woman managed to make herself extremely popular with the entire party. Nevertheless, he remained troubled by Alice's flamboyant flirtation with Nicholas Longworth, a worldly thirty-five-year-old congressman from Cincinnati with a reputation for numerous dalliances.

Taft was aware that Alice and Nick had been seeing one another before the cruise. He had heard stories about the "fast set" to which they belonged. "She seems to be so much taken up with Nick," he reported to Nellie, that she "pays little attention to anybody else." They took meals together, sat side by side on deck, and partnered on the dance floor, where Alice reportedly "looked almost unreal in her clinging gown, which matched the sea. As she glided through the dance, her long, spangled scarf wound itself around her, serpent like." Noting that the young couple appeared to revel in conversations "usually confined to husband and wife," Taft finally confronted Alice. "I think

I ought to know if you are engaged to Nick," he suggested in a gently paternal manner. Alice cryptically replied: "More or less, Mr. Secretary, more or less."

The arrival of the Taft party in Manila on August 4 inspired widespread celebration. Guns boomed and thousands filled the streets as the official delegation progressed to the Malacañan Palace for the welcoming ceremony. From the outset, Taft was determined to remedy the growing animosity between the Filipino people and the current insular government. The policy of the Roosevelt administration, he reiterated at every stop, was "the Philippines for the Filipinos. If the American officials were not in sympathy with this policy," he assured the islanders, "they would be recalled." While he continued to believe the Filipinos needed to prepare for independence, Taft officially announced that the long-anticipated popular assembly would be established in April 1907. The Filipino people, the *New York Tribune* reported, greeted this definitive proclamation with great enthusiasm.

Informed that the colonial administration considered Filipino families not "of sufficient rank to entertain Senators and Congressmen," Taft decided that he and Alice would move immediately from the palace to the home of a Filipino member of the commission, Benito Legarda. "I knew no way, but the direct way," he explained, "to show that we had no sympathy with the apparent desire to exclude Filipino hosts from those who should entertain the party." At a "very handsome ball" hosted by the Legardas, Taft and Alice delighted the Filipinos by joining in the native rigadon square dance. Taft had taken care to practice the complex steps with Alice and several other young ladies during the long ocean voyage. A number of similar receptions in the homes of local citizens went "a long way in cementing friendships."

Lodging with the Legardas also allowed Taft to meet with scores of disaffected Filipinos who would never have visited him at the palace with Governor General Wright present. "All day long," one observer recorded, "the great hall was occupied, the men sitting by the open windows disposing of one long cigar after another." Hearing their grievances, Taft reluctantly concluded that the majority of the commission—including the governor general—were "utterly lacking in the proper spirit" toward the native population. "They seem to think it does not make much difference whether they have the support of the Filipinos or not," he lamented. "To me it makes every difference in the success of the government." Indeed, he wrote to Nellie, many Filipinos insisted that if only the Tafts returned to Manila, they would soon "restore the old condition of things." The current situation was dispiriting, for it necessitated the removal of the governor general and possibly two other commission members, whom he considered friends.

Taft and his entourage "made the round" of the archipelago, traveling by small boats, bamboo rafts, carriages, and on horseback. They surveyed agricultural conditions where sugar, hemp, and rice were grown, meeting with tradesmen, government officials, educators, manufacturers, and farmers. Correspondents who accompanied the party noted "a happy sea change" in the attitudes of several protectionist congressmen, particularly Sereno Payne, chairman of the House and Ways Committee, and General Charles Grosvenor of Ohio. "It is already apparent," the *Tribune* editorialized, "that Sec. Taft's plan of enlarging the political and mental horizons of leading men of both parties as respects Philippine questions is working out admirably." Several legislators personally expressed their amazement and gratitude to Taft. "It was a great trip and cannot be otherwise than helpful to the Government," one member told him. "I never realized until this journey the magnitude of the Philippine problem, nor did I realize your devotion to the cause. I have heard a great many speeches made in my time, but never heard a series of better ones than were made by you while touring the islands. It is a miracle that so large a party was so harmonious, and the credit is due to your example."

Although Taft's primary mission was to the Philippines, the expedition also made stops in China and Japan, where Taft secretly met with Japan's prime minister, Taro Katsura. Undisclosed for the next twenty years, this meeting would have lasting consequences for the region. Long-standing hostilities between Russia and Japan had flared into war over competing territorial interests in Korea and China. Roosevelt had closely followed the evolution of this conflict, hoping he might mediate between the two warring powers. From the start, he had sympathized with Japan's desire to oversee affairs in Korea, to keep a strong hold on Port Arthur, and to return Manchuria to China. Still, he recognized that mounting Japanese victories would expand the imperial government's demands, upsetting the balance of power in the Far East. He was delighted, therefore, when Taft contacted him in late April to affirm that the Japanese were interested in having the U.S. president facilitate peace talks. In fact, Roosevelt was so enthusiastic that he curtailed his hunting expedition by a week to commence dialogue with the Japanese and Russian ministers.

Concealing the fact that the Japanese had initiated the process, Roosevelt sent identical letters to both sides. He requested that they "open direct negotiations for peace," offering his services "in arranging preliminaries as to time and place of meeting." When both the belligerents agreed, Roosevelt received accolades: "It is recognized all the world over as another triumph of Roosevelt the man," the *New York Tribune* editorialized. "It was America alone that assumed the responsibility. It is to America alone that the world will give the credit."

As preparations for a peace conference in Portsmouth, New Hampshire, began, Taft sailed into Yokohama, where his party received "a demonstrative welcome." Fireworks heralded the arrival of the ship, and thousands of citizens lined gaily decorated streets. From the harbor city, Taft journeyed to Tokyo for his confidential talk with Count Katsura. Taft assured Katsura that while he did not officially speak for the president, he was certain of Roosevelt's position. Katsura made it clear that "Korea being the direct cause of our war with Russia," it was "of absolute importance" that after the war, Japan should control Korea "to the extent of requiring that Korea enter into no foreign treaties without the consent of Japan." In return, Taft sought assurance that Japan did "not harbor any aggressive designs whatever on the Philippines."

Having reached agreement on both points, Taft informed Katsura that without the U.S. Senate's consent, the president could not enter into a formal alliance or even "a confidential informal agreement." Nevertheless, he expressed certainty that the two countries were in such fundamental accord on the issues discussed that the conversation could be treated "as if" a treaty had been signed. Taft promptly telegraphed a memo of the entire exchange to the president. "If I have spoken too freely or inaccurately or unwittingly," he concluded, "I know you can or will correct it." Roosevelt immediately dismissed his concerns, replying, "Your conversation with Count Katsura absolutely correct in every respect. Wish you would state to Katsura that I confirm every word you have said."

On August 5, accompanied by the sound of booming guns, the peace envoys from Russia and Japan met with the president aboard the presidential yacht *Mayflower*, anchored in Oyster Bay. After a buffet lunch served with cold white wine, the envoys proceeded to the U.S. Naval Base at Portsmouth. In the days that followed, agreements on Korea, Port Arthur, and Manchuria were reached with relative ease. Japan's insistence on some form of compensation from Russia threatened to torpedo the conference. The Russian envoys took the position that Russia had neither been conquered nor could be considered "prostrate in the enemy's hands." Therefore, they argued, Japan had no right to extract an "indemnity." Increasingly frustrated with mediating the dispute, Roosevelt confided to Kermit, "I am having my hair turned gray by dealing with the Russian and Japanese negotiators." In the end, the president persuaded the Japanese that prolonging the war simply to secure money would lose international support. A peace treaty was finally signed on

September 5, 1905, earning Roosevelt praise at home and abroad, as well as the Nobel Peace Prize.

⁓ ⁓

DESPITE SUCH INTERNATIONAL TRIUMPHS, PRESSING and complex domestic issues threatened the solidarity of the Republican Party. Once again, Taft had barely returned when he was recruited to suture the wound. Taft's three-month odyssey ended at 3:27 p.m. on October 2, 1905, when he stepped onto the platform at Union Station, appearing "hearty and vigorous" as he greeted colleagues with a big smile and a warm handshake. That evening, he dined with the president and first lady, along with Root, Garfield, and a few family friends. "We had a most interesting dinner," Garfield told his wife. "Mr. Taft is full of interesting accounts of the Orient."

Taft had little time to reacquaint himself with affairs in his department before he was called upon to deal with a troubling situation in Ohio. Factional disputes there threatened the reelection of Republican governor Myron Herrick. Earlier that summer, Lincoln Steffens had published his electrifying report contrasting Democrat Tom Johnson's principled governance of Cleveland with the venal mismanagement of Cincinnati's Republican boss Tom Cox. The piece revealed how Cox had become a millionaire twice over through corrupt alliances with traction companies, banks, and railroads. "The city is all one great graft," Steffens charged. "The reign of Cox is a reign of fear."

The exposé had created a sensation in Ohio. Although Cox claimed it was "full of falsehoods," the tale sparked public outrage and engendered bitter conflict within the Republican Party. Those beholden to the old machines dominated by corporations and political bosses inevitably opposed the progressive drive toward popular rule and governmental regulation. The growing split within the Republicans opened the door to Democrats, who successfully likened Governor Herrick's management of the state to Cox's grip on the city. In fact, they intimated that the governor had become "subservient" to Cox and his crowd, a participant in the systemic graft. "The stampede from Herrick is growing like a wild fire," one Ohio paper reported, "and so consuming is the anti-Cox, anti-bossism flame, that the disaffected thousands say they will vote the democratic ticket from top to bottom this year."

Believing that Ohio's gubernatorial race could influence the fortunes of the entire Republican Party, Roosevelt dispatched Taft to deliver a speech on Herrick's behalf. When Steffens learned of this step, he wrote an impassioned letter to the president, imploring him not to help the governor. "Governor Herrick is not a bad man," conceded Steffens, "he is simply weak. He is one of those men who can do dishonest things honestly." State politics could not be separated from Cincinnati's municipal situation, he insisted, arguing that the growing effort to vanquish Cox—whose candidates were on local ballots that accompanied the gubernatorial election—would be thwarted by the president's push to keep Republicans "in line" behind Herrick.

Caught in this hazardous political knot, Taft devised what newspapers called "a most adroit and ingenuous" speech. Voicing support for Herrick, whom he believed to be a decent man, he leveled a fierce barrage of criticism at the Cox regime. Public condemnation of Cox was "not pleasant" for Taft, particularly given that his brother Charley owned and edited the *Cincinnati-Times*, "the official organ" of the Cox regime. "Any pain you feel at the expressed difference of opinion between us finds a corresponding deep regret in my heart," Taft told Charley on the eve of his speech, "for I love you Charley as I love no one except my wife and children." Nevertheless, he felt bound to declare his opposition to Cox and his corrupt lieutenants.

Delivered before an overflowing audience in Akron, Ohio, the speech was termed "the most severe rebuke" ever suffered by the powerful boss. Accustomed to criticism leveled by his Democratic opponents and the progressive press, Cox now faced censure "from so prominent a Republican, a member of the president's cabinet." In straightforward language, Taft likened "Cox and Coxism" to "a curse" upon the people of Hamilton County, "a local despotism" designed for the financial benefit of the boss, his cronies, and the big corporations. He described the political machine's "distressing effect" on aspiring young Republicans, who were forced to submit "to the tyranny of the boss" or abandon public service altogether. If he were to vote in the upcoming race, Taft acknowledged, he would "vote against the municipal ticket nominated by the Republican organization."

Despite his condemnation, Taft "made clear the difference between Herrick—the clean-living, trusted and honored businessman and efficient executive of the State—and the foul boss of Cincinnati." While he refused to endorse the Republican ticket in Hamilton County, Taft declared that he would happily vote for Governor Herrick and hoped others would do the same. If he believed his visit to Ohio would perpetuate the Cox machine, Taft assured his listeners, he would never have come. But it would be unfair to abandon "a governor who has done well by his State and his party."

Although Taft had sought to rally support for Herrick, newspapers focused on his "scathing denunciation" of Cox, which fell upon the city and state "like the explosion of a bomb." Excerpts from the speech were carried in more than six hundred papers. Dozens of editorials and letters commended

Taft for his honesty and courage. "We had about come to the conclusion that there wasn't a man in Ohio who dared call his soul his own without the permission of George Cox," one Ohio citizen wrote. "You are the only man who can lead this city out of the slough of despond," another remarked. "You have done more good for your own town by that speech than you have any idea of," Taft's close friend Howard Hollister wrote. "The weakness and cowardice of a great many of our principal men have been a chief trouble here, and now they are encouraged to come out and talk and act like men. I hear it everywhere."

The elections that fall brought a crushing defeat for the Cox machine. But Taft's hope that voters would split their tickets, voting Democratic in the local election and Republican in the gubernatorial race, proved vain: John Pattison, the Democratic candidate for the governorship, defeated Myron Herrick by a wide margin. "Do not concern yourself about the stories that are afloat that you caused my defeat," Herrick graciously told Taft. "I know my friends and know you to be one whom I love and respect."

Buoyed by the demise of the Cox machine, young Republicans in Cincinnati formed a new Republican Club with a progressive agenda. Led by Howard Hollister, they called on members to stand unequivocally against bossism and machine politics and advocate a platform that included national regulation of railroads and tariff revision. At Hollister's request, both Taft and Roosevelt accepted honorary memberships in the "Roosevelt Republican Club." Only such clear dissociation from corrupt and self-serving elements of the Republican Party, Hollister argued, could "disabuse the public mind of the growing feeling of domination of the party by the corporations and money making commercial politicians."

⌒ ⌒

As THEODORE ROOSEVELT HAD SURMISED, the struggle against corruption and consolidation in Ohio reflected a burgeoning movement across the country. And the president was acutely aware of the difficult balance he would have to strike in order to realign his party without compromising the nation's prosperity. In the winter of 1905, a dramatic "Oil War" in the state of Kansas illuminated this intensifying conflict, captivating the interest of the entire country. "Kansas is in the clutches of the Standard Oil Company," the *Hutchinson News* reported, "and is howling for relief."

A year earlier, spectacular deposits that surpassed the total volume of the Pennsylvania oil fields had been discovered in Kansas and the Indian Territory in Oklahoma. "On the instant," Ida Tarbell recalled, "Kansas went oil-mad, practically every farmer in the state dreamed of flowing wells." The Standard

Oil Company immediately began furnishing tanks, building refineries, and constructing pipelines. Independent producers were placated with the promise that they would receive market price for their oil. Only when Standard had a total lock on refining and transportation, William Allen White explained, did the company "put on the screws." A barrel of oil that had yielded a dollar and eighteen cents in 1904 had dropped to thirty-seven cents a year later. With control of both in-state refineries and all the pipelines, Standard Oil had effectively become "the only transporter and buyer" of the region's crude oil, with power to set whatever price it chose.

Popular anger fueled the successful gubernatorial campaign of Kansas Republican Edward Hoch, who challenged the Republican machine with a platform calling for construction of "a first-class" state refinery that would force Standard "to be reasonable." In his inaugural address, Hoch proposed a series of additional measures to regulate the oil trade, including one to make pipelines common carriers, rendering them subject to the same state supervision as railroads. When the upper house passed the bill for the state refinery, Standard retaliated by boycotting Kansas oil entirely, leaving the producers "without a market" and throwing "a large number of men out of work." Standard's despotic tactics backfired when public recognition that the giant company "was *punishing* Kansas" generated such outrage that the refinery bill sailed through the lower chamber. Borne on a wave of defiance, the legislation even garnered support from conservatives, who felt the measure smacked of socialism. "Scare Kansas! Well, we'll see about that!"

At the White House, telegrams poured in, urging the president to protect the state "from oppression of the Standard Oil trust." Congressman Philip Campbell of southeast Kansas introduced a resolution requesting an investigation into "the unusually large margin" between the price of Kansas crude oil and the market price of refined products. It was "hardly a secret," one Kansas newspaper suggested, that the situation in Kansas presented President Roosevelt with the opening he was seeking to move against "the mother of all trusts." Indeed, some observers speculated that the resolution was instigated by the administration.

After discussing the situation with the Kansas representative, Roosevelt in February 1905 announced that he had directed Bureau of Corporations director James Garfield to undertake "a rigid and comprehensive review" of Standard Oil's methods of operation, "especially in the Kansas field." Garfield planned to travel to Kansas the following month to oversee a team of fifty special agents, ensuring a thorough investigation of the trust's practices. The president clearly understood, Campbell maintained, that this was the "most important investigation of the kind which has been undertaken." Although passage of the House resolution brought Standard's boycott in Kansas to an end, the fundamental problem of monopoly lingered.

Two days after the president's announcement, Ida Tarbell wrote to John Phillips: "What would you think of an article on Kansas & the Standard Oil Company?" Having spent nearly four years studying Standard Oil, Tarbell remained vitally interested in the company's activities. Her twenty-four-part magazine series had been republished as a two-volume book the previous November to great acclaim. One critic predicted it would "rank as one of the most complete and authoritative contributions to economic history written in the last quarter century." Miss Tarbell's study, another wrote, "is to the present time the most remarkable book of its kind ever written in this country." The oil war in Kansas promised to furnish a new and vital postscript.

When she wrote her proposal, Tarbell had returned home to Titusville to be with her father, who was suffering from stomach cancer. His death on March 1 had suddenly "darkened" her world, for he had "built himself into every crook and cranny" of her childhood home—indeed, of the entire town. Her family at the magazine did their best to console her. "I have thought a great deal of you in your sorrow," S. S. McClure wrote from Switzerland when the news reached him. "There are times when your face expresses a singular pathos & sense of suffering & I know how sad & heartbroken you have been." He hoped she found some solace in the fact that her father had seen "with his own eyes" how she had used her substantial gifts to dignify the Tarbell name.

Not long after the funeral, Ida left for Kansas, exhibiting what McClure termed her "pathetic & characteristic" impulse relentlessly to immerse herself in work. Though she set out "with a heavy heart," the monthlong journey proved to be "as exciting" as any she had undertaken. Independent oilmen hailed her arrival as the coming of "a prophet," certain that she would reveal Standard's "unfair and illegal methods" in Kansas to "all the world." Local journalists trailed her throughout the state, taking her picture and printing her remarks. Embarrassed by her celebrity, she told Albert Boyden she hoped "to Heaven . . . all the foolishness" published about her would not be taken seriously in the office. "Believe nothing," she entreated them, "until I have a hearing!"

Straightaway, Tarbell called on the governor. Initially skeptical about his plan for a state refinery, she came away convinced that the project would be "a good thing," and serve "as a measuring stick" for the public to determine the real costs of refining. In the long run, however, Standard's control over oil transport had to be addressed. "Build your own pipe line," she urged the oil producers; "build it to the seas." In addition, she recommended that they pressure Congress to pass a law "making all pipelines common carriers," subject to regulations that would ensure fair play.

Soon afterward, Tarbell joined Governor Hoch and Congressman Campbell at "the biggest mass meeting of oil producers ever known." Diffident when asked to speak before 3,000 people, she composed a letter to be delivered at the convention. She challenged Kansas "to play the oil game as well as the Standard Company plays it," but "with due regards for the rights of men, something the Standard has never done."

Next, Tarbell embarked on a ten-day field trip through the countryside to gauge for herself the extent of the new oil fields. Traveling by a two-horse open carriage over primitive roads, she encountered the worst dust storm in many years. Her driver, bellowing to be heard over the rising wind, roared: "Jehoshaphat! Wrap your head up." Even after the storm passed, Ida was unable to bathe for ten days because dust had seeped into the water supply, producing "a muddy liquid quite impossible to drink and hopeless for cleansing." Undeterred, she continued her mission. "The wonder is that discomfort doesn't count out here," she explained to John Phillips. All hardships were eclipsed by the contagious excitement of the farmers, by the promise that every little town would become "a world's center," every well "a gusher." One weekend, Tarbell crossed the Oklahoma border to see the oil fields in the Indian Territory. Everywhere she went, crowds gathered, bands serenaded her, and people gave her flowers and candy. In the "new town of Tulsa," she was "paraded up and down" the main thoroughfare. At the request of a local citizen in Muskogee, she "submitted to five sittings for her picture." From early morning until midnight, she was called upon to make little speeches.

Needful of respite, Tarbell spent a leisurely weekend in Emporia with William and Mary White. She had taken the "city-shy" boy "by the hand" when he first ventured into New York and had always appreciated "his affection and loyalty for his state." She was delighted now to see his home, his place of work, and his beloved town. In Emporia, Tarbell agreed to address a group of students at a chapel. "The new thing which Kansas has put in the fight against the evils of Standard monopoly," she told them, "is an ethical question. Here people say they oppose Standard's methods because they are wrong." Kansas was not merely motivated by the monopoly's impact on business— "Standard had never met with this spirit in any of its previous fights." After her departure, White wrote an editorial echoing her conviction that the problem with Standard Oil was "as much a moral issue as it is a financial one." The machinations Standard employed—bribing legislatures, tampering with juries, purchasing judges—constituted "the real danger to the country." Yet, he concluded, "because it is a corporation and has neither soul nor body," Standard had largely managed "to escape the vengeance which the law . . . would surely have visited upon natural persons guilty of similar practices."

As Tarbell passed through Kansas City on her way to New York, she stopped for a brief visit to express her gratitude and admiration for the state's spirit. She found that spirit so compelling that she extended her visit. "I stayed and stayed, and even now I am reluctant to return to the east," she later explained, describing how the nature of this fight set it apart: "The Kansans are not fighting now for the money they can make. They are not fighting because their oil doesn't market well. They're fighting because a monopoly, a trust, has sought to come into their state and dictate to them where their products shall go and what shall be paid for their products. It's the fight for justice and right."

In a two-part article, Tarbell argued that "if one wants a neat demonstration, complete to the last detail, that the Standard Oil Company is to-day, as always, 'a conspiracy in restraint of trade,' he should go to Kansas"; there, the company continued to perpetuate "exactly what it did" three decades earlier in Pennsylvania—crushing independents, fixing prices, operating pipelines as private fiefdoms, and colluding with railroads. Her revelations produced a growing demand for official action. If her charges proved accurate, the *Wall Street Journal* commented, "we take it that Commissioner Garfield will be honest enough to report the fact, and if the fact is reported, we believe that the administration is courageous enough to prosecute even the Standard Oil Company."

Early on, Garfield had decided to take on the daunting task of expanding the scope of his investigation beyond Kansas, to encompass Standard's methods of operation nationwide. He traveled to "nearly all of the great fields" and talked with hundreds of producers, refiners, and railroadmen. Special agents were dispatched throughout the United States and even to Europe. Garfield's wife, Helen, was anxious about the investigation. "Do read Ida Tarbell's McClure article," she urged her husband. "It is very cleverly written—I feel that the man and those in the ring will lie to you just as she says they have lied all along." She needn't have worried; not only had Garfield read the piece, he had borrowed Tarbell's collection of relevant sources and documentary evidence. "I shall try to find the truth," he reassured his wife.

Garfield's report was published in two parts. The first concluded that Standard Oil had continued to receive the same "unjust and illegal" preferences from the railroads outlined in Tarbell's exhaustive series and that these rebates, bribes, and kickbacks had facilitated development of the trust's extensive pipeline system. The second outlined the monopolistic position of Standard Oil in the petroleum industry. Roosevelt transmitted the first report to the Congress with a special message: "All the power of the government will be directed toward prosecuting the Rockefeller trust." Commentators agreed that the report, endorsed by the president, constituted "the most severe arraignment of a corporation" ever issued from such "a high official source."

"Garfield's Report Causes Sensation," blasted the *Laredo* (Texas) *Times*. "Makes Almost as Good Reading as Ida Tarbell's Magazine Articles." Indeed, public commentary invariably referenced Tarbell's earlier work. "All that Ida Tarbell told in McClure's Magazine is being reaffirmed," one newspaper remarked; another termed the report "a vindication" of her methods, validated now by the official seal. If the commissioner "can prove all he says," Tarbell herself told a reporter, "he has rendered one of the most important public services in the history of the country."

The Justice Department prepared two lines of attack corresponding to Garfield's report: the first alleged illegal rebates under the Elkins Act of 1903; the second charged "conspiracy in restraint of trade" based on violation of the Sherman Anti-Trust Act. "If my report affords the basis for making these prosecutions successful I shall be mightily pleased," Garfield wrote to Helen. While "conspiracy and monopoly" were difficult to prove, the rebate case promised to be relatively straightforward.

Judge Kenesaw Mountain Landis, a colorful jurist who would later become the first commissioner of baseball, presided over the first case, in which the government charged Standard of Indiana with receiving illegal rebates from the Chicago & Alton Railroad. On the day the ruling was handed down, hundreds of would-be spectators were denied entrance to the overcrowded courtroom. The ruling, which found Standard guilty of accepting rebates on 1,462 carloads of oil, required nearly two hours to read. Landis rendered the judgment with a series of dramatic "sledgehammer blows," drawing applause on two occasions for his condemnation of Standard's corrupting influence on its employees and the nation as a whole. Never before, one court reporter noted, had a judicial sentence featured such inflamed rhetoric.

Although the guilty verdict surprised few, the size of the resulting fine stunned the company and the country. For each of the 1,462 carloads of oil that had enjoyed an illegal rebate, Landis levied the highest possible fine, $20,000, generating a spectacular cumulative total of $29,240,000. Commenting on the hefty charge, Mark Twain drolly remarked that the sum evoked the bride's proverbial astonishment on the morning after her wedding: "I expected it but didn't suppose it would be so big."

Ida Tarbell optimistically declared that the decision presaged the "beginning of the end" for the "giant octopus." For thirty-five years, Rockefeller's corporation had absorbed small fines as the cost of doing business; this "Big Fine," she hoped, would mark the moment when Standard "must either conform" to "fair dealing" or face ruin. Despite such predictions, John D. Rockefeller remained sanguine about his company's prospects. He was on a golf course when word of the judgment reached him. "Judge Landis," he complacently predicted, "will be dead a long time before this fine is paid." Rockefeller's prophecy was confirmed eleven months later when Appeals Court Judge Peter Grosscup overturned the decision on a technicality. "It's nothing more than we expected," the Standard attorneys smugly proclaimed. Roosevelt publicly derided Grosscup's ruling as "a gross miscarriage of justice," further proof of "too much power in the bench."

His momentary frustration aside, Roosevelt remained optimistic about the administration's second and more trenchant line of attack. Six months after the publication of the Garfield Report, the attorney general filed suit in St. Louis, charging Standard Oil of New Jersey and its five dozen subsidiaries with conspiracy to monopolize the oil industry in violation of the Sherman Anti-Trust Act. With this prosecution, the *Des Moines Daily News* observed, "the government [had] finally attacked the very citadel of the Standard Oil Company." Again, reports invariably cited Tarbell's work as both inspiration and template for the government's case. "The petition of the US government for an injunction dissolving the Standard Oil Company of New Jersey reads like a chapter from Ida Tarbell," one commentator asserted. "Every essential charge made by Miss Tarbell in her exposé," another suggested, was "repeated and put into the form of a legal allegation," substantiating her crusade against bribery and spying, sham independent companies, preferential relationships with the railroads, and interlocking boards of directors. In sum, the editorial continued, "the person who more than any other started the government attack on the biggest trust in the world was Ida Tarbell."

This time, the federal court found in the government's favor. Two years later, in a decision that stunned the business world, the Supreme Court affirmed the lower court's ruling. The High Court condemned Standard Oil, "not because it is a trust, but because it has an infamous record," and delivered a warning to "every trust that is tempted to oppress and destroy." A few short weeks later, the Court drove the point home with a similar judgment against the American Tobacco Company. Standard Oil was given six months to dissolve. Once again, Rockefeller was in the middle of a golf game when the news arrived. "Buy Standard Oil," he curtly responded. Even when the corporate "octopus" was divided into thirty-eight parts, Standard Oil of New Jersey preserved its identity, eventually morphing into Exxon; Standard Oil of New York incorporated as Mobil; and Standard Oil of Indiana evolved into Amoco.

While Roosevelt exulted in each of his anti-trust victories, he continued to regard the judicial system as an ineffective arena for controlling giant corporations. For the Department of Justice simultaneously "to carry on more than a limited number" of major suits was "not feasible," and protracted delays meant that "even a favorable decree may mean an empty victory." Regulation, he believed, promised a far better remedy. "The design should be to prevent the abuses incident to the creation of unhealthy and improper combinations," he argued, "instead of waiting until they are in existence and then attempting to destroy them by civil or criminal proceedings."

Unlike anti-trust proceedings, federal regulation required approval in the House and Senate, where conservative Republicans remained a dominant force. After failing to defeat the Bureau of Corporations, this reactionary bloc was determined to prevent Roosevelt from miring the party and the country in policy it considered tantamount to socialism. "The fundamental idea on which our government was founded," conservatives argued, "was that the functions of the federal government were strictly limited, and that all regulations which most closely affect the lives of the people should be left in the hands of state and municipal bodies." Roosevelt's regulatory ideas would "extend the power of the federal government" to an unlimited degree. "Are we to have a national government as highly centralized as that of France or Germany?" opponents ominously queried, warning, "That is what we certainly shall have if we find no way of checking the tendencies in government of which Theodore Roosevelt is so conspicuous and enterprising an exponent."

CHAPTER SEVENTEEN

The American People Reach a Verdict

Roosevelt's looming visage frightens the U.S. Senate in a Feb. 7, 1906,
cartoon from *Puck*, entitled "The Latest Thing in Nightmares."

INCREASINGLY FRUSTRATED IN THE WINTER of 1905 by the
bickering in Washington and the rancor within his own party, Theodore
Roosevelt ranted to a friend that "there are several eminent statesmen at the
other end of Pennsylvania Avenue whom I would gladly lend to the Russian
Government, if they cared to expend them as bodyguards for grand dukes
whenever there was a likelihood of dynamite bombs being exploded!" His
sardonic suggestion targeted the coterie of conservative Republican senators
who opposed his signature plan to regulate the railroads.

The cost to both his party and the country would be immense, he believed,
if "the people at large" perceived "that the Republican party had become unduly subservient to the so-called Wall Street men—to the men of mere wealth,
the plutocracy." It would result in "a dreadful calamity," Roosevelt told a

conservative friend, to see the nation "divided into two parties, one containing the bulk of the property owners and conservative people, the other the bulk of the wageworkers and the less prosperous people generally; each party insisting upon demanding much that was wrong, and each party sullen and angered by real and fancied grievances."

In the struggle to avert this calamitous future, nothing was more essential, Roosevelt believed, than railroad regulation. His first address to Congress following his election victory had indicated his belief in the primacy of the issue. "Above all else," he declared, "we must strive to keep the highways of commerce open to all on equal terms." The most critical piece of legislation the country needed was an act to give the Interstate Commerce Commission the power to regulate railroad rates that gave an "unreasonable" advantage to the trusts.

As the battle lines formed that winter, S. S. McClure decided that the magazine's next series would concentrate on the railroads. His staff had already concluded that many of the country's gravest problems, from state and municipal corruption to the ascendancy of the trusts, could be traced to the railroads. Whereas earlier modes of transportation (the wagon roads and waterways) had been available to all on an equal basis, a small circle of private owners now controlled the transportation network essential to all commerce. This exclusive circle could effectively determine the fortunes of cities, towns, and companies, the futures of entire industries. Both the Grangers and the Populists had called for governmental regulation of the railroads, but despite the passage of the 1903 Elkins Act, the industry had remained essentially unregulated.

Ida Tarbell's study of Standard Oil had convinced her that Rockefeller had employed discriminatory freight rates as the primary instrument in his campaign to crush independent competitors. "Until the transportation problem is settled and settled right," she warned, "the monopolistic trust will be with us, a leech on our pockets, a barrier to our free effort." Steffens, too, had discovered that in every city and state he had explored, "the story was always the same": corruption "came from the top"—from the men who owned streetcar lines in the cities and railroads in the states. New Jersey's dominant railroad had "seized the government," and the Southern Pacific Railroad had become "the actual sovereign" of California. Like his colleagues, Baker's own countrywide investigations had persuaded him that "the Railroad problem is pretty nearly the basic problem of our life: and we know little or nothing about it!"

Having completed his labor series, and "eager for more dragons to slay," Ray Baker was thrilled to be chosen for the assignment. By supplying "the real facts," the nation's reporters could shape that essential discussion. The journalist, he passionately believed, is the "true servant of democracy." This new project on the railroads, he told his father, would be "far more important than anything [he had] ever done." Baker started by examining everything he could gather on the subject—pamphlets, congressional reports, local investigations, scholarly studies, and court testimonies. He read accounts of La Follette's titanic fight against the railroads in Wisconsin and sought guidance from experts on the railroad industry.

Upon learning that Baker had begun his investigation, Roosevelt invited him to Washington. Baker promptly replied that he hoped to take up the railroad problem "in some big, important, and impressive way." On January 28, 1905, Baker joined the president for a "simple and most informal" family lunch, after which the two men engaged in a private conversation. By this time, Baker had gained "a pretty good grip on the railway problem" and shared with the president a detailed outline of his planned series. Central was the argument that railroads were public highways that must be accessible to all on fair and equal terms. They should no longer enjoy peculiar charter rights from the government—including the right of eminent domain and the right to charge tolls.

For his part, Roosevelt was confident he could steer a bill through the House, where the members felt the direct pressure of growing agitation against the railroads. "His chief trouble," he told Baker, would be the Senate, where members were sent by the state legislatures and many owed their seats to corporate interests. His best chance lay in mobilizing the public so that the Senate could no longer refuse to act. Nevertheless, he urged the reporter to be fair; an analysis couched in demagogic rhetoric would not be trusted. "My job is not to assess blame on anyone," Baker countered. "I am trying to get at the facts and report them as truthfully as I can."

"It was altogether the most interesting meeting & talk with him that I ever had," Baker told his father. "I think he likes to get these things first hand." The president had asked Baker "to consult" with him often during the course of his research, promising to enable the magazine's effort to clarify the complex problem for the general public. "Facilities have been given me here as never before," Baker proudly noted, "the Inter State Commerce people even offering me a desk & stenographer, with full admission to all their published documents & letters. It certainly shows how . . . a greater care for truth & fairness, which I have tried to attain in my articles, gets hold of people."

Two days after meeting with Baker, Roosevelt began his own campaign for railroad regulation with a major speech before the Union League Club in Philadelphia. "Neither this people nor any other free people," he declared, "will permanently tolerate the use of the vast power conferred by vast wealth, and especially by wealth in its corporate form, without lodging somewhere in the government the still higher power of seeing that this power, in addition to being used in the interest of the individual or individuals possessing it, is also used for and not against the interests of the people as a whole." Calling again for a public tribunal with "power over rates," he argued once more that only the national government could "keep the great highways of commerce open alike to all on reasonable and equitable terms."

The next day, Roosevelt met with Baker for another luncheon discussion. He admonished the journalist once again to beware of demagogues, emphasizing that the web of corruption linking politicians and corporations was "due quite as much to the blackmailing demands of legislators as to the offered bribes of businessmen." That evening, Baker wrote a long passage in his notebook enumerating the obstacles to passing desperately needed railroad regulation. While it was certainly possible that some legislators were paid by corporations to oppose unwanted bills, the congressional failure to address the disease was more complex. In recent years, the country had witnessed "an enormous industrial development," marked by the growth of "railroads, trusts & inventions." Although these unprecedented changes required new thinking about the relationship of business and government, Baker reasoned, a "legislative lag" clearly existed. Laws generated fifty years earlier, rooted in laissez-faire philosophy, remained on the books. "Once let an idea really penetrate the mind of a people," as this ethic of non-interference in private enterprise had done, and it would require a massive educational effort to remove it. If he and his fellow journalists could enable the public to re-envision the role of government, Baker noted, there would be "no further difficulty in regulating the trusts & the railroads."

Yet encouraging a new way of thinking demanded time and hard work, and Baker was still in the early phase of his research when Congress took up the question of railroad regulation during its short session in the winter of 1905. An administration-backed bill granting the ICC power to regulate railroad rates passed the House, but the Senate deliberately scheduled its hearings after Congress had adjourned on March 3, ending any chance for the legislation to pass. Assessing his defeat, Roosevelt concluded that his influence had been stunted: once he relinquished the chance to run for a third term, the opposition concluded he "need not be regarded as a factor hereafter." Still, he believed that if the necessity for regulation could be "clearly drawn" in the months ahead, the Senate would eventually bow to public feeling.

Sentiment did indeed begin to shift, but not in the direction Roosevelt desired. Troubled by the passage of the regulatory bill in the House, the railroads launched a sweeping propaganda campaign to turn the country against regulation. Lengthy hearings before the Senate Interstate Commerce Committee provided the opening salvo. Organized by senators sympathetic to the railroads, the six-week proceeding featured a witness list stacked to thwart regulatory efforts. Over two thirds of the witnesses, one reporter from Utah noted, "were either friendly toward or in fear of the railroads and testified accordingly." One after another, railroad executives argued that Roosevelt's bill was misguided at best and unconstitutional at worst. They pointed out "how delicate and difficult a task it was to adjust a freight-rate, how it required long practical experience," intimating that disaster would follow if the government "should meddle" in the complex business. "Any tinkering with rates would raise Cain with stocks," one railway head warned. "It would mean a general unsettling of affairs."

Forced to travel to Washington at their own expense, the few witnesses who spoke in favor of regulation were mocked and labeled as agitators. Railroad king James J. Hill likened the commotion over regulation to "an attack of 'pink-eye' or the grippe," which would eventually run its course. Members of the Senate committee did nothing to stop such belittling attacks. Congressmen who had voted for Roosevelt's bill in the House were blacklisted from receiving any further free passes. Not surprisingly, newspapermen attending the hearings were influenced by the strength of the opposition, and the national coverage soon turned sharply negative. A prominent Republican senator claimed that the president was looking for a way out, that he had finally realized his ill-considered foray into this arena might "throw the country into a panic."

To counter rumors that he had ceded the possibility of reform, Roosevelt dispatched Taft to a conference of three hundred railway executives meeting at the Willard Hotel. Vehemently reinforcing the administration's commitment to regulation, Taft spoke of the certain advent of railway rate legislation, warning that "if the railway men of the country were wise they would aid and not hinder it." The industry must recognize, he insisted, "that railroads are a public institution—an institution which must be regulated by law. You cannot run the railroads as you would run a private business. You must respond to the public demand."

Taft's words were greeted with "absolute silence," until Stuyvesant Fish, president of the Railway Congress, jumped to his feet and exhaustively countered Taft's arguments. The laws already on the books were sufficient to deal with any difficulties, he declared, arguing that the action proposed would cause more harm than good. When he took his seat amid great applause, Taft respectfully asked: "May I have fifteen minutes to reply?" His rebuttal rendered an even more forceful defense of the necessity for a tribunal with powers to revise unfair rates. Taft's words, "driven directly into the ears of the men who are most determined that there shall be no railroad legislation," created "a sensation." Observers understood that the secretary's address "had been carefully prepared, and prepared with the intention of causing exactly the impression that was caused."

The following day, Roosevelt endorsed Taft's speech by flatly stating that his own stance on the subject of the railroads "could not have been better expressed." Railroad magnates needed to understand that it was "essential, in the interests of the public," that the government assume a regulatory power over them. Furthermore, he vowed that if this power were awarded, it would be exercised with justice to both the captains of industry and the American people. Roosevelt repeatedly stressed that "the spirit of demagoguery" must not dictate legislative policy. "If we attack unjustly the proper rights of others because they are wealthy," he was careful to maintain, "we shall do ourselves just as much damage as if we permitted an attack upon those who are poor, because they are poor." He recognized that "the rock of class hatred" was "the greatest and most dangerous rock in the course of any republic." But the time for action had come. If Congress refused to advance the administration's moderate proposal, more radical demands would inevitably gain momentum.

Convinced now of the president's resolve, editorials predicted "a fight to the finish between the railroads and the administration." Nonetheless, *The Washington Post* reported, "an impression prevailed during the summer that the railroad interests were making such a campaign . . . that there was very grave doubt of any legislation of that character passing in the coming Congress."

⤳ ⤲

By SUMMER'S END, BAKER HAD completed his research and commenced writing a six-part, 50,000-word series, entitled "The Railroads on Trial." To herald the upcoming articles, McClure published a lengthy editorial announcement claiming that "the vitality of democracy" depended on "popular knowledge of complex questions." With regulatory legislation that would impact the entire nation under debate in Congress, the public needed to understand how railroads determined differential rates, whether they conspired to stifle competition, how goods were classified, and how private cars and midnight tariffs operated. The American people, not economists and sociologists, would ultimately have to assess whether a few great men, "like the barons of old," had become "more powerful than the sovereign himself."

Mindful of the president's earlier request to look over his railroad articles before publication, Baker wrote in early September to ask if Roosevelt still wanted to review his first installment, scheduled to appear in the November issue. "Yes, I should greatly like to see the proof," Roosevelt assured him the very next day. "I have learned to look to your articles for real help. You have impressed me with your earnest desire to be fair, with your freedom from hysteria and with your anxiety to tell the truth." Baker later recalled his trepidation after sending off the piece, aware that the president's "approval might be the measure of the usefulness of the entire series [he] had planned." If Roosevelt found his arguments compelling, Baker could employ "the incomparable sounding board of the White House" in his endeavor to educate the public. Five days later, Baker was elated and much relieved by Roosevelt's response: "I haven't a criticism to suggest." Indeed, the president graciously acknowledged, "you have given me two or three thoughts for my own message."

In clear, powerful language, Baker explained how, despite the Elkins Act that barred cash rebates, the railroads still managed to build in special rates. They had devised a schedule that favored products carried by the trusts through clever classification of goods and commodities. "In the early days of the Railroad," Baker pointed out, "the Rate was fixed exactly as it was on a turnpike—a regular toll, for so many miles, so much of a charge." As railroads had begun to consolidate, however, the small circle of controlling owners adopted the principle of "charging what the traffic will bear," providing preferential treatment to the trusts while forcing exorbitant rates on small shippers. When great clients like the Armours, the Rockefellers, or the Morgans desired special privileges, they were easily arranged—given that such families generally sat on the boards of these very same railroads.

Although "the fundamental purpose of all law," Baker argued, "is to do justice between strong and weak, between large and small," the railroads and the trusts had conspired "to build up and enforce the old favoritism to the strong." For the first time, Baker boldly suggested that railroad rates had become the fulcrum of a new political contest that set "a progressive party seeking to give the government more power in business affairs" against "a conservative party striving to retain all the power possible in private hands."

In thanking the president for reviewing his proofs, Baker took the occasion to warn him that the mood in the Midwest had become highly volatile; failure to pass regulatory legislation, he predicted, would foment "violent agitation" and calls for radical action. "The country was never at a more critical point in its career," the reporter observed, nor had it "ever had a better opportunity of handling its problem correctly. I wish, Mr. President—and you will pardon my freedom—that there were a Taft for the Bureau of Commerce and Labor. To my thinking there is no more important place now in the gift of government."

A few weeks later, Baker was amazed to receive a letter from the president, containing a "strictly confidential" partial draft from his annual message dealing with the corporations. "Will you give me any comments," Roosevelt asked, "which your experiences teach you ought to be made thereon?" In eight weeks, the president would deliver his State of the Union speech, and Baker reflected solemnly upon "the seriousness of the responsibility" granted to him. "I knew perfectly well how little I really knew about the complicated problems involved in the new legislation," he later wrote; "but then, who was there at that time who did?"

The reporter carefully weighed Roosevelt's language. Heartened by the president's willingness to make railroad regulation his first priority, he found the tone of the draft message disappointing: "It was too general, there was too much of the President's favorite balancing of good and evil." Baker applauded Roosevelt's drive to empower the Interstate Commerce Commission to revise the disputed freight rates but deplored his proposal to limit the Commission's authority to merely prescribing a maximum rate limit. "I was terribly afraid that he was plumping for a solution that, while it might help a little, and look good politically, would fail to reach the heart of the matter," Baker recalled.

The research for Baker's second article, which detailed all manner of new rebate chicanery, had convinced him that the trusts didn't care what the rate was, so long as they enjoyed a better rate than everyone else. The differential provided their advantage and allowed them to crush their competitors. Beyond their clever freight classification schemes, railroads had implemented a host of "cunning devices"—including private cars, refrigerator charges, elevator allowances, underweighing of freight, and variable tariffs. Such measures were specifically designed to lower rates for the great shippers in beef, oil, and steel while raising them "for the farmer, the small struggling manufacturers and shippers." Believing he had gained a comprehensive understanding of the railroad conspiracy, Baker felt compelled to tell the president plainly that his approach was misguided.

"I have asked myself over and over," Baker wrote to Roosevelt on November 11, expressing his doubts "whether the power to fix a maximum rate, which you suggest, will touch this specific case of injustice." He had determined that it would not. The "evil power" of the trusts, he explained, lay in their ability to compel the railroads to give them a lower rate than everyone else. The problem therefore was "*not* a maximum rate but a minimum rate." The only solution was to allow the governmental tribunal to "fix a *definite* rate."

Roosevelt replied immediately, agreeing that "it would be better if the Commission had the power to fix a definite instead of a maximum rate." His attorney general had warned him, however, that fixing a definite rate might be unconstitutional. While the maximum rate might not alleviate all problems, he concluded, "we should have first a law that is surely constitutional." Baker persisted, reiterating in a second letter that merely limiting the maximum rate would not mitigate the terrible inequity in the entire system. "Is there not, then, some practical way," he entreated, "for reaching the real abuse?" Quoting the abolitionist Wendell Phillips's remark on historic reforms, Baker challenged the president's objection: "If they do not succeed with the Constitution, then they must succeed without it."

There followed "a long and rather heated correspondence" between the two men, spurred by a four-page letter from the president. "I think you are entirely mistaken in your depreciation of what is accomplished by fixing a maximum rate," Roosevelt declared, arguing that "the insistence upon having only the perfect cure often results in securing no betterment whatever." Furthermore, he added, "the railroads have been crazy in their hostility to my maximum rate proposition, and evidently do not share in the least your belief that nothing will result from it." In additional exchanges, Roosevelt branded Baker's continued fear that the proposed measure would prove insufficient "simply absurd." He ended the correspondence with a reminder that "it was Lincoln, not Wendell Phillips and the fanatical abolitionists, who was the effective champion of union and freedom." Confronted by Roosevelt's strident tone, Baker was certain that his "suggestion would come to nothing."

"What was my surprise," Baker later recalled, "when I read the message in its final form as delivered to Congress, to find that the President had inserted a paragraph, almost in my own words, regarding the regulation of minimum rates." After calling upon Congress to grant an impartial tribunal authority to set "a maximum reasonable rate" when an existing rate was deemed "unreasonable and unjust," Roosevelt laid out a far more comprehensive proposal: "It sometimes happens at present not that a rate is too high but that a favored shipper is given too low a rate. In such cases the commission would have the right to fix this already established minimum rate as the maximum; and it would need only one or two such decisions by the commission to cure railroad companies of the practice of giving improper minimum rates." Finally, he urged Congress to grant the ICC supervision of private-car lines, elevator allowances, refrigerator charges, and industrial roads—all the devices Baker had exposed as subtle mechanisms of discrimination.

〜 〜

ON JANUARY 4, 1906, COLONEL William Hepburn, chairman of the Interstate and Foreign Commerce Committee, reported the administration-backed railroad bill to the floor of the House. As Roosevelt had outlined in his annual message, the bill gave the ICC the authority to determine a "just and reasonable" maximum for disputed rates. Though it was essentially a moderate bill, it nonetheless challenged "the most hoary tenet of free private enterprise"—the right to independently set prices according to supply and demand.

While Speaker Joseph Cannon could have easily exercised his absolute control over House procedure to prevent the bill from reaching the floor, he had allowed it to move forward. In exchange, the president had agreed to preserve the protective tariff—an issue the Old Guard considered even more vital than railroad regulation. Popular resentment toward the railroads was such that once the bill reached the floor, the outcome was clear. The overwhelming vote to pass the Hepburn bill on February 8 "was in many ways the most spectacular piece of politics ever witnessed at the Capitol," *The Washington Post* remarked, noting that a bill vitally affecting over $15 billion of property had passed "without the addition of a single amendment."

The following day, Roosevelt invited Ray Baker to join him during his afternoon shave. Baker professed his belief that "this railroad legislation was the most important of the President's administration" but "only a first step" toward broader reform. His investigations throughout the West had convinced the journalist that the public was moving beyond the president's position, even pushing for "governmental ownership of the railroad." Roosevelt vehemently disagreed, twisting so abruptly toward Baker that the barber had to flinch quickly to avoid cutting the president's chin. "I do not represent public opinion: I represent the public," Roosevelt passionately countered, insisting, "I must represent not the excited opinion of the West but the real interests of the whole people." Those interests would be ill served, he curtly rejoined, by turning the operation of the railroads over to government employees, for "he knew better than anyone else could how inefficient & undependable" they were. The Hepburn bill, Roosevelt insisted, would address most of the problems. Rather than speculate on future steps, he must focus on the U.S. Senate, where he faced perhaps the climactic struggle of his administration.

A battle royal was predicted between the president and the conservative senators, led by Nelson Aldrich. Public pressure precluded an outright assault on the bill, yet Aldrich and his colleagues remained confident that they could produce a final bill "so whittled down" by amendments "as to be practically worthless." Roosevelt was clearly prepared for such tactics: "They are making every effort to have some seemingly innocent amendment put in," he explained to Kermit, "which shall destroy something of what I am endeavoring to accomplish."

To forestall these inevitable efforts to gut the bill, Roosevelt declared unequivocally that he wished the Senate to pass the Hepburn bill without amendments. His statement produced "great indignation among the conservative senators." The chief executive, they insisted, had no business meddling in their deliberations. His presumptuous intervention showed a woeful disregard of the Senate's historic role "as a check upon the half-baked and demagogic bills passed by the lower house."

Roosevelt's push to get the bill unamended through the Senate Interstate Commerce Committee rested on the leadership of Iowa's junior senator, Jonathan Dolliver. A young progressive, Dolliver worked doggedly to produce a majority vote and deliver what would become the Dolliver/Hepburn bill to the floor. Of the eight Republicans, he won the support of three—all from the West where agitation for railroad control was most intense. Combined with five Democrats who had long favored regulatory control, they formed the slim majority Dolliver needed to bring the bill to the floor.

Conceding that he had lost in committee, Aldrich deftly contrived a deal with the Democrats: He would give Benjamin Tillman, the ranking Democrat from South Carolina, the honor of leading the fight on the floor in Dolliver's place. In turn, Democrats agreed to report the unamended bill "without prejudice," thereby allowing amendments to be freely offered during debate on the floor. This gambit astonished even the most seasoned journalists. The fact that Roosevelt's "most outspoken opponent" was "put in charge of the administration's pet measure," one Ohio paper remarked, was "considered so audacious a piece of irony that it has made the country gasp." Fully aware that Republicans controlled nearly two thirds of the Senate, Tillman himself "scarcely had time to pinch himself to see if he were really awake."

The loyal Dolliver, who had justifiably assumed he would lead the fight, was humiliated. Worse still, the president confronted a truly awkward dilemma. During Roosevelt's first term, the hot-tempered, foul-mouthed, and slovenly Tillman, known as "Pitchfork Ben," had engaged in a fistfight with a colleague on the Senate floor. In the aftermath, Roosevelt had publicly withdrawn Tillman's invitation to a state dinner, incurring the senator's abiding animosity. The two men had not spoken since. Aldrich calculated that with the irascible Tillman as floor leader, Roosevelt's influence on the legislative process would be severely diminished. The press agreed. Roosevelt now suffered the indignity, declared the *Charleston* (South Carolina) *News and Courier*, of seeing his signal legislation "confided to the care of a man who is not only not of his own party, but one who entertains a personal antagonism toward him." The president's "old enemies" in the Republican Party, the *Indianapolis News* observed, seemed determined not only to defeat his legislation but also to "show at the same time that the President is not after all a formidable figure."

In the following weeks, pro-railroad Republicans took to the floor, proposing a range of amendments designed to shatter the commission's authority. They were particularly intent upon a provision granting the courts broad power to relitigate the commission's revised rates, essentially leaving the pro-railroad judiciary as the true arbiter of rates.

Roosevelt nevertheless remained hopeful that the Hepburn bill would emerge intact, trusting that "public opinion may be relied upon to keep the Senate straight." By the spring of 1906, public outrage over the railroads had indeed reached a crescendo. Hundreds of magazines and newspapers followed every aspect of the debate, clearly outlining what was at stake. These publications, one editorialist observed, were "never better," and "never more influential," than in their joint effort to foster an informed public opinion "compounded of knowledge, discrimination and judgment."

In March, Baker published the most consequential piece in his railroad series, an exposé of the techniques the railroads employed to malign and falsify the Hepburn bill. Acknowledging the right of the railroads, "in common with all other citizens, to present facts and arguments to the people," Baker proceeded to reveal the multifarious devices of the railroads' lavishly funded propaganda campaign. A team of agents determined whether newspaper editors were "good" or "bad" on the issue of the railroads, then distributed free passes to those adjudged favorably inclined, while subjecting those deemed unfriendly to underhanded personal attacks. In one instance, a former city newspaperman was hired to write a pamphlet posing as a representative of farmers against regulation. In another scheme, small newspapers were supplied with free reading supplements seeded with attacks on Roosevelt's railroad legislation. Subsidized pamphlets spread the rumor that if railroad discriminations were outlawed, separate Jim Crow cars for Negroes would be forbidden. If all such "ordinary devices" to co-opt the press failed, then the railroads purchased newspapers outright.

Baker's description of this onslaught of covert railroad propaganda acquainted more than half a million men and women with the true methods of the anti-regulatory campaign. "It is a little startling," one magazine editorialized, "to read how the railroad combines first to rob the country of millions, and then to use a portion of this fund stolen from the people to corrupt the sources of information and thus try to perpetuate their robbery through a blinded public opinion." New subscriptions and letters commending Baker poured in to *McClure's*. A Mississippi farmer wrote that "after plowing all day," he and his boys had read the entire piece aloud. If he had the funds, he told Baker, he would send a copy to every family in the country. "Every member of Congress," he added, "should have a chance to read this able presentation of the question between the people and the railroads." One Wisconsin resident telegraphed *McClure's* that he considered Baker's article "worth all the publication will cost me for the next ten years." The sensational article heightened public demand for regulation, much as the publication of the Standard Oil telegrams had done during the battle over the Bureau of Corporations.

To the dismay of Senator Aldrich, who had counted on Roosevelt's pride to prevent any overture to the man he loathed, the president soon made it clear that he "was of course entirely willing to see Mr. Tillman personally," or meet with any other party empowered to act on Tillman's behalf. "I did not care a rap about Mr. Tillman's getting credit for the bill, or having charge of it," he later recalled. "I was delighted to go with him or with anyone else just so long as he was traveling my way." Still unwilling to set foot in the White House, Tillman asked former senator William E. Chandler to serve as intermediary.

After a series of White House sessions with Chandler, Roosevelt agreed to support a Tillman-endorsed amendment that limited judicial review to a simple determination of whether the commission's rate revision procedures were fair. By moving "to the left of his original position," the president hoped to fashion a majority comprising both Republican progressives and Democratic populists. "The fight on the rate bill is growing hot," Roosevelt told Kermit, explaining his ongoing efforts to save it: "I am now trying to see if I cannot get it through in the form I want by the aid of some fifteen or twenty Republicans added to most of the Democrats."

"As for Tillman," William Allen White wrote in the *Emporia Gazette*, "no member of the President's own party could have pressed the bill more vigorously at all times. He demanded that all other state business be stopped until a rate bill was passed, and he kept the senate an hour earlier and an hour later than it was accustomed to sit." Handed the greatest responsibility of his career, Benjamin Tillman had determined, he said, to "pocket my pride and lay aside my just indignation" in order to aid the president in securing "a good railroad law." No better illustration of "the mysterious ways of Providence and politics" could be found, *The Washington Post* commented, than the alliance of "the pitchfork and the big stick."

Roosevelt would gladly have signed Tillman's more radical revision of the Hepburn bill if his new coalition of progressive Republicans and Democrats had produced sufficient numbers to override the conservative Republican bloc. But in the end, a number of southern senators balked, deeming the bill a violation of states' rights, and Tillman could not deliver enough Democratic votes to make it work. Roosevelt was left with no choice but to revert to the original Hepburn bill, which had simply assumed the constitutional guarantee of due process. Despite such setbacks, Roosevelt remained satisfied with this formulation. "The great object," he insisted, "was to avoid the adoption of any of the broad amendments."

But in order to forge a majority on the original bill, he would have to mollify moderate Republicans who feared that unless the courts were directly vested with judicial review, the bill might be held unconstitutional. To win over this reluctant bloc, Roosevelt called on two Old Guard senators, William Allison of Iowa and John Spooner of Wisconsin. Both had long been staunch lieutenants to Nelson Aldrich, and both were assumed to be supporters of his bid to emasculate the bill. The political landscape was shifting, however; in Iowa and Wisconsin, the momentum to regulate the railroads had reached a frantic pitch and the two senators understood that ignoring their constituents on this issue would put their Senate seats in grave jeopardy.

Allison and Spooner's unexpected cooperation with Roosevelt made headlines. Two of the original Big Four, this "little knot of men" had ruled the upper branch in harmony for years. Nelson Aldrich found the break with Allison especially painful, for he relied upon Allison's masterful knowledge of parliamentary procedure. "Everybody is now watching with eagerness to see which of the two great Senate chieftains will demonstrate superior generalship," commented the *New York Times*. From his post at the *Emporia Gazette*, William Allen White noted that Aldrich appeared befuddled over the fact that he could "neither control the legislation of the upper branch affecting financial interests nor count upon the men he regarded as allies." This rupture in the Senate oligarchy was widely regarded as "symbolic of the new popular alignment all over the country in preparation for the coming contest between the forces of amalgamated capital and those of popular will and sentiment."

Straightaway, Allison devoted himself to fashioning his own amendment to the Hepburn bill, which stipulated the right to judicial review of ICC rulings—but cleverly leaving the scope of that review undetermined. The ambiguous language of the Allison amendment allowed the senator to forge a majority. Although Roosevelt had hoped to limit the court's review to a determination of procedural fairness, he recognized that this compromise provided the only chance of passage. Once the amendment was accepted, Roosevelt later told White, "Aldrich and his people really threw up their hands." Their chance to obtain a broad review provision had been eliminated. Indeed, when the Hepburn bill finally reached the Senate floor for a vote, Aldrich and a number of his older colleagues were noticeably absent. The bill passed by an overwhelming vote on June 29, 1906.

"No given measure and no given set of measures will work a perfect cure for any serious evil," Roosevelt reminded critics of the compromised bill. Though flawed, the president maintained that the Hepburn Act represented "the longest step ever yet taken in the direction of solving the railway rate problem." The legislation not only brought the railroads under federal control; it "lifted the idea of nationality to a point never before reached." The authority granted the Interstate Commerce Commission became clearer in the months that followed as the first case involving rate revision reached the Supreme Court. By declining to review the specific facts, the High Court defined the scope of judicial review in favor of Roosevelt and the progressives.

The president enjoyed widespread credit for the passage of the bill, exhibiting, one Democratic newspaper remarked, "the politician's gift of knowing when to fight, and, as well, when to surrender." Roosevelt had sought a Republican majority for the original Hepburn bill; when his efforts were subverted by the leader of his own party, he had reached out to the Democrats; when that failed to produce a majority, he returned to his original provision, altered only slightly by Allison's amendment. Even Benjamin Tillman grudgingly acknowledged that "but for the work of Theodore Roosevelt, we would not have had any bill at all."

However astute Roosevelt proved in dealing with Congress, he would doubtless have failed to secure a meaningful bill without a galvanized public behind him. The combined efforts of Baker and his fellow journalists had generated a widespread demand for reform. "Congress might ignore a president," the *Fort Wayne* (Indiana) *Weekly Sentinel* observed, "but could not ignore a president and the people."

A letter discovered among Baker's papers testifies to the impact of investigative journalism on the passage of the Hepburn Bill: "It is through writers like yourself, Mr. Steffens and Miss Tarbell that the country as a whole is beginning to understand. In the future your influence on the life of the Republic will be held to be greater than that of the men who now rule our Senate and our House." Baker had reflected on their accomplishment and his growing confidence in the nation's future in a January letter to his father: "This crusade against special privilege in high places is real war, a real revolution," he wrote. "We may not have to go as far as you did, when you fought out the slavery question with powder & blood. At the present, when any of us is wounded we bleed nothing but ink. But ink may serve the purpose."

UPTON SINCLAIR, THE YOUNG NOVELIST and friend of Ray Baker and Lincoln Steffens, helped instigate the next battle in the crusade against special privilege. Sinclair thought very highly of the dramatic factual stories in *McClure's* that mobilized public opinion but reproached his comrades for failing to endorse the panacea of socialism. At the age of twenty-four, Sinclair had concluded with certainty that socialism was the answer to the country's ills; his experience of reading a socialist pamphlet in 1902, he later said, "was like the falling down of prison walls about my mind."

Thus, unlike the members of the McClure team, Sinclair was not struggling to discover remedies for specific ills. "Perhaps it'll surprise you," he wrote to Baker during the railroad struggle, "but we socialists don't agree with your rebate agony. The quicker the concentration of wealth is completed the better it suits us. . . . The point all you reforming folks seem to miss is that you are locking the stable doors after the horse is gone. *The trusts are formed. The big shipper has got the money*. Also with the money he's bought the government."

By twenty-five, Sinclair had already published two obscure novels when the editor of a popular socialist weekly, *Appeal to Reason*, offered to pay $500 for the right to publish his next fiction project in serial form. He quickly chose the "wage slavery" of industrial-era workers as his subject. The young socialist decided to set his novel in the Chicago stockyards, where an unsuccessful strike by workers in the meatpacking plants had aroused his sympathy. Dazzled by the brilliance of Frank Norris and a small cadre of writers devoted to realism, Sinclair took up residence in Packingtown, the stockyard district. For seven weeks, he recalled, "I sat at night in the homes of the workers, foreign-born and native, and they told me their stories, one after one, and I made notes of everything." Wandering around the yards during the day, he noted, "I was not much better dressed than the workers, and found that by the simple device of carrying a dinner pail I could go anywhere." Passing into rancid, hazardous places that outsiders rarely frequented, he watched with amazement as scraps of meat that were later sold to the public were swept from floors infested with rats and covered in human spit. The pressure to produce profits dictated that nothing was allowed to go to waste: condemned hogs were rendered into lard;

moldy meats were "dosed with borax" and ground into sausage; spoiled hams were pumped with chemicals to mask a smell "so bad that a man could hardly bear to be in the room with them."

After a month of watchfulness, Sinclair had collected the data but not yet conceived the protagonists for his novel. One Sunday afternoon, he chanced to attend the rollicking traditional wedding celebration of a young Lithuanian couple. Standing transfixed with his back to a wall as the festivities unfolded around him, Sinclair found his characters amid the whirl of music and dance—"the bride, the groom, the old mother and father, the boisterous cousin, the children, the three musicians, everybody."

The Jungle tells the story of the young couple and their extended family as they immigrate to Chicago in pursuit of plentiful jobs, decent wages, and the fulfillment of the American dream. No one subscribes more completely to the idea that decency and hard work will earn a place in America than the central character, Jurgis Rudkus. Confident in his ferocious strength and determination to provide for his family, Jurgis immediately lands a job. He is "the sort of man the bosses like to get hold of. . . . When he was told to go to a certain place, he would go there on the run. When he had nothing to do for the moment, he would stand round fidgeting, dancing, with the overflow of energy that was in him." Filled with optimism, Jurgis saves every cent to buy a home for his wife and children: "He would work all day," Sinclair wrote, "and all night too, if need be; he would never rest until the house was paid for and his people had a home."

Before long, the predatory machine of Packingtown begins to corrode Jurgis's optimism and assurance. For years, glib salesmen had counted upon the ignorance of the immigrants. If a single payment was missed, the house was lost, along with everything paid into it. Indeed, Sinclair observed, the houses "were sold with the idea that the people who bought them would not be able to pay for them." The unscrupulous salesman could always count on a new wave of immigrants, clamoring desperately for jobs and needful of food and housing.

The meatpacking plants grind up workers as surely as they grind up hogs and cattle. Sinclair details the brutal hours of work with no compensation for injury and little hope of evading the diseases legion in unsanitary surroundings. During the holiday "speeding up" on the slaughtering floor, Jurgis is hurt. Finally able to return to work, he discovers that his job has been given to another man. Once "fresh and strong," Jurgis becomes "a damaged article" his bosses no longer want. At once vividly individual and representative of an entire beleaguered class, Sinclair's characters are callously denied any real hope of a livelihood or future. The devastation of the entire family has been set in motion, their tragedy engendered not through personal failure but through the savage capitalist system that pits man against man. When his young wife and then his son die, Jurgis is crushed in body and spirit. Finding himself at a socialist rally, he is at last spiritually reborn, awakened to revolution.

After five publishers rejected Sinclair's manuscript outright, Doubleday finally considered publication. "The revelations in the story were so astounding," the New York Times reported, "that the publishers commissioned a lawyer to go to Chicago to make a personal investigation of the author's representations." When the attorney's report corroborated Sinclair, Doubleday agreed to move forward. In February 1906, as he nervously awaited official publication, Sinclair sent two advance copies to Ray Baker. One was autographed to the journalist; the second, Sinclair hoped, Baker might deliver to the White House and present to President Roosevelt.

The book created an immediate sensation. Although some reviews criticized the contrived socialist epiphany of the ending, millions of readers found Sinclair's cast of characters and the grotesque details of the meatpacking industry compelling. "Not since Byron awoke one morning to find himself famous," observed the New York *Evening World*, "has there been such an example of world-wide fame won in a day by a book as has come to Upton Sinclair."

James Garfield was the first in the White House to read the book. "Hideous," he termed the story, "but not more so than the place," which he had visited during the Bureau of Corporations' investigation of the beef trust. Sinclair, he wrote in his journal, had produced "a terrible and I fear too true account of the lives of many miserable men & women among the working class in our big cities." During a long walk with the president, Garfield described at length his response to the book.

Intrigued by Garfield's reaction, Roosevelt finished reading the novel and invited the author to the White House during the first week in April. Although he proceeded to disparage the socialist diatribe tacked on to the conclusion, Roosevelt assured Sinclair that "all this has nothing to do with the fact that the specific evils you point out shall, if their existence be proved, and if I have power, be eradicated."

By the time Sinclair arrived for lunch on April 4, a Department of Agriculture investigator was en route to the stockyards with an order from the White House to evaluate the novelist's charges. Sending a representative of the very agency that had failed properly to inspect the plants, Sinclair objected, "was like asking a burglar to determine his own guilt." His objections prompted Roosevelt to dispatch two additional investigators with no official ties to the department. He chose two well-respected men: Commissioner of Labor Charles P. Neill and Assistant Secretary of the Treasury James Bronson Reynolds. Sinclair was delighted, though he feared the investigators would focus on the diseased meats rather than the working conditions in the yard. "I have power to deal with one and not with the other," Roosevelt responded.

As the investigation got under way, the *Chicago Tribune* ran a series of articles citing "on excellent authority" that the president's team had already debunked the overwhelming majority of Sinclair's charges and claiming that Roosevelt intended to castigate the novelist in an upcoming speech. In a state of panic, Sinclair barraged the president with letters, a telegram, and a phone call. Roosevelt patiently explained that the newspaper story was simply fabricated. "It is absurd to become so nervous over such an article," he admonished. "Hundreds such appear about me all the time, with quite as little foundation." Chastened, Sinclair maintained that he "should never have dreamed of writing," except it seemed incomprehensible that a journalist "with a reputation to protect" would dare to disseminate false information in such an "explicit and positive way." Roosevelt immediately assuaged Sinclair's anxiety. "I understand entirely how you felt. Of course you have not had the experience I have had with newspapers. . . . Meanwhile, we will go steadily ahead with the investigation."

In fact, Roosevelt's inspectors found stockyard conditions comparable to those Sinclair had portrayed. Initial reports told "of rooms reeking with filth, of walls, floors, and pillars caked with offal, dried blood, and flesh, of unspeakable uncleanliness." These findings were more than sufficient to convince Roosevelt to take action. On May 22, Illinois senator Albert Beveridge introduced a White House–backed bill to institute a rigid federal inspection program covering all phases of the meatpacking industry, from animal slaughter to sausage and canned meat production. If products were "found healthful and fit for human food," a government label indicating "inspected and passed" would be attached; if not, the meat products would be marked "inspected and condemned."

Roosevelt warned Senate leaders friendly to the packers "that unless effective meat inspection legislation were enacted without loss of time," he would make the report public. Although he had no desire to harm the packing industry or the livestock producers, if the meatpackers moved to kill the legislation, he would feel compelled to expose the sickening work conditions. Fearing adverse publicity even more than the regulation, the packers retreated. Without "a dissenting vote" the Beveridge bill passed the Senate three days after it was introduced.

While Roosevelt was satisfied, Upton Sinclair remained disappointed by the bill's quick passage. To release the report, he told the president, would give the public "a shock it will never get over," prompting true, enduring reform through "an enlightened public opinion." Disregarding Roosevelt's directive to remain patient while the House took up the Senate bill, Sinclair leaked his information from the report to the *New York Times*. "I sincerely hope that the disturbance I have been making has not been an annoyance to you," he told the president. "I had to make up my mind quickly." Exasperated, Roosevelt wrote to Frank Doubleday: "Tell Sinclair to go home and let me run the country for awhile."

The legislation, meanwhile, foundered in the House Agricultural Committee, chaired by the wealthy stockbreeder James Wadsworth, a strong proponent of the beef trust. One after another, witnesses were paraded before the committee to argue that while isolated problems might exist, "conditions were as clean and wholesome as in the average restaurant, hotel and home kitchen. That there were offensive odors was natural—one ought not to expect to find a rosebud in a slaughtering house." A series of emasculating amendments was prepared, one negating the "mandatory character" of inspection and granting packers the right of court review.

"I am sorry to have to say," Roosevelt informed Congressman Wadsworth, "that it seems to me that each change is for the worse and that in the aggregate they are ruinous, taking away every particle of good from the suggested Beveridge amendment." Because the packers and their representatives had reneged, producing only "sham" legislation, the president felt he was not "warranted" any longer in holding back the unfinished Reynolds-Neill Report.

On June 4, the president transmitted what he called a "preliminary" report to Congress. "The conditions shown by even this short inspection," he avowed, were "revolting." His investigators had determined that "the stockyards and packing houses are not kept even reasonably clean, and that the method of handling and preparing food products is uncleanly and dangerous to health." Federal legislation was imperative to prevent continued abuses. If Congress failed in its responsibility, the full report would be made public.

Released to the newspapers, this preliminary assessment produced a national uproar. The *New York Post* captured the public mood in a sardonic jingle:

Mary had a little lamb,
And when she saw it sicken,
She shipped it off to Packingtown,
And now it's labeled chicken.

Faced with public outrage and disgust, the House could no longer keep the bill "chloroformed in the committees." The most egregious of Wadsworth's provisions were eliminated and the measure was sent to a conference committee. In the end, a fairly comprehensive meat inspection bill emerged. "We cannot imagine any other President whom the country has ever had, paying any attention at all to what was written in a novel," the New York *Evening Post* remarked. "In the history of reforms which have been enacted into law," Beveridge proudly noted, "there has never been a battle which has been won so quickly and never a proposed reform so successful in the first contest."

☞ ☜

THE MOMENTUM OF THE RAILROAD regulation fight and the meat inspection amendment propelled the passage of a third important bill—the Pure Food and Drug Act—producing a historic session of congressional reform. Crusaders like Dr. Harvey Wiley, chief chemist in the Department of Agriculture, had battled unsuccessfully for over a decade to secure federal legislation requiring proper labels on food and drugs. In the absence of such regulation, adulterated food products and bogus medicines flooded the market. Conservatives lampooned Wiley as "chief janitor and policeman of the people's insides." In the Senate, Nelson Aldrich emerged as the most vocal opponent of regulatory measures. "Are we going to take up the question as to what a man shall eat and what a man shall drink," he scornfully asked, "and put him under severe penalties if he is eating or drinking something different from what the chemists of the Agricultural Department think it is desirable for him to eat or drink?"

Pressure for reform began to build, however, with the publication of two groundbreaking articles in *Collier's* magazine. Interested in commissioning an investigative piece on the patent medicine industry, the editor of the *Ladies' Home Journal*, Edward Bok, reached out to S. S. McClure to find a writer capable of painstaking research. McClure introduced Bok to Mark Sullivan, a recent graduate of the Harvard Law School. Sullivan's article proved too technical and too extensive for the *Ladies' Home Journal*, but Bok brought it to *Collier's*, where it attracted widespread attention.

Sullivan's research yielded some stunning discoveries. The Lydia E. Pinkham Company, a celebrated patent medicine firm, advertised its numerous compounds for ailing women beneath the kindly and intelligent visage of Mrs. Pinkham—offering the promise that she would personally answer letters and dispense advice to inquiring customers. When Sullivan traveled to her hometown of Lynn, Massachusetts, and learned that she had been dead for over two decades, he took a picture of the inscription on her headstone: "Lydia E. Pinkham. Died May 17, 1883."

Less grimly humorous but far more pernicious was the young journalist's revelation that a secret clause had been written into the advertising contracts of thousands of newspapers across the country. At that time, patent medicines provided the largest source of advertising revenue for newspapers, and this clause stipulated that the contract would be canceled if material detrimental to the industry appeared anywhere in the paper. From William White, who had refused to take patent medicine ads in the *Emporia Gazette*, Sullivan obtained an original copy of the contract form.

The success of Sullivan's piece prompted *Collier's* to commission a ten-part investigative series on the patent medicine industry modeled after *McClure's* exposés. In fact, the writer of the series, Samuel Hopkins Adams, had been on *McClure's* staff before moving to *Collier's*. Adams procured experts to test more than two hundred patent medicines, a great majority of which were revealed as either "harmless frauds or deleterious drugs": an ointment containing clay and glycerin was marketed as a cancer cure; a pink starch and sugar pill promised to remedy paralysis; Isham's Spring Water claimed rheumatism would vanish within days. Even more worrisome, many concoctions were found to contain significant quantities of alcohol and narcotics, potentially leading the unwary toward addiction. Laboratories claiming to test these medicines turned out to be fraudulent or nonexistent.

For the first time, public pressure impelled a bill regulating food and drugs "to run the gauntlet of the upper house in safety." After reaching the House, however, "it slept. And it slept." For four months, Speaker Joe Cannon refused to bring the legislation to the floor for a vote. Finally, the national uproar over diseased meat forced his hand. On June 30, 1906, reformers were at last able to celebrate the passage of the Pure Food and Drug Act. The bill "would not have had the slightest chance" of surviving in the House, Senator Beveridge observed, had it not been for "the agitation" generated by the meat inspection amendment. This landmark bill authorized the federal government to examine the contents of processed food and patent medicines, forbade the sale of adulterated or misbranded food and drugs, and required that every package and bottle be properly labeled.

☙ ☙

"DURING NO SESSION OF CONGRESS since the foundation of the Government," the *New York Times* proclaimed, "has there been so much done, first, to extend the Federal power of regulation and control over the business of the country, and second, to cure and prevent abuses of corporation privileges." Had Congress accomplished even one of the three major steps toward railroad regulation, meat inspection, or food and drug oversight, one midwestern paper observed, the first session of the 59th Congress would have been historic. Taken together, these three monumental measures marked "the beginning of a new epoch in federal legislation—governmental regulations on corporations and the invocation of the police power, so to speak, to stay the hand of private greed" and protect the general welfare.

No sooner had journalists illuminated a problem than the fight to secure a remedy had begun. By the spring of 1906, it was virtually certain that Congress would pass measures to regulate the railroads and the food and drug industry; only the timing and nature of those regulations remained to be determined. "For pass them they must," McClure's biographer noted. "That verdict had already been reached by the people."

The momentum of the progressive agenda continued with an employer's liability law for the District of Columbia; the Antiquities Act that granted the president authority to declare national monuments on federal lands; and statehood bills for Arizona and New Mexico. Conservatives railed against "the most amazing program of centralization" ever enacted, and Wall Street warned that Roosevelt was only "sowing the seeds" of revolution. But the American people overwhelmingly agreed with the president's declaration that this Congress had accomplished "more substantive work for good than any Congress has done at any session since he became familiar with public affairs."

Even Democratic newspapers "reluctantly" acknowledged the unprecedented efficacy of the 59th Congress and the remarkable leadership of the president. "The public confidence has been greatly restored in our law-makers," observed the *Detroit Free Press*, "inasmuch as strongly reformative measures have been adopted in the face of tremendous private interests, the sole spur necessary being an insistent pubic demand, clearly defined."

Yet even as he gloried in the moment, Theodore Roosevelt sensed that he would never again achieve this magnitude of success in directing domestic policy. "I do not expect to accomplish very much in the way of legislation after this Congress, and perhaps after this session," he wistfully confided to Kermit. "By next winter people will begin to think more about the next man who is to be President; and then, too, by that time it is almost inevitable that the revulsion of feeling against me should have come. It is bound to come some time, and it is extraordinary that it has not come yet."

CHAPTER EIGHTEEN

"Cast into Outer Darkness"

In this 1906 cartoon, *Puck* portrays "The Muck Rakers"—including
Ida Tarbell and Ray Stannard Baker—in the aftermath of Roosevelt's
celebrated "Muckraking-Man" speech.

TO *MCCLURE'S* MATCHLESS TEAM OF journalists, the legislative
record of the 59th Congress represented not a fait accompli, but the first
successful skirmishes in a much larger war on the corrupt consolidation of
wealth and power. "Signs everywhere now show a great moral awakening,"
Baker told his father, "the cleaning out of rotten business & still more rotten
politics. But we've only begun!" For the first time, Baker explained, "men were
questioning the fundamentals of democracy, inquiring whether we truly had
self-government in America, or whether it had been corrupted by selfish interests." Most important, he continued, "this questioning came not alone from
what one might call the working class," but from middle America as well.

Investigative journalism, one historian has observed, had "assumed the
proportions of a movement," exerting an influence on the American consciousness "hardly less important than that of Theodore Roosevelt himself."
Magazines like *McClure's* had become so politically significant that William
Allen White quipped it was as if we had "Government by Magazine." During these heady days, Finley Peter Dunne's Irish bartender Mr. Dooley waxed
poetic on the power of the printed word, noting that it had the strength "to
make a star to shine on the lowliest brow" or to "blacken the fairest name in

Christendom." A mere three years before, Dooley explained, John D. Rock-efeller had enjoyed the reputation of undiluted success and civic rectitude, until, "lo and behold, up in his path leaps a lady with a pen in hand and off goes John D. for the tall timbers." More astonishingly, Dooley marveled, the same few years had seen a work of fiction rout the beef trust, and Ray Baker's lead pencil produce "a revolution" in Congress, and "when a state [wanted] to elect a governor or a city a mayor," it turned not to professional politicians but to Lincoln Steffens. "Yes," decried Mr. Dooley, "the hand that rocks the fountain pen is the hand that rules the world."

To outsiders, the solidarity of McClure's enterprise appeared impregnable. By 1906, Sam McClure was considered among the ten most important men in America. His gifted writers operated more like an intimate team, an extended family, than the staff of a magazine. For Ida Tarbell, now in her twelfth year at *McClure's*, the magazine provided freedom, security, and comradeship. "Here was a group of people I could work with, without sacrifice or irritation," Tarbell later reflected in her autobiography. "Here was a healthy growing undertaking which excited me, while it seemed to offer endless opportunity to contribute to the better thinking of the country." Ray Baker felt the same way, recognizing the "rare group" McClure had assembled—all "genuinely absorbed in life, genuinely in earnest in their attitude toward it, and yet with humor, and yet with sympathy, and yet with tolerance." The magazine was "a success," Lincoln Steffens recalled. "We had circulation, revenue, power. In the building up of that triumph we had been happy, all of us; it was fun, the struggle."

In the spring of 1906, however, just when "the future looked fair and per-manent," Ida reminisced, "the apparently solid creation was shattered and I found myself sitting on its ruins." Ray Baker's memoir registers similar grief and disbelief: "The institution that had seemed to me as permanent as any-thing could be in a transitory world—I mean *McClure's Magazine*—seemed to be crumbling under my feet." The schism that ended *McClure's* glorious era shocked the publishing world and devastated the staff.

Although McClure's team had long been accustomed to the rapid mood swings that drove Sam McClure into alternating periods of manic energy and pathological torpor, his creative wizardry had always compensated for his mercurial behavior. "Never forget," Ida Tarbell had counseled every time Mc-Clure riled the office with one of his outbursts, "that it was he & nobody else" who built the magazine, that all "the great schemes, the daring moves," the ideas that had propelled his writers' series and, finally, the writers themselves to national acclaim originated with him.

But in recent months the frenetic shifts from one grandiose plan to another had become more frequent, the melancholy periods infinitely darker. These radical vacillations in temperament compelled months of bed rest and even destroyed McClure's interest in the work he had always adored. While still capable of brilliance, McClure exhibited increasingly erratic behavior that took a cumulative toll on his colleagues. One of Sam McClure's escapades in the summer of 1903 had marked the first in a series of troubling events that became distressingly emblematic of the way his compulsions began to compromise the accomplishments and aspirations of his friends and colleagues at the magazine.

McClure had invited Ida to join him and his wife, Hattie, at Divonne-les-Bains, the popular spa town in eastern France on the border of Switzerland. Worried that her grinding work on the Standard Oil project was impacting her health, McClure hoped she would join them for the entire summer season. "You are infinitely precious to me," he told Ida. "I dreamed about you last night," he revealed, and "awoke this morning very anxious about you." If she found the pace of the series pressing her, he would gladly rein it in. "The truth is you have taken the forward place in my heart of all my friends," he wrote. "I want to live near you & be much with you during the coming years."

The prospect of a European vacation with Sam delighted Ida, but her work kept her in New York until July. In her absence, McClure invited a young poet, Florence Wilkinson, and a newly wed couple, Alice and Cale Rice, to accompany him to London and France. Wilkinson, a tall, dark-haired beauty, conducted poetry classes at her Greenwich Village studio. Four of her poems, at Sam's direction, had recently appeared in *McClure's*. The inclusion of Wilkinson's slight romantic verse in a magazine that had published the poetry of William Butler Yeats and A. E. Housman puzzled the staff, who suspected that their editor's fascination with the girl betrayed his usually impeccable judgment. The Rices would become well-known writers, but at the time Alice Hegan Rice had published her first novel and her husband had produced two slim volumes of poetry.

In London, McClure had arranged luxurious accommodations and memorable entertainment for his young friends, including a dinner at the Vagabondia with a circle of illustrious writers and an evening of theatre in the box of Bram Stoker, the author of *Dracula*. After arranging British publishers for the three aspiring writers, McClure brought them to Divonne. A week later, while Hattie stayed behind seeking relief for her rheumatism, the ever restless McClure set out with Wilkinson and the Rices for Chamonix and Mont Blanc. At the Hôtel du Paris, he selected a suite for the Rices on the second floor, while he and Florence Wilkinson stayed on the third. By the time Florence left the group for Bellagio, the intimacy that had developed between McClure and the young poet was apparent to the Rices.

When Ida Tarbell joined McClure and the Rices in the Swiss village of Gletsch, the newly organized traveling party set forth on a walking tour of the Alps. In the course of three weeks, they trekked from the valley of the Rhône to Lucerne and Zurich, and then on to the Engadine Valley in Italy, stopping at small inns along the way. Their "rollicking adventure," Alice Rice recalled, was directed by McClure, their "buccaneer leader," who "went through life like a tornado carrying everything in its wake." Reaching San Moritz in the late afternoon as fashionable carriages paraded along the thoroughfare, McClure was so exhilarated by the beauty of the mountain scene that he "lost his head completely," challenging Cale to scale a hill and then somersault down its slope. "So," Alice remembered, "to the utter amazement of the summer residents, taking their afternoon drive, two wild Americans came catapulting down the hillside, landing in the promenade almost under their horses' feet."

During that "never-to-be forgotten" European tour, Alice Rice and her husband forged a lifelong friendship with Ida Tarbell. Toward the end of their journey, the young couple, in all likelihood, confided the intimacy they had witnessed between Florence and Sam. Tensions grew until Ida could barely contain her tears when they parted, and McClure rightly feared that he had diminished himself in her eyes. "I have felt terribly sad since you left," he lamented in a subsequent letter. "I have no friend like you & I cannot endure to have hurt you & forfeited any of your confidence," he added, begging her forgiveness and promising never to "take another party to the Alps *of any kind*, just my family & you and other of my associates."

Ida's real distress was not driven by prudish disdain for his amorous entanglements; instead, she feared that Sam McClure's recklessness could tarnish the magazine with hypocrisy. In article after article, *McClure's* had exposed immoral businessmen and politicians. The authority of its painstaking investigations rested on the integrity of the writers and editors. Clearly, public scandal involving the magazine's charismatic founder would be a valuable weapon for those seeking to demean all their efforts.

After returning to New York that fall of 1903, Ida had shared her apprehensions with John Phillips. When Sam departed alone for a two-month European stay in November, they feared he planned to meet with Florence. His letters home revealed a mood of exultation: "I feel sure of myself as I haven't for many years. I am stronger on this trip than I was any time in ten years," he wrote from Berlin. Sam's buoyant tone persisted as he traveled through Germany and back to London. "I am so much keener & sharper than ever," he boasted. "I feel my vision broadened and feel strong physically and mentally." When McClure suddenly embarked on a solo holiday in the Appalachian Mountains in the spring, Tarbell and Phillips were convinced the sojourn was engineered to meet his lover.

In May 1904, the office erupted into turmoil when McClure directed the poetry editor, Witter Bynner, to purchase yet another of Florence's verses, this time a lover's poem that seemed directed to McClure himself. McClure composed a letter announcing its imminent publication by the magazine. He then asked Bynner to present the announcement to Miss Wilkinson personally, accompanied by a lavish arrangement of fresh flowers. When Tarbell and Phillips learned of these instructions, they upbraided Sam "like a naughty child." By this time, Hattie had learned about the affair, and turbulent days followed. A chastened McClure swore he would finally end the relationship and apparently informed Florence that they must sever all communication.

A week later, Sam left for Europe with his wife. Upon reaching Divonne, Hattie wrote Ida that something "very terrible" had come up during the ocean voyage: Sam had confessed to the existence of numerous letters written to Florence over the previous year. Immediately realizing "all the possibilities implied in that circumstance," Hattie urged her husband to have John Phillips retrieve his correspondence, but Sam "was wild at that idea." Instead, he sent off another letter to Florence, requesting the return of all his correspondence. "As the time approached when an answer could be expected," Hattie confided to Ida, Sam "fell into a terrible condition. He lost flesh, nearly a pound a day for nearly a week." Every day, he fretfully awaited the postman.

"I have so much to do right for," the overwrought McClure confessed to Ida during this interval. "I couldn't bear to lose you, not to speak of John or the others. . . . I am now at the bottom. I can go no further nor feel any sadder . . . I am about to take the desperate, but sure cure. Three weeks, in bed & milk." Realizing that their friend was ill equipped to resolve the situation, Tarbell and Phillips decided they must intervene. The awareness of extant letters exchanged between the illicit lovers confirmed their worst fears. "The Lord help us!" Ida exclaimed. Concluding that they must approach Florence Wilkinson directly, Ida considered visiting the Finger Lakes, where Florence was spending the summer. There, Ida would "make an appeal for courage," hopeful that the young woman would return the letters and refuse further contact with Sam. "I fear I would be hard on her," she admitted to John, as they considered their options, "but I will honestly try to put that out of my mind and help the girl if she will let me." In the end, Ida decided it might be wiser for Phillips to make the appeal, since it was "quite natural" that Florence should "feel resentment" toward her. The shy Phillips agreed to undertake the unpleasant task, meeting with Florence in upstate New York, where he secured her promise to return the letters and refrain from further communication with McClure.

Although Florence initially kept her part of the bargain, Sam could not keep his. "I have received six or seven letters and two cable messages," Florence informed Phillips. The letters, she told him, "I have returned mostly sealed as they came. It hurts me more than words can say." She had indeed sent a packet containing all McClure's correspondence, but Florence could not bear to reject unopened all his new letters. "I think his health is suffering unnecessarily under the strain of absolute silence," she wrote. "I think, too, he is in an agony of doubt as to my feelings toward him. I wish he could know that I love him as well as ever—though I am never to see him." Despite Phillips's concerns, she desperately wished to post one letter assuring Sam that "the love by itself is not wrong." Phillips should understand that "it was not humanly possible for his side to snap off so suddenly," though she would do her utmost to ease the situation.

McClure's longtime friend and London office manager Mary Bisland reported to Ida that Sam could not stop talking about Florence, protesting that he had been "wretched & restless" since the separation and insisting that he had "not the very vaguest idea of giving her up," though he feared she was now determined to end the affair. At times, McClure seemed to listen to reason, making "very solemn promises" to Hattie that he would devote himself to her and that she would once again work in the office by his side. But such pledges alternated with dark declarations that he would leave New York for a year or more, perhaps never to return. "He said he was a hurt animal who wanted to crawl into a hole and hide forever," Hattie sadly told Ida. "My heart is broken to see how weak he is. . . . He must learn over again to live with me and do right."

Yet even during his most depressed days in Europe, McClure never failed to follow every detail of the magazine's progress, continuing to provide valuable input. Writing to Tarbell in June 1904, he captured the vision articulated in recent articles: "The struggle for possession of absolute power which you find in your work among capitalists & Steffens finds among politicians & Baker finds among labor unions, is the age-long struggle & human freedom has been won only by continual & tremendous effort." Much as he admired Steffens's articles on corruption, he warned Phillips that they were "full of dynamite, far & away the most terrible stuff we can handle." Steffens "must never be rushed," he further cautioned, and his use of invective must be carefully curtailed. In the article on Wisconsin, for example, Steffens had accused Senator John Spooner of bribing state legislators to obtain his Senate seat. "Unless Spooner was elected by bribery, we must clear him," McClure instructed. "Either he or the magazine must be cleared." The article on Nelson Aldrich would be equally "sensational" and "must be very understated and very accurate." Compounding his unease, McClure intuited that the atmosphere at the magazine had become less collegial. He feared that with each writer "working in his own little cubicle, in his own little field," each would fail "to get the inspiration or the information that would vitalize his work, from other departments."

His perceptions were by and large astute, but Sam McClure also fired off a series of ill-tempered critiques that upset staffers in New York. They bristled at his particularly high-handed indictment of an internal advertisement extolling the magazine's growing reputation. "The man who is responsible for this advt is relieved from further ad writing absolutely," McClure haughtily ordered, complaining, "Why in the name of ordinary decency and modesty do we have to vaunt ourselves like this, saying we are the best. . . . We act like a spoiled, over-petted and over-praised, but ill-bred small boy." He implored Hattie to write a separate letter conveying to everyone in the office the depth of his displeasure. Henceforth, he demanded, not a single ad should be run without his express approval. Put to bed under doctor's orders to begin the dreaded milk cure yet again, Hattie reported, he had asked her to read some of the magazine's recent short stories, which she had concluded were "very poor, trashy, empty things . . . far below the old McClure standard." Future stories, he then insisted, should be sent to Divonne so Hattie could determine if they seemed "unworthy." Phillips patiently answered Sam's diatribes, but he began to wonder if his oldest friend would ever be healthy enough to return to full-time work.

Hattie's determination to forgive her husband's past indiscretions was severely tested in July 1904 when she received a shattering letter from Miss Wilkinson. Florence had learned that she was not the only "other" woman in Sam's life. Her "dearest" friend, Edith Wherry, had revealed her own romantic relationship with McClure, which had apparently developed after the fateful European vacation. Florence had written Hattie in a fit of jealous anger, intending to injure Sam in his wife's eyes. The distressing missive spurred Sam into belated recognition that he would have to take control of a quickly deteriorating situation. "Yesterday," he wrote to Phillips, "Mrs. McClure received a letter from Florence that brought about a condition that resulted in my making a complete finis to the terrible affair & I have so written Miss W. You have done nobly & Miss Tarbell but now the matter is finished absolutely. . . . There is no possible chance for further troubles."

McClure managed to convince his wife that Miss Wherry's confession was a mere figment of the young girl's imagination, and the troubled couple headed home with a commitment to resume their marriage. While Hattie admitted that her heart was still "wrung with the anguish of it all," she told Sam that she was willing to leave everything in the past now that he had ended his "strange wanderings."

Back home, Sam professed his resolve to abandon all distraction and phi-landering, insisting to Ida Tarbell that her devoted efforts had "saved" him. He was so "horrified at the awful course of the past year or two" that he dared not dwell on it, fearing he would "never again be first" in her esteem and af-fections. If he were unable to regain her confidence, he told her, that alone would serve as lasting "punishment" for all he had done. Despite his contri-tion, there remained a disagreeable postscript to the Wherry episode. When Sam was in Chicago months later, Edith Wherry sent a manuscript to Hattie with the alarming title "The Shame of S. S. McClure, Illustrated by Letters and Original Documents." Miss Wherry claimed that she was determined "to live henceforth in truth & honor." Accordingly, "the wall of lies" which had sheltered her liaison with Sam must be razed. Hattie brought the explosive manuscript to the office, seeking the counsel of Tarbell and Phillips. An urgent telegram was dispatched, urging McClure's immediate return to New York. When he arrived the next day, the staff drew up a plan of financial compensa-tion to suppress the manuscript.

McCLURE'S RETURN TO THE MAGAZINE seemed to revive him. Bursting with new concepts, he proposed that Steffens embark on an investigation of life insur-ance companies and that Tarbell take on the U.S. Senate, predicting that "the whole future" of the country would be determined by "that most powerful ruling body." During a trip through the Midwest in the summer of 1905, he stopped in Emporia to visit William Allen White and reported that he himself was "getting along splendidly" in both "his work and learning" and that he was poised "to do greater editing than ever before."

Relieved to witness the lift in McClure's spirits, Phillips and Tarbell nev-ertheless mistrusted his leadership after the enervating months of crises. Not only did Tarbell ignore his suggestion to study the Senate; she had also, McClure sorrowfully noted, neglected to write to him during his travels. "I thought when I came back," he told her, "I could stand the years of waiting until I earned your confidence and regained my place with you & Mr. Phillips." Now, McClure feared that things "would never be the same," and that realization placed "a heavy, heavy load" on his heart. "My mind constantly dwells in the past & more especially the first four years of the magazine," he plaintively confided to Ida. "They were the golden years of my life . . . I often dream of being back with you all. I feel also how much I have done to destroy the most precious possession of my life."

Impelled by a feverish desire to reclaim the affection and respect of his colleagues, McClure spent days and nights developing an elaborate plan for a new monthly companion magazine to *McClure's*. Transported by manic excitement, the publisher convinced himself that it would be "the greatest periodical ever published in America." Once his staff understood the brilliance of the scheme, he exulted, they would acknowledge that he was "a stronger and more productive man than ever." In late November 1905, he sent the finished prospectus to Tarbell. He was sharing "a tremendous secret," he wrote, which he hoped would mollify any anxieties she might continue to harbor.

McClure's Universal Journal, the second monthly he envisioned, would be larger than the current magazine, attracting the most famous novelists and short story writers in the world and featuring serious articles about current issues. Single copies would cost but five cents, one third the price of *McClure's* magazine. The lower price would be accomplished by utilizing less expensive paper and relying on pen-and-ink illustrations instead of costly copperplate engravings. McClure predicted a net yearly income of $2 million and proposed to found the company by issuing nearly $13 million in stock. The staff of *McClure's* would manage both the current magazine and the new journal.

But Sam McClure's extravagant ambitions were not confined to the publishing world. The new monthly would be affiliated with four interlocking, profitable enterprises that would help solve pressing social problems: a People's Bank; a People's Life Insurance Company; a People's University to issue textbooks on all subjects and develop correspondence courses; and a Universal Library to supply the public with affordable copies of great works of literature no longer covered by copyright. In addition to these boggling schemes, McClure planned to purchase 1,000 acres of land upon which to build a model community with affordable housing.

Far from being intrigued, Ida Tarbell considered McClure's grandiosity a manifestation of his illness, a manic projection that eclipsed the gratification of real accomplishment. His compulsion to "build a bigger, a more imposing House of McClure" would only jeopardize the magazine to which she had devoted her best years. *McClure's Universal Journal* would inevitably compete for the same readers as *McClure's* magazine, diminishing the value of her stock in the magazine and destabilizing the entire enterprise. Most troubling of all, whether the product of megalomania or the most beneficent of motives, McClure's scheme of consolidating different enterprises under the same roof echoed the very trusts against which she and her colleagues had waged war. Her instincts told her that this was "the plan which was eventually to wreck his enterprises."

When John Phillips saw McClure's prospectus, he understood more clearly than Tarbell that the company's finances would never support a venture of this magnitude. As the largest minority stockholder and managing editor during Sam's repeated absences, Phillips had "all the different branches of the work in his hand"—the advertising department, the editorial section, the book publishing arm, the printing press, the art department. Over the years, Sam's traveling expenses had been a continuing drain on the treasury. In his expansive moods, the publisher would impulsively purchase twice as many articles as the magazine could possibly use. He had signed deals to extend the company's operations that ultimately had to be abandoned at heavy cost. He had rewarded his writers and artists with money and generous gifts. Though the magazine itself continued to flourish, the company was under stress.

For more than a decade, the steadfast Phillips had anchored the magazine. While Sam wandered through Europe, the quiet editor remained at his desk from early morning until late at night, managing the business details and working intimately with each of the writers. Ray Baker later said that he had never known an editor "who had so much of the creative touch, a kind of understanding which surprised the writer himself with unexpected possibilities in his own subjects." An "uncompromising" critic, Phillips told his writers exactly why their articles did not work, often recommending remedies and suggesting "felicities of expression which the author would have liked to think of first." William Allen White declared that without Phillips, the staff "would not know where to go or what to do."

The dynamic between Phillips and McClure had been established for a quarter of a century: when McClure was editor-in-chief of the college newspaper, John kept the paper running while Sam disappeared for days at a time; in Boston, Phillips edited the bicycling magazine, the *Wheelman*, while Sam traveled around New England in search of writers and ideas; in the early days of their New York syndicate, Phillips managed operations while McClure crossed the ocean to meet with Kipling, James Barrie, and Conan Doyle. When they were young, John had so admired Sam's energy, his "push and business ability," that he would readily have changed places with him. As Sam's mood swings intensified over the years, Phillips willingly assumed more and more of his partner's responsibilities. Finally Phillips's vaunted patience snapped— the combined impact of the Wilkinson affair, the vituperative letters from Divonne, and Sam's preemptive hiring of a high-salaried art director for the new venture proved too much.

After that rash hiring decision, Tarbell and Phillips quickly resolved to work in tandem and persuade McClure to abandon his scheme. During the Wilkinson crisis, the two had formed a close bond. Faced with this new catastrophe, they spent many hours together, strategizing over lunches in the city and dinners in each other's homes. The affection and trust Tarbell had once reserved for McClure was now claimed by Phillips. "He is certainly the rarest and most beautiful soul on earth," she told Albert Boyden, *McClure's* managing editor. In mid-January 1906, craving respite from the office maelstrom, Tarbell joined John and Jennie Phillips on a trip to Kansas, Colorado, and the Grand Canyon. In Emporia, they stayed with William Allen White, who accompanied them for the remainder of the trip.

"It has been a glorious trip," Tarbell wrote cheerfully to Boyden. Their buoyant mood was soon spoiled when they received a series of letters forwarded from the office indicating that "the Chief" had defied their objections and moved ahead in their absence to incorporate the McClure's Journal Company. Phillips "as usual is an angel & has written [McClure] a beautiful letter," Tarbell reported to Boyden, but conditions in the office had reached a "diabolical" stage, requiring a unified action to stop the madness.

McClure informed Phillips that his letter had come the very morning that the new journal's art director arrived at the office. The distraction "thoroughly unfitted me for the work with him," Sam peevishly objected. "I'm engaging upon a tremendous task, a noble and splendid one. I have the greatest idea for a periodical ever invented, and am entering upon an enterprise that will benefit everyone also tremendously, and nothing but a large recovery of my original calmness of mind, and what at one time was unruffable good nature, will enable me to stand what are really petty and useless annoyances and opposition." As "one of the most successful business organizers in this country," he continued, "it never occurred to me that having founded one business I could not found another." McClure went on to assert that his mind was "settled." He would not only launch *McClure's Universal Journal*, but would create a weekly magazine in the near future. Phillips, McClure suggested, had "a tendency to look upon the dark side of things." He recommended that his oldest friend take a two-year paid vacation to gain perspective on his "ridiculous" concerns.

Additional letters from anxious staff members soon reached the vacationers, pleading with them to return before the enterprise suffered irreparable damage. "All S.S. wants is sympathy and a recognition of his genius," Dan McKinley wrote. Their editor, he continued, "feels he is not master in his own shop; he feels that his opinions and ideas are no longer considered worthy of serious thought." Albert Boyden acknowledged that those who remained in the office could no longer cope with the situation. "I wish we did have the brains and wisdom and patience to work it out without you," he wistfully wrote, "but we have not."

By the time the entire staff reconvened in New York, Phillips had reached a desperate resolution: If he could not persuade McClure to abandon his vainglorious scheme, he would resign. "It was a momentous decision for a man of forty-five to make," Phillips wrote in an unpublished memoir. "The impelling reasons were personal, almost spiritual . . . I felt that I could not submit to being wrenched into courses and proposed undertakings that would arouse inner dissension with no prospect of peace. As soon as the decision was made, there was a great calm, a serene contentment."

When McClure learned of Phillips's decision, he summoned Tarbell to his office and demanded to know whether "anybody else is going." She informed him that she, too, would resign. Staying on without Phillips, she insisted, "would be like living in a house with a corpse." At the prospect of her desertion, McClure broke down. "You, too, Ida Tarbell," he accused. Tarbell recorded in her diary that night that as McClure railed against their departure and reiterated his abiding love for her, all she could think of was "Napoleon at Fontainebleau." Her attempts to explain to McClure that for Phillips it was a question of "his own soul"—that it was no longer possible "to live in such humiliation as he has had to endure"—failed to penetrate his hysteria. Finally, she wrote, McClure "sprang up & flung his arms around me & kissed me—left weeping & I sat down sobbing hysterically but am more convinced than ever that we are right."

In the immediate aftermath of their declared intention to resign, a compromise was nearly reached. Phillips and Tarbell agreed to stay if McClure would "democratize" the management of the magazine by creating a board of directors and putting a portion of his stock into a trusteeship administered by Tarbell, Phillips, Steffens, and Baker. When McClure acquiesced, the three of them went off for an awkward lunch together. McClure returned to the office looking "cheerful" for the first time in weeks. An agreement was drawn up.

Then, just as swiftly as McClure had agreed, he changed his mind. The notion that the magazine had become an institution "beyond the ability of one man" to run, he now told Phillips, was "utterly absurd." Though he traveled a great deal, such excursions had always proved invaluable to the magazine. "My facilities for getting to know public opinion and the opinion of able thinkers is vastly greater than it was ten years ago," he insisted. "The management of this magazine is probably not one-thousandth as difficult as Abraham Lincoln's job; but Lincoln could never have managed his job had it not been for the extraordinary facilities that went with his position for sensing public opinion."

The more he contemplated the matter, the more he realized it would be "utterly impossible" for him to accept a lesser role in the magazine. "When you read history," he proclaimed, "you find that kings who have come to the end of their tether, as a rule would suffer death rather than give up part of their power." By grandiose analogy, he would rather sell his majority interests than relinquish control. Tarbell and Phillips immediately offered to purchase his *McClure's* stock. Even as this new document was generated, however, McClure again rescinded the decision. "I cannot leave the magazine," he declared to Tarbell. "I would soon lose my mind." Discussion then shifted to the possibility that he would buy out both Phillips's and Tarbell's stock, enabling them to start their own magazine.

Throughout these negotiations and reversals, Albert Brady's brother Curtis recalled, "the entire office was embroiled in the turmoil." Members of the staff "were compelled to take sides whether or not they wished to do so, but some did it secretly—afraid to express their opinions aloud. It was not unusual to see small groups of men, with their heads together, speaking in undertones, and then busy themselves when someone else came along." It soon became clear that the majority of the staff backed Phillips and Tarbell, including Steffens, Baker, Boyden, and John Siddall.

Explaining his decision to resign in a letter to his father, Steffens observed that McClure had been away for months, "playing and getting well." Then, upon his return, he had embarked upon "a big, fool scheme of founding a new magazine with a string of banks, insurance companies, etc., and a capitalization of $15,000,000. It was not only fool, it was not quite right." Indeed, it seemed "a speculative scheme," designed to extract money from investors that would never be repaid, much like the schemes *McClure's* magazine had been reporting on over the years. "Having built up *McClure's,* given it purpose and character, and increased its circulation so that it was a power as well as a dividend-payer," Steffens maintained, "we did not propose to stand by and see it exploited and used, even by the owner."

During this tumultuous period, Ray Baker had been absent from the office completing his railroad articles. Warned of the situation by a stream of alarming letters, he confided to his wife on March 9 that McClure had "become so utterly unbalanced & unreasonable that he is almost past working with." A week later he grimly concluded that "dynamite, nitroglycerine & black powder" had been laid and could not be defused. When the time came, Baker decided to join his departing associates, who, as he told his father, "are not only my friends, but who have contributed largely to whatever success I have attained." The departure left him painfully adrift: "I was left with no certainty, at the moment anyway, of continuing to do the work to which I was most deeply devoted; I was lost in a fog of contention and antagonism." Recalling the discord years later, Baker acknowledged that "in the afterlook these ills seem trivial enough: at that time, they were all but catastrophic."

⌒ ⌒

AS RUMORS SPREAD ABOUT THE impending breakup at *McClure's*, many in the press mistakenly attributed the schism to a memorable address that President Roosevelt delivered that same spring. Exasperated by a sensationalist attack on the U.S. Senate in a magazine owned by his hated political rival, William Randolph Hearst, Roosevelt denounced investigative journalists as muckrakers, bent on relentless negativity and dispiriting exploitation of the nation's ills. "In Bunyan's *Pilgrim's Progress*," he began, "you may recall the description of the Man with the Muck-rake, the man who could look no way but downward." Bunyan's muckraker, he suggested, "typifies the man who in this life consistently refuses to see aught that is lofty, and fixes his eyes with solemn intentness only on that which is vile and debasing."

The coincidence of this speech and the first reports of dissension at the magazine led reporters to speculate that McClure had responded to the president's denunciation of muckraking with a decision to soften future exposés. According to such accounts, Tarbell, Steffens, and Baker, unwilling to accept the change in policy, had deserted to form their own magazine. McClure unequivocally rejected reports that Roosevelt's speech had in any way "affected his views of what a magazine ought to be." *McClure's*, he insisted, would continue to "report the activities of contemporary life," as it had always done. Nonetheless, the lingering implication that the editor had planned "to muzzle his writers" exacerbated McClure's distress.

"The Treason of the Senate," the explosive series that aroused Roosevelt's ire, was conceived by William Randolph Hearst, who had long targeted the trust-dominated Senate in his newspapers. During Hearst's short career as a Democratic congressman from New York and throughout his failed presidential run in 1904, the flamboyant publisher had agitated for a constitutional amendment stipulating popular election of senators. A democratic process, he argued, should replace the current system of election by state legislatures. The 1905 purchase of his first monthly magazine, *The Cosmopolitan*, provided an ideal forum to continue his campaign. He offered David Graham Phillips, the best-selling progressive novelist, a handsome price and substantial research help to undertake an investigation of the Senate's betrayal of the public interest. The first of nine monthly installments appeared in March 1906, just as Roosevelt was battling to secure Senate approval of his signature bill to regulate the railroads.

"Treason is a strong word," the David Graham Phillips series began, "but not too strong, rather too weak, to characterize the situation in which the Senate is the eager, resourceful, indefatigable agent of interests as hostile to the American people as any invading army could be, and vastly more dangerous; interests that manipulate the prosperity produced by all, so that it heaps up riches for the few." In the course of the series, Phillips would sketch individual biographies of eighteen Republican and three Democratic senators. Each portrait revealed "a triangulation" between the senator's eagerness to assist corporations, the increase of his personal wealth, and the expansion of his influence in Washington. Though criticism of the Senate's hostility to progressive reform was not new, the scathing language and focused attack on the most powerful Republican leaders (including Lodge, Aldrich, Elkins, and Knox) attracted widespread attention. The circulation of *The Cosmopolitan* doubled overnight. Throughout the country, small daily and weekly newspapers reprinted individual articles. "Little wonder," the historian George Mowry observes, "that Theodore Roosevelt feared a general discrediting of his party, the national legislature, and indeed the administration if the effects of such charges were not somehow dissipated."

New York senator Chauncey Depew, who had nominated Roosevelt for governor in 1898, was targeted in the first piece. "For those who like the sight of a corpse well beaten up," one newspaper editorialized, this "mean" portrait deserved "the championship belt." Under a picture of Depew, the caption announced: "Here is the archetypal Face of the Sleek, Self-Satisfied American Opportunist in Politics and Plunder." Railroad barons Cornelius and William Vanderbilt were identified as the men who first enlisted Depew in "personal and official service. . . . And ever since then have owned [him] mentally and morally." Throughout the article, charges of "boodler" and "robber" were leveled, alongside the labels "coward" and "sniveling sycophant."

Although he never accused Depew of outright venality, Phillips argued that the New York senator, like many of his colleagues, was thoroughly beholden to the campaign contributions of the special interests.

The tone of the piece appalled Roosevelt. He told his journalist friend Alfred Henry Lewis that while he had the "heartiest sympathy and commendation" for responsible attacks on corruption, "hysteria and sensationalism" would fail to produce "any permanent good," and the country would conclude that "the liar is in the long run as noxious as the thief." The series produced outrage in the conservative press. *The Critic* accused Phillips of "sowing the seeds of anarchy." The New York *Sun* asserted that debasing an institution created by the founding fathers was tantamount to "playing with matches in dangerous proximity to a powder magazine." Speaking in defense of the Senate, Henry Cabot Lodge declared: "Slander and misrepresentation directed against individuals are not of much importance, but wise institutions and free systems of government, painfully wrought, tried in the fires of sacrifice and suffering, should endure."

Concerned that the "epidemic of Congress-baiting" would jeopardize his regulatory program, Roosevelt devised a clever counterstroke. On March 17, 1906, at the annual dinner of the Gridiron Club, an informal assembly of reporters, editors, cabinet officials, and leaders in business and academia, Roosevelt delivered his own piece of propaganda. After a series of humorous skits, the president spoke without notes for forty-five minutes, railing against "muckrakers," who saturated magazines and newspapers "with sensational articles," dredging all that was bleak and corrupt while "ignoring at the same time the good in the world." He had initially planned to indict David Graham Phillips, but Elihu Root persuaded him that a personal attack would only fuel the writer's celebrity. By avoiding a direct condemnation of the "Treason" series, however, Roosevelt inadvertently left the audience speculating about his intended targets.

In truth, the president's attack on the muckrakers reflected more than momentary anger at Hearst and David Graham Phillips. His exasperation with the proliferation of increasingly sensational and shoddily investigated exposure journalism had been slowly building. Although "the masters" at *McClure's* typically invested months and even years of careful research in their studies, a host of less meticulous and principled "imitators" had followed in their wake. In the competition for "hot stuff," politicians and businessmen were being "tried and found guilty in magazine counting rooms before the investigation is begun." The carefully documented quest for truth had been supplanted by slapdash, often slanderous accusations. Even when the articles rested on solid documentary evidence, Roosevelt feared that an incessant fixation on corruption had begun "to produce a very unhealthy condition of excitement and irritation in the public mind," leading to an "enormous increase in socialistic propaganda."

As usual, Peter Dunne's Mr. Dooley trenchantly captured public agitation. There once was a time, the Irish bartender opined, when reading popular magazines calmed the mind. Readers came away feeling that life was a "glad, sweet song." Indeed, one could drape his "watch on the knob" on an unlocked door, confident it would be there in the morning. Now, however, a reader turning the pages of any magazine would discover that "everything has gone wrong." Corruption and double-dealing today were so rampant that "the world is little better," Dooley concluded, "than a convict's camp." Roosevelt "immensely" enjoyed Mr. Dooley's outlook. "I get sick of people who are always insisting upon nothing but the dark side of life," he told Dunne. "There are a lot of things that need correction in this country; but there is not the slightest use of feeling over-pessimistic about it."

National fatigue with the ubiquitous literature of exposure had already set in when Roosevelt spoke to the Gridiron Club. "The public cannot stand at attention with its eyes fixed on one spot indefinitely," the literary critic Edwin E. Slosson shrewdly observed. "It is bound to get restive, and seek diversion in other interests." A Wisconsin municipal court judge expressed the resentment of many: "It is getting so nowadays that the man or corporation that accumulates property to any extent is made the subject of these attacks." Nor, a fellow Wisconsin citizen observed, should a man be considered "a criminal simply because he holds a public office."

↝ ↜

THE MORNING AFTER THE GRIDIRON speech, Lincoln Steffens called on the president. "Well," Steffens reproached, "you have put an end to all these journalistic investigations that have made you." Roosevelt insisted that he had not intended a general indictment of legitimate reporters like Steffens. He was simply defending "poor old Chauncey Depew" against a terribly unfair portrait in the Hearst press. Steffens remained unconvinced, correctly sensing the president's growing impatience with the never-ending exposés—even as he relied on them to mobilize public opinion.

In fact, on several occasions the previous year, Roosevelt had directly criticized Steffens for his tendency to "repeat as true unfounded gossip of a malicious or semimalicious character." It was "an absurdity," he had scolded Steffens, to claim that Senator Aldrich was "the boss of the United States."

Such a preposterous claim carried "a sinister significance," for "[we] suffer quite as much from exaggerated, hysterical, and untruthful statements in the press as from any wrongdoing by businessmen or politicians." Roosevelt had also decried Steffens's characterization of Postmaster General Henry C. Payne as the ringleader of a corrupt effort to fix legislators and thereby destroy Governor La Follette's legislative program. "Poor Payne is sick either unto death or nigh unto death," Roosevelt had complained to Lodge, two days before Payne died. "This attack on him in *McClure's Magazine* by Steffens was, I think, the immediate cause of breaking him down; and I am convinced that it is an infamously false attack."

Nevertheless, Steffens had continued to enjoy unusual access to the White House. When he arrived in Washington to investigate whether the corruption uncovered in city and state governments extended to the federal level, Roosevelt offered to help. The president provided the celebrated journalist with a card inscribed: "To any officer or employee of the Government, Please tell Mr. Lincoln Steffens anything whatever about the running of the government that you know (not incompatible with the public interest) and provided only that you tell him the truth—no matter what it may be—I will see that you are not hurt. T. Roosevelt."

The resultant syndicated series, however, nettled Roosevelt. To Steffens, the signal question America faced could not be answered with the passage of railroad regulation or food and drug laws, but only with fundamental change to the corrupt system that invested special interests with undue power at the expense of the people. "I'd rather make our government represent us than dig the canal; the President would rather dig the canal and regulate railway rates. So he makes his 'deal' with the speaker and I condemn it."

Roosevelt was especially angered by reformers' accusations that he was too compromising in his efforts to remedy the abuses of capitalism. "In stating your disapproval of my efforts to get results," he wrote Steffens, "which of course must be gotten by trying to come to a working agreement with the Senate and House and therefore by making mutual concessions, you have often said or implied that I ought to refuse to make any concessions, but stand uncompromisingly for my beliefs, and let the people decide. As a matter of fact I have come a great deal nearer getting what I wanted than, for instance, Governor La Follette."

Roosevelt grumbled that Steffens and his friends failed to understand the requisites of practical leadership—a sense of when to move forward, when to hold back, when to mobilize the public, when to negotiate behind closed doors. Leadership that led to genuine progress depended upon an acute sense of timing, a feel for both the public and the congressional pulse. Yet in recent months it had seemed that crusading writers were intent on usurping his authority, creating the intolerable impression that rather than "summoning," Roosevelt "was being dragged."

All these frustrations had informed Roosevelt's decision to castigate the "new journalism" at the Gridiron Club Dinner. Remarks at the informal club meeting were traditionally off the record, but word of the president's dramatic condemnation "spread like wildfire," along with speculation that he was referencing progressive writers such as Lincoln Steffens, Ray Baker, David Phillips, and Upton Sinclair. When Roosevelt announced his intention to reiterate his Gridiron message in a public address, Baker was dumbfounded, concerned that "such an attack might greatly injure the work which we were trying honestly to do." He finally decided to write a frank letter to the president. "I have been much disturbed at the report of your proposed address," Baker began. "Even admitting that some of the so-called 'exposures' have been extreme, have they not, as a whole, been honest and useful? and would not a speech, backed by all of your great authority, attacking the magazines, tend to give aid and comfort to these very rascals" whose activities were being exposed by hardworking journalists? Moreover, he warned, "the first to stop the work of letting in the light and air will be those who have been trying honestly to tell the whole truth, good and bad, and leave the field to the outright ranters and inciters."

Roosevelt was undeterred. "One reason I want to make that address," he replied the next day, "is because people so persistently misunderstand what I said." The president confided in Baker that "Hearst's papers and magazines" were his intended target and promised his speech would clarify that he abhorred "the whitewash brush quite as much as of mud slinging."

Roosevelt delivered his formal "Muckrake Man" address on April 14, 1906. That he seriously considered Baker's concerns is evident in his carefully measured speech. He cautioned that his words must not be distorted, insisting "at the risk of repetition" that the fight against corruption and exploitation must continue. Every word of reproach against the crusading journalists was counterbalanced with a word of commendation. He termed their investigations "indispensable," yet explained that when muckrakers penned "sensational, lurid and untruthful" articles, they became "potent forces for evil." In the end, however, Roosevelt's vivid portrait of the muckraker eclipsed his positive remarks about investigative journalism. His speech was widely received as an indiscriminate attack on all reform journalists.

Commentators reflected that the president could not publicly speak "upon a question which is shaking the country from center to circumference without exercising a powerful influence upon one side of the other." And despite his "almost nervous dread" of misinterpretation, Roosevelt had "put into the hands of every trust magnate, every insurance thief, and every political corruptionist a handy weapon which will be used unconscionably for their defense." All such interests, one journal predicted, would "now plead not guilty, point to the 'muck rake' and seek shelter behind the portly figure of the President."

Baker read the speech as a profound betrayal. He noted sadly that while Roosevelt had indeed employed his "familiar balance of approval and disapproval," he had failed to distinguish between the sensationalist yellow press and the responsible journalists. "He did not 'think it worthwhile' to acknowledge the service of those men who had been striving to tell the truth, honestly and completely, whose work he had repeatedly approved, and for whose help he had again and again expressed his appreciation," Baker later wrote. Instead, the indelible image of the muckraker "classed all of us together."

Baker's alarm proved well founded: *McClure's* magazine, the most illustrious journal, was "singled out" for a devastating satire in *Life* magazine. Each of the writers of "McSure's" magazine—Ida Tarbarrell, Ray Standard Fakir, Sinkem Beffens—was viciously mocked in turn. "I'm giving my whole life to breaking the butterfly of a John Rockefeller upon the wheel of my ponderous articles," Tarbell/Tarbarrell was quoted as saying. "He's got too much money. If that isn't a shame, I'd like to know what a shame is!" In another scathing send-up, Steffens/Beffens humbly submitted to a supposed interview: "I'm not really great. I'm only eminent, unparalleled, superlatively remarkable." Pondering such achievement, the interviewer highlighted Steffens's process: "With only his suit-case and his gold rake studded with diamonds, he can take the morning train for an unknown city, rake off in a few hours the thick slime of municipal corruption and have a shame-shrieking article ready for McSure's by night."

"These satirical jabs cut [Baker] deeply," his biographer claims. "The bubble of devoted public service that had developed around his work had been irreparably punctured." Deeply demoralized to find his name among those "cast into outer darkness," Baker would never forgive Roosevelt. "I met the President many times afterward and there were numerous exchanges of letters," he recalled, "but while I could wonder at his remarkable versatility of mind, and admire his many robust human qualities, I could never again give him my full confidence, nor follow his leadership."

In the wake of the president's speech, morale among conservatives and

corporate interests rallied. The New York *Sun* proclaimed that the muckrakers' era of exposure had come to an end: "It was a great day while it lasted, but
it became too hot. The Muck-rakers worked merrily for a time in their own
bright sunshine, and an unthinking populace applauded their performance.
Now there are few to do them reverence." It was said, only partly in jest, that
"rebaters and bribers" were "beginning to walk abroad with the old smile,"
sensing that "the tidal wave of magazine reform" was finally abating.

Progressives mounted an impassioned defense of the magazine crusaders.
One supporter argued that these journalists numbered among "the loftiest
and purest of living patriots, who have taken their professional and political
lives in their hands that they might serve as 'soldiers of the common good.' "
Their "long, laborious work" had initiated the "inspiring movement" for honest government; no fair-minded citizen could deny the "astonishingly great"
influence of Ida Tarbell, Lincoln Steffens, or Ray Baker. "The day will come,"
one sympathetic commentator correctly predicted, "when the 'muck rake' will
be borne through the streets as a triumphant emblem of reform," when the
epithet "muckraker" would become "a badge of honor."

ON MAY 11, 1906, FOUR weeks after the president's speech, the *New York Times*
confirmed that Phillips, Tarbell, Steffens, Baker, and Boyden were leaving *Mc-
Clure's*. Furthermore, it was understood that the five journalists were "quietly
planning to start a magazine venture of their own." After weeks of turmoil,
McClure had finally agreed to buy out Phillips and Tarbell, whose combined
stock was worth $187,000. He also promised each of them six months salary at
full pay. "I am certain that it is not in my power at the present time adequately
to reward them for their services, which no money could pay for," McClure
told a business associate. "They leave me retaining my deepest love and affection and esteem and confidence. I think I may say that it is the greatest
tragedy thus far of my life to lose them." With Baker and Steffens, he was
equally generous, continuing their salaries while they completed work on
already contracted projects. "I wish you all good fortune," he told Baker. "I
have always enjoyed working with you and your work has been very successful
in the magazine, and I am very sorry to lose you." Moved by his publisher's
remarkable magnanimity, Steffens observed: "There was nothing mean about
S. S. McClure."

In the aftermath of the schism, McClure lost not only his star writers but
his partner, managing editor, and three top business executives as well. While
some in the publishing world wondered if he could survive the loss of the in-

imitable team that had given the magazine "its chief features of life and popularity," Sam McClure proved surprisingly resilient in the face of catastrophe.
Necessity compelled him to abandon his "colossal scheme" and focus all his
energies on rebuilding the magazine. "I have really to look after almost every
department," he told Hattie, "and am getting up material for the fall prospectus. I am standing it splendidly; I rarely get tired." Without Phillips to maintain
daily operations, he could no longer escape responsibility and found himself
"working harder" than ever before. In the office by 8 a.m., McClure remained
at his desk long past midnight, sustaining himself on "three or four quarts of
milk a day." After midnight, he retired to an apartment on a floor above the
magazine's offices to read "masses of manuscripts," including portions of an
autobiography by Mark Twain which his syndicate had agreed to publish.

In a matter of weeks, McClure managed to assemble an almost completely
new roster of talent. Of the original team, only the poetry editor Witter Bynner,
the manuscript reader Viola Roseboro, and Albert Brady's younger brothers—
Curtis, Oscar, and Ed—remained. To replace Ida Tarbell, he relied upon Willa
Cather, a little known fiction writer who would become a world-class novelist.
He hired Will Irwin, a distinguished reporter from the New York *Sun*, as
managing editor. Two first-rate investigative reporters, George Kibbe Turner
and Burton Hendrick, joined the staff full time, along with Ellery Sedgwick,
the future editor of the *Atlantic Monthly*. "The very name, *McClure's Magazine*,
had an irresistible attraction for any young man," Sedgwick explained. Much
as Tarbell, Baker, and Steffens had described their Chief in happier years,
Sedgwick was mesmerized by McClure's "burning force," explaining how
"everyone about him caught fire and he would inflame the intelligence of his
staff into molten excitement."

Though his eager new writers lacked the renown of the original team,
McClure reasoned that before long he would "be able to repeat the process"
that had made Tarbell, Steffens, and Baker household names. The newly
constituted group did indeed produce a number of significant investigations in
the months that followed; but the tenor of the magazine, reflecting the temper
of the nation, had changed. Even before Roosevelt delivered his "Muckrake
Man" speech, McClure had sensed that public interest in the parade of public
and private misbehavior was waning. "To go on now with the heavy exposure
articles," he told his stockholders, "would not convert those who disagree with
us, and those who agree with us don't need conversion."

Furthermore, the new staff members brought differing sensibilities and
strategies to *McClure's*. Although Ellery Sedgwick had applauded the early

efforts of the crusading journalists, he believed the time had come "to halt and to think soberly." Too many editors, he charged, had lost "all sense of responsibility" in the race for circulation. Ida Tarbell's replacement, Willa Cather, also had a profound influence on the magazine's direction. She edited a superb series on the Christian Science founder Mary Baker Eddy; but Cather's real genius lay in literature, in historical narratives rather than accounts of present-day political struggles and economic analyses. Consequently, while the quality of fiction and poetry in *McClure's* remained high, the impact of the investigative pieces diminished. *McClure's* was not alone; a similar shift took place in popular publications across the country, a literature "of distraction" gradually replacing the literature of "inquiry."

If "an exhilarating sense of excitement and adventure" permeated the revivified magazine in the early months, it was not long before McClure's mercurial temperament produced unbearable tensions within the newly organized staff. As managing editor, Will Irwin found it impossible to deal with the endless intrigues McClure manufactured. "As a curb on genius," he acknowledged, "I was not a success." Sedgwick reported that "the staff worked under some natural law of desperation. The chief was forever interrupting, cutting every sequence into a dozen parts." The dynamic had become frustrating: "A week in the McClure office was the precise reversal of the six busy days described in the first chapter of Genesis. It seemed to end in a world without form and void. From Order came forth Chaos." In fifteen months, both Sedgwick and Irwin were fired.

McClure soldiered on. For years, the fiction and poetry that he scouted and commissioned would continue to set the literary standard for American magazines. He published early stories by Damon Runyan and Joseph Conrad, introduced A. E. Housman's *Shropshire Lad* to the American public, and provided a forum for the new work of William Butler Yeats and Moira O'Neill. The company eventually foundered, hampered by the costs of buying out the departing writers and constructing a new printing plant on Long Island. Forced to economize, McClure could no longer continue his penchant for liberal spending to attract the most gifted writers. Nor could he afford to keep his book publishing arm, which he sold to Doubleday, Page & Company. The magazine never recovered the strength or influence it had exerted during its heyday.

Public disenchantment with sensationalist journalism and Theodore Roosevelt's dramatic caricature of the muckrakers may have conspired to diminish the stature and power of *McClure's*. The real corrosion of the magazine's intensive energy happened from within, however, precipitated by the same force that had made the enterprise great: the outsized personality and manic power of S. S. McClure himself.

☙ ❧

THE SHIFTING PUBLIC MOOD ALSO presented difficulties for Phillips and the rest of the departing team. They had initially planned to launch their own venture, but when *The American Magazine*, a monthly "of good reputation," was offered for sale, they pooled their resources to meet the $400,000 price tag. At the time, *The American* was "just about holding its own, financially." By re-creating the publication as a writer's magazine, built upon their own good names, they hoped to raise the circulation and "make it profitable within a comparatively short time."

"All of us had plunged into the enterprise with astonishingly little regard for the future," Baker recalled. "No one of us had much money: we put into the common fund all we had and more." In addition, the friends decided to heavily cut their own paychecks until they turned a profit. If the magazine failed, Baker acknowledged, he stood "to lose everything." Still, he told his father, there was nothing "so dizzily stimulating" as building a new enterprise, "resting in complete confidence upon one's friends, devoted to what one considers high purposes, each sacrificing to the limit for the common cause."

For Steffens, too, trepidation mingled with excitement. "I feel as if I were at the crisis of my life," he wrote. "We are buying an old magazine which we propose to make the greatest thing of the kind that was ever made in this world—sincere, but good-natured; honest, but humorous; aggressive, but not unkind; a straight, hard fighter, but cheerful." Though Ida Tarbell seemed to Baker "the most dauntless of the adventurers," she fully recognized what was at stake. Each of them had "seen something in which they deeply believed go to pieces," she recalled. All of them "had been too cruelly bruised to take anything lightly."

William Allen White followed his friends to *The American Magazine*. Though not party to the bitter final months in the *McClure's* office, White had nevertheless determined long before that despite Sam McClure's "spark of genius," the magazine's stability and success had always relied upon the ballast of John Phillips. White chose to help finance the *The American* but maintained that he bore absolutely no ill will toward McClure or his magazine, where he had received "nothing but the kindest treatment." Indeed, even as he cast his lot with the new venture, he reached out to McClure. "You may draw on me whenever you will for whatever you will," he assured the editor.

Everyone recognized that creating cohesion, building a trusting yet playful atmosphere, would foster the success of *The American*. When Phillips and
Tarbell persuaded Finley Peter Dunne to join the group, Baker was thrilled:
"Everything amused him! We were youthful and dead in earnest—and he was
wise." Dunne proved himself a great companion, who "loved so much to talk"
that he could entertain his office mates for hours. "He had a wide knowledge
of men and their ways," Tarbell recalled. Whenever conflict arose within
the team, "Mr. Dooley" could be relied upon to lighten the heavy mood. As
managing editor, Albert Boyden "made it his business" to foster camaraderie
among his writers and contributors at the new magazine. At his fourth-floor
walk-up on Stuyvesant Square, he hosted regular dinners for a revolving
group of novelists, artists, politicians, and scientists. "What talk went on in that
high-up living room!" Tarbell recalled. "What wonderful tales we heard!"

The press assumed that with "all the muckrakers muckraking under one
tent," *The American Magazine* would provide "a helpful experiment" to determine whether the public appetite for exposure journalism had truly atrophied.
"Their muck-raking has been of the convincing rather than the frenzied variety and they have reputations for literary honesty to be maintained," the
Omaha *Evening World-Herald* observed. "This is undoubtedly the most notable combination that has ever launched any publication." The Boston *Journal
of Education* expressed certitude that the pioneers of authentic investigative
journalism would produce an outstanding magazine.

Although the new publishing team proudly proclaimed that they would
"not be deterred by adjectives or phrases," their first public announcement
nevertheless reflected anxiety about the shift in popular sentiment: "We shall
not only make this new *American Magazine* interesting and important in a
public way, but we shall make it the most stirring and delightful monthly book
of fiction, humor, sentiment and joyous reading that is anywhere published. It
will reflect a happy, struggling, fighting world, in which, as we believe, good
people are coming out on top. There is no field of human activity in which
we are not interested. Our magazine will be wholesome, hopeful, stimulating,
uplifting, and above all, it will have a human interest on every page."

The statement provoked a wave of positive commentary in the press, accompanied by pointed advice. "Reformers need relaxation," *The Outlook* observed, "and it has sometimes seemed of late as if, in his endeavor to secure
greatly needed righteousness, the ardent and patriotic American might lose his
ability to be at ease in a world in which there are so many sources of pleasure
as well as of pain." William Allen White, whose cheerful temperament had
never really suited him for muckraking, offered similar counsel. "It seems to

me the great danger," he told Phillips, "is that of being too Purposeful. People will expect the pale drawn face; the set lips and a general line of emotional insanity. You should fool 'em."

In the end, the new enterprise suffered not from a surfeit of purpose but from a lack of direction. Pressure to fill pages in the early months led to a publication without the focused passion and clear vision of the old *McClure's*. "We are editing in a very funny way," Boyden acknowledged. "We rush in every good thing every month and trust to the Lord to send more." Phillips implored each writer "to look into his literary cupboard" for half-finished work and send it pell-mell to New York. Consequently, those early issues comprised a miscellany: Tarbell submitted articles on Abraham Lincoln and John D. Rockefeller as she began a long series on the tariff; White contrasted Emporia and New York in one article, and the altruistic and egoistic spirit of man in another; Steffens profiled William Randolph Hearst and produced admiring portraits of several prominent progressives or "Upbuilders," including the timber fraud prosecutor Francis Heney and the idealistic millionaire Rudolph Spreckels; and Baker, while investigating the problem of race in America, contributed a long series of articles on the pastoral joys to be found outside the nation's growing cities.

The country life series proved a much-needed tonic for Ray Baker's life and career. "Utterly beaten down with weariness" following the disintegration of *McClure's*, he had returned to the "safe haven" of his country home in East Lansing, still a small village surrounded by farmhouses and "stretches of wilderness." Just as the rugged Arizona landscape had once provided solace during an earlier period of depression, so Michigan's "natural beauties" now absorbed his attention. For hours each day, he split cordwood, mulched fruit trees, and planted shrubs. Such "hard physical work" began to restore his body and mind.

When he received Phillips's request to rummage his literary cupboard, Baker turned to the private journals he had been keeping for nearly a decade. In these pages, he had recorded not only his thoughts on politics and economics but daily observations of rural life. Reading over these entries, he conceived the idea of a fictional alter ego: an educated, successful man who had abandoned his frenetic city life for the rigors and simple pleasures of life on a farm. When Baker sat down to organize his thoughts, memories of his childhood in the frontier town of St. Croix and winters working as a schoolteacher in small Michigan farming communities mingled with his recent experiences in East Lansing. Writing "more easily" than ever before, Baker completed six potential installments for the magazine in three weeks. Anxious that the portrait of country life would confound readers accustomed to his hard-hitting investigative journalism, he chose to solicit an opinion of his new work using the pen name "David Grayson." Swearing Phillips and the staff to secrecy, he mailed out the manuscript with a note: "Take care of my child." Though he later acknowledged how "ridiculous" his request must have appeared, this more intimate mode of writing was "something utterly different" from his previous successful work. Finally, after restless days spent rambling through the countryside, the editorial judgment from Phillips arrived by telegraph: "Manuscript a delight. Bully boy. Send more chapters."

The David Grayson stories instantly resonated with the reading public. Fan letters arrived by the thousands. "You have sublimated the *real* but commonplace experiences of life that we all enjoy," one admirer wrote, "but never take the time or have the talent to write about." David Grayson clubs sprang up in all sections of the country. Women dreamed of marrying a gentleman like David Grayson, a philosopher-farmer with a well-stocked library who had found happiness and peace in growing things, farm auctions, country fairs, schoolhouse meetings, and neighborly conversations. "David Grayson is a great man," Lincoln Steffens told Baker. "I never had realized there was in you such a sense of beauty, so much fine, philosophic wisdom and, most wonderful of all—serenity." Under such titles as *Adventures in Contentment* and *Adventures in Friendship*, the collected Grayson stories continued for decades, filling six books that sold over 2 million copies. Not until years later, when he discovered that imposters were presenting lectures and readings across the country under the name of David Grayson, did Baker finally claim Grayson's work as his own.

While Phillips delighted in the acclaim given the Grayson stories, he had advised Baker even before the series began that "people will be expecting something from you over your own name—something that is timely and notable and distinguished." The industrious Baker had no sooner completed his first Grayson installments than he embarked for San Francisco in early August 1906. There, he documented the aftermath of the devastating earthquake and fire of the previous spring before embarking on what critics considered his best magazine journalism, a "pioneer" study of "the Negro in American life."

His interest had been awakened by two previous articles on lynching he had produced for *McClure's*. Baker traveled extensively throughout the South and the North, talking with people, gathering statistics, reading local papers, and assembling data. Everywhere, he worked "to get at the *facts*," to create a dispassionate portrait of African-American life, of racial prejudice and Jim Crow, of southern moderates and northern philanthropists. Three decades later, in preparing *An American Dilemma*, Gunnar Myrdal relied on Baker's twelve-part series as "a major source." Still, this new work could not match the concrete impact of his earlier series on labor and the railroads. "The Riddle of the Negro" provided only the nebulous hope that "a clear statement of the case" would nudge Americans toward substituting "understanding and sympathy for blind repulsion and hatred." One Pennsylvania newspaper observed matter-of-factly that *The American* was "reporting the negro problem with no effort to solve it." The issue of race in America, the *Bedford Gazette* agreed, was simply "too complex to solve." In the first decade of the twentieth century, a fair-minded discussion of the racial problem represented a significant step forward. The issues containing Baker's series sold throughout the country. "Your work has been a wonderful thing for us," Tarbell assured Baker, "and I am proud of you." Phillips appreciatively told Baker that people everywhere were talking about his articles on race, with the consensus that they were "the best things running now in any magazine."

If Baker contributed disproportionately to the first issues of the new magazine, Lincoln Steffens seriously disappointed his colleagues. Initially inspired by the idea of a writer's magazine, Steffens soon chafed at the "consensus editing," allocation of space, demand for proof against libel, and hurried deadlines. "It does not matter," Phillips told Steffens, "how hard you work and write, if we don't get the material into the magazine when it needs it." The new magazine simply did not have the working capital *McClure's* had enjoyed to cover false starts or years of travel and research. Frayed by the production schedule, Boyden had little patience with Steffens's constant complaints that his articles were given less space in *The American* than they had been granted in *McClure's*. "You are crazy, Stef," Boyden testily replied, enclosing a comparison to show the griping was unfounded. Meanwhile, Boyden reminded Steffens, he had failed to answer a request for pictures to accompany one of his articles. "We don't need any sleeping partners in this concern," Peter Dunne grumbled.

Steffens shot off a resentful letter to Phillips, enumerating his grievances. "It is very difficult for me to write calmly after receiving a letter such as yours," Phillips responded. "It seems to me not only unsympathetic but unmanly. It repudiates all the terms of our association in its tone and its temper. It seems to me that you cannot stand on the threshold and speak spitefully through the door: that you should either come in or go out. . . . I could very easily by comparison show that you have had more out of this magazine than anybody else in proportion to what you have put in." Indeed, he pointed out, the magazine was covering not only Steffens's traveling expenses but those of his wife and her elderly mother. Most disappointing of all, Phillips rebuked his longtime friend and colleague, "you haven't confidence in us, and that is everything!"

Steffens remained oblivious to the vexation of the other staff members. He had money, celebrity, lecture invitations, and a new seaside estate near Cos Cob, Connecticut. "My husband has become famous," Josephine Steffens reflected sadly, "but at a high price." Steffens had issued a sanctimonious ultimatum to his partners: "Either I am to write as I please without being edited; or I quit." Six months later, he resigned from the magazine. At the time of his departure, Steffens argued that he must sell his stock in order to meet expenses while he sought a new position. His partners agreed to buy him out, further diminishing the working capital of the new enterprise.

Through all the hurly-burly at *The American*, Ida Tarbell remained the same stabilizing force she had always been at *McClure's*. Only later did she acknowledge how disorienting the transition had been. "I know now I should not have taken it as well as I did (and inwardly that was nothing to boast of) if it had not been cushioned by an engrossing personal interest," she recalled. Although her New York apartment had served as her "writing headquarters" for years, Ida had yearned for a country home. During the turbulent spring of 1906, she finally purchased an old farmhouse situated on forty acres of land in Redding Ridge, Connecticut. Initially, she planned to use the abandoned property as a retreat, doing only the most necessary maintenance. But soon she was tempted to start "borrowing and mortgaging" to fix the roof and wallpaper the rooms, taking on extra freelance work to pay for furniture, rugs, and antiques. Before long, Tarbell turned her energies to the land: she pruned apple trees, planted crops, created a new orchard, and bought chickens, a cow, a pig, and two horses. Ever practical, she reallocated money set aside for an evening gown to purchase some much-needed fertilizer for the garden. Encouraged by the warmth and camaraderie of her rural neighbors, she learned what Baker had already discovered—that "the most genuine of human dramas" could be found in the trials and triumphs of the surrounding countryside.

"All this was good for me," Ida reflected of her rural homemaking, "but while it was good for me it was not so good for my work on the magazine." Preoccupied with the engaging task of furnishing her new home, she found her research on the tariff increasingly tedious. By pursuing the subject in her first big series for *The American*, she had hoped to expose the special interests that lay behind the complicated schedules for wool, iron ore, coal, sugar, or flax. She loathed protectionism and intended to "get into the fight" for revision. Nevertheless, after months in Washington studying every issue of the

Congressional Record since the Civil War, Tarbell could not render the subject engaging or alive. Though she talked with senators and congressmen who had taken part in earlier tariff struggles, the debates that appeared "so important" to her were "a dead issue to them."

Tarbell's six-part series, "The Tariff in Our Times," ran from December 1906 through June 1907, with three additional installments published two years later. Critics lauded the "comprehensive and careful accumulation of chronological information," but most found the cumulative effect uninspiring. Tarbell dealt "exhaustively (and at times exhaustingly)" with events, one reviewer noted, yet the whole remained "invertebrate." She was the first to admit that her early installments lacked "vitality" and that she relied too heavily on "secondhand" material. The series had no "cohesive force," William Allen White told her candidly. "It is not written around the progressive narrative; it continues but doesn't get anywhere, there is no beginning, climax and end." It seemed to White that the project required exactly what McClure had prescribed as Tarbell researched the Standard Oil Company: "a central figure" that would "hold the reader." While Tarbell's series would eventually build momentum during the fiery debates over the Payne-Aldrich Tariff in 1909, her initial contribution did little to buoy the struggling fortunes of *The American Magazine*.

On July 1, 1907, Tarbell wrote a long letter to Bert Boyden offering her assessment of the magazine's first year. Something was missing, she conceded, "a certain hustle, ingenuity—a generalizing effort such as we used to get out of S.S. It's a talent—a genius, and we haven't it in the staff."

Uncannily, Ida Tarbell received a letter that same day from her old friend and former Chief. "I dreamed of you," McClure told her. "I thought I was telling you how I found out that by speaking slowly & calmly and acting calmly I found I had much greater influence on people (I am actually doing this) & I thought that I was standing by your chair & you drew me down & kissed me to show your approval. When you disapproved of me it nearly broke my heart," he confided, offering a final touching confession: "I never cease to love you as I have for many, many years. I wish you had not turned away."

The Roosevelt children, ranging here from five to nineteen years of age, unabashedly made the White House their own. Not since Willie and Tad Lincoln scampered through the halls had there been such a din in the executive mansion. "Places that had not seen a human being for years were made alive by the howls and laughter of these newcomers," observed the chief usher at the White House.

The Tafts, shown here circa 1904, traded their exotic life in the Malacañan Palace for a house on K Street in Washington. Their daughter Helen joined Ethel Roosevelt at the National Cathedral School, and seven-year-old Charlie became great friends with Quentin Roosevelt.

"Thank Heaven you are to be with me!" Roosevelt exclaimed in 1903, when Taft agreed to return home from the Philippines and become his secretary of war. The president knew that he could rely on Taft, pictured here at his desk in the War Department and on the telephone, as "a needed and valuable corrective to his own impetuosity."

The 1906 schism that ended *McClure's* magazine's glorious era shocked the publishing world. John Phillips, Ida Tarbell, Albert Boyden *(seated left to right)*, Ray Stannard Baker, and John Siddal *(standing left to right)* were no longer able to continue working with the mercurial S. S. McClure. Together they pooled their talents and resources to buy *The American Magazine*, which they recast as a writers' collective. "This is undoubtedly the most notable combination that has ever launched any publication," one journal commented.

After deciding not to seek a third term, Roosevelt told journalists that "he would crawl on his hands and knees from the White House to the Capitol" to secure the election of Taft (*left*) as his successor.

Turning the candidate's oversized physique into a metaphor for his inability to take Roosevelt's place, one cartoonist showed Taft vainly trying to stuff himself into Teddy's Rough Rider garments.

A cartoon from 1907 captured the president's determination. Its caption has Roosevelt asking: "Uncle Sam, can't you take him for my third term?"

Charley Taft's colonial mansion in Cincinnati, with its white pillars and sweeping green lawns, provided a perfect setting for his brother Will to officially accept his nomination as the Republican presidential candidate on July 28, 1908.

During the election campaign Roosevelt watched over Taft, one political correspondent observed, "like a hen over her chickens." Exultant over Taft's victory, Roosevelt is pictured here with his old friend at the White House on the morning of the new president's inauguration.

Defying inaugural tradition, Nellie decided to do what "no President's wife had ever done"—accompany her husband from the Capitol to the White House on March 4, 1909. "That drive was the proudest and happiest event of Inauguration Day," she recalled. "I was able to enjoy, almost to the full, the realization that my husband was actually President of the United States."

As first lady, Nellie, pictured *(above)* with Taft and his military aide Captain Archie Butt *(far left)*, introduced a series of Friday afternoon garden parties that quickly became, as one reporter observed, "the most popular form of official hospitality yet seen in Washington." But only ten weeks into her husband's administration, Nellie's career as a social leader in Washington was cut short by a devastating stroke that permanently robbed her of the ability to speak intelligibly. She spent months recuperating in a seaside mansion in Beverly, Massachusetts *(below)*. Surrounded by "parklike lawns" and adjacent to a country club, this residence was a favorite retreat of President Taft and quickly became known as "the Summer White House."

52

Roosevelt displayed no interest in what critics called "devil wagons," far preferring his horses *(left)*, but Taft *(below)* fell in love with automobiles "on the first whirl." As president, Taft converted the White House stables into an oversized garage for his collection of motorcars.

53

54

Taft exercised regularly while in the White House and worked with doctors to improve his diet, yet his weight remained a constant issue, affecting both his health and energy level, and skewing the public's perception of him. The bathtub *(left)*, easily holding four workmen, was specially designed to accommodate his huge frame.

Despite Roosevelt's caution that the working class looked upon golf as a "rich man's game," Taft loved nothing more than to spend the afternoon on the green.

Taft better served his public image when, on June 9, 1910, accompanied by the ever present Archie Butt, he threw out a ceremonial first pitch at a Washington Nationals game, establishing a tradition that has continued ever since.

In April 1910 Roosevelt met with the deposed forester Gifford Pinchot on the Italian Riviera. After receiving a full briefing from Pinchot about his battles with Taft over conservation, Roosevelt for the first time expressed open disappointment at the course of his successor's presidency.

The anguish that Taft (shown here signing a bill) felt over Roosevelt's disapproval would be temporarily dispelled by the nearly complete triumph of his administration's legislative agenda. "We never had such a towering wood pile of work from the congressional saw mill," one newspaper editorial observed.

When Roosevelt returned from Africa, he established a base of operations at the offices of the weekly public affairs magazine, *The Outlook*.

On August 23, 1910, Roosevelt boarded a private railroad car secured by *The Outlook* to begin a speaking tour through the West. One political question was on every reporter's mind: "On which side will the Colonel now align himself? What changes have taken place in his philosophy?"

Before every speech President Taft was beset by grave misgivings, acutely aware that his texts remained "infernally long" despite his efforts to prune his words. "Never mind if you cannot get off fireworks," Nellie consoled him. "That is not your style, and there is no use in trying to force it."

62

When he threw his hat into the ring in the 1912 race for the presidential nomination, Theodore Roosevelt's personal popularity had never been higher. Drawing enthusiastic crowds, he scored impressive victories in states where direct primaries were held.

"If they are anxious for a fight, they shall have it," thundered Roosevelt during the 1912 Republican campaign. Crowds cheered Roosevelt as if he were a boxer, urging him to attack Taft: "Hit him between the eyes!" and "Put him over the ropes!" Political cartoonists were quick to seize on the phenomenon, as in this cartoon of prizefighter Roosevelt working over a Taft-shaped punching bag.

Despite his popularity with rank-and-file Republicans, Roosevelt failed to capture his party's support for president at the Republican National Convention in Chicago in June 1912. The old system prevailed, and Taft was nominated to pursue a second term. The disappointed candidate is shown here arriving in New York after the convention with Edith Roosevelt at his side, firmly resolved to form a third party.

On October 14, 1912, a would-be assassin shot at Roosevelt while he campaigned in Milwaukee. The candidate's bundle of notes for his speech, stored in his coat, helped save his life: the bullet penetrated no farther than the ribcage, and Roosevelt, though in pain, was able to deliver his speech on schedule. Returning home after the shooting, he descends from the train in Oyster Bay, assisted by aides and doctors.

In later years, the members of the old *McClure's* magazine staff gathered to celebrate their birthdays. For Tarbell *(seated between Willa Cather and Will Irwin)*, these gatherings represented the "unbreakable quality in friendship" that healed old wounds. "We sat enthralled as in the old years while Mr. McClure *(at left)* enlarged on his latest enthusiasm, marveling as always at the eternal youthfulness in the man, the failure of life to quench him."

Theodore and Edith Roosevelt shared an enduring love affair over three eventful decades of marriage. They are pictured here in 1917, two short years before Roosevelt's death at age sixty. He repeatedly declared that she remained as pretty as on the day he married her.

In 1921, William Howard Taft finally achieved his life's ambition when he was appointed chief justice of the Supreme Court of the United States. The position was perfectly suited to his temperament: no professional assignment ever made him happier.

CHAPTER NINETEEN

"To Cut Mr. Taft in Two!"

This Mar. 18, 1906, cartoon, "Reinforcing the Bench," shows
Roosevelt using a "Big Stick" to persuade Taft to take a seat
on the Supreme Court bench.

I N EARLY JANUARY 1906, WHILE attending a party in the New Jersey home of his Yale classmate John Hammond, William Howard Taft received a long-distance phone call from the president, informing him that Associate Justice Henry Billings Brown planned to announce his retirement when he turned seventy years old. Brown deemed his weakening eyesight "a gentle intimation" that the time had come "to give place to another." Knowing that duty alone had led Taft to decline the appointment three years before, Roosevelt was delighted to present him with the open seat. Taft was disposed to claim the honor, though Nellie and other friends and advisers begged him to decline, insisting that he "would be shutting the door on any further political advancement" when he was considered "the logical candidate for president in 1908." Since no commitment was required until March, the matter rested until Justice Brown formally announced his decision.

In the interim, Taft focused on pushing the Philippine tariff bill through Congress. The legislation was designed to substantially lower rates on products imported from the islands, an allowance that Taft believed was absolutely critical to the future of the Philippine economy. For two consecutive years, the bill had fallen victim to the powerful sugar and tobacco lobbies and their "standpatter" allies, as the protectionist bloc in Congress was known. But with the help of Democratic votes in late January 1906, it passed the House by an overwhelming vote of 257 to 71. Lauding the victory, Taft happily noted that several key members of the Ways and Means Committee had shifted their stance after touring the islands with his congressional delegation the previous summer.

When the bill proceeded to the Senate, Taft testified for two full days before the Senate Committee on the Philippines, hopeful that "the tremendous vote" in the House would sway the upper chamber. Connecticut senator Frank Brandegee led the opposition, arguing that Taft was "sacrificing" American economic interests for his "sentimental" desire to aid the Filipinos. "I do not believe," the senator maintained, "that we are under any obligations whatever to the Filipino people to open our markets." Taft was furious with Brandegee, privately labeling him "an infernal ass." Despite Taft's persistent efforts, the protectionist bloc managed to kill the bill in committee. "We suffered a very serious blow," Taft related to his Filipino friends, "but I am not despairing." Several publications had pledged to reveal those who had conspired in "smothering" the tariff legislation, so he remained hopeful the bill would eventually reach the Senate floor.

When Justice Brown officially announced his retirement on March 8, the press immediately began speculating that Taft would not only replace Brown but soon thereafter—if seventy-three-year-old Melvin Fuller retired during Roosevelt's term—assume the position of chief justice. Had the tariff bill passed that spring, Taft later remarked, he would "undoubtedly have accepted," but he informed Roosevelt in early March that he was too deeply occupied by critical matters in both the Philippines and Panama to consider the position. At Taft's suggestion, the president offered the post to Philander Knox; when Knox declined, however, Roosevelt renewed the pressure on Taft.

Roosevelt foresaw that over the coming decades, as the federal government confronted the social and economic stresses born of the industrial age, the Court "would have as important decisions to face as [it] had in the days of Marshall." Roosevelt had discussed the matter at length with Henry Cabot

Lodge, who had impressed upon him the absolute necessity of Taft taking the appointment. The Court desperately needed "a big man—one who would fill the public eye and one in whom the public had confidence." With five of the nine justices in their late sixties or seventies, the current Court was clearly "running down." At such a critical juncture, the president claimed, he had no higher duty than to put the best man on the bench. On the following Friday, he intended to announce his nomination of William Howard Taft.

Before the decision was made public, Taft requested time to confer with his brothers in New York. He also confided to Roosevelt that Nellie "bitterly opposed" the appointment; in fact, she had warned that very morning that to accept would be "the great mistake of [his] life." Roosevelt promised to meet with her personally and "explain the situation" before he made anything official. To accommodate such a discussion, Nellie remained behind for a noon meeting with President Roosevelt rather than join her husband on the 9 a.m. train to New York for the family council.

Before boarding the train to New York, Taft sent an explanatory note to Roosevelt outlining Nellie's position. He had repeatedly assured his wife, he told Roosevelt, that he was so engaged in his cabinet duties and the management of his "three great trusts"—the Philippines, Panama, and the U.S. Army—that he "had concluded to stick to it and not seek at your hands or accept any appointment to the Bench." Despite this resolve, he trusted that the president could better weigh the cost of losing him in the cabinet against "the crying need for putting strength in the Supreme Court." If the president determined he could be most beneficial on the bench, he would "of course yield." Even as he declared his preference for remaining in the cabinet, Taft appeared tortured by second doubts and hopeful the president might decide the matter for him.

Conflicting counsel produced during Taft's conference with his brothers did little to clarify the situation. Charles thought he should take the nomination, so long as it was clearly understood (as Roosevelt had already promised) that he would be appointed to the chief justiceship once Fuller retired. Horace, long Nellie's closest ally in advocating against a judicial career, was adamantly opposed, believing that his brother stood an excellent chance of becoming president. Moreover, Horace argued, "quite apart from the Presidency," it would be a shame to have his "personality removed from politics." For his part, Harry found talk of the presidency flattering but felt that Taft was better suited to be chief justice.

When Taft returned to Washington the next morning, he found a remarkable letter from the president awaiting him. After conversing with Nellie the previous morning, Roosevelt believed he had misconstrued his friend's desires. All along, Roosevelt confessed, he had thought that Taft wanted the Court appointment and that all the president's urgings toward that end were consequent with Taft's deepest inclinations. But in the wake of his discussions of the matter with Nellie, he had resolved to leave the decision completely up to Taft himself. "My dear Will," he wrote, "it is preeminently a matter in which no other man can take the responsibility of deciding for you what is right and best for you to do. Nobody could decide for me whether I should go to the war or stay as Assistant Secretary of the Navy . . . whether I should accept the Vice-Presidency, or try to continue as Governor." In each defining situation, he concluded, "the equation of the man himself" must be "the vital factor."

Roosevelt proceeded to offer his heartfelt advice, carefully considering each of his friend's prospects. In the first place, he stated flatly, he considered Taft not only "the best man" to become the next president but the "most likely" to receive the Republican nomination and win the general election. (While Roosevelt held Elihu Root in equal esteem, he recognized that the conservative lawyer's long corporate ties made him unavailable as a candidate.) "The good you could do in four or eight years as the head of the Nation would be incalculable," Roosevelt asserted, adding that "the shadow of the presidency falls on no man twice, save in the most exceptional circumstances." Naturally, no election is guaranteed, the president qualified, adding that he hoped that Taft's "sweet and fine nature" would not "be warped" if he should fail. But even if the presidency did not materialize, Taft would enjoy "three years of vital service" in the cabinet and would certainly be "one of the great leaders for right in the tremendous contests" that lay ahead.

"First and infinitely foremost," Roosevelt wrote, stressing the benefits of assuming a place on the bench, at only forty-eight-years of age, Taft would have "the opportunity for a quarter of a century to do a great work as Justice of the greatest Court in Christendom (a court which sadly needs great men) on questions which seem likely vitally and fundamentally to affect the social, industrial and political structure of our commonwealth"; secondarily, declining this opportunity to join the Court would diminish or foreclose Taft's chance to serve as chief justice, for in order to fill the current vacancy with some other "big man," like Elihu Root, the president might have to utilize the option of the top post.

"Where you can fight best I cannot say, for you know what your soul turns to better than I," Roosevelt acutely observed in closing. "You have two alternatives before you, each with uncertain possibilities, and you cannot be sure that whichever you take you will not afterwards feel that it would have been better if you had taken the other. But whichever you take I know that you will render great and durable service to the Nation for many years to come."

Taft was deeply moved by Roosevelt's generous and candid endeavor to help him work through the momentous decision he faced. The letter was "all I could expect and more," he told Nellie. If forced to decide immediately, he would accept, he explained to Horace—otherwise he might well jeopardize his chance at the chief justiceship. He would talk with the president, he concluded, and ask to defer the decision, allowing him to continue the tariff fight until Congress adjourned in July. Displaying decisiveness in contrast to Taft's dilatory nature, Roosevelt agreed to release a statement explaining that since Brown would not retire until June and the Court not resume work until October, he had decided to postpone his nomination.

Throughout that spring, newspapers speculated on Taft's prospects. It was a "somewhat unusual experience," the New York *Sun* observed, "to possess a public servant whose usefulness and versatility are so generally recognized" that half his supporters hoped he would remain in politics, while the other half preferred to see him on the Supreme Court. Sadly, the *Sun* remarked with broad humor, it was "impossible, under the Constitution and laws, to cut Mr. Taft in two!" While the natural ambition of "the big, jovial, brainy" Taft might incline him toward the bench, the *Hutchinson* (Kansas) *News* suggested, he had now "tasted power," and perhaps an "easy berth" on the Court was no longer so appealing.

As early as the summer of 1906, editorials in Republican newspapers began touting Taft as the only man capable of defeating the Democratic front-runner, the charismatic William Jennings Bryan, in the upcoming presidential election. "He has done big things," the *Kansas City Star* noted, "is magnetic and popular" and "would come nearer to carrying forward the Roosevelt policies than any other Republican." The *Journal of Commerce* observed that "no American" stood higher "in the eyes of his countrymen" than the popular secretary of war. Day after day, Taft received letters begging him to look toward the presidency instead of the Court. "I do not see in the horizon any man in the Republican ranks except yourself who would give us good assurance of carrying the country," *Outlook* publisher Lyman Abbott urged. "For the love of Mike, do not go to the Supreme Bench," another friend pleaded; "there are certain lucky individuals who have a happy faculty of appealing to the imagination and the heart of the general public . . . and you are one of these lucky people."

Though Taft disavowed any desire for the presidency, the prospect inevitably informed his decision to refuse the Court nomination. In a lengthy letter to Roosevelt in mid-July, he insisted that while the bench remained his ultimate preference, the timing was once again wrong. News that Congress had adjourned without passing the tariff bill had produced "a most gloomy" spirit in the Philippines, and remaining in the cabinet would allow him to continue his fight in the next session. "p.s.," he humbly continued. "Please don't misunderstand me to think that I am indispensable or that the world would not run on much the same if I were to disappear in the St. Lawrence River, but circumstances seem to have imposed something in the nature of a trust on me." (Roosevelt eventually nominated Attorney General William Moody to fill the vacant seat.) In a second postscript, Taft contritely confessed that Nellie thought it "an outrage" to inflict such a long letter upon such a busy man!

"Now, you beloved individual," the president replied from Oyster Bay, "as for your long letter I enjoyed it thoroughly." At Sagamore Hill, he explained, he had plenty of time to read and relax; indeed, after only three weeks on vacation, he was "rather shocked" to discover how easily he had adapted. "Ten years ago I got uneasy if I was left with leisure on my hands," Roosevelt remarked, "and if I had no mental work I wished to be riding, chopping, rowing, or doing something of that kind all the time. Now I am perfectly content to sit still." Writing again a few weeks later, he exclaimed: "By George, I am as pleased as Punch that you are to stay in the Cabinet!"

Relieved to have the Court decision behind him, Taft happily anticipated a two-month vacation with Nellie and the children at Murray Bay. There, he intended to continue the diet and exercise regimen that had enabled him to lose over 75 pounds during the previous eight months, reducing his weight from 330 to 254 pounds. During this period, he had faithfully maintained a rigorous, doctor-prescribed diet that excluded sugar, fats, milk, cheese, cream, egg yolks, and bread. He was allowed only grilled fish, lean meat, egg whites, clear soup, salads, vegetables, some fruits, gluten biscuits, and sugarless wine. At his heaviest, Taft had been forced to send away for a new bathroom scale; those available in Washington, he told Charles, were "boys" scales, registering no more than 250 pounds. Having reached a manageable weight by July, he discovered that his new physique was "not an inexpensive luxury." His tailor had to completely reconstruct "twenty pairs of Trousers . . . twenty Waist Coats . . . two Prince Albert Coats . . . and five Sack Coats!" Horace was thrilled by his brother's progress: "It is the best thing you have done for many a day." Given his "infernally healthy" constitution, Horace jested, there was now "no reason why [you] should not live to be a hundred."

DURING THE SUMMER IN MURRAY BAY, Taft's customary day began at 7 a.m., with dictation to his private secretary Wendell W. Mischler. Still in his twenties when he joined the secretary of war Taft, Mischler would remain with Taft until his death. At nine o'clock, Taft joined his family for breakfast, then returned to work for another hour. Generating responses to the five thick batches of mail that arrived by train or steamship each day required three hours in the early morning and two more in the late afternoon. In the interim, Taft relished outdoor activities and socializing with his family—golf games with his brothers, trout fishing and rambles along the rocky shore, tennis and picnics with Nellie and the children. In one golf respite, Taft happened upon fellow Murray Bay vacationer Justice John Harlan "jumping up and down to coax a ball in that was hovering on the very edge of the first hole." Having no luck, Harlan called over to Taft: "Come on! You jump. That will do the business." The casual atmosphere of Murray Bay allowed Taft to dress in comfort, saving his "city clothes" for Sunday church. Without fancy dinners or formal receptions to attend, he could easily adhere to his diet. The nation's problems seemed to recede with each passing day, and friends and family could almost "see youth returning to him."

By the second week in August, as he began preparation for a major political speech, Taft's equanimity started to unravel. The chairman of the Republican State Committee had asked him to give the keynote address at an event in Maine early that September to open the party's midterm campaign. In a letter from Oyster Bay, Roosevelt underscored the importance of the speech. Taft organized his presentation around four topics: the legislative goals of Congress, questions surrounding labor unrest, the trusts, and the tariff. The first three issues gave him little trouble. He agreed wholeheartedly with Roosevelt's regulatory legislation, his position on labor, and his anti-trust initiatives. But he strongly wished to call for a downward revision of the tariff, a step that Roosevelt feared would split the party in two.

Taft's long struggle with conservative Republicans over the Philippine tariff had awakened him to the larger inequity of the entire domestic tariff structure—a system that created immense advantages for eastern manufacturers and massive corporations over western farmers and small business. He believed the tariff represented the "only weakness" in the Republican Party, and he wanted to address the problem publicly. Nonetheless, he remained well aware that he would be regarded as a spokesman for the administration, promising Roosevelt that he would revise his remarks if the draft seemed "too outspoken." Nellie had read an "outrageously long" early draft, which she deemed reminiscent of a "dull" opinion from the bench. He had compressed the entire speech. "One's wife is mighty useful under circumstances like this," he proudly acknowledged to Roosevelt.

"It's a bully speech," encouraged Roosevelt in reply. He was confident that Taft had safely navigated the tariff issue by stating that revision would be possible only when popular sentiment within the party crystallized. Personally, he did not believe that reform would be realized before the presidential election. Yet, if the Republicans were victorious, they would probably have to present a plan for revision immediately afterward. "I neither wish to split the Republican party," Roosevelt wrote, "nor to seem to promise something Congress would not do." In fact, he suggested that Taft show the speech to the conservative party leaders, Speaker Cannon and Charles Littlefield.

On the evening of September 5, 3,000 people gathered at the Alameda Opera House in downtown Bath, Maine, to hear Taft deliver "the first big Administration speech of the campaign." The audience enthusiastically cheered Taft's passionate defense of regulatory reforms and anti-trust initiatives. The president's historic work to strengthen the federal response to long-standing abuses, Taft declared, "is the issue of the campaign, its only issue; its only possible issue." Only when he turned to the tariff did Taft diverge from his central message. "With a frankness that is almost startling," *The Washington Post* observed, the likely 1908 Republican nominee voiced his opposition to the conservative "stand-pat attitude" of both the president and the Speaker of the House, proclaiming "that his party must face tariff revision squarely and unhesitatingly."

Reaction in the press was overwhelmingly favorable. The New York *Sun* called Taft's speech "the frankest, the ablest and the most manly and engaging deliverance that has ever come from any member of Mr. Roosevelt's Cabinet on any subject." The solicitor general, Henry Hoyt, told Taft that he had "never made a sharper speech," lauding it as "honest & courageous all the way through," and adding, "All of us in our hearts agree with you about tariff revision." Taft was delighted by the public praise but most anxiously awaited Roosevelt's response. "It is the great speech of the campaign," Roosevelt telegraphed him, "and I cannot imagine the people failing to recognize it as such." Taft humbly replied: "A man never knows exactly how the child of his brain will strike other people."

TAFT'S PLAN TO EXTEND HIS tranquil vacation at Murray Bay through September was abruptly cut short by turmoil in Cuba. Revolutionary forces, angered by electoral fraud during the 1905 presidential campaign, had taken control

of most of the island outside of Havana, leaving President Tomás Estrada
Palma in a precarious situation. Though the treaty ending the war with Spain
had bound the United States to respect Cuban sovereignty, the Platt Amendment stipulated that the United States retained power to take action whenever necessary to safeguard the independent status of the island nation, and
to support "a government adequate for the protection of life, property and
individual liberty."

"In Cuba what I have dreaded has come to pass," Roosevelt told George
Trevelyan on September 6: "A revolution has broken out, and not only do I
dread the loss of life and property, but I dread the creation of a revolutionary habit, and the creation of a class of people who take to disturbance and
destruction as an exciting and pleasant business." On September 13, President
Estrada Palma claimed he could not "prevent rebels from entering cities and
burning property" and secretly requested the landing of U.S. troops "to save
his country from complete anarchy." Roosevelt confided to Ambassador Henry
White that he was "so angry with that infernal little Cuban republic that I
would like to wipe its people off the face of the earth. All that we wanted from
them was that they would behave themselves," he added petulantly, "and be
prosperous and happy so that we would not have to interfere."

The following day, Roosevelt summoned Taft and Assistant Secretary of
State Robert Bacon to a conference at Oyster Bay. The two men would travel
to Cuba "as intermediaries," Roosevelt decided, hoping to effect a peaceful
solution. From Oyster Bay, Taft took the train to Washington, where he conferred with the judge advocate general to determine whether congressional
approval was necessary if the president decided to send troops. The judge
advocate general, Taft told Roosevelt, believed the treaty authorized presidential action without congressional approval. Nevertheless, Taft wished to
get Attorney General Moody's opinion. Roosevelt adamantly directed him not
to consult Moody. "If the necessity arises I intend to intervene," he explained,
"and I should not dream of asking the permission of Congress. That treaty
is the law of the land and I shall execute it." His decision was in the interest
of the country, he added, essential to "give independence to the Executive in
dealing with foreign powers." Furthermore, he was certainly "willing to accept
responsibility to establish precedents which successors may follow."

When Taft and Bacon reached Havana, they met with President Estrada
Palma and the leaders of his Moderate Party. Not a single delegate from the
Liberal Party, which represented Cuba's less privileged, was present. Pushing
for intervention to sustain their power, Estrada Palma and his supporters were
dismayed when Taft refused to act before meeting with rebels in the field to

fully evaluate the situation. The secretary of war had not traveled to Cuba intent on using American power to suppress the insurgents; he had come as an arbitrator hoping to reconcile differences peacefully.

Taft's "informal, straightforward and kindly manner," one reporter noted, "created a strong and favorable impression." Even as he privately lamented "the utter unfitness of these people for self government," Taft listened patiently to representatives from both sides. Reviewing the evidence regarding the 1905 election, he concluded that complaints of wholesale fraud were "well founded." To orchestrate a compromise, he suggested that if insurgents "laid down their arms and dispersed to their homes," a temporary executive acceptable to both sides would be appointed, the disputed legislative seats would be vacated, and planning would begin for a new election. The liberals agreed, but the moderates promptly sabotaged the possibility. Rather than accept the compromise terms, Palma announced that he, his cabinet, and every moderate congressman would resign, "leaving nothing of the Government."

Meanwhile, the fierce skirmishes outside Havana continued. Having nearly routed government forces in the countryside, the rebels stood poised to enter the capital. "The insurgents are all about Havana," Taft told Nellie nervously. "I don't know that I can save bloodshed." One insurgent encampment was situated only 1,200 yards from the house where Taft was staying. The rapidly shifting situation required William Taft to take decisive action without explicit guidance from the president. "Things are certainly kaleidoscopic," Roosevelt telegraphed. "I must trust to your judgment on the ground." The tense days during this standoff proved "the most unpleasant" Taft had ever experienced. "I am in a condition of mind where I can hardly do anything with sequence," he confessed to Nellie, adding, "I would give a great deal to talk it over with you." Unable to sleep, he found himself awake at three in the morning, watching a severe thunderstorm build and roll over Havana Bay. Were it not for Nellie and his family, Will reflected, he would not be sorry if one of the bolts flashing in the sky struck him dead.

After a week of rancorous negotiation, Taft finally brokered a four-point plan. President Estrada Palma would remain in office long enough to officially request American intervention. The United States would set up a provisional government, with Taft as the initial temporary governor general. The insurgents, secure in America's pledge that new elections would be held, would begin to disarm. And to keep the peace, American forces would land in Cuba. Taft wisely emphasized that this provisional government would "be maintained only long enough to restore order and peace and public confidence." The Cuban Constitution would remain in full force and Cuba's flag would continue to fly over government buildings. Once elections were held, the U.S. military would be withdrawn.

Taft anticipated that his course of action would be criticized back at home but took solace in the fact that "all parties here seem to be delighted." A resolution without further bloodshed and war, he assured Nellie, would "go a long way to make such attacks futile." A telegraph from Oyster Bay confirmed Taft's judgment: "I congratulate you most heartily upon the admirable way you have handled the whole matter," Roosevelt wrote, adding that he was "especially pleased with the agreement which the revolutionary committee signed."

As soon as the accord became public, the rebels began to disarm. Taft promptly cabled Nellie to join him in Havana, knowing her presence would bring him "great comfort." He planned to remain in Havana for several weeks, until Charles E. Magoon, the former governor of the Panama Canal Zone, could relieve him as governor general. Eager for adventure, Nellie decided instantly to go. Accompanied by Robert Bacon's wife, she sailed from Norfolk on a steamer escorted by a battleship and three hundred Marines. "For the first time in my life I felt as if we were actually 'going to war,' " she recalled. Her ceremonious reception as "the first lady of the land" was reminiscent of her days in Manila. On the day after their arrival, Nellie Taft and Mrs. Bacon hosted a splendid gala at the palace, with a guest list comprising more than three hundred Cubans from both sides of the dispute. "Everybody seemed to be especially happy and festive after the month of gloom," Nellie recalled, "and the pretty white gowns, the gay Cuban colours and the crisp smartness of American uniforms mingled together in the great rooms with quite brilliant effect." Once Magoon was sworn in as governor general, the Tafts made plans to depart Havana. "Upon my word you seem to have handled everything in a most masterly way," Roosevelt commended his secretary of war as he wrapped up his stay in Cuba. "I doubt whether you have ever rendered our country a greater service."

As the Tafts prepared to embark from the Havana dock on October 13, Magoon reported, "the shore of the Bay was lined with thousands of cheering people, all available water craft was pressed into service to escort the ships to the mouth of the harbor, the forts exchanged salutes with the vessels." Nellie recalled a widely printed cartoon depicting poor Magoon seated "in agony on a sizzling stove labeled 'Cuba,' while Mr. Taft appeared in the distance in a fireman's garb carrying a long and helpful-looking line of hose." Indeed, the political situation on the islands was far from resolved, and preparation for the new elections proved unexpectedly complex. In the end, Magoon would struggle for over two years to complete a new census and revise the electoral laws; not until early 1909 were national elections finally held. After the election, Magoon finally relinquished control to a newly elected liberal administration and the U.S. troops sailed for home.

Though many critics opposed the very concept of intervention in Cuban affairs, Taft's role in the crisis was generally praised. "Merely to record the movements and missions of the Secretary of War requires a nimble mind," the New York *Sun* remarked. Most men would have considered it "a labor of Hercules" to negotiate peace in the midst of a revolution: Taft—accustomed to settling volatile dilemmas from Manila to Panama, from Ohio to Maine— simply threw "a change of clothing into a traveling bag" as if he were setting forth on a holiday and "returned to his War Department duties." Taft himself presented a far less jaunty picture of his struggle to implement peace in Cuba: "If mental worry kept me down I should have lost 50 pounds in this crisis," he revealed to Charles. Instead, having sought comfort in food during "those awful twenty days," he had gained back 15 or 20 pounds, necessitating yet another alteration of his wardrobe.

☙   ❧

TAFT SCARCELY HAD TIME TO unpack before Roosevelt dispatched him on a three-week speaking tour through a dozen states in advance of the midterm elections. "The paramount issue," a midwestern editorial observed, was "whether the president shall be sustained during the remaining two years of his term by a republican congress." No one could present a better case for the Roosevelt administration than William Howard Taft, the most prominent cabinet member, "the jolly good fellow" most likely to secure the next Republican nomination.

All 5,000 seats at the Lyric Stage in Baltimore were filled, and hundreds more people stood in the back and packed the galleries when Taft stepped to the podium. Though he spoke for an hour and three quarters, defending the measured use of federal power to correct abuses of the industrial system, not one person rose to leave. "This is rather contrary to your theory that no audience can stand more than an hour," he teased Nellie, conceding wryly that a few might have "sneaked out saying to themselves that a man who has the egregious vanity to think he can entertain an audience for more than an hour ought not to be encouraged." In Cleveland, Danville, Decatur, Omaha, and Pocatello, Taft addressed similarly enthusiastic crowds. Seven thousand people thronged to hear him speak in Boise, Idaho, where he was met with sustained applause: "Hats were thrown up in the air, women stood up on the chairs and waved their handkerchiefs."

"The notices have all been favorable," Nellie informed him from home. Nonetheless, she was concerned that he seemed unable to forgo mention of the tariff, sparking an antagonism within the Republican Party that could cost him the nomination. Taft acknowledged the legitimacy of her political estimate but felt so strongly on the issue he would wage the fight notwithstanding. Furthermore, he hoped his wife wouldn't get "the blues" when he explained that despite feeling more "at home" with his audiences, he still found scant enjoyment in the political game and wished she could "put aside any hope in the direction of politics."

Despite her husband's protestations, Nellie was unwilling to relinquish the prospect of a Taft presidency. In Roosevelt, she found a powerful ally, though she continued to fear that he coveted another term for himself. On Saturday, October 27, with Taft in transit from Pittsburgh to Cleveland, Roosevelt invited Nellie to lunch at the White House. He confessed his concern to her, explaining that some Kentucky supporters had told him that Taft had flatly "turned them down" when they approached him about setting up an organization of support, maintaining that he was "not a candidate." If Taft could not be "more encouraging," Roosevelt continued, it might "become necessary for him to support someone else." When Roosevelt mentioned Charles Evans Hughes, the New York attorney who had successfully investigated the life insurance industry and was now running against William Randolph Hearst for governor, Nellie grew annoyed by the tone of conversation. "I felt like saying 'D—— you, support who you want, for all I care,' " she confessed to her husband, "but suffice it to say I did not."

"I think what the president is anxious to do," Taft cannily speculated to his wife after considering her account of the White House luncheon, "is to stir you up to stir me up to take more interest in the Presidential campaign, with a broad intimation that if I did not take more interest he would not." Taft also posted a letter to the president conveying his understanding that Roosevelt might have to support a Hughes candidacy. "If you do," Taft assured the president, "you may be sure it will awaken no feeling of disappointment on my part." In fact, Taft confirmed, his recent travels had convinced him that "the strong feeling" he had encountered everywhere was not for him, but for the renomination of Roosevelt himself. The people did not want a "substitute," he explained; they wanted a third term.

Taft, meanwhile, continued to speak before spirited crowds. In some states, he spoke seven or eight times a day as his train moved from city to city. Despite the frenetic pace, he took the time every few days to update Roosevelt on local and state issues. "I am immensely interested in your account of the campaign," Roosevelt responded. "I take the keenest pride in what you are now doing. Three cheers for 'offensive partisanship'!"

When the votes were tallied on November 6, Roosevelt was tremendously pleased. Republicans had expected significant losses in the midterm elections following their landslide victory two years before. Instead, the party retained a strong majority in the House, losing only twenty-eight seats, and actually added four seats in the Senate. "Our triumph at the elections has certainly been great," Roosevelt wrote to Kermit. His party's hold on Congress, he believed, would make the last two years of his term "very, very much easier than they otherwise would have been." Roosevelt readily acknowledged his debt to Elihu Root and especially to the dutiful William Howard Taft. "I am overjoyed," he told his secretary of war, enthusiastically praising Taft's efforts as he added, "I cannot sufficiently congratulate you upon the great part you have played in the contest." He was particularly pleased by Governor Frank Gooding's reelection in Idaho and the defeat of the "scandal-mongering" William Randolph Hearst in New York—a victory he considered nothing less than a triumph for civilization. "By George," he confided to Taft, "I sometimes wish I was not in the White House and could be on the stump."

━ ━

TWO DAYS AFTER THE ELECTION, the president and first lady embarked on a long-anticipated trip to Panama. "I'm going down to see how the ditch is getting along," Roosevelt shouted from the deck of the yacht set to carry him from the nation's capital down the Rappahannock River to the sea, where he would board the warship *Louisiana*. The "ditch," one reporter explained, referred to the massive artificial lake under construction on the Isthmus of Panama that promised to rival "the pyramids . . . the Colossus of Rhodes [or] the hanging gardens of Babylon." Roosevelt began the six-day sail in "particularly good spirits," delighted to be taking an unprecedented step in the history of the presidency—leaving the country to visit a foreign land. Indeed, when his trip was first announced, "a large portion of the public gasped," anxious that "such a jaunt would be contrary to law." The public was assured, however, that "modern inventions" would enable the president to keep abreast of the nation's business "no matter where he may be."

Roosevelt's three-day visit to Panama was packed with "a little of everything." Wishing to judge the progress of the construction firsthand, the president climbed atop a steam shovel and barraged the operator with dozens of questions about his work. He traveled by train to several excavation sites, observed drilling machines at work, and watched as dynamite charges were detonated. He met with laborers, toured their sleeping quarters and bathrooms, and listened to their complaints. He even dropped by the workers' mess rooms, insisting that he sample the food they were served. Overall, the *New York Tribune* reported, the president came away "well pleased with what he saw," and the men were well pleased to see him.

Although the Tafts had been invited to join the president and Edith on the Panama trip, Taft had already arranged to follow his western political tour with a weeklong inspection of half a dozen Army bases in Nebraska, Oklahoma, Illinois, Kansas, and Texas. At each base, he was received with elaborate ceremony. "Not in the history of the post at Fort Sill has there been accorded to an officer of the war department a larger reception," one reporter remarked. At Fort Leavenworth, "several thousand school children waved flags; whistles were blown, church bells rung and hundreds of cannon crackers were fired." After a final stop at Fort Sam Houston in San Antonio, Taft settled down for the long train ride home. "One trouble about travel," he wrote Nellie, "is that with nothing particular to do on the cars, meals assume an undue importance." And, indeed, Taft's extensive travels had prompted him to add 15 more pounds to his girth.

⌒ ⌒

WHEN TAFT ARRIVED AT HIS War Department office shortly after his return, he found himself thrust in the midst of a firestorm. During his lengthy absence from Washington, the president had made a unilateral decision on a matter he would normally have discussed with his secretary of war. Roosevelt had issued a sweeping presidential order discharging without honor an entire battalion of black soldiers for an incident three months earlier in Brownsville, Texas.

Racial tensions in the small southern city had been building since late July 1906, when the battalion first arrived at Fort Brown from Nebraska. Local papers had denounced the government's decision to transfer the troops to a region where privileges granted in the North "would certainly be denied them." A series of minor confrontations had taken place: black soldiers were forced off the sidewalk, hit with revolver butts, and denied access to public bars. Rumors of a black soldier assaulting a white woman in her home circulated. Then, just past midnight on August 14, a group of soldiers had allegedly entered town and fired into buildings, killing a saloonkeeper and so grievously injuring the chief of police that his arm was later amputated. Eyewitnesses produced contradictory accounts: some claimed that the townspeople had fired first; others pointed to "colored soldiers in khaki and blue shirts" as the aggressors. No one could identify any of the individual soldiers, all of whom had returned to their barracks immediately after the shootings.

With Taft en route to Cuba when the first official account reached Washington, Roosevelt took charge, ordering the inspector general of the Army to investigate the incident. Six days later, Major Augustus Blocksom wired an initial report. Even while acknowledging that racial prejudice had motivated townspeople to heap abuse upon the enlisted men, he nevertheless discounted the report that the citizens had fired first, blaming an unidentified group of about "nine to fifteen" soldiers for initiating the raid. Interviews with battalion members had failed to disclose the identities of those involved. Blocksom therefore recommended that if the soldiers continued to obstruct the investigation by refusing to cooperate, they should be collectively "discharged from the service." Because the townspeople of Brownsville remained "in a state of great nervous tension," with civilians patrolling the streets with guns "openly at night," he suggested the battalion be temporarily transferred to Fort Reno, Oklahoma. "It is very doubtful," the *Brownsville Herald* observed, "whether our people would ever tolerate the presence of negro soldiers here again."

Roosevelt accepted Blocksom's recommendation to remove the troops, ordering the inspector general, Ernest A. Garlington, to Fort Reno to conduct further interviews with the enlisted men. When Garlington arrived on October 18, he called the troops into formation on the Parade Grounds and read them an ultimatum from the president: If they continued to conceal the names of those involved in the raid, they would be discharged en masse. When not a single man broke rank, Garlington recommended that the entire battalion be dishonorably discharged at once. Although "this extreme penalty" undoubtedly meant that men with "no direct knowledge" of "who actually fired the shots" would be found guilty, because they stood together, he argued, "they should stand together when the penalty falls."

Taft was on the campaign trail in early November when Roosevelt accepted Garlington's recommendation. The president directed that all 167 men be dishonorably discharged from the Army, a status that not only prevented them from reenlistment but barred them from any civil service position. The battalion included several Medal of Honor winners, soldiers with a quarter of a century of distinguished service, and men who had fought beside Roosevelt in the Spanish-American War. To prevent negative publicity, the order was deliberately delayed until after the midterm elections.

When the order was finally revealed, telegrams and resolutions condemning the president's "despotic usurpation of power" flooded both the White House and the War Department. "Deep resentment" percolated in the black community, where Roosevelt had once been lionized for opening "the door of hope" by inviting Booker T. Washington to dinner and publicly fighting to confirm several high-level black appointees. The decision was deemed "a truckling to sectional prejudice" and a bid by the president to capitalize on newfound popularity in the South in the wake of his wildly successful trip through the region. "Once enshrined in our love as our Moses," one black preacher lamented, Roosevelt "is now enshrouded in our scorn as our Judas."

Reading through the pile of telegrams and petitions on the Saturday of his return, Taft consented to meet Mary Church Terrell—a leading black educator, graduate of Oberlin College, and member of New York's Constitutional League. All she wanted, Mrs. Terrell informed the secretary, was for him "to withhold the execution of that order" until a trial could be set to determine "the innocent ones." With "a merry twinkle in his eye," she recalled, Taft responded with gentle irony: "Is that *all* you want me to do?" She "realized for the first time what a tremendous request" she had made, Terrell explained, and "how difficult it would be to change the status of the soldiers' case." Still, there was something in Taft's "generous-hearted" manner that made her believe he would do what he could.

That very day, Taft cabled Roosevelt—then en route from Panama to Puerto Rico—that he intended to "delay the execution of the order" until he received a response. He did not think the president fully realized "the great feeling that has been aroused on the subject," or the negative impact on Army morale and racial relations. Taft always believed it better to reconsider a case when a decision raised serious questions. "If a rehearing shows that the original conclusion was wrong, it presents a dignified way of recalling it; and if it does not, it enforces the original conclusion."

Upon learning that Taft had delayed the order, reporters speculated that the terms of the soldiers' discharge might be modified. Taft publicly remarked that he would prefer honorable discharges, which would allow eventual reinstatement and access to the Soldiers' Homes. Furthermore, he questioned the president's legal power to preclude employment in the civil branch. The *New York Times* reported that the incident had placed such "a severe strain upon the relations between the President and his Secretary of War" that a new appointment to the cabinet might be required.

Taft heard nothing from Roosevelt over the weekend. On Monday, he left Washington for a daylong meeting at Yale, where he had been elected to the Yale Corporation. When he returned on Tuesday afternoon to find that there was still no response to his cable, he met with William Loeb, Roosevelt's private secretary. Loeb showed him a letter the president had written to Massachusetts governor Curtis Guild, Jr., just before leaving for Panama. "The order in question will under no circumstances be rescinded or modified," Roosevelt had declared. "There has been the fullest and most exhaustive investigation of the case." Viewing this document, Taft sadly concluded that he no longer had a right to delay the order. The next morning, a telegram from Roosevelt confirmed that he remained inflexible: "Discharge is not to be suspended," he wrote. "I care nothing whatever for the yelling of either the politicians or the sentimentalists. The offense was most heinous and the punishment I inflicted was imposed after due deliberation."

Criticism of the Brownsville order mounted into early December. When Congress convened on December 3, the conservative Republican senator Joseph Foraker introduced a resolution calling for a full investigation into the matter. Foraker's inquiry, which proposed to study whether the president's order overstepped his authority, provoked what the *New York Times* characterized as a "fighting mad" reaction from Roosevelt. Foraker had been among the most outspoken opponents of Roosevelt's railroad legislation; consequently, his resolution was seen as a blatant political maneuver to wrest control of the Republican Party from Roosevelt, Taft, and the progressives. "It is impossible to admit that he could be sincere in any belief in the troops' innocence," Roosevelt testily asserted.

In a letter to Congress "tingling with indignation," Roosevelt insisted that "he was not only acting well within his constitutional rights, but that it was his duty to strip the uniform" from "murderers, assassins, cowards and the comrades of murderers." The discrimination that the soldiers had endured at the hands of the townspeople offered no "excuse or justification for the atrocious conduct." Indeed, the president asserted that dismissal was "utterly inadequate"—had the murderers been identified and found guilty, they would have been executed. Several days later, Roosevelt underscored his defiant stand, informing reporters that he would "fight to the last ditch" rather than abandon his order. If Congress should adopt legislation to reinstate the soldiers, he would veto it. If the legislation passed over his veto, he would find another means to prevent the soldiers' reenlistment. "Not even the threat of impeachment proceedings," one paper remarked, "would deter him from the stand pat course he had decided to follow."

Roosevelt's strident response provoked both anger and sorrow in the black community. The Suffrage League of Boston predicted that his "extraordinary language" would likely incite "race hatred and violence" against 10 million innocent Negro citizens. The *Washington Bee* declared that "the colored man [would] be deceived no more," for Roosevelt, "intoxicated with peevishness and vindictiveness," had made it evident that he was no friend to their cause. "We shall oppose the renomination of Theodore Roosevelt," the *Bee* concluded, "or anyone named by him."

Though he maintained his public bravado, Roosevelt gradually softened his position, sending a new round of investigators to Brownsville to ask further questions. At Taft's urging, he even revoked the provision barring soldiers from civil jobs with the government. Eventually, he allowed individual soldiers to apply for reinstatement, though the burden to prove innocence concerning the raid and the raiders' identities lay with each applicant. Regardless of these concessions, Roosevelt's handling of the Brownsville affair became a permanent scar on his legacy. Six decades later, the U.S. Army finally "cleared the records" of all 167 soldiers "dishonorably discharged" in what had proved to be the "only documented case of mass punishment" in the institution's history.

Privately, Taft continued to believe that had he been present in Washington during the Brownsville incident, he might have prevented the president from issuing his draconian order. In other difficult situations, he had successfully mollified Roosevelt's pugnacity. Nevertheless, once the order was promulgated, Taft never wavered in his public support for the president. When Richard Harding Davis applauded his "courage and good judgment" in ordering the delay, Taft demurred, telling the reporter his action had "been misunderstood." Because of his absence at the time of the original decision, he maintained to Davis, he had simply not been aware of the facts or of the extensive investigation the president had already carried out.

Only his innermost circle was privy to Taft's continuing anxiety. "This Brownsville matter is giving me a great deal of trouble," he confessed to Howard Hollister, adding plaintively that he sometimes wished himself "out of it all" and engaged in "some quiet occupation which did not involve crimination and recrimination." William Taft understood that his chance for the Supreme Court had come and gone, that "when a man has got his face pointed in one direction the only manly way to do is to keep on and take the mud that is thrown." He fully recognized the futility of agonizing over lost possibilities, he assured Hollister, "but the difficulty with worry is that it does not disappear with argument."

CHAPTER TWENTY

Taft Boom, Wall Street Bust

On Dec. 11, 1907, *Puck* paired this image of Roosevelt struggling
to launch Taft's ponderous candidacy with the caption:
"How the Diabolo Can I Keep This Going Till Nomination Day?"

DURING THE SECOND SESSION OF the 59th Congress, which
stretched from December 3, 1906, to March 4, 1907, Theodore Roosevelt's long-standing apprehension over his waning influence on domestic
legislation proved justified. Of the nearly five dozen measures the president
had recommended in his annual December address, only a small number were
given "favorable consideration"—the rest were rejected outright or simply
"passed over in silence." Reporters considered the session "an uneventful and

poor spirited affair," despite the passage of two important measures that had been held over from the previous session: a bill banning corporate contributions in federal elections and legislation preventing railroads from "knowingly" working their employees for more than sixteen consecutive hours. Aside from these two achievements many critical bills were blocked by the conservative Republican leadership: the Philippine tariff law, a child labor law for the District of Columbia, the eight-hour workday bill, a national inheritance tax, a progressive income tax, and a federal licensing law for corporations.

In addition, Roosevelt was deeply frustrated by new threats to his hard-won conservation measures. On February 25, 1907, the Senate passed an amendment to the Agricultural Appropriations Act, rescinding the president's executive power to designate national forests in six western states. Thereafter, only an act of Congress could create a forest reserve, leaving "some sixteen million of acres," Roosevelt later contended, "to be exploited by land grabbers and by the representatives of the great special interests." Because a veto of the entire agricultural bill was not politically viable, Roosevelt and his chief of forestry, Gifford Pinchot, devised an ingenious remedy. With six days remaining before the bill would be signed, Pinchot mobilized his office to work round the clock, some employees toiling forty-eight hours without interruption to draft proclamations placing all 16 million acres into forest lands. No sooner was each proclamation completed than Roosevelt signed an executive order withdrawing the land from development. Through these orders, nearly three dozen new national forest reserves were designated in the American West, including Rainier and Cascade in Washington and Oregon, Bear Lodge in Wyoming, and Lewis and Clark in Montana. Only with the amendment rendered meaningless did Roosevelt sign the agricultural bill. "Opponents of the Forest Service," Roosevelt later boasted, "turned handsprings in their wrath."

Though he was pleased with this successful maneuvering, the president was painfully aware that his strength on Capitol Hill remained seriously compromised by his renunciation of a possible third term. Each passing day emboldened conservative members of Congress to challenge the administration's programs and policies. Looking ahead to the election, Roosevelt feared that if the reactionary wing of his party successfully nominated and elected one of their own, they would work to dilute or even repeal his historic regulatory bills and, in the end, gut his achievements and demolish his legacy.

Of paramount importance was a successor who would sustain and advance his agenda, and there was no man he trusted more to uphold the progressive cause than William Howard Taft. Reporters were fascinated by "the deep, unbroken friendship" the two shared, "like unsophisticated school-boys when together," one journalist expounded, "each apparently under the spell of a romantic affection, a strong, simple sense of knightly companionship in the great field of moral errantry and patriotic adventure." Roosevelt knew he would have to proceed carefully to help his friend get elected. "I am well aware," he told William Allen White, "that nothing would more certainly ruin Taft's chances than to have it supposed that I was trying to dictate his nomination." Nevertheless, he defiantly continued, "it is preposterously absurd to say that I have not the right to have my choice as regards the candidates for the Presidency, and that it is not my duty to try to exercise that choice in favor of the man who will carry out the governmental principles in which I believe with all my heart and soul."

To that end, Roosevelt launched a private campaign of persuasion, engineering a boom of support for Taft's candidacy. In personal letters and meetings, he repeatedly insisted that he would "do all in his power" for Taft, though he could say nothing in public. To visitors, he extolled Taft's "boundless courage," emphasizing his absolute freedom from "any possible corrupting or beguiling influence." In off-the-record conversations with journalist friends, he swore that "he would crawl on his hands and knees from the White House to the Capitol" to secure Taft's election, but if they quoted him, he warned, he would disavow any such statement. A ditty in the *Kansas City Times* compressed the president's stance perfectly:

IMPARTIAL MR. ROOSEVELT
Says Roosevelt: "I announce no choice,
To no man will I lend my voice,
I have no private candidate,
I care not whom you nominate—
Just so it's Taft."

Indeed, the ferocity of Roosevelt's desire for a Taft presidency far exceeded the candidate's own. Taft's declaration of his candidacy was so tepid, so lacking in conviction that it sounded as if he had decided *not* to run: "I wish to say," he began, "that my ambition is not political; that I am not seeking the presidential nomination, that I do not expect to be the Republican candidate." Still, he avowed, "I am not foolish enough to say that in the improbable event that the opportunity to run for the great office of President were to come to me, I should decline it, for this would not be true." This tentative announcement prompted speculation that an unwilling Taft had "been drawn into the maelstrom of Presidential politics," finally yielding to "the persistent pleading of the President and strong personal friends." Even after announcing his candidacy, Taft indicated a preference for working "behind the scenes" and pursuing his duties "irrespective of politics." He found the prospect of soliciting support repugnant and "was very much averse" to burdening his friends with requests for assistance. William Taft, observed a *Chicago Tribune* reporter, seemed to have "an almost morbid fear of being placed in the attitude of struggling for the Presidency."

Initially, Taft's reluctance appeared a winning quality, evidence that the office should seek the man rather than the man the office. "Taft is not a politician in the sense that he is a wire-puller and a seeker of power," commended *The Washington Post*, "but as a natural statesman and leader, he draws all men to him. Let him appear at a public reception, let him make a speech before a large audience, let him attend a private gathering and when he leaves, at least fifty percent of the people will be his friends." The *New York Times* too observed that while Taft might be ignorant of "the little details of politics, the methods of juggling a ward primary, and of playing horse with a caucus," he nevertheless commanded "a bigger, broader kind of politics . . . the kind that is frank and open."

Taft's peculiar diffidence over his presidential hopes also freed him to take a principled stand when faced with trouble brewing in Ohio. In late March 1907, Roosevelt's nemesis, the reactionary senator Joseph Foraker, openly assailed Taft's candidacy, declaring his intention to challenge Taft for the endorsement of the Republican State Committee. The press predicted that a state committee endorsement of Foraker for president could prove crippling to Taft's candidacy. Foraker "may cause trouble," Roosevelt acknowledged to Kermit, adding that in Ohio, the senator was already mustering "the fight against Taft, and incidentally against me."

When Foraker issued his statement, Taft was in the middle of a three-week trip to Panama, Cuba, and Puerto Rico. Speaking on his brother's behalf, Charles Taft accepted Foraker's challenge, suggesting that the question of Ohio's endorsement be put before the voters in a primary. "This is a direct contest between the friends of the Administration of President Roosevelt and his opponents," he argued, relaying Taft's readiness to let the voters decide: "We are willing to submit it to the Republican voters of Ohio and the sooner the better." Nellie found the confrontation unsettling and concurred with the president that Taft "had nothing to gain" from heeding Foraker's challenge and "much possibly to lose."

The decision to call Foraker's bluff, however, soon proved wise. Foraker understood that Roosevelt and Taft enjoyed more support among Ohio's voters and realized that if he manipulated an endorsement from the state committee and subsequently lost to Taft in an open primary or convention, he might jeopardize his Senate seat. Through intermediaries, he therefore offered to endorse Taft for president in exchange for his support in the approaching senatorial contest. Taft flatly refused. "I don't care for the Presidency if it has to come by compromise with Senator Foraker," Taft told Arthur Vorys, his Ohio campaign manager. As "a question of political principle," declared Taft, he could never strike a bargain to endorse a man who had consistently opposed the policies and programs of the Roosevelt administration. Furious, Foraker warned that henceforth, Taft should meet him in the political arena "with a drawn sword in his hand."

In a long letter to Roosevelt, Taft acknowledged that affairs in Ohio had "become somewhat acute." The state committee was scheduled to meet in late July, and Foraker might have sufficient votes to defeat a resolution endorsing Taft's nomination. Still, Taft insisted, he had no regrets. "Rather than compromise with Foraker, I would give up all hope for the Presidency," he stated. "I must explain to you that the Ohio brand of politics the last twenty years has been harmony and concession on the subject of principle to the last degree, provided it secured personal preferment and division of the spoil in a satisfactory way." If Foraker hoped to win, Taft concluded, the senator would have to engage in "a stand-up fight."

Roosevelt's reply demonstrated an admiration for his friend's character that far eclipsed any misgivings over his political acuity. "While under no circumstances," Roosevelt wrote, "would I have advised you to take the position you have taken in refusing to compromise with Foraker on the lines that the local politicians want, yet, now that you have taken it, I wish to say that I count it as just one of those fine and manly things which I would naturally expect from you, and I believe you are emphatically right."

Steeled for defeat when the state committee met to select candidates at the end of July, Taft enjoyed a stunning victory. The committee not only voted 15 to 6 to endorse Taft for president; they also refused to back Foraker in the Senate race. "I am hopeful that it will have a very good effect in other states," a relieved Taft told Howard Hollister. Foraker's political career came to an unceremonious end the following September, when William Randolph Hearst released letters suggesting he had received bribes from Standard Oil. Foraker later argued that the money was simply compensation for legal services, but the damage was done; he withdrew from the Senate race and never served in public office again.

DESPITE HIS VICTORY IN OHIO, Taft found the bitter struggle dispiriting. While Roosevelt reveled in the fight, urging his chosen successor to deliver a "mauling" to Foraker, Taft possessed no such bellicose spirit and could never forget that his "first substantial start in public life" was due to the early kindness of the now disgraced senator. The politics of personal destruction held no relish for a man "born with an instinct to be personally agreeable." Reporters described Will Taft as "the kindest man they [had] ever known in public life." Perhaps better than any other, Louise Taft understood the strengths and weaknesses of her favorite child. Asked what she thought of her son's presidential candidacy, she confessed that she shared Will's reluctance. "A place on the Supreme bench, where my boy would administer justice, is my ambition for him," she admitted. "His is a judicial mind, you know, and he loves the law." Though Taft had proven himself in the Philippines, Cuba, and Panama, the mother knew her son's disposition and the toll that political discord exacted. "Uneasy lies the head that wears a crown," she warned him when he declared his candidacy, shrewdly discerning that "Roosevelt is a good fighter and enjoys it, but the malice of the politicians would make you miserable."

As the months passed, public enchantment with Taft as the reluctant politician began to wane. "He wins the hearts of individuals, but he does not fire the heart of the sovereign multitude," observed reporter James Creelman of the weakening Taft boom. Taft's reluctance to passionately embrace his political ambition began to shift from a sign of moral strength to an indication of weakness: "The country respects and trusts his ability and integrity, but its attitude is that of passive recognition and approval, not the head-long affection that brings power to a political leader of the first rank." Why this "statesman of stainless name, unshakeable independence and creative and administrative abilities" had stirred "so little enthusiasm in the American people" had initially seemed a mystery to Creelman. The explanation, he finally suggested, lay in "the fact that the Secretary of War is not dowered with a political order of mind and is almost wholly devoid of political ambitions." The *New York Times* concurred, adding that people will not flock to a candidate who "can scarcely be said to have waved his standard and asked people to flock to it."

Though Taft had robustly stumped for Roosevelt, he did little in his own behalf to invigorate his popularity. As a candidate in his own right, Taft was expected to emerge as more than the genial defender and chief spokesman for the administration. Correspondents covering the campaign inevitably demanded the headline-generating phrasemaking and charismatic demeanor they had come to expect from Roosevelt. When Taft was criticized as not "fitted to say things that attract attention," his campaign manager urged him to include anecdotes and striking figures of speech in his oratory. "I am not sure that I can make the epigrams that you are hunting for," Taft responded disconsolately, turning to his habitual self-deprecating humor as he continued. "The truth is you have a pretty old horse to run and you've got to take me as I am." Before each address, he was beset by grave misgivings, acutely aware that his drafts remained "infernally long" despite all efforts to prune his words. "Never mind if you cannot get off fireworks," Nellie consoled him. "It must be known by this time that that is not your style, and there is no use in trying to force it. If people don't want you as you are they can leave you, and we shall both be able to survive it."

More problematic to critics than Taft's speaking style was his failure to present a political figure independent from Theodore Roosevelt. On tariff reduction, the sole issue on which he had publicly been at odds with Roosevelt's policy, he now softened his stance and repeated the president's view that "revision must wait until after the election." Though he did not echo Roosevelt's "ferocious denunciation" of business, Taft positioned himself squarely behind the anti-trust and regulatory policies designed to prevent corporate abuses and deflate "swollen fortunes." He passionately defended the railroad rate bill, the food and drug legislation, and the recent conservation measures. He called for a strengthened employer's liability law, a progressive income tax, and an inheritance tax. With only a few "minor exceptions," Taft proclaimed his "complete, thorough, and sincere sympathy" with Roosevelt's policies. The New York *Sun* carped that "there is not an original note" in any of Taft's speeches, jeering that "his ample corporeal capacity receives and contains all that Roosevelt has been, and is, and hopes to be."

Taft expressed bafflement at the press's surprise concerning his sympathy with Roosevelt's policies. "I am much amused at the attitude of the New York papers," he told Horace. "Did they suppose I was coming out to attack Roosevelt's policies? Did they suppose I had stayed in the Cabinet thus long and disapproved of them?" But even some of Taft's ardent backers wished that he would endeavor to set himself apart. "Is it possible," Taft asked one concerned supporter, "that a man shows lack of originality, shows slavish imitation because he happens to concur in the views of another who has the power to enforce those views? Mr. Roosevelt's views were mine long before I knew Mr. Roosevelt at all." He would not, he insisted, "be driven from adherence to those views" by unjust, nonsensical criticism.

Nonetheless, by midsummer of 1907, Taft's candidacy had stalled. A lingering problem, one supporter admitted, lay in "the feeling of uncertainty as to the President's real intentions." So long as the merest possibility remained that Roosevelt might rescind his pledge and run for a third term, many Republicans would not commit to anyone else. "The President is a hero in the eyes of the people," as a friend expressed this concern to Taft, "and they will not surrender his leadership unless they are compelled to." Particularly in the western states, a "well defined movement" had emerged "to force the nomination of Roosevelt." Straw votes taken in the Nebraska and South Dakota legislatures revealed "an almost unanimous sentiment for Roosevelt," and Kansas was reportedly poised to send a Roosevelt delegation to the convention whether he agreed to run or not. "It's hard to write snappy Taft stuff when every damned man I meet gives three cheers for Roosevelt and refuses to talk of any other candidate," another frustrated advocate acknowledged. "Nearly every man who says a good word for Taft doesn't want his name used for fear he may offend Roosevelt. . . . It's a plain, unabridged truth that 90 percent of the Taft sentiment I have found is second-hand or remnant Roosevelt sentiment."

Nellie Taft had never been able to shake her intuitive apprehension that Roosevelt would change his mind about his own candidacy. As calls for a third term gathered steam and newspapers began to suggest circumstances under which the president might enter the race, her concern escalated. While running would be an "almost grotesque" betrayal of his friendship with Taft, the New York *Sun* speculated, the president would doubtless "welcome a situation in which his candidacy might seem inevitable, demanded by the patriotic and imperative clamor of the entire nation." With sardonic, incisive humor, the editorial inquired: "May not the imaginative mind assemble conditions and considerations under which Mr. Taft will seem the victim of it all and also the appointed sacrifice to an illustrious Necessity?" The *Sun*'s piece further unsettled Nellie, who expressed her misgivings to Will: "How they hate him & they go farther than I in insinuating that this is all part of his scheme to get himself nominated as the only man," she wrote, anxiously explaining how easily her husband could be labeled "a martyr and a scapegoat."

In all likelihood, had Roosevelt not declared against a third term on the eve of his overwhelming victory in 1904, he would have pursued a third term. His White House years had been the most fulfilling of his life. Only forty-nine years old and in splendid health, Roosevelt was proud of his work and eager to expand his legacy. He reportedly boasted that he "could get the nomination by simply holding up [his] little finger." Even as he warmed to the popular clamor for a third term, Roosevelt suspected that many of those who called for his reelection "would feel very much disappointed" if he actually ran, and would conclude that he had fallen "short of the ideal they had formed" as to the integrity of his character and the credibility of his word.

Roosevelt told one Cincinnati reporter, Gus Karger, that his decision not to run was an unregrettable "personal sacrifice" so long as Taft secured the nomination. "But I do not wish to have made it in vain," he clarified, "by paving the way to the selection of a successor not in sympathy with the policies of this administration." In case Taft's canvass failed to take off, however, he would not foreclose the possibility of his candidacy. Moreover, Roosevelt argued, while a public reiteration of his vow not to run would rally support for Taft in the West, it might damage his cause in the East, and particularly in New York. Once he irrevocably stated that he would not join the race, he could no longer keep the party organization there from openly backing Governor Hughes. At least "for the moment," Roosevelt convinced himself—and Taft—that saying nothing was "the wisest course." Meanwhile, third-term proponents continued their vocal campaign; by late August, the odds in favor of Roosevelt's renomination had grown "shorter."

"Political affairs are kaleidoscopic," Roosevelt warned his secretary of war on September 3, 1907. Though he still claimed that Taft was "the man upon whom it was most desirable to unite," he acknowledged that his assessment might alter as the race evolved. Support for New York governor Hughes was growing; Treasury Secretary George Cortelyou was still hoping to run; Cannon and Fairbanks remained live possibilities. This unsettled situation made him "a little nervous," Roosevelt admitted to Taft, adding that it was "a matter of real difficulty to prevent certain people declaring for [him]." Taft of all people, he assumed, would appreciate "that the first thing to be considered was the good of the nation and the next thing the good of the party." After that, "any personal preference," he portentously concluded, "must come in the third place."

Just as Roosevelt's support for Taft showed distinct signs of faltering, Taft, ironically, began to feel more sanguine about his campaign. A three-week swing through the heartland and the Far West had gone surprisingly well. "So far as I am able to judge," he reported to Charles, "the trip I have made through the west has helped me." On a sweltering summer day in Columbus, more than 20,000 people had gathered to hear him speak. "It was as great a meeting as they ever had in Ohio," Taft happily noted. In Kentucky, he had spoken to "a fine audience of 4000 people"; in Oklahoma, an immense hall "was filled to suffocation"; and in Denver, he was greeted by "every politician in the state and every state officer." Not only had Taft's formal speeches gone more smoothly, but he had also become increasingly comfortable waving and making brief remarks to the crowds clustered at train stations along his route. "Personal contact," he acknowledged, "does a great deal." His clear blue eyes and famous smile, the *New York Times* reported, made all who met the man "feel glad and sociable and sincere."

Buoyed by his warm reception everywhere he traveled, Taft took Roosevelt's ominous musings in stride. "Nellie was out of patience with the President's letter," he told Charles, "but I understand exactly his state of mind. Under the hammering of the New York papers, and the disposition to press Hughes on, he has become a little more discouraged," Taft explained, claiming, "I don't think he knows as much about the matter as I do, for I have crossed the country and been in all parts of it." Regardless of his current optimism, he promised his brother that he was "not getting into a situation where a failure to get the nomination" would render him "bitter or indeed disappointed." Rather, he assured Charles, "I think that in your general earnestness and zeal on my behalf, a defeat would be more disappointing to you than to me."

The day before his scheduled departure for a long-promised visit to the Philippines, Taft responded to Roosevelt's letter. "I fully understand the difficulties of your position, and exactly how you feel in respect to the candidacy of myself and the others," he began; "I have been, however, agreeably surprised to receive the expressions of good will which I found in the trip across the Continent." Acknowledging that "one hears the things he likes to hear," he had found overwhelming evidence of "affirmative support" across the nation. Nonetheless, he was "prepared to learn at any time" during his Pacific journey that his "boom" had "busted." Whatever the outcome, Taft insisted, he would remain grateful "for the great compliment you have paid me in taking an interest in the matter, and for making my boom at all possible."

☞ ☜

WILL AND NELLIE, WITH TEN-YEAR-OLD Charlie in tow, sailed for the Philippines on September 13. Taft met with officials in Japan and China for several weeks before heading to Manila. The former governor general was scheduled to open the first Philippine Assembly. Taft had long considered creation of a popularly elected assembly a vital step toward eventual Filipino sovereignty. Though the Philippine Commission still exercised executive powers, the new assembly would have the "right to initiate legislation" or "to modify, amend, shape, or defeat legislation proposed by the Commission." As "the first parliament ever freely elected in Asia," the historian Stanley Karnow explains, the assembly "was a tribute to the liberalism of U.S. colonial rule," but "American democracy it was not." Only those who owned land, paid taxes, and demonstrated literacy were allowed to vote.

Taft feared he would encounter "a chill" upon reaching Manila rather than the exuberant welcome of two years earlier. Since that time, the movement for independence had gained momentum, casting an unfavorable light on his prediction that it would take generations to prepare the people for self-rule. But his misgivings proved unfounded. "The enthusiasm of the welcome," he related to Charles, exceeded anything he had experienced before, "and it was the more delightful in that it was unexpected." The reception was particularly gratifying, he added, because it showed that the "common people," along with the "wealthier classes," celebrated his role in creating the National Assembly.

He began his address by frankly admitting that he had not changed his mind about the duration required to achieve genuine sovereignty, but conceded that the question would be determined largely by the success of the new assembly. He wisely acknowledged that the United States, unused to the undertaking of colonial rule and lacking a "trained body of colonial administrators and civil servants," had made serious missteps. Adventurers and military men unsuited "by character or experience" for the serious work of public service had delayed effective government in the islands. In addition, he lamented the dilatory pace of American investment and roundly criticized the U.S. Congress for failing to reduce the tariff on the major Philippine exports of tobacco products and sugar. Yet, despite these obstacles, he believed the islands had made great advancements: hundreds of thousands of Filipino children were attending school; sanitation services and general public health had significantly improved; and a judicial system was now in place. Furthermore, he noted, miles of new roads and street railways had been built, a civil service had been established, and the problems with the Catholic Church had been largely settled. Taft ended his oration by extending his "congratulations upon the auspicious beginning of your legislative life" and conveying his "heartfelt sympathy in the work which you are about to undertake."

At the Inaugural Ball, Taft once again won hearts with his graceful execution of the complex national dance, the rigadon. Will and Nellie attended a "thousand and one events" in the days that followed, inspecting projects that had been completed since their last visit and renewing old friendships and acquaintances at a succession of dances, parties, and banquets. "Everybody," Nellie happily noted, "was glad to see us." The Tafts remained in the Philippines from mid-October through the first week of November, far removed from the stock market collapse that threatened both Roosevelt's legacy and Taft's candidacy.

In October, a series of difficulties on Wall Street escalated into what later became known as the Roosevelt Panic of 1907. Stock prices had been slumping since the previous March; in July and August, a number of companies, including a mining firm and a major street railway company, fell into bankruptcy. As industrial production slackened toward summer's end, experts calculated that stock market losses approached $1 billion. Wall Street blamed Theodore Roosevelt's "crusades against business" for the decline, arguing that his excessive regulation had paralyzed the economy. "By slow and insidious degrees," the *Sun* editorialized, "he has upset the public confidence, arrayed class against class, and fomented mistrust and hatred." The *New York Times* concurred, tracing the country's ills to the administration's "deep-seated, undiscriminating hostility" to business. By "going up and down the country, planting the doctrine of discontent," another critic charged, Roosevelt had "sowed the wind, and we will reap the whirlwind." Union Pacific Railroad president E. H. Harriman, a lifelong Republican, bitterly claimed that he would "take Bryan or Hearst rather than Roosevelt. We cannot be worse off than we are now with that man in the White House."

In a defiant rejoinder, Roosevelt dispensed with his characteristic even-handed rhetoric. He stridently railed against "certain malefactors of great wealth," who conspired "to bring about as much financial distress as they possibly can in order to discredit the policy of the government, and thereby to secure a reversal of that policy so that they may enjoy the fruits of their own evil-doing." These plutocrats, he charged, would even "welcome hard times or a panic" to install "a safe type" in the White House. "They are as blind to some of the tendencies of the time, as the French noblesse was before the French Revolution." Those business interests that shrank from regulation, the president suggested, should examine their own operations. He was "responsible for turning on the light," he noted proudly, not "for what the light showed." Curiously, Roosevelt omitted all mention of the muckraking journalists who had proven so instrumental in illuminating industrial abuses.

As summer turned to early fall, Roosevelt continued to frame the downturn as "a temporary period of weakness," part of a worldwide contraction after a period of great prosperity. Unwilling to cancel his agenda, he left Washington on September 29 to deliver a series of speeches in the West, a trip that would culminate in a ten-day bear hunt in northeast Louisiana. Yet, while Roosevelt hunted bear, the bear market savaged Wall Street and the financial crisis deepened.

In early October, banking moguls F. Augustus Heinze and Charles W. Morse drove up copper prices in an attempt to corner the market. Their sensational failure—and the resulting depression of stock value—might have remained an isolated incident if news had not leaked that their costly speculation had been funded by the stately Knickerbocker Trust Company, the second largest investment bank in New York. Spooked by rumors that the venerable institution might fail, investors stood in queues outside the bank doors from dawn till dusk attempting to reclaim their funds. On the afternoon of October 22, the Knickerbocker ran out of money and was forced to shutter its offices. Three weeks later, the bank's president, Charles T. Barney, committed suicide. Evidence that the respected firm had abandoned sound banking practices to gamble with customers' deposits shattered confidence in other financial institutions. In the days that followed, customers rushed to retrieve money, some standing all night on the sidewalks, others sleeping in the vestibules. Reports indicated that "hardly a bank or trust company" was spared, as the Panic threatened to compromise the nation's entire financial structure.

In the absence of a centralized banking system, seventy-year-old J. P. Morgan served as "a one-man Federal Reserve." The magnificent library at his Madison Avenue house was designated "Panic Headquarters." Surrounded by rare books, Renaissance paintings, and exquisite tapestries, Morgan and his partners met with a carefully selected group of leading bankers. Day after day, often late into the night, this financial cabal monitored the precarious situation, transferring monies from one bank to another, declaring which institutions to save and then raising sufficient funds to rescue them. Within two days the bankers had pledged nearly $10 million.

As Roosevelt hurried back to Washington, Treasury Secretary George Cortelyou took a day train to New York. Meeting with Morgan's group that evening, he promised that the government would add $25 million to the bankers' fund to be distributed at Morgan's discretion. "It was an extraordinary transference of power to a private banker," the biographer Ron Chernow observes. The next day, reporters noted that immense bags of bank securities were delivered to the U.S. subtreasury and J. P. Morgan's headquarters. This quick action saved dozens of banks and trust companies, including the venerable Trust Company of America.

Despite these efforts to stabilize the banking system, stock prices continued to tumble. On Thursday, October 24, the president of the New York Stock Exchange broke the news to Morgan that his brokers no longer had the cash to continue trading. Determined to avoid a shutdown that would likely precipitate the wholesale collapse of financial institutions across the city, Morgan called an emergency meeting. Less than thirty minutes had elapsed before a messenger brought word that Morgan's group had pledged $25 million to keep the exchange open. Elated at this reprieve, exuberant stockbrokers hooted and cheered, hailing J. P. Morgan as "the Man of the Hour." The crisis had proven that Morgan "was still the chief among the country's financiers," the New York *Evening Mail* observed, "the one leader who could inspire the confidence of the multitude and command the resources of the nation."

Just as one firestorm was contained a new blaze erupted. On November 1, Morgan learned that Moore & Schley, a leading brokerage house, was on the verge of bankruptcy. Understanding that the firm's failure "would bring down a few more stories of the tottering financial pyramid," Morgan evolved an ingenious plan. The troubled brokerage house owned a large stake in the Tennessee Coal and Iron Company (TC&I), one of the few significant combinations to escape the grip of United States Steel. In a meeting with U.S. Steel's chairman, Judge Elbert Gary, Morgan proposed that U.S. Steel purchase TC&I, exchanging its own solid bonds for TC&I bonds to redeem Moore & Schley. As a precondition, Gary insisted on Roosevelt's assurance that the purchase would not trigger an anti-trust suit. "Can you go at once?" Morgan demanded.

That evening, Judge Gary and Henry Clay Frick took the overnight train to Washington. Meeting with the president at eight o'clock the following morning, the two U.S. Steel representatives maintained that "under ordinary circumstances they would not consider purchasing the stock," which was priced "somewhat in excess" of the firm's true value. Nevertheless, they believed it was "to the interest of every responsible businessman" to avoid a "general industrial smashup." Roosevelt assured them that he "felt . . . no public duty" to file suit under the Sherman Anti-Trust Act.

The announcement of the deal not only saved Moore & Schley; it also helped restore confidence in the market. But when the terms of the TC&I purchase were made public, Roosevelt came under heavy criticism. John Moody, a respected financial analyst, termed the $45 million purchase price "the best bargain . . . ever made in the purchase of a piece of property"; the coal and iron ore deposits alone, he estimated, were worth "hardly less than $1 billion." Some suspected that Roosevelt had been hoodwinked into legitimizing U.S. Steel's bid to "swallow up a lively competitor, while wrapping itself in the cloak of public spirit."

Roosevelt adamantly denied such charges. "The Nation trembled on the brink," he contended, justifying his decision by pointing to the speed and volatility of the financial markets: "Events moved with such speed that it was necessary to decide and to act on the instant, as each successive crisis arose."

A decision had been necessary before the stock market opened that morning. "I would have showed myself a timid and unworthy public servant, if in that extraordinary crisis, I had not acted precisely as I did." In the years ahead, however, the contentious decision would open a painful rift in Roosevelt's friendship with William Howard Taft.

⌒ ⌒

ALTHOUGH THE IMMEDIATE DANGER OF the financial panic subsided, a general malaise began to seep into every sector of the economy, costing laborers their jobs and farmers their livelihood. "Whether I am or am not in any degree responsible for the panic, I shall certainly be held responsible," Roosevelt grumbled to his physician, Dr. Alexander Lambert. "The big moneyed men" had long since "reached a pitch of acute emotional insanity," he told Kermit. That anger-fueled hysteria would begin to infect even friends and supporters, he suspected, "because when the average man loses his money he is simply like a wounded snake and strikes right and left at anything, innocent or the reverse, that presents itself as conspicuous in his mind."

"From all sides," Ida Tarbell observed, "the business world, the press, leaders of public opinion—there came such a berating of the President as a man has rarely had to endure." No longer simply a "destroyer of credit," Roosevelt had now become an "assassin of property." From Kansas, William Allen White wrote to cheer his friend. "I feel personally hurt by all this abuse that is being heaped on you," he began. "The whole system is bending its energy to turn back the clock, and the prayers and the assistance of every good American should be with you in this crisis." Roosevelt found some consolation in White's words but remained pessimistic about his prospects. "I care a great deal more for such a letter as you have written to me than I do for the attacks that are being made upon me," he replied. "If there is much depression, if we meet hard times, then a great number of honest and well-meaning people will gradually come to believe in the truth of these attacks, and I shall probably end my term of service as President under a more or less dark cloud of obloquy. If so, I shall be sorry, of course; but I shall neither regret what I have done nor alter my line of conduct."

On the morning of November 16, Ray Baker arrived at the White House for a scheduled discussion about his series on race in America. Instead, when Baker noticed a thin red pamphlet called *The Roosevelt Panic* on the president's desk, the conversation quickly turned to the economy. Wall Street, Roosevelt explained, had circulated this incendiary tract "to destroy his program of reform." For two hours, Roosevelt shared his vantage on the troubling situation. "It looks now," he told Baker, "as though there would be let down in business throughout the country for some time to come. I shall be blamed for it: my enemies will make capital of it. It is probable that before next summer I shall be the bête noir of the country." While still hopeful for Taft's nomination, the president feared that "the country at the next election would have to choose between an extreme radical like Bryan and a republican reactionary; that in either event the moderate reform movement which he advocates would be lost sight of." Continuing the conversation with Baker the next morning, Roosevelt repeatedly insisted that "the fight must be carried through." The idea of either a reactionary or Bryan as the next president, Baker observed, seemed to set "his fighting blood to running!" The journalist departed with a growing conviction that Roosevelt was seriously considering another run. "A man may sometimes have to jeopardize his own soul," the president had cryptically commented, "when the interests of the country are at stake."

And in truth, Roosevelt was still brooding over the prospects of another term. "I hate for personal reasons to get out of the fight here," he told one friend. "I have the uncomfortable feeling that I may possibly be shirking a duty." The leader who quits "the fight before it is finished" deserves little respect, he confided to another supporter. Nevertheless, he countered, a political leader "must understand the temper and convictions of the people." And while he believed he could win the Republican nomination, Roosevelt had misgivings about the general election. Nothing would be more humiliating than to break his word and then lose.

The time had come, Roosevelt finally decided, to make clear that he would not seek a third term under any circumstance. On the evening of December 11, he released an unusually succinct statement: "On the night after my election I made the following announcement." Verbatim, he repeated his pledge renouncing a third term and concluded with an equally curt finality: "I have not changed and shall not change the decision thus announced."

Roosevelt's proclamation arrived "like a clap of thunder out of the clear sky," the *National Tribune* reported. "Washington has been throbbing with political gossip ever since." Derisive speculation abounded among the president's critics: "I suppose he has come to the conclusion that it would not be worthwhile for him to run," Democratic senator Tillman charged, stridently observing that "the pitiful condition into which he and Cortelyou have got things shows that he could not be elected." Although Roosevelt would undoubtedly "do his utmost to name the man who [would] carry out his policies,"

William Randolph Hearst noted, only time would tell whether the popularity he once enjoyed or the rejection he currently endured would prove more
potent for his chosen candidate.

In Republican circles, commentary focused primarily on Taft's brighten-
ing prospects. With Roosevelt "definitely and positively out of the Presidential race," party leaders were free "to come out squarely for Taft." California
senator Frank Flint insisted that the state had been for Taft "all along" and
could now openly declare its support. Kansas senator Chester Long concurred,
calling Taft's candidacy "the only one worth considering."

As the political world debated Taft's future, Will and Nellie crossed the
Atlantic on the SS *President Grant*. They had cut short their round-the-world
tour upon receiving news that Taft's mother was critically ill. Louise Taft had
been in splendid health until the previous summer, when she developed an
acute inflammation of the gall bladder. Before his departure for the Philippines, Taft had stopped at the old family mansion in Millbury, Massachusetts,
where his mother and her sister Delia resided together. Doctors considered
Louise's condition serious, yet Will and his brothers were convinced that her
cheerful nature and her "strength, constitution and courage" would carry
her through. She remained mentally clear and for a time seemed to be "on
the road to recovery." On her eightieth birthday in September, Annie Taft
reported, "her cheeks were as rosy as a young girl's and she was happy as a
child at seeing us. There was something marvelous about the youthfulness
of her face." As winter approached, however, she "slowly but steadily" lost
ground. On December 4, Charles telegraphed Will in St. Petersburg that the
end was near. "Still have hope that she will survive until you arrive," Charles
wrote two days later, but Taft's ship had left Hamburg, Germany, when he
received word that his mother was dead.

When the SS *President Grant* arrived at Quarantine in New York, a courier handed Taft a confidential letter from the president. "I hope you will say
nothing for publication until you see me," Roosevelt cautioned. "Things have
become somewhat intricate and you want to consider well what steps you
are to take before taking them," he explained. "A great many of your ardent
supporters became convinced that your canvass was being hurt by the refusal
of many people to accept my declination as final, and that numbers of people
who were sincerely attached to you, but who were even more devoted to me,
did not come out for you because they thought I was still a possibility . . .
I therefore decided to make one more public statement."

Neither politics nor strategy were foremost on William Taft's agenda. No
sooner had he landed than he made plans for an immediate trip to Cincinnati.

"I was very much pained not to be able to come here to attend the funeral," he told a friend. Missing the final "epoch" in his mother's life had left him with a terrible "sense of something wanting," a loss he hoped to mitigate by laying "a wreath on her grave and [calling] on her old friends." While his mother's death represented "a great change" for the entire family, he took solace in the knowledge that through eight decades, she had lived according to her own design, never riddled by a longing "for something else." Ever a force "to be reckoned with," Louise Taft had been a formative power within her own family, just as she had helped shape every community in which she lived. And although she would not see the new chapter that was beginning for her son William, Louise Taft had never doubted his devoted and amiable soul.

CHAPTER TWENTY-ONE

Kingmaker and King

In this Aug. 1, 1906, *Puck* cartoon—"The Crown Prince"—
Theodore Roosevelt wears an emperor's garb and holds aloft
his chosen successor: an infant Taft.

BY THE TIME HE RETURNED to Washington in the early winter of 1908, Taft found that the push for his nomination had "caught its second wind and straightened out for the home-stretch." In the wake of Roosevelt's reaffirmation that he would not run again, William Nelson of the *Kansas City Star* informed Taft that the state now regarded him "as its first and only choice"—a resolution in his favor had gone through "with a whoop." Furthermore, the Colorado State Committee endorsed Taft unanimously, and a poll among likely Michigan delegates showed him trouncing the field by a two to one margin.

Buoyed by the show of widening support, Taft began to actively engage in his campaign for the first time. On the eve of a Republican State Committee meeting in West Virginia, he assured Governor William Dawson that his endorsement would be a decisive blow, clinching not only West Virginia but neighboring states as well. "If you could bring this about," he encouraged the governor, "I shall be everlastingly grateful." He solicited activists for information on the political climate in their regions and responded to encouraging editorials with handwritten notes, telling the publisher of the *St. Paul Pioneer Press and Tribune* that the "friendly tone" of a recent editorial had made his "whole day and week brighter."

Increasingly comfortable at the podium, Taft responded to questions with "rapid-fire" retorts and "witty sallies." Asked at Cooper Union in New York why "a blacklisted laborer" should not "be allowed an injunction as well as a boycotted capitalist," he replied succinctly: "He should be. Were I on the bench I would give him one quickly." Explaining his preference for capitalism over socialism, Taft wryly observed that he did not trust a governmental committee "to determine the worth" of a lawyer, doctor, carpenter or judge—unless, of course, he himself was a member of that committee. Only once did Taft's words come back to haunt him. To the daunting question of what those unable to find work during the recession might do, he had earnestly answered, "God knows. . . . They have my deepest sympathy. It is an awful case when a man is willing to work and is put in this position." Critics seized upon the phrase "God knows" to suggest Taft's want of empathy for the laboring class. Nonetheless, when the long question-and-answer session came to an end, "it was the general verdict that the Secretary was entitled to the referee's decision, and when the gong rang the crowd swarmed into the ring to grasp the victor's hand."

By late January, New York governor Hughes was the sole remaining candidate with a national following who could potentially challenge Taft for the Republican nomination. Taft's supporters urged him to fight Hughes for the New York delegates, but Taft insisted that a nasty struggle in the governor's home fort would ultimately hurt Republican chances in the fall. This decision drew praise from party leaders, but Roosevelt continued to worry that Hughes was a threat. Aware that the governor intended to deliver a major campaign speech on January 31, Roosevelt deliberately chose that same date to present a special message to Congress. The president's words proved to be so "blistering," so "genuinely sensational," that they stole headlines from Hughes's "sane and sound" address.

Roosevelt's anger over the legislature's persistent refusal to act on his recommendations had been mounting for weeks. When the Supreme Court ruled the 1906 Employers' Liability Act unconstitutional in early January, the president was irate, calling it "a matter of humiliation to the Nation" that an employee who suffered an accident "through no fault of his own" would not be protected. "In no other prominent industrial country in the world," he charged, "could such gross injustice occur." He challenged Congress to enact a new liability law and take up his additional regulatory measures without delay. Any implication that such regulations had precipitated the recent panic was wrongheaded, he maintained; in fact, as far as individual blame could be ascribed, the collapse was "due to the speculative folly and flagrant dishonesty of a few men of great wealth, who seek to shield themselves from the effects of their own wrongdoing by ascribing its results to the actions of those who have sought to put a stop to the wrongdoing."

While critics accused Roosevelt of "prostituting his high office and the machinery of government in order to play petty and mean politics against Hughes," the substance of his speech garnered widespread approval. "It hurls defiance at a legislature that thought in its folly that the day of Roosevelt was done," the *Denver Post* observed, contending that "it appeals beyond Congress to the hearts of the American people." The *Boston Daily Globe* also praised the president's "sledgehammer eloquence," while the *Chicago Tribune* rated it "one of America's great state papers." Even those who considered its tone incongruous with "the preconceptions of presidential dignity" acknowledged that the message had caught everyone's attention. "It has maddened my enemies," Roosevelt told Kermit, but "I believe it has helped Taft's nomination."

A New York *World* cartoon aptly illustrated the strategic timing of the president's address: Hughes is pictured trying to deliver his speech while Roosevelt beats an enormous bass drum, drowning out the governor's words. Delighted by the image, Taft wrote to the *World* editor and requested the original caricature. "It records something which may prove to be an epoch in the campaign," he explained. "I should like very much to have it as a part of my memorabilia." By spring, the president noted with satisfaction that "the Hughes boom has collapsed," and Taft's nomination was all but "settled."

Still, Roosevelt continued to monitor every aspect of the campaign, counseling and comforting Taft through the inevitable vicissitudes. In March, for instance, a subordinate in his Columbus campaign office released a statement declaring that Taft would prove more acceptable to the business community than his predecessor. The statement reprinted a series of quotes from the *Wall Street Journal* touting Taft as deliberative and measured in his nature and training—a needful antidote to the impulsive, intemperate president. Both Taft's temperament and his record, the *Journal* had suggested, boded "distinctly against any conclusion that he would continue Mr. Roosevelt's methods." Taft immediately repudiated the release and fired the employee, but the incident continued to disturb him. "Good heavens, you beloved individual," Roosevelt placated him, "you'll have any number of such experiences," though not "as many as I have had; and, unlike you I have frequently been myself responsible!"

Far more troubling, Taft confided, was the "painful experience" of finding himself "held up to execration" as an enemy of the black race for his role as secretary of war during the Brownsville incident. From his abolitionist father, Taft had inherited a deep sympathy and support for the rights of the freed slaves. Indefatigably, he had worked in the Philippines "to oppose the color caste." Yet regardless of his record of combating inequality, scores of traditionally Republican black leaders now considered him "a menace" and declared they would "never, never" support him. While some in Taft's camp suggested he distance himself from the president by publicly discussing his attempt to delay the order, Taft refused; loyalty trumped political advantage. Roosevelt finally took action himself, issuing a formal statement claiming "entire responsibility for the dismissal of the negro troops" and absolving Taft of any role in the decision. As news of Roosevelt's statement spread through the black community, resistance to Taft's nomination dissipated. "We are satisfied," declared the editor of a popular black newspaper, that "President Roosevelt was responsible for the discharge of the soldiers and we believe that Mr. Taft had nothing at all to do with it."

In late spring, however, speaking at Grant's Tomb on Decoration Day, Taft inadvertently instigated his own controversy when he referred to the Civil War general's predilection "for strong drink," which had forced his resignation from the Union Army. Intended as a tribute to the "wonderful resolution, strength of character, and military genius" that allowed Grant to triumph over adversity, Taft's address sought to project a fallible exemplar for young people rather than a mythical figure, "painted as perfect without temptation." Whatever his intention, many veterans perceived Taft's depiction of Grant as a desecration: "I trust you will have the grace to go and hang yourself rather than attempt to belittle a nation by running for the presidency," the commander of the New Hampshire Sons of Veterans histrionically suggested. Across the country, outraged veterans accused Taft of insulting "the mighty dead" and warned that they would not forget his "heartless" remarks on election day. When Roosevelt and Taft reconvened, the president stood "at mock attention," solemnly exclaiming, "Viva Grant." He advised Taft not to fret: "It is not going to hurt you. I have got the public accustomed to hearing the truth from statesmen or politicians, whichever we might be termed, without it changing the destinies of the nation."

The president's confidence, it seemed, was well founded; such stumbles did little to stay the momentum of Taft's campaign. "All opposition to Taft has died down and he will be nominated easily," Roosevelt assured a friend at the end of May. The surge of support in recent months represented "an astonishing achievement for Mr. Taft," the *Chicago Evening Post* observed, affirming the candidate's ability to evade the many snares that had beset his campaign. "We doubt whether the history of the country has ever recorded a more remarkable feat by a presidential candidate than this utter routing of each and every anti-convention attack upon him."

ROOSEVELT'S SATISFACTION WITH THE PROGRESS of Taft's campaign as summer arrived could not mask his chagrin that Congress had refused to act on his proposals for a second straight year. "Congress is ending, by no means in a blaze of glory," the president complained to Whitelaw Reid, ambassador to Great Britain. The reigning conservatives in the House and Senate, he grumbled, "felt a relief that they did not try to conceal at the fact that I was not to remain as President." While a few significant measures had passed— including a revised employer liability act and a child labor bill for the District of Columbia—the core of Roosevelt's progressive recommendations had again been ignored. With "practical unanimity," journalists referred to the session as the "do nothing Congress."

In his frustration, Roosevelt failed to appreciate that conservatives were emboldened not only by his impending departure but also by the diminished power of the muckraking journalists, whose popular exposures of corporate abuse had played a collaborative role in pressuring Congress to act. Nor did the president acknowledge that his celebrated address castigating muckrakers had "crystallized" a nascent sentiment of disfavor toward the new journalism. Two years after Roosevelt's diatribe, a survey of leading monthlies revealed a sharp decline in the fiery investigative pieces that had fueled public demand for reform. "The noon of the muckraker's day is past," one Iowa newspaper declared. "Look upon these magazines now," observed the *New York Times*. "Read them from cover to cover. Where are the muckrakers?" Magazine publishers were acutely sensitive to capricious public sentiment, the *Times* concluded: "Like the manufacturers of print cloth and summer silks," they were "prepared to offer any pattern the reader desires. We judge that quiet patterns are now in favor."

While the country sought respite from grim catalogues of wrongdoing, members of the old *McClure's* team struggled with their vacillating feelings toward Theodore Roosevelt and the Square Deal. William Allen White remained the most passionate champion of the president. Embarking on a biographical sketch of Taft for the May issue of *The American Magazine*, White first consulted with Roosevelt. "Don't hold the knife edge of your balance so perfectly poised in this piece that your readers won't see your bias," Roosevelt had counseled him. White needed little prompting, for he had developed a genuine affection for Taft after spending several days with him on a train from Kansas City to Washington. In the weeks that followed, the two men continued to correspond as White sought to fill in details of Taft's career. In lengthy letters to White, Taft meticulously credited every mentor and benefactor who had helped facilitate his success. "The meanest man in the world," he remarked, "is the man who forgets the old friends that helped him on an early day and over early difficulties."

The resulting piece portrayed Taft as an "amiable giant," who had triumphed through the warmth of his personality, his "prodigious capacity for hard, consecutive work," and his judicial instinct to grapple with every issue "without resting and without fatigue until it is settled or solved." No political figure was better suited than Taft to pursue Roosevelt's "unfinished business," White argued, to push nearly a dozen pending anti-trust suits through the courts, to resolve the imperfections in recently enacted epoch-making laws. "The times demand not a man bearing promises of new things," White concluded, "but a man who can finish the things begun . . . who, with a steady hand, and a heart always kind and a mind always generously just, can clean off the desk." The piece delighted Roosevelt. "It would be impossible to get two men of fairly strong character and fairly marked individuality who would agree more closely," he responded to White, "unless it is either one of us and Taft!"

Ida Tarbell had long shared White's fascination with Roosevelt, though she found his pugnacity and relish for war distasteful. "I wabble terribly whenever I see him face to face," she confessed to Baker. "He seems so amazing." She had genuinely exulted in his crusade against the trusts, sharing his conviction that the government had a right and a duty to regulate corporations "for the sake of democracy." Roosevelt was "in the right," she insisted; "corporations exist not for themselves, but for the people." As Tarbell immersed herself in the tariff issue, however, she began to suspect that the president was a "less amazing" figure than she had initially imagined. Having envisioned Roosevelt as "the St. George" who would marshal popular support for downward tariff revision after the 1907 Panic, she was sorely disappointed by his unwilling-ness to risk Republican Party unity. Still, Tarbell remained a proponent of the Square Deal, trusting that investigation, legislation, regulation, and judicial proceedings could right the wrongs of the industrial world.

By 1908, Lincoln Steffens had arrived at very different conclusions. Steffens no longer trusted that the Square Deal could solve the nation's gross inequities of wealth and power, believing that more radical measures were necessary, including public ownership of corrupt railroads and trusts. "I certainly am socialistic," he told his sister, "but I'm not a Socialist." In the June issue of *Everybody's*, he published an article comparing the leadership styles of Theodore Roosevelt, Taft, and La Follette. Although he praised Roosevelt for galvanizing the public and predicted that Taft would faithfully follow his predecessor's regulatory course, he argued that La Follette alone was fighting against the system itself.

Roosevelt responded to Steffens with a 2,000-word rebuttal. "You contend," he began, "that Taft and I are good people of limited vision who fight against specific evils with no idea of fighting against the fundamental evil." After a quarter of a century in politics, Roosevelt observed, he had found that change was realized by "men who take the next step; not those who theorize about the 200th step." He pointed out that "it was Lincoln," not Wendell Phillips, who "saved the Union and abolished slavery." Indeed, history suggested that those, like La Follette, who fought "the system in the abstract," accomplished "mighty little good." Roosevelt closed by suggesting that Steffens visit the White House to continue their dialogue. Steffens replied that they had always argued about politics with such "mutual understanding" and "genuine affection" that he now felt closer to the president than to many who shared his own views.

By the final year of Roosevelt's presidency, Ray Baker too had come to question his leadership style, though he still continued to regard him as "the most interesting personality" in the country. In a 1908 article for *The American Magazine*, Baker located the source of the president's strength in what the philosopher William James termed "the art of energizing"—the ability to command ordinary talents to an extraordinary degree. Whereas most people never tapped their "vast stores of hidden energies," Baker contended that Roosevelt succeeded through "the simple device of self-control and self-discipline, of using every power he possesses to its utmost limit—a dazzling, even appalling spectacle of a human engine driven at full speed." Despite being an "ordinary shot," he had practiced methodically to become a world-class hunter. Lacking the succinct poetic clarity of Lincoln's literary genius, he had nonetheless produced an astonishingly versatile body of work. While preaching simple homilies and banal maxims, he had nonetheless reached the hearts of his countrymen and given the people voice.

After a decade of observation, however, Baker had reached a less flattering assessment of the president: "Roosevelt never leads; he always follows. He acts, but he acts only when he thinks the crowd is behind him. . . . Upon all the great issues which he has championed, the country was prepared before he entered the arena." Though he had pushed his agenda "valiantly and fearlessly," Baker argued, the times now demanded a thinker—someone who could deal with the unjust tariff structure and the underlying conflict between the rich and the poor, who could formulate a "European system of comprehensive social insurance to protect the injured, the sick and the aged."

Baker's musings provoked a lively correspondence with Roosevelt. "I think you lay altogether too much stress," Roosevelt told the reporter, "upon your theory that everywhere and at all times political thought divides itself into two opposing forces," driving what Baker had called "the fundamental conflict between the few and the many." In the South, Roosevelt pointed out, the tension between the races reached "immeasurably farther" into the souls of men than any struggle between the poor and the rich. Although he believed in "equal opportunities for all," he decried the inflammatory and unprofitable language of class warfare, which impeded the moral struggle to improve "man as a man."

"I wish as much as you do that we had reached the stage in our civilization where we could avoid the hatred and demagogy of ignorance and class strife," Baker promptly replied. In the present situation, he maintained, class action by unions and parties seemed indispensable. Would "any amount of effort to improve the Russian Jewish tailor of the East-side—as a man—make much headway," he wondered, "unless there is a determined effort to change his environment and the institutions which help to make him poor, downtrodden, outcast?"

One evening, less than a week after this exchange of letters, the two men talked at the White House until midnight, and for the first time in their long acquaintance, the ever exuberant president struck Baker as a weary man. Roosevelt disclosed his plans to spend a year big game hunting in "the wilds of Africa" when his term ended. "The best thing I can do is to go entirely away," he told Baker, "out of reach of everything here." He admitted that he believed his time had come and gone; that he was "through." When Baker suggested that "the people might not be through with him," the president responded "with a curious finality, a sort of sadness" unlike anything Baker had heard from him.

"New issues are coming up," Roosevelt acknowledged. "People are going to discuss economic questions more and more; the tariff, currency, banks. They are hard questions, and I am not deeply interested in them; my problems are moral problems, and my teaching has been plain morality." Never, Baker later reflected, had he seen the president "in a more human mood."

ROOSEVELT'S WISTFUL DEMEANOR ON THE eve of the Republican National Convention in June 1908 in Chicago revealed residual misgivings about his iron-clad pledge to forgo a third term. "When you see me quoted in the press as welcoming the rest I will have after March the 3d take no stock in it," he informed his military aide Archie Butt. "I have enjoyed every moment of this so-called arduous and exacting task." For all seven years of his tenure, he proudly told George Trevelyan, he had "*been* President, emphatically," utilizing "every ounce of power there was in the office." At times, he was plagued by "ugly qualms" about "abandoning great work" simply to be true to his word. Yet, if he did answer the call to run again, he feared that even those who had spurred him on would suffer a shock of "disappointment" at an unseemly quest to hold the office "longer than it was deemed wise that Washington should hold it."

Roosevelt was not the only one preoccupied by the tantalizing prospect of a third term. As Chicago began "to throb with the confusion and excitement of arriving throngs" in preparation for the convention, "a stampede" for Roosevelt remained a distinct possibility. "Taft has nothing to fear from any combination of opponents," *The Washington Post* remarked. "The only man who can defeat him is Pres. Roosevelt." In journalistic circles, the odds of a stampede to nominate Roosevelt at the first mention of his name proved "an unfailing topic for conjecture, and the explosive possibility of its injection at the psychological moment" was widely anticipated. Any large political gathering, the *San Francisco Chronicle* observed, can easily become "a mob, ready to accept what psychologists call 'suggestion.' "

As expectations began to mount, two antithetical factions enhanced the likelihood of a Roosevelt stampede. For progressive and moderate Republicans who "in their heart of hearts" preferred Roosevelt to anyone else, hope remained that if actually nominated, the president would feel compelled to accept the honor despite his repeated refusals. The agenda of the second group was far more calculating; for Taft's reactionary opponents, known as "the Allies," "a stampede" would be the "last card" in their effort to break Taft's majority on the first ballot. By pushing for a third term, they hoped "to create a diversion against Taft and weaken him as a candidate." If the president then refused to accept the nomination—as they anticipated—the door would open for a second or third ballot to nominate one of their own: Cannon, Knox, or Fairbanks.

The sky was "full of sunshine" on June 16, the first day of the convention. The band played patriotic airs as delegates found their seats on the floor and spectators piled into the galleries. Barely audible above the din, the presiding officer's tribute to "the glories of the party" did not seem designed "to set the blood tingling." Toledo mayor Brand Whitlock observed a restlessness in the gallery reminiscent of "that expectant interest in which multitudes view an animal trainer at work; down in their hearts the secret human wish, or half-wish, that the animals may turn and eat the trainer." The analogy, he said, served only to point out that "the spectators longed for something to happen. But nothing happened."

The agenda for the second day of the convention promised to sate the crowd's desire for excitement. Though Will and Nellie remained in Washington with their seventeen-year-old daughter Helen and ten-year-old son Charlie, the rest of the Taft clan descended upon Chicago. Two hours before the convention proceedings opened at 10 a.m., William Howard Taft arrived at his War Department office. His quarters at the Old Executive Building included a large reception room for visitors, an adjoining space for his secretary and two clerks, and a private office with a desk, couch, and several comfortable chairs. Electricians equipped the office to receive telegraph messages directly from the convention hall, and a long-distance telephone line allowed Frank Hitchcock, Taft's national campaign manager, to reach him from the floor of the Coliseum. To relieve his anxiety, Taft "plunged into the business of the day," reviewing routine matters with his secretary. When a photographer arrived and suggested that he pose expectantly by the telephone, Taft balked. "I do not sit at the telephone," he laughed, explaining that "telephone messages are taken by somebody else. I'll not do anything unnatural." Nellie arrived at noon, taking a seat at her husband's desk, while young Charlie stationed himself in the anteroom with the telegraph operator, ready to carry incoming messages to his mother. She read each dispatch aloud to the assembled gathering of associates and friends as Taft paced restlessly in and out of the office, intermittently occupying an easy chair by the window. Dozens of newspapermen and clerks gathered in the outer reception room.

At 1:30 p.m., the convention chairman Senator Henry Cabot Lodge approached the podium to deliver the keynote address. For half an hour, the senator held the 14,000 attendees rapt with a powerful critique of the Democrats and a stirring defense of Republican policies, carefully avoiding any mention of Theodore Roosevelt. When he finally introduced "the magic name," Lodge unleashed "a wild, frenzied uncontrollable stampede for Roosevelt." The point of Lodge's speech that touched a "burning fuse to dry powder" was the simple observation that to the great dismay of "vested abuses and profitable wrongs," the president had "fearlessly enforced the laws," becoming "the best abused and most popular man in the United States today." Delegates and spectators "exploded with a roar," clapping, whistling, stamping their feet. "Hats, fans, umbrellas, flags, newspapers, arms, coats were waved, flapped, brandished, jiggled" while the audience chanted: "Four Years More. Four Years More."

When Lodge attempted to continue, his words were drowned in "volleys of cheers" that echoed from floor to ceiling. "It seemed," one journalist remarked, "as if the roof would blow off." This disruption was merely "a trifle compared with what followed." After someone threw a four-foot Teddy bear into the air, delegates began tossing it from one state to another. "Each time it appeared above the heads of the delegates," *The Washington Post* reported, "it was a signal for another outburst." The convention was "on the verge of a good natured riot" when a national committeeman from Oklahoma captured and sat on the bear, successfully resisting all attempts to snatch it away.

Bulletins describing these outbursts on the convention floor understandably produced anxiety for the little group assembled in Taft's office. Fortunately, Taft had departed to meet with Secretary Root about an official matter just before the pandemonium erupted, but Nellie was unnerved. Her anxiety was somewhat mollified when Frank Hitchcock called from the floor assuring everyone that he was "not at all alarmed." The Taft delegates would remain firm.

Back in Chicago, the wild ovation persisted for a record forty-nine minutes, ceasing only when Lodge returned to the podium, wresting the crowd's attention "by the force of his personality" and the impact of his words. "That man is no friend to Theodore Roosevelt," he proclaimed, "who now, from any motive, seeks to urge him as a candidate for the great office which he has finally declined. The President has refused what his countrymen would gladly have given him; he says what he means and means what he says, and his party and his country will respect his wishes as they honor his high character and great public service." Aware that Lodge was the president's designated spokesman—and that he carried a letter confirming Roosevelt's refusal in case of his nomination—the gathering accepted the senator's words "as the voice of the President." The convention quieted; the possibility of the stampede, feared by some and desired by many, had come and gone.

Nellie was still seated at the desk receiving bulletins when Taft returned to the office. After learning of the excitement, he walked over to the White House, where the president and first lady were preparing for a horseback ride through Rock Creek Park. William Loeb, Roosevelt's secretary, remarked that the convention had simply needed "to blow off steam" before moving forward. Archie Butt had never seen Roosevelt more ebullient. Flattered by the emotional outpouring, the president recognized that the convention had paid him the highest possible compliment without forcing a decision that threatened both his party's prospects and the credibility of his word. Taft, too, was smiling. A reassuring telegram had arrived from Frank Hitchcock: "The cheers for Roosevelt today, will be for Taft tomorrow."

When the convention opened the following day, Nellie resumed her customary position at her husband's desk. Charlie happily continued serving as messenger, and Miss Helen Taft, scheduled to attend Bryn Mawr College in the fall, joined the group as the nominating speeches for favorite sons were set to begin. Journalists remarked on the solidarity of the Taft family, particularly noting Nellie's unusual role as one of her husband's "best advisers" in every aspect of the campaign. A *San Francisco Chronicle* reporter described the atmosphere in the room as "electric with excitement [and] suppressed nervous tension."

Nellie strove to remain calm as she relayed reports of the enthusiastic cheering that greeted Ohio congressman Theodore Burton's nominating speech for Taft. Delegates stood on their chairs as a large banner bearing Taft's picture was carried through the aisles, waving their hats and flags to a chorus of "Taft, Taft, Taft." A burst of good-natured laughter greeted a pair of ample trousers adorning a flagpole brandished by a member of the Texas delegation: "As pants the hart for cooling streams," they intoned, "so Texas pants for Taft!" To better view the animated demonstration, Charles Taft climbed a stepladder on the edge of the Ohio delegation. His "beaming smile" revealed pride and pleasure in the accomplishments of a younger brother whom he had mentored and supported since the death of their father. Though less protracted than the frenzy unleashed by Roosevelt's name on the previous day, the exuberant response buoyed the spirits of Taft's supporters.

By late afternoon, visitors inundated Taft's inner office, with reporters streaming in and out. Just before the balloting was set to begin, Nellie was handed a bulletin causing her to turn "white as marble." A large lithograph of Roosevelt had been carried onto the stage, she relayed to the gathering, and once again the audience had erupted into a frenzy that made it impossible for Chairman Lodge to restore order. "Scarcely a word was spoken," one correspondent noted. "Men who ordinarily are not affected by nervousness hung over the telegraph instrument as though their lives depended upon the words which the stolid telegrapher was ticking out." Silence prevailed for nearly fifteen minutes, until the next bulletin announced that twenty-six Massachusetts delegates had voted for Taft. No one could fathom how the roll call had reached Massachusetts until it was discovered that even as the demonstration continued unabated, Lodge had somehow proceeded with the vote. "Pay no attention to the crowd," he shouted to the clerk, declaring, "I shall not have the president made by a Chicago mob." Seven states managed to cast their votes before the mayhem finally subsided. "The scene was absolutely unique in American history," one correspondent noted, "the voting being taken during a terrific uproar in behalf of a man whose name was not before the convention."

Shortly before five-thirty, a telegram arrived declaring that the press associations had "flashed" the nomination of William Howard Taft. Her eyes "aglow with excitement," Nellie read the news to the assembled throng. "Bubbling over with happiness," she rose to embrace her husband, who "laughed with the joy of a boy." A "football rush" followed as Taft's colleagues in the War Department arrived en masse to extend their congratulations. Moments later, a bulletin confirmed that the nomination was declared unanimous, and Secretary of State Root appeared to accompany Taft to an appointment at the War College. "You know how happy I feel over this," Root told the new nominee. " I do," Taft replied, giving the secretary "a resounding whack on the back." The nominee warned Root that they would face a delay as he shook hands with the assembled reporters. "It will be a long time before you will be able to shake the newspapermen," Root quipped. Taft cordially greeted "the boys" in turn but declined to make a statement. "Words don't frame themselves for me now," he humbly insisted, "but I don't deny that I am very happy."

Roosevelt was engaged in a tennis game with Assistant Secretary of State Robert Bacon when he received word of Taft's nomination. He had prepared a formal statement, which he directed his secretary to release straightaway to the press. "The country is indeed to be congratulated upon the nomination of Mr. Taft. I have known him intimately for many years and I have a peculiar feeling for him, because throughout that time we have worked for the same object with the same purposes and ideals. I do not believe there can be found in the whole country a man so well fitted to be president."

That evening, against a backdrop of music and fireworks, Taft addressed hundreds of his neighbors and friends from his doorstep. "A great honor has fallen upon me today to lead a great political party in the contest that is to come," he solemnly acknowledged. He then turned to Nellie, "the real ruler of the family," acknowledging that "no greater need of approval could be desired." Reminded that his nine o'clock reception at the White House would begin in two minutes, he hastened off on foot in that direction. But when the crowd thwarted his progress, he was forced to recruit the Army Band's wagon. "Does this outfit belong to any one?" he inquired. "Everything belongs to you to-night," he was assured. He promptly jumped into the wagon and proceeded to the White House, where his old friend, the proud kingmaker, awaited.

The convention completed its business the following day, nominating the conservative New York congressman James Sherman for vice president. Neither Roosevelt nor Taft was particularly happy with the choice of "Sunny Jim." They had hoped to add a progressive from the West to the ticket, but when Albert Beveridge, Herbert Hadley, Jonathan Dolliver, and A. B. Cummins all refused, they had left the decision to the delegates. The platform approved by the delegates was equally unsatisfying. At Taft's insistence, it called for a special session to revise the tariff and create a postal savings bank system, but it diluted an anti-injunction plank and blamed Democrats for the failure to act on progressive measures, exonerating the Republican majority. While Senators La Follette and Beveridge expressed "disappointment," William Allen White defended the convention's work in an editorial. "We can't get all we desire," he maintained. "A party is no place for a crank. If he cannot compromise and go forward he should flock alone."

☙ ❧

"The next four months are going to be kind of a nightmare for me," Taft confessed to a friend shortly after the convention. Each morning he awakened "with a certain degree of nervous uneasiness of what may appear in the newspaper," he explained, and though he could handle attacks "manufactured out of whole cloth," those blending truth and falsehood were more troubling.

To fortify himself, Taft planned to spend July and August at the Homestead, a celebrated resort hotel in Hot Springs, Virginia, where he could work, relax, and replenish his energies for the fall campaign. Situated atop the Blue Ridge Mountains, a short horseback ride from waterfalls and ancient woodlands, the Homestead boasted a majestic high-ceilinged lobby, a wide veranda surrounding the entire building, and an eighteen-hole golf course. Nellie, Will, and Charlie occupied the Presidential Suite, with a private balcony overlooking the grassy links. In addition, a five-room office suite had been configured, providing two private chambers for the nominee, along with a reception area and workspace for his secretary and clerk. In the days that followed, dozens of senators, congressmen, cabinet officials, and members of the Republican National Committee made the train trip to Hot Springs. Overnight, the little town became the focus of national attention, just as Oyster Bay had been seven years earlier.

Despite the many diversions offered by the luxurious Homestead, Taft kept to a rigorous schedule. Typically awakened at seven by his Filipino valet, he favored a spare breakfast of dry toast and a single soft-boiled egg. By 8:30 a.m., he was bathed, shaved, and settled in his office, where he read and signed responses to more than 1,500 congratulatory notes in addition to general correspondence of nearly 150 letters every day. By ten, he was out on the eighteen-hole golf course with one or two invited guests. By 2 p.m., he had returned to his office, meeting with party leaders to determine strategy for each region of the country. In the late afternoon, he would devote several hours to working on his acceptance speech, scheduled for late July. At seven thirty, he and Nellie went to dinner in the public dining room with their visitors, before settling on the wide veranda that served as the "favorite promenade" for hotel guests.

The week after the Tafts arrived in Hot Springs, the Democratic Party held its convention in Denver. After the defeat of their previous nominee, conservative Judge Alton Parker, the party once again turned to the progressive hero William Jennings Bryan. Their platform demanded the passage of bills Roosevelt had failed to push through the Republican Congress—an eight-hour day, a general employers' liability act, a progressive income tax, and a child labor law. They further advocated the direct election of senators, a public record of campaign contributions, a federal guarantee of bank deposits, and a law removing tariff protection for the products of any corporation with a market share over 50 percent.

The Democratic platform, Taft confided to Roosevelt, left him in a quandary over his own acceptance speech, for while he disagreed vehemently with some of their pledges, he approved many of them. "We will be able to riddle it," Roosevelt assured him in reply. A few days later, the president forwarded specific suggestions on how to "slash savagely" at Bryan and his platform. After working steadily for another week, Taft sent his first draft to Roosevelt. "Both of the first two paragraphs should certainly be omitted," Roosevelt replied, but aside from a weak section on bank deposits, he found the remainder of the address "admirable." He added in closing: "I think that the number of times my name is used should be cut down. You are now the leader."

While Taft's continued desire for the counsel of the country's "most accomplished politician" was understandable, his "extraordinarily frank announcement" that he intended to bring his final draft to Oyster Bay for Roosevelt to review provoked scorn and concern. "I have the highest regard for the president's judgment," he told the press, justifying his apparent deference to Roosevelt's opinion, "and a keen appreciation of his wonderful ability for forceful expression." Editorial writers universally lambasted "the spectacle of Candidate Taft hurrying to Oyster Bay to submit his speech of acceptance." The *New York Times* likened his action to that of "a schoolboy about to submit his composition to the teacher before he read it in school," and observed that despite great admiration for Roosevelt, people would like their next president to demonstrate "an existence independent of his late chief." The New York *Sun* described the visit as a "humiliating pilgrimage," further evidence that Taft was "but the puppet of the White House Punch and Judy manipulator." Although the copy of the speech that Taft's secretary released to the press after Roosevelt's review revealed few substantial changes, the episode was "not calculated to inspire confidence in Republican breasts."

From New York, Taft traveled to his brother Charley's Cincinnati home, where the official notification ceremony and acceptance address would take place. The stately colonial mansion, with its white pillars and sweeping green lawns, provided a perfect setting for the festivities. Workers had constructed a platform and two temporary porches flanking the imposing entrance to accommodate members of the notification committee and distinguished visitors. A flagpole erected on the south lawn flew a silk flag which the local citizens had donated to honor Taft's visits to Cincinnati. The spacious grounds afforded standing room for nearly 1,500 spectators. "What we thought originally would be merely a formal affair, attended by a few people," Charley explained to a relative, "has developed into a big demonstration." Thousands streamed into Cincinnati from neighboring states to attend the open-air concerts, fireworks, receptions, and marching band performances that accompanied the main event. A large, enthusiastic crowd greeted Taft at the Cincinnati train station with an enormous banner bearing the words NO PLACE LIKE HOME. Charles was first to grasp his brother's hand, and they proceeded "arm in arm" to a waiting carriage. On the drive to the Pike Street home where he intended to spend a quiet weekend with Nellie before Tuesday's big event, Taft appreciated the city's "holiday attire"—flags waving, houses draped with bunting, streets adorned with colorful streamers.

On July 28, the designated Notification Day, "the booming of cannon" announced a two-hour parade through the city. From the reviewing stand, Taft was gratified to observe Democrats marching side by side with Republicans in a show of bipartisanship for their favorite son. The formal ceremony began at noon, with the head of the notification committee delivering the official announcement that the Republican Party had selected William Howard Taft "as its candidate for president—the highest honor that can be conferred by this constitutional republic." Taft "smiled cordially and looked as much astonished as he could be." And when his turn came to speak, the audience erupted in warm applause.

Disregarding Roosevelt's admonishment, Taft opened with a tribute to the president's "movement for practical reform," touting his leadership in securing long-overdue regulatory legislation over corporate behavior, the railroads, the food and drug industry, and the conservation of natural resources. These laws, Taft argued, offered a far more constructive avenue for curbing corporate abuses than Democratic proposals to dismantle large corporations simply because they were big. The Republican approach "would compel the trusts to conduct their business in a lawful manner," while Bryan and the Democrats would simply "destroy the entire business in order to stamp out the evils which they have practiced."

Having commended the high standard of morality set by Roosevelt's agenda, Taft was careful to delineate a policy of his own. "The chief function of the next Administration," he pledged, "is distinct from, and a progressive development of, that which has been performed by President Roosevelt. The chief function of the next Administration is to complete and perfect the machinery by which these standards may be maintained, by which the lawbreakers may be promptly restrained and punished, but which shall operate with sufficient accuracy and dispatch to interfere with legitimate business as little as possible. Such machinery is not now adequate." Furthermore, he expressed his personal support for two issues that conservative delegates had refused to sanction in the Republican Party platform: a progressive income tax and the direct election of senators.

After the official hour-long address, Taft spoke informally to friends and fellow citizens, expressing the gratitude and wonder he and Nellie felt at the spectacular reception. "Popular elections are uncertain," he concluded, "but whatever betide me as a candidate, we can never be deprived of the joy we feel at this welcome home." An elated Nellie added her own remarks: "Hasn't it been glorious!" she exclaimed. "I love public life. To me this is better than when Mr. Taft was at the bar and at the bench, for the things before him now and in which he takes part are live subjects."

After a luncheon party at the Country Club, the Tafts ended their long day on the *Island Queen*, escorted up the Ohio River by more than 150 smaller boats, "all ablaze with illumination." From the steamer's deck, Will and Nellie witnessed a magnificent display of fireworks. Three days later, the glow of his home city's "tremendous outpouring" remained with Taft. "No matter what may happen," he reflected to Roosevelt, "the joy we felt at our reception in Cincinnati was unalloyed."

"I congratulate you most heartily," the president wrote. "The speech is a great success and has achieved exactly the purposes you sought to obtain. Of course, the *Sun*, *Times*, and *Evening Post* are dreadfully pained at your having praised me," he gleefully observed, "or rather, as they phrase it, having submitted to my insistence that you should praise me. I am glad they did not see your speech before I got at it." In its revised form, Taft's speech garnered a positive response. The *Wall Street Journal* called it "an exceedingly able and shrewd political document." Though "not brilliant in the Roosevelt and Bryan sense," nor studded with "telling phrases," the *Journal* declared, it increased "the popular faith in Mr. Taft's fitness for the high office" and perfectly positioned him "in the middle of the road, avoiding alike the extreme of eastern conservatism and the extreme of western radicalism."

Relieved that his acceptance speech was behind him, Taft returned to Hot Springs for the month of August, intending to focus on a rigorous regime of dieting and exercise. By limiting his food consumption and walking three or four hours each day over the formidable fairways of the golf course, he hoped to shed the 50 pounds he had gained during the previous year. "I play golf just as I would take medicine," he conceded to reporters, and after a brief stint of this hiking and golfing regimen under the hot sun, he proudly reported to Roosevelt that he had already lost inches in his waist. Taft's other planned activity, trail riding, had to be abandoned after the ankles of his saddle horse proved too weak to carry his weight. "No man weighing 300 pounds has any business on a horse's back," declared the president of the Massachusetts Society for the Prevention of Cruelty to Animals upon reading of the animal's collapse, callously griping, "if he must ride let him use an automobile or an elephant." One Taft supporter offered to donate a 3,500-pound workhorse, one so large that "a special stall" would be built to accommodate the massive creature. Undeterred, Taft continued his daily exertions on the links.

With little hard news to report, correspondents resorted to detailed accounts of Taft's golf game, creating the unfortunate impression that the candidate engaged in little beyond recreation. The *Tribune* reporter, at least, observed that he played golf as he did "everything else, with the same steadiness and poise, and same equable temper, never becoming discouraged by any obstacle and never losing his temper or his nerve as a result of a bad play."

The rash of golfing anecdotes vexed Roosevelt. "It would seem incredible that anyone would care one way or the other about your playing golf," the president complained to Taft, but he had "received literally hundreds of letters from the West protesting about it." Because the working class looked upon golf as a "rich man's game," Roosevelt cautioned his friend to suppress future reports about his golf game. Nor should he even permit himself to be photographed on the golf course, for "the American people regard the campaign as a very serious business." Taft insisted that he was working "very hard" but acknowledged that appearances could be misleading.

As the general election drew near, Roosevelt continued to hover about Taft "like a hen over her chickens." Early on, Taft had pledged to make public all campaign contributions as soon as the election was over. Realizing such transparency might paralyze large donors, Taft told the president that he was "willing to undergo the disadvantage in order to make certain that in the future we shall reduce the power of money in politics." Republican fund-raising did, in fact, suffer. "I must tell you plainly," Taft's treasurer George Sheldon protested, that your pledge has "tied my hands and at least one of my legs and I am well nigh helpless." The nominee caused further consternation when he refused a $50,000 check from William Cromwell, a friend who had donated despite the knowledge that his contribution would be on public record. Taft told Cromwell he could not accept such a large sum from anyone outside his own family. Though he realized the gift was prompted by "nothing but the purest friendship," he feared its size would be "misunderstood." Roosevelt disagreed. "I have always said you would be the greatest President," he chided Taft, "but really I think you are altogether oversensitive. If I were in your place I should accept that contribution of Cromwell's with real gratitude." Taft finally agreed to accept a $10,000 check, with the understanding that the amount could be increased if necessary.

Facing a host of difficulties even before the traditional Labor Day opening for the fall campaign, Taft confessed to Roosevelt that he felt somewhat chagrined about his chances. "Don't get one particle discouraged," Roosevelt assured him; "you have exactly the right attitude of mind in the matter. In 1904 I never permitted myself to regard the election as anything but doubtful." In truth, Taft had reason to worry. Williams Jennings Bryan had become a far more formidable candidate since his previous runs in 1896 and 1900. In those earlier campaigns, the Chicago journalist Walter Wellman noted, many had viewed Bryan as "a dangerous man—revolutionary, socialist, and by some, almost an anarchist." But with the rise of Theodore Roosevelt and the progressive wing of the Republican Party, many policies championed by the Democratic candidate had become law. "No longer an outcast," Bryan

pronounced himself a more legitimate heir to Roosevelt than Taft, promising that a Democratic majority would break the stranglehold of Republican
conservatives on Congress.

Taft's political strategists were initially reluctant to send their candidate on
a speaking tour, preferring to run a front-porch campaign from his brother's
home in Cincinnati. They feared that Taft "would be placed at a disadvantage
appearing on the stump against the gifted Nebraskan." Once again, Taft's
principles collided with their strategy. "If the candidate does not go out and
work himself," he told Roosevelt, "the subordinates in the ranks are not liable to tear their shirts, whereas the personal presence of the man at the head
will have an encouraging and stimulating effect." At Taft's direction, party
strategists designed a strenuous tour, focused mainly in the West and Midwest,
where Bryan was gaining substantial momentum.

Fearing that Taft would be too reticent on the stump, Roosevelt barraged
him with incessant advice. "Do not *answer* Bryan; attack him!" he counseled
in early September, adding, "Don't let *him* make the issues." A week later,
the president resumed. "Hit them hard, old man," he encouraged, offering
a slew of new suggestions: "Let the audience see you smile *always*, because I
feel that your nature shines out so transparently when you do smile—you big,
generous, high-minded fellow. Moreover let them realize the truth, which is
that for all your gentleness and kindliness and generous good nature, there
never existed a man who was a better fighter when the need arose." Taft
promised to confront Bryan directly, but he remained reluctant to launch an
uncharacteristic, dramatic offensive. "I cannot be more aggressive than my
nature makes me," he told a concerned supporter. "That is the advantage and
the disadvantage of having been on the Bench. I can't call names and I can't
use adjectives when I don't think the case calls for them, so you will have to
get along with that kind of a candidate."

"I am not very pleased with the way Taft's campaign is being handled,"
Roosevelt complained to his son-in-law, Nicholas Longworth, adding, "I do
wish that Taft would put more energy and fight into the matter." Constitutionally incapable of remaining on the sidelines, Roosevelt decided "to put a
little vim into the campaign" with a series of public letters. The first of these
missives challenged Bryan's claim that he, rather than Taft, was the president's
"natural successor." "The true friend of reform," Roosevelt clarified, "is the
man who steadily perseveres in righting wrongs, in warring against abuses,
but whose character and training are such that he never promises what he cannot perform . . . and that, while steadily advancing, he never permits himself
to be led into foolish excesses." William Howard Taft "combines all of these

qualities to a degree which no other man in our public life since the Civil War has surpassed," he ardently insisted. "For the last ten years," he added, "I have been thrown into the closest intimacy with him, and he and I have on every essential point stood in heartiest agreement, shoulder to shoulder."

Bryan's further assertion that Roosevelt's views aligned more closely with the Democratic platform than with the agenda of his own Republican Party prompted a fiery exchange between the two men. "You say that your platform declares in favor of the vigorous enforcement of the law against guilty trust magnates and officials," Roosevelt noted, "and that the platform upon which Mr. Taft stands makes no such declaration. It was not necessary. That platform approved the policies of this administration." He pointed out that under Grover Cleveland, the last Democratic president, not a single anti-trust case was instituted—nor was action taken to stop rebates. Deeds, he argued in a further exchange, were far more important than words.

Roosevelt's fiery declarations put Bryan on the defensive, and spurred the sluggish Republican campaign. Bryan "walked into a trap," Taft gratefully told Roosevelt, "and that gave you an opportunity, at his instance, to hit him, two or three blows between the eyes." Throughout the West, Taft added, Bryan's "claim to be the heir of your policies is now the subject of laughter and ridicule rather than of serious weight."

Ascribing "the revival in the Republican campaign" to his pugnacious friend, Taft overlooked his own winning impression made at every stop. The "Taft Special," which carried him to twenty-one states in forty-one days, consisted of four cars: a private car for the nominee and his guests, a dining car, a sleeping car for the newspapermen, and a baggage car. Addressing friendly crowds at each city and town along the whistle-stop tour, Taft "proved to be a good deal more of a speaker than most of those present had counted on hearing." While he was in no sense "a professional entertainer," one reporter remarked, his words displayed such openness and were uttered with such conviction that "he strengthened himself in the hearts of his hearers." Audiences invariably came away persuaded that Taft was "on the level," that he told "the truth about himself," and stated his thoughts without equivocation. "That man has a fine face," one spectator enthused. "I would trust him anywhere." As the crowds continued to grow, Taft became more confident in his oratory. "I have been in real touch with the people," he proudly observed. "They have come to see me and hear me in numbers far beyond my anticipation, and what seems of even more importance, they have responded to what I have had to say in a way that I could feel their sympathy."

"You are making such a success with your speeches," Nellie wrote from

New York where she was busy settling her children into their various schools. For weeks, she had been nettled by gossip that Roosevelt was disappointed by Taft's inability to generate campaign momentum. Now, these sanguine reports of the whistle-stop tour left her "treading on air." The president, she informed her husband, had requested a meeting with her: "I can't imagine what Teddy wants," she wrote, " but probably only to complain of some thing." Nellie was mistaken. In fact, the president was growing more confident about Taft's prospects in the general election. Recognizing that Taft's speaking tour had invigorated the campaign, he simply wanted to share his enthusiasm with her. Nellie "had a most delightful time," Will wrote afterward to Roosevelt. "You gave her courage and hope."

Expressing a similar optimism to Kermit in late October, Roosevelt wrote that the political outlook had "changed materially for the better." He was now certain, he told his son, that Taft would be elected. To everyone's relief, the speaking tour had succeeded "tremendously," an achievement for which Roosevelt did not hesitate to take credit—forgetting that Taft had done yeoman work in both his 1904 and 1906 campaigns. Archie Butt told of his amusement at the president's skewed recounting of how he transformed Taft from a soporific lecturer into a popular draw: "I told him he simply had to stop saying what he had said in this or that decision," for at that point people "promptly begin to nod. I told him that he must treat the political audience as one coming, not to see an etching, but a poster. He must, therefore, have streaks of blue, yellow, and red to catch the eye, and eliminate all fine lines and soft colours. I think Mr. Taft thought I was a barbarian and a mountebank at first, but I am pleased to say that he is at last catching the attention of the crowd."

Such indiscretions invariably filtered into Taft's camp, fueling resentment at the president's condescending and potentially damaging self-aggrandizement. Taft's supporters had long felt that Roosevelt "was keeping himself too much in the limelight," creating the impression that Taft was incapable "of standing on his own feet." Always gracious, Taft assured Roosevelt that he did not know who had spread rumors that his people were rankled by the president's active role. Personally, he had been "very touched" by Roosevelt's speechmaking advice and "delighted" by everything done to support him.

Nellie joined Taft in Buffalo on the last day of his speaking tour. In western New York, Pennsylvania, and Ohio, they were met by "monster" crowds brimming with enthusiasm. Reporters noted that Nellie "seemed to enjoy it immensely." They reached Cincinnati at 8 a.m. on November 3, spending the day at Charley's home before going to vote in the afternoon. In preparation for receiving the election returns, Charley had converted the veranda into a telegraph room with wires directly connected to the national Republican headquarters in New York, Western Union, the Associated Press, and the United Press.

The extended family and friends gathered in the large drawing room, surrounded by the exquisite art collection Charles and Annie had assembled during their sojourns in Europe. Newspapermen who had traveled with the candidate on the whistle-stop tour joined them. Gus Karger, the *Cincinnati Times* reporter who had served as Taft's publicity agent during the campaign, read out the returns. Early reports from Massachusetts, Connecticut, New York, and Maryland soon indicated a magnificent victory for William Howard Taft.

The excited candidate paced throughout the evening, "exhibiting the finest specimen of that smile which the campaign had made famous." At 8:45 p.m., he finally agreed to make a statement: "Just say that everything looks favorable," he directed modestly. Nellie was more forthcoming, exclaiming, "I was never so happy in my life." Though Taft's popular margin was only half the size of Roosevelt's 1904 victory, he carried twenty-nine of the forty-six states, beating Bryan by over a million and a quarter votes. Later that night, Taft delivered a short speech with his distinctive, self-effacing sincerity: "I pledge myself to use all the energy and ability in me to make the next Administration a worthy successor to that of Theodore Roosevelt," he said. "I could have no higher aim than that."

At the White House, Archie Butt reported, Roosevelt "was simply radiant over Taft's victory, and made no attempt to disguise it," interpreting the victory as a vindication of his own policies. When the conversation turned to Taft's struggle to lose weight through golf and horseback riding, the president offered pithy advice: "If I were Taft, I would not attempt to take much exercise. I would content myself with the record I was able to make in the next four years or the next eight and then be content to die."

Taft addressed his very first letter as president-elect to his friend and mentor Theodore Roosevelt. "My selection and election are chiefly your work," he told him. "You and my brother Charley made that possible which in all probability would not have occurred otherwise." In later years, Roosevelt would express resentment at being yoked with Taft's brother as a joint benefactor, heedless that Charles's decades of financial support had enabled Will to sustain a career in public service. At that moment, however, Roosevelt responded with unalloyed joy. "You have won a great personal victory as well as a great victory for the party," the president wrote, "and all those who love you, who admire and believe in you, and are proud of your great and fine qualities, must feel a thrill of exultation."

CHAPTER TWENTY-TWO

"A Great Stricken Animal"

First Lady Nellie Taft, posed in formal attire
at the White House, ca. 1909.

HENRY ADAMS, SCION OF TWO presidents and an acute student of
American political life for nearly seven decades, called William Howard Taft "the best equipped man for the Presidency who had been suggested
by either party during his lifetime." A prominent New Yorker argued that
Taft was "the greatest all around man" ever to reach the White House. As
Congressman James E. Watson noted, "he had served with great success in
every subordinate post he had occupied."

From his early days as solicitor general to his governor generalship of the
Philippines to his tenure as secretary of war, Taft had proved himself reliable,
hardworking, and loyal. On those rare occasions when he disagreed with a
superior, he kept his dissent private. Nor had he objected when credit for his

achievements was extended to others. "The most difficult instrument to play in the orchestra is second fiddle," a celebrated conductor once noted, yet for nearly two decades, Taft had performed with unfailing mastery.

Whether the skills of this exemplary subordinate were the requisite skills to lead a nation remained the only unanswered question. Ray Baker suggested that sometimes the second fiddler may be a more accomplished musician than the first, "but he could not fill the first fiddler's place. He has not the audience-sense; he does not know how to handle men; he has not the ability to beat disharmonies into harmonies." As leadership scholars observe: "Not everyone was meant to be No. 1."

Within hours of his election triumph, Taft was already anguished that his nature was ill-suited to his new role. He "spoke like a man," one insider noted, "whose job had got him down even before he tackled it." In one of his first statements, Taft predicted that his friends and acquaintances would soon "shake their heads and say 'poor Bill.' " Not long afterward, he responded to confident remarks on the prospects of his administration with "a trembling fear" that in four years' time, he would "be like the man who went into office with a majority and went out with unanimity."

Yet with each substantial step in his successful career, Taft had overcome similar waves of grave doubt and anxiety. As solicitor general, despite fearing in his first days that the demand for a one-sided argument would prove incompatible with his temperament, he had quickly developed into an effective advocate, winning a large majority of the government's cases. When initially approached to govern the Philippines, he had protested that he was not the right man for the job. He left that position with an international reputation as a successful administrator. "Sitting on the lid" as acting president during Roosevelt's two-month vacation, he had deftly defused a number of potentially explosive situations. And painfully aware of his deficiencies as a campaigner, he had nevertheless bested all rivals to win both the Republican nomination and the general election. Through all these challenges Taft had relied on the guidance of a superior; now, for the first time, he was truly on his own.

FACED WITH THE COMPLICATED TASK of shaping a cabinet, Taft sought escape. He traveled first to Hot Springs, Virginia, and then to Augusta, Georgia, where he stayed for six weeks in a comfortable cottage adjacent to the luxury Bon Air Hotel, widely celebrated for its "splendid 18 hole golf course and the handsomest clubhouse in the South." While Nellie thought the location too remote to accurately gauge the tenor of Washington, Taft insisted on "getting away for a complete rest." He defiantly proposed to spend his time sleeping and playing golf. Clearly, there was much preparatory work for the presidency, but Taft's dilatory nature took hold and he refused to consider a single appointment until he was "good and ready." In the interim, he would do his part "to make golf one of the popular outdoor exercises" in the country.

Each evening, groups of leading citizens vied to entertain the Tafts. A committee in Atlanta decorated the city with flags and bunting in preparation for the president-elect's appearance at an elaborate "possum and taters" banquet. Newspapers described a specially constructed cage that housed each arriving batch of twenty possums until a hundred were gathered to feed six hundred guests. Featuring vaudeville acts, songs, and the release of doves, the gala evening was ranked the most brilliant event ever held in Atlanta, marking "a social epoch" in the history of the new South. A cartoon of Taft as Billy Possum prompted a toymaker to patent a new stuffed animal. But expectations that Billy Possum would rival the Teddy bear in popularity were swiftly dashed when the stuffed creature, resembling "a gigantic rat," caused children to cry.

Taft's sojourn at the Bon Air Hotel provided a happy respite, enabling him to enjoy "the honor without the responsibilities of the office." For the first time in months, the entire family was together: Robert and Helen arrived from Yale and Bryn Mawr, and the families of Charles and Harry Taft stayed for several weeks, along with Taft's good friend John Hays Hammond. Splendid weather afforded long hours on the golf links, daylong fishing excursions, and automobile rambles around the countryside. "He is so genial, so companionable, so gentlemanly," a woman remarked, "that one is apt to forget that he is the President-elect."

By postponing cabinet decisions, however, Taft inadvertently fueled speculation and rumor. Conventional wisdom suggested that after repeated pledges to support Roosevelt's policies, the new president would retain most of his predecessor's cabinet. Taft had even conveyed a message to Roosevelt for his cabinet colleagues: "Tell the boys I have been working with that I want to continue all of them. They are all fine fellows, and they have been mighty good to me. I want all them to stay just as they are."

In the months that followed, Taft began to recognize the necessity of establishing an independent identity, particularly after the barrage of criticism that accompanied his "humiliating pilgrimage" to Oyster Bay to consult Roosevelt on his acceptance speech. Throughout the campaign, Taft had stressed the very different challenges that would confront his own prospective administration. Roosevelt, Taft repeatedly explained, had launched a successful crusade against the abuses of industry and "aroused the people to demand reform." Now, Taft said, the time had come to perfect the necessary regulatory machinery and to craft amendments that would ensure proper enforcement. To accomplish these ends, a different sensibility and "different personnel" might be required.

Notwithstanding, the first man invited into Taft's cabinet was Roosevelt's trusted secretary of state, Elihu Root. In the cabinet's premier post, Root would provide the anchor in Roosevelt's absence. Looking back on his achievement in the Philippines, the president-elect attributed much of his success to the detailed instructions, goals, and framework Root had furnished. "I merely followed the way opened up by Root," he insisted. Indeed, after his election, Taft went so far as to tell an audience that the administration was topsy-turvy: Root "ought to be Pres.-elect," he insisted, "and I ought to be a prospective member of *his* Cabinet. Because I know how to serve under him." Such sentiments cannot be simply construed as extravagant humility or an odd, self-disparaging humor. Rather, like his chronic procrastination, they connote tentativeness, a want of confidence arising from underlying insecurity. Root was sorely tempted to accept Taft's offer. "I would rather stay here than do anything else," he told a friend, but "between rheumatism and the climate and the incessant and wearisome pressure of social duties I am satisfied that it would mean a complete breakdown of Mrs. Root's health."

With Root out of the running, Taft turned next to another intimate of his predecessor, Henry Cabot Lodge. Though "touched and gratified," Lodge nonetheless felt that he could be of greater service to the country by remaining in the Senate. After conferring with Roosevelt, Taft finally offered the post to former attorney general Philander Knox, then a Pennsylvania senator. "Knox called on me last night," Roosevelt informed Taft several days later. "I had a long talk over his accepting the position of Secretary of State and I am confident that he will do so." Five days later, Knox sent a telegram confirming his acceptance. Taft told Roosevelt he was planning to invite Knox to Augusta, hoping to secure guidance on his remaining choices. There, Knox would be joined by Taft's campaign chair, Frank Hitchcock, slated to become postmaster general. "Ha ha!" Roosevelt jested. "*You* are making up your Cabinet. *I* in a lighthearted way have spent the morning testing the rifles for my African trip. Life has compensations!"

Taft's initial assurance that he would retain the entire cabinet proved particularly troublesome when he subsequently decided to replace Luke Wright as secretary of war. When Taft had resigned his own cabinet post the previous July after securing the Republican nomination, Roosevelt had wanted Wright,

Taft's successor as governor general in the Philippines, to replace him. Worried that Wright would decline a term of only nine months, Roosevelt had asked Taft if he could offer the "inducement" of a longer tenure should he win the election. Taft had confirmed that he "would be more than pleased to continue Wright," and Roosevelt could relay that message. Once Taft had the choice in his hands, however, he hesitated, concerned that Wright was not "decisive" enough and tended "to let questions settle themselves without mental action by him." Instead, he selected another southern Democrat, Jacob Dickinson. While rethinking a key appointment was surely Taft's prerogative, he exacerbated the awkward situation and irritated Roosevelt by failing to inform Wright until mid-February 1909, just weeks before the inauguration.

In the end, no appointment would have more far-reaching consequences for Taft's administration than his decision to replace Interior Secretary James Garfield with Richard Ballinger. Roosevelt had pushed to retain Garfield from the outset. "I didn't have to be hit with a club ten times a day to understand the workings of his mind," Taft later remarked. No two young men in the Roosevelt administration had been closer to the president than Garfield and Gifford Pinchot. Pinchot had driven Roosevelt's conservation fight; Garfield had served for seven years, first as civil service commissioner, then as head of the Bureau of Corporations, and finally as secretary of the interior, where he worked closely with Pinchot. A "peculiar intimacy" bonded the trio, Roosevelt reflected, "because all three of us have worked for the same causes, have dreamed the same dreams, have felt a substantial identity of purpose."

Garfield had every reason to believe that Taft would ask him to stay. As one of Taft's staunchest supporters during the fight for nomination and election, Garfield had delivered scores of speeches in Ohio and chaired the convention in Columbus that provided an early boost to Taft's candidacy. Furthermore, Garfield was connected with Taft personally as well as politically: he and his wife, Helen, socialized with Will and Nellie, dining at each other's houses and vacationing together. Their son, John, attended Horace Taft's school in Connecticut. The press assumed that Garfield would not only stay on in Taft's cabinet, but would likely become an important member of the new president's inner circle.

Yet almost immediately after his election, Taft began searching for someone to replace Garfield. Although Taft considered Garfield an accomplished bureau chief, he did not think him "big enough" for a cabinet position. He was convinced that Pinchot dominated Garfield, and did not relish the thought of Pinchot running the Interior Department in addition to the Forestry Bureau. While he recognized Pinchot's vital role in securing Roosevelt's conservation legacy, Taft believed that some of his executive policies and land withdrawals had not merely strained but broken existing law. Geographic representation also weighed heavily in Taft's rationale. Garfield hailed from Ohio, the state of the president-elect himself, while the West Coast clamored for someone to represent their interests.

Taft's choice, Richard Ballinger, had been a reform mayor in Seattle before joining the Roosevelt administration as head of the Land Office, where he was regarded as an ardent conservationist and an excellent administrator. By the time Ballinger returned to his Seattle law practice in 1908, Garfield was deeply impressed with his work. "He has done admirably," he noted, "& leaves with a reputation for ability, industry & fairness." When first approached to join Taft's cabinet, Ballinger regretfully declined, citing "limited personal means" and the promise to his wife that they would remain in Seattle. After further conversations, however, he was finally persuaded.

Had Taft taken Garfield into his confidence early on, perhaps explaining the necessity of geographical balance, he might have avoided future conflict, but instead he said nothing. Beyond his initial choice of Knox and Hitchcock, Taft remained silent regarding further appointments until he could assemble a complete cabinet. In late December, rumors circulated that Garfield was "out of the running," leaving the interior secretary in an embarrassing position. "I am utterly at sea," Garfield recorded in his journal on January 11, observing with frustration, "if he wishes me to stay he should ask me soon—if not he surely owes it to me, because of our relations during many years & close association recently, to frankly tell me so." When no announcement was forthcoming by late January, the press speculated that Garfield might be chosen after all and attributed the delay to the difficult process of constructing a balanced, cooperative cabinet, a particular challenge for "a genial, agreeable man, averse to making enemies or disappointing ambition." Yet the longer Taft withheld selections, the more anxious Garfield grew. "Rumors & more rumors but he says nothing," he reported, calling Taft's procrastination "an astounding condition of affairs & wholly without reasonable explanation."

Garfield was not the only former Roosevelt cabinet officer bewildered and exasperated by Taft's inaction. Gossip filled the vacuum; word spread that Taft had "completely changed his mind," deciding "to keep no one" associated with his predecessor so that his administration could stand on its own merits. While Roosevelt publicly defended Taft's right to choose his own men in his own way, he advised the president-elect to inform those he did not intend to reappoint immediately. "They will be making their plans, and less than two months remains, and I do not think they ought to be left in doubt," Roosevelt told Taft. "Of course I am perfectly willing to tell them if you will write me to do so."

"I think I ought to do it myself," Taft replied, yet he continued to wait more than two weeks before sending a half-dozen letters simultaneously. Each began with the same stilted phrase: "The President has thought that you were entitled to the notice of my cabinet plans insofar as to advise you that in the list of my cabinet I have not been able to include your name." The recipients, all formerly Taft's intimate colleagues, were understandably hurt by this impersonal and awkward manner of address. In the end, despite the fact that two additional members of Roosevelt's cabinet—George Meyer and James Wilson—joined Secretary of State Philander Knox in the new administration, the overriding impression was of "a clean sweep" of Roosevelt's team.

"T.R.'s Trusty Aides All to Walk Plank," announced the *Cleveland Press*. "Taft Seems Bent Upon Dumping His Old Associates in his Cabinet." Taft asserted that he had simply examined each position and carefully considered the best men to comprise the new administration. "I have my own record to make," he maintained, "and my own place to secure in the confidence of the country." Proponents of Roosevelt's agenda, however, began to question the president-elect's strategy: "If Taft is going to fire all his old associates in the Roosevelt administration, how is he going to make good his pledge to carry on the Roosevelt policies? Why, if he intends to finish the Roosevelt program, does he get rid of all the men trained in the Roosevelt school?" In addition, Roosevelt supporters voiced concern over the preponderance of corporate lawyers in the new cabinet.

Roosevelt himself could not help but feel "a little cast down" by Taft's dealings and decisions as he assembled his cabinet. Still, he continued to profess belief in his old friend. "They little realize that Taft is big enough to carve out his own administration on individual lines," he told Archie Butt. "I predict a brilliant administration for him. I felt he was the one man for the Presidency, and any failure in it would be as keenly felt by me as by himself or his family." While Taft's "system may be different," the president predicted, "the results will be the same."

After announcing his cabinet choices, Taft wrote a long letter to Roosevelt. "People have attempted to represent that you and I were in some way at odds during this last three months," he explained, "whereas you know and I know that there has not been the slightest difference between us." Indeed, the two men had spent many hours together during the transition. Through conversations and correspondence, Taft had kept Roosevelt informed on each cabinet decision and had shared an early draft of his inaugural address. "How could I but be delighted with your Inaugural?" Roosevelt responded. "It is simply fine in every way . . . and it marks just exactly what your administration will be."

Taft's final letter to Roosevelt before he assumed the presidency expressed "renewed appreciation" for his old friend's "breadth of soul and mind and magnanimity." Roosevelt replied with an equal warmth and affection. "Your letter," he wrote, "[was] so very nice—nice isn't anything like a strong enough word, but at the moment to use words as strong as I feel would look sloppy."

ROOSEVELT MADE NO SECRET OF his reluctance to leave office. "If I had conscientiously felt at liberty to run again, and try once more to hold this great office," he acknowledged, "I should greatly have liked to do so and to continue to keep my hands on the levers of this mighty machine." In his last annual message to Congress, he had firmly declared that he felt "none of the weariness of public life" which seven tumultuous years might well have produced. Although conservative leaders in the House and Senate had successfully blocked most of his proposals for two straight years, Roosevelt remained undaunted. In a sweeping "valedictory message" of more than 21,000 words, the outgoing president expounded "his whole social philosophy" and urged Congress to "carry into effect the new spirit of democracy," reinforcing federal power to address "present day" social and economic problems.

"He is as voluminous as ever," the New York Tribune remarked. If only "a fraction" of the laws that Roosevelt advocated were passed, another reporter observed, "they would commit the country to a course of new experiments and make over the face of the social creation." He wanted authority over telegraph and telephone companies, along with railroads, placed in the hands of the Interstate Commerce Commission. He called for greater regulation of interstate corporations, prohibition of child labor, enforcement of an eight-hour workday, strengthening of workmen's compensation, the establishment of a postal savings system, and an inheritance tax. "The danger to American democracy lies not in the least in the concentration of administrative power in responsible and accountable hands," he argued. "It lies in having the power insufficiently concentrated, so that no one can be held responsible to the people for its use." What might have been interpreted as "an infringement upon liberty" before the Industrial Revolution and the rise of massive corporations "may be [the] necessary safeguard of liberty today." Within this new industrial context, he criticized the courts for ruling unconstitutional various state laws designed to remedy social problems, "arrogat[ing] to themselves functions which properly belong to legislative bodies."

Finally, Roosevelt rounded on Congress. For two decades, the executive departments had deployed members of the Secret Service to ferret out land frauds, violations in anti-trust laws, and, on rare occasions, illegal actions perpetrated by senators or congressmen themselves. The previous year, however, Congress had passed an amendment preventing the Secret Service from pursuing such investigations. Incensed, Roosevelt charged that no one but members of the criminal class could benefit from such an amendment; clearly, "Congressmen did not themselves wish to be investigated."

Roosevelt's comments provoked a "storm of censure" from Republicans and Democrats alike. Senator Aldrich introduced a resolution challenging the president to produce evidence of congressional misbehavior, while Senators Bailey and Tillman huffily defended the "self-respect and integrity" of fellow legislators. Adamantly refusing to retract his charge, Roosevelt fired off a 6,000-word response that targeted specific members of the Congress, including Minnesota representative James Tawney and Senators Tillman and Bailey. "Pandemonium broke loose," the *Times* reported. In return, Congress took a rare measure not utilized since Jackson's presidency, reprimanding Roosevelt with an overwhelming 212–35 vote to reject his message "on the ground that it lacked due respect."

Despite such overwhelming resistance, Roosevelt held fast to his position. "Congress of course feels that I will never again have to be reckoned with and that it is safe to be ugly with me," he confided to Kermit, admitting, "I am not having an easy time." Even as he acknowledged that "it is a President's duty to get on with Congress if he possibly can, and that it is a reflection upon him if he and Congress come to a complete break," he nevertheless insisted that he must continue to "fight hard" on the issue of corruption—a touchstone of his presidency—or "be put in a contemptible position." Although this bitter struggle ended his days in Washington on a disagreeable note, he took pride that he had exercised his presidential powers "right up to the end."

⌐ ⌐

DURING THE FINAL WEEKS OF the Roosevelt administration, a mood of sadness enveloped the White House. "I have never seen so much feeling in evidence in all my life," Archie Butt observed as this vital stage in the lives of both the president and his colleagues drew to a close. As the chief military aide, the forty-three-year-old Captain Butt had developed an intimate relationship with both the president and first lady. His warmth, flair for conversation, and love of books had made him a welcome companion at Sagamore Hill and scores of White House lunches and dinners. A graduate of the University of the South in Tennessee, Archie had worked as a journalist for nearly a decade before volunteering for service during the Spanish-American War. Remaining in the military, he had served in the Quartermaster Department in the Philippines, Cuba, and Washington before Roosevelt brought him to the White House. Butt had begun his duties "believing thoroughly in the real greatness" of the president, and the weeks and months spent with the family had not altered his original judgment. He had traveled with the Roosevelts on overnight trips, joined them for horseback rides, tennis games, and scrambles through Rock Creek Park—always assuming "his duties with a boyish delight and a relish for all the gay doings of the White House."

Archie Butt had grown especially close to Edith Roosevelt. "She is perfectly poised and nothing seems to annoy her," the forty-three-year-old bachelor told his mother, lauding Edith's "ever-softening influence" on her volatile husband. Even while drawing a protective curtain around her family, Edith had unfailingly carried out social obligations with natural elegance. Formerly, Butt remarked, the "smart element" of society had been "wont to sneer" at the garish nature of public entertainments at the White House. Under Edith Roosevelt, however, functions were smaller, less frequent, and more formal; guests were required to present cards, and soon, smart society clamored for invitations. Edith's Friday evening musicales attracted the nation's finest performers, including Ignace Jan Paderewski, the concert pianist, and the young cellist Pablo Casals. "If social affairs have thus become less democratic, they have also become more dignified," remarked one reporter. "Were we living in the days of chivalry," Butt confessed with grandiose nostalgia, "I could easily believe myself in the role of knight for a mistress so gentle, so sweet, and so altogether lovely."

"The ball rolls faster as it nears the bottom," Captain Butt observed as the Roosevelt administration drew to a close in early February. The White House calendar was "filled every minute" with brilliant but melancholy events—the last Army and Navy reception, the last meeting with the diplomatic corps. Several of the ministers and ambassadors "actually wept as they said goodbye," Butt recounted. The wife of the Japanese ambassador "could not say a word, but burst out crying, and the Ambassador was not much better." Later that same afternoon, Edith Roosevelt finally "had a good cry" of her own, but when the president attempted to comfort her, he "broke down himself."

For his final public journey, Roosevelt chose to deliver a speech at Knob Creek Farm in Kentucky, birthplace of his hero Abraham Lincoln. He had ordered his train route withheld from the newspapers, fearing he would be met with diminished enthusiasm as his presidency neared its end. "For the first hour there were no yells," Archie Butt recorded, and Roosevelt looked forlorn as he gazed out at calm streets and empty platforms. Before long, however, the train schedule leaked. Suddenly, throngs materialized at every spot along the way: families and children stood at tiny intersections; in larger towns, thousands assembled to wave and cheer, wishing their president a final farewell. "He jumped from his seat as readily for a half-dozen people at a road crossing as he would for a crowd at a station," Archie Butt marveled. At one point, Roosevelt rushed to the platform to greet a single woman in a field, prompting recollection of an earlier trip when "he found himself waving frantically at a herd of cows." With deadpan mirth, Roosevelt remembered that he had "met with an indifferent, if not a cold, reception."

On March 1, Roosevelt hosted perhaps the most colorful official luncheon on record. "The papers have made a good deal of fun of my tennis cabinet," he playfully observed, "but they have never known how extensive or what a part it has played in my administrations. It will be gathered together to-day for the first time." Thirty-one members of this fabulously eclectic "tennis cabinet"—Roosevelt's hunting companions, sparring partners, tennis mates, and fellow rock climbers—would attend. In order that "various elements" of this informal cabinet might "get acquainted," the president told Archie Butt to seat them "irrespective of rank." Jules Jusserand, the French ambassador, and cabinet members James Garfield, Truman Newberry, and George Meyer should enjoy the company of "the wolf hunters and the 'two-gun' men." Needless to say, this convergence of disparate worlds made quite an impression: "Is there any other man," Mme Jusserand exclaimed, who "could have had on one side of him the Ambassador of a great country and on the other a 'desperado' from Oklahoma?" Throughout the lunch, Roosevelt spoke of his relationship with each of the men in turn. According to Archie Butt, "there was not a dry eye around all that table."

The Roosevelts chose to spend March 3, 1909, their last night in the White House, with the Tafts. Arriving in the late afternoon, Will and Nellie were escorted to a bedroom suite on the second floor, later designated the Lincoln Bedroom. "It was a curious occasion," Alice Roosevelt Longworth recalled. "There were the Tafts, about to take over, obviously being tactful, soft pedaling their natural elation." For everyone else, "like an obscuring fog, was the inevitable melancholy of saying good-by, of closing the door on great times; the interest, the personal associations, the power—all over, gone." Even Archie Butt, who would remain at his post with the new president, "was frankly emotional," and Elihu Root was in such "low spirits" that tears brimmed from his eyes.

"The dinner would have been hopeless," Archie Butt remarked, "had it not been for the President," who lightened the mood with one entertaining story after another. Regardless of Roosevelt's efforts, everyone seemed relieved when the meal ended. In customary fashion, couples separated, the men going to the president's upstairs study while the women congregated in the library. Sometime after 10 p.m., Taft rose to keep his promised appearance at a Yale smoker in his honor at the Willard Hotel. His departure brought the evening to an end, leaving only Theodore, Edith, Nellie, and Captain Butt. "Mrs. Roosevelt finally arose," Butt wrote, "and said she would go to her room and advised Mrs. Taft to do the same. She took her hand kindly and expressed the earnest hope that her first night in the White House would be one of sweet sleep."

Taft remained at the smoker until midnight, his late return to the White House provoking a widely read spoof in the New York *Sun* the next day. A fictional dispatch portrayed a weary Taft trudging upstairs, whereupon a servant announced that the president awaited him. And there before him stood Roosevelt, broadsword in hand. "Thought you'd like a short bout before turning in," Roosevelt offered. "Here, get this mask and these pads on. Here are the gauntlets." Taft barely had time to don his equipment before Roosevelt struck three decisive blows. "Now we'll have a little wrestling," he suggested, and "as if by magic, the mattress was spread." Almost instantly, Taft was on his back. Exulting in triumph, Roosevelt asked the servants to set up the rings and parallel bars. For thirty minutes, they took turns until Roosevelt mercifully declared himself the clear victor. Finally, at 3 a.m., the *Sun* fancied, "the two athletes went to bed!"

In fact, by the time Taft returned to the White House, the Roosevelts had long since retired. Only Nellie, too excited to sleep, had waited up. For weeks, she had been preoccupied with the inaugural festivities and everything had been meticulously arranged—everything except the weather. A soggy wet snow had been falling all day. The storm was supposed to end by morning but the wind gusting over the water "shunted it back angrier than before" and the nation's capital found itself "bound hand and foot" by the worst blizzard since 1888. Gale winds howled, tree limbs cracked under the weight of the heavy snow, and streets were covered with a slick slush. "It was really very serious," Nellie recalled. "Railroad and telegraphic communications were paralyzed all along the Atlantic Coast."

On March 4, Inaugural Day, the president and president-elect met for an early breakfast. "The storm will soon be over," Roosevelt sardonically predicted. "As soon as I'm out where I can do no further harm to the Constitution it will cease." Taft suggested a different, if equally portentous interpretation. "You're wrong," he told his old friend. "It is my storm. I always said it would be a cold day when I got to be President."

The Street Department was already hard at work clearing snow from Pennsylvania Avenue, but there was no time to remove the "yellowish, slimy, shoe-penetrating mush" from the sidewalks. In front of every structure with windows on the street—"candy stores, pawnbrokers' shops, undertaking parlors, Chinese restaurants, machine shops"—carpenters had been busy all week long building seats which the owners planned to sell at a premium. By midmorning, melancholy enveloped the proprietors of the small shops along the parade route. With wet snow still blanketing the city, prices began to plummet. Seats expected to garner five dollars sold for one; sandwiches priced at a dime could be had for three cents. Despite the severe conditions, people "stood three deep on both sides of Pennsylvania Avenue," prepared to cheer and wave as the carriage bearing the president and president-elect moved slowly toward the Capitol. Unfortunately, hardly a glimpse of the two could be seen through the windows, for a driving snow had forced the coachmen to close the top of the carriage.

At the Capitol, more than 10,000 hearty souls waited to take their seats in the open stands to witness the inaugural ceremony. Inside, the Inaugural Committee debated whether to move the ceremony to the Senate chamber for the first time since President Jackson's second inaugural. Reluctant to disappoint the eager crowd, Taft fought to keep the ceremony on the Capitol Plaza. "If so many spectators could endure the cold merely to see the sight," he argued, "he certainly could endure it." The president-elect relented only when advised that the elderly chief justice and several members of Congress and the diplomatic corps might be imperiled by the exposure. The disheartening news was blared to the expectant crowd through megaphones: "All exercises will be conducted in the Senate chamber, and no one will be admitted there unless he has a ticket." No longer an open, public ceremony, the inaugural was attended by members of Congress, high government officials, Supreme Court justices, and ambassadors.

Cheers erupted when Roosevelt and Taft entered, walking "arm in arm" down the aisle. "Hale and hearty as Mr. Roosevelt looked," the *Sun* reported, "he was dwarfed by Mr. Taft's generous proportions." Appropriately, William Howard Taft took the oath of office on the same Bible used for decades to swear in Supreme Court justices. Then, speaking in "a slow, distinct voice, which carried to the furthest reaches of the chamber," he delivered his inaugural address. "For the first time in a century," correspondents observed, the assembled guests could actually hear the president's words.

While he felt the "heavy weight of responsibility" to preserve and enforce regulatory reforms initiated by "his distinguished predecessor," Taft simultaneously reassured those businesses companies "pursuing proper and progressive business methods." He pledged to secure amendments to both the anti-trust and interstate commerce laws that would make a distinction between "legitimate" combinations "and those formed with the intent of creating monopolies and artificially controlling prices." Pressing Roosevelt's agenda, he urged Congress to pass new conservation laws, consider a graduated inheritance tax, establish a postal savings bank system, and provide added protections to members of the working class. "The scope of a modern government," he maintained, "has been widened far beyond the principles laid down by the old 'laissez faire' school of political writers, and this widening has met popular approval." Finally, stepping into uncharted territory for his party, Taft called for a downward revision of the tariff and announced that he was summoning Congress into special session on March 15 for this purpose.

When Taft finished, Roosevelt jumped up and climbed the steps to the raised platform. "The new president turned to meet him," reporters observed, "with a smile that irradiated his face; the departing president grinned all over." Then, "with hands on each other's shoulders," they talked for several minutes. "God bless you, old man," Roosevelt exclaimed, calling his address "a great state document." Witnesses of the emotional scene "applauded like mad."

Rather than ride together back to the White House, as custom dictated, the two men parted. Months earlier, Roosevelt had decided to go straight from the inaugural ceremony to Union Station. There, he bid adieu to thousands of well-wishers with a short, heartfelt speech. A band played "Auld Lang Syne" and, amid "deafening" cheers, Roosevelt and Edith departed for Oyster Bay.

Since Roosevelt had abandoned tradition, Nellie followed suit, deciding to do what "no President's wife had ever done"—accompany her husband from the Capitol to the White House. "Some of the Inaugural Committee expressed their disapproval," she recalled, "but I had my way and in spite of protests took my place at my husband's side." Although a bitter wind still scoured the streets, the snow had stopped and the new president insisted the carriage top remain open. Drawn by four horses, the carriage elicited "a continuous cheer" from the thousands of visitors unable to witness either the oath of office or Taft's address. "Three cheers for the first lady," a voice shouted along their route. Seeing his wife's radiant smile, Taft took up the cheer himself and soon the entire crowd was hailing the first lady. "That drive was the proudest and happiest event of Inauguration Day," Nellie recalled. "My responsibilities had not yet begun to worry me, and I was able to enjoy, almost to the full, the realization that my husband was actually President of the United States."

NEWSPAPERS PREDICTED THE GENIAL NEW president would usher in an "era of good feelings." Taft "has no enemies of his own making; he is not taking over any of the enemies of his predecessor," observed Walter Wellman. The change of administration signaled "peace and reassurance" rather than the atmosphere of "vituperation and denunciation" that had marked the final months of Roosevelt's tenure. While progressives trusted Taft to continue his mentor's work, conservatives took comfort that "judicial poise had succeeded erratic temperament," that decisions would now be made with deliberation, not drama. "Never did any man," the *Sun* editorialized, arrive at the White House "with such universal good will."

Already questioning his own competence for the nation's highest office, Taft found such grand expectations unnerving. Asked a week after his inauguration how he liked being president, he confessed that he remained disoriented. "I hardly know yet. When I hear someone say Mr. President, I look around expecting to see Roosevelt, and when I read in the headlines of the morning papers that the President and Senator Aldrich and Speaker Cannon have had a conference, my first thought is, 'I wonder what they talked about.' So you can see that I have not gone very far yet."

Roosevelt's departure for Africa on March 23 signaled opportunity as well as anxiety for Taft. For years, Archie Butt observed, Taft had "been living on the steam of Theodore Roosevelt," propelled by the outsized personality and ambition of his friend and chief. "He will have to find his own fuel now," Butt conjectured, "and, like a child, will have to learn to walk alone. There is not the slightest doubt in my mind that he will learn to walk alone and will walk possibly all the better but it is going to be a readjustment just the same."

Initially, Captain Butt had hesitated to accept Taft's offer to remain in the White House, fearing he would not be able to serve the new president with the same devotion he continued to feel toward his predecessor. "The influence of Mr. Roosevelt over those around him is masterful and his friends become fanatical, e.g. to wit—I," he told his sister Clara. He had great admiration and liking for Taft, however, and considered Nellie "an intellectual woman and a woman of wonderful executive ability." He had been in the Philippines when Taft was governor general and had seen how the Filipino people had responded to the warmth and openness of the big man's personality. While

Butt acknowledged at the start that he missed Roosevelt's "marvelous wit," he found his new chief a most enjoyable companion. "He is essentially a gregarious animal," Butt reflected. "He likes to have someone in the car with him when he is reading or studying, and if he is at work, he works better if he has someone in the room with him."

Despite Taft's initial reservations, his first two months in office augured well for the new administration. Early on, he decided that his White House would be open to all: he would not, like Roosevelt, compile a "list of undesirables"; there would be no "abrupt and stormy attacks" on fellow politicians. Reflecting on the animosity between the president and Congress that had consumed the country since the previous December, Taft resolved to end such recrimination. "I hope that I shall never be called upon ever to say anything in disparagement of Senators and members of the House. I have no desire to belittle them."

As governor general of the Philippines, Taft had welcomed every political group at Malacañan Palace, making it "a rule never to pay any attention to personal squabbles and differences." He hoped to institute the same policy as president. Aware that access to the White House was an enormous political asset, Taft announced a series of a half-dozen formal dinner parties designed to unify "all the warring factions" in the House and Senate. "I am rather proud of these lists," he told Archie Butt. "I do not believe there were given six dinners at the White House where more thought has been expended than on these six." He was careful to include Senator Joseph Bailey, despite the fact that just a month earlier the Texas Democrat had pronounced Taft wholly unsuited for the presidency. And Bailey appeared to appreciate the gesture. "I have come to pay my tribute and respects to a most agreeable personality," Bailey declared at the event. Taft also lifted Roosevelt's ban on Senator Tillman of South Carolina and invited dozens of rank-and-file congressmen who had not previously attended a White House dinner. Where Roosevelt had dispensed White House invitations "to pay for favors already performed and loyalty which had been proven," Taft hoped his magnanimity would induce future cooperation.

The volatile guest list for the first of these affairs, which included Old Guard Republicans and their progressive antagonists, northern Democrats and southern Populists, created "the liveliest interest" in the capital. Fortunately, one reporter noted, ladies had been invited to keep these "belligerent Congressmen apart." Even with their mollifying influence, some suggested, the situation might "require all of President Taft's diplomacy to keep things going smoothly." In the end, good food, good wine, and the music of the Marine

Band made the first dinner a notable success, setting an agreeable precedent for the five events planned for the future. "It is undoubtedly Mr. Taft's purpose to conciliate," observed a northwestern paper. "He doesn't like discord. He thinks it will be possible to get all the good men of the country together on a common platform—the Roosevelt men and the anti-Roosevelt men."

During the weeks that followed, reporters kept a tally of "the undesirables" once again "finding their way" to the White House. Democratic senator Augustus Bacon of Georgia was "pleased as a boy" with his first invitation in seven years. Senators Hale, Aldrich, Payne, "and a lot of other ungodly standpatters" were again welcomed in the president's home, as were the most fervent Roosevelt men. Rather than wielding the "big stick through the press" to prod legislative action, Taft hoped that "personal appeal," reasoned arguments, and a spirit of hospitality would prevail.

Reporters too delighted in the "startling contrast" evident in Taft's method of handling the hundreds of audience-seekers from that of his predecessor. Senators, congressmen, and all manner of officials appeared during the morning hours between ten and twelve. To expedite matters, Roosevelt had kept his door open, entertaining a dozen or more callers simultaneously with his snappy banter, sending them "on their way out almost before they realized they were in." One visitor described his experience as being "caught in a strong draught." Taft possessed none of Roosevelt's "terminal facilities." He invited callers individually into his office, closed the door, and reportedly made everyone feel "so much at home" that they were inclined to linger all morning. At the pace he conducted business, Archie Butt worried, Taft would "be about three years behind" on the final day of his term.

Taft extended the window for callers an additional hour and a half, interrupting the flow of visitors only to take his lunch. Unlike Roosevelt, who famously invited people from all walks of life to his table, Taft generally ate alone. Forever struggling to lose weight, he limited his midday meal to an apple or a glass of water. One visitor, having reportedly waited three hours to see him, was finally invited into the president's office with an unceremonious greeting: "I am glad you have come in," Taft told him, "but you will have to wait until I have had my luncheon." When the weary caller asked how long it would be, Taft's only reply was to pick up a pitcher of water and pour himself a glass. When he finished drinking, he returned to his desk: "Now I am through, what do you want to tell me?"

Meetings with governmental officials and lawmakers often stretched until five o'clock, after which Taft, like Roosevelt, took time to exercise. "There the resemblance ended," one White House correspondent remarked. Roosevelt

took strenuous hikes or played in vigorous tennis matches; Taft much preferred a leisurely round of golf. As a horseman, Roosevelt "jumped hurdles,
forded creeks, and sought out unused bridle paths," another reporter noted,
while the new president trotted "along the river front or around the ellipse."
Before long, even these placid forays were replaced by late afternoon spins in
one of the three new White House automobiles. Roosevelt had displayed no
interest in what critics called "devil wagons," but "Taft fell in love with them
on the first whirl." In short order, he converted the stable, which had held
Roosevelt's "jumpers, pacers, and calipers," into an oversized garage for his
Model M steam touring convertible (capable of seating seven passengers); a
Pierce Arrow Limousine; and a Baker Queen Victoria electric, which Nellie
learned to drive.

Diverted by their superficial differences in style, the journalists initially
failed to recognize a far more consequential contrast between the two men—
their differing attitudes toward the press. More than any previous president,
Theodore Roosevelt had treated journalists as intimates; covering the White
House had been "a reporter's paradise" for seven years. "No president ever
lived on better terms with the newspapermen than did Roosevelt," reporter
Gus Karger proclaimed. He inquired after their families, shared confidential
anecdotes, and discussed their latest projects. Throughout his day, whether
he was being shaved, signing documents, or traveling from place to place, he
gave them unheard of access to his comings and goings. Most important, as
one historian wrote, "he made the White House hum with activity, and in
the process, gave the correspondents who covered him the best ongoing story
in generations." Now, that colorful story had come to an end. "There will be
some one at the White House whom you will like more than me," Roosevelt
had predicted during his final meeting with the press corps, "but not one who
will interest you more."

As secretary of war, Taft had enjoyed an easy rapport with members of
the press, who frequented his office to secure gossip, information, and anecdotes. "It was a favorite occupation for the correspondents," Oscar King Davis
recalled, "to 'go Tafting' "—to meet with the secretary in the late afternoon
for "a half-hour or so of very pleasant conversation which often furnished
a good deal of news." Always "a good scout," Taft had spoken frankly, and
depended on reporter friends to protect his occasional indiscretions. In his
first weeks as president, however, Taft discovered that "casual remarks" made
headlines, and quickly recognized "the necessity of care" in everything he
disclosed. Rather than hold informal daily discussions with members of the
press, he would see individual journalists by appointment only. Nonetheless,

the new president promised to meet with the entire group of correspondents on a weekly basis. Before he discontinued these press conferences, the White House reporters developed a genuine affection for "the big, good-humored man who had taken the place of the strident, dynamic Roosevelt."

Taft was beginning to create "his own atmosphere," Archie Butt remarked in late April. "People are forgetting that he is the residuary legatee, and his smile, good nature, and evenness of temper are winning hearts to him." The press and the public seemed to have reached a similar verdict about the new occupant of the White House. "Roosevelt made good with the people; and Taft promises to do likewise," one reporter noted. "Take it all and all," another concluded, "Washington is mighty happy in these opening days of the Taft administration."

If Taft professed to be "a fish out of water" in his new office, Nellie was finally entirely in her element. The new president frequently touted his wife's strengths, maintaining that without her guidance, he would never have sought and never gained the presidency. "I am no politician," he told a gathering in Georgia shortly after his election. "There," he proudly indicated Nellie, "is the politician of the family. If she had only let me alone, I guess I should now be dozing on the Circuit Court bench." Her acumen, he insisted proudly, had facilitated every critical step of his career. Indeed, he held that without her "tact and diplomacy," he would never have succeeded in the Philippines. Now he had faith that Nellie would "share the responsibilities" of his new office and once again prove instrumental in surmounting the "formidable" challenges he would face.

Journalists latched onto Taft's narrative, emphasizing Nellie's decisive role in her husband's political ascendancy. Their comradeship, the *Ladies' Home Journal* observed, was "like that of two men who are intimate chums." A portrait emerged of an ambitious wife who championed her viewpoints "with almost masculine vigor," while Taft assumed "his most judicial attitude." Article after article highlighted Nellie's role in her husband's choice to leave the Cincinnati Superior Court to become solicitor general, and then to relinquish his federal judgeship and become governor general of the Philippines. "Yes," Nellie acknowledged, "it is true that I urged Mr. Taft to give up his position on the bench and return to politics. I felt that while he honored and loved his legal position more than all else in his career, he might spend the younger years of his life in a wider field." Again, reporters observed, Nellie's "judgment prevailed" when Taft turned down Roosevelt's third offer for the Supreme Court to test the waters for the presidency. A week after his victory, Nellie was asked if she studied politics. "Indeed, I do," she replied in her usual forthright manner. "I have studied the situation gravely and I think I understand it well."

"Few women have gone into the White House so well equipped to meet the exactions" of the first lady's position, remarked the *New York Times*. As the governor general's wife, she had already served in a similar capacity; she acutely understood the importance of getting out among the people, appreciated the ceremonial aspects of her role, and was well versed in the rules of etiquette required for her position. Her knowledge of Spanish, French, and German enabled her to speak freely with the diplomats and natives of numerous countries. "You make me feel truly at home when you converse with me in French," Ambassador Jusserand told her. Nellie's extensive travels had provided her with myriad stories and anecdotes to entertain such dignitaries. The new first lady was "never at a loss for conversation," a reporter for the *New York Tribune* wrote. "Never within the recollection of Washingtonians of today," claimed another correspondent, had a first lady shown herself so conversant "on any subject of contemporaneous interest." Asked how she found time "to keep up so thoroughly" with world events, Nellie rejoined with droll simplicity: "By reading the daily papers."

His first interview with Nellie Taft left the *Ladies' Home Journal* reporter George Griswold Hill "impressed with her dignity." He remarked upon her unusual acuity and shrewd insight into people and situations. "She surveys the man or woman presented to her with a look so calm and deliberate," Hill observed, "that strangers sometimes are wont to describe her as cold." Beneath her "cloak of composure," however, Hill discerned a charming and sensitive woman. A *New York Times* reporter was similarly taken with the clever new first lady: "Her smile has the charm of intelligence," he reported, "that quick flash of recognition, distinct from the frozen, automatic smile peculiar to many women in official life."

As the president's wife, Nellie announced early on, she considered herself "a public personage" and would "cheerfully meet any demands the position [made] upon her." Her statement revealed a far different temperament from that of her predecessor. Even after seven years as first lady, Edith Roosevelt had remained "unwilling to look upon herself otherwise than as a private individual." Believing that "a woman's name should appear in print but twice—when she is married and when she is buried," Edith had refrained from publicly voicing political opinions and routinely declined interview requests. In a rare portrait piece, entitled "Mrs. Roosevelt. The Woman in the

Background," Mabel Daggett portrayed Edith Roosevelt as an intensely private and traditional wife and mother. She "presents none of the restless new woman attributes," Daggett wrote. "She throbs for no reforms. She champions no causes." Surrounded by her boisterous family, Edith was described as "a happy woman," adored by her husband. Edith Roosevelt, Daggett concluded, would intentionally "step out into history as one of the least known" first ladies.

Before she took up residence in the White House, Nellie Taft made it clear she would play a far different role. In December 1908, she agreed to become honorary chair of the Women's Welfare Department of the National Civic Federation (NCF)—a progressive organization founded to better the working lives of wage earners employed in government and industry positions. No previous first lady had taken "a commanding lead" in promoting controversial programs to improve public welfare. At the annual meeting, Nellie delivered a well-received speech calling for investigations into the working conditions of female employees in federal and state departments, post offices, public hospitals, and police stations. "She plainly showed," one attendee noted, "that she has brains and used them without in any sense being aggressive or pedantic." During the NCF banquet at the Waldorf-Astoria in New York the following evening, she was observed "in animated conversation" with the union leader Samuel Gompers. Not all Washingtonians approved of Nellie's unconventional activism. A traditionalist, Archie Butt predicted that Nellie would "make a fine mistress of the White House," but only if she would refrain from speaking publicly about "the betterment of the working girl class," and focus instead upon "the simple duties of First Lady."

Public policy affecting working women was not the only issue on which Nellie expressed a strong opinion. Asked about granting suffrage to women, she answered with her usual directness: "The woman's voice is the voice of wisdom and I can see nothing unwomanly in her casting the ballot." In fact, Nellie fervently rejected traditional restrictions on a woman's role in society, insisting that intellectual development in no way diminished her capabilities in the home. Nothing in a college education, she maintained, "makes a girl either unfit for domestic obligations or masculine in her tastes." Some women were "not called on to preside over a home," and for those who did marry and have children, education would "make them great in intellect and soul." Her daughter Helen, she noted with pride, had chosen to take "a full college course" at the National Cathedral School, then secured a prestigious scholarship to Bryn Mawr College. While Nellie appreciated "the distinct advantages for a young girl in the social life of the White House," she fully supported her daughter's decision to pursue her education elsewhere. With her progressive views, one reporter noted, Mrs. Taft had "endeared herself to that class of women who are sometimes slightingly referred to as 'strongminded.' "

Despite Captain Butt's concern, Nellie's political activities did nothing to interfere with her duties as mistress of the White House. In fact, the new first lady had ambitious plans to make the national capital the hub of American cultural life. The White House, she argued, belonged to the people, and she would conduct social affairs there "on a plane of the highest and broadest democracy." She hoped that Washington would someday supplant New York as the "real social center" of the country. In the capital, she envisioned "a national society" comprised "of the best people in the land, a society not founded on the dollar, but on culture, art, statesmanship." No other city, she maintained, "is more beautifully laid out or has more natural charm during the months given over to official and social life." New Yorkers reacted with scorn, calling the first lady's idea "as absurd as it is impracticable," insisting that New York "has been, and always will be the mecca of culture and wealth in our land."

Undeterred, Nellie embarked on her first major project. With the coming of spring, inspired by the Luneta, the popular municipal park in the heart of Manila where all classes of the citizenry could gather for outdoor concerts, she worked with a landscape architect to transform the south side of Washington's Tidal Basin into "one of the most famous esplanades of the world." She enlisted her husband to persuade Congress that $25,000 should be appropriated to beautify the area—to plant trees, improve both the bridle path and the roadway, build an octagonal wooden bandstand, and install hundreds of comfortable benches. During her travels in the Far East, Nellie had fallen under the enchantment of Japanese cherry trees. Discovering that "both the soil and climate" of Washington were suitable for their growth, she purchased 100 trees from nurseries around the country; when her plans became public, the mayor of Tokyo sent an additional 2,000 young cherry trees to Washington.

On April 17, the president and first lady officially dedicated "Potomac Park" with the first in a series of White House–sponsored public concerts to be held every Wednesday and Saturday afternoon from five to seven. Hours before the first notes of the inaugural concert, "vehicles of every description" began to arrive—"horse drawn victorias and landaus, electric and gasoline motor cars, taxicabs and nearly every type of carriage." Men and women on horseback lined the winding bridle path and thousands of pedestrians settled on the lawn near the river. All told, 10,000 people representing "every walk of life" had gathered in the new park.

Vigorous cheers greeted the president and first lady as they arrived in an open electric landaulet. They smiled and bowed "right and left," stopping frequently to speak with friends and acquaintances. The entire cabinet was present, along with dozens of ambassadors. "Everybody saw everybody that he or she knew," Nellie marveled, "and there was the same exchange of friendly greetings that had always made the Luneta such a pleasant meeting place." Though Nellie had taken pains to ensure that her municipal park would "acquire the special character" she so desired, she could hardly have envisioned the future of Potomac Park and the cherry blossom festival that one day would draw millions of visitors to the nation's capital.

In May, Nellie also introduced a series of Friday afternoon garden parties. After developing a "very strong liking" for open-air festivities in the Far East, she decided the south grounds of the White House would provide a perfect setting for similar events. The Marine Band was stationed on the lawn, a large refreshment tent was situated under the trees at the rear of the mansion, and iron benches were scattered around the grounds. The invitations, issued each week to more than five hundred people, asked men to attend in white "short coats, flannel trousers and straw hats," while women wore white dresses and carried "bright colored parasols." The president and first lady stood on a knoll to receive their guests, who were free to "roam at will in the private grounds of the President and sip tea and punch and eat sandwiches and ices under the historic trees." These picturesque gatherings, one reporter observed, "are as informal as any entertainment given in the name of the President and his wife can be." Nevertheless, they quickly became "the most popular form of official hospitality yet seen in Washington."

Taft expressed his immense pride in Nellie's accomplishments to Archie Butt. "It was a difficult thing for her to give any individuality to her entertainments following so close on the Roosevelt administration, which was so particularly brilliant," he acknowledged, but she had clearly managed to do so. Butt was equally impressed that she had managed to distinguish herself. "She possesses a nature which I think is going to unfold and enlarge itself as it adjusts itself to new and broader surroundings," he told his sister. "She really looks ten years younger since she entered the White House, and I think she has become more gracious and kinder toward all the world."

It was evident to all that the vivacious and self-possessed first lady would continue to be instrumental in all the new president's endeavors. "The complete social success of the Taft administration has been fully established," the *Kansas City Star* observed on May 16. "In the ten weeks of her husband's Administration," the *New York Times* agreed, "Mrs. Taft has done more for society than any former mistress of the White House has undertaken in as many months."

ON MAY 17, NELLIE AND William Taft hosted a small party on the presidential yacht, the *Sylph*. The guests included Attorney General George Wickersham and his wife; her sister Lady Hadfield and husband; the steel baron Sir Robert Hadfield; and Archie Butt. The *Sylph* set sail on the Potomac, heading toward Mt. Vernon, where a special tour of President Washington's home had been arranged. Nellie was talking with the attorney general when she suddenly grew faint and collapsed.

Crushed ice was pressed to her forehead and wrists, and the first lady "seemed to revive," Butt recalled, but she remained only "half conscious" and "did not speak." Taft raced to her side as the ship turned back and a message was dispatched directing Dr. Matthew Delaney to meet them at the White House. "The trip back seemed interminable," Butt recalled, because "no one could do anything." When they reached the White House, Taft and Butt each took one of Nellie's arms and "practically carried" her inside.

Nellie's right side was paralyzed, the right side of her face had fallen, and she remained unable to speak. Taft was devastated—he "looked like a great stricken animal," Archie Butt sorrowfully remarked. Never had he "seen greater suffering or pain shown on a man's face." The symptoms, Taft anxiously told his son Robert, indicated "a lesion in the brain." After examining Nellie, however, Dr. Delaney concluded that "because she could hear all right," she had suffered in all likelihood "a mere attack of nervous hysteria rather than a bursting of a blood vessel in the brain." With extended rest, he reassured the president, her symptoms might disappear.

The last of the six congressional dinners was scheduled for that very evening. Recognizing his obligation "in the face of sorrow," Taft circulated among his guests with a forced smile and friendly demeanor. "But what a dinner!" Butt observed. "Every mouthful seemed to choke him, yet he never wavered." He was "fighting her battle, for it would humiliate her terribly to feel that people were commiserating with her." While the men smoked cigars, Taft hastened to his wife's room and consulted with her doctor. Told that she had fallen peacefully asleep, he rejoined the party. The night was balmy, allowing the guests, as Nellie had planned, to move to the East Terrace. There, electric lights, covered with red paper and colorful flowers, created an atmosphere of enchantment. "The beauty of the scene cut the President like a knife," Butt sadly noted, who likewise recognized the hand of the stricken first lady in every carefully orchestrated detail.

After sixteen hours of sleep, Nellie finally awakened. "Her old will and determination asserted itself," Archie remarked, as she immediately tried to get out of bed and walk. By late afternoon, Taft reported to Robert, she had regained partial "control of her right arm and her right leg," though she remained mute. The doctor expressed his continued confidence that the paralysis of her vocal chords was temporary. The White House released a statement insisting there was "no cause for alarm." The first lady was simply enduring a "nervous attack"—the label then given to a range of amorphous afflictions brought on by exhaustion. Newspaper reports attributed the collapse to Nellie's "ceaseless and strenuous efforts to aid her husband." Her exertions, the *St. Louis Post Dispatch* suggested, were "more than one person could stand up under and she went to pieces."

Of the true severity of Nellie's illness and disability, the public remained uninformed. In his initial diagnosis, Dr. Delaney had failed to discern the serious stroke she had suffered. A blood vessel had burst in the area of her brain that controlled language and speech, producing what Taft later described as aphasia—the loss or partial loss of the ability to speak. While she remained alert and clearly comprehended verbal communication, she was unable to express her thoughts and ideas in words. Two weeks after her stroke, Nellie could venture hesitantly out of her bedroom and walk around the second floor. "She only comes into the corridor," observed Butt, "when she can do so without running any danger of seeing anyone." At the end of May, she remained unable to project her own thoughts into language, though she could "repeat almost anything" said to her. Nevertheless, the doctor remained optimistic, predicting it "merely a question of time and rest and practice until she regains her speech entirely."

Taft mobilized the entire family to help with Nellie's rehabilitation. Helen came home from Bryn Mawr to be with her mother, and Nellie's sisters—Eleanor More, Lucy Laughlin, and Jennie Anderson—took turns living in the White House. The stroke had not destroyed Nellie's ability to read or listen, so Helen spent hours reading aloud to her mother, then encouraging her to repeat the same passages. Very gradually, Nellie began to speak on her own, though her words were often jumbled and indistinct. At times, she tended "to say the opposite of what she meant" or speak with undue emphasis. "She gets pretty depressed about talking," Helen reported to her brother Robert in mid-June. "She tries very hard but it seems to be such an effort that I hate to make her." Eventually, the first lady learned to deliver stock phrases such as "Glad to see you," but complex expressions remained difficult and enunciation was a struggle. Consonants at the beginning of words presented a particular impediment. The housekeeper, Elizabeth Jaffray, recalled "scores of times" when Taft sat with Nellie, "his hands over hers, saying over and over again:

'Now, please, darling, try and say "the"—that's it, "the." That's pretty good, but now try it again.' "

"No one knows how [the president] suffers over his wife's illness," Butt lamented. "As the weeks go by and there does not seem to be any permanent improvement, his hope sinks pretty low." Despite an outward show of optimism, Taft slowly began to acknowledge "the tragedy" which had befallen his marriage, his family, and his presidency. In Nellie's presence, he remained resolutely cheerful, determined to buoy her spirits and make her laugh. But beneath this bright veneer, Butt detected "a world of misery in his mind." Whenever he was left alone, Taft would sit by the window, "simply looking into the distance."

Before her illness, Nellie had discovered an ideal summer home for the family in Beverly, Massachusetts. On July 3, the president and first lady, accompanied by Nellie's sister Eleanor, Dr. Delaney, and Captain Butt, boarded the *Colonial Express* to "take up their residence" in the seaside community. The grand house stood amid "parklike lawns, shrubs, trees and flower-beds" that lent "an English beauty to its surroundings." One porch faced the sea; the other looked to Beverly Cove. The three children could walk to the Montserrat Club to play tennis, swim, and enjoy all manner of social activities, and two excellent golf courses were close by—the Myopia Club and the Essex Club. But what should have been a relaxing retreat for the first family became a period of enforced inactivity for Nellie. Although the doctor now conceded that it would "take quite a time" for her to recover, he believed she would be immeasurably strengthened by "two months of entire rest." Newspapers reported that the first lady would be kept "in seclusion," that no visitors would be entertained, and that the Secret Service would "keep intruders away."

The president himself was able to stay in Beverly for only twenty-two hours, just long enough to get Nellie settled. He was needed in Washington, where the special session of Congress called to revise the tariff was culminating in a nasty battle. "The great tug will begin," he remarked as he returned to the White House, "and one of the crises of my life will be on." The tariff struggle would indeed become a defining event in Taft's young presidency, but the true crisis had already transpired. His eloquent and independent wife, the partner who had attended to every detail in the opening days of his administration, was permanently incapacitated. The fierce and loving voice that had counseled and prodded Taft to every achievement and consoled him through every insecurity and difficulty was silent.

CHAPTER TWENTY-THREE

A Self-Inflicted Wound

President William Howard Taft.

PRESIDENT TAFT WELL UNDERSTOOD THE political hazards of his pledge to pursue tariff reform. For more than a decade, the Republican establishment had trumpeted the reigning tariff structure as the engine of American prosperity, the key to the nation's burgeoning industry. Protectionism had become a central tenet of conservative Republican ideology. While Theodore Roosevelt had sympathized with progressive claims that high tariffs strengthened monopolies and artificially inflated prices, he had persistently evaded the issue, aware that a tariff battle would create a dangerous schism within the Republican Party, pitting western farmers against eastern manufacturers. During the final years of his administration, however, newly elected western progressives had passionately assailed the unjust advantages that the tariff granted the industrial East at the expense of their agrarian region.

As Taft took office, the battle could no longer be postponed. Sensitized to the inequities of the tariff system by his long and futile efforts to reduce the Philippine tariff, the new president was prepared to take the lead. Of all the members of Roosevelt's cabinet, Taft had espoused the most consistently progressive views on the tariff, tenaciously advocating for revision. Duties, he argued, should be levied simply to "equal the difference between the cost of production abroad and at home." When excessive duties were built into the tariff structure through the influence of powerful corporations, the system served only to spur monopoly, guarantee disproportionate profits, and raise prices for consumers. At Taft's insistence, the Republican platform "unequivocally" called for a "special session of Congress" to revise the tariff.

With the Old Guard still entrenched in both Houses, the president faced formidable opposition. Genuine downward revision, reporters predicted, would only be achieved by an "uprising and demonstration of popular opinion" similar to that which had propelled railroad regulation, meat inspection, and the Pure Food and Drug Act. To prompt them to take action, conservative Republican leaders would have to conclude that nothing short of "cataclysm" would result if they failed to alter their policy.

As the tariff struggle began in earnest in the spring of 1909, no journalist was better positioned to clarify the convoluted tariff system for the public— and expose the economic disparities and suffering wrought by that system— than Ida Tarbell. Two years of research and writing had convinced her that the tariff represented "the greatest issue before the people—the question of special privilege, and unequal distribution of wealth." She launched a passionate crusade "to humanize" the issue by dramatizing the tariff's role in consolidating wealth and imposing serious hardships on working Americans.

That spring, Tarbell published two influential articles in *The American Magazine* that framed the arcane tariff schedule as a simple moral issue. In "Where Every Penny Counts" and "Where the Shoe Is Pinched," she demonstrated how manufacturers' profits had ballooned under the protective tariff even as the wages of ordinary Americans failed to keep pace with the rising cost of living. Protectionists claimed it hardly mattered if "this or that duty made an article cost a cent or two more at retail," she observed; in fact, a cent or two clearly did make "a material difference" in the lives of "the vast majority of American families," who subsisted "on $500 or less a year." To support a family on an average wage of six or eight dollars a week, Tarbell pointed out, a man "must think before he buys a penny newspaper and he must save or plan for months to get a yearly holiday for the family at Coney Island." Faced with such limited choices, she continued, "there is practically no possibility of a nest egg, or of schooling for the children beyond fourteen years of age." Illness inevitably resulted in "debt or charity" for those in such dire circumstances, and "the accumulation of those things which make for comfort and beauty in a home is out of the question." For working-class families, "every penny added to the cost of food, of coal, of common articles of clothing means simply less food, less warmth, less covering."

Tarbell trenchantly illustrated this reality in her second article on the "vital importance" of shoes. For the average working-class family, she explained, the cost of buying and mending shoes made up more than a quarter of their total outlay for clothing. One could do without a hat, extra trousers, or a dress, she maintained, but not without footwear. "It was hard enough for the poor to buy shoes ten years ago before the Dingley tariff," she argued, "but with every year since it has been harder." In the last decade, the price of ordinary shoes and boots had risen 25 percent. "Why should shoes increase in cost?" she asked, pointing out that "they ought to decrease, such has been the extraordinary advance in shoe machinery and in methods." The answer, Tarbell demonstrated, lay in the duties on hides and thread—fees that benefited the Beef Trust, the United Shoe Company, and the Leather Trust at the expense of the consumer. For years, legislators had acquiesced to these duties in return for campaign contributions and support for their local machines.

"At a time when wealth is rolling up as never before," Tarbell concluded, "a vast number of hard-working people in this country are really having a more difficult time making ends meet than they have ever had before." Because wage increases were not keeping pace with the escalating cost of living, the workingman was left to feel that "no matter how much he earns he will still have to spend it all in the same hard struggle to get on, that there is no such thing for him as getting ahead." By focusing on workaday living and highlighting the immediate rather than dwelling on the abstract, Tarbell's articles proved a revelation for many. "I never knew what the tariff meant before," the pioneering social reformer Jane Addams told her.

⁂

DESPITE THE HEIGHTENED AWARENESS SPURRED by Ida Tarbell's thoughtful explications, President Taft still struggled to transform that growing public sentiment into political capital. The first skirmish in the tariff battle followed immediately upon his election. During the campaign, western proponents of reform had focused their ire on Speaker Joseph Cannon, high priest of protectionism and special interests in the House. The seventy-two-year-old Speaker held the House in an autocratic grasp: no bill could reach the floor without his approval; no member could be recognized to speak without his consent. Deploying his power to appoint all Republican committee members and their chairs, he routinely rewarded conservatives and punished progressives. Conceding Cannon's strength, Roosevelt had repeatedly bargained with him, pledging to preserve the protective tariff in return for Cannon's cooperation in allowing anti-trust and regulatory legislation to reach the floor. During the 1908 presidential campaign, however, the tariff issue had caught fire. "Cannonism" had become a successful rallying cry in western districts, prompting the ouster of a half-dozen Old Guard supporters. After the election, a rebellious group of thirty progressive Republicans initiated a revolt, hoping to assemble a majority capable of unseating the Speaker, or at least curtailing his powers when Congress convened in mid-March 1909.

Taft seriously considered backing these "insurgents," as Cannon's foes became known. He had "never liked" the Speaker, considering him a vulgar reactionary who consistently opposed "all legislation of a progressive character." Writing to Roosevelt immediately after his victory, Taft spoke of the movement to defeat Cannon's nomination. "If by helping it I could bring it about I would do so," he explained, "but I want to take no false step in the matter." Roosevelt cautioned against hasty action: "I do not believe it would be well to have [Cannon] in the position of the sullen and hostile floor leader bound to bring your administration to grief, even tho you were able to put someone else in as Speaker." Elihu Root was even more vehemently opposed to any intervention by Taft, counseling that "it would be very unfortunate to have the idea get about that you wanted to beat Cannon and are not able to do it."

Nonetheless, Taft remained "very much disposed to fight." Replying to Root, he cited a speech Cannon had recently delivered in Cleveland that seemed to repudiate the Republican platform's pledge to revise the tariff. "In our anxiety to get votes," Cannon had reportedly stated, "we sometimes put in our platform things that are not orthodox." Such "cynical references" to platform promises could prove "enough to damn the party if they are not protested against," Taft told Root: "I am willing to have it understood that my attitude is one of hostility to Cannon and the whole crowd unless they are coming in to do the square thing. If they don't do it, and I acquiesce, we are going to be beaten; and I had rather be beaten by not acquiescing than by acquiescing. You know me well enough to know that I do not hunt a fight just for the fun of it, but Cannon's speech at Cleveland was of a character that ought to disgust everybody who believes in honesty in politics and dealing with people squarely."

To better gauge the odds of defeating Cannon, Taft consulted leading Republican editors and state officials across the country, asking them how their local congressmen would likely vote on the issue. "A new irrepressible conflict has begun in earnest," the *New York Times* reported, "a conflict which has been threatening every session of Congress for the last four years, but which Mr. Roosevelt has never been able to make up his mind to undertake." The *Times* predicted "a desperate fight in all probability, for Speaker Cannon and the close friends around him are not quitters. It will leave deep scars and ensure a warfare that probably will endure throughout the Taft administration."

Roosevelt continued to caution against alienating Cannon. In a barrage of "urgent telegrams and letters," he informed Taft that Minnesota congressman James Tawney was "very anxious" to arrange a direct conversation between the president-elect and the Speaker. Roosevelt stressed the importance of the interview, adding that he would provide "a full statement of the facts" on Cannon as soon as Taft returned to Washington from Hot Springs.

As speculation in the press intensified, a delegation of Cannon's friends made a pilgrimage to Hot Springs to assure Taft that Cannon would "support genuine tariff revision" and "not stand in the way of carrying forward" the new president's legislative program. He was shown a full text of Cannon's Cleveland speech, which gave an "entirely different impression" from the troubling excerpt he had read. In fact, the Speaker had promised that within "a hundred days," Congress would pass a new tariff law. This new law would not be "perfect," Cannon explained, but it would be "the best revenue law ever written."

Meanwhile, Taft had received disheartening responses to his inquiries regarding the insurgents' prospects. On the east coast, Cannon's support was unshakable; even in Kansas, a center of progressivism, five of eight congressmen stood with the Speaker. Taft was forced to concede that unless he personally went after Cannon "hammer and tongs," using all the powers of his presidency to fashion a majority, Cannon would be reelected. And even if he prevailed, he would be left with the "factious and ugly Republican minority" that Roosevelt had warned of. In the end, Taft resolved to work through the existing party machinery to accomplish the passage of his legislative proposals.

In itself, Taft's decision to relinquish the effort to oust the Speaker would have aroused little criticism; the mistake that would haunt his presidency, however, was his public declaration of surrender from Hot Springs, which immediately eliminated any advantage over Cannon. Moreover, as Taft's biographer Henry Pringle observes, the public concession "sent a chill of discouragement over the valiant but futile band of House insurgents." After a subsequent meeting with Cannon and Republican members of the Ways and Means Committee, Taft had further dispirited reformers by expressing full confidence in the conservative leadership's promise "to prepare an honest and thorough revision of the present tariff." All hope of unseating Cannon vanished. When Congress convened on March 15, 1909, the Speaker easily won reelection.

Perhaps it was inevitable that Taft's temperament—his aversion to dissension and preference for personal persuasion—would ultimately lead him to work within the system rather than mobilize external pressure from his bully pulpit. But his conciliatory approach left his administration and the American people at the mercy of Joseph Cannon, "the most sophisticated" politician in the country, "the most familiar with every subterranean channel of politics, the most cunning in its devious ways, the most artful in the tricks of the craft."

⌒ ⌒

PROGRESSIVES NEVERTHELESS REMAINED HOPEFUL THAT the new president would provide vital leadership to combat the special interests controlling the congressional tariff-making process. On March 16, 1909, they waited expectantly for the president's message, which would signal the start of the special session. Theodore Roosevelt had used this forum as a powerful tool to focus public attention on his legislative agenda, spending weeks preparing each message. He had dictated "page after page, taking a theme and working it up, his mind glowing with the delight of expression." Though no one anticipated such a definitive or provocative communication from William Howard Taft, his decision to speak about the tariff in his first presidential message augured well. "The Senate and House were crowded," Robert La Follette recalled. "The attention was keen everywhere. The clerk began to read. At the end of two minutes he stopped. There was a hush, an expectation that he would resume. But he laid aside the paper."

As realization spread that the clerk was finished, one journalist reported, "statesmen almost fell out of their chairs." The presidential message, expected to be "historic," contained only 340 words. In truth, Taft had composed the entire text in fifteen minutes that morning. The address sounded "no clarion call to the people" and made "no allusion, direct or indirect, to the question of what kind of changes should be made." He simply and straightforwardly called on Congress to "give immediate consideration" to the tariff. Having already discussed the principles upon which revision "should proceed," Taft believed it unnecessary to reiterate his position. Without an inherent "flair for the dramatic" and hoping he might "avoid the bitter feuding with Congress that had marked Roosevelt's last days in office," he had chosen to launch his administration with "no loud noises, no explosions, no disturbances of the atmosphere."

Taft understood, he later said, that it was vital for a president to communicate "the facts and reasons sustaining his policies." Cultivating good relations with the press afforded "a great advantage" to a leader. Nevertheless, he confessed, from his first days in office he was "derelict" in his use of the bully pulpit. The weekly press conferences he had promised soon became a chore. "There was none of the give and take, the jokes, and the off-the-record comments" that had characterized Roosevelt's interactions with the journalists. Before long, Taft discontinued the weekly sessions, attributing his discomfort with the press to his years on the bench, where he was unaccustomed to freely expanding upon his positions. "When the judgment of the court was announced," he explained, "it was supposed that all parties in interest would inform themselves as to the reasons for the action taken."

Many of the reporters were eager to help him, Taft later acknowledged, "but they properly complained that I did not help them to help me." In the spring of 1909, William Allen White, Ray Baker, and Ida Tarbell all signaled their readiness to support and publicize tariff revision, postal savings, and the rest of the president's progressive agenda. "If ever at any time I may serve you in any way," White wrote after the inaugural, "kindly let me know." Taft thanked him for his offer, and the two men exchanged a few letters, but the president never found a way to properly utilize the Kansas editor. "I am not constituted as Mr. Roosevelt is," he explained to White, "in being able to keep the country advised every few days of the continuance of the state of mind in reference to reforms. It is a difference in temperament. He talked with correspondents a great deal. His heart was generally on his sleeve, and he must communicate his feelings. I find myself unable to do so. After I have made a definite statement, I have to let it go at that, until the time for action arises."

Baker, too, hoped to assist the president's endeavor to revise the tariff. "I knew what a hard fight he had ahead of him, and I wanted to help him, in my own small way, if I could, with my pen," the journalist remembered. Baker had become increasingly disillusioned with Roosevelt's failure to confront the issue. "Although the tariff storm was steadily rising," he lamented, "Roosevelt said not so much as a single word on the subject. Though the issue was driving his party straight upon the reefs, he offered no counsel, suggested no remedy. He left the brunt of the storm for poor Mr. Taft to meet." Now that the new president had made tariff reform his signature issue, Baker was anxious to meet with him and see how he might aid the cause.

An interview was arranged not long after the special legislative session had commenced. The Cabinet Room was filled with people waiting to see the president. Emerging from his private office, Taft asked that Baker "remain to the last," so they would have an opportunity to talk. "I had liked him on previous occasions when I had met him," Baker recalled. Now, watching "his frank, free, whole-hearted way of greeting his visitors," his expansive manner of draping "one of his great arms over the shoulder of a congress-man," the journalist liked him "better than ever." Entering the private office where he had previously met with Roosevelt, Baker was struck immediately by the contrast. The small room had formerly exuded "the air of a quiet study." Books of history, works of fiction, and volumes of poetry had been strewn upon the table, "a riding crop and a tennis racket leaning in the corner." Now, Taft had transformed the study into a staid law office: "On all sides of the room were cases filled with law-books, nothing but law books." The shift in decor was "not without significance," Baker concluded, revealing "the legal mind" of the new occupant, a temperament desiring "everything carried forward quietly; according to the rules of the court," without "emotional appeals" to the public.

Initially fearful that the new president's "dislike for publicity" would pre-vent him from mobilizing public opinion to pressure Congress, Baker was "impressed" by "the perfect freedom" with which Taft discussed the tariff. "He outlined his position with a degree of frankness and earnestness that left in my mind no doubt of his essential sincerity," Baker remarked, noting that the president evinced an "easy optimism" that admitted no doubt about the eventual outcome. "I went away from the White House that day fully con-vinced that Mr. Taft not only would do what he said he would, regarding the tariff, but that he *could* do it." In the wake of this encouraging visit, however, Taft never called on Baker as the battle dragged on and the prospects for significant revision diminished.

No journalist fathomed the history of corporate efforts to evade downward tariff revision better than Ida Tarbell. As the special session was getting under way, she published a revealing article called "Juggling with the Tariff" that used the example of the wool schedule to illustrate the arcane tariff-making process. "Fifty years ago wool was disposed of in perhaps fifty words, which anybody could understand," she wrote; "to-day it takes some three thousand, and as for intelligibility, nobody but an expert versed in the different grades of wools, of yarns, and of woolen articles could tell what the duty really is." If Congress actually relied on such "disinterested experts," the process might nevertheless produce a decent tariff; instead, Tarbell explained, "Congress consults the wool-growers, the top-maker, the spinner and the weaver, and these gentlemen, being particularly human, each asks for an amount which will give him the advantage in the business—and he who is cleverest gets it."

Not surprisingly, those who secured the desired duties also happened to be the largest campaign contributors to the congressmen and senators on the relevant committees. "Mr. Taft is right," she declared, laying out a blueprint of necessary proceedings for reform: "What is wanted in making the present bill is evidence—evidence of the cost of production here and abroad, gathered not by the interested, but by the disinterested, not by clerks, but by experts. When provision has been made for obtaining that, the first step toward putting an end to the present tariff juggling will have been taken."

Throughout the spring, Tarbell remained hopeful that the new president's leadership would help secure the first genuine revision. She considered William Howard Taft "one of the most kindly, modest, humorous, philosophical of human beings." At a cabinet dinner shortly after the election, she found herself seated next to him. "There was something very lovable about the way the President talked of his election—not at all of any pride or pleasure he had taking the place," but rather of the deep pleasure it had afforded his family. With her warm feelings toward Taft and passion for tariff reform, Tarbell would undoubtedly have supported the president in much the same way Baker had helped Roosevelt during the battle for railroad regulation—sharing extensive research, providing advance copies of upcoming articles, and collaborating through subsequent conversations. Yet there is no record that the president ever followed up their dinner meeting with correspondence or an invitation to the White House.

THE LEGISLATIVE BATTLE PLAYED OUT in three acts. Deliberations began in the House and moved on to the Senate, culminating in a conference committee to reconcile the bills produced by each chamber. Early on, Cannon and Aldrich advised Taft to wait until the final conference committee stage to exert his influence. Trusting that the two men would honor the party's pledge to revise the tariff downward, Taft agreed "to keep his distance" from the congressional deliberations. If adjustments were necessary, he could make a personal appeal afterward, persuading each side to do what was best for both party and country.

"I have got to regard the Republican party as the instrumentality through which to try to accomplish something," he explained to William Allen White, when cautioned that public sentiment in the West had turned against the traditional party leadership. Indeed, the resentment against Cannon and Aldrich was so strong, another friend warned, that "no matter what tariff bill passes, or what you do, you are bound to be soundly abused." Taft remained imperturbable in the face of such admonitions. "I am here to get legislation through," he countered, "not to satisfy particular parts of the country."

Taft considered the Payne bill, passed by the House on the evening of April 9, "a genuine effort in the right direction," though reductions were "not as great" as he anticipated. The bill put hides, oil, coal, tea, and coffee on the free list and reduced the duties on lumber, scrap iron, and a host of other items. To Taft's disappointment, the controversial wool schedule was not changed. The combination of "the Western wool growers and the Eastern wool manu-facturers," he lamented, rendered it "impossible" to get lower duties "through either the Committee or the House." The bill also made what the president considered "inappropriate" increases in food, spices, mustard, gloves, and hosiery. Despite these shortcomings, the free trade *Evening Post* judged the Payne bill "a more enlightened and promising measure than any tariff ever fathered by the Republican party." For the first time, the *Post* acknowledged, "the forgotten consumer is given a thought."

If the Senate retained all the reductions in the House bill and struck out the higher rates on food, hosiery, and gloves, Taft told the *New York Times*, the final product "would be satisfactory to him." He would not engage in a struggle with Congress "at this early stage." The measure had passed the House with an almost straight party-line vote of 217 to 161, a good omen for Republican unity. Now it was "up to the Senate"—or, as many believed, to a single senator. "The House makes the tariff," the *New York Press* quipped. "Senator Aldrich, pretty much single-handed, remakes it."

Taft had reason to be skeptical of Nelson Aldrich. He had witnessed the Senate leader's machinations during Roosevelt's fight to regulate the railroads and blamed Aldrich for the repeated failure to reduce the tariff on imports from the Philippines. Initial reports from the Finance Committee indicated that the senator had crafted hundreds of amendments to the House bill, the great majority cleverly constructed to raise, not lower, duties. "I fear Aldrich is ready to sacrifice the party, and I will not permit it," Taft told his secre-tary, George Meyer. Even more troubling, Aldrich soon openly revealed his antagonism to the president's agenda. On April 22, a scant two weeks after the Senate had taken up the Payne bill, Aldrich stood on the Senate floor and asked, "Where did we ever make the statement that we would revise the tariff downward?" This was the time when Taft should have summoned the press and upbraided Aldrich and his reactionary allies. But whereas Roosevelt spoiled for dramatic fights, public confrontation was not in the new president's disposition. "There is no use trying to be William Howard Taft with Roo-sevelt's ways," he conceded.

While Taft hesitated to challenge Aldrich openly, La Follette, Beveridge, Nelson, and a small group of progressive Republicans mobilized for a major intraparty battle against the Senate leader. Aware that Aldrich had abundant experience in devising obscure classifications for each of the 4,000 duties in the tariff schedule, they agreed to concentrate on a few major products. For efficiency, they divided the daunting research: Dolliver chose cotton, La Follette selected wool, A. B. Cummins focused on metal and glass, and Joseph Bristow tackled lead and sugar. Time was short, for Aldrich was determined to move the bill through the upper chamber as quickly as possible. "It has been tariff, tariff, all the time, literally morning, noon and night," Lodge reported to Roosevelt, complaining, "I have never been so worked in my life." It was often past midnight when the insurgents left their offices, only to continue sifting through hundreds of pages of material at home until the small hours of the morning. On weekends, they gathered in Albert Beveridge's apartment, sharing information and discussing strategy.

In private meetings, Taft encouraged the insurgents to "go ahead, criticize the bill, amend it, cut down the duties—go after it hard," promising, "I will keep track of your amendments. I will read every word of the speeches you make, and when they lay that bill before me, unless it complies with the platform, I will veto it." Had the president truly followed the devastating critique presented in the insurgents' extended speeches, he would have been far better equipped to influence the final shape of the bill. At the close of a harried day, however, Taft wanted nothing more than to provide Nellie with comfort and companionship, patiently working to help her regain her speech. By June, he confessed to a group of woolen manufacturers that he was "bewildered by the intricacies of the tariff measure" and would have more confidence if he possessed "more technical knowledge."

The Senate debate dragged on, becoming increasingly bitter and unprofitable. The insurgents blasted Aldrich and his lieutenants as "reactionary tools of the trusts and eastern corporations"; the Senate leader, in turn, accused the insurgents of treachery to the Republican Party. During one savage indictment of the cotton schedule, Aldrich attempted to bolt from the chamber. "The Senator will not turn his back upon what I have to say here without taking the moral consequences," Dolliver shouted at him. Taft worried that the insurgents were becoming "irresponsible," exposing the party's rift to the nation, and making compromise impossible.

Aldrich himself, the shrewdest and most discerning political animal in the Senate, knew precisely where to yield and where to hold fast. He bartered reductions on some schedules for increases in others, confident that in the end, the bill would emerge essentially his own. William Howard Taft was the only real obstacle that Aldrich faced. The president possessed the power to mobilize public opposition, use patronage as a club, and ultimately to withhold his signature from a bill. Accordingly, Aldrich set to work on the good-natured Taft. He spent relaxing mealtime hours repeatedly assuring him that the final tariff bill would be worthy of his support. On a number of items, Aldrich acknowledged, the Senate had restored duties cut by the House. When the bill reached the joint committee, however, he promised to "confer" with the president, assuring him that his suggestions would carry "great influence." Knowing Taft's enduring allegiance to the Philippines, he guaranteed that the islands would finally see the reductions Taft had long advocated. Moreover, he claimed to accept the president's plan for a tariff commission composed of experts who would furnish objective information during future debates. Most importantly, the senator pledged that once the tariff was settled, he and his lieutenants would cooperate to move forward the rest of the legislative program outlined in Taft's inaugural address relating to trusts, interstate commerce, postal savings, and conservation—all considered vital to the "general carrying out of the Roosevelt policies."

By early summer, as the futility of the insurgents' struggle on the Senate floor grew increasingly apparent, newspapers called on the president to intervene. "Mr. Taft is not proving a courageous captain," the *New York American* charged, extending the metaphor to suggest a purloined presidency: "His course was clearly charted and the prospect at the outset was for a quick and fair voyage. But he has surrendered the command to Senator Aldrich, and the latter, as was to be expected, is steering the vessel into pirate-infested seas." The president's sympathizers argued that it was premature "to form definite conclusions until results begin to show," suggesting that Taft's benign temperament and beaming smile might well "cloak a determination as unrelenting as Mr. Roosevelt's own."

In mid-June, Taft finally abandoned his "hands off" approach to the legislature, sending a special message to Congress on an issue intimately connected to tariff reduction. To balance the projected loss of federal revenue resulting from overall reductions, some additional form of taxation would be necessary. The House had proposed an inheritance tax, but the Senate roundly objected "on the ground that the States—some thirty-six of them—had already adopted inheritance taxes, and this would be a double tax." Hoping to resolve this contentious standoff, Taft called on Congress to pass both a tax on corporations and a constitutional amendment establishing an income tax. In principle, the president supported the progressives' preference for a bill to impose an immediate federal income tax. But in practice, he feared that the conservative Supreme Court, which had ruled the measure unconstitutional just a decade earlier, would refuse to "reverse itself," exposing the Court to severe criticism at a time when its reputation was "already at a low ebb." A constitutional amendment granting Congress power to levy an income tax would settle the question for good.

As he pursued his tax agenda with Aldrich, Taft engaged in "some pretty shrewd politics." He met individually with members of the Finance Committee and "committed them separately" to both tax propositions before dispatching his message to Congress. The corporate tax, he persuasively argued, would simultaneously provide needed revenue and empower the federal government to oversee the transactions of a wide range of corporations. It would "go a great way" toward securing the protection from "illegitimate schemes" and anti-trust violations that Roosevelt had long hoped to provide. During their previous conversations, Aldrich had reluctantly accepted the corporation tax, thinking that Taft had been persuaded to drop the income tax amendment. But with the president's support, Congress passed both measures. "Just when they thought they had him sleeping," Archie Butt observed, "he showed them he was never so alive in his life." Later that summer, the states began ratification of what would eventually become the sixteenth constitutional amendment; the process was completed before Taft's term came to an end.

With the revenue question resolved, the Senate's tariff bill passed just before midnight on July 8 by a margin of 9 votes. The Senate bill made some reductions that the House had neglected, but also restored duties on hides and raw materials and left intact the controversial wool and cotton schedules. The Democratic vote along party lines was expected; that ten Republican senators followed La Follette in joining the Democrats made headlines. These dissenting votes revealed the very party split Theodore Roosevelt had feared, and long carefully avoided, further complicating matters for Taft.

As the conference committee began its deliberations, Taft remained hopeful that he could persuade the dozen conferees to combine the best elements of both bills in a final product that both progressives and conservatives could support. Newspapers across the country called on the president to take charge. "Congress has had its inning," the *Baltimore Sun* observed. "It is now the President's inning, and he has the masses of the people behind him." The *Boston Journal* declared it time for the president "to make good," calling the proceedings "the greatest crisis of his career as Chief Magistrate." The final tariff legislation, press reports agreed, would be a defining moment in his young presidency. "If he allows a bill to come from conference which disappoints the country," the *Journal* concluded, "he will have forfeited a large share of the stock of popular confidence with which he was invested when he became President."

In the days that followed, Butt observed, Taft "used the White House as a great political adjunct." He invited Payne to dinner one night and Aldrich the next; both men dined with the president the following evening, then retired to the terrace where they continued their conversation until long after midnight. The president put his yacht "at the disposal of the conferees in the hope that they might take a comfortable trip down the Chesapeake and adjust some matters under the influence of such a favorable environment." He took breakfasts with the insurgents, lunches with the standpatters, and late evening automobile rides with Speaker Cannon.

Throughout these intensive negotiations, Taft found time for almost daily letters to Nellie. He was "longing" for her company, he assured her, and would proceed to Beverly the moment the tariff struggle ended. In the interim, he was "delighted" that Bob and Helen had arrived. "I hope that you will feel more like making the effort to talk with them than you have heretofore," he cajoled tenderly, "because it is practice that brings about the changes you seek." The pace of recovery might be frustrating, he acknowledged, but he predicted that progress would come "by jerks." Meanwhile, she was fortunate to enjoy the cooling onshore wind. "Last night was as hot a night as I have ever passed in Washington," he told her. "I slept in three beds, and changed because each time I waked up I found myself so bathed in perspiration that the bed was uncomfortable."

Taft's stream of letters, continuing through July and into the second week of August, provide insight into his strategy during the final stage of the tariff battle. The newspapers, he explained, had overstated the increases in the Senate bill, leading the public to view "the Senate bill as a very bad bill, and the House bill, by contrast as a good one." The primary difference between the two, he told Nellie, lay in the Senate's treatment of raw materials. If he could make the conferees return raw materials and hides to the free list and reduce the lumber rates, he believed he could "reconcile the country to the view that a substantial step downward has been taken."

On July 16, Taft made his first public move to influence the legislative process. Since he had called Congress into special session four months earlier, the president had patiently allowed lawmakers to work their will. Now, as tensions escalated within the conference committee, he issued a forceful statement that "he was committed to the principle of downward revision." Unless he was presented with evidence that the producers of oil, coal, or hides were unable "to compete successfully, without reduction of wages, then they did not need a duty and their articles should go on the free list." He understood that such action might hurt politicians in specific districts, but "with the whole people as his constituency," the president was obliged to provide a "broader point of view." The insurgents were "jubilant." Republican senator Bristow of Kansas commented that the president's statement "greatly strengthens the hands of the progressives." Congratulatory messages flooded the White House and newspapers predicted that the final product would be "the Taft tariff bill—not the Payne or the Aldrich, or the Payne-Aldrich bill."

Nellie was relieved to hear that her husband had intervened at last. "I see today you made a statement as to what you were going to stand for," she wrote. "I hope you won't have to come down much on it dear." While Nellie's handwriting remained poor, her desire to support her husband was fiercely conveyed. Indeed, as the trials of Taft's presidency commenced in earnest, the loss of her acute judgment and indomitable presence was a source of sorrow and frustration for both of them. For the first time in their marriage, Nellie was distracting Will from the difficulties he faced rather than offering sound guidance and solace.

The tariff situation, Taft acknowledged to his brother Horace, was "a good deal more of a muddle than the papers make out." Despite repeated promises to follow the president's lead in the conference proceedings, Aldrich refused Taft's request to commit himself "in writing" concerning free hides and raw materials. Although Taft had developed genuine respect for the Senate leader during the eighteen-week ordeal, he understood that he was dealing with "an expert and acute politician" and that he might "be deceived." He was particularly worried about the cotton schedule of duties. "Aldrich insists that it is not an increase," he confided to Nellie, "but I fear he is not borne out by the facts." Meanwhile, Speaker Cannon threatened to defeat the entire bill unless the conferees agreed to the House-sponsored duties on gloves and hosiery. Apparently, Aldrich explained to Taft, the Speaker felt he "owed his victory" to the glove manufacturer Lucius Littauer, "and therefore it was a personal matter with him" to keep the measure intact. The Speaker's blatant demand outraged Taft. "It is the greatest exhibition of tyranny that I have known," he declared. "Aldrich and I continue to be good friends although we differ somewhat, but he is a very different man from the Speaker."

On July 28, Taft sent an ultimatum to the conference committee, insisting that he would not sign any bill that did not contain both the free raw materials agreed upon by the House and the Senate reductions in gloves and hosiery. "They have my last word," he told Archie Butt, before departing for a round of golf followed by a dinner party. Ten minutes into dinner, Butt recorded, "the message came by phone from the White House that the conferees had agreed and had accepted the rates as laid down by the President. For a moment, Taft remained perfectly silent, staring incredulously at the paper before him." Then, smiling broadly, he shared his satisfaction: "Well, good friends, this makes me very happy." When the round of congratulations ended and the party drew to a close, Butt accompanied Taft to the White House. "There was no one waiting for him," Butt observed. He was "lonelier in his victory than he had been in his fight."

On the afternoon of Thursday, August 5, the president arrived to sign the Payne-Aldrich bill. The sun was shining on the Capitol; the president wore a "cut away suit" and carried "a straw hat in his hand," appearing "fairly radiant" to the assembled spectators. Cabinet officers along with members of Congress filled the president's chamber, where Taft's relief and good humor were evident to all. "Do you think I ought to adjourn Congress before I sign it?" he joked. "I certainly do not," Aldrich replied, as the audience broke into laughter.

For weeks, correspondents had speculated about the possibility of a presidential veto. Progressives, still desperately unhappy with the bill despite the last-minute improvements, had called upon Taft to reject this version and start over in the full session the following year. Well aware that he "could make a lot of cheap capital" and "popularize [himself] with the masses with a declaration of hostilities toward Congress," Taft felt that such an action "would greatly injure the party." Moreover, he was delighted by many aspects of the bill, including the reduced duties on raw materials, the formation of the tariff commission, the corporate tax, the income tax amendment, and the free trade provision for the Philippines. At this juncture, he had worked too hard and too long with congressional leaders to turn against them.

At six minutes after five o'clock, the president signed the Payne-Aldrich bill. Three minutes later, he appended his signature to a companion bill that established free trade with the Philippines, fulfilling a promise made long before. "A broad smile of satisfaction overspread his face," one reporter observed, "and he wrote his name with a flourish not in evidence when he signed the other bill."

In the midst of the ceremony, Butt recorded, "a terrific thunderstorm broke out." The room suddenly darkened. "Heavy black clouds rolled up, and the electric lights had to be turned on. Peals of thunder and vivid flashes of lightning came from the sky." Correspondents straightaway declared the storm a portent, auguring the "storm of protest" that would inevitably follow as the public understood the disappointing limitations of the bill. The measure was not "perfect," Taft admitted in a public statement, but it nevertheless represented "the result of a sincere effort on the part of the Republican party to make a downward revision and to comply with the promises of the platform." Later that night, he celebrated with cigars and wine at a White House dinner. "Practically all the prominent figures in the tariff fight" attended, the *New York Times* noted—"except the 'insurgents' in both branches of Congress." Trusting that the animosities of the debate would soon be forgotten, the president expressed sincere thanks to every member who had helped steer the measure through "its long and stormy journey."

Public reaction to Taft's role in the passage of the tariff bill was mixed. The *New York Tribune* offered a positive assessment, claiming that his "patient leadership" had "borne fruit in the many material concessions forced from the Senate," easing the way "for intelligent and fair-minded tariff legislation in the future." The *New York American* was less optimistic; while conceding that the president had made the final bill "less shocking," it insisted that slight improvements to a bad bill did not relieve him of his obligation to carry out his party's pledge. A tariff law that retained and even increased duties on "the necessities of the common people," such as cotton and wool, many editorials proclaimed, could only be judged an "empty victory." Most agreed that the president had "vindicated his personal sincerity," but the fact that "he erred in his strategy" could not be denied. It was "his own fault," the *New York Times* charged, that the final result had fallen short of his promised reform. "It is clear that he made the mistake of holding aloof too long; that he waited until after the horse was stolen before locking the stable door."

⤙ ⤚

THE DAY AFTER SIGNING THE bill, Taft departed for Beverly. He planned to spend five relaxing weeks with Nellie and the children before embarking on a two-month tour of the West. As the presidential train pulled into tiny Montserrat Station on the edge of town, Taft was thrilled to see Nellie waiting to greet him. The train had barely "come to a standstill," a reporter for the *New York Times* noted, "before he ran down the steps of the observation platform," pushing his way through the "enthusiastic" crowd to reach his wife. He embraced her with kisses "which could be heard by everyone present." While the president and his family motored to their seaside cottage, members of the White House staff drove to the office suites arranged at the Board of Trade building in Beverly. Once Taft escaped to the Myopia Hunt Golf Course that afternoon, the *Baltimore Sun* correspondent discerned an unmistakable message in his expression: "If anybody says the word tariff to me within the space of several days he will get hit with a golf stick."

Taft soon settled into a pleasant routine. After working with his secretary or meeting with visitors in the morning, he played a round of golf, returned to his papers and documents in early afternoon, and then gave "the rest of the day" to Nellie. He sat with her on the veranda, telling stories "to make her forget her illness," and when breezes cooled the late afternoons, he accompanied her on long drives in the countryside and along the shore. Seated beside his wife in the back of the open touring car, Taft directed the chauffeur to travel "over every beautiful road," trying each day "to find some new and pleasant route." They always returned from these forty- or fifty-mile excursions by seven-thirty, when their children joined them for "the family dinner hour" and everyone exchanged stories about the day's activities.

Taft watched the weeks slip by with growing dread, aware that at the end of his holiday his 13,000-mile western tour would commence. "If it were not for the speeches, I should look forward with the greatest pleasure to this trip," he told Captain Butt. "But without the speeches there would be no trip, and so there you are." During the Beverly respite, Taft had hoped to prepare four basic speeches, but as the end of August approached, he had not drafted a single one. "I would give anything in the world if I had the ability to clear away work as Roosevelt did," he confessed. "I have never known any one to keep ahead of his work as he did. It was a passion with him. I am putting off these speeches from day to day, and the result will be that I shall have to slave the last week I am here and get no enjoyment out of life at all." Three days before the trip began, Taft was still unprepared. "I do not know exactly what to say or how to say it," he told a friend. "I shall stagger through the matter some way, but not in any manner, I fear, to reflect credit on the Administration."

Before Taft set out on his trip, he explained to reporters that he hoped to "take the people into his confidence regarding the tariff contest." He would travel from the Alleghenies to the Rockies, where rebellion against the Republican Old Guard and the tariff was "rampant." He was optimistic that straightforward conversation with his critics might "prepossess them in favor of his standard." He would readily acknowledge that "the bill was unsatisfactory in many ways," but insisted that "it was the best he could obtain from the Congress under the circumstances." A future fight for deeper reductions loomed, for Taft believed that the American people had "learned a great deal about the tariff" and were prepared to elect new representatives pledged to remedy the "shortcomings" in the present bill. Most important, Taft believed this comprehensive tour would allow him to engage directly with "tens and hundreds of thousands" of his "fellow citizens," creating a "personal touch" between people in all sections of the country and their president.

In his strategy to realize this ambitious agenda, Taft stumbled badly from the outset. He opened his speaking tour at a black-tie banquet sponsored by the Boston Chamber of Commerce. The audience of nearly 2,000 included "cabinet members, diplomats, congressmen, clergymen and distinguished business leaders." The diners greeted him with hearty applause, but soon settled into a "grim silence" when he announced that he would refrain from any tariff discussion in order "to leave something" for future audiences. He chose instead to expound upon the Monetary Commission, appointed by Congress in the wake of the 1907 Panic. Chaired by Nelson Aldrich, the commission was leaning toward "a central bank" with sufficient reserves to meet future financial crises. The president characterized Aldrich as "one of the ablest statesmen in financial matters in either house," a leader eager "to crown his political career" with the creation of "a sound and safe monetary and banking system." While Aldrich would one day be credited as the "Father of the Federal Reserve Banking System," he was then regarded throughout the West as a servant of special privilege and the chief architect of the disappointing tariff bill. Taft's inept decision to lionize the senator in his very first speech cast a shadow on his tour before it had even started.

The president's train traveled from Boston to Illinois, making short stops along the way. Reaching Chicago that evening, he spoke at Orchestra Hall, where the massive crowd gave him a hearty reception. At Milwaukee the next day, he detailed his plans for postal savings legislation and dedicated a building in La Crosse before moving on to Winona, a small Minnesota city on the banks of the Mississippi, where he finally delivered his first statement on the tariff.

The choice of Winona, home to Representative James Tawney, was dictated, one correspondent noted, by Taft's "omnipresent good nature . . . his most endearing trait." Minnesota was a "hotbed of insurgency." Tawney, chairman of the Appropriations Committee, was the only member of the ten-person state delegation who had voted for the Payne-Aldrich tariff bill. The legislation was so unpopular in Minnesota that Tawney was in danger of losing his seat in the next election. Republican leaders in the House had implored the president to present a strong defense of Tawney's vote in the congressman's home district.

Though Taft knew that his first major speech on the tariff would be widely reported, he continued to procrastinate on the necessary preparation. The day before the scheduled address, he confessed his anxiety to Nellie: "Hope to be able to deliver a tariff speech at Winona but it will be a close shave." On the train from La Crosse to Winona, he finally settled down in his private state-room to work. He had "a mass of facts and figures before him," along with a lengthy statement prepared by Representative Payne. Two stenographers stood ready to take dictation. A draft was completed when the train reached Winona at eight o'clock that evening, but there was no time to solicit comments or make revisions. "Speech hastily prepared," he telegraphed Nellie, "but I hope it may do some good."

Speaking for over an hour, Taft touted the bill's merits and admitted its faults, particularly acknowledging its failure to reduce the wool schedule. Had he left the matter there, promising to revisit the tariff in the next congressional session, the speech would have stirred scant criticism. Instead, the president pressed on with a clumsy argument to vindicate the embattled Tawney. "What was the duty of a Member of Congress," he asked, who favored more dramatic reform but realized the genuine benefits of compromise? Taft was "glad to speak" in support of Tawney's decision to vote for the bill. In certain situations, party members had to "surrender their personal predilections" for the sake of unity. He would not criticize those Republican legislators who felt the divide between their desired course and the current bill "so extreme" that they "must in conscience abandon the party." In the end, however, he concurred with Representative Tawney that party unity trumped specific reductions "in one or two schedules." Party solidarity was essential to establishing the broader regulatory package that would "clinch the Roosevelt policies." This lumbering argument was effectively a reprise of Taft's earlier justification for his own decision against a veto. The real self-inflicted wound occurred in his twenty-four-word verdict on the bill itself: "On the whole," he concluded, "I am bound to say that I think the Payne tariff bill is the best bill that the Republican party ever passed."

This succinct, ill-considered statement made headlines across the country, obscuring the more nuanced argument presented in the president's address. By stating "without hesitation" that the bill represented the Republicans' signal legislative achievement, the *New York Times* charged, William Taft "has decided to abandon the cause of tariff reform." A majority of editorials echoed this view. "Western Republicans have made up their minds that they are not going to be ruled by New England," the *St. Paul Pioneer Press and Tribune* observed. "Instead of softening the antagonism between the two factions of his party, he has very clearly intensified it." His blundering Winona speech, the *Indianapolis Star* declared, proved that the president was "out of touch with American public sentiment on the tariff question." Even Horace Taft concurred with his brother's critics. "I did not write to you about it," he told

Will, "because my secretary is a lady and no language that suited the speech could be dictated. I will swear at you about it when I see you."

In Minnesota, Taft's "commendation" of Tawney was widely interpreted as an effort to undermine insurgent members of the state delegation. This surge of public resentment rekindled a sharp nostalgia for Taft's predecessor. "Theodore Roosevelt's good fortune has not deserted him," the *New York Times* observed. "The stars in their courses seem to fight for him. If he still cherishes an ambition to return to the White House, the path has been opened to him by President Taft, and no thoroughfare could be more inviting or easier to travel." If Roosevelt were to return and proclaim the tariff a failure to honor his party's pledge, the *Times* added, there would be no way of staying "the overwhelming demand" for his renomination in 1912. In actuality, Roosevelt fully endorsed the Payne-Aldrich tariff. "You have come out as well as we could hope on the tariff question," he told Lodge in a private letter. Like Taft, he regarded the corporate tax as a critical achievement, for it permanently established "the principle of national supervision." When Lodge lauded the critical role Nelson Aldrich had played in the passage of the bill, Roosevelt offered no objection. "I never appreciated his ability so fully before," Lodge wrote, calling Aldrich "a man of real power and force." Roosevelt replied that he was not "surprised" by Lodge's admiration, noting that his own inter-changes with Aldrich gave him "a steadily higher opinion of him." Roosevelt remained, of course, 10,000 miles away in "the wilds of Africa." None of these comments became public, and western insurgents continued to enshrine him as the exemplar of true reform, projecting their dissenting views of the tariff onto the former president.

Despite the onslaught of criticism, Taft trusted that the public would ul-timately recognize his Winona speech as a "truthful statement." Indeed, he insisted, compromise was "the only ground upon which the party [could] stand with anything like a united force and win victories." He remained convinced that the insurgents would relent when Congress convened in December, and began work on his proposed reform package to strengthen control over corpo-rate interests. In Iowa and California, he delivered rousing speeches designed to regain the confidence of the reformers. "Of course we want prosperity," Taft assured them, "but we wish prosperity in such a way . . . so that everybody will get his share, and that it shall not be confined to a few who monopolize the means of production or the means of transportation, and thus prevent that equality of distribution which we all like to see."

Indeed, it appeared the hostility might dissipate as the crowds grew in size and enthusiasm along the president's route. Nearly 7,000 people cheered him at the Armory in Portland; in Phoenix, he spoke "practically to the entire town of 20,000 people"; at the Seattle Exposition grounds, 80,000 poured through the gates. "Winning Taft Smile Spreads Radiance," the local paper in Albuquerque declared. "Taft's personality again has stood him in good stead," chimed the *Chicago Tribune*. "The distrust has faded." It was clear to those inside his administration that the president's desire to connect with the citizenry was unfeigned. He "really and sincerely likes people," Archie Butt observed. "He likes different types and he enjoys studying them. Whereas most people in his position try to avoid handshaking," the president "will stop a dozen times on his way in and out of a room to shake hands with anybody who calls to him."

Scarcely absent from Taft's side for the duration of the tour, Butt felt "more real affection" for the new chief than ever before. He noticed that Taft showed anger only on a few occasions when he had been savaged in newspaper editorials. Incensed, Taft gave instructions to stop sending him such clippings, particularly from the free trade *New York Times*. "They are prompted by such wild misconceptions and such a boyish desire to point the finger of scorn, that I don't think their reading will do me any particular good," he wrote, "and would only be provocative of that sort of anger and contemptuous feeling that does not do anybody any good." He assured Nellie that he could not have misread the friendly support he encountered everywhere. "Whatever their judgment as to particular things I have done," he told his wife, "I certainly up to this time have their good will, and that is a considerable asset."

Near the end of his transcontinental journey, Taft remarked that he had "enjoyed every moment of the trip." When people wondered how he endured the long days, filled with "266 speeches and 579 formal dinners, luncheons and breakfasts," he said it was a matter "of temperament, one of taste, and possibly one of disposition." For a person like him, who loved meeting with people and hearing about their lives, the trip was "as stimulating as champagne." When his train pulled into Union Station on the evening of November 10, an enthusiastic crowd, including members of his cabinet, was there to welcome him home. "Well, I'm back again," he announced with a broad smile, "feeling just as well as when I went away or even feeling better."

Behind the ebullience and the cheerful faces that greeted Taft when he stepped off the train, however, tensions were brewing that would prove calamitous for the new president's administration. Taft's optimism was soon punctured by the realization that his inner circle was "full of despair and predicting all sorts of evil"—harboring personal and political wounds that Taft's honorable nature had small hope of suturing.

CHAPTER TWENTY-FOUR

St. George and the Dragon

This cartoon, "An Off Day in the Jungle," imagines how
Roosevelt, on safari in Africa, heard the news that Gifford Pinchot
had been ousted from the Forest Bureau.

DURING TAFT'S FIFTY-SEVEN-DAY ABSENCE FROM Washington, a latent animosity between Chief Forester Gifford Pinchot, Roosevelt's closest ally in the conservation crusade, and Interior Secretary Richard Ballinger, Taft's choice to replace Garfield, flared into open discord. The conflict quickly escalated beyond the confines of "a mere personal squabble" into "a matter of state." With Roosevelt's allies falling in behind Pinchot, and Taft defending Ballinger, the controversy would pit the East of America versus the West, corporate interests against public rights, developers against conservationists—until all the divisive factions at play in the confrontation between Pinchot and Ballinger were framed as the opening volley in the battle for the 1912 presidential nomination. Noting the great dissatisfaction among progressives with the administration's actions on both conservation and the tariff, the *New York Times* cited the comment that if Roosevelt toured the country upon his return from Africa, "there would be such a fire behind him by the time he got across the continent that nothing could stand in front of it."

Contention over the regulation of waterpower had initially set Ballinger and Pinchot at odds. Near the end of his term, President Roosevelt had delivered a dramatic message to Congress on the future of hydroelectric power: America, he pronounced, was on the verge of a momentous development—the electrical transmission of waterpower over large distances. Although supplies of oil, gas, and coal would eventually be exhausted, hydroelectric power offered a source of renewable energy. The industry was "still in its infancy," yet Roosevelt warned that an "astonishing consolidation" had already occurred. Thirteen large corporations, led by General Electric and Westinghouse, controlled more than one third of the waterpower then in use. Unless potential power sites still owned by the government were leased to developers on terms consistent with "the public interest," the hydroelectric industry would follow the path of the oil industry: a great monopoly would develop, eradicating competition and dictating the price citizens paid for electricity in their homes and businesses. "I esteem it my duty," Roosevelt had concluded, "to use every endeavor to prevent this growing monopoly, the most threatening which has ever appeared, from being fastened upon the people of this nation."

With time running out on his administration, Roosevelt, together with Garfield and Pinchot, had come up with a plan. Acting without congressional authorization, Garfield issued executive orders to withdraw from private development more than 1.5 million acres of land situated along sixteen rivers in half a dozen western states. These protected lands included hundreds of thousands of acres with little connection to waterpower sites, but "there was no time," Pinchot explained, "to make detailed surveys." Under the pressing circumstances, the blanket withdrawal assured safety for the actual power sites. Roosevelt later justified these withdrawals, along with other controversial executive actions, arguing that the president "is the steward of the people, and that the proper attitude for him to take is that he is bound to assume that he has the legal right to do whatever the needs of the people demand, unless the Constitution or the laws explicitly forbid him to do it."

Within three weeks of assuming his post as the new interior secretary, Richard Ballinger restored the vast majority of Garfield's withdrawals to the public domain. A lawyer and former judge, Ballinger believed that the previous administration had acted illegally in making wholesale withdrawals without congressional authorization or even the requisite data to determine potential locations for hydroelectric development. Once the proper surveys were completed, he would ask Congress for legislation to protect the actual sites. Meanwhile, conservation efforts should not restrict legitimate development in the states of the Far West. Developers and businessmen in that region had long excoriated Roosevelt's conservation policies as a socialistic threat to "traditional western individualism." So many tracts of public land had been temporarily withdrawn from settlers and private developers, one critic sarcastically noted, "that a man could ride from the Missouri River to the Pacific Ocean and his horse need not once step a hoof outside government land."

While Taft considered himself a Roosevelt conservationist and recognized the vital work of Garfield and Pinchot, he fundamentally agreed with Ballinger's insistence that problems had to be resolved "on the basis of law." He would never endorse the cavalier attitude that "the end justified the means." In Taft's estimation, the "sweeping declaration of executive authority" used to justify the withdrawals misconceived "the entire theory of the Federal Constitution" which delegated specific powers to each of the three branches. "It is," he declared, "a very dangerous method of upholding reform to violate the law in so doing; even on the ground of high moral principle, or of saving the public." The Constitution granted Congress "the power to dispose of lands, not the Executive." Indeed, Taft believed that Roosevelt's conservation reforms would have been "further along" had he "taken a different way."

Ballinger's restoration orders provoked indignation among progressives, who feared that monopolies would grab thousands of invaluable water sites before the completion of the surveys. "Stop Ballinger," pleaded an editorial in the *Des Moines Daily News*. "Mr. Taft stop him! In the name of justice, if he is blind, see for him! If he is callous, feel for him! If he is without power to estimate the awfulness of this crime, think for him!" While more conservative commentators lauded the shift away from Roosevelt's "cowboy methods," progressives, educated by the former president to both the importance of conservation and the treachery of monopoly, reacted with outrage. "Attention! Land Thieves and Natural Resource Grabbers," the *Tacoma Times* announced: "Game is Soft Again." Under Roosevelt, the *Tacoma Times* declared, "any doubt about the power of the chief executive to make withdrawals of public land was resolved in favor of the people." Taft's administration had resolved the doubt "in favor of the predatory interests."

Gifford Pinchot was on an extended speaking tour in the West when Ballinger reversed Garfield's withdrawals. Returning to Washington in April 1909, he discovered "what was going on" and immediately called on President Taft. Largely uninvolved with conservation efforts during his years in the cabinet, Taft regarded Pinchot as an exemplary public servant but possessed of a fanatical strain, all too ready to attribute evil motives to anyone who opposed his ideas. Furthermore, Taft believed that Pinchot's intimacy with Roosevelt had endowed him with power far beyond his official responsibilities as the head of a single bureau in the Department of Agriculture. For two days running, Taft listened closely as Pinchot "protested as vigorously as [he] knew how against Ballinger's action," explaining why the restorations threatened public interest. "To his honor," Pinchot later said, Taft called in Ballinger and directed him to halt any further restorations and again re-withdraw any such "lands as were actually valuable for water-power purposes." Greatly relieved, Garfield maintained that Pinchot's intervention had forestalled disaster.

But Ballinger's concessions under pressure from the president did little to allay Pinchot's suspicions or satisfy the progressive press. "Everything is not yet altogether serene," the *Springfield* (Massachusetts) *Republican* reported. It remained to be seen whether the waterpower trust had capitalized on the "golden opportunities" provided by Ballinger's original restoration orders. In the absence of facts, rumors abounded. In May, the Philadelphia *Press* reported that "five million acres of publicly owned land" were being turned over to corporate interests. The continuing antagonism between Ballinger and Pinchot provided fodder for drastic speculation: some papers predicted that Ballinger would have to resign, others that Pinchot was on his way out. The future seemed equally murky to the protagonists themselves: "Was Conservation really in danger?" Had the president "gone over to the Old Guard?"

In early August, the controversy came to a head at the National Irrigation Conference in Spokane, Washington. As thousands of delegates from across the country poured into the Armory to discuss and debate reclamation, forests, waterways, and conservation, journalists predicted an open clash between Pinchot and Ballinger, both of whom were among the speakers. On August 9, the day before Pinchot was set to speak, the staff correspondent for the United Press released a sensational attack on Ballinger, claiming the secretary had used "one excuse or another" to delay Taft's re-withdrawal order, enabling General Electric, Guggenheim, and Amalgamated Copper to grab a total of 15,868 acres in Montana, including power sites worth millions upon millions of dollars. "This is a true story," the reporter contended, "of how the birth right of a great state" was lost to monopoly. "Richard Achilles Ballinger, stand up!" demanded the *Spokane Press* the next day. "You are accused of grave misadministration of your high office." Through Ballinger's actions, the state of Montana has been "eternally delivered into the hands of the power trust," the indictment continued. "President Taft cannot do anything about it now."

These spectacular charges set the stage for Gifford Pinchot's speech, which was widely construed as a direct attack on the embattled secretary. "The purpose of the Conservation movement," Pinchot declared at the outset, "is to make our country a permanent and prosperous home for ourselves and for our children and for our children's children." Pinchot "threw down the gauntlet" before Ballinger, stating "unequivocally" that a great waterpower trust was "in process of formation," aided by "strict construction" of the law, which inevitably championed "the great interests as against the people." The struggle over waterpower, he contended, was simply another chapter in "the everlasting conflict" between "the few" and "the many." This statement unleashed "a storm of applause," as did Pinchot's testimonial to Theodore Roosevelt. "I stand for the Roosevelt policies because they set the common good of all of us above the private gain of some of us," he reiterated, "because they recognize the livelihood of the small man as more important to the nation than the profit of the big man. . . . And I propose to stand for them while I have the strength to stand for anything." When he finished, the 1,200 delegates "cheered him for fully five minutes," clapping their hands and stomping the floor in "the wildest reception" accorded to any of the conference speakers. Later that day, Pinchot wrote to inform Taft of the "deplorable fact" he had just discovered, that monopolies had seized valuable waterpower sites in Montana "after the restoration and before the second withdrawal."

The delegates looked with "breathless interest" to Richard Ballinger's response to both the newspaper charges and Pinchot's speech. When the interior secretary stood at the podium the next day, he merely read a "routine dissertation on public-land matters," as if "the conflict" with Pinchot and the furor over his policies "had never been born." Furthermore, he declined to remain for questions after his prepared remarks, as every other speaker had done. "He picked up his hat," one reporter noted, "hustled into a waiting automobile, and hurried to his hotel." Former California governor George Pardee openly denounced Ballinger's decision to flee. "I have been in public office and have been criticized," Pardee derisively observed. "I do not object to it. A public official should be willing to be criticized. An agent of the people of this country should be called to account." Raucous cheers broke out in the hall along with rhythmic shouts of "Hit 'em again."

The United Press reporter who broke the story pressed Ballinger for an interview at his hotel. Refusing to "grant an audience," Ballinger finally agreed to talk by phone. "The dope you put out is all wrong and false," he began. When the reporter claimed to have records and maps substantiating the charges, Ballinger grew testy. "I'll have no conference with you," he responded, terminating the call. When another reporter "questioned and quizzed" the secretary about his actions, Ballinger became equally truculent. "See here. You don't understand this thing," he bellowed. "You are hindering the development of the West."

"Mr. Ballinger's silence is not reassuring," the *San Francisco Call* editorialized. "The country wants to know whether Ballinger is secretly fighting the policy of conservation." When Ballinger eventually put out a statement, he simply repeated that his decisions were fully warranted and his actions unreasonably maligned. "Gross misrepresentations have been sent out," he declared. "Criticisms have been pretty severe from some quarters, but knowing that I am absolutely right in the position I have taken, I have paid no attention to them. In time it will be shown beyond a doubt that my course has been absolutely right." In both his private and public life, Ballinger maintained, he had "always believed" in the tenet of "nonpublicity," confident that his actions would be vindicated "by the results accomplished."

Ballinger was, in fact, eventually able to prove that the Montana land grab story was riddled with error from start to finish. Only four tracts of 40 acres each were actually involved in the restoration, a total of 158.63 acres. Reporting the figure of 15,863 acres, the correspondent had misplaced the decimal point. Moreover, detailed surveys revealed that not a single valuable water site was contained in the restored land. Two of the tracts "did not touch the river at all," the third "touched the river only in its extreme corner," and the fourth had never been included in the Garfield withdrawals. Finally, not one of these entries had moved to actual patent. Pinchot eventually acknowledged that he had been mistaken when he charged that "monopolists had grabbed off" valuable waterpower sites in Montana. By then Ballinger had lost the public battle; the impression that he had betrayed Roosevelt's conservation policies was widespread. The controversy between Pinchot and Ballinger had "assumed a certain symbolic importance," with the chief forester advocating for the public and the interior secretary representing the corporations.

THE DISPUTE OVER WATERPOWER WAS soon "completely overshadowed" by dramatic developments in what was called the Cunningham coal scandal. Pinchot brought such grave allegations against the interior secretary that it was "taken for granted" that "either one side or the other must make good," leaving the other in abject humiliation. Capturing headlines for months, the scandal and ensuing congressional investigation would eventually become "the driving wedge," which "slowly but surely" created an unbridgeable "chasm" between William Howard Taft and Theodore Roosevelt.

Details of the coal case, "a slumbering volcano" in the Interior Department over the previous three years, first became public at the same Spokane conference that escalated the waterpower story. Louis R. Glavis, a twenty-seven-year-old field investigator for the General Land Office in the Interior Department, had approached Pinchot in desperation, fearing that the department, under pressure from Ballinger, was on the verge of handing over 5,000 acres of potentially rich coal land to a syndicate headed by a Seattle developer, Clarence Cunningham.

As the special agent assigned to investigate the validity of land claims in Alaska, Glavis had gradually accumulated evidence suggesting that Cunningham, acting as the agent for a group of wealthy clients, had acted illegally when he staked his thirty-three claims. The Alaska land laws, designed to protect small farmers and prevent monopoly, limited each individual to 160 acres. Individual settlers, who paid small fees for the land, were required to prove they were acting "in good faith," on their own behalf, when they staked claims for land. From the outset, Glavis believed, the Cunningham group had agreed to consolidate their claims "into one property," which would be "operated for the joint benefit of all." Indeed, he had uncovered a document proposing to give a Morgan-Guggenheim Company half the stock in return for $250,000 in cash investments to develop the coal property. Before completing his investigation, however, Glavis had been pulled from the case. Upon learning that the Land Office had scheduled a hearing on the Cunningham claims, half of which lay within the Chugach National Forest, he had turned to the chief forester for help.

Most troubling of all, Glavis reported, Ballinger had been "closely identified" with the members of the Cunningham group at various stages of the claims process. When Ballinger was land commissioner, he had shared all departmental correspondence on the case with Cunningham and had, at one point, actually ordered the claims to patent, pulling back only after an urgent telegram from Glavis. Then, in the summer of 1908, after leaving his post as land commissioner and returning home to Seattle, Ballinger had met with members of the Cunningham group, who had retained him as their "legal representative" before the government. Ballinger's actions, Glavis continued, flouted a three-decades-old ruling that no government employee could "act as counsel, attorney, or agent for prosecuting any claim against the government" within two years of leaving employment. Finally, when Ballinger returned to public service as interior secretary, he had urged the department to decide the Cunningham claims without further delay.

After hearing Glavis's account, Pinchot dispatched an urgent letter to Taft.

"I advised him to lay the whole matter before you without delay," he told the president. Immediate action was in order, Pinchot warned, because "many persons" already knew of "various parts" of the story and it would soon become "impossible to prevent its becoming public." Before Glavis even reached the "Summer Capital" in Beverly, in fact, sensational articles began to appear. "Ballinger Mixed in Alaska Frauds," headlined the *Salt Lake Tribune*. The fact that Ballinger had accepted fees from Cunningham during the year between his service as land commissioner and his return to Washington as secretary drew particular attention. Glavis reportedly had "a whole trunk full of documentary evidence" that would lead to the indictment of Ballinger and several other high officials in the Interior Department. It was later revealed that the publicity wing in the Forestry Bureau had leaked these reports.

When Glavis met with the president on August 18, he handed him a detailed statement on the coal case and his allegations against Ballinger. The following day, Taft discussed the charges with Attorney General George Wickersham, who was vacationing nearby. Wickersham reviewed the Glavis statement and "made notes upon his reading." The two men talked again the following afternoon and determined that Taft should forward the Glavis report to Ballinger and request a written reply. The president instructed Ballinger to answer each of the charges, "especially concerning [his] relation as counsel to the persons interested in the Cunningham coal claims." Taft "quite distinctly" recalled that Ballinger had told him the previous year that because of his "professional relation" with the Cunningham group, he had turned the case over to Assistant Secretary Frank Pierce; beyond that, he remembered little else about the situation. He would appreciate a written explanation "as full as possible." Taft also requested written statements from Frank Pierce and the chief of Field Service, H. H. Schwartz, under whom Glavis had worked.

The Interior Department officials responded quickly, providing a vigorous defense of Ballinger. Pierce insisted that Ballinger "has had nothing to do with these Cunningham cases since he became Secretary," adding that any "blame or criticism . . . should fall upon [him] and not upon the Secretary." Schwartz asserted that Glavis's decision to seek help from the Forestry Department was utterly unnecessary: at that juncture no one in the Interior Department was suggesting "issuance of patents, but only expedition of hearings." And based on the evidence already accumulated, the hearings would likely have resulted in an adverse decision to the claimants.

Meanwhile, Ballinger continued to toil over his own response. Asked about the allegations by the press, he remarked only that he intended "to kill some snakes." On September 4, he completed his 10,000-word document, taking up each one of the Glavis charges in turn. Before becoming land commissioner, Ballinger testified, he had no personal knowledge of the Cunningham claims, though as a twenty-year resident of Seattle he had developed friendships and acquaintances with a number of the claimants. He acknowledged that at one point he had clear-listed the claims, based upon a favorable report from another special agent. Upon receiving Glavis's telegram, however, he had acted immediately to stop the patents. The patents were still being held up when he left the land commissionership.

Ballinger did concede that in the summer of 1908, Cunningham had come to his house simply to complain of his treatment by Glavis. Cunningham told Ballinger that at one of his meetings with Glavis, he had allowed the agent to read a journal documenting each stage of the claims process. He claimed that Glavis had stolen one of the pages, which he was using out of context to demonstrate an illegal intent to consolidate. Cunningham argued that Glavis had interpreted the document incorrectly. When Cunningham learned that Ballinger would soon travel east, he asked him to carry an affidavit to Interior Secretary Garfield presenting his point of view. Ballinger gave the affidavit to Garfield, but the secretary told him that the claims would never be upheld unless the group was willing to apply under a recent law that forgave early signs of consolidation but severely limited the amount of money that could be raised to develop the property. Ballinger advised Cunningham accordingly. For his services and traveling expenses, Ballinger reported, he received $250. Since he had never been retained as a "legal representative," he argued, there had been no violation of the long-standing rule which, at any rate, applied only to monetary claims against the government. Furthermore, he labeled the charge that he had furnished Cunningham with departmental correspondence relating to the case a pure fabrication.

On Labor Day, September 6, Ballinger hand-delivered his written statement to Beverly, along with "several satchels full of documents." Oscar Lawler, the assistant attorney general assigned to the Interior Department, accompanied him. They joined the president for lunch at the Myopia Hunt Club, where Taft was scheduled to present victory cups for the annual horse show before a crowd of 5,000. That evening, Ballinger and Lawler conferred with the president for several hours. Taft later reported that he stayed up until three o'clock, "reading the answers and exhibits." When he reconvened with Ballinger and Lawler the following evening, the president had already determined that the Glavis report contained no hard evidence that Ballinger was dishonest, disloyal, or incompetent. "The cruel injustice which has been done to [Ballinger] makes me indignant," Taft declared. He told Lawler that he "was very anxious to write a full statement of the case," explaining his reasoning to the public. But because he was scheduled to leave in one week for his two-month tour around the country and still had a half-dozen speeches to write, he asked Lawler to prepare a draft statement "as if he were president."

The following Sunday, Wickersham and Lawler returned to Beverly with Lawler's draft. Taft asked Wickersham to spend the rest of the day reviewing the entire record. He continued to work on his own statement, using Lawler's draft as a starting point. After a second reading, Wickersham told Taft that he saw nothing in the record to incriminate Ballinger. Finding Wickersham "in substantial accord" with his own views, Taft completed his own statement and directed the attorney general to embody his notes and oral statement in a written analysis, to be filed with the documents. He should date the analysis prior to the publication of the president's statement, Taft continued, to demonstrate that his decision had been buttressed by the attorney general's "summary of the evidence and his conclusions."

Taft issued his statement on September 13, in the form of an official letter to Ballinger, which he furnished to the press as he boarded the train to begin his 13,000-mile journey. Having examined the documents, Taft wrote, he had concluded that the Glavis charges embraced "only shreds of suspicion without any substantial evidence to sustain his attack." Though he believed that "Glavis was honestly convinced of the illegal character of the claims in the Cunningham group, and that he was seeking evidence to defeat the claims," the record revealed an inordinate delay on his part. The claimants were entitled to a speedy hearing, which was all the Interior Department had requested. As for the charges against Ballinger himself, it was clear that since becoming secretary, he had "studiously declined to have any connection whatever with the Cunningham claims." Glavis was aware of this fact, Taft charged, along with several other pieces of exculpatory evidence, but "in his zeal to convict," he had not provided "the benefit of information" that might place the suspect transactions in a different and more favorable context. A subordinate who believes "his chief is dishonest," Taft asserted, has a responsibility "to submit that evidence to higher authority"; an employee who levels charges founded only on "suspicions" and "fails to give to his chief the benefit of circumstances within his knowledge that would explain his chief's action as on proper grounds," however, can no longer be trusted. He therefore granted Ballinger's request for "authority to discharge Mr. Glavis" for disloyalty to his superior officers in "making false charges against them."

By his own standards of jurisprudence, the president's precipitous decision to declare Ballinger innocent and Glavis guilty was seriously flawed. Taft had provided Glavis no chance to respond to Ballinger's countercharges, or even to see the documents upon which they were based. He had judged Glavis guilty of "misrepresentation," "suppression," and "culpable delay," without "an opportunity to be heard in his own defense." The president of the United States had questioned the young investigator's integrity, condemned his character, and broadcast his severance from public service to the nation at large.

The press greeted the president's statement as a victory for Ballinger and a defeat for Pinchot, who had pushed Glavis forward. "The Ballinger adherents threw their hats in the air and shouted that it is all over," the *New York Tribune* reported. "The Pinchot camp remained grimly silent and muttered threats in strict confidence." Correspondents speculated that Pinchot's resignation was imminent. Yet the chief forester's departure was the last thing Taft wanted. He fully understood that the public would interpret Pinchot's exit as evidence of the administration's opposition to Roosevelt's conservation policies.

To forestall "hasty action" on Gifford Pinchot's part, Taft wrote him a warm, personal letter. "My Dear Gifford," he began, "I write this to urge upon you that you do not make Glavis' cause yours." His decision to uphold Ballinger and discharge Glavis, he explained, was reached only after a careful study of documents Pinchot had never seen and carried no adverse judgment on his chief forester; on the contrary, "I have the utmost confidence in your conscientious desire to serve the Government and the public," and "I should consider it one of the greatest losses that my administration could sustain if you were to leave it." When a public servant had been so "unjustly treated," as Ballinger, he wrote, "it is my duty as his chief, with the knowledge I have of his official integrity and his lack of culpability, to declare it to the public." In the name of "teamwork," he hoped Pinchot and the members of the Forestry Bureau would refrain from further public argument with the Interior Department. "It is most demoralizing," the president concluded, "and subversive of governmental discipline."

After several conferences with Taft, Pinchot agreed to remain at his post. The president, in turn, promised to issue a statement of support for Pinchot to counter the reigning impression that "in holding Ballinger up," he was condemning his chief forester. "Never at any time," Taft said, had he "intended to reflect upon Mr. Pinchot." He also authorized publication of an excerpt from his personal letter, in which he assured the forester that he would deem his resignation "one of the greatest losses" his administration could endure. Pleased that a temporary truce had been established, Taft was nevertheless apprehensive, certain that Pinchot remained "as fanatical" as ever "in his chase after Ballinger." He feared Pinchot had reached "a state of mind" that would "lead to a break" at some point. "He is looking for martyrdom," Taft told Wickersham, "and it may be necessary to give it to him; but I prefer to let him use all the rope that he will."

Taft's instincts were correct. Pinchot had no intention of relinquishing the fight. Indeed, he was already engaged in a conspiracy to deliver the Glavis report to leading muckraking magazines. "I have been thinking this miserable business over," Assistant Forester Overton Price had written Pinchot three days after the president's dismissal of Glavis, "and this is the way I see the thing. . . . First, the most effective publicity possible to the Glavis side, and the Garfield side, of the case, preferably, in a special issue of a clean national magazine. . . . Second, a congressional investigation with an honest man at the head of it. . . . Third, a President discredited by the people and by the man who made him President." Pierce promised that he would attend to all the work himself, without directly implicating Pinchot. "Don't let them cloud the issue by laying yourself open to any charge of direct insubordination. . . . I can do a great deal without getting fired; that isn't your job. You have got a much bigger job."

In the weeks that followed, Overton Price and Alexander Shaw, the Forestry Bureau's legal officer, spent many hours with Glavis, determining how best to publicize his allegations. Price and Shaw later conceded that "as employees of subordinate rank" in the Agricultural Department, they were engaged in highly "irregular" conduct. Nevertheless, they believed that by exposing the head of the Interior Department, they would forestall the "grave and immediate danger" of losing invaluable public lands. In September, Price and Shaw met for six hours with Garfield, "going over in detail" every aspect of the Glavis report. Shaw then aided Glavis to transform his bureaucratic report into an accessible and engaging publishable article. As they prepared the piece, the Forestry Bureau leaked more material to the press, stimulating further criticism of the interior secretary. Such machinations within his administration were not lost on William Taft. "Pinchot has spread a virus against Ballinger," he told Nellie, "and has used the publicity department of his bureau for the purpose. He would deny it, but I can see traces in his talks with many newspapermen on the subject, who assume Ballinger's guilt, and having convicted him treat any evidence showing that he is a man of strength and honesty as utterly to be disregarded."

In late October, Glavis was introduced to Norman Hapgood, the publisher of *Collier's*. Another magazine had offered $3,000 for the piece, but Glavis refused payment for work he considered a public duty. Hapgood "read the article that night and accepted it the next day," proceeding immediately with plans for publication. No attempt was ever made to contact Ballinger or anyone within the Interior Department to verify the details or documents underlying the allegations.

Published in *Collier's* on November 13, the Glavis article renewed "the newspaper frenzy" that had temporarily subsided in the aftermath of Taft's September statement. The piece was carefully phrased throughout; Glavis later claimed he never intended to depict Ballinger as venal—he simply wanted to stop the exploitation of Alaska coal lands. Yet the headline blatantly placed Ballinger at the center of a ring of corruption. "The Whitewashing of Ballinger," read the streamer. "Are the Guggenheims in Charge of the Department of the Interior?" Section headings within the article extended the implication: "A Leak in the Land Office," "Ballinger Pushes Trial When Government Is Not Ready," "The Alaska Coal Lands Are in Danger in Ballinger's Hands." The potential purchase of coal lands by the Morgan-Guggenheim syndicate, which was already in possession of vast copper mines, smelters, steamship lines, and railroads in the West, raised the specter that one company would control all "the natural resources of Alaska."

With this invocation of monopoly, "the muckrake periodical press took off in full cry." Glavis was likened to Ida Tarbell, a dogged investigator fighting to expose corruption at the highest levels. While some of the ensuing articles reflected serious research, others, as Roosevelt had warned in his celebrated rebuke of the "Muckrake Man," simply repeated the most sensational rumors as fact. A piece by John Matthews in *Hampton's* charged that Taft himself was "a party to the conspiracy." Citing "circumstantial evidence," Matthews concocted the tale of a deal purportedly conceived at the 1908 Republican Convention, which would allow J. P. Morgan "on behalf of the Morgan-Guggenheim combination to name the Secretary of the Interior," with the assurance that once Ballinger was in place, "the Alaska coal grants" would be approved.

Ballinger refused to give a detailed statement in response to such distortions and outright slander. Instead, he launched a virulent attack on "literary apostles of vomit," who "imagine they can invent calumnies and pure fabrications so rapidly as to preclude reply." He labeled Matthews's charges "so asinine" they did not merit a rejoinder. "I have felt so thoroughly conscious of the justice of my position," he told the editor of the *Spokesman-Review*, "that I have felt assured that the public would ultimately understand the truth without the necessity of my entering upon a campaign of publicity." Taft, too, shied from the controversy, maintaining that both Ballinger and Pinchot were committed to Roosevelt's conservation policies, despite their divergent approaches to carrying them out.

When Ballinger released his first annual report to Congress on November 29, the chorus of outrage seemed to still. The report displayed a liberal stance on every issue, garnering widespread praise from conservationists. Even Pinchot and Garfield conceded that Ballinger had come out "in favor of all the things we fought for." While Pinchot dismissed Ballinger's motivation as "the goodness of a bad boy recently spanked," he predicted that "the whole controversy will pass quietly away, with the net result that Ballinger is forced completely over on to the Conservation side," leaving "the Administration . . . stronger for Conservation than it otherwise would have been."

More than anyone, Taft wanted the contentious ordeal to end. Ballinger, however, saw only one route to restore his honor and reputation: a full congressional inquiry into the activities of both his department and the Forest Bureau. For months, he had silently gathered ammunition, evidence that not only vindicated his own actions but implicated Pinchot and his subordinates in manufacturing malignant attacks. Aware of Taft's reluctance, Ballinger told the president "that the situation had become intolerable to him." Unless Taft consented to a congressional investigation, he would resign.

Friends and family urged the president to accept Ballinger's resignation and move on, but Taft felt compelled to defend his beleaguered cabinet official. Aware that an inquiry would prolong the struggle, overshadow his legislative program, and potentially compromise his administration, he nevertheless insisted that he would be "a coward or a white-livered skunk" if he deserted "an honest man" who had been subjected to venomous newspaper attacks. He had hoped that "the whole affair was a tempest in a teapot which soon would simmer down." Instead, leaked information fueled sensational headlines. Faced with Ballinger's ultimatum, the president agreed to the request for a congressional probe.

On December 23, after a series of conferences at the White House, Richard Ballinger sent a letter to Washington State's Republican senator Wesley Jones, demanding a complete investigation into the charges leveled against him. He petitioned that "any investigation of the Interior Department should embrace the Forest Service," as there was "reason to believe that the pernicious activity of certain of its officers has been the inspiration of these charges." Later that day, Senator Jones introduced a resolution asking the government "to transmit to Congress any reports, statements, papers, or documents" relating to the Glavis charges and the president's letter of exoneration. A special investigative committee, comprising six members from each House, was convened.

Pinchot's supporters feared that "all the power of the administration" would be deployed to secure "a packed investigating committee," groomed from the start to "glaze over the evidence against Ballinger," punish members of the Forest Bureau for leaking government files, and discredit Pinchot "before the people." A Washington "insider" warned Robert Collier that he had acquired "secret information" suggesting that once the committee had "whitewashed" Ballinger, the interior secretary would sue *Collier's* "for a million dollars on the ground of slander." Collier called Pinchot, Garfield, Hapgood, and Henry Stimson, Garfield's legal adviser, to an "emergency council of war" in New York. They agreed that Glavis needed an experienced lawyer to represent him at the hearing. Hapgood suggested Louis Brandeis, the prominent Boston attorney (and future Supreme Court justice). *Collier's* proposed to pay the jurist $25,000 "to conduct the defense." Brandeis readily accepted, beginning at once to pore over thousands of pages of documents.

Gifford Pinchot pursued a more public defense, delivering a speech in New York that attracted unprecedented attention. Framing his struggle with Ballinger as a battle "between special interests and equal opportunity," the chief forester declared conservation "a moral issue," a question of social justice. "Is it fair that thousands of families should have less than they need, in order that a few families should have swollen fortunes at their expense?" he asked. Pinchot, Taft told Horace with grave irritation, was "out again defying the lightning and the storm." While Ballinger was "busily engaged" in the practical endeavor of "drafting laws" to protect the public lands from exploitation, Pinchot was "harassing the wealthy" and "championing the cause of the oppressed." The outcome of this battle within the administration was undecided, however. "Will Pinchot remain the St. George and Ballinger the dragon?" Taft worriedly mused. "I don't know. Let us see."

⌐ ⌐

IN JANUARY 1910, WITH THE congressional investigation imminent, the *National Tribune* reported that both "the Ballingerites and the Pinchotites" were stockpiling ammunition. The Pinchotites were initially expected "to be on the defensive," working to deflect evidence that the Ballinger camp had gathered "to prove them as plotting against the Interior Department and as furnishing material for the muckraking magazines." When the time came for Ballinger's cross-examination, however, the Pinchotites were projected to gain advantage. "It will be a hot old political time," the *Tribune* predicted, relishing the controversy. "It remains true today as it was in the days of [the Roman emperors]," *Current Literature* observed, "that a gladiatorial combat is the quickest way to ensure tremendous public interest."

Surmising that the Ballingerites would "bring out, piece by piece, various bits of testimony" to shine "the worst possible light" on the Forest Bureau's involvement with Glavis, Pinchot decided "to lay our hand on the table, tell in advance all the facts, and assign the exact reasons for everything that had been done." He requested a report from Price and Shaw detailing their involvement in the release of "official information" about Ballinger and the Cunningham case. On January 5, three weeks before the hearings, he transmitted their report, along with his own commentary, to Senator Dolliver, Republican chair of the Committee on Agriculture and Forestry. Pinchot acknowledged that Price and Shaw had violated "the rules of official decorum" but argued that "their breach of propriety" was insignificant in comparison with "the imminent danger that the Alaska coal fields still in government ownership might pass forever into private hands with little or no compensation to the public." Appeals through official channels had failed. A final petition to the White House had been derailed by Taft's "mistaken impression of the facts," resulting in his decision to remove Glavis, "the most vigorous defender of the people's interests." Both Price and Shaw had "acted from a high and unselfish sense of public duty," intentionally choosing "to risk their official positions rather than permit what they believed to be the wrongful loss of public property."

Archie Butt was with Taft when news of Pinchot's letter to Congress reached the White House. "One trouble is no sooner over in this office than another arises," Taft declared in frustration. Though he regarded the letter "as a piece of insubordination almost unparalleled in the history of the government," the president realized that by dismissing Pinchot, the man most pivotal in securing Roosevelt's conservation legacy, he risked alienating Roosevelt himself. "I believe [Taft] loves Theodore Roosevelt," Butt attested, "and a possible break with him or the possible charge of ingratitude on his part is what is writhing within him now." Taft told Butt that no decision "had distressed him as much." As he weighed the consequences that afternoon, he looked to Butt "like a man almost ill." Discussing the matter with his cabinet, Taft learned that Pinchot had not cleared his letter with his boss, Agriculture Secretary James Wilson. The president sent for Senator Root, who initially warned against firing Pinchot. An examination of the correspondence, however, changed Root's mind: "There is only one thing for you to do now, and that you must do at once," he advised. Later that night, Taft directed Wilson to fire Pinchot, Price, and Shaw.

"The plain intimations in your letter," Taft wrote Pinchot, "are, first, that I had reached a wrong conclusion as to the good faith of Secretary Ballinger." Yet Pinchot "had only seen the evidence of Glavis, the accuser," and had no knowledge of the documentary evidence submitted to the White House. "Second," the president continued, Pinchot suggested that without public exposure, "the Administration, including the President," would have patented "fraudulent claims" to Alaska's rich coal lands. "I should be glad to regard what has happened only as a personal reflection, so that I could pass it over and take no official cognizance of it. But other and higher considerations must govern me." The people "placed me in an office of the highest dignity and charged me with the duty of maintaining that dignity and proper respect for the office on the part of my subordinates. . . . By your own conduct you have destroyed your usefulness as a helpful subordinate."

After this painful decision, Butt reported, Taft "looked refreshed and even fairly happy." The Washington papers generally agreed that the president "could have followed no other course," for Pinchot's letter "was too flagrant an offense to be overlooked." Pinchot, one editorial suggested, was "suffering from the same malady that overtook Mr. Glavis, a swollen idea of his own importance." It seemed initially that Pinchot's dismissal would precipitate little furor. In fact, Taft's own message on conservation policy two weeks later garnered universal praise. "Quite as admirable a message as Mr. Pinchot could have written," pronounced the New York *World*. The *New York Tribune* found the address "peculiarly satisfactory," noting Taft's "specific and practical" promotion of "new legislation to govern the disposal of the public lands." It was evident from his tone, *The Outlook* agreed, that Taft remained fully committed to "the Roosevelt policies." Furthermore, the appointment of Henry Graves to replace Pinchot clearly demonstrated Taft's commitment to preserve the nation's forests. Graves, the head of the Yale School of Forestry, was "a personal friend of Mr. Pinchot" and a widely respected conservationist.

Theodore Roosevelt was in the Congo when a runner brought him news of Pinchot's dismissal. "I cannot believe it," he wrote Pinchot. "The appointment in your place of a man of high character, a noted forestry expert, in no way, not in the very least degree, lightens the blow." Roosevelt would refrain from any overt criticism of his successor, but he offered Pinchot his sincere support and hoped later to discuss the whole matter in detail. "I do wish that I could see you. Is there any chance of your meeting me in Europe?" Overjoyed to hear from Roosevelt, Pinchot decided to set off as soon as he had completed his testimony before Congress.

First, however, the former forester was determined to use the hearings to vindicate his actions and crush Richard Ballinger. After his dismissal, hundreds of supportive letters and telegrams arrived from across the country urging him to continue the fight. "The people have faith in you, by the million," one telegram read. Freed from the constraints of office and all duties as a sub-

ordinate, Pinchot became "general-in-command of the anti-Ballinger forces."
Together with Garfield and Collier, he spent hours with Louis Brandeis, helping to prepare Glavis for the witness stand and reading through the mass of
material provided by the administration for documents that would buttress
their case. Glavis handled himself well on the stand. The *National Tribune*
reported that he had presented his case "in the most convincing way." For
those anticipating fireworks, however, the early phase of the inquiry proved
"a keen disappointment." In the absence of hard evidence of corruption on
Ballinger's part, the investigation seemed to show "the existence of a quarrel
rather than a scandal."

Public interest in the hearings heightened when Gifford Pinchot took
the stand. He "opened with a heavy volley," flatly charging that Ballinger
had "been unfaithful to his trust, disloyal to the President and an intentional
enemy to the conservation policy." Had the interior secretary not been checked
by "the public clamor against him," invaluable public lands would have been
lost forever to the special interests. "The imperative duty before this country,"
Pinchot declared, "is to get rid of an unfaithful public servant." After this
impressive start, however, he failed to substantiate his dramatic charges. Taft
was relieved. "Pinchot has distinctly discredited himself by his thundering,"
he told Horace, "and then falling down altogether in respect to his specifica-
tions." Horace agreed that Pinchot had "proven nothing at all."

After Pinchot left the stand, the hearings became "so tedious," the *Arizona
Republic* editorialized, "that auditors are unable to remain awake." The public was quickly becoming bored with the complex issue and even with Louis
Glavis, "of whom it had never heard before and of whom perhaps it will never
hear again." The "waning interest," the paper predicted, would soon take
the controversy off the front page. "Besides the baseball season is fairly under
way," and "the public eye" is turning toward Reno, Nevada, where "The Battle
of the Century" was scheduled to take place: the heavyweight fight between
the challenger, African-American Jack Johnson, and the reigning champion,
Jim Jeffries.

Many years later, Louis Brandeis acknowledged that they had not unearthed anything "really decisive" at that point in the investigation. He returned once again to the mountain of documents that the Taft administration
had delivered to Congress. The committee had requested the data upon which
the president had based his September 13 decision to exonerate Ballinger and
dismiss Glavis, and Brandeis focused particularly on the attorney general's
85-page report, dated September 11. Brandeis read the detailed report "ten,
fifteen, twenty times," and "saw that it was not a hastily thrown together

patchwork but a carefully prepared unit," so meticulously compiled that it seemed unlikely to have been generated in the brief interval after Taft met with Glavis. Brandeis "was certain that something was wrong, but he had to prove it." In several instances, he finally discovered, the report referenced facts and events that were not known or did not take place until weeks after September 11. The administration was claiming a document that did not exist at the time as the basis for the president's decision.

Brandeis revealed his discovery to *Collier's* Norman Hapgood and asked the editor to come to the hearings on April 22. On that day, Brandeis called Ballinger's assistant Edward Finney to the stand. He had designed a line of questioning that would make Finney realize that the predating had been discovered and asked Hapgood to monitor the expression on Finney's face during the proceedings. At lunch, Hapgood confirmed that Finney had appeared cognizant of his peril; Brandeis sharpened his questions when the session resumed, finally introducing into the record incidents mentioned in the September 11 report that had not yet occurred. He intimated that the document had been prepared after the fact "to make it appear" as if Taft had possessed more substantial documentary evidence when he passed judgment. Prevented by the rules of the investigation from issuing a subpoena to Wickersham, Brandeis leaked the story to the press. Attorney General Wickersham initially refused comment but eventually wrote to Congress that he had, indeed, backdated the report.

As the *National Tribune* observed, backdating documents was common practice in government. Had administration officials acknowledged the actual chronology when they sent the documents to the Congress, "there probably would have been no unfavorable comment." Their failure to do so invited speculation that they had falsified records in a deliberate attempt to deceive Congress and the country. The revelation revived interest in the hearings, accentuating "an attitude of suspicion" toward Ballinger, Wickersham, and Taft himself.

IF THE LENGTHY WICKERSHAM REPORT had not served as the basis for Taft's decision, Brandeis queried, what did? It turned out that the lawyer had known the answer for months, though he had bided his time before springing his discovery of the Lawler memo. In February, Brandeis had met with twenty-four-year-old Fred Kerby, one of the two stenographers who had taken Lawler's dictation. After the publication of Taft's celebrated letter the previous September, Kerby had "noted the similarities between the two documents," recognizing sections with identical wording.

Kerby agreed to meet Garfield and Brandeis at Pinchot's house, where he recounted the facts about preparing the memo. He recalled that Lawler, "in constant consultation" with various interior officials, including Ballinger, had written and revised the memo a half-dozen times. It was midnight on Saturday when the final version was completed. The rough drafts were "laid in the grate and a match put to the pile." Lawler placed the final memo "in his brief case" and joined Ballinger in the secretary's carriage. The two men then drove together to the station, catching the "Owl" to New York, where Wickersham would receive the memo to bring to Beverly. Kerby, still employed at the Interior Department and newly married, "asked that, if possible, they avoid calling [him] to testify." Brandeis promised that he would try to "get the facts into the record through cross-examination of Ballinger and thus compel production of the Lawler document."

In early March, Brandeis sent a letter to the attorney general and the Interior Department, requesting production of "the so-called memorandum prepared by Mr. Lawler at the request of the President." Department officials claimed they had searched the files, but it could not be found. A second request in April met with a similar response. Brandeis suspected that they were deliberately withholding the memo, aware that it might cast a shadow on the fairness of Taft's decision to exonerate Ballinger and dismiss Glavis.

When Ballinger took the stand, Brandeis directed a series of questions designed to extract information about the Lawler memo. Brandeis noted that in Ballinger's opening statement he had failed to mention that Lawler had accompanied him to Beverly. When Ballinger claimed he did not consider it "of any material moment," Brandeis pressed him further, asking if it was "not a matter of moment in view of the part that [Lawler] subsequently played?" Ballinger continued his evasive responses as Brandeis turned his questions to the contents of his companion's briefcase. Under repeated questioning, Ballinger said that Lawler had "a grip with some clothes in it," but he wasn't sure what else it contained. Finally, he acknowledged that Lawler had brought the president a memorandum, covering "a sort of resume of the facts." Ballinger appeared intensely nervous as the cross-examination persisted, his foot beating "a restless tattoo on the floor." At one point, he turned in anger toward Brandeis, calling his line of questioning "an insult." Ballinger refused any further questions that bore on the president's actions.

Having "exhausted all channels" to introduce the Lawler memo, Brandeis returned to Fred Kerby. Fully aware that he would compromise his career, Kerby agreed to give a public statement describing the preparation of the memo. In his written statement, Kerby explained that he had known of

Lawler's instructions to prepare a memo which Taft could use as a draft for his own opinion. He identified "certain portions" of the president's published letter that had been drawn from Lawler's draft, though the passages he cited were not substantial. He never suggested that Lawler had actually dictated the president's letter. To the contrary, he said that the draft had been "specifically" prepared in triple space to leave room for revision. The headlines accompanying the young stenographer's statement told a different story, however: "Ballinger Accused of Preparing Taft's Letter of Exoneration," announced the *Washington Times*. "President's Statement Giving Secretary Clean Bill Almost Identical in Verbiage with Notes in Shorthand Note Book which was Ordered Destroyed."

When the story broke on the afternoon of May 14, Taft was on the golf course. Ballinger and Lawler went at once to Wickersham's office, where they suddenly "found" the missing Lawler memo and sent it to the committee. This unexpected discovery "a few minutes after the Kerby story was printed, will go down in history," the *Washington Times* charged, "as one of the most remarkable coincidences of all time." Few questioned Ballinger's immediate dismissal of Kerby, but the secretary was widely criticized for his venomous public statement that charged the young stenographer with "treachery" and claimed that he was "unworthy" of public trust.

On Sunday, Taft finally took up the matter personally. He wrote a public letter to Senator Knute Nelson, chair of the investigating committee, describing in full detail the circumstances under which he had prepared his September 13 letter. He acknowledged that he had, indeed, asked Lawler for a draft statement, but insisted that the resulting memo "did not state the case in the way [he] wished it stated." It was filled with criticisms of both Pinchot and Glavis, which the president "did not think proper or wise to adopt." In the end, while he found the references to the documents helpful, he incorporated only a few general statements. "The conclusions which I reached were based upon my reading of the record," Taft maintained, "and were fortified by the oral analysis of the evidence and the conclusions, which the attorney general gave me." Desiring to have a full record of the circumstances reach the public, he had asked Attorney General Wickersham to incorporate his findings into "a written statement," backdated to September 11 and filed with the record. Occupied with other matters, Wickersham had not completed his analysis and summary until late October.

The press praised both the president's "manly" assumption of responsibility for the predating of the attorney general's summary and his characteristic candor in narrating "the sequence of events from his meeting with Glavis to his exoneration of Brandeis." A line-by-line comparison of the Lawler memo and Taft's letter corroborated the president's testimony that he had used only a few "unimportant" statements from the memo. "There was absolutely nothing wrong," the *Chicago Record-Herald* observed, "in instructing a subordinate to prepare an opinion." Nor was it questionable to use that opinion as a first draft, as was "done every day in public and private offices." Nonetheless, the press generally agreed that "the people who had charge of the management of the Ballinger-Pinchot investigation for the administration" had "simply blundered to the limit." Why did Wickersham wait to acknowledge the predating "until he was cornered?" Why was Ballinger so evasive on the witness stand? Why was the Lawler memo initially withheld from the committee? Why did Wickersham go to such lengths to conceal it? Why, if Kerby simply stated the facts that Taft himself later acknowledged, did Ballinger "fly into a rage" and call him a traitor? Each incident "came as a startling revelation," observed the *San Antonio Light and Gazette*; taken together, they "shattered the last vestige of confidence in the good faith" of those involved. Many were also dismayed by the serial dismissals of those who opposed the administration: first Glavis; then Pinchot, Price, and Shaw; and now Kerby.

When the hearings came to a close in late May, "the puzzled, unsatisfactory verdict" was that Interior Secretary Ballinger had "done nothing illegal." *The Washington Post* observed that "not a single fact has been produced to show that he was even derelict in duty, much less corrupt." Yet, as dozens of editorials pointed out, that finding could not restore the public confidence he had lost. "Rightly or wrongly," a midwestern newspaper declared, "the great mass of the American people have come to look upon him with deep distrust."

Reflecting widespread sentiment, the *Indianapolis Star* called on Ballinger to resign. "His presence in the cabinet is a drag upon the administration," the *Emporia Gazette* concurred. "He cannot be blind to the extraordinary courage which his chief has displayed in standing by him." He should voluntarily lift "the burden" which the president had "carried long and unflinchingly." *The Outlook* asserted that Ballinger could no longer "be regarded as a trustworthy custodian" of the public lands.

An indignant Ballinger announced that he had no intention of stepping down. He had done nothing wrong and therefore was fully "justified in remaining at the head of his department." Charley Taft tried to convince his brother to let Ballinger go, but the president refused. "Life is not worth living and office is not worth having," Taft maintained, "if, for the purpose of acquiring the popular support, we have to do a cruel injustice or acquiesce in it." The press, he believed, had "unjustly persecuted" a good man. The storm of criticism had "broken" Ballinger's health. He looked two decades older than when he joined the cabinet. Taft deemed it his presidential duty to stand by his controversial interior secretary until Ballinger himself chose to leave.

Nine additional months would pass before the secretary decided to resign. During that time, Taft and Ballinger finally succeeded in securing congressional support for a measure granting the president legal authority to withdraw public lands from private development. Backed by the new law, Taft's withdrawals in four years "almost equaled that of Roosevelt" in seven. Conservationists hailed Taft's appointment of Walter Fisher, head of the National Conservation League, to replace Ballinger. "His entrance into the Government service will unquestionably meet with strong public approval," Gifford Pinchot said. "I speak with confidence for we have been working together for years."

The damage to the president's political fortunes had been done, however. While some respected the loyalty the president had shown to his cabinet secretary, progressives believed that Taft should have dismissed Ballinger at the first sign of unfaithfulness to conservation causes. A president had "no right," they argued, to put his own feelings above "the public welfare." The bitter struggle had consumed the attention of the country for more than a year. Reformers' faith in the president, already weakened by the tariff struggle, had plummeted. The split in the Republican Party appeared irreparable.

<hr />

"IS THE REPUBLICAN PARTY BREAKING UP?"—Ray Baker's provocative title— headlined the first in a series of influential articles in *The American Magazine* in the winter and spring of 1910, designed both to chronicle and aid the growing insurgent movement within the party. For nearly three weeks, Baker traveled through what he called "the skirmish lines in the Insurgent territory— Minnesota, Iowa, Kansas, Wisconsin and Indiana." He met with the rebels who had fought against the tariff and criticized Ballinger—Murdock of Kansas, Cummins and Dolliver of Iowa, La Follette of Wisconsin, Clapp of Minnesota. Plans were evolving to run insurgent candidates against conservative Republicans in every district, even if the intraparty struggle ended up rewarding Democrats.

By wresting power from the Old Guard, the progressives aimed to regulate the economy in the interests of the many as opposed to the interests of the few. Although Roosevelt had occasionally "dragooned" the Congress into supporting progressive policies through outside pressure, the party organization remained in conservative hands. Western insurgents intended to finish the job Roosevelt had begun. The conflict within the Republican Party was no longer regional. When Baker traveled to New England, which gave "at first a decided impression of political quietude," he discovered that insurgency, while less developed in the East than in the West, was "following close behind."

From New England, he proceeded to Washington, just in time to witness the insurgents' unexpected triumph over Speaker Cannon. After failing to unseat Cannon the year before, the insurgents had regrouped around a resolution to divest the Speaker of his autocratic grip on the party. Capitalizing on a moment during a sparsely attended all-night session, George Norris of Nebraska introduced a resolution to rescind the Speaker's authority to appoint the Rules Committee. Instead, the entire House would elect the members of this most powerful body. The long debate that followed was "tense and dramatic." Everyone understood that Joseph Cannon was "fighting the fight of his life for his political future and the integrity of the party machinery." On the afternoon of March 19, Cannon "met his Waterloo." Forty-three insurgent Republicans cooperated with 150 Democrats to pass the resolution. Though Cannon would retain his position, his reign would never again be absolute.

"A real revolution is underway," an emotional Baker told his father, "and it will not stop until government by trusts & special interests is wiped out." In the months that followed, Baker continued to popularize the progressive cause. In a "case study" of Rochester, New York, home of the theologian Walter Rauschenbusch, a towering figure in the Social Gospel movement, Baker "noted with pleasure the existence of a strong religious element working successfully within the reform movement." This progressive uprising gave John Phillips what he had long been searching for—a central focus for the magazine. "We are naturally the insurgent magazine," he told William Allen White, "and we want to make The American Magazine more and more expressive in this movement." He hoped that White would help sustain the movement for reform by following Baker's lead with a series of "vigorous, stirring" political articles. He encouraged White to do anything possible to make the magazine "the organ and mouthpiece of the great liberal movement. This seems to me our opportunity."

White responded immediately to Phillips's request. Kansas was host to a dramatic battle for control of the statewide party. As precinct leader and state committeeman, White had been lining up insurgent candidates to run against standpatters at every level. He believed the Republican Party was doomed unless it changed from within. White strove to vividly articulate for readers the insurgents' vision of what the Republican Party stood for, even as he endeavored to gain control of the political machinery—through the insti tution of direct primaries, the initiative, the referendum, and the recall. Only an informed and empowered populace could truly win the battle to regulate and control capital in the interests of the country as a whole.

Ida Tarbell, too, lent her "powerful pen" to the insurgent cause. Unlike White, she never engaged directly in politics. Profoundly disappointed by the Payne-Aldrich tariff, which she considered "as hopeless a failure as a tariff could well be," she embarked on a new series designed to reveal how "the same old circus, the same old gilded chariots, the same old clowns" had managed once again to hoodwink America. Her only solace, she later wrote, came from the "rousing challenge" Republican progressives had issued to the Old Guard. She was thrilled by their new style of debate, which, her colleague Ray Baker noted, replaced "the hazy generalities on the advantages of a protective tariff" with a detailed presentation of facts and evidence akin to the muckrakers' investigative skills. During the long legislative struggle, Tarbell asserted, these insurgents had "crystallized into one of the most vigorous and intelligent fighting bands that had been seen for many years in Congress." Their struggle would be fierce, she knew. Political pandering to special interests did not end with the tariff; the same intellect that "argues and fights for a Ballinger" is furious when a railroad rate is questioned and "can be counted on to support anybody's privilege." It was against these "ways of thinking," prevalent in every realm of life, that progressives were fighting.

John Phillips heralded Tarbell's critique of the recent tariff-making process with a trenchant editorial: "The popular judgment of the Payne-Aldrich Tariff Bill grows more severe with each passing month," his piece began. "It is a bogus revision, and every man of sense knows that we will get no permanent settlement of this matter until a genuine, searching, informed revision has been made. He knows that by shirking this duty the Taft Administration has lost the country years of time. Here is the real basis of the anti-Taft sentiment—the good reason for insurgency."

While united in their support of the insurgents, the magazine's team differed in their opinion of William Howard Taft. John Phillips had been ambivalent about the new president from the beginning. "I thought that Taft might stand still," the editor remarked in September 1909. "I didn't think he'd go backwards." Five months later, Phillips observed that disappointment with Taft had kindled a newfound respect for Roosevelt, even among those who had "opposed him." The fact that the former president had never even tried to revise the tariff nor spoken out once against Cannon's regime "mattered little to the insurgents." His "crusading spirit" trumped any details of his actual policy. Tarbell had been more hopeful about Taft at the start, but turned against him with a vengeance when he signed the flawed Payne bill and then compounded his mistake by proclaiming it the best tariff ever passed. "Taft is done for, I fully believe," she told White. "Not a man of discernment, but what shakes his head over him."

William Allen White was slower than his colleagues to abandon faith in the president, still hoping in the spring of 1910 that Taft would succeed in getting his legislative agenda through Congress. White reminded Taft that the insurgents had been his allies in the fight for regulatory reform and postal savings banks. "But they will not work with Senator Aldrich and Mr. Cannon," he warned. "So an unhappy situation has arisen. The people have begun to confuse you with the leadership." Taft responded to White as he did to previous suggestions that he break with the Republican leadership. The idea that he could make enemies of the men with power over the fate of his legislative program made no sense. "I have confidence in the second judgment of the people based on what is done rather than what is proclaimed or what is suspected from appearances," he asserted, "and if I can make good in legislation, I shall rely on fair discussion to vindicate me."

On May 21, 1910, three weeks before Theodore Roosevelt's scheduled return from his African adventure, President Taft invited William Allen White to lunch. News of the invitation sparked hope among insurgents, who felt Taft had "foolishly and needlessly linked his fortunes" with men and influences at odds with the need for action. If the president truly listened to White, he would realize that the best chance of securing his legislative program lay with the growing band of insurgents, not the regulars.

"I could not have asked more courtesy, more consideration, more cordial hospitality," White reported after the meeting. For the first time in months, Taft told White, Nellie "had come to the table at the White House." The first lady had listened with attention, although it seemed to White that she suffered from "a curious amnesia." The reporter repeatedly tried "to steer the conversation" toward the insurgency, but Taft refused to take the bait. The two men talked of art and architecture, of movements in Europe and "everything under the sun but politics." They moved to a sunny porch after lunch and continued to talk. "We had a most amiable time," White reported, but he departed with the dispiriting conviction that he had come on "a fool's errand."

Of all the journalists at that time, Ray Baker had the most profound understanding of Taft's character and personal style. In January 1910, as the Ballinger hearings were getting under way, he began research for a lengthy assessment of the embattled president. "I trust you are gathering some gorgeous material on Taft," Phillips wrote. "The time is getting ripe. Everybody comes in with the same story"—they sense that the White House is occupied by "a jelly fish" incapable of real leadership. "The material is rich, and is getting richer. Somebody is going to make a bomb out of it one of these days," the editor predicted; "we want to be the fellows in charge of the fireworks." Refusing to succumb to pressure, Baker in "The Measure of Taft" produced a remarkably balanced piece, which revealed the president's considerable strengths along with his troubling weaknesses.

He began by noting that despite the progressives' disenchantment, the people by and large regarded the president with warmth. "There is one thing of which no popular criticism of a public man can wholly rob us," Baker maintained, "and that is our own vivid personal impression of him. We like him, personally, or we don't like him." And the public liked Taft. They appreciated the simple pleasure he took in walking about town, stopping in stores to chat with proprietors, visiting friends in their homes and hotels. They applauded his decision to hold receptions for visiting schoolchildren. While congressmen complained that he was wasting too much time shaking hands with the never-ending groups that deluged Washington during Easter break, Taft was adamant: "If these young visitors want to see the President, it is virtually their right." People everywhere were taken with his humble and accessible manner. "A mighty cheer swept across the crowd" at the Nationals' ballpark when the president, "with his good, trusty right arm," threw out the first ball for the first time in history and then chose to sit with ordinary fans instead of heading for the presidential box. "All his life long, Mr. Taft has been thus impressing the men he met with the charm of his personality," Baker noted. "Men have liked him instinctively, and they have not only liked him, but they have admired and respected his high ideals."

But the same "personal charm" that had propelled Taft to the presidency ultimately proved "dangerous" to him, Baker concluded. For far too long, his amiable nature had kept him from the rough-and-tumble of politics, from the need to fight for himself and his convictions. Had he come into the White House when McKinley first arrived, "when the Republican party stood like the Rock of Gibraltar," he might have sailed through his term "with smiling serenity"; instead, he found himself embroiled in a war within his party that threatened to rupture friendships and divide families. "In a war," Baker proclaimed, "the chief thing is to *fight*." The temperate Taft was ill-equipped to take up arms.

The most alarming trait Baker discerned in the president was his inability to accept honest criticism. Taft acknowledged that twelve years on the bench, the one place relatively "free from severe criticism by the press," had done little to prepare him for the onslaught from newspapers and magazines. Rather than accept that "criticism may spring from an honest difference in principles," the president sought to discredit the publications, implying that their critiques sprang from self-interest or malice. They were angry at him, he insisted, for proposing to increase second-class postal rates and for failing to lower the tariff on wood pulp, both measures that would hurt their bottom line.

Taft's loyal supporters further amplified this defensive, even paranoid stance toward the press. One proponent argued that the magazine writers had been "arrayed against" the administration "from the first," disseminating poison with their insidious literary tricks. This diatribe drew a powerful response from Sam McClure. Though McClure's empire was merely a "skeleton" of what it had once been, his words still carried weight. "In the first place," McClure argued, "the administration did not have the magazines against it from the start." On the contrary, the press was "eager to support him." Indeed, *McClure's* had sent George Kibbe Turner, one of its best writers, to the White House to conduct a wide-ranging interview with the president. The resulting piece, which attracted a large readership, was presented entirely in Taft's words, affording him an open platform to explain his views on every contentious subject. "I have trained most of the successful writers, on public questions, for the magazines in this country, and I know their methods and their quality as probably no other man living," McClure justifiably stated; no journalists could be found who "write with greater sincerity or who are more eager to get the truth." Taft's troubles, McClure concluded, stemmed from his own actions: first, the tariff and the Winona speech had spread across the landscape "like a frost"; then "the Alaska business" had begotten the president's relentless defense of Ballinger, "an unnecessary struggle against the people's wishes."

Roosevelt had learned little of Taft's troubles while he was in Africa. He had received an earful from Gifford Pinchot, however, when the latter came to see him on the Italian Riviera in mid-April. Pinchot arrived at Roosevelt's villa in the early morning, remained for lunch, and then accompanied the former president on a long trek over the Maritime Alps. Months earlier, Pinchot had enumerated Taft's failings in a letter, condemning the new president's decision to surround himself with corporate lawyers, his alliance to Cannon and Aldrich, his surrender of executive powers to Congress, and, most damningly, his appointment of Richard Ballinger. "We have fallen back down the hill you led us up," Pinchot had written, "and there is a general belief that the special interests are once more substantially in full control of both Congress and the Administration."

Pinchot carried with him a half-dozen letters from fellow progressives, all confirming his own estimate of Taft. Senator Dolliver spoke with sadness of his "disappointment" that the president had "lost the opportunity and wasted the prestige" Roosevelt had bequeathed him, warning that the corporate tyranny would triumph "unless a way could be found to overthrow the present management in Congress which is now the guardian of the President's opinions." Albert Beveridge provided a devastating narrative of Taft's first year as president. "The people at first received the President with good expectations," he informed Roosevelt, "then with tolerance, then with faint distrust, then with silent opposition and now with open and settled hostility." More telling than such general criticisms, however, was Pinchot's personal story of his acrimonious struggle with Ballinger. "We had one of the finest talks we have ever had," Pinchot eagerly relayed to Jim Garfield. Reporters, noting Pinchot's smile when he returned to his hotel, declared that "no event in Roosevelt's entire trip" held more political significance than this day-long conference.

In a grim letter to Henry Cabot Lodge that same day, Roosevelt expressed his first open disappointment in the course of his successor's presidency: "You do not need to be told that Taft was nominated solely on my assurance to the Western people especially, but almost as much to the people of the East, that he would carry out my work unbroken; not (as he has done) merely working for the same objects in a totally different spirit, and with . . . a totally different sense from that in which both I and the men who acted under my word understood it." Many now believed, Roosevelt lamented, that he had "deceived them." Still, "a good chance" remained that Taft could recover. "Everybody believes him to be honest, and most believe him to be doing the best he knows how." But for the moment at least, the former president would follow the course Lodge had prescribed and "keep absolutely still about home politics."

In preparation for Roosevelt's mid-June homecoming, Ray Baker wrote an ominous speculative piece entitled "The Impending Roosevelt." "As the fight deepens both sides are seen listening sharply for the first clashing sounds of the returning warrior," Baker noted. "He is more popular now than he was when he sailed for Africa." Despite his absence from the political scene for over a year, Theodore Roosevelt remained "the most interesting, amusing, thrilling figure in America." Would he endorse the Taft administration? Would he join the insurgent rebellion? "One thing may be set down as absolutely certain," Baker concluded. "Roosevelt will act. Roosevelt always acts. . . . And when he acts no stage smaller than that of the nation will serve him; he is of continental size."

"The Parting of the Ways"

This "Bronco Buster" cartoon illustrates the jolt
Roosevelt received when Democrats made huge gains
in the 1910 midterm elections.

THE PROSPECT OF THEODORE ROOSEVELT'S return to American soil on June 18, 1910, left William Howard Taft fraught with anxiety. He was perplexed, he confided to Archie Butt, why Roosevelt had never once written to him during his travels. The letter Butt had hand-delivered as the former president left for Africa in March 1909 more than a year earlier remained unanswered. Roosevelt had never acknowledged the farewell gift that accompanied the letter. Butt, who had helped Taft choose the present—a gold ruler extendable to eight inches at one end, with a pencil affixed to the other—was bewildered. "There is no doubt that he received it?" Taft asked. "None whatever," Butt assured him. "I gave it to him, and he held it up for the press men to see and sent his thanks by me and said he would answer it on his way over."

Unaccountably, a copy of a telegram from Roosevelt to Taft, written aboard the SS *Hamburg* on the day he sailed, remains in Roosevelt's own papers. "Am deeply touched by your gift and even more by your letter," Roosevelt had written. "Everything will surely turn out all right, old man." Perhaps, Butt speculated, "Roosevelt did write and gave the letter to someone to mail," who then kept it "as a souvenir." Perhaps Taft, expecting a letter, had forgotten receipt of the telegram. Either way, Taft waited stubbornly for the Colonel to reciprocate the correspondence and was deeply hurt when no letter came.

The lack of communication between the two men became public when Taft was forced to deny a newspaper report that Roosevelt had sent him a letter strongly endorsing the accomplishments of his administration. Upon further questioning, Taft had to admit that, in fact, he had "received no letters" from Roosevelt over the past year and a quarter. This was particularly striking, the *Indianapolis Star* noted, since "the colonel has kept up a pretty steady correspondence with many other persons." Indeed, all social connection between the two families seemed to have cooled. Taft found it hard to understand why Edith Roosevelt had remained "singularly silent during all the time of his wife's illness."

Taft was not the only party harboring hurt feelings. Roosevelt was angered by reports from home suggesting that family members had not been accorded proper treatment from the White House under Mrs. Taft. Edith complained that although eighteen-year-old Ethel had been invited to a garden party during a visit to Washington, the first lady apparently had not done enough to recognize her. Alice and Nick Longworth had received a number of dinner invitations, but Alice felt slighted, believing she should have been asked to greet the guests at the head of the receiving line. The haughty young woman interpreted such minor omissions as a deliberate intent on the first lady's part "to let the setting sun know its place." The Roosevelt children, Butt observed, were convinced that Taft occupied the presidency "solely as a result of their father's predetermination to put him there," placing the new president and his first lady under a special obligation to the entire Roosevelt family. Taft fully appreciated the central role Roosevelt had played in his election, but felt that he had done all he could, given Nellie's serious illness, to accommodate the family. "Everything which is done by either side is misconstrued," Archie Butt told his sister-in-law; the fact that such "petty personal jealousies" could tarnish the long-standing friendship between Roosevelt and Taft seemed to him inexplicable. Further aggravating matters, Roosevelt could not fathom why no "word of welcome" from the White House awaited him when he came out of the jungle and met with scores of correspondents and friends in Khartoum.

When Taft finally decided at the end of May to swallow his pride and write once more to Roosevelt, he described the painful calamity of Nellie's collapse openly. Her inability to speak, he confided, had been "nearly complete" for a prolonged period, requiring that everyone be "as careful as possible to prevent another attack." While she had slowly recovered her physical strength, Taft explained, a year later Nellie still could only "speak a formula of greeting" at large receptions. Dinners and social events that called for conversation had to be circumvented. On the political front, he acknowledged that "the Garfield Pinchot Ballinger controversy" had brought him "a great deal of personal pain and suffering," but he preferred not to "say a word" about the complex dispute. "You will have to look into that wholly for yourself," he told Roosevelt, "without influence by the parties if you would find the truth." Despite these personal and political difficulties, Taft hoped that his old friend would soon find time for an extended visit to the White House.

Concerned that his letter might not reach Roosevelt before he sailed from Europe, Taft made the decision to send Archie Butt to meet the *Kaiserin* in New York, where he might deliver a duplicate copy, along with a shorter note of welcome. To placate any wounded egos, Butt suggested to the president that Nellie also write her own note to Edith. That accomplished, Butt ventured, "you and Mrs. Taft have left nothing undone." If Edith, "not understanding Mrs. Taft's condition," did not feel that enough consideration had been given to her children, then this kindly explanatory note would straighten out the perceived neglect. To Butt's delight, Nellie agreed, though he privately worried that "when women get at cross purposes it is hard to get them straightened out again."

As an official representative of the president, Archie Butt was among the first to board the *Kaiserin*. "Oh, Archie, but this is fine," Roosevelt said, warmly clasping the hand of his former military aide. Archie dutifully delivered Taft's two letters to Roosevelt, explaining that the first was a duplicate of one previously sent, and the second a note of welcome. Roosevelt said he had received and answered the first letter just before setting sail from England, but opened the second one at once and read it through. "Please say to the President that I greatly appreciate this letter and that I shall answer it later," he replied. Butt then told Roosevelt about Nellie's stroke "and how she dreaded to see anyone whom she had known in the past." He trusted his account would explain why the first lady had not entertained the Roosevelt clan more expansively. Roosevelt said only "that he had heard much that had distressed him."

When Edith Roosevelt came in, Archie presented her with Nellie's letter, which she quickly tucked into her handbag. Distracted by the arrival of Alice and Kermit, Edith seemed to forget the correspondence—an oversight confirmed in a subsequent conversation with Archie Butt. Inviting Archie to Oyster Bay in July, Edith pointedly quipped, "if the master will let you off," adding, "Remember me to the President although you brought me no word." Archie reminded her that he had given her a letter; "she looked startled for a minute," only then recalling the note in her handbag. "Of course I will answer it," she recovered. "I appreciate it even if it has come a little bit late."

Archie caught the midnight train from New York and reached Washington in time for breakfast with Taft, providing a full account of his interactions with the Roosevelts. "I feel it is due largely to you that yesterday has passed off as it has," Taft said. "I want you to know that I am grateful." Butt learned that when Taft came back from his trip to Villanova the previous night, he had found Roosevelt's response to his first letter. In Butt's judgment, the response was "courteous," though it lacked the warmth that had characterized the friendship between the two men. "I am of course much concerned about some of the things I see and am told," Roosevelt wrote, "but what I have felt it best to do was to say absolutely nothing." Several days later, Taft received a second letter from Roosevelt thanking him for his "kind and friendly words of welcome." Nonetheless, he still avoided any commitment to a visit with his old friend. "Now, my dear Mr. President," Roosevelt wrote, "your invitation to the White House touches me greatly, and also what Mrs. Taft wrote to Mrs. Roosevelt. But I don't think it well for an ex-President to go to the White House, or indeed to go to Washington, except when he cannot help it." Overall, the feel of the letter disheartened both Taft and Butt. Former presidents, of course, frequently returned to the capital.

TAFT'S DISTRESS OVER ROOSEVELT'S COOLNESS was temporarily dispelled a week later by the nearly complete triumph of his administration's legislative agenda. Even in the face of intense "factional wrangling," the 61st Congress produced a splendid record, passing "more general legislation than any preceding session for many years." There had been many "dark days" during the winter and spring, the *New York Tribune* remarked, when almost everyone "lost faith" in the president's "ability to control and lead the dissident forces he had been called upon to command." Surprising many, the insurgents and the regulars had come together to enact a series of "strongly progressive" laws. "Taft a failure? Taft not effective?" one editorial remarked, aping the rhetoric of skepticism that had plagued Taft early on. "We never had such a towering wood pile of work from the congressional saw mill."

A new railroad bill bolstered the power of the Interstate Commerce Commission to initiate action against rate hikes, created a "special Commerce Court" to expedite judgments, and brought telegraph and telephone companies under the authority of the Interstate Commerce Act. These provisions strengthened federal control of railway rates, the historic program Roosevelt had begun. Publicizing campaign contributions both before and after congressional elections was mandated; individual statehood for Arizona and New Mexico granted; a Bureau of Mines created to improve the hazardous conditions in the mining industry; and money appropriated for the Tariff Board "to ascertain the difference in the cost of production, at home and abroad."

Passage of the postal savings bank bill, granting people of small means (who had generally hoarded their cash in fear of bank runs) the guarantee of the U.S. Treasury, was considered Taft's "crowning achievement." For nearly four decades, the big banks, stirring the specter of socialism, had defeated the idea of post office banks. "I am not in favor of having the government do anything that private citizens can do as well or better," Taft had repeatedly argued during his transcontinental trip the previous fall, but "the laissez-faire school, which believes that the government ought to do nothing but run a police force," had long fallen out of favor. When the bill finally passed, Taft declared, "I am as pleased as Punch," proudly touting it as "one of the great Congressional enactments. It creates an epoch."

The insurgents rightly took credit for adding amendments that improved each of these laws, but Taft deserved equal praise for corralling support from "Old Guard" Republicans, who at last fulfilled the promises they had made during the bitter tariff fight to support the rest of his legislative program. "When people come to write history fifty years from now," a *New York Times* reporter observed, "they might give credit to the worth of a plain-minded gentleman whose head wasn't thoroughly filled from the beginning with himself, but who really and honestly tried to enact into legislation the things he himself had written into his party's platform." Charley Taft was delighted by his brother's legislative success, writing to tell him, "I always had faith that it would come out that way, but it is a satisfaction to see it in black and white. . . . The record is immense; the accomplishments are tremendous."

Accompanied by Archie Butt and several of his cabinet members, Taft went to the president's room in the Senate on Sunday night, June 26, to sign the remaining bills before Congress adjourned. Members of both Houses "congratulated him on the fact that the measures on which he had been most insistent had been passed." He was "in a jovial mood," the *Washington Times* reported, "and seemed greatly pleased with the way the session was ending." Happy for his chief, Archie noted that "the only incident which marred the closing hours" was that not a single insurgent senator "came in to pay his respects or to say good-bye." Particularly in light of the party's legislative success, Taft was baffled by their continued hostility over the tariff struggle and the Ballinger-Pinchot episode. When the president had finished signing, he told Butt he was not ready to return to the White House, asking him to prepare the car "to take a joy ride." Soon, Archie wrote, they were "humming through the Soldiers' Home and down through the park." The following day, tired but happy, Taft left for his home in Beverly, where Nellie had settled for the summer.

UNLIKE TAFT, ROOSEVELT WAS INCAPABLE of extended periods of leisure; he rested at Sagamore Hill for a single day before heading to Manhattan to take up his duties as contributing editor to the weekly public affairs magazine *The Outlook*. Before leaving for Africa, he had signed a $12,000 annual contract with the publisher, Dr. Lawrence Abbott. *The Outlook* had appointed a three-room suite for Roosevelt: an office for his secretary, a waiting room for visitors, and a private room for the Colonel. Through a hidden wall, Roosevelt could escape to a side elevator without entering the main hall. Overall, the suite's "mahogany furniture, polished floors, and rich rugs" provided a "magnificence unusual for an office building."

Sorting through the 5,000 letters he had received during his absence, Roosevelt issued a statement expressing his "very real gratitude" to the many letter writers, along with his "real regret" that he could answer only "a small proportion." Asked by the newspapermen when he would comment on the current political situation, he declared that he would "not make a speech for two months" and that even then, his commentary would be "non-political." Indeed, he insisted, "I don't know that I will ever make a political speech again." Would he care to qualify that statement? one reporter queried. "Yes," Roosevelt laughingly said. "I won't say never."

And indeed, before a week had passed, Roosevelt had broken his resolve in dramatic fashion. Encountering New York governor Charles Evans Hughes at his thirtieth Harvard Reunion, Roosevelt was soon talking animatedly about how he could offer political support. Their discussion, observers noted, was "marked by frequent gestures"; Roosevelt repeatedly "brought his clenched fist down on the palm of his other hand." Throughout his governorship, Hughes had fought the party bosses, finally deciding to accept Taft's proffer of a Supreme Court seat rather than run for another term; but before leaving office, he hoped to pass a historic bill shifting the power of nomination from the party machine to the people. After listening to Hughes, Roosevelt impetuously agreed to back the governor's direct primary bill.

To substantiate his pledge, Roosevelt sent a telegram to the New York County Committee chair, Lloyd Griscom, roundly endorsing the direct primary bill. "I believe the people demand it," he maintained, and "I most earnestly hope that it will be enacted into law." With this action, Roosevelt "plunged into the very thick of the political controversy." He had taken "the helm and become the State leader in the approaching campaign." The Colonel's advocacy, the *New York Tribune* editorialized, "is likely to prove the most potent factor in determining the fate of that measure."

During Roosevelt's reemergence into the political arena, he carefully limited his contact with William Howard Taft. After spending the night at Henry Cabot Lodge's summer home in Nahant, Massachusetts, a small town only ten miles from Beverly, Roosevelt, most likely at Lodge's suggestion, called on the president at the Summer White House. Archie Butt and Secret Service agent Jimmy Sloan were on the porch when the big touring car carrying Roosevelt and Lodge arrived. Hearing the commotion, the president came outside. "Ah Theodore, it is good to see you," he said. "How are you, Mr. President," Roosevelt replied. "This is simply bully." Taking hold of Roosevelt's shoulders, Taft implored him to drop the formal title, but Roosevelt refused: "You must be Mr. President," he insisted, "and I am Theodore." Taft took Roosevelt's arm and led him to a wicker table on the veranda overlooking the water.

But despite Taft's efforts to revive their former cordiality, the atmosphere remained "strained," Archie Butt lamented. When the butler took drink orders, Roosevelt, who rarely drank anything stronger than wine, blurted out that "he needed rather than wanted a Scotch and soda." Assuming that the president and the Colonel would wish to talk in private, Butt was informed by Lodge that Roosevelt did not want "to be left alone with the President." Taft tried to set Roosevelt at ease, assuring him that he would "do all in his power" to help pass the direct primary bill in New York. When Nellie and Helen Taft joined the group, Roosevelt, aware of Nellie's condition, refrained from directing any questions to her. To alleviate the awkwardness, Taft asked Roosevelt to share stories about his recent encounters with the European kings and queens. Roosevelt happily obliged, regaling the little group with an hour of anecdotes until it was time to leave.

As Roosevelt and Lodge prepared to depart, Lodge proposed that they agree upon a statement for the swarm of two hundred journalists anxiously waiting for them at the gate. If the president did not object, Roosevelt suggested, he would simply say it had been "a most delightful afternoon." Taft readily agreed. "With nothing on which to hang a story," Archie Butt later observed, the reporters used their imaginations to concoct a compelling tale. "From beginning to end it was a love feast," one account ran; the warmth of their meeting was proof "that their friendship is of the stuff that endures," said another. "Just Like Old Times," the *New York Times* reported, fancifully adding that "for a full minute," the two old friends stood "with hands upon each other's shoulders, while evident delight shone in every line of their smile." The continuing "peals of laughter" and "slaps on the back," the *Times* concluded, made it abundantly clear that "rumors of coolness between them" were unfounded. Both men knew that such a convivial encounter was far from the truth. The self-conscious meeting had painfully exposed the widening rupture in their once intimate friendship. The *Times* did, however, get one detail right: when Roosevelt was asked when he intended to return for a second visit, he replied, "I don't know that I shall."

UNPLEASANT NEWS GREETED ROOSEVELT WHEN he got back to Sagamore Hill. That afternoon, the boss-controlled New York Senate, "in swift and emphatic fashion," had defeated the direct primary bill. "It is Mr. Roosevelt who is beaten," declared the New York *World*, while the *New York American* exulted that "for the first time in seven years the triumphant career of Theodore Roosevelt has had a serious backset." *The Literary Digest* predicted that "those who know the Colonel have little doubt" that such a "slap in the face" would propel him "back into the arena prepared for war." The prognosticators proved correct. "They made the fight on me," Roosevelt declared, "and I've got to vindicate myself."

Not surprisingly, Roosevelt's path to achieving vindication pitted him directly against the Old Guard Republican bosses who controlled the state machine. Fearing that reactionary forces would dominate the state convention that fall, Lloyd Griscom urged Roosevelt to run for the post of temporary convention chair. More powerful than its name suggested, the temporary chairman would deliver the keynote speech, exert influence over the platform, and play an important role in nominating the party's slate of candidates. A longtime acquaintance of Taft's, Griscom shortly afterward informed the president that Roosevelt had agreed to run. "It did not occur to me that any one would oppose" Roosevelt's candidacy, Taft later said. At Griscom's request, he sent a telegram to Vice President James Sherman the next day. The conservative New Yorker had been the party's choice, not Taft's, for the second spot. Taft instructed Sherman by telegram to tell the party bosses that they must avoid division at all costs, urging them to hold "a full conference" with Roosevelt and make "reasonable concessions with reference to platform and candidates."

Not until the following day did Taft learn that the Old Guard had decided to run its own candidate. Sherman attempted to enlist Taft's support behind an alternative candidate, such as Elihu Root. "Don't you know," Sherman cautioned, "that [Roosevelt] will make a speech against you and the Administration, and will carry the convention and prevent an endorsement, and take the machinery out of the hands of your friends?" When asked where he would "stand in such a fight," Taft momentarily wavered. Instead of using his influence to prevent opposition to Roosevelt, he simply said he should not be dragged into the battle. During the formal meeting of the Republican State Committee the next day, the bosses proposed the vice president as their candidate for temporary chair. With this clever move, they insinuated that Sherman had the backing of the administration. Griscom, who had not expected the vote that day, was taken aback. As a result, the panel chose Sherman by a 20–15 vote.

When Roosevelt received the news at the *Outlook* office, "he fumed and refused to believe the report." Later that afternoon, he issued a statement openly aligning himself with the progressive faction against the machine. "He was glad," he wrote, that the "State leaders had taken the course they did because it showed that he had tried to bring about harmony, and having failed to do so, he was now able to go in and fight for all he was worth." Indeed, he threatened he would take the fight to the floor of the convention, where the delegates had the power to overturn the committee choice. Bravado notwithstanding, Roosevelt was distressed by the newspaper reports. "Old Guard Is Jubilant," blared the *New York Times*. "The prestige of the former President has received several hard knocks" in the weeks since his return, the *Times* added, but this was "the heaviest blow yet."

When reports spread that Taft had conspired with the party bosses to bring about his defeat, Roosevelt was incensed. Apparently, several committee members had changed their votes after being erroneously told that Taft had endorsed Sherman's candidacy. As word reached the president that Roosevelt was planning to make a statement charging him "with treachery," Taft was beside himself. Unable to sleep, he would wander downstairs each morning at 5 a.m. to glean the latest from the newspapers. "No one knows just what

Mr. Roosevelt is going to do," Archie Butt observed, "and everyone about Beverly seems to be sitting over a volcano except the news paper men—and they, of course, fatten on what kills other people."

Though reluctant to respond to newspaper stories, Taft finally decided to issue a formal statement flatly denying that he had "ever expressed a wish to defeat Mr. Roosevelt" or "taken the slightest step to do so." On the contrary, he had sent the telegram to the New York leaders urging "the necessity for the fullest conference with Mr. Roosevelt." He was "indignant" to find that his request had been ignored. The *Washington Herald* reported that Roosevelt "was very glad to see President Taft's statement."

"As the waters of excitement recede," Butt reported to his sister-in-law, Clara, "it is evident that the last few days have left their permanent mark on the President. He looks ten years older." Taft admitted that he was "profoundly grieved" to learn that Roosevelt had thought, even for a moment, that he was capable of such treachery. "His whole attitude toward me since his return has been unfriendly," he told Archie, complaining that if Roosevelt felt disappointed, "the proper thing for him to have done was to give me the opportunity to explain my position and to thrash it out as we had done many times in the past." Archie Butt himself was equally disconsolate, fearing that the incident had further diminished the chances for reconciliation. "They are now apart," he lamented, "and how they will keep from wrecking the country between them I scarcely see."

LATE THAT SUMMER, COLONEL ROOSEVELT boarded a private railroad car secured by *The Outlook* to begin a three-week speaking tour through sixteen states, including Kansas, Nebraska, the Dakotas, and Minnesota. As he headed west for his first public appearances since returning from Africa, one political question was on everyone's mind: "On which side will the Colonel now align himself? What changes have taken place in his philosophy?" A resounding answer came on August 31, in Osawatomic, Kansas, as Roosevelt spoke at a ceremony dedicating the John Brown Memorial Park. The festive occasion, which brought more than 30,000 people, resembled that of "a county fair," with fireworks, a drum and fife corps, vendor booths, and food stands. Climbing onto a kitchen table that doubled as a speaking platform, Roosevelt delivered the most radical speech he had ever made, placing him ipso facto in "the front rank" of the insurgent forces. Entitled "The New Nationalism," the speech had gone through several drafts, with language and ideas provided by Gifford Pinchot, William Allen White, and *The New Republic* editor Herbert Croly, whose recent book, *The Promise of American Life*, had attracted Roosevelt's attention.

"The New Nationalism puts the national need before sectional or personal advantage," Roosevelt proclaimed. Such an approach, he explained, "regards the executive power as the steward of the public welfare. It demands of the judiciary that it shall be interested primarily in human welfare rather than in property." While he still stood for "the square deal," he now recognized that "fair play under the present rules of the game" was not enough; the rules themselves had to be "changed so as to work for a more substantial equality of opportunity and of reward for equally good service."

For this generation, Roosevelt maintained, "the struggle for freedom" demanded a fight for popular rule against the special interests. Though "every special interest is entitled to justice," he declared, "not one is entitled to a vote in Congress, to a voice on the bench, or to representation in any public office." To drive these "special interests out of politics," he called for the direct primary and for laws forbidding corporations from directly funding political objectives. "Every dollar received should represent a dollar's worth of service rendered—not gambling in stocks," Roosevelt further contended, calling for both an income tax and an inheritance tax on large fortunes. Finally, he pressed for new laws regulating child labor and women's work, enforcing better working conditions, and providing vocational training. "No matter how honest and decent we are in our private lives," he concluded, "if we do not have the right kind of law and the right kind of administration of the law, we cannot go forward as a nation."

As the crowd thundered its approval, Kansas governor Walter S. Stubbs jumped on the table. "My friends," he exclaimed, "we have just heard one of the greatest pronouncements for human welfare ever made. This is one of the big moments in the history of the United States!" Seated amid the emotional crowd, Gifford Pinchot was overjoyed, later declaring to Roosevelt that he was "the leader to whom all look." Headlines in progressive papers trumpeted Roosevelt's "Advanced Insurgent Stand," suggesting that the insurgent movement would now be "materially strengthened." During the remainder of his western tour, Roosevelt was repeatedly greeted with "frenzied applause" and "overpowering demonstrations of affection and devotion." No man in the present generation, one reporter suggested, "has ever been honored with so magnificent a tribute."

Whereas westerners ecstatically embraced Roosevelt's new radical stance, easterners reacted with "consternation and horror." The New York *Sun* called the New Nationalism doctrine "more nearly revolutionary than anything that ever proceeded from the lips of any American who has held high office in our Government." Conservative commentators warned against "this new Napoleon," who threatened to destroy the constitutional separation of powers. Steering clear of such incendiary labels, moderate and even some liberal Republicans criticized Roosevelt for making only "slight mention" of the president during his strenuous tour, regarding "his silence" as a "most adroit form of attack," ultimately designed to diminish Taft and raise his own prospects for 1912.

Reading reports of Roosevelt's speeches, Taft was genuinely disturbed. "He is going quite beyond anything that he advocated when he was in the White House," he told his brother Charley, "and has proposed a program which it is absolutely impossible to carry out except by a revision of the Federal Constitution. He has attacked the Supreme Court which came like a bolt out of a clear sky, and which has aroused great indignation throughout the country on the part of conservatives." Writing in a similar vein to Horace, he reported that Roosevelt's "wild ideas" had "frightened every lawyer" and startled every decent "conservative" in the East. Horace was saddened to see lines being drawn that positioned his brother "on the other side of the fence" from moderate progressives, making it seem as if he were defending the Old Guard and expounding the "kind of politics" he had always fought against. While Taft's positions had not materially changed since his days as a cabinet officer, Horace worried that many "good men fighting against machine politics" now regarded him as a member of the opposition.

Taft believed that with each "riotous reception" Roosevelt received, "his reasons for thinking I would not do as a candidate in 1912" had multiplied. "His present mental condition," he told Horace, "rejects me entirely and I think he occupies his leisure time in finding reasons why he is justified in not supporting me." He had heard from several sources, he told Charley, that Roosevelt was still angry over the fact that "I dared to include you in the same class with him as assisting me in my canvass for the presidency. I venture to think that swell-headedness could go no further than this." Gossipmongers exacerbated Taft's concerns, reporting letters they had seen in which Roosevelt described him as utterly unfit for the presidency, suggesting that he must be challenged for the nomination.

Archie Butt watched and worried as Taft's bitterness toward his predecessor grew; loyal to both men, Archie found the prospect of an open rupture heartbreaking. Taft sympathized with his aide's dilemma, observing, "I know how it distresses you, Archie, to see Theodore and myself come to the parting of the ways." Recognizing that it pained Archie to listen to conversations critical of Roosevelt, Taft greatly admired the "dignified silence" he maintained. "Your silence will never be misconstrued by me," Taft promised. With each passing month, he had come to rely more and more on Archie. "He told me," Archie recorded in September, "that he always loved to see me come and hated to see me go." Archie's reflections make clear that this feeling was reciprocated. "In many ways," Archie wrote, "he is the best man I have ever known, too honest for the Presidency, possibly, and possibly too good-natured or too trusting or too something on which it is hard just now for a contemporary to put his finger, but on which the finger of the historian of our politics will be placed."

Nellie, too, had grown increasingly dependent on Archie Butt. Though she had learned to communicate her thoughts and make her wishes known to family members, she remained incapable of conducting "a connected conversation with strangers." When the British ambassador and his wife called on the president and first lady, Butt served as "the buffer" between Nellie and Mrs. Bryce, enabling the flow of conversation whenever Nellie came "to a standstill." During a garden party when she "became separated" from the president, Butt again came to her rescue; being on her own, she told her son Robert, "was pretty awful," until Archie escorted her back to the mansion. After a series of fainting spells, Nellie's doctor advised her to reduce the rigorous schedule of musicales and garden parties she had planned for the 1910 social season. She refused, preferring, he interpreted, "to die in harness" rather than "remain in the background as an invalid." Assessing the full social schedule planned for the coming winter and spring, Helen Taft decided to assist her mother at the White House rather than return to Bryn Mawr in the fall.

Within the family circle, Nellie became less anxious about her inability to articulate her thoughts. On the contrary, she tended to blurt out whatever came to her mind without the restraint she had characteristically exercised. During a luncheon conversation, for example, she suddenly mentioned Mabel Boardman, head of the American Red Cross and a longtime family friend. Speaking with excessive emphasis, she told her husband he would never marry Miss Boardman. If he became a widower, she predicted, he would desire "something young and prettier."

Unsurprisingly, much of the first family's conversation in the months following Roosevelt's return centered on divining what he might do. After reading an account of Roosevelt's opposition to Ballinger, Nellie offered a prescient comment to her husband: "I suppose you will have to fight Mr. Roosevelt for the nomination, and if you get it he will defeat you. But it can't be helped. If possible you must not allow him to defeat you for the renomination. It does not make much difference about the reelection." Taft agreed with Nellie's assessment, surmising early on that Roosevelt would indeed challenge him in 1912. Numerous newspapers suggested that he should "step out of the way" for the former president, but he believed that "having once been nominated and elected," he was under obligation to his supporters to run for renomination— even if he faced certain defeat, which he would accept "like a gentleman."

RETURNING FROM HIS WESTERN TOUR in early September, Roosevelt had only two weeks to prepare for battle against Sherman and the Republican bosses at the state convention. The state party was "on the Eve of one of the bitterest factional fights" in a generation, and Roosevelt's contest with Sherman for the temporary chair stood at the center of the proceedings. The great underlying issue, Boss William Barnes declared, is "whether the Republican Party is to remain the party of conservatism or be carried away with radicalism."

Roosevelt felt that the conflict was beneath him. "Twenty years ago I should not have minded the fight in the least," he told Lodge. "It would have been entirely suitable for my age and standing. But it is not the kind of fight into which an ex-President should be required to go." Nonetheless, he confessed, "I could not help myself." Lloyd Griscom admitted to Roosevelt that he was having trouble rounding up votes for him among "good honest" party loyalists, who sympathized with his opposition to the bosses but were upset with his seeming hostility toward the president. A meeting with Taft to demonstrate they were "on good terms," Griscom advised, would be helpful. Roosevelt readily agreed, recognizing that a show of unity might "turn the scale" in a contest as close as this promised to be.

Griscom arranged a luncheon in New Haven, where Taft was attending a meeting of the Yale Corporation. After a general conversation with Griscom and Taft's newly appointed private secretary, Charles Norton, Taft and Roosevelt were left alone. Roosevelt later said he "made a point of being as pleasant as possible," but Taft saw beneath the mask, later divulging to Archie that he felt Roosevelt was "not genial and quite offish." Taft recognized immediately that Roosevelt was strategically waiting to bring up the New York situation so he could later claim that the president "had spoken first." His calculation worked. As the meeting drew to a close, Taft volunteered that he hoped Roosevelt would beat the bosses and was glad to offer his assistance.

Unlike Taft, his secretary was willing to engage in the political game, creating what Roosevelt considered a "very irritating experience." Norton, "a little too slick for genuine wisdom," told the newspapermen that the Colonel had requested the meeting to stave off trouble in New York and needed the president's backing. Roosevelt's opponents jumped on the story as a signal that he was worried about his chances at the convention. At once, Roosevelt put out a statement "emphatically" denying that he had sought the meeting or asked anything of Taft. At Roosevelt's bidding, Griscom followed up with a statement declaring that the meeting was his idea. Regardless of these attempts to reformulate the story, Roosevelt complained to Lodge, a general perception remained that he had come "to beg for assistance"—for this, he blamed Taft as well as Norton. As a result, Archie Butt lamented, Roosevelt and Taft grew "farther apart than ever."

The auditorium at the Saratoga town hall was jammed with 7,000 men and women on September 27 when Roosevelt came down the aisle. His appearance provoked a round of "riotous cheers" as delegates and spectators "shrieked and yelled and waved their hats and bonnets." When Vice President Sherman arrived shortly afterward, "the scene was repeated," setting the stage for a divisive public battle. The Old Guard had selected Colonel Abraham Gruber, "a little roly-poly" man, to deliver the attack against Roosevelt. Unable to make his way through the crowd, Gruber was "practically lifted over the heads of the army of humans and passed up to the platform." Labeling Roosevelt "an enemy of the nation" and a threat to "public safety," Gruber's mean-spirited diatribe provoked such deafening "catcalls" that he could not continue until Roosevelt jumped up, shouting, "I ask a full hearing for Col. Gruber."

Roosevelt's supporters were anxious when the balloting began, but he emerged victorious, receiving 567 votes against Sherman's 445. In a conciliatory speech intended to unify Republicans, Roosevelt listed the accomplishments of the last Congress, giving credit to Republican lawmakers and "to our able, upright, and distinguished Pres. William Howard Taft." Once installed as temporary chair, Roosevelt mustered the votes to get his fellow progressive Henry Stimson the nomination for governor and to pass a fairly progressive platform, including a plank calling for direct primaries. Parts of the platform disturbed him—including the endorsement of Taft in 1912 and approval of the tariff—but he believed that he had come out as well as possible.

While Roosevelt was at Saratoga, Taft was hosting a four-day sleepover for the members of his cabinet at the White House. Having spent the summer in Beverly, the president wanted to catch up on each department's work and make plans for his annual message. "The house party has been a great success," he reported to Nellie. "We have had a jolly time on the one hand, and we have been very hard working on the other." Normally, the unique situation of a cabinet house party would have attracted considerable newspaper attention, but all eyes—including those of the president and his cabinet—were directed to Saratoga and Roosevelt's fight against the Old Guard. "Bulletins were brought to the President as they arrived," Archie reported, and everyone "spent most of the day hearing and discussing the news from New York." On the day the platform was approved, Taft wrote to Nellie in Beverly, commenting, "I hope you saw the proceedings of the Saratoga Convention and the very satisfactory resolutions endorsing your husband. Roosevelt made a speech praising me also, which must have gone a little hard with him, but which indicated that he found it necessary." Overall, Taft's White House party was a distinct success, as evinced by a gracious note that George Wickersham wrote to Nellie: "We had a delicious table and nothing was lacking but the actual presence of its mistress to make the White House a perfect place of abode. It was a charming idea of the President to invite the Cabinet to stay there with him. It has served to draw us more together and to unite us absolutely in an enthusiastic love and admiration of our Chief."

Taft's surmise that necessity, not desire, had compelled both Roosevelt's speech and his acceptance of the tariff plank proved correct. Throughout his long career, Roosevelt had accepted the need for compromise. Though unhappy about the tariff plank, he believed he "should have lost everything" had he demanded its elimination. Hard-line insurgents fiercely disagreed with Roosevelt's flexibility. Gifford Pinchot refused to back the ticket, considering endorsement of the tariff offensive and objecting to Roosevelt's characterization of Taft as upright. Roosevelt fired back at progressive ideologues, defending Taft's honor even while questioning his leadership. "I think it absurd to say that Taft is not upright," though he may be a failed leader. To complaints by William Kent, a Republican congressman from California, that Stimson "was not radical enough," Roosevelt countered: "Among all men who are prominent here, Harry Stimson is the only man who is anywhere near as radical as I am." In a letter to his son Theodore Junior, Roosevelt poured out his frustrations: on the one hand, he pointed out, the traditional elements of the Republican Party—club members, big business, and Wall Street—"have been nearly insane over me." Yet, at the same time, "the wild-eyed radicals do not support us because they think we have not gone far enough. I am really sorry to say that good Gifford Pinchot has practically taken his place among the latter," he noted, finally recognizing the rigidity of Pinchot's views.

A week after the convention, Roosevelt reconnected with Ray Baker, inviting him to lunch at Oyster Bay. "I had one of the freest talks with him I ever had," Baker recorded in his journal. "Much of our talk covered the Saratoga fight. I told him frankly that I had thought that a defeat there on the platform would have been better for him than an organization victory." Appealing to

Baker as "a reasonable exponent of the extreme left wing of the party," Roosevelt defended his actions and "spoke exultantly" of Stimson's candidacy. When the discussion turned to Taft, he made it clear that "they had wholly parted company," fixating again on the letter Taft had written after his election, thanking both Charley and himself in equal measure! His pride clearly wounded, he proceeded to describe the humiliating reports that followed his meeting with Taft in New Haven. "It happened once: but never again! Never again!" When Baker asked if he intended to be a candidate in 1912, he answered frankly, "I don't know." At the present, he maintained that he was "not seeking a nomination," but "circumstances might force me to be a candidate."

After another conversation at the *Outlook* office two days later, Baker told Roosevelt that his words on the tariff lacked his "usual moral punch," that he "would have stood higher with the country" if he had fought against the tariff plank. "He took it all in very good part," Baker wrote, considering this ability to endure criticism "one of his finest characteristics." Nevertheless, the reporter was beginning to believe that Roosevelt would ultimately fail in his attempt to play "the old game" of serving "both party & principle." The tide was simply moving too fast for someone "trying to be both radical & conservative."

As summer turned to fall, Roosevelt spent his days and nights on the campaign trail, trying to keep the Republican Party unified for the midterm elections. He stumped for both progressives and conservatives—for Beveridge in Indiana, then Henry Cabot Lodge in Massachusetts. He traveled first to Georgia, Alabama, and Arkansas, and then to Missouri, Illinois, and Iowa. "I am being nearly worked to death," he admitted to Bamie in early October. "I only hope I can last until election day." In mid-October, he returned to his native state for the final push. Rallying huge audiences, his charismatic self had become the central issue of the campaign, leaving Henry Stimson in his shadow.

As the election neared, Republican prospects across the country darkened. After more than a decade of Republican rule, the people were frustrated by the cost of living, tired of high tariffs, and resentful of machine politics. When Democrats won an "unprecedented" victory in the October state elections in Maine, commentators predicted the midterms would result in a Democratic landslide.

"If Mr. Roosevelt can save New York while neighboring States are captured by the opposition," the *Springfield Republican* declared, "his own national leadership and influence will take on a finality unapproached even in his own career." If he triumphs, the *New York Times* agreed, "it will be practically impossible to prevent his seizing the nomination to the Presidency in 1912."

REPUBLICANS HAD EXPECTED TO LOSE ground during the midterm elections, but when the votes were totaled on November 8, the strength of the Democratic victory "stunned Washington." Democrats gained control of the House by a margin of nearly 60 votes, reduced the Republican majority in the Senate by ten seats, and elevated Democratic governors to power in twenty-six of the forty-eight states. In New Jersey, former university president Woodrow Wilson vanquished Republican Vivian Lewis by one of the widest margins in the state's history. In New York, the entire state ticket lost, including Henry Stimson and his own congressman, Charles Cocks. In Connecticut and Massachusetts, Democrats Simeon Baldwin and Eugene Foss easily trounced their opponents. In Ohio, Democrat Judson Harmon handily defeated Warren Harding. "The Democratic party in November of 1910," one historian has observed, "stood rehabilitated in the eyes of the country."

Despite the clear national trend, journalists interpreted the New York result as a "crushing rebuke" to Theodore Roosevelt. Had he kept his initial vow of silence after returning from Africa, one commentator observed, "defeat would have come to his party but a great cry for him as the only compeller of victory would have been heard." Instead, he had alienated the Old Guard at Saratoga, assumed personal control of the state party, and thrown his full weight behind the losing candidate, Henry Stimson. With the thrashing he took on his home turf, the *New York Times* declared, Roosevelt's "New Nationalism has been pitched into its grave." And beyond New York, there seemed "to be a fatal quality in his endorsement," one editorial observed, for "nearly every man whom he lauded in different parts of the country has been defeated," while the men he "singled out for vituperation" were "triumphantly elected."

Sensing blood, Roosevelt's opponents moved in for the kill. "The trail that Mr. Roosevelt has traveled for the last ten weeks can be traced by the battered wrecks of Republican hopes," declared the New York *World*. This "tremendous overthrow," proclaimed the *New York Herald*, "makes complete the defeat of his plans to make himself the next nominee for the Presidency and places upon a man once President a humiliation such as has never before been known by any one who has essayed the role of national leader of his party." Theodore Roosevelt, the New York *Evening Post* editorialized, is seen as "the chief architect of disaster. He has demonstrated that there are thousands of Republicans who will not vote for him or his nominees or his novel doctrines."

Roosevelt acknowledged that he had experienced "a smashing defeat" in New York, with troubling reverberations across the land. He recognized that he had lost support on all sides of the political spectrum: progressives claimed he had not been radical enough; conservatives charged he was too radical. Westerners condemned his failure to break with the administration, while easterners berated his unwillingness to endorse Taft. The time had come, he understood, for a new leader, "one who has aroused less envenomed hatred," to take up the causes he had championed. "The American people," he reluctantly admitted to William Allen White, "feel a little tired of me."

The decisive routing and overwhelming negative press hit the proud former president hard. On the weekend after the election, the journalist Mark Sullivan called on Roosevelt at Sagamore Hill. When Sullivan rose to leave after a good talk, Roosevelt pleaded: "Don't go. The time will come when only a few friends like you will come out to see me here." Roosevelt was still "in a most depressed state of mind" when Lloyd Griscom stopped by weeks later. "All his old buoyancy was gone," Griscom related to Archie Butt. "He really seemed to him to be a changed man." Regardless of his falling-out with Roosevelt, Taft was deeply affected when Archie shared Griscom's description of Roosevelt's isolation at Oyster Bay. "The American people are strange in their attitudes toward their idols," he mused. They lead them on and then "cut their legs from under them," simply "to make their fall all the greater." Given their former intimacy, he understood how hard it must be for Roosevelt "to feel everything slipping away from him, all the popularity, the power which he loved, and above all the ability to do what he thought was of real benefit to his country."

As president and head of the Republican Party, Taft was, of course, more responsible than anyone else for the magnitude of the Republican loss. "It was not only a landslide," he acknowledged, "but a tidal wave and holocaust all rolled into one general cataclysm." As early as the previous January, he had predicted that the "whole drift" of public sentiment was turning toward the Democrats. "Sooner or later I fear we have got to turn the government over to this element and let it demonstrate its incapacity to govern the country," he reflected, believing that only then would Republicans come back into power. When everyone in his inner circle "took a whack at the Colonel," placing all the blame "for the national disaster" on him, Taft cut the conversation short. "Roosevelt did not help the ticket very much," he said, "but I am inclined to think that even had he remained in Africa the result would have been the same."

Three days after the election, Taft headed for Panama to monitor progress on the building of the Canal. "The warmth of the tropics is in our veins again," Archie noted with delight. The balmy climate led Taft to express a similar release from anxiety: "What difference does it make to a man how Ohio went, when he can look at this scene and feel its warmth? Oh how it takes me back to the Philippines!" At every meal during the trip, Taft told nostalgic anecdotes of his time as governor general. "It is always back to the Philippines he likes to go when he reminisces," Archie observed. "The scenes which he pictures" and the events he describes "seem more real than any of the more recent years here in Washington."

While Taft was away, Roosevelt visited Washington to give a speech about his African safari to the National Geographic Society, inspect the collection of specimens he had sent to the Smithsonian, and meet with old friends. Though he knew the first lady was in New York, he stopped at the White House to pay his respects and leave his calling card. Greeted affectionately by the servants and employees, all of whose names he remembered, he expressed enthusiastic approval of the significant renovations Taft had made to the West Wing.

To accommodate the increased White House staff—which now numbered thirty clerks, in addition to the regular cadre of messengers and security guards—Congress had approved a budget of $40,000 to double the office space from six to twelve rooms. Positioned directly "in the center of the new addition" was a handsome new oval-shaped office for the president, replacing what had been a "severe rectangular room." As the former president entered the new Oval Office, he was informed that he was standing on what had been the site of the tennis court, where he and his playmates had spent many happy hours. "Oh, yes," he said wistfully, "the old tennis court."

The shared sense of loss created by the midterm rout engendered a brief period of rapprochement between Roosevelt and Taft. At Archie Butt's urging, Taft wrote to Roosevelt in November 1910, expressing his regret that he had missed his friend's visit to Washington. If he were coming back for the Gridiron Dinner, he added, "it would gratify me very much if you would come to the White House and stay with me." Roosevelt replied with more warmth than he had shown since his return. "You are a trump to ask me to come to the White House, and I should accept at once if I were going to the Gridiron dinner. But I am not going; I have repeatedly refused." Even while declining the invitation, Roosevelt proceeded to ask Taft about Panama and share his concerns about the California legislature, which was about to pass anti-Japanese legislation.

Taft wrote back the next day detailing the progress on the Canal, which was scheduled for completion in July 1913, at which time both of them would be "private citizens," able to go together to see the work begun by one and finished by the other. Roosevelt replied appreciatively, "I have always felt that the one thing for which I deserved most credit in my entire Administration was my action in seizing the psychological moment to get complete control of Panama. Incidentally, it was one of the things for which I was most attacked." And Taft wrote yet again, sending an advance copy of his annual message and letting Roosevelt know that he had discussed the California situation with his cabinet. "I have read your Message with great interest," Roosevelt replied. "There is nothing for me to say save in the way of agreement and commendation."

This cordial exchange of letters continued through the winter. "I see signs of the clouds which have been hanging over the President and Colonel Roosevelt breaking up," Archie happily observed, knowing that he was responsible for many small gestures that had helped to smooth "the rough edges." On Christmas Day, he showed the president a mahogany settee in the Red Room which Edith Roosevelt had purchased for the White House during her husband's first year as president. Sentimentally attached to the sofa because her children had "kneeled on it to look at the circus parades passing up and down Pennsylvania Avenue," Edith had hoped to take it with her to Sagamore Hill. A government bureaucrat summarily denied her request on the ground that it belonged to the White House. Hearing the story from Archie, Taft had the old sofa shipped to Oyster Bay as a New Year's gift, along with a letter, telling Edith he had purchased a substitute, thus making her old sofa his "to bestow by exchange." Both Theodore and Edith were touched by the thoughtful act. If the small sofa "brings the two families closer together," Archie remarked with his unerring emotional intelligence, "then it will indeed be worth preserving in a museum."

CHAPTER TWENTY-SIX

"Like a War Horse"

In the winter of 1911, Ray Stannard Baker observed that
Roosevelt seemed poised to fight for a third term, "like a war horse
beginning to sniff the air of distant battles."

WHILE TAFT AND ROOSEVELT RETREATED to nurse their
wounds, Senator La Follette and his dedicated band of insurgents
pressed their advantage, confident in their vision for the future of the Republican Party. In states where radicals controlled the nominating slates and
platforms, William Allen White pointed out, Republicans had triumphed; in
conservative states "where they compromised and pow-wowed and pussy-
footed," Republicans had met defeat. "I cannot get Roosevelt to see this,"
White lamented. "He thinks compromise is the only thing and he is going to
be everlastingly crucified by the American people unless he gets this compromise idea out of his head."

On January 21, 1911, La Follette hosted a gathering of progressive leaders at his Washington home. In the prior weeks he had called for the formation of a new organization that would redeem the party and restore popular rule long subverted by the special interests that controlled caucuses, nominating conventions, and the Republican Party organization. The National Progressive League promised to fight for a series of propositions: direct elections of U.S. senators; direct primaries to replace party caucuses; direct election of delegates to the party's national convention; and state constitutional amendments to provide for the initiative, referendum, and recall. The charter membership was impressive—"nine U.S. Senators, six governors and thirteen Congressmen." Nearly every leading progressive spokesman had signed on, including James Garfield, Gifford Pinchot, Louis Brandeis, Ray Baker, and William Allen White. The creation of the national organization spurred numerous states to set up their own Progressive Leagues.

In short order, a Progressive Federation of Publicists and Editors was founded. Its membership list, the *New York Times* remarked, was like "a roll call" of muckraker journalists, including S. S. McClure, Norman Hapgood, George Kibbe Turner, and Lincoln Steffens. La Follette was particularly thrilled to have the support of Lincoln Steffens. After leaving *The American*, the journalist had embarked on a series of disparate projects, among them a study of Boston's city government generously financed by the progressive merchant Edward Filene. A leader of the Good Government Association, Filene had engaged Steffens as "a sort of pathologist" to analyze the historic roots of Boston's corruption. During the two years Steffens lived on Beacon Hill, he had remained in close touch with La Follette. Their correspondence reveals an intimate friendship, different in kind from the mutually advantageous relationship Steffens had forged with Roosevelt. "I am hungry to see you," La Follette had written after a short absence. "How soon can you come to Washington and stay with us for a week?"

Despite their comprehensive reform agenda, the Washington press interpreted the activities of the National Progressive League as "an anti-Taft movement," designed to boost La Follette's prospects for the presidential nomination. "Nothing," the *Springfield Republican* agreed, "could be more reasonable than the supposition that the League will be in the thick of the fight over the Republican presidential nomination of 1912." Observers claimed that La Follette now had "a much larger following in the West than Roosevelt" and that he would be the "decided beneficiary if the Progressive League takes root and advances its schemes for direct nominations and popular government."

Before the inaugural meeting of the National Progressive League, La Follette had tried to enlist Roosevelt as a charter member. "Now, Colonel," La Follette had asked, "can't you consistently give this movement the benefit of your great name and influence?" The two men had never become friends. La Follette considered Roosevelt an opportunist who adapted his positions to accommodate public sentiment, while Roosevelt regarded the Wisconsin senator as "an extremist," with a "touch of fanaticism." Yet at this juncture, both men recognized the value of a show of cordiality. "That is a mighty nice letter of yours," Roosevelt replied, "and I appreciate it to the full." He heartily agreed with the league propositions, the Colonel told La Follette, though he considered them "merely a means and not an end." Nothing in the charter spoke of the economic issues he cared most deeply about—corporate control, the regulation of wealth, or the working conditions of the laboring man. Nevertheless, he intended to give the league his full support, not by joining but by endorsing its principles in *The Outlook*. After the midterm fiasco, he was "very anxious not to seem to take part prominently in any political movement."

ON MARCH 8, 1911, THEODORE Roosevelt embarked on a six-week train trip through the South and the Southwest that he presumed would be his last extensive speaking tour. He dreaded the daily grind of ceremonies, speeches, and dinners, worrying how he would be received. To friends and family members, Roosevelt claimed he did "not care a rap" about the "fairly universal" criticism directed toward him. "Such a revulsion was bound to come," he said. "The present feeling may wear itself out, or it may not. If it does, and I regain any influence and can use it to good purpose, I shall be glad; and if it does not, I shall be exceedingly happy here in my own home and doing my own work." In any case, he would proceed with his tour, honoring commitments made shortly after his return from Africa.

To Roosevelt's amazed delight, he was met everywhere with crowds as immense and adoring as any he had ever encountered. Eight thousand cheering spectators filled the Armory in Atlanta; 30,000 greeted him in Tacoma, Washington; and the applause from the Minnesota legislature was "as uproarious as in the days of yore." Though he appeared "heavier and slightly grayer," correspondents marveled at his continued ability to withstand rigorous days "without the slightest sign of tiring and without once deviating from the spirit of utmost good humor." Cities vied with one another to honor him. In Spokane, "all traffic was suspended; streetcars were stopped," and "every window, curbstone, cornice and even lofty roofs held their quota of cheering admirers." The Commercial Club in Portland was transformed into an African jungle, complete with live monkeys, parrots, and cockatoos. In Arizona, he formally dedicated the Roosevelt Dam, marking the completion of the immense reclamation project begun during his presidency. "If there could be any monument which would appeal to any man, surely it is this," he declared. "And I thank you from the bottom of my heart for the honor."

As the trip wound to a close, the Washington State *Leavenworth Echo* remarked, Roosevelt's "abiding popularity" would force opponents to revise the "ill-concealed delight" with which they had recently predicted his demise. "To borrow the humor of Mark Twain," the piece continued, "his political death appears to have been very much exaggerated." Indeed, "not another man since the death of Abraham Lincoln could have aroused one-half the popular enthusiasm that his recent trip around the United States created."

☞ ☜

ROOSEVELT RETURNED HOME FROM HIS tour to find that the president had engineered a resurgence of his own. For months, Taft had been working quietly on a plan he hoped would convince the American people that despite the complications of the Payne-Aldrich bill, he was a steadfast "low tariff and downward revision man." The previous summer, Taft had initiated negotiations with Canada for a reciprocity agreement that would eliminate or drastically lower tariffs on both sides of the border. In January 1911, negotiators had surprised Washington by announcing a sweeping agreement to be implemented by "concurrent legislation" in Congress and the Canadian Parliament rather than by treaty—requiring a two-thirds vote in the Senate. By providing free trade in agricultural products and reduced tariffs on manufactured goods, the agreement promised to halt the rising cost of living, a major source of public dissatisfaction.

An hour after the old Congress adjourned on March 4, Taft called for the new Congress to meet in special session a month later and consider the reciprocity legislation. Taft liked his chances with the new Congress, which ordinarily would not have convened until December, knowing that Democrats, long opposed to the Republican policy of protectionism, would enjoy a majority in the House and enlarged representation in the Senate. "At one stroke," the monthly periodical *Current Literature* observed, "the Taft administration has altered the whole aspect of political affairs in America, reversed political predictions, confused party ranks and stirred into quick activity industrial and commercial bodies all over the country." And "for the first time since he entered the White House," the writer added, "President Taft now assumes, in the mind of the people, the post of a real leader." No longer "following the lead of President Roosevelt or Senator Aldrich, or Senator La Follette, or any other man," William Taft was "striking out a policy of his own." Expressing similar optimism, the *New York Times* declared that not for a decade had there been such a "well-considered and heroic" break with the "stupid, sordid, greedy" policies of previous administrations. "Beyond all question he has the country behind him."

In contrast to the 1909 tariff fight, the president was clearly unwilling to "sit still and await results." Leaders of the House and Senate were summoned for "breakfast, lunch and dinner." Taft invited a group of ten senators for a "week-end sail" on the luxurious presidential yacht, the *Mayflower*. He composed a series of speeches, setting forth clear arguments for reciprocity. Tariffs were originally designed, he pointed out, to accommodate differences in the cost of production at home and abroad. Yet, between Canada and the United States, "linked together by race, language, political institutions and geographical proximity," there was essentially nothing to equalize. Given this situation, "the productive forces" of both countries should be allowed to operate freely.

Taft adroitly kept Theodore Roosevelt informed at every development, securing his invaluable support. Before he announced the agreement, the president had written a long letter to the Colonel, explaining his reasoning in full. "What you propose to do with Canada is admirable from every standpoint," Roosevelt had replied. "I firmly believe in Free Trade with Canada for both economic and political reasons." While it might "damage the Republican Party for awhile," he continued, it would "surely benefit the party in the end." That spring, Roosevelt "vigorously advocated" the reciprocity legislation in public speeches as well as private correspondence. Beyond the economic advantages, he argued, "it should always be a cardinal point in our foreign policy to establish the closest and most friendly relations of equal respect and advantage with our great neighbor on the North."

When debate opened in the House and Senate, Taft told Charley, he "expected the insurgents not only to support the bill but to claim that I was only trailing after them, and coming to their view." Lower tariffs had been the insurgents' rallying cry. Their passionate opposition to the Payne-Aldrich bill had launched them to national prominence: "Give us something," they had repeatedly argued, "which will decrease the cost of living and save the poor from starvation." The reciprocity agreement promised to address this underlying issue, but it placed the progressives in a serious, unanticipated bind. The majority of insurgents came from midwestern agricultural states. While public sentiment overwhelmingly favored reciprocity, farmers were among the special interests passionately opposed, fearing that free admission of Canada's agricultural products would reduce the demand for food products at home. Unwilling to antagonize their constituents, the insurgents led the attack against the bill.

The adage "politics makes strange bedfellows" was never more clearly illustrated than in the curious alliance that coupled insurgents with conservative "standpatters," who viewed reciprocity as the compromising breach in "the entire citadel of protection." The independent press, which had long admired the fighting spirit of the insurgents, now charged them with hypocrisy. "Washington grows weary of the insurgents," the *National Herald* declared. "This is something more than inconsistency." The "valiant little insurgent band" had shown themselves just "as selfish" as the Old Guard. Many of the derogatory comments were directed at Robert La Follette, who announced his candidacy for the Republican nomination in the midst of the reciprocity struggle. As the Wisconsin senator repeatedly sought to delay consideration of the popular bill, he was denounced for "trying to manufacture an issue for the Presidential campaign."

On April 21, 1911, the House passed a comprehensive reciprocity bill with strong Democratic support. Two months later, the Senate followed suit. Taft was thrilled, believing the legislation would signal the arrival of "a great epoch" for the country. The *Washington Times* agreed. "Today will be an important date in tariff history," the paper remarked; tariff duties, having reached their high point, would finally "descend on the other side." After the vote, Taft "extended his formal thanks to the Democrats," acknowledging that without their aid, "reciprocity would have been impossible."

Meanwhile, discussion of the legislation in the Canadian Parliament had descended into "hysteria." Conservative opponents issued dire warnings that reciprocity would inevitably lead to Canada's annexation by the United States. During the struggle in Congress, opponents had deliberately raised the specter of takeover, going so far as to introduce a resolution calling for negotiations to begin. Taft immediately reassured Canadian officials that no one in the administration had any thought of annexation. "Canada is now and will remain a political unit," he declared. Roosevelt underscored the president's efforts with an emphatic attack on the "bad faith" and "mean spirit" of those members of Congress who "sought to bar the path" to reciprocity by "pretending to look towards the annexation of Canada." With the Canadian debate spinning out of control, Liberal prime minister Sir Wilfrid Laurier decided to dissolve Parliament and take the case for reciprocity to the people in a September election. The great majority of Canadians, he believed, appreciated the tremendous economic advantages reciprocity would bring.

Taft's success with reciprocity had significantly altered the political landscape. The president "has gained remarkably in public estimation," one editorial observed, while "the insurgents have sagged steadily." Taft further consolidated his position when he offered to bring Henry Stimson into his cabinet as secretary of war. Stimson sought advice from Roosevelt, who "strongly urged" him to take the post and do everything possible to help the president. "If two years ago [Taft] had done some of the things he has done now, he would probably have saved himself from nine tenths of the blunders he has made," Roosevelt remarked. Nevertheless, the Colonel had no intention of supporting Taft or anyone else for the nomination. Henceforth, he intended to keep "as much aloof from politics as possible."

⟅ ⟆

WILL AND NELLIE WOULD LATER look back on June 19, 1911, as the happiest day of their White House years. Nellie had never forgotten the sense of wonder she experienced as a sixteen-year-old when she accompanied her parents to Washington for the elaborate festivities surrounding the silver wedding anniversary of Rutherford and Lucy Hayes. As her own silver anniversary approached that June, she began to coordinate an equally grand party that "would be remembered through life by all who were fortunate enough to be present."

The mansion and the gardens would be illuminated with 10,000 colored lights and hundreds of Japanese lanterns. Spotlights were positioned on the nearby rooftops to beam down on the fountains and the lawns. Weather permitting, the reception would be held on the South Lawn, followed by dinner and dancing in the East Room. Invitations were sent to all the members of official Washington: the cabinet, members of Congress, Army and Navy officers, the diplomatic corps, and many other distinguished guests. To give the affair "a unique distinction," Nellie invited the relatives of all former presidents—including kinsmen of Abraham Lincoln, Ulysses S. Grant, James Garfield, Grover Cleveland, Benjamin Harrison, and Theodore Roosevelt. All told, 5,000 invitations were issued.

On May 11, five weeks before the grand event, Nellie and Will went to New York to attend a banquet at the Hotel Astor. Watching over Nellie as Taft spoke, Butt noted how much her health seemed improved, "how truly pretty she was." After the dinner, the president and first lady, accompanied by the newly promoted Major Butt, went to Harry and Julia Taft's apartment, where they planned to spend the night. "For nearly an hour," Butt recalled, they enjoyed "Scotch and soda" and pleasant conversation before retiring. In the middle of the night, Archie heard Taft's voice in the hallway, shouting for help.

Nellie had suffered another stroke, "similar to the first one" though "less severe." Once again, she was unable "to articulate clearly or to find her words," Helen told her brother. Though her slow, hard-won progress was wiped away and "the defect in her speech" made her shrink from seeing anyone outside her family, Nellie refused to stay in bed. News that the first lady had "suffered a serious breakdown" brought "genuine regret and sympathy" from people across the country, along with speculation that the anniversary party would be canceled.

Determined to realize her dream, Nellie spent hours each day practicing a series of stock phrases she could use for the receiving line. She found the perfect dress for the occasion—a heavy white satin gown embroidered with silver flowers, fitted for her slender figure. Should the weather prove inclement, she outlined plans to move the entire party indoors. The president, too, was obsessed with "every detail," walking through the mansion and the grounds day after day to ensure that everything was "finished on time."

At 9 p.m., buglers trumpeted the start of the grand march, officially opening the anniversary celebration. Preceded by dozens of military aides clad in "immaculate white" and followed by the members of the cabinet, the president and first lady walked down the stairway to the sounds of Mendelssohn's "Wedding March." "A mighty shout went up" as they passed, a correspondent reported. "President Taft smiled and dimpled and bowed, and Mrs. Taft smiled and bowed, and everybody smiled." The applause continued as the couple made their way to the enclosed arbor, where Archie Butt stood ready to present each of the 5,000 guests to the president and first lady. Nineteen-year-old Helen remained close by, ready to take her mother's place at the first sign of trouble, but Nellie stayed on the receiving line until "the last hand was shaken."

Finally, Taft escorted the first lady to the mansion, where she relaxed on the portico to watch the dancing in the East Room while he returned to the garden. The president "skipped lightly from group to group," a Washington correspondent observed, "bringing personal messages of hospitality, enjoying himself to the fullest." He expressed his pride in Nellie's fortitude to all. She had stayed by his side "from start to finish," despite his repeated efforts "to make her sit down and save her strength." It appeared she thoroughly enjoyed herself, and that, above all, made him "happy as a boy."

THE PRESS TOOK NOTICE OF the conspicuous absence of Theodore and Edith Roosevelt at the silver anniversary party. Two weeks earlier, when Taft and Roosevelt attended the Jubilee celebration for Baltimore's Cardinal Gibbons, no hint of discord was evident as the two old friends "chatted, laughed and behaved just as they used to when Mr. Roosevelt was in the White House and Mr. Taft was Secretary of War." Roosevelt had promised they would try to attend the anniversary party, but at the last minute he declined. In the interim, a troubling incident had intervened, bringing an end to the temporary period of rapprochement between the two men. Elaborating on the visible rapport at Baltimore, "misguided friends" of the president had inspired an Associated Press story suggesting that Roosevelt had finally decided to endorse Taft, having determined that "under no circumstance" would he allow his own name to go before the convention. A "mutual friend" of both men had purportedly brought word of Roosevelt's endorsement to the White House. "This is the best political news Mr. Taft has received in many months," remarked the *Hartford Herald*, "and it comes to him in a manner that leaves no doubt as to its authenticity."

Asked to "affirm or deny" the report, Roosevelt simply answered, "I have made no such statement to the Associated Press or any paper. That is all I have to say." Taft's supporters hoped he would leave it at that, but as the hours went by, the Colonel became increasingly irritated. This was "too much like a repetition" of the New Haven incident, where he had been put in the embarrassing position of seeming to beg for Taft's aid. In his next go-round with the press, he flatly labeled the endorsement report "an unqualified falsehood." Still angry a week later, Roosevelt wrote to the editor of the Philadelphia *North American*. "It was outrageous for the Associated Press to fake that statement," he insisted. These vehement denials, the *Chicago Daily Tribune* declared, "threw a bombshell in political circles." While the disclaimer was "hailed with jubilation by the progressives," it engendered "considerable chagrin" among Taft's friends.

Resentment between the two men deepened later that summer when Roosevelt came out in striking public opposition to a peace project Taft had carefully developed. On August 4, after months of negotiation, representatives from the United States, England, and France gathered in the Oval Office to sign a comprehensive arbitration treaty. They had forged an agreement that every contentious issue that might arise, even those matters relating to national honor, would be "subject to arbitration." Taft believed that if the treaty emerged relatively intact from the Senate, it would be "the great jewel" of his administration, "the greatest act" of his tenure as president.

"The ideal to which we are all working," he declared, "is the ultimate establishment of an arbitral court to which we shall submit our international controversies with the same freedom and the same dependence on the judgment as in the case of domestic courts." No longer would "the interests of the great masses" be sacrificed to "the intrigues of statesmen unwilling to surrender their scepter of power." While he would never "minimize" the debt owed to the nation's soldiers, "when the books are balanced, the awful horrors" of war "far outweigh the benefits that may be traced to it." As the photographer prepared to capture the historic signing, Archie Butt deftly rearranged the president's desk so that a large photo of Nellie would be visible. "She meant so much in his life at all crucial times that I wanted her represented at this scene," Archie wrote.

Even before the treaty was signed, Roosevelt had positioned himself against the idea that countries could arbitrate questions of national honor. "No self-respecting nation," he wrote in *The Outlook*, "no nation worth calling a nation, would ever in actual practice consent to surrender its rights in such matters." Acquiescence, he maintained, would be tantamount to watching a man slap your wife and then depending upon an arbitrator to settle the matter. Archie Butt was "greatly disappointed" with Roosevelt's article. He considered the analogy puerile, "unworthy" of the man he revered. "For the first time," in discussion with Taft, he openly criticized his "old chief." Roosevelt had not yet exhausted his strident proclamations, however. When the president of the National Rifle Association wrote a scathing editorial criticizing Taft's "mushy" concern with "the horrors of war," Roosevelt expressed wholehearted approval. Roosevelt particularly savored the line which claimed that "death was not a dreadful thing. To me there is something unspeakably humiliating and degrading in the way in which men have grown to speak in the name of humanity of death as the worst of all possible evils. No man is fit to live," he asserted, "unless he is ready to quit life for adequate cause."

That September, as the Senate continued to debate the treaty, Roosevelt published a second article on the subject in *The Outlook*. "It is one of our prime duties as a nation to seek peace. It is an even higher duty to seek righteousness," he began. After detailing the treaty's numerous defects, he concluded that "there are some questions of national policy and conduct which no nation can submit to the decision of any one else." A president's willingness to countenance such outside arbitration "would be proof positive that he was not fit to hold the exalted position to which he had been elected."

Taft was not surprised by Roosevelt's bellicose attitude. "I am afraid the old fellow has made a grave mistake in this," he told Butt. "The fact of the matter is, Archie, the Colonel is not in favor of peace. He thinks that there are many worse things than wars, and he thinks war and a warlike spirit keeps up the virility of a people. He's a fighter, and he doesn't believe in peace."

☙ ☙

ON SEPTEMBER 15, AFTER CELEBRATING his fifty-fourth birthday with Nellie at the summer house in Beverly, President Taft boarded a special train to begin a two-month swing through the West. "The White House is once more on wheels," the *New York Tribune* reported. "The official address of the nation's head has again become 'Pres. Taft, en route.' " The presidential train was equipped with "every comfort that modern transportation by rail affords," including bathtubs, dining cars, drawing rooms, and "real beds" rather than conventional bunks. Though Taft likened delivering speeches to "taking medicine or standing a surgical operation," he had worked hard to prepare a series of talks on the major issues of the day, including peace and arbitration, the Tariff Board, conservation, the trusts, and reciprocity.

The first week of the trip proceeded smoothly. At the state fair in Syracuse, New York, he was greeted with "bright skies and a holiday crowd." At every stop in Pennsylvania and Michigan, people approached him with eager smiles. Even those "thought to be unfriendly" listened with respect to his speeches. "Go ahead, old man," they seemed to say. "We're going to see to it that you get a square deal." It comforted Taft that his speeches were "reported in full" in the papers of every city, allowing him to put his "case before the people."

As September 21 approached—the date on which the Canadian election would determine the fate of the reciprocity agreement—an anxious mood enveloped the train. "The bets seem to be so strongly in favor," Horace told his brother, "but the election has been so extraordinary and seems to have roused the people so deeply that it is hard to feel sure of anything." On the evening before the vote, Montreal was reportedly "ablaze with red fire and patriotism; alive with cheering thousands, and echoing with the oratory of the opposing hosts."

At a banquet in Kalamazoo, Taft was handed a telegram with the dismal results: "Laurier government and reciprocity beaten." By "an overwhelming majority," Canadians had thrown the Liberal government out of office. Pundits were "dumbfounded"; analysts concluded that the verdict was against "the bogey of annexation" rather than an actual "unfriendliness to reciprocity." The idea of "an Imperishable Canada" had won the day for the Conservative Party, leaving the prospect of free trade "dead as a ducat." The result was difficult for Taft to absorb. "We were hit squarely between the eyes," the president acknowledged. "I am very greatly disappointed." The extra session was "for naught," the *National Tribune* observed. After "toiling up the hill . . . we are back where we started, and possibly a little worse off." The New York *Evening Post* judged the outcome "a terrible blow" for Taft, perhaps "a fatal hurt." The *Boston Traveler* wryly observed that "it was very unkind of those Canadians to deprive President Taft of his best argument for reelection just when he needed it most."

Taft remained disconsolate for days, though he gamely pushed on with his impossible schedule, eventually covering twenty-eight states, making two hundred stops, and delivering nearly four hundred speeches. In Archie Butt's estimation, Taft's peace and arbitration talks, designed to spur public demand for the Senate to pass the treaties, were "by all odds" his best and most successful. Yet, even as his passionate appeals reached audiences, the Senate was busily crafting amendments to render the treaties impotent.

The rest of Taft's speeches, "dry and full of statistics," were not well received. Crowds often drifted off before he finished. "As I see him sometimes laboring to interest an audience and failing to do so," Butt lamented, "I feel so sorry for him I could almost cry." Correspondents generally deemed the trip a failure. And while people came "to see him and hear his voice," there was "no sign" that public opinion had shifted in his direction. "The Taft trip has proved," William Allen White proclaimed, "that he cannot regain the people's confidence, that he cannot know their language, and that he cannot hold their allegiance."

During the dispiriting days on his tour, Taft found comfort in food; by the time he returned home, he weighed 332 pounds. Butt worried constantly about the state of the president's health. His tendency to fall asleep during carriage rides or even in the midst of conversations had markedly increased. In church, where long sermons provoked drowsiness, Butt kept a watchful eye. If he saw the president's head beginning to nod, Butt would fall into a coughing spell to wake him up. Such discretion was not always possible; on one occasion, Butt recorded, "I had not suspected that he was falling asleep until I heard an audible snore, and then I punched him, and he woke with such a start as to attract the attention of everybody around him." After returning to the White House, Taft acknowledged to Aunt Delia that he was "too heavy," and intended to begin a new diet. "You will see I am not very ambitious," he confessed, "when I say that I shall be entirely satisfied if I can get down to three hundred pounds."

ROOSEVELT DELIVERED A HARSH ASSESSMENT of the president's tour. "I absolutely agree with everything you have written about poor Taft," he told California's progressive governor Hiram Johnson in late October. "When he started on this trip I still had some flickering hope that when he got out into the West, among the people who are heading the new movement . . . he would become infected with the spirit and would rise to a higher level than that on which he has carried on his presidency, but I am afraid it simply is not in him." Taft's problem, Roosevelt elaborated, was not that he had "gone wrong," but that he had stayed put while the country was moving ahead. "He never thinks at all of the things that interest us most," Roosevelt continued; "he does not appreciate or understand them." While he had been an exemplary lieutenant, serving the public well as governor general of the Philippines and as secretary of war, he appeared oblivious to the monumental changes taking place in his own country. "As for my ever having any enthusiasm for Taft again, it is utterly impossible," Roosevelt concluded. Nonetheless, "I shall support him if nominated because I do not believe that there is any ground for permanent hope in the Democratic Party."

The train of events that altered Roosevelt's perspective about the nomination began on October 27, his fifty-third birthday. Banner headlines across the country that day announced the Taft administration's anti-trust suit against the U.S. Steel Corporation, its allied holdings, and its officials, including J. P. Morgan, John D. Rockefeller, Andrew Carnegie, Judge Gary, George Perkins, and Henry Frick. Labeling U.S. Steel "a gigantic monopoly, acting illegally in restraint of trade, and attempting to stifle competition," the Justice Department sought "the dissolution" of the corporation's seventeen "constituent companies" and its twenty "subsidiaries." Citing a history of illegal actions, the government focused particularly on the acquisition of Tennessee Coal and Iron Company—the transaction President Roosevelt had sanctioned during the Panic of 1907. If the president had understood the facts of the situation, the petition read, he would have understood "that a desire to stop the panic was not the sole moving cause, but that there was also the desire and purpose to acquire control of a company that had recently assumed a position of potential competition of great significance."

This reference to the former president's decision generated a series of unflattering bylines: "Roosevelt Was Deceived"; "Roosevelt Fooled"; "Ignorance as a Defense." In essence, the *Philadelphia Record* observed, Roosevelt had "been named as a co-respondent in the Government's suit to divorce the Steel Corporation and Tennessee Iron. He cannot be indicted and fined; he cannot be enjoined and dissolved. But all the same he is on the defensive and on trial, and he is smarting as he has seldom smarted before. . . . Mr. Taft has kicked him on the shins and hustled him into the witness box for cross-examination." For those convinced that Roosevelt had exceeded his authority and facilitated an illegal merger, the government's brief promised vindication: "This is an official statement," the *St. Louis Post-Dispatch* rejoiced, "that, as president, Theodore Roosevelt was concerned in a lawless act."

Roosevelt was livid. "What I did was right," he truculently declared to a New York lawyer. "I would not only do it again under like conditions if I had the power, but I should esteem myself recreant to my duty if I failed to do it again." At the time, the crisis had spread rapidly and was threatening to destabilize the entire economy. "It was not a question of saving any bank or trust company from failure," he insisted; "the question was of saving the plain people, the common people, in all parts of the United States from dreadful misery and suffering; and this was what my action did." Moreover, the government's implication that he "was misled" by inaccurate facts was simply "not correct." The steel men had told "the truth" when they explained that the acquisition of Tennessee Coal would not produce a monopoly. U.S. Steel was not a monopoly then, nor was it one now. Indeed, Roosevelt pointed out, the market share controlled by U.S. Steel in 1911 was less that it had been in 1907.

The Colonel was particularly infuriated by the perceived hypocrisy of his successor. "Taft was a member of my cabinet when I took that action," he stressed. "We went over it in full and in detail, not only at one but at two or three meetings. He was enthusiastic in his praise of what was done." Any objections "should have been made instantly, or else from every consideration of honorable obligation never under any circumstances afterwards." While Taft might not have personally perused the final brief that cited Roosevelt's action, the Colonel's "own conception of the office of President is that he is responsible for every action of importance that his subordinates take." Roosevelt told his sister Corinne he could "never forgive" Taft for allowing this injustice. That it had "been done without his knowledge" was "the worst feature of the case."

Never content to remain in a defensive position, Roosevelt used the incident to launch a searing attack on the administration's entire anti-trust policy. During his three years in office, Taft had actually instituted more anti-trust suits than his predecessor. The Steel Corporation was simply the latest in a long series of enterprises—including the Electrical Trust, the Bath-Tub Trust, and the Tobacco Trust—that had "felt the heavy hand of the Government laid upon them." With Taft's wholehearted support, Attorney General Wickersham had "embarked upon a regular program of prosecutions and dissolutions and reorganizations." The Department of Justice had become a "juggernaut rolling over the trusts," winning one case after another. Earlier that fall, Wickersham had predicted that "probably one hundred additional corporations would be called to account under the Sherman Act, that their guilty officials would go to jail."

Though Roosevelt had gained great popularity as the nation's "trust-buster," Taft found himself the subject of constant criticism for pursuing the same objective. "The times have changed," one newspaper observed. Public expectation had moved beyond "old fashioned" trust busting, preferring government regulation designed to prevent the formation of monopolies in the first place. Litigation after the fact took on an aura of mean-spirited persecution. Roosevelt's indictment of Taft's anti-trust policy was perfectly timed to catch the shifting current in public opinion.

During his first years in the White House, Roosevelt explained in his *Outlook* article, corporations had viewed the Anti-Trust Law and the Interstate Commerce laws as "dead letters." He had instituted suits against Northern Securities and Standard Oil "because it was imperative to teach the masters of the biggest corporations" that they "would not be permitted to regard themselves as above the law." And when these corporations were truly "guilty of misconduct," these suits resulted in "a real and great good." He had never proceeded against corporations simply because they were big, but on evidence of "unfair practices." Moreover, he had expanded regulatory powers for the Bureau of Corporations as a better solution.

The Taft administration, by contrast, he argued, was apparently determined "to break up all combinations merely because they are large and successful." An endless "succession of lawsuits" threatened "to put the business of the country back into the middle of the eighteenth century." The "sharp practice" of corporate lawyers would inevitably delay decisions for years, ensuring insufficient punishment for the guilty and substantial harm to "the innocent." The job of controlling monopolies belonged to the federal executive, not the courts.

Roosevelt's first significant attack on the president made headlines: "Taft Wrong, Says Roosevelt"; "Colonel Finds Taft Policy Bad"; "Roosevelt Takes Issue with Taft." The entire edition of *The Outlook* immediately sold out and the publisher reprinted "tens of thousands" of copies to meet the overwhelming demand. "Roosevelt's broadside was the only topic of discussion today," reported the *Chicago Daily Tribune*. Progressive Republicans were thrilled that Roosevelt had finally declared publicly against Taft. More conservative Republicans, frightened by the Osawatomie speech, found comfort in the Colonel's carefully reasoned position on trusts. The *New York Times* reported "a striking revival of Roosevelt talk," and the *National Tribune* told of "a thousand questions" raised concerning his availability as a candidate. Roosevelt himself later credited the trust article for "bringing [him] forward for the Presidential nomination." The turbulence surrounding this piece, he believed, had lifted "a strong undercurrent of feeling" for him "to the surface."

⟡ ⟡

IN LATE NOVEMBER AND EARLY December 1911, public excitement for Roosevelt's candidacy began to develop "in an almost astonishing fashion." A poll taken by three leading Ohio papers revealed that of more than 16,000 Republican voters questioned, nearly three out of four supported Roosevelt, with the remaining votes scattered between Taft and La Follette. Nebraska Republicans announced that Roosevelt's name would be included on their presidential primary ballot. "Events in all parts of the country," a Pennsylvania paper observed, "point to a growing and irresistible demand on the part of his countrymen that Colonel Roosevelt again enter public life."

Though Roosevelt coyly continued to disclaim any intention of candidacy, his refusal to issue "a flat-footed denial" kept his name everywhere in contention. His sudden resurgence produced "anxious days" for La Follette, whose campaign was finally gathering steam. Earlier that fall, *The American Magazine* had begun publishing a ten-part series by the Wisconsin senator entitled "The Autobiography of an Insurgent." Written with the assistance of Ray Baker, the series proved immensely popular, generating support for both progressivism and its most notable champion. In mid-October, a Progressive Conference in Chicago had given La Follette its "almost unanimous" endorsement for president. At an Insurgents' Club dinner that fall, Gifford Pinchot had enthusiastically come out for La Follette, labeling him "the logical successor to Roosevelt." The mere mention of the senator's name had provoked "loud and prolonged applause." Yet, so long as Roosevelt's candidacy remained a possibility, however remote, La Follette found it challenging to raise funds or build a national organization.

On November 26, Ray Baker joined a small group of La Follette supporters for a dinner meeting at the senator's Washington home. "Will Roosevelt be a candidate? That is the great question," Baker recorded in his journal. If Roosevelt did run, Baker acknowledged, he would draw away much of La Follette's following, though the senator was "bearing the heavy brunt & toil of the work of making the progressive campaign." They would have to reach some resolution, for if both men "split the progressive vote," Taft might well "slip in." John Phillips was concerned that Roosevelt was playing a deft political game by "encouraging La Follette and the Progressives" with the idea of eventually moving in "and appropriating the goods." Conceding that Roosevelt remained one of the most "extraordinary, vital and energetic" people he had ever known, Phillips nonetheless considered Roosevelt's candidacy a powerful "setback for the Progressive or Liberal Movement."

Two weeks later, Baker traveled to New York to sound out the Colonel. Roosevelt still insisted that he was not a candidate, but he seemed to Baker "like a war horse beginning to sniff the air of distant battles." Roosevelt revealed "with evident delight" that two delegations, one from New Hampshire and the other from Ohio, had recently come to visit. Both were unhappy with Taft, but neither was prepared to support La Follette. Unless Roosevelt decided to run, both delegations would end up backing Taft. The conversation between Baker and Roosevelt continued as they walked from the *Outlook* office to the Long Island train station. "Fully a third of the people we met in the hurrying crowds," the journalist remarked, "recognized him & turned toward him or whispered to their companions." Roosevelt kept moving forward, shouldering his way through the crowded streets "as if he were in a football scrimmage." In parting, Baker reminded Roosevelt that the first presidential primaries were three months away. "Come to see me again in January," Roosevelt responded. Their conversation left it "absolutely plain" to Baker that "if the demand is loud and long enough, and if the prospects seem right . . . he will certainly jump into the game."

That same week, after lunching with her father at Oyster Bay, Alice Longworth carried a cryptic message to Archie Butt. "Now, Butt," Alice began, "you know that we are all devoted to you. Father looks upon you as a son, almost. Certainly I have never known him to be fonder of anyone outside his own family than he is of you, so you must understand what he meant when he told me to give you this message." Then she hesitated, afraid that Archie would not want to hear her out, but the major insisted she continue. "Alice, when you get the opportunity," Roosevelt had requested of his daughter, "tell Archie from me to get out of his present job. And not to wait for the convention or election, but do it soon."

"My Hat Is in the Ring"

In this Feb. 1912 cartoon, Roosevelt's hat dwarfs
all the others tossed in the "Presidential Ring."

THE COLONEL IS MUSSING UP the whole Progressive situation with his 'To be or not to be,' " fretted Lincoln Steffens in January 1912. "He won't make a statement. He talks to us privately, but not convincingly; at least not to all of us," he wrote to a friend, resolving that in all probability, Roosevelt "simply isn't clear himself. He's undecided; wabbles and, of course, the Taft side makes the most of it. La Follette is bully. He is for the cause, not himself, and wants to act, at once, and in the best interest of ultimate results." In truth, Roosevelt was far closer to a decision than Steffens realized. Continuing to insist that he would neither "seek the nomination" nor take a single step to secure it, Roosevelt softened his tone and told supporters that if "a genuine popular demand" for his nomination indicated conviction that he was "the man to do the job," he would "of course" accept.

"Events have been moving fast," Roosevelt told Michigan governor Chase Osborn in mid-January, noting that "it is impossible for me much longer to remain silent." Osborn was among more than half a dozen governors who were strongly urging him to run. In response, Roosevelt told Osborn he had come up with a plan: If the governors who had privately encouraged him would sign a joint public letter declaring their desire for him to run, he would answer their demand with an announcement of his candidacy. Roosevelt delegated the task of drafting the letter to Frank Knox, chairman of Michigan's state central committee; after the Colonel added several lines emphasizing that the governors were acting "not for his sake, but for the sake of the country," Knox was dispatched to secure the signatures.

Meanwhile, Roosevelt's friends began working surreptitiously to undermine La Follette's campaign. A convention of Ohio progressives, expected to endorse La Follette, decided on a last-minute substitute resolution that pronounced the Wisconsin senator "the living embodiment of progressive principles," but declined to express a preference "for a single candidate." La Follette was furious at his campaign manager for agreeing to the compromise.

On the night of January 22, La Follette spoke at Carnegie Hall before an overflow audience; crowds lining the streets had waited hours for the doors to open. "Carnegie Hall never held a bigger nor a more enthusiastic audience," the *New York Times* reported. Seated on the platform were more than two hundred Insurgents' Club members, including Gifford and Amos Pinchot, Ray Baker, Lincoln Steffens, and Francis Heney. The passionate orator "got on good terms with the audience at once and never lost it," the New York *World* observed. Afterward, a group of La Follette's friends gathered at the Plaza Hotel for dinner. The celebratory mood quickly dissipated when the conversation turned to Theodore Roosevelt. Earlier that day, the Pinchot brothers had gone to see the former president and were now convinced that the Colonel would run. They worried that if La Follette remained in the race, the two men would divide the progressive vote. William Allen White had already switched his allegiance to Roosevelt, arguing in the *Emporia Gazette* that only the former president could save the Republicans from massive defeat. "Roosevelt or bust!" he proclaimed. Perhaps the time had come, La Follette's friends suggested, for him to withdraw.

The senator could no longer suppress his rage that Roosevelt had been using him as "a stalking horse" all along, testing President Taft's political strength. "When Roosevelt left the White House," La Follette charged, "he had 1916 firmly in his mind." Yet the wild reception as the Colonel toured the country had "fired his blood. There were the old-time crowds, the music, the cheers. He began to think of 1912 for himself. It was four years better than 1916." Regardless of Roosevelt's ambitions, La Follette insisted, he would continue his own campaign.

A week later, during a "painful" conference at the senator's Washington home, the Pinchots redoubled their efforts to persuade La Follette to end his candidacy. The Pinchot brothers were among his most fervent supporters before Roosevelt's name surfaced, and La Follette viewed their entreaties as a bitter betrayal. He told them he would persevere, even if he had to "fight alone," even if he carried only Wisconsin. "When I gave my ultimatum, refusing to abandon the field," La Follette later said, "Gifford Pinchot left my house and never crossed the threshold again." The next morning, La Follette ordered his manager to release a statement: "Senator La Follette never has been and is not now a quitter," the communiqué read, concluding, "He will be there until the gavel falls in the convention announcing the nominee."

For La Follette, trouble soon piled on trouble. Although mentally and physically exhausted, he was scheduled to speak on February 2 in Philadelphia at the annual banquet of the Periodical Publishers' Association. There, he would join an impressive roster of speakers, including New Jersey's new governor Woodrow Wilson, California governor Hiram Johnson, and Philadelphia mayor Rudolph Blankenburg. But five days before the event, doctors diagnosed his thirteen-year-old daughter with tuberculosis in three glands near her jugular vein. An operation to cut off the affected tissue was scheduled for the morning after the banquet. La Follette considered withdrawing from the engagement but feared his failure to show would signal an intention to withdraw from the race.

La Follette arrived late, set to give the banquet's closing speech. Wilson had earlier delivered the evening's best speech, humorous, charming, and short. Before taking the stage at ten o'clock that night, La Follette "took a great gobletful of whiskey and swallowed it neat, as a stimulant." He had prepared a provocative message for the magazine publishers—a warning that the same "money power" that had gained domination over the newspaper industry in recent decades was now threatening to corrupt independent periodicals through "the centralization of advertising." After their staunch efforts to illuminate corruption, he trusted they would "not be found wanting" before this "final test." They alone promised "to hold aloft the lamp of truth, lighting the way for the preservation of representative government."

Had La Follette focused his speech solely on this challenge to magazine journalists, he might have found an appreciative audience; instead, he began with a long historical lecture on how corporate interests had seized control of the newspapers, reducing journalists to hirelings "who no longer express honest judgments and sincere conviction," writing only "what they are told to write." La Follette encountered a response significantly less sympathetic than he might have hoped. In the enervating days preceding the banquet, he had neglected to inquire about the composition of the audience of eight hundred people. This particular annual dinner had been specifically calculated "to bring together the newspaper and magazine publishers." For the first time, newspapermen made up a significant portion of the guests.

La Follette immediately alienated his listeners by announcing that he would read his speech and give it out for publication, since he was "frankly sick of being eternally misquoted." His voice grew "acid and raucous" as he berated the newspapermen as instruments of the "predatory interests." Dumbfounded at first, the audience quickly grew angry. Scores of newspapermen simply rose and left. La Follette "shook his fist at them," roaring: "There go some of the fellows I'm hitting. They don't want to hear about themselves." When another guest leaned over to whisper a comment to his neighbor, the senator pointed "his dagger-like forefinger" at the man, accusing him of accepting bribes from the trust, and hollered: "You've got to listen to me and hear the facts for once!" Attempting to return to his text after each of these fiery outbursts, La Follette repeatedly lost his place, rereading long passages he had already read. During the first two hours, he repeated one section seven times.

As midnight approached, La Follette's secretary, seated directly behind him, desperately tried to get him to stop. Increasing numbers left the room, and those who remained began to applaud with contempt, in hopes of bringing the interminable harangue to an end. "You can't drown me out!" he defiantly shouted, threatening with renewed belligerence, "If you don't shut up and listen I'll talk all night!" By the end of the ordeal, the *New York Times* reporter sardonically noted, he "was denouncing the empty chairs" and "calling the abandoned cups and cigar stubs minions of the trust." At twelve-thirty he collapsed in his chair, "with closed eyes and his chin sunk on his chest."

This humiliating episode was heartbreaking to Baker. He had expected La Follette to deliver "the greatest speech of his career—the speech with which he hoped to win the East." Instead, the gifted orator had utterly lost control of himself and his emotions. "To those of us who were there and who were La Follette's friends," Baker grimly recalled, "it was a tragedy beyond tears."

Rumors circulated that La Follette had suffered a nervous breakdown and headed for a sanitarium. Dispirited and exhausted, he was nevertheless not only able to attend his daughter's operation the following morning but also, after "a short rest," return to the Senate. The damage to his campaign, however, proved irreparable. As he later acknowledged, his supposedly "shattered health" provided a pretext for hundreds of his supporters who wanted to "switch to Roosevelt" but would have felt guilty doing so. In a dramatic statement that captured headlines, Gifford Pinchot announced that he was abandoning La Follette, whose "ill health" compromised the progressive cause. "I shall," he declared, "hereafter advocate the nomination of Colonel Roosevelt, whose duty I believe it is to take up the leadership of the progressive movement."

As La Follette and his wife, Belle, endured the gloomy days that followed, a gracious letter from Sam McClure provided a singular bright spot. "I want to let you know how much I sympathize with you and the Senator," McClure assured Belle, adding that he had "listened with eager interest to all that he said." Indeed, *McClure's* had recently published a seven-part series, the "last great series" Sam McClure would publish, exploring the increasing "concentration of capital in the hands of a few men" on Wall Street—the very "money power" theme at the center of La Follette's botched address.

The senator's speech, McClure told Mrs. La Follette, had simply started too late and lasted too long, preventing the crowd from giving it the "justice" it deserved. "Your letter," Belle replied, "was very helpful to me, and to Mr. La Follette." At its core, the speech had a powerful message, but her husband had been unable to deliver it due to his overwrought emotions. "I think in his state of over strain and exhaustion," she explained, "the hostility he felt in his audience must have caused him to lose all self possession. Of course, he realizes what it means and suffers accordingly . . . I shall always remember your kindness and think of you as a friend."

⌒ ⌒

"POOR SENATOR LA FOLLETTE," ROOSEVELT wrote to his publicity chief, newspaperman John Callan O'Laughlin, after the debacle, attempting to justify his own late entrance into the race. "It is perfectly silly of him to feel hurt at me, and I wish you could bring out the fact that I have done absolutely nothing, that if ever there was a perfectly spontaneous and genuinely popular movement, this has been one . . . each and every one of [the governors] wrote to me out of a clear sky, saying that he was for me. Between ourselves, in more than one case I did not even know the Governor's name until he wrote me." Roosevelt's protest was somewhat disingenuous. While the movement for his candidacy may have begun spontaneously, the Colonel was orchestrating every detail of how and when to respond publicly to the round-robin letter he himself had initiated. Having received an invitation to speak before the Ohio Constitutional Convention in Columbus two months earlier, he decided to use the occasion to present his platform before giving a formal answer to the governors' request.

By delaying his entry into the race, Roosevelt had similarly destabilized Taft's position. "The trouble with the Colonel" had long overshadowed the White House "like a big, black cloud." Throughout the early winter, Taft continued to hope that Roosevelt would ultimately decide against running. Otto Bannard, a friend to both men, believed that "the whole plan" was to effect Taft's voluntary withdrawal, that if Roosevelt had to face the "handicap" of taking the nomination from a sitting president, he would not run. Indeed, Taft had not been happy in the presidency and seriously dreaded the prospect of open conflict with his old friend. Moreover, if he deferred to Roosevelt, he might have another shot at the Supreme Court. But the dignity of the presidency—and his duty to the people who elected him—ultimately prevented such a move. "I hate to be at odds with Theodore Roosevelt, who made me President," he told Horace, to which he made an important addendum: "of course, he made me *President* and not *deputy*, and I have to be President; and I do not recognize any obligation growing out of my previous relations to step aside and let him become a candidate for a third term when he specifically declined a third term."

The period of uncertainty weighed with particular gravity on Archie Butt. "My devotion to the Colonel is as strong as it was the day he left," he told Clara, but "I would not ask to be relieved from the President now if my whole life was at stake." Day in and day out, Butt had been a constant companion to the president. Taft "is so honest, so big, and tries to be so just," Butt said of his boss, "that it is hard for the people to get a proper perspective of him." The affection, even love between the two men was mutual. "A President sees but very few people continuously in a confidential way," Taft explained, "and his Aide has to be with him all the time." For three years, Archie Butt had shared moments of sadness, anxiety, and joy. "I very much doubt whether I have ever known a man," Taft declared, with such an empathetic gift "to put himself in the place of another, and suffer and enjoy with that other, as Archie Butt."

A few weeks after the mysterious warning from Alice Roosevelt that he should leave the White House soon, Archie received an open invitation from Edith Roosevelt to join the family at Oyster Bay. He wrote back to propose a visit the last Sunday in January, when he would be in New York with the president. "Delighted," Edith responded by telegram. "Will expect you to lunch." Despite the tensions of the upcoming election, Archie did not conceal such correspondence from Taft, telling the president he would like to accept the invitation. "Go by all means," Taft replied. "It will cheer them, and I know will make you happy."

The visit, Archie recorded with delight, was "like a leaf out of an old book." Logs were "glowing" in every fireplace; dogs were running "all over the house," and the Colonel and Mrs. Roosevelt "were just the same dear people." Archie sat with Edith by the fire for some time before the Colonel arrived. "We settled down to an old-time gossip," Butt recalled, "Mrs. Roosevelt asking a hundred questions and I tripping up myself in my haste" to tell the latest stories of her Washington friends. Hearing their laughter, Roosevelt charged into the room, urging them to repeat their entertaining conversation. At lunch, Butt angled for some indication of Roosevelt's plans, but the Colonel never "mentioned the president" nor "even asked about him," leaping instead "from subject to subject with the agility of a flying squirrel."

"It is all a mystery to me," Archie told Taft later that night, "but the fact that he would not send a message to you by me was significant." No longer hopeful that Roosevelt would not run, Taft grew "more bitter every hour" about his former friend. "The clash which must follow between these two men is tragic," Archie lamented. "It is moving now from day to day with the irresistible force of the Greek drama, and I see no way for anything save divine Providence to interpose to save the reputation of either should they hurl themselves at each other."

꒰ ꒦

WHEN ROOSEVELT ARRIVED IN COLUMBUS, Ohio, on February 21, 1912, to deliver the speech heralded as his platform should he run for president, an enormous crowd of "cheering spectators" provided "a boisterous reception." Sustained applause greeted his entrance to the rotunda and continued as he took his seat. His face, the president of the constitutional convention declared by way of introduction, was "more familiar than the face of the man in the moon."

"We Progressives believe," Roosevelt began, "that human rights are supreme over all other rights; that wealth should be the servant, not the master, of the people." All those who sought reform were engaged in an epic battle "on behalf of the common welfare," a fight to ensure that the people's wishes, rather than the special interests, propelled governmental decisions. "Unless representative government does absolutely represent the people it is not representative government at all," he proclaimed. An advocate of "pure democracy," he fully embraced the campaign to put additional "weapons in the hands of the people," including direct primaries, the initiative, and the referendum.

To the dismay of the Pinchot brothers, Roosevelt then proceeded to deploy his characteristic "balanced statements": progressives must treat capital with the same justice as labor; they must "encourage legitimate and honest business," even as they attacked "injustice and unfairness and tyranny in the business world," and above all, he maintained, they must understand that "methods for the proper distribution of prosperity" were worthless "unless the prosperity is there to distribute." He renewed his call for federal laws to regulate child labor and women's working conditions, establish an income tax, and secure workmen's compensation—all measures that many moderate Republicans could support.

Near the end of his speech, however, Roosevelt introduced a radical proposal that demolished any prospect of securing support from a broad party base. "When a judge decides a constitutional question, when he decides what the people as a whole can or cannot do, the people should have the right to recall that decision if they think it wrong," he insisted. Time and again, he had witnessed "lamentable" judicial decisions by state courts, which had declared laws designed to secure better conditions for laborers unconstitutional. It was "foolish to talk of the sanctity of a judge-made law," he pointed out, when such cases were often the product of a divided bench, with "half of the judges" fervently condemning the outcome. "If there must be a decision by a close majority," Roosevelt suggested, "then let the people step in and let it be *their* majority that decides."

The "damaging effect" of Roosevelt's recall speech was soon evident. The proposition that "a plebiscite or popular referendum" could overturn "the highest appellate tribunals in the states," the New York *Sun* argued, had "revolutionary" consequences for the framework of America's government—creating nothing less than a "Court of the Crowd, with supreme jurisdiction." Acknowledging that Roosevelt had not included Supreme Court decisions in his proposal, the editorial predicted that such a policy would eventually compromise the highest court in the land as well. Why require the long, cumbersome procedure to secure a constitutional amendment? While the *Sun*'s opposition was predictable, many papers followed a similar line of reasoning. The Colonel's proposed judicial recall, declared the *St. Louis Republic*, revealed "Mr. Roosevelt's incapacity to grasp a legal proposition." The *World* characterized the speech as Roosevelt's attempt to "out demagogue all other demagogues." With this address, the *New York Times* predicted, the former president had effectively removed himself from his party, rendering his nomination impossible.

Beyond this outcry in the press, Roosevelt's inflammatory speech estranged him from several of his closest allies. "Theodore has gone off upon a perfectly wild program," Elihu Root told a friend, admitting that he had "been feeling very sad about [Roosevelt's] new departure." His fellow cabinet member Oscar Straus shared Root's consternation. Roosevelt had shown him a draft of the speech a week before, and Straus was appalled by the judicial recall proposition. His attempt to discuss the issue with Roosevelt, however, had been summarily rebuffed. "That was so unlike the Roosevelt I knew," Straus added, "that I was quite disappointed and somewhat taken aback."

While Straus kept his objections private, Henry Cabot Lodge felt compelled to declare his disapproval publicly. "I am opposed to the constitutional changes advocated by Colonel Roosevelt," he told the *New York Times*. Though the two men had been "close and most intimate friends" for three decades, he could not remain silent when "the sanctity of the judiciary" was under attack. "I have had my share of mishaps in politics but I never thought that any situation could arise which would have made me so miserably unhappy as I have been during the past week," Lodge wrote to Roosevelt, following his public statement. "I knew of course that you and I differed on some of these points but I had not realized that the difference was so wide." Roosevelt replied the next day: "My dear fellow, you could not do anything that would make me lose my warm personal affection for you."

The swirling controversy only reinforced Edith Roosevelt's chagrin over her husband's decision to engage in what would undoubtedly prove a ferocious fight with Taft for the nomination. The previous six months had not been easy for her. In September 1911, riding "at a gallop" with Theodore, she had been thrown on the hard macadam road when her favorite horse suddenly "swerved and wheeled." The concussion and dislocation of three vertebrae that resulted required three weeks of bed rest. "She is very much shattered," Roosevelt confided to a friend a month later. Her convalescence had just begun when Theodore seriously started to entertain the idea of running. "Politics are hateful," Edith despaired in a letter to Kermit. "Father thinks he must enter the fight definitely . . . and there is no possible result which could give me aught but keen regret." Three days after the Columbus speech, Edith and her daughter Ethel sailed to South America. "At the worst of it I was forced to be away," she wrote a friend, admitting that "in all my life I was never more unhappy."

Few were more vexed by Roosevelt's determination to run than his son-in-law, Congressman Nicholas Longworth, whose family had known the Tafts for decades. In her memoir Alice recorded "the quandary" her husband faced: "On the one hand his friendship with Mr. Taft and the fact that he came from

Mr. Taft's own district; on the other his affection for and his admiration of Father, made his position almost intolerable. I have never been so sorry for any one." Roosevelt sympathized with Nick's uncomfortable position. "Of course you must be for Taft," he told Nick on the eve of his announcement. Still, his son-in-law found the situation painful, particularly as Alice grew "single-minded in enthusiasm" for her father's campaign, evincing more emotion and interest in politics than ever before. This newfound political passion stirred domestic strife: at dinner parties with members of Nick's family, Alice fought back whenever they criticized her father. "I got furious," she confided in her diary after one unpleasant exchange. "Poor Nick angry—Says I must 'shut up.' "

If family and friends were foiled by Roosevelt's decision, the Colonel himself embraced the looming battle with gusto. "It is not the critic who counts," he had famously preached upon his return from his African safari, "not the man who points out how the strong man stumbles, or where the doer of deeds could have done better. The credit belongs to the man who is actually in the arena, whose face is marred by dust and sweat and blood; who strives valiantly; who errs, and comes short again and again, because there is no effort without error and shortcoming; but who does actually strive to do the deeds; who knows the great enthusiasms, the great devotions; who spends himself in a worthy cause."

Indeed, his exuberance for battle manifested itself three days before his planned announcement, when he answered a question about his intentions with a spontaneous declaration: "My hat is in the ring." The tradition of "shying the hat" went back to a time when men either fought in a ring "with bare knuckles" or flung a hat at a rooster that would only fight when goaded. The former president's reference to fisticuffs and cockfighting, the New York *Evening World* commented, undoubtedly heralded "some brutality in the contest."

On Sunday evening, February 25, Roosevelt's New York office released the governors' request that "in the interests of the people as a whole," the Colonel should respond affirmatively to the "unsolicited and unsought" demand that he enter the race. "I deeply appreciate your letter," Roosevelt publicly replied, affirming, "I will accept the nomination for President if it is tendered to me, and I will adhere to this decision until the convention has expressed its preference."

That same night, before news of his decision had become public, Roosevelt attended a Porcellian Club Dinner and a meeting of the Harvard Overseers, after which he went to the home of his old college friend, Judge Robert Grant. At Roosevelt's request, Grant had invited another college friend, the historian William Roscoe Thayer, and William Allen White to dinner. While Roosevelt showed "no signs" of agitation about the upcoming struggle, his friends expressed misgivings about his decision to run and the backlash from the Columbus speech. White continued to believe that public sentiment stood "overwhelmingly" with Roosevelt but doubted whether the political system was "flexible enough to register that sentiment." If presidential primaries existed across the nation, he was confident Roosevelt would win, but the convention system had myriad ways of thwarting public desire. Grant believed Roosevelt was making "an unnecessary and possibly fatal blunder" by challenging a sitting president instead of waiting for an open field four years later. And Thayer begged him, "for the sake of his own future, not to engage in a factional strife which might end his usefulness to the country."

The Colonel blithely deflected their arguments with animation and good humor. Never losing his composure when Thayer as a historian defended the judiciary and argued that Roosevelt's platform would "destroy representative government" in favor of "the whims of the populace," Roosevelt countered that he could identify nearly four dozen senators who obtained their offices through the influence of Wall Street. "Do you call that popular, representative government?" he queried in response. And when Grant wondered if he would have the backing of party leaders, Roosevelt acknowledged that he had "none of them; not even Lodge." Instead, he counted on a cadre of young leaders, like Governor Robert Bass of New Hampshire.

As the lively conversation broke up around midnight, Grant made one final attempt to dissuade Roosevelt from running, emphasizing that people would think him disloyal to the president. About to retire to the guest room upstairs, Roosevelt angrily declared: "What do I owe to Taft? It was through me and my friends that he became President. I had him in the hollow of my hand and he would have dropped out." To illustrate his point, he withdrew his pocketknife from his pocket, balanced it in the palm of his hand, then let it clatter to the floor.

THE PRESIDENT, THE FIRST LADY, and a few guests, including Archie Butt, were at dinner in the White House when a messenger brought Roosevelt's letter declaring his candidacy. Reading it aloud to those at the table, Taft remarked that it was more definite than he had expected. Assuming it would be laden "with conditions and explanations," he was surprised to find a clear "rallying cry to the Progressives." Nellie turned to her husband. "I told you so four years ago, and you would not believe me," she chided. Her husband gave a good-natured laugh. "I know you did, my dear, and I think you are perfectly happy now. You would have preferred the Colonel to have come out against me than to have been wrong yourself."

Archie was less able to make light of the revelation, tossing in his bed that night unable to sleep. A week earlier, with the president's blessing, he had made plans for a short European vacation with his good friend, the painter and sculptor Frank Millet. Archie had driven himself "like a steam engine" through the continuous round of dinners and receptions marking the winter social season, and now felt "tired all the time." They were planning to sail on the *Berlin*. "If the old ship goes down," he wrote his sister-in-law, Clara, "you will find my affairs in shipshape condition."

As he lay in his bed that night, Archie had second thoughts about the trip. "It seems to me that the President will need every *intime* near at hand now. If we are ever to be of any real comfort to him, this is the time," he reflected. "I can see he hates to see me go, and I feel like a quitter in going." That morning, he canceled his sailing orders and told the president of his intention to remain in Washington. "He would not hear of it," Archie told his Aunt Kitty, "and insisted on my going on the ground this was the only time I could get away."

On Saturday, March 2, Archie Butt sailed for Europe. He hated "to leave the Big White Chief," he told Clara, but he'd be back in six weeks, returning to the White House in plenty of time to support the president during "the fight of his life for the nomination."

⌒　⌒

"BY A STRANGE COINCIDENCE," *The Washington Post* reported, both Taft and Roosevelt opened their national headquarters on the same day. The Taft men commandeered twelve luxurious rooms in the Raleigh Hotel, while two blocks away, the Roosevelt headquarters occupied the tenth floor of the Munsey Building. To head his campaign, the Colonel chose Montana senator Joseph M. Dixon, an energetic young man with "a very pleasant and winning personality, easy manners, and attractive address." Taft selected Illinois congressman William Brown McKinley, chairman of the Republican National Committee. No relation to the assassinated president, McKinley had made a fortune in traction corporations before entering Congress in 1905. For both campaigns, major financial backers helped furnish "the sinews of war." Roosevelt would enjoy the support of two multimillionaires—Frank Munsey, the publisher of newspapers and magazines, and George Perkins, who had departed the house of Morgan "to devote himself to public affairs." Taft could rely on traditional Republican Party stalwarts, including the financiers Otto Bannard and Chauncey Depew. And once again, Charley Taft contributed handsomely to his brother's campaign.

As the battle for the nomination began, Taft was immensely relieved that the Colonel's radical Columbus speech provided the opportunity to distinguish his own position "without indulging in any personal attack." Though he agreed with many of the Colonel's proposals on capital and labor, he had felt that the initiative and the referendum were problematic and was "unalterably opposed" to "the recall of judicial decisions." In a letter to Charley, he noted that Roosevelt had "stirred up a veritable hornet's nest of disapproval." The issues were now "sharply defined," clearing "the political atmosphere wonderfully." Meeting with Roosevelt's friend Henry White in early March, Taft vowed that his campaign would remain a battle of ideas. Indeed, he hoped that "when all this turmoil of politics had passed," he and Roosevelt "would get together again and be as of old."

Speaking in New York, Boston, and Toledo in the late winter and early spring, Taft deployed a series of metaphors to illuminate the inherent dangers in subjecting judicial decisions to "the momentary passions of a people." In one late winter speech, he warned that judicial recall would topple "the pillars of the temple." In subsequent addresses that spring, the president warned that such action threatened to smash "the ark of the covenant" and that it laid "the axe at the foot of the tree of well ordered freedom." Defending his beloved judiciary, Taft found his voice. At the State House in Boston, he enjoyed the most "genuine ovation" of his speaking career. "One cannot adequately describe," he told Charley, "the manner in which my speech was received without using extravagant expressions."

"Taft has behaved with dignity and amiable forbearance since the announcement," Roosevelt's friend Judge Grant told the historian James Ford Rhodes at the end of March, noting that he had "become almost an idol, even in circles where a few months ago he was reviled." If Taft triumphed, Grant continued, it would be "on the crest of the wave of revolt from and denunciation of Roosevelt." In recent weeks, suspicion that Roosevelt had not granted the president "quite the square deal seems to have taken hold of the public mind," and "the abuse" of the Colonel in the New York and Massachusetts newspapers had been "overwhelming and bitter."

When the election year opened, only one eastern state—New Jersey—and five western states—Wisconsin, Nebraska, Oregon, North Dakota, and California—made use of the direct primary. Everywhere else, delegates would be selected at district and state conventions, where local machines and the power of federal patronage gave the president a decided advantage.

Taft's campaign had already established control of most southern state conventions before Roosevelt formally entered the race. Fearful that the region's running totals would make Taft's lead appear impregnable before delegates from the rest of the country were selected, an enterprising Roosevelt supporter organized groups of men to contest the results of conventions throughout the South. Even if it was later determined that legitimate Taft majorities existed, the newspapers would be forced to list the results as contested rather than straight Taft victories. When rumors reached Roosevelt that bribes were being employed, he wrote his overenthusiastic organizer that while he was "absolutely sure that there was not a particle of truth" to the accusations, he nonetheless wanted "assurance" that no "improper" tactics were being used "to influence any man."

At state conventions in the North and West, brutal altercations broke out, swiftly dispelling Taft's hope for a high-minded campaign based on the issues. In Michigan, Taft's forces secured a victory after what one newspaper described as "the worst riots that ever occurred in a political gathering in the state." More than 1,800 men arrived at the Bay City Armory to claim 1,400 seats. The Taft men, the *New York Times* reported, were admitted first and filled the hall "despite the frantic efforts of the Roosevelt men to gain entrance through side doors, windows, and the basement." With the aid of the state militia, delegates without proper credentials were "seized bodily" and thrown to the back of the crowd. Eventually, four hundred Roosevelt supporters were admitted, and "then the fireworks began." When the chairman of the Taft delegation attempted to open the meeting, the Colonel's men "set up a roar," making it impossible for him to continue. One Roosevelt advocate rushed the platform only to be flung backward, landing atop the newspapermen's table. More than a hundred men joined the fight before police "charged on the combatants and restored order with their clubs." The Roosevelt faction promptly selected their own delegates before leaving the hall, "yelling and jeering at their foes." The Taft faction then moved forward with the regular order of business.

Violence erupted at conventions in many other states as well, including Missouri and Oklahoma. In the third Missouri district, the Taft contingent, positioned at the only open door with "clubs and baseball bats," prevented Roosevelt supporters from entering. Pandemonium broke out in Oklahoma City when a Roosevelt man wearing a Rough Rider outfit entered the hall on a horse and "rode down the aisle to the rostrum." Before an hour had passed, a series of "dynamite explosions" shook the convention hall. A few weeks later, at a district convention in Guthrie, Oklahoma, a Roosevelt supporter held a loaded gun to the head of the chairman of Taft's delegation. He wanted to be fully prepared, he declared, in case "any chicanery" occurred. Before the "all-night session" came to a close, one delegate had "dropped dead" from an apparent apoplexy.

⌒ ⌒

EVEN BEFORE OFFICIALLY THROWING HIS hat in the ring, Roosevelt realized that his only chance for the nomination lay in expanding the direct primary beyond the half-dozen states that had adopted the system. In his letter to the governors, he had voiced his "hope that so far as possible the people may be given the chance, through direct primaries, to express their preference as to who shall be the nominee." Initially led by La Follette and his band of insurgents, the movement for direct primaries had been slow to catch on. Two years earlier, Roosevelt had unsuccessfully tried to persuade the New York state legislature to change its nominating system. As a presidential candidate, however, he transformed the "sluggishly moving cause" into "a torrential crusade."

"Get the Direct Primary for Your State," proclaimed a Roosevelt supporter in *Collier's Weekly*, alerting constituents that "the Presidential primary means that you can go to the polls (if you are a Republican) and say whether you want Taft or Roosevelt. If you don't do the choosing the bosses will." Roosevelt operatives pressured legislatures in one state after another to change their rules. "Don't let the politicians tell you it is too late," the progressive journalist Mark Sullivan proclaimed. "The Presidential primary can be got for every State if the people demand it."

The call for a popular voice in party nominations was a delicate issue for the Taft campaign. While the president's strength lay in the old convention system, the political climate made public opposition to direct primaries awkward. Nor did Taft oppose the concept in principle; he told Horace that he had "no objection at all" to Republican primaries, so long as the law provided safeguards to prevent Democrats from voting. Meanwhile, his managers did everything possible to prevent states from adopting primaries. "Legislatures are being dragooned, officeholders are being set at work," the *Washington Times* reported, "and big business is using its influence at every point." Challenged to explain why Taft's campaign organizers were leading the fight, William McKinley flatly stated: "I do not favor changes in the rules of the game while the game is in progress. To propose the recall of conventions in the midst of the campaign is contrary to the dictates of fair play." It appeared the campaign would progress smoothly, Taft assured Horace, if he could "only keep my people from talking too much."

Roosevelt sounded the central theme of his own campaign in a speech at Carnegie Hall on March 20. Every seat was occupied; the speaker's platform was jammed with chairs; women in evening gowns crowded the upper boxes. Five thousand people had to be turned away. Roosevelt "waved his hand energetically" to stop the "wild cheers" that greeted him as he entered, but the demonstration only escalated when someone in the back began the singsong refrain: "What's the matter with Roosevelt?" To which the crowd chanted: "He's all right!" At last, the audience reluctantly quieted and Roosevelt began to speak.

"The great fundamental issue now before the Republican party and before our people can be stated briefly," he thundered, posing the rhetorical question: "Are the American people fit to govern themselves, to rule themselves, to control themselves? I believe they are. My opponents do not." Declaring that he stood by the sentiments in his Columbus speech, Roosevelt adroitly folded his proposal for the recall of judicial decisions into the larger issue of popular rule. Any attack on his proposal, he maintained, was in effect "a criticism of all popular government," grounded in "the belief that the people are fundamentally unworthy."

For the first time, the *New York Times* reported, Roosevelt proceeded to pour "ridicule" on the president, deriding his misguided interpretation of the principles of American government. Unlike Abraham Lincoln, who believed in "government of the people, by the people, for the people," Roosevelt charged that Taft ostensibly held that "our government is and should be a government of all the people by a representative part of the people," the very definition of "oligarchy." Where progressives trusted that the entire voting republic would rule correctly most of the time, Taft rested his hope in the courts—"a special class of persons wiser than the people." In recent years, Roosevelt pointed out, these very courts had proved "the most serious obstacles" to social justice— repeatedly striking down legislation designed to better the working conditions of ordinary citizens. "Our task as Americans is to strive for social and industrial justice, achieved through the genuine rule of the people," he urged. "We, here in America, hold in our hands the hope of the world." The destiny of "our great experiment" would mean nothing, he warned, "if on this new continent we merely build another country of great but unjustly divided material prosperity," rather than a genuine democracy based on "the rule of all the people."

As spring commenced, vigorous efforts by the Roosevelt campaign to spread the direct primary system had succeeded in Pennsylvania, Massachusetts, Maryland, Ohio, South Dakota, Illinois, and New York, bringing the number of participating states to thirteen. The New York struggle resulted in multiple litigations regarding the format of the ballot and the placement of the delegates' names, but the primary was finally set for March 26. In Illinois, the *Chicago Tribune* led a successful campaign to force the reluctant governor to call a special legislative session to pass the bill. With primaries scheduled nearly every week between mid-March and early June, the first presidential campaign conducted under this new system generated widespread interest and high emotions.

The primary season opened on March 12 in North Dakota, where Robert La Follette still "had his fighting clothes on," determined to prove that he was the sole progressive in the race. Roosevelt, he charged, was merely a "switch engine" that ran on "one track, and then on another." Aware that La Follette was generating widespread enthusiasm, Roosevelt's managers published a last-minute appeal in newspapers across the state: "Today's primary crucial. On the returns," the statement advised, "will depend whether Col. Theodore Roosevelt is to be further considered as a factor in the fight for the nomination."

In Washington, Alice Roosevelt Longworth waited anxiously. After placing repeated telephone calls to her father's campaign manager, she finally received the "very bad news" that La Follette had beaten Roosevelt by a margin of 58 percent to 39 percent. Though Taft garnered but a miserable 3 percent of the vote, Roosevelt had predicted that if he did not win, "the East will construe it not as a defeat for Taft but as a defeat for me." *The Washington Post* confirmed Roosevelt's assessment: "The small vote count for President Taft means very little, as he was not fighting for recognition of the primaries as were Roosevelt and La Follette." Moreover, Taft could not anticipate much support in a state on the Canadian border, where many farmers still resented his advocacy for reciprocity. "In a nutshell," the *Post* concluded, the outcome in North Dakota "is decidedly embarrassing to Roosevelt, encouraging to La Follette and the subject of mixed amusement and satisfaction to Taft."

A week later, Roosevelt suffered a far more significant loss when Taft crushed him by a margin of eight to one in New York's "first trial of the new primary law," securing eighty-three out of ninety district delegates. "They are stealing the primary election from us," Roosevelt protested. It was evident that "an entire breakdown of the election machinery" in New York had occurred. Litigation by both the Taft and Roosevelt campaigns had delayed getting the ballots to the printer. In some districts, they arrived only after the polling had closed; in others, the long ballots had been so badly folded that the bottom section bearing the delegates' names became detached. Despite these technical difficulties, the press reported "the indisputable fact" that Taft had scored a decisive victory over Roosevelt.

The day after the New York primary, Roosevelt boarded a train to begin a weeklong swing through the West in anticipation of the Illinois primary. Having studied the returns from New York, he reached Chicago "in a fighting mood." Discarding his prepared speeches, he "raised the cry of fraud," claiming that the Taft men in New York "had cheated the people out of their will by the grossest corruption" since "the days of Tweed." Had he simply been unable to gain support for his political philosophy, the Colonel maintained, he "should be sorry" but would not complain. "If the politicians subvert the will of the people," however, he would "have a great deal to say." Buoyed by immense crowds yelling "Teddy, Teddy, hooray for Teddy," Roosevelt escalated his rhetoric against bosses, machines, and William Howard Taft. "Our fight," he claimed, "is the biggest fight the Republican Party has been in since the Civil War." Before a packed Decatur crowd, he linked Taft directly to Republican William Lorimer, who would soon be expelled from the Senate for bribing members of the Illinois state legislature to obtain his Senate seat. Generating wild applause, he proclaimed: "As an American citizen, it is a shock to me to see the name of Lincoln desecrated by its use as a mask for Mr. Lorimer."

"Easter came on April seventh that year," Alice Roosevelt recalled, "but all that I could think of was the Illinois primary, two days off." A loss in Illinois after his humiliating New York defeat would cripple the Roosevelt movement. But before midnight on April 9, it became clear that Roosevelt had won a sweeping victory, "carrying every district in the State but one, and electing fifty-six of the fifty-eight delegates." His campaign secretary, Oscar King Davis, later designated April 9 as "the day on which the Roosevelt 'band wagon' got its real start, and from then on there was a rush to get aboard it." Well aware that he had benefited from widespread anti-Lorimer sentiment, Roosevelt claimed the stunning victory as "a stinging rebuke to the alliance between crooked business and crooked politics." As he headed toward Pennsylvania, where voters would go to the polls in four days, he wore his broadest smile. "We slugged them over the ropes," he told supporters. The outcome was almost "too good to believe," Alice Roosevelt recorded in her diary. "How wonderfully happy I am."

A somber mood enveloped the Taft camp. Taft confided to Howard Hollister that the Illinois defeat had "given his campaign a heavy jolt." More frustrating than the loss itself, Taft told his friend, was the unjust way that the Lorimer issue had been used to debase him. Roosevelt knew that Taft had never supported Lorimer; indeed, he and the Colonel had exchanged letters, working together to determine how they might persuade a reluctant Senate to expel one of its own. Despite the blow suffered in Illinois, Taft assured Hollister, the campaign could easily "recover by a good result in Pennsylvania."

On Saturday, April 13, the people of Pennsylvania crushed Taft's hope "for turning the avalanche of sentiment" that Roosevelt had unleashed. "It was long after midnight," the *Washington Times* reported, "before the weary managers quit bringing their discouraging telegrams and Mr. Taft sought a few hours rest." By Sunday morning, it was clear that Roosevelt had achieved another staggering triumph, gaining sixty-eight of seventy-six delegates. After hearing the final tally, Taft wrote a long letter to his brother Horace. "One of the burdens that a man leading a cause has to carry is the disappointment that his friends and sympathizers feel at every recurring disaster," he began. With every unfavorable report in the papers, that load grew heavier. "I felt more sorrow at Nellie's disappointment and yours, and that of all who have become absorbed in the fight on my behalf than I did myself," he explained. Nevertheless, he assured his brother, he had no plans to withdraw. Nor did he intend to "make any personal attacks on Roosevelt." If Roosevelt persisted in his "lies and unblushing misrepresentations," however, he could not prevent his campaign managers "from pointing out his mendacity."

"I wish I could help," Horace replied. "I can't manage to think of much else. I don't see how you stand it. I don't mind a licking. I can get used to anything. But the continued uncertainty is hard to bear." No matter the eventual outcome, Horace told his brother, William Taft would never lose the affection and respect of "the thinking men," the men who understood the fight being waged for the Constitution. Hoping to cheer his brother, Horace recounted a conversation with Taft's eldest son, Robert, who had "never loved him so much" and expressed certainty "that his place in history is sure if he never does another lick."

"The stampede is on," the *Pittsburgh Press* proclaimed. "Those who have been led to believe that Roosevelt has been fighting a lost cause will have to change their minds. Theodore Roosevelt is stronger today than he has been at any time since his hat was cast into the ring." Optimism reigned too at Roosevelt's headquarters in Washington. "Of course, Pennsylvania settles it," *Chicago Tribune* correspondent Cal O'Laughlin wrote to Roosevelt on April 14. "I am absolutely convinced that you will be nominated hands down at Chicago," noting with satisfaction that "the gloom around the White House to-day was so thick, it could be cut with a knife."

⌒ ⌒

KEEPING ABREAST OF THE INCREASINGLY bitter nomination struggle from abroad, Major Butt decided to cut his vacation a little short, "anxious to be home," where he could offer comfort and companionship to his beleaguered Chief.

On April 10, 1912, he boarded the White Star Line's palatial new ocean liner, RMS *Titanic*, for her maiden crossing of the North Atlantic.

On Monday morning, April 15, the press reported that the *Titanic*, carrying more than 2,300 passengers and crew, had struck a giant iceberg. The first reports erroneously suggested that the great ship had been "held afloat by her water-tight compartments" and was "slowly crawling" toward Halifax. Relieved to hear that "all onboard had been saved," Taft went to see the comedy *Nobody's Widow* at Poli's Theatre that evening. Learning at around 11 p.m. that the ship had actually gone down in the early morning hours, "he looked," one reporter observed, "like a man that had been stunned by a heavy blow." He rushed back to his office, where he closeted himself in the telegraph room to read the latest bulletins. Shortly before midnight, he dispatched a telegram to the White Star offices in New York: "Have you any information concerning Major Butt? If you communicate at once I will greatly appreciate." The response offered little reason for optimism. There was "no definite information" available. Before returning to the mansion, Taft instructed the telegraph operator to bring him the most recent news regardless of how late it arrived.

The days that followed would drive Taft down into a profound state of grief. By early Tuesday morning, White Star officials had compiled a list of over seven hundred survivors, mainly women and children, who had been loaded into lifeboats and taken aboard the nearby *Carpathia*. At noon, the *Washington Times* reported, the president's telegraph operator received a message from the White Star office, expressing their profound "regret that Major Butt's name" was not to be found on any list of survivors. "Even with the list of the rescued made public," the press reported, "Washington found it hard to realize that the President's military aide, the tall, stalwart, light-hearted man who won such popularity, who knew pretty nearly everybody in the Capital, and was loved by all of them is really dead." The White House canceled all social activities as "news of the disaster swallowed up all such temporary minor considerations as politics and official business."

Both the president and the first lady were "greatly depressed," *The Washington Post* reported; "in fact, the entire White House staff was plunged into sorrow." With tears in his eyes, Taft told callers he considered Archie a member of his family and felt "his loss as if he had been a younger brother." To his friend Mabel Boardman, Taft confessed that it was impossible to believe he would never see Archie again. "I miss him every minute," he wrote; "every house, and every tree, and every person suggests him. Every walk I take somehow is lacking his presence, and every door that opens seems to be his coming."

As survivors began talking about their ordeal, Taft absorbed stories about

Archie's last hours. Marian Thayer, a Philadelphia Main Liner whose husband had perished on the ship, sent a heartfelt letter to the president. "In my own grief I think often of yours," she told him, "and feel I must write to tell you how I spent the last Sunday evening with Major Butt." She had dined with Archie at a small dinner party in honor of the *Titanic*'s captain, Edward J. Smith, and could not forget "how devoted he was to you and what a lovely noble man he was!" Archie had told Mrs. Thayer about the scores of letters he had written to his mother and his sister-in-law over the recent years and shared his hope that if published posthumously, this correspondence might leave "his mark and memorial of truth to the world." He admitted that he was "very nervous" about returning home, Marian confided to Taft, knowing that the nomination battle between "you and someone else he loved but I do not" was in full swing. "Oh, how he loved you" she added, "and how frightfully you will miss his care—such a true, devoted, close more-than-friend."

According to reports, Archie had been in the smoking room enjoying a game of cards at 11:40 p.m. when the *Titanic* hit the iceberg. "A slight rocking of the ship" followed, but the passengers remained unaware of danger until forty minutes later, when a steward announced: "The captain says that all passengers will dress themselves warmly, bring life preservers and go up to the top deck." Over the next two hours, as water continued to flood the vessel, women and children were lowered into lifeboats. Mrs. Henry Harris, wife of the celebrated theatrical producer who died on board, recalled that Archie Butt had been "the real leader" during the rescue operation. A male passenger who survived by jumping at the last moment told reporters: "My last view of Major Butt—one that will live forever in my memory—was of that brave soldier coolly aiding the officers of the boat in directing the dis-embarkation of the women from the doomed ship." Even before the limited survivor list and the testimony of witnesses reached him, William Taft was grimly certain of his companion's fate: "After I heard that part of the ship's company had gone down, I gave up hope for the rescue of Major Butt, unless by accident. I knew that he would certainly remain on the ship's deck until every duty had been performed and every sacrifice made."

Theodore Roosevelt was on a whirlwind speaking tour through the West when the tragic news of the disaster reached him. From Lindsberg, Kansas, he "paid tribute" to his former aide. "Major Butt was the highest type of officer and gentleman. He met his end as an officer and gentleman should, giving up his own life that others might be saved. I and my family all loved him sincerely." For Alice Roosevelt, who was especially close to Archie, the loss was particularly painful. "I can't believe it," she repeatedly recorded in her diary. "I can't believe it."

Taft immediately prepared for the journey to Augusta, Georgia, where he would speak at the memorial service in his devoted aide's hometown. Shops were closed, flags flew at half-mast, and thousands gathered around the Grand Opera House hoping to hear the president speak. "Everybody knew Archie as Archie," Taft began. "I cannot go into a box at a theater; I cannot turn around in my room; I can't go anywhere without expecting to see his smiling face or to hear his cheerful voice in greeting. The life of the President is rather isolated, and those appointed to live with him come much closer to him than anyone else." Before reaching the end of his prepared remarks, he broke down and could not finish.

☙ ❧

HEAVYHEARTED, TAFT ENDEAVORED TO RETURN to "a rush of activities" in preparation for the April 30 Massachusetts primary, which the press had deemed "the Gettysburg of the Republican presidential test." If the president could not win the Bay State, "the very heart of the section where he is supposed to be the strongest," commentators noted, "the curtain will ring down on his candidacy." Fully aware of the stakes, Taft decided to buck the tradition that kept sitting presidents from campaigning on their own behalf, announcing that he would deliver his message "in person" to the people of Massachusetts.

For weeks, Taft's campaign advisers had argued that it was "absolutely essential" for him to "open fire" on the former president. Taft had refused, believing it undignified "to get down into the ring of crimination and recrimination." The walloping he suffered in Illinois and Pennsylvania, however, persuaded him that the time had come to answer Roosevelt's charges. His campaign announced that Taft would "explode a bomb" that would level Roosevelt's false accusations. When he finished drafting his speeches, Taft circulated them to his cabinet at an "all night" session. Apparently, one Washington correspondent reported, "the President's idea of severity was not as strong as that of some of his advisers." Informed of the proposed attack, Roosevelt laughed. "Frightful," he mockingly replied.

The president's train reached Springfield, Massachusetts, in the early afternoon of April 25. Speaking in a half-dozen small towns en route to Boston, where he would deliver his principal address that evening, Taft revealed acute discomfort at the need to defend himself "against the accusations of an old friend," whom he "greatly admired and loved," a man who had helped make him president. "This wrenches my soul," he admitted. If the fight were purely personal, he would have remained silent, but it was his duty to represent "the cause of constitutionalism," and he could not allow Roosevelt's false charges to go unanswered. When he arrived at South Station, he learned that an immense crowd had already filled the new Boston Arena, with thousands more packed into Symphony Hall. Anticipation that he would deliver a fighting speech had revitalized his supporters.

"Mr. Roosevelt," Taft began, claims to believe "that every man is entitled to a square deal. I propose to examine the charges he makes against me, and to ask you whether in making them he is giving me a square deal." With emotion in his voice, "throwing aside official reserve," Taft proceeded to tell "the cold, naked truth about Theodore Roosevelt," presenting hard evidence to counter each of his rival's major accusations. He began by producing a transcript to prove that he had never stated, as Roosevelt repeatedly claimed, that "our Government is and *should be* a government of all the people by a representative part of the people." In fact, he had pointed out that major segments of the population remained voiceless, while "the people" included only adult males, since women were not allowed to vote. Nor had he ever been a supporter of the disgraced Senator Lorimer, as Roosevelt well knew. To prove his point, Taft read out the letter to the Colonel in which he had suggested a joint strategy for removing Lorimer from the Senate. Yet another letter revealed Roosevelt's dishonorable opportunism: while the reciprocity agreement was being hammered out with Canada, Roosevelt had written to tell Taft that it was "admirable from every standpoint." Yet facing the opposition of angry farmers, the Colonel had hastily revised his position. Taft pushed relentlessly onward, refuting each of eleven accusations Roosevelt had made against him in the course of the campaign.

Nearly two hours had passed before Taft reached his peroration, which included "a solemn warning to the American people" regarding "the danger of a third presidential term." Mr. Roosevelt, he stated, "is convinced that the American people think that he is the only one to do the job." Though Roosevelt had never articulated "exactly" what that job entailed, the ambitious plans outlined in his Columbus platform could not possibly be completed in four years. "We are left to infer, therefore, that 'the job' which Mr. Roosevelt is to perform is one that may take a long time, perhaps the rest of his natural life. There is not the slightest reason why, if he secures a third term, and the limitation of the Washington, Jefferson, and Jackson tradition is broken down, he should not have as many terms as his natural life will permit." Taft concluded with an ominous question, implying the full danger of granting Roosevelt an unprecedented third term: "If he is necessary now to the Government, why not later?"

The audience, which had "loudly cheered" Taft throughout the entire speech as "each item was submitted to the square deal balance and found wanting," received his final words "with a storm of endorsement." As his advisers had urged, William Taft had finally struck back. "He had cause for exhilaration," his biographer remarked, but "weariness and depression were the only sensations he felt." Informed that evening that several hundred bodies, recovered from the icy waters near the site where the *Titanic* went down, were being taken to Halifax, Taft had dispatched an Army official to the city wharf "to scrutinize" every victim, "in the hope of recovering" the body of Archie Butt. After his speech at the Arena, Taft stopped at Symphony Hall to meet the overflow crowd. It was after midnight by the time he returned to his private car. Spent, he "slumped over," and despite the presence of a journalist, "began to weep."

In sharp contrast, Theodore Roosevelt was in great spirits as he prepared his own Boston speech, scheduled for delivery at Mechanics Hall the very next night. "If they are anxious for a fight they can have it," he blasted, as he flung aside his earlier draft to respond to Taft's allegations. Incited by his belligerent tone, "the crowd was keyed up" from the start. They stamped in unison, shouting: "Hit him between the eyes! Soak him! Put him over the ropes!" The Colonel did not disappoint, delivering what the *New York Times* called a "merciless denunciation" of his former friend, "flaying the President in one scathing sentence after another." With each thrust Roosevelt delivered, the audience "howled with delight," spurring him onward. Roosevelt dismissed Taft's square deal comment out of hand. "Taft has not only been disloyal to our past friendship, but he has been disloyal to every canon of decency and fair play," he countered. "He only discovered I was dangerous to the people when I discovered he was useless to the people." Insisting that a gentleman's unpardonable sin is to publish a letter marked "confidential," the Colonel claimed that the president was guilty of "the crookedest kind of deal." Categorically, he stated, "I care nothing for Taft's personal attitude toward me."

"This is our first presidential campaign under the preference primary plan," the *New York Times* editorialized two days later. "We hope it may be our last. The spectacle presented by the fierce fight for the nomination is one that must be amazing to foreigners, it is one that should bring a blush of shame to the cheek of every American." The old system, the *Times* continued, under which candidates were "content to await the action of the convention" and appeal to the people in a formal acceptance speech, "was a rational, a seemly procedure." Under this new system, "we are no longer a people, but a mob."

On April 30, the Massachusetts voters granted Taft a narrow victory, but

six days later, Roosevelt captured Maryland, and the following week California. Then came the battle for Ohio, which brought both men to the Buckeye
State for ten days of hard campaigning. Traveling thousands of miles by train
from one corner of the state to the other, Taft and Roosevelt sometimes found
themselves playing "rival matinees in the same towns." With each passing day,
the tone of the campaign degenerated further. Roosevelt called the president
a "puzzlewit" and a "fathead," while Taft railed against his rival's egotism.
"You'd suppose there was not anybody in the country to do this job he talks
about but himself," the president ridiculed. "It's I, I, I, all the time with him."
Robert La Follette, having traveled to Ohio after a surprisingly good showing
in California, joined in the bitter attacks, focusing most of his ire on Roosevelt.
While some people found "the spectacle of a President and ex-President hurl-
ing personal abuse at each other" unseemly, "the attacks of one on the other
won the loudest applause everywhere."

"It is about as painful for me as it possibly could be," Taft confessed as the
contest in Ohio drew near. "At least, if it is settled against me, it will be finally
settled," he told his Aunt Delia. "I have had a long and, I hope, an honorable
career, and one in which good fortune has been with me at many crises. If
now, fortune is to desert me for a time or permanently, it is my business to
stand it, and I hope I have the courage to do so." Roosevelt, by contrast, found
pleasure in every aspect of the campaign. He reveled in the sight of the enormous crowds that greeted him at every stop; he enjoyed going after his rival,
bantering with the press, talking with local officials. "He is having a perfectly
corking time," one reporter noted, "and has said so a dozen times."

On May 21, a jubilant Roosevelt carried the state of Ohio by a margin of
55 percent to 39 percent of the popular vote. Beating Taft in his own state
had "settled the contest," he predicted. "It will be hopeless to try to beat us"
at the convention. A week later, Roosevelt carried both New Jersey and South
Dakota, bringing the primary season to an end. In nine of the thirteen states
where direct primaries had been held, Roosevelt had won overwhelming victories. Taft had carried only New York and Massachusetts. La Follette had
secured North Dakota and Wisconsin. The total popular vote for Roosevelt
stood at 1,214,969, while Taft secured 865,835 votes and La Follette 327,357.

"I have had so many jolts," the despondent Taft told Horace—bespeaking
a battering far beyond the political arena, to intimate his sorrow over the ugly
estrangement from Theodore Roosevelt and a profound grief for his lost companion Archie Butt—"that I am not worrying over it."

CHAPTER TWENTY-EIGHT

"Bosom Friends, Bitter Enemies"

"His Back to the Wall," a June 3, 1912, *New York World* cartoon,
dramatizes the tumultuous battle between Taft and Roosevelt
for the Republican presidential nomination.

TO OBSERVERS ACROSS THE NATION and even overseas, it was clear an unprecedented challenge to President Taft was well under way. "A month ago practically every impartial observer believed that Mr. Roosevelt had no chance," *The Times* of London noted as the primary season drew to an end. "Now, however, it is admitted on all hands that he has a chance." As Republicans completed preparations to meet in Chicago in mid-June to choose their nominee for president, William Jennings Bryan predicted that the Republican National Convention of 1912 would be "the most exciting ever held in the history of the country." Not only were the main contenders "once bosom friends" who had become "bitter enemies," but the country had "never before" witnessed a fight for the nomination between a president and an ex-president.

"Each side makes confident assertions," one correspondent for the *New York Tribune* remarked, "but each side secretly is scared stiff." Roosevelt steadfastly maintained that the people had already spoken. The vast majority of primary voters had chosen him, furnishing a significant percentage of the 540 delegates he needed to secure the nomination; the convention, he confidently asserted, would "not dare to oppose the will of the majority," because to do so "would mean ruin to the Republican Party." The president, however, had far greater support in states where party organizations retained control of the selection process. Taft believed he had accumulated enough delegates in non-primary states to win at Chicago. In truth, neither campaign arrived in the Windy City with enough votes to take the nomination on the first ballot. "No man in this city, nor any man in this hemisphere," the *Tribune* reporter figured, "knows absolutely who will be nominated for President."

Before the convention could begin its proceedings, the Republican National Committee had to settle disputes over 254 seats. These contested seats represented more than half the votes necessary for victory and the turbulent nomination fight had generated scores of rival delegations. Meeting in Chicago twelve days before the convention, the committee was charged with determining the legitimacy of the competing claims. Lawyers from both sides were prepared with detailed affidavits, but there, the New York *Sun* noted, resemblance to a civilized courtroom setting would likely end. Emotions were running high, the paper declared, and "the lawyers and witnesses and contestants are liable to break out into fisticuffs and thump each other around the committee room." There were "some contests, of course, Roosevelt ought to win," Taft acknowledged, but he believed the vast majority of the disputes brought by the Colonel's campaign had been intended merely to generate publicity. Most important, the National Committee comprised loyal Taft supporters whom Roosevelt would not be able to "frighten or bulldoze."

To Roosevelt's detriment, the first contests to be decided were from the South, where Taft had legitimately secured most of the delegates before his opponent even entered the race. The Roosevelt campaign had never expected to win these contests; indeed, they had been instituted simply to keep Taft's delegate count from appearing insurmountable before the northern primaries commenced. When these early cases came before the committee, even Roosevelt's men voted to seat the Taft delegates, conceding that in most instances "the contestants had failed to make out a case."

In Oyster Bay, Roosevelt followed the hearings with dismay, anxious that decisions in Taft's favor would begin to sound all too "familiar." In one Alabama district where Roosevelt had a reasonable case for seating two of his delegates, the committee nonetheless assigned the two places to Taft, confirming his fears. Roosevelt issued a fierce denouncement of the decision, charging that men had "been sent to the penitentiary for less reprehensible election frauds than the theft of that delegation." The Colonel's bombastic statement succeeded in riveting public attention on the actions of the National Committee. While the public outcry stiffened the spine of his supporters, it simultaneously hardened the attitudes of the Taft committeemen. On subsequent rulings in critical contests in Washington, Indiana, Texas, and California, the committee divided along straight partisan lines, with thirty-nine members consistently voting for Taft's delegates, fourteen for Roosevelt's.

Even impartial observers agreed that in the cases of Washington and Indiana, the committee's decisions complied with "neither justice nor logic." In Washington, the first primaries ever held in Spokane, Tacoma, and Seattle favored Roosevelt by two-to-one and sometimes ten-to-one margins. Overwhelming support in these populous areas should have secured him a majority of the state's fourteen delegates; but when evidence of fraud and "irregularities" in the city primaries surfaced at the hearings, the National Committee decided it had no choice but to stand by the proceedings of the state party organization, which had selected Taft. In Indiana, the committee "reversed itself," declining to examine a series of questionable district primaries in which Taft had emerged the clear victor. Though Roosevelt's team demonstrated that repeat voting had occurred and that some Indianapolis ballots had not been counted, the committee claimed that it was too late to relitigate the election results.

The National Committee's decision to award the majority of the Texas delegates to Taft represented what many considered the most glaring violation of "fair play." Texas was the sole southern state where the leader of the state party, Cecil Andrew Lyon, was a Roosevelt man. Lyon had accompanied the Colonel on his hunting trip in 1905 and remained a personal friend. At the state convention, Lyon engineered a solid victory for Roosevelt. The committee acknowledged that the Roosevelt delegation had been legally chosen according to party rules but claimed that the rival Taft delegation, selected at a rump convention, had greater popular support. Seating the Taft delegation, the committee argued, was an important step toward eliminating "boss rule" in the state of Texas. California was one of the last contests the committee considered. The hearing should have been simple: the California legislature had passed a primary law calling for delegates to be elected at large. Roosevelt, who had won the state by a margin of 77,000 votes, argued he was entitled to all twenty-six of the state's delegates. Taft had carried one district—the

4th congressional district of San Francisco. The committee gave the two San Francisco seats to Taft.

The rhetoric from both campaigns grew more vitriolic with each passing day. Taft's campaign manager, William McKinley, claimed that the Roosevelt forces were taking "desperate measures" to forestall the inevitability of Taft's nomination on the first ballot. It was "common knowledge," McKinley asserted, that several Negro delegates from the South had been "brazenly approached" by Roosevelt men "with offers of money" to switch their allegiance to the Colonel. "I dare them to name any of our men involved in bribery," Senator Joseph Dixon retorted. "McKinley is like a cuttlefish," he added, "that muddies the water that its own hideousness may not be seen."

Of the 254 seats, the National Committee finally awarded 235 to Taft and only 19 to Roosevelt. While most analysts agree that Taft rightfully won the great majority of the southern contests, which yielded over 150 delegates, the 100 remaining seats are subject to debate. Roosevelt likely deserved to win somewhere between thirty and fifty. Even with fifty additional delegates, however, he would have been short of a majority. Still, with the help of La Follette's delegates, Taft's nomination on the first ballot might be prevented—and then, anything was possible.

As the committee hearings wound to a close, Roosevelt's campaign managers decided that they must do something "to crystallize the public spirit, to force public indignation, or arouse enough public sentiment to compel the nomination of Roosevelt." The temporary roll of delegates established by the National Committee still had to be sanctioned by the convention's Committee on Credentials and voted upon by the delegates as a whole. Aware that time was running out, Senator Dixon prevailed upon Roosevelt to take the unprecedented step of coming to Chicago in person.

Roosevelt needed little encouragement. On June 14, he and Edith drove together to his *Outlook* office in New York. Reporters noted that "he seemed in a gay mood," sporting "a new sombrero, with a five-inch brim." The old hat he had worn when he gave his controversial Columbus speech, he quipped, "had been kicked around the ring enough to warrant a new one." The Colonel sequestered himself in his office for several hours before appearing in the lobby with a prepared statement: "A small knot of professional politicians," he charged, were trying "to steal" the right of the people "to make their own nomination." The rank and file of Republican voters, having clearly expressed their will in the primaries, were "not in the mood to see their victory stolen from them."

On the day Roosevelt boarded the *Lake Shore Limited* bound for Chicago, the president issued a brief statement from the White House. "All the information I get is that I will be nominated on the first ballot with votes to spare," Taft announced. He had remained silent during the proceedings of the National Committee, leaving Washington correspondents to chronicle his social life: a trip with Nellie to present diplomas to Annapolis cadets; a sail on the *Mayflower* to Hampton Roads; a dinner for Guatemala's minister of foreign affairs; an evening party on Capitol Hill; and a golf game at Chevy Chase.

While Taft remained tight-lipped, his campaign spokesmen made headlines, depicting Roosevelt's journey to Chicago as "an undeniable admission of defeat." Recalling the Colonel's assertion that he would not go unless it proved "absolutely necessary," William McKinley claimed that the trip represented "the last hope of a lost cause." New York boss William Barnes issued an acid personal attack: "Mr. Roosevelt's departure for Chicago was inevitable. Undignified as it is, and impotent as it will prove to be, its chief interest lies in the disclosure of the mania for power over which Mr. Roosevelt has no control."

The people of Chicago greeted the arrival of Theodore Roosevelt quite differently; word that Roosevelt was en route drove the city "plum crazy" with excitement. Ordinary business was suspended as tens of thousands made plans to celebrate Roosevelt's arrival. In the Loop district, one reporter observed, "there wasn't an office boy on the job." It seemed that "everyone had lost a grandmother and had failed to show up for work." Scuffles erupted in hotel lobbies as Roosevelt delegates routinely cried out "thief" at men sporting Taft badges. Armed with megaphones, Roosevelt supporters belted out songs for "Teddy," only to be met with "jeers and hoots" by equal numbers of Taft men. A bartender at one of the leading hotels offered a special "campaign drink" garnished with a lemon peel cut to resemble a Rough Rider hat. The circumference of the cocktail glass symbolized the political ring into which the Colonel had metaphorically flung his hat. Patrons who kept the lemon peel in the glass as they consumed the gin and vermouth concoction were Roosevelt men; those who discarded it supported Taft.

Hours before Roosevelt's train arrived at La Salle Station, three bands and an immense crowd, waving "Teddy" flags and wearing Roosevelt buttons, had gathered at the railway yards. "The sight of the Colonel, teeth agleam, romantic headgear, burly arms waving greetings, was catalytic," reported Mark Sullivan. "A mob, shouting, laughing, cheering, shoving, engulfed the police and took Roosevelt to its bosom." Thousands of screaming men and women lined the streets as the former president rode in an open car to the Congress Hotel. So frenzied was the crowd in the lobby that it took a team of five men using "football tactics" to propel Roosevelt to the elevator.

No sooner had the Colonel reached the quiet of his room than he clambered from a window onto a balcony over Michigan Avenue, anxious to satisfy the expectations of the waiting crowd. "His appearance was the signal for a roar," the *New York Times* reported. Smiling broadly and waving his hat, he initiated the wild acclaim of the people for several minutes before leaning over the stone railing to speak. "Chicago is a mighty poor place in which to try and steal anything," he roared. "Give it to 'em, Colonel," the crowd thundered in return. "Knock 'em out." In answer to their entreaties, he went directly after the president. "The receiver of stolen goods is no better than the thief," he fiercely pronounced. "The people will win. We have won in every State where the people could express themselves 3 to 1 and sometimes 8 to 1. This is a naked fight against corrupt politicians and thieves and the thieves will not win."

Before Roosevelt went to dinner that night, a newspaperman asked whether he was prepared "to stand up to the rigors of what lay ahead." His answer provided the enduring symbol of his campaign. "I'm feeling like a bull moose," he replied, invoking the antlered king of the northern woods whose supposed instinct "to gore his antagonist" reflected Roosevelt's combative mood. "He is essentially a fighter," Elihu Root said of his old friend, "and when he gets into a fight he is completely dominated by the desire to destroy his adversary." The bull moose icon captured the imagination of the American people. Images of the massive creature suddenly appeared on posters and placards all across the country, while button manufacturers desperately tried to keep up with demand. The Teddy bear had been supplanted by a far more imposing and belligerent mascot.

The following Monday, June 17, Roosevelt "put in one of the busiest days of his life—a very frenzy of activity, which amazed and startled even his close associates." He met with streams of supporters, interviewed Taft delegates who might be persuaded to change their minds, conferred with the seven governors, and talked with reporters, all the while continuing to draft the address he would deliver that evening to a mass audience. It was evident, a *Chicago Daily Tribune* reporter marveled, that the Colonel had not lost any of his "magnetism." And he had retained the gift for making every caller feel that he was "at that moment the exact person of all the world's population he loved and most desired to see."

More than 20,000 people clamored for tickets to hear Roosevelt's final speech of the nominating campaign. His managers had reserved the Auditorium, advertised as "the largest theater in the United States west of the Alleghenies," though, in actuality, it seated only 4,200. At 6 p.m., police shut down all the surrounding streets, allowing only ticket holders to enter the cordoned area. Hundreds of eager bystanders without tickets deployed all manner of "ingenious" schemes to gain entrance: women claimed their husbands and children were already inside; men insisted they were members of the glee club or the platform committee. All were steadfastly denied by the police. Every seat was filled long before Roosevelt arrived. An organist played patriotic tunes while the audience sang along. "A great roar" greeted the Colonel's entrance, and the "avalanche of applause" continued for nearly five minutes. At last, Roosevelt stretched out his arms and began delivering what critics considered not only "the most moving speech of his career" but "one of the most dramatic speeches ever made."

He had decided to run, Roosevelt explained, only when "convinced that Mr. Taft had definitely and completely abandoned the cause of the people and had surrendered himself wholly to the biddings of the professional political bosses and of the great privileged interests standing behind them." He entreated those still backing Senator La Follette to join with him, for he had honestly earned "the overwhelming majority" of the votes of the Republican progressive vote, and he alone could win the fight against Taft. He then set forth two maxims: first, those delegates "fraudulently put on the temporary roll by the dishonest action of the majority of the national committee" must be barred from voting; second, if they were allowed to participate, then progressives would not be bound by the actions of the convention.

Buoyed by the thunderous approval of the crowd, Roosevelt rolled toward his final call to arms. "A period of change is upon us," he proclaimed, warning that "our opponents, the men of reaction, ask us to stand still. But we could not stand still if we would; we must either go forward or go backward. . . . It would be far better to fail honorably for the cause we champion than it would be to win by foul methods the foul victory for which our opponents hope. But the victory shall be ours, and it shall be won as we have already won so many victories, by clean and honest fighting for the loftiest of causes. We fight in honorable fashion for the good of mankind; fearless of the future; unheeding of our individual fates; with unflinching hearts and undimmed eyes; we stand at Armageddon, and we battle for the Lord."

The hall erupted in tumultuous, sustained applause. "There is no question," William Allen White observed, "that the psychology of the situation, the enthusiasm of the crowds, the lonesomeness at Taft headquarters and the energy of the Roosevelt workers all point to Roosevelt's nomination." Still, White reflected, "it is delegates rather than psychology that make nominations."

By the commencement of the Republican National Convention on June 18, the atmosphere was so tense that "extraordinary preparations" were made "to preserve the peace." More than 1,000 policemen were deployed to the Coliseum, a massive stone structure "two squares in length and one in width," capable of seating more than 12,000 people. "Passions have been unloosed, anger has been unbridled," *The Washington Post* reported. "It is almost incredible to hear at a national convention the question seriously discussed if there will be firearms used and whether blood will be shed, but one can hear this at every step in the frightful jam and welter in the hotel lobbies."

In the comfort of the White House that morning, Taft was detached both physically and emotionally from the turmoil in Chicago. "Whatever happens," he wrote to Horace, "I shall be glad to have the strain over." With each passing month, the gulf between Taft and Roosevelt had grown. Taft had long considered himself a moderate progressive, aligned almost perfectly with the sentiments and policies of his old friend. In the throes of the brutal campaign, however, he had withdrawn increasingly from more progressive ideas. "If I am nominated, I shall have to take my stand as the representative of the conservative, sober, second thought of the people of the United States," he told one friend. "I may go down to defeat if a bolt is started by Roosevelt," the president acknowledged to another, "but I will retain the regular organization of the party as a nucleus about which the conservative people who are in favor of maintaining constitutional government can gather."

Before convening his cabinet at ten that morning, Taft spoke by long-distance telephone to his campaign team. McKinley and Charles Hilles were hopeful that they had the votes from the temporary list of delegates to win the crucial election of the convention's presiding officer, known as the temporary chair. Taft's candidate was New York senator Elihu Root, perhaps the shrewdest decision of his entire campaign. William Allen White described the sixty-seven-year-old Root as the "most learned, even erudite, distinguished, and impeccable conservative," a "calm, serene, and sure" leader, capable of dominating any gathering. Indeed, Roosevelt himself had once described his former secretary of state as "the ablest man that has appeared in the public life of any country in any position in my time." Such praise came before Elihu Root had backed William Taft through the bitter primary season. Now, Roosevelt announced his blistering opposition to Root's candidacy for the chairmanship, declaring: "Mr. Root stands as the representative of reaction. He is put forward by the bosses and the representatives of special privilege. He has ranged himself against the men who stand for progressive principles." Roosevelt's vituperative charges, Root's biographer observes, "were cruel thrusts at an old friend and Root felt them."

In an equally canny move, the Roosevelt team chose Wisconsin governor Francis McGovern as their candidate for the chairmanship. A few weeks earlier, Roosevelt had asked Dixon to "think over whether it would not be (a good play) wise to have McGovern of Wisconsin Permanent Chairman." Not only was Wisconsin's popular governor "a fine fellow," but "our choice of him would emphasize, as nothing else would, the fact that we wish all Progressives to stand together." Three days later, Roosevelt approached McGovern directly: "I assume that you will make the nominating speech for La Follette. And this would leave all the La Follette men at entire liberty to stand by him." If McGovern then ran for chair with the backing of the Roosevelt team, the progressives would present "a united front." When McGovern agreed, Roosevelt was delighted, hoping that "state pride" would lead La Follette's twenty-six delegates to support the selection of McGovern for chair.

At noon, Republican national chair Victor Rosewater called the convention to order. Rosewater had been designated to take charge of the proceedings until the election of the chair. But before Rosewater had the chance to call for nominations for the position, Roosevelt's floor leader, Missouri's Herbert Hadley, rose and motioned that seventy-two of the most fiercely contested Taft delegates, fraudulently included in the temporary roll by the National Committee, should be replaced by "honestly elected" Roosevelt delegates.

The method by which the Roosevelt team arrived at the figure of seventy-two remains a matter of conjecture. Three years later, a disaffected former intimate of the Colonel informed Taft that Hadley had approached Roosevelt, suggesting a determined fight on twenty-four or twenty-eight seats that had clearly been stolen from them in states such as Texas, Washington, California, and Indiana. Roosevelt, "with characteristic emphasis and energy," immediately tripled that figure, knowing how many votes he needed to control the convention.

Hadley's motion to bar participation of the seventy-two contested delegates brought great cheers from Roosevelt supporters. After silence was restored, Indiana's James Watson, a Taft spokesman, insisted that Hadley's motion "was not in order, on the ground that the convention itself had no chairman as yet," and therefore could not take up any business. Rosewater allowed forty minutes of debate on the motion before rendering the critical ruling that Hadley's motion was, indeed, out of order, and straightaway opened nominations for the chairmanship. As expected, Root's nomination was greeted with cheers from

Taft's supporters while McGovern drew equal enthusiasm from the Roosevelt side. A wave of surprise swept the hall, however, when La Follette's manager, Walter Houser, stood and forcibly insisted that McGovern's candidacy was "not with La Follette's consent." La Follette, he continued, would strike no deal whatsoever with Roosevelt. Houser's words propelled La Follette boosters to their feet, waving a large banner bearing the words: "We'll heed not Taffy's smile / Nor Teddy's toothsome grin / For it's La Follette once, La Follette twice / And La Follette till we win!" It seemed, the *New York Tribune* observed, that La Follette preferred "to see Senator Root elected rather than to see Colonel Roosevelt win the initial contest of the convention." Roosevelt's failure to reconcile with La Follette would prove costly.

So raucous was the atmosphere in the hall that nearly three hours passed before the voting was completed. When Rosewater announced that Root had defeated McGovern by a narrow margin of 558 to 501, pandemonium erupted. Pennsylvania's William Flinn marched up onto the platform, jabbed a finger at Root, and screamed out: "Receiver of stolen goods!" This brazen accusation prompted a series of fistfights that would have escalated into wholesale rioting without police intervention. Root approached the speaker's table to deliver his keynote address, apparently unperturbed by "the sweating wrathful faces in the pit." Marveling at the senator's comportment, William White reflected that "hundreds of [Root's] outraged fellow Republicans, men who had once been his friends, were glaring at him with eyes distraught with hate." Still, White observed, "Root's hands did not tremble, his face did not flicker."

That afternoon, in lieu of an anxious White House vigil for convention bulletins, Taft and Nellie had motored to the ballpark to attend a Nationals baseball game. When the president entered the stadium, the exuberant crowd of more than 20,000 "loudly cheered him for five minutes, the men throwing their hats into the air and the women waving their handkerchiefs." In a brief speech, Taft congratulated the team on their astonishing record—winning sixteen games in a row—before settling into his box to enjoy the action. So absorbed did he become in the game, which the Nationals won, that he never called for any updated bulletins. Returning to the White House, he discovered, to his great satisfaction, that Elihu Root had defeated Francis McGovern.

Roosevelt, meanwhile, had monitored every twist and turn of the proceedings by wire and telephone. All afternoon, hundreds of supporters had gathered in the Florentine Room of the Congress Hotel, where news from the convention floor was relayed by telephone to a man with a megaphone. "It was his duty," one journalist for the *New York Times* recorded, "to shout out the various incidents of the Colonel's triumphant progress" to those packing the room and the noisy throng assembled in the hallways and the lobby below. "There were frequent cheers from the crowd," the *Times* reporter wrote, "but as it progressed and the tide began to fall, threatening to leave the Colonel stranded on the political sands, the megaphone man lost his enthusiasm and his voice." When word spread that Roosevelt "had lost his preliminary skirmish," the crowd "fell silent."

The Colonel "remained in seclusion" for a short time while he and Dixon debated their next move. Later that night, he called a meeting of his delegates. Infusing them with his own energy and defiance, he "urged them to stand by him" as he resumed the fight to purge the tainted delegate roll once the convention came to order the following morning.

As DELEGATES AND SPECTATORS GATHERED for the second day of the convention, June 19, "electricity filled the air." The Coliseum was "a powder mine." With the chairman in place and the convention open for business, Hadley once again moved to replace the seventy-two contested Taft delegates with Roosevelt men. Chairman Root allowed three hours of debate on the motion. Watson, speaking for the Taft campaign, persuasively countered Hadley's motion, insisting that the full convention had "no knowledge" and was "in no temper to pass upon these contests." Evaluating the merits of the National Committee's controversial decisions belonged finally to the Committee on Credentials, which would be officially appointed later that day. After conferring with Hadley, Watson announced that a compromise had been reached and that Hadley would "consent to refer the resolution to the Committee on Credentials." The news thrilled Republicans on both sides of the bitter divide. A Pennsylvania delegate dashed to the stage, shouting, "Hadley, the next president of the United States," triggering a boisterous Hadley demonstration. Delegations marched about the hall exulting in the sudden possibility of a compromise candidate who might unite the party.

Just as suddenly, the spell was broken. An attractive young woman in a white dress, with a "radiant and infectious smile," stood up in the gallery blowing kisses and waving a large Roosevelt poster. The band began playing; shouts of "Teddy, Teddy, Teddy" rose from every corner in the hall. The woman made her way to the floor, escorted through the aisles "with the Roosevelt State delegations and placards falling in line." For forty-two minutes, the crowd followed her lead. Regardless of whether, as some speculated, this lady had been cued to begin blowing kisses and rallying support for the Colonel, the emotional Roosevelt demonstration ended the prospect of bringing Hadley to the stage as a compromise candidate.

When Root finally restored order, Hadley stood up, returning the convention's focus to the delegate confirmation process for the contested seats. While both he and Root agreed that "no man can be permitted to vote upon the question of his own right to a seat in the convention," Hadley stridently argued that the entire group of contested delegates should be barred from determining the composition of the vital Credentials Committee. Root, however, adhering to congressional parliamentary procedure, maintained that "the rule does not disqualify any delegate whose name is on the roll from voting upon the contest of any other man's right, or participating in the ordinary business of the convention so long as he holds his seat." This pivotal ruling, which allowed all the contested delegates to participate in the makeup of the Credentials Committee, essentially delivered control of the convention to Taft.

The committee members began their deliberations that night. Outnumbered thirty-one to twenty-one, the Roosevelt men soon realized that the Taft contingency had no intention of relitigating the National Committee's seating decisions. It was evident that most, if not all, of the contested delegates from the temporary roll would retain their seats, thereby providing Taft a clear majority. At midnight, a message arrived from the Colonel himself. "We are requested to go at once to the Florentine room of the Congress hotel," California's Francis Heney shouted, dismissively observing, "We can't get a square deal here." Back at the hotel, rebellious delegates and regular party members debated whether to bolt. While talk of a new party had been in the air since the convention opened, they now faced the difficult reality of engineering a split and financing a new creation. Suddenly the "prospect of leaving party lines, even to support Colonel Roosevelt," did not seem "half as attractive" as from "some miles further away." If the prospective members were "to be anything other than ridiculous figures in their state campaigns," this new party would require "time and money and effort," with money the paramount resource.

Amos Pinchot would long recall "the moment when the third party was born." At two o'clock in the morning, Roosevelt's inner circle gathered in his bedroom suite. "A dozen were seated around the table, the rest in armchairs or leaning against the wall," Pinchot wrote. "Roosevelt was walking rapidly up and down in silence." All eyes were on Frank Munsey and George Perkins, who whispered together in the corner. Without the financial support of these two wealthy men, there was little hope that a new party could be organized in time for the fall election. "Suddenly, the whispered talk ceased," Pinchot recollected, as both Munsey and Perkins "moved over to Roosevelt, meeting him in the middle of the room. Each placed a hand on one of his shoulders, and one, or both of them, said, 'Colonel, we will see you through.' " Munsey, the more effusive of the two magnates, added: "My fortune, my magazines and my newspapers are with you."

Returning to the conference room, Roosevelt read a short announcement to his delegates and supporters. If the convention refused to purge the tainted roll, the Colonel had resolved to "lead a fight for his principles in defiance of any action of the regular Republican convention." He expressed his thanks "to those who had come thus far in his fight, but who might not care to continue with him further." He would release these men, parting from them "on terms of friendship and undiminished gratitude." Those who chose to stay, he invited to participate in the birth of a new party. "Grizzled veterans wiped tears from their eyes," observed a reporter for the *Washington Times*, "making no effort to conceal their emotions."

As word spread that Roosevelt might come in person to deliver a statement that next day, the convention hall was "jammed to its fullest capacity." Minutes after Root gaveled the convention to order, Taft's floor leader called for a recess, explaining that the report of the Credentials Committee was not ready. A later four o'clock session lasted only a minute because the committee was still not ready. After this second delay, the convention was adjourned until the following day. Leaving the hall, delegates and spectators "gathered in knots," trying to piece together what was happening. Word circulated that men on both sides had revived the search for a compromise candidate—perhaps Cummins or Hughes or Hadley. It was rumored but later denied that Taft had agreed "to withdraw his candidacy providing Colonel Roosevelt would do the same." Details of the dramatic midnight session in Roosevelt's suite gradually began to surface—foremost Roosevelt's pledge to continue fighting if the Credentials Committee refused to seat his "honestly elected" delegates.

The mayhem in Chicago attracted unprecedented attention in the press. Correspondents covered every reversal, every sensational, rancorous moment, with relish. Reporters from dozens of national and regional publications were busy "politicking, filing correspondence, intriguing, pretending they were making a president." Sam McClure, who had come to the convention on his own, "stood on the edges" of the clusters of journalists, feeling "like a cipher." He had been "shorn" as editor of his once celebrated magazine a month earlier when his accumulated debt had finally forced him to lease and then sell

McClure's. The buyer had originally promised to retain McClure as editor, but the final deal left S.S., in his own words, "unhorsed." He had come to Chicago in search of work. At the convention hall and in the lobbies of the hotels, the fifty-five-year-old McClure met up with scores of old friends. For the first time in his life, observing the hurly-burly of the convention, Sam McClure found himself on the periphery of the action.

At noon on Friday, June 21, after two straight nights with little sleep, the Credentials Committee was finally ready to issue state-by-state reports on the contested seats. Proceeding alphabetically with Alabama, the committee chairman announced that the majority had voted to sustain the original decision of the National Committee and seat the two Taft delegates. A minority report introduced by the Roosevelt members was immediately voted down by a safe Taft majority. "A storm of hisses and booing" broke out, but Root swiftly restored order, calling on Arizona and then Arkansas. As one state after another voted to seat the Taft delegates, a voice from the gallery rose from the din: "Roll the steamroller some more!" As each new case was decided in favor of Taft's delegates, "a thousand toots and imitation whistles of the steamroller engine pierced the air." Bedlam followed as the galleries "caught the spirit," rhythmically shouting "Toot Toot" and "Choo Choo." The police removed a man who interrupted the proceedings by repeatedly crying: "All aboard." As he was escorted out, he grinned and waved, provoking "a great uproar." The convention was adjourned until the following day when, amid "a chorus of shrieks, whistles, groans and catcalls," the remainder of the states followed suit, granting Taft all seventy-two contested delegates.

With Taft's nomination on the first ballot virtually guaranteed, Henry Allen, a Roosevelt delegate from Kansas, asked to read a statement from the Colonel. "The Convention has now declined to purge the roll of the fraudulent delegates," Roosevelt's announcement began. "This action makes the convention in no proper sense any longer a Republican convention, representing the real Republican Party, therefore I hope that the men elected as Roosevelt delegates will now decline to vote on any matter before the Convention. . . . Any man nominated by the Convention as now constituted would be merely the beneficiary of this successful fraud." Roosevelt's inflammatory words provoked near riot on the convention floor. Taft delegates physically attacked Roosevelt delegates; brawls erupted throughout the galleries. Although police stopped dozens of scuffles, they were unable "to keep track of them all."

It was nearly 7:30 p.m. on Saturday night before the roll call for the nomination began. At 9:28 p.m., William Howard Taft was officially proclaimed the victor, with 561 votes. Three hundred forty-four Roosevelt delegates had followed the Colonel's request, designating themselves "present but not voting." An additional 107 delegates insisted on following the command of their primaries, casting their votes for Roosevelt. Of the remaining votes, La Follette received 41, Senator Cummins 17, and Justice Hughes 2.

☙ ❧

THE WHITE HOUSE WAS so quiet on the night the convention concluded, one reporter remarked, that "no one would have suspected that under the same roof was the man who had been named as candidate of the ruling party." During the balloting, Taft had been with Nellie and their children in the living quarters. Young Charlie Taft was once again in charge of carrying the up-to-date bulletins from the telegraph office. Reporters noted that the fourteen-year-old was "all grin" when word came that his father had secured a majority vote for the nomination. But unlike the "electric" excitement that had filled the room four years earlier, when Nellie had sparkled with happiness and Taft had "laughed with the joy of a boy," both the president and first lady clearly understood that the divisive convention had rendered Republican chances for election in November almost impossible. "No Republican convention ever adjourned," observed the *New York Tribune*, "leaving so many sores and with so little prospect that the wounds would be healed."

"I am not afraid of defeat in November," Taft repeatedly said in the days that followed his nomination. He believed he had already achieved the victory he wanted by preventing Roosevelt from taking over the Republican Party and moving it in an incomprehensibly radical direction that threatened to upset the constitutional separation of powers and destroy "the absolute independence of the judiciary." In the course of the campaign, he had come to regard Roosevelt as "a real menace to our institutions." The central issue "at stake," he declared in his first public statement after his nomination, "was whether the Republican party" would remain "the chief conservator" of the country's constitutional guarantees. His victory, he proudly noted, had "preserved the party organization as a nucleus for conservative action."

☙ ❧

THE ROOSEVELT DELEGATES HAD BEGUN their exodus from the Coliseum even before the finalization of Taft's nomination. A "mass meeting" had been called at Orchestra Hall a short distance away to begin the process of forming a new national party. Great applause greeted Edith and the Roosevelt children as they took their seats in a box near the platform. News that conservative Vice President James Sherman had been renominated added to the "delight" of the

Roosevelt men, who had worried that Taft might try to bolster the Republican ticket by selecting a progressive for the second spot. As they waited for the various state delegations to arrive from the convention, the audience joined in a spirited rendition of "America." When the California delegation paraded into the hall bearing its distinctive Golden Bear banner, the crowd erupted with "wild enthusiasm." A new round of cheers began a few minutes later when the Ohio delegation entered the room. "Here comes Texas," screamed a man in the audience as the Lone Star delegation marched in, followed in short order by Oklahoma. Similar waves of cheering met each of the delegations as they entered the room, creating a jubilant atmosphere.

California governor Hiram Johnson opened the formal proceedings of the new Progressive Party. "We came here," he declared, "to carry out the mandate of the people to nominate Theodore Roosevelt. By a fraud he has been robbed of that which was his. We, the delegates free and untrammeled, have come here to nominate him tonight." After a nominating resolution was unanimously passed, a notification committee composed of representatives from twenty-two states escorted Roosevelt into the hall. "The people leaped to their feet with a shout and for five minutes there was pandemonium," the *New York Tribune* reported. Another demonstration ensued when Roosevelt mounted the stage to declare his acceptance. He charged supporters to go home, "find out the sentiment of the people," and then reconvene a few weeks later at "a mass convention" to nominate "a progressive candidate on a progressive platform" that would truly represent people in all sections of the country. "If you wish me to make the fight I will make it," he promised, "even if only one State should support me. The only condition I impose, is that you shall be free when you come together to substitute any other man in my place if you deem it better for the movement and in such case I will give him my heartiest support."

The enthusiasm that had sustained the Roosevelt Progressives all week reached a peak that evening at Orchestra Hall. That a split party had little prospect for victory in November seemed irrelevant to the exuberant crowd, though not to former Republican senator Chauncey Depew, who offered a widely quoted comment as the 1912 Republican National Convention came to a close. "The only question now," he said, "is which corpse gets the most flowers."

⤞ ⤝

DURING THE LAST WEEK OF June, as Democrats gathered in Baltimore to choose their nominee for president, reporters asked Roosevelt for his thoughts on the leading contenders—Speaker Champ Clark and New Jersey governor Woodrow Wilson. "I'm in the fight for an independent Republican party," Roosevelt defiantly declared, "and whatever the Democrats do will make no difference with me." Bluster aside, Roosevelt knew he had a much greater chance of victory if the Democrats chose the more conservative Clark over Wilson, who had emerged as a Progressive champion. "Pop's been praying for Clark," Kermit Roosevelt disclosed, revealing a Roosevelt far from indifferent to the outcome.

Like the Republicans, the Democrats quickly evidenced party discord in their own battle to appoint the temporary chair. Clark, with the backing of Tammany Hall, won that "first skirmish," but progressives refused to accept his nominee, overturning the result when the time came to choose a permanent chair. "Everybody's doing it. Doesn't it remind you of Chicago?" Roosevelt gleefully asked reporters. When the balloting began for the nomination, Clark took an early lead, reaching a majority vote on the tenth ballot. Democratic Party rules required a two-thirds vote for victory, however; by the fourteenth ballot, the momentum had shifted to Wilson. Sixteen ballots later, Wilson held a slight majority, but it was not until the forty-sixth ballot, eight turbulent days after the Democratic National Convention opened, that the New Jersey governor finally secured the nomination. The suspenseful events in Baltimore had transfixed the nation's attention. All week long, William White reported, "the country was standing around the billboards of newspapers in great crowds," waiting for the latest news from that city.

Throughout the dramatic ordeal, Wilson appeared impassive. "You must sometimes have wondered why I did not show more emotions as the news came in from the convention," he told reporters when word of his victory finally arrived, "and I have been afraid that you might get the impression that I was so self-confident and sure of the result that I took the steady increase in the vote for me complacently and as a matter of course. The fact is that the emotion has been too deep to come to the surface."

Wilson's nomination immediately affected Roosevelt's campaign prospects. Chase Osborn, one of the seven governors who had originally urged the Colonel to run, announced that he intended to support New Jersey's Democratic governor. With a progressive in the field, he explained, there was "no necessity for a new political party." The president of Minnesota's Progressive League agreed with Osborn, declaring that his organization would back Wilson. To illustrate that Wilson's appeal crossed party lines, his campaign cited more than 2,000 letters from Republicans pledging support. "Warmest congratulations from a Roosevelt Progressive Republican, who will vote for Wilson," one Californian had written. "I most gladly leave my old party—the party of my father—and join your cause," declared a lawyer from West Virginia.

Robert La Follette was delighted to support Woodrow Wilson. Still consumed with anger toward Roosevelt for projecting his personal ambition for a third term onto "a strong and rapidly growing" Progressive movement within the Republican Party, La Follette insisted that he would devote his days to "exposing the Roosevelt fraud." Calling the Colonel's primary battle "the most extravagant in American history," La Follette vowed to travel through the West, convincing farmers and laborers alike that "men notoriously identified with the Steel Trust and the Harvester Trust" were among Roosevelt's chief financial backers. Wilson gratefully acknowledged La Follette's support, lauding the Wisconsin senator as a courageous leader—"taunted, laughed at, called back, going steadfastly on."

"If Wilson had been nominated first," Roosevelt privately conceded, he might never have initiated the movement for a third party. "But it was quite out of the question," he told a friend, "after having led my men into the fight, that I should then abandon them." Now, supporters would conclude that he "was flinching from the contest," that he "was not game enough to stand punishment and face the possibility of disaster." Moreover, Roosevelt contended, while Wilson might be an "excellent man," supporting him "would mean restoring to power the Democratic bosses in Congress and in the several States, and I don't think that we can excuse ourselves for such action."

The die was cast. On July 7, Roosevelt's campaign manager Senator Dixon released "a call to the people of the United States," designating August 5 for a convention in Chicago of the newly formed National Progressive Party in Chicago. Each state was asked to send a bloc of delegates equal to the total of its senators and representatives, selected by whatever method the state leaders desired. The call urged all those in all sections of the country who believed in "a national progressive movement" to rally together "to secure the better and more equitable diffusion of prosperity," and to "strike at the roots of privilege" in both industry and politics.

Sixty-three prominent Republicans in forty states signed the declaration, but to Roosevelt's chagrin, many of his once most fervent supporters held back. Those who were running for office faced a difficult choice: forsake their hero or join an untested party with little time to develop the machinery to get out the vote. In the end, Montana senator Joseph Dixon was the only senator or governor up for reelection who took the leap of joining the Progressive Party. Senators Cummins, Hadley, Borah, and Nelson declared their opposition to Taft but declined to desert the Republican Party, promising instead to reform it from within. These defections both saddened and irritated Roosevelt, who believed the national cause should hold precedence. "I feel that Cummins naturally belongs to us," he lamented to one friend, while confessing to another, "I greatly regret that Hadley was so foolish as not to come with us."

Carefully observing Roosevelt's efforts to establish his "Bull Moose" party—the name the newspapers gave to the new organization—Taft felt the Colonel's campaign was "sagging." With a trace of sympathy, he remarked to Nellie that the Colonel was "up against now what I have always had to contend against, to wit, the selfishness of local candidates, and he is feeling the effects I suppose of a tendency to regularity that a third party always has to fight." Nonetheless, Taft predicted, Roosevelt was "such a persistent talker" that he would compel "the courage of his followers." Though he believed Roosevelt "utterly unscrupulous" at times, Taft marveled at his "method of stating things, and his power of attracting public attention."

Despite the historic dominance of the two-party system, the Colonel remained confident that once "the object and purposes of his campaign" were made clear, many voters would "be won over," in particular, those "holding back for a nicer definition of his aims." During the final two weeks in July, Roosevelt canceled public appearances and refused visitors, closeting himself "hour after hour" in his private study at Sagamore Hill to prepare both the planks of the new party's platform and the keynote address he would deliver on August 5, the first day of the convention. Fully aware that "a great measure of his party's success" would depend upon "the strength and solidity" of its principles and platform, he promised that his speech would represent "the greatest effort of [his] life."

When he finished the first draft of the platform, Roosevelt took a single day off, amusing reporters with his characteristically frenetic style of relaxation: "Got up with the sun; worked in the library until breakfast; took Mrs. Roosevelt for a long walk toward Cold Spring Harbor; rowed about twelve miles; went horseback riding after luncheon and played six sets of tennis on his return." The next morning, he was back at his desk, reinvigorated, to complete his projected 15,000-word keynote speech on schedule.

⁙ ⁙

IN THE WAKE OF THE contentious Republican National Convention, President Taft wisely decided that "simplicity" should be "the distinguishing feature" of his notification ceremony, scheduled for August 1. There would be none of the fireworks, open-air concerts, booming cannons, parades, or decorated streets that had made Cincinnati so festive four years earlier. Marked by "unusual informality," the ceremony would be held in the White House, with only four hundred persons in attendance—primarily cabinet officials, members of Congress, and prominent Republican figures. During the last week in July, Taft worked "an average of sixteen hours a day" on his acceptance speech, designed as a defense of the Republican Party, the Constitution, judicial independence, private property, and civil liberty. "Roosevelt proposes to give out a radical platform that will startle some people," he told his Aunt Delia, recognizing exactly where he stood in the current political landscape. "Wilson says that his letter of acceptance is going to be radical, so between the two I have no part to play but that of a conservative, and that I am going to play."

The notification ceremony took place at noon in the East Room. The seats had been positioned in a semicircle around a raised platform. Stationed in the adjoining hallway, the Marine Band played patriotic airs. Warm applause greeted Nellie as she walked in and took her seat on the dais. Shortly thereafter, President Taft, accompanied by members of the Notification Committee, entered "amid loud shouts and handclapping." Following tradition, the chair of the Notification Committee, Elihu Root, delivered the official news of Taft's nomination.

In his brief remarks, Root referred to the turmoil surrounding the contested delegates. Speaking with force and authority, Root assured the president that as the convention's presiding officer, he had followed "long-established and unquestioned rules of law governing the party" at every step along the way. "Your title to the nomination is as clear and unimpeachable as the title of any candidate of any party since political conventions began." Root's testimonial provided tremendous comfort to Taft, who worried that Roosevelt's continued "harping" on the seating of delegates had persuaded people that his campaign had "committed great frauds," and that he had, in effect, stolen the nomination.

Taft accepted the nomination on behalf of a Republican Party "through which substantially all the progress and development in our country's history in the last fifty years has been finally effected." Our party, he declared, stands for "the right of property" and "the right of liberty," for institutions that have "stood the test of time," and for an economic system that rewards "energy, courage, enterprise, attention to duty, hard work, thrift, and providence" rather than "laziness, lack of attention, lack of industry, the yielding to appetite and passion." While he hoisted the conservative banner, Taft also spoke with genuine pride of the progressive legislation passed in recent years—the railroad legislation, the postal banking system, workers' compensation, an eight-hour day for all government contracts, and, most recently, the Children's

Bureau, the first federal agency dedicated to the social welfare of children. Even as the Republican Party protected the traditions of the past, he argued, it must remain sensitive to the shifting views of the role of government. "Time was," he explained, "when the least government was thought the best, and the policy which left all to the individual, unmolested and unaided by the government, was deemed the wisest." As industry consolidation and wealth disparity grew apace, however, it was "clearly recognized" that the government had a responsibility "to further equality of opportunity in respect of the weaker classes in their dealings with the stronger and more powerful." In sum, Taft did not intend to take the country backward, but rather to protect it against the demagogic proposals of his adversaries.

Asked to comment on Taft's speech, Roosevelt initially told reporters he preferred to answer the president in his own upcoming address at the Progressive Party Convention. "On second thought," he proved "unable to restrain himself," derogating Taft's words as "fatuous, inadequate, conservative," and ignorant of all "the live issues."

CHAPTER TWENTY-NINE

Armageddon

A Nov. 16, 1912, *Harper's Weekly* cartoon distilled the election's outcome:
In the original caption, Taft, as the GOP elephant, says to his opponent,
Bull Moose Roosevelt: "Well, you've helped rip me apart and 'downed' yourself!
Now I hope you're satisfied!"

A S MEMBERS OF THE PROGRESSIVE Party began filling Chicago's hotels in preparation for the August 5, 1912, opening of the "Bull Moose Convention," journalists remarked that "no man could go through the lobbies" without confronting a gathering of people that "looked less like the average Republican or Democratic Convention than anything you ever saw." There was "not a saloon-keeper in the crowd"; the delegates were younger and more earnest than the usual convention goers. Petticoats were everywhere. Hundreds of social workers, suffragettes, and advocates for working girls' rights had enlisted in the new party. "Instead of forcing your way through a crowd of tobacco-stained political veterans," the *New York Times* observed, "you raise your hat politely and say, 'Pardon me, Madam.' "

A sense of "great adventure" was in the air, William Allen White observed in the *Boston Daily Globe*, despite the certainty of "a convention seemingly without contest or climax, a convention apparently devoid of chance or speculation." No one questioned who the nominee would be or how it would come about. There would be "no dead places" in the convention hall, "no blocks of delegates seated with arms folded, with faces set and sullen while other delegates behaved like dancing dervishes." There was little dissent on any major issue; almost everyone believed in the Social Gospel. They had come to Chicago as crusaders, "satisfied that they were in the right."

Roosevelt had already contrived his response to the only issue that threatened this near-perfect accord. Though the new party embraced a number of Negro delegates from the North ("more, in fact," he noted, "than ever before figured in a National convention"), there would not be a single Negro delegate from the South. The Colonel had given southern progressives permission to send solely white delegations. Hoping to break into the "Solid South," he had persuaded himself that true justice would only come to Negro residents of old Confederate states by enlisting the efforts of "high-minded white men." Roosevelt's policy "was riddled with contradictions and paradoxes," as the historian John Gable succinctly observes. "He wanted to establish the New Nationalism on a nationwide basis by using a sectionalist approach; he sought to bring an end to racism by a racist strategy." When word of Roosevelt's "lily-white" delegations leaked, discord surfaced among party members attending the convention. But once Roosevelt made it clear that he absolutely would "not budge," the issue quickly faded from discussion. It was evident to all that Roosevelt himself was "the whole show," the rhyme and reason for the new party.

Once again, Chicago went mad with Theodore Roosevelt's arrival. The streets were blocked, all work came to a halt, and the sidewalks were filled with thousands of people. Standing in the rear of an open automobile as he made his way to the same hotel suite where he had stayed during the Republican Convention, Roosevelt was buoyant: "My friends," he proclaimed, "it is a great pleasure for me to be in Chicago again, and this time at the birth of a new party and not at the death of an old party." Reaching the Congress Hotel, he settled in to work on his all-important speech. He had deliberately scheduled his address before the platform was voted on, informing delegates that he would accept their nomination only if the party's agenda corresponded to the views he intended to outline in his "Confession of Faith."

When Roosevelt stepped onto the stage of the Coliseum, he received perhaps one of "the greatest personal demonstrations that has ever been given
a man in public life." Seasoned reporters were long accustomed to staged
political rallies. Over the years, they had witnessed "hundreds of men marching about with signs and banners, and shouting themselves hoarse"; but this
display of genuine emotion was unprecedented. The men and women gathering in Chicago had left past affiliations behind, having decided to "cast their
lots together" under the banner of a fledgling movement. They signaled their
collective identity with a unique "battle flag"—a red bandanna, chosen to
represent "the plain people," the heart of the country. Every man wore the
party's emblem around his neck; every woman had one around her wrist. One
delegate had even fastened a red bandanna around the neck of a stuffed bull
moose, strategically placed at the front of the auditorium.

Roosevelt "stood smiling in the center of the storm," waving his bandanna
at friends in various delegations. Twenty thousand voices spontaneously rose
in "The Battle Hymn of the Republic," the assembled crusaders finding courage and unity in the stirring words and soaring melody. During the nearly
hour-long demonstration, Roosevelt's managers invited a procession of people
onto the platform to shake hands with the Colonel. When Jane Addams was
led to the stage, the delegates "sprang to their feet and yelled," offering a
moving tribute to the settlement house worker who had committed her life to
helping the poor and the underprivileged. "I have been fighting for progressive principles for thirty years," she said. "This is the first time there has been
a chance to make them effective. This is the biggest day of my life."

When it seemed that the ecstatic tumult would never end, Roosevelt looked
toward his wife, seated in a box near the stage. While Edith had dreaded her
husband's entry into the race, she knew that once he had committed himself to
the fight, he had to carry it through. Noting her "jovial smile and bright eye,"
Roosevelt beamed. He took off his hat and hailed her, inspiring the delegates
to follow suit. Then, en masse, they gave homage to the former first lady, doffing their hats and cheering with abandon. "Mrs. Roosevelt shrank into her
chair," Richard Harding Davis reported. "Her confusion, her pleasure, her
distress, were as pretty as was the compliment the men strove to pay her. Before their onslaught of good will and admiration she blushed and looked like
a young girl." The cheering continued unabated until she rose from her seat
and bowed to the crowd. "That curtsy she made," exclaimed a correspondent
who had covered the Roosevelt family since their days in Albany, "was the
most prominent part I ever saw Mrs. Roosevelt take in public life!"

At last, the crowd composed itself enough for Roosevelt to speak. "At present," he began, "both the old parties are controlled by professional politicians in the interests of the privileged classes." Together, they would forge a new Progressive Party, based on "the right of the people to rule." Though the delegates cheered the familiar litany of progressive proposals to establish popular sovereignty through presidential primaries, direct election of senators, and the publication of campaign contributions, they reserved their most sustained applause for the Colonel's pledge to secure women the right to the vote. "In most cases where men applaud the mention of woman suffrage, they do it with a grin," one reporter remarked, but at this convention, "old men and young men alike got up on their chairs, yelled like wild Indians and waved anything available and portable."

Each new reform that Roosevelt projected, the *New York Times* noted, even the most radical, "fell on willing ears"—the call for "a living wage," the prohibition of child labor, federal regulation of interstate corporations, a graduated inheritance tax, an eight-hour workday for women, new standards for workmen's compensation, and, finally, a system of social insurance designed to protect citizens against "the hazards of sickness . . . involuntary unemployment, and old age" to which employers and employees would both contribute. "Surely there never was a fight better worth making than the one in which we are engaged," Roosevelt proclaimed. "Whatever fate may at the moment overtake any of us, the movement itself will not stop." He closed his two-hour address with the same stirring lines he had uttered seven weeks earlier in Chicago: "We stand at Armageddon, and we battle for the Lord."

The following day, the platform—"a purely Rooseveltian document," embracing everything the Colonel wanted—was approved. Nominations followed for the presidency. Jane Addams was among those who seconded Roosevelt's nomination, marking "the first time a woman ever had made a seconding speech in a national convention of a big party." After Roosevelt's unanimous election, the delegates chose California governor Hiram Johnson as the vice-presidential nominee. When the two men entered the hall, "wave upon wave of emotion swept over the audience." And when Roosevelt, equally moved, began to speak, "his voice trembled and he seemed to forget all the little tricks" he commonly deployed when trying to reach an audience. He simply thanked the delegates from the bottom of his heart, saying, "I have been President and I measure my words when I say I hold it by far the greatest honor and the greatest opportunity that has ever come to me to be called by you to the leadership for the time being of this great movement."

"The Bull Moose party has attained more strength & following than I thought possible at first," Ray Baker recorded in his journal not long after Roosevelt's powerfully emotional speech. "It includes no small number of high idealistic sincere men. Its platform is excellent. I can accept the planks nearly every one. A great figure in it is Miss Addams. It has aroused in some quarters almost a fanatical interest." Despite—or perhaps because of—his allegiance to the new party's principles, Baker could not shake a sense of disenchantment with its presidential nominee. "It is odd to me—as though the scales had suddenly fallen from my eyes," he reflected, "to see how different I regard T.R. from what I did a few years ago. There was no more enthusiastic & earnest admirer of him than I was. I felt that he was doing a great work—as I still believe he did do—the work of a great moral revivalist." But at this juncture, Baker believed, the Progressive movement needed a steadier hand, a leader "great enough to forget himself" in service of the cause. Roosevelt's titanic persona, the reporter lamented, "obscures everything," reducing the campaign to a referendum on his personal popularity rather than a discussion of vital reform issues.

In the end, Baker's concern over Roosevelt's distracting cult of personality was strong enough to shift his political allegiance. "As for me," Baker declared that August, "I shall vote for Wilson. I distrust the old party behind him & some of the things it stands for, but I have great confidence in the man and in the faction of the party (the progressive-Bryan faction) which he represents. And I like his clear, calm way of putting things." Baker had first encountered Woodrow Wilson two years earlier as he prepared an article on the forerunners of the 1912 campaign. "I left Princeton," he recalled years later, "convinced that I had met the finest mind in the field of statesmanship to be found in American public life." After that striking first impression, Baker followed Wilson's "meteoric career" with great interest; "overjoyed" by Wilson's subsequent nomination for the presidency, Baker "even dared to make speeches" on the Democratic nominee's behalf.

William Allen White had initially shared Baker's concerns, believing that the Progressive Party would be diminished if conceived as "a personal party." He had advised Roosevelt against bolting from the Republicans, preferring that he remain an "ace" for the future, when the new party had developed more fully. On a personal level, White found Wilson "a cold fish," with "a highty tighty way." The hand Wilson extended when the two men first met felt "like a ten-cent pickled mackerel in brown paper—irresponsive and lifeless." Nevertheless, White recognized that Wilson "had done a fine liberal job" as governor of New Jersey and would most likely make a good president.

Once Roosevelt mortgaged his own future to the new party, however, White never looked back. He quit his post as Republican national committeeman, joined the Progressive Party, and resolved to do everything possible for his hero and the Progressive cause. Playing a central role on the platform committee, White spent "four days and the better part of three nights" at the Congress Hotel in the week prior to the convention, drafting and reworking every section of the document before the delegates arrived. "Our social philosophy," he proudly remarked, could be "simmered down" to a single phrase—"using government as an agency of human welfare!"

Witnessing Roosevelt during the heady days of the Bull Moose Convention, White was impressed anew with his old friend's remarkable vitality—"He seemed full of animal spirits, exhaustless at all hours, exuding cheer and confidence." The rage that had consumed the Colonel during the Republican National Convention seemed transformed into ebullience with the birth of the new party: "What if he was a little obvious now and then as he grabbed the steering wheel of events and guided that convention not too shyly?" White later reflected, explaining, "I felt the joy and delight of his presence and, knowing his weakness, still gave him my loyalty—the great rumbling, roaring, jocund tornado of a man."

While White was transfixed by Roosevelt's performance during the Bull Moose Convention, his colleague Ida Tarbell was stuck in Europe. "It makes me crazy to get back," she wrote to Bert Boyden. "Of course T.R. is a wonder. But what about those Negro delegates? It looks to us here like a suicidal operation. But of course nothing he does counts." Though Tarbell had long been ambivalent about Roosevelt, she believed the financial and industrial powers arrayed against him were "a thousand times more dangerous than he." Months earlier, she had written to John Phillips suggesting that the magazine ought to address the widespread fearmongering that equated Roosevelt's pursuit of a third term with a slide into absolute monarchy. "Why stop with a third term?" opponents repeatedly warned. "The same reasons will apply for a fourth term, or for any number of terms." Without term limits, they argued, Roosevelt would simply stay in power for life. "We've got a King now," Tarbell parried, "this Wall Street—petty boss—Tammany—High Protection crowd. It's a real king—not a possible one like T.R. It's not one man; it's a tight combine of men. It's not impulsive, generous, full of human faults, but always for the human right." The priority, implored Tarbell, must be to destroy "this very able alliance that's got us all in its grip . . . that must be made clear. Then if T.R. needs to be batted a bit—we can do it." *The American Magazine* never ran a specific piece to counter criticism of "King Roosevelt," but John Phillips, Albert Boyden, John Siddall, and Finley Peter Dunne all finally supported Roosevelt and the Progressive Party.

Another of McClure's old team, Lincoln Steffens, was less well disposed toward Theodore Roosevelt when the campaign season opened. Months earlier, the two men had crossed swords over the sensational trial of two union leaders, the brothers John and James McNamara, who had been accused of setting off a bomb at the Los Angeles Times building. The blast, directed at the anti-union newspaper publisher Harrison Gray Otis, killed twenty-one workingmen and injured one hundred others. Labor leaders across the country rose to the defense of the two union men. Steffens publicly defended the brothers, labeling the bombing an act of "social revolution" rather than a crime. Roosevelt was disgusted by such a justification. "It seems to me that Steffens made an utter fool of himself," he told a California friend. "Murder is murder," he proclaimed in an *Outlook* editorial, "and the foolish sentimentalists or sinister wrong-doers who try to apologize for it as 'an incident of labor warfare' are not only morally culpable but are enemies of the American people, and, above all, are enemies of American wage-workers."

But even fierce disagreement with Roosevelt over the culpability of the McNamara brothers did not prevent Steffens from sympathizing with both the Progressive Party and the Colonel's continuing struggle against the titans of Wall Street. "It looks like Wilson out here," the journalist reported to his brother-in-law after canvassing a wide range of opinion; "all the interests are determined to beat T.R. at any rate. They have given up Taft, and they don't care for Wilson, but the man they hate is the Bull Moose and they are bound to beat him if they can. It's personal, you see."

⌒ ⌒

EARLY ON, WILLIAM TAFT MADE it clear that he had no plans to engage in "a whirlwind campaign." Though he planned to deliver a few prepared speeches in Washington or Beverly, he would observe the time-honored precedent that "a President who is a candidate for reelection should remain at home and leave it to the judgment of the people to decide whether or not his record of achievement" deserved a second term. He believed "in his heart" that he had executed his office with dignity and fairness, endeavoring in a judicial manner to decide all issues on their merits without regard to personal advantage. He had revitalized an aging Supreme Court by appointing a staggering six justices to the bench—all distinguished lawyers, half of them Democrats. Most important, Taft's countrymen had enjoyed four years of peace and prosperity under his administration. While the federal government could not bid "the rain to fall, the sun to shine, or the crops to grow," Taft remarked, it could, by pursuing wrongheaded policies, "halt enterprise, paralyze investment," or cause "hundreds of thousands of workingmen" to lose their jobs. William Taft trusted that "the negative virtue of having taken no step to interfere with the coming of prosperity and the comfort of the people is one that ought highly to commend an administration, and the party responsible for it, as worthy of further continuance of power."

Taft's campaign managers accepted his refusal to go on the stump, but worried that both Roosevelt and Wilson would dominate the headlines while their candidate seemed detached from the battle. Without active leadership from the White House, RNC chairman Charles Hilles found it difficult to raise funds, engage surrogate speakers, or keep the public's attention on the president. "It always makes me impatient," Taft confided in Nellie, "as if I were running a P. T. Barnum show, with two or three shows across the street, as if I ought to have as much advertising as the rest." When advisers suggested that he replicate the aggressive demeanor of the Bull Moose, he circuitously declared: "I couldn't if I would and I wouldn't if I could."

Clearly, the campaign had savagely exacerbated existing tensions between Taft and Theodore Roosevelt. "As the campaign goes on," Taft told Nellie, "it is hard for me to realize that we are talking about the same man as that man whom we knew in the Presidency." As for his "personal relations" with his erstwhile friend, Taft bluntly added, "they don't exist." Seriously hurt by the rift, Taft preferred to recall his old friend and mentor as almost a separate person from the belligerent, insult-hurling foe against whom he currently contended. He now looked upon Roosevelt simply "as an historical character of a most peculiar type in whom are embodied elements of real greatness, together with certain traits that have now shown themselves in unfitting him for any trust or confidence." Taft was particularly incensed by the open contempt Roosevelt displayed both toward him personally and for the nation's highest office. When an audience member solicited comment on the president, Roosevelt mockingly replied: "I never discuss dead issues." Before another audience, he repeated a variation of this jest, observing that all the old Republican bosses were shifting allegiance to Wilson, recognizing that the president "was a dead cock in the pit." Nor, Roosevelt elaborated, was the Republican platform even "worthy of serious discussion," given that it was adopted at a convention "organized by theft."

The fall campaign was already in full swing before the president yielded to his supporters' pleas. Standing before an audience of 2,500 cheering Republicans on the lawn of his summer home in Beverly, he delivered a spirited attack on Roosevelt's third party. One issue stood above all others, he declared, eclipsing the traditional partisan wrangling between Republicans and Democrats over the tariff and the trusts—the issue of "the preservation of the institutions of civil liberty as they were handed down to us by our forefathers." Splitting away from the Republican Party, a third party had been created "merely to gratify personal ambition and vengeance." In the pursuit of votes, this new party had employed "every new fad and theory, some of them good, some of them utterly preposterous and impracticable, some of them as Socialistic as anything that has been proposed in the countries of Europe"; all had been stuffed into the Progressive platform. Taken together, the president warned, these reforms suggested "an entire willingness to destroy every limitation of constitutional representative government." So long as Republicans remained true to their heritage, he predicted, this radical movement would surely fail. "The great bulk of our people are not emotional, undiscriminating, superficially minded, non-thinking, or hero worshipping," he asserted; "they have the virtue of second sober thought."

Expanding on the same theme two days later at the Beverly Republican Club, Taft predicted that the secession of the third party would prompt a "new vitality" among traditional Republicans. "We know that we are a better set of men than we are now called by those who were very glad at one time to be known as leading Republicans. No student of history can deny that the grandeur of this Nation, and the height that it has reached among the Nations during the last sixty years, has been due to the guidance, and the force, and the energy, and the enterprise of the Republican Party."

~ ~

WELL AWARE FROM THE OUTSET that the Republican split made victory in November "very improbable," Roosevelt nevertheless resolved to give every ounce of his energy to the campaign. He embarked upon an unprecedented speaking tour, covering forty states in every region of the country, including the solid Democratic South. He planned to travel by train, making whistle-stops at hundreds of small towns along the way. Although he anticipated a "deluge of travel and dust and howling and irritated fatigue," he would willingly invest "a tremendous amount of very hard work" so long as there was "a chance" of victory. In addition to three or four prepared addresses each day, he agreed to appear on the train's rear platform wherever a crowd assembled, to ride in parades, attend banquets, and meet with local committeemen. "I am perfectly happy," he told his British friend Arthur Hamilton Lee, "for I have never in my life been in a movement into which I could enter as heartily as into this."

The Colonel opened his campaign in Providence, Rhode Island. Journalists noted with amazement that even in this "boss-ridden" and "rock-ribbed" Republican state, immense crowds welcomed him. The 7,000 cheering people who thronged the streets, mostly workers from the textile mills and nearby shops, were markedly different from the usual Republican crowds. Speaking that evening to an overflow audience at Infantry Hall, Roosevelt decried the "rule of the bosses," beseeching his listeners to help establish "the rule of the people" in its place. Echoing the crusading spirit of the Progressive Convention, the audience launched into "The Battle Hymn of the Republic" and "Onward, Christian Soldiers." A massive banner above the speaker's rostrum bore the legend: "We stand at Armageddon and we battle for the Lord." Buoyed by his enthusiastic reception, Roosevelt predicted that Progressives could triumph anywhere "if they could get the people to realize what they were trying to accomplish."

Governor Wilson had initially hoped to confine his campaign appearances to a few well-prepared speeches. "My private judgment," he told a *Washington Times* correspondent, "is that extended stumping tours are not the most effective method of conducting a campaign. You must remember that I am governor of New Jersey and that I must keep in touch with the business of the State." He hoped to reach the public through a reasoned discussion of the issues and a clear explication of his political philosophy. He had no appetite for the kind of whistle-stop tour that would require him to stand on a train platform and shout extemporaneous remarks to a boisterous crowd.

Convinced from the beginning that Taft would run third, Woodrow Wilson viewed Roosevelt as his chief adversary. "I am by no means confident," he admitted to a friend. "He appeals to their imagination; I do not. He is a real, vivid person, whom they have seen and shouted themselves hoarse over and voted for, millions strong; I am a vague, conjectural personality, more made up of opinions and academic prepossessions than of human traits and red corpuscles." The Colonel's headlong campaign would demand sustained exertion. "I haven't a Bull Moose's strength," Wilson reflected, "as Roosevelt seems to have."

Despite his reservations, Wilson eventually agreed to make an extensive tour of the Midwest during the month of September, followed by a second trip "as far west as Colorado" in October. The governor "had, in reality, only one speech to make," Baker observed, and "he made it again and again." He urged listeners to envision a more expansive future for themselves and their country. He delivered his words with "such consummate skill as an orator" that each audience came away convinced that the candidate had spoken directly to their hopes and needs. "Wilson was a new personality in American public life," Ray Baker explained. "He profited by antithesis. He had the unfamiliar glamour, to the popular eye, of the scholar, the thinker, the historian. There had been enough heat in politics; what was needed now was light. Wilson was expository rather than denunciatory. He was asking the country to look at its problems: he was not offering panaceas." With disarming honesty, the candidate repeatedly stated: "I do not want to promise heaven unless I can bring it to you. I can only see a little distance up the road."

Positive responses from both audiences and the traveling press corps bolstered the governor's confidence. Speaking at Boston's Tremont Temple on September 27, he relaxed enough to offer a playful barb at Roosevelt's expense: "Suppose you choose the leader of the third party as President. Don't you think he will be pretty lonely? Not that he'll mind it, because I believe he finds himself rather good company." Wilson's lighthearted ribbing of Roosevelt's majestic ego underscored a serious point—without a majority party behind him in Congress, the Colonel would likely find it difficult to get anything done.

꘏ ꘎

RETIRING TO THE COPLEY PLAZA Hotel after his speech, Wilson discovered that President Taft was in the banquet hall for a dinner address to the International Congress of Chambers of Commerce. The governor sent word that he would be "very glad of the opportunity" to meet with the president before the evening ended. Shortly before midnight, a meeting was arranged in a private suite on the fifth floor. "I hope the campaigning has not worn you out," Taft remarked. "It has been quite a hard week," the governor acknowledged. Indeed, his voice had gotten "a bit husky" from overuse. "Well," Taft cordially responded, "there are three men that can sympathize with you, Mr. Bryan, Mr. Roosevelt, and myself." The mutual regard between Taft and Wilson was evident as the conversation continued. "It was a very delightful meeting," Wilson told reporters waiting in the corridor. "I am very fond of President Taft."

The natural warmth President Taft showed to Governor Wilson reflected an odd tranquility about the election. While Taft occasionally detected "currents of air" that seemed to be "blowing in the right direction," he acknowledged to friends that he would "probably be defeated." Winning the nomination had been the all-important victory—and not simply because he had bested Roosevelt. He had long believed that a loss at the convention would have been regarded as a personal rejection, whereas defeat in the fall election reflected a more general reverse for the party. "I seem to think that we have won what there was to fight about, and that what follows is less important," he told Nellie without a trace of defensive rationalization.

Nellie shared her husband's equanimity. "I wanted him to be re-elected, naturally," she later wrote, "but I never entertained the slightest expectation of it and only longed for the end of the turmoil when he could rest his weary mind and get back into association with the pleasant things of life." In the aftermath of Nellie's stroke, her close family circle had sustained her. Her children were thriving: Robert was an editor of the *Harvard Law Review*; Helen would soon be returning to Bryn Mawr; and irrepressible Charlie was getting excellent grades at the Taft School in Connecticut, where Horace kept a watchful eye over him. As the election approached, Nellie remained in Beverly, content to be removed from the political fray. "She is in a condition where defeat will not disappoint her, if at all," Taft reported to Horace. "I am glad to say she is in a happy frame of mind."

As THE BULL MOOSE CANDIDATE headed west through Iowa and North Dakota to Oregon and California, he continued to attract huge crowds; nonetheless, his managers fretted that he "was going stale," repeating tired arguments about the Republican Convention, the collusion of business and politics, and the dangers of vesting too much power in the courts. Instead of "rehashing" these matters, they pressed him to engage Woodrow Wilson directly. To prepare for such a confrontation, Roosevelt commenced to study the governor's record, receiving daily briefings on his speeches and closely following his rival's campaign. A select group at Roosevelt's headquarters prepared a lengthy report that outlined Wilson's positions on every question—from the minimum wage and woman suffrage to labor and the trusts. From that point forward, remarked Roosevelt's publicity chief, Oscar King Davis, "it was Wilson, Wilson, Wilson, all the time in the private car, and nothing but Wilson and his record in the Colonel's talks."

Roosevelt launched the "first direct assault" on his Democratic opponent in San Francisco, with what the *New York Times* deemed the "most important speech of his campaign since his 'Confession of Faith.'" His criticism addressed the fundamental role of the government in a democratic society. "Mr. Wilson is fond of asserting his platonic devotion to the purposes of the Progressive Party," Roosevelt began, "but such platonic devotion is utterly worthless from a political standpoint because he antagonizes the only means by which those purposes can be made effective." Roosevelt claimed that "the key to Mr. Wilson's position" could be found in a single line he had recently voiced in New York: "The history of liberty," Wilson had stated, "is the history of the limitation of governmental power, not the increase of it." Such an understanding, Roosevelt charged, was a reincarnation of the old "laissez faire doctrine," which, if restored, would mean "the undoing of every particle of social and industrial advance we have made." Under Wilson's theory of limited governmental power, Roosevelt charged, "every railroad must be left unchecked, every great industrial concern can do as it chooses with its employees and with the general public; women must be permitted to work as many hours a day as their taskmasters bid them." By contrast, his own party would build on laws recently established to protect the nation's consumers and workers. His "New Nationalism" proposed "to use the whole power of the Government to protect all those who, under Mr. Wilson's laissez-faire system, are trodden down in the ferocious, scrambling rush of an unregulated and purely individualistic industrialism."

Of course, the single line excerpted from Wilson's address did not represent the full measure of the candidate's thinking about governmental power. In other speeches, Wilson articulated his conviction that "freedom to-day is something more than being let alone." In the modern industrial world, he explained, laws were needed to ensure "fair play." In keeping with the traditional Democratic philosophy Wilson insisted that these laws should emanate from state capitals, not Washington. He understood that the expansion of federal power was anathema to the southern base of the Democratic Party, where states' rights safeguarded segregation. Despite his more progressive personal views, Wilson could not abandon his party's historic commitment to the Jeffersonian ideal of a smaller, less expansive federal government.

Roosevelt's "declaration of war" against his opponent's concept of limited national government prompted Wilson to articulate a more positive strategy to expand the nation's prosperity. In a speech at Indianapolis, he called upon his countrymen to "open again the fields of competition, so that new men with brains, new men with capital, new men with energy in their veins, may build up enterprises in America." While Roosevelt accepted trusts as inevitable and strove, through centralized federal power, to regulate them in the interests of the public, Wilson argued that the very size of the corporations posed a problem. He called upon the American people "to organize the forces of liberty in our time to make conquest of a new freedom."

Wilson's "New Freedom" slogan caught on, providing a counterpoint to Roosevelt's "New Nationalism." Expanding on his theme as the campaign progressed, Wilson argued that "the wealth of America" lay in its small businesses, its towns and villages. "Its vitality does not lie in New York, nor in Chicago," he asserted; "it will not be sapped by anything that happens in St. Louis. The vitality of America lies in the brains, the energies, the enterprise of the people throughout the land; in the efficiency of their factories and in the richness of the fields that stretch beyond the borders of the town." By reinforcing the anti-trust law and by "abolishing tariff favors" and "credit denials," he would return genuine free enterprise to America.

Never one to shy from a fight, Roosevelt delighted in the escalating policy debate with Wilson, vigorously defending his regulatory approach and claiming that Wilson's proposal to break up big corporations defied the realities of modern life. Drawing on his own experience, he pointed out that when the Supreme Court dissolved Standard Oil, the company simply "split up into a lot of smaller companies," which continued to operate "in such close alliance" that they remained, in effect, under Standard's control. The result was higher prices for the consumer and even lower wages for the workers. Only the owners had benefited: "The price of the stock has gone up over 100 percent," Roosevelt observed, "so that Mr. Rockefeller and his associates have actually seen their fortunes doubled by the policy which Mr. Wilson advocates and which Mr. Taft defends." Little wonder, the Colonel sardonically concluded, that Wall Street prayed for either Wilson or Taft's policies in preference to his own commitment to put all these companies under a powerful Federal Commission.

By early October, it was "becoming more and more plain that the fight was between Wilson and Roosevelt," Oscar Davis remarked. "Taft was steadily fading into the background." The Republican Party receded as both front-runners directed their energies to the task of distinguishing the New Freedom from the New Nationalism. The two doctrines "were as close as fraternal twins" compared with the platform embraced by the Socialist Party candidate, Eugene Debs. On the presidential ballot for a fourth time, Debs maintained that the capitalist system was "utterly incapable" of dealing with the problems of the industrial age. His Socialist Party platform called for "the collective ownership" of transportation and communication, of land (wherever it was practical), and of the banking system. To ensure more direct democracy, the Socialist platform proposed the abolition of the U.S. Senate, the elimination of the president's veto power, and the removal of the Supreme Court's power to declare laws passed by Congress unconstitutional.

ON THE NIGHT OF MONDAY, October 14, Roosevelt was scheduled to deliver a speech to a large Milwaukee audience. Two days earlier, as a bitter wind blew through the open flaps of "a mammoth tent" on Chicago's west side, he had shouted himself so hoarse that he could barely speak beyond a whisper. But over the emphatic resistance of Dr. Scurry Terrell, his throat specialist, Roosevelt insisted on honoring his commitment to the people of Milwaukee— which included participating in a parade through the city streets, a banquet at the Gilpatrick Hotel, and a public address. "I want to be a good Indian," he declared.

An open touring car stood in front of the hotel, waiting to convey the Roosevelt party to the Auditorium after dinner. Roosevelt entered first, followed by Henry Cochems, head of the Progressive Party's speaker's bureau. Gathered on the opposite curb, the crowd started clapping and cheering. Roosevelt acknowledged the ovation by standing and doffing his hat. At that moment, a man at the front of the crowd raised a large pistol and fired. "It was point-blank range," Oscar Davis observed, "and almost impossible to miss." As the bullet hit the right side of the Colonel's chest, he lurched and collapsed on the seat. Just as the man with the pistol prepared to fire a second shot, Roosevelt's stenographer, Elbert Martin, leapt on the assailant. A former football player, Martin quickly disarmed the man and began to strangle him. "I wasn't trying to take him prisoner," Martin later admitted, "I was trying to kill him." The inflamed crowd spurred him on, shouting, "Lynch him," "Kill him." In the midst of the chaos, Roosevelt struggled to his feet and called out to Martin, "Bring him here," he ordered, "don't hurt him." The stenographer grudgingly obeyed, dragging the man toward the car. Roosevelt lifted his would-be assassin's head to look directly at his face. "What did you do it for?" he asked, but marking the dead expression in the man's eyes, he added, "Oh, what's the use. Turn him over to the police."

Falling back on his seat once again, Roosevelt ordered the chauffeur to go straight to the Auditorium, against the insistence of Dr. Terrell, who demanded that they stop first at the emergency room of the hospital to have him examined. "You get me to that speech," Roosevelt shouted. Only when they reached the green room in the Auditorium did Roosevelt allow the doctor to look closely at the wound, which was located just under his right nipple. "It was bleeding slightly," Oscar Davis noted, "the blood-spot on his white shirt being about the size of a man's hand." Unable to determine where the bullet had lodged, Dr. Terrell again demanded a thorough hospital examination. "It's all right," Roosevelt said, inhaling deeply several times. "I don't get any pain from this breathing." And with a handkerchief secured to his chest as a bandage, he headed for the stage.

When told of the shooting, the audience cried out in shock, but Roosevelt quieted them down. "It's true," he informed them, "but it takes more than that to kill a bull moose." He withdrew his spectacles and his speech from the inside pocket of his coat. The speech had been typed on fifty heavy sheets of paper folded in half to fit into his breast pocket. Seeing the hole the bullet had ripped through the pages, and the dented spectacle case, Roosevelt suddenly understood "how narrowly he had escaped." Indeed, the bullet would have gone "straight into his heart" if it had not been deflected upward by the buffering combination of his thick manuscript and metal eyeglass case; instead, it struck the fourth rib on the right side, fracturing the bone but coming to a halt.

Roosevelt had spoken for about half an hour when Oscar Davis, standing at the side of the stage, noticed that the color had drained from his face and he was "laboring very hard to go on." He approached, suggesting that the Colonel bring the speech to a close. "No, sir," Roosevelt replied, with a ferocious expression. "I will not stop until I have finished." Though "his heart was racing," he ignored the "knifelike pain in his ribs" and continued to speak for an additional hour. Finally reaching the last page of the script, he turned to Dr. Terrell and murmured, "Now I am ready to go with you and do what you want."

While Roosevelt was being examined at Milwaukee Hospital, police interrogated the attacker, John F. Schrank. A thirty-six-year-old former saloonkeeper from the East Side of Manhattan, Schrank produced a written manifesto that described a dream in which President McKinley had risen from his coffin and indicted Roosevelt as his murderer. He told police that he had first begun "to think seriously" of Roosevelt "as a menace to his country" when he heard the Colonel shout "Thief" at the Republican Convention and announce his decision to run for a third term on a new party. "Any man looking for a third term ought to be shot," Schrank declared. He was fully persuaded, he added, "that if Colonel Roosevelt was defeated at the fall election he would again cry 'Thief!' and that his action would plunge the country into a bloody civil war." Schrank confessed that he had followed Roosevelt to Charleston, New Orleans, Atlanta, and Chattanooga with the intention of shooting him, but the right opportunity had never presented itself.

At Milwaukee Hospital, Roosevelt was in good spirits, joking with doctors as they examined the wound and took X-rays to reveal the location of the bullet. The decision was made to transfer him to Mercy Hospital in Chicago, where chest surgeons would determine if they needed to operate to remove the bullet. "There are only three possible dangers," Roosevelt explained to reporters when he reached Mercy Hospital, "pleurisy, pneumonia, and blood poisoning. If we can get safely past these three there isn't a thing in the world to prevent me from resuming my campaign."

President Taft was at the Hotel Astor in New York to attend a banquet in honor of his cabinet when the head of the Associated Press approached his table with news of the shooting. "All over the room conversation died down," the *New York Tribune* reported; "whispers of 'Roosevelt!' and 'Impossible!' were heard." The dinner guests got up from their tables to rush to the telephones. Later that night, Taft issued a short statement to the press, and the following morning he sent a sympathetic telegram to Roosevelt. Woodrow Wilson offered to suspend his campaign while his opponent remained hospitalized, but Roosevelt swiftly declined his offer: "The fight should go on to its conclusion, just as it would in case of battle," he argued, "even though the commanding general might be struck down."

Edith Roosevelt had been enjoying a musical comedy in New York when she received word of the attack on her husband. She left the theatre and straightaway made arrangements to travel to Chicago the following day, accompanied by Theodore Junior, Ethel, and the family doctor, Alexander Lambert. "It's the best news I've heard since I got here," Roosevelt said. Edith took command as soon as she reached the hospital, consulting with the medical staff, limiting visits, and making sure that her husband followed the doctors' orders. "He has been as meek as a lamb since the Boss arrived," noted the *New York Times* correspondent. Despite Roosevelt's pleas to let more people into his room, she insisted that he needed rest. "This thing about ours being a campaign against boss rule is a fake," he said with chagrin. "I never was so boss ruled in my life as I am at this moment."

By the following Saturday, doctors determined that the danger of infection was past, that the bullet was lodged "outside of the rib" and could most likely "be allowed to live there permanently." The Colonel's color and appetite had returned, though his broken rib continued to make it painful to breathe. So long as he remained "in absolute quiet" for several days, the hospital medical staff agreed to release him after the weekend. By Monday morning, he was cleared to leave. An ambulance transferred him to his railroad car, where he slept and read until the train reached New York.

"I am in fine shape," he reported to Bamie a few days later. Though his wound remained "open" and the doctors would not allow him to return to the campaign trail, the indomitable Colonel still hoped to make one final appearance at Madison Square Garden at the end of October, the week before the election.

The shooting forced the cancelation of scores of campaign events, yet the dramatic attack upon the stalwart and stoic former president had rekindled the nation's empathy, and speculation swirled about how it might reshape the election. "Encouraging reports are coming in from all over," Ethel Roosevelt noted to Bamie; "things look better for us than they ever have." While immense crowds continued to cheer Governor Wilson at every stop of his final campaign tour, a Democratic speaker at an Oakland rally articulated the worst fears of the Wilson camp. "The bullet that rests in Roosevelt's chest has killed Wilson for the Presidency," he said. Taft recognized the difficulty of anticipating the political impact of such an event. With his usual equanimity, he took a more philosophical approach to the furor. "What effect the incident will have on the election," he remarked, "is difficult to conjecture."

SPECIAL PRECAUTIONS WERE TAKEN TO protect Roosevelt from "the rush of the crowd" as he made his way to Madison Square Garden on October 30 to deliver his "farewell manifesto." At dinner with Edith and Dr. Lambert earlier that evening, the Colonel had expressed surprise that the simple journey to the city had fatigued him, but he "looked to the excitement of the moment to carry him through." Aware that his voice had not "regained its accustomed power," he was anxious to begin speaking as soon as he took the stage. Catching sight of him, however, the audience of 16,000 poured forth a spontaneous and emotional tribute for forty-two minutes, despite Roosevelt's best efforts to dampen the crowd.

"Perhaps once in a generation," Roosevelt at last began, "there comes a chance for the people of a country to play their part wisely and fearlessly in some great battle of the age-long warfare for human rights." Perhaps less dramatic than the struggles their fathers and forefathers had faced, the battle for social justice was "well-nigh as important." If the problems created by the industrial age were left unattended, Roosevelt cautioned, America would eventually be "sundered by those dreadful lines of division" that set "the *haves*" and the "*have-nots*" against one another.

"We know that there are in life injustices which we are powerless to remedy," Roosevelt acknowledged, "but we know also that there is much injustice which can be remedied." The Progressive Party, he pledged, would harness the "collective power of the people through their governmental agencies" to move the country forward. "We propose to lift the burdens from the lowly and the weary, from the poor and the oppressed," he asserted. "We propose to stand for the sacred rights of childhood and womanhood. Nay, more, we propose to see that manhood is not crushed out of the men who toil, by excessive hours of labor, by underpayment, by injustice and oppression. . . . Surely, there never was a fight better worth making than this." And, finally, contemplating this cause so much larger than any individual, Roosevelt concluded: "Win or lose I am glad beyond measure that I am one of the many who in this fight have stood ready to spend and be spent."

Throughout, his face and manner had revealed strain, but the voice was "as clear as a bell." Those who had witnessed scores of earlier appearances felt they heard "a new Roosevelt" on this night, free from "the old violence and the old sarcasm." He uttered not a single word against his opponents, focusing his remarks solely on the principles for which the Progressive Party stood. Even his nemesis, the New York *Sun*, praised his lyrical and passionate presentation, lauding the "good taste" he exhibited in avoiding the "temptation to misuse an unparalleled opportunity for self-exhibition."

On the Friday before the election, President Taft sat down with New York *World* reporter Louis Seibold for an extended interview. Aware that his chance for outright victory was small, Taft nevertheless hoped to outpoll Roosevelt. A frank discussion of the circumstances surrounding his break with Roosevelt, the reporter suggested, might help to influence public opinion. Taft was "in excellent spirits," Seibold later recalled. The lengthy conversation, transcribed by the president's stenographer, was scheduled to run the following day—not only in the *World* but in newspapers across the country through release to the Associated Press.

When he entered the presidency, Taft explained, he had been "anxious to carry out the promises of the platform," but he was hindered by long-developing factions within the Republican Party. Asked by Seibold if Roosevelt had "fomented" these factions, Taft cast no blame. "No," he replied, "the party naturally divided itself." The rupture was caused by a widening division between eastern manufacturing interests, desiring a high protective tariff, and western farmers, calling for serious tariff reductions. He had moved "in the right direction" when he signed the Payne Bill, but "the genius of publicity," the president admitted, was an attribute he never possessed. "The training of a Judge is something that leads you to depend upon the opinion published and the decree entered as speaking for themselves," he reflected, endeavoring to justify his lack of engagement with the press. As a result, he never properly educated the country about the benefits of the tariff bill, the corporation tax, or any of the other measures he was proud to have passed.

When the reporter sought Taft's comment on anything "beyond the personal ambition of Mr. Roosevelt" that had propelled the former president into the race, Taft demurred. There had been "personalities enough in the preconvention campaign," he cryptically remarked. Under Seibold's persistent probing to explain the bitterness of Roosevelt's commentary during the primary contest, Taft eventually offered a benign explanation: "Mr. Roosevelt is so constituted that it is impossible for him to go into a controversy without becoming personal." Roosevelt had once told him that in every fight he strove to "get close up to a man," attacking "not only the man's argument but the man himself. He could not ascribe to the man differing from him radically any other than an improper motive."

Would Roosevelt have entered the race if he had foreseen "the wrecking of the Republican party," Seibold wondered. "I can not tell," Taft replied, loath to publicly ascribe malicious motives to his adversary. "I don't think he went deliberately into it that way," noting that Roosevelt was not "a planner" but simply a man who "acts from day to day." Taft himself remained "in a philosophical state" as he considered the upcoming election. "I have had to be. The experience I have had in the Presidency has made me so," he explained, "and what I am very hopeful is that whatever happens, the country will go on to ultimate happiness."

After the interview, Seibold was told he could have the transcript upon its completion, but later that afternoon he received word that the president wanted time to make "minor corrections." Taft invited the reporter to join him on the evening train to New York, as the presidential party traveled to attend the funeral of Vice President James Sherman, who had died from heart disease two days earlier. Seibold agreed but emphasized the practical need to get the interview into production; "space was being saved in every newspaper." Still Taft procrastinated, insisting that he needed time for edits, and furthermore wanted to consult Root and Wickersham when the train reached New York. "I'm afraid that's too late," Seibold warned. "But Roosevelt was my closest friend," Taft objected.

The interview never ran.

⁐ ⁐

ON ELECTION EVE, TAFT ARRIVED in his home city of Cincinnati following a twenty-eight-hour train ride from New York. He had chosen a "leisurely" route through Ohio, allowing him to greet and visit the friendly crowds gathered at train stations along the way. He refrained from mentioning politics, indulging instead in pleasantries about the prosperous economy and local events. Upon reaching Cincinnati, he went directly to his brother Charley's mansion, where he would receive election returns among family and friends. Nellie had not made the trip, choosing instead to accompany Helen and young Charlie to New York, where the Republican National Committee chairman had arranged a small dinner party.

On election day, November 5, Taft reportedly "slept late, ate a good breakfast, smiled profusely and acted generally as though some sixteen million men were not voting on the subject of his political fate." At noon, he motored to his regular polling place on Madison Road, stopping first to visit Nick Longworth, who was in a tight race to retain his congressional seat. The polling place was crowded, but the president "stood in line and waited his turn," chatting with friends and posing for pictures. After casting his vote, he spent a quiet afternoon at his brother's Pike Street house.

Roosevelt passed "a busy morning" catching up on his voluminous correspondence; at noon, he motored to the small firehouse in Oyster Bay where he traditionally cast his vote. Accompanied by his gardeners, coachman, and chauffeur, he was greeted with cheers from "a crowd of villagers." After signing the register, he headed toward the booth. "Here goes another Bull Mooser vote," a man shouted, eliciting a broad smile from the Colonel. That afternoon, Theodore and Edith took "a long ramble in the woods" before returning to dress for dinner and prepare for the election returns.

After a final campaigning push the night before the election, Woodrow Wilson returned home to Princeton, thrilled to be back with his family on election day. "He felt like a boy out of school on a lark," he told reporters that morning, relieved that for once "he didn't have to jump out and make a speech somewhere." After breakfast, Wilson walked to his polling place at the Chambers Street fire station. Directly across the street stood the boardinghouse where he had lived more than three decades earlier when he came to Princeton as a college freshman. Wilson had spent the better part of his life in Princeton, Ray Baker noted, and he knew "every nook and corner of the old town." After casting his vote, the governor had lunch with his wife and daughters, answered letters, posed for press photographs, and took a walk through the countryside with his secretary and an old friend.

The small dinner party at Wilson's home that night, the *New York Times* reported, "was much in the nature of a celebration, for every minute or two it was interrupted by messages from the telegraph room, every one of which brought news that the tide was running strongly in the Governor's favor." Before long, such bulletins made it clear to both the president and the former

president that neither man could win the election. By the time Taft and Roosevelt each sat down for dinner, "an air of gloom and despondency" pervaded
Pike Street and Sagamore Hill alike.

Official word of Governor Wilson's victory was confirmed after 10 p.m.
via telegraph. Ellen Wilson delivered the welcome news to her husband, who
stood talking to friends before a bright fire in the parlor. "My dear," she said,
kissing him, "I want to be the first to congratulate you." The bells atop historic
Nassau Hall began to ring, and soon several thousand Princeton students
arrived at Wilson's house, waving flags and carrying torches. Speaking with
"great emotion, even with tears in his eyes," Wilson told the students that he
understood the serious challenges he faced. "I look almost with pleading to
you, the young men of America, to stand behind me, to support me in the
new administration."

Wilson had achieved an immense victory in the Electoral College. He captured forty of the forty-eight states, bringing him 435 electoral votes; Roosevelt
took six states, producing 88 votes; Taft won only Vermont and Utah, for a
total of 8 electoral votes. The popular vote was somewhat less emphatic. Wilson won nearly 6.3 million votes, compared to 4.1 million for Roosevelt, and a
little short of 3.5 million for Taft. Eugene Debs secured over 900,000 votes, the
highest total the Socialist Party had ever reached. The split between Taft and
Roosevelt had clearly hurt both men: their combined vote exceeded Wilson's
by nearly 1.3 million. And together, they had captured over 50 percent of the
electorate, leaving only 41.9 percent with the new president, Woodrow Wilson.

At 11:30 p.m., President Taft sent a warm congratulatory telegram to Governor Wilson, extending his "best wishes for a successful Administration."
By then, it was already clear that Taft had suffered an overwhelming defeat,
coming in third. Four years earlier, he had celebrated victory with dozens
of jubilant friends. On that auspicious night, "several thousand of his fellow
townsmen with blatant horns and red fire thronged about the mansion." On
this night, "the streets were deserted and the only persons in the vicinity were
the policemen on guard around the house."

As news of Wilson's victory came over the wires, Roosevelt sent word to
the press that he would receive them at eleven o'clock. "They went in rather
more subdued than usual," the New York Times reported, "filled with a great
curiosity to see just how he was taking the defeat." He was seated at his desk,
"with a log wood blaze shining softly from the big fireplace," when the group
of journalists arrived. "Now old friends," Roosevelt remarked, "I'm really
glad to see you." He then proceeded to recite from memory the telegram he

had sent to the president-elect: " 'The American people, by a great plurality, have conferred upon you the highest honor in their gift. I congratulate you thereon.' " After finishing, he laughed softly and said: "That's all."

         ⌒ ⌒

NOT SURPRISINGLY, ROOSEVELT WAS HIT harder by the defeat than the president, who appeared to make a quick recovery. As Taft boarded the train for his return to Washington, he "chatted as gaily as he did before the election," appearing to reporters as if "a great load had been taken from his shoulders." He acknowledged that while he had been "hopeful" that he might secure victory in a close election, he had not been "so hopeful" that he had experienced "any shock of real disappointment." To a lifelong friend he humbly explained his composure: "The people of the United States did not owe me another election. I hope that I am properly grateful for the one term of the Presidency which they gave me, and the fact that they withheld the second is no occasion for my resentment or feeling of injustice." Most important, he reflected to another friend: "As I look back over the record of the administration, I feel very well satisfied that a great deal was accomplished which will be useful to the people in the future, and that, after all, is the only real satisfaction one gets out of any public service."

Although Roosevelt had been realistic about his chances, he was deeply unsettled by the magnitude of the loss. In the two weeks following the attempt on his life, there had been such an outpouring of "popular feeling," Edith explained to Kermit, that Progressive leaders felt victory might truly be possible—not only for Roosevelt but for the party. When the election returns were fully counted, the Progressives actually captured just a single governorship and a dozen congressional seats. The Democrats not only increased their majority in the House but also seized control of the Senate for the first time in nearly two decades. "There is no use disguising the fact that the defeat at the polls is overwhelming," a disappointed Roosevelt wrote his British friend Arthur Hamilton Lee, allowing that he "had expected we would make a better showing." Several days later, his assessment appeared darker as he told Gifford Pinchot: "We must face the fact that our cutting loose from the Republican Party was followed by disaster to the Progressive cause in most of the States where it won two years ago."

Only in time would Roosevelt's perspective on the defeat grow more sanguine. "It was a phenomenal thing to be able to bring the new party into second place and to beat out the Republicans," he told Henry White that November, recognizing the remarkable achievement of an association that had, in a mere three months, managed to gather more support than a sitting president, and defeat a political party that had held sway over national politics for fifty years.

In the aftermath of the election, Roosevelt reiterated to reporters his view that "the leader for the time being is of little consequence, but the cause itself must triumph, for its triumph is essential to the wellbeing of the American people." Rather than a rationalization to assuage the bitterness of his loss, his statement would prove remarkably prescient. Although the Progressive Party met defeat, the progressive causes would continue to influence American politics for years to come. Within the coming decade alone, three signal amendments would be added to the Constitution: the Sixteenth, giving the national government the power to levy a progressive income tax, without which many of the New Deal's social programs might not have been possible; the Seventeenth, providing for the popular election of U.S. senators; and the Nineteenth, finally granting American women the right to vote.

While William Howard Taft had embraced the role of the conservative during the presidential race, he, too, had long since rejected the laissez-faire philosophy that had dominated politics since the Civil War, committing himself instead to the core progressive belief that government had a responsibility to remedy social problems, improve working conditions, safeguard public health, and protect our natural heritage. Though the two men had strikingly different temperaments—Roosevelt's original and active nature at odds with Taft's ruminative and judicial disposition—their opposing qualities actually proved complementary, allowing them to forge a powerful camaraderie and rare collaboration. There was a time, at the height of their careers, when Theodore Roosevelt and William Howard Taft stood shoulder to shoulder as they charted a different role for the U.S. government that would fundamentally enlarge the bounds of economic opportunity and social justice.

ON MAY 26, 1918, SIX years after the election that ended his presidency and fractured his party, William Howard Taft arrived for a conference at Chicago's Blackstone Hotel. As Taft was retiring to his room upstairs, the elevator operator informed him that Colonel Roosevelt was presently seated alone in the dining room. "I hear he's leaving right away," the young man remarked. Taft did not hesitate. "Then I'll ask you to take me back downstairs," he responded.

After the White House, Taft had become the Kent Professor of Constitutional Law at Yale, a position that offered intellectual engagement, the camaraderie of a cherished college campus, and the freedom to lecture around the country. Roosevelt had found his own solace through a combination of writing, public speaking, and intense physical activity. The election no sooner behind him, he had begun work on his autobiography. Completing that project within ten months, he embarked on an expedition to explore the River of Doubt, an uncharted tributary of the mighty Amazon. Returning home, he occupied himself writing dozens of articles and delivering scores of speeches each year. He had stopped at the Blackstone Hotel on his way to Des Moines, where the following day he was scheduled to deliver three speeches.

Over the years since the contentious 1912 election, mutual friends and political allies had repeatedly tried to reunite Roosevelt and Taft, but their infrequent meetings had been neither "cordial" nor "intimate," marked by what Taft deemed "armed neutrality." In 1915, they had both served as honorary pallbearers at the funeral of Yale professor Thomas Lounsbury. Taft made the first overture, extending his hand to Roosevelt. "How are you, Theodore?" he asked. The Colonel merely "shook hands silently without smiling," and "no further communication passed between them." A year later, in early October 1916, Elihu Root had arranged for the two men to appear at a Union League Club reception for Republican presidential nominee Charles Evans Hughes. Organized with the goal of "cementing the union of Progressives and Republicans" against Woodrow Wilson, Republicans hailed the event as a "Big Love

Feast." Though Roosevelt's presence was calculated to symbolize his return to "the Republican fold," Taft told Nellie they simply "shook hands with a Howdy do and that was all."

Only when grave illness hospitalized Roosevelt in early February 1918 did the possibility open for a genuine reconciliation. Learning that the Colonel was enduring an operation to remove a fistula much like the ordeal he had suffered through when he was governor general, Taft sent him a sympathetic telegram. "I know something of the pain and discomfort he is passing through," Taft wrote to Nellie, adding that from "the tone of the dispatches," he suspected that Roosevelt's condition was far more serious than his own had been. In fact, the Colonel had never recovered from malaria contracted during his expedition to the River of Doubt, leaving him prone to fever and infection. During this most recent bout of fever, a rectal abscess had developed, along with abscesses in both ears. The surgery to remedy these conditions proved successful, but persistent fever and severe nausea required him to remain in the hospital for almost a month. His first communication was a telegram to Taft. "Am rather rocky, but worth several dear Men," he jested. "Greatly touched and Pleased by Your Message."

This written exchange, the first in six years, led Roosevelt to send Taft a draft of a speech he would deliver in late March. An indictment of Wilson's handling of America's participation in World War I, the piece was entitled "Speed up the War and Take Thought for After the War." It criticized the administration for "sluggishness in making war," and called "for longer hours of work in war plants" as well as for "universal military training—to be continued after the war." Taft wholeheartedly concurred with Roosevelt's critique of Wilson's wartime leadership. He carefully read the draft and made two recommendations. "I have embodied both of those suggestions," Roosevelt wrote in response. "I think them capital. I am rather ashamed I never thought of them myself, and I am malevolently pleased that neither Root nor Lodge thought of them!"

These cordial exchanges renewed Taft's optimism that Roosevelt might finally be ready to reconcile. Hurrying across the Blackstone's dining room, which was bustling with nearly a hundred diners, he spotted the Colonel at a small table by the corner window. "Theodore!" he exclaimed. "I am glad to see you!" Roosevelt rose from his seat and grasped Taft's shoulders. "Well, I am indeed delighted to see you. Won't you sit down?" All across the room, customers rose from their dinners and waitstaff paused, "recognizing the significance of the meeting." Suddenly, the chamber erupted into applause. *New York Tribune* reporter John Leary, who was traveling with Roosevelt, heard the loud ovation from the lobby. Joined by curious members of the hotel staff, he started up the stairs leading to the dining room. Encountering a patron who had witnessed the hoopla, he asked what had incited the outburst. "T.R. and Taft's got together," the man explained. "They're holding an old-home week."

"By Godfrey, I never was so surprised in my life," Roosevelt later told Leary. "I no more thought of him being in Chicago than in Timbuctoo. But wasn't it a gracious thing for him to do?" There was so much commotion when they first greeted each other, he explained, that he could hardly hear what Taft was saying. "I don't mind telling you how delighted I am," Roosevelt added. "I never felt happier over anything in my life. It was splendid of Taft."

The two men talked together "like a pair of happy schoolboys" until Roosevelt had to depart to catch the night train to Des Moines. "Taft was beaming," one witness reported, "and Colonel Roosevelt, leaning half across the table, was expressing himself very earnestly." Meeting Leary on the way out, Taft could not disguise his elation. "Isn't he looking splendid?" he said. "I never saw him looking much better." Asked about the nature of their conversation, Taft simply replied that they "discussed patriotism and the state and welfare of the Nation." His smile suggested that a far more important exchange had occurred. Describing the meeting a week later to Henry Stimson, Roosevelt confided that at long last they had "completely renewed the old friendly relations."

⌒ ⌒

SEVEN MONTHS LATER, ON CHRISTMAS Day, 1918, after a six-week hospital stay for a severe attack of inflammatory rheumatism, Theodore Roosevelt returned to convalesce at Sagamore Hill. Though delighted to be back in his beloved home, he was still in considerable pain. Doctors predicted a full recovery, but Edith hired a nurse to attend to his medical needs and contacted James Amos, the black valet who had served Roosevelt in the White House. Her husband, she explained to Amos, would not allow "anyone else" to help, but they understood that it might be difficult for him to come. Amos never hesitated. He packed a suitcase and made arrangements to remain by Roosevelt's side as long as he was needed.

By the following Sunday morning, January 5, 1919, Roosevelt "seemed better again." Comfortably situated in "the warmest room in the house," the large bedroom that had once been the children's nursery, he dictated letters and proofread an editorial for *Metropolitan* magazine, calling on the country to give women the right to vote. "There should be no further delay," he emphatically stated. The war was over. The time had come to focus on domestic issues. "It is an absurdity to longer higgle about the matter."

Together, Edith and Theodore passed "a happy and wonderful day," she later recalled. He had long treasured the view of the water from that corner room, and "as it got dusk, he watched the dancing of waves & spoke with happiness of being home and made little plans for me. I think he had made up his mind," she wrote, "that he would have to suffer for some time to come and with his high courage had adjusted himself to bear it. He was very sweet all day."

At around ten o'clock that night, Theodore told Edith he felt a curious "sensation of depression about the chest," almost as though his heart were preparing to stop. "I know it is not going to happen," he assured her, "but it is such a strange feeling." Edith called their family physician, Dr. George Faller, who "examined him carefully, found no indication of anything wrong with heart and lungs, and after giving him a slight stimulant, left him." While Edith prepared to retire, Amos helped Roosevelt get settled for the night. The Colonel remained for a short time on the sofa before turning to his valet. "James, don't you think I might go to bed now?" Amos took off Roosevelt's robe and "had almost to lift him into bed." Edith returned to give her husband a good night kiss, after which Roosevelt said, "James, will you please put out the light?"

Edith came to check on her husband shortly after midnight, and again two hours later. Finding him in a "peaceful slumber," she departed for her room. Amos rested in a chair not far from the bed. Shortly before four o'clock, the valet was alarmed by the sound of "irregular breathing." Roosevelt's respiration "seemed to stop," he later said. "Then it resumed again and paused again." Amos rushed to summon the nurse and alerted Mrs. Roosevelt. By the time Edith reached his room, Theodore was dead. Doctors later confirmed that Roosevelt had died in his sleep from a coronary embolism. "Death had to take him sleeping," Vice President Thomas Marshall cabled from Washington, "for if Roosevelt had been awake, there would have been a fight."

☙ ❧

RAY BAKER, IDA TARBELL, AND William Allen White were all in Paris on separate assignments covering the Armistice and the Versailles Peace Conference when news of Roosevelt's death reached Europe. Their "brave little adventure" in creating a writer's magazine dedicated to serious public issues had failed. Relentless money troubles had forced John Phillips to sell *The American Magazine* to a big publishing house, which pressured the writers to satisfy advertisers' demands for popular pieces. "The test of the stories," Baker lamented, became not whether they were "good literature" or important contributions to national discourse, but whether they would attract 600,000 readers. Prize contests were introduced, along with stories of romance and marriage. Baker had been tempted to leave in 1912, when the new publishers demanded that he remove a sentence critical of the business community. Loyalty to his colleagues had kept him on board for three additional years until he could no longer abide the way his literary ambitions were continuously "strangled by commercial considerations" and finally resigned. In short order, Tarbell, Phillips, and White also resigned.

White and Tarbell had been sent to Paris by the *Red Cross Magazine*, where John Phillips was now the editor. Ray Baker was serving President Wilson as press liaison, assigned to give daily briefings to over one hundred American correspondents who had journeyed overseas to report on the peace conference. Tarbell observed that Baker managed his demanding job with such "absolute fairness" that even "the tongues of some of the most bumptious" journalists were "silenced." The three old colleagues had taken rooms in the Hôtel de Vouillemont, located just off the Place de la Concorde not far from the headquarters of the American Peace Commission. "There were hours when it seemed like a gathering in the office of the old *American Magazine*," Tarbell recalled, "so natural and intimate it was."

White was at breakfast when he read of Theodore Roosevelt's death in the Paris *Herald*'s morning edition. "Again and again I looked at the headlines to be sure that I was reading them correctly," he recalled. Just then, Ray Baker arrived, carrying the same paper. "Ray, Ray, the Colonel is dead—Roosevelt!" White cried. "Yes, Will," Baker responded, sadly embracing him. "It's a great blow. We are all sorry." Soon Ida Tarbell joined them, White recalled, and the three "sat down to talk it all over, and get used to a world without Roosevelt in it."

⌒ ⌒

WILLIAM HOWARD TAFT WAS AMONG the five hundred guests invited to attend Roosevelt's private funeral service, held in the modest Episcopal church in Oyster Bay. "It was my father's wish," Archie Roosevelt explained, "that the funeral service be conducted entirely by those friends among whom he had lived so long and happily." After their fortuitous meeting at the Blackstone Hotel, Roosevelt and Taft had resumed their old habit of intimate, friendly correspondence, sending each other drafts of speeches, commenting on articles, sharing thoughts on the central issues of the day. Visiting Roosevelt in the hospital in late November, Taft had discovered with delight that they were in essential accord on the need for a league of nations to enforce the postwar peace. Snow had fallen the morning that Theodore Roosevelt was laid to rest, but the sun had come out by the time Taft arrived at the church. "You're a dear personal friend," Archie said, taking him by the hand and directing him to a pew in the front. Though the half-hour service had "no pomp, no ceremony," no singing or music, its very simplicity, one mourner observed, made it "profoundly impressive."

The village bells tolled as mourners followed the casket up the hill to the gravesite where "a mound of flowers hid the freshly-turned earth." According to an old "widow's custom," Edith Roosevelt attended neither funeral nor burial. Though she would live to the age of eighty-seven, she had lost the only man she would ever love, the man, she had told Theodore, she loved "with all the passion of a girl who had never loved before."

As Theodore Roosevelt's casket was lowered into the ground, "an isolated figure" stood "quite apart from the others," William Howard Taft, softly crying. "I want to say to you," Taft later told Roosevelt's sister Bamie, "how glad I am that Theodore and I came together after that long painful interval. Had he died in a hostile state of mind toward me, I would have mourned the fact all my life. I loved him always and cherish his memory."

⌒ ⌒

At noon on October 3, 1921, sixty-four-year-old William Howard Taft finally secured the position he had long desired "as strongly as a man can ever want anything." The death of Chief Justice Edward White the previous May had created a vacancy that President Warren Harding was happy to fill with the former chief executive. In a ceremony witnessed by Nellie and dozens of old friends, Taft took the judicial oath "to administer justice without respect to persons, and do equal right to the poor and to the rich." Reporters noted that "the famous Taft Smile" was irresistible as friends and colleagues "rushed up to congratulate him." After the ceremony, Taft and Nellie joined the other justices and their families at a White House reception. "This is the greatest day of my life," the new chief justice of the United States declared.

"The people of the United States greet Mr. Taft in his new role," *The Washington Post* editorialized the following day. "Their good wishes will not be inspired solely by their abiding faith in his wisdom and justice, but also by the fact that they like him personally. His popularity throughout the country has grown from the day, nearly ten years ago, when the fortunes of political warfare went overwhelmingly against him and, instead of permitting defeat to sour his nature or crush his spirit, he accepted his lot philosophically and with a smile."

The public trust was not misplaced. Under Taft's able leadership, "antiquated" court procedure was streamlined, "speeding up" and greatly improving the delivery of justice throughout "the whole system of federal courts." And through his "great skill and patience," Taft finally secured from Congress the funds to construct a separate building for the Supreme Court, allowing the justices to move from the "old Senate chamber" to the classic marble structure that graces Washington today. As Taft had always suspected, the position of chief justice was more suited to his mind and temperament than the presidency had ever been. Fulfilled at work and happy at home, he embarked upon a successful regime of diet and exercise, bringing his weight down to less than 250 pounds, a reasonable weight for a man of his stature and proportions. Years of obesity, however, had already damaged his health. On February 3, 1930, escalating heart trouble forced his resignation from the job he had loved more than any other. "We call you Chief Justice still," Justice Oliver Wendell Holmes wrote a week later on behalf of his colleagues, "for we cannot give up the title by which we have known you all these later years and which you have made so dear to us . . . you showed us in new form your voluminous capacity for getting work done, your humor that smoothed the tough places, your golden heart that brought you love from every side and most of all from your brethren whose tasks you have made happy and light."

Just over a month after he left the bench, on March 8, 1930, William Howard Taft was dead. Nellie Taft, whose catastrophic illness had left her husband bereft of his most valuable ally and altered his presidency in ways the public never comprehended, would live thirteen years more, dying just short of her eighty-second birthday.

☞ ☜

During the 1920s and the 1930s, the members of the original *McClure's* magazine staff continued to celebrate each other's birthdays. Such was the "unbreakable quality in friendship," Ida Tarbell marveled, that despite the bitter 1906 split, the core group could not be permanently alienated. "You pick up at the day when the friendship was—not broken but interrupted," she observed. Year after year, the "old Crowd" would convene, reviving "a hundred, yes a thousand memories" of the days that had proved the most fulfilling of their lives—the idealistic time when they genuinely believed, in Ray Baker's words, that they were "saving the world." Sustained by passion and optimism, they "muck-raked never to destroy, but with utter faith in reason and progress"; they "criticized in full confidence that, once understood, evils would be speedily corrected." None of them had truly realized, Baker later acknowledged to Lincoln Steffens, how "hard-boiled" the world really was.

At each of these collective birthday celebrations, Sam McClure, then in his seventies and eighties, was "the star of the evening." He would recount his personal history with such charm—his impoverished youth, his marriage to Hattie when his weekly salary was only twelve dollars, his eventual triumph "storming the sacred citadels in the publishing business"—that his listeners were riveted as if the tale were novel. His "old fire" flared up, Tarbell was happy to see. "We sat enthralled," she wrote, as McClure "enlarged on his latest enthusiasm, marveling as always at the eternal youthfulness in the man, the failure of life to quench him."

After John Phillips was unable to attend one of these gatherings, Tarbell wrote to tell him how much he had been missed, how they all realized that he was the one, during all those years, who had kept the *McClure's* "flame steady and lasting." Revisiting "that wonderful adventure we all had together," Phillips confessed to Ray Baker, was "almost like a physical pain—not because of you and me and so on. But because of this country, and because those sincere attempts, to do something in reporting and interpretation of what was good and sound and progressive, seemed lost and forgotten." Still, he hoped that other "times of awakening" lay ahead, that a new generation of journalists would be drawn to the work that "seemed once almost a mission and a call."

⤳ ACKNOWLEDGMENTS ⤶

At the outset, I wish to acknowledge my debt to a remarkable circle of biographers and historians whose studies of Theodore Roosevelt, William Howard Taft, the muckraking journalists, and the Progressive era provided the background I needed to begin thinking about this project.

Dedicated staff members of numerous libraries have provided invaluable help in my search for primary sources and pictures. I particularly want to thank Joshua Caster, Heather Cole, Wallace Finley Dailey, Zachary Downey, Mary Haegert, E. Ray Henderson, Isabel Planton, Jane Westenfeld, and Cherry Williams.

In Massachusetts, I am grateful to the Theodore Roosevelt Collection at Houghton Library, Harvard University; the Sophia Smith Collection at Smith College, Northampton; and the Jones Library at Amherst. In Ohio, the Cincinnati History Library and Archives at the Cincinnati Museum Center, and the William Howard Taft National Historical Site, National Park Service. In Washington, D.C., the Manuscript Division of the Library of Congress. In Pennsylvania, the Pelletier Library, Allegheny College, Meadville. In New York, the Rare Book and Manuscript Library at Columbia University. And in Indiana, the Lilly Library at Indiana University, Bloomington.

Each of the past seven summers, I have participated in the intern program at Harvard's Institute of Politics, working with a truly wonderful group of students, including Alex Burns, Welton Blount, Samuel Jacobs, Arjun Ramamurti, Sam Barr, James McAuley, and Amanda McGowan. For reading all or parts of the manuscript, I wish to thank Lindsay Hosmer Goodwin, John Hill, Beth Laski, and Frank Phillips. I am grateful to Gary Zola for squiring me through Taft's Cincinnati, and to Paul Grondahl for guiding me through Roosevelt's Albany.

I am especially indebted to Michelle Krowl and Camille Larson for their phenomenal work in searching through the archives at the Library of Congress, where the treasure trove of primary materials that form the bedrock of this book is housed—letters, diaries, newspaper articles, periodical pieces, memoirs, office files, and pamphlets.

My longtime agent Binky Urban gave her wholehearted support to this project from simply the germ of an idea to its completion. There is no one better.

And I owe more than I can express to Beth Laski, my manager, my publicist, my great friend. It is impossible to imagine my life without her.

There is no way this project would have been completed on time without Nora Titone. She worked with me on *Team of Rivals* and then went on to write a wonderful book on Edwin and John Wilkes Booth. She returned these last ten months to help in a thousand ways, tying together all the loose ends with an attention to detail that is simply astonishing. With good cheer and endless enthusiasm, she is an absolute joy to work with. She is a true champion.

How lucky I have been that Simon & Schuster has been my publisher for more than a quarter of a century. Even as I list the following names, I feel as if I am listing members of my family: Jonathan Karp, Carolyn Reidy, Richard Rhorer, Jackie Seow, Joy O'Meara, George Turianski, Gina DiMascia, Julia Prosser, Stephen Bedford, W. Anne Jones. For managing the voyage during these last hectic months, I am particularly grateful to Ann Adelman, my incomparable copy editor; to Jonathan Cox, Alice Mayhew's indefatigable assistant; and to Lisa Healy and Irene Kheradi, who finally brought the book home.

And of course, there is no one like Alice Mayhew, my editor, counselor, and guide, to whom I proudly dedicate this book. She saw the story I wanted to tell from the start, offering critical advice and ideas at every stage. She has been my indispensable partner throughout my writing career. She is a publishing legend. She is my treasured friend.

This book is also dedicated to my research assistant, Linda Vandegrift. We have worked together for nearly thirty years. Every book has benefited greatly from her extraordinary talent, organizational skills, and unfailing good judgment; but from the start, this story engaged her heart and mind more than any other. She became a true collaborator, without whom the book would simply not have been possible.

And finally, words cannot fully convey my gratitude to my husband, Richard Goodwin, and our best friend, Michael Rothschild, who read every draft of every chapter, providing loving and constructive ideas, comments, and criticisms at every step along the way of this seven-year journey.

⇒ NOTES ⇐

Abbreviations used in the notes:

Names

AB	Archibald Willingham Butt		**LTT**	Louise Torrey Taft
ARC	Anna Roosevelt Cowles		**MAH**	Marcus Alonzo Hanna
ARL	Alice Roosevelt Longworth		**RBH**	Rutherford Birchard Hayes
CRR	Corinne Roosevelt Robinson		**RHD**	Richard Harding Davis
DCT	Delia Chapin Torrey		**RLF**	Robert M. La Follette
EKR	Edith Kermit Carow Roosevelt		**RSB**	Ray Stannard Baker
HCL	Henry Cabot Lodge		**TR**	Theodore Roosevelt
HHM	Harriet Hurd McClure		**TR, JR.**	Theodore Roosevelt, Jr.
HHT	Helen Herron Taft		**UBS**	Upton Beall Sinclair
IMT	Ida Minerva Tarbell		**WAW**	William Allen White
JSP	John Sanborn Phillips		**WHT**	William Howard Taft
LS	Lincoln Steffens		**WW**	Woodrow Wilson

Journals and Collected Works

LTR: Theodore Roosevelt, Elting E. Morison, John M. Blum, and John J. Buckley, eds. *The Letters of Theodore Roosevelt*. 8 vols. Cambridge, MA: Harvard University Press, 1951–54.

NYT: *New York Times*
WTR: Theodore Roosevelt and Hermann Hagedorn, eds. *The Works of Theodore Roosevelt*. 24 vols. New York: Charles Scribner's Sons, 1923–26.

Papers and Collections

AB Letters: Archibald Willingham Butt Letters, Manuscript, Archives, and Rare Book Library, Emory University

ARC Papers: Anna Roosevelt Cowles Papers (MS Am 1834.1), Theodore Roosevelt Collection, Houghton Library, Harvard University

ARL Papers: Alice Roosevelt Longworth Papers, 1888–1942, Manuscript Division, Library of Congress, Washington, DC

CPT Papers: Charles P. Taft Papers, Manuscript Division, LC

CRR Papers: Corinne Roosevelt Robinson Papers (MS Am 1785–1785.7), Theodore Roosevelt Collection, Houghton Library, Harvard University

Derby Papers: Ethel Roosevelt Derby Papers (*87M-100, etc.), Theodore Roosevelt Collection, Houghton Library, Harvard University

Dunne Papers: Finley Peter Dunne Papers, Manuscript Division, LC

Garfield Papers: James Rudolph Garfield Papers, Manuscript Division, LC

Ida Tarbell Papers: Ida Tarbell Papers, Sophia Smith Collection, Smith College, Northampton, MA

IMTC: The Ida M. Tarbell Collection, Pelletier Library, Allegheny College, Meadville, PA

KR Papers: Kermit and Belle Roosevelt Papers, Manuscript Division, LC

LS Papers: Lincoln Steffens Papers, Rare Book & Manuscript Library, Columbia University in the City of New York

McClure MSS: Samuel Sidney McClure Manuscripts, The Lilly Library, Indiana University, Bloomington, IN

O'Laughlin Papers: John Callan O'Laughlin Papers, Manuscript Division, LC

Phillips MSS: John Sanborn Phillips Manuscripts, The Lilly Library, Indiana University, Bloomington, IN

Pinchot Papers: Gifford Pinchot Papers, Manuscript Division, LC

Pringle Papers: Henry F. Pringle Papers, Manuscript Division, LC

RBH Papers: Rutherford Birchard Hayes Papers, Manuscript Division, LC

RSB Papers: Ray Stannard Baker Papers, Manuscript Division, LC

RSB Papers II: Ray Stannard ("David Grayson") Baker Papers, The Jones Library, Amherst, MA

Taft-Karger Corr.: William H. Taft and Gustav J. Karger Correspondence, Cincinnati History Library and Archives, Cincinnati Museum Center

TRC: Theodore Roosevelt Collection, Houghton Library, Harvard University

TRJP: Theodore Roosevelt, Jr. Papers, Manuscript Division, LC

TRP: Theodore Roosevelt Papers, Manuscript Division, LC

White Papers: William Allen White Papers, Manuscript Division, LC

WHTP: William H. Taft Papers, Manuscript Division, LC

PREFACE

Page

xi "He had just finished": Lyman Abbott, "A Review of President Roosevelt's Administration: IV—Its Influence on Patriotism and Public Service," *Outlook*, Feb. 27, 1909, p. 430.

xii "a spark of genius": William Allen White to Charles Churchill, Aug. 9, 1906, William Allen White Papers, Manuscript Division, LC.

xii "The story is the thing": "Interview with S. S. McClure," *The North American* (Philadelphia), Aug. 15, 1905.

xii "muckraker . . . a badge of honor": Patricia O'Toole, *When Trumpets Call: Theodore Roosevelt after the White House* (New York: Simon & Schuster, 2005), p. 30.

xiii "It is hardly an exaggeration": Richard Hofstadter, *The Age of Reform: From Bryan to F.D.R.* (New York: Alfred A. Knopf, 1955), pp. 186–87.

xiii "Oh, things will be all right": *Van Wert* [OH] *Daily Bulletin*, April 5, 1905.

xiii "derelict": WHT, "Personal Aspects of the Presidency," *Saturday Evening Post*, Feb. 28, 1914.

xiv "not constituted": William Howard Taft to William Allen White, Mar. 20, 1909, White Papers.

xiv "vitality of democracy . . . complex questions": S. S. McClure, "The Railroads on Trial: Editorial Announcement of a New Series by Ray Stannard Baker," *McClure's* (October 1905), p. 673.

xiv "the mission of raising": William James, *Memories and Studies* (New York: Longmans, Green & Co., 1911), p. 323.

xiv "There is no one left . . . none but all of us": S. S. McClure, "Concerning Three Articles . . . and a Coincidence That May Set Us Thinking," *McClure's* (January 1903), p. 336.

CHAPTER ONE: The Hunter Returns

Page

1 ROOSEVELT IS COMING HOME: *Boston Daily Globe*, June 16, 1910.

1 "the wise custom" . . . take his pledge back: Herman H. Kohlsaat, *From McKinley to Harding: Personal Recollections of Our Presidents* (New York: Charles Scribner's Sons, 1923), pp. 137–38; *Oshkosh* [WI] *Daily Northwestern*, Nov. 9, 1904; *NYT*, Nov. 8, 1904.

2 "the greatest office . . . every hour": Oscar S. Straus, *Under Four Administrations: From Cleveland to Taft* (Boston: Houghton Mifflin, 1922), p. 251.

2 "dull thud . . . break his fall": Archibald W. Butt to "My Darling Mother," June 19, [1908], in Lawrence F. Abbott, ed., *The Letters of Archie Butt, Personal Aide to President Roosevelt* (Garden City, NY: Doubleday, Page & Co., 1924), p. 42.

2 "impenetrable spot": Elmer J. Burkett, "Theodore Roosevelt," *The Independent*, June 9, 1910, p. 1270.

2 "Even at this moment": TR to John Appleton Stewart, Mar. 19, 1910, in Elting E. Morison, ed., *The Days of Armageddon, 1909–1914*, Vol. 7 of *The Letters of Theodore Roosevelt* [hereafter *LTR*] (Cambridge, MA: Harvard University Press, 1951–54), p. 59.

2 "My political career . . . engulfing him": Lawrence F. Abbott, *Impressions of Theodore Roosevelt* (Garden City, NY: Doubleday, Page & Co., 1923), p. 53.

2 a six-week tour . . . Kings and queens: *Baltimore Sun*, June 18, 1910.

2 "People gathered . . . viva Roosevelt!": Lawrence F. Abbott, "Mr. Roosevelt in Europe," *Outlook*, June 4, 1910, pp. 249–50.

2 "No foreign ruler . . . class of society": *NYT*, June 10, 1910.

2 "I don't suppose . . . all about the man": AB to Clara, April 19, 1910, in Archibald Willingham Butt, *Taft and Roosevelt: The Intimate Letters of Archie Butt, Military Aide,* Vol. 1 (Garden City, NY: Doubleday, Doran & Co., 1930), p. 332.

3 "royal progress . . . American ever received": "A Welcome to Mr. Roosevelt from the President of the United States," *Outlook*, June 18, 1910, p. 342.

3 "a holiday appearance": *Evening Tribune* (Marysville, OH), June 19, 1910.

3 "as diversely typical . . . native born and aliens": Editorial, *Evening Star* (Washington, DC), June 18, 1910.

3 More than two hundred vessels: *NYT*, June 17, 1910.

3 "Flags floated . . . draped with bunting": *Evening Tribune*, June 19, 1910.

3 The night before . . . special duty: *NYT*, June 17, 1910; *Philadelphia Inquirer*, June 18, 1910.

3 "The United States . . . excitement of anticipation": *Atlanta Constitution*, June 15, 1910.

3 "If it were not . . . I am done for": Edith Kermit Carow Roosevelt to Kermit Roosevelt, April 7, 1909, KR Papers.

4 "would do anything in the world": Edith Kermit Carow to TR, June 8 [1886], in Sylvia Jukes Morris, *Edith Kermit Roosevelt: Portrait of a First Lady* [hereafter *EKR*] (New York: Coward, McCann & Geoghegan, 1980), p. 86.

4 They had been intimate childhood . . . broke down in tears: TR, *Diaries of Boyhood and Youth* (New York: Charles Scribner's Sons, 1928), p. 13.

4   a regular guest at "Tranquillity": David McCullough, *Mornings on Horseback* (New York: Simon & Schuster, 1981), pp. 142–43.
4   "the prettiest girls they had met": Morris, *EKR*, p. 53.
4   mysterious "falling out" . . . at the estate's summerhouse: Carleton Putnam, *Theodore Roosevelt: The Formative Years, 1858–1886* (New York: Charles Scribner's Sons, 1958), pp. 170, 556.
4   The conflict . . . "his very intimate relations": TR to ARC, Sept. 20, 1886, TRC.
4   "both of us had": TR to ARC, Sept. 20, 1886, TRC.
4   his "whole heart and soul": TR, Personal Diary, Jan. 25, 1880, TRP.
4   "I do not think . . . mistress of the White House": TR to Maria Longworth Storer, Dec. 8, 1902, in Elting E. Morison, ed., *The Square Deal, 1901–1903*, Vol. 3 of *LTR*, p. 392.
5   their fellow passengers, some 3,000: *NYT*, June 19, 1910.
5   massive battleship *South Carolina*: *Boston Daily Globe*, June 19, 1910.
5   "By George!": *Washington Post*, June 19, 1910.
5   "Flags were broken out . . . an eight-pounder": *Boston Daily Globe*, June 19, 1910.
5   "to add dignity": AB to Clara, June 19, 1910, in AB, *Taft and Roosevelt*, Vol. 1, pp. 394, 400.
5   "just as prominent": *Evening Bulletin* (Philadelphia), June 19, 1910.
5   he stopped his hectic motions: *NYT*, June 19, 1910.
5   "love of the hurly-burly . . . and Mr. Roosevelt": Arthur R. Colquhoun, "Theodore Roosevelt," *Living Age*, May 28, 1910, p. 519.
5   "pugilists, college presidents . . . noise and excitement": Edward G. Lowry, "The White House Now," *Harper's Weekly*, May 15, 1907, p. 7.
6   the Roosevelts' youngest sons . . . Nicholas Longworth: *Chicago Tribune*, June 19, 1910.
6   Eleanor Roosevelt; and her husband, Franklin: Joseph L. Gardner, *Departing Glory: Theodore Roosevelt as ex-President* (New York: Charles Scribner's Sons, 1973), p. 170.
6   Roosevelt busily shook hands: *Boston Daily Globe*, June 19, 1910.
6   "Come here, Theodore . . . anything else": AB to Clara, June 19, 1910, in AB, *Taft and Roosevelt*, Vol. 1, p. 399.
6   "the round face": *Chicago Tribune*, June 19, 1910.
6   "to kiss pop first": *Atlanta Constitution*, June 19, 1910.
6   "the Colonel spread his arms . . . pandemonium broke loose": *Chicago Tribune*, June 19, 1910.
6   "there came from the river": *NYT*, June 19, 1910.
6   "everywhere flags": *Atlanta Constitution*, June 19, 1910.
6   executed a "flying leap" . . . with every crew member: *Fort Wayne* [IN] *Sentinel*, June 18, 1910.
7   "an explosive word . . . meaning of the words": *NYT*, June 19, 1910.
7   "This takes me back . . . tell you how I feel": *Chicago Tribune*, June 19, 1910.
7   "Fine! Fine!": *NYT*, June 19, 1910.
7   "George, this is bully!": *Boston Daily Globe*, June 19, 1910.
7   Roosevelt hesitated . . . "shake hands with them": *NYT*, June 19, 1910.
7   "Boys, I am *glad*": *NYT*, June 19, 1910.
7   "We're mighty glad": *Washington Post*, June 19, 1910.
8   Reporters . . . remarked how "hale and hearty": *Evening Tribune* (Marysville, OH), June 19, 1910.
8   "It is true": *Evening Bulletin* (Philadelphia), June 19, 1910.
8   "the same bubbling": *Boston Daily Globe*, June 19, 1910.
8   detected "something different . . . more encompassing": AB to Clara, June 19, 1910, in AB, *Taft and Roosevelt*, Vol. 1, p. 396.
8   "You come back here . . . a look at Teddy": *Washington Post*, June 19, 1910.
8   "There he is!" . . . "Home, Sweet Home": *NYT*, June 19, 1910.
8   "the man of the hour": *Washington Post*, June 19, 1910.
8   "echoing boom": *Boston Daily Globe*, June 19, 1910.
8   "Turn around . . . all waiting for him": *Washington Post*, June 19, 1910.
8   "unnumbered thousands" . . . surrounding streets: *Boston Daily Globe*, June 19, 1910.
9   "a life-size Teddy bear": *NYT*, June 19, 1910.
9   "Delighted": *NYT*, June 18, 1910.
9   "from street level to skyline": New York *Sun*, June 19, 1910.
9   "Is there a stenographer": *Evening Tribune*, June 19, 1910.
9   "No man could . . . the American people": *Washington Post*, June 19, 1910.
9   A five-mile parade . . . lining the streets: *Evening Post* (Washington, DC), June 18, 1910.
9   "The sidewalks": *Chicago Tribune*, June 19, 1910.
9   Rough Rider unit . . . escort of honor: *Boston Daily Globe*, June 19, 1910.
9   "incomparably the largest": *Evening Star*, June 18, 1910.
9   Placards with friendly . . . front of the building: *Chicago Tribune*, June 19, 1910.
10   "You could not move": New York *Evening Post*, July 18, 1910.

10   "the malefactors of great wealth": *St. Louis Times*, June 19, 1910.

10   "Teddy! Teddy!": *Washington Post*, June 19, 1910.

10   "unconcealed delight . . . Not a bit": *NYT*, June 19, 1910.

10   with tears in his eyes: *Boston Daily Globe*, June 19, 1910.

10   a frightening storm: *Chicago Tribune*, June 19, 1910; *Los Angeles Times*, June 19, 1910.

10   "Everyone began talking": AB to Clara, June 19, 1910, in AB, *Taft and Roosevelt*, Vol. 1, p. 402.

10   a festive meal: AB to Clara, June 19, 1910, in ibid., p. 401.

10   The severe rainstorm . . . "to the ground": *Washington Post*, June 19, 1910.

10   "triumphal arches": *NYT*, June 19, 1910.

10   "to live among you again": *Washington Post*, June 19, 1910.

11   "the slightest trace of fatigue": *NYT*, June 19, 1910.

11   "We lived in . . . sweet intimacy": William Howard Taft, "My Predecessor," *Collier's*, Mar. 6, 1909, p. 25.

11   "the foremost member": TR to WHT, June 9, 1903, in *LTR*, Vol. 3, p. 486.

11   his daily "counsellor": TR to WHT, Feb. 14, 1903, in ibid., p. 426.

11   "I am quite as nervous": TR to WHT, Sept. 19, 1907, in Elting E. Morison, ed., *The Big Stick, 1905–1907*, Vol. 5 of *LTR*, p. 796.

11   When Taft was elected . . . a "beloved" friend: TR to WHT, Aug. 2, 1906, in ibid., p. 341.

12   "Taft is as fine a fellow": TR to Arthur Hamilton Lee, Dec. 20, 1908, in Elting E. Morison, ed., *The Big Stick, 1907–1909*, Vol. 6 of *LTR*, pp. 1432–33.

12   "I do not know any man": TR to Gifford Pinchot, Jan. 17, 1910, Pinchot Papers.

12   asked Pinchot to meet him in Europe: TR to Gifford Pinchot, Mar. 1, 1910, Pinchot Papers.

12   all expressing a belief . . . Roosevelt's hard-won advances: Albert J. Beveridge to Gifford Pinchot, Mar. 24, 1910; Jonathan P. Dolliver to Gifford Pinchot, Mar. 25, 1910, TRP.

12   On his final day: TR to Trevelyan, Oct. 1, 1911, in *LTR*, Vol. 7, p. 415.

12   "Roosevelt's spirit was much troubled": Edward Grey, *Twenty-five Years, 1892–1916* (New York: Frederick A. Stokes Co., 1925), Vol. 2, pp. 93–94.

12   "What will Mr. Roosevelt do?": *Advocate* (Newark, NJ), June 19, 1910.

13   the intensifying struggle . . . dividing the Republican Party: Ray Stannard Baker, "The Measure of Taft," *The American Magazine* (July 1910), p. 362.

13   "There is one thing": *NYT*, June 19, 1910.

13   "He looks haggard and careworn": AB to Clara, Jan. 7, 1910, in AB, *Taft and Roosevelt*, Vol. 1, p. 254.

13   faded to a sickly pale: AB to Clara, Easter [n.d.], 1910, in ibid., p. 312.

13   "It is hard . . . murmur against the fate": AB to Clara, Easter [n.d.], 1910, in ibid., p. 313.

13   "a man of tremendous . . . to show no resentment": AB to Clara, Feb. 9, 1910, in ibid., p. 278.

13   his "secondary role": AB to Clara, Feb. 13, 1910, in ibid., p. 281.

13   "he loves Theodore Roosevelt": AB to Clara, Jan. 7, 1910, in ibid., p. 254.

13   "He is going to be": AB, Dec. 10, 1908, in Abbott, ed., *Letters of Archie Butt*, Vol. 1, pp. 232–33.

13   "America incarnate": William Allen White, "Taft: A Hewer of Wood," *The American Magazine* (April 1908), p. 20.

13   a man who could "finish the things" . . . would "do much": Ibid., pp. 31, 32.

14   "by flashes or whims . . . long, logical habit": "Six Months of President Taft," *The World's Work* (September 1909).

14   "a great crusade . . . in the form of law": George Kibbe Turner, "How Taft Views His Own Administration," *McClure's* (June 1910), p. 211.

14   "intense desire . . . for legal method": WHT, "My Predecessor," *Collier's*, Mar. 6, 1909, p. 25.

14   Roosevelt had ended his presidency: TR to Kermit Roosevelt, May 10, 1908, in TR, Kermit Roosevelt, and Will Irwin, eds., *Letters to Kermit from Theodore Roosevelt, 1902–1908* (New York: Charles Scribner's Sons, 1946), p. 242.

14   "with the tools": "Six Months of President Taft," *The World's Work* (September 1909).

14   He had "great misgivings": WHT to HHT, Aug. 11, 1907, WHTP.

14   acceptance speech . . . "like a nightmare": WHT to TR, July 12, 1908, TRP.

14   He feared . . . "make many people mad": WHT to HHT, Aug. 13, 1907, WHTP.

14   negative press left him "very, very discouraged": *Nevada State Journal*, Mar. 23, 1910.

15   refused to read unfavorable articles: AB to Clara, Nov. 14, 1909, in AB, *Taft and Roosevelt*, Vol. 1, p. 206.

15   "But I am made this way": WHT to HHT, Aug. 15, 1907, WHTP.

15   his "campaign manager": *Syracuse* [NY] *Herald*, June 14, 1908.

15   "I pinch myself": WHT to Henry A. Morrill, Box 29, Pringle Papers.

15   "would rather be Chief Justice . . . to bear and undergo": AB to Clara, Mar. 4, 1910, in AB, *Taft and Roosevelt*, Vol. 1, p. 294.

15   "overcome the obstacles": WHT to Henry A. Morrill, Box 29, Pringle Papers.

15 Their sisters had been "schoolmates . . . forty years": Helen Herron Taft, *Recollections of Full Years* (New York: Dodd, Mead & Co., 1914), p. 7.

15 "with such high feeling . . . during that period": Ibid., p. 11.

15 "the deeper grew my respect": WHT to Alphonso Taft, July 12, 1885, WHTP.

16 a "merciless but loving critic": WHT to Nellie, June 28, 1895, WHTP.

16 "two men who are intimate chums": Betty Boyd Caroli, *First Ladies* (New York: Oxford University Press, 1987), p. 130.

16 "the Taft Administration will be brilliant": *NYT*, Mar. 4, 1909.

16 insisting "upon complete racial equality": Carl Sferrazza Anthony, *Nellie Taft: The Unconventional First Lady of the Ragtime Era* (New York: HarperCollins, 2005), p. 148.

16 Taft turned "deathly pale": AB to Clara, May 17, 1909, in AB, *Taft and Roosevelt*, Vol. 1, p. 88.

16 "great soul . . . wrapped in darkness": AB to Mrs. John D. Butt, June 8, 1909, in ibid., p. 101.

16 "I have had a hard time . . . at the White House": WHT to TR, May 26, 1910, TRP.

17 "this demonstration of amity . . . with the former President": *Indianapolis Star*, June 12, 1910.

17 "charged with the dignity . . . to any man": AB to Clara, June 16, 1910, in AB, *Taft and Roosevelt*, Vol. 1, p. 389.

17 "When you are being hammered": WHT, Speech, Mar. 22, 1910, Series 9, reel 567, WHTP; *Nevada State Journal*, Mar. 23, 1910.

17 he "read with deep interest": *Evening Star* (Washington, DC), June 18, 1910.

17 all "the members of the faculty . . . tremendous yell": *The North American* (Philadelphia), June 19, 1910.

18 gaily decorated . . . 2,500 invited guests: *Evening Bulletin* (Philadelphia), June 18, 1910.

18 "The Roosevelt luck" . . . decision to speak indoors: *Philadelphia Inquirer*, June 19, 1910.

18 the entire audience rose: *The North American*, June 19, 1910.

18 a "flying visit": *Evening Bulletin*, June 18, 1910.

18 "He came to me": *Evening Star* (Washington, DC), June 18, 1910.

18 "Banks, office buildings": *Philadelphia Inquirer*, June 18, 1910.

18 "a terrific electrical storm": Ibid.

18 "I thank you sincerely for coming": WHT, "Speech at Lincoln University, June 18, 1910," WHTP.

18 "one of the greatest men" . . . nation's racial problems: *Evening Star* (Washington, DC), June 19, 1910.

18 the press could not resist drawing comparisons: *The North American*, June 19, 1910.

19 Taft was "travel-stained": *New York Herald*, June 19, 1910.

19 exhausted when he boarded the train: *Fort Wayne* [IN] *Journal-Gazette*, June 19, 1910.

19 "in a free state of perspiration": *Galveston* [TX] *Daily News*, June 19, 1910.

19 "ready and eager": *Waterloo* [IA] *Times-Tribune*, June 19, 1910.

19 his bill . . . was awaiting his signature: *New York Herald*, June 19, 1910.

19 "an abiding faith . . . take care of itself ultimately": WHT to R. L. O'Brien, June 28, 1910, in Donald F. Anderson, *William Howard Taft: A Conservative's Conception of the Presidency* (Ithaca, NY: Cornell University Press, 1973), p. 218.

19 "the first positive step": "Six Months of President Taft," *The World's Work* (September 1909).

19 "for the first time, the power": George Kibbe Turner, "How Taft Views His Own Administration; An Interview with the President," *McClure's* (June 1910), p. 215.

19 a postal savings bill "fought at every step": *Evening Bulletin* (Philadelphia), June 18, 1910.

19 a secure place to deposit their money: WHT to William B. McKinley, Aug. 20, 1910, WHTP.

19 Taft "had unquestionably strengthened": *Evening Bulletin* (Philadelphia), June 18, 1910.

20 "their laughs would mingle": AB to Clara, June 15, 1912, in AB, *Taft and Roosevelt*, Vol. 2, p. 813.

20 "No other friendship": William Allen White, "Taft: A Hewer of Wood," *The American Magazine* (April 1908), pp. 23–24.

20 "The whole country waits and wonders": *Baltimore Sun*, June 18, 1910.

CHAPTER TWO: Will and Teedie

Page

21 "Louise is getting . . . clamorous appetite": Alphonso Taft to Increase N. Talbot, Sept 21, 1857, WHTP.

21 "very large . . . made with belts": LTT to DCT, Nov. 8, 1857, WHTP.

22 "took great comfort . . . boys growing up together": LTT to Susan Torrey, November [n.d.], 1857, WHTP.

22 "He spreads his hands . . . dimple in one cheek": Henry F. Pringle, *The Life and Times of William Howard Taft* [hereafter *Life and Times*] (New York: Farrar & Rinehart, 1939), Vol. 1, p. 3.

22 "deeply, darkly, beautifully blue": LTT to DCT, November [n.d.], 1857, WHTP.

22 "healthy, fast-growing boy": Alphonso Taft to DCT, Dec. 13, 1857, WHTP.

22 "upon being held . . . take care of himself": LTT to DCT, November [n.d.], 1857, WHTP.

22 children "are treasures . . . too much": LTT to Susan Torrey, Feb. 6, 1860, WHTP.

22   To her "great disappointment" . . . town of Millbury, Massachusetts: Horace Dutton Taft, *Memories and Opinions* (New York: The Macmillan Co., 1942), p. 3.

22   "She has great mental . . . synonymous with unhappiness": Ishbel Ross, *An American Family: The Tafts, 1678 to 1964* (Cleveland, OH: World Publishing Co., 1964), p. 18.

23   "If 'ladies of strong minds' ": Ibid., p. 24.

23   "One day in an oat field . . . college was sacred in his eyes": Taft, *Memories and Opinions*, pp. 4–5.

23   "I feel well assured": Alphonso Taft to Frances Phelps, Oct. 9, 1838, WHTP.

23   "There are no such high . . . comparatively few": Alphonso Taft to Sylvia Howard Taft, Nov. 15, 1838, WHTP.

23   "honourably famous": Charles Dickens, *American Notes*, Vol. 11 of *The Writings of Charles Dickens* (New York: Houghton Mifflin, 1894), p. 514.

23   "I have not spent": Alphonso Taft to Peter Rawson Taft, Mar. 30, 1839, WHTP.

24   her "noble husband . . . quiet joy": LTT to DCT, Jan. 4, 1854, WHTP.

24   "I do feel under": Pringle, *Life and Times*, Vol. 1, p. 13.

24   "the best husband": Ross, *An American Family*, p. 20.

24   "Oh, Louise": DCT to LTT, Jan. 18, 1854, WHTP.

24   "I had more pride": LTT to Samuel Torrey, June 6, 1866, WHTP.

24   "Willie is foremost": Alphonso Taft to Samuel Torrey, Oct. 16, 1872, WHTP.

24   "simplicity, courage": Taft, *Memories and Opinions*, p. 5.

24   "If flattery or admiration": Ibid., p. 106.

24   "It was very hard": Ibid., p. 115.

24   "Scarcely a night": Pringle, *Life and Times*, Vol. 1, p. 6.

25   "We might almost as well ask": DCT to LTT, Jan. 17, 1859, WHTP.

25   "spread out before you like a map": Alphonso Taft to Frances Phelps, Nov. 12, 1838, WHTP.

25   "the advantages of both . . . or to rough it": Taft, *Memories and Opinions*, p. 13.

25   "wholesome and natural": Ibid., p. 16.

25   "the city fairly blossomed . . . one end to the other": LTT to Anna Torrey, April 18, 1865, WHTP.

25   "He was . . . a born judge": Taft, *Memories and Opinions*, p. 11.

26   "the Constitution of the State": S. B. Nelson & Co., *History of Cincinnati and Hamilton County, Ohio; Their Past and Present, Including . . . Biographies and Portraits of Pioneers and Representative Citizens, Etc.* (Cincinnati: S. B. Nelson, 1894), p. 189.

26   "the school board": Martha Willard, "Notes for a Biographer," unpublished MS, 1935, p. 92, WHTP.

26   "To be Chief Justice": Ross, *An American Family*, p. 47.

26   "No leader of the Bar . . . patience and kindness": Taft, *Memories and Opinions*, p. 11.

26   "rich real estate holders": Lewis Alexander Leonard, *Life of Alphonso Taft* (New York: Hawke Publishing Co., 1920), p. 48.

26   "the path of virtue and integrity": Ibid., p. 54.

26   "these children are unfortunate . . . cruel circumstances": Ibid.

26   his unblemished reputation . . . "the day is long": *NYT*, March 8, 1876.

26   "reform element . . . old regime": Murat Halstead to Alphonso Taft, Mar. 7, 1876, WHTP.

27   a "fatty": Bessie White Smith, *Boyhoods of the Presidents* (Boston: Lothrop, Lee & Shepard Co., 1929), p. 251.

27   a "lubber": Pringle, *Life and Times*, Vol. 1, p. 20; Eugene P. Lyle, Jr., "Taft: A Career of Big Tasks, His Boyhood and College Days," *The World's Work* (July 1907).

27   "If you can't walk": Smith, *Boyhoods of the Presidents*, p. 251.

27   At the age of seven . . . "arithmetic and writing": Ross, *An American Family*, p. 40.

27   "He means to be a scholar": Ibid.

27   "Mediocrity will not do": Pringle, *Life and Times*, Vol. 1, p. 22.

27   "His average was 95": Alphonso Taft to DCT, Dec. 24, 1869, WHTP.

27   "We felt that the sun": Taft, *Memories and Opinions*, p. 11.

27   "Love of approval": AB to Clara, Aug. 10, 1910, in AB, *Taft and Roosevelt,* Vol. 2, p. 472.

28   "read up in the Gazetteer . . . impressive to him": LTT to Anna Torrey, July 18, 1869, WHTP.

28   Alphonso re-created for Will: Alphonso Taft to WHT, Aug. 1, 1869, WHTP.

28   "a mastery of fact": David H. Burton, *The Learned Presidency: Theodore Roosevelt, William Howard Taft, Woodrow Wilson* (Rutherford, NJ: Fairleigh Dickinson University Press, 1988), p. 91.

28   "the most conspicuous": Taft, *Memories and Opinions*, p. 26.

28   "the great social event": Ross, *An American Family*, p. 58.

28   the splendid Sinton mansion: HHT, *Recollections of Full Years*, p. 4.

29   the *Times-Star*, a Taft family holding: Ross, *An American Family*, p. 67.

29   "The result of coeducation": WHT, "Woman Suffrage," 1874, WHTP.

29   "from their constitutional peculiarities": LTT to DCT, Aug. 16, 1874, WHTP.

29   "Give the woman the ballot . . . this great reform": WHT, "Woman Suffrage," 1874, WHTP.

29 the only obstacle . . . was laziness: Pringle, *Life and Times*, Vol. 1, p. 21.

29 Will stood over six feet . . . nickname "Big Bill": David H. Burton, *Taft, Roosevelt and the Limits of Friendship* (Madison, NJ: Fairleigh Dickinson University Press, 2005), p. 21.

29 "To see his large bulk . . . a dreadnaught launched": Edward H. Cotton, *William Howard Taft: A Character Study* (Boston: Beacon Press, 1932), p. 21.

29 "dragged bodily" . . . to victory: Oscar King Davis, *William Howard Taft, the Man of the Hour; His Biography and His Views on the Great Questions of Today* (Philadelphia: P. W. Ziegler Co., 1908), p. 40.

29 "I begin to see": WHT to Alphonso Taft, Sept. 12, 1874, WHTP.

29 "It is not more": LTT to DCT, Oct. 22, 1874, WHTP.

30 "Another week of this . . . your expectations": WHT to Alphonso Taft, September [n.d.], 1874, WHTP.

30 His father "had other ideas": WHT, "College Athletic," *American Physical Education Review* (April 1916), p. 225.

30 "I doubt that such popularity": Pringle, *Life and Times*, Vol. 1, p. 35.

30 "If a man has to be isolated": WHT to LTT, Nov. 4, 1874, WHTP.

30 settled into a structured regimen: WHT to Alphonso Taft, Oct. 1, 1874, WHTP.

30 "As a scholar . . . moral force": Herbert Wolcott Bowen, *Recollections, Diplomatic and Undiplomatic* (New York: F. H. Hitchcock, 1926), pp. 52–53.

30 He was the class leader: Herbert S. Duffy, *William Howard Taft* (New York: Minton, Balch & Co., 1930), pp. 5–6.

30 "safe and comforting": Lyle, "Taft: A Career of Big Tasks . . . ," *The World's Work* (July 1907).

30 appointed him "father" of their graduating year: Cotton, *William Howard Taft, a Character Study*, p. 4.

30 "was the most admired": Bowen, *Recollections, Diplomatic and Undiplomatic*, p. 53.

30 "there was little . . . way to a degree": David H. Burton, *William Howard Taft, in the Public Service* (Malabar, FL: Robert E. Krieger Publ. Co., 1986), p. 6.

31 "a course of outside reading . . . stick to the course": Lyle, "Taft: A Career of Big Tasks . . . ," *The World's Work* (July 1907).

31 "hard common sense": WHT, "The Vitality of the Democratic Party, Its Causes," Pringle Papers.

31 "Taft was judicial . . . before anything else": Pringle, *Life and Times*, Vol. 1, p. 44.

31 "had more to do with stimulating": Ibid., p. 34.

31 Considered one of the most gifted . . . "secret of his success": Dumas Malone, ed., *Dictionary of American Biography* (New York: Charles Scribner's Sons, 1935), Vol. 9, p. 218.

31 Sumner was an apostle: Robert Green McCloskey, *American Conservatism in the Age of Enterprise: A Study of William Graham Sumner, Stephen J. Field and Andrew Carnegie* (Cambridge, MA: Harvard University Press, 1951), pp. 30–32.

31 "If we should set a limit": Ibid., p. 50.

31 he argued that "princely profits": WHT, "The Right of Private Property," *Michigan Law Journal* (August 1894), p. 223.

32 "the highest pinnacle": McCloskey, *American Conservatism in the Age of Enterprise*, p. 83.

32 "the lawyer who makes": WHT, "The Professional and Political Prospects of the College Graduate," in Harry Clark Coe and William Howard Taft, *Valedictory Poem and Oration Pronounced Before the Senior Class in Yale College, Presentation Day, June 25, 1878* (New Haven, CT: Morehouse & Taylor, 1878).

32 "the greatest prize in college": Pringle, *Life and Times*, Vol. 1, p. 41.

32 "He has in this . . . & practiced": Alphonso Taft to DCT, Oct. 21, 1877, WHTP.

32 "We shall regret that . . . reputation every time": Alphonso Taft to DCT, Dec. 16, 1877, WHTP.

32 "coming on slowly": WHT to Alphonso Taft, Mar. 11, 1878, WHTP.

32 "finding it rather difficult": WHT to Alphonso Taft, April 14, 1878, WHTP.

32 "The sound of approaching music . . . manly sincerity": *NYT*, June 26, 1878.

33 "I wish you could get": WHT to Alphonso Taft, April 14, 1878, WHTP.

33 "Peter continues so strange . . . to Tillie's wishes": LTT to DCT, Jan. 22, 1878, WHTP.

33 "I am doing my best . . . above all others": Peter Rawson Taft to Alphonso Taft, April 19, 1878, WHTP.

33 "I have a kind of presentiment": WHT to HHT, May 10, 1891, WHTP.

34 "a sickly and timid boy": TR to Edward S. Martin, Nov. 26, 1900, in Elting E. Morison, ed., *The Years of Preparation, 1898–1900*, Vol. 2 of *LTR*, p. 1443.

34 "Nobody seemed to think": New York *World*, Nov. 16, 1902.

34 "Theodore Roosevelt, whose name": Corinne Roosevelt Robinson, *My Brother, Theodore Roosevelt* (New York: Charles Scribner's Sons, 1921), p. 1.

34 "great and loving care . . . walk up and down with me": TR to Edward S. Martin, Nov. 26, 1900, in *LTR*, Vol. 2, p. 1443.

34 "I could breathe": Lincoln Steffens, *The Autobiography of Lincoln Steffens* (New York: Harcourt, Brace & Co., 1931), p. 350.

34 "My father": Ibid.

34 "one of the five richest": Nathan Miller, *The Roosevelt Chronicles* (New York: Doubleday & Co., 1979), p. 117.

34 feared would "spoil" him: New York *World*, Feb. 11, 1878.

35 "I am trying to school": Theodore Roosevelt, Sr., to Martha Bulloch Roosevelt, June 10, 1853, TRC.

35 now "confident . . . only live in your being": Martha Bulloch Roosevelt to Theodore Roosevelt, Sr., July 26, 1853, in CRR, *My Brother*, pp. 13–14.

35 "the blood rush . . . I love you!": Theodore Roosevelt, Sr., to Martha Bulloch Roosevelt, Aug. 3, 1853, in ibid., p. 15.

35 "If I may judge": Martha Elliott Bulloch to Susan West, Nov. 16, 1861, TRC.

36 "I shudder to think": AB to Clara, January 8, 1909, in Abbott, ed., *Letters of Archie Butt*, p. 279.

36 Thee suppressed . . . "absolute fighting forces": Anna Roosevelt Cowles, "The Story of the Roosevelt Family," unpublished MS, n.d., CRR Papers.

36 "the most dominant figure": CRR, *My Brother*, p. 9.

36 "the most intimate friend": Ibid., p. 7.

36 "we used to wait": TR, *An Autobiography* (New York: Charles Scribner's Sons, 1920), p. 8.

36 "there was never anyone": ARC, "The Story of the Roosevelt Family," CRR Papers.

36 "he was one of those rare": McCullough, *Mornings on Horseback*, p. 31.

36 He tutored them . . . "the dead limbs": CRR, *My Brother*, p. 8.

36 "turn aside from his business": DCT to LTT, Jan. 17, 1859, WHTP.

36 "I never knew anyone": TR, *An Autobiography*, p. 9.

36 "not so much for what it was": Theodore Roosevelt, Sr., to Martha Bulloch Roosevelt, Sept. 28, 1873, TRC.

37 improving the lives of tenement children: TR, *An Autobiography*, p. 10; CRR, *My Brother*, pp. 4–5.

37 "Father was the finest man": Jacob A. Riis, *Theodore Roosevelt: The Citizen* (New York: Grosset & Dunlap, 1907), p. 446.

37 to arrange home tutoring . . . Mittie's sister, Anna: TR, *An Autobiography*, pp. 12–13.

37 their mother provided: Ibid., p. 4; ARC, "The Story of the Roosevelt Family," CRR Papers.

37 "From the very fact . . . power of concentration": William Draper Lewis, *The Life of Theodore Roosevelt* (Philadelphia: John C. Winston Co., 1919), p. 36.

37 "men who were fearless": TR, *An Autobiography*, p. 27.

37 "I can see him now . . . month to month": CRR, *My Brother*, pp. 1–2.

37 "anything less tranquil": Ibid., p. 89.

38 "riding, driving . . . the 'divine fire' ": Frances Theodora Parsons, *Perchance Some Day* (New York: Privately printed, 1951), pp. 26, 29.

38 "Roosevelt Museum of Natural History": TR, *An Autobiography*, p. 14.

38 "He loves the woods": WHT, "My Predecessor," *Collier's*, Mar. 6, 1909, p. 25.

38 "Sit down, Will . . . domestic affairs": Edward George Lowry, "The White House Now," *Harper's*, May 15, 1909, p. 7.

38 "a great little home-boy": CRR, *My Brother*, p. 45.

39 He traversed fields . . . of the Vatican: TR, *Diaries of Boyhood and Youth*, pp. 18–19, 150, 181; CRR, *My Brother*, pp. 46, 49.

39 "we three": TR, *Diaries of Boyhood and Youth*, pp. 63, 109.

39 "that a real education": Kathleen Mary Dalton, "The Early Life of Theodore Roosevelt," PhD diss., Johns Hopkins University, 1979, p. 188.

39 "Theodore, you have the mind . . . *I'll make my body*": CRR, *My Brother*, p. 50.

39 to expand "his chest": Ibid.

39 "the strenuous life": Ibid.

39 two "mischievous" boys . . . "perceptible improvement whatever": TR, *An Autobiography*, pp. 27–28.

40 his "timid" nature: Parsons, *Perchance Some Day*, p. 28.

40 "There were all kinds of things": Edward Wagenknecht, *The Seven Worlds of Theodore Roosevelt* (New York: Longmans, Green & Co., 1958), p. 3.

40 "by constantly forcing": Parsons, *Perchance Some Day*, p. 28.

40 "a matter of habit": TR, *An Autobiography*, p. 32.

40 "We arrived in sight of Alexandria": TR, *Diaries of Boyhood and Youth*, p. 276.

40 "first real collecting": TR, *An Autobiography*, p. 19.

40 a private vessel . . . thirteen-man crew: McCullough, *Mornings on Horseback*, p. 123.

40 "I had no idea": TR, *An Autobiography*, p. 18.

40 "My first knowledge": Ibid., p. 19.

40 "an almost ruthless single-mindedness": Putnam, *Theodore Roosevelt: The Formative Years*, p. 99.

41 "And of course": CRR, *My Brother*, p. 80.

41 "This trip . . . formed": TR, *An Autobiography*, p. 19.

41 "lamentably weak in Latin": Ibid., p. 21.

41 "The young man never": Putnam, *Theodore Roosevelt: The Formative Years*, p. 127.

41 "What will I become . . . but it is hard": McCullough, *Mornings on Horseback*, p. 144.

42 "It produced congestion": Theodore Roosevelt, Sr., to Martha Bulloch Roosevelt, Nov. 9, 1874, in ibid., p. 145.

42 "I jump involuntarily": Elliott Roosevelt to Theodore Roosevelt, Sr., Nov. 22, 1874, in ibid., p. 146.

42 "could make more friends . . . in many respects": Elliott Roosevelt to Theodore Roosevelt, Sr., Mar. 6, 1875, in Joseph P. Lash, *Eleanor and Franklin* (New York: W. W. Norton & Co., 1971), p. 7.

42 "During my Latin lesson": Ibid.

42 "fainted just after leaving": Ibid., p. 8.

42 "Is it not splendid": TR to ARC, July 25, 1875, in Elting E. Morison, ed., *The Years of Preparation, 1868–1898*, Vol. 1 of *LTR*, p. 13.

42 "a slender nervous young man": Donald G. Wilhelm, *Theodore Roosevelt as an Undergraduate* (Boston: J. W. Luce & Co., 1910), p. 31.

42 He worried initially: TR to CRR, Nov. 26, 1876, TRC.

42 "studious, ambitious": Henry F. Pringle, *Theodore Roosevelt: A Biography* (New York: Harcourt, Brace & Co., 1931), p. 33.

42 "It was not often . . . again and again": Paul Grondahl, *I Rose Like a Rocket: The Political Education of Theodore Roosevelt* (New York: Free Press, 2004), p. 45.

42 "Now look here, Roosevelt": Wilhelm, *Theodore Roosevelt as an Undergraduate*, p. 35.

43 he would retreat to a corner: Ibid., p. 24.

43 "No man ever came": Ibid.

43 "My library has been": TR to Theodore Roosevelt, Sr., and Martha Bulloch Roosevelt, Feb. 11, 1877, in *LTR*, Vol. 1, p. 26.

43 "the greatest of companions": Wagenknecht, *Seven Worlds*, p. 44.

43 "As I talked the pages": Frederick S. Wood, *Roosevelt as We Knew Him: The Personal Recollections of One Hundred and Fifty of His Friends and Associates* (Philadelphia: John C. Winston Co., 1927), p. 361.

43 "He always carried a book": Wagenknecht, *Seven Worlds*, p. 46.

43 Roosevelt's ability to concentrate . . . "not be diverted": Charles Grenfell Washburn, *Theodore Roosevelt: The Logic of His Career* (Boston: Houghton Mifflin, 1916), p. 3.

43 Preparing so far ahead "freed his mind": Straus, *Under Four Administrations*, p. 256.

43 finished a complete draft: Ibid., pp. 255–56.

43 "I never knew a man": WHT, "My Predecessor," *Collier's*, Mar. 6, 1909, p. 25.

44 exercising rigorously day after day: TR, *Diaries of Boyhood and Youth*, pp. 355–56, 363.

44 "he danced just as you'd expect": Putnam, *Theodore Roosevelt: The Formative Years*, p. 166.

44 "His college life broadened": Lewis, *Life of Theodore Roosevelt*, p. 51.

44 "Funnily enough": TR to Martha Bulloch Roosevelt, Oct. 8, 1878, in *LTR*, Vol. 1, p. 34.

44 "As I saw the last of the train": Grondahl, *I Rose Like a Rocket*, pp. 41–42.

44 "I do not think": TR to Theodore Roosevelt, Sr., Oct. 22, 1876, in *LTR*, Vol. 1, p. 18.

45 The Senate rejected Roosevelt's nomination: *NYT*, Oct. 30 & Dec. 4, 1877; *Galveston* [TX] *Daily News*, Dec. 13, 1877.

45 "The machine politicians": Dalton, "The Early Life of Theodore Roosevelt," p. 282.

45 an advanced stage of bowel cancer: McCullough, *Mornings on Horseback*, p. 181.

45 "very much better": TR, *Diaries of Boyhood and Youth*, p. 364.

45 "Today he told me": TR, Personal Diary, Jan. 2, 1878, TRP.

45 His groans reverberated: Elliott Roosevelt, unpublished MS, n.d., TRC.

45 his dark hair turned gray: Putnam, *Theodore Roosevelt: The Formative Years*, p. 148.

45 Elliott stayed by his father's side: Elliott Roosevelt, undated memorandum, TRC.

45 His grief was "doubly bitter . . . dearest on earth died": TR to Henry Davis Minot, July 5, 1880, TRC.

45 "I never was able": TR, Personal Diary, June 20, 1878, TRP.

45 "The death of Mr. Roosevelt": *NYT*, Feb. 13, 1878.

45 "Flags flew . . . wept over him": Riis, *Theodore Roosevelt: The Citizen*, p. 447.

45 "There was truly no end": *NYT*, Feb. 12, 1878.

46 "He has just been buried": TR, Personal Diary, Feb. 12, 1878, TRP.

46 still struck him "like a hideous dream": Ibid.

46 "It has been a most fortunate thing": TR, Personal Diary, Mar. 11, 1878, TRP.

46 "If I had very much time": TR, Personal Diary, Mar. 6, 1878, TRP.

46 "every nook and corner": TR, Personal Diary, June 6, 1878, TRP.

46 "Am leading the most intensely": TR, Personal Diary, June 21, 1878, TRP.

46 "the only human being": TR, Personal Diary, April 18, 1878, TRP.

46 "it was a real case": TR, Personal Diary, Jan. 30, 1880, TRP.

46 he vowed "to win her": TR, Personal Diary, Jan. 25, 1880, TRP.

47 "made everything subordinate": TR to Henry Davis Minot, Feb. 13, 1880, in *LTR*, Vol. 1, p. 43.

47   mesmerized her young brother: Pringle, *Theodore Roosevelt: A Biography*, p. 42.
47   "the tortures" he was suffering: TR, Personal Diary, Jan. 30, 1880, TRP.
47   "I have hardly had": Ibid.
47   "I am so happy": TR, Personal Diary, Jan. 25, 1880, TRP.
47   "I do not believe": TR, Personal Diary, Mar. 11, 1880, TRP.
47   "nothing on earth left to wish for": TR, Personal Diary, July 29, 1880, TRP.
47   a "royally good time": TR, Personal Diary, June 28, 1879, TRP.
47   "As regards the laws": Richard Welling, "Theodore Roosevelt at Harvard," *Outlook*, Oct. 27, 1920,
      p. 367.
47   "only one gentleman": TR to ARC, Oct. 13, 1879, in *LTR*, Vol. 1, p. 42.
47   "I have certainly lived": TR, Personal Diary, May 5, 1880, TRP.
48   "do my best, and work": TR, Personal Diary, Mar. 25, 1880, TRP.
48   "Natural history was to remain": Putnam, *Theodore Roosevelt: The Formative Years*, p. 179.
48   "great sorrow and great joy . . . overbalanced the sorrow": TR to Henry Davis Minot, July 5, 1880,
      TRC.

CHAPTER THREE: The Judge and the Politician

Page
50   "a judicial habit of thought and action": Francis E. Leupp, "Taft and Roosevelt: A Composite Study,"
      The Atlantic Monthly (November 1910), p. 650.
50   an "old style" institution: Pringle, *Life and Times*, Vol. 1, p. 49.
51   "more about the workings of the law": Burton, *The Learned Presidency*, p. 96.
51   "struck and scratched him": *Cincinnati Commercial*, Nov. 6, 1878.
51   to complete these accounts before dinner: Pringle, *Life and Times*, Vol. 1, p. 53.
51   "Washington will remain . . . metropolis of America": Daniel Hurley and the Cincinnati Historical
      Society, *Cincinnati: The Queen City* (Cincinnati, OH: Cin. Hist. Soc., 1988), p. 73.
51   "large, handsome and fair": Pringle, *Life and Times*, Vol. 1, p. 61.
52   "a capital opportunity . . . to have you lose it": Alphonso Taft to WHT, July 1, 1879, WHTP.
52   "agreed on a settlement": Alphonso Taft to WHT, July 2, 1879, WHTP.
52   "This gratifying your fondness": Alphonso Taft to WHT, July 2, 1879, WHTP.
52   "I do not think": Alphonso Taft to WHT, July 3, 1879, WHTP.
52   "he would not be seen in public": Pringle, *Life and Times*, Vol. 1, p. 52.
53   a salary of $1,500 a year: Ibid., pp. 53–54.
53   "its talons deep in the judiciary": Duffy, *William Howard Taft*, p. 10.
53   "was able to secure any verdict": *NYT*, Mar. 30, 1884.
53   took "a sensational turn": *Cin. Com.*, Dec. 7, 1880.
53   he "fell in" with Miller Outcault: WHT to WAW, Feb. 26, 1908, White Papers.
53   "standing upon the railing": *Cin. Com.*, Dec. 14, 1880.
53   "nasty torrent of abuse": *Cin. Com.*, Dec. 11, 1880.
53   "the bitterest invective . . . three-cornered fight": *Cin. Com.*, Dec. 9, 1880.
53   to dismiss prosecutor Drew: *Titusville* [PA] *Morning Herald*, Dec. 16, 1880.
53   "the experience he had": HHT, *Recollections of Full Years*, p. 9.
54   "a Theodore Roosevelt might . . . personally or politically ambitious": Pringle, *Life and Times*, Vol. 1,
      p. 55.
54   "He was on his legs": Taft, *Memories and Opinions*, p. 110.
54   he canvassed the city . . . remained involved: WHT to WAW, Feb. 26, 1908, White Papers.
54   "I attended all . . . on good terms": Ibid.
54   "the most popular young man": LTT to DCT, Jan. 26, 1882, WHTP.
54   "was known to be a bruiser": Duffy, *William Howard Taft*, p. 7.
54   a "terrible beating": *Petersburg* [VA] *Index and Appeal*, April 22, 1879.
54   "lifted him up and dashed him": Lyle, "Taft: A Career of Big Tasks," *The World's Work* (August 1907).
54   "The feeling among all": *Bismarck* [ND] *Tribune*, April 26, 1879.
54   "I want him to . . . do it well": Alphonso Taft to DCT, Oct. 17, 1880, WHTP.
55   aghast to see his name . . . throughout the city: LTT to DCT, September [n.d.], 1880, WHTP.
55   "Don't allow yourself": Alphonso Taft to WHT, Sept. 10, 1880, WHTP.
55   "He finds the farmers . . . not embarrassed": LTT to DCT, September [n.d.], 1880, WHTP.
55   "There is every . . . first class lawyer, too": Alphonso Taft to DCT, Oct. 17, 1880, WHTP.
55   "If you will appoint": Taft, *Memories and Opinions*, p. 111.
55   "I did not wish": LTT to DCT, Jan. 26, 1882, WHTP.
55   Taft was "too young": Ibid.
55   collecting over $10 million: Lyle, "Taft: A Career of Big Tasks," *The World's Work* (August 1907).
55   "had no political enemies": WHT to WAW, Feb. 28, 1908, White Papers.

55 He detested the prominence of the position: WHT to Alphonso Taft, June 4, 1882, WHTP.
55 too "thin-skinned" for "public life": James David Barber, *The Presidential Character: Predicting Performance in the White House* (Englewood Cliffs, NJ: Prentice-Hall, 1985), p. 152.
56 "but announced . . . the course he followed": Taft, *Memories and Opinions*, p. 111.
56 the "bulldozer" tone of the letter: WHT to Alphonso Taft, July 24, 1882, WHTP.
56 "are among the best . . . in regard to Civil Service": WHT to Thomas Young, July 29, 1882, WHTP.
56 "I would much rather resign": WHT to Alphonso Taft, July 24, 1882, WHTP.
56 "The men whose removal . . . down to business": WHT to Alphonso Taft, Oct. 28, 1882, WHTP.
56 "I am mighty glad . . . Reformer in practice": Horace Taft to LTT, Sept. 5, 1882, WHTP.
57 "It is the opening": WHT to Alphonso Taft, Oct. 28, 1882, WHTP.
57 "to work at the law": Alphonso Taft to Charles P. Taft, Jan. 10, 1883, WHTP.
57 "younger by several years": Annie Sinton Taft to Alphonso Taft, May 6, 1883, WHTP.
57 "I wish you could look": WHT to Frances L. Taft, Jan. 26, 1883, WHTP.
57 "I hope you will make": Ross, *An American Family*, p. 71.
57 "glad to get home": WHT to LTT, Oct. 5, 1883, WHTP.
57 "Will is working well": H. P. Lloyd to Alphonso Taft, Dec. 13, 1883, WHTP.
57 "makes friends wherever": WHT to Frances L. Taft, Jan. 6, 1882, WHTP.
57 "grow large enough": Ibid.
57 he was "no nearer matrimony": WHT to LTT, Sept. 10, 1882, WHTP.
58 a different girl each evening: WHT to LTT, Feb. 2, 1883, WHTP.
58 "I see Father shake his head": WHT to Frances L. Taft, Feb. 11, 1883, WHTP.
58 A wave of ghastly murders: Hurley, *Cincinnati: The Queen City*, p. 90.
58 "a series of events": Ibid., p. 92.
58 "were filled with Christmas presents": *NYT*, Mar. 30, 1884.
58 "cold-blooded butchery": Duffy, *William Howard Taft*, p. 10.
58 "to plead guilty . . . absolute and unquestioned": Ibid.
58 Cincinnati residents were stunned: *NYT*, Mar. 31, 1884.
58 "The people of Cincinnati": Pringle, *Life and Times*, Vol. 1, p. 85.
58 "Justice": *NYT*, Mar. 31, 1884.
59 "become the mere agents": *Elyria* [OH] *Republican*, April 10, 1884.
59 "Hang the jury! . . . boisterous element remained": *NYT*, Mar. 30, 1884.
59 the mob divided into three groups: Ibid.
59 Berner . . . transferred to another jail: Pringle, *Life and Times*, Vol. 1, p. 87.
59 "the bloodiest affair": *NYT*, Mar. 30, 1884.
59 "to obtain testimony": WHT to Alphonso Taft, May 10, 1884, WHTP.
59 "conducted the defense": WHT to Alphonso Taft, June 15, 1884, WHTP.
59 "I shall do everything": WHT to Alphonso Taft, May 10, 1884, WHTP.
60 "was an extraordinary honor": Taft, *Memories and Opinions*, p. 112.
60 fearing even for his son's physical safety: WHT to Alphonso Taft, May 10, 1884, WHTP.
60 "thrown the bar": WHT to LTT, April 21, 1884, WHTP.
60 "for men to have backbone": WHT to Alphonso Taft, May 10, 1884, WHTP.
60 his brother was instrumental: Taft, *Memories and Opinions*, p. 112.
60 "a thankless task": Alphonso Taft to WHT, May 21, 1884, WHTP.
60 "I find that the Campbell . . . hoarse for Blaine": WHT to Alphonso Taft, June 15, 1884, WHTP.
60 "Your son Will did splendid": Benjamin Butterworth to Alphonso Taft, Jan. 5, 1885, WHTP.
60 "This is my last election": WHT to LTT, Oct. 26, 1884, WHTP.
61 "The investigation": WHT to Alphonso Taft, Nov. 23, 1884, WHTP.
61 "suddenly emerging": Pringle, *Life and Times*, Vol. 1, p. 89.
61 "actuated by no other motive . . . member of the Bar": *Cin. Com. Gazette*, Jan. 6, 1885.
61 "There was not a vindictive word . . . all is gone": *Cin. Com. Gaz.*, Jan. 8, 1885.
62 "Tom Campbell controls": Benjamin Butterworth to Alphonso Taft, Jan. 5, 1885, WHTP.
62 exonerated Campbell of all charges: *Cin. Com. Gaz.*, Feb. 4, 1885.
62 "It was disastrous": WHT to Alphonso Taft, Feb. 8, 1885, WHTP.
62 "whatever may be said": Benjamin Butterworth to Alphonso Taft, Jan. 5, 1885, WHTP.
62 "I am very glad now . . . it could be tried": WHT to Alphonso Taft, Feb. 8, 1885, WHTP.
62 "I was very much pleased": Alphonso Taft to WHT, Mar. 3, 1885, WHTP.
62 "It is the beginning . . . his feeling toward me": WHT to Alphonso Taft, Mar. 27, 1885, WHTP.
62 "I should not bow my head": WHT to HHT, July 4, 1885, WHTP.
62 "double-faced Campbell man": WHT to HHT, July 10, 1885, WHTP.
63 "instant sympathy . . . his type of mind": Julia B. Foraker, *I Would Live It Again: Memories of a Vivid Life* (New York: Harper & Bros., 1932), p. 305.

63   "knew him well enough": Joseph B. Foraker, *Notes of a Busy Life* (Cincinnati, OH: Stewart & Kidd Co., 1916), p. 237.

63   "a very bright young man": Duffy, *William Howard Taft*, p. 14.

63   "Considering the opportunity": Foraker, *Notes of a Busy Life*, p. 238.

63   "the welcome beginning": HHT, *Recollections of Full Years*, p. 22.

64   "hands full attending to various affairs": TR, Personal Diary, Oct. 18, 1880, TRP.

64   "It almost frightens me": TR, Personal Diary, Oct. 17, 1880, TRP.

64   "Our intense happiness": TR, Personal Diary, Oct. 27, 1880, TRP.

64   "equally matched" lawn tennis: TR, Personal Diary, Nov. 3, 1880, TRP.

64   reading poetry: TR to Martha Bulloch Roosevelt, Oct. 31, 1880, in *LTR*, Vol. 1, p. 47.

64   "an energetic questioner" . . . in his classmates: Putnam, *Theodore Roosevelt: The Formative Years*, p. 219.

64   "some of the teaching": TR, *An Autobiography*, p. 54.

64   "we are concerned": Robert Charles, "Legal Education in the Late Nineteenth Century, Through the Eyes of Theodore Roosevelt," *American Journal of Legal History* (July 1993), p. 247.

64   more than 1,000 pages: Ibid., p. 246.

64   he impressed professors: Putnam, *Theodore Roosevelt: The Formative Years*, p. 219.

64   "I tried faithfully": Riis, *Theodore Roosevelt*, pp. 36–37.

65   a volume in the Porcellian Club library: Ibid., p. 39.

65   "afflicted with a hatred": Hermann Hagedorn, ed., *The Naval War of 1812*, Vol. 6 of *The Works of Theodore Roosevelt* [hereafter *WTR*] (New York: Charles Scribner's Sons, 1926), p. 14.

65   "I spend most of my spare time": TR, Personal Diary, May 2, 1881, TRP.

65   "a wonderfully open": Christopher Gray, "Streetscapes: The Old Astor Library," *NYT*, Feb. 10, 2002.

65   American historians, desiring to embellish: Riis, *Theodore Roosevelt*, pp. 39–40.

65   "We're dining out": Owen Wister, *Roosevelt: The Story of a Friendship, 1880–1919* (New York: The Macmillan Co., 1930), p. 24.

65   "Alice is the best": TR, Personal Diary, May 25, 1881, TRP.

65   "Altogether it would be difficult": TR to CRR, June 16, 1881, in *LTR*, Vol. 1, pp. 48–49.

65   "I was anxious to go . . . to make it exciting": TR to ARC, Aug. 5, 1881, in ibid., p. 49.

66   "You would be amused": TR to ARC, Aug. 21, 1881, in ibid., p. 50.

66   "Am working fairly": TR, Personal Diary, Oct. 17, 1881, TRP.

66   "were so dry": TR, *An Autobiography*, p. 22.

66   "The volume is an excellent one": *NYT*, June 5, 1882.

66   "a comparison with": George T. Temple, "The Naval War of 1812," *The Academy*, July 22, 1882.

66   "in the very first class": TR to S. Van Duzer, in *LTR*, Vol. 1, p. 136.

66   "the first really satisfactory": Frederick Jackson Turner, "The Winning of the West," *The Dial* (August 1889).

67   "Everything was of interest": John A. Gable, ed., *The Man in the Arena: Speeches and Essays by Theodore Roosevelt* (Oyster Bay, NY: Theodore Roosevelt Assoc., 1987), p. 1.

67   the "barn-like room over a saloon": TR, *An Autobiography*, p. 56.

67   "to help the cause": William Roscoe Thayer, *Theodore Roosevelt: An Intimate Biography* (Boston: Houghton Mifflin, 1919), p. 21.

67   district politics were "low . . . of the governing class": TR, *An Autobiography*, p. 56.

67   "I went around there often": Ibid., p. 57.

67   "He looked like a dude": Hermann Hagedorn, *The Boys' Life of Theodore Roosevelt* (New York: Harper & Bros., 1918), pp. 66–67.

67   "a fine head": Ibid., p. 67.

67   "He was by nature": TR, *An Autobiography*, p. 59.

68   the college-educated men and "the swells": Hagedorn, *The Boys' Life*, p. 70.

68   "of high character": Thayer, *Theodore Roosevelt: An Intimate Biography*, p. 30.

68   the youngest president: While John F. Kennedy was the youngest man elected to the presidency, TR was still younger when he assumed the office after McKinley's assassination.

68   "My first days": TR, *An Autobiography*, p. 63.

68   "He came in as if": Hermann Hagedorn, Isaac Hunt, and George F. Spinney, "Memorandum of Conversation at Dinner at the Harvard Club, 27 West 44th Street, New York City, September 20, 1923," p. 42, TRC.

68   "He was like Moses": Ibid., p. 17.

68   "an analysis of the character": Ibid., p. 1.

68   "bad enough": TR, Diary, Jan. 7, 1882, in *LTR*, Vol. 2, p. 1469.

68   "totally unable to speak": TR, Diary, Jan. 24, 1882, in ibid., p. 1470.

69   "By God! . . . let me alone": Hagedorn et al., "Memorandum of Conversation," pp. 84–85, TRC.

69   "Why don't your mother . . . The third quit cold": Ethel Armes, "When T.R. Qualified as a Boxer," unpublished MS, pp. 1–2, TRC.

69   "When Taft gives way": Leupp, "Taft and Roosevelt: A Composite Study," *Atlantic Monthly* (November 1910), p. 649.

69   "very good men . . . very bad men": TR, "Phases of State Legislation," *Century Illus. Monthly Mag.* (April 1885), p. 820.

69   About thirty reporters . . . in the back of the chamber: "Diagrams of Senate and Assembly Chambers," in *Manual for the Use of the Legislature of the State of New York for the Year 1884* (Albany, NY: Weed, Parsons & Co., 1884), n.p.

70   "good-hearted man . . . honest laugh": Hagedorn et al., "Memorandum of Conversation," p. 49, TRC.

70   "vigor, thoroughness": Leupp, "Taft and Roosevelt: A Composite Study," *Atlantic Monthly* (November 1910), p. 649.

70   "He grew like . . . ninety percent of them did": Hagedorn et al., "Memorandum of Conversation," p. 41, TRC.

70   "a mighty tree": *Watertown* [NY] *Daily Times*, May 13, 1939.

70   "He would go away . . . grew right away from me": Hagedorn et al., "Memorandum of Conversation," pp. 40–41, TRC.

70   "It was Roosevelt's habit": William C. Hudson, *Random Recollections of an Old Political Reporter* (New York: Cupples & Leon, 1911), pp. 144–45.

71   Judge Westbrook's collusion: *NYT*, Dec. 27, 1881.

71   "We went after him": Hagedorn et al., "Memorandum of Conversation," p. 13, TRC.

71   Gould had amassed railroads . . . system for the city: Matthew Josephson, *The Robber Barons: The Great American Capitalists, 1861–1901* (New York: Harcourt, Brace & Co., 1964), pp. 194–95, 209.

71   A burdensome lawsuit: Ibid., p. 209.

71   the Gould syndicate began buying . . . rose sharply: *NYT*, Dec. 27, 1881.

71   who "prostituted" himself . . . "the wolf the sheep": *Brooklyn Eagle*, Dec. 30, 1881, reprinted in *NYT*, Dec. 31, 1881, Clipping Scrapbook, TRC.

71   "dignity and respect . . . rings and cliques": *Auburn* [NY] *Advertiser*, Dec. 28, 1881, reprinted in *NYT*, Dec. 30, 1881, Clipping Scrapbook, TRC.

72   "remain silent": *Waterbury* [CT] *Republican-American*, Dec. 28, 1881, reprinted in ibid.

72   Hunt suggested that Roosevelt: Hagedorn et al., "Memorandum of Conversation," p. 1, TRC.

72   "but would not take it up": Ibid., pp. 7–8.

72   "an energetic . . . cross-questioned him": Pringle, *Theodore Roosevelt: A Biography*, p. 71.

72   "the presses in the basement": George F. Spinney, "The Westbrook Scandal," p. 5, TRC.

72   "I am willing to go": TR, *An Autobiography*, p. 75.

72   "never been explained": New York *Evening Post*, Mar. 30, 1882, Clipping Scrapbook, TRC.

72   "By Jove!": Hagedorn et al., "Memorandum of Conversation," p. 9, TRC.

72   "Mr. Roosevelt correctly states": *NYT*, Mar. 30, 1882.

72   "Roosevelt suddenly interrupted . . . grew silent": Spinney, "The Westbrook Scandal," p. 7, TRC.

73   "slowly and clearly": Ibid., pp. 7–8.

73   "The men who . . . demand such an investigation": Ibid., pp. 10–11.

73   "Beyond a shadow . . . to be trifled with": Ibid., pp. 11–12.

73   "the day's proceedings": Ibid., p. 13.

73   "I have drawn blood": TR to Alice Hathaway Lee Roosevelt, April 5, 1882, in Nathan Miller, *Theodore Roosevelt: A Life* (New York: William Morrow, 1992), p. 135.

74   "Mr. Roosevelt has a most refreshing": *NYT*, April 6, 1882, Clipping Scrapbook, TRC.

74   "Before any official . . . in a newspaper": New York *World*, April 12, 1882, Clipping Scrapbook, TRC.

74   "like water poured": Hagedorn et al., "Memorandum of Conversation," p. 16, TRC.

74   "it was a good thing . . . business, or politics": TR, *An Autobiography*, p. 77.

74   "By the time": Hagedorn et al., "Memorandum of Conversation," p. 12, TRC.

74   Hunt later alleged . . . $2,500 each: Hermann Hagedorn and Isaac Hunt, "Conversation Re: Westbrook Affair," unpublished MS, p. 2, TRC.

75   "was dancing and jumping": Ibid., p. 4.

75   "To you, members": Putnam, *Theodore Roosevelt: The Formative Years*, p. 271.

75   "deathless silence": Hagedorn and Hunt, "Conversation Re: Westbrook Affair," p. 4, TRC.

75   "It was apparent": Spinney, "The Westbrook Scandal," p. 24, TRC.

75   "The action of the Assembly": *New York Herald*, June 1, 1882, Clipping Scrapbook, TRC.

75   "A Miscarriage of Justice . . . the general verdict": Quoted in *NYT*, June 2, 1882.

75   "won his spurs . . . anybody's esteem": Hagedorn and Hunt, "Conversation Re: Westbrook Affair," pp. 2, 4, TRC.

75   "Roosevelt's name": Spinney, "The Westbrook Scandal," p. 29, TRC.

75   "I rose like a rocket . . . not all-important": TR to TR, Jr., Oct. 20, 1903, in *LTR*, Vol. 3, p. 635.

76   "My head was": Riis, *Theodore Roosevelt*, p. 58.

76   "a perfect nuisance": Hagedorn et al., "Memorandum of Conversation," p. 26, TRC.

76 "so explosive": Ibid., p. 19.
76 "a damn fool": Ibid., p. 16.
76 "he yelled . . . the venom imaginary": Ibid.
76 "as a paper of . . . rotten": Ibid., p. 4.
76 "down the roll from Polk": TR, Mar. 9, 1883, in Hermann Hagedorn, ed., *Campaigns and Controversies*, Vol. 14 of *WTR*, p. 19.
76 "absolutely deserted . . . powerless to accomplish": Riis, *Theodore Roosevelt*, p. 59.
76 "I thereby learned": TR, *An Autobiography*, p. 85.
76 "I turned in to help": Riis, *Theodore Roosevelt*, p. 59.
76 "exceedingly unattractive persons . . . conditions of laborers": TR, "A Judicial Experience," *Outlook*, Mar. 13, 1909, p. 563.
77 "one of the most dreadful": Samuel Gompers and Stuart B. Kaufman, eds., *The Making of a Union Leader, 1850–1886*, Vol. 1 of *The Samuel Gompers Papers* (Urbana: University of Illinois Press, 1986), p. 172.
77 "actual character of the evils": Ibid.
77 Gompers . . . published comprehensive reports: Samuel Gompers, *Seventy Years of Life and Labor; An Autobiography* (New York: E. P. Dutton, 1925), p. 59.
77 "a breeding ground . . . to a sewer": Gompers and Kaufman, eds., *The Making of a Union Leader*, p. 174.
77 "dark and gloomy" . . . seemed like night: Ibid., p. 176.
77 "if the conditions described": Gompers, *Seventy Years of Life and Labor*, p. 60.
77 "a good deal shocked": TR, "A Judicial Experience," *Outlook*, Mar. 13, 1909, p. 563.
77 "overwhelming majority . . . scraps of food": TR, *An Autobiography*, p. 80.
77 "convinced beyond": TR, "A Judicial Experience," *Outlook*, Mar. 13, 1909, p. 564.
77 "a dangerous departure": Howard L. Hurwitz, *Theodore Roosevelt and Labor in New York State, 1880–1900* (New York: Columbia University Press, 1942), p. 82.
78 "fundamental rights": Ibid., p. 85.
78 "injurious to the public health": *NYT*, Jan. 30, 1884; George F. Spinney, "Memorandum on the Tenement-house Cigar Manufacturing Measure," unpublished MS, n.d., TRC.
78 "a disinfectant": Hurwitz, *Theodore Roosevelt and Labor*, p. 85.
78 "It was this case . . . reform ever received": TR, *An Autobiography*, p. 81.
78 "do for the City": *NYT*, April 10, 1883.
78 "he would deliver": Hagedorn et al., "Memorandum of Conversation," p. 39, TRC.
78 "only chance lay": TR, *An Autobiography*, p. 87.
79 his patrician circle . . . "have been nominated": Ibid., pp. 86–87.
79 "to accomplish far more": Ibid., p. 86.
79 "the creatures of the local ward bosses": Ibid., p. 82.
79 "I feel now": TR to Alice Hathaway Lee Roosevelt, Jan. 22, 1884, in *LTR*, Vol. 1, p. 64.
79 "great night . . . he'd had enough": Armes, "When T.R. Qualified as a Boxer," pp. 1–2, TRC.
79 "in my own lovely": TR, Personal Diary, Jan. 3, 1883, TRP.
80 "How I did . . . be with you again": TR to Alice Hathaway Lee Roosevelt, Feb. 6, 1884, in *LTR*, Vol. 1, p. 65.
80 "hated" to see him . . . "little new baby soon": Michael Teague, "Theodore Roosevelt and Alice Hathaway Lee: A New Perspective," *Harvard Library Bulletin* (Summer 1985), pp. 237–38.
80 Alice was thrilled: Anna Bulloch Gracie, "Account of Alice Roosevelt's Birth, March 25, 1884," TRC.
80 "He was full of life and happiness": Putnam, *Theodore Roosevelt: The Formative Years*, pp. 382–83.
80 "only fairly well": Grondahl, *I Rose Like a Rocket*, p. 129.
80 signs of acute Bright's disease: J. O. Affleck, "Bright's Disease," in T. S. Baynes, D. O. Kellogg, and W. R. Smith, eds., *Encyclopaedia Britannica* (New York: Werner Co., 1898), Vol. 4, pp. 345–46.
81 "somewhat insidiously . . . coma vigil": J. O. Affleck, "Typhus, Typhoid and Relapsing Fevers," in ibid., pp. 678–80.
81 "suicidal . . . and dismal": *NYT*, Feb. 13, 1884.
81 Visibility was . . . off its tracks: *NYT*, Feb. 14, 1884.
81 "There is . . . something": *NYT*, Feb. 13, 1884.
81 "There is a curse": Pringle, *Theodore Roosevelt: A Biography*, p. 51.
81 "The light has gone out of my life": TR, Personal Diary, Feb. 14, 1884, TRP.
81 "Seldom, if ever": New York *World*, Feb. 15, 1884.
81 "wholly unprecedented . . . has ever been held": TR, *In Memory of My Darling Wife, Alice Hathaway Roosevelt, and of My Beloved Mother, Martha Bulloch Roosevelt, Who Died in the Same House and on the Same Day on February 14, 1884* (New York: G. P. Putnam's Sons, n.d.), TRC.
82 "in a dazed, stunned . . . does or says": Putnam, *Theodore Roosevelt: The Formative Years*, p. 390.
82 "I fear he sleeps little": McCullough, *Mornings on Horseback*, p. 286.
82 "If I had very much time": TR, Personal Diary, Mar. 6, 1878, TRP.

82 "I shall come back": TR to Andrew Dickson White, Feb. 18, 1884, in *LTR*, Vol. 1, p. 65.

82 "a changed man . . . in his own soul": Hagedorn et al., "Memorandum of Conversation," p. 68, TRC.

82 "We spent three years": TR, Personal Diary, Feb. 17, 1884, TRP.

82 referred to her simply as "Baby Lee": TR to ARC, various dates, in *LTR*, Vol. 1, pp. 71, 79.

82 "There can never be": TR to Henry Davis Minot, Feb. 21 & Mar. 9, 1884, TRC.

82 "both weak and morbid": TR to CRR, Mar. 7, 1908, in *LTR*, Vol. 6, p. 966.

82 shared her birthday: Grondahl, *I Rose Like a Rocket*, p. 129.

83 an intense connection with his dead son: Doris Kearns Goodwin, *Team of Rivals: The Political Genius of Abraham Lincoln* (New York: Simon & Schuster, 2005), p. 443.

83 "to treat the past": TR to CRR, Mar. 7, 1908, in *LTR*, Vol. 6, p. 966.

83 "We are now holding": Putnam, *Theodore Roosevelt: The Formative Years*, p. 395.

83 "Reform Without Bloodshed": *Harper's Weekly*, April 19, 1884.

84 "prolonged and expensive . . . won't have it": Hudson, *Random Recollections of an Old Political Reporter*, pp. 148–49.

84 "As debate is . . . field of national politics": *Daily Freeman* [n.p.], April 12, 1883, Clipping Scrapbook, TRC.

84 "by far the most objectionable": TR to ARC, June 8, 1884, in *LTR*, Vol. 1, pp. 70–71.

84 "Our defeat is . . . a historic scene": TR to ARC, June 8, 1884, in ibid.

84 "Although not a very": TR to Simon North, April 30, 1884, in ibid., p. 66.

85 a "great school" for Roosevelt: Hagedorn et al., "Memorandum of Conversation," p. 73, TRC.

85 "We did not agree": Riis, *Theodore Roosevelt*, p. 59.

85 "Words with me are instruments": Gable, ed., *The Man in the Arena: Speeches and Essays*, p. 12.

85 "There is little use": Ibid., p. 55.

85 "only through strife": Ibid., p. 42.

86 this intuitive emotional intelligence: Daniel Goleman, *Emotional Intelligence: Why It Can Matter More than IQ* (London: Bloomsbury, 1996), p. 39.

CHAPTER FOUR: Nellie Herron Taft

Page

87 "It was at a coasting party": HHT, *Recollections of Full Years*, p. 7.

87 "Tall and slender . . . her whole countenance": *Washington Post*, May 5, 1907.

88 Harriet moved to Ohio . . . lawyer John Herron: HHT, *Recollections of Full Years*, pp. 5–6.

88 "Quite like living": RBH Diary, Jan. 8, 1850, RBH Papers.

88 "had no other friend": Harriet Collins Herron to RBH, July 8, 1889, RBH Papers.

88 "to go for money": Anthony, *Nellie Taft*, p. 30.

88 "I wish I could accept": John Herron to RBH, Dec. 18, 1875, RBH Papers.

88 "not particularly . . . finely kept shrubbery": HHT, *Recollections of Full Years*, pp. 3–4.

88 "A book . . . has more": HHT Diary, Aug. 23, 1880, WHTP.

89 The curriculum at The Nursery: Anthony, *Nellie Taft*, pp. 28–29.

89 "the inspiration": HHT, *Recollections of Full Years*, p. 7.

89 planned to celebrate their silver wedding anniversary: RBH Diary, Jan. 12, 1878, RBH Papers; *NYT*, Jan. 1, 1878.

89 "her baby has": John Herron to RBH, Dec. 26, 1877, RBH Papers.

89 "I feel very much": Anthony, *Nellie Taft*, p. 31.

89 "profusely decorated": *NYT*, Jan. 1, 1878; *Dubuque* [IA] *Herald*, Jan. 1, 1878.

89 brought "the house alive": Anthony, *Nellie Taft*, p. 32.

89 "to marry a man . . . marry an Ohio man": *Alton* [IL] *Evening Telegraph*, Dec. 2, 1908.

89 "Nothing in my life": *Washington Post*, May 5, 1907.

90 "She was intoxicated": RSB, "The Measure of Taft," *The American Magazine* (July 1910), p. 366.

90 to "receive attentions": HHT Diary, Sept. 5, 1879, WHTP.

90 "exceedingly . . . valiantly to each other": HHT Diary, Mar. 10, 1880, WHTP.

90 "I am blue . . . as if I were fifty": HHT Diary, July 13, 1880, WHTP.

90 "be busy and accomplish something": HHT Diary, Sept. 5, 1879, WHTP.

90 more than her father would pay: HHT Diary, Oct. 21, 1879, WHTP.

90 "I would much rather": Ibid.

90 "enjoy all the comforts": Anthony, *Nellie Taft*, p. 27.

90 "a repressed nervousness": Ibid.

90 "I am beginning": HHT Diary, June 4, 1880, WHTP.

91 "that adorable . . . he strikes me with awe": HHT to Alice Keys, July 5, 1880, WHTP.

91 her "stupid state": HHT Diary, Aug. 17, 1880, WHTP.

91 gambled at cards . . . late at night: HHT Diary, Aug. 17 & 27, 1880, WHTP.

91 the first visit by a president to the west coast: HHT Diary, Aug. 21, 1880, WHTP.

91   Nellie was left behind: HHT Diary, Aug. 28, 1880, WHTP.
91   "I have not read": HHT Diary, Sept. 1, 1880, WHTP.
91   "He is very sympathetic . . . as much as yours": HHT Diary, Jan. 15, 1881, WHTP.
92   "I am perfectly delighted": HHT Diary, Sept. 6, 1883, WHTP.
92   "drank beer . . . like a comrade & man": HHT Diary, Sept. 6, 1883, WHTP.
92   "Do you realize": Harriet Collins Herron to HHT, Mar. 19, 1882, CPT Papers.
92   "two dreadful letters . . . congenial work": HHT Diary, May 5, 1882, WHTP.
93   "The meeting at Miss Herron's": WHT to Frances Taft, Jan. 6, 1883, WHTP.
93   They resolved daily to read aloud: HHT Diary, July 9, 1883, WHTP.
93   "long and very tough": HHT Diary, Aug. 6, 1883, WHTP.
93   "repair" their "exhausted intellects": HHT Diary, Aug. 8, 1883, WHTP.
93   "Mamma thinks": HHT Diary, Sept. 29, 1883, WHTP.
93   "Why should I take": Ibid.
93   "All week I have been": HHT Diary, Oct. 6, 1883, WHTP.
94   "Nellie Herron has made": WHT to Frances Taft, Feb. 28, 1884, WHTP.
94   "that sweet school": WHT to HHT, Mar. 12, 1884, WHTP.
94   "very heated especially": WHT to LTT, Mar. 2, 1884, WHTP.
94   "I am not satisfied": WHT to HHT, Mar. 29, 1884, WHTP.
94   Will played the beautiful princess: HHT, *Recollections of Full Years*, p. 8.
94   "the only notable exception . . . social career": WHT to Frances Taft, Feb. 11, 1883, WHTP.
94   "the greatest credit . . . act on that theory": WHT to LTT, Mar. 2, 1884, WHTP.
95   "After awhile I found": WHT to Alice Keys, Aug. 19, 1885, WHTP.
95   "Trollope is a great favorite": WHT to HHT, Aug. 9, 1884, WHTP.
95   "my own appreciation": WHT to LTT, Mar. 8, 1885, WHTP.
95   "It seems . . . to the fact that I loved her": WHT to Alphonso Taft, July 12, 1885, WHTP.
95   "with overwhelming force": WHT to HHT, June 17, 1885, WHTP.
96   "I never have been certain": Anthony, *Nellie Taft*, p. 73.
96   "I love you Nellie": WHT to HHT, May 10, 1885, WHTP.
96   "My love for you grew . . . won in a moment": WHT to HHT, June 17, 1885, WHTP.
96   "You know": Pringle, *Life and Times*, Vol. 1, p. 108.
96   "The more I knew her": WHT to Alphonso Taft, July 12, 1885, WHTP.
97   "Your sweet smile . . . by Fate today": WHT to HHT, July 2, 1885, WHTP.
97   "The only real pleasure": WHT to HHT, July 16, 1885, WHTP.
97   "It is the one who stays": WHT to HHT, July 4, 1885, WHTP.
97   "I long to settle down": WHT to HHT, July 6, 1885, WHTP.
97   "we must continue the salon": WHT to HHT, July 20, 1885, WHTP.
97   "I shall have the greatest": WHT to HHT, July 6, 1885, WHTP.
97   "comfortably and cosily . . . intelligence of the wife": WHT to HHT, July 5, 1885, WHTP.
98   "His temperament": RSB, "The Measure of Taft," *The American Magazine* (July 1910), p. 366.
98   "guide, counsellor and friend": WHT to Delia Herron, Nov. 1, 1885, WHTP.
98   "You are becoming": WHT to HHT, July 20, 1885, WHTP.
98   "It is hard for me": WHT to HHT, July 11, 1885, WHTP.
98   "an equal partnership": WHT to HHT, July 15, 1885, WHTP.
98   "business had been . . . as much work": WHT to HHT, July 20, 1885, WHTP.
98   "a good and just member of society": Anthony, *Nellie Taft*, p. 73.
98   "a very hastily . . . no credit": WHT to LTT, April 16, 1885, WHTP.
98   "As usual": Horace Taft to LTT, April 19, 1885, WHTP.
98   "Each day has found . . . by George Eliot": WHT to LTT, Aug. 2, 1885, WHTP.
98   "I knew you would be": WHT to Alice Keys, Aug. 16, 1885, WHTP.
99   "How much I appreciate": Alice Keys to WHT, Aug. 31, 1885, WHTP.
99   "What a pair": Horace Taft to WHT, Sept. 2, 1885, WHTP.
99   "I went to the gymnasium . . . I felt lazy": WHT to HHT, Feb. 22, 1886, WHTP.
100 "I have given up": WHT to HHT, Feb. 26, 1886, WHTP.
100 "a superbly-fashioned satin": Anthony, *Nellie Taft*, p. 83.
100 "I hope you will think": WHT to HHT, Mar. 6, 1886, WHTP.
100 "The parlor is unchanged": WHT to HHT, Mar. 10, 1886, WHTP.
100 "a brilliant reception" . . . embark for Europe: Pringle, *Life and Times*, Vol. 1, p. 81.
100 "my first taste": HHT, *Recollections of Full Years*, p. 16.
100 "just one thousand dollars": Ibid., p. 17.
100 "gentle beyond anything . . . catholic sympathies": Ibid., pp. 18–19.
101 home overlooking . . . the Ohio River: Alphonso Taft to WHT, July 5, 1886, WHTP.
101 he had proudly amassed a catalogue: Anthony, *Nellie Taft*, p. 87.

101   "Nellie," he coyly questioned . . . "so unexpectedly": HHT, *Recollections of Full Years*, pp. 21–22.

101   "Wasn't it immense": Horace Taft to HHT, Feb. 4, 1887, WHTP.

101   "was not a matter . . . of the Bench": HHT, *Recollections of Full Years*, p. 22.

102   "did not share this feeling": Ibid.

102   Taft sustained the lower court decision: "Moore's & Co. v. Bricklayers' Union et al.," *Weekly Law Bulletin & Ohio Law Journal*, 23 (Columbus, OH: Capital Printing & Publ. Co., 1890), pp. 665–75.

102   Decades later, it remained: Frederick N. Judson, "The Labor Decisions of Judge Taft," *American Monthly Review of Reviews* (August 1907), p. 213.

102   "right to work . . . combine to do": "Moore's & Co. v. Bricklayers' Union et al.," *Weekly Law Bulletin & Ohio Law Journal*, 23, pp. 668–69.

103   "no freight moved": Hurley, *Cincinnati: The Queen City*, p. 94.

103   the strikers' "revolutionary fervor": Bruce C. Levine, *Who Built America? Working People and the Nation's Economy, Politics, Culture and Society* (New York: Pantheon Books, 1992), p. 73.

103   "If the little ones": *Ohio Educational Monthly & National Teacher*, 43 (1894), pp. 413–14.

103   Nellie devoted herself to teaching: HHT, Diary notebook, Dec. 1887, WHTP.

104   "were conspiring against him": Annie Sinton Taft to Horace Taft, June [n.d.], 1889, WHTP.

104   "You may rely upon": Ross, *An American Family*, p. 81.

104   "the highest rank . . . his father was": Annie Sinton Taft to Horace Taft, June [n.d.], 1889, WHTP.

104   "Poor Peter! . . . wisely to remove him": Henry W. Taft to Alphonso Taft, June 3, 1889, WHTP.

104   "Every time the telephone": WHT to Horace Taft, June 17, 1889, WHTP.

104   he had abandoned Cincinnati: Ross, *An American Family*, pp. 101–02.

104   "My chief regret": Taft, *Memories and Opinions*, p. 60.

105   he opened a private school: Ibid., p. 70.

105   "Nellie took the pain . . . happy she is": WHT to Alphonso Taft, Sept. 10, 1889, WHTP.

105   "On the whole": Ibid.

105   "I suppose you wish": Horace Taft to WHT, Oct. 22, 1889, WHTP.

105   "He breathes good will": Richard V. Oulahan, "William H. Taft as a Judge on the Bench," *American Monthly Review of Reviews* (August 1907), p. 208.

105   "upheld by the State Supreme Court": Pringle, *Life and Times*, Vol. 1, p. 100.

105   "would be satisfactory": Ibid., p. 107.

105   "pretty hopeful . . . a fine old Justice": Horace Taft to WHT, May 7, 1889, WHTP.

106   "O Yes": WHT to Alphonso Taft, August [n.d.], 1889, WHTP.

106   "chances of going": WHT to Alphonso Taft, Aug. 24, 1889, WHTP.

106   "It is a great event": Alphonso Taft to WHT, Feb. 3, 1890, WHTP.

106   "but it was I . . . a new interest in life": LTT to WHT, Feb. 3, 1890, WHTP.

106   "I was very glad". HHT, *Recollections of Full Years*, p. 24.

106   Only Will was reluctant . . . "one side of a case": Peri E. Arnold, *Remaking the Presidency: Roosevelt, Taft and Wilson, 1901–1916* (Lawrence: University Press of Kansas, 2009), p. 77.

107   "entirely unfamiliar . . . very little familiarity": WHT to Alphonso Taft, Feb. 26, 1890, WHTP.

107   "Go ahead, & fear not": Alphonso Taft to WHT, Feb. 1, 1890, WHTP.

107   "You will have": Alphonso Taft to WHT, Feb. 3, 1890, WHTP.

107   "To a large extent": Alphonso Taft to WHT, Feb. 7, 1890, WHTP.

107   "You have learned": LTT to WHT, Feb. 3, 1890, WHTP.

107   "I believe you are": Alphonso Taft to WHT, Feb. 7, 1890, WHTP.

107   a "brilliant reception" at the Lincoln Club: *Sandusky* [OH] *Daily Register*, Feb. 11, 1890.

107   "He arrived at six o'clock . . . why on earth he had come": HHT, *Recollections of Full Years*, p. 25.

108   "It is not a large house": WHT to H. D. Peck, April 26, 1890, WHTP.

108   "one of the nicest": John W. Herron to HHT, April 18, 1890, WHTP.

108   "Our house is what . . . at night at home": WHT to Alphonso Taft, April 18, 1890, WHTP.

CHAPTER FIVE: Edith Carow Roosevelt

Page

109   "vast silent spaces . . . lonely rivers": TR, *An Autobiography*, p. 93.

109   domestic bliss was "lived out": TR, Personal Diary, Feb. 17, 1884, TRP.

109   "any man ever loved a woman": TR, Personal Diary, Mar. 11, 1880, TRP.

109   he resigned himself: Hermann Hagedorn, Interview with William Merrifield, June [n.d.], 1919, TRC.

110   "the head of a great buffalo bull": TR to Alice Lee Roosevelt, Sept. 20, 1883, in H. W. Brands, *T.R.: The Last Romantic* (New York: Basic Books, 1997), p. 158.

110   the Elkhorn and the Chimney Butte: TR, Hermann Hagedorn, and G. B. Grinnell, *Hunting Trips of a Ranchman; Ranch Life and the Hunting Trail* (New York: Charles Scribner's Sons, 1927), p. 10.

110   the sum his father bequeathed: Morris, *EKR*, p. 77.

110   "The plains stretch": TR, *Hunting Trips*, pp. 151–52.

110   "noontide hours . . . hopeless, never-ending grief": Ibid., pp. 309–10.

110   on his horse sixteen hours a day: Hermann Hagedorn, *Roosevelt in the Bad Lands* (Boston: Houghton Mifflin, 1921), p. 156.

110   "hardest work . . . gathered for market": TR, *Hunting Trips*, p. 13.

110   "preparing breakfast": Ibid., p. 327.

110   "These long, swift rides": Ibid., p. 329.

111   "Black care": Ibid.

111   "enough excitement . . . sleep well at night": TR to ARC, Sept. 20, 1884, in *LTR*, Vol. 1, p. 81.

111   "The story-high house": TR, *Hunting Trips*, p. 10.

111   "Parkman and Irving": Hagedorn, *Roosevelt in the Bad Lands*, p. 108.

111   steadily before "the flickering firelight": TR, *Hunting Trips*, p. 305.

111   he relaxed in his rocking chair . . . "cool breeze": Ibid., p. 10.

111   As the crisp autumn . . . rounding up cattle: Ibid., p. 306.

111   "Where everything before . . . withered grass": Ibid., p. 126.

111   "dwindled to . . . never-ending" nights: Ibid., p. 341.

112   gathered round the fireplace . . . hermit thrushes and meadowlarks: Ibid., pp. 305–7, 12.

112   "will take a leading": *NYT*, July 13, 1885.

112   house stood atop a hill: TR, *An Autobiography*, p. 318.

112   "no day was long enough": Parsons, *Perchance Some Day*, p. 26.

112   "Especially memorable . . . just around the corner": Ibid., p. 63.

113   "She was the only one . . . oh so attractive!": Michael Teague, *Mrs. L: Conversations with Alice Roosevelt Longworth* (New York: Doubleday & Co., 1981), p. 10.

113   "had an extraordinary gift": Hermann and Mary Hagedorn, "Interview with Mrs. Nicholas Longworth, November 9, 1954," TRC.

113   Had "she been a man": Hermann and Mary Hagedorn, "Interview with Mr. and Mrs. Sheffield Cowles and Mrs. Joseph Alsop, Jr., November 22, 1954," TRC.

113   the two were secretly engaged: Hermann Hagedorn, *The Roosevelt Family of Sagamore Hill* (New York: The Macmillan Co., 1954), p. 426.

113   "You know all about": EKR to TR, June 8, 1886, Derby Papers, TRC.

113   Her father, Charles Carow: Morris, *EKR*, p. 10.

114   a fortune in iron manufacturing: EKR, *American Backlogs: The Story of Gertrude Tyler and Her Family, 1660–1860* (New York: Charles Scribner's Sons, 1928), pp. 32, 34.

114   "find great attention . . . an ornament to society": Daniel Tyler to Gertrude Tyler, Aug. 14, 1852, in ibid., pp. 86–87.

114   "Do not doubt": Gertrude Tyler to [her mother], Sept. 20, 1852, in ibid., p. 93.

114   "My dear Sir": Charles Carow to Daniel Tyler, Mar. 7, 1859, in ibid., p. 233.

114   "the risk of sailing": John Lynch, *Causes of the reduction of American Tonnage and the decline of navigation interests, being a report of a Select committee made to the House of Representatives of the United States, on February 17, 1870* (Washington, DC: Government Printing Office, 1870), pp. ix–x.

115   "My dear little girl . . . up in the morning": Charles Carow to EKR, May [n.d.], 186[?], TRC.

115   "precious little monkey": EKR, "Second Composition Book," May 18, 1875, TRC.

115   "Almost the first thing . . . light and colour": EKR to TR, June 8, 1886, TRC.

115   "a passion for fairy tales": Ibid.

115   "Oh fairy tales": EKR, "Fairy Tales" in P.O.R.E. Notebook, Jan. 6, 1877, TRC.

115   "I got your letter": Charles Carow to EKR, [n.d.], 1871, TRC.

115   he took Edith on long walks: Sylvia Jukes Morris, "Portrait of a First Lady," in Natalie A. Naylor, Douglas Brinkley, and John Allen Gable, eds., *Theodore Roosevelt: Many-Sided American* (Interlaken, NY: Heart of the Lakes Publ., 1992), p. 64.

116   "pledged friends": CRR, *My Brother*, p. 44.

116   hide her "old and broken toys": EKR, "In Memory of Corinne Roosevelt Robinson," TRC.

116   "the school room": Ibid.

116   *Our Young Folks*: TR, *An Autobiography*, p. 16.

116   "at the cost of . . . girls' stories": Ibid.

116   "I think imagination": EKR to TR, June 8, 1886, TRC.

116   "It was verry": TR, *Diaries of Boyhood and Youth*, p. 13.

116   "homesickness and longings": Ibid., p. 103.

116   "Whenever they see": EKR to CRR, Feb. 1, 1870, Derby Papers, TRC.

116   a bankruptcy warrant was issued: *NYT*, Mar. 1, April 1, & April 27, 1871.

117   "terrifying charm . . . clear-cut features": Parsons, *Perchance Some Day*, p. 20.

117   The curriculum included: Morris, *EKR*, p. 33.

117   "When I come home . . . hope to get them": EKR, "First Composition Book," Nov. 28, 1871, TRC.

117   "I have gone back": EKR to Kermit Roosevelt, Feb. 24, 1938, KR Papers.

117   to quote extensively from Wordsworth: EKR to Theodore Roosevelt, Jr., Mar. 6, 1942, in TRJP.
117   "indifference . . . a trick of manner": EKR to Kermit Roosevelt, Feb. 24, 1938, KR Papers.
117   "Girls . . . I believe": Hagedorn, *The Roosevelt Family of Sagamore Hill*, p. 10.
117   "the happiness of . . . difficult and critical teacher": EKR, "In Memory of Corinne Roosevelt Robinson,"
      TRC.
118   "little group of girls": Parsons, *Perchance Some Day*, p. 36.
118   " 'Consequences,' 'Truth' ": Ibid., p. 35.
118   "the happy six": CRR, *My Brother*, p. 90.
118   whom he "much worshipped": TR, Personal Diary, Aug. 20, 1878, TRP.
118   "In the early days": Parsons, *Perchance Some Day*, p. 30.
118   "I cannot believe": Anna Louisa Bulloch Gracie to EKR, Aug. 6, 1876, TRC.
118   On New Year's Day: CRR, Journal, Jan. 1, 1877, TRC.
118   "dimly and suggestively lit . . . tete-a-tete": CRR, Journal, Jan. 10, 1877, TRC.
118   "Edith revealed": Betty Boyd Caroli, *The Roosevelt Women* (New York: Basic Books, 1989), p. 190.
119   "To my castles . . . Sad and slow": EKR, "My Dream Castles," in P.O.R.E. Notebook, Jan. 27, 1877,
      TRC.
119   "I sit alone": EKR, "Memories," in P.O.R.E. Notebook, April [n.d.], 1876, TRC.
120   "She reads more": CRR, Journal, Nov. 12, 1876, TRC.
120   her "clever" friend: Ibid.
120   "tall and fair": CRR, Journal, Oct. 6, 1876, TRC.
120   "I have a feeling": CRR, Journal, Nov. 12, 1876, TRC.
120   "What fun we did have" . . . Lamson and Harry Jackson: CRR, Journal, May 10, 1877, TRC.
120   "The family all": TR, *Diaries of Boyhood and Youth*, p. 359.
120   "enjoyed . . . perfectly happy days": EKR to TR, May 29, 1877, Derby Papers, TRC.
120   "Edith looking prettier": TR to CRR, June 3, 1877, in *LTR*, Vol. 1, p. 28.
120   "Oh Edith": Morris, *EKR*, p. 57.
120   days spent sailing with Edith: TR, Private Diaries, Aug. 19, 1878, TRP.
120   rowing with her to the harbor: TR, Private Diaries, Aug. 20, 1878, TRP.
120   "spending a lovely morning": TR, Private Diaries, Aug. 21, 1878, TRP.
121   "Afterwards Edith": TR, Private Diaries, Aug. 22, 1878, TRP.
121   tempers "that were far": TR to ARC, Sept. 20, 1886, TRC.
121   "at first sight": TR, Pocket Diaries, Jan. 30, 1880, TRP.
121   campaign "to win her": Ibid.
121   in mid-February, Theodore wrote: Mabel Potter Daggett, "Mrs. Roosevelt," *The Delineator* (March
      1909).
121   the "shock" Edith experienced: Morris, *EKR*, p. 530.
121   another woman would be Theodore's constant: TR, Pocket Diaries, July 1 & 5, 1880, TRP.
121   "We had great fun . . . wild spirits": Parsons, *Perchance Some Day*, p. 43.
121   "danced the soles off": Morris, *EKR*, p. 64.
122   "All yesterday I": EKR to CRR, April 29, 1882, Derby Papers, TRC.
122   might marry "for money": Putnam, *Theodore Roosevelt: The Formative Years*, p. 555.
122   "someday, somehow": Morris, *EKR*, p. 67.
122   "the most cultivated": TR, Personal Diary, Nov. 16, 1879, TRP.
122   "argued weakness": TR to ARC, Sept. 20, 1886, TRC.
123   Respecting their secret even in his private diary: TR, Personal Diary, Feb. 20, 1886; Mar. 5, 6, 9, 10,
      12 & 14, 1886, TRP.
123   seventeen letters from Theodore: EKR to TR, June 8, 1886, Derby Papers, TRC.
123   "How fond one is": EKR, "Second Composition Book," May 18, 1875, TRC.
123   "with all the passion": EKR to TR, June 8, 1886, Derby Papers, TRC.
123   "heart on paper . . . so much to see you . . . digging": Ibid.
123   "He is middle aged": Ibid.
124   "read it through . . . as repulsive as her brother, Stiva": TR to CRR, April 12, 1886, in *LTR*, Vol. 1,
      p. 96.
124   He began to muse on: TR to ARC, June 19, 1886, in ibid., pp. 103–4.
124   an offer from Mayor William Grace: TR to HCL, June 23, 1885, & July 5, 1886, in ibid., p. 91.
124   "I would like a chance": TR to HCL, Aug. 20, 1886, in ibid., p. 109.
125   "Darling Bamie . . . *Forever your loving brother*": TR to ARC, Sept. 20, 1886, TRC.
125   "It looked to me . . . the happiest time": William Wingate Sewall, *Bill Sewall's Story of Theodore Roo-
      sevelt* (New York: Harper Bros., 1919), pp. 92, 95.
125   "fellow ranchmen . . . the most educational asset": TR and Ernest Hamlin Abbott, *The New National-
      ism* (New York: The Outlook Co., 1909), p. 105.
126   "It is a mighty good": Ibid., p. 105.

126 "to speak the same language": TR, *An Autobiography*, p. 57.

126 "to interpret the spirit": CRR, *My Brother*, p. 150.

126 "was visited . . . perfectly hopeless contest": TR to HCL, Oct. 17, 1886, in *LTR*, Vol. 1, p. 111.

126 "enormous increase . . . compelled to toil": Henry George, *Progress and Poverty* (New York: Cosimo Classics, 2005), pp. 10–11.

126 "the want and injustice . . . would be unknown": Ibid., p. 396.

126 "the mass of": *NYT*, Oct. 24, 1886.

127 "The best I can hope . . . Republican party": TR to Frances Smith Dana, Oct. 21, 1886, in *LTR*, Vol. 1, p. 113.

127 many of his "should-be supporters": TR to HCL, Oct. 20, 1886, in ibid., p. 112.

127 "I am a strong party man": *NYT*, Oct. 28, 1886.

127 "It is such happiness": ARC to EKR, Oct. 23, 1886, Derby Papers, TRC.

128 "Fighting is fun": Edmund Morris, *The Rise of Theodore Roosevelt* (New York: Coward, McCann & Geoghegan, 1979), p. 349.

128 "I read them all": TR to CRR, Jan. 22, 1887, in *LTR*, Vol. 1, p. 119.

128 "remember them all": Morris, *EKR*, p. 105.

128 "that wonderful silky": Ibid., p. 4.

128 "blue-eyed darling": Teague, *Mrs. L: Conversations with Alice Longworth Roosevelt*, p. 13.

128 "I hardly know": TR to ARC, Jan. 10, 1887, TRC.

128 "It almost broke my heart": ARC, "Memoir," p. 3, TRC.

128 she avoided further emotional attachments: Ibid., p. 84.

128 "the lovely smell": Teague, *Mrs. L: Conversations with Alice Roosevelt Longworth*, p. 22.

128 "I in my best dress": Alice Roosevelt Longworth, *Crowded Hours: Reminiscences of Alice Roosevelt Longworth* (New York: Charles Scribner's Sons, 1933), p. 8.

129 "mother who is in heaven": Ibid.

129 "In fact . . . he never ever": Teague, *Mrs. L: Conversations with Alice Roosevelt Longworth*, pp. 4–5.

129 "Where she was reserved": Nicholas Roosevelt, *Theodore Roosevelt: The Man as I Knew Him* (New York: Dodd, Mead & Co., 1967), p. 23.

129 "rowing over": TR to HCL, June 11, 1887, in *LTR*, Vol. 1, p. 128.

129 "She was extremely plucky": TR to ARC, Sept. 18, 1887, in Morris, *EKR*, p. 112.

129 "I have a small son now": TR to Jonas S. Van Duzer, in *LTR*, Vol. 1, p. 136.

130 "Theodore" . . . "put his foot down": Hermann and Mary Hagedorn, Interview with Mrs. Nicholas Longworth, Nov. 9, 1954, TRC.

130 "temptation . . . Father would not allow it": Morris, *EKR*, p. 114.

130 "the place where she kept" . . . permission to enter: *Sagamore Hill National Historic Site Pamphlet* (Lawrenceburg, IN: The Creative Co., 2000), p. 11.

130 "immense fun": TR to HCL, Oct. 19, 1888, in *LTR*, Vol. 1, p. 148.

130 "Mr. T.R.'s temperament . . . hold of the helm": William Henry Harbaugh, *Power and Responsibility: The Life and Times of Theodore Roosevelt* (New York: Farrar, Straus & Cudahy, 1961), p. 74.

131 "I am the new . . . began at that moment": Matthew F. Halloran, *The Romance of the Merit System: Forty-five Years' Reminiscences of the Civil Service* (Washington, DC: Judd & Detweiler, 1929), p. 56.

131 "He is equally at home": *Decatur* [IL] *Republican*, May 16, 1889.

131 "It has been a hopeless": EKR to ARC, Aug. 31, 1889, Derby Papers, TRC.

132 "Edie has occasional fits": TR to ARC, Jan. 4, 1890, in *LTR*, Vol. 1, p. 208.

133 "A very long way": Margaret Chanler, *Roman Spring: Memoirs* (Boston: Little, Brown, 1934), p. 203.

CHAPTER SIX: The Insider and the Outsider

Page

134 "Washington is just": TR to ARC, Feb. 11, 1894, in *LTR*, Vol. 1, p. 364.

134 "where everything throbs with . . . precedence over work": Frank George Carpenter and Frances Carpenter, eds., *Carp's Washington* (New York: McGraw-Hill Book Co., 1960), pp. 8–9.

134 managed to quit work early: TR to ARC, June 23, 1893, TRC.

134 "a streetcar will not . . . in which to live": Carpenter and Carpenter, eds., *Carp's Washington*, pp. 8–9.

135 "Common views and . . . Civil Service reform": WHT to Mark Sullivan, July 18, 1926, WHTP.

135 "hated the whole reform": TR, *An Autobiography*, p. 135.

135 "It will be a long, hard": WHT, "Civil Service Reform Applied to Municipal Government," Dec. 28, 1893, WHTP.

135 "One of the first observations": *NYT*, Aug. 30, 1890.

135 Roosevelt busily scanned "everything and everybody": Ibid.

136 "absorbed in work . . . not know it": WAW, "Taft, A Hewer of Wood," *The American Magazine* (April 1908), p. 23.

136 "Externally Taft is . . . settled or solved": Ibid.

136   Taft had no interest . . . dull and slow: WHT, "My Predecessor," *Collier's*, Mar. 6, 1909.

136   "they established": WAW, "Taft, A Hewer of Wood," *The American Magazine* (April 1908), p. 23.

136   "Mr. Taft . . . and she'd *get* it": Lyman Abbott, "William H. Taft," *Outlook*, April 4, 1908.

136   "One loves him": AB to Clara, Dec. 10, 1909, in AB, *Letters of Archie Butt*, p. 233.

136   "can get along": Abbott, "William H. Taft," *Outlook*, April 4, 1908.

136   "good nature": Ibid.

136   "a capacity . . . we do not possess": RSB, "The Measure of Taft," *The American Magazine* (July 1910), pp. 367–68.

137   "Each party profited": TR, *An Autobiography*, p. 131.

137   "For the last few years": TR to James Brander Matthews, July 31, 1889, in *LTR*, Vol. 1, p. 177.

137   "the fellow with no pull": Riis, *Theodore Roosevelt*, p. 106.

137   unqualified friends and kinsmen . . . "undemocratic": TR, "The Spoils System in Operation," in Hagedorn, ed., *Campaigns and Controversies*, *WTR*, Vol. 14, p. 89.

137   "To the victor belongs . . . so nakedly vicious": TR, *An Autobiography*, p. 130.

137   "Yes, TR is a breezy": Reprinted in *Galveston* [TX] *Daily News*, May 21, 1889.

138   "Until he began": Pringle, *Theodore Roosevelt: A Biography*, p. 123.

138   "to secure proper administration": TR, *An Autobiography*, p. 131.

138   "going to be enforced": TR to HCL, June 29, 1889, in *LTR*, Vol. 1, p. 167.

138   "so-called voluntary contributions": *Galveston* [TX] *Daily News*, Jan. 27, 1890.

138   "he was wrecking": Taft, *Memories and Opinions*, p. 111.

138   "to a poor clerk": *Galveston* [TX] *Daily News*, Jan. 27, 1890.

138   "to point out infractions": TR to Lucius Burrie Swift, May 16, 1889, in *LTR*, Vol. 1, pp. 162–63.

139   "Give me all": TR to Lucius Burrie Swift, May 16, 1889, in ibid., p. 162.

139   "I have to be sure": TR to Lucius Burrie Swift, May 7, 1892, in ibid., p. 280.

139   "We stirred things up well": TR to HCL, June 24, 1889, in ibid., p. 166.

139   "a model of fairness and justice": William Dudley Foulke, *Fighting the Spoilsmen: Reminiscences of the Civil Service Reform Movement* (New York: G. P. Putnam's Sons, 1919), p. 53.

139   "If he is not dismissed": TR to HCL, July 28, 1889, in *LTR*, Vol. 1, p. 175.

139   John Wanamaker . . . contempt for civil service reformers: Ibid., p. 171.

139   "It was a golden": TR to HCL, Aug. 8, 1889, in ibid., p. 186.

140   "a bribery chest": *Washington Post*, May 3, 1892.

140   "unfair and partial": TR to John Wanamaker, May 16, 1892, in *LTR*, Vol. 1, p. 281.

140   "head devil" of the spoilsmen: TR to Cecil Spring Rice, May 3, 1892, in ibid., p. 277.

140   "gross impertinence and impropriety": TR to John Wanamaker, May 16, 1892, in ibid., p. 282.

140   "It is war": *Washington Post*, May 26, 1892.

140   "not remember an instance": *NYT*, May 26, 1892, Clipping Scrapbook, TRC.

140   "put a padlock": *Ohio Democrat*, Nov. 27, 1890.

140   "like a person": *Washington Post*, April 29, 1892.

140   "He came into official life": *Washington Post*, May 6, 1890.

140   "utterly useless": TR to HCL, Oct. 19, 1889, in *LTR*, Vol. 1, p. 199.

140   Thompson . . . an "excellent" fellow: Ibid.

140   "My two colleagues": TR to ARC, May 24, 1891, in TR, *Letters from Theodore Roosevelt to Anna Roosevelt Cowles, 1870–1918* (New York: Charles Scribner's Sons, 1924), pp. 117–18.

140   "I have been continuing": TR to ARC, Feb. 1, 1891, in *LTR*, Vol. 1, p. 237.

141   "high regard . . . done before sundown": E. W. Halford, "Roosevelt's Introduction to Washington," *Frank Leslie's Illustrated Weekly*, Mar. 1, 1919, p. 314.

141   the House committee concluded: Joseph B. Bishop, *Theodore Roosevelt and His Time Shown in His Own Letters*, Vol. 1 (New York: Charles Scribner's Sons, 1920), p. 48.

141   "Mr. Roosevelt is": *Evening Times*, Oct. 29, 1890, Clipping Scrapbook, TRC.

141   "Cabot has been a real": TR to ARC, Feb. 12, 1893, TRC.

141   recite Shakespeare "almost by heart": John A. Garraty, *Henry Cabot Lodge: A Biography* (New York: Alfred A. Knopf, 1953), p. 102.

141   "You know, old fellow": TR to HCL, Nov. 1, 1886, in *LTR*, Vol. 1, p. 115.

142   Adams felt . . . especially "sympathetic": Henry Adams to Elizabeth Cameron, May 19, 1889, in Henry Adams and Worthington Chauncey Ford, eds., *Letters of Henry Adams* (Boston: Houghton Mifflin, 1930), Vol. 1, p. 398.

142   "Her taste in books": Chanler, *Roman Spring*, p. 203.

142   "Edith is really enjoying Washington": TR to ARC, Jan. 24, 1890, TRC.

142   "One night we dined": TR to ARC, Jan. 4, 1890, in *LTR*, Vol. 1, p. 208.

142   "Nannie has been a dear": EKR to ARC, Jan. 5, 1891, Derby Papers, TRC.

142   "Sunday-evening suppers . . . ineluctable will power": Chanler, *Roman Spring*, pp. 195, 203.

142   "Edith and I meet": TR to ARC, Feb. 11, 1894, in *LTR*, Vol. 1, p. 364.

143   "curled up . . . Theodore was the spinner": Miller, *Theodore Roosevelt: A Life*, p. 222.

143   "tendency to criticise . . . very entertaining": TR to ARC, April 1, 1894, in *LTR*, Vol. 1, p. 370.

143   not "succeeded in stopping . . . the wrong-doers": *Boston Herald*, Feb. 21, 1893; TR, "Civil Service Reform," in Hagedorn, ed., *Campaigns and Controversies*, *WTR*, Vol. 14, pp. 158–59.

143   "got on Harrison's . . . highest ideals": Abbott, "William H. Taft," *Outlook*, April 4, 1908.

143   "I did not find myself": WHT to Alphonso Taft, April 18, 1890, WHTP.

143   "They seem to think": WHT to Alphonso Taft, May 6, 1890, WHTP.

144   "opportunities for professional . . . case at Court": WHT to Paul Charlton, April 23, 1890, Pringle Papers.

144   "a few days in Cincinnati": WHT to Hiram D. Peck, April 26, 1890, WHTP.

144   "Don't be discouraged": Alphonso Taft to WHT, May 12, 1890, WHTP.

144   "Members waste": LTT to WHT, May 16, 1890, WHTP.

144   steadfastly "philosophical . . . improving it": WHT to Alphonso Taft [n.d.], WHTP.

144   "the very fact": WHT to Paul Charlton, April 23, 1890, Pringle Papers.

144   "somewhat more satisfaction . . . soporific power": WHT to Alphonso Taft [n.d.], WHTP.

144   "gain a good deal": WHT to Alphonso Taft, May 6, 1890, Pringle Papers.

144   "rather overwhelming" workload: WHT to Alphonso Taft, Feb. 26, 1890, WHTP.

144   "Each time a case": WHT to Alphonso Taft, Jan. 23, 1891, WHTP.

144   "So . . . you see": WHT to Alphonso Taft, Feb. 9, 1891, WHTP.

145   "the year's experience has been valuable": WHT to Alphonso Taft, Feb. 14, 1891, WHTP.

145   "the inattention . . . custom of the Bench": WHT to Alphonso Taft, Feb. 10, 1891, WHTP.

145   "new field": WHT to Alphonso Taft, Feb. 14, 1891, WHTP.

145   "made some very valuable . . . considerate of me": Ibid.

145   "The novelty of it": WHT to Charles P. Taft, May 2, 1890, Pringle Papers.

145   "The first duty": WHT to Alonzo Meyers, May 2, 1890, Pringle Papers.

145   "I shall sleep in a room": WHT to HHT, Aug. 27, 1890, WHTP.

145   "every evening . . . a great privilege": LTT to WHT, May 21, 1890, WHTP.

145   "come into exceedingly pleasant": WHT to Alphonso Taft, Feb. 14, 1891, WHTP.

146   "It has been": WHT to Alphonso Taft, Mar. 31, 1891, WHTP.

146   "scattered over . . . in the Supreme Court": WHT to Alphonso Taft, Feb. 14, 1891, WHTP.

146   "the heaviest weight": Alphonso Taft to WHT, Mar. 9, 1891, WHTP.

146   "There were fifty . . . becoming to her": WHT to Alphonso Taft, April 18, 1890, WHTP.

146   "Do write me": Agnes Davis Eckstein to HHT, April 15, 1890, WHTP.

146   "In the East room": *Washington Post*, Jan. 2, 1891.

147   "She had a very": WHT to Alphonso Taft, Jan. 6, 1891, WHTP.

147   "Tom Mack is with us": WHT to Alphonso Taft, Jan. 23, 1891, WHTP.

147   "throngs of buyers": *Illustrated Washington: Our Capital* (New York: American Publ. & Engraving Co., 1890), p. 75.

147   "The true Washingtonian . . . morning visitors": Constance McLaughlin Green, *Washington: A History of the Capitol, 1800–1950* (Princeton, NJ: Princeton University Press, 1963), p. 80.

147   "never ripened into intimacy": Charles Selden, "Six White House Wives and Widows," *Ladies' Home Journal* (June 1927).

147   "I don't like Mrs. Roosevelt": Anthony, *Nellie Taft*, p. 100.

147   "those who were actually": Robert V. Remini, *The House: The History of the House of Representatives* (New York: Smithsonian Books in assoc. with HarperCollins, 2006), p. 248.

148   "I suppose I ought": WHT to Alphonso Taft, Jan. 23, 1891, WHTP.

148   "I do not object": WHT to Alphonso Taft, April 18, 1891, WHTP.

148   "Your letters are": Alphonso Taft to WHT, May 28, 1890, WHTP.

148   "I am greatly exhilarated": Alphonso Taft to WHT, June 6, 1890, WHTP.

148   "The morning is": Charles P. Taft to WHT, Nov. 28, 1890, WHTP.

148   "Except when he is . . . always entertain him": LTT to WHT, April 13, 1891, WHTP.

149   the accomplishments of his boys: Charles P. Taft to WHT, May 21, 1890, WHTP.

149   "Can you not": Alphonso Taft to WHT, Jan. 10, 1891, WHTP.

149   "His vitality": WHT to HHT, May 18, 1891, WHTP.

149   "He seems to trust me": WHT to HHT, May 10, 1891, WHTP.

149   "noble boy . . . avoided this by suicide": WHT to HHT, May 29, 1891, WHTP.

149   did not want the general public to be inconvenienced: *Sandusky* [OH] *Daily Register*, June 4, 1891.

149   "I trust you": Charles Taft to WHT, April 4, 1891, WHTP.

150   a "ludicrous . . . rapidity of movement": WHT to HHT, June 1, 1891, WHTP.

150   "Springy and I": TR to ARC, June 20, 1891, in TR, *Letters from Theodore Roosevelt to Anna Roosevelt Cowles*, p. 118.

150   "We are just as": TR to HCL, July 1, 1891, in *LTR*, Vol. 1, p. 255.

150 "I see that I got ahead": Pringle, *Life and Times*, Vol. 1, p. 120.

150 "nervous and fidgety" assistance: TR to HCL, June 19, 1891, in *LTR*, Vol. 1, p. 253.

150 "Can you dine": TR to WHT, Aug. 19, 1891, in ibid., p. 258.

150 "It is a perfect nightmare": TR to ARC, Jan. 24, 1890, TRC.

150 "Elliott must be put": TR to ARC, May 2, 1890, TRC.

151 "He is evidently": TR to ARC, June 17, 1891, TRC.

151 ELLIOTT ROOSEVELT: Blanche Wiesen Cook, *Eleanor Roosevelt*, Vol. 1: *1884–1933* (New York: Viking, 1992), p. 67.

151 "emphatically . . . adjudge him one": Cited in *Washington Post*, Aug. 22, 1891.

151 "The horror": TR to ARC, Sept. 1, 1891, TRC.

151 "jumped out of the": CRR to ARC, Aug. 15, 1894, ARC Papers.

151 "the sunniest" child: Henry Taft to Alphonso Taft, June 3, 1889, WHTP.

151 "great comfort . . . whom everyone loved": TR to CRR, Aug. 29, 1894, in *LTR*, Vol. 1, p. 397.

151 "of whom we are really fond": TR to ARC, Jan. 7, 1894, in ibid., p. 345.

151 "merry blue eyes": WAW, "Taft, A Hewer of Wood," *American Magazine* (April 1908), p. 24.

152 "in the line of promotion": WHT to Alphonso Taft, Mar. 18, 1891, WHTP.

152 "have stirred up": Ibid.

152 "the man whom . . . years of hard work": WHT to Howard Hollister [n.d.], WHTP.

152 "would be very glad": Ibid.

152 "entirely philosophical . . . legion": WHT to Alphonso Taft, Mar. 18, 1891, WHTP.

152 "settled for good": HHT, *Recollections of Full Years*, p. 22.

152 "fixed in a groove": Ibid., p. 30.

152 "very much opposed": WHT to Alphonso Taft, Mar. 7, 1891, WHTP.

152 "It seems to me now": WHT to HHT, June 1, 1891, WHTP.

152 "If you get your heart's": HHT to WHT, July 18, 1891, WHTP.

153 "hardly a soul": WHT to HHT, July 18, 1891, WHTP.

153 "You will regard my failure": WHT to HHT, May 10, 1891, WHTP.

153 "I hate that": HHT to WHT, July 14, 1891, WHTP.

153 "It would be very easy": Ibid.

153 "I am not a bit happy": HHT to WHT, Aug. 18, 1890, WHTP.

153 "I love you ever": HHT to WHT, Aug. 27, 1890, WHTP.

153 "when we were first married": HHT to WHT, May 23, 1893, WHTP.

153 "simply crazy about": HHT to WHT, Sept. 7, 1890, WHTP.

153 "the dearest child": HHT to WHT, Sept. 1, 1891, WHTP.

153 His eating habits: HHT to WHT, Aug. 18, 1890, WHTP.

153 "I seem to care much more": HHT to WHT, July 13, 1891, WHTP.

153 "Don't make your brief": HHT to WHT, Sept. 21, 1891, WHTP.

154 "The press notices": Henry W. Taft to WHT, Dec. 18, 1891, WHTP.

154 "one of the most popular": *Washington Post*, Dec. 17, 1891.

154 "no man could have been": *Washington Post*, Dec. 20, 1891.

154 "Aside from": Horace Taft to WHT, Jan. 12, 1892, WHTP.

154 "One of the sweetest things": WHT to Howard Hollister, Dec. 21, 1891, WHTP.

154 "I feel so good": WHT to HHT, Mar. 17, 1892, WHTP.

154 "The two years": WHT to William Miller, March [n.d.], 1892, WHTP.

154 relinquish the "pleasant life": EKR to Emily Carow, Mar. 7, 1893, TRC.

154 "Our places are still": EKR to Emily Carow, Mar. 7, 1893, TRC.

155 "elected by the people" to Congress: EKR to Emily Carow, Nov. 14, 1893, TRC.

155 "a dream never to be realized": EKR to Emily Carow, Oct. 16, 1892, TRC.

155 "He is now": Ibid.

155 "nonsense" . . . his true concerns: Ibid.

155 "could do most . . . success awaits me": TR to ARC, Aug. 16, 1893, TRC.

155 "the moving spirit . . . to deal with Democrats": New York *Evening Post*, May 5, 1893, Clipping Scrapbook, TRC.

155 "It was practically": EKR to ARC, Feb. 3, 1894, Derby Papers, TRC.

155 "hope of going on": TR to HCL, Oct. 24, 1894, in TR and H. W. Brands, eds., *The Selected Letters of Theodore Roosevelt* (New York: Cooper Square Press, 2001), p. 96.

155 "they simply could not . . . lost the election?": Lilian Rixey, *Bamie: Theodore Roosevelt's Remarkable Sister* (New York: David McKay Co., 1963), p. 81.

156 "big, bustling New York": EKR to HCL, Oct. 27, 1895, Lodge-Roosevelt Correspondence, Massachusetts Hist. Soc.

156 "into one of her reserved": Rixey, *Bamie*, p. 81.

156 "The last four weeks": TR to HCL, Oct. 24, 1894, in *The Selected Letters of Theodore Roosevelt*, p. 96.

156   "I cannot begin": EKR to ARC, Sept. 28, 1894, Derby Papers, TRC.
156   his "one golden chance": TR to HCL, Oct. 24, 1894, in *The Selected Letters of Theodore Roosevelt*, p. 96.

CHAPTER SEVEN: The Invention of *McClure's*

Page
157   "We plow new fields . . . becoming harder": Cited in Eric F. Goldman, *Rendezvous with Destiny* (New
      York: Alfred A. Knopf, 1952), p. 32.
158   "the steamship . . . with their hand-looms": Henry George, *Progress and Poverty* (New York: Cosimo
      Classics, 2005), p. 7.
158   "the gulf between": Cited in Goldman, *Rendezvous with Destiny*, p. 33.
158   in a seminal paper: Frederick J. Turner, "The Significance of the Frontier in American History," in
      Annual Report of the Amer. Hist. Assoc. for the Year 1893 (Washington, DC: U.S. Government Printing
      Office, 1894), pp. 199–227.
158   "It was a time": Frank B. Latham, *The Panic of 1893: A Time of Strikes, Riots, Hobo Camps, Coxey's
      "Army," Starvation, Withering Droughts and Fears of "Revolution"* (New York: F. Watts, 1971), p. 4.
159   "My men here": TR to ARC, May 15, 1886, in *LTR*, Vol. 1, pp. 100–101.
159   "foulest of criminals": TR, "The Menace of the Demagogue," speech before the American Republican
      College League, Oct. 15, 1896, in Hagedorn, ed., *Campaigns and Controversies, WTR*, Vol. 14, p. 265.
159   "wild and illogical doctrines": TR, "The City in Modern Life," *Atlantic Monthly* (April 1895),
      p. 556.
159   "that at this stage": TR, "The Menace of the Demagogue," in Hagedorn, ed., *Campaigns and Contro-
      versies, WTR*, Vol. 14, pp. 264–65.
159   more than 4 million jobs: Latham, *The Panic of 1893*, p. 4.
160   This acclaimed muckraking journal: John Chamberlain, *Farewell to Reform: The Rise, Life and Decay
      of the Progressive Mind in America* (Chicago: Quadrangle Books, 1965), p. 128.
160   "genius . . . of excitable energy": RSB, *American Chronicle: The Autobiography of Ray Stannard Baker*
      (New York: Charles Scribner's Sons, 1945), p. 95.
160   "a vibrant, eager": Ida M. Tarbell, *All in the Day's Work: An Autobiography* (Urbana: University of Il-
      linois Press, 2003), p. 119.
160   "a bundle of tensions": Peter Lyon, *Success Story: The Life and Times of S. S. McClure* (New York:
      Charles Scribner's Sons, 1963), p. 11.
160   "a stream of words": Ibid., p. 14.
160   "like a caged lion": Robert Louis Stevenson and Lloyd Osbourne, *The Wrecker* (London: Oxford
      University Press, 1954), p. 107.
160   "lasted some twelve": Lyon, *Success Story*, p. 123.
160   "That was the first": Willa Cather and S. S. McClure, *The Autobiography of S. S. McClure* (Lincoln:
      University of Nebraska Press, 1997), p. 9.
161   "For a long while": Ibid., p. 17.
161   the Bible . . . *Book of Martyrs*: Lyon, *Success Story*, p. 5.
161   "opening those boxes": Cather and McClure, *The Autobiography*, p. 19.
161   "seemed to die down": Ibid., p. 18.
161   "began for the first time": Ibid., p. 27.
161   "a kind of 'arithmetic' . . . no text-book": Ibid., pp. 40–41.
162   "I used to waken": Ibid., p. 28.
162   "attacks of restlessness . . . all my life": Ibid., pp. 57, 59.
162   "I was seventeen . . . felt complete self-reliance": Ibid., p. 62.
162   had "never seen so": Lyon, *Success Story*, p. 13.
162   "Everything went well . . . blank stretch": Cather and McClure, *The Autobiography*, p. 18.
162   "the most beautiful": Lyon, *Success Story*, p. 17.
162   A brilliant student . . . top of her class: Cather and McClure, *The Autobiography*, p. 88.
162   "Don't cry for the moon": Lyon, *Success Story*, p. 17.
163   "My feeling for her": Cather and McClure, *The Autobiography*, p. 96.
163   "You mustn't write": Lyon, *Success Story*, p. 23.
163   "was easily the best": Cather and McClure, *The Autobiography*, p. 134.
163   At Phillips's house . . . William Dean Howells: Harold S. Wilson, *McClure's Magazine and the Muckrak-
      ers* (Princeton, NJ: Princeton University Press, 1970), p. 19.
163   "close acquaintance": Cather and McClure, *The Autobiography*, p. 130.
164   "He works by": Wilson, *McClure's Magazine and the Muckrakers*, p. 19.
164   "The three together": RSB, *American Chronicle*, p. 95.
164   "My present": McClure to Harriet Hurd, Dec. 23, 1881, McClure MSS.
164   "Mr. McClure": Lyon, *Success Story*, p. 32.
164   "would never receive": Ibid., p. 39.

164 "his personal appearance . . . his acquaintance": Albert Hurd to Harriet Hurd, April 29, 1883, McClure MSS.
165 "I do not love you": Lyon, *Success Story*, p. 33.
165 "This dismissal": Cather and McClure, *The Autobiography*, p. 143.
165 "weave the bicycle": Lyon, *Success Story*, p. 36.
165 "You are the surest": Ibid., p. 37.
165 "among the most attractive": Ibid., p. 38.
165 McClure took to the road: Wilson, *McClure's Magazine and the Muckrakers*, p. 35.
165 "I was in the big game": Cather and McClure, *The Autobiography*, pp. 150–51.
165 "When I have passed . . . identity with that boy": Ibid., p. 151.
166 "*could not* . . . love you still": Lyon, *Success Story*, p. 39.
166 "I saw it": Cather and McClure, *The Autobiography*, p. 164.
166 "a month's vacation": Jeanette L. Gilder, "When *McClure's* Began," *McClure's* (August 1912), p. 70.
166 "a handsome profit": Ibid.
166 "a dozen, or twenty": Lyon, *Success Story*, p. 57.
167 "distributing fifty thousand": Ibid., p. 74.
167 "much better fitted . . . as Mr. Phillips had": Cather and McClure, *The Autobiography*, p. 181.
167 "from one end of the country . . . in his teeth": Gilder, "When *McClure's* Began," *McClure's* (August 1912), p. 71.
167 "McClure was a Columbus": Ibid.
167 "dignified and conservative": Theodore P. Greene, *America's Heroes: The Changing Models of Success in American Magazines* (New York: Oxford University Press, 1970), p. 63.
167 "My qualifications": Lyon, *Success Story*, p. 94.
167 "He secured the best": "Mr. McClure and His Magazine," *American Monthly Review of Reviews* (July 1893), p. 99.
167 "before the name": J. L. French, "The Story of *McClure's*," *Profitable Advertising*, Oct. 5, 1897, p. 140.
167 purchased a dozen Sherlock Holmes: Cather and McClure, *The Autobiography*, p. 204.
167 "To find the best authors": French, "The Story of *McClure's*," *Profitable Advertising*, Oct. 5, 1897, p. 140.
168 "I propose to down . . . like champagne": Wilson, *McClure's Magazine and the Muckrakers*, p. 55.
168 "I would rather edit": Lyon, *Success Story*, p. 109.
168 "a reasonable profit": *Trenton* [NJ] *Times*, June 14, 1894.
168 "moneyed and well-educated . . . the upper classes": Frank Luther Mott, *A History of American Magazines, Vol. 4: 1885–1905* (Cambridge, MA: Harvard University Press, 1957), p. 2.
168 "within reach of": *Reno* [NV] *Evening Gazette*, July 6, 1893.
168 "The impregnability": Cather and McClure, *The Autobiography*, pp. 207–08.
168 "to make pictures": Ibid., p. 208.
169 "There was certainly": Ibid., p. 211.
169 "the good will of thousands": Gilder, "When *McClure's* Began," *McClure's* (August 1912), p. 72.
169 Conan Doyle invested $5,000: Lyon, *Success Story*, p. 133.
169 "It is not often . . . among the winners": "Mr. McClure and His Magazine," *American Monthly Review of Reviews* (July 1893), p. 99.
169 "no little of a": *Providence* [RI] *Journal*, June 4, 1893, in *McClure's* (August 1893), p. 6.
169 the "front rank at once": *Philadelphia Public Ledger*, June 13, 1893, in ibid.
169 "unusually brilliant": *Atlanta Constitution*, May 1, 1893.
169 "the first issue": TR to McClure, May 29, 1893, McClure MSS.
169 "a unity": Lyon, *Success Story*, p. 129.
169 "almost invented" it: John E. Semonche, *Ray Stannard Baker: A Quest for Democracy in Modern America, 1870–1918* (Chapel Hill: University of North Carolina Press, 1969), p. 76.
169 "in line with": Lyon, *Success Story*, p. 130.
170 "to deal with important": S. S. McClure, "The Making of a Magazine," *McClure's* (May 1924), p. 9.
170 "a power . . . for good": William Archer, "The American Cheap Magazine," *Fortnightly Review* (May 1910), p. 922.
170 the "mother hen": Wilson, *McClure's Magazine and the Muckrakers*, p. 96.
170 "This girl can write . . . exactly the qualities": Cather and McClure, *The Autobiography*, p. 218.
170 "unknown to half . . . enthusiasm and confidence": IMT, *All in the Day's Work*, pp. 118–19.
171 "more than he could ever": Ibid., p. 19.
171 "confident of . . . we had never heard of": Ibid., p. 22.
171 "nothing they did not . . . throttle their future": IMT and David M. Chalmers, *The History of the Standard Oil Company* (New York: Harper & Row, 1966), p. 21.
171 railroads arbitrarily doubled: Kathleen Brady, *Ida Tarbell: Portrait of a Muckraker* (Pittsburgh: University of Pittsburgh Press, 1989), p. 21.
171 His "big scheme": IMT, *All in the Day's Work*, p. 23.

171   "started the Standard Oil": Ibid., p. 219.

171   "There were nightly . . . during the day": Ibid., pp. 23–24.

172   "all pretty hazy . . . privilege of any sort": Ibid., pp. 25–26.

172   "readjustment of her status . . . sternest of problems": Ibid., p. 31.

172   "would never marry" . . . entreated God to prevent her ever marrying. Ibid., p. 36.

172   "classifying them": Ibid., p. 81.

172   "luminous eyes": Brady, *Ida Tarbell*, p. 29.

172   "an invader": IMT, *All in the Day's Work*, p. 40.

172   "the companionship": Ibid., pp. 39–40.

172   "shy and immature . . . reverence for Nature": Ibid., p. 41.

172   "She would arise . . . interested in people": Brady, *Ida Tarbell*, p. 28.

173   "go abroad and study": IMT, *All in the Day's Work*, p. 40.

173   "My early absorption . . . as of botany": Ibid., pp. 80–81.

173   "ardent supporters . . . laundries and bakeshops": Ibid., p. 82.

173   "a trilogy of . . . natural resources": Robert C. Kochersberger, *More Than a Muckraker: Ida Tarbell's Lifetime in Journalism* (Knoxville: University of Tennessee Press, 1994), p. xlvi.

173   "My life was busy": IMT, *All in the Day's Work*, pp. 78–79.

173   "disorderly fashion": Ibid., p. 73.

173   "secretly, very secretly": Ibid., p. 78.

174   "How will you support . . . You'll starve": Ibid., p. 87.

174   "There were a multitude": Ibid., p. 92.

174   "There were few mornings": Ibid., p. 103.

174   "It was not much": Ida M. Tarbell to [Tarbell family], Nov. 13, 1891, IMTC.

174   "bohemian poverty": Brady, *Ida Tarbell*, p. 51.

174   "a good dinner": IMT to [Tarbell family], Dec. 20, 1891, IMTC.

174   "happy evenings": IMT, *All in the Day's Work*, p. 105.

174   "Think of us": IMT to [Tarbell family], October [n.d.], 1891, IMTC.

175   "not a morsel more": IMT to [Tarbell family], Aug. 25, 1891, IMTC.

175   "a single egg": IMT, *All in the Day's Work*, pp. 90–91.

175   "It is the most heartless": IMT to [Tarbell family], November [n.d.], 1891, IMTC.

175   At night she wore everything: IMT to [Tarbell family], Dec. 20, 1891, IMTC.

175   "It isn't money": IMT to [Tarbell family], Dec. 27, 1891, IMTC.

175   "I think after . . . heart and hope": IMT to [Tarbell family], Dec. 7, 1891, IMTC.

175   *Scribner's* paid . . . first months in Paris: IMT to [Tarbell family], Sept. 21, 1891, IMTC.

175   "What excitement": IMT, *All in the Day's Work*, p. 98.

175   "Writing $5 . . . one's living": IMT to [Tarbell family], May 2, 1892, IMTC.

175   "I must go . . . never think of it again": IMT, *All in the Day's Work*, pp. 119–20.

176   "We all hope": McClure to IMT, Mar. 2, 1894, IMTC.

176   "All of the articles": McClure to IMT, Jan. 6, 1894, IMTC.

176   "actually starving . . . by force, if it must be": Esther Tarbell to IMT, Aug. 6, 1893, in Wilson, *McClure's Magazine and the Muckrakers*, p. 67.

176   "on the ragged edge . . . as a cricket": IMT to [Tarbell family], Mar. 16, 1894, IMTC.

176   "The little magazine": IMT to [Tarbell family], [n.d.], 1893, IMTC.

176   "so contemptuously anti-Napoleon": IMT, *All in the Day's Work*, p. 147.

177   "biography on the gallop": Ibid., p. 151.

177   "the best short life": Brady, *Ida Tarbell*, p. 91.

177   "I have often wished": IMT, *All in the Day's Work*, p. 152.

177   "His insight told him": Ibid., p. 161.

177   "could think of nothing": Gilder, "When *McClure's* Began," *McClure's* (August 1912), p. 75.

177   "Out with you": Lyon, *Success Story*, p. 134.

177   "all there was worth . . . so hopeless an assignment": IMT, *All in the Day's Work*, p. 163.

177   "They got a girl": Lyon, *Success Story*, p. 135.

177   "plan of campaign . . . humble and unknown": IMT, *All in the Day's Work*, p. 164.

178   McClure covered all her expenses . . . scrutinized multiple drafts: Brady, *Ida Tarbell*, p. 99.

178   "It is not only": "Miss Tarbell's Life of Lincoln," *McClure's* (January 1896), p. 206.

178   *McClure's* circulation . . . reached a quarter of a million: Lyons, *Success Story*, p. 137.

178   exceeding both the *Century* and *Harper's Monthly*: Brady, *Ida Tarbell*, p. 98.

178   "great power to stir": IMT, *All in the Day's Work*, p. 154.

178   "Here's a man": Ibid., p. 156.

178   "that Sam had three hundred": Brady, *Ida Tarbell*, p. 113.

178   "I found the place": IMT, *All in the Day's Work*, p. 160.

178   allowed her to get on "capitally": IMT to [Tarbell family], Feb. 26, 1893, IMTC.

178 "came and went": IMT, *All in the Day's Work*, p. 159.
178 blue eyes "glowed and sparkled": Ibid., p. 119.
179 "a stroke of genius": Ibid., p. 154.
179 "the sense of vitality . . . good comradeship": Ibid., p. 153.
179 The next "permanent acquisition": Ibid., p. 196.
179 "an honest paper": Semonche, *Ray Stannard Baker*, p. 77.
179 "farmers, tinkers": Ray Stannard Baker, *Native American: The Book of My Youth* (New York: Charles Scribner's Sons, 1942), p. 244.
179 "every human being": Ibid., p. 22.
179 "a wider field . . . import and value": RSB to his father, Jan. 16, 1898, RSB Papers.
179 "a devoted admirer . . . alive and talking": RSB, *American Chronicle*, p. 77.
179 "something fresh": Ibid., p. 78.
179 "To say that I was awed": Ibid., pp. 78–79.
179 "It took my breath . . . or anywhere else": Ibid., pp. 79–80.
180 "It 'breaks me all up' ": RSB to J. Stannard Baker, Feb. 1, 1898, RSB Papers.
180 "This is a magnificent": RSB to J. Stannard Baker, Mar. 25, 1898, RSB Papers.
180 "I like them": RSB to J. Stannard Baker, Sept. 17, 1898, RSB Papers.
180 "a capital team worker . . . anything else about him": IMT, *All in the Day's Work*, pp. 196–97.
180 "fishing and hunting . . . lumber camps": RSB, *Native American*, p. 11.
180 he married Alice Potter . . . "resident agent": Robert C. Bannister, Jr., *Ray Stannard Baker: The Mind and Thought of a Progressive* (New Haven, CT: Yale University Press, 1966), p. 4.
180 "Ours was a house": RSB, *Native American*, p. 38.
181 "How well I remember": Ibid., p. 26.
181 "a prodigious story-teller": Ibid., p. 48.
181 "into the lives and sorrows": Ibid., p. 45.
181 "My reading was always": Ibid., p. 47.
181 Ray assumed responsibility: Semonche, *Ray Stannard Baker*, p. 21.
181 "It went through me": RSB, *Native American*, p. 128.
181 "a great waste of time": Ibid., p. 163.
182 "details and facts": Ibid., p. 164.
182 "the one thing I needed": Ibid., p. 169.
182 well liked in college . . . at the top of his class: Semonche, *Ray Stannard Baker*, pp. 34, 40.
182 "When the time comes . . . successful in any employment": RSB, *Native American*, p. 220.
182 "I felt as though": Ibid., p. 223.
182 "Experience soon fades": Ibid., p. 237.
182 until his brother Harry . . . replaced him: Semonche, *Ray Stannard Baker*, p. 44.
183 "good working order" of society: Bannister, *Ray Stannard Baker*, p. 39.
183 Baker signed up . . . to question the laissez-faire economic principles: Semonche, *Ray Stannard Baker*, p. 50.
183 "anathema" to his father: RSB, *Native American*, pp. 284–85.
183 "with the greatest fervor . . . thirsty spirit": Ibid., p. 255.
183 "I did not make this": Ibid., p. 256.
183 "Great stuff, Baker": Ibid., p. 297.
184 "glimpses, street scenes": Ibid., pp. 291–92.
184 Ray tried to convince his father: RSB to J. Stannard Baker, Dec. 21, 1892, RSB Papers.
184 "There are thousands": RSB to J. Stannard Baker, Dec. 15, 1893, RSB Papers.
184 "plenty of people . . . plenty of work": RSB, *Native American*, pp. 286–87.
184 "The miserable living conditions": Ibid., p. 288.
184 "in the event . . . feels in the same way": RSB to J. Stannard Baker, Jan. 3, 1894, RSB Papers.
185 "I began to know . . . earn a living": Vivian Graff Rosenberg, *Turn of the Century American Journalist, Home-Spun Philosopher, Ray Stannard Baker* (Privately printed, 1977), p. 69.
185 incredible "power of the press": RSB, *American Chronicle*, p. 12.
185 "there appeared": Ibid., pp. 17–18.
185 "a grand adventure": Ibid., p. 27.
185 "the police seemed": Rosenberg, *Turn of the Century American Journalist*, p. 72.
185 "Coxey's eventful march . . . an act of God": Louis L. Snyder and Richard B. Morris, eds., *A Treasury of Great Reporting: "Literature Under Pressure" from the Sixteenth Century to Our Own Time* (New York: Simon & Schuster, 1962), p. 222.
185 "vanished in thin air": RSB, *American Chronicle*, p. 25.
186 "benevolent-looking, bearded": Ibid., p. 35.
186 "the wildest confusion": Ibid.
186 it was later proved . . . $25 million: Pringle, *Life and Times*, Vol. 1, p. 132.

186   the predatory hold of the Pullman monopoly must be broken: RSB, *American Chronicle*, p. 38.
186   "nothing to arbitrate . . . business of the company": Ibid., p. 38.
186   "putting the torch": Ibid., p. 39.
186   "It does seem": J. Stannard Baker to RSB, July 6 & 10, 1894, in Bannister, *Ray Stannard Baker*, p. 51.
186   "in the midst of the mob . . . toughs and outsiders": Testimony of RSB, *Hutchinson* [KS] *News*, Aug. 21, 1894.
187   "honeymoon as a newspaper . . . the trouble ended": RSB, *American Chronicle*, pp. 45–46.
187   "the greatest popular orator": Ibid., p. 62.
187   "The essential impression": Ibid., p. 63.
187   "the commonplace" . . . "the spectacular": Ibid., p. 45.
187   "somewhat low . . . as a writer": Ibid., p. 77.
187   "Suddenly and joyously . . . to write about it": Ibid., p. 84.
187   "What's the Matter with Kansas?" . . . "wild-eyed" rhetoric: WAW, *The Autobiography of William Allen White* (New York: The Macmillan Co., 1946), p. 281.
188   "That's the stuff!": Ibid., p. 282.
188   "more widely than any other . . . in a dozen years": Ibid., p. 284.
188   "I had seen cities . . . English poets were their friends": Ibid., pp. 300–301.
188   "the smile of . . . a poet": Walter Johnson, *William Allen White's America* (New York: Henry Holt & Co., 1947), p. 19.
188   "his affection and loyalty": IMT, *All in the Day's Work*, p. 259.
188   White's "love of life . . . high spirits": RSB, *American Chronicle*, p. 224.
188   "call on them whenever": Lyon, *Success Story*, p. 150.
189   "The McClure group . . . had real influence": WAW, *The Autobiography*, p. 301.
189   "never yielded . . . went back to Kansas": RSB, *American Chronicle*, p. 223.
189   His family lived in "the best house": WAW, *The Autobiography*, p. 69.
189   "I look back upon": Ibid., p. 61.
189   "to get a breeze": Ibid., p. 42.
189   "somebody . . . to the ruling class": Ibid., pp. 61–62.
189   "devoted and adoring . . . bowed down": Ibid., p. 25.
189   "In that Elysian childhood": Ibid., p. 26.
189   "He was so good-natured": Johnson, *William Allen White's America*, p. 10.
189   Summer days were spent . . . a boy's paradise: WAW, *The Autobiography*, pp. 45–46.
190   "I remember as a child": Johnson, *William Allen White's America*, pp. 19–20.
190   "distinguished citizens": WAW, *The Autobiography*, p. 67.
190   "I was not without": Ibid., p. 83.
190   "Here . . . was a novel . . . a new door": Ibid., p. 106.
190   his "life's calling": Ibid., pp. 109, 113.
190   "establish a home": Ibid., p. 136.
190   "a babble of clamoring voices": Ibid., p. 144.
191   "natural laws . . . the laboring classes": Goldman, *Rendezvous with Destiny*, p. 113.
191   "As I look back": WAW, *The Autobiography*, pp. 143–44.
191   "ceased to be a student": Ibid., p. 176.
191   "We have three crops": Latham, *The Panic of 1893*, p. 15.
192   "police power . . . with a public interest": Kermit L. Hall, ed., *The Oxford Guide to the United States Supreme Court Decisions* (New York: Oxford University Press, 1999), p. 203.
192   The justices denied the state's regulatory power: Ibid., p. 321.
192   "reasonable and just": Interstate Commerce Commission Act of 1887 (24 Stat. 379).
192   "It satisfies the public": Gary M. Walton and Hugh Rockoff, *History of the American Economy* (San Diego, CA: Harcourt Brace Jovanovich, 1990), p. 338.
192   "Liberty produces wealth . . . instead of servant": Henry Demarest Lloyd, *Wealth Against Commonwealth* (New York: Harper & Bros., 1902), pp. 2, 494.
192   "Wall Street owns . . . wages deny them!": Mary K. Lease, quoted in Levine, *Who Built America?*, p. 147.
193   "We meet in the midst . . . people must own the railroads": Edward McPherson, *A Handbook of Politics for 1892* (Washington, DC: J. J. Chapman, 1892), pp. 269ff.
193   "We prideful ones": WAW, *The Autobiography*, p. 183.
193   "demagogic rabble-rousing . . . blinded by my birthright": Ibid., p. 187.
193   "pinheaded, anarchistic crank[s]": Miller, *Theodore Roosevelt: A Life*, p. 218.
194   "representatives of those forces": TR, "The Menace of the Demagogue," in *WTR*, Vol. 14, p. 264.
194   "The 'best citizens' ": WAW, *The Autobiography*, p. 191.
194   "the first wave": Ibid., pp. 193–94.
194   "the black hand . . . for fifty years": Ibid., pp. 215–16.

194 becoming his "own master": Ibid., p. 256.
194 "I want to live": Johnson, *William Allen White's America*, p. 76.
194 "The new editor": WAW, *The Autobiography*, pp. 260–61.
195 "the best-known": Johnson, *William Allen White's America*, p. 4.
195 "was the beginning": WAW, *The Autobiography*, p. 286.
195 "seems big . . . just our size": McClure to John S. Phillips, April 21, 1897, Phillips MSS.
195 "one of the best journalists": C. C. Regier, *The Era of the Muckrakers* (Gloucester, MA: Peter Smith, 1957), p. 59.
195 "Jaccaci probed . . . clinched" the deal: LS, *The Autobiography*, p. 358.
196 "like springing up": Ibid., p. 359.
196 "He was a flower . . . compromise and peace": Ibid., pp. 361–64.
196 "young, handsome . . . society, the press": IMT, *All in the Day's Work*, pp. 198–99.
196 "entirely in harmony": Ibid., p. 199.
196 "associates in the . . . long friendship": RSB, *American Chronicle*, p. 221.
196 "as a kind of Socratic": Ibid., p. 221.
196 "his most consistent pose": Robert Stinson, *Lincoln Steffens* (New York: Frederick Ungar, 1979), p. 1.
196 "My story is": LS, *The Autobiography*, p. 3.
196 "paints, oils and glass": Ibid., p. 7.
197 "palatial residence": Justin Kaplan, *Lincoln Steffens: A Biography* (New York: Touchstone, 1974), p. 17.
197 "If I left home promptly": LS, *The Autobiography*, p. 34.
197 befriended a bridge-tender: Ibid., p. 28.
197 "in on the know . . . big killings": Ibid., p. 37.
197 "Bribery!": Ibid., p. 48.
197 "Nothing was what": Ibid., p. 47.
197 "the best private school": Ibid., p. 112.
197 "brought up to do their duty": Ibid., p. 111.
197 "stored in compartments . . . to anything else": Ibid., p. 119.
198 "My father listened . . . his interest and retire": Ibid., p. 128.
198 having received love "so freely": Ibid., p. 77.
198 Not until his own son was born: Kaplan, *Lincoln Steffens*, p. 21.
198 "She stands next": LS to Elizabeth Steffens, Feb. 1, 1891, LS Papers.
198 "My dear son": LS, *The Autobiography*, p. 169.
199 "on space . . . he told me his": Ibid., pp. 172–73.
199 "I came to love . . . a live city": Ibid., pp. 180–81.
199 "cool, dull": Ibid., p. 184.
199 "was a dismal time . . . in the ruin": Ibid., p. 187.
199 "successful men . . . stop to question": Ibid., p. 192.
199 "the gentleman reporter . . . accuracy and politeness": LS to Joseph Steffens, Jan. 18, 1893, in Lincoln Steffens, Ella Winter, Granville Hicks, and Carl Sandburg, eds., *The Letters of Lincoln Steffens*, Vol. 1 (New York: Harcourt, Brace & Co., 1938), pp. 88–89.
200 "confide in me . . . worth it all": LS to Joseph Steffens, Mar. 18, 1893, in ibid., pp. 91–92.
200 "The Evening Post . . . my field, my chance": LS to Joseph Steffens, Nov. 3, 1893, in ibid., pp. 97–98.
200 Long opposed to the Tammany regime . . . were delighted to document Parkhurst's findings: LS, *The Autobiography*, p. 193.
201 "a vigilant and well-informed press": "Interview with S. S. McClure," *The North American* (Philadelphia), August [n.d.], 1905.

CHAPTER EIGHT: "Like a Boy on Roller Skates"

Page
203 Lincoln Steffens was relaxing: LS, *The Autobiography*, p. 257.
203 Jacob Riis heralded . . . of Little Italy: Morris, *The Rise of Theodore Roosevelt*, p. 482.
203 "head forward": LS, "The Real Roosevelt," *Ainslee's Magazine* (December 1898), p. 481.
203 "Hello, Jake . . . "What do we do first?'": LS, *The Autobiography*, p. 257.
204 "It was all breathless": Ibid., p. 258.
204 An immigrant from Denmark . . . the same year: Thaddeus Seymour, Jr., "A Progressive Partnership: Theodore Roosevelt and the Reform Press—Riis, Steffens, Baker and White (Muckrakers)," PhD diss., University of Wisconsin, Madison, 1985, p. 35.
204 his "life-work" in journalism: Jacob A. Riis, *The Making of an American* (New York: Grosset & Dunlap, 1901), p. 197.
204 "Being the 'boss'": Ibid., p. 202.
204 "The sights I saw there": Ibid., p. 267.

204   neglected "repairs and": Jacob Riis, *How the Other Half Lives: Studies Among the Tenements of New York* (New York: Charles Scribner's Sons, 1890), p. 4.
204   "Only Riis wrote": LS, *The Autobiography*, p. 204.
204   "beautiful stories": Ibid., p. 205.
204   When he narrated . . . the problems were redressed: Ibid., p. 204.
204   "Why" he asked: Riis, *The Making of an American*, p. 349.
205   "The remedy": Riis, *How the Other Half Lives*, p. 4.
205   "Truly, I lay no claim": Riis, *The Making of an American*, pp. 309, 317.
205   "I cannot conceive": JRL quoted in Riis, *The Making of an American*, p. 308.
205   "both an enlightenment": TR, *An Autobiography*, p. 169.
205   "go a long way": TR, "Reform Through Social Work: Some Forces That Tell for Decency in New York City," *McClure's* (March 1901), p. 453.
205   "hysterical . . . sentimental excess": Ibid.
205   read the book and "had come": Jacob Riis, "Theodore Roosevelt," *American Monthly Review of Reviews* (August 1900), p. 182.
205   "exposing jobbery" . . . city's closets: Ibid., p. 181.
205   "I loved him": Jacob Riis, *The Making of an American*, p. 328.
205   "one of my truest": TR, "Jacob Riis," *Outlook*, June 6, 1914, p. 284.
205   "two sides . . . were hardest": TR, *An Autobiography*, p. 170.
205   "He had the most flaming . . . mere preacher": TR, "Jacob Riis," *Outlook*, June 6, 1914, p. 284.
206   "who looked at life": TR, *An Autobiography*, p. 169.
206   "He is a personal friend": TR to Horace E. Scudder, Aug. 16, 1895, in *LTR*, Vol. 1, p. 472.
206   his "state of mind" . . . "wise" mentors: Stinson, *Lincoln Steffens*, p. 143.
206   "With astonishment": LS, *The Autobiography*, p. 248.
207   "One police captain": LS to Joseph Steffens, Dec. 15, 1894, in LS et al., *Letters of Lincoln Steffens*, Vol. 1, p. 107.
207   a sizable fortune of $350,000: Morris, *The Rise of Theodore Roosevelt*, p. 485.
207   Alec "Clubber" Williams . . . the Lexow Committee: LS, *The Autobiography*, p. 252.
207   "supreme gift . . . explain themselves": *NYT*, Aug. 10, 1936.
207   "a clean breast . . . the whole rotten business": LS, *The Autobiography*, p. 273.
207   "on the square": Ibid.
207   "full publicity": Bishop, *Theodore Roosevelt and His Time*, Vol. 1, p. 59.
207   "in almost daily": Ibid., p. 62.
207   "There began between": Ibid., p. 58.
208   "No political influence": LS, "The Real Roosevelt," *Ainslee's Magazine* (December 1898), p. 481.
208   "would spare no man": LS, Scrapbook 1, LS Papers.
208   a route mapped out in advance: Riis, *The Making of an American*, p. 330.
208   those whom he discovered sleeping: New York *Sun*, June 8, 1895.
208   "What's that . . . fan him to death": Pringle, *Theodore Roosevelt, A Biography*, p. 139.
208   "A sorrier-looking set": New York *Evening Post*, June 7, 1895.
208   "Roosevelt on Patrol": New York *Sun*, June 8, 1895, Clipping Scrapbook, TRC.
208   "patrolman hunt . . . a new epoch": New York *Sun*, June 8, 1895, Clipping Scrapbook, TRC.
208   "Police Commissioner Roosevelt": *San Antonio* [TX] *Daily Light*, June 14, 1895.
208   became an alluring subject: Morris, *The Rise of Theodore Roosevelt*, p. 495.
209   "A pair of gold-mounted": New York *Sun*, June 23, 1895.
209   "Few men": Chanler, *Roman Spring*, p. 196.
209   "These midnight rambles": TR to ARC, June 23, 1895, in *LTR*, Vol. 1, p. 463.
209   "though each meant": TR to ARC, June 16, 1895, in ibid., p. 462.
209   "It is one thing": TR, *An Autobiography*, p. 200.
209   "tore down unfit": Riis, *The Making of an American*, p. 344.
209   "the tap-root" of corruption: Riis, *Theodore Roosevelt*, p. 138.
209   "The corrupt would never": LS, "The Real Roosevelt," *Ainslee's Magazine* (December 1898), p. 483.
209   it "is altogether too strict": TR to ARC, June 30, 1895, in *LTR*, Vol. 1, p. 464.
209   "Is there any other way": LS, "The Real Roosevelt," *Ainslee's Magazine* (December 1898), p. 483.
209   harbor "no protected class": TR, *An Autobiography*, p. 191.
210   "to a most limited extent": TR to HCL, Aug. 22, 1895, in TR and Henry Cabot Lodge, *Selections from the Correspondence of Theodore Roosevelt and Henry Cabot Lodge, 1884–1918* (New York: Charles Scribner's Sons, 1925), Vol. 1, p. 165.
210   "The police force became": Riis, *The Making of an American*, p. 329.
210   "I have never been": TR to HCL, July 20, 1895, in *LTR*, Vol. 1, p. 469.
210   "You are the biggest   wrecked the Republican Party": Avery Andrews, "Citizen in Action: The Story of T.R. as Police Commissioner," Unpublished typescript, n.d., TRC.

210   Reports surfaced: *The Journal* (New York), Aug. 6, 1895, Clipping Scrapbook, TRC.

210   "the next bomb": New York *World*, Aug. 7, 1895, in Clipping Scrapbook, TRC.

210   Rumors circulated: *NYT*, Jan. 4, 1896, Clipping Scrapbook, TRC.

210   "Roosevelt is like a boy": *Ohio Democrat* (New Philadelphia, OH), July 18, 1895.

210   "This was a fight": Bishop, *Theodore Roosevelt and His Time*, Vol. 1, p. 58.

210   "in windows . . . mounted paraders": New York *World*, Sept. 26, 1895.

210   "laughed louder . . . Certainly": *NYT*, Sept. 26, 1895.

210   "That is the . . . Millionaire's Club": New York *Sun*, Sept. 26, 1895.

210   "a striking resemblance": New York *World*, Sept. 26, 1895.

211   "That is really a good stroke": New York *Sun*, Sept. 26, 1895.

211   "shrieking with rage": TR to HCL, July 20, 1895, in *LTR*, Vol. 1, p. 469.

211   "It looked almost": New York *World*, Sept. 26, 1895.

211   "Bully for Teddy! . . . a man!": *Daily Republican* (Decatur, IL), Sept. 27, 1895.

211   "Cheered by Those": *Chicago Evening Journal*, Sept. 26, 1895, reprinted in *Daily Republican*, Sept. 27, 1895.

211   "a hundred parades": New York *World*, Sept. 26, 1895.

211   "are on the verge": TR to HCL, Oct. 3, 1895, in TR and HCL, *Selections from the Correspondence*, Vol. 1, p. 181.

211   "has actually been endeavoring": TR to HCL, Oct. 11, 1895, in *LTR*, Vol. 1, pp. 484–85.

211   "Thinks he's the whole board": LS, *The Autobiography*, p. 258.

211   "He talks, talks . . . parted rather coldly": Bishop, *Theodore Roosevelt and His Time*, Vol. 1, p. 63.

211   "armed combat": Morris, *The Rise of Theodore Roosevelt*, p. 529.

212   "His wife and children": Morris, *EKR*, p. 163.

212   "Their gay doings": Ibid.

212   "overstrained . . . the world should stop": HCL to ARC, December [n.d.], 1895, in Rixey, *Bamie*, p. 89.

212   "a chocolate éclair backbone": Wister, *Roosevelt: The Story of a Friendship*, p. 50.

212   "who want to strike down": TR to Cecil Spring Rice, Oct. 8, 1896, in *LTR*, Vol. 1, p. 562.

212   "years of social misery": TR to Cecil Spring Rice, Aug. 5, 1896, in ibid., p. 554.

212   "The halls were jammed": TR to ARC, Oct. 4, 1896, in TR, *Letters from Theodore Roosevelt to Anna Roosevelt Cowles*, p. 194.

213   "He gave all of his time": Wood, *Roosevelt As We Knew Him*, p. 42.

213   "the happiest . . . really worth living": Riis, *Theodore Roosevelt*, p. 131.

213   "had no heart in it": Ibid., p. 151.

213   "reform was . . . did come back": LS, *The Autobiography*, p. 181.

213   "The end of the reign . . . 'reform cop' is retired": New York *Evening Post*, April 15, 1897.

213   "the proudest single . . . brain and will power": LS, "The Real Roosevelt," *Ainslee's Magazine* (December 1898), p. 480.

213   people who had "failed in life": Morris, *The Rise of Theodore Roosevelt*, p. 550.

213   "I became more set": TR, *An Autobiography*, p. 201.

214   loosening the "steel chain": Goldman, *Rendezvous with Destiny*, p. 85.

214   "more than any he has ever": HHT, *Recollections of Full Years*, p. 30.

214   "Perhaps it is the comfort": Pringle, *Life and Times*, Vol. 1, p. 148.

214   "I have been . . . want of time": WHT to HHT, Dec. 10, 1892, WHTP.

214   "The Bar here . . . body of men": WHT to HHT, Nov. 26, 1895, WHTP.

214   "They have eight bedrooms": WHT to HHT, Nov. 21, 1892, WHTP.

214   "He is absolutely": Lyle, "Taft: A Career of Big Tasks," *The World's Work* (September 1907).

215   "Stop that! . . . to the case": Pringle, *Life and Times*, Vol. 1, p. 126.

215   Taft edited the document himself: Lyle, "Taft: A Career of Big Tasks," *The World's Work* (September 1907).

215   "over again and again": Ibid.

215   "holding that city . . . a civil war": WHT to HHT, July 9, 1984, WHTP.

215   killed "to make an impression": WHT to HHT, July 8, 1894, WHTP.

216   "I hate the . . . nothing to reporters": WHT to HHT, July 4, 1894, WHTP.

216   packing the court "to suffocation": WHT to HHT, July 11, 1894, WHTP.

216   "the last sentence": WHT to HHT, July 13, 1894, WHTP.

216   took almost an hour: Ibid.

216   "had the right to organize . . . employment are unsatisfactory": "Thomas vs. Cincinnati, New Orleans & Texas Pacific Railway Company," *Federal Reporter*, Vol. 62 (St. Paul: West Publishing Co., 1894), pp. 817–18.

216   "urged a peaceable . . . against their employers": Ibid.

217   not "as Police Commissioner": Hurwitz, *Theodore Roosevelt and Labor*, p. 172.

217   "applauded him to the echo": Riis, *The Making of an American*, p. 333.

217 "one railroad worker": John Fabian Witt, "Toward a New History of American Accident Law: Classical Tort Law and the Cooperative First-Party Insurance Movement," *Harvard Law Review* (January 2001), pp. 694–95, 719–20.

217 he would later be vindicated when in 1908: Pringle, *Life and Times*, Vol. 1, p. 139.

218 One brakeman was working: See "Narramore v. Cleveland, Cincinnati, Chicago and St. Louis Railway Company," *Federal Reporter*, Vol. 96 (1899).

218 "a dead letter": Pringle, *Life and Times*, Vol. 1, p. 141.

218 injured employees successfully cited: Witt, "Toward a New History of American Accident Law," *Harvard Law Review* (January 2001), pp. 776–77.

218 "to give the defendants": Pringle, *Life and Times*, Vol. 1, p. 145.

218 "Iron Pipe Trust Illegal": Arnold, *Remaking the Presidency,* p. 78.

218 "precisely the same": New York *World*, Feb. 15, 1898.

219 "The deanship is": WHT to HHT, July 1, 1897, WHTP.

219 "I wish I could make": WHT to HHT, Nov. 26, 1895, WHTP.

219 "a bad taste": WHT to HHT, Nov. 23, 1894, WHTP.

219 "something to say": HHT to WHT, June 23, 1895, WHTP.

219 "I shall use you": WHT to HHT, June 28, 1895, WHTP.

219 "the prominent names . . . fizzle of mine": WHT to HHT, July 13, 1895, WHTP.

219 "a happy summer home": Mabel Boardman, "The Summer Capital," *Outlook*, Sept. 25, 1909.

219 "whole cargo of Tafts": Robert Lee Dunn, *William Howard Taft, American* (Boston: Chapple, 1908), pp. 34, 43.

219 "He played eighteen . . . has got to burn around me": Taft, *Memories and Opinions*, pp. 107–09.

220 Nellie Taft . . . immersed herself in the civic life: HHT to WHT, Nov. 19, 1892; June 5, 1893; Nov. 11, 16, 20, & 24, 1893; Dec. 4, 1893, WHTP.

220 Nellie found time . . . president of the Orchestral Association: Anthony, *Nellie Taft*, pp. 110–20.

220 "My love for . . . me to know": WHT to HHT, Feb. 6, 1894, WHTP.

220 fancied herself "the new woman": WHT to HHT, June 27, 1897, WHTP.

220 "It is so delightful": HHT to WHT, July 6, 1896, WHTP.

221 "I should have much preferred": WHT to HHT, Mar. 26, 1896, WHTP.

221 "I want peace": Mrs. Bellamy (Maria Longworth) Storer, "How Theodore Roosevelt Was Appointed Assistant Secretary of the Navy: A Hitherto Unrelated Chapter of History," *Harper's Weekly*, June 1, 1912.

221 "The truth is": AB, *Taft and Roosevelt*, Vol. 2, p. 441.

221 "Judge Taft": HCL to TR, Mar. 8, 1897, in TR and HCL, *Selections from the Correspondence*, Vol. 1, p. 252.

222 "Give him a chance": Storer, "How Theodore Roosevelt Was Appointed . . . ," *Harper's Weekly*, June 1, 1912.

222 "more than once": AB, *Taft and Roosevelt*, Vol. 2, p. 441.

222 "would rather welcome a foreign war": Wagenknecht, *Seven Worlds*, p. 247.

222 "soldierly virtues . . . slothful, timid": *NYT*, June 3, 1897.

222 "The victories of peace": Wagenknecht, *Seven Worlds*, p. 248.

222 "seen the dead piled up": Evan Thomas, *The War Lovers: Roosevelt, Lodge, Hearst, and the Rush to Empire, 1898* (Boston: Little, Brown, 2010), p. 229.

222 "Every man": TR, "A Colonial Survival," in Hermann Hagedorn, ed., *Literary Essays*, Vol. 12 of *WTR*, p. 306.

222 "became convinced": TR, *An Autobiography*, p. 208.

222 incarcerating nearly a third: James Bradley, *The Imperial Cruise: A Secret History of Empire and War* (Boston: Little, Brown, 2009), p. 71.

222 "on the ground of . . . material gain": Pringle, *Theodore Roosevelt: A Biography*, p. 176.

222 exercised a "free hand": TR to ARC, Aug. 21, 1897, in TR, *Letters from Theodore Roosevelt to Anna Roosevelt Cowles*, p. 208.

222 He generated war plans: RSB, "Theodore Roosevelt: A Character Sketch," *McClure's* (November 1898), p. 23.

223 "I am having immense": TR to Bellamy Storer, Aug. 19, 1897, in *LTR*, Vol. 1, p. 655.

223 "it is not easy": Pringle, *Theodore Roosevelt: A Biography*, p. 175.

223 "There isn't the slightest": TR to John Davis Long, June 22, 1897, in *LTR*, Vol. 1, pp. 630–31.

223 "You must be tired": Thomas, *The War Lovers*, p. 174.

223 "stay there just exactly": TR to John Davis Long, Aug. 26, 1897, in *LTR*, Vol. 1, p. 662.

223 fortunate to avoid Washington: TR to John Davis Long, Sept. 15, 1897, in ibid., p. 675.

223 "an act of friendly courtesy": Morris, *The Rise of Theodore Roosevelt*, p. 596.

223 "an act of . . . Havana tomorrow": TR to Benjamin Harrison Diblee, Feb. 16, 1898, in *LTR*, Vol. 1, p. 775.

223 "It seemed as . . . General Miles": IMT, *All in the Day's Work*, pp. 189–90.

223 "vacillated between": Ibid., p. 189.

223 "suspension of judgment": IMT, "President McKinley in War Times," *McClure's* (July 1898), p. 211.

223 "excited goings-on . . . an invading army": IMT, *All in the Day's Work*, pp. 189–90.

224 Roosevelt's "amazing" personality: IMT to RSB, May 3, 1911, RSB Papers.

224 "I am more grieved": TR to William Sheffield Cowles, Mar. 30, 1898, in *LTR*, Vol. 2, p. 804.

224 "weakness . . . ludicrous than painful": "Theodore Roosevelt's Diaries—IV," *Personality* (July 1928), p. 65.

224 "The only effective forces": Bishop, *Theodore Roosevelt and His Time*, Vol. 1, pp. 90–91.

224 "warlike element": IMT, "President McKinley in War Times," *McClure's* (July 1898), p. 221.

224 "too much" for McKinley: IMT, *All in the Day's Work*, p. 189.

224 "He steadily grew paler": IMT, "President McKinley in War Times," *McClure's* (July 1898), p. 223.

224 "proceed at once . . . utmost endeavor": H. W. Brands, *Bound to Empire: The United States and the Philippines* (New York: Oxford University Press, 1992), p. 23.

224 "Keep full of . . . the Asiatic coast": TR to George Dewey, Feb. 25, 1898, in *LTR*, Vol. 1, p. 784.

224 "if it had not been": AB, *Taft and Roosevelt*, Vol. 2, p. 441.

224 "In all its earlier . . . best of the old": IMT, *All in the Day's Work*, pp. 195–96.

225 "a continuous flow of war articles": Ibid., p. 196.

225 "The editors of *McClure's* . . . historical value": "McClure's Magazine in War Times," *McClure's* (June 1898), p. 206.

225 "could not run away . . . to serve it?" IMT, *All in the Day's Work*, p. 195.

225 "a triumph of the new journalism": Hofstadter, *The Age of Reform: From Bryan to F.D.R.*, p. 191.

225 Baker calculated . . . every transmitted word: RSB, "How the News of the War Is Reported," *McClure's* (September 1898), pp. 491–94.

226 "It is a little short": RSB to to J. Stannard Baker, May 1, 1898, RSB Papers.

226 his paper . . . collapsed into insolvency: Thomas, *The War Lovers*, p. 271.

226 "Populists stopped . . . flags fluttering everywhere": WAW, "When Johnny Went Marching Out," *McClure's* (September 1898), pp. 199–203.

226 "have not been . . . entire four years": George B. Waldron, "The Cost of War," *McClure's* (June 1898), pp. 169–70.

227 "day and night": "McClure's Magazine in War Times," *McClure's* (June 1898), p. 206.

227 "Having tasted blood": IMT, *All in the Day's Work*, p. 196.

227 "For weeks we could not tell": TR to Brooks Adams, Mar. 21, 1898, in *LTR*, Vol. 1, p. 798.

227 A dangerous operation: TR to ARC, Mar. 7, 1898, in ibid., p. 790.

227 "kind of a nervous breakdown": TR to William Sheffield Cowles, Mar. 29, 1898, in *LTR*, Vol. 2, p. 803.

227 "You know what": AB to his mother, Oct. 21, 1908, in Abbott, ed., *Letters of Archie Butt*, p. 146.

227 "that a war hardly seemed": Arthur Lubow, *The Reporter Who Would Be King: A Biography of Richard Harding Davis* (New York: Scribner, 1992), front matter.

228 "We knew his face": Ibid., p. 1.

228 "queer, strained humility": TR, "A Colonial Survival," in *WTR*, Vol. 12, p. 301.

228 "He apparently considered . . . table during dinner": TR to James Brander Matthews, Dec. 6, 1892, in *LTR*, Vol. 1, p. 299.

228 "absolutely the very best": Richard Harding Davis and Charles Belmont Davis, *Adventures and Letters of Richard Harding Davis* (New York: Charles Scribner's Sons, 1917), p. 191.

228 "This is the best crowd": Ibid., pp. 195–96.

229 "jumped up . . . Americans in Cuba": Edward Marshall, *The Story of the Rough Riders, 1st U.S. Volunteer Cavalry: The Regiment in Camp and on the Battle Field* (New York: G. W. Dillingham Co., 1899), p. 104.

229 "He was suffering": Richard Harding Davis, *The Cuban and Porto Rican Campaigns* (New York: Charles Scribner's Sons, 1898), p. 163.

229 "If the men . . . 'shown more courage'": RHD and Davis, *Adventures and Letters*, pp. 196–97.

230 "No one who saw": Lubow, *The Reporter Who Would Be King*, p. 185.

230 "charging the rifle-pits": RHD, *The Cuban and Porto Rican Campaigns*, p. 217.

230 "Up, up they went . . . never quite to be got over": Quoted in Riis, *Theodore Roosevelt*, pp. 168–70.

230 "had single-handedly": Lubow, *The Reporter Who Would Be King*, p. 195.

230 "Except for Roosevelt": Ibid.

231 lived in constant anxiety: Morris, *EKR*, p. 181.

231 "These dreadful days": Rixey, *Bamie*, p. 123.

231 "for the sake of the children": Thomas, *The War Lovers*, p. 317.

231 "I do not want": Ibid., p. 279.

231 "looked the picture . . . the Cuban campaign": *NYT*, Aug. 15, 1898.

231 "bubbled over . . . could have been with us": New York *World*, Aug. 6, 1898.

231 "the sober judgment . . . any bloodshed": RSB to J. Stannard Baker, Mar. 8, 1898, RSB Papers.

231 "War excitement here . . . jostling crowds": RSB to J. Stannard Baker, May 1, 1898, RSB Papers.

231 "the thrill": RSB, *American Chronicle*, p. 84.

231 "It was the . . . time usually wasted": Ibid., p. 191.

232 "roomy, comfortable house . . . amassing a fortune": RSB, "Theodore Roosevelt: A Character Sketch," *McClure's* (November 1898), p. 32.

232 "I talked with a number": Ibid., p. 31.

232 "a magnificent example . . . joyousness of disposition": Ibid., pp. 32, 23, 24.

232 "rare power . . . active strength": Ibid., pp. 31–32.

232 "president of the": RSB to J. Stannard Baker, Aug. 30, 1898, RSB Papers.

232 "I want to thank you": TR to RSB, Nov. 4, 1898, RSB Papers.

232 "I was to write": RSB, *American Chronicle*, p. 84.

233 "one of his finest characteristics": RSB, Notebook J, Oct. 6, 1910, RSB Papers.

233 "Once a friend": RSB, "Theodore Roosevelt: A Character Sketch," *McClure's* (November 1898), p. 31.

233 "what was really interesting": Baker, *American Chronicle*, p. 95.

233 "outpouring of marvelous": Ibid., p. 85.

233 most amazing invention "since the days of Jonah": *Sioux Valley News* (Canton, SD), Jan. 5, 1899.

233 "simpler in construction . . . without recharging": RSB, "The Automobile in Common Use," *McClure's* (July 1899), pp. 7, 10.

233 "the first fully verified": Baker, *American Chronicle*, p. 153.

233 "one of the few thinkers": Ibid., p. 110.

233 "My life was being": Ibid., p. 116.

233 "I have been spreading": Ibid., p. 115.

233 "It seemed to me": Ibid., p. 120.

234 McClure's "affectionate interest": IMT to RSB, Sept. 13, 1899, RSB Papers.

234 "I cannot think": Baker, *American Chronicle*, p. 117.

234 "Do only what . . . friends they were": Ibid., p. 123.

234 "as far away as possible": Ibid.

234 "At first": Ibid., p. 124.

234 "across bare ridges . . . sense of freedom": Ibid., p. 125.

234 "I rode or tramped": Ibid., p. 129.

234 "I began again": Ibid.

234 "This being true . . . see and think": Ibid., p. 132.

234 "not a leader . . . live together peaceably": Ibid., pp. 132–33.

235 "one by one": LS, "Theodore Roosevelt, Governor," *McClure's* (May 1899), p. 57.

235 "Should I run?" . . . predicted victory: LS, *The Autobiography*, pp. 342–43.

235 "Take an independent . . . will end him": LS, "Theodore Roosevelt, Governor," *McClure's* (May 1899), p. 58.

235 "I am not a Republican": LS to Joseph Steffens, Oct. 18, 1894, in LS, et al., eds., *Letters of Lincoln Steffens*, Vol. 1, p. 106.

236 "I'm a practical man": LS, *The Autobiography*, p. 346.

236 "good public service . . . by bettering it": LS, "Theodore Roosevelt, Governor," *McClure's* (May 1899), p. 58.

236 "What's the difference? . . . when I'm governor": Ibid., p. 59.

236 "Roosevelt most positively": *NYT*, Sept. 18, 1898.

236 "Oh, what a howl": LS, "Theodore Roosevelt, Governor," *McClure's* (May 1899), p. 58.

236 "received with becoming meekness": *Commercial Advertiser* (New York), Sept. 19, 1898.

236 "Rough Rider . . . taken prisoner": Ibid.

236 "the master mind . . . damning words": Ibid.

237 "He was pacing . . . of his independence": LS, *The Autobiography*, p. 346.

237 "an inspired account": Harry H. Stein, "Theodore Roosevelt and the Press: Lincoln Steffens," *Mid-America* (April 1972), p. 95.

237 "no one asked": *Commercial Advertiser*, Sept. 20, 1898.

237 "Before you say anything": LS, "Theodore Roosevelt, Governor," *McClure's* (May 1899), p. 59.

237 "that he would be unable": *Commercial Advertiser*, Sept. 20, 1898.

237 "It is hard": LS, "Theodore Roosevelt, Governor," *McClure's* (May 1899), p. 60.

237 "It looked as though . . . allowed to go his way": Ibid.

238 "He stumped the State": Ibid.

238 "The fire and school bells": *NYT*, Oct. 27, 1898.

238 "seventeen feet": *Commercial Advertiser*, Oct. 26, 1898.

238 his "presence was everything": William T. O'Neil to J. S. Van Duzer, Nov. 1, 1898, in *LTR*, Vol. 2, pp. 885–86.

238 "that indefinable 'something' ": *Commercial Advertiser*, Oct. 26, 1898.

238 "probable size . . . an omen of victory": Riis, *Theodore Roosevelt*, pp. 204–05.

238 "Young gentlemen": LS, "The Real Roosevelt," *Ainslee's Magazine* (December 1898), p. 484.

CHAPTER NINE: Governor and Governor General

Page

239 the day Roosevelt was inaugurated: *New York Tribune*, Jan. 3, 1899.

239 "There never was such a mass": New York *World*, Jan. 3, 1899.

239 "the desks and seats": *NYT*, Jan. 3, 1899.

239 "A deafening outburst": Ibid.

239 "stood for a moment . . . touch of human nature": *Boston Daily Globe*, Jan. 3, 1899.

240 "He is a party man . . . first consideration": *New York Tribune*, Jan. 3, 1899.

240 "if we do not work . . . of the people": *NYT*, Jan. 3, 1899.

240 "It was a solemn": EKR to Emily Carow, Jan. 3, 1899, TRC.

240 "physically to cringe . . . as well as the guinea pigs": New York *Sun*, Jan. 1, 1899.

240 "usually an extremely . . . down the room": Parsons, *Perchance Some Day*, p. 123.

240 transforming . . . into a comfortable family home: Morris, *EKR*, p. 193.

241 "If only I could wake": EKR to HCL, January [n.d.], 1899, Lodge-Roosevelt Correspondence, Mass. Hist. Soc.

241 "Edith will never enjoy": TR to Maria Longworth Storer, Feb. 18, 1899, in *LTR*, Vol. 2, p. 949.

241 "perfect taste . . . her mind is made up": *Hayward* [CA] *Review*, Feb. 10, 1899.

241 "Everything about her speaks": *Des Moines* [IA] *Daily News*, Dec. 7, 1900.

241 "There's honor even . . . respect that wish": *Lima* [OH] *Daily News*, Mar. 9, 1899.

241 "represented him": *Sandusky* [OH] *Star*, May 24, 1899.

241 "ever on his feet . . . knows the Governor": "A Day with Governor Roosevelt," *NYT Illustrated Magazine*, April 23, 1899.

242 "plunge at once . . . affairs of the State": Ibid.

242 he would visit New York City: *Commercial Advertiser*, Jan. 23, 1899.

242 "touch Platt": New York *Evening Post*, Oct. 2, 1899.

242 "so belittled . . . some party boss": *The Argus* (Albany, NY), Dec. 14, 1899.

242 "the irrational independents": TR to Maria Longworth Storer, Dec. 2, 1899, in *LTR*, Vol. 2, p. 1101.

242 "solemn reformers . . . sinister": TR, *An Autobiography*, p. 288.

242 "I have met many": TR to Lucius Burrie Swift, Feb. 13, 1900, in *LTR*, Vol. 2, p. 1182.

243 "an understanding . . . reasons for them": LS, *The Autobiography*, p. 351.

243 "T.R. was a very practical": Ibid., p. 349.

243 "appealing directly . . . over the heads": TR, *An Autobiography*, p. 280.

243 "the séance . . . information to draw upon": *Commercial Advertiser*, Jan. 16, 1899.

243 workers would most benefit: G. Wallace Chessman, *Governor Theodore Roosevelt: The Albany Apprenticeship, 1898–1900* (Cambridge, MA: Harvard University Press, 1965), p. 202.

244 "I think that perhaps": TR to Jacob Riis, May 2, 1900, in *LTR*, Vol. 2, p. 1284.

244 "It was on one . . . living in the rooms": Riis, *Theodore Roosevelt*, p. 217.

244 "I do not think . . . in any shape": Ibid., p. 219.

244 to revise the code: Janet B. Pascal, *Jacob Riis: Reporter and Reformer* (Oxford: Oxford University Press, 2005), pp. 145–48.

244 "the grudging and querulous": TR, *An Autobiography*, p. 288.

244 legislation establishing an eight-hour . . . considerable progress: Ibid., p. 289.

245 "We arrived just as": Gifford Pinchot, *Breaking New Ground* (New York: Harcourt, Brace, & Co., 1947), p. 145.

245 "had the honor": Ibid.

245 "was the most important": Douglas Brinkley, *The Wilderness Warrior: Theodore Roosevelt and the Crusade for America* (New York: Harper, 2009), p. 356.

245 "as if it were . . . the Audubon Movement": Ibid., p. 358.

245 "I need hardly say . . . Polybius or Livy": TR to Frank M. Chapman, Feb. 16, 1899, in *LTR*, Vol. 2, p. 948.

246 "got on fairly well": TR, *An Autobiography*, p. 290.

246 "the storm of protest": Ibid., p. 298.

246 "only imperfectly understood . . . the good of the party": Ibid., p. 274.

246 "gentlemen's understanding . . . invisible empire": Ibid., p. 275.

246 "that it was a matter": Ibid., p. 298.

246 "had been suffered": Ibid.

246 "into sudden prominence": *NYT*, Mar. 21, 1899.

246 "radical legislation . . . as its champion": Thomas Platt to TR, May 6, 1899, TRC.
246 "consider the whole question": Ibid.
247 "The time to tax": *New York Tribune*, Mar. 29, 1900.
247 "Roosevelt Stops Franchise Tax": Chessman, *Governor Theodore Roosevelt*, p. 139.
247 "could get a show": TR, *An Autobiography*, p. 302.
247 "It was said to-day . . . He appreciates courage": *Commercial Advertiser*, April 28, 1899.
247 "Right in the solar plexus": Ibid.
247 the stock market suffered a significant drop: Chessman, *Governor Theodore Roosevelt*, p. 147.
247 "You will make . . . not to sign": Thomas Platt to TR, May 6, 1899, TRC.
247 "When the subject . . . various altruistic ideas": Ibid.
247 "Communistic or Socialistic": TR, *An Autobiography*, p. 299.
248 "created a good . . . State of New York": Thomas Platt to TR, May 6, 1899, TRC.
248 "I do not believe . . . the public burdens": TR to Thomas Platt, May 8, 1899, TRC.
248 "under no circumstances": Ibid.
248 "Some of the morning newspapers": *Commercial Advertiser* (New York), May 20, 1899.
249 "any taxes": Chessman, *Governor Theodore Roosevelt*, p. 152.
249 "Persistent efforts . . . just and reasonable": *Commercial Advertiser*, May 29, 1899.
249 "Passage of the amended": Ibid.
249 "Would you let me": TR to WAW, May 25, 1899, in *LTR*, Vol. 2, p. 1015.
249 "a young fellow named": WAW, *The Autobiography*, p. 297.
249 "a tallish . . . physical joy of life": WAW, "Remarks at the Theodore Roosevelt Memorial Association, New York, N.Y.," Oct. 27 [n.y.], White Papers.
250 "We walked": Ibid.
250 "the yearnings . . . of wealth and income": Ibid.
250 "He sounded": WAW, *The Autobiography*, p. 297.
250 "youth . . . into the new": Ibid., p. 298.
250 "the splendor . . . never shall again": Ibid., p. 297.
250 "Between his newspaper": Thaddeus Seymour, Jr., *A Progressive Partnership: Theodore Roosevelt and the Reform Press*, (Madison, WI: University of Wisconsin Press, 1985), pp. 159–60.
250 "I read it with": WAW, *The Autobiography*, p. 299.
250 "with the zeal": Seymour, "A Progressive Partnership: Theodore Roosevelt and the Reform Press," p. 163.
251 In Topeka . . . "a rousing reception": *Kansas City Star*, June 24, 1899.
251 "cannon boomed": Ibid.
251 hatbands promoting Roosevelt: Kohlsaat, *From McKinley to Harding*, p. 77.
251 "No public man": *Emporia* [KS] *Gazette*, June 29, 1899.
251 "Governor Roosevelt": *Kansas City Star*, June 26, 1899.
251 "had a larger crowd": *Emporia* [KS] *Gazette*, June 29, 1899.
251 "without either wiring . . . same thing for me": Kohlsaat, *From McKinley to Harding*, p. 78.
251 "telling of the sentiment": Ibid.
251 "Oh mentor!": TR to Herman H. Kohlsaat, Aug. 12, 1899, in ibid., p. 83.
251 "Was my McKinley": Ibid., p. 81.
252 Roosevelt wrote a warm letter to White: TR to WAW, July 1, 1899, in *LTR*, Vol. 2, p. 1028.
252 "we were planning for 1904": WAW, *The Autobiography*, p. 327.
252 "bearing great fruit . . . of their wisdom": WAW to TR, June 29, 1899, White Papers.
252 "When the war": WAW to TR, Aug. 29, 1901, in WAW and Johnson, eds., *Selected Letters of William Allen White*, p. 41.
252 "I think the 'Man' ": TR to WAW, Oct. 28, 1899, in *LTR*, Vol. 2, p. 1091.
252 "You are among the men": TR to WAW, Feb. 6, 1900, in ibid., p. 1169.
253 "in a great quandary": TR to WAW, Aug. 15, 1899, TRC.
253 "growth of popular unrest": TR to Herman H. Kohlsaat, Aug. 12, 1899, in *LTR*, Vol. 2, p. 1045.
253 "surprised to find . . . the quack": TR to HCL, Aug. 10, 1899, in ibid., p. 1048.
253 "such a good fellow . . . vanished": Ibid., p. 1047.
253 "by means which are utterly": Elihu Root to TR, Dec. 13, 1899, in Philip Jessup, *Elihu Root* (New York: Dodd, Mead & Co., 1938), Vol. 1, p. 209.
253 "Oh, Lord!": TR to Elihu Root, Dec. 15, 1899, in ibid., p. 210.
253 "In our great cities . . . remedies can be applied": *NYT*, Jan. 4, 1900.
254 "The first essential . . . which we can now invoke": Ibid.
254 "the adoption of": Ibid.
254 "the party of . . . enlightened conservatism": Chessman, *Governor Theodore Roosevelt*, p. 157.
254 Odell warned . . . leave New York State: Pringle, *Theodore Roosevelt: A Biography*, p. 211.
254 information on "their structure and finance": Chessman, *Governor Theodore Roosevelt*, p. 174.

255 Platt's "right-hand" man: TR, *An Autobiography*, p. 290.

255 "no matter what": *Commercial Advertiser*, Dec. 12, 1898.

255 "issued an ultimatum . . . made up my mind": TR, *An Autobiography*, p. 291.

255 "Why does he . . . cheek by jowl?": New York *Evening Post*, Jan. 19, 1900.

256 "thoroughly upright and capable": TR to Henry L. Sprague, Jan. 26, 1900, in *LTR*, Vol. 2, p. 1141.

256 "I have always . . . triumph for rascality": TR to Henry L. Sprague, Jan. 26, 1900, in ibid.

256 "The outcome of": *Commercial Advertiser*, Jan. 25, 1900.

256 "honest administration . . . the Colonel before Santiago": New York *Evening Post*, Jan. 29, 1900.

256 "Could they assail . . . they have Roosevelt": *Commercial Advertiser*, Jan. 24, 1900.

256 "the dogs of the *Evening Post*": TR to ARC, Feb. 27, 1900, in TR and ARC, *Letters from Theodore Roosevelt to Anna Roosevelt Cowles*, p. 238.

256 "I value you": TR to Joseph Bucklin Bishop, April 17, 1899, in *LTR*, Vol. 2, pp. 989–90.

256 Roosevelt encouraged Bishop to visit: TR to Joseph Bucklin Bishop, Feb. 16, 1899, in ibid., pp. 947–48.

257 "I will explain": TR to Joseph Bucklin Bishop, April 18, 1899, TRC.

257 "with the most unaffected dread": *NYT*, April 12, 1899.

257 "emphatically not one of the 'fool reformers' ": TR to Joseph Bucklin Bishop, April 14, 1899, in *LTR*, Vol. 2, p. 987.

257 "positive orders to . . . to break down Roosevelt": TR to Lucius Burrie Smith, Feb. 13, 1900, in ibid., p. 1182.

257 "You are about fourteen": TR to Joseph Bucklin Bishop, April 13, 1900, TRC.

257 "I thank Heaven": TR to Joseph Bucklin Bishop, May 2, 1900, TRC.

257 "Good Lord": Ibid.

257 "I need not tell you": TR to Joseph Bucklin Bishop, May 4, 1900, in *LTR*, Vol. 2, p. 1286.

257 "first acquaintance": Finley Peter Dunne, "Remembrance of Theodore Roosevelt," Unpublished MSS, Dunne Papers.

257 "Tis Th' Biography": "Mr. Dooley," *Harper's Weekly*, Nov. 25, 1899.

258 "I regret to state": TR to Finley Peter Dunne, Nov. 28, 1899, in *LTR*, Vol. 2, p. 1099.

258 "I shall be very happy": Finley Peter Dunne to TR, Jan. 10, 1900, TRP.

258 "I never knew": Finley Peter Dunne, "Remembrance of Theodore Roosevelt," Dunne Papers.

258 "Oh, Governor . . . *Alone in Cuba*": Elmer Ellis, *Mr. Dooley's America: A Life of Finley Peter Dunne* (New York: Alfred A. Knopf, 1941), p. 146.

258 "an experiment": LS, "Governor Roosevelt—As an Experiment: Incidents of Conflict in a Term of Practical Politics," *McClure's* (June 1900), p. 109.

258 "the organization doesn't": Ibid., p. 112.

258 "obvious solution . . . and successful too": Ibid.

259 "Your TR article": McClure to LS, Mar. 14, 1899, LS Papers.

259 "would be tempting . . . the party men": TR to George Hinckley-Lyman, Jan. 25, 1900, in *LTR*, Vol. 2, p. 1140.

259 Only "great luck . . . own throat": TR to Henry Clay Payne, Feb. 2, 1900, in ibid., p. 1162.

259 was a fait accompli: TR to George Hinckley-Lyman, Jan. 25, 1900, in ibid., pp. 1139–40.

259 "not an office . . . should achieve nothing": TR to Thomas Platt, Feb. 1, 1900, in ibid., p. 1156.

259 "tempting Providence": TR to ARC, Feb. 2, 1900, in ibid., p. 1159.

259 "the true stepping stone": HCL to TR, Feb. 2, 1900, in TR and HCL, *Selections from the Correspondence*, Vol. 1, p. 444.

259 "in New York . . . figurehead": TR to HCL, Feb. 2, 1900, in *LTR*, Vol. 2, p. 1160.

259 "the money question . . . up all winter": TR to HCL, Jan. 30, 1900, in ibid., p. 1153.

259 a great "comfort": EKR to Emily Carow, Oct. 15, 1899, TRC.

260 "would be a . . . continual anxiety": TR to HCL, Jan. 30, 1900, in *LTR*, Vol. 2, p. 1153.

260 languished in "oblivion": Diana D. Healy, *America's Vice-Presidents: Our First Forty-three Vice-Presidents and How They Got to Be Number Two* (New York: Atheneum, 1984), p. 133.

260 "if the Vice-Presidency": TR to HCL, Jan. 30, 1900, in *LTR*, Vol. 2, p. 1154.

260 "prove to the . . . alone as a nation": TR to H. K. Love, Nov. 24, 1900, in ibid., p. 1442.

260 "a violent departure": *Woodland* [CA] *Daily Democrat*, Dec. 29, 1900.

260 "little better than traitors": TR to HCL, Jan. 26, 1899, in *LTR*, Vol. 2, p. 923.

260 "We shall be branded": TR, "Address on the occasion of the presentation of a sword to Commodore Philip, New York," Feb. 3, 1899, in *WTR*, Vol. 14, p. 312.

260 "would not be pleasant": TR to Maria Longworth Storer, Dec. 2, 1899, in *LTR*, Vol. 2, p. 1101.

260 "emphatically worth doing": TR to HCL, January 22, 1900, in TR and HCL, *Selections from the Correspondence*, Vol. 1, p. 437.

260 "the chief pleasure": TR to Frédéric René Coudert, July 3, 1901, in *LTR*, Vol. 3, p. 105.

261 "if we shrink": TR, *The Strenuous Life: Essays and Addresses* (New York: The Century Co., 1902), pp. 20–21.

261 "the ideal man": HCL to TR, Jan. 27, 1900, in TR and HCL, *Selections from the Correspondence*, Vol. 1, p. 440.

261 irreversibly "planted": TR to HCL, Dec. 11, 1899, in ibid., p. 1107.

261 "declare decisively": TR to HCL, Feb. 2, 1900, in *LTR*, Vol. 2, p. 1160.

261 "There are lots": HCL to TR, April 16, 1900, in TR and HCL, *Selections from the Correspondence*, Vol. 1, p. 459.

261 "You will have . . . office of Vice-President": Wood, *Roosevelt As We Knew Him*, pp. 72–73.

262 "You disagreeable thing . . . not come true": Ibid., pp. 73–74.

262 she and Theodore had had more time together: Morris, *EKR*, p. 200.

262 "I really think": TR to HCL, Aug. 28, 1899, in *LTR*, Vol. 2, p. 1062.

262 "the county fair business": TR to Bellamy Storer, Sept. 11, 1899, in ibid., p. 1068.

262 "You gave my wife . . . every word": Wood, *Roosevelt As We Knew Him*, p. 74.

262 "an even chance . . . any outside ambition": TR to ARC, April 30, 1900, in *LTR*, Vol. 2, p. 1277.

262 "vociferous applause . . . Teddy, Teddy, Teddy": *Washington Times*, June 17, 1900.

262 "There'll Be a Hot": *St. Louis Republic*, June 17, 1900.

262 "he had reason . . . invaded" his room: *New York Tribune*, June 18, 1900.

263 "Round and round . . . drum and bugle": CRR, *My Brother*, p. 197.

263 "Don't you realize": TR to William McKinley, addendum, June 21, 1900, in *LTR*, Vol. 2, p. 1337.

263 "There is not a man": *Washington Times*, June 18, 1900.

263 "These fellows have . . . 'Vice-President'": New York *World*, June 18, 1900.

263 "If you decline": Ibid.

263 "the sun shone brightly": New York *Sun*, June 20, 1900.

263 "the magic . . . of the tumult": *NYT*, June 22, 1900.

263 "when he caught": *New York Tribune*, June 22, 1900.

263 the demonstration subsided: *NYT*, June 22, 1900.

263 "We stand on": TR, "Speech Before the Twelfth Republican National Convention, Philadelphia, Pa., June 21, 1900," in *WTR*, Vol. 14, p. 345.

263 "of rounded periods . . . was beyond them": *New York Tribune*, June 22, 1900.

264 "a little melancholy": TR to Henry White, July 7, 1900, in *LTR*, Vol. 2, p. 1349.

264 "should be a conceited fool": TR to HCL, June 25, 1900, in ibid., p. 1340.

264 "His friends were in despair": Riis, *Theodore Roosevelt*, p. 236.

264 "Oh, how I hate": Parsons, *Perchance Some Day*, p. 134.

264 "had hoped to the last": Hagedorn, *The Roosevelt Family of Sagamore Hill*, p. 89.

264 "get the rest": EKR to Emily Carow, June 22, 1900, TRC.

264 a telegraph boy knocked: WHT, "Address before the National Geographic Society," Washington, DC, Nov. 14, 1913, WHTP.

264 "important business . . . suppose that means?": HHT, *Recollections of Full Years*, p. 32.

264 "He might as well": Pringle, *Life and Times*, Vol. 1, p. 160.

264 "strongly opposed": HHT, *Recollections of Full Years*, p. 32.

264 "contrary to our traditions": Pringle, *Life and Times*, Vol. 1, p. 160.

264 "beside the question . . . governing themselves": HHT, *Recollections of Full Years*, pp. 33–34.

265 "under the most sacred": Pringle, *Life and Times*, Vol. 1, p. 160.

265 "Well . . . you'll be here": WHT to Henry W. Taft and Horace Taft, Jan. 28, 1900, Pringle Papers.

265 "You have had": HHT, *Recollections of Full Years*, p. 34.

265 "didn't sleep a wink . . . climate of Manila": Charles E. Barker, *With President Taft in the White House: Memories of William Howard Taft* (Chicago: A. Kroch & Son, 1947), pp. 23–24.

265 "so grave . . . impeachment": HHT, *Recollections of Full Years*, p. 33.

265 "Yes, of course . . . novel experience": Ibid.

265 "You can do more good": Horace Taft to WHT, Jan. 31, 1900, WHTP.

265 "the rest of . . . [his] colleagues": Henry W. Taft to WHT, Jan. 30, 1900, WHTP.

266 "responsible for success or failure": Pringle, *Life and Times*, Vol. 1, p. 161.

266 "the hardest thing he ever did": HHT, *Recollections of Full Years*, p. 35.

266 "the Philippines business": TR to HCL, Feb. 3, 1900, in *LTR*, Vol. 2, p. 1166.

266 "a very hard . . . to advise with": TR to WHT, Jan. 31, 1899, in ibid., p. 927.

266 "I wish there was": TR to Maria Longworth Storer, Dec. 2, 1899, in ibid., p. 1101.

266 rejoiced in his "final triumph": WHT to TR, Feb. 15, 1900, TRP.

266 "Curiously enough": TR to WHT, Feb. 7, 1900, in *LTR*, Vol. 2, p. 1175.

266 "That it was alluring": HHT, *Recollections of Full Years*, p. 33.

267 "Robert was ten": Ibid., pp. 36–37.

267 "We soon became": Ibid., p. 39.

267 "the most interesting years": Ibid., p. 40.

267 "one of the ablest": Ibid., p. 41.

267 a New England judge . . . and a historian: Ibid., pp. 41–45.

267 relished "the bonds of friendship": Ibid., p. 40.

267 "The populace": Pringle, *Life and Times*, Vol. 1, p. 169.

268 "as a personal reflection": WHT, "Address before the National Geographic Society," Washington, DC, Nov. 14, 1913, WHTP.

268 "We are civil officers . . . as to anyone": Press statement enclosed in WHT to Charles P. Taft, June 2, 1900, WHTP.

268 "the precise kind . . . loftiest of motives": *Harper's Weekly* clipping enclosed in Horace Taft to WHT, July 14, 1900, WHTP.

268 "high canopied . . . would be served": HHT, *Recollections of Full Years*, pp. 102–3, 105.

268 "homely and unpalatial abode": Ibid., p. 211.

269 the large library of books on civil law: WHT to Charles Taft, June 23, 1900, WHTP.

269 At ten o'clock . . . "who wish[ed] to see them": WHT to Charles Taft, July 25, 1900, WHTP.

269 At one o'clock . . . foot for their homes: WHT to Harriet Herron, Jan. 19, 1901, WHTP.

269 "The walk is about . . . strong at meals": Ibid.

269 "policy of conciliation": WHT, "Address before the National Geographic Society," Washington, DC, Nov. 14, 1913, WHTP.

269 "our little brown brothers . . . no friend of mine!": HHT, *Recollections of Full Years*, p. 125.

269 "agitation and discontent": Pringle, *Life and Times*, Vol. 1, p. 177.

269 to treat the Filipinos as "niggers": WHT to Charles P. Taft, June 2, 1900, WHTP.

269 "It is a great mistake": HHT to WHT, July 21, 1900, WHTP.

270 "except a select military circle": HHT, *Recollections of Full Years*, p. 109.

270 "even small gestures": Anthony, *Nellie Taft*, p. 141.

270 "made it a rule": HHT, *Recollections of Full Years*, p. 114.

270 "We always had": Ibid., p. 125.

270 insistence "upon complete racial equality": HHT quoted in Anthony, *Nellie Taft*, p. 248.

270 Filipinos of "wealth and position": WHT to HHT, July 8, 1900, WHTP.

270 "To say that": WHT to Charles P. Taft, June 13, 1901, WHTP.

270 spending a small inheritance: Anthony, *Nellie Taft*, p. 141.

270 "giving [the] wealthy": Pringle, *Life and Times*, Vol. 1, p. 194.

270 "precursors of . . . and binoculars": Stanley Karnow, *In Our Image: America's Empire in the Philippines* (New York: Random House, 1989), p. 196.

270 "enter upon some work": WHT to HHT, July 2, 1900, WHTP.

270 Philippine Constabulary Band . . . international renown: Anthony, *Nellie Taft*, pp. 156–57.

271 the reduction of infant mortality in Manila: Ibid., p. 155.

271 "in the interest of": Ibid., p. 154.

271 He likened her activism: WHT to HHT, June 12, 1900, WHTP.

271 "I wish to record": WHT to HHT, June 18 & 19, 1900, WHTP.

271 "with undisguised surprise": WHT to Charles P. Taft, Aug. 31, 1900, WHTP.

271 had met "congenial companions": HHT, *Recollections of Full Years*, p. 217.

271 "everybody in the world": Ibid., p. 98.

271 Charlie, nicknamed "the tornado": Ibid., p. 54.

271 "an old fashioned quadrille": Ibid., p. 166.

271 "literally dancing": Walter Wellman, "Taft, Trained to Be President," *American Review of Reviews* (June 1908).

271 "unusual size . . . superiority": LTT to WHT, July 9, 1900, WHTP.

272 "a good government . . . prosperous" economy: WHT to HHT, June 15, 1900, WHTP.

272 "ignorant, superstitious people": Pringle, *Life and Times*, Vol. 1, p. 173.

272 "Not that I am": WHT to Annie Roelker, Jan. 19, 1901, WHTP.

272 "a good deal to carry . . . to the campaign": WHT to Charles P. Taft, June 30, 1900, WHTP.

272 "draw in line": Charles P. Taft to WHT, June 23, 1900, WHTP.

272 "I could wish . . . Filipinos as well": WHT to TR, June 27, 1900, TRP.

272 "any help . . . be vice-president": TR to WHT, Aug. 6, 1900, in *LTR*, Vol. 2, p. 1377.

272 "as strong as . . . up to the limit": TR to MAH, June 27, 1900, in ibid., p. 1342.

272 "No candidate . . . on the American stump": Thomas Collier Platt and Louis J. Lang, *The Autobiography of Thomas Collier Platt* (New York: B. W. Dodge & Co., 1910), pp. 396–97.

273 Throughout the evening: *NYT*, Nov. 7, 1900.

273 "tiptoes with excitement . . . McKinley": HHT, *Recollections of Full Years*, p. 141.

273 "My dear Theodore": WHT to TR, Nov. [n.d.], 1900, TRP.

273 "Hardly a day passed": HHT, *Recollections of Full Years*, p. 147.

273 "The attitude of the native": WHT to Charles P. Taft, Jan. 29, 1901, WHTP.
273 "The leaders in Manila . . . welcome a change": WHT to HCL, Jan. 7, 1901, WHTP.
274 "Of course" . . . they came along as well: WHT to Charles Taft, Mar. 17, 1901, WHTP.
274 "greatly pleased . . . friendliest kind of attitude": HHT, *Recollections of Full Years*, p. 154.
274 The desire . . . "manifest on every side": WHT to Horace Taft, April 25, 1901, WHTP.
274 "the streets were crowded": HHT, *Recollections of Full Years*, p. 162.
274 "Spectacular" festivities . . . celebrated their progress: Ibid., pp. 162–65.
274 "a singular experience": Ibid., p. 181.
274 "The responsibilities . . . taking control of things": WHT to TR, May 12, 1901, TRP.
274 "I envy you . . . justifying my existence": TR to WHT, Mar. 12, 1901, in *LTR*, Vol. 3, p. 11.
274 "sympathize with . . . top to the bottom": TR to Maria and Bellamy Storer, April 17, 1901, in ibid., p. 56.
275 "ought to be abolished . . . any advice": TR to Leonard Wood, April 17, 1901, in ibid., p. 59.
275 "I am rather . . . unwarrantable idleness": TR to WHT, April 26, 1901, in ibid., pp. 68–69.
275 "I look forward": WHT to TR, May 12, 1901, TRP.
275 "I doubt if . . . old man": TR to WHT, Mar. 12, 1901, in *LTR*, Vol. 3, p. 12.
275 "music, fireworks": *New Castle [PA] News*, July 3, 1901.
275 "an occasion of . . . his natural size": HHT, *Recollections of Full Years*, pp. 206–7.
276 "a new step . . . popular basis": WHT, "Inaugural Address as Civil Governor of the Philippines," Manila, July 4, 1901, WHTP.
276 democracy "from the top down": Bradley, *The Imperial Cruise*, p. 121.
276 "feudal oligarchy . . . rich and poor": Karnow, *In Our Image*, p. 198.
276 "the wildest . . . of the new governor": *Daily Northwestern* (Oshkosh, WI), July 5, 1901.
276 "In some ways . . . was actually established": HHT, *Recollections of Full Years*, pp. 211–12.
276 "the idea of living": Ibid., p. 212.
276 "all of them . . . bank of the Pasig": Ibid., p. 213.
276 "Army and Navy people . . . among our guests": Ibid., p. 217.
277 "a great society beau": HHT to Harriet Herron, Sept. 2, 1901, WHTP.
277 "You would be amused": HHT to Jennie Anderson, July 17, 1901, in Phyllis Robbins, *Robert A. Taft, Boy and Man* (Cambridge, MA: Dresser, Chapman & Grimes, 1963), p. 67.
277 "It seems idle . . . to say this in public": TR to WHT, July 15, 1901, in *LTR*, Vol. 3, pp. 120–21.
277 professor of history at a university: TR to Hugo Munsterberg, May 7, 1901, in ibid., p. 72.
278 "Of course, I may": TR to Leonard Wood, Mar. 27, 1901, in ibid., p. 39.

CHAPTER TEN: "That Damned Cowboy Is President"

Page
279 "The ship of state": "President McKinley's Death," *The Nation*, Sept. 19, 1901, p. 218.
279 "What changes": *Washington Post*, Sept. 15, 1901, in Arnold, *Remaking the Presidency*, p. 39.
279 "Will he continue": *Minneapolis Journal*, Sept. 15, 1901.
279 prove a "bucking bronco": Kohlsaat, *From McKinley to Harding*, p. 98.
280 "first great duty": New York *Sun*, Sept. 15, 1901, in Mark Sullivan, *Our Times: The United States, 1900–1925* (New York: Charles Scribner's Sons, 1926), Vol. 2, p. 403.
280 presidents had been captive: See Arnold, *Remaking the Presidency*, p. 3.
280 "not depend on": New York *Sun*, Sept. 15, 1901, in Sullivan, *Our Times*, Vol. 2, p. 403.
280 "The conservative policy": *Boston Sunday Globe*, Sept. 15, 1901.
280 "dreaded radicalism . . . was progressive": TR, *An Autobiography*, p. 351.
280 "push . . . the masters of both of us": Ibid., p. 352.
280 "active support": Ibid., p. 354.
280 "one in purpose": *Atlanta Constitution*, Sept. 14, 1901.
280 "In this hour": *New York Tribune*, Sept. 17, 1901.
280 "an unusual request": George Juergens, "Theodore Roosevelt and the Press," *Daedalus* (Fall 1982), p. 113.
281 "keep them posted . . . not to be published": David S. Barry, *Forty Years in Washington* (Boston: Little, Brown, 1924), p. 268.
281 "I am President": Ibid., p. 267.
281 "pop-eyed . . . burning candor": WAW, "Remarks," Oct. 27 [n.y.], White Papers.
281 "be different . . . absolutely unchanged": Ibid.
281 "embarrass him sorely": Rixey, *Bamie*, p. 172.
281 "give the lie": Ibid.
281 "cataract solo of talk": WAW, "Remarks," Oct. 27 [n.y.], White Papers.
281 "Imagine me": Ibid.
281 "the old cannon": WAW, *The Autobiography*, p. 339.

281 "Here you are": TR to WAW, Mar. 12, 1901, in *LTR*, Vol. 3, pp. 10–11.

282 "a frowzy little . . . North at that time": WAW, *The Autobiography*, p. 335.

282 "about his own . . . wreck the machines": Ibid.

282 "untrammeled" greed: WAW, *Emporia* [KS] *Gazette*, Sept. 7, 1901, cited in Johnson, *William Allen White's America*, p. 127.

282 "We reformers . . . that had come to him": LS, *The Autobiography*, pp. 502–3.

282 "Unconsciously . . . a bitter piece": WAW, *The Autobiography*, pp. 339–40.

283 "too scorching": WAW to August Jaccaci, Oct. 23, 1901, in WAW and Johnson, eds., *Selected Letters of William Allen White*, p. 45.

283 "to bring order . . . purchase of privileges": WAW, "Platt," *McClure's* (December 1901), pp. 149–50.

283 an earthworm, "boring . . . inexorable, grinding": Ibid., pp. 148, 153.

283 "to haul both author": *Titusville* [PA] *Morning Herald*, Dec. 19, 1901.

283 "I will get": WAW to John S. Phillips, Dec. 17, 1901, White Papers.

283 "to bring about": Johnson, *William Allen White's America*, p. 135.

283 "who told him the lies": New York *World*, Dec. 19, 1901.

283 "No friend of mine": *Washington Post*, Dec. 18, 1901.

283 "I am perfectly . . . this business out": WAW to TR, Dec. 17, 1901, White Papers.

284 "Not one syllable . . . by the president": WAW to George B. Cortelyou, Dec. 18, 1901, TRC.

284 "The only damage": TR to WAW, Dec. 31, 1901, in *LTR*, Vol. 3, p. 214.

284 "they would welcome": Johnson, *William Allen White's America*, p. 135.

284 "a kind of nervous . . . you all out so": WAW to August Jaccaci, Jan. 21, 1902, White Papers.

284 "Probably no administration": Irwin H. Hoover, *Forty-two Years in the White House* (Boston: Houghton Mifflin, 1934), p. 27.

284 "While he is in": Sullivan, *Our Times*, Vol. 3, pp. 72–73.

284 "The infectiousness": Ibid., Vol. 2, p. 399.

285 "Where Mr. McKinley . . . never means to do so": Walter Wellman, *Chicago Record-Herald*, reprinted in the *Piqua* [OH] *Daily Call*, Nov. 20, 1901.

285 "a right good laugh . . . listens to nobody": Ibid.

285 "darts into the": LS, "The Overworked President," *McClure's* (April 1902), p. 485.

285 "one letter after another": Parsons, *Perchance Some Day*, p. 141.

285 "The room is": LS, "The Overworked President," *McClure's* (April 1902), p. 486.

285 "an overflowing stream": Ibid., p. 489.

285 "to try the President's": *NYT*, Sept. 29, 1901.

285 the "barber's hour": LS, *The Autobiography*, p. 509.

286 "A more skillful": Louis Brownlow, *A Passion for Politics: The Autobiography of Louis Brownlow: First Half* (Chicago: University of Chicago Press, 1955), p. 399.

286 Only "when the barber": LS, *The Autobiography*, p. 510.

286 "Western bullwackers": WAW, *Masks in a Pageant* (New York: The Macmillan Co., 1928), p. 306.

286 "Whether the subject . . . equally at home": Wagenknecht, *Seven Worlds*, p. 32.

286 "point to point . . . down over it": Ibid., p. 14.

286 "finger-marks": Jacob Riis, "Mrs. Roosevelt and Her Children," *Ladies' Home Journal* (August 1902), p. 6.

286 "this or that general": AB to his mother, Oct. 10, 1908, in Abbott, ed., *Letters of Archie Butt*, p. 119.

286 "in afternoon dress . . . should meet ladies": Thayer, *Theodore Roosevelt: An Intimate Biography*, pp. 262–63.

287 "by far the best . . . under discussion": Oscar King Davis, *Released for Publication: Some Inside Political History of Theodore Roosevelt and His Times, 1898–1918* (Boston: Houghton Mifflin, 1925), p. 128.

287 "allowed to become": Riis, "Mrs. Roosevelt and Her Children," *Ladies' Home Journal* (August 1902), p. 5.

287 "I play bear": TR to Alice Lee Roosevelt, Nov. 29, 1901, in *LTR*, Vol. 3, p. 203.

287 "It was the gloomiest": "Mrs. Roosevelt's Address," Oct. 20, 1933, *Roosevelt House Bulletin* (Fall 1933), pp. 2–3.

287 The children . . . pony to ride the elevator: Hoover, *Forty-two Years in the White House*, p. 29; Juergens, "Theodore Roosevelt and the Press," *Daedalus* (Fall 1982), p. 124; Isabella Hagner James, "Memoirs of Isabella Hagner, 1901–1905," *White House History: Journal of the White House Historical Association*, No. 26, p. 61.

287 "Places that had not": Hoover, *Forty-two Years in the White House*, p. 28.

287 "done more to brighten": *Atlanta Constitution*, Oct. 24, 1901.

287 Taft was certain that Roosevelt: WHT to William C. McFarland, Sept. 20, 1901, WHTP.

288 "impulsiveness and": WHT to Joseph Bucklin Bishop, Sept. 20, 1901, in Pringle, *Life and Times*, Vol. 1, p. 211.

288 citing the fortitude, honesty, and intelligence: WHT to Elihu Root, Sept. 26, 1901, in ibid.; WHT to Rev. Rainsford, Sept. 20, 1901, Pringle Papers.

288 to see "the consummation": TR to Joseph Bucklin Bishop, Sept. 20, 1901, in Pringle, *Life and Times*, Vol. 1, p. 210.

288 "In so far as the work": HHT, *Recollections of a Full Life*, p. 224.

288 "only a strenuous man": Horace Taft to WHT, Oct. 14, 1901, WHTP.

288 "I dislike speaking . . . incredibly difficult work": TR, "Governor William H. Taft," *Outlook* (September 1901), p. 166.

288 Unbeknownst to the Americans: Karnow, *In Our Image*, p. 189.

288 hundreds of insurrectionists suddenly charged: Ibid., p. 190.

289 "It was a disaster . . . in our beds any night": HHT, *Recollections of a Full Life*, p. 225.

289 "silly talk": Karnow, *In Our Image*, p. 191.

289 "no prisoners . . . Ten years": Ibid.

289 "Disastrous Fight . . . Slaughtered by Filipinos": *New York Tribune*, Sept. 30, 1901; *Houston Daily Post*, Sept. 30, 1901.

289 "the first severe reverse": *The News* (Frederick, MD), September 30, 1901.

289 "One of the Republicans": WHT to Charles P. Taft, Oct. 15, 1901, WHTP.

289 "in all other parts": WHT to Murat Halstead, Sept. 20, 1901, WHTP.

289 "to such a pitch": WHT to Charles P. Taft, Oct. 15, 1901, WHTP.

289 "Officers take": TR to Horace Taft, Oct. 21, 1901, in Pringle, *Life and Times*, Vol. 1, p. 213.

290 "a dreadful depression": WHT to TR, Sept. 13, 1902, TRP.

290 roving outlaw bands . . . new Board of Health: WHT to Murat Halstead, Sept. 20, 1901, WHTP.

290 "Altogether": WHT to Charles P. Taft, Oct. 15, 1901, WHTP.

290 "While I have none": WHT to Horace Taft, Oct. 21, 1901, WHTP.

290 Helen burst into tears: WHT to Charles P. Taft, Nov. 8, 1901, WHTP.

290 "Come dear am sick": WHT to HHT, Oct. 25, 1901, in Pringle, *Life and Times*, Vol. 1, p. 214.

290 "hire a hall and make a speech": WHT to Charles P. Taft, Nov. 8, 1901, WHTP.

290 "Much better": WHT to HHT, Oct. 26, 1901, in Pringle, *Life and Times*, Vol. 1, p. 214.

290 "peace of mind": WHT to Charles P. Taft, Nov. 8, 1901, WHTP.

290 promising them he would return: James A. Leroy, "Governor Taft's Record in the Philippines," *The Independent*, Jan. 28, 1904, p. 194.

291 "the high summer" . . . Hundreds . . . consolidated into single corporations: George E. Mowry, *Theodore Roosevelt and the Progressive Movement* (Madison: University of Wisconsin Press, 1946), p. 12.

291 "I intend to work": Bishop, *Theodore Roosevelt and His Time*, p. 150.

291 These organizations: WAW, "Platt," *McClure's* (December 1901), p. 150.

291 "just as he would": *NYT*, Jan. 17, 1890.

292 "Wake up . . . lots in the Senate": Lewis L. Gould, *The Most Exclusive Club: A History of the Modern United States Senate* (New York: Basic Books, 2005), p. 10.

292 the title of "national boss": Samuel J. Blythe, "The Passing of the Big Bosses," *Saturday Evening Post*, Feb. 25, 1922, p. 9.

292 "the liaison": Sullivan, *Our Times*, Vol. 2, p. 372.

292 not a single anti-trust suit: Ibid.

292 "In the final analysis": LS, "Great Types of Modern Business & Politics," *Ainslee's Magazine* (October 1901), p. 216.

292 "I told William . . . of the United States!": Sullivan, *Our Times*, Vol. 2, p. 380.

292 "it would be a great": TR to LS, June 24, 1905, in *LTR*, Vol. 4, p. 1254.

292 "would be as foolhardy": New York *World*, Nov. 29, 1901.

292 share an intimacy similar: Sullivan, *Our Times*, Vol. 2, p. 392.

292 "Go slow": Bishop, *Theodore Roosevelt and His Time*, Vol. 1, p. 154.

292 "It would not": TR to MAH, Oct. 16, 1901, in *LTR*, Vol. 3, p. 176.

292 "his was the rising": Sullivan, *Our Times*, Vol. 2, p. 400.

293 "I hope to keep": Nathaniel Wright Stephenson, *Nelson W. Aldrich: A Leader in American Politics* (New York: Charles Scribner's Sons, 1930), p. 175.

293 "a very pretty scene": *Piqua* [OH] *Daily Call*, Nov. 20, 1901.

293 "made more progress": *Decatur* [IL] *Daily Review*, Nov. 2, 1901.

293 "Many scribes": *Daily Nevada State Journal* (Reno, NV), Nov. 21, 1901.

293 "one hair's breadth": TR to Douglas Robinson, Oct. 17, 1901, in *LTR*, Vol. 3, p. 177.

293 "More and more": *Galveston* [TX] *Daily News*, Sept. 3, 1901.

293 "going so far as": Louis A. Coolidge, *An Old-Fashioned Senator: Orville H. Platt, of Connecticut* (New York: G. P. Putnam's Sons, 1910), pp. 445–46.

294 "furnish ammunition . . . in corporate control": Pringle, *Theodore Roosevelt: A Biography*, p. 244.

294 "very fond . . . companies as a right": TR to Douglas Robinson, Oct. 4, 1901, in *LTR*, Vol. 3, pp. 159–60.

294   "not prying into": Eric F. Goldman, "Public Relations and the Progressive Surge, 1898–1917," Institute for Public Relations, Annual Address, Nov. 19, 1965.

294   "I much enjoyed": TR to Douglas Robinson, Oct. 4, 1901, in *LTR*, Vol. 3, p. 160.

294   "the proposition . . . to undertake it": Paul Dana to TR, Nov. 15, 1901, WHTP.

294   "Your letter causes": TR to Paul Dana, Nov. 18, 1901, in *LTR*, Vol. 3, p. 200.

295   "A hush immediately . . . unusual attention": *Washington Times*, Dec. 4, 1901.

295   "with scant courtesy": Bishop, *Theodore Roosevelt and His Time*, Vol. 1, p. 161.

295   "a professed anarchist . . . good and bad alike": TR, "First Annual Message," in Hermann Hagedorn, ed., *State Papers as Governor and President*, Vol. 15 of *WTR*, pp. 84, 81.

295   "The captains of industry . . . reasonable limits controlled": Ibid., pp. 88–89, 90–91.

295   "Th' trusts": Sullivan, *Our Times*, Vol. 2, p. 411.

296   "It is no limitation" . . . touched "the hearts": TR, "First Annual Message," *WTR*, Vol. 15, pp. 91–92, 93, 138.

296   "No other message": "President Roosevelt's Message," *The Independent*, Dec. 12, 1901, p. 2967.

296   "characteristic of the man": *Public Opinion*, Dec. 12, 1901.

296   "skeptical of any . . . over the trusts": *Public Opinion*, Sept. 4, 1901.

296   "refreshing": *Public Opinion*, Dec. 12, 1901.

297   this vast new combination . . . touched a nerve: *New York Herald*, Feb. 20, 1902.

297   "had come to see . . . and financial side": RSB, *American Chronicle*, p. 165.

297   "revolutionary . . . crusading": Ibid., p. 166.

297   "a yearly income . . . the highest purpose": RSB, "J. Pierpont Morgan," *McClure's* (October 1901), pp. 2, 10.

297   "were unquestionably . . . ever been seen before": RSB, "What the U.S. Steel Corporation Really Is, and How It Works," *McClure's* (November 1901).

298   "the contestants gathered . . . the wreath of power?": RSB, "The Great Northern Pacific Deal," *Collier's*, Nov. 30, 1901.

298   "more powerful than": Sullivan, *Our Times*, Vol. 2, pp. 417–18.

298   Roosevelt asked . . . Philander C. Knox: *NYT*, Feb. 20, 1902.

298   A brilliant lawyer: Anita T. Eitler, *Philander Chase Knox, First Attorney-General of Theodore Roosevelt, 1901–1904* (Washington, DC: Catholic University of America Press, 1959), pp. 1–2.

298   "the view that Taft": Pringle, *Theodore Roosevelt: A Biography*, p. 255.

299   "to test the validity": *New York Herald*, Feb. 20, 1902.

299   "like a thunderbolt": *Washington Post*, Feb. 21, 1902.

299   "a wholesale war . . . it was wholly unprepared": *New York Herald*, Feb. 21, 1902.

299   "If we have done . . . a big rival operator": Bishop, *Theodore Roosevelt in His Own Time*, Vol. 1, pp. 184–85.

299   "It really seems hard": Sullivan, *Our Times*, Vol. 2, p. 415.

299   "an unknown country . . . is ended": Bishop, *Theodore Roosevelt in His Own Time*, Vol. 1, p. 183.

299   "the power of the mighty": TR, *An Autobiography*, pp. 423–24.

299   "served notice": Wister, *Roosevelt, The Story of a Friendship*, p. 210.

299   "that he was President": William H. Harbaugh, *Power and Responsibility: The Life and Times of Theodore Roosevelt* (New York: Farrar, Straus & Cudahy, 1961), p. 160.

299   turned his attention to the beef trust: *NYT*, April 15, 1902.

300   "an atrocious conspiracy": New York *World*, April 26, 1902.

300   "that such absolute control": New York *World*, April 30, 1902.

300   "This is the right course": New York *World*, April 26, 1902.

300   "more dangerous to": TR, "Speech in Providence, R.I., August 23, 1902," in *Outlook*, Sept. 13, 1902, p. 113.

300   distinguish *good* trusts . . . from *bad* trusts: TR, *An Autobiography*, p. 433.

300   "with the path": George E. Mowry, *The Era of Theodore Roosevelt* (New York: Harper Bros., 1958), p. 133.

300   "a period of": HHT, *Recollections of Full Years*, p. 233.

300   "opened and drained": WHT to Horace Taft, Jan. 6, 1902, WHTP.

300   their cross-country trip . . . had died the previous day: HHT, *Recollections of Full Years*, pp. 233–34.

301   "just the same . . . looks or manner": WHT to HHT, Jan. 30, 1902, WHTP.

301   without an invitation to dine: WHT to HHT, Feb. 20, 1902, WHTP.

301   "If General Chafee": *Chillicothe* [MO] *Constitution*, Jan. 17, 1902.

301   "compassion and merciful": WHT to Horace Taft, Jan. 30, 1902, WHTP.

301   "I have much more": Henry F. Graff, ed., *American Imperialism and the Philippine Insurrection: Testimony Taken from Hearings on Affairs in the Philippine Islands Before the Senate Committee on the Philippines, 1902* (Boston: Little, Brown, 1969), p. 121.

301   "flying in the face": Ibid., p. 46.

301   "somewhat intimate relations": Ibid., p. 155.
301   "but we are there": Ibid., p. 48.
301   America's primary responsibility: Ibid., p. 37.
302   "too progressive . . . educational school": WHT, "Civil Government in the Philippines," *Outlook*, May 31, 1902, pp. 313–14.
302   "that cruelties have been": Graff, ed., *American Imperialism*, p. 92.
302   uncommon "compassion" and "restraint": Ibid., p. 95.
302   "Following his appearance . . . task in hand": Leroy, "Governor Taft's Record in the Philippines," *The Independent*, Jan. 28, 1904, p. 195.
302   "there was not anything": WHT to HHT, Feb. 24, 1902, WHTP.
302   "I have been hacked": WHT to HHT, Feb. 3, 1902, WHTP.
302   "the cure seems to be complete": WHT to Horace Taft, April 20, 1902, WHTP.
302   "the crown of Spain . . . were imprisoned": WHT, "Civil Government in the Philippines," *Outlook*, May 31, 1902, p. 319.
303   "What a splendid": HHT to WHT, Feb. 24, 1902, WHTP.
303   In the weeks before the planned trip: Anthony, *Nellie Taft*, p. 167.
303   "What a disarrangement": WHT to HHT, April 23, 1902, WHTP.
303   "Within twenty-four hours . . . pleasure and pride": HHT, *Recollections of Full Years*, p. 237.
303   "lively . . . with humor": Pringle, *Life and Times*, Vol. 1, p. 228.
303   "in a broad spirit": WHT to HHT, June 10, 1902, WHTP.
304   Weeks went by . . . negotiations were suspended: Pringle, *Life and Times*, Vol. 1, p. 230.
304   "would have run its course": HHT, *Recollections of Full Years*, p. 250.
304   "I don't know how": WHT to HHT, July 26, 1902, WHTP.
304   "I can not tell": WHT to HHT, Aug. 5, 1902, WHTP.
304   Taft's arrival triggered: *Minneapolis Journal*, Aug. 23, 1902.
304   Thirty thousand Filipinos . . . "the government was assured": *Washington Times*, Aug. 23, 1902.
304   "as a real effort": WHT to TR, Sept. 13, 1902, WHTP.
304   he promised to work unremittingly: *Sandusky* [OH] *Star*, May 24, 1899.
304   "universal, earnest . . . the Filipino people": *Salt Lake Tribune*, Aug. 24, 1902.
305   "I am in the worst . . . calumnies": TR to H. H. Kohlsaat, Aug. 4, 1902, in Kohlsaat, *From McKinley to Harding*, pp. 110–11.
305   "As things have turned out": TR to WHT, July 31, 1902, WHTP.
305   "While the result": WHT to TR, Sept. 13, 1902, WHTP.
305   "no house of representatives . . . they sang 'Dixie' ": *The News* (Frederick, MD), July 2, 1902.
306   "By far the most important": TR, *An Autobiography*, p. 512.
306   "a keen personal pride": TR to Ethan A. Hitchcock, June 17, 1902 in *LTR*, Vol. 3, p. 277.
306   to enable small farmers to settle: TR, *An Autobiography*, p. 396.
306   "I regard": TR to Ethan A. Hitchcock, June 17, 1902 in *LTR*, Vol. 3, p. 277.
306   more than half a million dollars: Abby G. Baker, "The White House of the Twentieth Century," Oct. 22, 1903, *The Independent*, p. 2499.
306   "trembled when one walked": William Seale, *The President's House: A History* (Washington, DC: White House Hist. Assoc., 1988), Vol. 2, p. 657.
306   "had the determination": Morris, *EKR*, p. 242.
306   The plans . . . a library, and a den: *The New North* (Rhinelander, WI), June 12, 1902.
307   "I ask that": *Post-Standard* (Syracuse, NY), June 14, 1902.
307   "Their conduct": Joseph Bucklin Bishop to TR, June 21, 1902, WHTP.
307   "in alliance with the trusts": *The Indianapolis Sentinel*, Sept. 4, 1902.
307   "destroy all our prosperity": TR, "Speech in Fitchburg, Mass., August 23, 1902," *Outlook*, Sept. 13, 1902, p. 120.
307   "the average man . . . standard of comfort": TR, "Speech in Providence, R.I., August 23, 1902," *Outlook*, Sept. 13, 1902, p. 114.
307   "a sympathetic ear . . . unfocused discontent": Leroy G. Dorsey, "Reconstituting the American Spirit: Theodore Roosevelt's Rhetorical Presidency," PhD diss., Indiana University, 1993, pp. 181–82.
308   "full power . . . self-restraint": TR, "Speech in Providence, R.I., August 23, 1902," in *Outlook*, Sept. 13, 1902, p. 115.
308   From Rhode Island . . . overwhelming fervor: *Public Opinion*, Sept. 4, 1902.
308   "The booming . . . their holiday clothes": *Daily Times* (New Brunswick, NJ), Aug. 27, 1902.
308   "when the streets were not": *Boston Daily Globe*, Aug. 24, 1902.
308   "small towns": *Galveston* [TX] *Daily News*, Aug. 24, 1902.
308   William Craig, was caught: New York *World*, Sept. 4, 1902; *Washington Times*, Sept. 4, 1902.
308   "It was a dreadful": New York *World*, Sept. 4, 1902.
308   "I'm all right . . . too bad, too bad": *Washington Times*, Sept. 4, 1902.

308 "Gallop ahead": New York *World*, Sept. 4, 1902.

308 a "memorable conference": Stephenson, *Nelson W. Aldrich*, p. 194.

309 a resolution . . . that linked tariffs to trusts: *Sioux County Herald* (Orange City, IA), Sept. 19, 1902.

309 "The tariff must . . . hell will be to pay": Walter Wellman to TR, April 18, 1902, WHTP.

309 the "dynamite . . . to the Republican party": TR to Nicholas M. Butler, Aug. 12, 1902, in *LTR*, Vol. 3, p. 312.

309 "As long as I remain": Edmund Morris, *Theodore Rex* (New York: Random House, 2001), p. 145.

309 "make no attempt": Stephenson, *Nelson W. Aldrich*, p. 455, n. 54.

309 "I do not wish": TR to Nicholas M. Butler, Aug. 12, 1902, in *LTR*, Vol. 3, p. 312.

309 "a three weeks' ": TR to John Hay, Sept. 18, 1902, in ibid., p. 326.

309 "like that of a man": *Public Opinion*, Sept. 25, 1902.

310 crowds "in comparative silence": "President Roosevelt at Cincinnati," *Outlook*, Sept. 27, 1902, p. 205.

310 "There are a good many": TR to John Hay, Sept. 18, 1902, in *LTR*, Vol. 3, p. 326.

310 "a threatening abscess . . . before the needle was removed": New York *World*, Sept. 24, 1902; *Racine* [WI] *Daily Journal*, Sept. 24, 1902.

310 "Tell it not": TR to Orville H. Platt, Oct. 2, 1902, in *LTR*, Vol. 3, p. 335.

310 books that would feed: TR to Herbert Putnam, Oct. 6, 1902, in ibid., p. 343.

310 "Exactly the books": TR to Herbert Putnam, Oct. 8, 1902, in ibid., pp. 344–45.

311 "the most formidable": Walter Wellman, "The Progress of the World," *American Monthly Review of Reviews* (October 1902).

311 140,000 anthracite coal miners . . . panic was setting in: Sullivan, *Our Times*, Vol. 2, p. 427.

311 "the sorrows": John Mitchell, "The Mine Worker's Life and Aims," *The Cosmopolitan* (October 1901), p. 630.

311 "the average magazine": Ibid., p. 622.

311 "yet at the . . . precarious elevators": Stephen Crane, "In the Depths of a Coal Mine," *McClure's* (August 1894).

311 "on the descent": Mitchell, "The Mine Worker's Life and Aims," *Cosmopolitan*, Oct. 1901, p. 629.

312 "children were brought": Gompers, *Seventy Years of Life and Labor*, p. 154.

312 "reaping the reward": "Progress of the World," *American Monthly Review of Reviews* (November 1902).

312 estimated profit of $75 million: Walter Wellman, "The Inside History of the Coal Strike," *Collier's*, Oct. 18, 1902.

312 "When President McKinley": LS, "A Labor Leader of To-Day: John Mitchell and What He Stands For," *McClure's* (August 1902), p. 355.

312 "No better strike . . . bitterness or retort": "Progress of the World," *American Monthly Review of Reviews* (November 1902).

313 "was only a common": Wellman, "The Inside History of the Coal Strike," *Collier's*, Oct. 18, 1902.

313 "I beg of you": Sullivan, *Our Times*, Vol. 2, p. 426.

313 "The doctrine of the divine": Ibid.

313 "It will take a load": *New York Tribune*, Aug. 22, 1902.

313 "The coal business . . . you can appear to do?": HCL to TR, Sept. 27, 1902, in TR and HCL, *Selections from the Correspondence*, Vol. 1, pp. 531–32.

313 "I am at my wit's": Pringle, *Theodore Roosevelt: A Biography*, p. 269.

313 "Of course, we have": TR to MAH, September 27, 1902, in *LTR*, Vol. 3, pp. 329–30.

314 "no warrant . . . constitutional duties": "Progress of the World," *American Monthly Review of Reviews* (November 1902).

314 "the Jackson-Lincoln theory": TR, *An Autobiography*, p. 464.

314 "the failure of the": TR to John Mitchell, et al., Oct. 1, 1902, in *LTR*, Vol. 3, p. 334.

314 "For the first time": Wellman, "The Inside History of the Coal Strike," *Collier's*, Oct. 18, 1902.

314 "luxurious private cars . . . a cheap hotel": Ibid.

314 footmen in "plum-colored livery": New York *World*, Oct. 4, 1902.

314 "three parties affected . . . general good": Ibid.

315 "literally jumped . . . clear as a bell": Ibid.

315 "I had not expected . . . may discuss them": TR's question and Baer's insolent reply, reported in ibid., are not included in the official transcript, which TR later acknowledged did not include "all the invectives of the operators." See TR to Winthrop Crane, Oct. 22, 1902, in *LTR*, Vol. 3, p. 359.

315 "The duty of the hour": "President Roosevelt and the Coal Strike," *The Independent*, Oct. 9, 1902, p. 2383.

315 "extraordinary stupidity . . . irritate Mitchell": TR to Winthrop Crane, Oct. 22, 1902, in *LTR*, Vol. 3, pp. 360–61.

315 "insolent . . . offensive to me": TR, *An Autobiography*, p. 466.

315 "they insulted me": TR to MAH, Oct. 3, 1902, in *LTR*, Vol. 3, p. 338.

315 "Mitchell behaved": TR to Winthrop Crane, Oct. 22, 1902, in ibid., p. 360.

315   "appeared to such advantage": TR to MAH, Oct. 3, 1902, in ibid., p. 337.

315   "towered above": TR to Robert Bacon, Oct. 5, 1902, in ibid., p. 340.

315   "a set of outlaws": Morris, *Theodore Rex*, p. 160.

315   "by the seat": Wood, *Roosevelt As We Knew Him*, p. 109.

315   "to have any dealings": New York *World*, Oct. 4, 1902.

316   "If this is the case": Ibid.

316   "Well, I have tried": TR to MAH, Oct. 3, 1902, in *LTR*, Vol. 3, p. 337.

316   reveled "in the fact": TR, *An Autobiography*, p. 467.

316   "uncontrollable penchant": Sullivan, *Our Times*, Vol. 2, p. 431.

316   "a sorry mess": *Public Opinion*, Oct. 16, 1901.

316   "respectful, placable": *Public Opinion*, Oct. 9, 1902.

316   "ugly talk . . . would otherwise come": TR to Winthrop Crane, Oct. 22, 1902, in *LTR*, Vol. 3, p. 362.

316   "absolutely out of touch . . . misery and death": TR to ARC, Oct. 16, 1902, in TR, *Letters from Theodore Roosevelt to Anna Roosevelt Cowles*, pp. 252–53.

316   "a first-rate general . . . Commander-in-Chief": Sullivan, *Our Times*, Vol. 2, p. 436.

316   if "the operators went": Bishop, *Theodore Roosevelt and His Time*, Vol. 1, p. 212.

317   "Don't hit till": Wellman, "The Settlement of the Coal Strike," *American Monthly Review of Reviews* (November 1902).

317   "Theodore was a bit": Jessup, *Elihu Root*, Vol. 1, p. 275.

317   "The one condition": Sullivan, *Our Times*, Vol. 2, p. 438.

317   it would be the original architect: Wellman, "The Inside History of the Coal Strike," *Collier's*, Oct. 18, 1902.

317   Root would make it clear: Jessup, *Elihu Root*, Vol. 1, p. 275.

317   "It was a damned lie": Ibid., p. 276.

317   "was one of the": Wellman, "The Settlement of the Coal Strike," *American Monthly Review of Reviews* (November 1902).

317   the composition of the panel: TR to Winthrop Crane, Oct. 22, 1902, in *LTR*, Vol. 3, p. 359.

318   "Suddenly . . . accept with rapture": TR, *An Autobiography*, p. 468.

318   For three months the commission heard: *Public Opinion*, Dec. 18, 1902.

318   "The American people . . . triumph of peace": *Public Opinion*, Oct. 23, 1902.

318   "was won by popular": Ibid.

318   "the people's attorney": WAW, "The President," *Saturday Evening Post*, April 4, 1903.

318   "steady pressure": *Public Opinion*, Oct. 23, 1902.

318   "was all ready to . . . in less drastic fashion": TR, *An Autobiography*, pp. 475–76.

319   "My dear sir": TR to J. P. Morgan, Oct. 16, 1902, in *LTR*, Vol. 3, p. 353.

319   "May Heaven preserve me": TR to ARC, Oct. 16, 1902, in TR, *Letters from Theodore Roosevelt to Anna Roosevelt Cowles*, p. 254.

319   "Mother and I": TR to Kermit Roosevelt, Nov. 6, 1902, in *LTR*, Vol. 3, p. 374.

319   "doomed to failure . . . thousands of votes": "Progress of the World," *American Monthly Review of Reviews* (November 1902).

319   "a steady stream . . . samples of rugs": Seale, *The President's House: A History*, Vol 2, p. 674.

319   designing a garden . . . and a tennis court: Morris, *EKR*, pp. 248, 254.

319   "If Roosevelt had": Ellen Maury Slayden, *Washington Wife: Journal of Ellen Maury Slayden from 1897–1919* (New York: Harper & Row, 1963), p. 46.

319   "remarkable coping . . . and start again": Mac Keith Griswold, "First Lady Edith Kermit Roosevelt's 'Colonial Garden' at the White House," *White House History*, No. 23, p. 5.

319   "She is an old-fashioned": *New York Herald Tribune*, Oct. 30, 1932.

320   "By nature and inclination . . . dignity and charm": Isabella Hagner James, "Memoirs of Isabella Hagner, 1901–1905," *White House History*, No. 26, p. 63.

320   She was "at home" . . . at afternoon teas: *Logansport* [IN] *Journal*, Dec. 13, 1902.

320   "the chief end": Riis, "Mrs. Roosevelt and Her Children," *Ladies' Home Journal* (August 1902), p. 5.

320   "For the first time": *Newark* [OH] *Advocate*, Nov. 10, 1902.

320   immediate access to the president . . . and telephones: *Fort Wayne* [IN] *News*, Nov. 10, 1902.

320   "The public man": *Newark* [OH] *Advocate*, Nov. 10, 1902.

320   "had any right . . . the given conditions": TR to Maria Longworth Storer, Dec. 8, 1902, in *LTR*, Vol. 3, p. 392.

320   "It is very curious . . . uniformly good-natured": Bishop, *Theodore Roosevelt and His Time*, Vol. 1, p. 240.

320   a mid-November bear hunt . . . in honor of Teddy Roosevelt: New York *Sun*, Nov. 15, 1902; *NYT*, Nov. 19, 1902.

321   "I'd rather be *elected* . . . Hanna and that crowd": Pringle, *Theodore Roosevelt: A Biography*, p. 339.

321   "I do not think": *Woodland* [CA] *Daily Democrat*, Nov. 24, 1902.

321   "the monied interests" . . . opposition party: *Ottumwa* [IA] *Daily Courier*, Jan. 9, 1903.

321   the vehement reaction: TR to Lucius N. Littauer, Oct. 24, 1901, in *LTR*, Vol. 3, p. 181.

321   "Social equality": *Public Opinion*, Oct. 31, 1901, p. 556.

321   "The action of President": Ben Tillman, in Dewey W. Grantham, Jr., "Dinner at the White House," *Tennessee Historical Quarterly* (June 1958), p. 117.

321   "not nearly so strong": *Sandusky [OH] Daily Star*, Dec. 3, 1902.

321   "The plain people . . . against the trusts": TR, "Second Annual Message," Dec. 2, 1902, in *WTR*, Vol. 15, pp. 140–41, 144.

322   "It appears that": *Indiana [PA] Democrat*, Dec. 3, 1902.

322   "a very lame message": *Cincinnati Enquirer*, cited in *Racine [WI] Journal*, Dec. 5, 1902.

322   "A milk and water": *Indiana [PA] Democrat*, Dec. 3, 1902.

322   "We are bound to believe": New York *Evening Post*, cited in *Racine Journal*, Dec. 5, 1902.

CHAPTER ELEVEN: "The Most Famous Woman in America"

Page

324   "groundbreaking trio": David M. Chalmers, *The Muckrake Years* (New York: D. Van Nostrand Co., 1974), p. 24.

324   "Capitalists, workingmen . . . but all of us": McClure, "Concerning Three Articles in This Number of *McClure's*, and a Coincidence That May Set Us Thinking," *McClure's* (January 1903), p. 336.

325   "A lesser editor": Lyon, *Success Story*, p. 204.

325   "shameful facts . . . to the American pride": *Boston Daily Globe*, May 22, 1904.

325   "for the first time": Goldman, *Rendezvous with Destiny*, p. 74.

325   "the greatest success": Lyon, *Success Story*, p. 206.

325   Editorials . . . praised the quality of the research: *Salt Lake Tribune*, Jan. 4, 1903; *Los Angeles Times*, Feb. 15, 1903.

325   "Of course": New York *World*, cited in *Boston Daily Globe*, May 22, 1904.

326   "prophets crying": RSB, *American Chronicle*, p. 183.

326   "It is hardly": Hofstadter, *The Age of Reform*, pp. 186–87.

326   "gradual rise . . . intense human interest": Wilson, *McClure's Magazine and the Muckrakers*, p. 134.

327   "The great feature is Trusts . . . a good circulation": McClure to John S. Phillips, Sept. 14, 1899, McClure MSS.

327   While Phillips embraced McClure's idea: Wilson, *McClure's Magazine and the Muckrakers*, p. 136.

327   "The Pulpit, the Press": Frank Norris, *The Responsibilities of the Novelist, and Other Literary Essays* (New York: Doubleday, Page & Co., 1903), p. 10.

327   "the destruction of once": Benjamin O. Flower, "The Trust in Fiction: A Remarkable Social Novel, *The Octopus*," *The Arena* (May 1902), p. 547.

328   "the iron-hearted Power": Frank Norris, *The Octopus: A Story of California* (New York: Doubleday, Page & Co., 1910), p. 51.

328   "*The Octopus* is": Flower, "The Trust in Fiction," *The Arena* (May 1902), pp. 547–48.

328   "The string of triumphs": Lyon, *Success Story*, p. 173.

328   McClure overreached: Ibid., p. 166.

328   Frank Doubleday . . . six months after it was signed: Ibid., p. 172.

328   "raw milk is": Ronald F. Schmid, *The Untold Story of Milk: The History, Politics and Science of Nature's Perfect Food: Raw Milk from Pasture-Fed Cows* (Washington, DC: NewTrends, 2009), p. 76.

329   "unmelodious" clamor . . . "rhythmical" sounds: George Miller Beard, *American Nervousness: Its Causes and Consequences; a Supplement to Nervous Exhaustion (Neurasthenia)* (New York: G. P. Putnam's Sons, 1881), p. 106.

329   "local horrors": Ibid., p. 134.

329   "the ultracompetitive": David G. Schuster, "Neurasthenia and a Modernizing America," *Journal of the American Medical Association* 290, Nov. 5, 2003, pp. 2327–28.

329   "the repulsion . . . and got it": Cather and McClure, *The Autobiography*, pp. 254–55.

329   "When I get rested . . . worse than ever": McClure to JSP, Oct. 30, 1900, Phillips MSS.

329   "I am simply heart-broken": McClure to JSP, Oct. 30, 1900, Phillips MSS.

330   "The great issue": Lyon, *Success Story*, p. 190.

330   "the way to handle . . . the oil region": Cather and McClure, *The Autobiography*, p. 238.

330   "the unfairness of the situation": Mary Caroline Crawford, "The Historian of Standard Oil," *Public Opinion*, May 27, 1905.

330   "the bottom had dropped out": IMT, *All in the Day's Work*, p. 204.

330   "there must be two . . . the other side": Crawford, "The Historian of Standard Oil," *Public Opinion*, May 27, 1905.

330   "the all-seeing eye . . . ruin the magazine": IMT, *All in the Day's Work*, pp. 206–07.

330   "the audacity of the thing": Crawford, "The Historian of Standard Oil," *Public Opinion*, May 27, 1905.

331   "Go over": IMT, *All in the Day's Work*, p. 205.

331   "Come instantly . . . a good time": McClure to IMT, Sept. 30, 1901, IMTC.
331   Hattie, too, welcomed: Brady, *Ida Tarbell*, p. 122.
331   "You've never been there . . . in the Pantheon": IMT, *All in the Day's Work*, p. 206.
331   The image . . . incongruous and hilarious: Ibid.
331   "I lean on you": McClure to IMT, Dec. 30, 1901, IMTC.
331   he decided to stop . . . Greece for another time: IMT, *All in the Day's Work*, p. 206.
331   "It was always so . . . wild editor": LS, *The Autobiography*, pp. 363, 361.
332   "a way to compromise": Ibid., pp. 363, 364.
332   "absolutely incompetent . . . words passed": Lyon, *Success Story*, p. 195.
332   Mary Bisland . . . wrote a distressed letter: Ibid., pp. 195–96.
332   "Things will come out . . . that one hundredth idea!": IMT to Albert Boyden, April 26, 1902, in ibid.,
        p. 199.
333   "a particular industry": Mary E. Tomkins, *Ida M. Tarbell* (New York: Twayne Publishers, 1974), p. 60.
333   "exactly the quality": IMT, *All in the Day's Work*, p. 208.
333   almost lost her eyesight: *Atlanta Constitution*, Jan. 11, 1903.
333   "turn up" . . . curiously disappeared: IMT, *All in the Day's Work*, p. 209.
333   "Her sources of information": Cather and McClure, *The Autobiography*, p. 239.
334   "get his fun . . . a continuous joy": IMT, *All in the Day's Work*, p. 209.
334   "was as illustrious a meeting": Brady, *Ida Tarbell*, p. 125.
334   "Someone once asked me": Ibid., p. 126.
334   "I was a bit scared . . . face to face": IMT, *All in the Day's Work*, p. 212.
335   "a heavy shock of . . . the world, I thought": Ibid., pp. 212–13.
335   "documents, figures": Ibid., p. 215.
335   "unimpeachable accuracy": Cather and McClure, *The Autobiography*, p. 240.
335   "deep into appalling heaps . . . of your story": August F. Jaccaci to IMT, Nov. 23, 1901, Phillips MSS.
335   "hurt your health . . . for next fall": McClure to IMT, Dec. 2, 1901, IMTC.
335   "separated so completely": IMT to Harriet Hurd McClure, Nov. 8, 1902, McClure MSS.
335   "They are in such shape": IMT to JSP, May 26, 1902, Phillips MSS.
335   her deep respect for Phillips's opinion: Brady, *Ida Tarbell*, p. 130.
336   "be satisfied and thrilled": Ibid., p. 133.
336   "moderately comfortable . . . for the Alps": IMT to John M. Siddall, June 24, 1902, in ibid., p. 130.
336   "irrepressible energy . . . refine for the world": IMT, "The Birth of an Industry," *McClure's* (November
        1902), in IMT and David Mark Chalmers, *The History of the Standard Oil Company* (Mineola, NY:
        Dover Books, 1966), pp. 18, 17, 1, 16.
336   Rockefeller's "genius for detail": IMT, "The Legitimate Greatness of the Standard Oil Company,"
        McClure's (October 1904), in ibid., p. 202.
336   "in energy, in intelligence": Ibid., p. 196.
336   "You will have but one . . . swooped down": IMT, "John D. Rockefeller, A Character Study," *McClure's*
        (July 1905).
337   "There is no chance": IMT, "The Rise of the Standard Oil Company," *McClure's* (December 1902), in
        IMT and Chalmers, *History of the Standard Oil Company*, p. 32.
337   Within three months, twenty-one: Ibid., p. 33.
337   "They were there at the mouth": Ibid., p. 27.
337   "the railroad held its right . . . without discrimination": IMT, "John D. Rockefeller, A Character
        Study," *McClure's* (July 1905).
337   "from hopelessness . . . for principle": IMT, "The Great Consummation," *McClure's* (June 1903), in
        IMT and Chalmers, *History of the Standard Oil Company*, p. 99.
337   "To the man who had begun": IMT, "The Price of Trust Building," *McClure's* (March 1903), in ibid.,
        p. 66.
337   "the quantity, quality": IMT, "Cutting to Kill," *McClure's* (February 1904), in ibid., p. 123.
337   "her firm had a customer": Ibid., p. 115.
337   Of all the machinations: Ibid., p. 124.
338   "The unraveling of this espionage": IMT, "Speech to Rachel Crothers' Group" [n.d.], IMTC; see also
        Brady, *Ida Tarbell*, p. 145.
338   "had completed one": IMT, "The Troubles of a Trust," *McClure's* (March 1904), in IMT and Chalmers,
        History of the Standard Oil Company, p. 151.
338   "competition practically out": IMT, "The Price of Oil," *McClure's* (September 1904), in ibid., p. 185.
338   "Human experience": Ibid., p. 194.
338   "legitimate greatness . . . daring to lay hold of them": IMT, "The Legitimate Greatness of the Standard
        Oil Company," in ibid., p. 196.
338   "these qualities alone": IMT, "Conclusion," *McClure's* (October 1904), in ibid., p. 216.
338   "At the same time": Ibid., pp. 216–17.

338 "every great campaign": Ibid., p. 222.

338 "And what are we going . . . Standard Oil Company": Ibid., p. 227.

339 "You are today . . . afraid of you": McClure to IMT, April 6, 1903, IMTC.

339 "a Joan of Arc . . . against trusts and monopolies": Jeannette L. Gilder, "Some Women Writers," *Outlook*, October 1904, p. 281.

339 "The New Woman": *Logansport* [IN] *Pharos*, July 26, 1904.

339 "At least one American": *Lowell* [MA] *Sun*, June 11, 1904.

339 "the strongest intellectual force": *Los Angeles Times*, Feb. 14, 1906.

339 "proven herself to be": *Washington Times* quoted in "On the Making of McClure's Magazine," *McClure's* (November 1904), p. 107.

339 "the woman who talks": *Boston Daily Globe*, April 7, 1904.

339 "so feminine as to appear": Brady, *Ida Tarbell*, p. 157.

339 publishers' dinner: *Washington Post*, April 8, 1904.

339 "It is the first time": IMT to RSB, April 5, 1904, RSB Papers.

339 "that Mr. Rockefeller": *Washington Post*, July 8, 1905.

340 "Miss Ida Tarbell goes": *Chicago Daily Tribune*, Dec. 31, 1902.

340 "the net of avarice . . . sordid to benevolent": *Washington Post*, Nov. 26, 1905.

340 "accumulation of facts . . . in their significance": *Webster City* [IA] *Tribune*, Nov. 27, 1903.

340 "intimate style": *Outlook*, Oct. 1, 1904.

340 "remarkable for being nearly": *Chicago Daily Tribune*, Dec. 28, 1903.

340 "in a state of lively suspense": *Chicago Daily Tribune*, June 8, 1903.

340 "She never rants": *Webster City Tribune*, Nov. 27, 1903.

340 "an almost universal practice": Chalmers, *The Muckrake Years*, p. 94.

340 "excellent journalism": *Boston Evening Transcript*, Jan. 6, 1904.

340 "a quiet, modest": IMT, "John D. Rockefeller: A Character Study, Part Two," *McClure's* (August 1905), p. 397.

340 "willing to strain": *Fort Wayne* [IN] *Journal-Gazette*, Feb. 9, 1903.

340 "Rockefeller was known": *Alton* [IL] *Evening Telegraph*, Dec. 21, 1904.

341 "as expressionless . . . worthy of citizenship": IMT, "John D. Rockefeller: A Character Study, Part Two," *McClure's* (August 1905), pp. 386, 387, 398.

341 "were Mr. Rockefeller": Ibid., pp. 398–99.

341 "no cure": IMT, "Conclusion," *McClure's* (October 1904), in IMT and Chalmers, *History of the Standard Oil Company*, p. 222.

341 "an increasing scorn": Ibid.

341 board members "closely allied": *Daily Californian* (Bakersfield, CA), April 28, 1904.

341 "Your monumental work": McClure to IMT [n.d.], 1904, IMTC.

341 "one of the most remarkable": "On the Making of McClure's Magazine," *McClure's* (November 1904), p. 107.

341 "up to magazines": Brady, *Ida Tarbell*, p. 139.

341 "that the two things": *Outlook*, Oct. 1, 1904.

342 "You cannot imagine": McClure to IMT, Mar. 18, 1903, IMTC.

342 "the most genuinely creative": IMT, *All in the Day's Work*, p. 199.

342 to compel congressional action against monopolies: *Daily Northwestern* (Oshkosh, WI), Dec. 23, 1902.

342 "must stand . . . a tower of strength": *Logansport* [IN] *Journal*, Feb. 10, 1903.

342 the "only question": *Daily Northwestern*, Dec. 23, 1902.

342 "no time for anti-trust": *New York Tribune*, Jan. 6, 1903.

342 "I pass my days": TR to Kermit Roosevelt, Jan. 17, 1903, in TR et al., *Letters to Kermit from Theodore Roosevelt*, pp. 24–25.

342 "the ancient and honorable . . . the two stools": *Washington Post*, Feb. 19, 1903.

342 "The party had promised": Ibid.

343 an extra session "on extraordinary occasions": U.S. Constitution, art. II, sec. 3.

343 "While I could not force": TR to Lawrence Fraser Abbott, Feb. 3, 1903, in *LTR*, Vol. 3, p. 416.

343 That single word, "rebate . . . interests of the country": *Fort Wayne* [IN] *Journal-Gazette*, Feb. 9, 1903.

343 "no respectable railroad": TR to Lawrence Fraser Abbott, Feb. 3, 1903, in *LTR*, Vol. 3, p. 417.

343 By 1903, the railroads themselves actually favored: Gabriel Kolko, *Railroads and Regulation, 1877–1916* (New York: W. W. Norton & Co., 1970), pp. 94–95.

343 "grown beyond any effects": *Washington Post*, Feb. 8, 1903.

343 "the highways of commerce": TR to Lyman Abbott, Sept. 5, 1903, in *LTR*, Vol. 3, p. 592.

343 "equal rights for all": *Logansport* [IN] *Journal*, Feb. 10, 1903.

344 "violent opposition . . . sullenly acquiesced in": TR to Lawrence Fraser Abbott, Feb. 3, 1903, in *LTR*, Vol. 3, p. 417.

344   "the subconscious moral sense": WAW, "The Balance-Sheet of the Session," *Saturday Evening Post*,
       Mar. 28, 1903.

344   "the first essential . . . overcapitalization": TR, "First Annual Message," in *NYT*, Jan. 4, 1900.

344   The amendment . . . the abuses uncovered: Arthur M. Johnson, "Theodore Roosevelt and the Bureau
       of Corporations," *Mississippi Valley Historical Review* 45 (March 1959), p. 576.

344   "The Standard Oil Company": *Wall Street Journal*, Nov. 28, 1903.

345   "a disposition in some quarters": *New York Tribune*, Jan. 8, 1903.

345   "joked with the girls . . . would never, never do": *Logansport* [IN] *Pharos*, Feb. 18, 1903.

345   "I have been worked": TR to Kermit Roosevelt, Feb. 15, 1903, in TR et al., *Letters to Kermit from
       Theodore Roosevelt*, p. 29.

345   Singlestick . . . required him to shake left-handed: TR to Kermit Roosevelt, Jan. 25, 1903, in ibid.,
       p. 26.

345   "The Most Wounded President": *Minneapolis Journal*, Mar. 7, 1903.

345   rode a horse . . . for exercise: TR to Kermit Roosevelt, Feb. 19, 1903, in TR et al., *Letters to Kermit from
       Theodore Roosevelt*, p. 30.

345   "not suffice": *Boston Traveler*, quoted in *Hutchinson* [KS] *News*, Feb. 3, 1903.

345   a single objective: Ibid.

345   with "peremptory" instruction: *NYT*, Feb. 10, 1903.

346   "unalterably opposed": *Logansport* [IN] *Pharos*, Feb. 13, 1903.

346   "must be stopped": *Logansport* [IN] *Pharos*, Feb. 10, 1903.

346   "We own the Republican party": Ibid.

346   he would surely insist on the extra session: *Washington Post*, Feb. 8, 1903.

346   "a decided sensation": *NYT*, Feb. 9, 1903.

346   "for fear": *Eau Claire* [WI] *Leader*, Feb. 14, 1903.

346   "no surprise . . . nothing more": *Fort Wayne* [IN] *Journal-Gazette*, Feb. 9, 1903.

346   "This is no more than . . . promptly to right-about": *Los Angeles Times*, Feb. 14, 1903.

346   "from the standpoint": TR to Nicholas M. Butler, Aug. 29, 1903, in *LTR*, Vol. 3, p. 580.

347   "Taken as a whole": TR to David Bremner Henderson, Mar. 4, 1903, in ibid., p. 438.

347   "a great many people . . . consensus of opinion": TR to Nicholas M. Butler, Aug. 29, 1903, in ibid.,
       p. 580.

347   "gotten the trust legislation": TR to Joseph Bucklin Bishop, Feb. 17, 1903, in ibid., p. 429.

347   "not sufficiently far-reaching": *Washington Post*, Feb. 19, 1903.

347   "no single legislative act . . . will not be retracted": WAW, "The Balance-Sheet of the Session," *Saturday
       Evening Post*, Mar. 28, 1903.

CHAPTER TWELVE: "A Mission to Perform"

Page

348   Roosevelt embarked . . . upon the longest tour: *Boston Daily Globe*, April 2, 1903.

348   "Look out for": New York *World*, April 2, 1903.

349   "the handsomest ever": *Washington Times*, Mar. 31, 1903.

349   This "traveling palace" . . . a rear platform: New York *World*, April 1, 1903.

349   The remaining cars included: *Washington Times*, Mar. 31, 1903.

349   "gave himself very freely . . . have another chance": John Burroughs, *Camping and Tramping with
       Roosevelt* (Boston: Houghton Mifflin, 1907), pp. 8, 9, 12.

349   "to see the President . . . proprietary interest in him": TR to John Hay, Aug. 9, 1903, in *LTR*, Vol. 3,
       pp. 550–51, 555.

349   to gain "the people's trust": WAW, "Swinging 'Round the Circle with Roosevelt," *Saturday Evening Post*,
       June 27, 1903.

349   an array of bizarre gifts: TR to John Hay, Aug. 9, 1903, in *LTR*, Vol. 3, p. 555; "Survey of the World:
       End of Mr. Roosevelt's Tour," *The Independent*, June 11, 1903.

350   "Great heavens and earth!": *Anaconda* [MT] *Standard*, May 6 & 28, 1903.

350   "These were not epoch-making . . . original": WAW, "Swinging 'Round the Circle with Roosevelt,"
       Saturday Evening Post, June 27, 1903.

350   "the thick of civilization . . . the same ideals": TR to John Hay, Aug. 9, 1903, in *LTR*, Vol. 3, p. 548.

350   "Roosevelt Gems": *Daily Journal* (Salem, OR), May 28, 1903.

350   "make a fool wise . . . cannot be done": TR, "Speech in Aberdeen, S.D., April 7, 1903," in TR and
       Alfred H. Lewis, *A Compilation of the Messages and Speeches of Theodore Roosevelt, 1901–1905,* (New
       York: Bureau of National Literature and Art, 1906), pp. 263, 265.

350   "I do not like": *Daily Journal* (Salem, OR), May 28, 1903.

350   "Speak softly": *Fort Wayne* [IN] *Journal-Gazette*, April 3, 1903.

350   "sudsy metaphors . . . from a clothesline": WAW, "Swinging 'Round the Circle with Roosevelt," *Sat-
       urday Evening Post*, June 27, 1903.

350   "a square deal . . . rich or poor": TR, "Speech at Lynn, Mass., August 25, 1902," in TR and Lewis, *A Compilation of the Messages and Speeches*, p. 74.

350   "They were good enough": TR, "Speech at Grand Canyon, Ariz., May 26, 1903," in ibid., p. 328.

350   the black troops who fought beside him: *Anaconda* [MT] *Standard*, May 28, 1903.

350   he elaborated on the concept: *Atlanta Constitution*, Sept. 8, 1903.

351   "We must treat": *Anaconda* [MT] *Standard*, May 27, 1903.

351   "a great boy . . . waiting for him to fall": *Desert Evening News* (Salt Lake City, UT), Mar. 28, 1903.

351   "a man of such abounding": Burroughs, *Camping and Tramping with Roosevelt*, pp. 4, 80.

351   He arrived at the Grand Canyon: Douglas Brinkley, *The Wilderness Warrior: Theodore Roosevelt and the Crusade for America* (New York: HarperCollins, 2009), p. 527.

351   "Leave it as it is": *Salt Lake Tribune*, May 7, 1903; TR, "Speech at Grand Canyon, Ariz., May 6, 1903," in TR and Lewis, *A Compilation of the Messages and Speeches*, p. 327.

351   "great wonder of nature": *Salt Lake Tribune*, May 7, 1903.

351   "If Roosevelt had done nothing": Brinkley, *The Wilderness Warrior*, p. 528.

351   San Lorenzo Valley, home to: *Evening Herald* (Syracuse, NY), May 12, 1903.

352   "I am, oh, so glad": TR, "Speech at the Big Grove Tree, Santa Cruz, Cal., May 11, 1903," in TR and Lewis, *A Compilation of the Messages and Speeches*, p. 360.

352   "to protect these mighty": TR, "Speech at Leland Stanford, Jr., University, Palo Alto, Cal., May 12, 1903," in ibid., p. 370.

352   "a tree which was old . . . higher emotions in mankind": Ibid., p. 368.

352   "the great monarchs of the woods": Ibid., p. 370.

352   "not to preserve forests": TR, "Speech at the Meeting of the Society of American Foresters, Washington, D.C., March 26, 1903," in ibid., p. 208.

352   "a steady and continuous": *Salt Lake Tribune*, May 30, 1903.

352   already "seriously depleted": TR, "Speech at a Meeting of the Society of American Foresters, Washington, D.C., March 26, 1903," in TR and Lewis, *A Compilation of the Messages and Speeches*, p. 210.

352   "rushing away . . . the flow of streams": "How Our National Forests Conserve Irrigation and Water Power," *Literary Digest*, April 26, 1919, p. 117.

352   "a veritable garden of Eden": *Arizona Republican* (Phoenix, AZ), May 26, 1903.

352   "small irrigated farms": TR, "Speech at Denver, Colo., May 4, 1903," in TR and Lewis, *A Compilation of the Messages and Speeches*, p. 323.

352   "We do not ever": TR, "Speech at Leland Stanford, Jr., University, Palo Alto, Cal., May 12, 1903," in ibid., p. 370.

352   "come into the hands": *Salt Lake Tribune*, May 30, 1903.

353   THE DAY OF DELIVERANCE: *Arizona Republican*, May 19, 1903.

353   "the greatest in the world": *Arizona Republican*, May 26, 1903.

353   "make the community": *Reno* [NV] *Evening Gazette*, May 14, 1903.

353   The estimated cost of the five projects: *The Weekly Gazette* (Colorado Springs, CO), July 23, 1903.

353   "any other material movement": TR, "Speech at Grand Canyon, Ariz., May 6, 1903," in TR and Lewis, *A Compilation of the Messages and Speeches*, p. 327.

353   "a new type . . . a million inhabitants": TR to John Hay, Aug. 9, 1903, in *LTR*, Vol. 3, p. 558.

353   an "educational effect upon . . . great national forests": "The President's Trip and the Forests," *Century Illustrated Magazine* (August 1903), pp. 634–35.

353   Roosevelt had delivered 265 speeches: "Survey of the World: End of Mr. Roosevelt's Tour," *The Independent*, June 11, 1903.

353   "as fresh and unworn": Burroughs, *Camping and Tramping with Roosevelt*, p. 61.

354   "blossom like a rose": *Minneapolis Journal*, July 30, 1903.

354   "irrigate no public lands": *Anaconda Standard*, May 21, 1903.

354   Roosevelt had followed the reporter's career: RSB, *American Chronicle*, p. 170.

354   short notes commending: TR to RSB, Nov. 4, 1898; Feb. 2, 1900, Baker Papers.

354   "We intend to do": TR to George Hoar, Oct. 17, 1902, in *LTR*, Vol. 3, p. 354.

354   "ammunition for mere": RSB, *American Chronicle*, p. 168.

354   Baker had finally moved: Ibid., p. 161.

354   "never . . . forget": Ibid.

355   "the first desk": Ibid., p. 162.

355   "I actually thought . . . serpent in my new Eden!": Ibid., p. 163.

355   "What sort of men": "Interview with S. S. McClure," *The North American* (Philadelphia), Aug. 15, 1905.

355   "was generally hostile": RSB, *American Chronicle*, p. 166.

355   "only one aspect": Ibid., p. 168.

355   the more curious he grew: Ibid., p. 167; TR to Winthrop Crane, Oct. 22, 1902, in *LTR*, Vol. 3, p. 361.

355   Baker sought out people: RSB, *American Chronicle*, p. 167.

356   "low wages": Ibid., p. 163.
356   "singularly steady-headed": Ibid., pp. 166–67.
356   "What men I met": Ibid., p. 167.
356   "Don't, my dear boy": McClure to RSB, Nov. 5, 1902, RSB Papers.
356   "the feuds in . . . death can heal": McClure to LS, Nov. 10, 1902, LS Papers; *NYT*, Nov. 10, 1902.
356   "become the most . . . done magnificently!": McClure to RSB, Nov. 14, 1902, RSB Papers.
356   "is beginning to distinguish": McClure, "Editor's Note," in RSB, "The Right to Work: The Story of
      the Non-Striking Miners," *McClure's* (January 1903), p. 323.
356   "the rights of labor . . . even real danger": RSB, "The Right to Work," *McClure's* (January 1903), p. 323.
356   "the best position . . . crushed all family feeling": Ibid., pp. 334–35.
357   "All these things": Ibid., pp. 327–28.
357   clubbed to death: Ibid., pp. 330–33.
357   "only a few among scores": Ibid., p. 336.
357   "on fire . . . all winter long": RSB, *American Chronicle*, p. 168.
357   "Everything has borne out": McClure to RSB, Jan. 23, 1903, RSB Papers.
358   an entire series on labor: Ibid.
358   unable "to write fiction": RSB, *American Chronicle*, p. 173.
358   "a powerful new": Ibid., p. 179.
358   "I doubt whether": Ibid., p. 169.
358   "I have wondered": Ibid., p. 99.
358   "We were friends . . . rewriting his story": Ibid., pp. 94–95.
358   "the Chief . . . she has the punch": *Minneapolis Journal*, Feb. 26, 1906.
358   "so warmly . . . good sense and humor": RSB, *American Chronicle*, pp. 98, 99.
359   "Why bother": Ibid., p. 179.
359   a more obscure series: Ibid., pp. 143–45.
359   "no sign of living creatures . . . a man's heart": RSB, "The Great Southwest. III. Irrigation," *Century
      Illustrated Magazine* (July 1902), p. 361.
359   "My dear Mr. Baker": TR to RSB, June 25, 1903, *LTR*, Vol. 3, p. 504.
359   "get at the exact . . . suspicious in the extreme": RSB to TR [draft letter, n.d.], RSB Papers.
360   "I suppose . . . our getting the proof": TR to RSB, July 4, 1903, in *LTR*, Vol. 3, p. 510.
360   "I was so eager": RSB, *American Chronicle*, p. 170.
360   "I was determined": Ibid.
360   "If ever men . . . implacable desert": RSB, "The Great Southwest. III. Irrigation," *Century Illustrated
      Magazine* (July 1902), pp. 361–63.
361   the four men crowded: RSB, Notebook, July 15, 1903, RSB Papers.
361   "The President lives": RSB to J. Stannard Baker, July 16, 1903, RSB Papers.
361   "Robust, hearty": RSB, *American Chronicle*, p. 171.
361   "takes an extraordinary interest": RSB to J. Stannard Baker, July 16, 1903, RSB Papers.
361   "I don't care": RSB, *American Chronicle*, p. 172.
361   "on the market at reasonable": *Minneapolis Journal*, July 30, 1903.
361   "Who is the chief . . . get together on these subjects": RSB, *American Chronicle*, p. 172.
362   "As the time drew near": Ibid.
362   Baker's meticulous research . . . cleared Charles Walcott: RSB to Gifford Pinchot, July 17, 1903, RSB
      Papers.
362   Pinchot expressed great satisfaction: Gifford Pinchot to RSB, July 23, 1903, RSB Papers.
362   "I am immensely": TR to RSB, Oct. 15, 1903, TRC.
362   Investigating . . . Steffens had unearthed evidence: LS, *The Autobiography*, p. 521.
362   Fuller Construction Company was providing: *Wall Street Journal*, Oct. 24, 1903.
363   "riding about in his cab . . . $1500 or less": RSB, "The Trust's New Tool—The Labor Boss," *McClure's*
      (November 1903), pp. 30–31.
363   "starting with no . . . hand of the Trust": Ibid., pp. 39–40.
363   "Curiously enough": Ibid., p. 41.
363   "Worse still": Ibid., p. 33.
363   Jerome finally indicted Parks: Ibid.
364   "the need of . . . perpetrated by labor men": TR to RSB, Oct. 21, 1903, RSB Papers.
364   "When I get back East . . . to do so": RSB to TR, Nov. 10, 1903, TRC.
364   "When the corporations": *Wall Street Journal*, Oct. 24, 1904.
364   John Brooks publicly endorsed: Semonche, *Ray Stannard Baker*, p. 113.
364   flocked . . . "the greatest reporter": Louis Filler, *The Muckrakers* (Stanford, CA: Stanford University
      Press, 1993), p. 87.
364   "You have gone": John S. Phillips to RSB, Nov. 10, 1903, RSB Papers.
364   "a man can have . . . your perfect honesty": LS to RSB, Nov. 8, 1903, RSB Papers.

365   "were tired at night": RSB, "The Trust's New Tool—The Labor Boss," *McClure's* (November 1903), p. 34.

365   Neidig . . . built up a following: RSB, "The Lone Fighter," *McClure's* (December 1903), p. 195.

365   "We hear of": RSB, "The Trust's New Tool—The Labor Boss," *McClure's* (November 1903), p. 35.

365   "threatened with": RSB, "The Lone Fighter," *McClure's* (December 1903), p. 195.

365   "The 'lone fighter' ": C. S. Booth to RSB, Dec. 28, 1903, RSB Papers.

365   "a true and faithful . . . hands of workingmen": George O'Kane to RSB, Nov. 1, 1903, RSB Papers.

365   "splendid . . . sound and honest basis": Robert E. Neidig to RSB, Feb. 18, 1904, RSB Papers.

365   "My present work": RSB to J. Stannard Baker, Jan. 31, 1904, RSB Papers.

365   "probably doing more": RSB to J. Stannard Baker, Mar. 27, 1904, RSB Papers.

CHAPTER THIRTEEN: Toppling Old Bosses

Page

366   "mighty little letup . . . kind of a summer": TR to CRR, Sept. 23, 1903, in *LTR*, Vol. 3, pp. 604–5.

366   "I suppose young girls . . . even in Tammany": TR to Edward Stanton Martin, July 30, 1903, in ibid., p. 535.

367   "little mother . . . comforts to her": TR to EKR, Nov. 14, 1903, Derby Papers.

367   "looks so young and pretty": TR to Emily Carow, Aug. 6, 1903, in *LTR*, Vol. 3, p. 544.

367   "watched the white": TR to HCL, Sept. 30, 1903, in ibid., p. 606.

367   "Whether I shall": TR to CRR, Sept. 23, 1903, in ibid., p. 605.

367   "determined foes . . . of real moment": TR to George Trevelyan, May 28, 1904, in *LTR*, Vol. 4, pp. 806–7.

368   "flesh of": WAW, "Seconding the Motion," *Saturday Evening Post*, July 23, 1904, p. 4.

368   "pass the word . . . leave the president": WAW, "The President: The Friends and Enemies He Has Made," *Saturday Evening Post*, April 4, 1903.

368   "reform was . . . bobbing up in Congress": WAW, *The Autobiography*, p. 368.

368   "war on the railroads": LS, *The Struggle for Self-Government* (New York: McClure, Phillips & Co., 1906), p. 79.

368   "You may be an editor": LS, *The Autobiography*, p. 364.

369   "My business is to find": LS to Joseph Steffens, May 18, 1902, in LS et al., eds., *Letters of Lincoln Steffens*, Vol. 1, p. 156.

369   "If I should be": IMT, *All in the Day's Work*, p. 201.

369   Joe Folk and the investigations: "An Exposer of Municipal Corruptions," *The Bookman* (November 1903), pp. 247–48.

369   pervasive corruption: LS, *The Autobiography*, p. 368.

369   "safe . . . man of thirty-three": Johnson and Malone, eds., *Dictionary of American Biography* (New York: Charles Scribner's Sons, 1931), Vol. 3, p. 490.

369   "of bribing . . . no names were mentioned": LS, *The Autobiography*, p. 370.

370   "to the full extent . . . and confessed": Ibid., p. 371.

370   the money "was theirs": Lincoln Steffens, *The Shame of the Cities* (New York: Hill & Wang, 1904), pp. 86, 82.

370   "So long has": Ibid., p. 22.

370   "the greatest oak . . . oath of office": Ibid., p. 39.

370   due to receive over $200,000: Ibid., pp. 88–89.

370   "Missouri, Missouri": Ibid., p. 96.

371   Steffens drafted a new version: LS, *The Autobiography*, pp. 373–74.

371   "so frightened": LS, *The Shame of the Cities*, p. 34.

371   These spoils were divided: Ibid., pp. 48–50.

371   "Your article is": McClure to LS, Nov. 7, 1902, LS Papers.

371   "We'll call it": LS, *The Autobiography*, p. 374.

371   "You have made": McClure to LS, Nov. 10, 1902, LS Papers.

371   "Mr. Steffens's": "Tammany Outdone in St. Louis," *Outlook*, Jan. 10, 1903, p. 106.

372   "doing a public . . . wave of reform": *Arizona Republic* (Phoenix, AZ), Jan. 6, 1903.

372   "The newsstand had": LS, *The Autobiography*, p. 392.

372   a London editor . . . on the box lid: LS to Joseph Steffens, Dec. 13, 1903, in LS et al., *Letters of Lincoln Steffens*, Vol. 1, p. 160.

372   test his "dawning theory": LS, *The Autobiography*, p. 393.

372   "was not merely": LS, *The Shame of the Cities*, p. 9.

372   Wary of "philosophical generalizations": LS, *The Autobiography*, p. 393.

372   McClure feared: McClure to John S. Phillips, Mar. 20, 1903, Phillips MSS.

372   "facts, startling facts": LS, *The Autobiography*, p. 393.

372   "The disagreement became . . . stick to facts": Ibid., pp. 392–93.

373   Butler had directed the nominations: LS, *The Struggle for Self-Government*, pp. 7–8.
373   the presiding justice publicly called: Joseph W. Folk to LS, Mar. 19, 1903, LS Papers.
373   All the felons were back: LS, *The Shame of the Cities*, pp. 98, 100.
373   "Your narrative lacks . . . working out the article": McClure to LS, Jan. 20, 1903, LS Papers.
373   200,000 people sported: LS, *The Shame of the Cities*, pp. 14–15.
373   "Your article is . . . commencing to speak": Joseph W. Folk to LS, Mar. 28, 1903, LS Papers.
373   "The permanent remedy": Joseph W. Folk to LS, April 15, 1903, LS Papers.
373   "I must tell you": McClure to LS, June 17, 1903, LS Papers.
373   "the candidate . . . any other organ": McClure to LS, May 27, 1903, LS Papers.
374   "just chew[ing] the rag": LS, *The Autobiography*, p. 416.
374   "wise guys" in Minneapolis: Ibid., pp. 386, 382.
374   "Thieves, politicians . . . might as well talk": Ibid., p. 386.
374   "the best interviewer . . . a demi-god": Stephen J. Whitfield, "Muckraking Lincoln Steffens," *Virginia Quarterly Review* (Winter 1978), p. 87.
374   not "a temporary evil": LS, *The Autobiography*, p. 413.
374   "buying boodlers": LS, *The Shame of the Cities*, p. 3.
374   "public spirit became": Ibid., p. vii.
374   Steffens was hailed: *New York Tribune*, April 10, 1904.
374   agitator William Lloyd Garrison: *Congregationalist and Christian World*, April 9, 1904.
374   "a new kind" of journalist: "A Master Journalist," *Current Literature* (June 1904), p. 610.
374   "Instead of having": Richard Duffy, "Lincoln Steffens," *The Critic* (May 1904), p. 402.
374   "correctly diagnosed": "The Diagnosis and Cure of Municipal Corruption," *Outlook*, April 16, 1904, p. 917.
374   "into the wards": "William Allen White on Mr. Steffens's Book," *McClure's* (June 1904), pp. 220–21.
375   "have done more": "A Master Journalist," *Current Literature* (June 1904), p. 611.
375   "the political . . . stream of pollution": LS, *The Struggle for Self-Government*, p. 3.
375   "almost any State": Ibid., p. 5.
375   "the System": Ibid., p. 11.
375   "this paper government": Ibid., p. 15.
375   "appealing his case": Ibid., p. 16.
375   "that corruption": Ibid., p. 36.
375   a sweeping bribery scheme: Ibid., pp. 35–36.
375   "brilliant reductions": Kaplan, *Lincoln Steffens*, p. 125.
375   "a striking article . . . of his fellow-men": *NYT*, Mar. 30, 1904.
375   "Your last article . . . bloodless political revolution": Joseph W. Folk to LS, April 17, 1904, LS Papers.
376   "fixed . . . him with defeat": LS, *The Struggle for Self-Government*, p. 108.
376   "To have you turn": Belle La Follette to LS, Aug. 14, 1904, LS Papers.
376   his "long, hard fight": LS, *The Struggle for Self-Government*, p. 118.
376   "La Follette's people": LS to Joseph Steffens, Oct. 2, 1904, in LS et al., *Letters of Lincoln Steffens*, Vol. 1, p. 168.
376   "met a friendly legislature": Thomas Malone, ed., *Dictionary of American Biography* (New York: Charles Scribner's Sons, 1933), Vol. 5, p. 544.
376   "gone through the fire": Robert La Follette to LS, Nov. 14, 1904, LS Papers.
376   "No one will . . . court of last resort": Ibid.
376   "The President has": William Loeb to LS, Aug. 24, 1903, LS Papers.
377   renewing a friendship: *Racine [WI] Daily Journal*, Aug. 31, 1903; LS to Joseph Steffens, Oct. 17, 1903, LS Papers.
377   distance "as a political critic": H. H. Stein, "Theodore Roosevelt and the Press: Lincoln Steffens," *Mid-America* (April 1972), p. 98.
377   "He is a Democrat": LS to TR, Sept. 28, 1903, LS Papers.
377   "I wonder if you realize": LS to TR, Sept. 30, 1903, LS Papers.
377   "he and the President": LS to Joseph Steffens, Oct. 17, 1903, LS Papers.
377   "a complete destroying . . . on our part": TR to Thomas Jasper Akins, April 5, 1904, in *LTR*, Vol. 4, p. 771.
377   choosing to nominate Cyrus P. Walbridge: Steven L. Piott, *Holy Joe: Joseph W. Folk and the Missouri Idea* (Columbia: University of Missouri Press, 1997), p. 86.
377   was delighted when William Allen White: WAW to Samuel Adams, Nov. 9, 1904, White Papers.
377   "with the boodlers . . . traitor to a state": *Emporia [KS] Gazette*, reprinted in *Chicago Tribune*, July 22, 1904.
378   "a state of violent": *Washington Post*, July 25, 1904.
378   Folk ran a superb campaign . . . 30,000 votes: Piott, *Holy Joe*, p. 89.
378   "It must make you feel": Joseph W. Folk to LS, Nov. 9, 1905, LS Papers.

378 He reiterated the profound obligation: Joseph W. Folk to LS, April 17 & May 22, 1904, LS Papers.
378 "one of the greatest moral": *The Arena* (August 1904), p. 91.
378 "discovered that": New York *World*, reprinted in *Minneapolis Daily Times*, May 16, 1904.
378 "a powerful exponent": *The North American* (Philadelphia), Aug. 15, 1905.
378 "must-read" pieces: Winston Churchill in Semonche, *Ray Stannard Baker*, p. 120.
378 "distinctly literary . . . go wrong in the end": *Daily Northwestern* (Oshkosh, WI), Mar. 8, 1905.
378 for a potential series of articles: LS to Joseph Steffens, Oct. 17, 1903, LS Papers.
378 McClure preferred to continue: Lyon, *Success Story*, p. 222.
379 "assume the responsibilities": Herbert Croly, *Marcus Alonzo Hanna, His Life and Work* (New York: The Macmillan Co., 1912), p. 426.
379 "When you know": MAH to TR, May 23, 1903, TRC.
379 "the time had come . . . as a boon": TR to HCL, May 27, 1903, in *LTR*, Vol. 3, pp. 481–82.
379 "Your telegram received": TR to MAH, May 25, 1903, in ibid., p. 481.
379 "In view of": MAH to TR, May 27, 1903, in ibid., p. 481.
379 "It was surrender": *Oxnard* [CA] *Courier*, June 6, 1903.
379 "Hanna Backs Down . . . President's Wishes": *Fort Wayne* [IN] *Journal-Gazette* and *Trenton* [NJ] *Times*, May 27, 1903.
379 "I hated to . . . half hours chat": TR to MAH, May 29, 1903, TRJP.
380 "the most arduous": Croly, *Marcus Alonzo Hanna*, p. 450.
380 "an overwhelming personal victory": *Minneapolis Journal*, Nov. 5, 1903.
380 "almost unique . . . discredited leader": New York *Sun*, Nov. 6, 1903.
380 "There is alarm": *Stark County Democrat* (Canton, OH), Nov. 6, 1903.
380 "the turning point . . . from Theodore Roosevelt": Cited in New York *Sun*, Nov. 6, 1903.
380 "The wealthy capitalists": TR to Nicholas M. Butler, Nov. 4, 1903, in *LTR*, Vol. 3, p. 641.
380 "by the bushel":New York *Sun*, Nov. 6, 1903.
380 "It is agreed": *Stark County Democrat*, Nov. 6, 1903.
380 Roosevelt had "lost his popularity in": *Daily Telegram* (Eau Claire, WI), Dec. 12, 1903.
380 "the general idea . . . out on the plains!": Henry Hoyt to WHT, Oct. 19, 1903, WHTP.
381 "worried lest Hanna . . . getting the delegates": *Davenport* [IA] *Weekly Leader*, Dec. 11, 1903.
381 "hoping to get Hanna": LS to Joseph Steffens, Dec. [n.d.], 1903, in LS et al., *Letters of Lincoln Steffens*, Vol. 1, p. 162.
381 "If I am to have": LS to Joseph Steffens, Dec. 13, 1903, in ibid., p. 160.
381 "for a short confab . . . the heaviest blows": LS to Joseph Steffens, Dec. [n.d.], 1903, in ibid., p. 162.
381 "Hanna is my villain . . . may do good": LS to Joseph Steffens, January 26, 1904, in ibid., p. 184.
381 "above the danger mark": LS to Joseph Steffens, Dec. [n.d.], 1903, in ibid., p. 162.
381 "degraded the municipal": LS, *The Struggle for Self-Government*, p. 165.
381 "He wanted to have a President": Ibid., p. 168.
382 "legislators were kidnapped": Ibid., pp. 179–80.
382 "government of the people": Ibid., p. 168.
382 "was the choice": Ibid., p. 162.
382 "the senator's advanced age": *Minneapolis Journal*, Feb. 5, 1904.
382 "For some inexplicable": TR to Elihu Root, Feb. 16, 1904, in *LTR*, Vol. 4, p. 730.
382 "My Dear Mr. President . . . friendship as ever": *New York Tribune*, Feb. 24, 1904.
382 "The illness of Hanna": LS to Joseph Steffens, Feb. 14, 1904, in LS et al., *Letters of Lincoln Steffens*, Vol. 1, p. 165.
382 the old senator seemed to rally: *Washington Times*, Feb. 12, 1904; *St. Louis Republic*, Feb. 13, 1904.
382 "Today he is . . . decide his fate": LS to Joseph Steffens, Feb. 14, 1904, in LS et al., *Letters of Lincoln Steffens*, Vol. 1, p. 165.
382 after "a brave struggle," he died: James Rudolph Garfield, Diary, Feb. 15, 1904, Garfield Papers.
382 "all talk": *Daily Northwestern*, Feb. 21, 1904.
382 open resistance to Roosevelt: John Morton Blum, *The Republican Roosevelt* (Cambridge, MA: Harvard University Press, 1961), p. 54.
382 "Of course, Hanna's death": Albert Boyden to RSB, Feb. 15, 1904, RSB Papers.
383 "the best-governed": LS, "Ohio: A Tale of Two Cities," *McClure's* (July 1905), p. 293.
383 "appeared just": Brand Whitlock, *Forty Years of It* (New York: D. Appleton & Co., 1914), pp. 168, 167.
383 "My feeling": Tom L. Johnson to LS, Oct. 8, 1908, LS Papers.
383 "The day of the American . . . McClure and Lincoln Steffens": Cited in *Congregationalist and Christian World*, Nov. 18, 1905.
383 "To you, more than": Publicity copy, *McClure's* (November, 1905).
383 "very much like": Kaplan, *Lincoln Steffens*, p. 125.
383 "The story is": "Interview with S. S. McClure," *The North American*, Aug. 15, 1905.
383 "mold it into a story . . . vital interest": *Minneapolis Journal*, Feb. 26, 1906.

383   "We were ourselves": RSB, *American Chronicle*, p. 183.
384   "Month after month": Ibid., p. 184.
384   "a medal of honor . . . being accomplished": *Minneapolis Tribune*, May 16, 1904.
384   "when the historian": "The Literature of Exposure," *The Independent*, Mar. 22, 1906, p. 690.

CHAPTER FOURTEEN: "Thank Heaven You Are to Be with Me!"

Page
385   "You have been . . . absolutely cut off": Horace Taft to WHT, Nov. 2, 1903, WHTP.
386   "it would be impossible": TR, *An Autobiography*, p. 430.
386   "guilty of an irreparable . . . in Judge Holmes' favor": TR to HCL, July 10, 1902, in *LTR*, Vol. 3, pp. 288–89.
386   "the hearty approval": *Logansport* [IN] *Journal*, Sept. 9, 1902.
386   "no small amount of praise": *Daily Californian* (Bakersfield, CA), Sept. 5, 1902.
386   "of utmost importance": TR to WHT, Oct. 25, 1902, TRP.
386   Taft's views on economic matters: TR to HCL, July 10, 1902, in *LTR*, Vol. 3, p. 288.
386   "the blindness and greed . . . freedom of contract": WHT to TR, Nov. 9, 1902, TRP.
386   "I hesitated long": TR to WHT, Oct. 21, 1902, in *LTR*, Vol. 3, p. 358.
387   "All his life": HHT, *Recollections of Full Years*, p. 263.
387   "Great honor deeply": WHT to TR, Oct. 28, 1902, in ibid., p. 264.
387   "I am disappointed": TR to WHT, Oct. 29, 1902, in *LTR*, Vol. 3, p. 372.
387   "unanswerable": HHT, *Recollections of Full Years*, p. 266.
387   "I am awfully sorry": TR to WHT, Nov. 26, 1902, in *LTR*, Vol. 3, p. 382.
387   "He is extremely . . . satisfied with your decision": Henry W. Taft to WHT, Jan. 10, 1903, WHTP.
388   "really leaves me": WHT to Charles P. Taft, Jan. 7, 1903, WHTP.
388   "within a few months" Taft would resign: *Washington Times*, Dec. 9, 1902.
388   "heaved a sigh . . . one more protest": HHT, *Recollections of Full Years*, p. 266.
388   "Recognize soldiers duty . . . I bow to it": WHT to TR, Jan. 8. 1903, TRP.
389   "proudest and happiest" moments: Pringle, *Life and Times*, Vol. 1, p. 245.
389   "flags flying" . . . WE WANT TAFT: HHT, *Recollections of Full Years*, p. 267.
389   "This is a spontaneous . . . all Philippine questions": Ibid., p. 268.
389   "the thousands of people": *Daily Kennebeck Journal* (Augusta, ME), Jan. 12, 1903.
389   "All right stay": TR to WHT, Jan. 13, 1903, in HHT, *Recollections of Full Years*, p. 269.
389   "very sorry . . . take you away": TR to WHT, Jan. 29, 1903, in *LTR*, Vol. 3, p. 413.
389   "with renewed vigour": HHT, *Recollections of Full Years*, p. 269.
389   "working for other people": WHT to William Worthington, Feb. 6, 1904, WHTP.
390   "I was not a month": *Cedar Rapids* [IA] *Evening Gazette*, Jan. 25, 1904.
390   "There is not": TR, "Speech at Fargo, N.D., April 7, 1903," in TR and Lewis, *A Compilation of the Messages and Speeches*, p. 269.
390   "a personality which . . . administrative and legislative": Henry Taft to WHT, Jan. 10, 1903, WHTP.
390   "Stood trip well . . . How is the horse?": *Boston Daily Globe*, Jan. 31, 1904.
390   "a magnificent animal": Pringle, *Life and Times*, Vol. 1, p. 236.
390   "You will think I am . . . to leave me next fall": TR to WHT, Feb. 14, 1903, in *LTR*, Vol. 3, pp. 425–26.
390   "the wisest": Sullivan, *Our Times*, Vol. 3, p. 279.
391   "I wish to heaven . . . questions that come up": TR to WHT, Feb. 14, 1903, in *LTR*, Vol. 3, pp. 425–26.
391   "If only there were": Ibid., p. 426.
391   "In view of your desire . . . a definite answer": WHT to TR, April 3, 1903, TRP.
391   "in line with the kind": HHT, *Recollections of Full Years*, p. 269.
392   "prophesied on the day": WHT to Horace Taft, Aug. 19, 1903, WHTP.
392   "If I were to go . . . live in a boarding house": WHT to Charles P. Taft, Mar. 27, 1903, WHTP.
392   Taft's mother . . . urged his return: Charles P. Taft to WHT, May 8, 1903, WHTP.
392   the family was unanimous: Henry Taft to WHT, June 16, 1903, WHTP.
392   "I should prefer": Charles P. Taft to WHT, May 8, 1903, WHTP.
392   to give up so "great a work": Horace Taft to WHT, May 13, 1903, WHTP.
392   If acceptance of the secretaryship seemed inconsistent: Henry Taft to WHT, June 16, 1903, WHTP.
392   "earnest desire . . . embarrass your candidacy": WHT to TR, April 27, 1903, TRP.
393   "You don't know . . . Civil Service Commissioner": TR to WHT, June 9, 1903, in *LTR*, Vol. 3, pp. 485–86.
393   "should feel independent": WHT to HHT, Feb. 2, 1904, WHTP.
393   "struck me all in a heap": WHT to Charles P. Taft, Feb. [n.d.], 1904, WHTP.
393   "The President is very . . . the step at once": Henry Taft to WHT, June 16, 1903, WHTP.
393   "keep out of politics": WHT to Howard Hollister, Sept. 21, 1903, Pringle Papers.

393 "Thank Heaven": TR to WHT, June 9, 1903, in *LTR*, Vol. 3, p. 486.

393 "I have an additional . . . much to tell you": TR to WHT, Oct. 13, 1903, in ibid., p. 629.

394 "too amazed . . . a sacred potentate": *Davenport* [IA] *Weekly Leader*, Jan. 29, 1904.

394 "was most enjoyable": WHT to HHT, Feb. 1, 1904, WHTP.

394 the president stayed for hours: James Rudolph Garfield, Diary, Jan. 27, 1904, Garfield Papers.

394 affectionately known as "Big Bill": *Cedar Rapids* [IA] *Evening Gazette*, Jan. 25, 1904.

394 "Two men were never": *Washington Times*, Jan. 31, 1904.

394 "Taft is a splendid fellow": TR to Theodore Roosevelt, Jr., Feb. 6, 1904, TRJP.

394 "too much like" her husband: Ibid.

394 "As the people loved . . . his own impetuosity": Sullivan, *Our Times*, Vol. 3, pp. 16, 18.

395 "It was good": WHT to HHT, Feb. 1, 1904, WHTP.

395 "felt like crying": Horace Taft to WHT, Feb. 4, 1904, WHTP.

395 "democratic manner . . . breezy informality": *Washington Times*, Jan. 31, 1904.

395 "I'm mighty glad": *Cedar Rapids* [IA] *Evening Gazette*, Jan. 25, 1904.

395 "he found time": *Washington Times*, Jan. 31, 1904.

395 "He looks like": Sullivan, *Our Times*, Vol. 3, p. 15.

395 bombarded by dinner invitations: WHT to HHT, Mar. 4, 1904, WHTP.

395 "I went down": WHT to HHT, Feb. 12, 1904, WHTP.

395 "The President seems . . . opportunities of observation": WHT to HHT, Mar. 18, 1904, WHTP.

395 "coarse and brazen" divorced wife: WHT to HHT, Mar. 3, 1904, WHTP.

395 "the Chief of the Pawnees": WHT to HHT, April 16, 1904, WHTP.

395 Alice Roosevelt . . . poker with men: Stacy A. Cordery, *Alice: Alice Roosevelt Longworth, from White House Princess to Washington Power Broker* (New York: Viking, 2007), pp. 65–66, 74, 78.

396 "a great deal of criticism . . . much troubled": WHT to HHT, April 5, 1904, WHTP.

396 "Isn't there anything": Hagedorn, *The Roosevelt Family of Sagamore Hill*, p. 186.

396 "I do not feel": WHT to HHT, Mar. [n.d.], 1904, WHTP.

396 "loaded tons of work . . . for the Administration": Arthur Wallace Dunn, *From Harrison to Harding, A Personal Narrative, Covering a Third of a Century, 1888–1921* (New York: G. P. Putnam's Sons, 1922), p. 67.

396 a "trouble-shooter . . . there Taft was sent": Sullivan, *Our Times*, Vol. 3, p. 12.

396 "extremely popular both . . . as the other": *Iowa Postal Card* (Fayette, IA), April 28, 1904.

396 "Things have quieted down": A. B. Fergusson to WHT, Dec. 30, 1903, WHTP.

397 loath to invest "so far from home": *NYT*, Mar. 11 & April 11, 1904.

397 vital infrastructure projects would be undertaken: *Janesville* [WI] *Daily Gazette*, Mar. 25, 1904; *NYT*, April 11, 1904.

397 Cannon's approval of the railroad bill: WHT to HHT, Mar. 31, 1904, WHTP.

397 "All in favor . . . the bill is passed": *Waterloo* [IA] *Daily Reporter*, May 20, 1904.

397 "I have been working": WHT to HHT, Mar. 31, 1904, WHTP.

397 the bill finally passed: *NYT*, Feb. 7, 1905.

397 "it would seem": *Logansport* [IN] *Pharos*, Feb. 2, 1904.

397 allies of the sugar and tobacco industries vowed: *Post-Standard* (Syracuse, NY), Mar. 3, 1904.

397 "I can see": WHT to TR, Jan. 27, 1903, TRP.

398 "The interest of dollars": Lyman Abbott to WHT, Feb. 20, 1903, WHTP.

398 "You are unjust . . . skillful and resolute": TR to WHT, Mar. 19, 1903, in *LTR*, Vol. 3, p. 450.

398 as word spread . . . seating was filled to capacity: New York *Sun*, Mar. 15, 1904.

398 "nervous expectancy": *Boston Daily Globe*, Mar. 15, 1904; *NYT*, Mar. 15, 1904.

398 "paper and pencil . . . against daring financiers": *Boston Daily Globe*, Mar. 15, 1904.

398 "Oyez, Oyez, Oyez": Ibid.

398 "being an Ohio man . . . was the alternative": WHT to Joseph B. Bishop, Jan. 24, 1903, WHTP.

399 "How eminently characteristic": TR to Joseph B. Bishop, Mar. 10, 1903, TRP.

399 "everyone was alert": *Boston Daily Globe*, Mar. 15, 1904.

399 "No scheme or device": *Northern Securities Company v. United States*, 193 U.S. 197 (1904).

399 "holding companies . . . of the entire country": New York *World*, Mar. 15, 1904.

399 "it was all over": *Boston Daily Globe*, Mar. 15, 1904.

399 If "Congress can strike": *Northern Securities Company v. United States*, 193 U.S. 197 (1904).

399 "the surprise of the day . . . champion of labor": *Boston Daily Globe*, Mar. 15, 1904.

399 "while the merger": New York *Sun*, Mar. 15, 1904.

399 "I could carve out . . . it was never the same": Harbaugh, *Power and Responsibility*, p. 162.

399 "put aside all else": *Washington Post*, Mar. 15, 1904.

399 "hardly be exaggerated": New York *World*, Mar. 15, 1904.

400 "more to the people . . . greater than the law": *Public Opinion*, Mar. 24, 1904, p. 356.

400 the great "trust-buster": Hofstadter, *The Age of Reform*, p. 238.
400 "run amuck": *Public Opinion*, Mar. 24, 1904, p. 357.
400 "this power": "Mr. Roosevelt's Platform," *Outlook*, July 2, 1904, p. 481.
400 "If a corporation": TR to RSB, Aug. 27, 1904, in *LTR*, Vol. 4, p. 909.
400 "the selfish rich . . . lunatic fringe": Blum, *The Republican Roosevelt*, p. 60.

CHAPTER FIFTEEN: "A Smile That Won't Come Off"

Page
402 Strikers, he reported . . . were in peril: James H. Peabody to TR, Nov. 16 & 18, 1903, in Carroll D. Wright, *A Report on Labor Disturbances in the State of Colorado: From 1880 to 1904, Inclusive, with Correspondence Relating Thereto* (Washington, DC: Government Printing Office, 1905), pp. 9–10.
402 "no lawful authority . . . to control": Elihu Root to James H. Peabody, Nov. 17 & 19, 1903, in ibid., pp. 9, 11.
402 "corruption & bribery": RSB to J. Stannard Baker, Nov. 18, 1903, RSB Papers.
402 "had a pad . . . conditions in the West": RSB to Jessie Baker, Dec. 3, 1903, RSB Papers.
402 "I believe in": TR to RSB, Oct. 21, 1903, TRP.
402 With the president's blessing: TR to RSB, Nov. 25, 1903, TRP.
402 "everything the men wanted" . . . to stem the corruption and violence: RSB, "The Reign of Lawlessness: Anarchy and Despotism in Colorado," *McClure's* (May 1904), pp. 43–53.
403 "I have endeavored": RSB to TR, April 19, 1904, TRP.
403 "the most masterly": *The Arena* (August 1904), p. 191.
403 "This language is not": *Wall Street Journal*, April 25, 1904.
404 Roosevelt . . . had it circulated among officials: TR to Carroll D. Wright, Aug. 13, 1904, in *LTR*, Vol. 4, p. 891.
404 On June 6 . . . the "dastardly crime": Wright, *A Report*, p. 247.
404 "the least anarchistic expression": *Weekly Gazette* (Colorado Springs, CO), June 9, 1904.
404 "wives and sisters": *Boston Daily Globe*, June 11, 1904.
404 "in the name of law and order": *Reno [NV] Evening Gazette*, June 10, 1904.
404 "Having refused": TR to Carroll D. Wright, Aug. 5, 1904, in *LTR*, Vol. 4, p. 883.
404 "If it becomes necessary": TR to Carroll D. Wright, Aug. 13, 1904, in ibid., p. 891.
404 "the basis of": RSB to J. Stannard Baker, Jan. 29, 1905, RSB Papers.
404 "as the representative": TR to Philander C. Knox, Nov. 10, 1904, in *LTR*, Vol. 4, p. 1024.
405 "He was most . . . correct & fair": RSB to J. Stannard Baker, Jan. 29, 1905, RSB Papers.
405 the mine owners finally agreed: Wright, *A Report,* p. 32.
405 Governor Peabody was forced out of office: *New York Tribune*, Mar. 18, 1905.
405 the state legislature passed a state law: *Laws Passed at the Fifteenth Session of the General Assembly . . .* (Denver, CO: Smith-Brooks Printing Co., 1905).
405 "barring a cataclysm . . . sullen grumbling": TR to Kermit Roosevelt, June 21, 1904, in *LTR*, Vol. 4, p. 840.
405 "the thunderous demonstration": *San Francisco Chronicle*, June 22, 1904.
405 "a lifeless gathering": Francis E. Leupp, "The Republican Convention," *Outlook*, July 2, 1904, p. 490.
405 "sober and unhysterical": *New York Tribune*, June 22, 1904.
405 An enormous portrait of Hanna: *New York Tribune*, June 21, 1904.
405 "because they had to": Leupp, "The Republican Convention," *Outlook*, July 2, 1904, p. 489.
405 "shadow of the chance . . . he can overcome the people": WAW, "Seconding the Motion," *Saturday Evening Post*, July 23, 1904, pp. 4–5.
406 this spirit of rebellion . . . to realize "a better world": WAW, *The Autobiography*, p. 88.
406 "a new element . . . for his times": WAW, "Americans Look to Roosevelt to Solve New Perils to Nation," *Chicago Tribune*, Oct. 24, 1904.
406 "more than he needed the party": *Minneapolis Journal*, Nov. 9, 1904.
406 "professional politicians . . . grip of power": Leupp, "The Republican Convention," *Outlook*, July 2, 1904, p. 491.
406 taking control of . . . growl behind them": Ibid.
406 With his reputation for honesty: *New York Tribune*, Nov. 2, 1904.
406 "People may as well . . . irrevocable": TR to George Von Legerke Meyer, June 17, 1904, in *LTR*, Vol. 4, pp. 838–39.
406 "a formidable weapon": TR to Joseph Wharton, Nov. 22, 1904, in ibid., p. 1039.
406 "a cardinal policy": Milton W. Blumenberg, *Official Proceedings of the Thirteenth Republican National Convention: Held in the City of Chicago, June 21, 22, 23, 1904* (Minneapolis: Harrison & Smith Co., 1904), p. 134.
406 "four years more": *Public Opinion*, June 30, 1904, p. 806.

406 Roosevelt hesitated: TR to Nicholas M. Butler, Dec. 2, 1904, in *LTR*, Vol. 4, p. 838.

407 "of all men": TR to Theodore Roosevelt, Jr., May 14, 1904, TRJP.

407 "affectionate congratulations . . . his personal friends": *Post-Standard* (Syracuse, NY), June 24, 1904.

407 "in exceptionally good humor": *Trenton* [NJ] *Times*, June 24, 1904.

407 "With genial raillery": *Post-Standard* (Syracuse, NY), June 24, 1904.

407 "the hero . . . in their hearts": WAW, "The Great Political Drama in St. Louis," *Collier's*, July 12, 1904.

407 "eight-year reign was over": New York *World*, July 13, 1904.

408 "robbery of the many": Milton W. Blumenberg, *Official Report of the Proceedings of the Democratic National Convention Held in St. Louis, Mo., July 6, 7, 8, and 9, 1904* (New York: Press of the Publishers' Printing Co., 1904), p. 148.

408 the nominee was not apprised of his victory: *NYT*, July 10, 1904.

408 "the gold standard . . . decline the nomination": Blumenberg, *Official Report of the Proceedings of the Democratic National Convention*, p. 276.

408 no longer "an issue at this time": *Boston Daily Globe*, July 10, 1904.

408 "was most adroit . . . a clever politician": TR to John Hay, July 11, 1904, in *LTR*, Vol. 4, p. 852.

408 "all of Cleveland's": TR to HCL, July 14, 1904, in ibid., p. 858.

408 "was stronger": WHT to TR, July 16, 1904, TRP.

408 "a hard and uphill fight": TR to HCL, July 14, 1904, in *LTR*, Vol. 4, p. 858.

408 "I always like": TR to HCL, July 14, 1904, in ibid.

408 "was received . . . logical, convincing": *Minneapolis Journal*, July 28, 1904.

409 "characteristically forceful": *Titusville* [PA] *Herald*, July 28, 1904.

409 "keen and polished": HCL to TR, July 29, 1904, in TR and HCL, *Selections from the Correspondence*, Vol. 2, p. 92.

409 "used few gestures": *Washington Post*, Aug. 11, 1904.

409 mustered no "bugle call": *Boston Evening Transcript*, Aug. 27, 1904.

409 would not run for a second term: *Washington Post*, Aug. 11, 1904.

409 "shifty and tricky" gambit: TR to Joseph B. Bishop, Aug. 13, 1904, TRP.

409 failed to "straddle": TR to HCL, August 11, 1904, in *LTR*, Vol. 4, p. 887.

409 Taft's assessment had been correct: TR to HCL, July 22, 1904, in ibid., p. 863.

409 "His opponents may": WHT to HHT, Aug. 18, 1904, WHTP.

409 Roosevelt also circulated drafts: TR to John Hay, July 11, 1904, in *LTR*, Vol. 4, p. 853.

409 "I went at": William Dudley Foulke, *Lucius B. Swift, A Biography* (Indianapolis: Bobbs-Merrill Co. for the Indiana Hist. Soc., 1930), p. 73.

409 "Remarkable": *NYT*, Sept. 27, 1904.

409 "a veritable keynote": *Washington Post*, Sept. 12, 1904.

409 "the challenge contained . . . the Democrats have": WHT to TR, Sept. 14, 1904, TRP.

409 "the issues of the campaign": *Washington Post*, Sept. 27, 1904.

409 "a great paper . . . of the people": *NYT*, Sept. 27, 1904.

410 "heart to . . . his campaign": TR to Joseph B. Bishop, Sept. 28, 1904, TRP.

410 "take the offensive . . . sit still": TR to Kermit Roosevelt, Oct. 26, 1904, in *LTR*, Vol. 4, pp. 992–93.

410 "It seems strange": WHT to Howard Hollister, Sept. 21, 1903, WHTP.

410 "mere political discussion": WHT to HHT, Feb. 2, 1904, WHTP.

410 "I rather think": WHT to HHT, Sept. 27, 1904, WHTP.

410 "right down to": WHT to Charles P. Taft, June 23, 1904, WHTP.

410 "a great public document": TR to HCL, June 28, 1904, in *LTR*, Vol. 4, p. 849.

410 "a masterly argument . . . a truly great man": Garfield Diary, June 26 & Feb. 11, 1904, Garfield Papers.

410 presented his speech . . . at Sanders Theatre: *New York Tribune*, June 29, 1904.

410 Taft simply but clearly . . . "Philippines for the Filipinos": *Cincinnati Enquirer*, June 29, 1904.

411 Olney's rebuttal . . . "for they love him": Ibid.

411 "I fired my gun": WHT to TR, July 3, 1904, TRP.

411 "magical place": *Cincinnati Magazine* (August 1979), p. 72.

411 "The air is bracing": WHT to TR, July 3, 1904, TRP.

411 "The next ten days": WHT to HHT, Aug. 15, 1904, WHTP.

411 "a bit rusty": WHT to HHT, Aug. 3, 1904, WHTP.

411 "the Bench disqualifies": WHT to HHT, Aug. 15, 1904, WHTP.

412 "the size of her": WHT to Horace Taft, Aug. 4, 1904, WHTP.

412 Taft chose . . . a spirited defense: *NYT*, Aug. 28, 1904.

412 "When Theodore Roosevelt . . . previously formed opinion": Ibid.

412 "It was a success": WHT to HHT, Aug. 28, 1904, WHTP.

412 "It would be . . . support of his administration": *Titusville* [PA] *Herald*, July 29, 1904.

412 "a text-book for": Ibid.

412 a "glorious" triumph: WHT to TR, Sept. 7, 1904, TRP.
412 "I am pleased": TR to WHT, Sept. 10, 1904, in *LTR*, Vol. 4, p. 919.
412 "a rather gloomy letter": TR to Eugene Hale, Aug. 4, 1904, in ibid., p. 880.
412 "to speak without notes": WHT to HHT, Aug. 30, 1904, WHTP.
412 "great surprise" . . . proposed toasts: WHT to Howard Hollister, Sept. 16, 1904, WHTP.
413 "Mrs. Taft says": WHT to TR, Sept. 14, 1904, WHTP.
413 Roosevelt complained freely: TR to WHT, Sept. 5, 1904, WHTP.
413 Taft described a new diet: WHT to TR, Sept. 2, 1904, TRP.
413 "infernal liars . . . a corruption fund": TR to WHT, Sept. 10, 1904, in *LTR*, Vol. 4, p. 919.
413 "playing golf": WHT to TR, Sept. 7, 1904, TRP.
413 Taft was immediately dispatched: WHT to TR, Sept. 20, 1904, TRP.
413 "Do not in any speech": TR to WHT, Sept. 29, 1904, in *LTR*, Vol. 4, p. 960.
413 "the most auspicious in years": *Washington Post*, Oct. 2, 1904.
413 "After reading": Ibid.; *Hutchinson* [KS] *News*, Nov. 8, 1904.
413 In daily letters, she related: HHT to WHT, Oct. 3, 4 & 5, 1904, WHTP.
414 "I hope Charley's": WHT to HHT, Oct. 3, 1904, WHTP.
414 "I wish I could": WHT to HHT, Oct. 8, 1904, WHTP.
414 "I don't think": WHT to HHT, Oct. 6, 1904, WHTP.
414 "could not but smile": HHT to WHT, Oct. 7, 1904, WHTP.
414 a delegation of cigar and tobacco manufacturers: *NYT*, Oct. 10, 1904.
414 "to control cigar makers": WHT to HHT, Oct. 8, 1904, WHTP.
414 "just at the anxious time": WHT to HHT, Oct. 10, 1904, WHTP.
414 "I feel sure . . . emphasize the issue": WHT to TR, Oct. 10, 1904, TRP.
414 "Fiddle-dee-dee! . . . or something": TR to WHT, Oct. 11, 1904, in *LTR*, Vol. 4, p. 980.
414 "would not run": WHT to HHT, Oct. 12, 1904, WHTP.
415 "a man who never . . . liberty and equality": *Valentine* [NE] *Democrat*, Oct. 13, 1904.
415 "It is the culmination . . . utterly ignored": *Anaconda* [MT] *Standard*, Oct. 9, 1904.
415 conceding the region to Democrats: Ibid.
415 "full dinner pail": *Atlanta Constitution*, Oct. 18, 1904.
415 "He is on the side": New York *Sun*, July 30, 1904.
415 populist publications reviled him: TR to Joseph G. Cannon, Aug. 3, 1904, in *LTR*, Vol. 4, p. 880.
415 "without exception" . . . the closed shop: RSB, "Parker and Roosevelt on Labor: Real Views of the Two Candidates on the Most Vital National Problem," *McClure's* (November 1904), pp. 41–42.
415 "Personally he is": RSB to J. Stannard Baker, Sept. 8, 1904, RSB Papers.
416 "I cannot help feeling . . . but *no* easier": TR to RSB, Aug. 27, 1904, in *LTR*, Vol. 4, pp. 908, 910–11.
416 "I am perfectly astonished": RSB to TR, Sept. 6, 1904, TRP.
416 "a clear idea . . . preaches class hatred": RSB, "Parker and Roosevelt on Labor," *McClure's* (November 1904), pp. 51–52.
417 "thorough and painstaking" methods: *Los Angeles Times*, Nov. 3, 1904.
417 "the bulk of the voters . . . mass of voters": TR to Kermit Roosevelt, Oct. 26, 1904, in *LTR*, Vol. 4, p. 992.
417 "The steady advance": *NYT*, Oct. 2, 1904.
417 "would make the millions . . . a tremendous reform": LS to TR, Sept. 21, 1905, in LS et al., *Letters of Lincoln Steffens*, Vol. 1, p. 170.
417 "most emphatically" . . . or take executive action: TR to LS, Sept. 25, 1905, in *LTR*, Vol. 5, p. 36.
417 "entirely legitimate": TR to George B. Cortelyou, Oct. 26, 1904, in *LTR*, Vol. 4, p. 995.
418 Roosevelt willingly received hundreds of thousands of dollars: Morris, *Theodore Rex*, pp. 359–60.
418 "In view of the open": TR to George B. Cortelyou, Oct. 27, 1904, in *LTR*, Vol. 4, p. 998.
418 "big business corporations . . . entirely proper": TR to George B. Cortelyou, Oct. 26, 1904, in ibid., pp. 995–96.
418 "The fact that": *NYT*, Oct. 2, 1904.
418 corporations . . . "contributed to both campaign funds": *New York Tribune*, Nov. 1, 1904.
418 "in a conspiracy": *NYT*, Nov. 4, 1904.
418 "like a big stick": *Anaconda* [MT] *Standard*, Oct. 9, 1904.
418 "the prostitution": Ibid.
418 Cortelyou and Garfield were reluctant: Garfield Diary, Nov. 3, 1904, Garfield Papers.
418 "I don't see why": WHT to HHT, Nov. 3, 1904, WHTP.
419 "I am the man": TR to George B. Cortelyou, Nov. 2, 1904, in *LTR*, Vol. 4, pp. 1009–12.
419 to take the midnight train: Garfield Diary, Nov. 3, 1904, Garfield Papers.
419 "Blood Money . . . drew out of sight": *St. Louis Post-Dispatch*, Nov. 4, 1904.
419 "direct and fierce . . . in a few moments": *NYT*, Nov. 5, 1904.

419   "The gravamen of these charges . . . *unqualifiedly and atrociously false*": *NYT*, Nov. 5, 1904 (italics in the original).

420   "he had made no": *Post-Standard* (Syracuse, NY), Nov. 7, 1904.

420   "Parker fails to furnish proofs": TR to William Loeb, Nov. 6, 1904, in *LTR*, Vol. 4, p. 1015.

420   "has knocked Parker flat": Garfield Diary, Nov. 5, 1904, Garfield Papers.

420   "Parker's attacks": TR to Kermit Roosevelt, Nov. 6, 1904, in TR et al., eds., *Letters to Kermit from Theodore Roosevelt*, p. 83.

420   "he had never wanted . . . the United States": CRR, *My Brother*, p. 217.

420   "a first-class run": TR to Rudyard Kipling, Nov. 1, 1904, TRP.

420   "felt soured": TR to Kermit Roosevelt, June 21, 1904, in *LTR*, Vol. 4, p. 840.

420   a crowd of "home folk": *St. Louis Republic*, Nov. 9, 1904.

420   "sprang briskly": *Post-Standard* (Syracuse, NY), Nov. 9, 1904.

420   he caught the 1:14 train: *Washington Post*, Nov. 8, 1904.

420   "not to think of": TR to Kermit Roosevelt, Nov. 10, 1904, in *LTR*, Vol. 4, p. 1024.

420   "a plurality": *Oshkosh* [WI] *Daily Northwestern*, Nov. 9, 1904.

421   "a tremendous drift . . . very proud and happy": TR to Kermit Roosevelt, Nov. 10, 1904, in *LTR*, Vol. 4, p. 1024.

421   "no attempt . . . on the mantel shelf": *Oshkosh* [WI] *Daily Northwestern*, Nov. 9, 1904.

421   "I am deeply sensible": Kohlsaat, *From McKinley to Harding*, p. 137.

421   "a bid for votes": TR to Arthur Von Brisen, Oct. 27, 1904, in *LTR*, Vol. 4, p. 1000; *St. Paul* [MN] *Globe*, Nov. 10, 1904.

421   "use the office": TR, *An Autobiography*, p. 387.

421   "I feel very strongly . . . a new start": TR to George Otto Trevelyan, Nov. 4, 1904, in *LTR*, Vol. 4, pp. 1045–46.

422   "the greatest popular majority": TR to Kermit Roosevelt, Nov. 10, 1904, in TR et al., eds., *Letters to Kermit from Theodore Roosevelt,* p. 84.

422   He had won all . . . unexpected coup: Arthur Wallace Dunn, *How Presidents Are Made* (New York: Funk & Wagnalls, 1920), p. 85.

422   "I am stunned": TR to Kermit Roosevelt, Nov. 10, 1904, in *LTR*, Vol. 4, p. 1024.

422   "has had a smile": WHT to Charles P. Taft, Nov. 17, 1904, WHTP.

422   "The document that gave": Murat Halstead to WHT, April 17, 1905, WHTP.

422   "thousands of votes . . . willing to admit": Howard Hollister to WHT, Nov. 10, 1904, WHTP.

422   "the victory is . . . of the President": WHT to Henry Hoyt, Nov. 12, 1904, WHTP.

422   "It is no unheard of thing . . . must be protected": *Cincinnati Enquirer*, Nov. 11, 1904; *The News* (Frederick, MD), Nov. 11, 1904.

422   "Unless the Republican party": Henry Hoyt to WHT, Nov. 11, 1904, WHTP.

423   "pregnant with promise . . . history of the republic": *Minneapolis Journal*, Nov. 9, 1904.

423   "to the best": *St. Paul Globe*, Nov. 10, 1904.

423   "nothing but praise": *Public Opinion*, Nov. 17, 1904.

423   "to his everlasting honor" . . . his last: New York *Sun*, Nov. 9, 1904.

423   willingly cut off his hand at the wrist: Kohlsaat, *From McKinley to Harding*, p. 138.

CHAPTER SIXTEEN: "Sitting on the Lid"

Page

424   "blue, flecked . . . Roosevelt weather": *Boston Daily Globe*, Mar. 5, 1905.

424   "the morning sun": *Washington Post*, Mar. 5, 1905.

424   "supremely happy . . . moment of our lives": *Boston Daily Globe*, Mar. 5, 1905.

425   "a friendly little . . . truculent note": *Public Opinion*, Mar. 18, 1905.

425   "Much has been given . . . great wealth": TR, "Inaugural Address," March 4, 1905, in *WTR*, Vol. 15, pp. 267–69.

425   characteristic "earnestness": *Boston Daily Globe*, Mar. 5, 1905.

425   "tempestuous doings": See *Public Opinion*, Nov. 24, 1904.

425   "The Republican party": WAW, "The Reorganization of the Republican Party," *Saturday Evening Post*, Dec. 3, 1904.

425   "Everybody rejoices": *Ohio State Journal* (Columbus, OH), cited in *Van Wert* [OH] *Daily Bulletin*, April 5, 1905.

426   a "handsomely fitted" train: *NYT*, April 4, 1905.

426   "like a small boy" . . . office seekers: *Washington Post*, April 4, 1905.

426   "much more pleasant . . . the everlasting suspicion": TR to Kermit Roosevelt, April 14, 1905, in TR et al., eds., *Letters to Kermit from Theodore Roosevelt,* p. 97.

426   "wild enthusiasm . . . genuine pleasure": TR to John Hay, April 2, 1905, in *LTR*, Vol. 4, pp. 1159, 1156.

426 "in the saddle ... wolf hunter": TR to Kermit Roosevelt, April 14, 1905, in TR et al., eds., *Letters to Kermit from Theodore Roosevelt*, p. 98.

426 "up at daybreak ... band of huntsmen": New York *Sun*, April 21, 1905.

426 "roughened by wind": TR to Kermit Roosevelt, May 7, 1905, in TR et al., eds., *Letters to Kermit from Theodore Roosevelt*, pp. 99–100.

426 "Oh, things ... sitting on the lid": *NYT*, April 4, 1905; *Van Wert* [OH] *Daily Bulletin*, April 5, 1905.

426 "grave and exacting problems": *Washington Times* and *Van Wert* [OH] *Daily Bulletin*, April 5, 1905.

426 "Chair of the President ... Sec'y of War": *Harper's Weekly*, April 15, 1905.

426 "acting President ... all executive departments": *Van Wert* [OH] *Daily Bulletin*, April 5, 1905.

427 "the unusual sight": *NYT*, April 4, 1905.

427 "William Howard Taft": *Cleveland Leader*, cited in *Van Wert* [OH] *Daily Bulletin*, April 5, 1905.

427 a treaty was negotiated: TR, "Message to Congress," Dec. 3, 1903, in *WTR*, Vol. 15, pp. 202–12.

427 "I took the Canal Zone": Bishop, *Theodore Roosevelt and His Time*, Vol. 1, p. 308.

427 "that Roosevelt had ... value to the country": Viola Roseboro to Ada Pierce McCormick [n.d.], 1929, IMTC.

427 "You cannot conceive": *Baltimore Sun*, Feb. 22, 1904.

427 "He had an enormous": Burton, *William Howard Taft, in the Public Service*, p. 44.

427 the commission was authorized to establish: TR to WHT, May 9, 1904, in *LTR*, Vol. 4, pp. 788–89.

427 "really enough to occupy": Pringle, *Life and Times*, Vol. 1, pp. 280, 284.

427 "an independent colony": TR to WHT, Oct. 18, 1904, in *LTR*, Vol. 4, p. 986.

428 A small band of soldiers: WHT to Charles P. Taft, Nov. 17, 1904, WHTP.

428 "The whole atmosphere ... cries of 'Viva!' ": HHT, *Recollections of Full Years*, pp. 284, 287–89.

428 merely "experimental": David McCullough, *The Path Between the Seas: The Creation of the Panama Canal, 1870–1914* (New York: Simon & Schuster, 1977), p. 449.

428 When a virulent outbreak: Ibid., p. 452.

428 "Here again": TR to WHT, April 20, 1905, in *LTR*, Vol. 4, p. 1165.

428 eventually called for Wallace to resign: McCullough, *The Path Between the Seas*, p. 457.

428 "You are handling everything": TR to WHT, April 8, 1905, in *LTR*, Vol. 4, p. 1158.

428 "keeping the lid on": TR to WHT, April 20, 1905, in ibid., p. 1161.

428 "You are on the ground": Ibid., p. 1165.

429 "I wish you knew Taft": TR to George Trevelyan, May 13, 1905, in ibid., p. 1173.

429 "Taft, by the way": TR to John Hay, May 6, 1905, in ibid., p. 1168.

429 "everything was in good": T. H. Pardo de Tavera to WHT, May 6, 1905, WHTP.

429 lost its "Pole star": WHT to TR, Jan. 19, 1905; WHT to HHT, Sept. 24, 1905, WHTP.

429 "discontent": T. H. Pardo de Tavera to WHT, Feb. 5, 1905, WHTP.

429 "the only man who can": T. H. Pardo de Tavera to WHT, May 6, 1905, WHTP.

429 Taft assembled a party of eighty people: WHT to Charles P. Taft, July 24, 1905, WHTP.

429 "I doubt if so formidable": WHT to H. C. Corbin, Mar. 14, 1905, in Pringle, *Life and Times*, Vol. 1, p. 293.

429 "Just heard sad news": WHT to TR, July 1, 1905, TRP.

429 "If it were not" ... ask Elihu Root to take Hay's place: TR to WHT, July 3, 1905, in *LTR*, Vol. 4, p. 1260.

430 "hesitated a little ... no room for doubt": TR to HCL, July 11, 1905, in ibid., p. 1271.

430 Taft dispelled any qualms: Ibid., p. 1272.

430 "My dear fellow": TR to WHT, July 6, 1905, in ibid., p. 1261.

430 "I do not think": ARL, *Crowded Hours*, p. 69.

430 "The party has been": WHT to TR, July 13, 1905, TRP.

430 Friends and family had warned Taft: Horace Taft to WHT, Mar. 7, 1905; HHT to WHT, July 13, 1905, WHTP.

430 "She is quite amenable" ... Nevertheless, he remained troubled: WHT to HHT, Sept. 24, 1905, WHTP.

430 stories about the "fast set": WHT to HHT, Mar. 28, 1904, WHTP.

430 "She seems to be": WHT to HHT, July 31, 1905, WHTP.

430 "looked almost unreal": *Boston Daily Globe*, Aug. 8, 1905.

430 "usually confined to husband": WHT to HHT, Sept. 24, 1905, WHTP.

431 "I think I ought to know ... more or less": ARL, *Crowded Hours*, p. 88.

431 Guns boomed ... for the welcoming ceremony: *Galveston* [TX] *Daily News*, Aug. 8, 1905.

431 "the Philippines for ... would be recalled": *San Francisco Call*, Aug. 12, 1905.

431 The Filipino people: *New York Tribune*, Aug. 13, 1905.

431 "of sufficient rank ... entertain the party": WHT to HHT, Sept. 24, 1905, WHTP.

431 a "very handsome ball": Ibid.

431 "a long way in cementing": Mabel T. Boardman, "A Woman's Impressions of the Philippines," *Outlook*, Feb. 24, 1906.

431 Lodging with the Legardas: WHT to HHT, Sept. 24, 1905, Taft WHTP.

431 "All day long": Boardman, "A Woman's Impressions," *Outlook*, Feb. 24, 1906.

431 "utterly lacking in . . . of the government": WHT to HHT, Sept. 24, 1905, WHTP.

431 "restore the old condition" . . . considered friends: Ibid.

432 Taft and his entourage "made the round": *New York Tribune*, Aug. 24, 1905.

432 small boats . . . and farmers: Boardman, "A Woman's Impressions," *Outlook*, Feb. 24, 1906.

432 "a happy sea change . . . working out admirably": *New York Tribune*, Aug. 24, 1905.

432 "It was a great trip . . . due to your example": S. Young to WHT, Sept. 11, 1905, WHTP.

432 Taft secretly met . . . lasting consequences for the region: Bradley, *The Imperial Cruise*, pp. 249–50.

432 Roosevelt had closely followed: Howard K. Beale, *Theodore Roosevelt and the Rise of America to World Power* (Baltimore: Johns Hopkins University Press, 1956), p. 242.

432 From the start, he had sympathized: TR to WHT, April 20, 1905, in *LTR*, Vol. 4, pp. 1162–63.

432 he recognized . . . upsetting the balance of power: TR to WHT, April 8, 1905, in ibid., pp. 1158–59.

432 He was delighted . . . facilitate peace talks: WHT to TR, April 25, 1905, TRP.

432 curtailed his hunting expedition: TR to WHT, April 27, 1905, in *LTR*, Vol. 4, p. 1167.

432 Concealing the fact that the Japanese had initiated: TR to HCL, June 5, 1905, in ibid., p. 1202.

432 "open direct negotiations . . . and place of meeting": *Literary Digest*, June 17, 1905.

432 "It is recognized": *New York Tribune*, cited in ibid.

433 "a demonstrative welcome": *Minneapolis Tribune*, July 25, 1905.

433 "Korea being the direct cause . . . without the consent of Japan": WHT to TR, July 29, 1905, TRP.

433 "not harbor any . . . I know you can or will correct it": Ibid.

433 "Your conversation with Count Katsura": TR to WHT, July 31, 1905, in *LTR*, Vol. 4, p. 1293.

433 the peace envoys . . . met with the president: *Newark* [OH] *Advocate*, Aug. 5, 1905.

433 a buffet lunch: Morris, *Theodore Rex*, p. 407.

433 "prostrate in the enemy's hands" . . . extract an "indemnity": *San Francisco Call*, Aug. 12, 1905.

433 "I am having my hair": TR to Kermit Roosevelt, Aug. 25, 1905, in TR et al., *Letters to Kermit from Theodore Roosevelt*, p. 109.

433 In the end, the president persuaded the Japanese: Beale, *TR and the Rise of America,* pp. 255–62.

434 "hearty and vigorous": *Galveston* [TX] *Daily News*, Oct. 3, 1905; New York Sun, Oct. 3, 1905.

434 "We had a most interesting": James R. Garfield to Helen N. Garfield, Oct. 3, 1905, Garfield Papers.

434 "The city is all one": LS, "Ohio: A Tale of Two Cities," *McClure's* (July 1905), pp. 310–11.

434 "full of falsehoods": *Lima* [OH] *Daily News*, June 26, 1905.

434 "subservient" to Cox . . . systemic graft: *Washington Times*, Oct. 22, 1905.

434 "The stampede from": *Lima* [OH] *Daily News*, July 24, 1905.

434 "Governor Herrick . . . in line": LS to TR, Aug. 7, 1905, TRP.

435 "a most adroit": *Lima* [OH] *Times-Democrat*, Oct. 25, 1905.

435 Public condemnation . . . "not pleasant" for Taft: WHT to Howard Hollister, Oct. 3, 1905, WHTP.

435 "the official organ": *New Castle* [PA] *News*, July 26, 1905.

435 "Any pain you feel": WHT to Charles P. Taft, July 26, 1905, WHTP.

435 felt bound to declare: WHT to HHT, Oct. 5, 1905, WHTP.

435 Delivered before an overflowing audience: *Washington Post*, Oct. 22, 1905.

435 "the most severe rebuke . . . president's cabinet": *Hamilton* [OH] *Democrat*, Oct. 23, 1905.

435 "Cox and Coxism": *Elyria* [OH] *Republican*, Oct. 26, 1905.

435 "a local despotism": *Washington Times*, Oct. 22, 1905.

435 "distressing effect . . . the Republican organization": Ibid.; Pringle, *Life and Times*, Vol. 1, p. 269.

435 "made clear the difference" . . . others would do the same: *Van Wert* [OH] *Daily Bulletin*, Oct 24, 1905.

435 perpetuate the Cox machine . . . "his State and his party": *Washington Times*, Oct. 22, 1905.

435 "scathing denunciation": *Lima* [OH] *Times-Democrat*, Oct. 25, 1905.

435 "like the explosion": *Newark* [OH] *Advocate*, Oct. 23, 1905.

436 "We had about come": Benjamin Butterworth to WHT, Oct. 26, 1905, WHTP.

436 "You are the only man": Powel Crosley to WHT, Oct. 24, 1905, WHTP.

436 "You have done more good": Howard Hollister to WHT, Oct. 23, 1905, WHTP.

436 But Taft's hope . . . proved vain: LS, *The Struggle for Self-Government*, p. 208.

436 "Do not concern yourself": Myron Herrick to WHT, Nov. 15, 1905, WHTP.

436 a new Republican Club: Howard Hollister to WHT, Dec. 6 & 15, 1905, Feb. 1, 1906, WHTP; *Van Wert* [OH] *Daily Bulletin*, Mar. 14, 1906.

436 "Roosevelt Republican Club": *Van Wert* [OH] *Daily Bulletin*, Mar. 14, 1906.

436 "disabuse the public mind": Howard Hollister to WHT, Sept. 28, 1905, WHTP.

436   a dramatic "Oil War": IMT, "Roosevelt vs. Rockefeller," *The American Magazine* (December 1907), p. 119.

436   "Kansas is in the clutches": *Hutchinson* [KS] *News*, Feb. 2, 1905.

436   "On the instant": IMT, *All in the Day's Work*, p. 244.

437   "put on the screws" . . . a year later. WAW, "The Kansas Conscience," *The Reader* (October 1905), p. 489.

437   "the only transporter and buyer": IMT, "Roosevelt vs. Rockefeller," *The American Magazine* (December 1907), p. 119.

437   "a first-class" state refinery . . . "to be reasonable": IMT, *All in the Day's Work*, p. 249.

437   "without a market . . . men out of work": *Colorado Springs Gazette*, Mar. 13, 1905.

437   "was *punishing* Kansas . . . Well, we'll see about that!": IMT, "Kansas and the Standard Oil Company: A Narrative of Today, Part II," *McClure's* (October 1905), p. 618.

437   "from oppression" . . . refined products: *Atlanta Daily Democrat*, Feb. 20, 1905.

437   "hardly a secret" . . . instigated by the administration: *Hutchinson* [KS] *News*, Feb. 17, 1905.

437   "a rigid and . . . in the Kansas field": *Janesville* [WI] *Daily Gazette*, Feb. 18, 1905.

437   Garfield planned to travel to Kansas: *Syracuse* [NY] *Herald*, June 14, 1908.

438   "most important investigation": *Literary Digest*, Mar. 4, 1905.

438   Although passage of the House resolution: *Waterloo* [IA] *Times-Tribune*, Feb. 21, 1905.

438   "What would you think": IMT to JSP, Feb. 18, 1905, Phillips MSS.

438   "rank as one": *San Francisco Call*, Aug. 12, 1905.

438   "is to the present time": *The Critic*, April 1905, p. 287.

438   "darkened" her world: IMT, *All in the Day's Work*, p. 245.

438   "built himself into": IMT to Jessie Baker, Jan. 1, 1910, RSB Papers.

438   "I have thought" . . . dignify the Tarbell name: McClure to IMT, Mar. 29, 1905, IMTC.

438   "pathetic & characteristic" impulse: Ibid.

438   "with a heavy heart" . . . coming of "a prophet": IMT, *All in the Day's Work*, pp. 245, 247.

438   "unfair and illegal . . . all the world": *Iola* [KS] *Daily Register*, Mar. 15, 1905.

438   Local journalists trailed her: IMT to Albert Boyden, April 4, 1905, IMT Papers.

438   she hoped "to Heaven" . . . "until I have a hearing!": IMT to Albert Boyden, Mar. 20, 1905, IMT Papers.

438   would be "a good thing": *Iola* [KS] *Daily Register*, Mar. 16, 1905.

438   serve "as a measuring stick": IMT, *All in the Day's Work*, p. 249.

438   "Build your own . . . all pipelines common carriers": *Marysville* [OH] *Tribune*, April 20, 1905.

439   "the biggest mass meeting . . . has never done": *Lima* [OH] *Times-Democrat*, Mar. 20, 1905.

439   "Jehoshaphat! . . . hopeless for cleansing": IMT, *All in the Day's Work*, pp. 245–46.

439   "The wonder is . . . a gusher": IMT to JSP, Mar. 28, 1905, Phillips MSS.

439   "new town of Tulsa . . . paraded up and down": IMT, *All in the Day's Work*, pp. 247–48.

439   "submitted to five sittings": *Muskogee* [OK] *Democrat*, Mar. 27, 1905.

439   she was called upon: Albert Boyden to RSB, Mar. 21, 1905, RSB Papers.

439   "city-shy" boy . . . "loyalty for his state": IMT, *All in the Day's Work*, p. 259.

439   "The new thing . . . in any of its previous fights": *Emporia* [KS] *Gazette*, April 3, 1905.

439   "as much a moral issue . . . guilty of similar practices": *Emporia* [KS] *Gazette*, April 10, 1905.

440   "I stayed and stayed": *Marysville* [OH] *Tribune*, April 20, 1905.

440   "if one wants" . . . colluding with railroads: IMT, "Kansas and the Standard Oil Company: A Narrative of Today, Part I," *McClure's* (September 1905), p. 470.

440   "we take it": *Wall Street Journal*, Aug. 26, 1905.

440   "nearly all of the great fields": U.S. Government and James Rudolph Garfield, *Report of the Commissioner of Corporations on the Transportation of Petroleum: May 2, 1906* [hereafter *Garfield Report*] (Washington, DC: Government Printing Office, 1906), p. xix.

440   "Do read": Helen N. Garfield to James R. Garfield, April 13, 1905, Garfield Papers.

440   he had borrowed Tarbell's collection: James R. Garfield to IMT, June 11, 1906, IMTC.

440   "I shall try to find the truth": James R. Garfield to Helen N. Garfield, July 16, 1905, Garfield Papers.

440   "unjust and illegal": *Garfield Report*, pp. xx–xxi.

441   "All the power": *Estherville* [IA] *Enterprise*, May 9, 1906.

441   "the most severe arraignment": *The News* (Frederick, MD), May 12, 1906.

441   "a high official source . . . Ida Tarbell's Magazine Articles": *Laredo* [TX] *Times*, May 9, 1906.

441   "All that Ida Tarbell told": *Alton* [IL] *Evening Telegraph*, May 14, 1906.

441   "a vindication" of her methods: *Estherville* [IA] *Enterprise*, May 9, 1906.

441   validated now by the official seal: *Laredo* [TX] *Times*, May 9, 1906.

441   "can prove all he says": *Boston Daily Globe*, May 5, 1906.

441   "If my report affords . . . conspiracy and monopoly": James R. Garfield to Helen N. Garfield, June 24, 1906, Garfield Papers.

441   On the day the ruling was handed down. *Daily Californian* (Bakersfield, CA), Aug. 3, 1907.

441 "sledgehammer blows": *San Antonio* [TX] *Light*, Aug. 4, 1907.

441 Standard's corrupting influence: *Oakland* [CA] *Tribune*, Aug. 4, 1907.

441 Never before . . . such inflamed rhetoric: *San Antonio* [TX] *Light*, Aug. 4, 1907.

441 Landis levied the highest possible fine: Allan Nevins, *John D. Rockefeller* (New York: Charles Scribner's Sons, 1959), p. 325.

441 "I expected it": Ron Chernow, *Titan: The Life of John D. Rockefeller, Sr.* (New York: Random House, 1998), p. 541.

442 "beginning of the end" . . . or face ruin: *Logansport* [IN] *Journal*, Aug. 11, 1907.

442 "Judge Landis": Daniel Yergin, *The Prize: The Epic Quest for Oil, Money, and Power* (New York: Simon & Schuster, 1991), p. 92.

442 "It's nothing more than we expected": *Emporia* [KS] *Gazette*, July 26, 1908.

442 "a gross miscarriage of justice": *Cedar Rapids* [IA] *Evening Gazette*, Sept. 19, 1908.

442 "too much power in the bench": IMT, *All in the Day's Work*, p. 259.

442 "the government [had] finally": *Des Moines Daily News*, Nov. 19, 1906.

442 "The petition of the US government": *Paducah* [KY] *Evening Sun*, Nov. 15, 1906.

442 "Every essential charge . . . was Ida Tarbell": *Des Moines Daily News*, Nov. 19, 1906.

442 "not because it is a trust": *Indianapolis Star*, May 17, 1911.

442 a similar judgment: Pringle, *Life and Times*, Vol. 2, p. 665.

442 Standard Oil was given six months to dissolve: *Portsmouth* [OH] *Daily Times*, May 16, 1911.

442 "Buy Standard Oil": Chernow, *Titan*, p. 554.

442 Even when the corporate "octopus": Brady, *Ida Tarbell*, p. 158.

443 "to carry on . . . by civil or criminal proceedings": TR, "Seventh Annual Message, December 3, 1907," in *WTR*, Vol. 15, p. 420.

443 "The fundamental idea . . . enterprising an exponent": *Hartford* [CT] *Times*, cited in *Public Opinion*, Dec. 15, 1904.

CHAPTER SEVENTEEN: The American People Reach a Verdict

Page

444 "there are several eminent": TR to Cecil Spring Rice, Feb. 27, 1905, in *LTR*, Vol. 4, p. 1129.

444 "the people at large . . . the plutocracy": TR to Cecil Spring Rice, Dec. 27, 1904, in ibid., p. 1083.

444 "a dreadful calamity . . . grievances": TR to Philander Chase Knox, Nov. 10, 1904, in ibid., p. 1023.

445 "Above all else": TR, "Fourth Annual Message, Dec. 6, 1904," in *WTR*, Vol. 15, pp. 226–27.

445 This exclusive circle could effectively determine: Baker speech, *Boston Daily Globe*, Dec. 17, 1905; *New York Tribune*, Dec. 19, 1905.

445 the industry had remained essentially unregulated: George E. Mowry, *The Era of Theodore Roosevelt, 1900–1912* (New York: Harper & Bros., 1958), pp. 198–99.

445 "Until the transportation problem": IMT, "The History of the Standard Oil Company: Conclusion," *McClure's* (October 1904), p. 671.

445 "the story was always the same": Patrick F. Palermo, *Lincoln Steffens* (Boston: Twayne Publishers, 1978), p. 42.

445 "came from the top": Ibid., p. 42.

445 "seized the government": LS, *The Struggle for Self-Government*, p. 209.

445 "the actual sovereign": LS, *The Autobiography*, p. 564.

445 "the Railroad problem": RSB to J. Stannard Baker, Sept. 14, 1905, RSB Papers.

445 "eager for more dragons": RSB, *American Chronicle*, p. 190.

445 "the real facts . . . servant of democracy": RSB, Notebook [n.d.], 1905, RSB Papers.

446 "far more important": RSB to J. Stannard Baker, Mar. 1, 1905, RSB Papers.

446 Baker started by examining . . . on the railroad industry: RSB, *American Chronicle*, p. 190.

446 Roosevelt invited him to Washington: TR to RSB, Jan. 2, 1905, RSB Papers.

446 "in some big": RSB to TR, Jan. 10, 1905, RSB Papers.

446 "simple and most informal": RSB, Notebook C, Jan. 28, 1905, RSB Papers.

446 engaged in a private conversation: RSB, *American Chronicle*, p. 192.

446 "a pretty good grip": RSB to Albert Boyden, Jan. 12, 1905, RSB Papers.

446 the argument that railroads were public highways: Semonche, *Ray Stannard Baker*, p. 131.

446 "His chief trouble . . . as truthfully as I can": RSB, *American Chronicle*, pp. 192–93.

446 "It was altogether . . . gets hold of people": RSB to J. Stannard Baker, Jan. 29, 1905, RSB Papers.

447 "Neither this people . . . equitable terms": TR, "Speech at the Union League Club of Philadelphia, January 30, 1905," in TR and Lewis, *A Compilation of the Messages and Speeches*, pp. 551–53.

447 "due quite as much": RSB, Notebook C, Jan. 31, 1905, RSB Papers.

447 "an enormous industrial . . . regulating the trusts & the railroads": Ibid.

447 "need not be regarded . . . clearly drawn": TR to Joseph B. Bishop, Mar. 23, 1905, in *LTR*, Vol. 4, pp. 1144–45.

448   "were either friendly": *Truth* (Salt Lake City, UT), June 10, 1905.

448   "how delicate . . . should meddle": RSB, "Railroads on Trial, Part III," *McClure's* (January 1906), p. 327.

448   "Any tinkering with rates": *Truth*, June 10, 1905.

448   "an attack of 'pink-eye' ": RSB, "Railroads on Trial, Part V," *McClure's* (March 1906), p. 543.

448   Congressmen who had voted: *Galveston* [TX] *Daily News*, July 4, 1905.

448   the national coverage soon turned: RSB, "Railroads on Trial, Part V," *McClure's* (March 1906), pp. 544–49.

448   "throw the country into a panic": RSB, *American Chronicle*, p. 197.

448   "if the railway men . . . the public demand": *Sandusky* [OH] *Star-Journal*, May 10, 1905.

448   "absolute silence": *Salt Lake Tribune*, May 10, 1905.

448   Stuyvesant Fish . . . "May I have fifteen minutes": *Sandusky Star-Journal*, May 10, 1905.

449   "driven directly": *Alexandria* [DC] *Gazette*, May 11, 1905.

449   "a sensation": *Fort Wayne* [IN] *Weekly Sentinel*, May 17, 1905.

449   "had been carefully prepared": *Alexandria* [DC] *Gazette*, May 11, 1905.

449   "could not have been . . . of the public": TR, "Speech at the Iroquois Club Banquet, Chicago, Ill., May 10, 1905," in TR and Lewis, *A Compilation of the Messages and Speeches*, pp. 620, 619.

449   "the spirit of demagoguery . . . they are poor": TR, "Speech at the Chamber of Commerce Banquet, Denver, Colo., May 8, 1905," in ibid., p. 616.

449   "the rock of class hatred": TR, "Speech at the Iroquois Club Banquet, Chicago, Ill., May 10, 1905," in ibid., p. 620.

449   "a fight to the finish": *Alexandria* [DC] *Gazette*, May 11, 1905.

449   "an impression prevailed": *Washington Post*, Aug. 20, 1905.

449   "the vitality of democracy . . . than the sovereign himself": S. S. McClure, "Editorial Announcement of a New Series of Articles by Ray Stannard Baker: The Railroads on Trial," *McClure's* (October 1905), pp. 673, 672.

450   Baker wrote in early September: RSB to TR, Sept. 7, 1905, TRP.

450   "Yes, I should greatly like": TR to RSB, Sept. 8, 1905, TRP.

450   "approval might be the measure . . . of the White House": RSB, *American Chronicle*, p. 194.

450   "I haven't a criticism to suggest . . . my own message": TR to RSB, Sept. 13, 1905, in *LTR*, Vol. 5, p. 25.

450   "In the early days . . . what the traffic will bear": RSB, "The Railroad Rate: A Study in Commercial Autocracy," *McClure's* (November 1905), p. 50.

450   families generally sat on the boards: RSB, "Railroads on Trial, Part III," *McClure's* (January 1906), pp. 318–24.

450   "the fundamental purpose . . . in private hands": RSB, "The Railroad Rate: A Study in Commercial Autocracy," *McClure's* (November 1905), pp. 57, 47.

450   "violent agitation . . . in the gift of government": RSB to TR, Sept. 18, 1905, TRP.

451   "strictly confidential . . . to be made thereon?": TR to RSB, Oct. 16, 1905, TRP.

451   "the seriousness . . . at that time who did?": RSB, *American Chronicle*, pp. 197–98.

451   "It was too general": Ibid., p. 198.

451   "I was terribly afraid": Ibid.

451   "cunning devices . . . manufacturers and shippers": RSB, "Railroad Rebates," *McClure's* (December 1905), pp. 185, 180.

451   "I have asked myself . . . fix a *definite* rate": RSB to TR, Nov. 11, 1905, TRP.

452   "it would be better . . . is surely constitutional": TR to RSB, Nov. 13, 1905, TRP.

452   "Is there not . . . succeed without it": RSB to TR, Nov. 17, 1905, RSB Papers.

452   "a long and rather heated": RSB, *American Chronicle*, p. 199.

452   "I think you are entirely": TR to RSB, Nov. 20, 1905, in *LTR*, Vol. 5, p. 83.

452   "the railroads have been crazy": Ibid., p. 84.

452   "simply absurd": TR to RSB, Nov. 22, 1905, in ibid., p. 88.

452   "it was Lincoln": TR to RSB, Nov. 28, 1905, in ibid., p. 101.

452   "suggestion would come": RSB, *American Chronicle*, p. 200.

452   "What was my surprise": Ibid.

452   "a maximum reasonable rate . . . improper minimum rates": TR, "Fifth Annual Message, Dec. 5, 1905," in *WTR*, Vol. 15, pp. 275–76.

453   On January 4, 1906 . . . "just and reasonable": John Ely Briggs, *William Peters Hepburn* (Iowa City: State Hist. Soc. of Iowa, 1919), p. 264.

453   "the most hoary tenet": Blum, *The Republican Roosevelt*, p. 91.

453   to preserve the protective tariff: John M. Blum, "Theodore Roosevelt and the Hepburn Act: Toward an Orderly System of Control," in *LTR*, Vol. 6, Appendix 2, pp. 1561–62.

453   "was in many ways": *Washington Post*, Feb. 9, 1906.

453   "this railroad legislation . . . how inefficient & undependable": RSB, Notebook C, Feb. 9, 1906, RSB Papers.

453 A battle royal: *Public Opinion*, Dec. 9, 1905.

454 "so whittled down": *Public Opinion*, Nov. 11, 1905.

454 "They are making": TR to Kermit Roosevelt, Mar. 4, 1905, in TR et al., eds., *Letters to Kermit from Theodore Roosevelt,* p. 130.

454 "great indignation": *NYT*, Feb. 23, 1906.

454 "as a check": *Current Literature* (March 1906), p. 232.

454 the leadership of Iowa's junior senator: *NYT*, Feb. 24, 1906.

454 agreed to report the unamended bill "without prejudice": *Public Opinion*, Mar. 3, 1906.

454 "most outspoken opponent . . . the country gasp": *Elyria* [OH] *Chronicle*, Mar. 10, 1906.

454 "scarcely had time": *Washington Post*, Feb. 24, 1906.

454 "Pitchfork Ben" . . . a fistfight . . . would be severely diminished: *NYT*, April 5, 1906.

455 "confided to the care": *News and Courier* (Charleston, SC), cited in *Public Opinion*, Mar. 10, 1906.

455 "old enemies": *Indianapolis News*, cited in *Current Literature* (March 1906), p. 233.

455 judiciary as the true arbiter of rates: Blum, "TR and the Hepburn Act," in *LTR*, Vol. 6, pp. 1565–66.

455 "public opinion": TR to John Lee Strachey, Feb. 12, 1906, in *LTR*, Vol. 5, p. 150.

455 "never better . . . discrimination and judgment": "The Evolution of Public Opinion," *The Independent*, June 14, 1906.

455 "in common with all other" . . . "good" or "bad": RSB, "Railroads on Trial, Part V," *McClure's* (March 1906), pp. 535, 548.

455 a former city newspaperman was hired: RSB to TR, Oct. 13, 1905, TRP.

455 small newspapers were supplied . . . purchased newspapers outright: RSB, "Railroads on Trial, Part V," *McClure's* (March 1906), pp. 545, 548.

455 acquainted more than half a million: Semonche, *Ray Stannard Baker*, p. 142.

456 "It is a little startling": *Fairhope Courier* (Des Moines, IA), Mar. 9, 1906, Clipping, RSB Papers.

456 "after plowing all day . . . the people and the railroads": John Gladney to *McClure's*, Mar. 7, 1906, RSB Papers.

456 "worth all the publication": Emmet Zook to *McClure's*, March [n.d.], 1906, RSB Papers.

456 "was of course entirely": TR to William Boyd Allison, May 14, 1906, in *LTR*, Vol. 5, p. 270.

456 "I did not care a rap": TR, *An Autobiography*, p. 436.

456 "to the left of his original position": Blum, *The Republican Roosevelt*, p. 100.

456 "The fight on the rate bill": TR to Kermit Roosevelt, April 1, 1906, in *LTR*, Vol. 5, p. 204.

456 "As for Tillman": *Emporia* [KS] *Gazette*, May 19, 1906.

456 "pocket my pride": Sullivan, *Our Times*, Vol. 3, p. 254.

456 "the mysterious ways": *Washington Post*, Feb. 26, 1906.

457 a number of southern senators balked: Blum, *The Republican Roosevelt*, p. 101.

457 "The great object": TR to William Boyd Allison, May 5, 1906, in *LTR*, Vol. 5, p. 258.

457 Republicans who feared . . . held unconstitutional: TR to HCL, May 19, 1906, in ibid., pp. 273–74.

457 The political landscape was shifting . . . in grave jeopardy: Blum, "TR and the Hepburn Act," in *LTR*, Vol. 6, pp. 1562–63.

457 "little knot of men . . . superior generalship": *NYT*, April 5, 1906.

457 "neither control": *Emporia* [KS] *Gazette*, May 4, 1906.

457 "symbolic of the new": *Public Opinion*, April 21, 1906.

458 this compromise provided the only chance: TR to William Boyd Allison, May 14, 1906, in *LTR*, Vol. 5, p. 270.

458 "Aldrich and his people": TR to WAW, July 31, 1906, TRP.

458 The bill passed: *Salt Lake Tribune*, May 19, 1906.

458 "No given measure": TR to RSB, Nov. 20, 1905, in *LTR*, Vol. 5, p. 84.

458 "the longest step": Blum, *The Republican Roosevelt*, p. 104.

458 "lifted the idea": *Public Opinion*, June 2, 1906.

458 the High Court defined the scope: Blum, *The Republican Roosevelt*, p. 103.

458 "the politician's gift": *The Independent*, May 24, 1906.

458 "but for the work": Ibid.

458 "Congress might ignore": *Fort Wayne* [IN] *Weekly Sentinel*, July 4, 1906.

458 "It is through writers": Elwood Mead to RSB, June 9, 1906, RSB Papers.

459 "This crusade against": RSB to J. Stannard Baker, Jan. 23, 1906, RSB Papers.

459 "was like the falling down": Edmund Wilson, "Lincoln Steffens and Upton Sinclair," *The New Republic*, Sept. 28, 1932.

459 "Perhaps it'll surprise you": UBS to RSB, Dec. 2, 1905, RSB Papers.

459 By twenty-five . . . in serial form: Upton Sinclair, *Autobiography* (New York: Harcourt, Brace & World, 1962), pp. 108–9.

459 the "wage slavery": Anthony Arthur, *Radical Innocent: Upton Sinclair* (New York: Random House, 2006), p. 41.

459 The young socialist decided: UBS, *Autobiography*, p. 109.
459 "I sat at night . . . could go anywhere": Ibid.
460 "dosed with borax . . . in the room with them": Upton Sinclair, *The Jungle* (New York: Modern Library, 2006), pp. 148–49.
460 "the bride, the groom": UBS, *Autobiography*, p. 110.
460 "the sort of man": UBS, *The Jungle*, p. 23.
460 "He would work all day": Ibid., p. 54.
460 "were sold with the idea": Ibid., p. 72.
460 the holiday "speeding up" . . . no longer want: Ibid., p. 136.
461 "The revelations": *NYT*, Jan. 27, 1906; Isaac F. Marcosson, *Adventures in Interviewing* (New York: John Lane Co., 1919), pp. 282–84.
461 Sinclair sent two advance copies: UBS to RSB, Feb. 2, 1906, RSB Papers.
461 "Not since Byron awoke": Upton Sinclair, *My Lifetime in Letters* (Columbia: University of Missouri Press, 1960), p. ix.
461 "Hideous": James Rudolph Garfield, Diary, Mar. 2, 1906, Garfield Papers.
461 "a terrible and I fear": James Rudolph Garfield, Diary, Mar. 3, 1906, Garfield Papers.
461 Roosevelt . . . invited the author: TR to UBS, Mar. 9, 1906, TRP.
461 Although he proceeded . . . "be eradicated": TR to UBS, Mar. 15, 1906, in *LTR*, Vol. 5, pp. 178, 180.
461 "was like asking a burglar": UBS, *Autobiography*, p. 118.
462 He chose two well-respected men: Marcosson, *Adventures in Interviewing*, pp. 285–86.
462 "I have power": TR to UBS, April 9, 1906, TRP.
462 "on excellent authority" . . . intended to castigate the novelist: *Chicago Tribune*, April 10 & 11, 1906.
462 "It is absurd": TR to UBS, April 11, 1906, in *LTR*, Vol. 5, p. 209.
462 "should never have dreamed . . . explicit and positive way": UBS to TR, April 12, 1906, TRP.
462 "I understand entirely": TR to UBS, April 13, 1906, TRP.
462 conditions comparable to those Sinclair had portrayed: *The Independent*, May 31, 1906.
462 "of rooms reeking": *Public Opinion*, June 9, 1906.
462 "found healthful . . . inspected and condemned": *Outlook*, June 9, 1906.
462 "that unless effective": *Chicago Tribune*, May 26, 1906.
462 Without "a dissenting vote" the Beveridge bill passed: *The Independent*, May 31, 1906.
463 "a shock it will never": *NYT*, May 26, 1906.
463 Sinclair leaked his information: *NYT*, May 28, 1906.
463 "I sincerely hope": UBS to TR, May 29, 1906, TRP.
463 "Tell Sinclair": Arthur, *Radical Innocent*, p. 77.
463 "conditions were as clean": *Chicago Tribune*, June 9, 1906.
463 A series of emasculating amendments . . . the "mandatory character": *NYT*, May 29, 1906.
463 "I am sorry": TR to James Wolcott Wadsworth, May 31, 1906, in *LTR*, Vol. 5, p. 291.
463 "sham" legislation: TR to James Wolcott Wadsworth, June 15, 1906, in ibid., p. 299.
463 not "warranted" any longer: TR to James Wolcott Wadsworth, May 31, 1906, in ibid., p. 291.
463 On June 4 . . . a "preliminary" report: James Reynolds and Charles Patrick Neill, *Conditions in Chicago Stock Yards: Message from the President, June 4, 1906. The Roosevelt Policy; Speeches, Letters and State Papers, Relating to Corporate Wealth and Closely Allied Topics, of Theodore Roosevelt, President of the United States* (New York: Current Literature Publ. Co., 1908), Vol. 2, p. 386.
463 "The conditions . . . dangerous to health": Ibid., p. 387.
463 If Congress failed: Ibid., 389.
463 "Mary had a little lamb": Sullivan, *Our Times*, Vol. 2, p. 541.
464 "chloroformed in the committees": Ibid., p. 544.
464 "We cannot imagine": New York *Evening Post*, cited in *The Bookman* (July 1906), pp. 481–83.
464 "In the history of reforms": *Chicago Tribune*, June 30, 1906.
464 "chief janitor and policeman": Sullivan, *Our Times*, Vol. 2, p. 520.
464 "Are we going to take up": Nathaniel W. Stephenson, *Nelson W. Aldrich, a Leader in American Politics* (New York: Charles Scribner's Sons, 1930), p. 234.
464 McClure introduced Bok: Lyon, *Success Story*, pp. 233–34.
464 Bok brought it . . . widespread attention: Mark Sullivan, *The Education of an American* (New York: Doubleday, Doran & Co., 1938), p. 191.
464 Sullivan's research . . . "Died May 17, 1883": Ibid., pp. 187–88.
465 a secret clause . . . an original copy of the contract form: Ibid., p. 189.
465 a ten-part investigative series . . . "or deleterious drugs": Robert Morse Crunden, *Ministers of Reform: The Progressives' Achievement in American Civilization, 1889–1920* (New York: Basic Books, 1982), p. 180.
465 an ointment . . . fraudulent or nonexistent: Samuel Hopkins Adams, "The Great American Fraud," *Collier's Weekly*, Oct. 7, 1905, Jan. 13, 1906, & Feb. 17, 1906.
465 "to run the gauntlet": *Current Literature* (April 1906).

465 "it slept": Sullivan, *Our Times*, Vol. 2, p. 534.

465 On June 30, 1906: William Lamartine Snyder, *Supplement to Snyder's Interstate Commerce Act and Federal Anti-Trust Laws* (New York: Baker, Voorhis & Co., 1906), pp. 136–44.

465 "would not have had . . . the agitation": *Chicago Tribune*, June 30, 1906.

465 This landmark bill: Snyder, *Supplement to Snyder's Interstate Commerce Act*, pp. 136–44.

465 "During no session": *NYT*, June 30, 1906.

466 "the beginning of a new epoch": *Iowa Postal Card* (Fayette, IA), July 12, 1906.

466 "For pass them they must": Lyon, *Success Story*, p. 250.

466 "the most amazing program": Joshua David Hawley, *Theodore Roosevelt: Preacher of Righteousness* (New Haven: Yale University Press, 2008), p. 161.

466 only "sowing the seeds": Benjamin Wheeler to TR, July 1, 1906, TRP.

466 "more substantive work": *Postville* [IA] *Review*, July 6, 1906.

466 Even Democratic newspapers: *The Literary Digest*, July 7, 1906.

466 "The public confidence": Quoted in ibid.

466 "I do not expect": TR to Kermit Roosevelt, June 13, 1906, in TR et al., eds., *Letters to Kermit from Theodore Roosevelt*, p. 149.

CHAPTER EIGHTEEN: "Cast into Outer Darkness"

Page

467 "Signs everywhere": RSB to J. Stannard Baker, Jan. 23, 1906, RSB Papers.

467 "men were questioning": RSB, Notebook: "General Recollection of the Era," RSB Papers.

467 "assumed the proportions": Frank Luther Mott, *A History of American Magazines* (Cambridge, MA: Belknap Press, 1957), Vol. 4, pp. 207, 607.

467 "Government by Magazine": WAW to JSP, May 25, 1908, White Papers.

467 "to make a star to shine . . . that rules the world": Finley Peter Dunne, "Mr. Dooley on the Power of the Press," *The American Magazine* (October 1906). (Dunne's passage has been translated from dialect.)

468 Sam McClure was considered: WAW, *The Autobiography*, p. 386.

468 "Here was a group": IMT, *All in the Day's Work*, p. 254.

468 the "rare group . . . yet with tolerance": RSB, *American Chronicle*, p. 226.

468 "a success": LS, *The Autobiography*, p. 535.

468 "the future looked fair": IMT, *All in the Day's Work*, p. 254.

468 "The institution that had seemed": RSB, *American Chronicle*, p. 213.

468 "Never forget . . . the daring moves": IMT to Albert Boyden, April 26, 1902, in Lyon, *Success Story*, p. 199.

469 "You are infinitely precious . . . during the coming years": McClure to IMT, Mar. 18, 1903, IMTC.

469 Wilkinson . . . conducted poetry classes: Lucy Dow Cushing, ed., *The Wellesley Alumnae Quarterly* (Concord, NH: Wellesley College Alumnae Assoc., 1917), Vol. 2, p. 190.

469 who suspected that their editor's fascination: Lyon, *Success Story*, p. 207.

469 an evening of theatre: McClure to HHM, June 15, 1903, McClure MSS.

469 McClure brought them to Divonne: McClure to HHM, June 11, 1903; Mary Bisland to HHM, July 6, 1903, McClure MSS.

470 he and Florence Wilkinson stayed on the third: Lyon, *Success Story*, p. 256.

470 Their "rollicking adventure . . . under their horses' feet": Alice Hegan Rice, *The Inky Way* (New York: D. Appleton-Century Co.,1940), pp. 65–66.

470 During that "never-to-be forgotten" European tour: Ibid., p. 65; Cale Young Rice, *Bridging the Years* (New York: D. Appleton-Century, 1939), p. 63.

470 Ida could barely contain her tears: McClure to IMT [n.d., Saturday], 1905, IMTC; Brady, *Ida Tarbell*, p. 149.

470 "I have felt terribly sad": McClure to IMT [n.d.], 1903, IMTC.

470 McClure's recklessness could tarnish the magazine: Lyon, *Success Story*, pp. 258–59.

470 they feared he planned to meet with Florence: Ibid., pp. 257–58.

470 "I feel sure of myself": McClure to HHM, Nov. 21, 1903, McClure MSS.

471 "I am so much keener": McClure to HHM, Nov. 29, 1903, McClure MSS.

471 "I feel my vision broadened": McClure to HHM, Nov. [n.d.] 1903, McClure MSS.

471 When McClure suddenly embarked: Lyon, *Success Story*, p. 259.

471 McClure directed the poetry editor: See Florence Wilkinson, "Three Poems," *McClure's* (June 1904), p. 166.

471 upbraided Sam "like a naughty child": Lyon, *Success Story*, p. 260.

471 A chastened McClure swore: Florence Wilkinson to JSP, June [n.d.], 1904, in JSP to IMT [n.d.], 1904, IMTC.

471 something "very terrible . . . for nearly a week": HHM to IMT, June 24, 1904, IMTC.

471 "I have so much to do": McClure to IMT, June 22, 1904, IMTC.

471   "The Lord help us! . . . feel resentment": IMT to JSP, June [n.d.], 1904, IMTC.

472   "I have received six . . . to snap off so suddenly": Florence Wilkinson to JSP, June [n.d.], 1904, IMTC.

472   "wretched & restless . . . idea of giving her up": Mary Bisland to IMT, July 7, 1904, in Lyon, *Success Story*, p. 262.

472   "very solemn promises": HHM to JSP, July 30, 1904, IMTC.

472   "He said he was a hurt animal": HHM to IMT, June 24, 1904, IMTC.

472   "The struggle for possession": McClure to IMT, June 22, 1904, IMTC.

472   "full of dynamite . . . the magazine must be cleared": McClure to JSP, Oct. 15, 1904, Phillips MSS.

473   "sensational . . . very accurate": McClure to IMT, June 22, 1904, IMTC.

473   "working in his own little cubicle": McClure to IMT, Oct. 6, 1904, IMTC.

473   "The man who is responsible": McClure to Albert Boyden [n.d.], 1904, IMTC.

473   "Why in the name of ordinary": McClure to Albert Boyden [n.d.], 1904, IMTC.

473   "very poor, trashy . . . unworthy": HHM to JSP, June 9, 1904, IMTC.

473   Phillips patiently answered: JSP to HHM, Aug. 5, 1904, McClure MSS.

473   she was not the only "other" woman . . . Her "dearest" friend: Florence Wilkinson to HHM, Sept. 25, 1903, McClure MSS.

473   revealed her own romantic relationship: IMT to JSP, Sept. 7, 1904, McClure MSS.

473   "Yesterday": McClure to JSP, July 26, 1904, IMTC.

474   "wrung with the anguish . . . strange wanderings": HHM to McClure, Aug. 26, 1904, McClure MSS.

474   her devoted efforts had "saved" him . . . "punishment" for all he had done: McClure to IMT [n.d.], 1904, IMTC.

474   "The Shame of S. S. McClure . . . the wall of lies": IMT, "Notes of L'Affaire," July [n.d.], 1906, IMTC.

474   the staff drew up a plan: Lyon, *Success Story*, p. 277.

474   "the whole future . . . powerful ruling body": McClure to IMT, Mar. 29, 1905, IMTC.

474   "getting along splendidly . . . than ever before": McClure to HHM, July 5, 1905, McClure MSS.

475   "I thought when I came back . . . heavy heavy load": McClure to IMT [n.d., Saturday], 1905, IMTC.

475   "My mind constantly dwells": McClure to IMT, Mar. 29, 1905, IMTC.

475   developing an elaborate plan: Lyon, *Success Story*, p. 280.

475   "the greatest periodical": McClure to IMT, Nov. 27, 1905, IMTC.

475   "a stronger and more productive man": IMT, *All in the Day's Work*, p. 225.

475   "a tremendous secret" . . . *McClure's Universal Journal*: McClure to IMT, Nov. 27, 1905, IMTC.

475   Sam McClure's extravagant ambitions . . . affordable housing: IMT, *All in the Day's Work*, p. 256; Lyon, *Success Story*, p. 283; Albert Boyden to JSP, Feb. 6, 1906, IMTC.

475   Tarbell considered McClure's grandiosity: IMT, *All in the Day's Work*, p. 257.

475   "build a bigger": Ibid., p. 255.

476   McClure's scheme . . . echoed the very trusts: Ibid., p. 256.

476   "the plan which was eventually": Ibid.

476   "all the different branches": IMT to McClure, Oct. 18, 1904, IMTC.

476   "who had so much of the creative touch": RSB, Notebook, Dec. 1936, RSB Papers.

476   An "uncompromising" critic: RSB, *American Chronicle*, p. 94.

476   "felicities of expression": RSB to F. E. Dayton, Dec. 5, 1936, RSB Papers.

476   "would not know where to go": WAW to JSP, Mar. 17, 1906, in Lyon, *Success Story*, p. 285.

476   John had so admired Sam's energy, his "push and business ability": Lyon, *Success Story*, p. 37.

477   they spent many hours together . . . in each other's homes: JSP to IMT, November [n.d.], 1905, IMTC.

477   "He is certainly the rarest": IMT to Albert Boyden, July 20, 1905, IMTC.

477   "It has been a glorious trip": IMT to Albert Boyden, Feb. 11, 1905, IMTC.

477   a series of letters forwarded: Robert Mather to McClure, Feb. 2, 1906, IMTC.

477   "as usual is an angel" . . . a "diabolical" stage: IMT to Albert Boyden, Feb. 11, 1905, IMTC.

477   "thoroughly unfitted me" . . . his "ridiculous" concerns: McClure to JSP, Feb. 17, 1906, IMTC.

478   "All S.S. wants is sympathy": Daniel McKinley to JSP, Feb. 2, 1906, IMTC.

478   "I wish we did have the brains": Albert Boyden to JSP, Feb. 6, 1906, IMTC.

478   "It was a momentous decision": Lyon, *Success Story*, p. 286.

478   whether "anybody else is going . . . that we are right": IMT Diary, Mar. 22, 1906, IMTC.

478   if McClure would "democratize": Lyon, *Success Story*, pp. 286–87; IMT Diary, Mar. 22, 1906, IMTC.

478   "cheerful" for the first time in weeks: IMT Diary, Mar. 23, 1906, IMTC.

478   "beyond the ability of one man . . . sensing public opinion": McClure to JSP, April 5, 1906, McClure MSS.

479   "utterly impossible": McClure to JSP, April 5, 1906, McClure MSS.

479   "I cannot leave the magazine": McClure to IMT, April 7, 1906, IMTC.

479   "the entire office was embroiled . . . someone else came along": Curtis P. Brady, "The High Cost of Impatience," unpublished typescript, p. 266, McClure MSS.

479   "playing and getting well . . . even by the owner": LS to Joseph Steffens, June 3, 1906, in LS et al., eds., *Letters of Lincoln Steffens*, Vol. 1, p 173.

480   "become so utterly unbalanced": RSB to Jessie Baker, Mar. 9, 1906, in Bannister, *Ray Stannard Baker*, p. 110.

480   "dynamite, nitroglycerine & black powder": Robert William Stinson, "S. S. McClure and His Magazine: A Study in the Editing of 'McClure's,' 1893–1913," PhD diss., Indiana University, 1971, p. 249.

480   "are not only my friends": RSB to J. Stannard Baker, May 3, 1906, RSB Papers.

480   "I was left with no certainty . . . all but catastrophic": RSB, *American Chronicle*, p. 213.

480   "In Bunyan's *Pilgrim's Progress*": TR, "The Man with the Muck-Rake," *Putnam's Monthly* (October 1906), p. 42.

480   The coincidence . . . to form their own magazine: *New York Tribune*, May 11, 1906; *Life*, May 24, 1906.

480   "affected his views of . . . of contemporary life": "Magazines' Heads at War," unidentified newspaper clipping [n.d.], 1906, RSB Papers.

480   planned "to muzzle his writers": Lyon, *Success Story*, p. 294.

480   William Randolph Hearst, who had . . . agitated for a constitutional amendment: Judson A. Grenier and George E. Mowry, introduction, in David Graham Phillips, J. A. Grenier, and G. E. Mowry, *The Treason of the Senate* (Chicago: Quadrangle Books, 1964), p. 20.

481   He offered David Graham Phillips: Ibid., p. 21.

481   "Treason is a strong word": David Graham Phillips, "The Treason of the Senate: I," *The Cosmopolitan* (March 1906), p. 488.

481   Each portrait revealed "a triangulation": Grenier and Mowry, introduction, in Phillips, Grenier, and Mowry, *The Treason of the Senate*, p. 29.

481   The circulation of *The Cosmopolitan* doubled: Ibid.

481   "Little wonder": Ibid., p. 30.

481   "For those who like the sight": *Hutchinson* [KS] *News*, Feb. 22, 1906.

481   "Here is the archetypal Face . . . mentally and morally": Phillips, "The Treason of the Senate: I," *The Cosmopolitan* (March 1906), pp. 489, 588.

481   "boodler . . . sniveling sycophant": *Hutchinson* [KS] *News*, Feb. 22, 1906.

482   Although he never accused . . . contributions of the special interests: Phillips, "The Treason of the Senate: I," *The Cosmopolitan* (March 1906), p. 488.

482   "heartiest sympathy . . . noxious as the thief": TR to Alfred Henry Lewis, Feb. 17, 1906, in *LTR*, Vol. 5, pp. 156–57.

482   "sowing the seeds of anarchy": *The Critic* (June 1906), p. 512.

482   "playing with matches": Quoted in Grenier and Mowry, introduction, in Phillips, Grenier, and Mowry, *The Treason of the Senate*, p. 38.

482   "Slander and misrepresentation": *Public Opinion*, April 7, 1906.

482   "epidemic of Congress-baiting": *Current Literature* (March 1906), p. 231.

482   "muckrakers . . . with sensational articles": *Daily Telegraph* (Atlantic, IA), April 9, 1906.

482   "ignoring at the same time": *NYT*, April 6, 1906.

482   He had initially planned: Grenier and Mowry, introduction, in Phillips, Grenier, and Mowry, *The Treason of the Senate*, p. 34.

482   "the masters" at *McClure's* . . . "imitators" had followed in their wake: Edwin E. Slosson, "The Literature of Exposure," in Filler, *The Muckrakers*, p. 258.

482   "hot stuff . . . before the investigation is begun": *Washington Post*, April 11, 1906.

483   "to produce a very unhealthy . . . socialistic propaganda": TR to WHT, Mar. 15, 1906, in *LTR*, Vol. 5, p. 183.

483   "glad, sweet song . . . than a convict's camp": Mott, *A History of American Magazines, 1885–1905*, Vol. 4, p. 209. (Dunne's passage has been translated from dialect.)

483   "immensely" enjoyed . . . "feeling over-pessimistic about it": TR to Finley Peter Dunne, Dec. 15, 1905, TRP.

483   "The public cannot stand": Slosson, "The Literature of Exposure," in Filler, *The Muckrakers*, p. 258.

483   "It is getting so nowadays . . . holds a public office": *Oshkosh* [WI] *Daily Northwestern*, April 17, 1906.

483   "Well . . . poor old Chauncey Depew": LS, *The Autobiography*, p. 258.

483   Steffens remained unconvinced . . . mobilize public opinion: Ibid.

483   "repeat as true . . . businessmen or politicians": TR to LS, June 24, 1905, in *LTR*, Vol. 4, p. 1254.

484   "Poor Payne is sick": TR to HCL, Oct. 2, 1904, in ibid., p. 965.

484   "To any officer or employee": TR to "Any officer . . . ," Jan. 9, 1906, LS Papers.

484   To Steffens, the signal question: *Syracuse* [NY] *Herald*, Jan. 14, 1906.

484   "I'd rather make our government": LS, *Boston Daily Globe*, Feb. 11, 1906.

484   "In stating your disapproval": TR to LS, Feb. 6, 1906, in *LTR*, Vol. 5, pp. 147–48.

485   rather than "summoning . . . being dragged": Lyon, *Success Story*, p. 250.

485   All these frustrations . . . the "new journalism": *Washington Post*, April 11, 1906.

485   Remarks at the informal club . . . "spread like wildfire": RSB, *American Chronicle*, p. 201.
485   speculation that he was referencing: *Daily Telegraph* (Atlantic, IA), April 9, 1906; *Daily Times-Tribune* (Waterloo, IA), April 14, 1906.
485   "such an attack": RSB, *American Chronicle*, p. 202.
485   "I have been much disturbed": RSB to TR, April 7, 1906, in ibid., pp. 202–3.
485   "One reason I want . . . as much as of mud slinging": TR to RSB, April 9, 1906, in ibid., p. 203.
485   "at the risk of repetition . . . potent forces for evil": TR, "Speech at the Laying of the Corner-Stone of the Office Building of the House of Representatives, April 14, 1906," in TR, *Presidential Addresses and State Papers, April 14, 1906 to January 14, 1907* (New York: Review of Reviews Co., 1910), Vol. 5, pp. 713–15.
486   "upon a question which is shaking . . . portly figure of the President": *Nevada State Journal*, April 22, 1906.
486   "familiar balance of approval . . . classed all of us together": RSB, *American Chronicle*, pp. 203–4.
486   *McClure's* . . . was "singled out": Semonche, *Ray Stannard Baker*, p. 151.
486   "I'm giving my whole life to . . . ready for McSure's by night": Mrs. Woodrow, "A Rake's Progress," *Life*, May 5, 1906, pp. 639–40.
486   "These satirical jabs cut": Semonche, *Ray Stannard Baker*, pp. 151–52.
486   "cast into outer darkness . . . nor follow his leadership": RSB, *American Chronicle*, p. 204.
487   "It was a great day": New York *Sun*, cited in *Literary Digest*, April 21, 1906.
487   "rebaters and bribers . . . wave of magazine reform": Samuel Merwin, "The Magazine Crusade," *Success Magazine* (June 1906), p. 394.
487   "the loftiest and purest": *Nevada State Journal*, April 22, 1906.
487   "long, laborious work . . . astonishingly great": Merwin, "The Magazine Crusade," *Success Magazine* (June 1906), pp. 452, 449.
487   "The day will come . . . emblem of reform": *Nevada State Journal*, April 22, 1906.
487   "a badge of honor": *When Trumpets Call: Theodore Roosevelt After the White House*, p. 30.
487   "quietly planning to start": *NYT*, May 11, 1906.
487   After weeks of turmoil . . . worth $187,000: JSP and IMT to McClure, April 12, 1906, McClure MSS.
487   "I am certain that": McClure to Robert Mather, April 14, 1906, McClure MSS.
487   "I wish you all": McClure to RSB, May 10, 1906, RSB Papers.
487   "There was nothing mean": LS, *The Autobiography*, p. 536.
488   "its chief features of life and popularity": *Riverside* [CA] *Enterprise*, June 23, 1906.
488   Necessity compelled him . . . "colossal scheme": Alice Hegan Rice to IMT, June 14, 1906, IMTC.
488   "I have really to look": McClure to HHM, July 2, 1906, McClure MSS.
488   "working harder": McClure to HHM, June 27, 1906, McClure MSS.
488   "three or four quarts of milk": Lyon, *Success Story*, p. 298.
488   "masses of manuscripts" . . . an autobiography by Mark Twain: McClure to HHM, June 30, 1906, McClure MSS.
488   Of the original team, only . . . remained: Brady, "The High Cost of Impatience," p. 226, McClure MSS.
488   To replace Ida Tarbell . . . editor of the *Atlantic Monthly*: Lyon, *Success Story*, pp. 296–98.
488   "The very name": Ellery Sedgwick, *The Happy Profession* (Boston: Little, Brown & Co., 1946), p. 144.
488   "burning force . . . into molten excitement": Ibid., p. 139.
488   "be able to repeat the process": Lyon, *Success Story*, p. 296.
488   "To go on now": Ibid., p. 294.
489   "to halt and to think soberly . . . of responsibility": *Washington Post*, April 11, 1906.
489   She edited . . . investigative pieces diminished: Robert Cantwell, "Journalism: The Magazines," in Harold Stearns, *America Now: An Inquiry into Civilization in the United States by Thirty-Six Americans* (New York: Charles Scribner's Sons, 1938), pp. 348–49.
489   "of distraction" . . . of "inquiry": Ibid., p. 352.
489   "an exhilarating sense of excitement": Lyon, *Success Story*, p. 296.
489   "As a curb on genius": Will Irwin, *The Making of a Reporter* (New York: G. P. Putnam's Sons, 1942), p. 137.
489   "the staff worked under . . . came forth Chaos": Sedgwick, *The Happy Profession*, p. 142.
489   In fifteen months, both . . . were fired: Lyon, *Success Story*, p. 304.
489   Damon Runyan . . . and Moira O'Neill: Ibid., p. 296; Mott, *A History of American Magazines*, Vol. 4, p. 602.
489   The company eventually foundered: McClure to JSP, Oct. 17, 1906, McClure MSS.
489   Forced to economize: Lyon, *Success Story*, pp. 311–12.
489   Nor could he afford: *Centralia* [WA] *Daily Chronicle*, Dec. 1, 1908.
490   "of good reputation . . . comparatively short time": "Solicitation Letter," July [n.d.], 1906, RSB Papers.
490   "All of us had plunged": RSB, *American Chronicle*, p. 228.
490   stood "to lose everything": RSB to J. Stannard Baker, June 30, 1906, RSB Papers.

490   "so dizzily stimulating . . . for the common cause": RSB, *American Chronicle*, p. 228.

490   "I feel as if I were at the crisis": LS to Joseph Steffens, June 30, 1906, in LS et al., eds., *Letters of Lincoln Steffens*, Vol. 1, p. 174.

490   "the most dauntless": RSB, *American Chronicle*, p. 228.

490   "seen something in which": Tarbell, *All in the Day's Work*, p. 259.

490   "spark of genius . . . the kindest treatment": WAW to Charles Churchill, Aug. 9, 1906, White Papers.

490   "You may draw on me": WAW to McClure, Aug. 27, 1906, McClure MSS.

491   "Everything amused him! . . . loved so much to talk": RSB, *American Chronicle*, p. 225.

491   "He had a wide knowledge": Tarbell, *All in the Day's Work*, pp. 260–61.

491   "made it his business . . . wonderful tales we heard!": Ibid., pp. 261–62.

491   "all the muckrakers muckraking": *The Independent* (Kansas City, MO), July 8, 1906.

491   "a helpful experiment": *Erie* [PA] *Evening Herald*, June 29, 1906.

491   "Their muck-raking has been": *Evening World-Herald* (Omaha, NE), June 30, 1906.

491   "This is undoubtedly the most notable": *Journal of Education* (Boston), July 6, 1906.

491   "not be deterred": "Editorial Announcement," *The American Magazine* (October 1906).

491   "We shall not only make": "Solicitation Letter," July [n.d.], 1906, RSB Papers.

491   "Reformers need relaxation": *Outlook*, July 14, 1906, p. 589.

491   William Allen White . . . offered similar counsel: Johnson, *William Allen White's America*, p. 138.

491   "It seems to me": WAW to JSP, July 6, 1906, White Papers.

492   "We are editing in": Albert Boyden to RSB, Nov. 13, 1906, RSB Papers.

492   "to look into his literary": RSB, *American Chronicle*, p. 228.

492   "Utterly beaten down . . . hard physical work": Ibid., pp. 213–14.

492   "more easily . . . Send more chapters": Ibid., pp. 229, 231–34.

493   "You have sublimated": Ibid., p. 244.

493   "David Grayson is a great man": LS to RSB, July 25, 1906, in ibid., p. 239.

493   Under such titles as: Ibid., pp. 240, 247–48.

493   "people will be expecting": JSP to RSB, July 26, 1906, RSB Papers.

493   a "pioneer" study: Dewey Grantham, Jr., introduction, in Ray Stannard Baker, *Following the Color Line; American Negro Citizenship in the Progressive Era* (New York: Harper & Row, 1964), pp. x, xiii.

493   "to get at the *facts* . . . a major source": Ibid., pp. vii, x.

494   "a clear statement of the case": *Bedford* [PA] *Gazette*, Feb. 22, 1907.

494   "understanding and sympathy": Semonche, *Ray Stannard Baker*, p. 201.

494   "reporting the negro problem": *Bedford* [PA] *Gazette*, Feb. 22, 1907.

494   "too complex to solve": Ibid.

494   "Your work has been a wonderful thing": IMT to RSB, Aug. 9, 1907, RSB Papers.

494   "the best things running": JSP to RSB, May 22, 1907, RSB Papers.

494   chafed at the "consensus editing": Kaplan, *Lincoln Steffens*, p. 164.

494   "It does not matter": JSP to LS, May 11, 1907, LS Papers.

494   "You are crazy, Stef": Albert Boyden to LS, June 18, 1907, LS Papers.

494   he had failed to answer a request: Albert Boyden to LS, April 5, 1905, LS Papers.

494   "We don't need any": John E. Semonche, "The American Magazine of 1906–1915: Principle vs. Profit," *Journalism Quarterly* (Winter 1963), p. 38.

494   "It is very difficult for me": JSP to LS, Feb. 28, 1907, LS Papers.

494   the magazine was covering: Brady, *Ida Tarbell*, p. 183.

495   "you haven't confidence": JSP to LS, Feb. 28, 1907, LS Papers.

495   Steffens remained oblivious . . . near Cos Cob, Connecticut: Peter Hartshorn, *I Have Seen the Future: A Life of Lincoln Steffens* (Berkeley, CA: Counterpoint, 2011), pp. 148–49.

495   "My husband has become famous": Kaplan, *Lincoln Steffens*, p. 160.

495   "Either I am to write": LS to Joseph Steffens, Aug. 27, 1907, in LS et al., eds., *Letters of Lincoln Steffens*, Vol. 1, p. 188.

495   At the time of his departure, Steffens argued . . . the new enterprise: Brady, *Ida Tarbell*, p. 184.

495   "I know now I should not . . . most genuine of human dramas": IMT, *All in the Day's Work*, pp. 262–64.

495   "All this was good for me": Ibid., p. 267.

495   to "get into the fight": Ibid.

496   debates that appeared "so important": Ibid., p. 269.

496   "comprehensive and careful . . . invertebrate": *Life*, Feb. 8, 1912, p. 308.

496   lacked "vitality" . . . "secondhand" material: IMT, *All in the Day's Work*, p. 271.

496   no "cohesive force" . . . "hold the reader": WAW to JSP, June 22, 1907, White Papers.

496   "a certain hustle": IMT to Albert Boyden, July 1, 1907, McClure MSS.

496   "I dreamed of you": McClure to IMT, July 1, 1907, McClure MSS.

CHAPTER NINETEEN: "To Cut Mr. Taft in Two!"

Page

497 while attending a party . . . turned seventy years old: John Hays Hammond, *The Autobiography of John Hays Hammond* (New York: Farrar & Rinehart, Inc., 1935), Vol. 2, p. 532.

497 "a gentle intimation . . . to another": Henry Billings Brown and Charles A. Kent, *Memoir of Henry Billings Brown: Late Justice of the Supreme Court of the United States* (New York: Duffield, 1915), p. 32.

497 "would be shutting the door . . . in 1908": Hammond, *The Autobiography*, Vol. 2, p. 532.

498 In the interim . . . the previous summer: WHT, Professional Diaries [hereafter WHT Diaries], Jan. 22, 1906, WHTP.

498 "the tremendous vote": Ibid.

498 Taft was "sacrificing . . . to open our markets": *New York Tribune*, Mar. 17, 1906.

498 "an infernal ass": WHT to Horace Taft, Jan. 29, 1906, WHTP.

498 "We suffered a very" . . . reach the Senate floor: WHT to Henry Clay Ide, Mar. 17 & 21, WHTP.

498 the press immediately began: *Washington Post*, reprinted in *Syracuse* [NY] *Herald*, Mar. 10, 1906.

498 would "undoubtedly have accepted": WHT quoted in James Creelman, "The Mystery of Mr. Taft," *Pearson's Magazine* (May 1907), p. 529.

498 At Taft's suggestion . . . renewed the pressure on Taft: WHT Diaries, Mar. 10, 1906, WHTP.

498 "would have as important": TR quoted in WHT to TR, Mar. 14, 1906, WHTP.

499 "a big man": WHT Diaries, Mar. 10, 1906, WHTP.

499 "running down" . . . best man on the bench: TR quoted in WHT to TR, Mar. 14, 1906, WHTP.

499 he intended to announce his nomination: *NYT*, Mar. 14, 1906.

499 "bitterly opposed . . . explain the situation": WHT Diaries, Mar. 10, 1906, WHTP.

499 "three great trusts" . . . would "of course yield": WHT to TR, Mar. 14, 1906, WHTP.

499 Charles thought he should take: Charles P. Taft to WHT, Mar. 10, 1906, WHTP.

499 "quite apart from": Horace Taft to WHT, Mar. 13, 1906, WHTP.

499 Harry . . . better suited to be chief justice: Ross, *An American Family*, p. 183.

500 "My dear Will . . . for many years to come": TR to WHT, Mar. 15, 1906, in *LTR*, Vol. 5, pp. 183–86.

501 "all I could expect" . . . until Congress adjourned in July: WHT to HHT, Mar. 15, 1906, WHTP.

501 Displaying decisiveness . . . postpone his nomination: *Racine* [WI] *Daily Journal*, Sept. 24, 1902.

501 "somewhat unusual . . . Mr. Taft in two!": New York Sun, Mar. 17, 1906, in WHT Diaries, WHTP.

501 "the big, jovial, brainy" . . . no longer so appealing: *Hutchinson* [KS] *News*, Aug. 21, 1894.

501 "He has done big things": *Kansas City Star*, June 21, 1906; WHT Diaries, June 23, 1906, WHTP.

501 "no American . . . eyes of his countrymen": Clipping, in James Macusker to WHT, July 23, 1906, WHTP.

501 "I do not see": Lyman Abbott to WHT, Aug. 4, 1906, WHTP.

501 "For the love of Mike": Creighton Webb to WHT, May 29, 1906, WHTP.

502 "a most gloomy" . . . such a busy man!: WHT to TR, July 30, 1906, WHTP.

502 "Now, you beloved": TR to WHT, Aug. 2, 1906, in *LTR*, Vol. 5, pp. 341–43.

502 "rather shocked . . . to sit still": TR to WHT, July 21, 1906, in WHT Diaries, WHTP.

502 "By George": TR to WHT, Aug. 20, 1906, in ibid.

502 a rigorous, doctor-prescribed diet: W. E. Zouke Davie to WHT, Oct. 27, 1905, WHTP.

502 a new bathroom scale . . . 250 pounds: WHT to Charles P. Taft, Dec. 3, 1905, WHTP.

502 "not an inexpensive luxury": WHT to HHT, July 15, 1906, WHTP.

502 "twenty pairs of Trousers": Receipt from Owen, Tailor for Men and Women, to Fred W. Carpenter, July 11, 1906, WHTP.

502 "It is the best thing": Horace Taft to WHT, Dec. 13, 1905, WHTP.

503 Taft's customary day: Wendell W. Mischler to [unknown], Aug. 23, 1906, WHTP.

503 Taft relished . . . and the children: Robert Lee Dunn, *William Howard Taft, American* (Boston: Chapple Publ. Co., 1908), pp. 43–44; "Murray Bay," *Cincinnati Magazine* (August 1979), p. 72.

503 "jumping up and down . . . will do the business": Dunn, *William Howard Taft, American*, pp. 44–45.

503 saving his "city clothes": Ibid., p. 32.

503 "see youth returning": Ibid.

503 The chairman . . . to give the keynote: WHT to TR, Aug. 6, 1906, in WHT Diaries, WHTP.

503 In a letter from Oyster Bay: TR to WHT, Aug. 8, 1906, in ibid.

503 Taft organized his presentation: "Mr. Taft on the Present Issues," *Outlook*, Sept. 15, 1906, p. 95.

503 the "only weakness": WHT to TR, Aug. 21, 1906, WHTP.

503 if the draft seemed "too outspoken": WHT to TR, Aug. 28, 1906, WHTP.

503 "outrageously long . . . circumstances like this": WHT to TR, Aug. 28 & 29, 1906, WHTP.

504 "It's a bully speech": TR to WHT, August [n.d.], 1906, in WHT Diaries, WHTP.

504 "I neither wish": TR to WHT, Sept. 1, 1906, in *LTR*, Vol. 5, p. 392.

504 he suggested that Taft show: TR to WHT, Sept. 4, 1906, in WHT Diaries, WHTP.

504 "the first big Administration": *NYT*, Sept. 6, 1906.

504 "is the issue": New York *Sun*, Sept. 6, 1906, in WHT Diaries, WHTP.
504 "With a frankness . . . and unhesitatingly": *Washington Post*, Sept. 6, 1906.
504 "the frankest": New York *Sun*, Sept. 6, 1906, in WHT Diaries, WHTP.
504 "never made a sharper speech": Henry Hoyt to WHT, Sept. 6, 1906, WHTP.
504 "It is the great speech": TR to WHT, Sept. 6, 1906, in WHT Diaries, WHTP.
504 "A man never knows": WHT to TR, Sept. 8, 1906, WHTP.
504 Revolutionary forces . . . a precarious situation: *Newark* [NJ] *Advocate*, Sept. 14, 1906.
505 "a government adequate": Pringle, *Life and Times*, Vol. 1, pp. 305–06.
505 "In Cuba": TR to George Trevelyan, Sept. 9, 1906, in *LTR*, Vol. 5, p. 401.
505 could not "prevent rebels": Consul-General Steinhart to Acting Secretary of War, Sept. 13, 1906, in United States, *Papers Relating to the Foreign Relations of the United States, with the Annual Message of the President Transmitted to Congress December 3, 1906, Part 1* (Washington, DC: Government Printing Office, 1909), pp. 477–78.
505 "so angry with": Cited in Morris, *Theodore Rex*, p. 456.
505 "as intermediaries" . . . a peaceful solution: Bruce A. Vitor II, *Under the Shadow of the Big Stick: U.S. Intervention in Cuba, 1906–1909* (Fort Leavenworth, KS: U.S. Army Command & General Staff College, 2009), p. 12.
505 From Oyster Bay . . . Attorney General Moody's opinion: WHT to TR, Sept. 16, 1906, WHTP.
505 "If the necessity arises": TR to WHT, Sept. 17, 1906, in *LTR*, Vol. 5, p. 514.
505 When Taft and Bacon . . . reconcile differences peacefully: Duffy, *William Howard Taft*, pp. 187–88.
506 "informal, straightforward": *Racine Daily Journal*, Sept. 19, 1906.
506 "the utter unfitness": WHT to HHT, Sept. 20, 1906, WHTP.
506 "well founded . . . to their homes": WHT to Charles E. Magoon, Nov. 22, 1906; TR to WHT, Sept. 21, 1906, both in *LTR*, Vol. 5, p. 418.
506 "leaving nothing of the Government": WHT to TR, Sept. 25, 1906, WHTP.
506 "The insurgents": WHT to HHT, Sept. 23, 1906, WHTP.
506 One insurgent encampment: WHT to HHT, Sept. 22, 1906, WHTP.
506 "Things are certainly": TR to WHT, Sept. 26, 1906, in *LTR*, Vol. 5, p. 426.
506 "the most unpleasant": WHT to HHT, Sept. 27, 1906, WHTP.
506 he found himself awake . . . struck him dead: Ibid.
506 After a week . . . would land in Cuba: TR to WHT, Sept. 30, 1906, in *LTR*, Vol. 5, p. 435.
506 "be maintained only": Vitor, *Under the Shadow of the Big Stick*, p. 31.
506 The Cuban Constitution . . . would be withdrawn: Morris, *Theodore Rex*, p. 461.
507 "all parties here . . . such attacks futile": WHT to HHT, Sept. 30, 1906, WHTP.
507 "I congratulate you": TR to WHT, Sept. 30, 1906, in *LTR*, Vol. 5, p. 435.
507 promptly cabled Nellie . . . "great comfort": WHT to HHT, Sept. 29, 1906, WHTP.
507 "For the first time . . . quite brilliant effect": HHT, *Recollections of Full Years*, pp. 297, 299.
507 "Upon my word": TR to WHT, Oct. 4, 1906, in WHT Diaries, WHTP.
507 "the shore of the Bay": Dunn, *William Howard Taft, American*, p. 182.
507 "in agony on": HHT, *Recollections of Full Years*, p. 301.
508 "Merely to record . . . to his War Department duties": New York *Sun*, Oct. 27, 1906.
508 "If mental worry": WHT to Charles P. Taft, Oct. 4, 1906, WHTP.
508 "those awful twenty days": HHT, *Recollections of Full Years*, p. 295.
508 "The paramount issue . . . the jolly good fellow": *Omaha* [NE] *Daily Bee*, Oct. 31 & Nov. 2, 1906.
508 "This is rather contrary": WHT to HHT, Nov. 4, 1907, WHTP.
509 "Hats were thrown": *Salt Lake Herald*, Nov. 4, 1906.
509 "The notices have all been": HHT to WHT, Oct. 31, 1906, WHTP.
509 she was concerned . . . cost him the nomination: HHT to WHT, Oct. 27 & 29, 1906, WHTP.
509 "the blues . . . the direction of politics": WHT to HHT, Nov. 1, 1906, WHTP.
509 "turned them down . . . I did not": HHT to WHT, Oct. 27, 1906, WHTP.
509 "I think what": WHT to HHT, Oct. 31, 1906, WHTP.
509 "If you do" . . . a "substitute": WHT to TR, Oct. 31, 1906, WHTP.
510 "I am immensely": TR to WHT, Nov. 5, 1906, in *LTR*, Vol. 5, p. 487.
510 "Our triumph . . . would have been": TR to Kermit Roosevelt, Nov. 7, 1906, in TR et al., eds., *Letters to Kermit from Theodore Roosevelt*, p. 487.
510 "I am overjoyed . . . scandal-mongering": TR to John St. Loe Strachey, Oct. 25, 1906, in *LTR*, Vol. 5, p. 468.
510 "By George": TR to WHT, Nov. 8, 1906, in ibid., p. 492.
510 "I'm going down": *Los Angeles Herald*, Nov. 9, 1906.
510 The "ditch . . . gardens of Babylon": *New York Tribune*, Nov. 12, 1906.
510 "particularly good spirits": *Los Angeles Herald*, Nov. 9, 1906.
510 "a large portion . . . where he may be": *San Antonio* [TX] *Daily Light*, Nov. 11, 1906.

510   "a little of everything": *NYT*, Nov. 14, 1906.

510   Wishing to judge . . . about his work: *NYT*, Nov. 17, 1906.

511   He met with laborers . . . "what he saw": *New York Tribune*, Dec. 16, 1906.

511   Although the Tafts . . . Kansas, and Texas: WHT to TR, Nov. 4, 1906, WHTP.

511   "Not in the history": *Ada* [OK] *Evening News*, Nov. 9, 1906.

511   "several thousand": *Emporia* [KS] *Gazette*, Nov. 10, 1906.

511   "One trouble about travel": WHT to HHT, Nov. 16, 1906, WHTP.

511   During his lengthy absence . . . Brownsville, Texas: *Chicago Tribune*, Nov. 21, 1906.

511   "would certainly be denied them": *Brownsville* [TX] *Daily Herald*, Aug. 14, 1906.

511   A series of . . . public bars: United States, *Hearings Before the Committee on Military Affairs, United States Senate, Concerning the Affray at Brownsville, Tex., on the Night of August 13 and 14, 1906* (Washington, DC: Government Printing Office, 1908), Vol. 1, pp. 462–63.

511   Rumors . . . circulated: *Washington Post*, Aug. 15, 1906.

512   "colored soldiers" . . . after the shootings: United States and Ernest A. Garlington, *The Brownsville Affray: Report of the Inspector General of the Army; Order of the President Discharging Enlisted Men of Companies B, C, and D, Twenty-Fifth Infantry; Messages of the President to the Senate; and Majority and Minority Reports of the Senate Committee on Military Affairs* (Washington, DC: Government Printing Office, 1908), pp. 302–03.

512   Major Augustus Blocksom . . . "nine to fifteen": *Washington Post*, Aug. 22, 1906.

512   "discharged from the service": Morris, *Theodore Rex*, p. 455.

512   "in a state . . . openly at night": *Washington Post*, Aug. 22, 1906.

512   "It is very doubtful": *Brownsville Daily Herald*, Aug. 22, 1906.

512   If they continued to conceal: *NYT*, Oct. 18, 1906.

512   "this extreme penalty . . . when the penalty falls": *NYT*, Nov. 7, 1906.

512   The president directed . . . any civil service position: Ibid.; *Cleveland Journal*, Nov. 10, 1906.

512   The battalion included . . . Spanish-American War: *Cleveland Journal*, Nov. 24, 1906.

513   "despotic usurpation of power": *Arizona Silver Belt* (Globe City, AZ), Nov. 11, 1906.

513   "Deep resentment": *NYT*, Nov. 19, 1906.

513   "the door of hope": *NYT*, Nov. 21, 1906.

513   "a truckling": *NYT*, Nov. 19, 1906.

513   "Once enshrined": Ibid.

513   Taft consented to meet Mary Church Terrell: *NYT*, Nov. 18, 1906.

513   "to withhold the execution . . . generous-hearted": Mary Church Terrell, "Taft and the Negro Soldiers," *The Independent*, July 23, 1908.

513   "delay the execution . . . on the subject": Pringle, *Life and Times*, Vol. 1, pp. 324–25.

513   the negative impact: WHT to Louise T. Taft, Jan. 15, 1907, in WHT Diaries, WHTP.

513   "If a rehearing shows": WHT to CPT, Jan. 1, 1907, WHTP.

513   Upon learning that Taft . . . the civil branch: *Cleveland Journal*, Nov. 24, 1906.

513   "a severe strain upon": *NYT*, Nov. 21, 1906.

514   "The order in question": TR to Curtis Guild, Jr., Nov. 7, 1906, in *LTR*, Vol. 5, p. 489.

514   "Discharge is not": TR to WHT, Nov. 21, 1906, in WHT Diaries, WHTP.

514   When Congress convened . . . overstepped his authority: New York *Sun*, Dec. 4, 1906.

514   a "fighting mad" reaction: *NYT*, Dec. 23, 1906.

514   "It is impossible": TR to RSB, Mar. 30, 1907, in *LTR*, Vol. 5, p. 634.

514   "tingling with . . . comrades of murderers": *The News* (Frederick, MD), Dec. 20, 1906.

514   "excuse or justification . . . utterly inadequate": *New York Tribune*, Dec. 20, 1906.

514   "fight to the last . . . decided to follow": New York *Sun*, Dec. 23, 1906.

514   "extraordinary language . . . hatred and violence": *The News* (Frederick, MD), Dec. 20, 1906.

515   "the colored man": *Washington* [DC] *Bee*, Dec. 29, 1906.

515   sending a new round: *Bisbee* [AZ] *Daily Review*, Dec. 30, 1906.

515   At Taft's urging: *Chicago Tribune*, Jan. 15, 1907.

515   Eventually, he allowed: *NYT*, Mar. 12, 1908.

515   "cleared the records": *NYT*, Sept. 29, 1972.

515   Privately, Taft continued: WHT to Charles P. Taft, Jan. 1, 1907, WHTP.

515   "courage and good judgment" . . . already carried out: WHT to Richard Harding Davis, Nov. 24, 1906, WHTP.

515   "This Brownsville matter . . . disappear with argument": WHT to Howard Hollister, Dec. 25, 1906, in WHT Diaries, WHTP.

CHAPTER TWENTY: Taft Boom, Wall Street Bust

Page
516   "favorable consideration . . . in silence": *Fort Wayne* [IN] *Journal-Gazette*, Mar. 7, 1907.
516   "an uneventful and poor": *Post-Standard* (Syracuse, NY), Mar. 5, 1906.
517   a bill banning corporate contributions: *NYT*, Jan. 22, 1907.
517   "knowingly" . . . sixteen consecutive hours: *The Railway Age*, Mar. 8, 1907, p. 323.
517   many critical bills . . . law for corporations: *Fort Wayne* [IN] *Journal-Gazette*, Mar. 7, 1907.
517   "some sixteen million": TR, *An Autobiography*, p. 404.
517   Pinchot mobilized his office . . . into forest lands: Pinchot, *Breaking New Ground*, p. 300.
517   Through these orders: Brinkley, *The Wilderness Warrior*, pp. 677–78.
517   "Opponents of the Forest Service": TR, *An Autobiography*, pp. 404–05.
518   "the deep, unbroken friendship": James Creelman, "The Mystery of Mr. Taft," *Pearson's* (May 1907), p. 530, in WHT Diaries, WHTP.
518   "I am well aware": TR to WAW, July 30, 1907, WHTP.
518   "do all in his power": *Evening Independent* (Massillon, OH), April 23, 1907.
518   "boundless courage . . . beguiling influence": *San Antonio* [TX] *Gazette*, June 25, 1907.
518   "he would crawl": John Callan O'Laughlin, "The Next President," *Outlook*, Mar. 30, 1907, p. 749.
518   he would disavow any such statement: "TR: Press Agent," *Harper's Weekly*, Sept. 28, 1907, p. 1410.
518   IMPARTIAL MR. ROOSEVELT: *Kansas City Times*, April 16, 1907, in WHT Diaries, WHTP.
518   "I wish to say": *Cleveland Leader*, Dec. 29, 1906, in WHT Diaries, WHTP.
518   "been drawn into . . . irrespective of politics": O'Laughlin, "The Next President," *Outlook*, Mar. 30, 1907, p. 747.
519   "was very much averse": WHT to Edward Colston, Mar. 22, 1907, WHT Diaries, WHTP.
519   "an almost morbid fear": O'Laughlin, "The Next President," *Outlook*, Mar. 30, 1907, p. 747.
519   "Taft is not a politician": *Washington Post*, Jan. 27, 1907.
519   "the little details": *Washington Post*, April 25, 1907.
519   The press predicted: *The Independent* (NY), April 4, 1907, pp. 757–58.
519   "may cause trouble": TR to Kermit Roosevelt, April 11, 1907, in TR et al., eds., *Letters to Kermit from Theodore Roosevelt*, p. 188.
519   "This is a direct contest": New York *Sun*, Mar. 31, 1907, in WHT Diaries, WHTP.
519   "had nothing to gain . . . possibly to lose": HHT to WHT, April [n.d., "Easter Sunday"], 1907, WHTP.
519   The decision . . . soon proved wise: WHT to Charles P. Taft, May 8, 1907, WHTP.
520   Through intermediaries . . . senatorial contest: *New York Tribune*, May 11, 1907.
520   "I don't care . . . political principle": WHT to Arthur Vorys, Jan. 20, 1907, WHT Diaries, WHTP.
520   "with a drawn sword in his hand": WHT to Gustav J. Karger, May 14, 1907, Taft-Karger MSS, CMC.
520   "become somewhat . . . a stand-up fight": WHT to TR, July 23, 1907, WHTP.
520   "While under no circumstances": TR to WHT, July 26, 1907, in *LTR*, Vol. 5, pp. 726–27.
520   Steeled for defeat . . . in the Senate race: *New York Tribune*, July 30, 1907, in WHT Diaries, WHTP.
520   "I am hopeful": WHT to Howard C. Hollister, July 31, 1907, WHTP.
520   Foraker's political career . . . in public office again: Pringle, *Life and Times*, Vol. 1, pp. 371–72; *Fort Wayne Journal-Gazette*, Sept. 8, 1908.
521   Despite his victory . . . a "mauling": TR to WHT, Aug. 3, 1907, in *LTR*, Vol. 5, p. 741.
521   "first substantial start": WHT to Joseph B. Foraker, Aug. 24, 1908, in Pringle, *Life and Times*, Vol. 1, p. 371.
521   "born with an instinct": Creelman, "The Mystery of Mr. Taft," *Pearson's* (May 1907), p. 512, in WHT Diaries, WHTP.
521   "the kindest man": Lyle, "Taft: A Career of Big Tasks," *The World's Work* (November 1907).
521   "A place on the Supreme": Unidentified newspaper clipping, Los Angeles, May [n.d.], 1907, in WHT Diaries, WHTP.
521   "Uneasy lies the head": LTT to WHT, Jan. 21, 1907, WHTP.
521   "He wins the hearts . . . devoid of political ambitions": James Creelman, "The Mystery of Mr. Taft," *Pearson's* (May 1907), pp. 511, 505, in WHT Diaries, WHTP.
521   "can scarcely be said": *NYT*, Aug. 18, 1907.
522   "fitted to say things": *Mansfield* [OH] *News*, May 2, 1907.
522   "I am not sure": WHT to Arthur Vorys, Aug. 6, 1907, WHTP.
522   his drafts remained "infernally long": WHT to TR, Aug. 10, 1907, WHTP.
522   "Never mind if": HHT to WHT, Aug. 18, 1907, WHTP.
522   "revision must wait": New York *Sun*, Aug. 20, 1907.
522   "ferocious denunciation . . . and sincere sympathy": *NYT*, Aug. 20, 1907.
522   "there is not": New York *Sun*, Aug. 20, 1907.
522   "I am much amused": WHT to Horace Taft, Sept. 10, 1907, WHTP.
522   "Is it possible . . . adherence to those views": WHT to Charles H. Heald, Dec. 25, 1907, WHTP.

522   "the feeling of . . . are compelled to": Charles Nagel to WHT, May 6, 1907, WHT Diaries, WHTP.

523   "well defined movement": *Cedar Rapids* [IA] *Evening Gazette*, Nov. 8, 1907.

523   "an almost unanimous sentiment": *Chicago Record-Herald*, Mar. 5, 1907, in WHT Diaries, WHTP.

523   "It's hard to write . . . Roosevelt sentiment": C. S. Watts to N. Wright, in Charles P. Taft to WHT, May 21, 1907, WHTP.

523   "almost grotesque . . . an illustrious Necessity?": New York *Sun*, Mar. 31, 1907.

523   "How they hate him": HHT to WHT, Mar. 31, 1907, WHTP.

523   "could get the nomination": Gustav J. Karger to Joseph Garretson, Oct. 30, 1907, Taft-Karger MSS, CMC.

523   "would feel very much . . . they had formed": TR to Kermit Roosevelt, May 15, 1907, in TR, et al., eds., *Letters to Kermit from Theodore Roosevelt*, p. 195.

524   "personal sacrifice . . . this administration": Gustav J. Karger to Joseph Garretson, Oct. 30, 1907, Taft-Karger MSS, CMC.

524   In case Taft's canvass . . . backing Governor Hughes: TR to WHT, Sept. 3, 1907, in *LTR*, Vol. 5, pp. 780–82.

524   "for the moment . . . the wisest course": TR to WHT, Sept. 3, 1907, in ibid., p. 781.

524   by late August . . . had grown "shorter": *Galveston* [TX] *Daily News*, Aug. 31, 1907.

524   "Political affairs . . . in the third place": TR to WHT, Sept. 3, 1907, in *LTR*, Vol. 5, pp. 780–82.

524   "So far as I am able": WHT to Charles P. Taft, Sept. 11, 1907, WHTP.

524   "It was as great": WHT to Charles P. Taft, Aug. 21, 1907, WHTP.

524   "a fine audience of 4000 people": WHT to TR, Aug. 30, 1907, WHTP.

524   "was filled to suffocation": WHT to LTT, Aug. 30, 1907, WHT Diaries, WHTP.

524   "every politician": WHT to TR, Aug. 30, 1907, WHTP.

525   "Personal contact": WHT to Charles P. Taft, Sept. 11, 1907, WHTP.

525   "feel glad": *NYT*, Aug. 18, 1907.

525   "Nellie was out . . . to you than to me": WHT to Charles P. Taft, Sept. 11, 1907, WHTP.

525   "I fully understand . . . my boom at all possible": WHT to TR, Sept. 11, 1907, WHTP.

525   "right to initiate . . . by the Commission": "Address by Wm. H. Taft, Secretary of War, at the Inauguration of the Philippine Assembly, October 16, 1907," in United States and WHT, *Special Report of Wm. H. Taft, Secretary of War, to the President, on the Philippines* (Washington, DC: Government Printing Office, 1908), p. 98.

525   "the first parliament": Karnow, *In Our Image*, p. 238.

526   "a chill . . . wealthier classes": WHT to Charles P. Taft, Oct. 23, 1907, WHTP.

526   He began his address . . . "about to undertake": See WHT, *Special Report . . . on the Philippines*, pp. 86, 89, 102.

526   "thousand and one events": HHT, *Recollections of Full Years*, p. 315.

526   "Everybody": Anthony, *Nellie Taft*, p. 205.

527   stock market losses approached $1 billion: Jean Strouse, *Morgan: American Financier* (New York: Random House, 1999), p. 573.

527   "crusades against business" . . . paralyzed the economy: *Chicago Record-Herald*, Feb. 2, 1907, cited in Pringle, *Theodore Roosevelt: A Biography*, p. 434.

527   "By slow and insidious": New York *Sun*, Dec. 6, 1907.

527   "deep-seated, undiscriminating": *Current Literature* (October 1907), p. 352.

527   By "going up and down": *Current Literature* (December 1907), p. 596.

527   "take Bryan or Hearst": Creelman, "Theodore the Meddler," *Pearson's* (January 1907), p. 4.

527   "certain malefactors": *The News* (Frederick, MD), Aug. 21, 1907.

527   "welcome hard times": TR to William E. Dodd, Jan. 30, 1907, in *LTR*, Vol. 5, p. 575.

527   "They are as blind": TR to William H. Moody, Sept. 21, 1907, in ibid., p. 802.

527   "responsible for turning on": *Current Literature* (December 1907), p. 597.

527   "a temporary period of weakness": TR to Henry L. Higginson, Aug. 12, 1907, in *LTR*, Vol. 5, p. 746.

528   Their sensational failure . . . investment bank in New York: *Current Literature* (December 1907), p. 585.

528   Spooked by rumors . . . shutter its offices: Strouse, *Morgan: American Financier*, p. 577.

528   Evidence that the respected firm: *Current Literature* (December 1907), p. 594.

528   In the days that followed: Ibid., pp. 586–87, 590.

528   "hardly a bank": Ibid., p. 590.

528   "a one-man Federal Reserve": Frederick Lewis Allen, *The Great Pierpont Morgan* (New York: Harper & Row, 1949), p. 265.

528   "Panic Headquarters": Ida May Tarbell, *The Life of Elbert H. Gary: The Story of Steel* (New York: D. Appleton, 1925), p. 199.

528   Within two days the bankers: Jean Strouse, "The Brilliant Bailout," *The New Yorker*, Nov. 23, 1998, p. 69.

528   "It was an extraordinary": Chernow, *The House of Morgan*, p. 124.

528 The next day . . . Morgan's headquarters: *Racine* [WI] *Daily Journal*, Oct. 23, 1907; *Galveston Daily News*, Oct. 24, 1907.

528 On Thursday . . . to keep the exchange open: Strouse, *Morgan: American Financier*, p. 580.

529 "the Man of the Hour": *Literary Digest*, Nov. 9, 1907, p. 676.

529 "was still the chief": Ibid.

529 "would bring down": IMT, *Life of Elbert H. Gary*, p. 196.

529 "Can you go at once?": Ibid., p. 200.

529 "under ordinary circumstances": TR to Charles J. Bonaparte, Nov. 4, 1907, in *LTR*, Vol. 5, p. 831.

529 "somewhat in excess": Mowry, *The Era of Theodore Roosevelt*, p. 218.

529 "to the interest . . . no public duty": TR to Charles J. Bonaparte, Nov. 4, 1907, in *LTR*, Vol. 5, p. 831.

529 But when the terms: Chernow, *The House of Morgan*, p. 128.

529 "the best bargain . . . less than $1 billion": Pringle, *Theodore Roosevelt: A Biography*, p. 444.

529 "swallow up a lively": Allen, *The Great Pierpont Morgan*, p. 261.

529 "The Nation trembled . . . crisis arose": TR, *An Autobiography*, p. 438.

530 "I would have showed": Ibid., p. 442.

530 a general malaise began . . . their livelihood: TR to Cecil Spring Rice, Dec. 21, 1907, in *LTR*, Vol. 6, p. 870.

530 "Whether I am": TR to Alexander Lambert, Nov. 1, 1907, in *LTR*, Vol. 5, p. 826.

530 "The big moneyed men": TR to Kermit Roosevelt, Dec. 8, 1907, in ibid., p. 226.

530 "because when the average": TR to Alexander Lambert, Nov. 1, 1907, in ibid., p. 826.

530 "From all sides": IMT, *Life of Elbert H. Gary,* p. 192.

530 "destroyer of . . . of property": *Literary Digest* (December 1907), p. 594.

530 "I feel personally": WAW to TR, Nov. 22, 1907, White Papers.

530 "I care a great deal more": TR to WAW, Nov. 26, 1907, in *LTR*, Vol. 5, pp. 855–56.

530 "to destroy his . . . blood to running!": RSB to J. Stannard Baker, Nov. 17, 1907, RSB Papers.

531 "A man may sometimes": RSB, Notebook, Nov. 16, 1907, and RSB to J. Stannard Baker, Nov. 16, 1907, RSB Papers.

531 "I hate for personal reasons": TR to Frederic Harrison, Dec. 18, 1907, in *LTR*, Vol. 6, p. 866.

531 "the fight before . . . of the people": TR to Arthur Hamilton Lee, Dec. 26, 1907, in ibid., pp. 874–75.

531 "On the night after . . . gossip ever since": *National Tribune* (Washington, DC), Dec. 19, 1907.

531 "I suppose he has come": *NYT*, Dec. 12, 1907.

531 "do his utmost": Ibid.

532 "definitely and positively": New York *Sun*, Dec. 13, 1907.

532 "to come out squarely": *Sandusky* [OH] *Star-Journal*, Dec. 13, 1907.

532 Frank Flint . . . "all along": *New York Tribune*, Dec. 13, 1907.

532 "the only one worth considering": *NYT*, Dec. 12, 1907.

532 "strength, constitution and courage": Horace Taft to WHT, Aug. 20, 1907, WHTP.

532 "on the road to recovery": Charles P. Taft to Delia Torrey, Nov. 21, 1907, WHTP.

532 "her cheeks were": Anne Taft to WHT, Dec. 20, 1907, WHTP.

532 "slowly but steadily": WHT to Mrs. Samuel Carr, Dec. 24, 1907, WHTP.

532 "Still have hope": Charles P. Taft to WHT, Dec. 6, 1907, WHTP.

532 Taft's ship . . . his mother was dead: WHT Diaries, Dec. 7, 1907, WHTP.

532 "I hope you will say . . . public statement": TR to WHT, Dec. 12, 1907, in *LTR*, Vol. 5, p. 864.

533 "I was very much . . . a great change": WHT to Mrs. Samuel Carr, Dec. 24, 1907, WHTP.

533 "for something else . . . reckoned with": WHT to Therese McCagg, Dec. 26, 1907, WHTP.

CHAPTER TWENTY-ONE: Kingmaker and King

Page

534 "caught its second wind": *The North American* (Philadelphia), June 21, 1908.

534 "as its first . . . with a whoop": William Nelson to WHT, Jan. 22, 1908, WHTP.

534 endorsed Taft unanimously: D. C. Bailey to WHT, Feb. 12, 1908, WHTP.

534 a poll . . . two to one margin: *Van Wert* [OH] *Daily Bulletin*, Feb. 4, 1908.

535 "If you could bring": WHT to William Dawson, Jan. 16, 1908, WHTP.

535 He solicited activists: WHT to Thomas Latta, Feb. 11, 1908, WHTP.

535 "friendly tone . . . brighter": WHT to Tams Bixby, Mar. 26, 1908, WHTP.

535 "rapid-fire . . . witty sallies": *Washington Post*, Feb. 12, 1908.

535 "a blacklisted laborer": Dunn, *William Howard Taft, American*, p. 175.

535 "to determine" . . . of that committee: WHT, "Cooper Union Speech of January 10, 1908," WHTP.

535 "God knows": *Washington Post*, Jan. 11, 1908.

535 "it was the general verdict": *Outlook*, Jan. 18, 1908, p. 108.

535 By late January . . . chances in the fall: WHT to Herbert Parsons, Jan. 23, 1908.

535 so "blistering . . . sensational": Davis, *Released for Publication*, p. 71.

535 "sane and sound" address: Henry C. Ide to WHT, Feb. 2, 1908, WHTP.

536 "a matter of humiliation . . . a stop to the wrongdoing": United States, *Special Message of the President of the United States, Communicated to the Two Houses of Congress on January 31, 1908* (Washington, DC: Government Printing Office, 1908), pp. 2, 26–27.

536 "prostituting his high office": Davis, *Released for Publication*, p. 71.

536 "It hurls defiance" . . . caught everyone's attention: Cited in *Chicago Tribune*, Feb. 2, 1908.

536 "It has maddened": TR to Kermit Roosevelt, Feb. 10, 1908, in TR et al., eds., *Letters to Kermit from Theodore Roosevelt*, p. 231.

536 "It records something": WHT to Frank T. Cobb, Feb. 3, 1908, WHTP.

536 "the Hughes boom . . . settled": TR to Kermit Roosevelt, April 11, 1908, in TR et al., eds., *Letters to Kermit from Theodore Roosevelt*, p. 238.

537 "distinctly against any": New York *Sun*, Mar. 9, 1908, WHTP.

537 Taft immediately repudiated . . . to disturb him: WHT to TR, Mar. 9, 1908, WHTP.

537 "Good heavens . . . myself responsible!": TR to WHT, Mar. 9, 1908, WHTP.

537 "painful experience . . . execration": WHT to Nahum Brascher, Jan. 19, 1908, WHTP.

537 From his abolitionist father: WHT to Robert Barnes, April 26, 1908, WHTP.

537 "to oppose the color caste": "Professor DuBois's Advice," *The Independent*, April 2, 1908, p. 768.

537 "a menace": *Washington Bee*, Dec. 29, 1906.

537 "never, never" support him: "The Negroes and Secretary Taft," *The Independent*, Feb. 13, 1908, p. 374.

537 "entire responsibility": *NYT*, Aug. 8, 1906.

537 "We are satisfied": Ibid.

537 predilection "for strong drink": W. E. Chandler to WHT, June 5, 1908, WHTP.

537 "wonderful resolution": WHT to W. E. Chandler, June 6, 1908, WHTP.

537 "painted as perfect": *Current Literature* (July 1908), p. 10.

537 "I trust you will": Frank H. Challis to WHT, June 2, 1908, WHTP.

537 "the mighty dead . . . heartless": *Los Angeles Herald*, June 2, 1908.

537 "at mock attention . . . destinies of the nation": AB to his mother, June 8, 1908, in Abbott, ed., *Letters of Archie Butt*, p. 23.

538 "All opposition to Taft": TR to Whitelaw Reid, May 25, 1908, in *LTR*, Vol. 6, p. 1036.

538 "an astonishing achievement": *Chicago Evening Post*, April 13, 1908.

538 "Congress is ending": TR to Whitelaw Reid, May 25, 1908, in *LTR*, Vol. 6, p. 1036.

538 "practical unanimity . . . do nothing Congress": *Syracuse* [NY] *Herald*, June 1, 1908.

538 "crystallized" a nascent sentiment: Semonche, *Ray Stannard Baker*, p. 151.

538 "The noon of the muckraker's day": *Waterloo* [IA] *Semi Weekly Courier*, Nov. 27, 1908.

538 "Look upon these . . . now in favor": *NYT*, July 23, 1908.

539 "Don't hold the knife": Johnson, *William Allen White's America*, p. 165.

539 White needed . . . to Washington: WAW to WHT, Jan. 22, 1908, White Papers.

539 In lengthy letters . . . his success: WAW to WHT, Feb. 26, 1908, White Papers.

539 "The meanest man": WHT to Miller Outcault, Mar. 23, 1908, WHTP.

539 an "amiable giant . . . clean off the desk": WAW, "Taft: A Hewer of Wood," *The American Magazine* (April 1908), pp. 19, 23, 31, 32.

539 "It would be impossible": TR to WAW, June 26, 1908, White Papers.

539 "I wabble terribly . . . seems so amazing": IMT to RSB, May 3, 1911, RSB Papers.

539 "for the sake of . . . but for the people": IMT, "Roosevelt vs. Rockefeller," *The American Magazine* (February 1908), p. 434.

539 "less amazing" figure: IMT to RSB, May 3, 1911, RSB Papers.

539 "the St. George": IMT, *All in the Day's Work*, p. 271.

540 "I certainly am socialistic": Palermo, *Lincoln Steffens*, p. 69.

540 Although he praised . . . the system itself: LS, "Roosevelt—Taft—La Follette: On What the Matter Is in America, and What to Do About It," *Everybody's Magazine* (June 1908), pp. 725, 732, 736.

540 "You contend . . . mighty little good": TR to LS, June 5, 1908, in *LTR*, Vol. 6, pp. 1051, 1053.

540 "mutual understanding . . . genuine affection": LS to TR, June 9, 1908, TRP.

540 "the most interesting . . . valiantly and fearlessly": RSB, "The Powers of a Strenuous President," *The American Magazine* (April 1908), pp. 555–56, 559.

541 a "European system": Semonche, *Ray Stannard Baker*, p. 213.

541 "I think you lay . . . man as a man": TR to RSB, June 3, 1908, in *LTR*, Vol. 6, pp. 1047–49.

541 "I wish as much . . . downtrodden, outcast?": RSB to TR, June 8, 1908, TRP.

541 "the wilds of Africa . . . plain morality": RSB, "The New Roosevelt: A Sketch from Life from an Unpublished Letter," *The American Magazine* (September 1908), p. 472.

542 "in a more human mood": Ibid.

542 "When you see me": AB to his mother, May 15, 1908, in Abbott, ed., *Letters of Archie Butt*, p. 7.

542 "*been* President . . . should hold it": TR to George Trevelyan, June 19, 1908, in *LTR*, Vol. 6, pp. 1087, 1086, 1089.

542 "to throb with . . . Pres. Roosevelt": *Washington Post*, June 14, 1908.

542 "an unfailing topic": *Emporia* [KS] *Gazette*, June 16, 1908.

542 "a mob": *San Francisco Chronicle*, June 17, 1908.

542 "in their heart of hearts": *Des Moines Daily News*, June 16, 1908.

542 "a stampede . . . last card": *Washington Post*, June 14, 1908.

542 "to create a diversion": *The North American*, June 21, 1908.

543 "full of sunshine": *Outlook*, June 27, 1908, p. 420.

543 The band played: *Emporia* [KS] *Gazette*, June 16, 1908.

543 "the glories of . . . blood tingling": *New York Tribune*, June 18, 1908.

543 "that expectant interest": *Des Moines Daily News*, June 17, 1908.

543 His quarters at . . . comfortable chairs: *NYT*, March 29, 1908.

543 Electricians equipped . . . the Coliseum: *New York Tribune*, June 18, 1908.

543 "plunged into the . . . do anything unnatural": *Emporia* [KS] *Gazette*, June 18, 1908.

543 Nellie arrived at noon . . . outer reception room: *Washington Post*, June 19, 1908.

544 "the magic name": *Outlook*, June 27, 1908, p. 417.

544 "a wild, frenzied": *Des Moines Daily News*, June 17, 1908.

544 "burning fuse to dry powder": *New York Tribune*, June 19, 1908.

544 "vested abuses . . . United States today": Republican National Convention and Milton W. Blumenberg, *Official Report of the Proceedings of the Fourteenth Republican National Convention: Held in Chicago, Illinois, June 16, 17, 18 and 19, 1908: Resulting in the Nomination of William Howard Taft, of Ohio, for President* (Columbus, OH: F. J. Heer, 1908), p. 87.

544 "exploded with a roar . . . Four Years More": *Outlook*, June 27, 1908, p. 417.

544 "volleys of cheers . . . would blow off": *New York Tribune*, June 18, 1908.

544 "a trifle . . . for another outburst": *Washington Post*, June 18, 1908.

544 "on the verge": *New York Tribune*, June 18, 1908.

544 Fortunately, Taft . . . pandemonium erupted: WHT Diaries, June 17, 1908, WHTP.

544 Nellie was unnerved: Joseph Bucklin Bishop, *Presidential Nominations and Elections: A History of American Conventions, National Campaigns, Inaugurations and Campaign Caricature* (New York: Charles Scribner's Sons, 1916), p. 74.

544 "not at all alarmed": WHT Diaries, June 17, 1908, WHTP.

544 "by the force of his": *Outlook*, June 27, 1908, p. 417.

544 "That man is no friend": RNC and Blumenberg, *Official Report of the Proceedings of the Fourteenth Republican National Convention*, p. 88.

544 "as the voice of the President": *Washington Post*, June 18, 1908.

545 "to blow off steam": *New York Tribune*, June 18, 1908.

545 Archie Butt had never: AB to his mother, June 19, 1908, in Abbott, ed., *Letters of Archie Butt*, p. 39.

545 "The cheers for Roosevelt": *Des Moines Daily News*, June 17, 1908.

545 one of her husband's "best advisers": *Washington Post*, June 19, 1908.

545 "electric with": *San Francisco Chronicle*, June 19, 1908.

545 Nellie strove to remain calm: Bishop, *Presidential Nominations and Elections*, p. 73.

545 "Taft, Taft, Taft . . . beaming smile": *Galveston* [TX] *Daily News*, June 19, 1908.

545 Though less protracted: *Boston Daily Globe*, June 19, 1908.

545 "white as marble": Bishop, *Presidential Nominations and Elections*, pp. 74–75.

545 "Scarcely a word": *San Francisco Chronicle*, June 19, 1908.

546 "Pay no attention": *Galveston* [TX] *Daily News*, June 19, 1908.

546 Seven states managed: *Current Literature* (July 1908), p. 1.

546 "The scene was absolutely": *Galveston* [TX] *Daily News*, June 19, 1908.

546 "flashed . . . aglow with excitement": *Washington Post*, June 19, 1908.

546 "Bubbling over with . . . joy of a boy": *San Francisco Chronicle*, June 19, 1908.

546 A "football rush": *Washington Post*, June 19, 1908.

546 "You know how . . . I am very happy": Ibid.

546 Roosevelt was engaged: *San Francisco Chronicle*, June 19, 1908.

546 "The country is indeed": *Boston Daily Globe*, June 19, 1908.

546 "A great honor . . . to you to-night": New York *Evening World*, June 19, 1908.

547 The convention completed . . . "Sunny Jim": ARL, *Crowded Hours*, p. 151.

547 They had hoped . . . to the delegates: TR to HCL, June 15, 1908, in *LTR*, Vol. 6, p. 1077; WHT to TR, June 15, 1908, WHTP.

547 diluted an anti-injunction plank: *Des Moines Daily News*, June 17, 1908.

547 expressed "disappointment": *Des Moines Daily News*, June 19, 1908; Pringle, *Life and Times*, Vol. 1, pp. 354–55.

547 "We can't get all": *Emporia* [KS] *Gazette*, June 22, 1908.

547 "The next four months": WHT to Charles E. Magoon, July 10, 1908, WHTP.

547 "with a certain degree . . . out of whole cloth": WHT to John Rodgers, July 19, 1908, WHTP.

547 the Presidential Suite . . . secretary and clerk: *Washington Times*, July 12, 1908.

547 In the days . . . seven years earlier: *Fort Wayne* [IN] *Journal-Gazette*, June 19, 1910.

548 Typically awakened . . . settled in his office: *Albuquerque* [NM] *Citizen*, July 21, 1908.

548 more than 1,500 congratulatory . . . letters every day: *Racine* [WI] *Journal*, July 7, 1908; *Bemidji Daily Pioneer* (St. Paul, MN), July 14, 1908.

548 By ten . . . "favorite promenade": *Washington Times*, July 12, 1908.

548 After the defeat . . . over 50 percent: *Greenville* [PA] *Evening Record*, July 11, 1908.

548 The Democratic platform: WHT to TR, July 13, 1908, TRP.

548 "We will be able": TR to WHT, July 13, 1908, WHTP.

548 how to "slash savagely": TR to WHT, July 17, 1908, in *LTR*, Vol. 6, p. 1132.

548 "Both of the first . . . now the leader": TR to WHT, July 21, 1908, in ibid., pp. 1139–40.

548 "most accomplished . . . frank announcement": *NYT*, July 23, 1908.

549 "I have the highest": *Marion* [OH] *Weekly Star*, July 25, 1908.

549 "the spectacle": *New Castle* [PA] *News*, July 24, 1908.

549 "a schoolboy . . . his late chief": *NYT*, July 23, 1908.

549 "humiliating pilgrimage": New York *Sun*, July 24, 1908.

549 "but the puppet": *Pensacola* [FL] *Journal*, July 24, 1908.

549 "not calculated": *New Castle* [PA] *News*, July 24, 1908.

549 The stately colonial mansion . . . distinguished visitors: *Alexandria* [DC] *Gazette*, July 26, 1908.

549 A flagpole: *Piqua* [OH] *Leader-Dispatch*, July 28, 1908.

549 The spacious grounds: *Alexandria* [DC] *Gazette*, July 26, 1908.

549 "What we thought": Charles P. Taft to William Edwards, July 25, 1908, WHTP.

549 NO PLACE LIKE HOME . . . "arm in arm": *New York Tribune*, July 26, 1908.

549 the city's "holiday attire": *Coshocton* [OH] *Daily Age*, July 28, 1908.

549 "the booming of cannon": *Piqua* [OH] *Leader-Dispatch*, July 28, 1908.

549 From the reviewing stand: *Alexandria* [DC] *Gazette*, July 26, 1908.

550 "as its candidate": *Piqua* [OH] *Leader-Dispatch*, July 28, 1908.

550 "smiled cordially": *Alexandria* [DC] *Gazette*, July 26, 1908.

550 "movement for practical reform . . . is not now adequate": WHT, "Speech Accepting the Republican Nomination, July 28, 1908," in *Republican Campaign Text-Book, 1908* (Philadelphia: Dunlap Printing Co., 1908), p. 3.

550 "Popular elections": *Cincinnati Price Current*, July 30, 1908.

550 "Hasn't it been glorious!": Anthony, *Nellie Taft*, p. 215.

550 After a luncheon party . . . "all ablaze with illumination": *Alexandria* [DC] *Gazette*, July 26, 1908.

550 From the steamer's deck: *Piqua* [OH] *Leader-Dispatch*, July 28, 1908.

551 "tremendous outpouring . . . was unalloyed": WHT to TR, July 31, 1908, TRP.

551 "I congratulate you": TR to WHT, July 30, 1908, in *LTR*, Vol. 6, p. 1144.

551 "an exceedingly able . . . western radicalism": *Wall Street Journal*, July 29, 1908.

551 he hoped to shed the 50 pounds: *Waterloo* [IA] *Semi Weekly Courier*, July 7, 1908.

551 "I play golf": *Bemidji* [MN] *Daily Pioneer*, July 14, 1908.

551 after a brief stint . . . in his waist: WHT to TR, July 12, 1908, TRP.

551 "No man weighing 300": *NYT*, Aug. 18, 1908.

551 a 3,500-pound workhorse . . . "a special stall": *NYT*, Aug. 26, 1908.

551 "everything else": *New York Tribune*, Aug. 14, 1908.

551 "It would seem incredible": TR to WHT, Sept. 14, 1908, in *LTR*, Vol. 6, p. 1234.

552 a "rich man's game": *New York Tribune*, Aug. 14, 1908.

552 "the American people": TR to WHT, Sept. 5, 1908, in *LTR*, Vol. 6, pp. 1209–10.

552 "very hard" . . . could be misleading: WHT to TR, Sept. 21, 1908, TRP.

552 "like a hen over her chickens": Charles Willis Thompson, *Presidents I've Known and Two Near Presidents* (Indianapolis: Bobbs-Merrill, 1929), p. 225.

552 "willing to undergo": WHT to TR, July 9, 1908, TRP.

552 "I must tell you": George Sheldon to WHT, Sept. 28, 1908, WHTP.

552 "nothing but the . . . misunderstood": WHT to William N. Cromwell, Aug. 6, 1908, WHTP.

552 "I have always said": TR to WHT, Aug. 7, 1908, in *LTR*, Vol. 6, p. 1157.

552 Taft finally agreed . . . chagrined about his chances: WHT to TR, Aug. 10, 1908, WHTP.

552 "Don't get one particle": TR to WHT, Aug. 24, 1908, in *LTR*, Vol. 6, pp. 1196, 1195.

552 "a dangerous man . . . No longer an outcast": *Fort Wayne* [IN] *Journal-Gazette*, Aug. 8, 1908.

553 "would be placed": *Evening Independent* (Massillon, OH), Oct. 1, 1908.

553 "If the candidate": WHT to TR, Sept. 11, 1908, TRP.

553 "Do not *answer*": TR to WHT, Sept. 1, 1908, in *LTR*, Vol. 6, p. 1204.

553 "Hit them hard": TR to WHT, Sept. 11, 1908, in ibid., p. 1231.

553 Taft promised to confront Bryan directly: WHT to TR, Sept. 14, 1908, TRP.

553 "I cannot be more": WHT to E. N. Huggins, Aug. 11, 1908, WHTP.

553 "I am not very pleased . . . into the campaign": TR to Nicholas Longworth, Sept. 21, 1908, in *LTR*, Vol. 6, pp. 1244–45.

553 the president's "natural successor": *Galveston* [TX] *Daily News*, Sept. 14, 1908.

553 "The true friend . . . shoulder to shoulder": TR to Conrad Kohrs, Sept. 9, 1908, in *LTR*, Vol. 6, p. 1213.

554 "You say that": TR to William Jennings Bryan, Sept. 27, 1908, in *LTR*, Vol. 6, p. 1259.

554 Deeds, he argued: TR to William Jennings Bryan, Sept. 23, 1908, in ibid., pp. 1253–54.

554 "walked into a trap": WHT to TR, Oct. 9, 1908, TRP.

554 "claim to be the heir": WHT to TR, Oct. 3, 1908, TRP.

554 "the revival": WHT to TR, Oct. 9, 1908, TRP.

554 The "Taft Special" . . . forty-one days: *Van Wert* [OH] *Daily Bulletin*, Oct. 6, 1908.

554 consisted of four cars: *Racine* [WI] *Daily Journal*, Sept. 23, 1908.

554 "proved to be . . . a professional entertainer": *Current Literature* (December 1908), p. 621.

554 "he strengthened himself": *Lawrence* [KS] *Daily World*, Oct. 5, 1908.

554 "on the level . . . trust him anywhere": *Evening Independent* (Massillon, OH), Oct. 1, 1908.

554 "I have been in real touch": *NYT*, Oct. 2, 1908.

554 "You are making such . . . treading on air": HHT to WHT, Sept. 24, 1908, WHTP.

555 "I can't imagine": HHT to WHT, Sept. 25, 1908, WHTP.

555 "had a most delightful time": WHT to TR, Oct. 3, 1908, TRP.

555 "changed materially": TR to Kermit Roosevelt, Oct. 24, 1908, in *LTR*, Vol. 6, p. 1318.

555 To everyone's relief . . . "tremendously": TR to HCL, Oct. 21, 1908, in ibid., p. 1314.

555 "I told him he simply": AB to his mother, Oct. 21, 1908, in Abbott, ed., *Letters of Archie Butt*, pp. 143–44.

555 "was keeping himself . . . on his own feet": Hammond, *The Autobiography*, Vol. 2, p. 537.

555 "very touched . . . delighted": WHT to TR, Sept. 14 & Nov. 1, 1908, TRP.

555 "monster" crowds . . . "enjoy it immensely": *Cincinnati Inquirer*, Nov. 3, 1908.

555 They reached Cincinnati . . . in the afternoon: WHT Diaries, Nov. 3, 1908, WHTP.

555 In preparation for . . . the United Press: *Lima* [OH] *Daily News*, Nov. 4, 1908.

556 "exhibiting the finest specimen": Ibid.

556 "Just say that": Ibid.

556 "I was never so happy": HHT to WHT, Nov. 3, 1908, WHTP.

556 Though Taft's popular margin . . . a million and a quarter votes: Pringle, *Life and Times*, Vol. 1, p. 377.

556 "I pledge myself": New York *Sun*, Nov. 4, 1909.

556 "was simply radiant . . . content to die": AB to Clara, Nov. 5, 1908, in Abbott, ed., *Letters of Archie Butt*, pp. 153, 156.

556 "My selection and election": WHT to TR, Nov. 7, 1908, TRP.

556 "You have won": TR to WHT, Nov. 10, 1908, in *LTR*, Vol. 6, p. 1340.

CHAPTER TWENTY-TWO: "A Great Stricken Animal"

Page

557 "the best equipped man": HCL to WHT, June 22, 1908, WHTP.

557 "the greatest all around man": *NYT*, Feb. 28, 1909.

557 "he had served with great": James Eli Watson, *As I Knew Them: Memoirs of James Watson, Former United States Senator from Indiana* (Indianapolis: Bobbs-Merrill Co., 1936), p. 134.

558 "The most difficult instrument": David A. Heenan and Warren G. Bennis, *Co-Leaders: The Power of Great Partnerships* (New York: John Wiley & Sons, 1999), p. 23.

558 "but he could not fill": RSB, "The Measure of Taft," *The American Magazine* (July 1910), pp. 366–67.

558 "Not everyone was meant": Heenan and Bennis, *Co-Leaders*, p. 270.

558 "spoke like a man": Pinchot, *Breaking New Ground*, p. 381.

558 "shake their heads": *Syracuse* [NY] *Herald*, Nov. 6, 1908.

558 "a trembling fear . . . out with unanimity": WHT to Rufus Rhodes, Jan. 2, 1909, WHTP.

558 "splendid 18 hole": *Boston Evening Transcript*, Dec. 17, 1903.

558 While Nellie thought the location: Mowry, *The Era of Theodore Roosevelt, 1900–1912*, p. 233.

558 "getting away for a complete rest": *Piqua* [OH] *Leader-Dispatch*, Nov. 5, 1908.

559 He defiantly proposed: *Fort Wayne* [IN] *Journal-Gazette*, Nov. 8, 1908.

559 "good and ready": *Washington Post*, Jan. 21, 1909.

559 "to make golf": *Syracuse* [NY] *Herald*, Nov. 9, 1908.

559 "possum and taters" banquet: *Atlanta Constitution*, Jan. 4, 1909; *Lima* [OH] *Daily News*, Jan. 1, 1909.

559 a specially constructed cage . . . six hundred guests: *Atlanta Constitution*, Jan. 4, 1909.

559 marking "a social epoch": *Atlanta Constitution*, Jan. 16, 1909.

559   A cartoon of Taft: *Atlanta Constitution*, Jan. 27, 1909.

559   "a gigantic rat" . . . children to cry: Ibid.

559   "the honor without": *Atlanta Constitution*, Jan. 24, 1909.

559   Robert and Helen . . . Bryn Mawr: WHT to Mabel Boardman, Dec. 24, 1908, WHTP.

559   the families of Charles . . . John Hays Hammond: *NYT*, Jan. 11, 1909.

559   "He is so genial": "Mr. Taft's Visit to the South," *The Independent*, Jan. 28, 1909.

559   "Tell the boys": Sullivan, *Our Times*, Vol. 4, p. 321.

559   his "humiliating pilgrimage": New York *Sun*, July 24, 1908.

560   "aroused the people": Pringle, *Life and Times*, Vol. 1, p. 382.

560   "different personnel": WHT to George B. Cortelyou, Jan. 22, 1909, WHTP.

560   "I merely followed": AB, *Taft and Roosevelt*, Vol. 1, p. 345.

560   "ought to be Pres.-elect": *NYT*, Feb. 27, 1909.

560   "I would rather stay here": Jessup, *Elihu Root*, Vol. 2, p. 138.

560   "touched and gratified" . . . in the Senate: HCL to WHT, Dec. 9, 1908, WHTP.

560   "Knox called on me": TR to WHT, Dec. 15, 1908, in *LTR*, Vol. 6, p. 1423.

560   planning to invite Knox . . . his remaining choices: WHT to TR, Dec. 22, 1908, TRP.

560   Frank Hitchcock . . . postmaster general: *Atlanta Constitution*, Jan. 24, 1909.

560   "Ha ha!": TR to WHT, Dec. 31, 1908, in *LTR*, Vol. 6, p. 1454.

561   "inducement . . . to continue Wright": Sullivan, *Our Times*, Vol. 4, p. 320.

561   not "decisive . . . action by him": WHT to Philander C. Knox, Dec. 22, 1908, WHTP.

561   he exacerbated . . . before the inauguration: AB to Clara, Feb. 14, 1908, in Abbott, ed., *Letters of Archie Butt*, p. 338.

561   "I didn't have to be hit": Gustav J. Karger, "Memorandum #5," Mar. 12, 1910, Taft-Karger MSS, CMC.

561   A "peculiar intimacy": TR to Gifford Pinchot, Jan. 24, 1909, TRP.

561   Garfield had every reason . . . to Taft's candidacy: James R. Garfield, Diary, Mar. 3, 1908, Garfield Papers.

561   he and his wife . . . vacationing together: James R. Garfield, Diary, Sept. 3, 1908, Garfield Papers.

561   Their son, John: James R. Garfield, Diary, Mar. 28, 1908, Garfield Papers.

561   The press assumed: *Syracuse* [NY] *Herald*, Dec. 22, 1908.

561   "big enough" . . . the Forestry Bureau: Gustav J. Karger, "Memorandum #5," Mar. 12, 1910, Taft-Karger MSS, CMC.

561   While he recognized . . . represent their interests: Pringle, *Life and Times*, Vol. 1, p. 478.

562   "He has done admirably": James R. Garfield, Diary, Mar. 2, 1908, Garfield Papers.

562   "limited personal means" . . . finally persuaded: Hammond, *The Autobiography*, Vol. 2, p. 543.

562   that Garfield was "out of the running": *Syracuse* [NY] *Herald*, Dec. 22, 1908.

562   "I am utterly at sea": James R. Garfield, Diary, Jan. 11, 1909, Garfield Papers.

562   "a genial, agreeable man": *Jefferson City* [MO] *Tribune*, Jan. 20, 1909.

562   "Rumors & more rumors": James R. Garfield, Diary, Jan. 18, 1909, Garfield Papers.

562   "an astounding condition": James R. Garfield, Diary, Jan. 12, 1909, Garfield Papers.

562   Gossip filled the vacuum: AB to Clara, Jan. 5, 1909, in Abbott, ed., *Letters of Archie Butt*, pp. 271–72.

562   "completely changed . . . to keep no one": James R. Garfield, Diary, Jan. 4, 1909, Garfield Papers.

562   "They will be making": TR to WHT, Jan. 4, 1909, in *LTR*, Vol. 6, p. 1458.

563   "I think I ought": WHT to TR, Jan. 8, 1909, CPT Papers.

563   "The President has thought": WHT to George B. Cortelyou, Jan. 22, 1909, WHTP.

563   The recipients . . . manner of address: James R. Garfield, Diary, Jan. 27, 1909, Garfield Papers.

563   "a clean sweep": Ibid.

563   "T.R.'s Trusty Aides . . . in the Roosevelt school?": *Cleveland Press*, Feb. 11, 1909, clipping in James R. Garfield, Diary, Garfield Papers.

563   "a little cast down": AB to Clara, Jan. 30, 1909, in Abbott, ed., *Letters of Archie Butt,* p. 313.

563   "They little realize": AB to Clara, Jan. 30, 1909, in ibid., p. 314.

563   Taft's "system may be different": AB to Clara, Jan. 11, 1909, in ibid., p. 283.

563   "People have attempted": WHT to TR, Feb. 25, 1909, TRP.

563   "How could I but be": TR to WHT, Feb. 26, 1909, in *LTR*, Vol. 6, p. 1538.

564   "renewed appreciation . . . and magnanimity": WHT to TR, Feb. 25, 1909, TRP.

564   "Your letter": TR to WHT, Feb. 26, 1909, in *LTR*, Vol. 6, p. 1538.

564   "If I had conscientiously": TR to George Otto Trevelyan, Nov. 6, 1908, in ibid., p. 1329.

564   "none of the weariness": *New York Tribune*, Dec. 9, 1908.

564   a sweeping "valedictory message": See *Current Literature* (January 1909), p. 14.

564   "his whole social . . . as voluminous as ever": *New York Tribune*, Dec. 9, 1908.

564   "a fraction . . . the social creation": *Literary Digest*, Dec. 19, 1908.

564   "The danger to American . . . wish to be investigated": TR, "Eighth Annual Message," in *WTR*, Vol. 15, pp. 498, 508, 512, 528.

565   a "storm of censure": *NYT*, Dec. 17, 1908.

565   "self-respect . . . Pandemonium broke loose": *NYT*, Jan. 9, 1909.

565   Congress took a rare measure: Pringle, *Theodore Roosevelt: A Biography*, p. 485.

565   "on the ground": *NYT*, Jan. 9, 1909.

565   "Congress of course feels": TR to Kermit Roosevelt, Jan. 14, 1909, in *LTR*, Vol. 6, p. 1475.

565   "it is a President's . . . up to the end": TR to TR, Jr., Jan. 31, 1909, in ibid., pp. 1498–99.

565   "I have never seen": AB to Clara, Mar. 2, 1909, in Abbott, ed., *Letters of Archie Butt*, p. 376.

566   "believing thoroughly": AB to his mother, April 8, 1908, in ibid., p. 1.

566   "his duties with a boyish": Introduction, in ibid., p. xxiii.

566   "She is perfectly poised": AB to his mother, July 27, 1908, in ibid., p. 75.

566   "ever-softening influence": Ibid.

566   "smart element . . . wont to sneer": AB to his mother, Oct. 19, 1908, in ibid., p. 134.

566   garish nature of . . . clamored for invitations: Mabel Potter Daggett, "Mrs. Roosevelt: The Woman in the Background," *The Delineator* (March 1909), p. 394.

566   Edith's Friday evening . . . Pablo Casals: Morris, *EKR*, p. 236.

566   "If social affairs": Daggett, "Mrs. Roosevelt," *The Delineator* (March 1909), p. 394.

566   "Were we living": AB to Clara, March 2, 1909, in Abbott, ed., *Letter of Archie Butt*, p. 380.

566   "The ball rolls . . . every minute": AB to Clara, Feb. 7, 1909, in ibid., p. 326.

566   "actually wept as . . . broke down himself": AB to Clara, Mar. 2, 1909, in ibid., pp. 376–77.

566   "For the first hour . . . if not a cold, reception": AB to Clara, Feb. 14, 1909, in ibid., pp. 335–36.

567   "The papers have made . . . from Oklahoma?": AB to Clara, Mar. 1, 1909, in ibid., pp. 365–69.

567   "there was not a dry eye": Ibid., p. 368; *Oelwein* [IA] *Daily Register*, Mar. 2, 1909.

567   "It was a curious . . . low spirits": ARL, *Crowded Hours*, pp. 164–65.

568   "The dinner would have been": AB to Clara, Mar. 2, 1909, in Abbott, ed., *Letters of Archie Butt,* p. 378.

568   "Mrs. Roosevelt finally arose": Ibid., p. 380.

568   "Thought you'd like . . . went to bed!": New York *Sun*, Mar. 5, 1909.

568   "shunted it back": *Current Literature* (April 1909), p. 347.

568   "bound hand and foot": *NYT*, Mar. 5, 1909.

568   Gale winds howled: *NYT*, Mar. 4, 1909.

568   "It was really very serious": HHT, *Recollections of Full Years*, p. 328.

568   "The storm will soon . . . got to be President": Ibid.

569   "yellowish, slimy" . . . had for three cents: *NYT*, Mar. 5, 1909.

569   "stood three deep": Ibid.

569   Unfortunately, hardly . . . top of the carriage: Ibid.

569   the Inaugural Committee debated: *Current Literature* (April 1909), p. 348.

569   "If so many spectators": Ibid.; HHT, *Recollections of Full Years*, p. 329.

569   "All exercises will be": *NYT*, Mar. 5, 1909.

569   No longer an open . . . justices, and ambassadors: Ibid.

569   walking "arm in arm": Ibid.

569   "Hale and hearty": New York *Sun*, Mar. 5, 1909.

569   "a slow, distinct voice": *NYT*, Mar. 5, 1909.

570   "For the first time": Ibid.

570   "heavy weight of responsibility . . . met popular approval": William Howard Taft, *Presidential Addresses and State Papers of William Howard Taft, from March 4, 1909, to March 4, 1910* (New York: Doubleday, Page, 1910), pp. 53–56.

570   "The new president . . . each other's shoulders": *NYT*, Mar. 5, 1909.

570   "God bless you . . . state document": HHT, *Recollections of Full Years*, p. 331.

570   "applauded like mad": *NYT*, Mar. 5, 1909.

570   amid "deafening" cheers: *Current Literature* (April 1909), p. 349.

570   "no President's wife . . . my husband's side": HHT, *Recollections of Full Years*, p. 331.

570   "a continuous cheer": *NYT*, Mar. 5, 1909.

570   "Three cheers for the first lady": New York *Sun*, Mar. 5, 1909.

570   "That drive was the proudest": HHT, *Recollections of Full Years*, p. 332.

571   an "era of good feelings": *Current Literature* (April 1909), p. 347.

571   "has no enemies . . . and denunciation": *Los Angeles Times*, Mar. 4, 1909; New York *World*, Mar. 5, 1909.

571   "judicial poise had succeeded": Dunn, *From Harrison to Harding*, Vol. 2, p. 103.

571   decisions would now be made: New York *World*, Mar. 5, 1909.

571   "Never did any man": New York *Sun*, Mar. 5, 1909.

571   "I hardly know yet": AB to Clara, Mar. 11, 1909, in AB, *Taft and Roosevelt*, Vol. 1, p. 9.

571   "been living on . . . just the same": AB to Clara, Mar. 22, 1909, in ibid., p. 27.

571   Captain Butt had hesitated . . . toward his predecessor: AB to Clara, Nov. 30, 1908, in Abbott, ed., *Letters of Archie Butt,* p. 207.

571   "The influence of": AB to Clara, Jan. 5, 1909, in ibid., p. 273.

571   "an intellectual woman": AB to Clara, Nov. 16, 1908, in ibid., p. 173.

572   "marvelous wit": AB to Clara, Mar. 16, 1908, in AB, *Taft and Roosevelt*, Vol. 1, p. 14.

572   "He is essentially": AB to Clara, Mar. 21, 1910, in ibid., p. 308.

572   "list of undesirables . . . stormy attacks": *Oshkosh* [WI] *Daily Northwestern*, April 21, 1909.

572   "I hope that I shall never": AB to Clara, April 15, 1909, in AB, *Taft and Roosevelt*, Vol. 1, p. 308.

572   "a rule never to pay": AB to Clara, Mar. 28, 1909, in ibid., p. 32.

572   "all the warring factions": *Atlanta Constitution*, Mar. 27, 1909.

572   "I am rather proud": AB to Clara, April 24, 1909, in AB, *Taft and Roosevelt*, Vol. 1, p. 60.

572   "I have come to pay": Edward Lowry, "The White House Now," *Harper's Bazaar*, May 15, 1909.

572   Taft also lifted . . . on Senator Tillman: *NYT*, April 25, 1909.

572   invited dozens . . . White House dinner: AB to Clara, April 24, 1909, in AB, *Taft and Roosevelt*, Vol. 1, p. 60.

572   "to pay for favors": AB to Clara, April 27, 1909, in ibid., p. 63.

572   "the liveliest interest . . . things going smoothly": *NYT*, March 27, 1909.

573   "It is undoubtedly": *Oshkosh* [WI] *Daily Northwestern*, April 7, 1909.

573   "the undesirables . . . finding their way": Lowry, "The White House Now," *Harper's Bazaar*, May 15, 1909.

573   "pleased as a boy": AB to Clara, April 8, 1909, in AB, *Taft and Roosevelt*, Vol. 1, p. 44.

573   "and a lot of other": Dunn, *From Harrison to Harding*, Vol. 2, p. 102.

573   the "big stick . . . personal appeal": *Daily Gleaner* (Kingston, Jamaica), April 7, 1909.

573   "startling contrast": *Lawrence* [KS] *Daily World*, Mar. 30, 1909.

573   "on their way . . . terminal facilities": Lowry, "The White House Now," *Harper's Bazaar*, May 15, 1909.

573   "so much at home": *NYT*, April 25, 1909.

573   "be about three years behind": AB to Clara, Mar. 10, 1909, in AB, *Taft and Roosevelt*, Vol. 1, p. 3.

573   "I am glad . . . want to tell me?": Lowry, "The White House Now," *Harper's Bazaar*, May 15, 1909.

573   "There the resemblance . . . around the ellipse": Ibid.

574   "devil wagons . . . pacers, and calipers": *Lawrence* [KS] *Daily World*, Mar. 30, 1909.

574   his Model M . . . Nellie learned to drive: Michael L. Bromley, *William Howard Taft and the First Motoring Presidency, 1909–1913* (Jefferson, NC: McFarland & Co., 2003), pp. 100, 103–4.

574   "a reporter's paradise": Juergens, "Theodore Roosevelt and the Press," *Daedalus* (Fall 1982), p. 114.

574   "No president ever lived": James E. Pollard, *The Presidents and the Press* (New York: The Macmillan Co., 1947), p. 583.

574   "he made the White House": Juergens, "Theodore Roosevelt and the Press," *Daedalus* (Fall 1982), p. 120.

574   "There will be some one": Gustav J. Karger, "Memorandum #3," Mar. 1, 1909, p. 25, Taft-Karger MSS, CMC.

574   "It was a favorite . . . a good scout": Davis, *Released for Publication*, p. 94.

574   "casual remarks . . . necessity of care": *Daily Gleaner* (Kingston, Jamaica), April 7, 1909.

575   "the big, good-humored": Delbert Clark, *Washington Dateline* (New York: Frederick A. Stokes Co., 1941), p. 58.

575   "his own atmosphere . . . hearts to him": AB to Clara, April 27, 1909, in AB, *Taft and Roosevelt*, Vol. 1, p. 68.

575   "Roosevelt made good": *Lawrence* [KS] *Daily World*, Mar. 30, 1909.

575   "Take it all and all": Lowry, "The White House Now," *Harper's Bazaar*, May 15, 1909.

575   "a fish out of water": WHT to Henry A. Morrill, Dec. 2, 1908, Pringle Papers.

575   "I am no . . . Circuit Court bench": L. P. Winter, "Mr. Taft's Visit to the South," *The Independent*, Oct. 9, 1902, p. 178.

575   "tact and diplomacy . . . the responsibilities": *Syracuse* [NY] *Herald*, Mar. 12, 1909.

575   "formidable" challenges: WHT to Henry A. Morrill, Dec. 2, 1908, Pringle Papers.

575   "like that of two men . . . most judicial attitude": George Griswold Hill, "The Wife of the New President," *Ladies' Home Journal* (March 1909), p. 6.

575   Article after article . . . the Philippines: *Milford* [IA] *Mail*, July 16, 1908.

575   "Yes . . . it is true": *Lima* [OH] *Daily News*, Nov. 9, 1909.

575   Nellie's "judgment prevailed": *Milford* [IA] *Mail*, July 16, 1908.

576   "Indeed, I do": *Des Moines Capital*, Nov. 13, 1908.

576   "Few women have gone": *NYT*, Nov. 15, 1909.

576   As the governor general's wife: Hill, "The Wife of the New President," *Ladies' Home Journal*, Mar. 1909, p. 6.

576   "You make me feel": *Oakland* [CA] *Tribune*, Sept. 20, 1908.

576   "never at a loss": *New York Tribune*, May 31, 1908.

576   "Never within the recollection": *Omaha* [NE] *Daily Bee*, Mar. 14, 1909.

576   "to keep up so . . . daily papers": *Ada* [OK] *Evening News*, March 23, 1909.

576   "impressed . . . cloak of composure": Hill, "The Wife of the New President," *Ladies' Home Journal*, Mar. 1909, p. 6.

576   "Her smile has": *NYT*, Nov. 15, 1908.

576   "a public personage . . . private individual": *Syracuse* [NY] *Herald*, Mar. 12, 1909.

576   "a woman's name . . . the least known": Daggett, "Mrs. Roosevelt: The Woman in the Background," *The Delineator* (March 1909), p. 393.

577   to become honorary chair: Mrs. John Hays Hammond, "The Woman's Welfare Department of the National Civic Federation," in Henry R. Mussey, ed., *Proceedings of the Academy of Political Science in the City of New York* (New York: Columbia University Press, 1912), Vol. 2, p. 99.

577   "a commanding lead": *Ada* [OK] *Evening News*, Mar. 23, 1909.

577   controversial programs to improve: Anthony, *Nellie Taft*, p. 250.

577   At the annual meeting . . . police stations: New York *Sun*, Dec. 15, 1908.

577   "She plainly showed": *Ada* [OK] *Evening News*, Mar. 23, 1909.

577   "in animated conversation": *NYT*, Dec. 16, 1908.

577   "make a fine . . . First Lady": AB to [unknown] [n.d.], AB Letters.

577   "The woman's voice": *Des Moines Capital*, Nov. 13, 1908.

577   "makes a girl . . . full college course": *Washington Post*, May 5, 1907.

577   "the distinct advantages": Hill, "The Wife of the New President," *Ladies' Home Journal*, Mar. 1909, p. 6; *Washington Post*, June 24, 1908.

578   "endeared herself": *Ada* [OK] *Evening News*, Mar. 23, 1909.

578   "on a plane": *NYT*, Mar. 14, 1909.

578   the "real social . . . art, statesmanship": *Washington Post*, Nov. 14, 1908.

578   "is more beautifully": *Washington Post*, Mar. 9, 1909.

578   "as absurd . . . wealth in our land": *Washington Post*, Mar. 14, 1909.

578   "one of the most famous": *Hamilton* [OH] *Evening Journal*, April 9, 1909.

578   She enlisted . . . comfortable benches: AB to Clara, April 13, 1909, in AB, *Taft and Roosevelt*, Vol. 1, pp. 51–52; *Kansas City Star*, May 16, 1909.

578   "both the soil and climate": HHT, *Recollections of a Full Life*, p. 362.

578   when her plans . . . to Washington: AB, "1909 Social Diary of Archibald Willingham Butt," WHTP.

578   "Potomac Park . . . every type of carriage": New York *Sun*, April 18, 1909.

578   "every walk of life": *Washington Times*, April 18, 1909.

578   bowed "right and left": *New York Tribune*, April 18, 1909.

579   "Everybody saw . . . special character": HHT, *Recollections of a Full Life*, p. 362.

579   "very strong liking": Ibid., p. 365.

579   "short coats, flannel trousers": *Syracuse* [NY] *Herald*, May 15, 1909.

579   "bright colored parasols": HHT, *Recollections of a Full Life*, p. 368.

579   "roam at will": *Washington Herald*, May 15, 1909.

579   "are as informal . . . seen in Washington": *Kansas City Star*, May 16, 1909.

579   "It was a difficult thing": AB to Clara, May 12, 1909, in AB, *Taft and Roosevelt*, Vol. 1, p. 86.

579   "She possesses a nature": AB to Clara, April 13, 1909, in ibid., p. 54.

579   "The complete social": *Kansas City Star*, May 16, 1909.

579   "In the ten weeks": *NYT*, May 19, 1909.

580   On May 17 . . . President Washington's home: AB to Clara, May 17, 1909, in AB, *Taft and Roosevelt*, Vol. 1, p. 87.

580   Nellie was talking . . . and collapsed: Lewis L. Gould, *Helen Taft: Our Musical First Lady* (Lawrence: University Press of Kansas, 2010), p. 51.

580   "seemed to revive . . . shown on a man's face": AB to Clara, May 17, 1909, in AB, *Taft and Roosevelt*, Vol. 1, p. 88.

580   "a lesion in the brain . . . in the brain": WHT to Robert Taft, May 18, 1909, WHTP.

580   With extended rest . . . symptoms might disappear: AB to Clara, May 18, 1909, in AB, *Taft and Roosevelt*, Vol. 1, p. 92.

580   "in the face . . . like a knife": AB to Clara, May 17, 1909, in ibid., pp. 89–90.

580   "Her old will": AB to Clara, May 18, 1909, in ibid., pp. 91–92.

581   partial "control of her right arm": WHT to Robert Taft, May 18, 1909, WHTP.

581   "no cause for alarm . . . nervous attack": *NYT*, May 18, 1909.

581   "ceaseless and strenuous . . . went to pieces": *St. Louis Post-Dispatch*, June 18, 1909.

581   what Taft later described as aphasia: WHT to TR, May 26, 1910, TRP.

581   "She only comes into": AB to Clara, June 1, 1909, in AB, *Taft and Roosevelt*, Vol. 1, p. 108.

581   she remained unable to project: WHT to Horace Taft, May 28, 1909, WHTP.

581   "repeat almost anything": Helen Taft Manning to Robert A. Taft, May [n.d.], 1909, WHTP.

581   "merely a question of time": Ibid.

581   Taft mobilized . . . to repeat the same passages: WHT to Frances Taft Edwards, June 25, 1909, WHTP.
581   "to say the opposite": Seth Taft, *Going Like 80: A Biography of Charles P. Taft II* (private printing, 2004). Presented to the author by Frances and Seth Taft.
581   "She gets pretty depressed": Helen Taft Manning to Robert A. Taft, June [n.d.], 1909, WHTP.
581   Eventually, the first lady . . . particular impediment: AB to Clara, Jan. 2, 1910, AB Letters.
581   "scores of times . . . 'now try it again' ": Elizabeth Jaffray, *Secrets of the White House* (New York: Cosmopolitan Book Corp., 1927), p. 25.
582   "No one knows": AB to Clara, [Easter] 1909, in AB, *Taft and Roosevelt*, Vol. 1, p. 313.
582   acknowledge "the tragedy": AB to Clara, May 17, 1909, in ibid., p. 89.
582   "a world of misery": AB to Mrs. John D. Butt, June 8, 1909, in ibid., p. 101.
582   "simply looking into the distance": AB to Clara, May 27, 1909, in ibid., p. 99.
582   "take up their residence": AB, "1909 Social Diary of Archibald Willingham Butt," WHTP.
582   "parklike lawns" . . . the Essex Club: Mabel T. Boardman, "The Summer Capital," *Outlook*, Sept. 25, 1909, pp. 176–78.
582   "take quite a time": WHT to Mabel Boardman, June 27, 1909, WHTP.
582   "two months of entire rest": WHT to Frances Taft Edwards, June 25, 1909, WHTP.
582   "in seclusion . . . intruders away": *NYT*, July 7, 1909.
582   "The great tug will begin": WHT to HHT, July 7, 1909, WHTP.

CHAPTER TWENTY-THREE: A Self-Inflicted Wound

Page
583   Protectionism had become a central tenet: Jonathan Lurie, *William Howard Taft: The Travails of a Progressive Conservative* (New York: Cambridge University Press, 2012), p. 103.
583   While Theodore Roosevelt had sympathized . . . inflated prices: RSB, Notebook, Nov. 17, 1907, RSB Papers.
583   During the final years . . . agrarian region: Stanley D. Solvick, "William Howard Taft and Cannonism," *Wisconsin Magazine of History* (Autumn 1964), pp. 51–52.
584   "equal the difference": WHT, "Address Accepting the Republican Nomination for President, Cincinnati, Ohio, July 28, 1908," WHTP.
584   When excessive duties were built . . . prices for consumers: Ibid.; WHT, *Presidential Addresses and State Papers*, pp. 55–56; WHT to Horace Taft, June 27, 1909, WHTP.
584   "unequivocally . . . special session of Congress": RNC and Blumenberg, *Official Report of the Proceedings of the Fourteenth Republican National Convention*, p. 117.
584   "uprising and demonstration . . . cataclysm": *Waterloo* [IA] *Times-Tribune*, Mar. 16, 1909.
584   "the greatest issue" . . . to "humanize": *Washington Times*, June 24, 1910.
584   "this or that duty . . . less or covering": IMT, "Where Every Penny Counts," *The American Magazine* (March 1909), pp. 437–38.
585   "vital importance" of shoes: *Atlanta Constitution*, April 25, 1909.
585   "It was hard enough . . . and in methods": IMT, "Where Every Penny Counts," *The American Magazine* (March 1909), p. 440.
585   For years, legislators had acquiesced: IMT, "Juggling with the Tariff: A Sidelight on the Most Lively Question Now Before Congress," *The American Magazine* (April 1909), p. 578.
585   "At a time when . . . getting ahead": IMT, "Where Every Penny Counts," *The American Magazine* (March 1909), p. 439.
585   "I never knew": IMT, *All in the Day's Work*, p. 273.
586   "Cannonism" had become . . . convened in mid-March 1909: Pringle, *Life and Times*, Vol. 1, pp. 402–3; Solvick, "William Howard Taft and Cannonism," *Wisconsin Magazine of History* (Autumn 1964), pp. 52–53.
586   Taft seriously considered backing: WHT to WAW, Mar. 12, 1909, White Papers.
586   "never liked" the Speaker: AB to Clara, April 5, 1911, in AB, *Taft and Roosevelt*, Vol. 2, p. 609.
586   "all legislation of a progressive character": WHT to TR, Oct. 9, 1908, TRP.
586   "If by helping it": WHT to TR, Nov. 7, 1908, TRP.
586   "I do not believe": TR to WHT, Nov. 10, 1908, TRP.
586   "it would be very unfortunate": Elihu Root to WHT, Nov. 23, 1908, in Pringle, *Life and Times*, Vol. 1, p. 405.
586   "very much disposed to fight": WHT to William N. Cromwell, Nov. 22, 1908, WHTP.
586   "In our anxiety": *Salt Lake Tribune*, Nov. 18, 1908.
586   "cynical references . . . with people squarely": WHT to Elihu Root, Nov. 25, 1908, WHTP.
586   To better gauge the odds: WHT to J. N. Dolley, Nov. 23, 1908, and WHT to Frank L. Dingley, Nov. 23, 1908, WHTP.
586   "A new irrepressible   Taft administration": *NYT*, Nov. 24, 1908.

587   "urgent telegrams and letters": WHT to Horace Taft, June 27, 1909, WHTP.
587   "very anxious . . . of the facts": TR to WHT, Nov. 28, 1908, in *LTR*, Vol. 6, p. 1389.
587   "support genuine tariff . . . carrying forward": *Waterloo* [IA] *Daily Courier*, Dec. 2, 1908.
587   "entirely different impression": *Washington Post*, Dec. 11, 1908.
587   "a hundred days . . . perfect": *Waterloo* [IA] *Times-Tribune*, Nov. 18, 1908.
587   "the best revenue law": Pringle, *Life and Times*, Vol. 1, p. 403.
587   "hammer and tongs . . . Republican minority": WHT to Joseph L. Bristow, Dec. 5, 1908, WHTP.
587   the mistake that would haunt his presidency: *Waterloo* [IA] *Daily Courier*, Dec. 2, 1908.
587   "sent a chill of": Pringle, *Life and Times*, Vol. 1, p. 407.
587   "to prepare an honest": *Washington Post*, Dec. 11, 1908.
588   All hope of unseating . . . won reelection: *NYT*, Mar. 16, 1909.
588   "the most sophisticated": Sullivan, *Our Times*, Vol. 4, p. 374.
588   "page after page": *Decatur* [IL] *Daily Review*, Mar. 16, 1909.
588   "The Senate and House": Robert M. La Follette, *La Follette's Autobiography: A Personal Narrative of Political Experiences* (Madison, WI: Robert M. La Follette Co., 1919), p. 438.
588   "statesmen almost fell": *Washington Times*, Mar. 17, 1909.
588   expected to be "historic": Claude Gernade Bowers, *Beveridge and the Progressive Era* (Boston: Houghton Mifflin, 1932), p. 334.
588   Taft had composed the entire text: *Decatur Daily Review*, Mar. 18, 1909.
588   "no clarion call": Bowers, *Beveridge and the Progressive Era*, p. 340.
588   "no allusion": *New York Tribune*, Mar. 16, 1909.
588   "give immediate consideration . . . should proceed": WHT, "Message to Congress, March 16, 1909," in WHT, *Presidential Addresses and State Papers*, Vol. 1, p. 69.
588   "flair for . . . days in office": Stanley D. Solvick, "William Howard Taft and the Payne-Aldrich Tariff," *Mississippi Valley Historical Review* (December 1963), p. 428.
588   "no loud noises": *Current Literature* (June 1909), p. 579.
589   "the facts and reasons . . . derelict": WHT, "Personal Aspects of the Presidency," *Saturday Evening Post*, Feb. 28, 1914.
589   The weekly press conferences: F. B. Marbut, *News from the Capital; The Story of Washington Reporting* (Carbondale: Southern Illinois University Press, 1971), p. 171.
589   "There was none": J. Frederick Essary, "Thirty-two Years as a Washington Correspondent," *Editor and Publisher*, May 31, 1941, p. 13.
589   "When the judgment . . . to help me": WHT, "Personal Aspects of the Presidency," *Saturday Evening Post*, Feb. 28, 1914.
589   "If ever at any time": WAW to WHT [n.d.], 1909, White Papers.
589   "I am not constituted": WHT to WAW, Mar. 20, 1909, White Papers.
589   "I knew what a hard": RSB, *American Chronicle*, p. 254.
589   "Although the tariff storm": RSB, "Theodore Roosevelt," unpublished MSS, 1910, RSB Papers.
589   "remain . . . not without significance": RSB, "The Measure of Taft," *The American Magazine* (July 1910), p. 363.
590   "the legal mind . . . dislike for publicity": RSB, "Taft—So Far," *The American Magazine* (July 1909), p. 312.
590   "impressed . . . *could* do it": RSB, "The Measure of Taft," *The American Magazine* (July 1910), pp. 363–64.
590   "Fifty years ago . . . will have been taken": IMT, "Juggling with the Tariff," *The American Magazine* (April 1909), pp. 578–79, 586.
591   "one of the most . . . taking the place": IMT, "William Howard Taft," unpublished MSS [n.d.], IMTC.
591   "to keep his distance": Lurie, *William Howard Taft*, p. 104.
591   If adjustments were necessary: Solvick, "William Howard Taft and the Payne-Aldrich Tariff," *Mississippi Valley Historical Review* (December 1963), pp. 431–33.
591   "I have got to regard": WHT to WAW, Mar. 12, 1909, White Papers.
591   "no matter what tariff bill": William Dudley Foulke to WHT, Mar. 10, 1909, WHTP.
592   "I am here to get": WHT to William Dudley Foulke, Mar. 12, 1909, WHTP.
592   "a genuine effort . . . inappropriate": WHT to Horace Taft, June 27, 1909, WHTP.
592   "a more enlightened . . . given a thought": Cited in *Current Literature* (May 1909), p. 468.
592   "would be satisfactory . . . this early stage": *NYT*, April 21, 1909.
592   "up to the Senate . . . remakes it": *Current Literature* (May 1909), p. 465.
592   Taft had reason . . . from the Philippines: WHT to TR, Jan. 27, 1903, TRP.
592   "I fear Aldrich is ready": AB to Clara, April 4, 1909, in AB, *Taft and Roosevelt*, Vol. 1, p. 41.
592   "Where did we ever": Pringle, *Life and Times*, Vol. 1, p. 429.
592   This was the time: Ibid., p. 430.

592 "There is no use": AB to Clara, Dec. 19, 1909, in AB, *Taft and Roosevelt*, Vol. 1, p. 236.
593 While Taft hesitated . . . against the Senate leader: Mowry, *The Era of Theodore Roosevelt*, pp. 244–45.
593 Aware that Aldrich . . . tackled lead and sugar: Bowers, *Beveridge and the Progressive Era*, p. 339.
593 "It has been tariff": HCL to TR, June 21, 1909, in TR and HCL, *Selections from the Correspondence*, Vol. 2, pp. 337–38.
593 It was often past midnight . . . discussing strategy: Bowers, *Beveridge and the Progressive Era*, pp. 346–48.
593 to "go ahead . . . I will veto it": La Follette, *La Follette's Autobiography*, p. 440.
593 "bewildered by the intricacies": *NYT*, June 9, 1909.
593 "more technical knowledge": WHT to HHT, July 8, 1909, WHTP.
593 "reactionary tools": Mowry, *The Era of Theodore Roosevelt*, p. 245.
593 "The Senator will not turn": Kenneth W. Hechler, *Insurgency: Personalities and Politics of the Taft Era* (New York: Russell & Russell, 1964), p. 121.
593 Taft worried . . . becoming "irresponsible": Bowers, *Beveridge and the Progressive Era*, p. 343.
594 to "confer . . . the Roosevelt policies": WHT to Horace Taft, June 27, 1909, WHTP.
594 "Mr. Taft is not proving . . . pirate-infested seas": *Current Literature* (June 1909), p. 580.
594 "to form definite . . . Mr. Roosevelt's own": Ibid.
594 his "hands off" approach: *NYT*, June 15, 1909.
594 "on the ground that": WHT to Horace Taft, June 27, 1909, WHTP.
595 refuse to "reverse itself": *NYT*, June 20, 1909.
595 "already at a low ebb": *NYT*, June 16, 1909.
595 "some pretty shrewd . . . separately": AB to Clara, June 20, 1909, in AB, *Taft and Roosevelt*, Vol. 1, pp. 124–25.
595 "go a great way . . . illegitimate schemes": George Kibbe Turner, "How Taft Views His Own Administration: An Interview with the President," *McClure's* (June 1910), p. 214.
595 "Just when they thought": AB to Clara, June 20, 1909, in AB, *Taft and Roosevelt*, Vol. 1, p. 125.
595 These dissenting votes revealed: *Current Literature* (August 1909), pp. 3–5.
595 "Congress has had": *Literary Digest*, July 24, 1909.
595 "to make good . . . he became President": Ibid.
596 "used the White House": AB to Clara, Aug. 17, 1909, in AB, *Taft and Roosevelt*, Vol. 1, p. 178.
596 He invited Payne to dinner . . . after midnight: WHT to HHT, July 18, 1909, WHTP.
596 "at the disposal": WHT to HHT, July 17, 1909, in William Howard Taft and Lewis L. Gould, *My Dearest Nellie: The Letters of William Howard Taft to Helen Herron Taft, 1909–1912* (Lawrence: University Press of Kansas, 2011), pp. 46–47.
596 "longing" for her company: WHT to HHT, Aug. 3, 1909, WHTP.
596 "delighted . . . changes you seek": WHT to HHT, July 11, 1909, WHTP.
596 progress would come "by jerks": WHT to HHT, July 18, 1909, WHTP.
596 "Last night was as hot": WHT to HHT, July 13, 1909, in WHT and Gould, *My Dearest Nellie*, p. 39.
596 "the Senate bill . . . has been taken": WHT to HHT, July 11, 1909, WHTP.
596 "he was committed . . . broader point of view": *Decatur* [IL] *Daily Review*, July 17, 1909.
597 "jubilant . . . of the progressives": *Fort Wayne* [IN] *News*, July 17, 1909.
597 Congratulatory messages flooded: *New York Tribune*, July 26, 1909.
597 "the Taft tariff bill": *NYT*, July 18, 1909.
597 "I see today you made": HHT to WHT, July 17, 1909, WHTP.
597 "a good deal more of a muddle": WHT to Horace Taft, July 21, 1909, WHTP.
597 Despite repeated promises . . . "in writing": WHT to HHT, July 11, 1909, WHTP.
597 "an expert and acute . . . be deceived": Solvick, "William Howard Taft and the Payne-Aldrich Tariff," *Mississippi Valley Historical Review* (December 1963), p. 437.
597 "Aldrich insists that": WHT to HHT, July 22, 1909, WHTP.
597 "owed his victory . . . personal matter with him": AB to Clara, July 23, 1909, in AB, *Taft and Roosevelt*, Vol. 1, p. 154.
597 "It is the greatest exhibition": WHT to HHT, July 26, 1909, WHTP.
597 "They have my last . . . in his fight": AB to Clara, July 23, 1909, in AB, *Taft and Roosevelt*, Vol. 1, pp. 163–65.
598 a "cut away suit . . . fairly radiant": *Washington Post*, Aug. 6, 1909.
598 "Do you think . . . certainly do not": *Eau Claire* [WI] *Leader*, Aug. 6, 1909.
598 "could make . . . injure the party": AB to Clara, July 16, 1909, in AB, *Taft and Roosevelt*, Vol. 1, p. 144.
598 "A broad smile": *Eau Claire* [WI] *Leader*, Aug. 6, 1909.
598 "a terrific thunderstorm": AB to Clara, Aug. 6, 1909, in AB, *Taft and Roosevelt*, Vol. 1, p. 170.
598 "Heavy black clouds": *Washington Post*, Aug. 6, 1909.
598 the "storm of protest": AB to Clara, Aug. 6, 1909, in AB, *Taft and Roosevelt*, Vol. 1, p. 170.
599 "perfect . . . branches of Congress": *NYT*, Aug. 6, 1909.
599 "its long and stormy journey": Ibid.

599 "patient leadership . . . in the future": *Literary Digest*, Aug. 7, 1909.
599 made the final bill "less shocking": Ibid.
599 "the necessities of the common people": *Tacoma* [WA] *Times*, Aug. 6, 1909.
599 judged an "empty victory": *NYT*, Aug. 6, 1909.
599 "vindicated his personal . . . in his strategy": *Literary Digest*, Aug. 7, 1909.
599 "his own fault . . . the stable door": *NYT*, Aug. 6, 1909.
599 "come to a standstill . . . enthusiastic": *NYT*, Aug. 8, 1909.
599 "which could be heard": AB to Clara, Aug. 10, 1909, in AB, *Taft and Roosevelt*, Vol. 1, p. 173.
599 While the president and his family . . . in Beverly: *NYT*, Aug. 8, 1909.
600 "If anybody says": *Baltimore Sun*, Aug. 8, 1909.
600 Taft soon settled into: Boardman, "The Summer Capital," *Outlook*, Sept. 25, 1909, p. 177.
600 "the rest . . . forget her illness": AB to Clara, Aug. 10, 1909, in AB, *Taft and Roosevelt*, Vol. 1, p. 173.
600 "over every beautiful . . . pleasant route": *National Tribune* (Washington, DC), Aug. 25, 1909.
600 "the family dinner hour": Boardman, "The Summer Capital," *Outlook*, Sept. 25, 1909, p. 179.
600 "If it were not . . . out of life at all": AB to Clara, Aug. 24, 1909, in AB, *Taft and Roosevelt*, Vol. 1, p. 185.
600 "I do not know exactly": WHT to Nancy Roelker, Sept. 11, 1909, in Anderson, *William Howard Taft*, p. 206.
600 "take the people into": *New York Tribune*, Sept. 10, 1909.
600 "rampant . . . favor of his standard": *National Tribune*, Aug. 25, 1909.
600 "the bill was unsatisfactory . . . under the circumstances": *New York Tribune*, Sept. 10, 1909.
600 A future fight . . . loomed: *NYT*, Sept. 14, 1909.
600 "learned a great . . . shortcomings": *New York Tribune*, Sept. 10, 1909.
600 "tens and hundreds . . . personal touch": WHT, "Speech at the Boston Chamber of Commerce, Sept. 14, 1909," WHTP.
601 "cabinet members . . . and banking system": *Register and Leader* (Des Moines, IA), Sept. 15, 1909.
601 "Father of the Federal": *NYT*, Nov. 19, 1914.
601 Reaching Chicago . . . a hearty reception: *New York Tribune*, Sept. 17, 1909.
601 At Milwaukee . . . first statement on the tariff: *New York Tribune*, Sept. 18, 1909.
601 "omnipresent good nature": Thompson, *Presidents I've Known*, p. 218.
601 "hotbed of insurgency": *Current Literature* (November 1909), p. 480.
601 Republican leaders in the House . . . home district: Thompson, *Presidents I've Known*, p. 218.
601 "Hope to be able": WHT to HHT, Sept. 16, 1909, in Pringle, *Life and Times*, Vol. 1, p. 453.
602 "a mass of facts": *Washington Post*, Sept. 18, 1909.
602 "Speech hastily prepared": WHT to HHT, Sept. 17, 1909, in Pringle, *Life and Times*, Vol. 1, p. 453.
602 "What was the duty . . . Republican party ever passed": William Howard Taft and David Henry Burton, *The Collected Works of William Howard Taft* (Athens: Ohio University Press, 2001), pp. 179, 181, 177.
602 "without hesitation": *NYT*, Sept. 19, 1909.
602 "Western Republicans . . . on the tariff question": All cited in *Literary Digest*, Oct. 2, 1909, p. 511.
602 "I did not write to you": Horace Taft to WHT, Oct. 8, 1909, WHTP.
603 "commendation" of Tawney: *Current Literature* (November 1909), p. 478.
603 "Theodore Roosevelt's . . . overwhelming demand": *Literary Digest*, Oct. 2, 1909.
603 "You have come out . . . national supervision": TR to HCL, Sept. 10, 1909, in TR and HCL, *Selections from the Correspondence*, Vol. 2, p. 346.
603 "I never appreciated . . . power and force": HCL to TR, April 29, 1909, in ibid., pp. 333–34.
603 "surprised . . . opinion of him": HCL to TR, Sept. 10, 1909, in ibid., p. 346.
603 "the wilds of Africa": RSB, Notebook K, June 13, 1908, RSB Papers.
603 "truthful statement . . . win victories": WHT to Robert Taft, Oct. 28, 1909, in Pringle, *Life and Times*, Vol. 1, p. 456.
603 "Of course we want": *NYT*, Oct. 7, 1909.
603 Nearly 7,000 . . . in Portland: WHT to HHT, Oct. 2, 1909, WHTP.
604 in Phoenix . . . through the gates: AB, "Record of the Trip of President Taft," in WHT Diaries, WHTP.
604 "Winning Taft Smile": *Albuquerque* [NM] *Morning Journal*, Oct. 16, 1909.
604 "Taft's personality": *Current Literature* (November 1909), p. 476.
604 "really and sincerely . . . more real affection": AB to Clara, Nov. 14, 1909, in AB, *Taft and Roosevelt*, Vol. 1, p. 205.
604 He noticed that Taft: AB to Clara, Nov. 14, 1909, in ibid., p. 206.
604 "They are prompted": WHT to Frederick Carpenter, Oct. 24, 1909, WHTP.
604 "Whatever their judgment": WHT to HHT, Oct. 24, 1909, WHTP.
604 "enjoyed every moment": WHT, "Speech at Charleston, South Carolina, Nov. 5, 1909," WHTP.
604 "266 speeches": *Current Literature* (December 1909), p. 8.
604 "of temperament": WHT, "Speech at Charleston, SC, Nov. 5, 1909," WHTP.

604   "as stimulating as champagne": *Albuquerque* [NM] *Morning Journal*, Oct. 16, 1909.
604   "Well, I'm back again": *New York Tribune*, Nov. 11, 1909.
604   "full of despair": AB to Clara, Nov. 14, 1909, in AB, *Taft and Roosevelt*, Vol. 1, p. 208.

CHAPTER TWENTY-FOUR: St. George and the Dragon

Page
605   "a mere personal . . . matter of state": *Logansport* [IN] *Reporter*, Nov. 18, 1909.
605   falling in behind Pinchot: AB to Clara, Nov. 14, 1909, in AB, *Taft and Roosevelt*, Vol. 1, p. 203.
605   the opening volley: *New York Tribune*, Nov. 10, 1909.
606   "there would be such a fire": *Current Literature* (December 1909), p. 592.
606   "still in its infancy . . . astonishing consolidation": *New York Daily Tribune*, Jan. 16, 1909.
606   "the public interest": *Emporia* [KS] *Gazette*, April 29, 1909.
606   "I esteem it my duty": *New York Daily Tribune*, Jan. 16, 1909.
606   "there was no time": Pinchot, *Breaking New Ground*, p. 408.
606   "is the steward": TR, *An Autobiography*, p. 464.
606   Within three weeks . . . to the public domain: *Salt Lake Herald*, April 22, 1909.
606   the previous administration had acted illegally: *Washington Times*, April 27, 1909.
607   Once the proper surveys . . . the Far West: *Times-Herald* (Burns, OR), April 3, 1909.
607   threat to "traditional western individualism": Mowry, *The Era of Theodore Roosevelt*, p. 251.
607   "that a man could ride": *Times-Herald*, April 3, 1909.
607   "on the basis of law": WHT to William Kent, June 29, 1909, in Pringle, *Life and Times*, Vol. 1, p. 480.
607   "the end justified the means": *Springfield* [MA] *Daily Republican*, April 30, 1909.
607   "sweeping declaration": Knute Nelson, Louis R. Glavis, et al., *Investigation of the Department of the Interior and of the Bureau of Forestry* [hereafter *Investigation*] (Washington, DC: Government Printing Office, 1911), Vol. 7, p. 4203.
607   "It is . . . not the Executive": WHT to William Kent, June 29, 1909, in Pringle, *Life and Times*, Vol. 1, p. 481.
607   "further along . . . a different way": Ibid., p. 476.
607   "Stop Ballinger": *Des Moines Daily News*, May 2, 1909.
607   "cowboy methods": *Current Literature* (December 1909), p. 592.
607   progressives, educated by . . . treachery of monopoly: *Times-Herald*, April 3, 1909.
607   "Attention! Land Thieves . . . predatory interests": *Tacoma* [WA] *Times*, May 4, 1909.
607   "what was going on": Pinchot, *Breaking New Ground*, p. 409.
608   Taft regarded Pinchot . . . a fanatical strain: WHT to Lawrence F. Abbott, Aug. 31, 1909, WHTP.
608   all too ready to attribute: WHT to HHT, Oct. 3, 1909, WHTP.
608   "protested as vigorously . . . water-power purposes": Pinchot, *Breaking New Ground*, p. 409.
608   Greatly relieved, Garfield maintained: James R. Garfield, Diary, May 8, 1909, Garfield Papers.
608   "Everything is not . . . golden opportunities": *Springfield Daily Republican*, April 30, 1909.
608   "five million acres": Stephen Ponder, " 'Nonpublicity' and the Unmaking of a President: William Howard Taft and the Ballinger-Pinchot Controversy of 1909–1910," *Journalism History* (Winter 1994), p. 114.
608   "Was Conservation . . . the Old Guard?": Pinchot, *Breaking New Ground*, p. 417.
608   "one excuse or another": *Spokane* [WA] *Press*, Aug. 9, 1909.
608   enabling General Electric . . . millions of dollars: *New York Tribune*, Aug. 14, 1909.
608   "This is a true story": *Spokane* [WA] *Press*, Aug. 9, 1909.
608   "Richard Achilles Ballinger . . . about it now": *Spokane* [WA] *Press*, Aug. 10, 1909.
609   Pinchot's speech . . . on the embattled secretary: *NYT*, Aug. 12, 1909.
609   "The purpose of . . . the gauntlet": Pinchot, *Breaking New Ground*, p. 417.
609   "unequivocally . . . in process of formation": *The North American* (Philadelphia), Aug. 11, 1909.
609   "strict construction . . . the many": Pinchot, *Breaking New Ground*, p. 418.
609   "a storm of applause . . . wildest reception": *The North American*, Aug. 11, 1909.
609   "deplorable fact . . . the second withdrawal": Gifford Pinchot to WHT, Aug. 10, 1909, in *Investigation*, Vol. 2, p. 63.
609   "breathless interest . . . never been born": Pinchot, *Breaking New Ground*, p. 419.
609   "He picked up his hat": *Spokane* [WA] *Press*, Aug. 14, 1909.
609   "I have been in": *Seattle Star*, Aug. 12, 1909.
609   "Hit 'em again . . . no conference with you": *Spokane* [WA] *Press*, Aug. 14, 1909.
610   "questioned and quizzed . . . of the West": *Washington Post*, Nov. 18, 1909.
610   "Mr. Ballinger's silence": *San Francisco Call*, Aug. 31, 1909.
610   "Gross misrepresentations": *The Ranch* (Seattle, WA), Sept. 1, 1909.
610   "always believed . . . results accomplished": Richard Ballinger to William Cowles, Dec. 9, 1909, in Ponder, " 'Nonpublicity' and the Unmaking of a President," *Journalism History* (Winter 1994), p. 117.

610   misplaced the decimal point: *New York Tribune*, Aug. 14, 1909.

610   "did not touch . . . its extreme corner": *Investigation*, Vol. 2, p. 719.

610   "monopolists had grabbed off": *National Tribune* (Washington, DC), Mar. 10, 1909.

610   "assumed a certain": Chester Rowell to WHT, Aug. 27, 1909, WHTP.

610   "completely overshadowed": *Washington Times*, Aug. 25, 1909.

610   "taken for granted . . . make good": *Washington Post*, Aug. 26, 1909.

610   "the driving wedge . . . chasm": Mowry, *The Era of Theodore Roosevelt*, p. 258.

611   "a slumbering volcano": *Tacoma* [WA] *Times*, Aug. 24, 1909.

611   in desperation: L. R. Glavis to WHT, Aug. 11, 1909, in *Investigation*, Vol. 2, pp. 4–23.

611   acting "in good faith": Gifford Pinchot to WHT, Nov. 4, 1909, in Vol. 4, p. 1224.

611   "into one property . . . benefit of all": *NYT*, Jan. 2, 1911.

611   to give a Morgan-Guggenheim company . . . coal property: John Lathrop and George Kibbe Turner, "Billions of Treasure: Should the Mineral Wealth of Alaska Enrich the Guggenheim Trust or the U.S. Treasury?," *McClure's* (January 1910), p. 347.

611   "closely identified" with the members: *Washington Times*, Aug. 22, 1909.

611   "legal representative": L. R. Glavis to WHT, Aug. 11, 1909, in *Investigation*, Vol. 2, p. 10.

611   "act as counsel": Louis R. Glavis, "The Whitewashing of Ballinger," *Collier's*, Nov. 13, 1909, p. 16.

612   "I advised him . . . becoming public": Gifford Pinchot to WHT, Aug. 10, 1909, in *Investigation*, Vol. 2, p. 63.

612   "Ballinger Mixed . . . evidence": *Salt Lake Tribune*, Aug. 14, 1909.

612   would lead to the indictment of Ballinger: *Washington Post*, Aug. 26, 1909.

612   It was later revealed: Overton W. Price and A. C. Shaw to Gifford Pinchot, Jan. 5, 1910, in *Investigation*, Vol. 4, p. 1275.

612   "made notes upon his reading": *Titusville* [PA] *Herald*, May 16, 1910.

612   "especially concerning . . . professional relation": WHT to Richard Ballinger, Aug. 22, 1909, in *Investigation*, Vol. 2, p. 64.

612   he remembered little else: Gustav J. Karger, "Conversation with William Howard Taft, March 12, 1910," Taft-Karger MSS, CMC.

612   "as full as possible": WHT to Richard Ballinger, Aug. 22, 1909, in *Investigation*, Vol. 2, p. 64.

612   "has had nothing to do": Frank Pierce to WHT, Sept. 1, 1909, in ibid., p. 188.

612   "issuance of patents": H. H. Schwartz to WHT, Sept. 1, 1909, in ibid., p. 218.

612   "to kill some snakes": *Washington Post*, Sept. 4, 1909.

612   On September 4 . . . left the land commissionership: Richard Ballinger to WHT, Sept. 4, 1909, in *Investigation*, Vol. 2, pp. 66–75.

613   in the summer of 1908 . . . "legal representative": Richard Ballinger to WHT, Sept. 4, 9, & 10, 1909, in ibid., Vol. 2, pp. 68–70, 97, 100.

613   "several satchels": *Oakland* [CA] *Tribune*, Sept. 6, 1909.

613   Myopia Hunt Club: *Indiana* [PA] *Evening Gazette*, Sept. 6, 1909.

613   "reading the answers": *Titusville* [PA] *Herald*, May 16, 1910.

613   "The cruel injustice": WHT to Horace Taft, Sept. 11, 1909, WHTP.

614   "was very anxious . . . the evidence and his conclusions": *Titusville Herald*, May 16, 1910.

614   "only shreds of . . . making false charges against them": WHT to Richard Ballinger, Sept. 13, 1909, WHTP.

615   "misrepresentation . . . in his own defense": These arguments were later made by Louis D. Brandeis on May 5, 1910, in *Investigation*, Vol. 7, pp. 3872–3874.

615   "The Ballinger adherents": *New York Tribune*, Sept. 17, 1909.

615   "hasty action . . . of governmental discipline": WHT to Gifford Pinchot, Sept. 13, 1909, WHTP.

615   "in holding Ballinger up": WHT to Charles Nagel, Sept. 24, 1909, WHTP.

615   "Never at any . . . greatest losses": *Nevada State Journal*, Sept. 26, 1909.

615   "as fanatical . . . after Ballinger": WHT to George Wickersham, Oct. 7, 1909, WHTP.

615   "a state of . . . a break": WHT to Charles Nagel, Sept. 24, 1909, WHTP.

616   "He is looking": WHT to George Wickersham, Oct. 7, 1909, WHTP.

616   "I have been thinking": Overton W. Price to Gifford Pinchot, Sept. 16, 1909, Pinchot Papers.

616   In the weeks . . . publicize his allegations: James R. Garfield, Diary, Sept. 21, 1909, Garfield Papers.

616   "as employees . . . immediate danger": Overton W. Price and A. C. Shaw to Gifford Pinchot, Jan. 5, 1910, in *Investigation*, Vol. 4, p. 1279.

616   "going over in detail": James R. Garfield, Diary, Sept. 21, 1909, Garfield Papers.

616   Shaw then aided Glavis: Norman Hapgood, *The Changing Years, Reminiscences of Norman Hapgood* (New York: Farrar & Rinehart, 1930), p. 182.

616   "Pinchot has spread": WHT to HHT, Oct. 15, 1909, WHTP.

616   "read the article": Hapgood, *The Changing Years*, p. 182.

617   No attempt was ever made: Pringle, *Life and Times*, Vol. 1, p. 498.

617 "the newspaper frenzy": Ponder, " 'Nonpublicity' and the Unmaking of a President," *Journalism History* (Winter 1994), p. 116

617 "The Whitewashing . . . in Ballinger's Hands": Glavis, "The Whitewashing of Ballinger," *Collier's*, Nov. 13, 1909, pp. 16–18.

617 The potential purchase of coal lands . . . railroads in the West: James L. Penick, *Progressive Politics and Conservation: The Ballinger-Pinchot Affair* (Chicago: University of Chicago Press, 1968), pp. 82–83.

617 "the natural resources of Alaska": Pinchot, *Breaking New Ground*, p. 427.

617 "the muckrake periodical": Mowry, *The Era of Theodore Roosevelt*, p. 257.

617 Glavis was likened to Ida Tarbell: *Fairbanks* [AK] *Daily News-Miner*, Dec. 17, 1909.

617 "a party to the conspiracy": Filler, *The Muckrakers*, p. 333.

617 "circumstantial evidence . . . Alaska coal grants": John Matthews to Gifford Pinchot, Jan. 8, 1910, Pinchot Papers.

617 Ballinger refused to give a detailed statement: *Washington Post*, Nov. 18, 1909.

617 "literary apostles . . . so asinine": Richard Ballinger, "Press Release, Nov. 20, 1909," Pinchot Papers.

617 "I have felt so thoroughly": Richard Ballinger to William Cowles, Dec. 9, 1909, in Ponder, " 'Nonpublicity' and the Unmaking of a President," *Journalism History* (Winter 1994), p. 117.

618 "in favor of all": James R. Garfield, Diary, Nov. 30, 1909, Garfield Papers.

618 "the goodness of a bad": Gifford Pinchot to James R. Garfield, Dec. 4, 1909, Pinchot Papers.

618 "the whole controversy": Gifford Pinchot to Charles R. Crane, Nov. 29, 1909, Pinchot Papers.

618 "that the situation had become": *Washington Post*, Dec. 21, 1909.

618 "a coward . . . an honest man": WHT to Reuben Melville, Dec. 24, 1909, WHTP.

618 "the whole affair": *Washington Post*, Aug. 30, 1909.

618 Faced with Ballinger's ultimatum: *Washington Times*, Dec. 22, 1909.

618 "any investigation . . . papers, or documents": Pinchot, *Breaking New Ground*, p. 443.

618 "all the power . . . before the people": Phillip Wells to William Kent, Dec. 22, 1909, WHTP.

619 A Washington "insider . . . to conduct the defense": Filler, *The Muckrakers*, pp. 334–35.

619 "between special . . . at their expense?": Pinchot, *Breaking New Ground*, pp. 444–45.

619 "out again defying . . . Let us see": WHT to Horace Taft, Dec. 27, 1909, WHTP.

619 "the Ballingerites . . . old political time": *National Tribune* (Washington, DC), Dec. 30, 1909.

619 "It remains true": *Current Literature* (June 1910), p. 588.

619 "bring out . . . worst possible light": *Washington Times*, Jan. 7, 1910.

620 the Forest Bureau's involvement: Gifford Pinchot to Jonathan P. Dolliver, Jan. 5, 1910, in *Investigation*, Vol. 4, pp. 1283–85.

620 "to lay our hand": Gifford Pinchot to W. K. Kavanaugh, Jan. 20, 1910, Pinchot Papers.

620 "official information . . . of public property": Gifford Pinchot to Jonathan P. Dolliver, Jan. 5, 1910, in *Investigation*, Vol. 4, pp. 1283–84.

620 "One trouble . . . within him now": AB to Clara, Jan. 7, 1910, in AB, *Taft and Roosevelt*, Vol. 1, pp. 253–54.

620 "had distressed him as much": AB to Clara, Jan. 9, 1910, in ibid., p. 256.

620 "like a man almost ill": AB to Clara, Jan. 7, 1910, in ibid., p. 254.

620 "There is only one": AB to Clara, Jan. 9, 1910, in ibid., p. 256.

620 Taft directed Wilson to fire: *El Paso* [TX] *Herald*, Jan. 8, 1910.

620 "The plain intimations . . . a helpful subordinate": WHT to Gifford Pinchot, Jan. 7, 1910, WHTP.

621 "looked refreshed": AB to Clara, Jan. 9, 1910, in AB, *Taft and Roosevelt*, Vol. 1, p. 255.

621 "could have followed . . . to be overlooked": *La Crosse* [WI] *Tribune*, Jan. 8, 1910.

621 "suffering from the same": *Post-Standard* (Syracuse, NY), Jan. 8, 1910.

621 "Quite as admirable . . . public lands": *Literary Digest*, Jan. 22, 1910, p. 128.

621 "the Roosevelt policies . . . friend of Mr. Pinchot": *Outlook*, Jan. 22, 1910, p. 141.

621 "I cannot believe it": TR to Gifford Pinchot, Jan. 17, 1910, Pinchot Papers.

621 "The appointment . . . meeting me in Europe?": TR to Gifford Pinchot, Mar. 1, 1910, Pinchot Papers.

621 "The people have faith": Pinchot, *Breaking New Ground*, p. 457.

622 "general-in-command . . . most convincing way": *National Tribune*, Feb. 3, 1910.

622 "a keen disappointment . . . than a scandal": *Literary Digest*, Feb. 12, 1910, p. 269.

622 "opened with a heavy volley": *National Tribune*, Mar. 3, 1910.

622 had "been unfaithful": *Indianapolis Star*, Feb. 28, 1910.

622 "the public clamor . . . unfaithful public servant": *National Tribune*, Mar. 3, 1910.

622 "Pinchot has distinctly": WHT to Horace Taft, Mar. 5, 1910, WHTP.

622 "proven nothing at all": Horace Taft to WHT, Mar. 9, 1910, WHTP.

622 "so tedious" . . . Jim Jeffries: *Arizona Republican* (Phoenix, AZ), April 18, 1910.

622 "really decisive . . . he had to prove it": Gifford Pinchot, "Interview with Louis D. Brandeis, March 3, 1940," Pinchot Papers.

623 he finally discovered . . . after September 11: Frederick Kerby, "The Inside Story of How a Private Secretary Wrecked an Administration," Unpublished ms [n.d.], enclosed in Frederick Kerby to Gifford Pinchot, Jan. 28, 1941, Pinchot Papers.

623 Brandeis revealed his discovery . . . cognizant of his peril: Pinchot, "Interview with Louis D. Brandeis, March 3, 1940," Pinchot Papers.

623 "to make it appear": New York *Sun*, April 23, 1910.

623 Prevented by the rules . . . leaked the story to the press: *Washington Post*, April 24, 1910.

623 Wickersham initially refused . . . backdated the report: *Newport* [RI] *Daily News*, May 12, 1910.

623 "there probably would": *National Tribune*, May 19, 1910.

623 Their failure to do so . . . Congress and the country: *Le Mars* [IA] *Globe-Post*, May 16, 1910.

623 "an attitude of suspicion": *National Tribune*, May 19, 1910.

623 "noted the similarities . . . match put to the pile": Kerby, "The Inside Story," Pinchot Papers.

624 "in his brief case . . . of the Lawler document": Ibid.

624 "the so-called memorandum": G. W. Wickersham to Knute Nelson, May 14, 1910, in *Investigation*, Vol. 7, p. 4364.

624 "of any material . . . resume of the facts": *Investigation*, Vol. 7, pp. 3862, 3865–66.

624 "a restless tattoo": *New Castle* [PA] *News*, April 30, 1910.

624 "an insult": *Investigation*, Vol. 7, p. 3868.

624 "exhausted all channels": Kerby, "The Inside Story," Pinchot Papers.

625 He identified "certain portions": *Washington Times*, May 14, 1910.

625 "specifically" prepared: *Washington Times*, May 15, 1910.

625 "Ballinger Accused": *Washington Times*, May 14, 1910.

625 the story broke . . . on the golf course: Kerby, "The Inside Story," Pinchot Papers.

625 suddenly "found . . . coincidences of all time": *Washington Times*, May 16, 1910.

625 "treachery . . . unworthy": Ibid.; *Fort Wayne* [IN] *Weekly Sentinel*, May 18, 1910.

625 "did not state . . . a written statement": *Titusville* [PA] *Herald*, May 16, 1910.

625 "manly" assumption: *Waterloo* [IA] *Evening Courier*, May 18, 1910.

625 "the sequence of events": *Fort Wayne* [IN] *Weekly Sentinel*, May 18, 1910.

626 "unimportant" statements: *Washington Herald*, May 15, 1910.

626 "There was absolutely . . . private offices": Cited in *Waterloo* [IA] *Evening Courier*, May 18, 1910.

626 "the people who had": *National Tribune*, May 19, 1910.

626 "until he was . . . fly into a rage": *Waterloo* [IA] *Evening Courier*, May 18, 1910.

626 "came as a startling . . . the good faith": *San Antonio* [TX] *Light and Gazette*, May 16, 1910.

626 "the puzzled . . . done nothing illegal": Stewart Edward White, "The Ballinger Case," *The American Magazine* (March 1910), p. 687.

626 "not a single fact": *Literary Digest*, May 14, 1910.

626 "Rightly or wrongly": *Emporia* [KS] *Gazette*, May 26, 1910.

626 Reflecting widespread sentiment . . . to resign: *Indianapolis Star*, June 10, 1910.

626 "His presence . . . long and unflinchingly": *Emporia* [KS] *Gazette*, May 26, 1910.

626 "be regarded as": "The Ballinger Case: A Review," *Outlook*, June 11, 1910, p. 295.

626 "justified in remaining": *Indianapolis Star*, June 10, 1910.

626 Charley Taft tried . . . the president refused: AB to Clara, May 5, 1910, in AB, *Taft and Roosevelt*, Vol. 1, p. 347.

626 "Life is not worth": WHT to P. A. Baker, May 21, 1910, in Pringle, *Life and Times*, Vol. 2, p. 558.

626 "unjustly persecuted" a good man: AB to Clara, June 22, 1910, in AB, *Taft and Roosevelt*, Vol. 1, p. 408.

627 "broken" Ballinger's health: *Literary Digest*, May 28, 1910, p. 1067.

627 "almost equaled": Paolo E. Coletta, *The Presidency of William Howard Taft* (Lawrence: University Press of Kansas, 1973), p. 98.

627 "His entrance into": Gifford Pinchot, "Statement, March 7, 1911," Pinchot Papers.

627 "no right . . . the public welfare": *Indianapolis Star*, June 10, 1910.

627 "Is the Republican Party" . . . occasionally "dragooned": RSB, "Is the Republican Party Breaking Up? The Story of the Insurgent West," *The American Magazine* (February 1910), pp. 435–39.

628 "at first a decided": RSB, "Is the East Also Insurgent?," *The American Magazine* (March 1910), pp. 579, 587.

628 From New England . . . over Speaker Cannon: Semonche, *Ray Stannard Baker*, pp. 236–37.

628 "tense and dramatic": *Washington Times*, Mar. 19, 1910.

628 "fighting the fight": *Washington Times*, Mar. 18, 1910.

628 "met his Waterloo": *Washington Times*, Mar. 19, 1910.

628 Forty-three insurgent Republicans . . . pass the resolution: Remini, *The House*, p. 275.

628 "A real revolution": RSB to J. Stannard Baker, Mar. 27, 1910, RSB Papers.

628 "case study . . . within the reform movement": Semonche, *Ray Stannard Baker*, p. 238.

628 "We are naturally . . . our opportunity": JSP to WAW, Aug. 9, 1910, White Papers.

628   As precinct leader . . . changed from within: WAW, *The Autobiography*, p. 424.
628   the insurgents' vision: WAW, "The Insurgence of Insurgency," *The American Magazine* (December 1910), p. 171.
629   her "powerful pen . . . could well be": *Washington Times*, June 24, 1910.
629   "the same old circus": IMT, *All in the Day's Work*, p. 272.
629   the "rousing challenge": Ibid., p. 273.
629   "the hazy generalities": RSB, "On the Political Firing Line," *The American Magazine* (November 1910), p. 9.
629   "crystallized into one": IMT, *All in the Day's Work*, p. 274.
629   "argues and fights . . . ways of thinking": IMT, "The Standpat Intellect," *The American Magazine* (May 1911), p. 40.
629   "The popular judgment": JSP, Editorial, *The American Magazine* (September 1910), p. 707.
629   "I thought that Taft": JSP to WAW, Sept. 18, 1909, White Papers.
629   "opposed him": JSP to RSB, Feb. 24, 1910, RSB Papers.
629   "mattered little . . . crusading spirit": Hechler, *Insurgency*, p. 13.
630   "Taft is done for": IMT to WAW, Sept. 29, 1909, White Papers.
630   "But they will not work": WAW to WHT, Feb. 3, 1910, in Johnson, *Selected Letters of William Allen White*, p. 105.
630   Taft responded to White . . . made no sense: WAW to Guy W. Mallon, Jan. 13, 1910, WHTP.
630   "I have confidence": WHT to WAW, Mar. 20, 1909, White Papers.
630   "foolishly and needlessly": *NYT*, April 20, 1910.
630   "I could not have asked . . . steer the conversation": WAW, *The Autobiography*, p. 425.
630   "everything under the sun": WAW to J. Haskel, June 6, 1910, White Papers.
630   "We had . . . a fool's errand": WAW, *The Autobiography*, pp. 425–26.
630   "I trust you are . . . the fireworks": JSP to RSB, Feb. 24, 1910, RSB Papers.
631   "There is one thing": RSB, "The Measure of Taft," *The American Magazine* (July 1910), p. 362.
631   They appreciated . . . homes and hotels: *National Tribune*, Jan. 6, 1910.
631   "If these young visitors": *National Tribune*, Mar. 31, 1910.
631   "A mighty cheer . . . trusty right arm": *Washington Post*, April 15, 1910.
631   "All his life long . . . chief thing is to *fight*": RSB, "The Measure of Taft," *The American Magazine* (July 1910), pp. 364–65, 367–68.
631   "free from severe criticism": WHT, "Speech to the New York Press Club," Mar. 22, 1910, WHTP.
632   "criticism may spring": RSB, "The Measure of Taft," *The American Magazine* (July 1910), p. 369.
632   "arrayed against . . . from the first": Paul Kester to HHT, Sept. 22, 1910, WHTP.
632   "skeleton" . . . still carried weight: Lyon, *Success Story*, p. 322.
632   "In the first place . . . against the people's wishes": McClure to Charles Norton, Oct. 11, 1910, McClure MSS.
632   Pinchot arrived at Roosevelt's villa . . . over the Maritime Alps: *San Francisco Call*, April 12, 1910.
632   "We have fallen back": Gifford Pinchot to TR, Dec. 31, 1909, TRP.
633   "disappointment . . . the President's opinions": Jonathan P. Dolliver to Gifford Pinchot, Mar. 25, 1910, TRP.
633   "The people at first": Albert J. Beveridge to Gifford Pinchot, Mar. 24, 1910, TRP.
633   "We had one of the finest": Gifford Pinchot to James R. Garfield, April 27, 1910, Pinchot Papers.
633   "no event in": *San Francisco Call*, April 12, 1910.
633   "You do not need . . . the best he knows how": TR to HCL, April 11, 1910, in *LTR*, Vol. 7, pp. 71, 70.
633   "keep absolutely still": TR to HCL, Mar. 4, 1910, in ibid., p. 52.
633   "As the fight deepens . . . of continental size": RSB, "The Impending Roosevelt," *The American Magazine* (April 1910), pp. 735, 737.

CHAPTER TWENTY-FIVE: "The Parting of the Ways"

Page
634   He was perplexed: AB to Clara, June 5, 1910, in AB, *Taft and Roosevelt*, Vol. 1, p. 364.
634   a gold ruler: AB to Clara, Mar. 22, 1909, in ibid., p. 25.
634   "There is no doubt . . . his way over": AB to Clara, June 5, 1910, in ibid., p. 364.
635   "Am deeply touched": TR to WHT, Mar. 23, 1909, in *LTR*, Vol. 7, pp. 3–4.
635   "Roosevelt did write": AB to Clara, June 6, 1910, in AB, *Taft and Roosevelt*, Vol. 1, p. 367.
635   The lack of communication . . . accomplishments of his administration: *Mansfield* [OH] *News*, June 15, 1910.
635   "received no letters . . . other persons": *Indianapolis Star*, June 12, 1910.
635   "singularly silent": AB to Clara, Feb. 14, 1910, AB Letters.
635   although eighteen-year-old Ethel . . . to recognize her: EKR to Kermit Roosevelt, May 12, 1909, KR Papers.

635 "to let the setting sun": Nicholas Longworth to TR, April 27, 1910, TRP.
635 "solely as a result": AB to Clara, May 17, 1910, in AB, *Taft and Roosevelt*, Vol. 1, p. 352.
635 "Everything which is . . . personal jealousies": AB to Clara, May 17, 1910, AB Letters.
636 no "word of welcome" . . . in Khartoum: AB to Clara, June 6, 1910, in AB, *Taft and Roosevelt*, Vol. 1, p. 367.
636 "nearly complete . . . would find the truth": WHT to TR, May 26, 1910, TRP.
636 Taft made the decision . . . note of welcome: WHT to TR, June 14, 1910, TRP.
636 "you and Mrs. Taft . . . out again": AB to Clara, June 16, 1910, in AB, *Taft and Roosevelt*, Vol. 1, p. 392.
636 "Oh, Archie . . . answer it later": AB to Clara, June 19, 1910, in ibid., p. 398.
636 "and how she dreaded . . . had distressed him": AB to Clara, June 19, 1910, in ibid., p. 402.
637 "if the master . . . a little bit late": AB to Clara, June 19, 1910, in AB Letters.
637 "I feel it is . . . courteous": AB to Clara, June 19, 1910, in AB, *Taft and Roosevelt*, Vol. 1, pp. 394–95, 403.
637 "I am of course much concerned": TR to WHT, June 8, 1910, in *LTR*, Vol. 7, p. 88.
637 "kind and friendly . . . cannot help it": TR to WHT, June 20, 1910, in ibid., p. 93.
637 Overall, the feel of the letter: AB to Clara, June 24, 1910, in AB, *Taft and Roosevelt*, Vol. 1, p. 411.
637 intense "factional wrangling": *National Tribune* (Washington, DC), June 23, 1910.
637 "more general legislation": *Washington Times*, June 26, 1910.
637 "dark days . . . to command": *New York Tribune*, June 26, 1910.
637 "strongly progressive . . . congressional saw mill": *Eau Claire* [WI] *Leader*, June 25, 1910.
638 a "special Commerce Court . . . at home and abroad": *New York Tribune*, June 26, 1910.
638 Taft's "crowning achievement": *Eau Claire* [WI] *Leader*, June 25, 1910.
638 "I am not in favor": *Los Angeles Herald*, Sept. 18, 1909.
638 "I am as pleased": WHT to [Otto] Bannard, June 11, 1910, in Pringle, *Life and Times*, Vol. 1, p. 519.
638 "one of the great Congressional": WHT to [William B.] McKinley, Aug. 20, 1910, WHTP.
638 The insurgents rightly took credit: *National Tribune*, June 23, 1910.
638 "Old Guard" Republicans . . . the promises: *Eau Claire* [WI] *Leader*, June 25, 1910.
638 "When people come": *NYT*, June 26, 1910.
638 "I always had faith": Charles P. Taft to WHT, July 2, 1910, WHTP.
638 "congratulated him . . . session was ending": *Washington Times*, June 26, 1910.
639 "the only incident . . . through the park": AB to Clara, June 26, 1910, in AB, *Taft and Roosevelt*, Vol. 1, pp. 413–14.
639 he rested at Sagamore Hill . . . *The Outlook*: *Burlington* [VT] *Weekly Free Press*, June 23, 1910.
639 Before leaving for Africa, he had signed: *NYT*, Mar. 11, 1909.
639 a three-room suite . . . "an office building": *Burlington* [VT] *Weekly Free Press*, June 23, 1910.
639 "very real . . . small proportion": "Mr. Roosevelt to The Outlook's Readers," *Outlook*, July 2, 1910, p. 462.
639 "not make a speech . . . I won't say never": *New York Tribune*, June 24, 1910.
639 "marked by frequent . . . his other hand": *NYT*, June 30, 1910.
639 Throughout his governorship . . . direct primary bill: Edmund Morris, *Colonel Roosevelt* (New York: Random House, 2010), pp. 94–95.
640 "I believe the people": *NYT*, June 30, 1910.
640 "plunged into the very thick": *Boston Daily Globe*, June 30, 1910.
640 taken "the helm . . . in the approaching campaign": *NYT*, June 30, 1910.
640 "is likely to prove": *New York Tribune*, June 30, 1910.
640 "Ah Theodore . . . nothing on which to hang a story": AB to Clara, June 30, 1910, in AB, *Taft and Roosevelt*, Vol. 1, pp. 418–20, 431.
641 "From beginning to end": *New York Tribune*, July 1, 1910.
641 "that their friendship": *Washington Post*, July 2, 1910.
641 "Just Like Old Times . . . don't know that I shall": *NYT*, July 1, 1910.
641 "in swift and emphatic fashion": *Boston Daily Globe*, July 1, 1910.
641 "It is Mr. Roosevelt . . . prepared for war": Cited in *Literary Digest*, July 9, 1910, p. 43.
641 "They made the fight": Pringle, *Life and Times*, Vol. 2, p. 563.
641 More powerful than . . . slate of candidates: Lewis L. Gould, *The William Howard Taft Presidency* (Lawrence: University Press of Kansas, 2009), p. 113.
641 "It did not occur . . . platform and candidates": WHT to Lloyd Griscom, Aug. 20, 1910, WHTP.
642 "Don't you know . . . such a fight": WHT to Charles Norton, Aug. 21, 1910, WHTP.
642 Taft momentarily wavered . . . dragged into the battle: AB to Clara, Aug. 17, 1910, in AB, *Taft and Roosevelt*, Vol. 2, p. 479.
642 the panel chose Sherman: Gould, *The William Howard Taft Presidency*, p. 114.
642 "he fumed . . . the heaviest blow yet": *NYT*, Aug. 17, 1910.

642 Roosevelt was incensed . . . endorsed Sherman's candidacy: WHT to Charles P. Taft, Sept. 10, 1910, and WHT to Lloyd Griscom, Aug. 20, 1910, WHTP.

642 "with treachery . . . kills other people": AB to Clara, Aug. 18, 1910, in AB, *Taft and Roosevelt*, Vol. 2, p. 488.

643 "ever expressed . . . conference with Mr. Roosevelt": *Washington Herald*, Aug. 23, 1910.

643 He was "indignant": WHT to Charles Norton, Aug. 22, 1910, WHTP.

643 "was very glad to see": *Washington Herald*, Aug. 23, 1910.

643 "As the waters of excitement": AB to Clara, Aug. 21, 1910, in AB, *Taft and Roosevelt*, Vol. 2, p. 493.

643 "profoundly grieved": AB to Clara, Aug. 18, 1910, in ibid., p. 488.

643 "His whole attitude . . . in the past": AB to Clara, Aug. 19, 1910, in ibid., p. 484.

643 "They are now apart": AB to Clara, Aug. 20, 1910, in ibid., p. 492.

643 "On which side": Amos E. Pinchot, *History of the Progressive Party, 1912–1916* (New York: New York University Press, 1958), p. 115.

643 "a county fair": Robert S. La Forte, "Theodore Roosevelt's Osawatomie Speech," *Kansas Historical Quarterly* (Summer 1966), pp. 195, 196–97.

643 with fireworks . . . food stands: *New York Tribune*, Sept. 1, 1910.

643 Climbing onto a kitchen table . . . "the front rank": *Washington Times*, Sept. 1, 1910.

643 the speech had gone . . . Herbert Croly: Pinchot, *History of the Progressive Party*, pp. 112–13.

644 "The New Nationalism . . . go forward as a nation": Theodore Roosevelt, *The New Nationalism* (New York: Outlook, 1910).

644 "My friends": La Forte, "Theodore Roosevelt's Osawatomie Speech," *Kansas Historical Quarterly* (Summer 1966), p. 197.

644 he was "the leader": Char Miller, *Gifford Pinchot and the Making of Modern Environmentalism* (Washington, DC: Island Press/Shearwater Books, 2001), pp. 235–36.

644 "Advanced Insurgent . . . materially strengthened": *Washington Times*, Sept. 1, 1910.

644 "frenzied applause . . . in our Government": Sydney Brooks, "The Confusion of American Politics," *Fortnightly Review* (October 1910), pp. 648–49.

645 "this new Napoleon": La Forte, "Theodore Roosevelt's Osawatomie Speech," *Kansas Historical Quarterly* (Summer 1966), p. 198.

645 "slight mention . . . form of attack": *National Tribune*, Sept. 8, 1910.

645 "He is going quite beyond": WHT to Charles P. Taft, Sept. 10, 1910, WHTP.

645 "wild ideas" . . . decent "conservative": WHT to Horace Taft, Sept. 16, 1910, WHTP.

645 "on the other side . . . against machine politics": Horace Taft to WHT, Sept. 15, 1910, WHTP.

645 "riotous reception . . . not supporting me": WHT to Horace Taft, Sept. 16, 1910, WHTP.

645 "I dared to include": WHT to Charles P. Taft, Sept. 10, 1910, WHTP.

645 Gossipmongers exacerbated . . . the nomination: AB to Clara, Sept. 17, 1910, in AB, *Taft and Roosevelt*, Vol. 2, pp. 514–15.

645 "I know how . . . misconstrued by me": AB to Clara, September [n.d.], 1910, in ibid., pp. 529–30.

646 "He told me . . . will be placed": AB to Clara, Sept. 17, 1910, in ibid., p. 515.

646 "a connected conversation": AB to Clara, Jan. 2, 1910, AB Letters.

646 "the buffer . . . to a standstill": AB to Clara, Aug. 4, 1910, AB Letters.

646 "became separated . . . pretty awful": Anthony, *Nellie Taft*, p. 280.

646 "to die in harness": AB to Clara, April 14, 1910, AB Letters.

646 "something young and prettier": AB to Clara, Oct. 4, 1910, AB Letters.

646 "I suppose you will have": AB to Clara, July 6, 1910, in AB, *Taft and Roosevelt*, Vol. 2, p. 436.

647 "step out of the way . . . like a gentleman": WHT to Horace Taft, Sept. 16, 1910, WHTP.

647 "on the Eve . . . away with radicalism": *Washington Times*, Sept. 24, 1910.

647 "Twenty years ago . . . on good terms": TR to HCL, Sept. 21, 1910, in *LTR*, Vol. 7, pp. 135–36.

647 unity might "turn the scale": TR to TR, Jr., Sept. 21, 1910, in ibid., p. 133.

647 "made a point of being": TR to HCL, Sept. 21, 1910, in ibid., pp. 135–36.

647 "not genial and quite offish": AB to Clara, Sept. 20, 1910, in AB, *Taft and Roosevelt*, Vol. 2, p. 524.

647 "had spoken first": WHT to HHT, Sept. 24, 1910, WHTP.

647 "very irritating . . . genuine wisdom": TR to HCL, Sept. 21, 1910, in *LTR*, Vol. 7, p. 135.

648 Roosevelt's opponents jumped on the story: *New York Tribune*, Sept. 20, 1910.

648 a statement "emphatically" denying: *Times Dispatch* (Richmond, VA), Sept. 21, 1910.

648 "to beg for assistance": TR to HCL, Sept. 21, 1910, in *LTR*, Vol. 7, p. 135.

648 "farther apart than ever": AB to Clara, Sept. 20, 1910, in AB, *Taft and Roosevelt*, Vol. 2, p. 518.

648 "riotous cheers . . . passed up to the platform": *Washington Herald*, Sept. 28, 1910.

648 "an enemy of the nation . . . public safety": *New York Tribune*, Sept. 27, 1910.

648 "catcalls . . . for Col. Gruber": *San Francisco Call*, Sept. 28, 1910.

648 Roosevelt's supporters were anxious: *Washington Herald*, Sept. 28, 1910.

648 567 votes against . . . 445: Morris, *Colonel Roosevelt*, p. 114.

648   "to our able, upright": *Omaha* [NE] *Daily Bee*, Sept. 28, 1910.

648   "The house party has been": WHT to HHT, Sept. 28, 1910, WHTP.

649   "Bulletins . . . from New York": AB to Clara, Sept. 27, 1910, in AB, *Taft and Roosevelt*, Vol. 2, p. 531.

649   "I hope you saw": WHT to HHT, Sept. 28, 1910, WHTP.

649   "We had a delicious table": George Wickersham to HHT, Oct. 2, 1910, WHTP.

649   "should have lost everything": TR to TR, Jr., Oct. 3, 1910, TRJP.

649   Pinchot refused to back the ticket: TR to TR, Jr., Oct. 19, 1910, in *LTR*, Vol. 7, p. 145.

649   "I think it absurd . . . as radical as I am": TR to William Kent, Nov. 28, 1910, in ibid., p. 176.

649   "have been nearly insane": TR to Theodore Roosevelt, Jr., Sept. 21, 1910, in ibid., p. 133.

649   "the wild-eyed radicals": TR to TR, Jr., Oct. 19, 1910, in ibid., p. 145.

649   "I had one . . . force me to be a candidate": RSB, Notebook, Oct. 5, 1910, RSB Papers.

650   "usual moral punch . . . finest characteristics": RSB, Notebook, Oct. 6, 1910, RSB Papers.

650   "the old game . . . radical & conservative": RSB, Notebook, Oct. 8, 1910, RSB Papers.

650   "I am being nearly worked": TR to ARC, Oct. 7, 1910, TRC.

650   When Democrats won an "unprecedented" victory: *National Tribune*, Oct. 27, 1910.

650   "If Mr. Roosevelt can save": *Literary Digest*, Nov. 5, 1910, p. 775.

650   "it will be practically": *NYT*, Oct. 5, 1910.

651   the strength of the Democratic victory "stunned Washington": *National Tribune*, Nov. 17, 1910.

651   Democrats gained control . . . the forty-eight states: Andrew Busch, *Horses in Midstream: U.S. Midterm Elections and Their Consequences, 1894–1998* (Pittsburgh: University of Pittsburgh Press, 1999), p. 85; Sullivan, *Our Times*, Vol. 4, p. 452.

651   "The Democratic party": Mowry, *Theodore Roosevelt and the Progressive Movement*, p. 156.

651   "crushing rebuke" to Theodore: *NYT*, Nov. 9, 1910.

651   "defeat would have come": *Literary Digest*, Nov. 19, 1910, p. 917.

651   "New Nationalism has been pitched": *NYT*, Nov. 9, 1910.

651   "to be a fatal . . . triumphantly elected": *Literary Digest*, Nov. 19, 1910, p. 917.

651   "The trail that Mr. Roosevelt": *Current Literature* (December 1910), p. 585.

651   This "tremendous overthrow": *Literary Digest*, Nov. 19, 1910, p. 916.

651   "the chief architect": Ibid., p. 917.

651   "a smashing defeat": TR to Arthur Hamilton Lee, Nov. 11, 1910, in *LTR*, Vol. 7, p. 163.

651   He recognized that he had lost support . . . "envenomed hatred": TR to Benjamin Ide Wheeler, Nov. 21, 1910, in ibid., p. 173.

652   "The American people": TR to WAW, Dec. 12, 1910, in ibid., p. 182.

652   "Don't go": Sullivan, *Our Times*, Vol. 4, p. 453.

652   "in a most depressed . . . benefit to his country": AB to Clara, Jan. 19, 1910, in AB, *Taft and Roosevelt*, Vol. 2, pp. 579–81.

652   "It was not only a landslide": AB to Clara, Nov. 9, 1910, in ibid., p. 556.

652   "whole drift . . . govern the country": AB to Clara, Jan. 30, 1910, in ibid., Vol. 1, p. 272.

652   "took a whack . . . would have been the same": AB to Clara, Nov. 9, 1910, in ibid., Vol. 2, p. 555.

652   "The warmth of . . . the Philippines!": AB to Clara, Nov. 11, 1910, in ibid., pp. 556–57.

653   "It is always back . . . here in Washington": AB to Clara, Nov. 24, 1910, in ibid., p. 563.

653   While Taft was away, Roosevelt . . . meet with old friends: *Washington Times*, Nov. 17 & 19, 1910.

653   he stopped at the White House: New York *Sun*, Nov. 20, 1910.

653   To accommodate the increased . . . security guards: *Evening Independent* (Massillon, OH), Oct. 18, 1909.

653   "in the center": William Seale, *The President's House: A History*, Vol. 2 (Washington, DC: White House Hist. Assoc. with the cooperation of the National Geographic Society, 1986), pp. 756–58.

653   "severe rectangular room": *Evening Independent*, Oct. 18, 1909.

653   "Oh, yes": New York *Sun*, Nov. 20, 1910.

653   "it would gratify me": WHT to TR, Nov. 25, 1910, TRP.

653   "You are a trump": TR to WHT, Nov. 28, 1910, WHTP.

653   would be "private citizens": WHT to TR, Nov. 30, 1910, TRP.

653   "I have always felt": TR to WHT, Dec. 8, 1910, WHTP.

654   And Taft wrote yet again: WHT to TR, Dec. 2, 1910, WHTP.

654   "I have read your Message": TR to WHT, Dec. 8, 1910, WHTP.

654   "I see signs of the clouds": AB to Clara, Dec. 26, 1910, in AB, *Taft and Roosevelt*, Vol. 2, p. 570.

654   smooth "the rough edges": AB to Clara, Jan. 7, 1911, AB Letters.

654   On Christmas Day . . . first year as president: AB to Clara, Dec. 26, 1910, in AB, *Taft and Roosevelt*, Vol. 2, p. 570.

654   "kneeled on it to look": AB to Clara, Jan. 7, 1911, AB Letters.

654   "to bestow by exchange": WHT to EKR, Dec. 31, 1910, in Morris, *EKR*, p. 338.

654   Both Theodore and Edith were touched: TR to WHT, Jan. 7, 1911, in *LTR*, Vol. 7, p. 204.

654   "brings the two families . . . in a museum": AB to Clara, Dec. 26, 1910, in AB, *Taft and Roosevelt*, Vol. 2, p. 570.

CHAPTER TWENTY-SIX: "Like a War Horse"

Page
655   "where they compromised . . . out of his head": WAW to Mark Sullivan, Nov. 22, 1910, White Papers.
656   On January 21 . . . the initiative, referendum, and recall: Robert M. La Follette [hereafter RLF] to LS, Jan. 14, 1911, LS Papers.
656   "nine U.S. Senators": *Current Literature* (March 1911).
656   Progressive Federation of Publicists and Editors: Mowry, *Theodore Roosevelt and the Progressive Movement*, p. 173.
656   "a roll call" . . . Lincoln Steffens: *NYT*, Jan. 14, 1911.
656   "a sort of pathologist": Kaplan, *Lincoln Steffens*, p. 167.
656   "I am hungry": RLF to LS, Nov. 6, 1909, LS Papers.
656   "an anti-Taft movement": *National Tribune*, Feb. 2, 1911.
656   "Nothing . . . could be more reasonable": *Current Literature* (March 1911).
656   "a much larger . . . popular government": *National Tribune*, Feb. 2, 1911.
657   "Now, Colonel . . . name and influence?": RLF to TR, Jan. 9, 1911, TRP.
657   La Follette considered Roosevelt an opportunist: RLF, *La Follette's Autobiography*, pp. 215–18.
657   "an extremist . . . fanaticism": TR to TR, Jr., Nov. 21, 1910, TRP.
657   "That is a mighty nice letter": TR to RLF, Jan. 24, 1911, in *LTR*, Vol. 7, p. 214.
657   "merely a means": TR to RLF, Jan. 3, 1911, in ibid., p. 202.
657   "very anxious not to seem": TR to RLF, Jan. 24, 1911, in ibid., p. 215.
657   On March 8, 1911, Theodore Roosevelt embarked: *New York Tribune*, Mar. 7, 1911.
657   "not care a rap": TR to Lady Delamere, Mar. 7, 1911, TRC.
657   "fairly universal . . . my own work": TR to William Dudley Foulke, Jan. 2, 1911, in *LTR*, Vol. 7, p. 196.
657   Eight thousand . . . in Atlanta: *Times Dispatch* (Richmond, Va.), Mar. 9, 1911.
657   30,000 . . . in Tacoma, Washington: *San Juan Islander* (Friday Harbor, WA), April 14, 1911.
657   "as uproarious as": *Bemidji Daily Pioneer* (St. Paul, MN), April 15, 1911.
657   "heavier and slightly grayer": *Seattle Star*, April 7, 1911.
657   "without the slightest sign": *San Francisco Call*, Mar. 24, 1911.
657   "all traffic was . . . cheering admirers": *San Juan Islander* (Friday Harbor, WA), April 14, 1911.
657   The Commercial Club . . . and cockatoos: *Arizona Republican* (Phoenix, AZ), April 4, 1911.
658   "If there could be any monument": *Bisbee* [AZ] *Daily Review*, Mar. 19, 1911.
658   "abiding popularity . . . the United States created": *Leavenworth* [WA] *Echo*, April 14, 1911.
658   "low tariff and downward revision man": WHT to TR, Jan. 10, 1911, TRP.
658   "concurrent legislation": Pringle, *Life and Times*, Vol. 2, p. 587.
658   "At one stroke . . . policy of his own": *Current Literature* (March 1911).
659   "well-considered . . . country behind him": Ibid., p. 6.
659   "sit still and await results": *Washington Times*, Jan. 30, 1911.
659   "breakfast, lunch and dinner": AB to Clara, June 27, 1911, AB Letters.
659   a "week-end sail": *National Tribune*, June 13, 1911.
659   "linked together . . . the productive forces": *Current Literature* (March 1911), p. 4.
659   "What you propose . . . party in the end": TR to WHT, Jan. 12, 1911, WHTP.
659   Roosevelt "vigorously advocated": *Chicago Daily Tribune*, Feb. 23, 1911.
659   "it should always be": Extract from a speech delivered by Theodore Roosevelt in New York City on Feb. 13, 1911, WHTP.
659   "expected the insurgents": WHT to Charles P. Taft, July 22, 1911, WHTP.
659   "Give us something": *New York Tribune*, Jan. 28, 1911.
660   "politics makes . . . citadel of protection": *Current Literature* (March 1911), p. 2.
660   "Washington grows weary . . . as selfish": *Washington Herald*, July 6, 1911.
660   La Follette . . . announced his candidacy: *Washington Times*, June 17, 1911.
660   "trying to manufacture": *Washington Herald*, July 6, 1911.
660   "a great epoch": WHT to Charles P. Taft, July 22, 1911, WHTP.
660   "Today will be . . . have been impossible": *Washington Times*, July 24, 1911.
660   Canadian Parliament had descended into "hysteria": Pringle, *Life and Times*, Vol. 2, p. 597.
660   Conservative opponents . . . negotiations to begin: *Washington Times*, July 24, 1911.
660   "Canada is now": New York *Evening World*, Feb. 15, 1911.
660   "bad faith . . . annexation of Canada": *Chicago Daily Tribune*, Feb. 23, 1911.
661   "has gained remarkably": *Washington Herald*, July 24, 1911.
661   Roosevelt, who "strongly urged" him: Henry L. Stimson and McGeorge Bundy, *On Active Service in Peace and War* (New York: Harper Bros., 1948), p. 28.

661 "If two years ago": TR to James R. Garfield, April 28, 1911, in *LTR*, Vol. 7, p. 246.
661 "as much aloof": TR to TR, Jr., June 20, 1911, in *LTR*, Vol. 2, p. 293.
661 "would be remembered": *National Tribune*, June 22, 1911.
661 The mansion and the gardens . . . many other distinguished guests: *Washington Times*, June 19, 1911.
661 "a unique distinction": *Washington Herald*, June 19, 1911.
661 Nellie invited . . . Theodore Roosevelt: *Salt Lake Tribune*, June 17, 1911.
661 "how truly pretty" . . . shouting for help: AB to Clara, May 14, 1911, in AB, *Taft and Roosevelt*, Vol. 2, pp. 650–51.
662 "similar to the first . . . to find her words": Helen Taft Manning to Robert Taft, May 15, 1911, in Anthony, *Nellie Taft*, p. 304.
662 "the defect in her speech": WHT to Horace Taft, May 25, 1911, WHTP.
662 "suffered a serious . . . regret and sympathy": *Emporia* [KS] *Gazette*, May 18, 1911.
662 Determined to realize . . . her slender figure: *Washington Herald*, June 20, 1911.
662 "every detail . . . finished on time": New York *Sun*, June 19, 1911.
662 aides clad in "immaculate white": *Washington Herald*, June 20, 1911.
662 "A mighty shout . . . everybody smiled": *National Tribune*, June 29, 1911.
662 The applause continued: *Washington Herald*, June 20, 1911.
662 "the last hand was shaken": *National Tribune*, June 29, 1911.
662 "skipped lightly . . . happy as a boy": *Washington Herald*, June 29, 1911.
663 "chatted, laughed . . . Secretary of War": William Manners, *TR and Will: A Friendship That Split the Republican Party* (New York: Harcourt, Brace & World, 1969), p. 192.
663 Roosevelt had promised . . . he declined: William H. Cowles to Henry L. Stimson, June 7, 1911, WHTP.
663 "misguided friends" of the president: *Chicago Daily Tribune*, June 7, 1911.
663 "under no circumstance . . . mutual friend": *Atlanta Constitution*, June 7, 1911.
663 "This is the best political": *Hartford Herald*, June 14, 1911.
663 "affirm or deny . . . like a repetition": *San Francisco Chronicle*, June 8, 1911.
663 "an unqualified falsehood": *NYT*, June 7, 1911.
663 "It was outrageous": TR to Edward A. Van Valkenburg, June 14, 1911, in *LTR*, Vol. 7, p. 286.
663 "threw a bombshell . . . considerable chagrin": *Chicago Daily Tribune*, June 7, 1911.
663 forged an agreement . . . "subject to arbitration": *Salt Lake Tribune*, Aug. 5, 1911.
663 "the great jewel . . . the greatest act": AB to Clara, April 30, 1911, in AB, *Taft and Roosevelt*, Vol. 2, p. 635.
663 "The ideal to which": *San Francisco Call*, Sept. 8, 1911.
664 "the interests of": *New York Tribune*, Oct. 18, 1911.
664 "minimize . . . be traced to it": *Daily Kennebec Journal* (Augusta, ME), May 31, 1911.
664 "She meant so much": AB to Clara, Aug. 4, 1911, in AB, *Taft and Roosevelt*, Vol. 2, pp. 730–31.
664 "No self-respecting nation": TR, "The Arbitration Treaty with Great Britain," *Outlook*, May 20, 1911, p. 97.
664 "greatly disappointed . . . old chief": AB to Clara, May 18, 1911, AB Letters.
664 "mushy . . . for adequate cause": TR to James A. Drain, June 19, 1911, in *LTR*, Vol. 7, p. 287.
664 "It is one of our prime duties": TR, "The Peace of Righteousness," *Outlook*, Sept. 9, 1911, pp. 66, 69, 70.
664 "I am afraid the old fellow": AB to Clara, Sept. 8, 1911, in AB, *Taft and Roosevelt*, Vol. 2, p. 753.
665 On September 15 . . . through the West: *Los Angeles Herald*, Nov. 12, 1911.
665 "The White House is once more": *New York Tribune*, Sept. 17, 1911.
665 "every comfort . . . real beds": *Washington Times*, Sept. 13, 1911.
665 "taking medicine": WHT to Otto Bannard, Sept. 10, 1911, WHTP.
665 he had worked hard . . . and reciprocity: WHT to Charles P. Taft, Sept. 16, 1911, WHTP.
665 "bright skies": *Marion* [OH] *Daily Mirror*, Sept. 16, 1911.
665 "thought to be . . . a square deal": Gustav J. Karger, "Report from Taft's Western Trip," Sept. 1911, Taft-Karger MSS, CMC.
665 "reported in full . . . before the people": WHT to J. C. Hemphill, Nov. 16, 1911, WHTP.
665 "The bets seem to be": Horace Taft to WHT, Sept. 21, 1911, WHTP.
665 "ablaze with red fire": *Washington Herald*, Sept. 20, 1911.
665 "Laurier government": Pringle, *Life and Times*, Vol. 2, p. 598.
665 "an overwhelming . . . to reciprocity": *National Tribune*, Sept. 28, 1911.
665 "an Imperishable Canada": *Times Dispatch*, Sept. 23, 1911.
665 "dead as a ducat": *National Tribune*, Sept. 28, 1911.
665 "We were hit squarely": WHT to Horace Taft, Sept. 26, 1911, WHTP.
666 "for naught . . . little worse off": *National Tribune*, Sept. 28, 1911.
666 "a terrible blow . . . needed it most": Cited in the *Salt Lake Tribune*, Sept. 29, 1911.
666 Taft remained disconsolate . . . four hundred speeches: AB to Clara, Nov. 20, 1911, in AB, *Taft and Roosevelt*, Vol. 2, p. 765.

666   "by all odds" . . . most successful: AB to Clara, Sept. 8, 1911, in ibid., p. 762.

666   "dry and full . . . could almost cry": AB to Clara, Oct. 5, 1911, in ibid., p. 757.

666   "to see him . . . no sign": "The President's Journey," *Outlook*, Nov. 11, 1911, p. 606.

666   "The Taft trip has proved": *NYT*, Oct. 29, 1911.

666   he weighed 332 pounds: Manners, *TR and Will*, p. 210.

666   Butt worried constantly . . . markedly increased: AB to Clara, Nov. 20, 1911, in AB, *Taft and Roosevelt*, Vol. 2, p. 765.

666   "I had not suspected": AB to Clara, Nov. 27, 1911, in ibid., pp. 769–70.

666   "too heavy . . . three hundred pounds": WHT to Delia Torrey, Nov. 29, 1911, WHTP.

667   "I absolutely agree . . . the Democratic Party": TR to Hiram Warren Johnson, Oct. 27, 1911, in *LTR*, Vol. 7, pp. 419–20.

667   Banner headlines . . . Henry Frick: "The Government and the Steel Corporation," *Outlook*, Nov. 4, 1911, p. 547.

667   "a gigantic monopoly": *Manchester Guardian* (UK), Oct. 27, 1911.

667   "the dissolution . . . subsidiaries": *The Independent*, Nov. 2, 1911.

667   "that a desire to stop": *St. Louis* [MO] *Post-Dispatch*, Oct. 28, 1911.

667   "Roosevelt Was Deceived": Manners, *TR and Will*, p. 200.

667   "Roosevelt Fooled": Pringle, *Life and Times*, Vol. 2, p. 670.

667   "Ignorance as a Defense": *St. Louis* [MO] *Post-Dispatch*, Oct. 28, 1911.

667   "been named as a": *New York Herald*, Nov. 18, 1911.

668   "This is an official statement": *Philadelphia Record,* cited in *St. Louis Post-Dispatch*, Oct. 28, 1911.

668   "What I did": TR to Everett P. Wheeler, Oct. 30, 1911, in *LTR*, Vol. 7, p. 430.

668   "It was not a question": TR, "The Steel Corporation and the Panic of 1907," *Outlook*, Aug. 19, 1911, p. 866.

668   "was misled . . . the truth": TR, "The Trusts, the People, and the Square Deal," *Outlook*, Nov. 18, 1911, pp. 650–51.

668   "Taft was a member": TR to James R. Garfield, Oct. 31, 1911, in *LTR*, Vol. 7, pp. 430–31.

668   "should have been . . . his subordinates take": TR to Everett P. Wheeler, Oct. 30, 1911, in ibid., p. 430.

668   "never forgive . . . of the case": AB to Clara, Jan. 15, 1912, in AB, *Taft and Roosevelt*, Vol. 2, p. 813.

668   Never content to remain . . . anti-trust policy: TR, "The Trusts, the People, and the Square Deal," *Outlook*, Nov. 18, 1911, p. 649.

668   "felt the heavy hand": TR, "The Government and the Steel Corporations," *Outlook*, Nov. 4, 1911, p. 574.

668   "embarked upon . . . rolling over the trusts": *National Tribune*, Oct. 19, 1911.

669   "probably one hundred": Pringle, *Life and Times*, Vol. 2, pp. 668–69.

669   "The times have . . . old-fashioned": *National Tribune*, Oct. 19, 1911.

669   "dead letters" . . . harm to "the innocent": TR, "The Trusts, the People, and the Square Deal," *Outlook*, Nov. 18, 1911, pp. 651–52, 653, 656.

669   "Taft Wrong, Says Roosevelt": New York *Sun*, Nov. 17, 1911.

669   "Colonel Finds": *Boston Herald*, Nov. 17, 1911.

669   "Roosevelt Takes Issue": *Chicago Record-Herald*, Nov. 17, 1911.

669   "tens of thousands": TR to Charles D. Willard, Dec. 11, 1911, in *LTR*, Vol. 7, p. 454.

669   "Roosevelt's broadside": *Chicago Daily Tribune*, Nov. 18, 1911.

669   More conservative Republicans . . . position on trusts: Mowry, *Theodore Roosevelt and the Progressive Movement*, pp. 192–93.

670   "a striking revival": *NYT*, Dec. 22, 1911.

670   "a thousand questions": *National Tribune*, Dec. 21, 1911.

670   "bringing [him] forward . . . to the surface": TR to William Bailey Howland, Dec. 23, 1911, in *LTR*, Vol. 7, p. 466.

670   "in an almost astonishing fashion": James R. Garfield to Gifford Pinchot, Nov. 28, 1911, Garfield Papers.

670   A poll taken . . . Taft and La Follette: *New Castle* [PA] *News*, Dec. 8, 1911.

670   Nebraska Republicans . . . primary ballot: *NYT*, Dec. 22, 1911.

670   "Events in all parts": *New Castle* [PA] *News*, Dec. 8, 1911.

670   "a flat-footed denial . . . anxious days": *National Tribune*, Dec. 21, 1911.

670   "The Autobiography of an Insurgent": RSB, Notebook, September [n.d.], 1911, RSB Papers.

670   "almost unanimous" endorsement: James R. Garfield, Diary, Oct. 16, 1911, Garfield Papers.

670   "the logical . . . and prolonged applause": *NYT*, Nov. 28, 1911.

670   La Follette found it challenging: Pinchot, *History of the Progressive Party,*, pp. 42–43.

670   "Will Roosevelt be . . . slip in": RSB, Notebook, Nov. 26, 1911, RSB Papers.

671   "encouraging La Follette . . . Liberal Movement": JSP to WAW, Jan. 5, 1912, White Papers.

671   "like a war horse . . . again in January": RSB, Notebook, Dec. 8, 1911, RSB Papers.

671 "absolutely plain . . . into the game": RSB to RLF, Dec. 8, 1911, La Follette Papers.
671 "Now, Butt . . . but do it soon": AB to Clara, Dec. 4, 1911, in AB, *Taft and Roosevelt*, Vol. 2, p. 776.

CHAPTER TWENTY-SEVEN: "My Hat Is in the Ring"

Page
672 "The Colonel is . . . of ultimate results": LS to Allen H. Suggett, Jan. 24, 1912, in LS et al., eds., *Letters of Lincoln Steffens*, Vol. 1, p. 287.
672 "seek the nomination": TR to Frank Andrew Munsey, Jan. 16, 1912, in *LTR*, Vol. 7, p. 479.
672 "a genuine popular . . . do the job": TR to Herbert Spencer Hadley, Jan. 23, 1912, in ibid., p. 489.
673 he would "of course" accept: TR to Henry Beach Needham, Jan. 9, 1912, in ibid., p. 475.
673 "Events have been moving": TR to Chase Salmon Osborn, Jan. 18, 1912, in ibid., p. 484.
673 If the governors . . . announcement of his candidacy: Ibid., p. 485.
673 "not for his sake": Harold Howland, *Theodore Roosevelt and His Times: A Chronicle of the Progressive Movement* (New Haven: Yale University Press, 1921), p. 210.
673 "the living embodiment . . . a single candidate": *NYT*, Jan. 2, 1912.
673 La Follette was furious: Nancy C. Unger, *Fighting Bob La Follette: The Righteous Reformer* (Chapel Hill: University of North Carolina Press, 2000), p. 201.
673 "Carnegie Hall . . . never lost it": Cited in Belle Case La Follette and Fola La Follette, *Robert M. La Follette, June 14, 1855–June 18, 1925* (New York: The Macmillan Company, 1953), Vol. 1, pp. 388–90.
673 They worried . . . divide the progressive vote: Pinchot, *History of the Progressive Party, 1912–1916*, p. 133.
673 "Roosevelt or bust!": *Chicago Tribune*, Jan. 11, 1912; La Follette, *La Follette's Autobiography*, p. 579.
673 "a stalking horse": Pinchot, *History of the Progressive Party, 1912–1916*, p. 133.
674 "When Roosevelt left . . . better than 1916": *NYT*, Oct. 4, 1912.
674 "painful" conference . . . to "fight alone": Pinchot, *History of the Progressive Party, 1912–1916*, p. 134.
674 "When I gave": Unger, *Fighting Bob La Follette*, p. 202.
674 "Senator La Follette": *Logansport* [IN] *Pharos-Tribune*, Jan. 30, 1912.
674 doctors diagnosed . . . tuberculosis . . . the morning after the banquet: La Follette and La Follette, *Robert M. La Follette*, Vol. 1, pp. 399, 404; Unger, *Fighting Bob La Follette*, pp. 202–3.
674 Wilson had earlier delivered . . . charming, and short: *NYT*, Oct. 21, 1917.
674 "took a great gobletful": WAW, *The Autobiography*, p. 449.
674 "money power . . . what they are told to write": La Follette, *La Follette's Autobiography*, pp. 607–8, 605.
675 "to bring together": La Follette and La Follette, *Robert M. La Follette*, Vol. 1, p. 403.
675 "frankly sick": *NYT*, Oct. 21, 1917.
675 "acid and raucous": Wister, *Roosevelt: The Story of a Friendship*, p. 300.
675 "predatory interests": *NYT*, Oct. 21, 1917.
675 "shook his fist . . . about themselves": Wister, *Roosevelt: The Story of a Friendship*, p. 300.
675 "his dagger-like forefinger . . . facts for once!": *NYT*, Oct. 21, 1917.
675 During the first two hours: *NYT*, Feb. 3, 1912.
675 As midnight approached . . . to get him to stop: Pinchot, *History of the Progressive Party, 1912–1916*, pp. 134–35.
675 "You can't drown . . . minions of the trust": *NYT*, Oct. 21, 1917.
675 "with closed eyes": Pinchot, *History of the Progressive Party, 1912–1916*, p. 135.
675 "the greatest speech . . . tragedy beyond tears": RSB, *American Chronicle*, pp. 267–68.
676 "a short rest . . . switch to Roosevelt": La Follette, *La Follette's Autobiography*, p. 610.
676 "ill health . . . progressive movement": *Washington Herald*, Feb. 19, 1912.
676 "I want to let you know": McClure to Belle Case La Follette, Feb. 6, 1912, McClure MSS.
676 "last great series . . . a few men": Lyon, *Success Story*, p. 326.
676 the "justice" it deserved: McClure to Belle Case La Follette, Feb. 6, 1912, McClure MSS.
676 "Your letter . . . you as a friend": Belle Case La Follette to McClure, Feb. 9, 1912, McClure MSS.
676 "Poor Senator La Follette": TR to John Callan O'Laughlin, Feb. 8, 1912, in *LTR*, Vol. 7, pp. 499–500.
677 "The trouble with . . . big, black cloud": AB to Clara, Dec. 19, 1911, in AB, *Taft and Roosevelt*, Vol. 2, p. 794.
677 "the whole plan . . . handicap": AB to Clara, Dec. 20, 1911, in ibid., p. 798.
677 "I hate to . . . a third term": WHT to Horace Taft, Feb. 15, 1912, WHTP (italics added).
677 "My devotion to the Colonel": AB to Clara, Jan. 13, 1912, in AB, *Taft and Roosevelt*, Vol. 2, p. 812.
677 "is so honest": AB to Clara, Dec. 19, 1911, in ibid., p. 794.
677 "A President sees . . . as Archie Butt": WHT, "Tribute to Major Butt," in Archie Butt and William Howard Taft, *Both Sides of the Shield* (Philadelphia: J. B. Lippincott Co., 1912), pp. vii, x.
678 "Delighted": AB to Clara, Jan. 27, 1912, in AB, *Taft and Roosevelt*, Vol. 2, p. 827.
678 "Go by all means . . . make you happy": Ibid.
678 "like a leaf . . . by me was significant": AB to Clara, Jan. 29, 1912, in ibid., pp. 828–29, 831, 833, 835.

678 "more bitter . . . at each other": AB to Clara, Feb. 14, 1912, in ibid., pp. 843–44.

678 "cheering spectators . . . a boisterous reception": *Marion* [OH] *Daily Mirror*, Feb. 21, 1912.

678 "more familiar than": *Evening Standard* (Ogden City, UT), Feb. 21, 1912.

678 "We Progressives believe . . . in the hands of the people": TR, "A Charter of Democracy," in *WTR*, Vol. 17, *Social Justice and Popular Rule* (New York: Charles Scribner's Sons, 1976), p. 119–20.

679 his characteristic "balanced statements": Pinchot, *History of the Progressive Party, 1912–1916*, p. 141.

679 "encourage legitimate . . . let it be *their* majority that decides": TR, "A Charter of Democracy," in *WTR*, Vol. 17, pp. 124, 125, 139, 142, 146 (italics added).

679 The "damaging effect": *NYT*, Feb. 26, 1912.

679 "a plebiscite . . . supreme jurisdiction": New York *Sun*, Feb. 22, 1912.

679 "Mr. Roosevelt's incapacity" . . . rendering his nomination impossible: Cited in *New York Tribune*, Feb. 22, 1912.

680 "Theodore has gone off": Jessup, *Elihu Root*, Vol. 2, p. 180.

680 "That was so unlike": Straus, *Under Four Administrations*, pp. 310–11.

680 "I am opposed . . . most intimate friends": *NYT*, Feb. 26, 1912.

680 "the sanctity of the judiciary": Garraty, *Henry Cabot Lodge: A Biography*, p. 287.

680 "I have had my share": TR to HCL, Feb. 28, 1912, in TR and HCL, *Selections from the Correspondence*, Vol. 2, pp. 423–24.

680 "My dear fellow": TR to HCL, Mar. 1, 1912, in *LTR*, Vol. 7, p. 515.

680 "at a gallop . . . swerved and wheeled": TR to HCL, Oct. 3, 1911, in ibid., p. 400.

680 The concussion . . . three weeks of bed rest: TR to ARC, Oct. 5, 1911, TRC.

680 "She is very much shattered": TR to William Cowles, Oct. 27, 1911, in TR, *Letters from Theodore Roosevelt to Anna Roosevelt Cowles, 1870–1918*, p. 297.

680 "Politics are hateful": EKR to Kermit Roosevelt, Feb. 11, 1912, in Morris, *EKR*, p. 376.

680 "At the worst of it": EKR to Arthur Lee, April (n.d.), 1912, in ibid., pp. 550–51.

680 "the quandary . . . sorry for any one": ARL, *Crowded Hours*, pp. 185–86.

681 "Of course you must be": TR to Nicholas Longworth, Feb. 13, 1912, in *LTR*, Vol. 7, p. 503.

681 "single-minded in enthusiasm": ARL, *Crowded Hours*, p. 186.

681 "I got furious": Cordery, *Alice*, p. 223.

681 "It is not the critic": TR, "Citizenship in a Republic: An Address at the Sorbonne, Paris, April 23, 1910," in *WTR*, Vol. 13, *American Ideals* (New York: Charles Scribner's Sons, 1926), p. 510.

681 "My hat is in the ring . . . in the contest": New York *Evening World*, Feb. 22, 1912.

681 "in the interests . . . unsolicited and unsought": William Ellsworth Glasscock et al. to TR, Feb. 10, 1912, in *LTR*, Vol. 7, p. 511.

681 "I deeply appreciate": TR to William Ellsworth Glasscock et al., Feb. 24, 1912, in ibid., p. 511.

682 "no signs" . . . the Columbus speech: Robert Grant to James Ford Rhodes, Mar. 22, 1912, in Elting E. Morison, ed., *The Days of Armageddon, 1914–1918*, Vol. 8 of *LTR*, pp. 1456–57.

682 "overwhelmingly . . . register that sentiment": WAW to TR, Feb. 2, 1912, White Papers.

682 "an unnecessary and possibly": Robert Grant to James Ford Rhodes, Mar. 22, 1912, in *LTR*, Vol. 8, pp. 1460–61.

682 "for the sake of his own future . . . popular, representative government?": Thayer, *Theodore Roosevelt: An Intimate Biography*, pp. 352–54.

682 "none of them . . . would have dropped out": Robert Grant to James Ford Rhodes, Mar. 22, 1912, *LTR*, Vol. 8, p. 1457.

682 "with conditions . . . been wrong yourself": AB to Clara, Feb. 25, 1912, in AB, *Taft and Roosevelt*, Vol. 2, p. 850.

683 tossing in his bed that night unable to sleep: AB to Clara, Feb. 26, 1912, in ibid., p. 851.

683 "like a steam engine . . . shipshape condition": AB to Clara, Feb. 23, 1912, in ibid., pp. 847–48.

683 "It seems to me": AB to Clara, Feb. 26, 1912, in ibid., p. 851.

683 "He would not hear of it": AB to Kitty, Feb. 27, 1912, in ibid., pp. 851–52.

683 "to leave . . . for the nomination": AB to Clara, Feb. 23, 1912, in ibid., pp. 847–48.

683 "By a strange coincidence": *Washington Post*, Feb. 15, 1912.

683 The Taft men . . . the Munsey Building: *Indianapolis Star*, Feb. 16, 1912.

683 "a very pleasant and winning": Davis, *Released for Publication*, p. 267.

683 Taft selected . . . William Brown McKinley: *California Outlook* (Los Angeles), Feb. 17, 1912.

683 "the sinews of war": *Indianapolis Star*, Feb. 16, 1912.

683 "to devote himself": Gardner, *Departing Glory*, p. 226.

683 And once again, Charley Taft . . . his brother's campaign: *Mt. Sterling* [KY] *Advocate*, June 19, 1912.

684 "without indulging . . . judicial decisions": *Waterloo* [IA] *Daily Reporter*, Feb. 22, 1912.

684 "stirred up . . . atmosphere wonderfully": WHT to Charles P. Taft, Feb. 28, 1912, WHTP.

684 "when all this turmoil": Pringle, *Theodore Roosevelt: A Biography*, p. 556.

684 "the momentary passions . . . of the temple": *NYT*, Feb. 13, 1912.

684 "the ark of the covenant": "The Ark of the Covenant," *Outlook*, April 20, 1912, p. 847.

684 "the axe at the foot": *Washington Post*, Mar. 9, 1912.

684 "genuine ovation . . . extravagant expressions": WHT to Charles P. Taft, Mar. 20, 1912, WHTP.

684 "Taft has behaved . . . overwhelming and bitter": Robert Grant to James Ford Rhodes, Mar. 22, 1912, in *LTR*, Vol. 8, pp. 1460–61.

684 When the election year opened . . . the direct primary: Sullivan, *Our Times*, Vol. 4, p. 494.

684 Fearful that the region's . . . rather than straight Taft victories: Gardner, *Departing Glory*, pp. 228–29.

685 "absolutely sure . . . influence any man": TR to Ormsby McHarg, Mar. 4, 1912, in *LTR*, Vol. 7, p. 516.

685 "the worst riots": *Washington Herald*, April 12, 1912.

685 "despite the frantic . . . jeering at their foes": *NYT*, April 12, 1912.

685 "clubs and baseball bats": *Jasper* [IN] *Weekly Courier*, Mar. 22, 1912.

685 "rode down . . . dynamite explosions": *NYT*, Jan. 24, 1912.

685 in case "any chicanery" occurred: Mowry, *Theodore Roosevelt and the Progressive Movement*, p. 232.

686 "all-night session . . . dropped dead": *El Paso* [TX] *Herald*, Mar. 15, 1912.

686 his "hope that so far": TR to William Ellsworth Glasscock et al., Feb. 24, 1912, in *LTR*, Vol. 7, p. 511.

686 "sluggishly moving cause . . . crusade": Sullivan, *Our Times*, Vol. 4, p. 492.

686 Get the Direct . . . "people demand it": Ibid., pp. 492–93.

686 "no objection at all": WHT to Horace Taft, Mar. 7, 1912, WHTP.

686 "Legislatures are being": *Washington Times*, Mar. 7, 1912.

686 "I do not favor changes": *Washington Herald*, Mar. 8, 1912.

686 "only keep my people": WHT to Horace Taft, Mar. 7, 1912, WHTP.

687 "waved his hand . . . He's all right!": *NYT*, Mar. 21, 1912; TR to Joseph Moore Dixon, Mar. 21, 1912, in *LTR*, Vol. 7, p. 511.

687 "The great . . . fundamentally unworthy": TR, "The Right of the People to Rule: An Address at Carnegie Hall, New York City, March 20 . . ." *Outlook*, Mar. 23, 1912, pp. 618, 620.

687 "ridicule" . . . principles of American government: *NYT*, Mar. 21, 1912.

687 "our government is . . . rule of all the people": TR, "The Right of the People to Rule," *Outlook*, Mar. 23, 1912, pp. 621, 625.

687 As spring commenced . . . finally set for March 26: *Washington Times*, Mar. 27, 1912.

688 the *Chicago Tribune* led a successful campaign: Davis, *Released for Publication*, p. 273.

688 "had his fighting . . . then on another": Unger, *Fighting Bob La Follette*, pp. 215–16.

688 "Today's primary crucial": *Washington Post*, Mar. 19, 1912.

688 the "very bad news": ARL Diary, Mar. 19, 1912, ARL Papers.

688 Though Taft garnered: Unger, *Fighting Bob La Follette*, p. 216.

688 "the East will construe": TR to William Franklin Knox, Mar. 12, 1912, in *LTR*, Vol. 7, p. 525.

688 "The small vote count": *Washington Post*, Mar. 20, 1912.

688 Taft could not anticipate . . . advocacy for reciprocity: *Washington Post*, Mar. 19, 1912.

688 "In a nutshell": *Washington Post*, Mar. 20, 1912.

688 "first trial of the new primary law": *Atlanta Constitution*, Mar. 27, 1912.

688 "They are stealing": Gardner, *Departing Glory*, p. 231.

688 "an entire breakdown": *Atlanta Constitution*, Mar. 27, 1912.

688 "the indisputable fact": *New York Tribune*, Mar. 28, 1912.

689 "in a fighting mood . . . cry of fraud": *NYT*, Mar. 27, 1912.

689 "had cheated . . . days of Tweed": New York *Sun*, Mar. 28, 1912.

689 "should be sorry . . . since the Civil War": *Chicago Daily Tribune*, Mar. 28, 1912.

689 "As an American citizen": *Decatur* [IL] *Daily Review*, April 8, 1912.

689 "Easter came": ARL, *Crowded Hours*, p. 190.

689 "carrying every district . . . to get aboard it": Davis, *Released for Publication*, p. 280.

689 "a stinging rebuke": TR to Joseph Medill McCormick, April 10, 1912, in *LTR*, Vol. 7, p. 533.

689 "We slugged them": *Washington Times*, April 10, 1912.

689 "too good . . . happy I am": ARL Diary, April 9, 1912, ARL Papers.

689 "given his campaign . . . in Pennsylvania": WHT to Howard Hollister, April 9, 1912, WHTP.

690 "for turning the . . . a few hours rest": *Washington Times*, April 14, 1912.

690 "One of the burdens . . . his mendacity": WHT to Horace Taft, April 16, 1912, WHTP.

690 "I wish . . . does another lick": Horace Taft to WHT, April 16, 1912, WHTP.

690 "The stampede . . . into the ring": *Pittsburgh Press*, April 15, 1912.

690 "Of course, Pennsylvania . . . with a knife": John Callan O'Laughlin to TR, April 14, 1912, John Callan O'Laughlin Papers, Manuscript Division, LC [hereafter O'Laughlin Papers].

690 "anxious to be home": Butt to WHT [n.d.], included in letter from Edward Butt to WHT, Oct. 17, 1918, cited in Anthony, *Nellie Taft*, p. 335.

691 "held afloat . . . slowly crawling": *Washington Times*, April 15, 1912.

691 "all onboard . . . no definite information": *NYT*, April 16, 1912.

691 over seven hundred survivors, mainly women and children: *New York Tribune*, April 16, 1912.

691 "regret that Major Butt's name": *Washington Times*, April 16, 1912; telegram from P. A. S. Franklin to President William H. Taft, April 16, 1912, WHTP.

691 "Even with the list": *Washington Post*, April 17, 1912.

691 "news of the disaster": *Washington Post*, April 16, 1912.

691 "greatly depressed": *Washington Post*, April 19, 1912.

691 "his loss as if he had been": *Washington Times*, April 19, 1912.

691 "I miss him every minute": WHT to Mabel Boardman, April 22, 1912, WHTP.

692 "In my own grief . . . close more-than-friend": Marian Thayer to WHT, April 21, 1912, in Hugh Brewster, *Gilded Lives, Fatal Voyage: The Titanic's First-Class Passengers and Their World* (New York: Crown, 2012), pp. 309–10.

692 "A slight rocking of the ship": Marshall Everett, ed., *The Story of the Wreck of the Titanic: Eyewitness Accounts from 1912* (Mineola, NY: Dover Books, 2011), p. 21.

692 "The captain says": Brewster, *Gilded Lives, Fatal Voyage*, p. 167.

692 "the real leader": *Narka* [KS] *News*, April 26, 1912.

692 "My last view . . . every sacrifice made": *Washington Times*, April 19, 1912.

692 "paid tribute . . . loved him sincerely": *NYT*, April 20, 1912.

693 "I can't believe it": ARL Diary, April 16 & 17, 1912, ARL Papers.

693 "Everybody knew Archie" . . . and could not finish: *NYT*, May 6, 1912.

693 "a rush of activities . . . open fire": *Indianapolis Star*, April 21, 1912.

693 "to get down into the ring": WHT to J. C. Hemphill, April 12, 1912, WHTP.

693 "explode a bomb": *NYT*, April 23, 1912.

693 "all night . . . some of his advisers": *NYT*, April 24, 1912.

693 "Frightful": *NYT*, April 23, 1912.

693 "against the accusations": WHT, "Address at Palmer, Mass., April 25, 1912," WHTP.

693 "greatly admired and loved": WHT, "Address at West Brookfield, Mass., April 25, 1912," WHTP.

693 "This wrenches my soul": *NYT*, April 25, 1912.

694 "the cause of constitutionalism": WHT, "Address at Palmer, Mass., April 25, 1912," WHTP.

694 When he arrived at South Station . . . revitalized his supporters: *Chester* [PA] *Times*, April 26, 1912.

694 "Mr. Roosevelt . . . a square deal": *NYT*, April 26, 1912.

694 "throwing aside . . . Theodore Roosevelt": *Lowell* [MA] *Sun*, April 26, 1912.

694 "our Government is . . . danger of a third presidential term": *NYT*, April 26, 1912.

694 "is convinced that" . . . be completed in four years: WHT, "Address at Boston, Mass., April 26, 1912," WHTP.

694 "We are left . . . why not later?": *NYT*, April 26, 1912.

695 "loudly cheered . . . storm of endorsement": *Lowell* [MA] *Sun*, April 26, 1912.

695 "He had cause": Pringle, *Life and Times*, Vol. 2, p. 781.

695 Informed that evening . . . being taken to Halifax: New York *Sun*, April 26, 1912.

695 "to scrutinize . . . recovering": *Atlanta Constitution*, April 26, 1912.

695 "slumped over . . . began to weep": Pringle, *Life and Times*, Vol. 2, pp. 781–82.

695 "If they are anxious": *NYT*, April 25, 1912.

695 "the crowd was keyed up": *Boston Post*, April 27, 1912.

695 "Hit him between the eyes!": Sullivan, *Our Times*, Vol. 4, p. 485.

695 "merciless denunciation": *NYT*, April 27, 1912.

695 "howled with delight": *Boston Daily Globe*, April 27, 1912.

695 "Taft has not only been . . . attitude toward me": *NYT*, April 27, 1912.

695 "This is our first . . . but a mob": *NYT*, April 28, 1912.

696 "rival matinees": *Washington Times*, May 14, 1912.

696 "puzzlewit . . . fathead": TR to Nicholas Longworth, May 9, 1912, in *LTR*, Vol. 7, p. 541n.

696 "You'd suppose there was not": *El Paso* [TX] *Herald*, May 13, 1912.

696 Robert La Follette . . . after a surprisingly good showing: *Bakersfield* [OH] *Morning Echo*, May 15, 1912.

696 focusing most of his ire: *Washington Herald*, May 13, 1912.

696 "the spectacle of a President": New York *Sun*, May 15, 1912.

696 "It is about as painful . . . courage to do so": WHT to Delia Torrey, May 12, 1912, WHTP.

696 "He is having": *Cleveland Plain Dealer*, May 16, 1912.

696 "settled the contest . . . to beat us": *Emporia* [KS] *Gazette*, May 21, 1912.

696 In nine of the thirteen states: "Appendix B: Republic Primary Results, 1912," in Lewis L. Gould, *Four Hats in the Ring: The 1912 Election and the Birth of Modern American Politics* (Lawrence: University Press of Kansas, 2008), p. 190.

696 "I have had so many": WHT to Horace Taft, May 29, 1912, WHTP.

CHAPTER TWENTY-EIGHT: "Bosom Friends, Bitter Enemies"

Page
697 "A month ago": *The Times* (London), May 23, 1912.
697 "the most exciting . . . never before": *Washington Times*, June 6, 1912.
698 "Each side makes": *New York Tribune*, June 16, 1912.
698 "not dare to oppose": TR to T. R. McAnally, May 24, 1912, in *LTR*, Vol. 7, p. 548.
698 The president, however, had far . . . to win at Chicago: WHT to William Worthington, May 29, 1912, WHTP.
698 "No man in this city": *New York Tribune*, June 16, 1912.
698 "the lawyers and witnesses": New York *Sun*, April 21, 1912.
698 "some contests . . . frighten or bulldoze": WHT to William Worthington, May 29, 1912, WHTP.
698 "the contestants had failed": *Washington Times*, June 7, 1912.
698 all too "familiar": Ibid.
699 "been sent to the penitentiary": *Washington Times*, June 10, 1912.
699 "neither justice nor logic": John A. Gable, *The Bull Moose Years: Theodore Roosevelt and the Progressive Party* (Port Washington, NY: Kennikat Press, 1978), p. 15.
699 two-to-one and sometimes ten-to-one margins: TR, "Thou Shalt Not Steal," *Outlook*, July 13, 1912, p. 574.
699 "irregularities" . . . the committee "reversed itself": Mowry, *Theodore Roosevelt and the Progressive Movement*, p. 239.
699 Though Roosevelt's team demonstrated . . . election results: *Washington Times*, June 10, 1912.
699 Texas delegates . . . "fair play": Sidney M. Milkis, *Theodore Roosevelt, the Progressive Party, and the Transformation of American Democracy* (Lawrence: University Press of Kansas, 2009), p. 109.
699 eliminating "boss rule": Gable, *The Bull Moose Years*, p. 15.
700 gave the two San Francisco seats to Taft: *Salt Lake Tribune*, June 13, 1912.
700 "desperate measures . . . offers of money": Ibid.
700 "I dare them . . . may not be seen": *Washington Times*, June 13, 1912.
700 Roosevelt likely deserved . . . between thirty and fifty: Mowry, *Theodore Roosevelt and the Progressive Movement*, pp. 238–39.
700 "to crystallize": *Chicago Daily Tribune*, June 16, 1912.
700 Aware that time was running out . . . in person: Milkis, *Theodore Roosevelt, the Progressive Party, and the Transformation of American Democracy*, p. 110.
700 "he seemed in . . . stolen from them": *NYT*, June 15, 1912.
701 "All the information I get": *Chicago Daily Tribune*, June 15, 1912.
701 leaving Washington correspondents . . . at Chevy Chase: *New York Tribune*, June 8, 9, 13 & 15, 1912.
701 "an undeniable admission": *Chicago Daily Tribune*, June 15, 1912.
701 "absolutely necessary": Ibid.
701 "the last hope of a lost cause": *New York Tribune*, June 16, 1912.
701 "Mr. Roosevelt's departure": *Chicago Daily Tribune*, June 15, 1912.
701 "plum crazy . . . to show up for work": *Washington Times*, June 15, 1912.
701 cried out "thief": Manners, *TR and Will*, p. 235.
701 songs for "Teddy . . . jeers and hoots": *NYT*, June 15, 1912.
701 a special "campaign drink": Manners, *TR and Will*, p. 235.
701 waving "Teddy" flags . . . at the railway yards: *New York Tribune*, June 16, 1912.
701 "The sight of the Colonel . . . to its bosom": Sullivan, *Our Times*, Vol. 4, pp. 505–6.
701 "football tactics": *NYT*, June 16, 1912.
702 "His appearance was . . . steal anything": Ibid.
702 "Give it to 'em . . . Knock 'em out": New York *Sun*, June 16, 1912.
702 "The receiver of stolen": Manners, *TR and Will*, p. 237.
702 "The people will win": *Washington Times*, June 16, 1912.
702 "to stand up . . . like a bull moose": New York *Sun*, June 16, 1912.
702 "to gore his antagonist": *Cedar Rapids* [IA] *Republican*, June 1, 1912.
702 "He is essentially": Elihu Root to E. S. Martin, Mar. 9, 1912, in Jessup, *Elihu Root*, Vol. 2, p. 180.
702 The bull moose icon: Sullivan, *Our Times*, Vol. 4, pp. 506–7.
702 "put in one of": *New York Tribune*, June 16, 1912.
702 "magnetism . . . most desired to see": *Chicago Daily Tribune*, June 17, 1912.
702 "the largest theater" . . . seated only 4,200: *Chicago Daily Tribune*, June 17, 1912.
703 "ingenious" schemes . . . "avalanche of applause": *Chicago Daily Tribune*, June 18, 1912.
703 "the most moving speech": Sullivan, *Our Times*, Vol. 4, p. 508.
703 "one of the most dramatic": *Washington Times*, June 18, 1912.
703 "convinced that Mr. Taft . . . we battle for the Lord": TR, "The Case against the Reactionaries," in *WTR*, Vol. 17, pp. 205–6, 212–13, 228, 231.

703   "There is no question . . . that make nominations": WAW, Literary MSS, 1912, White Papers.

704   "extraordinary preparations" . . . 12,000 people: *National Tribune* (Washington, DC), June 23, 1912.

704   "Passions have been . . . hotel lobbies": *Washington Post*, June 18, 1912.

704   "Whatever happens": TR to Horace Taft, June 18, 1912, WHTP.

704   "If I am nominated": WHT to Felix Agnus, Feb. 29, 1912, WHTP.

704   "I may go down": WHT to William Worthington, May 29, 1912, WHTP.

704   Before convening his cabinet . . . his campaign team: *New York Tribune*, June 19, 1912.

704   McKinley and Charles Hilles . . . the temporary chair: Sullivan, *Our Times*, Vol. 4, p. 514. Technically, as Sullivan points out, the presiding officer was known as the temporary chair until the final day of the convention, when he became the permanent chair; but to avoid confusion, I am following Sullivan's lead by calling him the permanent chair, or the chair, throughout the story of the convention.

704   "most learned . . . and sure": WAW, *The Autobiography*, pp. 469–70.

704   "the ablest man": Sullivan, *Our Times*, Vol. 4, p. 516.

704   "Mr. Root stands": Ibid., p. 498.

705   "were cruel thrusts": Jessup, *Elihu Root*, Vol. 2, p. 202.

705   "think over whether . . . to stand together": TR to Joseph Dixon, May 25, 1912, in *LTR*, Vol. 7, p. 548.

705   "I assume that . . . a united front": TR to Francis McGovern, May 28, 1912, in ibid., p. 548n.

705   hoping that "state pride" would lead: Sullivan, *Our Times*, Vol. 4, p. 515.

705   At noon . . . "honestly elected" Roosevelt delegates: *New York Tribune*, June 19 & 21, 1912.

705   Three years later . . . "emphasis and energy": Nicholas Butler to WHT, Nov. 12, 1915, Pringle Papers.

705   "was not in order": *New York Tribune*, June 19, 1912.

705   Rosewater allowed . . . out of order: *NYT*, June 19, 1912.

705   Root's nomination . . . the Roosevelt side: Ibid.

706   "not with La Follette's consent": Gardner, *Departing Glory*, p. 248.

706   La Follette . . . would strike no deal whatsoever: *New York Tribune*, June 19, 1912.

706   "We'll heed not": Ibid.

706   "to see Senator Root": *New York Tribune*, June 15, 1912.

706   "Receiver of stolen goods!": Gardner, *Departing Glory*, p. 248.

706   "the sweating wrathful . . . did not flicker": WAW, *The Autobiography*, p. 470.

706   "loudly cheered him": *New York Tribune*, June 19, 1912.

706   their astonishing record: *The Day Book* (Chicago), June 19, 1912.

706   Returning to the White House . . . Francis McGovern: *Washington* (DC) *Herald*, June 19, 1912.

706   "It was his duty" . . . the crowd "fell silent": *NYT*, June 19, 1912.

707   "remained in seclusion . . . stand by him": Ibid.

707   "electricity filled" . . . debate on the motion: *Washington Times*, June 19, 1912.

707   "no knowledge . . . upon these contests": *NYT*, June 20, 1912.

707   "consent to refer . . . Hadley, the next": Ibid.

707   "radiant and infectious . . . falling in line": Sullivan, *Our Times*, Vol. 4, pp. 528, 530.

708   "no man can . . . he holds his seat": RNC and Milton W. Blumenberg, *Official Report of the Proceedings of the Fifteenth Republican National Convention, Held in Chicago, Illinois, June 18, 19, 20, 21 and 22, 1912* (New York: Tenny Press, 1912), p. 160.

708   Outnumbered thirty-one . . . seating decisions: *NYT*, June 20, 1912.

708   "We are requested . . . square deal here": *Chicago Daily Tribune*, June 19, 1912.

708   "prospect of leaving . . . money and effort": *New York Tribune*, June 20, 1912.

708   "the moment when . . . 'we will see you through' ": Pinchot, *History of the Progressive Party, 1912–1916*, p. 165.

709   "My fortune": Stoddard, *As I Knew Them*, p. 306.

709   "lead a fight . . . conceal their emotions": *Washington Times*, June 21, 1912.

709   "jammed to its fullest capacity": *NYT*, June 21, 1912.

709   Minutes after . . . was not ready: *Chicago Daily Tribune*, June 20, 1912.

709   A later four o'clock session . . . the following day: *NYT*, June 21, 1912.

709   spectators "gathered in knots": *Washington Times*, June 20, 1912.

709   "to withdraw . . . honestly elected" delegates: *New York Tribune*, June 21, 1912.

709   "politicking . . . like a cipher . . . shorn": Lyon, *Success Story*, p. 341.

709   his accumulated debt . . . "unhorsed": Ibid., pp. 334–37.

710   "A storm of hisses . . . steamroller some more!": *NYT*, June 21, 1912.

710   "a thousand toots": WAW, *The Autobiography*, pp. 471–72.

710   "caught the spirit . . . Choo Choo": *Evening Standard* (Ogden City, UT), June 22, 1912.

710   "All aboard . . . a great uproar": *NYT*, June 21, 1912.

710   "a chorus of shrieks": *Evening Standard*, June 22, 1912.

710   "The Convention has now ... this successful fraud": TR to the Republican National Convention, June 22, 1912, in *LTR*, Vol. 7, pp. 562–63.

710   "to keep track of them all": Manners, *TR and Will*, p. 262.

710   It was nearly 7:30 p.m. ... with 561 votes: *NYT*, June 22, 1912.

711   "present but not" ... Justice Hughes 2: *New York Tribune*, June 22, 1912.

711   "no one would have suspected": *Washington Herald*, June 23, 1912.

711   the fourteen-year-old was "all grin": Ibid.

711   "electric" excitement ... "joy of a boy": *San Francisco Chronicle*, June 19, 1908.

711   both the president and first lady ... almost impossible: WHT to Mabel Boardman, June 23, 1912, WHTP.

711   "No Republican convention": *New York Tribune*, June 23, 1912.

711   "I am not afraid": WHT to Fred Carpenter, June 27, 1912, WHTP.

711   "the absolute independence": *New York Tribune*, June 23, 1912.

711   "a real menace": WHT to Fred Carpenter, June 27, 1912, WHTP.

711   "at stake ... the chief conservator": *New York Tribune*, June 23, 1912.

711   "preserved the party organization": WHT to Fred Carpenter, June 27, 1912, WHTP.

711   A "mass meeting": Davis, *Released for Publication*, p. 314.

711   Great applause greeted Edith ... "Here comes Texas": *New York Tribune*, June 23, 1912.

712   "We came here ... there was pandemonium": Ibid.

712   "find out ... my heartiest support": *Washington Times*, June 23, 1912.

712   "The only question now": Sullivan, *Our Times*, Vol. 4, p. 531.

713   "I'm in the fight": *New York Tribune*, June 28, 1912.

713   "Pop's been praying": Quoted in *NYT*, July 4, 1912.

713   "first skirmish ... you of Chicago?": *New York Tribune*, June 26, 1912.

713   When the balloting began ... finally secured the nomination: Gould, *Four Hats in the Ring*, pp. 92–93.

713   "the country was standing": WAW, *The Autobiography*, p. 478.

713   "You must sometimes": *Times Dispatch* (Richmond, VA), July 3, 1912.

713   "no necessity for": *New York Tribune*, July 4, 1912.

713   "Warmest congratulations ... join your cause": *Washington Herald*, July 22, 1912.

714   "a strong and rapidly growing": *New York Tribune*, June 29, 1912.

714   "exposing the Roosevelt fraud": *Washington Herald*, July 17, 1912.

714   "the most extravagant ... the Harvester Trust": *New York Tribune*, June 29, 1912.

714   "taunted, laughed at": Unger, *Fighting Bob La Follette*, p. 232.

714   "If Wilson had ... abandon them": TR to Alfred Warriner Cooley, July 10, 1912, in *LTR*, Vol. 7, p. 575.

714   "was flinching from ... of disaster": TR to Chase Salmon Osborn, June 28, 1912, in ibid., p. 566.

714   "excellent man ... for such action": TR to Chase Salmon Osborn, July 5, 1912, in ibid., p. 569.

714   "a call to ... roots of privilege": *Washington Times*, July 8, 1912.

714   Senators Cummins, Hadley ... to desert the Republican Party: *LTR*, Vol. 7, p. 573n.

714   promising instead to reform it from within: Pringle, *Theodore Roosevelt: A Biography*, pp. 565–66.

715   "I feel that Cummins": TR to John C. Kelly, July 10, 1912, in *LTR*, Vol. 7, p. 575.

715   "I greatly regret": TR to William Rockhill Nelson, July 30, 1912, in ibid., p. 583.

715   "sagging ... courage of his followers": WHT to HHT, July 20, 1912, WHTP.

715   "utterly unscrupulous ... public attention": WHT to HHT, July 15, 1912, WHTP.

715   "the object and purposes ... definition of his aims": *Washington Times*, July 8, 1912.

715   "hour after hour ... and solidity": *New York Tribune*, July 20, 1912.

715   "the greatest effort": *NYT*, Aug. 2, 1912.

715   Roosevelt took a single day ... "tennis on his return": *Washington Herald*, July 25, 1912.

715   "simplicity ... unusual informality": *New York Tribune*, July 31, 1912.

716   the ceremony would be held ... four hundred persons in attendance: WHT to Frances Taft Edwards, Aug. 2, 1912, WHTP.

716   "an average of sixteen": *Washington Herald*, July 29, 1912.

716   "Roosevelt proposes ... going to play": WHT to DCT, Aug. 1, 1912, WHTP.

716   The notification ceremony ... "loud shouts and handclapping": *NYT*, Aug. 2, 1912.

716   "long-established ... political conventions began": WHT and Elihu Root, *Speech of William Howard Taft Accepting the Republican Nomination for President of the United States, Together with the Speech of Notification by Senator Elihu Root, Delivered at Washington, D.C., August 1, 1912* (Washington, DC: Government Printing Office, 1912), p. 3.

716   "harping" ... stolen the nomination: WHT to HHT, July 15, 1912, WHTP.

716   Taft accepted the nomination ... "with the stronger and more powerful": WHT and Elihu Root, *Speech of William Howard Taft*, p. 5.

717   Asked to comment . . . Progressive Party Convention: *New York Tribune*, Aug. 2, 1912.
717   "On second thought . . . the live issues": *New York Tribune*, Aug. 3, 1912.

CHAPTER TWENTY-NINE: Armageddon

Page
718   "no man could go": *Washington* [DC] *Times*, Aug. 4, 1912.
718   "looked less like": *NYT*, Aug. 6, 1912.
718   "not a saloon-keeper": William Menkel, "The Progressives at Chicago," *American Review of Reviews*
       (September 1912).
719   "Instead of forcing": *NYT*, Aug. 5, 1912.
719   "great adventure . . . chance or speculation": *Boston Daily Globe*, Aug. 4, 1912.
719   "no dead places . . . in the right": Richard Harding Davis, "The Men at Armageddon," *Collier's*, Aug.
       24, 1912.
719   "more, in fact": *NYT*, Aug. 2, 1912.
719   "high-minded white men": TR, "The Progressives and the Colored Man," *Outlook*, Aug. 24, 1912,
       p. 911.
719   "was riddled . . . a racist strategy": Gable, *The Bull Moose Years*, pp. 65–66.
719   "lily-white" delegations: *New York Tribune*, Aug. 2, 1912.
719   would "not budge": *NYT*, Aug. 6, 1912.
719   "the whole show": *NYT*, Aug. 7, 1912.
719   Once again, Chicago went . . . thousands of people: *Washington Times*, Aug. 5, 1912.
719   "My friends": Ibid.
719   "Confession of Faith": *New York Tribune*, Aug. 5, 1912.
720   "the greatest personal": *Washington* [DC] *Herald*, Aug. 7, 1912.
720   "hundreds of men . . . cast their lots together": Ernest Hamlin Abbott, "The Progressive Convention,"
       Outlook, Aug. 17, 1912, pp. 858–59.
720   "battle flag . . . the plain people": *Emporia* [KS] *Gazette*, June 24, 1912.
720   Every man wore . . . around her wrist: *Washington Herald*, Aug. 6, 1912.
720   a red bandanna around: *NYT*, Aug. 7, 1912.
720   "stood smiling": *Chicago Tribune*, Aug. 7, 1912.
720   Twenty thousand voices . . . soaring melody: *NYT*, Aug. 7, 1912.
720   "sprang to their feet": Davis, "The Men at Armageddon," *Collier's*, Aug. 24, 1912.
720   "I have been fighting": *NYT*, Aug. 7, 1912.
720   When it seemed . . . he had to carry it through: Manners, *TR and Will*, p. 268.
720   "jovial smile and bright eye": *NYT*, Aug. 7, 1912.
720   "Mrs. Roosevelt shrank . . . in public life!": Davis, "The Men at Armageddon," *Collier's*, Aug. 24,
       1912.
720   "At present . . . people to rule": TR, "A Confession of Faith," in *Social Justice and Popular Rule*, *WTR*,
       Vol. 17, pp. 257–58.
721   Though the delegates . . . the right to the vote: *NYT*, Aug. 7, 1912.
721   "In most cases": *NYT*, Aug. 6, 1912.
721   "fell on willing ears": *NYT*, Aug. 7, 1912.
721   "a living wage . . . we battle for the Lord": TR, "A Confession of Faith," in *WTR*, Vol. 17, pp. 268–69,
       298–99.
721   "a purely Rooseveltian document": *Washington Herald*, Aug. 8, 1912.
721   "the first time a woman": *Chicago Tribune*, Aug. 7, 1912.
721   "wave upon wave . . . this great movement": *Washington Times*, Aug. 8, 1912.
722   "The Bull Moose party": RSB, Notebook L, Aug. 31, 1912, RSB Papers.
722   "It is odd to me . . . to forget himself": RSB, Notebook M, Aug. 8, 1912, RSB Papers.
722   Roosevelt's titanic persona . . . "obscures everything": RSB, Notebook L, Aug. 31, 1912, RSB
       Papers.
722   "As for me": RSB, Notebook M, Aug. 8, 1912, RSB Papers.
722   "I left Princeton . . . dared to make speeches": RSB, *American Chronicle*, pp. 273–75.
722   "a personal party" . . . an "ace" for the future: WAW, *The Autobiography*, p. 474.
722   "a cold fish . . . a fine liberal job": Ibid., p. 479.
723   "four days . . . of human welfare!": Ibid., pp. 484–85, 487–88.
723   "He seemed full . . . tornado of a man": Ibid., p. 490.
723   "It makes me crazy": IMT to Albert Boyden, Aug. 23, 1905, Ida Tarbell Papers.
723   "a thousand times": IMT to JSP, n.d., Ida Tarbell Papers.
723   "Why stop with": Harry Pratt Judson, "Mr. Roosevelt and the Third Term," *The Independent*, Mar. 28,
       1912.
723   "We've got a King . . . we can do it": IMT to JSP, n.d., Ida Tarbell Papers.

723   *The American Magazine* . . . Progressive Party: RSB, Notebook L, Aug. 31, 1912, RSB Papers.

724   Months earlier . . . injured one hundred others: Robert E. Weir, *Workers in America: A Historical Encyclopedia* (Santa Barbara, CA: ABC-CLIO, 2013), p. 438.

724   an act of "social revolution": *Hawaiian Gazette* (Honolulu), July 23, 1912.

724   "It seems to me": TR to Charles D. Willard, Dec. 11, 1912, in *LTR*, Vol. 7, p. 453.

724   "Murder is murder": TR, "Murder Is Murder," *Outlook*, Dec. 16, 1911, p. 902.

724   "It looks like . . . personal, you see": LS to Allen H. Suggett, Sept. 12, 1912, in *The Letters of Lincoln Steffens*, Vol. 1, p. 308.

724   "a whirlwind campaign": *NYT*, Aug. 13, 1912.

724   "a President who is": *New York Tribune*, July 14, 1912.

724   He believed "in his heart": *NYT*, Aug. 13, 1912.

724   six justices to the bench . . . half of them Democrats: Jonathan Lurie, *William Howard Taft: The Travails of a Progressive Conservative* (New York: Cambridge University Press, 2012), p. 121.

725   "the rain to fall . . . continuance of power": *NYT*, Sept. 29, 1912.

725   "It always makes": WHT to HHT, July 22, 1912, WHTP.

725   "I couldn't if I would": *NYT*, Aug. 13, 1912.

725   "As the campaign . . . trust or confidence": WHT to HHT, Aug. 26, 1912, WHTP.

725   "I never discuss dead issues": *New York Tribune*, Aug. 18, 1912.

725   "was a dead cock": *NYT*, Sept. 18, 1912.

725   "worthy of . . . organized by theft": TR, "A Speech at Grand Forks, North Dakota, 6 September 1912," in TR and Lewis L. Gould, *Bull Moose on the Stump: The 1912 Campaign Speeches of Theodore Roosevelt* (Lawrence: University Press of Kansas, 2008), pp. 75–76.

726   "the preservation of . . . second sober thought": *NYT*, Sept. 29, 1912.

726   "new vitality . . . of the Republican Party": *NYT*, Oct. 1, 1912.

726   Well aware . . . "very improbable": TR to Arthur Hamilton Lee, Aug. 14, 1912, in *LTR*, Vol. 7, p. 598.

726   He embarked upon an unprecedented . . . solid Democratic South: *New York Tribune*, Aug. 13, 1912.

726   "deluge of travel": TR to Ethel Roosevelt, Aug. 21, 1912, TRC.

726   "a tremendous amount": Davis, *Released for Publication*, p. 345.

726   "a chance" of victory: TR to Arthur Hamilton Lee, Aug. 14, 1912, in *LTR*, Vol. 7, p. 598.

726   "I am perfectly happy": Ibid.

727   Journalists noted . . . this "boss-ridden": *Washington Times*, Aug. 17, 1912.

727   "rock-ribbed . . . what they were trying to accomplish": *NYT*, Aug. 8, 1912.

727   "My private judgment": *Washington Times*, Aug. 24, 1912.

727   He hoped to reach the public . . . his political philosophy: *NYT*, Aug. 8, 1912.

727   He had no appetite . . . boisterous crowd: August Heckscher, *Woodrow Wilson* (New York: Scribner, 1991), p. 258.

727   "I am by no means": WW to Mary A. Hulbert, Aug. 25, 1912, in Ray Stannard Baker, *Governor, 1910–1913*, Vol. 3 of *Woodrow Wilson: Life and Letters* (Garden City, NY: Doubleday, Page & Co., 1927), p. 390.

727   "I haven't a": WW to Frank P. Glass, Sept. 6, 1912, in ibid., p. 400.

727   "as far west as Colorado": *American Review of Reviews* (November 1908).

727   "had, in reality . . . skill as an orator": RSB, *Governor, 1910–1913*, p. 377.

728   "Wilson was a new . . . distance up the road": Ibid., p. 391.

728   "Suppose you choose": WW, "How Shall We Use the Government?," in WW and John Wells Davidson, *A Crossroads of Freedom: The 1912 Campaign Speeches* (New Haven, CT: Yale University Press, 1956), p. 295.

728   "very glad of the opportunity . . . fond of President Taft": *NYT*, Sept. 27, 1912.

728   "currents of air . . . the right direction": WHT to Henry Taft, Sept. 18, 1912, WHTP.

728   "probably be defeated": WHT to Gustav J. Karger, Sept. 7, 1912, Taft-Karger Corr., CMC.

728   Winning the nomination . . . a more general reverse for the party: AB to Clara, Nov. 24, 1911, in AB, *Taft and Roosevelt*, Vol. 2, p. 768.

729   "I seem to think": WHT to HHT, July 23, 1912, WHTP.

729   "I wanted him to be": HHT, *Recollections of Full Years*, p. 393.

729   "She is in a condition": WHT to Horace Taft, Nov. 1, 1912, WHTP.

729   "was going stale . . . rehashing": Davis, *Released for Publication*, p. 353.

729   "it was Wilson": Ibid., p. 360.

729   "first direct assault . . . 'Confession of Faith' ": *NYT*, Sept. 15, 1912.

729   "Mr. Wilson is fond . . . advance we have made": TR, "Address at the San Francisco Coliseum, Sept. 14, 1912," in TR and Gould, *Bull Moose on the Stump,* pp. 110–11.

730   "every railroad must": Ibid., p. 113.

730 "to use the whole power": Ibid., pp. 116–17.
730 "freedom to-day . . . fair play": WW and William Bayard Hale, *The New Freedom; A Call for the Emancipation of the Generous Energies of a People* (New York: Doubleday, Page & Co., 1913), p. 284.
730 In keeping with . . . less expansive federal government: Gould, *Four Hats in the Ring*, p. 163.
730 Roosevelt's "declaration of war": *NYT*, Sept. 15, 1912.
730 "open again the fields": John Milton Cooper, *Woodrow Wilson: A Biography* (New York: Alfred A. Knopf, 2009), p. 168.
730 While Roosevelt accepted . . . posed a problem: Ibid., p. 167.
730 "to organize the forces": Ibid., p. 168.
731 "the wealth of America . . . borders of the town": WW, "The Wealth of America: Address at Kokomo, Indiana, October 4, 1912," in Wilson and Davidson, *A Crossroads of Freedom*, p. 333.
731 "abolishing tariff favors" and "credit denials": Wilson and Hale, *The New Freedom*, p. 292.
731 "split up into a lot . . . which Mr. Taft defends": TR, "Speech at the San Francisco Coliseum, Sept. 14, 1912," in TR and Gould, *Bull Moose on the Stump,* pp. 113–14.
731 "becoming more and more plain": Davis, *Released for Publication*, p. 360.
731 "were as close as fraternal twins": Manners, *TR and Will*, p. 268.
731 "utterly incapable" . . . to declare laws passed by Congress unconstitutional: "The Socialist Party Platform: May 12, 1912," in *1900–1936*, Vol. 3 of Arthur M. Schlesinger, Jr., and Fred L. Israel, eds., *History of American Presidential Elections, 1789–1968* (New York: Chelsea House, 1971), pp. 2198, 2200–2.
732 as a bitter wind blew: Davis, *Released for Publication*, pp. 366, 368.
732 "a mammoth tent": *Chicago Daily Tribune*, Oct. 13, 1912.
732 Roosevelt insisted . . . "I want to be a good Indian": Davis, *Released for Publication*, pp. 371–72.
732 An open touring car . . . and began to strangle him: Ibid., pp. 374–76.
732 "I wasn't trying to take him": Thompson, *Presidents I've Known*, p. 148.
732 "Lynch him," "Kill him": *Washington [DC] Times*, Oct. 15, 1912.
732 "Bring him here . . . Turn him over to the police": Thompson, *Presidents I've Known*, p. 148.
732 "You get me to that speech . . . pain from this breathing": Davis, *Released for Publication*, pp. 378–80.
733 "It's true": Morris, *Colonel Roosevelt*, p. 245.
733 "how narrowly he had escaped" . . . but coming to a halt: Davis, *Released for Publication*, pp. 381–82.
733 Oscar Davis, standing . . . "until I have finished": Ibid., pp. 383–84.
733 "his heart was racing . . . do what you want": Morris, *Colonel Roosevelt*, pp. 245–46.
733 While Roosevelt was being examined . . . as his murderer: *Chicago Daily Tribune*, Oct. 15, 1912.
733 "to think seriously" . . . the right opportunity had never presented itself: *New York Tribune*, Oct. 15, 1912.
733 At Milwaukee Hospital . . . location of the bullet: *Washington Times*, Oct. 15, 1912.
734 "There are only three possible": Thompson, *Presidents I've Known*, p. 153.
734 "All over the room" . . . to rush to the telephones: *New York Tribune*, Oct. 15, 1912.
734 "The fight should go on": Davis, *Released for Publication*, p. 396.
734 Edith Roosevelt . . . attack on her husband: *Chicago Daily Tribune*, Oct. 15, 1912.
734 She left the theatre . . . Alexander Lambert: *Washington Times*, Oct. 15, 1912.
734 "It's the best news": *Washington Times*, Oct. 16, 1912.
734 "He has been as meek . . . I am at this moment": Thompson, *Presidents I've Known*, p. 151.
734 "outside of the rib . . . live there permanently": EKR to Kermit Roosevelt, Oct. 21, 1912, KR Papers.
734 "in absolute quiet": *Washington Post*, Oct. 20, 1912.
734 By Monday morning . . . until the train reached New York: EKR to Kermit Roosevelt, Oct. 16, 1912, KR Papers.
734 "I am in fine shape": TR to ARC, Oct. 27, 1912, in *LTR*, Vol. 7, p. 632.
734 still hoped to make one final appearance: Ibid.
735 "Encouraging reports are coming in": Ethel Roosevelt to ARC, October [n.d.], 1912, ARC Papers.
735 "The bullet that rests": *NYT*, Oct. 27, 1912.
735 "What effect the incident": WHT to Mabel Boardman, Oct. 17, 1912, WHTP.
735 "the rush of the crowd": *Chicago Daily Tribune*, Oct. 30, 1912.
735 "farewell manifesto": *NYT*, Oct. 30, 1912.
735 "looked to the excitement": New York *Sun*, Oct. 31, 1912.
735 "regained its accustomed power": *New York Tribune*, Oct. 30, 1912.
735 he was anxious to begin speaking: *Washington Post*, Oct. 31, 1912.
735 "Perhaps once in a generation . . . to spend and be spent": TR, "Address at Madison Square Garden, Oct. 30, 1912," in TR and Gould, *Bull Moose on the Stump,* pp. 187, 188, 190, 191–92.
736 "as clear as a bell . . . the old sarcasm": *NYT*, Oct. 27, 1912.
736 "good taste . . . for self-exhibition": New York *Sun*, Oct. 31, 1912.
736 President Taft sat down: Memorandum of Louis Seibold interview, Oct. 26, 1912, WHTP.
736 Taft nevertheless hoped to outpoll: WHT to Horace Taft, Nov. 1, 1912, WHTP.

736 "in excellent spirits" . . . the Associated Press: Pringle, *Life and Times*, Vol. 2, p. 837.

736 "anxious to carry out . . . the country will go on to ultimate happiness": WHT and Louis Seibold interview, Nov. 1, 1912, WHTP.

737 "minor corrections . . . my closest friend": Pringle, *Life and Times*, Vol. 2, pp. 837–38.

737 a "leisurely" route . . . the prosperous economy and local events: *San Francisco Call*, Nov. 5, 1912.

738 Upon reaching Cincinnati . . . a small dinner party: *Washington* [DC] *Herald*, Nov. 5, 1912.

738 "slept late, ate a good breakfast": *Evening World* (New York), Nov. 5, 1912.

738 At noon, he motored . . . his congressional seat: *New York Tribune*, Nov. 6, 1912.

738 "stood in line and waited": *Evening World*, Nov. 5, 1912.

738 "a busy morning . . . Bull Mooser vote": *Washington Times*, Nov. 5, 1912.

738 "a long ramble . . . and make a speech somewhere": *NYT*, Nov. 6, 1912.

738 Wilson walked to his polling place . . . "every nook and corner": RSB, *Governor, 1910–1913*, p. 407.

738 After casting his vote . . . an old friend: *NYT*, Nov. 6, 1912.

738 "was much in the nature": Ibid.

739 "an air of gloom": Ibid.; *Washington* [DC] *Herald*, Nov. 6, 1912.

739 "My dear": *Washington Times*, Nov. 6, 1912.

739 "great emotion . . . the new administration": RSB, *Governor, 1910–1913*, p. 409.

739 Wilson had achieved an immense victory . . . leaving only 41.9 percent: Gould, *Four Hats in the Ring*, pp. 174, 176.

739 "best wishes . . . guard around the house": New York *Sun*, Nov. 6, 1912.

739 "They went in . . . from the big fireplace": *NYT*, Nov. 6, 1912.

739 "Now old friends . . . That's all": *Evening World*, Nov. 6, 1912.

740 "chatted as gaily . . . from his shoulders": *Washington Herald*, Nov. 7, 1912.

740 "hopeful . . . shock of real disappointment": WHT to Horace Taft, Nov. 8, 1912, WHTP.

740 "The people of": WHT to Mrs. Buckner A. Wallingford, Jr., Nov. 9, 1912, WHTP.

740 "As I look back": WHT to Otto Bannard, Nov. 10, 1912, in Pringle, *Life and Times*, Vol. 2, p. 603.

740 "popular feeling": EKR to Kermit Roosevelt, Nov. 6, 1912, KR Papers.

740 "There is no use . . . a better showing": TR to Arthur Hamilton Lee, Nov. 5, 1912, in *LTR*, Vol. 7, p. 633.

740 "We must face": TR to Gifford Pinchot, Nov. 13, 1912, in ibid., p. 642.

740 "It was a phenomenal thing": TR to Henry White, Nov. 12, 1912, in ibid., p. 639.

741 "the leader for the time": *Evening World*, Nov. 6, 1912.

741 the core progressive belief that government . . . our natural heritage: Richard Hofstadter, *The Progressive Movement, 1900–1915* (Englewood Cliffs, NJ: Prentice-Hall, 1963), pp. 3, 4.

Epilogue

Page

743 "I hear he's leaving . . . back downstairs": *New York Tribune*, May 27, 1918.

743 After the White House, Taft had become: Frederick C. Hicks, *William Howard Taft, Yale Professor of Law & New Haven Citizen: An Academic Interlude in the Life of the Twenty-Seventh President of the United States and the Tenth Chief Justice of the Supreme Court* (New Haven: Yale University Press, 1945), pp. 1, 80.

743 he had begun work on his autobiography: Morris, *Colonel Roosevelt*, p. 256.

743 to explore the River of Doubt: Johnson and Malone, eds., *Dictionary of American Biography*, Vol. 8, p. 143.

743 and delivering scores of speeches each year: "Chronology," Appendix IV, in *LTR*, Vol. 8, pp. 1480–94.

743 He had stopped at the Blackstone Hotel: John J. Leary, *Talks with T.R., from the Diaries of John J. Leary, Jr.* (Boston: Houghton Mifflin Co., 1920), p. 200.

743 neither "cordial" nor "intimate": WHT to Gustav J. Karger, April 14, 1915, in Taft-Karger Corr., CMC.

743 "armed neutrality": WHT to Mabel Boardman, April 19, 1915, Mabel Thorp Boardman Papers, Manuscript Division, LC.

743 "How are you . . . between them": William Lyons Phelps, *Autobiography with Letters* (New York: Oxford University Press, 1939), p. 618.

743 "cementing the union": WHT to Gustav J. Karger, Sept. 26, 1915, in Taft-Karger Corr., CMC.

743 a "Big Love Feast": *Daily Capital Journal* (Salem, OR), Oct. 4, 1916.

744 "the Republican fold": *Bridgeport* [CT] *Telegram*, May 29, 1918.

744 "shook hands with": WHT to HHT, Oct. 5, 1916, WHTP.

744 "I know something . . . the dispatches": WHT to HHT, Feb. 9, 1918, WHTP.

744 The surgery to remedy . . . almost a month: Morris, *Colonel Roosevelt*, pp. 517–18.

744 "personally sent . . . by Your Message" TR telegram to WHT, Feb. 12, 1918, WHTP.

744 "sluggishness . . . after the war": TR to WHT, Mar. 4, 1918, in *LTR*, Vol. 8, p. 1294n.

744   Taft wholeheartedly concurred: WHT to TR, Mar. 11, 1918, WHTP.

744   "I have embodied . . . thought of them!": TR to WHT, Mar. 16, 1918, in *LTR*, Vol. 8, p. 1301.

744   "Theodore!" . . . erupted into applause: *New York Tribune*, May 27, 1918.

745   "T.R. and Taft's got together": Leary, *Talks with T.R.*, pp. 201–2.

745   "By Godfrey . . . splendid of Taft": Ibid., p. 204.

745   "like a pair of happy schoolboys": *New York Tribune*, May 27, 1918.

745   "Taft was beaming . . . welfare of the Nation": Leary, *Talks with T.R.*, pp. 202–3.

745   "completely renewed": TR to Henry Stimson, June 5, 1918, in *LTR*, Vol. 8, p. 1337.

745   "anyone else" . . . as long as he was needed: James Amos and John T. Flynn, "The Beloved Boss," *Collier's*, Aug. 7, 1926, p. 40.

745   "seemed better again": CRR, *My Brother*, p. 363.

745   "the warmest room" . . . *Metropolitan* magazine: Morris, *Colonel Roosevelt*, pp. 549–50.

746   "There should be . . . higgle about the matter": *New York Tribune*, Jan. 7, 1919.

746   "a happy and wonderful day": EKR to TR, Jr., Jan. 12, 1919, TRJP.

746   "as it got dusk": Ibid.

746   "sensation of depression": *New York Tribune*, Jan. 7, 1919.

746   his heart were preparing to stop: *NYT*, Jan. 7, 1919.

746   "I know it is not": EKR to KR, Jan. 12, 1919, KR and Belle Roosevelt Papers.

746   "examined him carefully": *New York Tribune*, Jan. 7, 1919.

746   "James, don't you . . . put out the light?": Amos and Flynn, "The Beloved Boss," *Collier's*, Aug. 7, 1926, p. 40.

746   Edith came to check: EKR to Kermit Roosevelt, Jan. 12, 1919, KR Papers.

746   a "peaceful slumber" . . . Theodore was dead: Amos and Flynn, "The Beloved Boss," *Collier's*, Aug. 7, 1926, p. 40.

746   "Death had to take him": Edward Renehan, Jr., *The Lion's Pride: Theodore Roosevelt and His Family in Peace and War* (New York: Oxford University Press, 1998), p. 222.

746   "brave little adventure": Finley Peter Dunne to IMT, [n.d.], IMTC.

746   Relentless money troubles: John E. Semonche, "The American Magazine, 1906–1915," *Journalism and Mass Communication Quarterly* (Winter 1963), pp. 40–42.

747   "The test of" . . . 600,000 readers: RSB, Notebook V, April 14, 1915, RSB Papers.

747   Prize contests . . . and marriage: Semonche, "The American Magazine, 1906–1915," *Journalism and Mass Communication Quarterly* (Winter 1963), p. 43.

747   "strangled by commercial considerations": RSB, Notebook V, April 14, 1915, RSB Papers.

747   White and Tarbell had been sent to Paris: IMT, *All in the Day's Work*, pp. 336–37.

747   Ray Baker was serving President Wilson: WAW, *The Autobiography*, p. 546.

747   over one hundred American correspondents: *Bridgeport* [CT] *Telegram*, Jan. 15, 1919.

747   "absolute fairness . . . intimate it was": IMT, *All in the Day's Work*, p. 350.

747   "Again and again . . . without Roosevelt in it": WAW, *The Autobiography*, p. 551.

747   "It was my father's wish": Morris, *Colonel Roosevelt*, p. 554.

748   Taft had discovered with delight: WHT to Irving Fisher, Dec. 1, 1922, WHTP.

748   "You're a dear personal friend": WHT to HHT, Jan. 9, 1919, WHTP.

748   "no pomp . . . profoundly impressive": "Theodore Roosevelt's Funeral: An Impression," *Outlook*, Jan. 22, 1919.

748   "a mound of flowers": *New York Tribune*, Jan. 9, 1919.

748   "widow's custom": Morris, *EKR*, p. 437.

748   "with all the passion": EKR to TR, June 8, 1886, Derby Papers.

748   "an isolated figure . . . from the others": *Bisbee* [AZ] *Daily Review*, Jan. 9, 1919.

748   "I want to say to you": WHT to ARC, July 26, 1921, in Pringle, *Life and Times*, Vol. 2, p. 913.

748   At noon on October 3, 1921: *Washington* [DC] *Times*, Oct. 3, 1921.

748   "as strongly as a man": HHT, *Recollections of a Full Life*, p. 263.

748   "to administer justice": "Judiciary Oath," U.S. Code, Title 28, Part 1, chap. 21, sect. 453.

748   "the famous Taft . . . greatest day of my life": *Sweetwater* [TX] *Daily Reporter*, Oct. 4, 1921.

748   "The people of the United States": *Washington Post*, Oct. 4, 1921.

749   "antiquated . . . federal courts": Allen Edgar Ragan and Harlow Lindley, *Chief Justice Taft* (Columbus: Ohio State Arch. & Hist. Soc., 1938), p. 104.

749   "great skill . . . old Senate chamber": Robert Post, "The Supreme Court Opinion as Institutional Practice: Dissent, Legal Scholarship, and Decisionmaking in the Taft Court," *Minnesota Law Review* 85 (2011), pp. 1267–68.

749   "We call you Chief Justice": Oliver Wendell Holmes et al., to WHT, Feb. 10, 1930, in Pringle, *Life and Times*, Vol. 2, p. 1079.

749   "unbreakable quality . . . but interrupted": IMT, *All in the Day's Work*, p. 406.

749   the "old Crowd": RSB to IMT, Oct. 30, 1917, IMTC.

749 "a hundred, yes a thousand": IMT to Alice and Cale Rice, Jan. 21, 1933, IMTC.

749 "saving the world": RSB to LS, April 28, 1930, RSB Papers.

749 "muck-raked never to . . . speedily corrected": RSB, Notebook LIV, [n.d.], p. 22, RSB Papers.

750 how "hard-boiled" the world really was: RSB to LS, April 28, 1930, RSB Papers.

750 "the star . . . the publishing business": IMT to Viola Roseboro, Nov. 6, 1937, IMTC.

750 His "old fire": IMT to JSP, Oct. 6, 1937, IMTC.

750 "We sat enthralled": IMT, *All in the Day's Work*, p. 406.

750 Tarbell wrote . . . "flame steady and lasting": IMT to JSP, Oct. 6, 1937, IMTC.

750 "that wonderful adventure . . . a mission and a call": JSP to RSB, Dec. 20, 1920, RSB Papers.

ILLUSTRATION CREDITS

Numbers in bold roman type refer to illustrations in the inserts; numbers in bold italics refer to book pages.

The Bancroft Library, University of California, Berkeley: **15**

Culver Pictures, Inc.: **54**

Courtesy of the Ida M. Tarbell Collection, Pelletier Library, Allegheny College: *324*, **19**, **24**, **43**

Kansas State Historical Society: **21**

Library of Congress, Prints and Photographs Division: **87**, LC-DIG-hec-15220; *239 (right)*, PR 13 CN 1980: 167 Container (AA) 3; **557**, LC-DIG-hec-15221; *583*, LC-USZ62-121727; **25**, LC-USZ62-132301; **30**, PR 13 CN 1980: 167 Container (AA) 4; **38**, LC-DIG-ppmsca-26036; **40**, LC-USZ62-48773; **41**, LC-USZ62-48769; **42**, LC-USZ62-95893; **44**, LC-USZ627757; **49**, LC-USZ62-7634; **50**, LC-DIG-hec-01006; **51**, LC-USZ62-95701; **53**, LC-DIG-hec-01007; **55**, LC-USZ62-53971; **56**, LC-USZ62-10309; **58**, LC-DIG-hec-15169; **61**, LC-DIG-hec-07123; **68**, LC-DIG-hec-15127; *back endpaper*, LC-USZ62-32737

Courtesy, The Lilly Library, Indiana University, Bloomington, Indiana: *157*, **16**, **17**, **18**, **20**, **66**

Courtesy of Mark Rohling and the Taft Museum of Art, Cincinnati, Ohio: **47**

Theodore Roosevelt Collection, Houghton Library, Harvard University [photographs]: *1*, TRC-PH-1 560.62; *21 (left)*, TRC-PH-2 520.11-003; *109*, TRC-PH-2 570.R67ed-003; *134*, TRC-PH-2 520.21-001; *239 (left)*, TRC-PH-2 560.41-020; *385*, TRC-PH-4 560.52 1906-072; *401*, Roosevelt R500.P69a-088; *655*, Roosevelt R560.6.C71; **1**, TRC-PH-2 520.12-003; **4**, TRC-PH-4 560.11-018; **5**, TRC-PH-2 520.11-009; **6**, MS Am 1541.9 (136); **7**, TRC-PH-1 570.1 R67r 1878; **8**, *87M-102; **10**, TRC-PH-1 520.13-003a; **11**, TRC-PH-2 560.14-149; **12**, 520.14-001; **14**, TRC-PH-1 560.22-001; **22**, TRC-PH-2 520.23-007; **27**, TRC-PH-2 560.41-066; **32**, TRC-PH-1 560.41-057; **33**, Roosevelt R500.P69a-050; **34**, TRC-PH-1 560.51 1902-156; **35**, TRC-PH-1 560.51 1903-115; **36**, TRC-PH-1 560.52 1905-002; **37**, TRC-PH-5 560.52 1905-019a; **39**, TRC-PH-3 541.51-001; **48**, TRC-PH-1 560.52 1909-017; **52**, Roosevelt R500.P69a-064; **57**, Roosevelt R500.R67-056; **59**, TRC-PH-2 560.6; **60**, Roosevelt R560.6.C71; **62**, TRC-PH-1 560.7; **64**, TRC-PH-1 560.7; **65**, TRC-PH-1 560.7; **67**, TRC-PH-2 541.9-010; *front endpaper*, TRC-PH-1 560.52 1905-012

Theodore Roosevelt Collection, Houghton Library, Harvard University [political cartoons]: *203*, TRC-PH-1 560.23; *279*, *348*, *366*, *444*, *467*, *497*, *516*, *534*, *605*, *634*, *672*, *697*, *718*; **13**, **23**, **31**, **45**, **46**, **63**, preceding illustrations TRC-CT-1

Courtesy of the University of Chicago Library: *50*, **26**

Courtesy of the U.S. Army Heritage and Education Center: **29**

Courtesy of the William Howard Taft National Historic Site, National Park Service: *21 (right)*, **2**, **3**, **9**, **28**

≈ INDEX ≈

On March 4, 1909, the day of William Howard Taft's inauguration, Washington, D.C., was hit by its worst blizzard in decades. "I always said it would be a cold day when I got to be President," Taft told Roosevelt.